Legal Environment

WITH BUSINESS ETHICS CASES

Jeffrey F. Beatty | Susan S. Samuelson | Marianne M. Jennings

CENGAGE
Learning™

Australia • Brazil • Japan • Korea • Mexico • Singapore • Spain • United Kingdom • United States

CENGAGE
Learning™

Legal Environment: With Business Ethics Cases

Jeffrey F. Beatty | Susan S. Samuelson
Marianne M. Jennings

Executive Editors:
 Michele Baird

 Maureen Staudt

 Michael Stranz

Project Development Manager:
 Linda deStefano

Senior Marketing Coordinators:
 Sara Mercurio

 Lindsay Shapiro

Production/Manufacturing Manager:
 Donna M. Brown

PreMedia Services Supervisor:
 Rebecca A. Walker

Rights & Permissions Specialist:
 Kalina Hintz

Cover Image:
 Getty Images*

* Unless otherwise noted, all cover images used by Custom Solutions, a part of Cengage Learning, have been supplied courtesy of Getty Images with the exception of the Earthview cover image, which has been supplied by the National Aeronautics and Space Administration (NASA).

© 2008, Cengage Learning

ALL RIGHTS RESERVED. No part of this work covered by the copyright herein may be reproduced, transmitted, stored or used in any form or by any means graphic, electronic, or mechanical, including but not limited to photocopying, recording, scanning, digitizing, taping, Web distribution, information networks, or information storage and retrieval systems, except as permitted under Section 107 or 108 of the 1976 United States Copyright Act, without the prior written permission of the publisher.

For product information and technology assistance, contact us at
Cengage Learning Customer & Sales Support, 1-800-354-9706

For permission to use material from this text or product,
submit all requests online at **cengage.com/permissions**
Further permissions questions can be emailed to
permissionrequest@cengage.com

Library of Congress Control Number: 0000000000

ISBN-13: 978-0-324-68422-3

ISBN-10: 0-324-68422-3

Cengage Learning
5191 Natorp Boulevard
Mason, Ohio 45040
USA

Cengage Learning is a leading provider of customized learning solutions with office locations around the globe, including Singapore, the United Kingdom, Australia, Mexico, Brazil, and Japan. Locate your local office at:
international.cengage.com/region

Cengage Learning products are represented in Canada by Nelson Education, Ltd.

For your lifelong learning solutions, visit **custom.cengage.com**

Visit our corporate website at **cengage.com**

Printed in the United States of America

Contents: Overview

Contents

UNIT 2
Contracts & the UCC 209

UNIT 3
Agency & Employment 339

Unit 4

Business Organizations 429

Preface

When we began work on the first edition of this textbook, our publisher warned us that our undertaking was risky because there were already so many Legal Environment texts. Despite these warnings, we were convinced that there was a market for a Legal Environment book that was different from all the others. Our goal was to capture the passion and excitement—the sheer enjoyment—of the law. Business law is notoriously complex, and as authors we are obsessed with accuracy. Yet this intriguing subject also abounds with human conflict and hard-earned wisdom, forces that can make a law book sparkle.

Now, as the third edition goes to press, we think of the students who have said to us, "This is the best textbook I have ever read," and "I had no idea business law could be so interesting." We recall the faculty who have told us, "Until I read your book I never really understood UCC 2-207" and "With your book, we have great class discussions." Comments such as these never cease to thrill us and to make us grateful that we persisted in writing a Legal Environment text like no other—a book that is precise and authoritative *yet a pleasure to read.*

Comprehensive

Staying comprehensive means staying current. This third edition contains over 50 new cases. Almost all were reported within the last two or three years. We never include a new court opinion merely because it is recent, but the law evolves continually, and our willingness to toss out old cases and add important new ones ensures that this book—and its readers—remain on the frontier of legal developments.

Look, for example, at the important field of corporate governance. All texts cover par value, and so do we. Yet a future executive is far likelier to face conflicts over Sarbanes-Oxley, executive compensation, and shareholder proposals. We present a clear path through this thicket of new issues. We want tomorrow's business leaders to anticipate the challenges that await them and then use their knowledge to avert problems.

We have greatly rewritten many chapters for this third edition to ensure full coverage of rapidly evolving issues, such as cyberlaw, securities law, UCC revisions, and the Bankruptcy Abuse Prevention and Consumer Protection Act of 2005. However, we have kept the strong narrative flow from the earlier edition. Like you, we are here to teach. We do not use boxes because, in our experience, they disrupt the flow of the text. Students inform us that a box indicates peripheral material, that is, material they routinely skip; we prefer to give them an uncluttered whole. Each chapter also contains several Internet addresses, offering students a quick link to additional knowledge.

These addresses, however, are woven into the body of the tε
that new technology and research methods are an integral parε
For example, page 371 in Chapter 15 on employment law contains
Website where the Labor Department answers questions about ε
Medical Leave Act. We believe that a well-written chapter is seamless aι

Strong Narrative

The law is full of great stories, and we use them. Your students and ours should come to class excited. In Chapter 3 on dispute resolution (page 43), we explain litigation by tracking a double-indemnity lawsuit. An executive is dead. Did he drown accidentally, obligating the insurance company to pay? Or did the businessman commit suicide, voiding the policy? The student follows the action from the discovery of the body, through each step of the lawsuit, to the final appeal. The chapter offers a detailed discussion of dispute resolution, but it does so by exploiting the human drama that underlies litigation.

Students read stories and remember them. Strong narratives provide a rich context for the remarkable quantity of legal material presented. When students care about the material they are reading, they persevere. We have been delighted to find that they also arrive in class eager to question, discuss, and learn.

Precise

The great joy of using English accurately is the power it gives us to attack and dissect difficult issues, rendering them comprehensible to any lay reader. This text takes on the most complex legal topics of the day, yet it is appropriate for *all college and graduate level students*. Accessible prose goes hand in hand with legal precision. We take great pride in walking our readers through the most serpentine mazes this tough subject can offer. UCC section 2-207, on "battle of forms" conflicts, is hardly sexy material, but it is important. We spotlight the real-world need for section 2-207, and then use pinpoint directions to guide our readers through its many switchbacks, arriving at a full understanding with sanity and good humor intact. (See page 223.)

As we explore this extraordinary discipline, we lure readers along with quirky anecdotes and colorful diagrams. (Notice that the color display on page 470 clarifies the complex rules of the duty of care in the business judgment rule.) However, before the trip is over we insist that students:

- gauge policy and political considerations,

- grapple with legal and social history,

- spot the nexus between disparate doctrines, and

- confront tough moral choices.

Beyond that, we ask students to figure out how to avoid the very problems that have generated our law.

Authoritative

We insist, as you do, on a lawbook that is indisputably accurate. A professor must teach with assurance, confident that every paragraph is the result of exhaustive research and meticulous presentation. Dozens of tough-minded people spent thousands of hours reviewing this book, and we are delighted with the stamp of approval we have received from trial and appellate judges, working attorneys, scholars, and teachers.

We reject the cloudy definitions and fuzzy explanations that can invade judicial opinions and legal scholarship. To highlight the most important rules, we use bold print, and then follow with vivacious examples written in clear, forceful English. (See, for example, the discussion of factual cause on page 143.) We cheerfully venture into contentious areas, relying on very recent appellate decisions. (Can computer software be patented? See page 565.) Where there is doubt about the current (or future) status of a doctrine, we say so. In areas of particularly heated debate, we footnote our work: we want you to have absolute trust in this book.

A Book for Students

We have written this book as if we were speaking directly to our students. We provide black letter law, but we also explain concepts in terms that hook students. Over the years, we have learned how much more successfully we can teach when our students are intrigued. No matter what kind of a show we put on in class, *they are only learning when they want to learn.*

Every chapter begins with a story, either fictional or real, to illustrate the issues in the chapter and provide context. Chapter 21 on cyberlaw begins with the true story of a college student who discovers nude pictures of himself online. These photos had been taken in the locker room without his knowledge. What privacy rights do any of us have? Does the Internet jeopardize them? Students want to know—right away.

Most of today's undergraduates were not yet born when Jimmy Carter was president. They come to college with varying levels of preparation; many now arrive from other countries. We have found that to teach business law most effectively we must provide its context. Chapter 19 on securities regulation begins with a brief but graphic description of the 1929 stock market crash and the Great Depression (page 487). Only with this background do students grasp the importance and impact of our securities laws.

At the same time, we enjoy offering "nuts and bolts" information that grabs students: how much money corporate directors earn or how scam artists create car accidents in order to file fraudulent insurance claims. In Chapter 24 on consumer law, we bring home the issue of credit history by providing Websites that students can use to check their own credit reports (page 627).

Students respond enthusiastically to this approach. One professor asked a student to compare our book with the one that the class was then using. This was the student's reaction: "I really enjoy reading the [Beatty & Samuelson] textbook and I have decided that I will give you this memo ASAP, but I am keeping the book until Wednesday so that I may continue reading. Thanks! :-)"

Along with other professors, we have used this text in courses for undergraduates, MBAs, and executive MBAs, with the students ranging in age from 18 to 55. The book works, as some unsolicited comments indicate:

- An undergraduate wrote, "This is the best textbook I have had in college, on any subject."

- A business law professor stated that the "clarity of presentation is superlative. I have never seen the complexity of contract law made this readable."

- An MBA student commented, "I think the textbook is great. The book is relevant, easy to understand and interesting."

- A state supreme court justice wrote that the book is "a valuable blend of rich scholarship and easy readability. Students and professors should rejoice with this publication."

- A Fortune 500 vice president, enrolled in an Executive MBA program, commented, "I really liked the chapters. They were crisp, organized and current. The information was easy to understand and enjoyable."
- An undergraduate wrote, "The textbook is awesome. A lot of the time I read more than what is assigned—I just don't want to stop."

Humor

Throughout the text we use humor—judiciously—to lighten and enlighten. Not surprisingly, students have applauded—but is wit appropriate? How dare we employ levity in this venerable discipline? We offer humor because we take law seriously. We revere the law for its ancient traditions; its dazzling intricacy; its relentless, though imperfect, attempt to give order and decency to our world. Because we are confident of our respect for the law, we are not afraid to employ some levity. Leaden prose masquerading as legal scholarship does no honor to the field.

Humor also helps retention. We have found that students remember a contract problem described in a fanciful setting, and from that setting recall the underlying principle. By contrast, one widget is hard to distinguish from another.

FEATURES

We chose the features for our book with great care. As mentioned above, all features are considered an essential part of the text and are woven into its body. Also, each feature responds to an essential pedagogical goal. Here are some of those goals and the matching feature.

New Feature: Devil's Advocate

GOAL: Challenge the court's conclusions. In this feature we provide short critical commentary on the decision just reported. We are reminding students that the court's holding is the work of mortals. There is generally a very respectable counter-argument, which at least some people will find more persuasive. Students should consider the opposing view, and should practice formulating their own positions, independent of the judges' reasoning. A student who concludes, after analyzing alternative views, that the court got it right understands the holding more comprehensively than one who never considered the other side.

For example, in Chapter 7 on criminal law, we include the famous *Ewing* case (pages 177–178) on cruel and unusual punishment, but follow it with a Devil's Advocate feature arguing against a sentence of 25 years to life in a recidivist shoplifting case.

New Feature: Public Policy

GOAL: Provide context for understanding the law. What are the policies underlying this case or statute? Why is the law this way? What is the impact of the law? In Chapter 13 on secured transactions and bankruptcy, we discuss Congress's goals in passing the Bankruptcy Abuse Prevention and Consumer Protection Act of 2005 and then ask students to consider whether the statute is likely to be effective in achieving these goals (page 322).

For cases, we consider the impact of the court's decision on the rest of us who were not parties to the litigation. This feature reminds students that a decision prompted by one dispute between two litigants may have dramatic consequences for local communities, companies, families, employees, voters, and many others. What are the financial implications of the holding? Will business costs be passed on to unsuspecting citizens? Who is harmed, who is helped? Is this the *best* possible decision? How would you improve it?

You Be the Judge

GOAL: Get students to think independently. When reading case opinions, students tend to accept the court's "answer." Judges, of course, try to reach decisions that appear indisputable, when in reality they may be controversial—or wrong. From time to time we want students to think through the problem and reach their own answer. Virtually every chapter contains a You Be the Judge feature, providing the facts of the case and conflicting appellate arguments. The court's decision, however, appears only in the Instructor's Manual.

Because students do not know the result, discussions tend to be more free-flowing. For instance, many commentators feel that *Smith v. Van Gorkom*, the landmark case on the business judgment rule, was wrongly decided. However, when students read the court's opinion, they rarely consider the opposing side. Now, with the case presented as You Be the Judge in Chapter 18 (page 470), the students disagree with the court at least half the time. They are thinking.

Economics & the Law

GOAL: Understand the economic impact of the law. This feature helps students understand how laws do (or, in some cases, do not) make economic sense. For example, in Chapter 19 on securities (page 507), we explain why insider trading causes harm and therefore why the law prohibits it. Conversely, Chapter 25 on environmental law (page 649) explains why political considerations often interfere with the most rational environmental decisions.

Newsworthy

GOAL: Prove that the law touches each of us every day. Students are intrigued to see the relevancy of what they are learning. Each chapter contains at least one Newsworthy feature—a newspaper or magazine article illustrating the legal issue under discussion. Thus, in Chapter 14 on agency law (page 342), an article about an American diplomat killed by terrorists demonstrates that an agency relationship exists only when the principal has control over its agent.

Cyberlaw

GOAL: Master the present and anticipate the future. The computer has changed all of our lives forever, and the courts and statute books are full of fascinating cyberlaw issues. Do employers have the right to read workers' e-mail? When does an electronic signature satisfy the statute of frauds? Can a company hold its shareholder meetings in cyberspace? Cyberlaw is fully discussed in Chapter 21: Cyberlaw and Chapter 22: Intellectual Property. Finally, throughout the text we discuss still more cyberlaw issues as they relate to the particular topic; icons highlight those sections.

At Risk

GOAL: Help managers stay out of court. As every lawyer knows, the best lawsuit is the one that never happens. Some of our students are already in the workforce, and the rest soon will be, so we offer ideas on avoiding legal disputes. Sometimes we provide detailed methods to avoid the particular problem; other times we challenge the students to formulate their own approach to dispute prevention. For example, this feature in Chapter 14 on agency law (page 357) explains what an agent must do to avoid personal liability when signing a contract on behalf of a principal.

Ethics

GOAL: Make ethics real. We ask ethical questions about cases, legal issues, and commercial practices. Is it fair for one party to void a contract by arguing, months after the fact, that there was no consideration? Do managers have ethical obligations to older workers for whom employment opportunities may be limited? What is wrong with bribery? What is the ethical obligation of developed nations to dispose of toxic waste from computers? We do not have definitive answers but believe that asking the questions and encouraging discussion reminds students that ethics is an essential element of justice and of a satisfying life.

Update

GOAL: To keep students current. As we go to press, this book is accurate and up-to-date. Inevitably, however, during the book's three-year life span some laws will change. Courts will decide cases; legislatures will pass statutes. When we can foresee that the law is likely to change in a particular area, we ask the students to research the latest developments. For example, in Chapter 21 on cyberlaw, we reported that Congress was considering legislation to require companies to notify customers if their personal information was stolen and ask students to research the status of this law. (See page 558.)

Cases

GOAL: Let the judges speak. Each case begins with a summary of the facts and a statement of the issue. Next comes a tightly edited version of the decision, in the court's own language, so that students "hear" the law developing in the diverse voices of our many judges. We cite cases using a modified bluebook form. In the principal cases in each chapter, we provide the state or federal citation, the regional citation, and the LEXIS or Westlaw citation. We also give students a brief description of the court. Because many of our cases are so recent, some will have only a regional reporter and a LEXIS or Westlaw citation.

Practice Tests

GOAL: Encourage students to practice! At the end of the chapters we challenge the students with ten or more problems, including the following:

- *Internet Research Problem.* This question sends students to an Internet address where they can explore issues from the chapter.

- *You Be the Judge Writing Problem.* The students are given appellate arguments on both sides of the question and must prepare a written opinion.

- *Ethics*. This question highlights the ethical issues of a dispute and calls upon the student to formulate a specific, reasoned response.
- *CPA Questions*. For topics covered by the CPA exam administered by the American Institute of Certified Public Accountants; the practice tests include questions from previous CPA exams.
- *Role Reversal*. Students are asked to formulate their own test questions. Crafting questions is a good way to reinforce what they already understand and recognize areas that they need to review.

TEACHING MATERIALS

For more information about any of these ancillaries, contact your South-Western Legal Studies in Business sales representative for more details, or visit the Beatty Legal Environment Website at **academic.cengage.com/blaw/beatty**.

Instructor's Resource CD (IRCD)

The IRCD contains the Instructor's Manual in Microsoft Word files. This manual includes special features to enhance class discussion and student progress:

- Dialogues. These are a series of questions-and-answers on pivotal cases and topics. The questions provide enough material to teach a full session. In a pinch, you could walk into class with nothing but the manual and use the Dialogues to conduct an exciting class.
- Action learning ideas: interviews, quick research projects, drafting exercises, classroom activities, commercial analyses, and other suggested assignments that get students out of their chairs and into the diverse settings of business law.
- Skits. Various chapters have lively skits that students can perform in class, with no rehearsal, to put legal doctrine in a real-life context.
- A chapter theme and a quote of the day.
- Updates of text material.
- New cases and examples.
- Answers to You Be the Judge cases from the text and to the Practice Test questions found at the end of each chapter.

    The IRCD also includes the ExamView testing software files, the test bank in Microsoft Word files, and the Microsoft PowerPoint lecture slides.

ExamView Testing Software—Computerized Testing Software

This testing software contains all of the questions in the printed test bank. This easy-to-use test creation software program is compatible with Microsoft Windows. Instructors can add or edit questions, instructions, and answers and select questions by previewing them on the screen, selecting them randomly, or selecting them by number. Instructors can also create and administer quizzes online, whether over the Internet, a local area network (LAN), or a wide area network (WAN). The ExamView testing software is available on the Instructor's Resource CD.

Test Bank

The test bank offers hundreds of essay, short answer, and multiple choice problems and may be obtained on the IRCD.

Microsoft PowerPoint® Lecture Review Slides

PowerPoint slides are available for use by students as an aid to note-taking and by instructors for enhancing their lectures. Download these slides at academic.cengage.com/blaw/beatty.

Business Law Digital Video Library

Featuring 60+ segments on the most important topics in Business Law, the Business Law Digital Video Library helps students make the connection between their textbook and the business world. Access to the Business Law Digital Video Library is free when bundled with a new text, and students with used books can purchase access to the video clips online. New to this edition are LawFlix, twelve scenes from Hollywood movies with instructor materials for each film clip. The accompanying instructor materials include elements such as goals for the clips, questions for students (with answers for the instructor), background on the film and the scene, and fascinating trivia about the film, its actors, and its history. For more information about the Business Law Digital Video Library, visit http://digitalvideolibrary.westbuslaw.com.

South-Western Legal Studies in Business Resource Center

This Website offers a unique, rich, and robust online resource for instructors and students. The address academic.cengage.com/blaw provides customer service and product information, links to all text-supporting Websites, and other cutting-edge resources such as NewsEdge and Court Case Updates.

Cengage Learning Custom Solutions

Whether you need print, digital, or hybrid course materials, Cengage Learning Custom Solutions can help you create your perfect learning solution. Draw from Cengage Learning's extensive library of texts and collections, add or create your own original work, and create customized media and technology to match your learning and course objectives. Our editorial team will work with you through each step, allowing you to concentrate on the most important thing—your students. Learn more about all our services at www.custom.cengage.com.

CaseNet

CaseNet is Cengage Learning's legal and business case collection featuring selections from the South-Western Legal Studies in Business case database and other prestigious partners. Using TextChoice you can search, preview, arrange cases, and add your original material or legal cases from your state to create the perfect case resource for your course. To start building your casebook, visit CaseNet at http://www.textchoice.com/casenet or contact your local South-Western Legal Studies sales representative.

Interaction with the Authors

This is our standard: Every professor who adopts this book must have a superior experience. We are available to help in any way we can. Adopters of this text often call or e-mail us to ask questions, obtain a syllabus, offer suggestions, share pedagogical concerns, or inquire about ancillaries. One of the pleasures of working on this project has been our discovery that the text provides a link to so many colleagues around the country. We value those connections, are eager to respond, and would be happy to hear from you.

TO THE STUDENT

Each Practice Test contains one Role Reversal feature in which we challenge you to create your own exam question. Your professor may ask you to submit the questions in writing or electronically or to prepare an overhead slide. The goal is to think creatively and accurately. The question should be challenging enough that the average student will need to stop and think, but clear enough that there is only one answer. Questions can be formatted as essay, short answer, or multiple choice.

For a multiple choice question, the first step is to isolate the single issue that you want to test. For example, in the unit on contract law, you do not want to ask a question that concerns five different aspects of forming an agreement. A good question will focus exclusively on one issue, for example, whether a job offer has to be in writing (some do, others do not). Create a realistic fact pattern that raises the issue. Provide one answer that is clearly correct. Add additional answers that might seem plausible but are definitely incorrect.

Some exam questions are very direct and test whether a student knows a definition. Other questions require deeper analysis. Here are two multiple choice questions. The first is direct.

Question: Which contract is governed by the Uniform Commercial Code?

a. An agreement for an actor to appear in a movie for a $600,000 fee.
b. An agreement for an actor to appear in a movie for a fee of $600,000 plus 2% of box office.
c. An agreement for the sale of a house.
d. An agreement for the sale of 22,000 picture frames.
e. An agreement for the rental of an apartment.

As you will learn later on, the correct answer is (d), because the Code applies to the sale of goods, not to employment contracts or real estate deals.

The next question is more difficult, requiring the student to spot the issue of law involved (product liability), remember how damages are awarded in such cases (generally, without regard to fault), and make a simple calculation.

Question: Lightweight Corp. manufactures strings of Christmas tree lights and sells 3.5 million sets per year. Every year, between 10 and 20 of the company's strings have a manufacturing defect that causes a consumer injury. Maxine receives a severe shock from a Lightweight string of lights. She sues. The evidence at trial is that: 1) Lightweight's safety record is the best in the industry; 2) all competing companies have a higher rate of injuries; 3) the lights that injured Maxine arrived at her house in the factory box, untouched by anyone outside of Lightweight; 4) Maxine operated the lights properly.

Maxine's medical bills amount to $200,000; her lost income is $100,000; and her pain and suffering amounts to $600,000. What is the probable outcome at trial?

a. Maxine will win $200,000.
b. Maxine will win $100,000.
c. Maxine will win $900,000.
d. Maxine will win nothing.
e. Lightweight might win damages for a frivolous lawsuit.

As you will learn, the correct answer is (c). Lightweight is responsible under product liability law regardless of its careful work and excellent record. Maxine is entitled to all of her damages. Notice that the same question could be used in essay format, simply by deleting the multiple choice answers.

ACKNOWLEDGMENTS

We are grateful to the following reviewers who gave such helpful comments on the first two editions of this book:

Lois Beier
Kent State University

William C. Kostner
Doane College

Teri Elkins
University of Houston

Russ Meade
Gardner-Webb University

Lizbeth G. Ellis
New Mexico State University

Bruce L. Rockwood
Bloomsburg University

Paul Fiorelli
Xavier University

Daphyne Saunders Thomas
James Madison University

Gary Greene
Manatee Community College

Jeffrey F. Beatty
Phone: (617) 353-6397
E-mail: jfbeatty@bu.edu

Susan S. Samuelson
Phone: (617) 353-2033
E-mail: ssamuels@bu.edu

THE LEGAL ENVIRONMENT

© GLEN ALLISON/PHOTODISC/GETTY IMAGES

Introduction to Law

© DAVID TOASE/PHOTODISC/GETTY IMAGES

The Pagans were a motorcycle gang with a reputation for violence. Two of its rougher members, Rhino and Backdraft, entered a tavern called the Pub Zone, shoving their way past the bouncer. The pair wore gang insignia, in violation of the bar's rules. For a while, all was quiet, as the two sipped drinks at the bar. Then they followed an innocent patron toward the men's room, and things happened fast.

"Wait a moment," you may be thinking. "Are we reading a chapter on business law or one about biker crimes in a roadside tavern?" Both.

Law is powerful, essential, and fascinating. We hope this book will persuade you of all three ideas. Law can also be surprising. Later in the chapter we will return to the Pub Zone (with armed guards) and follow Rhino and Backdraft to the back of the pub. Yes, the pair engaged in street crime, which is hardly a focus of this text. However, their criminal acts will enable us to explore one of the law's basic principles, negligence. Should a pub owner pay money damages to the victim of gang violence? The owner herself did nothing aggressive. Should she have prevented the harm? Does her failure to stop the assault make her liable?

We place great demands on our courts, asking them to make our large, complex, and sometimes violent society into a safer, fairer, more orderly place. The Pub Zone case is a good example of how judges reason their way through the convoluted issues involved. What began as a gang incident ends up as a matter of commercial liability. We will traipse after Rhino and Backdraft because they have a lesson to teach anyone who enters the world of business. ◼

THREE IMPORTANT IDEAS ABOUT LAW

Power

The strong reach of the law touches us all. To understand something that powerful is itself power. Suppose that, some years after graduation, you are a mid-level manager at Sublime Corp., which manufactures and distributes video games and related hardware and software. You are delighted with this important position in an excellent company—and especially glad you bring legal knowledge to the job. Sarah, an expert at computer-generated imagery, complains that Rob, her boss, is constantly touching her and making lewd comments. That is sexual harassment, and your knowledge of *employment law* helps you respond promptly and carefully. You have dinner with Jake, who has his own software company. Jake wants to manufacture an exciting new video game in cooperation with Sublime, but you are careful not to create a binding deal (*contract law*). Jake mentions that a similar game is already on the market. Do you have the right to market one like it? That answer you already know (*intellectual property law*).

The next day a letter from the Environmental Protection Agency asks how your company disposes of toxic chemicals used to manufacture computer drives. You can discuss it efficiently with in-house counsel, because you have a working knowledge of *environmental law* and *administrative law*. You may think your corporation is about to surge ahead in its field, and you would like to invest in its stock. But wait! Are you engaging in insider trading? Your training in *securities law* will distinguish intelligent investment from felony.

It is not only as a corporate manager that you will confront the law. As a voter, investor, juror, entrepreneur, and community member, you will influence and be affected by the law. Whenever you take a stance about a legal issue, whether in the corporate office, in the voting booth, or as part of a local community group, you help to create the social fabric of our nation. Your views are vital. This book will offer you knowledge and ideas from which to form and continually reassess your legal opinions and values.

Importance

Law is also essential. Every society of which we have any historical record has had some system of laws. Naturally, the systems have varied enormously.

An extraordinary example of a detailed written law comes from the Visigoths, a nomadic European people who overran much of present-day France and Spain during the fifth and sixth centuries A.D. Their code admirably required judges to be "quick of perception, clear in judgment, and lenient in the infliction of penalties." It detailed dozens of crimes. For example, a freeman who kidnapped the slave of another had to repay the owner with four slaves and suffer 100 lashes. If he did not have four slaves to give, the kidnapper was himself reduced to slavery. Sadly, the code explicitly permitted torture of slaves and lower-class freemen, while prohibiting it for nobles.[1] The Iroquois Native Americans, disregarded by many historians, in fact played a role in the creation of our own government. Five major nations made up the Iroquois group: the Mohawk, Cayuga, Oneida, Onondaga, and Seneca. Each nation governed itself regarding domestic issues. But each nation also elected "sachems" to a League of the Iroquois. The league had authority over any matters that were common to all, such as

---

[1] S.P. Scott, *Visigothic Code (Forum Judicum)* (Littleton, CO: Fred B. Rothman & Co., 1982), pp. 3, 45.

relations with outsiders. Thus, by the fifteenth century, the Iroquois had solved the problem of *federalism:* how to have two levels of government, each with specified powers. Their system impressed Benjamin Franklin and others and influenced the drafting of our Constitution, with its powers divided between state and federal governments.[2] As European nations today seek to create a more united Europe, they struggle with the same problem.

The greatest of all Chinese lawgivers disliked written law altogether. Confucius, who lived from 551 to 479 B.C.E., understood law within a broader social perspective. He considered good rulers, strong family ties, and an enlightened nobility to be the surest methods to a good society. "As a judge, I decide disputes, for that is my duty; but the best thing that could happen would be to eliminate the causes for litigation!" Although he spoke 2,500 years ago, the distinction Confucius described is still critically important in our society: Which do we trust more—a written law or the people who enforce it?

Fascination

In 1835 the young French aristocrat Alexis de Tocqueville traveled through the United States, observing the newly democratic people and the qualities that made them unique. One of the things that struck de Tocqueville most forcefully was the American tendency to file suit: "Scarcely any political question arises in the United States that is not resolved, sooner or later, into a judicial question."[3] De Tocqueville got it right: For better or worse, we do expect courts to solve many problems.

Not only do Americans litigate—they watch each other do it. Every television season offers at least one new courtroom drama to a national audience breathless for more cross-examination. Almost all the states permit live television coverage of real trials. The most heavily viewed event in the history of the medium was the O.J. Simpson murder trial. Nonetheless, cameras in the courthouse are still controversial. Federal courts generally prohibit them. Only a small (but growing) number of foreign countries allows coverage of some judicial proceedings, including Australia, Canada, France, Hong Kong, Israel, Italy, the Netherlands, Norway, the Philippines, and Spain. Proponents urge that televising trials increases awareness of social ills and reduces the chances of judicial unfairness. Opponents argue that the camera transforms a dignified search for truth into a carnival show of publicity gimmicks.

Regardless of where we allow cameras, it is an undeniable benefit of the electronic age that we can obtain information so quickly. From time to time we will mention Websites of interest. Some of these are for nonprofit groups, while others are commercial sites. We do not endorse or advocate on behalf of any group or company but simply wish to alert you to what is out there. The commercial site of a cable television company devoted to trial broadcasts, http://www.courttv.com/, includes up-to-the-minute information on current cases, often including trial testimony, appeal briefs, and other timely data.

The law is a big part of our lives, and it is wise to know something about it. Within a few weeks, you will probably find yourself following legal events in the news with keener interest and deeper understanding. In this chapter, we develop the background for our study. We look at where law comes from: its history and its present-day institutions. In the section on jurisprudence, we examine different theories about what "law" really means. And finally we see how courts—and students—analyze a case.

---

2 Jack Weatherford, *Indian Givers* (New York: Fawcett Columbine, 1988), pp. 133–150.
3 Alexis de Tocqueville, *Democracy in America* (1835), Vol. 1, Ch. 16.

ORIGINS OF OUR LAW

It would be nice if we could look up "the law" in one book, memorize it, and then apply it. But the law is not that simple, and *cannot* be that simple, because it reflects the complexity of contemporary life. In truth, there is no such thing as "the law." Principles and rules of law actually come from many different sources. Why is this so? In part because we inherited a complex structure of laws from England. We will see that by the time of the American Revolution, English law was already an intricate system.

Additionally, ours is a nation born in revolution and created, in large part, to protect the rights of its people from the government. The Founding Fathers created a national government but insisted that the individual states maintain control in many areas. As a result, each state has its own government with exclusive power over many important areas of our lives. To top it off, the Founders guaranteed many rights to the people alone, ordering national *and* state governments to keep clear. This has worked, but it has caused a multilayered system, with 50 state governments and one federal government all creating and enforcing law.

A summary of English legal history will show the origin of our legal institutions. This brisk survey will also demonstrate that certain problems never go away. Anglo-Saxon England, about 1,000 years ago, was a world utterly different from our own. Yet we can see uncanny foreshadowings of our own unfinished efforts to create a peaceful world.

English Roots

England in the tenth century was a rustic agricultural community with a tiny population and very little law or order. Danes and Swedes invaded repeatedly, terrorizing the Anglo-Saxon peoples. Criminals were hard to catch in the heavily forested, sparsely settled nation. The king used a primitive legal system to maintain a tenuous control over his people.

England was divided into shires, and daily administration was carried out by a "shire reeve," later called a sheriff. The shire reeve collected taxes and did what he could to keep peace, apprehending criminals and acting as mediator between feuding families. Two or three times a year, a shire court met; lower courts met more frequently.

Contemporary law: Mediation lives on. As we discuss in Chapter 3, on dispute resolution, lawsuits have grown ever more costly. Increasingly, companies are turning to mediation to settle disputes. The humble shire reeve's work is back in vogue.

Because there were so few officers to keep the peace, Anglo-Saxon society created an interesting method of ensuring public order. Every freeman (nonslave) belonged to a group of 10 freemen known as a "tithing," headed by a "tithingman." If anyone injured a person outside his tithing or interfered with the king's property, all 10 men of the tithing could be forced to pay.

Contemporary law: Today, we still use this idea of collective responsibility. In a business partnership, all partners are personally responsible for the debts of the partnership. They could potentially lose their homes and all assets because of the irresponsible conduct of one partner. That liability has helped create new forms of business organization, including limited liability companies, which we discuss in Chapter 17 on starting a business.

When cases did come before an Anglo-Saxon court, the parties would often be represented either by a clergyman, by a nobleman, or by themselves. There were few professional lawyers. Each party produced "oath helpers," usually 12, who would swear that one version of events was correct. The court explicitly gave greater credence to oath helpers from the nobility.

Contemporary law: The Anglo-Saxon oath helpers were probably forerunners of our modern jury of 12 persons. But as to who is telling the truth, that is a question that will never disappear. We deny giving a witness greater credence because of his or her status. But is that accurate? Some commentators believe that jurors are overly impressed with "expert witnesses," such as doctors or engineers, and ignore their own common sense when faced with such "pedigreed" people.

In 1066 the Normans conquered England. William the Conqueror made a claim never before made in England: that he owned all the land. The king then granted sections of his lands to his favorite noblemen, as his tenants in chief, creating the system of feudalism. These tenants in chief then granted parts of their land to *tenants in demesne*, who actually occupied a particular estate. Each tenant in demesne owed fidelity to his lord (hence "landlord"). So what? Just this: Land became the most valuable commodity in all of England, and our law still reflects that.

Contemporary law: One thousand years later, American law still regards land as special. The statute of frauds, which we study in the section on contracts, demands that contracts for the sale or lease of property be in writing. And landlord-tenant law, vital to students and many others, still reflects its ancient roots. Some of a landlord's rights are based on the 1,000-year-old tradition that land is uniquely valuable.

In 1250, Henry de Bracton (d. 1268) wrote a legal treatise that still influences us. *De Legibus et Consuetudinibus Angliae (On the Laws and Customs of England)*, written in Latin, summarized many of the legal rulings in cases since the Norman Conquest. de Bracton was teaching judges to rule based on previous cases. He was helping to establish the idea of *precedent.* **The doctrine of precedent, which developed gradually over centuries, requires that judges decide current cases based on previous rulings.**

Contemporary law: This vital principle is the heart of American common law. Precedent ensures predictability. Suppose a 17-year-old student promises to lease an apartment from a landlord but then changes her mind. The landlord sues to enforce the lease. The student claims that she cannot be held to the agreement because she is a minor. The judge will look for precedent—that is, older cases dealing with the same issue—and he will find many holding that a contract generally may not be enforced against a minor. That precedent is binding on this case, and the student wins. The accumulation of precedent, based on case after case, makes up the **common law.**

During the next few centuries, judges and lawyers acquired special training and skills. Some lawyers began to plead cases full-time and gained unique skill—and power. They represented only those who could pay well.

Parliament passed an ever greater number of laws, generally called **statutes,** the word we still use to mean a law passed by a legislative body. Parliament's statutes swelled in number and complexity until they were unfathomable to anyone but a lawyer.

Contemporary law: Our society still struggles with unequal access to legal talent. Rich people often fare better in court than poor. And many Americans regard law as byzantine and incomprehensible. A primary purpose of this text is to remove the mystique from the law and to empower you to participate in legal matters.

As lawyers became more highly skilled, they searched ever wider for ways to defeat the other side. One method was by attacking the particular writ in the case. The party bringing the case was called the plaintiff. His first task was to obtain a **writ,** which was a letter from the central government ordering a court to hear the case. Each type of lawsuit required a different writ. For example, a landlord's lawsuit against a tenant required one kind of writ, whereas a claim of assault needed a different one. If a court decided that the plaintiff's lawyer had used the wrong writ, it would dismiss the lawsuit. This encouraged lawyers for the defendant to attack the writ itself, claiming it was inappropriate. By doing that, they could perhaps defeat the case without ever answering who did what to whom.

Contemporary law: This is the difference between procedure and substance, which will become clear during the course. **Substantive** rules of law state the rights of the parties.

For example, it is substantive law that if you have paid the purchase price of land and accepted the deed, you are entitled to occupy the property. **Procedural** rules tell how a court should go about settling disputes. For example, what evidence can be used to establish that you *did* pay for the property? How much evidence is necessary? Who may testify about whether you paid? Those are all issues of procedural law. To this day, lawyers attack procedural aspects of an opponent's case before dealing with the substantive rights.

Here is an actual case from more than six centuries ago, in the court's own language. The dispute illustrates that some things have changed but others never do. The plaintiff claims that he asked the defendant to heal his eye with "herbs and other medicines." He says the defendant did it so badly that he blinded the plaintiff in that eye.

THE OCULIST'S CASE (1329)

LI MS. Hale 137 (1), fo. 150, Nottingham*

Attorney Launde [for defendant]: Sir, you plainly see how [the plaintiff claims] that he had submitted himself to [the defendant's] medicines and his care; and after that he can assign no trespass in his person, inasmuch as he submitted himself to his care: but this action, if he has any, sounds naturally in breach of covenant. We demand [that the case be dismissed].

Excerpts from Judge Denum's Decision: I saw a Newcastle man arraigned before my fellow justice and me for the death of a man. I asked the reason for the indictment, and it was said that he had slain a man under his care, who died within four days afterwards. And because I saw that he was a [doctor] and that he had not done the thing feloniously but [accidentally] I ordered him to be discharged. And suppose a blacksmith, who is a man of skill, injures your horse with a nail, whereby you lose your horse: you shall never have recovery against him. No more shall you here.

Afterwards the plaintiff did not wish to pursue his case any more. ■

This case from 1329 is an ancient medical malpractice case. Defendant's lawyer makes a procedural argument. Attorney Launde does not deny that his client blinded the plaintiff. He claims that the plaintiff has brought the wrong kind of lawsuit. Launde argues that the plaintiff should have brought a case of "covenant"— that is, a lawsuit about a contract.

Judge Denum decides the case on a different principle. He gives judgment to the defendant because the plaintiff voluntarily sought medical care. He implies that the defendant would lose only if he had attacked the plaintiff. As we will see when we study negligence law, this case might have a different outcome today. Note also the informality of the judge's ruling. He rather casually mentions that he came across a related case once before and that he would stand by that outcome. The idea of precedent is just beginning to take hold.

Sometimes a judge refused to hear a case, ruling that no such claims were legal. The injured party might then take his case to the Chancellor, in London, whose status in the king's council gave him unique, flexible powers. This *Court of Chancery* had no jury.

---

* J. Baker and S. Milsom, *Sources of English Legal History* (London: Butterworth & Co., 1986).

The court's duty was to accomplish what "good conscience" required—that is, an *equitable* result—and so this more creative use of a court's power became known as **equity.**

Contemporary law: In present-day America, judges still exercise equity powers, based on those cases the Chancery Court accepted. For example, a court today might issue an injunction requiring a factory owner to stop polluting the air. The injunction (order to stop) is an equitable remedy. Only a judge can exercise equitable powers because historically Chancery had no jury. If a judge grants an injunction, she is said to be exercising equitable powers.

Parliament added statutes on more and more matters, at times conflicting with common-law rulings of the various judges. What should a court do when faced with a statute that contradicts well-established precedent? In the seventeenth century, one of England's greatest judges, Lord Coke, addressed the problem. In *Dr. Bonham's Case,* Lord Coke ruled that "when an Act of Parliament is against Common right and reason, or repugnant, or impossible to be performed, the Common Law will control it and adjudge such Act to be void."[4]

Audacious man! In a decision of breathtaking strength, Lord Coke declared that a single judge could overrule the entire Parliament, based on what the judge might consider "Common right and reason." This same tension carries on today between elected officials, such as state legislators, and courts, which sometimes declare acts of the legislatures void.

Of course, by the time Lord Coke was on the bench, in the seventeenth century, English common law had also spread across the ocean to the newly created colonies. We will pick up the story in America.

Law in the United States

The colonists brought with them a basic knowledge of English law, some of which they were content to adopt as their own. Other parts, such as religious restrictions, were abhorrent to them. Many had made the dangerous trip to America precisely to escape persecution, and they were not interested in recreating their difficulties in a new land. Finally, some laws were simply irrelevant or unworkable in a world that was socially and geographically so different. American law ever since has been a whitewater river created from two strong currents: One carries the ancient principles of English common law, the other, a zeal and determination for change.

During the nineteenth century, the United States changed from a weak, rural nation into one of vast size and potential power. Cities grew, factories appeared, and sweeping movements of social migration changed the population. Changing conditions raised new legal questions. Did workers have a right to form industrial unions? To what extent should a manufacturer be liable if its product injured someone? Could a state government invalidate an employment contract that required 16-hour workdays? Should one company be permitted to dominate an entire industry?

In the twentieth century, the rate of social and technological change increased, creating new legal puzzles. Were some products, such as automobiles, so inherently dangerous that the seller should be responsible for injuries even if no mistakes were made in manufacturing? Who should clean up toxic waste if the company that had caused the pollution no longer existed? If a consumer signed a contract with a billion-dollar corporation, should the agreement be enforced even if the consumer never understood it? As we venture into this millennium, new and startling questions are certain to confront us. Before we can begin to examine the answers, we need to understand the sources of contemporary law.

---

[4] Eng. Rep. 638 (C.P. 1610).

SOURCES OF CONTEMPORARY LAW

During the colonial period, there were few trained lawyers and fewer law books in America. After the Revolution that changed, and law became a serious, professional career. The first great legal achievement was the adoption of the United States Constitution.

Constitutions

United States Constitution

The United States Constitution, adopted in 1788 by the original 13 colonies, is the supreme law of the land.[5] Any law that conflicts with it is void. This Federal Constitution, as it is also known, does three basic things. First, it establishes the national government of the United States, with its three branches. The Constitution creates the Congress, with a Senate and a House of Representatives, and prescribes what laws Congress may pass. The same document establishes the office of the president and the duties that go with it. And it creates the third branch of government, the federal courts, describing what cases they may hear.

Second, the Constitution ensures that the states retain all power not given to the national government. This simple idea has meant that state governments play an important role in all of our lives. Major issues of family law, criminal law, property law, and many other areas are regulated predominantly by the various states.

Third, the Constitution guarantees many basic rights to the American people. Most of these rights are found in the amendments to the Constitution. The First Amendment guarantees the rights of free speech, free press, and the free exercise of religion. The Fourth, Fifth, and Sixth Amendments protect the rights of any person accused of a crime. Other amendments ensure that the government treats all people equally and that it pays for any property it takes from a citizen. Merely by creating a limited government of three branches and guaranteeing basic liberties to all citizens, the Constitution became one of the most important documents ever written.

State Constitutions

In addition to the Federal Constitution, each state has a constitution that establishes its own government. All states have an executive (the governor), a legislature, and a court system. Thus there are two entire systems of government affecting each of us: a federal government, with power over the entire country, and a state government, exercising those powers that the United States Constitution did not grant to the federal government. This is federalism at work.

Statutes

The second important source of law is statutory law. The Constitution gave to the United States Congress the power to pass laws on various subjects. These laws are statutes, like those passed by the English Parliament. For example, the Constitution allows Congress to pass statutes about the military: to appropriate money, reorganize divisions, and close bases. You can find any federal statute, on any subject, at the Website of the United States House of Representatives, which is http://www.house.gov/.

State legislatures also pass statutes. Each state constitution allows the legislature to pass laws on a variety of subjects. All state legislatures, for example, may pass statutes about family law issues such as divorce and child custody.

---

[5] The complete text of the Constitution appears in Appendix A.

Common Law

As we have seen, the common law originated in England as lawyers began to record decisions and urge judges to follow earlier cases. As judges started to do that, the earlier cases, called *precedent*, took on steadily greater importance. Eventually, judges were *obligated* to follow precedent. **The principle that precedent is binding on later cases is *stare decisis*, which means "let the decision stand."** *Stare decisis* makes the law predictable, and this in turn enables businesses and private citizens to plan intelligently.

Equity

Principles of equity, created by the Chancellor in England, traveled to the colonies along with the common-law rules. All states permit courts to use equitable powers. An example of a contemporary equitable power is an *injunction*, a court order that someone stop doing something. Suppose a music company is about to issue a new compact disc by a well-known singer, but a composer claims that the recording artist has stolen his song. The composer, claiming copyright violation, could seek an injunction to prevent the company from issuing the compact disc. Every state has a trial court that can issue injunctions and carry out other equitable relief. As was true in medieval England, there is no jury in an equity case.

Administrative Law

In a society as large and diverse as ours, the executive and legislative branches of government cannot oversee all aspects of commerce. Congress passes statutes about air safety, but U.S. senators do not stand around air traffic towers, serving coffee to keep everyone awake. The executive branch establishes rules concerning how foreign nationals enter the United States, but presidents are reluctant to sit on the dock of the bay, watching the ships come in. **Administrative agencies** do this day-to-day work.

Most administrative agencies are created by Congress or by a state legislature. Familiar examples at the federal level are the Federal Communications Commission (FCC), which regulates most telecommunications; the Federal Trade Commission (FTC), which oversees interstate trade; and the Internal Revenue Service, whose feelings are hurt if it does not hear from you every April 15. At the state level, regulators set insurance rates for all companies in the state, control property development and land use, and regulate many other issues.

Other Sources of Law

Treaties

The Constitution authorizes the president to make treaties with foreign nations. These must then be ratified by the United States Senate. When they are ratified, they are as binding upon all citizens as any federal statute. In 1994 the Senate ratified the North American Free Trade Agreement (NAFTA) with Mexico and Canada. NAFTA was controversial then and remains so today—but it is now the law of the land.

Executive Orders

In theory all statutes must originate in Congress or a state legislature. But in fact, executives also legislate by issuing executive orders. For example, in 1970 Congress authorized

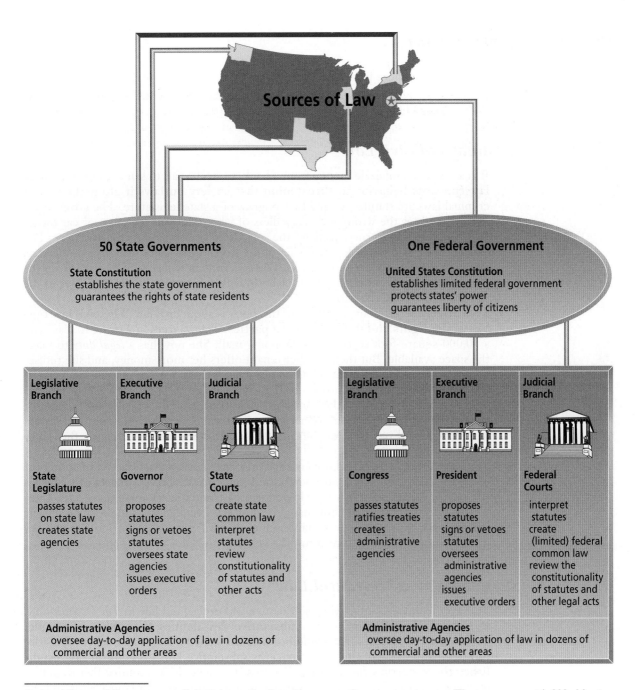

Sources of Law

50 State Governments

State Constitution
establishes the state government
guarantees the rights of state residents

Legislative Branch

State Legislature

passes statutes
  on state law
creates state
  agencies

Executive Branch

Governor

proposes
  statutes
signs or vetoes
  statutes
oversees state
  agencies
issues executive
  orders

Judicial Branch

State Courts

create state
  common law
interpret
  statutes
review
  constitutionality
  of statutes and
  other acts

Administrative Agencies
oversee day-to-day application of law in dozens of
commercial and other areas

One Federal Government

United States Constitution
establishes limited federal government
protects states' power
guarantees liberty of citizens

Legislative Branch

Congress

passes statutes
ratifies treaties
creates
  administrative
  agencies

Executive Branch

President

proposes
  statutes
signs or vetoes
  statutes
oversees
  administrative
  agencies
issues
  executive orders

Judicial Branch

Federal Courts

interpret
  statutes
create
  (limited) federal
  common law
review the
  constitutionality
  of statutes and
  other legal acts

Administrative Agencies
oversee day-to-day application of law in dozens of
commercial and other areas

Federal Form of Government. Principles and rules of law come from many sources. The government in Washington creates and enforces law throughout the nation. But 50 state governments exercise great power in local affairs. And citizens enjoy constitutional protection from both state and federal government. The Founding Fathers wanted this balance of power and rights, but the overlapping authority creates legal complexity.

President Nixon to issue wage-price controls in an effort to stabilize the economy. This was a colossal grant of power, allowing the president personally to regulate the nation's economy. Critics charge that Congress should not give away the powers that the people have granted to it, and such delegations of authority have led to extensive lawsuits.

CLASSIFICATIONS OF LAW

We have seen where law comes from. Now we need to classify the law into different types. We use three main classifications throughout this book: criminal and civil law, substantive and procedural law, and public and private law.

Criminal and Civil Law

It is a crime to embezzle money from a bank, to steal a car, to sell cocaine. **Criminal law concerns behavior so threatening that society outlaws it altogether.** Most criminal laws are statutes, passed by Congress or a state legislature. The government itself prosecutes the wrongdoer, regardless of what the bank president or car owner wants. A district attorney, paid by the government, brings the case to court. The injured party—for example, the owner of the stolen car—is not in charge of the case, although she may appear as a witness. The government will seek to punish the defendant with a prison sentence, a fine, or both. If there is a fine, the money goes to the state, not to the injured party.

Civil law is different, and most of this book is about civil law. **The civil law regulates the rights and duties between parties.** Tracy agrees in writing to lease you a 30,000-square-foot store in her shopping mall. She now has a *legal duty* to make the space available. But then another tenant offers her more money, and she refuses to let you move in. Tracy has violated her duty, but she has not committed a crime. The government will not prosecute the case. It is up to you to file a civil lawsuit. Your case will be based on the common law of contract. You will also seek equitable relief, namely, an injunction ordering Tracy not to lease to anyone else. You should win the suit, and you will get your injunction and some money damages. But Tracy will not go to jail.

Some conduct involves both civil and criminal law. Suppose Tracy is so upset over losing the court case that she becomes drunk and causes a serious car accident. She has committed the crime of driving while intoxicated, and the state will prosecute. Tracy may be fined or imprisoned. She has also committed negligence, and the injured party will file a lawsuit against her, seeking money. We will again see civil and criminal law joined together when we return to the *Pub Zone* case, later in the chapter.

Substantive and Procedural Law

We saw the distinction between substantive and procedural law in *The Oculist's Case*, and it remains important today. **Substantive law defines the rights of people.** Substantive law requires that a landlord who has signed a lease must deliver the store to her tenant. Most of this book concerns substantive law. **Procedural law establishes the processes for settling disputes.** Procedural law requires that to get an injunction against Tracy, you must first notify her in writing of your claims and the time and place of the hearing on the injunction.

Public and Private Law

Public law refers to the rights and obligations of governments as they deal with the nation's citizens. For example, when the Federal Trade Commission prohibits deceptive advertising, that is public law. **Private law** regulates the duties between individuals. Landlord-tenant law is private law.

JURISPRUDENCE

We have had a glimpse of legal history and a summary of the present-day sources of American law. But what *is* law? That question is the basis of a field known as **jurisprudence.** How do we distinguish a moral rule from a legal rule? What is the real nature of law? Can there be such a thing as an "illegal" law?

Law and Morality

Law is different from morality, yet the two are obviously linked. There are many instances when the law duplicates what all of us would regard as a moral position. It is negligence to drive too fast in a school district, and few would dispute the moral value of that law. And similarly with contract law: If the owner of land agrees in writing to sell property to a buyer at a stated price, the seller must go through with the deal, and the legal outcome matches our moral expectations.

On the other hand, we have had laws that we now clearly regard as immoral. At the turn of the century, a factory owner could typically fire a worker for any reason at all—including, for example, his religious or political views. Today we would say it is immoral to fire a worker because she is Jewish—and the law prohibits it.

Finally, there are legal issues where the morality is not so clear. You are walking down a country lane and notice a three-year-old child playing with matches near a barn filled with hay. Are you obligated to intervene? No, says the law, though many think that is preposterous. (See Chapter 4 on common law for details.) A company buys property and then discovers, buried under the ground, toxic waste that will cost $300,000 to clean up. The original owner has gone bankrupt. Should the new owner be forced to pay for the cleanup? If the new owner fails to pay for the job, who will? (See Chapter 25, on environmental law.)

Legal Positivism

This philosophy can be simply stated: Law is what the sovereign says it is. The **sovereign** is the recognized political power whom citizens obey, so in the United States, both state and federal governments are sovereign. A legal positivist holds that whatever the sovereign declares to be the law *is* the law, whether it is right or wrong.

The primary criticism of legal positivism is that it seems to leave no room for questions of morality. A law permitting a factory owner to fire a worker because she is Catholic is surely different from a law prohibiting arson. Do citizens in a democracy have a duty to consider such differences?

NEWS*worthy*

Most states allow citizens to pass laws directly at the ballot box, a process called voter referendum. California voters often do this, and during the 1990s, they passed one of the state's most controversial laws. Proposition 187 was designed to curb illegal immigration into the state by eliminating social spending for undocumented aliens. Citizens debated the measure fiercely but passed it by a large margin. One section of the new law forbade public schools from educating illegal immigrants. The law obligated a principal to inquire into the immigration status of all children enrolled in the school and to report undocumented students to immigration authorities. Several San Diego school principals rejected the new rules, stating that they would neither inquire into immigration status nor report undocumented aliens. Their statements produced a heated response. Some San Diego residents castigated the school officials as lawbreakers, claiming that

- A school officer who knowingly disobeyed a law was setting a terrible example for students, who would assume they were free to do the same;
- The principals were advocating permanent residence and a free education for anyone able to evade our immigration laws; and
- The officials were scorning grass-roots democracy by disregarding a law passed by popular referendum.

Others applauded the principals' position, asserting that

- The referendum's rules would transform school officials from educators into border police, forcing them to cross-examine young children and their parents;
- The new law was foolish because it punished innocent children for violations committed by their parents; and
- Our nation has long respected civil disobedience based on humanitarian ideals, and these officials were providing moral leadership to the whole community.

Ultimately, no one had to decide whether to obey Proposition 187. A federal court ruled that only Congress had the power to regulate immigration and that California's attempt was unconstitutional and void. The debate over immigration reform—and ethics—did not end, however. Congress periodically considers proposals to cut social benefits for illegal immigrants. ◆

Natural Law

St. Thomas Aquinas (1225–1274) answered the legal positivists even before they had spoken. In his *Summa Theologica*, he argued that an unjust law is no law at all and need not be obeyed. It is not enough that a sovereign makes a command. The law must have a moral basis.

Where do we find the moral basis that would justify a law? Aquinas says that "good is that which all things seek after." Therefore, the fundamental rule of all laws is that "good is to be done and promoted, and evil is to be avoided." This sounds appealing but also vague. Exactly which laws promote good and which do not? Is it better to have a huge corporation dominate a market or many smaller companies competing? Did the huge company get that way by being better than its competitors? If Wal-Mart moves into a rural area, establishes a mammoth store, and sells inexpensive products, is that "good"? Yes, if you are a consumer who cares only about prices. No, if you are the owner of a Main Street store driven into bankruptcy. Maybe, if you are a resident who values small-town life but wants lower prices.

Natural law debates are eternal. One of the greatest of the ancient Greek dramatists, Sophocles (496–406 B.C.E.), touches upon the subject in one of his famous plays, *Antigone*. Oedipus's two sons, Eteocles and Polyneices, have arranged to rule Thebes in rotation, but when Eteocles refuses to give up the throne, Polyneices and his many supporters attack the city. Both brothers are killed in the battle. Creon, who inherits the crown, declares that Eteocles will receive a hero's burial but that Polyneices must lie exposed in the dust. Anyone attempting to bury him will be executed. Antigone, the sister of the dead men, is horrified. Declaring that religious beliefs compel her to rescue her brother's soul from perpetual torment, she attempts to bury Polyneices. Antigone admits to Creon that she understood his ruling, but retorts, in the language of natural law:

> [Your] order did not come from God. Justice,
> That dwells with the gods below, knows no such law.
> I did not think your edicts strong enough

To overrule the unwritten unalterable laws
Of God and heaven, you being only a man.
They are not of yesterday or to-day, but everlasting,
Though where they came from, none of us can tell.[6]

Creon, a legal positivist, responds simply and forcefully that "Our country is our life." Any attack upon the city-state warrants death, as does any disobedience of its laws. Ultimately, he orders Antigone to her death and then, inevitably, regrets his decision.

Two thousand five hundred years later, we still debate the meaning and significance of natural law. Court cases and political debates about abortion, stem cell research, school prayer, evolution, and euthanasia all echo the themes disputed by Creon and Antigone.

What does natural law tell us about abortion? Abortion supporters, or those advocating free choice, will say that natural law protects a woman's reproductive rights and that it is violent and unnatural for any government to tell a woman what to do with her body. Opponents of abortion reach the opposite conclusion, arguing that no good can come from terminating the life of a fetus and that a law permitting abortion is no law at all. What do you think?

Legal Realism

Legal realists take a very different tack. They claim it does not matter what is written as law. What counts is who enforces that law and by what process. All of us are biased by issues such as income, education, family background, race, religion, and many other factors. These personal characteristics, they say, determine which contracts will be enforced and which ignored, why some criminals receive harsh sentences while others get off lightly, and so on.

Judge Jones hears a multimillion dollar lawsuit involving an airplane crash. Was the airline negligent? The law is the same everywhere, but legal realists say that Jones's background will determine the outcome. If she spent 20 years representing insurance companies, she will tend to favor the airline. If her law practice consisted of helping the "little guy," she will favor the plaintiff.

Other legal realists argue, more aggressively, that those in power use the machinery of the law to perpetuate their control. The outcome of a given case will be determined by the needs of those with money and political clout. A court puts "window dressing" on a decision, they say, so that society thinks there are principles behind the law. A problem with legal realism, however, is its denial that any lawmaker can overcome personal bias. Yet clearly some do act unselfishly.

Summary of Jurisprudence	
Legal Positivism	Law is what the sovereign says.
Natural Law	An unjust law is no law at all.
Legal Realism	Who enforces the law counts more than what is in writing.

No one school of jurisprudence is likely to seem perfect. We urge you to keep the different theories in mind as you read cases in the book. Ask yourself which school of thought is the best fit for you.

---

6 Sophocles, *Antigone*, translated by E.F. Watling in *Sophocles, The Theban Plays* (New York: Penguin, 1964).

WORKING WITH THE BOOK'S FEATURES

In this section we introduce a few of the book's features and discuss how you can use them effectively. We will start with *cases.*

Analyzing a Case

A law case is the decision a court has made in a civil lawsuit or criminal prosecution. Cases are the heart of the law and an important part of this book. Reading them effectively takes practice. Let us return to the Pub Zone tavern, which we visited in the chapter's opener, and see what we can learn about courts and the law.

KUEHN V. PUB ZONE

364 N.J. Super. 301, 835 A.2d 692
Superior Court of New Jersey, Appellate Division, 2003

Facts: Maria Kerkoulas owned the Pub Zone bar. She knew that several motorcycle gangs frequented the tavern. From her own experience tending bar, and conversations with city police, she knew that some of the gangs, including the Pagans, were dangerous and prone to attack customers for no reason. Kerkoulas posted a sign prohibiting any motorcycle gangs from entering the bar while wearing "colors," that is, insignia of their gangs. She believed that gangs without their colors were less prone to violence, and experience proved her right.

Rhino, Backdraft, and several other Pagans, all wearing colors, pushed their way past the tavern's bouncer and approached the bar. Although Kerkoulas saw their colors, she allowed them to stay for one drink. They later moved toward the back of the pub, and Kerkoulas believed they were departing. In fact, they followed a customer named Karl Kuehn to the men's room, where without any provocation they savagely beat him. Kuehn was knocked unconscious and suffered brain hemorrhaging, disc herniation, and numerous fractures of facial bones. He was forced to undergo various surgeries, including eye reconstruction.

Although the government prosecuted Rhino and Backdraft for their vicious assault, our case does not concern that prosecution. Kuehn sued the Pub Zone, and that is the case we will read. The jury awarded him $300,000 in damages. However, the trial court judge overruled the jury's verdict. He granted a judgment for the Pub Zone, meaning that the tavern owed nothing. The judge ruled that the pub's owner could not have foreseen the attack on Kuehn and had no duty to protect him from an outlaw motorcycle gang. Kuehn appealed, and the appeals court's decision follows:

Issue: Did the Pub Zone have a duty to protect Kuehn from the Pagans' attack?

Excerpts from Judge Payne's Decision: Whether a duty exists depends upon an evaluation of a number of factors including the nature of the underlying risk of harm, that is, its foreseeability and severity, the opportunity and ability to exercise care to prevent the harm, the comparative interests of and the relationships between or among the parties, and, ultimately, based on considerations of public policy and fairness, the societal interest in the proposed solution.

Since the possessor [of a business] is not an insurer of the visitor's safety, he is ordinarily under no duty to exercise any care until he knows or has reason to know that the acts of the third person are occurring, or are about to occur. He may, however, know or have reason to know, from past experience, that there is a likelihood of conduct on the part of third persons in general which is likely to endanger the safety of the visitor, even though he has no reason to expect it on the part of any particular individual.

We find the totality of the circumstances presented in this case give rise to a duty on the part of the Pub Zone to have taken reasonable precautions against the danger posed by the Pagans as a group. In this case, there was no reason to suspect any particular Pagan of violent conduct. However, the gang was collectively known to Kerkoulas to engage in

▼

random violence. Thus, Kerkoulas had knowledge as the result of past experience and from other sources that there was a likelihood of conduct on the part of third persons in general that was likely to endanger the safety of a patron at some unspecified future time. A duty to take precautions against the endangering conduct thus arose.

We do not regard our recognition of a duty in this case to give rise to either strict or absolute liability on the part of the Pub Zone. To fulfill its duty in this context, the Pub Zone was merely required to employ "reasonable" safety precautions. It already had in place a prohibition against bikers who were wearing their colors, and that prohibition, together with the practice of calling the police when a breach occurred, had been effective in greatly diminishing the occurrence of biker incidents on the premises. The evidence establishes that the prohibition was not enforced on the night at issue, that three Pagans were permitted entry while wearing their colors, and the police were not called. Once entry was achieved, the Pub Zone remained under a duty to exercise reasonable precautions against an attack.

The jury's verdict must therefore be reinstated. ∎

Analysis

Let's take it from the top. The case is called *Kuehn v. Pub Zone*. Karl Kuehn is the **plaintiff,** the person who is suing. The Pub Zone is being sued and is called the **defendant.** In this example, the plaintiff's name happens to appear first but that is not always true. When a defendant loses a trial and files an appeal, *some* courts reverse the names of the parties.

The next line gives the legal citation, which indicates where to find the case in a law library. We explain in the footnote how to locate a book if you plan to do research.[7]

The *Facts* section provides a background to the lawsuit, written by the authors of this text. The court's own explanation of the facts is often many pages long and may involve complex matters irrelevant to the subject covered in this book, so we relate only what is necessary. This section will usually include some mention of what happened at the trial court. Lawsuits always begin in a trial court. The losing party often appeals to a court of appeals, and it is usually an appeals court decision that we are reading. The trial judge ruled in favor of Pub Zone, but later, in the decision we are reading, Kuehn wins.

The *Issue* section is very important. It tells you what the court had to decide—and also why you are reading the case. In giving its decision, a court may digress. If you keep in mind the issue and relate the court's discussion to it, you will not get lost.

Excerpts from Judge Payne's Decision begins the court's discussion. This is called the *holding*, meaning a statement of who wins and who loses. The holding also includes the court's *rationale*, which is the reasoning behind the decision.

The holding that we provide is an edited version of the court's own language. Some judges write clear, forceful prose; others do not. Either way, their words give you an authentic feel for how judges think and rule, so we bring it to you in the original. Occasionally we use brackets, "[ ]," to substitute our language for that of the court, either to condense or to clarify. Notice the brackets in the second paragraph of

---

[7] If you want to do legal research, you need to know where to find particular legal decisions. A case citation guides you to the correct volume(s). The full citation of our case is *Kuehn v. Pub Zone*, 364 N.J. Super. 301, 835 A.2d 692. The string of numbers identifies two different books in which you can find the full text of this decision. The first citation is to "N.J. Super," which means the official court reporter of the state of New Jersey. New Jersey, like most states, reports its law cases in a series of numbered volumes. This case appears in volume 364 of the New Jersey Superior Court reporters. If you go to a law library and find that book, you can then turn to page 301 and—*voila!*—you have the case. The decision is also reported in another set of volumes, called the regional reporters. This series of law reports is grouped by geographic region. New Jersey is included in the Atlantic region, so our case appears in reporters dedicated to that region. The "A" stands for Atlantic. After a series of reporters reaches volume 999, a second set begins. Our case appears in volume 835 of the second set of the Atlantic reporters ("A.2d"), at page 692. In addition, most cases are now available online, and your professor or librarian can show you how to find them electronically.

the Pub Zone decision. Judge Payne explains the point at much greater length, so we have condensed some of his writing into the phrase "of a business."

We omit a great deal. A court's opinion may be three pages or it may be 75. We do not use ellipses (. . .) to indicate these deletions, because there is more taken out than kept in, and we want the text to be clean. When a court quotes an earlier decision verbatim but clearly adopts those words as its own, we generally delete the quotation marks, as well as the citation to the earlier case. If you are curious about the full holding, you can always look it up.

Let us look at a few of Judge Payne's points. The holding begins with a discussion of *duty*. The court explains that whether one person (or bar) owes a duty to protect another depends upon several factors, including whether the harm could be foreseen, how serious the injury could be, and whether there was an opportunity to prevent it.

Judge Payne then points out that the owner of a business is not an insurer of a visitor's safety. Typically, the owner has a duty to a visitor *only* if he has a reason to know that some harm is likely to occur. How would a merchant know that? Based on the character of the business, suggests the judge, or the owner's experience with particular people.

The judge then applies this general rule to the facts of this case. He concludes that the Pub Zone did in fact have a duty to protect Kuehn from the Pagans' attack. Based on Kerkoulas's experience and warnings received from the police, she knew that the gang was dangerous and should have foreseen that admitting them in their "colors" greatly increased the chance of an attack.

Next, the court points out that it is not requiring the Pub Zone to *guarantee* everyone's safety. The bar was merely obligated to do a *reasonable* job. The prohibition on colors was a good idea, and calling the police had also proven effective. The problem, of course, was that in this case Kerkoulas ignored her own rule about gang insignia and failed to call the police.

Based on all the evidence, the jury's finding of liability was reasonable, and its verdict must be reinstated. In other words, Kuehn, who lost at the trial, wins on appeal. What the court has done is to *reverse* the lower court's decision, meaning to turn the loser into the winner. In other cases we will see an appellate court *remand* the case, meaning to send it back down to the lower court for additional steps. Or the appellate judges could *affirm* the lower court's decision, meaning to leave it unchanged.

Devil's Advocate

Each chapter has several cases. After some of them, a "Devil's Advocate" feature offers you a contrasting view of the legal issue. This is not part of the case but is instead a suggestion of another perspective on the problem discussed. The authors take no position for or against the court's decision, but merely want you to consider an alternate view and decide which analysis of the law makes more sense to you—that of the court or the Devil's Advocate. Is the following view persuasive?

Devil's Advocate

A court should not force small businesses to guarantee their customers' safety. Two or three violent men, whether motorcycle gang members or frustrated professors, could enter a grocery store or clothing retailer at any time and mindlessly attack innocent visitors. Random attacks are just that—random, unforeseeable. No merchant should be required to anticipate them. Send the criminals to jail, but do not place the burden on honest business people. ◆

Update

In this feature we ask students to find a current article on an issue discussed in the text. The goal is for you to apply the principles of this course to current events—this material is very real! You may use periodicals from the library or articles from any electronic database. The article should be dated within the past two months.

uPdate

Find an article online concerning a tavern's liability for a criminal assault. What did the bar allegedly do or fail to do? Is this a civil or criminal case? What outcome do you anticipate? How could the owner have avoided the problem? ◆

You Be the Judge

Many cases involve difficult decisions for juries and judges. Often both parties have legitimate, opposing arguments. Most chapters in this book will have a feature called "You Be the Judge," in which we present the facts of a case but not the court's holding. We offer you two opposing arguments based on the kinds of claims the lawyers made in court. We leave it up to you to debate and decide which position is stronger or to add your own arguments to those given. The following case is another negligence lawsuit, with issues similar to those in the Pub Zone case. A suicide caused a distraught family to sue a rock singer and music producer. Once again the defendants asked the judge to dismiss the case. They pointed out, correctly, that a negligence case requires a plaintiff to prove that the defendant *could have foreseen the type of harm that occurred*. Could Ozzy Osbourne have foreseen this sad outcome to one of his songs? You be the judge.

YOU BE THE JUDGE

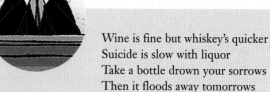

MCCOLLUM V. CBS, INC.

202 Cal. App. 3d 989, 249 Cal. Rptr. 187, 1988 Cal.
App. LEXIS 909, California Court of Appeal, 1988

Facts: John McCollum, 19 years old, was an alcoholic with serious emotional problems. He listened over and over to music recorded by Ozzy Osbourne on CBS records, particularly two albums called *Blizzard of Oz* and *Diary of a Madman*. He usually listened to the music on the family stereo in the living room because the sound was most intense there. One Friday evening, though, he went to his bedroom and lay on his bed, listening to more Osbourne music. He placed a loaded .22-caliber handgun to his right temple and pulled the trigger.

McCollum's parents sued Osbourne and CBS records, claiming that they negligently aided and encouraged John to commit suicide. The parents' argument was that Osbourne's songs were designed to appeal to unstable youths and that the message of some of his music explicitly urged death. One of the songs John had listened to before his death was "Suicide Solution," which included these lyrics:

Wine is fine but whiskey's quicker
Suicide is slow with liquor
Take a bottle drown your sorrows
Then it floods away tomorrows
Now you live inside a bottle
The reaper's traveling at full throttle
It's catching you but you don't see
The reaper is you and the reaper is me
Breaking law, knocking doors
But there's no one at home
Made your bed, rest your head
But you lie there and moan
Where to hide, Suicide is the only way out
Don't you know what it's really about.*

The trial court dismissed the lawsuit, ruling that the plaintiff had not made out a valid negligence claim. The court ruled that the First Amendment's free speech provision protected the rights of Osbourne and CBS to publish any music they wanted. In addition, the court found that the defendants could not have foreseen that anyone would respond to the ▼

lyrics by taking his own life. With no foreseeability, the court ruled, the plaintiffs' case must fail. The parents appealed.

You Be the Judge: **Was McCollum's suicide foreseeable?**

Argument for the Parents: Your honors, for years Ozzy Osbourne has been well known as the "madman" of rock 'n' roll. The words and music of his songs revolve around bizarre, antisocial beliefs, emphasizing death and satanic worship. Many of his songs suggest that life is hopeless and that suicide is not only acceptable but desirable. Now one of his devoted fans has acted on Osbourne's advice and killed himself. The defendants share responsibility for this tragic death.

Osbourne and CBS knew that many of Osbourne's fans struggled with self-identity, alienation, and substance abuse. Both defendants aggressively targeted this market and reaped enormous profits. They realized that the confused youths who adored Osbourne were precisely those most vulnerable to vicious advice. Yet in spite of their knowledge, both defendants churned out songs such as "Suicide Solution," urging troubled, chemically addicted young people to kill themselves. Not only was it *foreseeable* that one of Osbourne's fans would sooner or later take his life,

it was *inevitable*. The only way to ensure that this doesn't occur again is to permit a jury to hear the parents' case and, if it is persuaded by the evidence, to award the grieving parents damages.

Argument for Osbourne and CBS: Your honors, we all agree that this death was tragic and unnecessary. But the plaintiffs delude themselves if they think that Mr. Osbourne and CBS bear any responsibility. The fact is that John McCollum was deeply troubled and alcoholic. He was responsible for his life—and for his own death. Next to the young man himself, of course, those who bear the greatest responsibility for his sad life and gruesome end are his parents, the plaintiffs in this case. Mr. Osbourne and CBS sympathize with the parents' bereavement, but not with their attempt to foist responsibility onto others.

If the plaintiffs' far-fetched foreseeability argument were the law—which it is not—every singer, writer, and film and television producer would be at risk of several thousand lawsuits every year. Under their theory, a producer who made a bank robbery movie would be liable for every robbery that took place afterward, as would every author or singer who ever mentioned the subject. The First Amendment was written to ensure that we *do* have access to arts and entertainment, and to prohibit efforts at silencing artists with outlandish lawsuits. This death was never foreseeable and no jury should ever hear the case. ●

Chapter Conclusion

We depend upon the law to give us a stable nation and economy, a fair society, a safe place to live and work. These worthy goals have occupied Anglo-Saxon kings and twenty-first-century lawmakers alike. But although law is a vital tool for crafting the society we want, there are no easy answers about how to create it. In a democracy, we all participate in the crafting. Legal rules control us, yet *we* create *them*. A working knowledge of the law can help build a successful career—and a solid democracy.

Chapter Review

1. Our federal system of government means that law comes from a national government in Washington, D.C., and from 50 state governments.

2. The history of law foreshadows many current legal issues, including mediation, partnership

liability, the jury system, the role of witnesses, the special value placed on land, the idea of precedent, and the difference between substantive and procedural law.

3. The primary sources of contemporary law are

- the United States Constitution and state constitutions

- Statutes, which are drafted by legislatures

- Common law, which is the body of cases decided by judges, as they follow earlier cases, known as precedent; and

- Administrative law, the rules and decisions made by federal and state administrative agencies.

4. Other sources of contemporary law include

- Treaties

- Executive orders

5. Criminal law concerns behavior so threatening to society that it is outlawed altogether. Civil law deals with duties and disputes between parties, not with outlawed behavior.

6. Substantive law defines the rights of people. Procedural law describes the processes for settling disputes.

7. Jurisprudence is concerned with the basic nature of law. Three theories of jurisprudence are

- Legal positivism: The law is what the sovereign says it is.

- Natural law: An unjust law is no law at all.

- Legal realism: Who enforces the law is more important than what the law says.

Practice Test

1. Can one person really understand all the legal issues mentioned at the beginning of this chapter? For example, can a business executive know about insider trading and employment law and environmental law and tort law and all the others? Will a court really hold one person to such knowledge?

2. Why does our law come from so many different sources?

3. The stock market crash of 1929 and the Great Depression that followed were caused in part because so many investors blindly put their money into stocks they knew nothing about. During the 1920s, it was often impossible for an investor to find out what a corporation was planning to do with its money, who was running the corporation, and many other vital things. Congress responded by passing the Securities Act of 1933, which required a corporation to divulge more information about itself before it could seek money for a new stock issue. What kind of law did the Congress create? Explain the relationship between voters, Congress, and the law.

4. Union organizers at a hospital wanted to distribute leaflets to potential union members, but hospital rules prohibited leafleting in areas of patient care, hallways, cafeterias, and any areas open to the public. The National Labor Relations Board (NLRB) ruled that these restrictions violated the law and ordered the hospital to permit the activities in the cafeteria and coffee shop. The NLRB cannot create common law or statutory law. What kind of law was it creating?

5. Leslie Bergh and his two brothers, Milton and Raymond, formed a partnership to help build a fancy saloon and dance hall in Evanston, Wyoming. Later, Leslie met with his friend and drinking buddy, John Mills, and tricked Mills into investing in the saloon. Leslie did not tell Mills that no one else was investing cash or that the entire enterprise was already insolvent. Mills mortgaged his home, invested $150,000 in the saloon—and lost every penny of it. Mills sued all three partners for fraud. Milton and Raymond defended on the ground that they didn't commit the fraud, only Leslie did. The defendants lost. Was that fair? By holding them liable, what general idea did the court rely on? What Anglo-Saxon legal custom did the ruling resemble?

6. ETHICS Confucius did not esteem written laws, believing instead that good rulers were the best guarantee of justice. Does our legal system rely primarily on the rule of law or the rule of people? Which do you instinctively trust more? Legal realists argue that the "rule of law" is a misleading term. What point are they making, and how does it relate to Confucius's principles? Confucius himself was an extraordinarily wise man, full of wisdom about life and compassion for his fellow citizens. Because he was extraordinary, what does that tell us about other rulers by contrast? How does that affect Confucius's own views?

7. Tommy Parker may have been involved in some unsavory activities as an officer in a failed savings and loan institution. A federal agency, the Office of Thrift Supervision (OTS), ordered Tommy not to spend or waste any of his own assets while it was investigating him. Later, Tommy and his wife, Billie, got divorced and divided their property. On February 18, the OTS filed papers in court asking for an order that *Billie* not spend any of her assets. Billie received a copy of the papers on February 20, and the hearing took place on February 24, without Billie in attendance. The court ordered Billie not to spend any assets except for essential living expenses. Billie appealed, claiming that under court rules she was entitled to five days' notice before the hearing took place and that weekend days are not counted. She had had only two business days' notice. Assume that her counting of the days was correct (which it was). Explain the difference between procedural law and substantive law. Which type of law was Billie relying on? Should her appeal be granted?

8. Plaintiff Miss Universe, Inc., owns the trademark "Miss U.S.A." For decades, the company has produced the Miss U.S.A. beauty pageant, seen by many millions of people in the United States. William Flesher and Treehouse Fun Ranch began to hold a nude beauty pageant in California. They called this the "Miss Nude U.S.A." pageant. Most of the contestants were from California; the majority of states were not represented in the contest. Miss Universe sued Flesher and Treehouse, claiming that the public would be confused and misled by the similar names. The company sought an *equitable remedy* in this lawsuit. What does "equitable" mean? What equitable remedy did Miss Universe seek? Should it win?

9. Bill and Diane are hiking in the woods. Diane walks down a hill to fetch fresh water. Bill meets a stranger, who introduces herself as Katrina. Bill sells a kilo of cocaine to Katrina, who then flashes a badge and mentions how much she enjoys her job at the Drug Enforcement Agency. Diane, heading back to camp with the water, meets Freddy, a motorist whose car has overheated. Freddy is late for a meeting where he expects to make a $30 million profit; he's desperate for water for his car. He promises to pay Diane $500 tomorrow if she will give him the pail of water, which she does. The next day, Bill is in jail and Freddy refuses to pay for Diane's water. Explain the criminal law/civil law distinction and what it means to Bill and Diane. Who will do what to whom, with what results?

10. *YOU BE THE JUDGE* WRITING PROBLEM Should trials be televised? Here are a few arguments to add to those in the chapter. You be the judge. **Arguments against Live Television Coverage:** We have tried this experiment, and it has failed. Trials fall into two categories: Those that create great public interest, and those that do not. No one watches dull trials, so we do not need to broadcast them. The few that are interesting have all become circuses. Judges and lawyers have shown that they cannot resist the temptation to play to the camera. Trials are supposed to be about justice, not entertainment. If a citizen seriously wants to follow a case, she can do it by reading the daily newspaper. **Arguments for Live Television Coverage:** It is true that some televised trials have been unseemly affairs, but that is the fault of the presiding judges, not the media. Indeed, one of the virtues of television coverage is that millions of people now understand that we have a lot of incompetent people running our courtrooms. The proper response is to train judges to run a tight trial by prohibiting the grandstanding in which some lawyers may engage. Access to accurate information is the foundation on which a democracy is built, and we must not eliminate a source of valuable data just because some judges are ill trained.

11. In his most famous novel, *The Red and the Black*, the French author Stendhal (1783–1842) wrote: "There is no such thing as 'natural law': this expression is nothing but old nonsense. Prior to laws, what is natural is only the strength of the lion, or the need of the creature suffering from hunger or cold, in short, need." What do you think?

12. *ROLE REVERSAL* Each Practice Test contains one Role Reversal feature, in which we challenge you to create your own exam question. The goal is to think creatively and accurately. Crafting questions is a good way to reinforce what you understand and recognize the areas

you need to review. Your professor may ask you to submit the questions in writing or electronically or to prepare an overhead slide.

The question should be challenging enough that the average student will need to stop and think, but clear enough that there is only one answer. Useful questions can be formatted as essay, short answer, or multiple choice. Notice that some exam questions are very direct, while others require deeper analysis. Here are two examples. The first focuses on a definition.

Question: Legal positivism is:

a. A decision by an appeals court *affirming* the trial court.

b. A decision by an appeals court *reversing* a trial court.

c. A theory of jurisprudence insisting that the law is what the sovereign says it is.

d. A theory of law requiring that current cases be decided based on earlier decisions.

e. A theory of law requiring that current cases be decided by a majority vote of the judges.

As you know, the correct answer is "c."

The next question demands that the student spot the issue of law involved (foreseeability) and correctly apply it to the facts provided.

Question: Marvin asks Sheila, a qualified auto mechanic, to fix his engine, which constantly stalls (stops) while driving. When Marvin returns, Sheila informs him that the engine is now "perfect—runs like a top." Marvin drives home along Lonesome Highway. Suddenly the car stalls. Sheila has not fixed it. Marvin pulls over and begins the long walk to the nearest telephone. A blimp flies overhead, advertising "Top" brand tires. Tragically, the blimp suddenly plummets to earth and explodes 20 feet from Marvin, seriously injuring him. Marvin sues Sheila. Sheila's best defense is that:

a. The falling blimp is so bizarre that Sheila could never have foreseen it.

b. Sheila made *reasonable efforts* to fix the engine.

c. Marvin should have checked the engine himself.

d. Marvin should have carried a cell phone with him in case of emergencies.

e. Sheila is a qualified mechanic and her work is presumptively sufficient.

The correct answer is "a." Notice that the same facts could be used as an essay question, simply by deleting the multiple-choice answers. Now it is your turn for Role Reversal: Draft a multiple-choice question focusing on *legal realism*.

Internet Research Problem

Go to **academic.cengage.com/blaw/beatty** to find two current cases that interest you: one civil, one criminal. Explain the different roles played by each type of law, and summarize the issues in the respective cases.

You can find further practice problems at **academic.cengage.com/blaw/beatty.**

CHAPTER 2

Business Ethics and Social Responsibility

© MEL CURTIS/PHOTODISC/GETTY IMAGES

Arthur Haupt is a 79-year-old retired waiter who lives with his black cat, Max, in a tidy 650-square-foot apartment in Chicago's Rienzi Plaza apartment building.

He works 20 hours a week, shelving books at Loyola University's law library, earning $6.95 an hour. He also gets Social Security and two modest pensions. His total income last year was $18,713. His monthly rent in this federally subsidized apartment is $352. Market rent for an equivalent apartment would be as high as $1,644.

Last fall, Haupt's landlord notified him that he might be evicted. Nationally, landlords have taken about 125,000 units out of the federal subsidy program. At the same time, demand for subsidized housing is rising, in part because big cities such as Chicago are tearing down their old public-housing projects and telling residents to find subsidized apartments instead. Where will Arthur Haupt go?

The landlord, Sheldon Baskin, is not a bad guy. Twenty years ago, he and his partners signed a contract with the federal government, promising to build and maintain an apartment building for low-income Chicagoans. In exchange, the government guaranteed a steady stream of rent. But now the contract on Rienzi Plaza is set to expire. Baskin could make a larger profit on the building by selling it, converting it to condominiums, or renting to unsubsidized tenants who could pay more. What does Baskin owe to his investors?

The Rienzi tenants and community groups have begun looking for a white knight—someone who could buy the building and preserve its low-income housing. Two for-profit organizations that specialize in investing in "affordable" housing expressed interest in buying Rienzi, but neither has made an offer.

Meanwhile, Baskin asked government officials how much more rent they would pay if he extended his contract for five years. Officials said they would have to hire an outside consultant to do a market study, a task that would take months—long past the deadline by which federal regulations require Baskin to announce his decision.[1] ▪

---

[1] Based on Jonathan Eig, "Landlord's Dilemma: Help Poor Tenants or Seek More Profits," *Wall Street Journal*, July 17, 2001, p. 1. Republished with permission of *The Wall Street Journal*; permission conveyed through the Copyright Clearance Center, Inc.

Business is an enormously powerful tool that corporate managers can use to accomplish many goals. They may wish to earn a good living, even to become wealthy, but they can also use their business skills to cure the ill, feed the hungry, entertain the bored, and in many other ways affect their community, their country, and their world.

This book is primarily about the impact of law on business. But law is only one set of rules that governs business; ethics is another. **Ethics is the study of how people ought to act.** Law and ethics are often in harmony. Most reasonable people agree that murder should be prohibited. But law and ethics are not always compatible. In some cases, it might be *ethical* to commit an *illegal* act; in others, it might be *unethical* to be *legal*. Here are two examples in which law and ethics might conflict:

George Hart, a 75-year-old man confined to a wheelchair, robbed a bank in San Diego of $70 so that he could buy heart medicine. He entered a branch of the HomeFed Bank, where he had $4 in his account, and apologized while demanding $70 from a teller, threatening to blow up the bank if she did not comply. Hart was arrested minutes later when he tried to buy a $69 bottle of heart medicine at a nearby drugstore. Hart said he "hated to have to go to this extreme," but insisted he had tried every other way to find money to buy the medicine.[2]

In 1963, Martin Luther King, Jr., was arrested in Birmingham, Alabama, for leading illegal sit-ins and marches to protest laws that discriminated against African Americans. When eight local clergymen criticized his activities, King offered this defense:

> We know through painful experience that freedom is never voluntarily given by the oppressor; it must be demanded by the oppressed. . . . Perhaps it is easy for those who have never felt the stinging darts of segregation to say "Wait. . . ." [W]hen you see the vast majority of your 20 million Negro brothers smothering in an air-tight cage of poverty in the midst of an affluent society; when you suddenly find your tongue twisted as you seek to explain to your six-year-old daughter why she can't go to the public amusement park that has just been advertised on television, and see tears welling up when she is told that Funtown is closed to colored children. . . . [W]hen you take a cross-country drive and find it necessary to sleep night after night in the uncomfortable corners of your automobile because no motel will accept you. . . . How can [we] advocate breaking some laws and obeying others? The answer lies in the fact that there are two types of laws: just and unjust. I agree with St. Augustine that "an unjust law is not law at all."[3]

Could one argue in the case of the bank robber that his actions, although illegal, were ethical? Would the argument be stronger if he had been stealing the money to help someone else? In the case of Martin Luther King, Jr., would it be reasonable to conclude not only that breaking the law was ethical but also that *obeying* the law would have been *unethical?* Were the eight clergymen who criticized King behaving unethically by upholding these odious laws?

The other chapters of this book focus on legal issues, but this chapter concentrates on ethics. In all the examples in this chapter, the activities are *legal*, but are they *ethical?*

WHY BOTHER WITH ETHICS?

Business schools teach students how to maximize the profitability of an enterprise, large or small. Does ethical behavior maximize profitability? Some people argue that, in the long run, ethical behavior does indeed pay. But they must mean the very long

---

2 "Bank Robber in Wheelchair Has an Alibi: His Medicine," *New York Times,* Jan. 18, 1991, p. A16.
3 Martin Luther King, Jr., "Letter from Birmingham Jail," *The Christian Century,* June 12, 1963.

run, because to date there is little evidence that ethical behavior *necessarily* pays financially, either in the short or the long run.

For instance, when a fire destroyed the Malden Mills factory in Lawrence,
Massachusetts, its 70-year-old owner, Aaron Feuerstein, could have shut down the
business, collected the insurance money, and sailed off into retirement. But a layoff of
the factory's 3,000 employees would have been a major economic blow to the region.
So instead Feuerstein kept the workers on the payroll while he rebuilt the factory.
These actions gained him a national reputation as a business hero. Many consumers
promised to buy more of the company's patented Polartec fabric. In the end, however,
the story did not have a fairy-tale ending: Five years after the fire, Malden Mills filed
bankruptcy papers. The company was not able to pay off the loans it had incurred to
keep the business going.

In contrast, unethical companies may perform well financially. Mutuals.com offers
shares in Vice Funds, a mutual fund that invests in "booze, bets, bombs, and butts"
(alcohol, gambling, defense contractors, and cigarettes). Over the past five years, these
industries have earned better returns than the Standard & Poor's 500. Even for individuals, unethical behavior is no bar to financial success. The first antitrust laws in
America were designed, at least in part, to restrain John D. Rockefeller's unethical
activities. Yet, four generations later, his name is still synonymous with wealth and his
numerous heirs can live comfortably on their inheritance from him.[4]

If ethical behavior does not necessarily pay and unethical behavior sometimes
does, why bother with ethics?

Society as a Whole Benefits from Ethical Behavior

John Akers, the former chairman of IBM, argues that without ethical behavior, a society cannot be economically competitive. He puts it this way:

> Ethics and competitiveness are inseparable. We compete as a society. No society anywhere
> will compete very long or successfully with people stabbing each other in the back; with
> people trying to steal from each other; with everything requiring notarized confirmation
> because you can't trust the other fellow; with every little squabble ending in litigation; and
> with government writing reams of regulatory legislation, tying business hand and foot to
> keep it honest. That is a recipe not only for headaches in running a company; it is a recipe
> for a nation to become wasteful, inefficient, and noncompetitive. There is no escaping this
> fact: the greater the measure of mutual trust and confidence in the ethics of a society, the
> greater its economic strength.[5]

People Feel Better When They Behave Ethically

Every businessperson has many opportunities to be dishonest. Consider how one
person felt when he resisted temptation:

> Occasionally a customer forgot to send a bill for materials shipped to us for processing. . . .
> It would have been so easy to rationalize remaining silent. After all, didn't they deserve to
> lose because of their inefficiency? However, upon instructing our staff to inform the parties
> of their errors, I found them eager to do so. They were actually bursting with pride. . . . Our

---

4 Chapter 20, on antitrust, discusses Rockefeller's career at greater length.

5 David Grier, "Confronting Ethical Dilemmas," unpublished manuscript of remarks at the Royal
Bank of Canada, Sept. 19, 1989.

honesty was beneficial in subtle ways. The "inefficient" customer remained loyal for years. . . . [O]ur highly moral policy had a marvelously beneficial effect on our employees. Through the years, many an employee visited my office to let me know that they liked working for a "straight" company.[6]

Profitability is generally not what motivates managers to care about ethics. Managers want to feel good about themselves and the decisions they have made; they want to sleep at night. Their decisions—to lay off employees, install safety devices in cars, burn a cleaner fuel—affect peoples' lives. When two researchers asked businesspeople why they cared about ethics, the answers had little to do with the profitability:

> The businesspeople we interviewed set great store on the regard of their family, friends, and the community at large. They valued their reputations, not for some nebulous financial gain but because they took pride in their good names.[7]

The Web site http://www.yourtruehero.org offers examples of ordinary people who have inspired others with their ethical behavior.

Unethical Behavior Can Be Very Costly

Unethical behavior is a risky business strategy—it may lead to disaster. An engaged couple made a reservation and put down a $1,500 deposit to hold their wedding reception at a New Hampshire restaurant. Tragically, the bride died of asthma four months before the wedding. Invoking the terms of the contract, the restaurant owner refused to return the couple's deposit. In a letter to the groom, he admitted, "Morally, I would of course agree that the deposit should be returned." When newspapers reported this story, customers deserted the restaurant and it was forced into bankruptcy—over a $1,500 disagreement.[8] Unethical behavior does not always damage a business, but it certainly has the potential of destroying a company overnight. So why take the risk?

Even if unethical behavior does not devastate a business, it can cause other, subtler damage. In one survey, a majority of those questioned said that they had witnessed unethical behavior in their workplace and that this behavior had reduced productivity, job stability, and profits. Unethical behavior in an organization creates a cynical, resentful, and unproductive workforce.

So why bother with ethics? Because society benefits when managers behave ethically. Because ethical managers have happier, more satisfying lives. And because unethical behavior can destroy a business faster than a snake can bite.

WHAT IS ETHICAL BEHAVIOR?

It is one thing to decide, in theory, that being ethical is good; in practice, it can be much more difficult to make the right decisions. Supreme Court Justice Potter Stewart once said that he could not define pornography, but he knew it when he saw it. Many people

---

[6] Hugh Aaron, "Doing the Right Thing in Business," *Wall Street Journal,* June 21, 1993, p. A10.

[7] Amar Bhide and Howard H. Stevenson, "Why Be Honest if Honesty Doesn't Pay?" *Harvard Business Review,* Sept.–Oct. 1990, pp. 121–129, at 127.

[8] John Milne, "N.H. Restaurant Goes Bankrupt in Wake of Wedding Refund Flap," *Boston Globe,* Sept. 9, 1994, p. 25.

feel the same way about ethics—that somehow, instinctively, they know what is right and wrong. In real life, however, ethical dilemmas are often not black and white, but many shades of gray. The purpose of this section is to analyze the following ethics checklist as an aid to managers in making tough decisions:

- What are the facts?
- What are the critical issues?
- Who are the stakeholders?
- What are the alternatives?
- What are the ethical implications of each alternative?
- Is it legal?
  - How would it look in the light of day?
  - What are the consequences?
  - Does it violate important values?
- Does it violate the Golden Rule?
  - Is it just?
  - Has the process been fair?
- Is more than one alternative right?
  - Which values are in conflict?
  - Which of these values are most important?
  - Can you find an alternative that is consistent with your values?

Analyzing the Ethics Checklist

What Are the Facts?

Although this question seems obvious, people often forget in the heat of battle to listen to (and, more importantly, to *hear*) all the different viewpoints. Instead of relying on hearsay and rumor, it is crucial to discover the facts, firsthand, from the people involved. There is always another side to the story. It may be easy to condemn a bank robber, until learning the money was needed to buy medicine.

What Are the Critical Issues?

In analyzing ethical dilemmas, expand your thinking to include *all* the important issues. Avoid a narrow focus that encompasses only one or two aspects. In the case of the New Hampshire restaurant that refused to refund a deposit, the owner focused on the narrow legal issue. His interpretation of the *contract* was correct. But if the owner had expanded his thinking to include consideration for his customers, he might have reached a different decision.

Who Are the Stakeholders?

Stakeholders are all the people potentially affected by the decision. That list might include subordinates, bosses, shareholders, suppliers, customers, members of the community in which the business operates, society as a whole, or even more remote stakeholders, such as future generations. The interests of these stakeholders often conflict. Current shareholders may benefit from a company's decision to manufacture a product that contributes to global warming, while future generations are left to contend with a potential environmental nightmare.

What Are the Alternatives?

The next step is to list the reasonable alternatives. A creative manager may find a clever solution that is a winner for everyone. What alternatives might be available to Sheldon Baskin, the landlord who faced a dilemma in the opening scenario?

What Are the Ethical Implications of Each Alternative?

Is the Alternative Legal?   Illegal may not always be synonymous with unethical, but, as a general rule, you need to think long and hard about the ethics of any illegal activities.

How Would the Alternative Look in the Light of Day?   If your activities were reported on the evening news, how would you feel? Proud? Embarrassed? Horrified? Undoubtedly, sexual harassment would be virtually eliminated if people thought that their parents, spouse, or partner would shortly see a video replay of the offending behavior.

What Are the Consequences of This Alternative?   Ask yourself: Am I hurting anyone by this decision? Which alternative will cause the greatest good (or the least harm) to the most people? For example, you would like to fire an incompetent employee. That decision will clearly have adverse consequences for him. But the other employees in your division will benefit and so will the shareholders of your company. Overall, your decision will cause more good than harm.

You should look with a particularly critical eye if an alternative benefits you while harming others. Suppose that you become CEO of a company whose headquarters are located in a distant suburb. You would like to move the headquarters closer to your home to cut your commuting time. Of course, such a decision would be expensive for shareholders and inconvenient for other employees. Do you simply impose your will on the company or consider the consequences for everyone?

This approach to decision making was first developed by two nineteenth-century English philosophers, Jeremy Bentham and John Stuart Mill. They argued that all decisions should be evaluated according to how much happiness they create. This philosophy is called **utilitarianism.** Some commentators have criticized utilitarianism on practical grounds—benefit and harm are difficult to measure. Others also argue that not all happiness is equal. A band of robbers may receive more benefit from stealing money than the victim suffers harm, but most people would nonetheless argue that the decision to steal is wrong. Despite these criticisms, it is wise at least to consider the costs and benefits of a decision.

Does the Alternative Violate Important Values?   In addition to consequences, consider fundamental values. It is possible to commit an act that does not harm anyone else but is still the wrong thing to do. Suppose, for instance, that you are away from home and have the opportunity to engage in a temporary sexual liaison. You are absolutely certain that your spouse will never find out and your partner for the night will have no regrets or guilt. There would be no negative consequences, but you believe that infidelity is wrong, *regardless of the consequences*, so you resist temptation.

Some people question whether, as a diverse, heterogeneous society (not to mention world), we have common values. But throughout history and across many different cultures, common values do appear. The following values are almost universal:

- *Consideration* means being aware of and concerned about other people's feelings, desires, and needs. The considerate person is able to imagine how he would feel in someone else's place.

- *Courage* is the strength to act in the face of fear and danger. Courage can require dramatic action (saving a buddy on a battlefield) or quiet strength (doing what you think is right, despite opposition from your boss).

- *Integrity* means being sincere, honest, and loyal. If you have integrity, you do not criticize others behind their back or take credit for their ideas and efforts.

- *Responsibility* means being trustworthy and dependable. The responsible person meets her commitments and lives up to her promises. If you promise to finish a project by a certain date, your colleagues can count on that pledge.

- *Self-control* is the ability to resist temptation. The person with self-control does not drink or eat too much, party too hard, watch too much television, or spend too much money.

Although reasonable people may disagree about a precise list of important values, most would agree that values matter. Try compiling your own list of values and then check it periodically to see if you are living up to it in your business and personal life. In one survey, business executives reported that the values they respected most were responsibility and honesty.

Does the Alternative Violate the Golden Rule?   We all know the Golden Rule: Do unto others as you would have them do unto you. If one of the alternatives you are considering would be particularly unpleasant when done to you, reconsider.

Immanuel Kant, an eighteenth-century German philosopher, took the Golden Rule one step further with a concept he called the **categorical imperative.** According to Kant, you should not do something unless you would be willing for everyone else to do it too (not just to you). Imagine that you could cheat on an exam without getting caught. You might gain some short-term benefit—a higher grade. But what would happen if everyone cheated? The professor would have to make the exams harder or curve everyone's grade down. If your school developed a reputation for cheating, you might not be able to find a job after graduation. Cheating works only if most people are honest. To take advantage of everyone else's honesty is contemptible.

Is the Alternative Just?   Are you respecting individual rights such as liberty (privacy, free speech, and religious freedom), welfare (employment, housing, food, education), and equality? Would it be just to fire an employee because her political views differ from your own?

Has the Process Been Fair?   Unequal outcomes are acceptable, provided they are the result of a fair process. At the end of a poker game, some players have won and others lost, but no one can complain that the result was unfair, unless players cheated. In a business context, a fair process means applying the same set of rules to everyone. If three of your subordinates are vying for the same promotion, it would be unfair to let one state her case to you but not the others.

Is More Than One Alternative Right?

Thus far, the ethics checklist has served two purposes. It helps to clarify the issues at stake. It also filters out decisions that are downright wrong. Have you considered lying to a customer about product specifications? For a start, such an action violates principles of integrity, not to mention the Golden Rule. Nor would you want your activity to be revealed on the front page of the local newspaper.

Often, the most difficult decisions arise not in cases of right versus wrong but in situations of right versus right.[9] President Harry Truman's decision to drop atomic bombs on two Japanese cities is a classic example of right versus right. He argued that if he had not ended the war by using nuclear weapons, more Americans and Japanese would have died during a land invasion. Looking simply at the consequences, he concluded that the terrible suffering by the Japanese people was justified because, ultimately, fewer people died overall. At the same time, Truman's decision violated the Golden Rule and Kant's categorical imperative. Indeed, since the end of World War II, the United States has worked hard to ensure that no one else ever deploys nuclear weapons. The ethics checklist presents no clear-cut answer. In the end, Truman decided that the most right (or least wrong) choice was to end the war quickly.

Nuclear weapons make a dramatic example, but what about a more typical business decision? AT&T adopted a policy of cutting costs to maximize its stock price. To implement this policy, the company laid off 40,000 people, despite record profits. Even as workers suffered, shareholders benefited because the company's stock price rose in response to the layoff announcement. But is stock price the only issue? Does the company have an obligation to protect employee jobs? Is one right more important than another?

Which Values Are in Conflict?   There are many ways to justify a decision to lay off workers, even 40,000 of them. If managers avoid layoffs, then profits suffer, stock prices fall, companies merge, and executives lose their own jobs. In business school and on the job, managers learn how to analyze, compete, and win. Competing— and winning—are important. But what about other values, such as compassion and caring? Do the individual people affected by this decision matter too?

Which of These Values Are Most Important?   Suppose that, growing up, you had seen family members or neighbors suffering through bouts of unemployment. That experience might have taught you that compassion is a high priority. Managers must determine which values are important in their own lives.

Can You Find an Alternative That Is Consistent with Your Values? The decision you make not only determines the kind of person you are now, but also sets your course for the future. Can you reach a decision that is consistent with the kind of person you are or want to be? Instead of announcing massive layoffs, some companies offer generous severance packages, retraining programs, and other voluntary methods of reducing the workforce. Shareholders may receive less benefit, but employees suffer less harm.

The following article discusses the importance of values in achieving personal fulfillment.

ECONOMICS
& the LAW

Once upon a time, there was a game that Wall Street traders and investment bankers liked to play—often on the commute home to Greenwich, Connecticut, or Short Hills, New Jersey, after a particularly profitable or trying day. It was called "What's Your Number?" The answer—in millions of dollars—was the amount you would want to have socked away before you could ditch your high-pressure job and lead the life you really wanted.

The breathtaking part of this game was not the numbers. And it was not that the question was asked by men and women in their 20s, 30s, and 40s. No, the remarkable part of this diversion was that the players kept increasing their numbers. There never seemed to be a high enough answer to "How much is enough?"

---

[9] For a thoughtful discussion of right versus right, see Joseph L. Badaracco, Jr., *Defining Moments: When Managers Must Choose between Right and Right* (Boston: Harvard Business School Press, 1997).

And there was a price to pay for all this money. "If your sense of accomplishment is all wrapped up in a bank account, it's going to affect your relationships," said Dr. Stephen Goldbart, a codirector of the Money, Meaning & Choices Institute, a consulting and training firm in San Francisco. "Absorption with money is going to make the human side of you unavailable. Our society has mixed up what it means to feel fulfilled and successful with making a lot of money."

As you might have guessed, this fable seems to have a moral. After the World Trade Center attacks, many of Wall Street's gold hoarders said they then realized what was really important: family, friends, and health. But meaningful work and personal fulfillment can't be ordered like pizza. They don't come conveniently attached to certain jobs or careers. The hardest thing about abandoning money as a scorecard for success and fulfillment is that there is no handy replacement, no way to advertise your newfound virtue. The second hardest thing is realizing that if your fulfillment needs to be advertised, you have simply traded one game for another.[10] ◆

Applying the Ethics Checklist: Making Decisions

An organization has responsibilities to customers, employees, shareholders, and society generally, both here and overseas. Employees also have responsibilities to their organizations. The purpose of this section is to apply the ethics checklist to actual business dilemmas. The checklist does not lead to one particular solution; rather it is a method to use in thinking through ethics problems. The goal is for you to reach a decision that satisfies you.

Organization's Responsibility to Society

Facts.   In the United States, teenagers routinely list alcohol commercials among their favorite advertisements. Adolescents who frequently see ads for alcohol are more likely to believe that drinkers are attractive, athletic, and successful. They are also more likely to drink, drink excessively, and drink in hazardous situations, such as driving a car.

While Secretary of Health and Human Services, Louis W. Sullivan publicly denounced the test marketing of Uptown, a high-tar cigarette targeted at African Americans. He called it "contemptible that the tobacco industry has sought to increase their market" among minorities because this population was "already bearing more than its fair share of smoking-related illness and mortality." Comedian Jay Leno joked that R. J. Reynolds named the cigarette Uptown "because the word 'Genocide' was already taken."[11]

A promotion for Request Jeans shows a man pinning a naked woman against a shower wall. Another advertisement featured childlike model Kate Moss lying naked on a couch. Above the couch was a picture of the product being promoted—Calvin Klein's Obsession for Men. Or how about the ad for a stereo that has a picture of a woman with these words: "She's terrific in bed, she's witty and intelligent, but she didn't have a Linn hi-fi. Her sister did and I married her sister."

Critical Issues.   What are the obligations of advertising executives and marketing managers to those who see their ads? Is it ethical to sell jeans by glorifying rape? Are men more likely to commit rape as a result of seeing one of these advertisements?

---

10 Ellyn Spragins, "When Numbers Cease to Matter," New York Times, Oct. 7, 2001, §4, p. 8. Copyright © 2001 by The New York Times Co. Reprinted by permission.

11 Richard W. Pollay, Jung S. Lee, and David Carter-Whitney, "Separate, But Not Equal: Racial Segmentation in Cigarette Advertising," *Journal of Advertising*, Mar. 1992, vol. 21, no. 1, p. 45.

Is it ethical to entice teenagers into drinking or African Americans into smoking? If these ads sell product, is that justification enough?

Stakeholders. Ad designers are primarily responsible to their firms and the firms' clients. After all, designers are paid to sell products, not to make the world a better place. But what about the people who see the advertisements? Do the designers have any responsibility to them? Or to society as a whole?

Alternatives. Firms have at least four alternatives in dealing with issues of ethics in advertising. They can

- Ignore ethics and simply strive to create promotions that sell the most product, whatever the underlying message;

- Try, in a general way, to minimize racism, sexism, and other exploitation;

- Include, as part of the development process, a systematic, focused review of the underlying messages contained in their advertisements; or

- Refuse to create any ads that are potentially demeaning, insensitive, or dangerous, recognizing that such a stand may lead to a loss of clients.

Ethical Implications. All these alternatives are perfectly legal. And, far from the ad executives being embarrassed if the ads see the light of day, the whole purpose of ads is to be seen. As for the consequences, the ads may help clients sell their products. But the ads may also harm those who see them by encouraging, among other things, drinking, smoking, sexual assault, and promiscuity. A manager might question whether these ads violate fundamental values. Are they showing consideration for others? Do they encourage self-control? As for the Golden Rule, how would an advertising executive feel about an ad in which he was being sexually assaulted? Or a promotion in which he was assumed to be less valuable than a stereo system? Are these ads just? Do they violate principles of equality? Is the process by which they have been created fair? Have those who may be adversely affected by them had an opportunity to be heard?

Right versus Right. In a country with rampant anorexia among teenage girls, is it ethical to run ads with emaciated girls as role models? Is it ethical to run ads for lottery tickets when these tickets are largely purchased by those who can least afford to gamble? If you worked in an advertising agency or marketing department, you might feel a strong sense of loyalty to your company. But what about consideration for those who could be harmed by your ads? You must decide which values are important to you and look for solutions that enable you to live by these values.

Some of the ads described in this section appear stunningly tasteless. They could have been worse, however. The Ad Graveyard **(http://zeldman.com/ad.html)** offers examples of proposed ads that never saw the light of day, for very obvious reasons.

Organization's Responsibility to Its Customers

In this chapter's opening scenario, Sheldon Baskin faces a dilemma: Now that his contract with the federal government has expired, he can raise rents by as much as 500 percent at Rienzi Plaza, home to 140 poor and elderly tenants. Moving would be difficult for the elderly tenants, especially because they are unlikely to find another apartment in the neighborhood. They might end up in homeless shelters. But what about Baskin's partners? Is it fair to them if he decides to subsidize the rents of low-income tenants? Does he owe his partners the highest return on their investment?

What would you do if you were Sheldon Baskin? He is concerned about several important stakeholders—his partners and his tenants. What about the community?

Does it benefit from having elderly members? Will the community be harmed if some of these elderly become homeless? How will Baskin feel about himself if he puts these elderly tenants out on the street? Or if *The Wall Street Journal* runs a front-page article about his eviction plans? On the other hand, could he argue that it is the government's responsibility to house the poor and elderly? What decision would be best for Baskin? The tenants? His partners? The community?

Organization's Responsibility to Its Employees

Enron

Which deal would you rather have?

- *Plan A:* Your company has a 401(k) pension plan. Federal law permits you to contribute a certain amount tax free each year. You can then invest that money in a choice of mutual funds. In addition, for every dollar you put in, your employer will contribute a dollar of company stock. The good news is that, if the stock market—and your company—prosper, your retirement years will indeed be golden. The downside is that if the stock market or your company declines, you could be like one of the tenants in Rienzi Plaza, unable to pay your rent.

- *Plan B:* The amount of your annual pension is guaranteed by the company, regardless of how the market performs. This guarantee is backed up by a federal agency. In addition to your regular pension plan, you have the right to invest in a special 401(k) plan, for which the company guarantees a minimum annual return of 12 percent.

Enron Corp. offered Plan A to its rank-and-file employees; Plan B was reserved for top executives. At one point, 60 percent of the assets in the Plan A 401(k) were invested in Enron stock. Then the stock plummeted in value from $80 a share to under $1. As the stock price sank, the company imposed a month-long "blackout" prohibiting all employees from selling any stock in the 401(k) while a new plan administrator took over. Less than a month after the blackout ended, the company filed for bankruptcy. As a result, the 401(k) plans lost $1.3 billion of their $2.1 billion worth.

The fate of Enron raises two issues:

1. *Equality of treatment within the company.* Is it ethical for top executives to set up two such different pension/savings plans for company employees? Should top executives be entitled to guaranteed retirement pay while rank-and-filers are at the mercy of stock market fluctuations?

    Alternatively, could one argue that offering top executives a better pension is no more unfair than paying them higher wages? What difference does it make if the disparity in pay between the top and bottom takes the form of higher current compensation, a better pension, or a fancier executive dining room?

2. *The ethics of pension plans versus 401(k) plans.* A traditional pension plan (such as top Enron officials had) guarantees a certain annual payment for the life of the employee. Under federal law, companies must set aside money to meet these promises. If, for whatever reason, the company fails to do so, a federal agency guarantees the payments (up to certain limits). These traditional pension plans are more expensive for companies to operate. To avoid this financial commitment, many companies have switched to 401(k) plans in which all the risk is borne by the employee.

    Supporters of 401(k) plans argue that these plans are better than nothing, which is what companies would offer if 401(k) plans were not available. After all, tax advantages and employer matching contributions entice many workers into saving money that they might otherwise just spend. Moreover, the younger employees whom companies want to attract rarely object to a 401(k) pension plan because they tend not to think long-term and they do not appreciate these plans' significant disadvantages (nor have these companies been eager to educate them).

What will you do when you become a top executive in a large company? Is it enough just to meet the minimum requirements of the pension laws? Should the employee plan look like yours? Does your obligation to shareholders require you to save money by offering the cheapest possible pension plan to employees? Would a generous pension plan for all employees benefit the company by attracting valuable workers or harm the company by decreasing its profits?

Gillette

When James Kilts became CEO of Gillette Co., the consumer products giant had been a mainstay of the Boston community for a hundred years. But the organization was going through hard times: Its stock was trading at less than half its peak price and some of its storied brands of razors were wilting under intense competitive pressure. In four short years, Kilts turned Gillette around—strengthening its core brands, cutting jobs, and paying off debt. With its stock up 61 percent, Kilts had added $20 billion in shareholder value.

Then suddenly Kilts sold Gillette to Procter & Gamble Co. for $57 billion. So short was Kilts's stay in Boston that he never moved his family from their home in Rye, New York. The deal was sweet for Gillette shareholders—the company's stock price went up 13 percent in one day. And tasty also for Kilts—his payoff was $153 million, including a $23.9 million reward from P&G for having made the deal and a "change in control" clause in his employment contract that was worth $12.6 million. In addition, P&G agreed to pay him $8 million a year to serve as vice-chairman after the merger. When he retires, his pension will be $1.2 million per year. Moreover, two of his top lieutenants were offered payments totaling $57 million.

Any downside to this deal? Four percent of the Gillette workforce—6,000 employees—were to be fired. If the payouts to the top three Gillette executives were divided among these 6,000, each unemployed worker would receive $35,000. The loss of this many employees (4,000 of whom live in New England) will have a ripple effect throughout the area economy. Although Gillette shareholders have certainly benefited in the short run from the sale, their profit would have been even greater without this $210 million payout to the executives. Moreover, about half the increase in Gillette revenues during the time that Kilts was running the show are attributable to currency fluctuations. A cheaper dollar increased revenue overseas. If the dollar had moved in the opposite direction, there might not have been any increase in revenue. Indeed, for the first two years after Kilts joined Gillette, the stock price declined. It wasn't until the dollar turned down that the stock price improved.

Some commentators have asked: (1) Do CEOs who receive sweeteners have too strong an incentive to sell their companies; and (2) Is it unseemly for them to be paid so much when many employees will lose their jobs? As one observer put it, "People think they are joining a company for the long haul and boom, the rug is pulled out from under them because the CEO wants a quick payday."[12] One study found that

---

[12] Mark Maremont, "No Razor Here: Gillette Chief to Get A Giant Payday," *Wall Street Journal,* Jan. 31, 2005, p. 1.

CEOs who receive sweeteners negotiate a lower sale price than those who do not.[13] But another commentator said of Kilts, "His incentives were based on performance, and he performed. Look at his track record. There's a market for CEOs and he's one of the best."[14]

Organization's Responsibility to Its Shareholders

Ford Motor Company was founded by William C. Ford, Jr.'s great-grandfather Henry. The younger Ford is an avid environmentalist and also chairman of the company that bears his name. He shares the concern of many environmentalists that automobile exhaust contributes to global warming. Under the younger Ford's leadership, the company decided to increase the fuel economy of its sports utility vehicles (SUVs) by 25 percent (about five miles per gallon). This decision came shortly after Congress, partly in response to lobbying by automobile manufacturers, refused to increase national fuel economy standards.

Ford Motor was a leader in the development of SUVs, which comprised about a fifth of its output each year. Because these heavy cars are gas inefficient, Ford was barely able to meet existing federal standards. To achieve higher fuel economy, the company had to make more auto parts out of lighter aluminum and redesign the SUV engines. The cost of implementing these changes was substantial, but the company decided not to pass the costs on to consumers. The plan was controversial within the company itself, because some insiders believe that consumers would prefer more powerful cars to more gas-efficient ones.

Milton Friedman, a Nobel Laureate in economics, famously observed, "The one and only social responsibility of business is to increase its profits."[15] He argued that an executive should act for the benefit of the owners of the company. His primary responsibility is to them. If an individual wishes to support other responsibilities, such as a charity, a church, a city, or a country, let him do so with his own time and money, not that of the shareholders.

If you were a shareholder of Ford Motor Company, would you support the fuel efficiency initiative? Perhaps you would prefer to earn higher returns on your stock so that you could give money to other projects you consider more compelling (finding an AIDS vaccine, for example). Should William Ford, who inherited his company stock, have the right to spend company funds to support his pet projects? If the air needs to be cleaner or the schools richer, why shouldn't private donors or public institutions be responsible, not one company's shareholders?[16]

Do executives have an obligation to be socially responsible? Ford officials argued that their fuel economy initiative might be profitable—it might increase sales enough to make up for the lower profit per car. Moreover, an environmentally friendly image might help sales on all its cars, not just SUVs. By voluntarily increasing its own fuel standards, Ford might head off tighter federal regulation.

---

13 *Ibid.*

14 *Ibid.*

15 Milton Friedman, "The Social Responsibility of Business Is to Increase Its Profits," *New York Times Magazine*, Sept. 13, 1970, p. 32.

16 See, for instance, David Henderson, "Misguided Virtue: False Notions of Corporate Social Responsibility," Hobart Paper 142, Institute of Economic Affairs, London, cited in *The Economist*, Nov. 17, 2001, p. 70.

Organization's Responsibility Overseas

An American company's ethical obligations do not end at the border. What ethical duties does an American manager owe to stakeholders in countries where the culture and economic circumstances are very different?

Here is a typical story from Guatemala:

> My father left home a long time ago. My mother supported me and my five brothers and sisters by selling tortillas and corn. Our house was a tin shack on the side of the road. We were crowded with all of us in one room, especially when it rained and the roof and sides leaked. There were hundreds of squatters in the neighborhood, but one day the police came and cleared us all out. The owners of the land said we couldn't come back unless we paid rent. How could we afford that? I was 12 and my mother said it was time for me to work. But most people won't hire children. Lots of other kids shine shoes or beg, but I heard that the maquila [clothing factory] was willing to hire children if we would work as hard as older people.
>
> I can keep up with the grown-ups. We work from 6:00 in the morning to 6:30 at night, with half an hour break at noon. We have no other breaks the whole rest of the day. If I don't work fast enough, they hit me, not too hard, and threaten to fire me. Sometimes, if there is too much work to do, they'll lock the doors and not let us out until everything is finished.
>
> I'm always really tired at the end of the day and in the morning, too. But I earn $30 a week and without that money, we would not have enough to eat. My mother hopes all of my brothers and sisters can get jobs in the factory, too.
>
> Of course, I'd rather be in school where I could wear a uniform and have friends. Then I could get a job as a clerk at the medical clinic. I would find people's files and tell them how long before the doctor could see them.

This description paints a distasteful picture indeed: children being beaten as they work 12-hour days. Should American companies (and consumers) buy goods that are produced in sweatshop factories? Jeffrey Sachs, a leading economist and adviser to developing nations, says, "My concern is not that there are too many sweatshops but that there are too few."[17] Why would he support sweatshops and child labor?

Historically, poor children have worked. Indeed, for many people and for many centuries, the point of having children was to create a supply of free labor to help support the family. In England in 1860, almost 40 percent of 14-year-old boys worked, and that was not just a few hours at Burger Box, but more likely 60 hours a week. That percentage is higher than in Africa or India today. For a child in a desperately poor family, the choice is not work or school, it is work, starvation, or prostitution. (For a history of sweatshops in America, work your way over to http://americanhistory.si.edu; search for "Sweatshops.")

Industrialization has always been the first stepping stone out of dire poverty—it was in England, it is now in the Third World. Eventually, higher productivity leads to higher wages. In China, factory managers have complained that their employees want to work even longer hours to earn more money. The results in China have been nothing short of remarkable—if each of China's provinces were counted as a separate country, then 20 of the world's fastest growing economies between 1978 and 1995 would have been Chinese. During the Industrial Revolution in England, per capita output doubled in 58 years. In China, it took only 10 years.

---

17 Allen R. Meyerson, "In Principle, A Case for More 'Sweatshops,'" *New York Times*, June 22, 1997, p. E5.

During the past 50 years, Taiwan and South Korea welcomed sweatshops. During the same period, India resisted what it perceived to be foreign exploitation. Although all three countries started at the same economic level, Taiwan and South Korea today have much lower levels of infant mortality and much higher levels of education than India.[18]

When governments or customers try to force Third World factories to pay higher wages, the factory owners typically either relocate to lower-wage countries or mechanize, thereby reducing the need for workers. In either case, the local economy suffers.

The difference, however, between the twenty-first and the nineteenth centuries is that now there are wealthy countries able to help their poorer neighbors. In the nineteenth century, England was among the richest countries, so it was on its own to solve its economic problems. Is America ethically obligated to assist the people around the world who live in abject poverty? Already, owing to pressure from activists, many companies have introduced better conditions in their factories. Workers are less likely to be beaten. They can go to the bathroom without asking permission. They might even receive rudimentary medical care. Manufacturing processes use fewer dangerous chemicals. Factories are cleaner, with better lighting and more ventilation. But hours are still long and wages low.

Companies argue that higher wages lead to increased prices, which, in their turn, drive away customers. Many of these sweatshops produce clothing. As a consumer, how much would be you willing to pay in higher clothing prices to eliminate sweatshops and child labor? As a taxpayer, how much are you willing to pay in taxes to subsidize Third World incomes so that sweatshops and child labor are no longer necessary?

Employees' Responsibility to Their Organization

Darby has been working for 14 months at Holden Associates, a large management consulting firm. She is earning $65,000 a year, which *sounds* good but does not go very far in New York City. It turns out that her peers at competing firms are typically paid 20 percent more and receive larger annual bonuses. Darby works about 60 hours a week, more if she is traveling. A number of times she has had to reschedule her vacation or cancel personal plans to meet client deadlines. She hopes to go to business school in a year and has already begun the application process.

Holden has a policy that permits any employee who works as late as 8:00 P.M. to eat dinner at company expense. The employee can also take a taxi home. Darby is in the habit of staying until 8:00 P.M. every night, whether or not her workload requires it. Then she orders enough food for dinner, with leftovers for lunch the next day. She has managed to cut her grocery bill to virtually nothing. Sometimes she invites her boyfriend to join her for dinner. As a student, he is always hungry and broke. Darby often uses the Holden taxi to take them back to his apartment, although the cab fare is twice as high as to her own place.

Sometimes Darby stays late to work on her business school applications. Naturally she uses Holden equipment to print out and photocopy the finished applications. Darby has also been known to return catalog purchases through the Holden mailroom on the company dime. Many employees do that, and the mailroom staff does not seem to mind.

Is Darby doing anything wrong? How would you behave in these circumstances?

---

[18] The data in this and the preceding paragraph are from Nicholas D. Kristof and Sheryl WuDunn, "Two Cheers for Sweatshops," *New York Times Magazine*, Sept. 24, 2000, p. 70.

Chapter Conclusion

Even employees who are ethical in their personal lives may find it difficult to uphold their standards at work if those around them behave differently. Managers wonder what they can do to create an ethical environment in their companies. To help foster a sense of ethics within their organizations, many U.S. companies have developed their own formal ethics codes. For instance, Johnson & Johnson's corporate credo states that managers must take actions that are "just and ethical" and all employees must be "good citizens." (For a closer look at this credo, go to http://www.jnj.com; click on "View Our Credo.") Many companies have also instituted formal ethics training programs for their employees.

In the end, however, the surest way to infuse ethics throughout an organization is for top executives to behave ethically themselves. Few employees will bother to "do the right thing" unless they observe that their bosses value and support such behavior. To ensure a more ethical world, managers must be an example for others, both within and outside their organizations.

For further discussion and updates on ethical issues, check in at http://ethics.acusd.edu/index.html.

Chapter Review

1. There are at least three reasons to be concerned about ethics in a business environment:

   - Society as a whole benefits from ethical behavior.
   - People feel better when they behave ethically.
   - Unethical behavior can be very costly.

2. The ethics checklist:

   - What are the facts?
   - What are the critical issues?
   - Who are the stakeholders?
   - What are the alternatives?
   - What are the ethical implications of each alternative?

   - Is it legal?
   - How would it look in the light of day?
   - What are the consequences?
   - Does it violate important values?
   - Does it violate the Golden Rule?
   - Is it just?
   - Has the process been fair?
   - Is more than one alternative right?
   - Which values are in conflict?
   - Which of these values are most important?
   - Can you find an alternative that is consistent with your values?

Practice Test

1. A Harvard Business School alumna told this story about her life as an MBA student in the 1980s:

   During the spring of my first year, I took a Business Policy class. One of the young men in the class hung a bigger than life-size poster in the back of the room. It was a naked woman chained to a tree next to a Paul Bunyan-type man, fully clothed in a flannel jacket, with a chain saw. He was starting to de-limb her. The class broke up. The professor was standing there doubled over in laughter. There were 85 men guffawing away as if it were the funniest thing they'd ever seen. The women just sat there with their mouths open.

Did this professor and these students behave ethically? What would you consider to be ethical behavior in this circumstance for the men, the women, and the professor?

2. Joya is the head of the personal insurance division of a large insurance company. Six months before, she was almost promoted to vice-president, but she lost out to Bill, a colleague from another division. Bill has now called a meeting to discuss who should be promoted to head the marine insurance division. In Joya's opinion, Ichiro is the most qualified person. However, she knows that Bill will not support him because he is Japanese and a relatively recent immigrant to the United States. Nonetheless, Joya is astonished at the meeting when Bill announces that the staff in the marine insurance division strongly objects to Ichiro because of his drinking problem. Joya knows that Ichiro does not have a drinking problem and that the staff in his department thinks he would be a terrific choice. Based on Bill's false information, those at the meeting agree that the promotion should go to Jim, who happens to be a friend of Bill's. Joya knows that Jim is unpopular in his division because of his harsh, demanding style. She thinks that his appointment as department head will be disastrous. At the end of the meeting, Bill says that he will report the sense of the meeting to the CEO. Joya knows the CEO (they exchange pleasantries when passing in the hallways), but they have no regularly scheduled meetings. Nor is Joya likely to have the opportunity to mention Bill's behavior in a casual way. She is concerned that if she reports Bill is lying, the CEO will think she is causing trouble out of jealousy that Bill got the job she wanted. What should Joya do?

3. Executives were considering the possibility of moving their company to a different state. They wanted to determine if employees would be willing to relocate, but they did not want the employees to know the company was contemplating a move because the final decision had not yet been made. Instead of asking the employees directly, the company hired a firm to carry out a telephone survey. When calling the employees, these "pollsters" pretended to be conducting a public opinion poll and identified themselves as working for the new state's Chamber of Commerce. Has this company behaved in an ethical manner? Would there have been a better way to obtain this information?

4. Mark is an executive for a multinational office equipment company that would like to enter the potentially vast Chinese market. The official tariffs on office equipment imported into China are so high that these goods are uncompetitive in the local market. Mark discovers, however, that many companies sell their goods to importers offshore. These importers then negotiate "special" tariff rates with Chinese officials. Because these custom officials are under pressure to meet revenue targets, sometimes they are willing to negotiate lower, unofficial rates. What would you do if you were Mark?

5. Rap artist Ice-T and his band, Body Count, recorded a song called *Cop Killer* in which the singer gleefully anticipates slitting a policeman's throat. (The lyrics to this song are available at **http://www.cleat.org/remember/ TimeWarner/lyrics.html**.) Time Warner, Inc., produced this song and other gangsta rap recordings with violent and sexually degrading lyrics. Recorded music was an important source of profits for the company, which was struggling with a $15 billion debt and a depressed stock price. If Time Warner renounced rap albums, its reputation in the music business— and future profits—might have suffered. This damage could spill over into the multimedia market, which is crucial to Time Warner's future. The company was concerned about several important stakeholders—shareholders, consumers, suppliers (rap musicians). What decision would you have made if you had been CEO of Time Warner?

6. H. B. Fuller Co. of St. Paul is a leading manufacturer of industrial glues. Its mission statement says that the company "will conduct business legally and ethically." It has endowed a university chair in business ethics and donates 5 percent of its profits to charity. But now it is under attack for selling its shoemakers' glue, Resistol, in Central America. Many homeless children in these countries have become addicted to Resistol's fumes. So widespread is the problem that glue-sniffers in Central America are called "resistoleros."

Glue manufacturers in Europe have added a foul-smelling oil to their glue that discourages abusers. Fuller fears that the smell may also discourage legitimate users. What should Fuller do?

7. According to the Electronic Industries Association, questionable returns have become the toughest problem plaguing the consumer electronics industry. Some consumers purchase electronic equipment to use once or twice for a special occasion and then return it—a radar detector for a weekend getaway or a camcorder to record a wedding. Or a customer might return a cordless telephone because he cannot figure out how it works. The retailer's staff lacks the expertise to help, so they refund the customer's money and ship the phone back to the manufacturer labeled as defective. Excessive and unwarranted returns force manufacturers to repackage and reship perfectly good products, imposing extra costs that squeeze their profits and raise prices to consumers. One retailer returned a cordless telephone that was two years old and had been chewed up by a dog. What ethical obligations do consumers and retailers have in these circumstances?

8. Consider this complaint from an ethics professor:

   I make my living teaching and writing about ethics. . . . But in our own world—in our departments of philosophy and religious studies and medical humanities and ethics institutes—what happens?

   - Job openings [for instructors] are announced for positions that are already earmarked for specific persons. . . . [O]ver half the positions announced in the official employment newsletter for the American Academy of Religion were not "real."

   - It is extremely common for letters of application, even those responding to announced openings, to go without acknowledgment.

   - There are numerous instances of candidates who are brought to campus for interviews and who wait in vain to hear anything from their prospective employers. When the candidates finally call, embarrassed but

desperate, they are told, "Oh, that position has been filled."

Do recruiters have any ethical obligations to job candidates?

9. Six months ago, Todd, David, and Stacey joined a large, prestigious accounting firm in Houston. On paper, these three novices look similar and each graduated from a top MBA program. All three were assigned to work for the same client, a national restaurant chain. They quickly became friends and often lunched together. One day, a senior manager in the firm stopped by the conference room where Todd and David were working to ask if they would like to join him for lunch at the posh Hunter Club nearby. David said, "Thanks, that'd be great, but we usually eat lunch with Stacey. Could she come, too?" The manager hemmed and hawed for a minute, shifted his weight from one foot to the other, and finally said, "The Hunter Club doesn't allow women at lunch." What should Todd and David do?

10. Genentech, Inc., manufactured Protropin, a genetically engineered version of the human growth hormone. This drug's purpose was to enhance the growth of short children. Protropin was an important product for Genentech, accounting for more than one third of the company's total revenue of $217 million. Although the drug was approved for the treatment of children whose bodies made inadequate quantities of growth hormone, many doctors prescribed it for children with normal amounts of growth hormone who simply happened to be short. There was no firm evidence that the drug actually increased growth for short children with normal growth hormone. Moreover, many people questioned whether it is appropriate to prescribe such a powerful drug for cosmetic reasons, especially when the drug might not work. Nor was there proof that it was safe over the long term. Was Genentech behaving ethically? Should it have discouraged doctors from prescribing the drug to normal, short children?

11. **ROLE REVERSAL** Write one or two paragraphs that could be used as an essay question describing an ethical dilemma that you have faced in your own life.

Internet Research Problem

Go to **academic.cengage.com/blaw/beatty** and click on "Ethics Tools: Resolving Ethical Dilemmas (with Real-to-Life Examples)." Outline the steps you would take to resolve one of these dilemmas. Use the ethics checklist in this chapter to guide you.

You can find further practice problems at **academic.cengage.com/blaw/beatty.**

Dispute Resolution

© AKIRA KAEDE/PHOTODISC/GETTY IMAGES

Tony Caruso had not returned for dinner, and his wife, Karen, was nervous. She put on some sandals and hurried across the dunes, a half mile to the ocean shore. She soon came upon Tony's dog, Blue, tied to an old picket fence. Tony's shoes and clothing were piled neatly nearby. Karen searched frantically throughout the evening, helped by her friends. A little past midnight, Tony's body washed ashore, his lungs filled with water. A local doctor concluded he had accidentally drowned.

Karen and her friends were not the only ones distraught. Tony had been partners with Beth Smiles in an environmental consulting business, Enviro-Vision. They were good friends, and Beth was emotionally devastated. When she was able to focus on business issues, Beth filed an insurance claim with the Coastal Insurance Group. Beth hated to think about Tony's death in financial terms, but she was relieved that the struggling business would receive $2 million on the life insurance policy.

Several months after filing the claim, Beth received this reply from Coastal: "Under the policy issued to Enviro-Vision, we are conditionally liable in the amount of $1 million in the event of Mr. Caruso's death. If his death is accidental, we are conditionally liable to pay double indemnity of $2 million. But pursuant to section H(5), death by suicide is not covered. After a thorough investigation, we have concluded that Anthony Caruso's death was an act of suicide, as defined in section B(11) of the policy. Your claim is denied in its entirety." Beth was furious. She was convinced Tony was incapable of suicide. And her company could not afford the $2 million loss. She decided to consult her lawyer, Chris Pruitt. ■

THREE FUNDAMENTAL AREAS OF LAW

This case is a fictionalized version of several real cases based on double indemnity insurance policies. In this chapter we follow Beth's dispute with Coastal from initial interview through appeal, using it to examine three fundamental areas of law: alternative dispute resolution, the structure of our court systems, and civil lawsuits. But first we need to look at the best sort of dispute—the kind that is avoided.

Dispute Prevention

Over the years, one of the important services attorney Chris Pruitt has done for Enviro-Vision is *prevent disputes*. It is vital to understand and apply this concept in business and professional work and in everyday life. There is an old saying that you have a chance to go broke twice in your life: once when you lose a lawsuit, the other time when you win. The financial and emotional costs of litigation are extraordinarily high.

at RISK

You can avoid disputes in many different ways. Throughout the text we specify an array of preventive steps as they relate to the different legal problems posed. Here we can mention a few of the potential disputes Enviro-Vision avoided by thinking ahead.

When Beth and Tony started Enviro-Vision, Chris pointed out that, as business partners, the best way to protect both their friendship and their business was with a detailed partnership agreement. Although Beth and Tony found it tedious to create, the agreement helped them avoid problems such as those concerning capital contributions to the partnership, about who owns what, and about hiring and firing employees. Further, Enviro-Vision avoids unjustified firings by giving all employees written job descriptions. It educates employees about sexual harassment. When drafting a contract, Beth has learned to be sure that the client knows exactly what it is getting, when the work is due, what the risks are, and how much it will cost. Each of these practices has prevented potential lawsuits. ◆

When Beth Smiles meets with her lawyer, Chris Pruitt brings a second attorney from his firm, Janet Booker, who is an experienced **litigator**—that is, a lawyer who handles court cases. If they file a lawsuit, Janet will be in charge, so Chris wants her there for the first meeting. Janet probes about Tony's home life, the status of the business, his personal finances, everything. Beth becomes upset that Janet doesn't seem sympathetic, but Chris explains that Janet is doing her job: She needs all the information, good and bad.

Litigation versus Alternative Dispute Resolution

Janet starts thinking about the two methods of dispute resolution: litigation and alternative dispute resolution. **Litigation** refers to lawsuits, the process of filing claims in court, and ultimately going to trial. **Alternative dispute resolution** is any other formal or informal process used to settle disputes without resorting to a trial. It is increasingly popular with corporations and individuals alike because it is generally cheaper and faster than litigation.

ALTERNATIVE DISPUTE RESOLUTION

Janet Booker knows that even after expert legal help, vast expense, and years of work, litigation may leave clients unsatisfied. If she can use alternative dispute resolution (ADR) to create a mutually satisfactory solution in a few months, for a fraction of the cost, she is glad to do it. We will look at different types of ADR and analyze their strengths and weaknesses.

Negotiation

In most cases the parties negotiate, whether personally or through lawyers. Fortunately, the great majority of disputes are resolved this way. Negotiation often begins as soon as a dispute arises and may last a few days or several years.

Mediation

Mediation is the fastest growing method of dispute resolution in the United States. Here, a neutral person, called a mediator, attempts to coax the two disputing parties toward a voluntary settlement. (In some cases, there may be two or more mediators, but we will use the singular.) Generally, the two disputants voluntarily enter mediation, although some judges order the parties to try this form of ADR before allowing a case to go to trial.

A mediator does not render a decision in the dispute but uses a variety of skills to prod the parties toward agreement. Often a mediator will shuttle between the antagonists, hearing their arguments, sorting out the serious issues from the less important, prompting the parties and lawyers alike to consider new perspectives, and looking for areas of agreement. Mediators must earn the trust of both parties, listen closely, try to diffuse anger and fear, and build the will to settle. Good mediators do not need a law degree, but they must have a sense of humor and low blood pressure.

Mediation has several major advantages. Because the parties maintain control of the process, the two antagonists can speak freely. They need not fear conceding too much, because no settlement takes effect until both parties sign. All discussions are confidential, further encouraging candid talk. This is particularly helpful in cases involving proprietary information that might be revealed during a trial.

Of all forms of dispute resolution, mediation probably offers the strongest "win–win" potential. Because the goal is voluntary settlement, neither party needs to fear that it will end up the loser. This is in sharp contrast to litigation, where one party is very likely to lose. Removing the fear of defeat often encourages thinking and talking that are more open and realistic than negotiations held in the midst of a lawsuit. Studies show that more than 75 percent of mediated cases do reach a voluntary settlement. Such an agreement is particularly valuable to parties that wish to preserve a long-term relationship. Consider two companies that have done business successfully for 10 years but now are in the midst of a million-dollar trade dispute. A lawsuit could last three or more years and destroy any chance of future trade. However, if the parties mediate the disagreement, they might reach an amicable settlement within a month or two and could quickly resume their mutually profitable business.

This form of ADR works for disputes both big and small. Two college roommates who cannot get along may find that a three-hour mediation session restores tranquility in the apartment. On a larger scale, consider the work of former United States Senator George Mitchell, who mediated the Anglo-Irish peace agreement, setting Northern Ireland on the path to peace for the first time in three centuries. Like most good mediators, Mitchell was remarkably patient. In an early session, Mitchell permitted the head of one militant party to speak without interruption—for seven straight hours. The diatribe yielded no quick results, but Mitchell believed that after Northern Ireland's tortured history, any nonviolent discussions represented progress.

Arbitration

In arbitration, another form of ADR, the parties agree to bring in a neutral third party, but with a major difference: the arbitrator has the power to impose an award. The arbitrator allows each side equal time to present its case and, after deliberation, issues a binding decision, generally without giving reasons. Unlike mediation, arbitration ensures that there will be a final result, although the parties lose control of the outcome. Arbitration is generally faster and cheaper than litigation.

Parties in arbitration give up many rights that litigants retain, including discovery and class action. *Discovery*, as we see later, allows the two sides in a lawsuit to obtain, before trial, documentary and other evidence from the opponent. Arbitration permits both sides to keep secret many files that would have to be divulged in a court case, potentially depriving the opposing side of valuable evidence. A party may have a stronger case than it realizes, and the absence of discovery may permanently deny it that knowledge. A *class action* is a suit in which one injured party represents a large group of people who have suffered similar harm. For example, in an employment discrimination case, a large group of employees who claim similar injury might band together to bring the case, giving themselves much greater clout. Arbitration eliminates this possibility, because injured employees face the employer one at a time. Finally, the fact that an arbitrator may not provide a written, public decision bars other plaintiffs, and society generally, from learning what happened.

Mandatory Arbitration

Mandatory arbitration is a variation that contains one big difference: the parties agree *in advance* to arbitrate any disputes that may arise. For example, a consumer who purchases a computer or hires a real estate agent may sign an agreement requiring arbitration of any disputes; a customer opening an account with a stockbroker or bank—or health plan—may sign a similar form, often without realizing it. The good news is fewer lawsuits; the bad news is you might be the person kept out of court.

Assume that you live in Miami. Using the Internet, you order a $2,000 ThinkLite laptop computer, which arrives in a carton, loaded with six fat instructional manuals and many small leaflets. You read some of the documents and ignore others. For four weeks you struggle to make your computer work, to no avail. Finally, you telephone ThinkLite and demand a refund, but the company refuses. You file suit in your local court, at which time the company points out that buried among the hundreds of pages it mailed you was a *mandatory arbitration form.* This document prohibits you from filing suit against the company and states that if you have any complaint with the company, you must fly to Chicago; pay a $2,000 arbitrator's fee; plead your case before an arbitrator selected by the Laptop Trade Association of America; and, in the event you lose, pay ThinkLite's attorney's fees, which could be several thousand dollars. Is that mandatory arbitration provision valid? It is too early to say with finality, but thus far the courts that have faced such clauses have enforced them.[1]

To return to our hypothetical case, Janet Booker proposes to Coastal Insurance that they use ADR to expedite a decision in their dispute. Coastal rejects the offer. Coastal's lawyer, Rich Stewart, says that suicide is apparent. He does not want a neutral party to split the difference and award $1 million to Enviro-Vision. Janet reports

---

[1] See, e.g., Hill v. Gateway 2000, 105 F.3d 1147, 1997 U.S. App. LEXIS 1877 (7th Cir. 1997), upholding a similar clause.

this explanation to Beth but adds that she does not believe it. She thinks that Coastal wants the case to drag on as long as possible in the hopes that Enviro-Vision will ultimately settle cheap.

It is a long way to go before trial, but Janet has to prepare her case. The first thing she thinks about is where to file the lawsuit.

COURT SYSTEMS

The United States has more than 50 *systems* of courts. One nationwide system of *federal* courts serves the entire country. In addition, each *state* has its court system. The state and federal courts are in different buildings, have different judges, and hear different kinds of cases. Each has special powers and certain limitations.

State Courts

The typical state court system forms a pyramid, as Exhibit 3.1 shows. You may use the Internet to learn the exact names and powers of the courts in your state. Go to http://www.state.[two-letter abbreviation for state].us/, and click on "agencies," "courts," or a similar link.

Trial Courts

Almost all cases start in trial courts, the ones endlessly portrayed on television and in film. There is one judge, and there will often (but not always) be a jury. This is the only court to hear testimony from witnesses and receive evidence. **Trial courts determine the facts of a particular dispute and apply to those facts the law given by earlier appellate court decisions.**

In the Enviro-Vision dispute, the trial court will decide all important facts that are in dispute. Did Tony Caruso die? Did he drown? Assuming he drowned, was his death accidental or suicide? Once the jury has decided the facts, it will apply the law to those facts. If Tony Caruso died accidentally, contract law provides that Beth Smiles is entitled to double indemnity benefits. If the jury decides he killed himself, Beth gets nothing.

Facts are critical. That may sound obvious, but in a course devoted to legal principles, it is easy to lose track of the key role that factual determinations play in the resolution of any dispute. In the Enviro-Vision case, we will see that one bit of factual evidence goes undetected, with costly consequences.

Jurisdiction **refers to a court's power to hear a case.** In state or federal court, a plaintiff may start a lawsuit only in a court that has jurisdiction over that kind of case. Some courts have very limited jurisdiction, whereas others have the power to hear almost any case.

Trial Courts of Limited Jurisdiction. These courts may hear only certain types of cases. Small claims court has jurisdiction only over civil lawsuits involving a maximum of, say, $2,500 (the amount varies from state to state). Municipal court has jurisdiction over traffic citations and minor criminal matters. A juvenile court hears only cases involving minors. Probate court is devoted to settling the estates of deceased persons, though in some states it will hear certain other cases as well. Land court focuses on disputes about title to land and other real property issues. Domestic relations court resolves marital disputes and child custody issues.

Trial Courts of General Jurisdiction. Trial courts of general jurisdiction, however, can hear a very broad range of cases. The most important court, for our

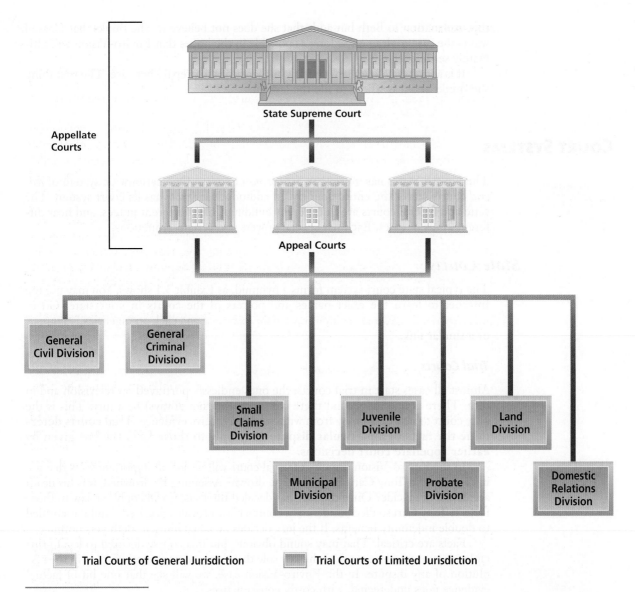

State Supreme Court

Appellate Courts

Appeal Courts

General Civil Division

General Criminal Division

Small Claims Division

Municipal Division

Juvenile Division

Probate Division

Land Division

Domestic Relations Division

Trial Courts of General Jurisdiction   Trial Courts of Limited Jurisdiction

Exhibit 3.1

purposes, is the general civil division. This court may hear virtually any civil lawsuit. In one day it might hear a $450 million shareholders' derivative lawsuit, an employment issue involving freedom of religion, and a foreclosure on a mortgage. Most of the cases we study start in this court.[2] If Enviro-Vision's case against Coastal goes to trial in a state court, it will begin in the trial court of general jurisdiction.

[2] Note that the actual name of the court will vary from state to state. In many states it is called superior court, because it has power superior to the courts of limited jurisdiction. In New York it is called supreme court (anything to confuse the layperson); in some states it is called court of common pleas; in Oregon and other states it is a circuit court. They are all civil trial courts of general jurisdiction. Within this branch, some states are beginning to establish specialized business courts, to hear complex commercial disputes. At least one state has created a cybercourt for high-tech cases. Lawyers will argue their cases by teleconference and present evidence via streaming video.

Appellate Courts

Appellate courts are entirely different from trial courts. Three or more judges hear the case. There are no juries, ever. These courts do not hear witnesses or take new evidence. They hear appeals of cases already tried below. **Appeals courts generally accept the facts given to them by trial courts and review the trial record to see if the court made errors of law.**

Generally, an appeals court will accept a factual finding unless there was *no evidence at all* to support it. If the jury decides that Tony Caruso committed suicide, the appeals court will normally accept that fact, even though the appeals judges consider the jury's conclusion dubious. On the other hand, if a jury concluded that Tony had been murdered, an appeals court would overturn that finding if neither side had introduced any evidence of murder during the trial.

An appeals court reviews the trial record to make sure that the lower court correctly applied the law to the facts. If the trial court made an **error of law,** the appeals court may require a new trial. Suppose the jury concludes that Tony Caruso committed suicide, but votes to award Enviro-Vision $1 million because it feels sorry for Beth Smiles. That is an error of law: if Tony committed suicide, Beth is entitled to nothing. An appellate court will reverse the decision. Or suppose that the trial judge permitted a friend of Tony's to state that he was certain Tony would never commit suicide. Normally, such opinions are not permissible in trial, and it was a legal error for the judge to allow the jury to hear it.

Court of Appeals.   The party that loses at the trial court may appeal to the intermediate court of appeals. The party filing the appeal is the **appellant.** The party opposing the appeal (because it won at trial) is the **appellee.**

This court allows both sides to submit written arguments on the case, called **briefs.** Each side then appears for oral argument, usually before a panel of three judges. The appellant's lawyer has about 15 minutes to convince the judges that the trial court made serious errors of law, and that the decision should be **reversed,** that is, nullified. The appellee's lawyer has the same time to persuade the court that the trial court acted correctly and that the result should be **affirmed,** that is, permitted to stand.

State Supreme Court.   This is the highest court in the state, and it accepts some appeals from the court of appeals. In most states there is no absolute right to appeal to the supreme court. If the high court regards a legal issue as important, it accepts the case. It then takes briefs and hears oral argument just as the appeals court did. If it considers the matter unimportant, it refuses to hear the case, meaning that the court of appeals' ruling is the final word on the case.[3]

In most states seven judges, often called justices, sit on the supreme court. They have the final word on state law.

Federal Courts

As discussed in Chapter 1, federal courts are established by the United States Constitution, which limits what kinds of cases can be brought in any federal court. (See Exhibit 3.2.) For our purposes, two kinds of civil lawsuits are permitted in federal court: federal question cases and diversity cases.

---

[3] In some states with smaller populations, there is no intermediate appeals court. All appeals from trial courts go directly to the state supreme court.

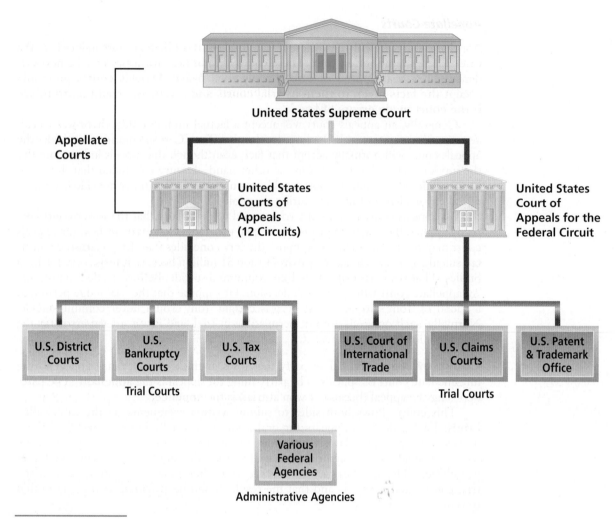

United States Supreme Court

Appellate Courts

United States Courts of Appeals (12 Circuits)

United States Court of Appeals for the Federal Circuit

U.S. District Courts

U.S. Bankruptcy Courts

U.S. Tax Courts

Trial Courts

U.S. Court of International Trade

U.S. Claims Courts

U.S. Patent & Trademark Office

Trial Courts

Various Federal Agencies

Administrative Agencies

Exhibit 3.2

Federal Question Cases

A claim based on the United States Constitution, a federal statute, or a federal treaty is called a federal question case.[4] Federal courts have jurisdiction over these cases. If the Environmental Protection Agency orders Logging Company not to cut in a particular forest, and Logging Company claims that the agency has wrongly deprived it of its property, that suit is based on a federal statute and is thus a federal question. If Little Retailer sues Mega Retailer, claiming that Mega has established a monopoly, that claim is also based on a statute—the Sherman Antitrust Act—and creates federal question jurisdiction. Enviro-Vision's potential suit merely concerns an insurance contract. The federal district court has no federal question jurisdiction over the case.

---

[4] 28 U.S.C. §1331 governs federal question jurisdiction and 28 U.S.C. §1332 covers diversity jurisdiction.

Diversity Cases

Even if no federal law is at issue, federal courts have **diversity jurisdiction** when (1) the plaintiff and defendant are citizens of different states *and* (2) the amount in dispute exceeds $75,000. The theory behind diversity jurisdiction is that courts of one state might be biased against citizens of another state. To ensure fairness, the parties have the option of federal court.

Enviro-Vision is located in Oregon and Coastal Insurance is incorporated in Georgia.[5] They are citizens of different states and the amount in dispute far exceeds $75,000. Janet could file this case in United States District Court based on diversity jurisdiction.

Trial Courts

United States District Court.   This is the primary trial court in the federal system. The nation is divided into about 94 districts, and each has a district court. States with smaller populations have one district. States with larger populations have several districts; Texas is divided geographically into four districts.

Other Trial Courts.   There are other, specialized trial courts in the federal system. Bankruptcy court, tax court, and the United States Court of International Trade all handle name-appropriate cases. The United States Claims Court hears cases brought against the United States, typically on contract disputes.

Judges.   The President of the United States nominates all federal court judges, from district court to the Supreme Court. The nominees must be confirmed by the Senate.

Appellate Courts

United States Courts of Appeals.   These are the intermediate courts of appeals. As the map on p. 52 shows, they are divided into "circuits," which are geographical areas. There are 11 numbered circuits, hearing appeals from district courts. For example, an appeal from the Northern District of Illinois would go to the Court of Appeals for the Seventh Circuit. You will find an interactive map of the District and Circuit Courts at http://www.uscourts.gov. Click on "Court Links."

A twelfth court, the Court of Appeals for the District of Columbia, hears appeals only from the district court of Washington, D.C. This is a particularly powerful court because so many suits about federal statutes begin in the district court for the District of Columbia. Also in Washington is the thirteenth court of appeals, known as the Federal Circuit. It hears appeals from specialized trial courts, as shown in Exhibit 3.2.

Within one circuit there are many circuit judges, up to about 30 judges in the largest circuit, the ninth. When a case is appealed, three judges hear the appeal, taking briefs and hearing oral argument.

United States Supreme Court.   This is the highest court in the country. There are nine justices on the Court. One justice is the chief justice, and the other eight are associate justices. When they decide a case, each justice casts an equal vote. The chief justice's special power comes from his authority to assign opinions to a

---

[5] For diversity purposes, a corporation is a citizen of the state in which it is incorporated and the state in which it has its principal place of business.

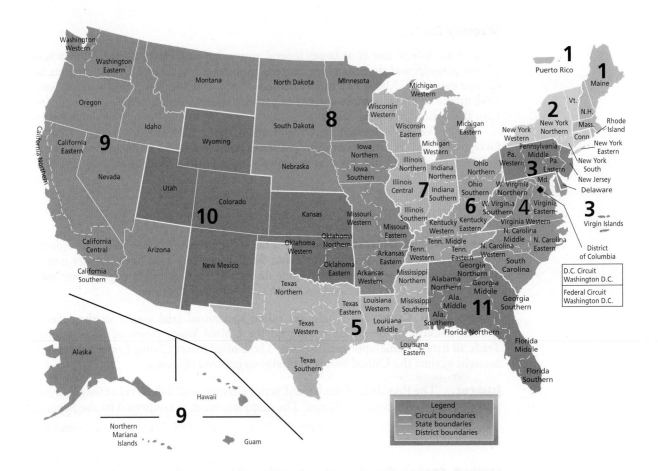

given justice. The justice assigned to write an opinion has an opportunity to control the precise language and thus to influence the voting by other justices. For a face-to-face meeting with Supreme Court justices, past and present, introduce yourself to http://www.oyez.org.

The Supreme Court has the power to hear appeals in any federal case and in certain cases that began in state courts. Generally, it is up to the Court whether or not it will accept a case. A party that wants the Supreme Court to review a lower court ruling must file a petition for a **writ of certiorari,** asking the Court to hear the case. The Court receives about 8,000 of these requests every year but currently accepts fewer than 100. Most cases accepted involve either an important issue of constitutional law or an interpretation of a major federal statute.

LITIGATION

Janet Booker decides to file the Enviro-Vision suit in the Oregon trial court. She thinks that a state court judge may take the issue more seriously than a federal district court judge.

Pleadings

The documents that begin a lawsuit are called the **pleadings.** These consist of the complaint, the answer, and sometimes a reply.

Complaint

The plaintiff files in court a **complaint,** which is a short, plain statement of the facts she is alleging and the legal claims she is making. The purpose of the complaint is to inform the defendant of the general nature of the claims and the need to come into court and protect his interests.

Janet Booker files the complaint, as shown in the following. Because Enviro-Vision is a partnership, she files the suit on behalf of Beth personally.

STATE OF OREGON
CIRCUIT COURT

Multnomah County   Civil Action No. _____

_____

Elizabeth Smiles,
Plaintiff

JURY TRIAL DEMANDED

v.

Coastal Insurance Company, Inc.,
Defendant

_____

COMPLAINT

Plaintiff Elizabeth Smiles states that:
1. She is a citizen of Multnomah County, Oregon.
2. Defendant Coastal Insurance Company, Inc., is incorporated under the laws of Georgia and has as its usual place of business 148 Thrift Street, Savannah, Georgia.
3. On or about July 5, 2006, plaintiff Smiles ("Smiles"), Defendant Coastal Insurance Co, Inc. ("Coastal") and Anthony Caruso entered into an insurance contract ("the contract"), a copy of which is annexed hereto as Exhibit "A." This contract was signed by all parties or their authorized agents, in Multnomah County, Oregon.
4. The contract obligates Coastal to pay to Smiles the sum of two million dollars ($2 million) if Anthony Caruso should die accidentally.
5. On or about September 18, 2006, Anthony Caruso accidentally drowned and died while swimming.
6. Coastal has refused to pay any sum pursuant to the contract.
7. Coastal has knowingly, willingly and unreasonably refused to honor its obligations under the contract.

WHEREFORE, plaintiff Elizabeth Smiles demands judgment against defendant Coastal for all monies due under the contract; demands triple damages for Coastal's knowing, willing, and unreasonable refusal to honor its obligations; and demands all costs and attorney's fees, with interest.

ELIZABETH SMILES,
By her attorney,
[Signed]
Janet Booker
Pruitt, Booker & Bother
983 Joy Avenue
Portland, OR
October 18, 2006

Service

When she files the complaint in court, Janet gets a summons, which is a paper ordering the defendant to answer the complaint within 20 days. A sheriff or constable then *serves* the two papers by delivering them to the defendant. Coastal's headquarters are in Georgia, so the state of Oregon has required Coastal to specify someone as its agent for receipt of service in Oregon.

Answer

Once the complaint and summons are served, Coastal has 20 days in which to file an answer. Coastal's answer, shown below, is a brief reply to each of the allegations in the complaint. The answer tells the court and the plaintiff exactly what issues are in dispute. Because Coastal admits that the parties entered into the contract that Beth claims they did, there is no need for her to prove that in court. The court can focus its attention on the disputed issue: whether Tony Caruso died accidentally.

STATE OF OREGON
CIRCUIT COURT

Multnomah County   Civil Action No. 06-5626

Elizabeth Smiles,
Plaintiff
v.
Coastal Insurance Company, Inc.,
Defendant

ANSWER
Defendant Coastal Insurance Company, Inc., answers the complaint as follows:
1. Admit.
2. Admit.
3. Admit.
4. Admit.
5. Deny.
6. Admit.
7. Deny.
COASTAL INSURANCE COMPANY, INC.,
By its attorney,
[Signed]
Richard B. Stewart
Kiley, Robbins, Stewart & Glote
333 Victory Boulevard
Portland, OR
October 30, 2006

If the defendant fails to answer in time, the plaintiff will ask for a **default judgment,** meaning a decision that the plaintiff wins without a trial.

Counter-Claim

Sometimes a defendant does more than merely answer a complaint, and files a **counter-claim,** meaning a second lawsuit by the defendant against the plaintiff. Suppose that after her complaint was filed in court, Beth had written a letter to the newspaper, calling Coastal a bunch of "thieves and scoundrels who spend their days mired in fraud and larceny." Coastal would not have found that amusing. The company's answer would have included a counter-claim against Beth for libel, claiming that she falsely accused the insurer of serious criminal acts. Coastal would have demanded money damages.

If Coastal counter-claimed, Beth would have to file a **reply**, which is simply an answer to a counter-claim. Beth's reply would be similar to Coastal's answer, admitting or denying the various allegations.

Class Actions

Suppose Janet uncovers evidence that Coastal denies 80 percent of all life insurance claims, calling them suicide. She could ask the court to permit a **class action.** If the court granted her request, she would represent the entire group of plaintiffs, including those who are unaware of the lawsuit or even unaware they were harmed. Class actions can give the plaintiffs much greater leverage, because the defendant's potential liability is vastly increased. In the back of her mind, Janet has thoughts of a class action *if* she can uncover evidence that Coastal has used a claim of suicide to deny coverage to a large number of claimants.

ECONOMICS *& the* LAW	From his small town in Maine, Ernie decides to get rich quickly. On the Internet he advertises "Energy Breakthrough! Cut your heating costs 15 percent for only $25." One hundred thousand people send him their money. In return, they receive a photocopied graph, illustrating that if you wear two sweaters instead of one, you will feel 15 percent warmer. Ernie has deceitfully earned $2,500,000 in pure profit. What can the angry homeowners do? Under the laws of fraud and consumer protection, they have a legitimate claim to their $25, and perhaps even to treble damages ($75). But few will sue, because the time and effort required would be greater than the money recovered.

Economists analyze such legal issues in terms of *efficiency*. The laws against Ernie's fraud are clear and well intended, but they will not help in this case because it is too expensive for 100,000 people to litigate such a small claim. The effort would be hugely *inefficient*, both for the homeowners and for society generally. The economic reality may permit Ernie to evade the law's grasp.

That is one reason we have class actions. A dozen or so "heating plan" buyers can all hire the same lawyer. This attorney will file court papers in Maine on behalf of *everyone*, nationwide, who has been swindled by Ernie—including the 99,988 people who have yet to be notified that they are part of the case. Now the con artist, instead of facing a few harmless suits for $25, must respond to a multimillion-dollar claim being handled by an experienced lawyer. Treble damages become menacing: three times $25 times 100,000 is no joke, even to a cynic like Ernie. He may also be forced to pay for the plaintiffs' attorney, as well as all costs of notifying class members and disbursing money to them. With one lawyer representing an entire class, the legal system has become fiercely efficient.

Congress recently passed a statute designed to force large, multi-state class actions out of state courts, into federal. Proponents of the new law complained that state courts often gave excessive verdicts, even for frivolous lawsuits. They said the cases hurt businesses while enriching lawyers. Opponents argued that the new law was designed to shield large corporations from paying for the harm they cause by sending the cases into a federal system that is often hostile to them. ◆

Judgment on the Pleadings

A party can ask the court for a judgment based simply on the pleadings themselves, by filing a motion to dismiss. **A motion is a formal request to the court** that the court take some step or issue some order. During a lawsuit the parties file many motions. A **motion to dismiss** is a request that the court terminate a case without permitting it to go further. Suppose that a state law requires claims on life insurance contracts to be filed within three years, and Beth files her claim four years after Tony's death. Coastal would move to dismiss based on this late filing. The court might well agree, and Beth would never get into court.

Discovery

Few cases are dismissed on the pleadings. Most proceed quickly to the next step. **Discovery is the critical, pre-trial opportunity for both parties to learn the strengths and weaknesses of the opponent's case.**

The theory behind civil litigation is that the best outcome is a negotiated settlement and that parties will move toward agreement if they understand the opponent's case. That is likeliest to occur if both sides have an opportunity to examine most of the evidence the other side will bring to trial. Further, if a case does go all the way to trial, efficient and fair litigation cannot take place in a courtroom filled, like a piñata, with surprises. On television dramas, witnesses say astonishing things that amaze the courtroom (and keep viewers hooked through the next commercial). In real trials the lawyers know in advance the answers to practically all questions asked because discovery has allowed them to see the opponent's documents and question its witnesses. The following are the most important forms of discovery.

Interrogatories.   These are written questions that the opposing party must answer, in writing, under oath.

Depositions.   These provide a chance for one party's lawyer to question the other party, or a potential witness, under oath. The person being questioned is the **deponent.** Lawyers for both parties are present. During depositions, and in trial, good lawyers choose words carefully and ask questions calculated to advance their cause. A fine line separates ethical, probing questions from those that are tricky, and a similar line divides answers that are merely unhelpful from perjury.

Production of Documents and Things.   Each side may ask the other side to produce relevant documents for inspection and copying; to produce physical objects, such as part of a car alleged to be defective; and for permission to enter on land to make an inspection, for example, at the scene of an accident.

Physical and Mental Examination.   A party may ask the court to order an examination of the other party, if his physical or mental condition is relevant, for example, in a case of medical malpractice.

Requests for Admission.   Either party can insist that the opposing party admit or deny certain facts, to avoid wasting time on points not in dispute. In a medical malpractice case, the plaintiff would request that the doctor admit he performed the surgery and admit what would be the normal level of care a surgeon would provide for such a case (while not expecting the surgeon to admit that he erred).

Janet Booker begins her discovery with interrogatories. Her goal is to learn Coastal's basic position and factual evidence and then follow up with more detailed questioning during depositions. Her interrogatories ask for every fact Coastal relied on in denying the claim. She asks for the names of all witnesses, the identity of all documents, the description of all things or objects that they considered. She requests the names of all corporate officers who played any role in the decision and of any expert witnesses Coastal plans to call. Interrogatory No. 18 demands extensive information on all *other* claims in the past three years that Coastal has denied based on alleged suicide. Janet is looking for evidence that would support a class action.

Beth remarks on how thorough the interrogatories are. "This will tell us what their case is." Janet frowns and looks less optimistic: she's done this before.

Coastal has 30 days to answer Janet's interrogatories. Before it responds, Coastal mails to Janet a notice of deposition, stating its intention to depose Beth Smiles. Beth and Janet will go to the office of Coastal's lawyer, and Beth will answer questions under oath. But at the same time Coastal sends this notice, it sends *25 other notices of deposition.* The company will depose Karen Caruso as soon as Beth's deposition is over. Coastal also plans to depose all seven employees of Enviro-Vision; three neighbors who lived near Tony and Karen's beach house; two policemen who participated in the search; the doctor and two nurses involved in the case; Tony's physician; Jerry Johnson, Tony's tennis partner; Craig Bergson, a college roommate; a couple who had dinner with Tony and Karen a week before his death; and several other people.

Beth is appalled. Janet explains that some of these people might have relevant information. But there may be another reason that Coastal is doing this: the company wants to make this litigation hurt. Janet will have to attend every one of these depositions. Costs will skyrocket.

Janet files a **motion for a protective order.** This is a request that the court limit Coastal's discovery by decreasing the number of depositions. Janet also calls Rich Stewart and suggests that they discuss what depositions are really necessary. Rich insists that all of the depositions are important. This is a $2 million case and Coastal is entitled to protect itself. As both lawyers know, **the parties are entitled to discover anything that could reasonably lead to valid evidence.**

Before Beth's deposition date arrives, Rich sends Coastal's answers to Enviro-Vision's interrogatories. The answers contain no useful information whatsoever. For example, Interrogatory No. 10 asked, "If you claim that Anthony Caruso committed suicide, describe every fact upon which you rely in reaching that conclusion." Coastal's answer simply says, "His state of mind, his poor business affairs, and the circumstances of his death all indicate suicide."

Janet calls Rich and complains that the interrogatory answers are a bad joke. Rich disagrees, saying that it is the best information they have so early in the case. After they debate it for 20 minutes, Rich offers to settle the case for $100,000. Janet refuses and makes no counteroffer.

Janet files a **motion to compel answers to interrogatories,** in other words, a formal request that the court order Coastal to supply more complete answers. Janet submits a **memorandum** with the motion, which is a supporting argument. Although it is only a few pages long, the memorandum takes several hours of library research and writing to prepare—more costs. Janet also informs Rich Stewart that Beth will not appear for the deposition, since Coastal's interrogatory answers are inadequate.

Rich now files *his* motion to compel, asking the court to order Beth Smiles to appear for her deposition. The court hears all of the motions together. Janet argues that Coastal's interrogatory answers are hopelessly uninformative and defeat the whole purpose of discovery. She claims that Coastal's large number of depositions creates a huge and unfair expense for a small firm.

Rich claims that the interrogatory answers are the best that Coastal can do thus far and that Coastal will supplement the answers when more information becomes available. He argues against Interrogatory No. 18, the one in which Janet asked for the names of other policyholders whom Coastal considered suicides. He claims that Janet is engaging in a fishing expedition that would violate the privacy of Coastal's insurance customers and provide no information relevant to this case. He demands that Janet make Beth available for a deposition.

These discovery rulings are critical because they will color the entire lawsuit. A trial judge has to make many discovery decisions before a case reaches trial. At times the judge must weigh the need of one party to see documents against the other side's need for privacy. One device a judge can use in reaching a discovery ruling is an **in camera inspection,** meaning that the judge views the requested documents alone, with no lawyers present, and decides whether the other side is entitled to view them. The following case illustrates a common discovery problem: refusal by one side to provide answers. The decision also demonstrates why such aggressive conduct can backfire disastrously.

AMERICAN CASH CARD CORP. V. AT&T CORP.

210 F.3d 354, 2000 WL 357670
United States Court of Appeals for the Second Circuit, 2000

Facts: The American Cash Card Corp. ("Amcash") sued AT&T, claiming that AT&T had promised to provide a long distance service at a special low rate, but had in fact charged much more. AT&T filed a counterclaim, saying that it had provided the promised telephone service but that Amcash had failed to pay its (very large) bills.

The trial court ordered that all discovery be finished by August 16, 1996. AT&T served its first request for documents and its first interrogatories in May of that year. Amcash requested two extensions of its response deadline, but then failed to produce documents or answers. In August, the court ordered Amcash to respond promptly or face sanctions. Amcash produced only a few answers to interrogatories. The court issued a second order, requiring a full response by October 8, 1996, threatening to dismiss Amcash's case if it failed to answer. Amcash withheld all papers concerning finances and other key issues.

In January 1997, the trial judge ordered Amcash to produce the financial records, including customer information, no later than January 31. The court also ordered Amcash to pay $7,500 to AT&T for that company's expenses in obtaining discovery orders.

Amcash produced a few records, but retained many more. The company's general manager, Vicki Zakaria, admitted in a deposition that Amcash's attorney had never asked her to look for documents concerning AT&T, or to conduct an electronic search for relevant information, even though her computer contained substantial data relating to the phone company. She even mentioned that she had additional AT&T documents in her home, which she had never furnished.

In February, the trial court dismissed Amcash's claims and awarded AT&T $108,394,969 on its counterclaims. Amcash appealed.

Issue: Did the trial court abuse its discretion by dismissing Amcash's claims and allowing AT&T's claims?

Excerpts from the Court's Summary Order: Although entry of a default judgment is an extreme measure, discovery orders are meant to be followed. When we review a district court's entry of default judgment as a sanction, the question is not whether the Court of Appeals would as an original matter have entered such a judgment; it is whether the district court abused its discretion in so doing.

First, [Amcash contends], the district court abused its discretion because of the severity of the effects of entering default judgment in this case. But here, as in other areas of the law, the most severe in the spectrum of sanctions provided by statute or rule must be available to the district court in appropriate cases, not merely to penalize those whose conduct may be deemed to warrant such a sanction, but to deter those who might be tempted to such conduct in the absence of such a deterrent.

Second, Appellants seem to maintain that the district court abused its discretion because its finding of

▼

bad faith was incorrect. The district court's finding in this respect is, however, a factual determination, subject to reversal only upon a showing of clear error. The district court's conclusions concerning Appellant's bad faith is, instead, amply supported by the facts in the record. Appellants try to avoid responsibility for their failure to obey the district court's discovery orders by shifting the blame to the incompetence of their trial counsel. But even if this were the case, the defense would not be availing. For a litigant chooses counsel at his peril, and here, as in countless other contexts, counsel's disregard of his professional responsibilities can lead to extinction of his client's claim.

Affirmed. ■

Public Policy

Public policy refers to the interest that society has in any dispute. In appellate cases, judges routinely consider not only the interests of the two parties, but also the effect that their ruling will have on the general population. Notice two public policy concerns in the *American Cash Card* case. First, the judges dismiss the plaintiff's suit partly for deterrent effect. What does that mean? Is that motive wise? Second, the judges decide the case based on *procedural*, rather than *substantive*, issues. Is it proper to decide a $100 million dispute without holding a trial? What is the public policy effect of this ruling? As you answer, take into account the importance of discovery in resolving disputes. ◆

In the Enviro-Vision case, the judge rules that Coastal must furnish more complete answers to the interrogatories, especially as to the factual basis of its denial. However, he rules against Interrogatory No. 18, the one concerning other claims Coastal has denied. This simple ruling kills Janet's hope of making a class action of the case. He orders Beth to appear for the deposition. As to future depositions, Coastal may take any 10, but then may take additional depositions only by demonstrating to the court that the deponents have useful information.

Rich proceeds to take Beth's deposition. It takes two full days. He asks about Enviro-Vision's past and present. He learns that Tony appeared to have won their biggest contract ever from Rapid City, Oregon, but that he then lost it when he had a fight with Rapid City's mayor. He inquires into Tony's mood, learns that he was depressed, and probes in every direction he can to find evidence of suicidal motivation. Janet and Rich argue frequently over questions and whether Beth should have to answer them. At times Janet is persuaded and permits Beth to answer; other times she instructs Beth not to answer. For example, toward the end of the second day, Rich asks Beth whether she and Tony had been sexually involved. Janet instructs Beth not to answer. This fight necessitates another trip into court to determine whether Beth must answer. The judge rules that Beth must discuss Tony's romantic life only if Coastal has some evidence that he was involved with someone outside his marriage. The company lacks any such evidence.

Crucial Clue.   Now limited to 10 depositions, Rich selects his nine other deponents carefully. For example, he decides to depose only one of the two nurses; he chooses to question Jerry Johnson, the tennis partner, but not Craig Bergson, the former roommate; and so forth. When we look at the many legal issues this case raises, his choices seem minor. In fact, unbeknownst to Rich or anyone else, his choices may determine the outcome of the case. As we will see later, Craig Bergson has evidence that is possibly crucial to the lawsuit. If Rich decides not to depose him, neither side will ever learn the evidence and the jury will never hear it. A jury can only decide a case based on the evidence presented to it. *Facts are elusive—and often controlling.*

In each deposition, Rich carefully probes with his questions, sometimes trying to learn what he actually does not know, sometimes trying to pin down the witness to a specific version of facts so that Rich knows how the witness will testify at trial. Neighbors at the beach testify that Tony seemed tense; one testifies about seeing Tony, unhappy, on the beach with his dog. Another testifies he had never before seen Blue tied up on the beach. Karen Caruso admits that Tony had been somewhat tense and unhappy the last couple of months. She reluctantly discusses their marriage, admitting there were problems.

Other Discovery. Rich sends Requests to Produce Documents, seeking medical records about Tony. Once again, the parties fight over which records are relevant, but Rich gets most of what he wants. Rich sends Requests for Admission, forcing Beth to commit herself to certain positions, for example, that Tony had lost the Rapid City contract and had been depressed about it.

Plaintiff's Discovery. Janet does less discovery than Rich because most of the witnesses she will call are friendly witnesses. She can interview them privately without giving any information to Coastal. With the help of Beth and Karen, Janet builds her case just as carefully as Rich, choosing the witnesses who will bolster the view that Tony was in good spirits and died accidentally.

She deposes all of the officers of Coastal who participated in the decision to deny insurance coverage. She is particularly aggressive in pinning them down as to the limited information they had when they denied Beth's claim.

Summary Judgment

When discovery is completed, both sides may consider seeking summary judgment. **Summary judgment is a ruling by the court that no trial is necessary because there are no *essential* facts in dispute.** The purpose of a trial is to determine the facts of the case, that is, to decide who did what to whom, why, when, and with what consequences. If there are no relevant facts in dispute, then there is no need for a trial.

Suppose Joe sues EZBuck Films, claiming that the company's new movie, Lover Boy, violates the copyright of a screenplay that he wrote, called Love Man. Discovery establishes that the two stories are suspiciously similar. But EZBuck's lawyer also learns that Joe sold the copyright for *Love Man* to HotShot Pix. EZBuck may or may not have violated a copyright, but there is no need for a trial because Joe *cannot win* even if there is a copyright violation. He does not own the copyright. The court will grant summary judgment for EZBuck.

In the following case, the defendant won summary judgment, meaning that the case never went to trial. And yet, this was only the beginning of trouble for that defendant, William Jefferson Clinton.

JONES V. CLINTON

990 F. Supp. 657, 1998 U.S. Dist. LEXIS 3902
United States District Court for the Eastern District of Arkansas, 1998

Facts: In 1991, Bill Clinton was governor of Arkansas. Paula Jones worked for a state agency, the Arkansas Industrial Development Commission (AIDC). When Clinton became president, Jones sued him, claiming that he had sexually harassed her. She alleged that, in May 1991, the governor arranged for her to meet him in a hotel room in Little Rock, Arkansas. When they were alone, he put his hand on her leg and slid it toward her pelvis. She escaped from his grasp, exclaimed, "What are you doing?" and said she was "not that kind of girl." ▼

She was upset and confused, and sat on a sofa near the door. She claimed that Clinton approached her, "lowered his trousers and underwear, exposed his penis and told her to kiss it." Jones was horrified, jumped up and said she had to leave. Clinton responded by saying, "Well, I don't want to make you do anything you don't want to do," and pulled his pants up. He added that if she got in trouble for leaving work, Jones should "have Dave call me immediately and I'll take care of it." He also said, "You are smart. Let's keep this between ourselves." Jones remained at AIDC until February 1993, when she moved to California because of her husband's job transfer.

President Clinton denied all of the allegations. He also filed for summary judgment, claiming that Jones had not alleged facts that justified a trial. Jones opposed the motion for summary judgment.

Issue: Was Clinton entitled to summary judgment or was Jones entitled to a trial?

Excerpts from Judge Wright's Decision: [To establish this type of a sexual harassment case, a plaintiff must show that her refusal to submit to unwelcome sexual advances resulted in a tangible job detriment, meaning that she suffered a specific loss. Jones claims that she was denied promotions, given a job with fewer responsibilities, isolated physically, required to sit at a workstation with no work to do, and singled out as the only female employee not to be given flowers on Secretary's Day.]

There is no record of plaintiff ever applying for another job within AIDC, however, and the record shows that not only was plaintiff never downgraded, her position was reclassified upward from a Grade 9 classification to a Grade 11 classification, thereby increasing her annual salary. Indeed, it is undisputed that plaintiff received every merit increase and cost-of-living allowance for which she was eligible during her nearly two-year tenure with the AIDC and consistently received satisfactory job evaluations.

Although plaintiff states that her job title upon returning from maternity leave was no longer that of purchasing assistant, her job duties prior to taking maternity leave and her job duties upon returning to work both involved data input. That being so, plaintiff cannot establish a tangible job detriment. A transfer that does not involve a demotion in form or substance and involves only minor changes in working conditions, with no reduction in pay or benefits, will not constitute an adverse employment action, otherwise every trivial personnel action that an irritable employee did not like would form the basis of a discrimination suit.

Finally, the Court rejects plaintiff's claim that she was subjected to hostile treatment having tangible effects when she was isolated physically, made to sit in a location from which she was constantly watched, made to sit at her workstation with no work to do, and singled out as the only female employee not to be given flowers on Secretary's Day. Plaintiff may well have perceived hostility and animus on the part of her supervisors, but these perceptions are merely conclusory in nature and do not, without more, constitute a tangible job detriment. Although it is not clear why plaintiff failed to receive flowers on Secretary's Day in 1992, such an omission does not give rise to a federal cause of action.

In sum, the Court finds that a showing of a tangible job detriment or adverse employment action is an essential element of plaintiff's sexual harassment claim and that plaintiff has not demonstrated any tangible job detriment or adverse employment action for her refusal to submit to the Governor's alleged advances. The President is therefore entitled to summary judgment [on this claim]. ■

In other words, the court acknowledged that there were factual disputes, but concluded that even if Jones proved each of her allegations, she would *still* lose the case, because her allegations fell short of a legitimate case of sexual harassment. Jones appealed the case. Later the same year, as the appeal was pending and the House of Representatives was considering whether to impeach President Clinton, the parties settled the dispute. Clinton, without acknowledging any of the allegations, agreed to pay Jones $850,000 to drop the suit.

Janet and Rich each consider moving for summary judgment, but both correctly decide that they would lose. There is one major fact in dispute: Did Tony Caruso commit suicide? Only a jury may decide that issue. As long as there is *some evidence* supporting each side of a key factual dispute, the court may not grant summary judgment.

Final Preparation

Well over 90 percent of all lawsuits are settled before trial. But the parties in the Enviro-Vision dispute cannot seem to compromise, so each side gears up for trial. The attorneys make lists of all witnesses they will call. They then prepare each witness very carefully, rehearsing the questions they will ask. It is considered ethical and proper to rehearse the questions, provided the answers are honest and come from the witness. It is unethical and illegal for a lawyer to tell a witness what to say. The lawyers also have colleagues cross-examine each witness, so that the witnesses are ready for the questions the other side's lawyer will ask.

This preparation takes hours and hours, for many days. Beth is frustrated that she cannot do the work she needs to for Enviro-Vision, because she is spending so much time preparing the case. Other employees have to prepare as well, especially for cross-examination by Rich Stewart, and it is a terrible drain on the small firm. More than a year after Janet filed her complaint, they are ready to begin trial.

TRIAL

Adversary System

Our system of justice assumes that the best way to bring out the truth is for the two contesting sides to present the strongest case possible to a neutral factfinder. Each side presents its witnesses and then the opponent has a chance to cross-examine. The adversary system presumes that by putting a witness on the stand and letting both lawyers "go at" her, the truth will emerge.

The judge runs the trial. Each lawyer sits at a large table near the front. Beth, looking tense and unhappy, sits with Janet. Rich Stewart sits with a Coastal executive. In the back of the courtroom are benches for the public. On one bench sits Craig Bergson. He will watch the entire proceeding with intense interest and a strange feeling of unease. He is convinced he knows what really happened.

Janet has demanded a jury trial for Beth's case, and Judge Rowland announces that they will now impanel the jury.

Right to Jury Trial

Not all cases are tried to a jury. As a general rule, both plaintiff and defendant have a right to demand a jury trial when the lawsuit is one for money damages. For example, in a typical contract lawsuit, such as Beth's insurance claim, both plaintiff and defendant have a jury trial right whether they are in state or federal court. Even in such a case, though, the parties may *waive* the jury right, meaning they agree to try the case to a judge.

If the plaintiff is seeking an equitable remedy, such as an injunction, there is no jury right for either party. Equitable rights come from the old Court of Chancery in England, where there was never a jury. Even today, only a judge may give an equitable remedy.

Voir Dire

The process of selecting a jury is called **voir dire,** which means "to speak the truth."[6] The court's goal is to select an impartial jury; the lawyers will each try to get a jury as favorable to their side as possible.

Potential jurors are questioned individually, sometimes by the judge and sometimes by the two lawyers, as each side tries to ferret out potential bias. Each lawyer may make any number of **challenges for cause,** claiming that a juror has demonstrated probable bias. For example, if a prospective juror in the Enviro-Vision case works for an insurance company, the judge will excuse her on the assumption that she would be biased in favor of Coastal. If the judge perceives no bias, the lawyer may still make a limited number of **peremptory challenges,** entitling him to excuse that juror for virtually any reason, which need not be stated in court. For example, if Rich Stewart believes that a juror seems hostile to him personally, he will use a peremptory challenge to excuse that juror, even if the judge sensed no animosity. The process continues until 14 jurors are seated. Twelve will comprise the jury; the other two are alternates who hear the case and remain available in the event one of the impaneled jurors is taken ill. For a discussion of the jury's responsibility, see http://www.placer.ca.gov and click on "Jury Duty," then on "General Information."

Although jury selection for a case can sometimes take many days, in the Enviro-Vision case the first day of the hearing ends with the jury selected. In the hallway outside the court, Rich offers Janet $200,000 to settle. Janet reports the offer to Beth and they agree to reject it. Craig Bergson drives home, emotionally confused. Only three weeks before his death, Tony had accidentally met his old roommate and they had had several drinks. Craig believes that what Tony told him answers the riddle of this case.

Opening Statements

The next day, each attorney makes an opening statement to the jury, summarizing the proof he or she expects to offer, with the plaintiff going first. Janet focuses on Tony's successful life, his business and strong marriage, and the tragedy of his accidental death.[7]

Rich works hard to establish a friendly rapport with the jury. He expresses regret about the death. Nonetheless, suicide is a clear exclusion from the policy. If insurance companies are forced to pay claims never bargained for, everyone's insurance rates will go up.

Burden of Proof

In civil cases, the plaintiff has the burden of proof. That means that the plaintiff must convince the jury that its version of the case is correct; the defendant is not obligated to disprove the allegations.

The plaintiff's burden in a civil lawsuit is to prove its case by a **preponderance of the evidence.** It must convince the jury that its version of the facts is at least *slightly more likely* than the defendant's version. Some courts describe this as a "51–49" persuasion, that is, that plaintiff's proof must "just tip" credibility in its favor. By contrast, in a criminal case, the prosecution must demonstrate **beyond a reasonable doubt** that the defendant is guilty. The burden of proof in a criminal case is much tougher because the likely consequences are, too. See Exhibit 3.3.

---

6 Students of French note that *voir* means "to see" and assume that *voir dire* should translate, "to see, to speak." However, the legal term is centuries old and derives not from modern French but from Old French, in which *voir* meant "truth."

7 Janet Booker has dropped her claim for triple damages against Coastal. To have any hope of such a verdict, she would have to show that Coastal had no legitimate reason at all for denying the claim. Discovery has convinced her that Coastal will demonstrate some rational reasons for what it did.

Exhibit 3.3
Burden of proof. In a civil lawsuit, a plaintiff wins with a mere preponderance of the evidence. But the prosecution must persuade a jury beyond a reasonable doubt in order to win a criminal conviction.

Plaintiff's Case

Since the plaintiff has the burden of proof, Janet puts in her case first. She wants to prove two things. First, that Tony died. That is easy, since the death certificate clearly demonstrates it and since Coastal does not seriously contest it. Second, in order to win double indemnity damages, she must show that the death was accidental. She will do this with the testimony of the witnesses she calls, one after the other. Her first witness is Beth. When a lawyer asks questions of her own witness, it is **direct examination.** Janet brings out all the evidence she wants the jury to hear: that the business was basically sound, though temporarily troubled, that Tony was a hard worker, why the company took out life insurance policies, and so forth.

Then Rich has a chance to **cross-examine** Beth, which means to ask questions of an opposing witness. He will try to create doubt in the jury's mind. He asks Beth only questions for which he is certain of the answers, based on discovery. Rich gets Beth to admit that the firm was not doing well the year of Tony's death; that Tony had lost the best client the firm ever had; that Beth had reduced salaries; and that Tony had been depressed about business.

Rules of Evidence

The lawyers are not free simply to ask any question they want. The law of **evidence** determines what questions a lawyer may ask and how the questions are to be phrased, what answers a witness may give, and what documents may be introduced. The goal is to get the best evidence possible before the jurors so they can decide what really happened. In general, witnesses may only testify about things they saw or heard.

These rules are complex, and a thorough explication of them is beyond the scope of this chapter; however, they can be just as important in resolving a dispute as the underlying substantive law. Suppose a plaintiff's case depends upon the jury hearing about a certain conversation, but the rules of evidence prevent the lawyer from asking about it. That conversation might just as well never have occurred.

Janet calls an expert witness, a marine geologist, who testifies about the tides and currents in the area where Tony's body was found. The expert testifies that even experienced swimmers can be overwhelmed by a sudden shift in currents. Rich objects strenuously that this is irrelevant, because there is no testimony that there *was* such a current at the time of Tony's death. The judge permits the testimony.

Karen Caruso testifies that Tony was in "reasonably good" spirits the day of his death, and that he often took Blue for walks along the beach. Karen testifies that Blue was part Newfoundland. Rich objects that testimony about Blue's pedigree is irrelevant, but Janet insists it will show why Blue was tied up. The judge allows the testimony. Karen says that whenever Blue saw them swim he would instinctively go into the water and pull them to shore. Does that explain why Blue was tied up? Only the jury can answer.

Cross-examination is grim for Karen. Rich slowly but methodically questions her about Tony's state of mind and brings out the problems with the company, his depression, and tension within the marriage. Janet's other witnesses testify essentially as they did during their depositions.

Motion for Directed Verdict

At the close of the plaintiff's case, Rich moves for a **directed verdict,** that is, a ruling that the plaintiff has entirely failed to prove some aspect of her case. Rich is seeking to win without even putting in his own case. He argues that it was Beth's burden to prove that Tony died accidentally and that she has entirely failed to do that.

A directed verdict is permissible only if the evidence so clearly favors the defendant that reasonable minds could not disagree on it. If reasonable minds could disagree, the motion must be denied. Here, Judge Rowland rules that the plaintiff has put in enough evidence of accidental death that a reasonable person could find in Beth's favor. The motion is denied.

Defendant's Case

Rich now puts in his case, exactly as Janet did, except that he happens to have fewer witnesses. He calls the examining doctor, who admits that Tony could have committed suicide by swimming out too far. On cross-examination, Janet gets the doctor to acknowledge that he has no idea whether Tony intentionally drowned. Rich also questions several neighbors as to how depressed Tony had seemed and how unusual it was that Blue was tied up. Some of the witnesses Rich deposed, such as the tennis partner Jerry Johnson, have nothing that will help Coastal's case, so he does not call them.

Craig Bergson, sitting in the back of the courtroom, thinks how different the trial would have been had he been called as a witness. When he and Tony had the fateful drink, Tony had been distraught: business was terrible, he was involved in an extramarital affair that he could not end, and he saw no way out of his problems. He had no one to talk to and had been hugely relieved to speak with Craig. Several times Tony had said, "I just can't go on like this. I don't want to, anymore." Craig thought Tony seemed suicidal and urged him to see a therapist Craig knew and trusted. Tony had said that it was good advice, but Craig is unsure whether Tony sought any help.

This evidence would have affected the case. Had Rich Stewart known of the conversation, he would have deposed Craig and the therapist. Coastal's case would have been far stronger, perhaps overwhelming. But Craig's evidence will never be heard. Facts are critical. Rich's decision to depose other witnesses and omit Craig may influence the verdict more than any rule of law.

Closing Argument

Both lawyers sum up their case to the jury, explaining how they hope the jury will interpret what they have heard. Janet summarizes the plaintiff's version of the facts, claiming that Blue was tied up so that Tony could swim without worrying about him. Rich claims that business and personal pressures had overwhelmed Tony. He tied up his dog, neatly folded his clothes, and took his own life.

Jury Instructions

Judge Rowland instructs the jury as to its duty. He tells them that they are to evaluate the case based only on the evidence they heard at trial, relying on their own experience and common sense.

He explains the law and the burden of proof, telling the jury that it is Beth's obligation to prove that Tony died. If Beth has proven that Tony died, she is entitled to $1 million; if she has proven that his death was accidental, she is entitled to $2 million. However, if Coastal has proven suicide, Beth receives nothing. Finally, he states that if they are unable to decide between accidental death and suicide, there is a legal presumption that it was accidental. Rich asks Judge Rowland to rephrase the "legal presumption" part but the judge declines.

Verdict

The jury deliberates informally, with all jurors entitled to voice their opinion. Some deliberations take two hours; some take two weeks. Many states require a unanimous verdict; others require only, for example, a 10 to 2 vote in civil cases.

This case presents a close call. No one saw Tony die. Yet even though they cannot know with certainty, the jury's decision will probably be the final word on whether he took his own life. After a day and a half of deliberating, the jury notifies the judge that it has reached a verdict. Rich Stewart quickly makes a new offer: $350,000. Beth hesitates but turns it down.

The judge summons the lawyers to court, and Beth goes as well. The judge asks the foreman if the jury has reached a decision. He states that it has: the jury finds that Tony Caruso drowned accidentally and awards Beth Smiles $2 million.

Motions after the Verdict

Rich immediately moves for a **judgment *non obstante veredicto*** (JNOV), meaning a judgment notwithstanding the jury's verdict. He is asking the judge to overturn the jury's verdict. Rich argues that the jury's decision went against all of the evidence. He also claims that the judge's instructions were wrong and misled the jury.

Judge Rowland denies the JNOV. Rich immediately moves for a new trial, making the same claim, and the judge denies the motion. Beth is elated that the case is finally over—until Janet says she expects an appeal. Craig Bergson, leaving the courtroom, wonders if he did the right thing. He felt sympathy for Beth and none for Coastal. Yet now he is neither happy nor proud.

APPEALS

Two days later, Rich files an appeal to the court of appeals. The same day, he phones Janet and increases his settlement offer to $425,000. Beth is tempted but wants Janet's advice. Janet says the risks of an appeal are that the court will order a new trial, and they would start all over. But to accept this offer is to forfeit over $1.5 million. Beth is unsure what to do. The firm desperately needs cash now. Janet suggests they wait until oral argument, another eight months.

Rich files a brief arguing that there were two basic errors at the trial: first, that the jury's verdict is clearly contrary to the evidence; and second, that the judge gave the wrong instructions to the jury. Janet files a reply brief, opposing Rich on both issues. In her brief, Janet cites many cases that she claims are **precedent:** earlier decisions by the state appellate courts on similar or identical issues. Although the following case is from a different jurisdiction, it is an example of the kind of case that she will rely on.

HERNANDEZ V. MONTVILLE TOWNSHIP BOARD OF EDUCATION

354 N.J. Super. 467, 808 A.2d 128
Superior Court of New Jersey, Appellate Division, 2002

Facts: Victor Hernandez had worked for more than 20 years as a custodian at a public power plant. He had received training in health and safety rules from the Occupational Safety and Health Administration (OSHA).

Hernandez took a second job as night custodian at an elementary school. Shortly after he started work, the school board fired him for alleged poor job performance. Hernandez filed suit, claiming that the real reason for his termination was that he had repeatedly notified his superiors of health and safety violations in the schools, including missing bulbs in emergency exit lights and toilets that backed up for long periods, spilling foul matter on the floor. He argued that his termination violated the state's Conscientious Employee Protection Act (CEPA), which is designed to protect whistleblowers who report violations of health laws.

The jury awarded Hernandez $44,000 for lost wages and $150,000 for emotional distress. The jury had not been permitted to hear his claim for punitive damages (those designed to punish a defendant for exceptionally bad conduct). The trial judge then granted a judgment notwithstanding the verdict (JNOV) to the school board, meaning that Hernandez won nothing. The trial judge stated:

"Talk about trivial. By the time the jury went out, I should have concluded that the plaintiff simply had not made out a case, under the CEPA law, because he never disclosed or threatened to disclose to his supervisor an activity, policy, practice of an employer that the employee reasonably believed was in violation of law or a rule. There simply was none. But in addition to that, there isn't any other evidence adduced by anyone in the case that these things that he's complaining about ever occurred. I didn't believe anything [plaintiff] said. [This is] trivialization beyond belief."

Hernandez appealed.

Issue: Did the trial court err by rejecting punitive damages, or by granting the JNOV?

Excerpts from Judge Axelrad's Decision: Plaintiff knew there were regulations and policies against exposing schoolchildren to urine and feces and against unlit exit signs, particularly in an elementary school setting. Plaintiff was informed by defendant's safety representative that OSHA's general standards require washing facilities to be maintained in a sanitary condition. Moreover, the staff handbook provided to plaintiff stressed the importance of safety.

Contrary to the court's finding in granting JNOV, it is irrelevant to plaintiff's CEPA claim whether there was independent corroboration of the overflowing toilets. Under the JNOV standard the court must accept as true plaintiff's testimony, which the jury clearly found credible. Moreover, [Facilities Manager] Vandeneulebroeke acknowledged that on more than one occasion if parts were not in stock it took a week to repair a toilet.

Until plaintiff began complaining, he had a good work record. There was ample evidence in the

▼

record for the jury to conclude defendant's proffered reason for termination was a pretext and that the whistleblowing itself was a substantial factor in the termination. Thus, this was not a "runaway jury" as categorized by the court. Accordingly, it was error for the court to substitute its judgment for that of the jury and reverse the jury verdict.

Furthermore, the punitive damage claim should have been submitted to the jury. Plaintiff claims that [all of his superiors] lied in their testimony. He further testified that Foschini, the other janitor, warned him "to keep [his] mouth shut" because if he said anything about unsafe conditions and health hazards,

he would get fired. Based upon the compensatory damage verdict, it appears that the jury agreed. Our Supreme Court [has] made it clear that "punitive damages, which are available under CEPA against public entities, should be determined by a jury as the trier of fact." There is no reason to remove this issue from the jury.

Because plaintiff presented sufficient evidence to sustain the jury verdict, we reverse the trial court's grant of a JNOV and reinstate the verdict on compensatory damages. We remand for a new trial on punitive damages and consideration of interest, attorney's fees and costs. ■

Eight months later, the lawyers representing Coastal and Enviro-Vision appear in the court of appeals to argue their case. Rich, the appellant, goes first. The judges frequently interrupt his argument with questions. Relying on decisions like *Hernandez*, they show little sympathy for his claim that the verdict was against the facts. They seem more sympathetic with his second point, that the instructions were wrong.

When Janet argues, all of their questions concern the judge's instructions. It appears they believe the instructions were in error. The judges take the case under advisement, meaning they will decide some time in the future—maybe in two weeks, maybe in five months.

Appeals Court Options

The court of appeals can **affirm** the trial court, allowing the decision to stand. The court may **modify** the decision, for example, by affirming that the plaintiff wins but decreasing the size of the award. (That is unlikely here; Beth is entitled to $2 million or nothing.) The court might **reverse and remand,** nullifying the lower court's decision and returning the case to the lower court for a new trial. Or it could simply **reverse,** turning the loser (Coastal) into the winner, with no new trial.

What will it do here? On the factual issue it will probably rule in Beth's favor. There *was* evidence from which a jury could conclude that Tony died accidentally. It is true that there was also considerable evidence to support Coastal's position, but that is probably not enough to overturn the verdict. As we saw in the *Hernandez* case, if reasonable people could disagree on what the evidence proves, an appellate court generally refuses to change the jury's factual findings. The court of appeals is likely to rule that a reasonable jury *could* have found accidental death, even if the appellate judges personally suspect that Tony may have killed himself.

The judge's instructions raise a more difficult problem. Some states would require a more complex statement about "presumptions."

What does a court of appeals do if it decides the trial court's instructions were wrong? If it believes the error rendered the trial and verdict unfair, it will remand the case, that is, send it back to the lower court for a new trial. However, the court may conclude that the mistake was **harmless error.** A trial judge cannot do a perfect job, and not every error is fatal. The court may decide the verdict was fair in spite of the mistake.

Janet and Beth talk. Beth is very anxious and wants to settle. She does not want to wait four or five months, only to learn that they must start all over. Janet urges that they wait a few weeks to hear from Rich: they don't want to seem too eager.

A week later, Rich telephones and offers $500,000. Janet turns it down, but says she will ask Beth if she wants to make a counter-offer. She and Beth talk. They agree that they will settle for $1 million. Janet then calls Rich and offers to settle for $1.7 million. Rich and Janet debate the merits of the case. Rich later calls back and offers $750,000, saying he doubts that he can go any higher. Janet counters with $1.4 million, saying she doubts she can go any lower. They argue, both predicting that they will win on appeal.

Rich calls, offers $900,000 and says, "That's it. No more." Janet argues for $1.2 million, expecting to nudge Rich up to $1 million. He doesn't nudge, instead saying, "Take it or leave it." Janet and Beth talk it over. Janet telephones Rich and accepts $900,000 to settle the case.

If they had waited for the court of appeals decision, would Beth have won? It is impossible to know. It is certain, though, that whoever lost would have appealed. Months would have passed waiting to learn if the state supreme court would accept the case. If that court had agreed to hear the appeal, Beth would have endured another year of waiting, brief writing, oral argument, and tense hoping. The high court has all of the options discussed: to affirm, modify, reverse and remand, or simply reverse.

Chapter Conclusion

No one will ever know for sure whether Tony took his own life. Craig Bergson's evidence might have tipped the scales in favor of Coastal. But even that is uncertain, because the jury could have found him unpersuasive. After two years, the case ends with a settlement and uncertainty—both typical lawsuit results. The missing witness is less common but not extraordinary. The vaguely unsatisfying feeling about it all is only too common and indicates why litigation is best avoided—by dispute prevention.

Chapter Review

1. Alternative dispute resolution (ADR) is any formal or informal process to settle disputes without a trial. Mediation, arbitration, and other forms of ADR are growing in popularity.

2. There are many *systems* of courts, one federal and one in each state. A federal court will hear a case only if it involves a federal question or diversity jurisdiction.

3. Trial courts determine facts and apply the law to the facts; appeals courts generally accept the facts found by the trial court and review the trial record for errors of law.

4. A complaint and an answer are the two most important pleadings, that is, documents that start a lawsuit.

5. Discovery is the critical pre-trial opportunity for both parties to learn the strengths and weaknesses of the opponent's case. Important forms of discovery include interrogatories, depositions, production of documents and objects, physical and mental examinations, and requests for admission.

6. A motion is a formal request to the court.

7. Summary judgment is a ruling by the court that no trial is necessary because there are no essential facts in dispute.

8. Generally, both plaintiff and defendant may demand a jury in any lawsuit for money damages.

9. Voir dire is the process of selecting jurors in order to obtain an impartial panel.

10. The plaintiff's burden of proof in a civil lawsuit is preponderance of the evidence, meaning that its version of the facts must be at least slightly more persuasive than the defendant's. In a criminal prosecution, the government must offer proof beyond a reasonable doubt in order to win a conviction.

11. The rules of evidence determine what questions may be asked during trial, what testimony may be given, and what documents may be introduced.

12. The verdict is the jury's decision in a case. The losing party may ask the trial judge to overturn the verdict, seeking a judgment *non obstante veredicto* or a new trial. Judges seldom grant either.

13. An appeals court has many options. The court may affirm, upholding the lower court's decision; modify, changing the verdict but leaving the same party victorious; reverse, transforming the loser into the winner; and/or remand, sending the case back to the lower court.

Practice Test

1. You plan to open a store in Chicago, specializing in beautiful rugs imported from Turkey. You will work with a native Turk who will purchase and ship the rugs to your store. You are wise enough to insist on a contract establishing the rights and obligations of both parties and would prefer an ADR clause. But you want to be sensitive to different cultures and do not want a clause that will magnify a problem or alienate the parties. Is there some way you can accomplish all of this?

2. Solo Serve Corp. signed a lease for space in a shopping center. The lease contained this clause: "Neither Landlord nor tenant shall engage in or permit any activity at or around the Demised Premises which violates any applicable law, constitutes a nuisance, or is likely to bring discredit upon the Shopping Center, or discourage customers from patronizing other occupants of the Shopping Center by other than activities customarily engaged in by reputable businesses." Westowne Associates, the landlord, later leased other space in the center to The Finish Line, an off-track betting business that also had a license to sell food and liquor. Solo Serve sued, claiming that Westowne had breached the lease. Solo Serve requested either a permanent injunction barring The Finish Line from using the center or that The Finish Line pay the cost of relocating its own business.

   The case raises two questions. The minor one is, did Westowne violate the lease? The major one is, how could this dispute have been prevented? It ultimately went to the United States Court of Appeals, costing both sides much time and money.

3. State which court(s) have jurisdiction as to each of these lawsuits:

   a. Pat wants to sue his next-door neighbor Dorothy, claiming that Dorothy promised to sell him the house next door.

   b. Paula, who lives in New York City, wants to sue Dizzy Movie Theatres, whose principal place of business is Dallas. She claims that while she was in Texas on holiday, she was injured by their negligent maintenance of a stairway. She claims damages of $30,000.

   c. Phil lives in Tennessee. He wants to sue Dick, who lives in Ohio. Phil claims that Dick agreed to sell him 3,000 acres of farmland in Ohio worth over $2 million.

   d. Pete, incarcerated in a federal prison in Kansas, wants to sue the United States government. He claims that his treatment by prison authorities violates three federal statutes.

4. Probationary schoolteachers sued the New Madrid, Missouri, school district, claiming that the school district refused to give them permanent jobs because of their union organizing activity. The defendant school district claimed that each plaintiff was refused a permanent job because of inferior teaching. During discovery, the plaintiffs asked for the personnel files of probationary teachers who *had* been offered permanent jobs. The school district refused to provide them, arguing that the personnel files did not indicate the union status of the teachers and therefore would not help the plaintiffs. The trial court ruled that the school district need not release the files. On appeal, the plaintiffs argue that this hindered their ability to prove the real reasons they had been fired. How should the appeals court rule?

5. Students are now suing schools for sexual harassment. The cases raise important issues about the limits of discovery. In a case in Petaluma, California, a girl claimed that she was harassed for years and that the school knew about it and failed to act. According to press reports, she alleges that a boy stood up in class and asked, "I have a question. I want to know if [Jane Doe] has sex with hot dogs." In discovery, the school district sought the parents' therapy records, the girl's diary, and a psychological evaluation of the girl. Should they get those things?

6. British discovery practice differs from that in the United States. Most discovery in Britain concerns documents. The lawyers for the two sides, called solicitors, must deliver to the opposing side a list of all relevant documents in their possession. Each side may then request to look at and copy those it wishes. Depositions are rare. What advantages and disadvantages are there to the British practice?

7. **ETHICS** Trial practice also is dramatically different in Britain. The parties' solicitors do not go into court. Courtroom work is done by different lawyers, called barristers. The barristers are not permitted to interview any witnesses before trial. They know the substance of what each witness intends to say but do not rehearse questions and answers, as in the United States. Which approach do you consider more effective? More ethical? What is the purpose of a trial? Of pretrial preparation?

8. Claus Scherer worked for Rockwell International and was paid more than $300,000 per year. Rockwell fired Scherer for alleged sexual harassment of several workers, including his secretary, Terry Pendy. Scherer sued in United States District Court, alleging that Rockwell's real motive in firing him was his high salary.

   Rockwell moved for summary judgment, offering deposition transcripts of various employees. Pendy's deposition detailed instances of harassment, including comments about her body, instances of unwelcome touching, and discussions of extramarital affairs. Another deposition, from a Rockwell employee who investigated the allegations, included complaints by other employees as to Scherer's harassment. In his own deposition, which he offered to oppose summary judgment, Scherer testified that he could not recall the incidents alleged by Pendy and others. He denied generally that he had sexually harassed anyone. The district court granted summary judgment for Rockwell. Was its ruling correct?

9. Lloyd Dace worked for ACF Industries as a supervisor in the punchpress department of a carburetor factory. ACF demoted Dace to an hourly job on the assembly line, and Dace sued, claiming that ACF discriminated on the basis of age. At trial, Dace showed that he had been 53 years old when demoted and had been replaced by a man aged 40. He offered evidence that ACF's benefits supervisor had attended the meeting at which his demotion was decided and that the benefits supervisor was aware of the cost savings of replacing Dace with a younger man.

   At the end of Dace's case, ACF moved for a directed verdict and the trial court granted it. The judge reasoned that Dace's entire case was based on circumstantial evidence. He held that it was too speculative for the jury to infer age discrimination from the few facts that Dace had offered. Was the trial court correct?

10. **YOU BE THE JUDGE** WRITING PROBLEM Apache Corp. and El Paso Exploration Co. operated a Texas gas well that exploded, burning out of control for over a year. More than 100 plaintiffs sued the two owners, claiming damage to adjoining gas fields. The plaintiffs also sued Axelson, Inc., which manufactured a valve whose failure may have contributed to the explosion. Axelson, in turn, sued Apache and El Paso. Axelson sought discovery from both companies about an internal investigation they had conducted, before the blowout, concerning kickbacks (illegal payments) at the gas field. Axelson claimed that the investigation could shed light on what caused the explosion, but the trial court ruled that the material was irrelevant, and denied discovery. Axelson appealed. Is the investigation discoverable? **Argument for Axelson:** If the companies investigated kickbacks, they were concerned about corruption and mismanagement—both of which can cause employees to cut corners, ignore safety concerns, fabricate reports, and so forth. All of those activities have the potential to cause a serious accident. All parties are entitled to discover material that may lead to relevant evidence, and that could easily happen here. **Argument for Apache and El Paso:** This is a fishing expedition. The investigation was completed before the explosion and is completely unrelated. Any internal investigation has the potential (a) to reveal valuable

business or trade secrets and (b) to prove embarrassing to the companies investigated. Axelson's motive is to force the two owners to settle in order to avoid such revelations. Discovery is not supposed to be a weapon.

11. Imogene Williams sued the U.S. Elevator Corp. She claimed that when she entered one of the company's elevators, it went up three floors but failed to open, fell several floors, stopped, and then continued to erratically rise and fall for about 40 minutes. She claimed physical injuries and emotional distress. At trial, U.S. Elevator disputed every allegation. When the judge instructed the jury, he asked them to decide whether the company had been negligent. If it had, the jury was to decide what physical injuries

Williams had suffered. The judge also instructed them that she could receive money for emotional damages only if the emotional damages resulted from her physical injury. The jury found for U.S. Elevator, deciding that it had not been negligent.

On appeal, Williams argues that the judge was wrong in stating that the emotional injuries had to result from the physical injuries. The court of appeals agreed that the instruction was incorrect. There could be emotional damages even if there were no physical injuries. What appellate remedy is appropriate?

12. **ROLE REVERSAL** Write a multiple-choice question that illustrates the unique significance of summary judgment: that there is no need for a trial because there are no essential facts in dispute.

Internet Research Problem

You may be called for jury duty before long. Read the summary of the juror's responsibilities at academic.cengage.com/blaw/beatty. Some people try hard to get out of jury duty. Why is that a problem in a democratic society?

You can find further practice problems at academic.cengage.com/blaw/beatty.

Common Law, Statutory Law, and Administrative Law

Jason observes a toddler wander onto the railroad tracks and hears a train approaching. He has plenty of time to pull the child from the tracks with no risk to himself but chooses to do nothing. The youngster is killed. The child's family sues Jason for his callous behavior, and a court determines that Jason owes— nothing.

"Why can't they just fix the law?" students and professionals often ask, in response to Jason's impunity and countless other legal oddities. Their exasperation is understandable. This chapter cannot guarantee intellectual tranquility, but it should diminish the sense of bizarreness that law can instill. We will look at three sources of law: common law, statutory law, and administrative law. Most of the law you learn in the course comes from one of these sources. The substantive law will make more sense when you have a solid feel for how it was created. ∎

© PHILIP COBLENTZ/PHOTODISC/GETTY IMAGES

Common Law

Jason and the toddler present a classic legal puzzle: What, if anything, must a bystander do when he sees someone in danger? We will examine this issue to see how the common law works.

The common law is judge-made law. It is the sum total of all the cases decided by appellate courts. The common law of Pennsylvania consists of all cases decided by appellate courts in that state. The Illinois common law of bystander liability is all the cases on that subject decided by Illinois appellate courts. Two hundred years ago, almost all law was common law. Today, most new law is statutory. But common law still predominates in tort, contract, and agency law, and it is very important in property, employment, and some other areas.

We focus on appellate courts because they are the only ones to make rulings of law, as discussed in Chapter 3. In a bystander case, it is the job of the state's highest court to say what legal obligations, if any, a bystander has. The trial court, on the other hand, must decide *facts:* Was this defendant able to see what was happening? Was the plaintiff really in trouble? Could the defendant have assisted without peril to himself?

Stare Decisis

Nothing perks up a course like Latin. ***Stare decisis*** means "let the decision stand." It is the essence of the common law. The phrase indicates that once a court has decided a particular issue, it will generally apply the same rule in future cases. Suppose the highest court of Arizona must decide whether a contract for a new car, signed by a 16-year-old, can be enforced against him. The court will look to see if there is **precedent,** that is, whether the high court of Arizona has already decided a similar case. The Arizona court looks and finds several earlier cases, all holding that such contracts may not be enforced against a minor. The court will apply that precedent and refuse to enforce the contract in this case. Courts do not always follow precedent, but they generally do: *stare decisis.*

Two words explain why the common law is never as easy as we might like: *predictability* and *flexibility.* The law is trying to accommodate both goals. The need for predictability is apparent: people must know what the law is. If contract law changed daily, an entrepreneur who leased factory space and then started buying machinery would be uncertain if the factory would actually be available when she was ready to move in. Will the landlord slip out of the lease? Will the machinery be ready on time? The need for predictability created the doctrine of *stare decisis.*

Yet there must also be flexibility in the law, some means to respond to new problems and changing social mores. In this new millennium, we cannot be encumbered by ironclad rules established before electricity was discovered. These two ideas may be obvious but they also conflict: the more flexibility we permit, the less predictability we enjoy. We will watch the conflict play out in the bystander cases.

Bystander Cases

This country inherited from England a simple rule about a bystander's obligations: you have no duty to assist someone in peril unless you created the danger. In *Union Pacific Railway Co. v. Cappier,*[1] through no fault of the railroad, a train struck a man, severing an arm and a leg. Railroad employees saw the incident happen but did nothing to assist him. By the time help arrived, the victim had died. In this 1903 case the court held that the railroad had no duty to help the injured man:

---

[1] 66 Kan. 649, 72 P. 281 (1903).

With the humane side of the question courts are not concerned. It is the omission or negligent discharge of legal duties only which come within the sphere of judicial cognizance. For withholding relief from the suffering, for failure to respond to the calls of worthy charity, or for faltering in the bestowment of brotherly love on the unfortunate, penalties are found not in the laws of men but in [the laws of God].

As harsh as this judgment might seem, it was an accurate statement of the law at that time in both England and the United States: bystanders need do nothing. Contemporary writers found the rule inhumane and cruel, and even judges criticized it. But—*stare decisis*—they followed it. With a rule this old and well established, no court was willing to scuttle it. What courts did do was seek openings for small changes.

Eighteen years after the Kansas case of *Cappier*, the court in nearby Iowa found the basis for one exception. Ed Carey was a farm laborer, working for Frank Davis. While in the fields, Carey fainted from sunstroke and remained unconscious. Davis simply hauled him to a nearby wagon and left him in the sun for an additional four hours, causing serious permanent injury. The court's response:

> It is unquestionably the well-settled rule that the master is under no legal duty to care for a sick or injured servant for whose illness or injury he is not at fault. Though not unjust in principle, this rule, if carried unflinchingly and without exception to its logical extreme, is sometimes productive of shocking results. To avoid this criticism [we hold that where] a servant suffers serious injury, or is suddenly stricken down in a manner indicating the immediate and emergent need of aid to save him from death or serious harm, the master, if present is in duty bound to take such reasonable measures as may be practicable to relieve him, even though such master be not chargeable with fault in bringing about the emergency.[2]

And this is how the common law changes: bit by tiny bit. In Iowa, a bystander could now be liable *if* he was the employer and *if* the worker was suddenly stricken and *if* it was an emergency and *if* the employer was present. That is a small change but an important one.

For the next 50 years, changes in bystander law came very slowly. Consider *Osterlind v. Hill*, a case from 1928.[3] Osterlind rented a canoe from Hill's boatyard, paddled into the lake, and promptly fell into the water. For *30 minutes* he clung to the side of the canoe and shouted for help. Hill heard the cries but did nothing; Osterlind drowned. Was Hill liable? No, said the court: a bystander has no liability. Not until half a century later did that same state supreme court reverse its position and begin to require assistance in extreme cases—a long time for Osterlind to hold on.[4]

In the 1970s, changes came more quickly.

TARASOFF V. REGENTS OF THE UNIVERSITY OF CALIFORNIA

17 Cal. 3d 425, 551 P.2d 334, 131 Cal. Rptr. 14
Supreme Court of California, 1976

Facts: On October 27, 1969, Prosenjit Poddar killed Tatiana Tarasoff. Tatiana's parents claimed that two months earlier Poddar had confided his intention to kill Tatiana to Dr. Lawrence Moore, a psychologist employed by the University of California at Berkeley. They sued the university, claiming that Dr. Moore should have warned Tatiana and/or should have arranged for Poddar's confinement.

▼

---

[2] Carey v. Davis, 190 Iowa 720, 180 N.W. 889 (1921).

[3] 263 Mass. 73, 160 N.E. 301 (1928).

[4] Pridgen v. Boston Housing Authority, 364 Mass. 696, 308 N.E.2d 467 (1974).

Issue: Did Dr. Moore have a duty to Tatiana Tarasoff, and did he breach that duty?

Excerpts from Justice Tobriner's Decision: Although under the common law, as a general rule, one person owed no duty to control the conduct of another, nor to warn those endangered by such conduct, the courts have carved out an exception to this rule in cases in which the defendant stands in some special relationship to either the person whose conduct needs to be controlled or in a relationship to the foreseeable victim of that conduct. Applying this exception to the present case, we note that a relationship of defendant therapists to either Tatiana or Poddar will suffice to establish a duty of care.

We recognize the difficulty that a therapist encounters in attempting to forecast whether a patient presents a serious danger of violence. Obviously we do not require that the therapist, in making that determination, render a perfect performance; the therapist need only exercise that reasonable degree of skill, knowledge, and care ordinarily possessed and exercised by members of [the field] under similar circumstances.

In the instant case, however, the pleadings do not raise any question as to failure of defendant therapists to predict that Poddar presented a serious danger of violence. On the contrary, the present complaints allege that defendant therapists did in fact predict that Poddar would kill, but were negligent in failing to warn.

In our view, once a therapist does in fact determine, or under applicable professional standards reasonably should have determined, that a patient poses a serious danger of violence to others, he bears a duty to exercise reasonable care to protect the foreseeable victim of that danger.

[The Tarasoffs have stated a legitimate claim against Dr. Moore.] ■

The *Tarasoff* exception applies when there is some special relationship, such as therapist-patient. What if there is no such relationship? The 1983 case of *Soldano v. O'Daniels*[5] arose when a patron in Happy Jack's bar saw Villanueva threaten Soldano with a gun. The patron dashed next door, into the Circle Inn bar, told the bartender what was happening, and urged him to call the police. The bartender refused. The witness then asked to use the phone to call the police himself, but the bartender again refused. Tragically, the delay permitted Villanueva to kill Soldano.

As in the earlier cases we have seen, this case presented an emergency. But the exception created in *Carey v. Davis* applied only if the bystander was an employer, and that in *Tarasoff* only for a doctor. In *Soldano* the bystander was neither. Should the law require him to act—that is, should it carve a new exception? Here is what the California court decided:

> Many citizens simply "don't want to get involved." No rule should be adopted [requiring] a citizen to open up his or her house to a stranger so that the latter may use the telephone to call for emergency assistance. As Mrs. Alexander in Anthony Burgess' *A Clockwork Orange* learned to her horror, such an action may be fraught with danger. It does not follow, however, that use of a telephone in a public portion of a business should be refused for a legitimate emergency call.
>
> We conclude that the bartender owed a duty to [Soldano] to permit the patron from Happy Jack's to place a call to the police or to place the call himself. It bears emphasizing that the duty in this case does not require that one must go to the aid of another. That is not the issue here. The employee was not the good samaritan intent on aiding another. The patron was.

Do these exceptions mean that the bystander rule is gone? *Parra v. Tarasco*[6] provides a partial answer. Ernesto Parra was a customer at the Jiminez Restaurant when

---

[5] 141 Cal. App. 3d 443, 190 Cal. Rptr. 310, 1983 Cal. App. LEXIS 1539 (1983).
[6] 230 Ill. App. 3d 819, 595 N.E.2d 1186.

food became lodged in his throat. The employees did not use the Heimlich maneuver or any other method to try to save him. Parra choked to death. Was the restaurant liable? No, said the Illinois Appeals Court. The restaurant had no obligation to do anything.

The bystander rule, that hardy oak, is alive and well. Various initials have been carved into its bark—the exceptions we have seen and a variety of others—but the trunk is strong and the leaves green. Perhaps someday the proliferating exceptions will topple it, but the process of the common law is slow and that day is nowhere in sight. In the meantime, it is nice to be reminded that even without a legal obligation, some citizens do choose to get involved.

NEWS*worthy*

As the freight train rumbled through rural Indiana, conductor Robert Mohr looked ahead and saw what seemed to be a puppy. Then the "puppy" sat up straight and shook her blond curls. Nineteen-month-old Emily Marshall had wandered away from her mother and was playing on the tracks, dead ahead. Engineer Rodney Lindley jammed on the brakes but could not possibly stop the 96-car, 6,000-ton train. There was no time to jump off and sprint ahead to the girl. Mohr, aged 49, hustled onto the engine's catwalk and clambered forward, as Lindley slowed the train to 10 miles per hour. Gripping a guard rail, Mohr leaned perilously far forward, waited until the engine loomed directly above the child— and deftly booted her to safety. Emily bounced up with nothing worse than a chipped tooth and forehead cuts, and Mohr, the merrier, was a Hoosier hero. ◆

STATUTORY LAW

Most new law is statutory law. Statutes affect each of us every day, in our business, professional, and personal lives. When the system works correctly, this is the one part of the law over which we the people have control. We elect the local legislators who pass state statutes; we vote for the senators and representatives who create federal statutes. If we understand the system, we can affect the largest source of contemporary law. If we live in ignorance of its strengths and pitfalls, we delude ourselves that we participate in a democracy.

As we saw in Chapter 1, there are many systems of government operating in the United States: a national government and 50 state governments. Each level of government has a legislative body. In Washington, D.C., Congress is our national legislature. Congress passes the statutes that govern the nation. In addition, each state has a legislature, which passes statutes for that state only. In this section we look at how Congress does its work creating statutes. State legislatures operate similarly, but the work of Congress is better documented and obviously of national importance.[7]

---

[7] See the chart of state and federal governments in Chapter 1. A vast amount of information about Congress is available on the Internet. The House of Representatives has a Web page at http://www. house.gov/. The Senate's site appears at http://www.senate.gov. Each page provides links to current law, pending legislation, votes, committees, and more. If you do not know the name of your representative or senator (shame!), the Web page will provide that information. Most state legislatures have Websites, which you can reach from links found at http://www.ncsl.org/public/sitesleg.htm. These sites typically permit you to read statutes, research legislative history, examine the current calendar, and note upcoming events. For example, the Website http://housegop.state.il.us/ brings you to the Republican caucus in the Illinois House of Representatives, while the site http://www.housedem. state.il.us/ will take you to the same body's Democratic caucus. Many of these Websites enable you to e-mail your local representatives.

Bills

Congress is organized into two houses, the House of Representatives and the Senate. Either house may originate a proposed statute, which is called a **bill.** The bill must be voted on and approved by both houses. Once both houses pass it, they will send it to the president. If the president signs the bill, it becomes law and is then a statute. If the president opposes the bill, he will **veto** it, in which case it is not law.[8]

Committee Work

If you visit either house of Congress, you will probably find half a dozen legislators on the floor, with one person talking and no one listening. This is because most of the work is done in committees. Both houses are organized into dozens of committees, each with special functions. The House currently has about 27 committees (further divided into about 150 subcommittees), and the Senate has approximately 20 committees (with about 86 subcommittees). For example, the armed services committee of each house oversees the huge defense budget and the workings of the armed forces. Labor committees handle legislation concerning organized labor and working conditions. Banking committees develop expertise on financial institutions. Judiciary committees review nominees to the federal courts. There are dozens of other committees, some very powerful, because they control vast amounts of money, and some relatively weak.

When a bill is proposed in either house, it is referred to the committee that specializes in that subject. Why are bills proposed in the first place? For any of several reasons:

- *New Issue, New Worry.* If society begins to focus on a new issue, Congress may respond with legislation. We consider next, for example, the congressional response to employment discrimination.

- *Unpopular Judicial Ruling.* If Congress disagrees with a judicial interpretation of a statute, the legislators may pass a new statute to modify or "undo" the court decision. For example, if the Supreme Court misinterprets a statute about musical copyrights, Congress may pass a new law correcting the Court's error. However, the legislators have no such power to modify a court decision based on the Constitution. When the Supreme Court ruled that lawyers had a right *under the First Amendment* to advertise their services, Congress lacked the power to change the decision.

- *Criminal Law.* Statutory law, unlike common law, is prospective. Legislators are hoping to control the future. And that is why almost all criminal law is statutory. A court cannot retroactively announce that it *has been* a crime for a retailer to accept kickbacks from a wholesaler. Everyone must know the rules in advance because the consequences—prison, a felony record—are so harsh.

Discrimination: Congress and the Courts

The civil rights movement of the 1950s and 1960s convinced most citizens that African Americans continued to suffer relentless discrimination in jobs, housing, voting, schools, and other basic areas of life. Demonstrations and boycotts, marches and counter-marches, church bombings and killings persuaded the nation that the problem was vast and urgent.

In 1963 President Kennedy proposed legislation to guarantee equal rights to African Americans in these areas. The bill went to the House Judiciary Committee, which heard testimony for weeks. Witnesses testified that blacks were often unable to vote because of their race, that landlords and home sellers adamantly refused to sell or

---

[8] Congress may, however, attempt to override the veto. See the discussion on p. 84.

rent to blacks, that education was still grossly unequal, and that blacks were routinely denied good jobs in many industries. Eventually, the Judiciary Committee approved the bill and sent it to the full House.

The bill was dozens of pages long and divided into "titles," with each title covering a major issue. Title VII concerned employment. We will consider the progress of Title VII in Congress and in the courts. Here is one section of Title VII, as reported to the House floor[9]:

> Sec. 703(a). It shall be an unlawful employment practice for an employer—
>
> (1) to fail or refuse to hire or to discharge any individual, or otherwise to discriminate against any individual with respect to his compensation, terms, conditions, or privileges of employment, because of such individual's race, color, religion, or national origin; or
>
> (2) to limit, segregate, or classify his employees in any way which would deprive or tend to deprive any individual of employment opportunities or otherwise adversely affect his status as an employee, because of such individual's race, color, religion, or national origin.

Debate

The proposed bill was intensely controversial and sparked angry argument throughout Congress. Here are some excerpts from one day's debate on the House floor, on February 8, 1964[10]:

> MR. WAGGONNER. I speak to you in all sincerity and ask for the right to discriminate if I so choose because I think it is my right. I think it is my right to choose my social companions. I think it is my right if I am a businessman to run it as I please, to do with my own as I will. I think that is a right the Constitution gives to every man. I want the continued right to discriminate and I want the other man to have the right to continue to discriminate against me, because I am discriminated against every day. I do not feel inferior about it.
>
> I ask you to forget about politics, forget about everything except the integrity of the individual, leaving to the people of this country the right to live their lives in the manner they choose to live. Do not destroy this democracy for a Socialist government. A vote for this bill is no less.
>
> MR. CONTE. If the serious cleavage which pitted brother against brother and citizen against citizen during the tragedy of the Civil War is ever to be justified, it can be justified in this House and then in the other body with the passage of this legislation which can and must reaffirm the rights to all individuals which are inherent in our Constitution.
>
> The distinguished poet Mark Van Doren has said that "equality is absolute or no, nothing between can stand," and nothing should now stand between us and the passage of strong and effective civil rights legislation. It is to this that we are united in a strong bipartisan coalition today, and when the laws of the land proclaim that the 88th Congress acted effectively, judiciously, and wisely, we can take pride in our accomplishments as free men.

Other debate was less rhetorical and aimed more at getting information. The following exchange anticipates a 30-year controversy on quotas:

> MR. JOHANSEN. I have asked for this time to raise a question and I would ask particularly for the attention of the gentleman from New York [MR. GOODELL] because of a remark he made—and I am not quarreling with it. I understood him to say there is no plan for balanced employment or for quotas in this legislation . . . I am raising a question as to whether

---

[9] The section number in the House bill was actually 704(a); we use 703 here because that is the number of the section when the bill became law and the number to which the Supreme Court refers in later litigation.

[10] The order of speakers is rearranged, and the remarks are edited.

in the effort to eliminate discrimination—and incidentally that is an undefined term in the bill—we may get to a situation in which employers, and conceivably union leaders, will insist on legislation providing for a quota system as a matter of self-protection.

Now let us suppose this hypothetical situation exists with 100 jobs to be filled. Let us say 150 persons apply and suppose 75 of them are Negro and 75 of them are white. Supposing the employer . . . hires 75 white men and 25 Negroes. Do the other 50 Negroes or anyone of them severally have a right to claim they have been discriminated against on the basis of color?

MR. GOODELL. It is the intention of the legislation that if applicants are equal in all other respects there will be no restriction. One may choose from among equals. So long as there is no distinction on the basis of race, creed, or color it will not violate the act.

The debate on racial issues carried on. Later in the day, Congressman Smith of Virginia offered an amendment that could scarcely have been smaller—or more important:

Amendment offered by MR. SMITH of Virginia: On page 68, line 23, after the word "religion," insert the word "sex."

In other words, Smith was asking that discrimination on the basis of sex also be outlawed, along with the existing grounds of race, color, national origin, and religion. Congressman Smith's proposal produced the following comments:

MR. CELLER. You know, the French have a phrase for it when they speak of women and men. They say "vive la difference." I think the French are right. Imagine the upheaval that would result from adoption of blanket language requiring total equality. Would male citizens be justified in insisting that women share with them the burdens of compulsory military service? What would become of traditional family relationships? What about alimony? What would become of the crimes of rape and statutory rape? I think the amendment seems illogical, ill timed, ill placed, and improper.

MRS. ST. GEORGE. Mr. Chairman, I was somewhat amazed when I came on the floor this afternoon to hear the very distinguished chairman of the Committee on the Judiciary [MR. CELLER] make the remark that he considered the amendment at this point illogical. I can think of nothing more logical than this amendment at this point.

There are still many States where women cannot serve on juries. There are still many States where women do not have equal educational opportunities. In most States and, in fact, I figure it would be safe to say, in all States—women do not get equal pay for equal work. That is a very well known fact. And to say that this is illogical. What is illogical about it? All you are doing is simply correcting something that goes back, frankly to the Dark Ages.

The debate continued. Some supported the "sex" amendment because they were determined to end sexual bias. But politics are complex. Some *opponents* of civil rights supported the amendment because they believed that it would make the legislation less popular and cause Congress to defeat the entire Civil Rights bill.

That strategy did not work. The amendment passed, and sex was added as a protected trait. And, after more debate and several votes, the entire bill passed the House. It went to the Senate, where it followed a similar route from Judiciary Committee to full Senate. Much of the Senate debate was similar to what we have seen. But some senators raised a new issue concerning §703(2), which prohibited *segregating or classifying* employees based on any of the protected categories (race, color, national origin, religion, or sex). Senator Tower was concerned that §703(2) meant that an employee in a protected category could never be given any sort of job test. So the Senate amended §703 to include a new subsection:

Sec. 703(h). Notwithstanding any other provision of this title, it shall not be an unlawful employment practice for an employer . . . to give and to act upon the results of any professionally developed ability test provided that such test . . . is not designed, intended or used to discriminate because of race, color, religion, sex or national origin.

With that amendment, and many others, the bill passed the Senate.

Conference Committee

Civil rights legislation had now passed both houses, but the bills were no longer the same due to the many amendments. This is true with most legislation. The next step is for the two houses to send representatives to a House–Senate Conference Committee. This committee examines all the differences between the two bills and tries to reach a compromise. With the Civil Rights bill, Senator Tower's amendment was left in; other Senate amendments were taken out. When the Conference Committee had settled every difference between the two versions, the new, modified bill was sent back to each house for a new vote.

The House of Representatives and the Senate again angrily debated the compromise language reported from the Conference Committee. Finally, after years of violent public demonstrations and months of debate, each house passed the same bill. President Johnson promptly signed it. The Civil Rights Act of 1964 was law. (See Exhibit 4.1.)

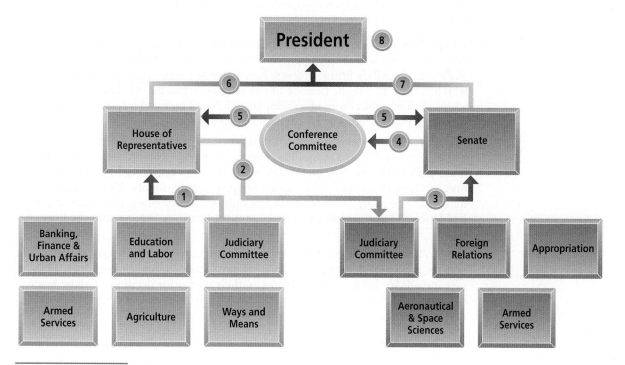

Exhibit 4.1

The two houses of Congress are organized into dozens of committees, a few of which are shown here. The path of the 1964 Civil Rights Act (somewhat simplified) was as follows: (1) The House Judiciary Committee approved the bill and sent it to the full House; (2) the full House passed the bill and sent it to the Senate, where it was assigned to the Senate Judiciary Committee; (3) the Senate Judiciary Committee passed an amended version of the bill and sent it to the full Senate; (4) the full Senate passed the bill with additional amendments. Because the Senate version was now different from the bill the House passed, the bill went to a Conference Committee. The Conference Committee (5) reached a compromise and sent the new version of the bill back to both houses. Each house passed the compromise bill (6 and 7) and sent it to the president, who signed it into law (8).

Title VII of the Civil Rights Act obviously prohibited an employer from saying to a job applicant, "We don't hire blacks." In some parts of the country, that had been common practice; after the Civil Rights Act passed, it became rare. Employers who routinely hired whites only, or promoted only whites, found themselves losing lawsuits.

A new group of cases arose, those in which some job standard was set that appeared to be racially neutral yet had a discriminatory effect. In North Carolina, the Duke Power Co. required that applicants for higher paying, promotional positions meet two requirements: they must have a high school diploma, and they must pass a standardized written test. There was no evidence that either requirement related to successful job performance. Blacks met the requirements in lower percentages than whites, and consequently whites obtained a disproportionate share of the good jobs.

Title VII did not precisely address this kind of case. It clearly outlawed overt discrimination. Was Duke Power's policy overt discrimination, or was it protected by Senator Tower's amendment, §703(h)? The case went all the way to the Supreme Court, where the Court had to interpret the new law.

Statutory Interpretation

Courts are often called upon to interpret a statute, that is, to explain precisely what the language means and how it applies in a given case. There are three primary steps in a court's statutory interpretation:

- *Plain Meaning Rule.* When a statute's words have ordinary, everyday significance, the court will simply apply those words. Section 703(a)(1) of the Civil Rights Act prohibits firing someone because of her religion. Could an employer who had fired a Catholic because of her religion argue that Catholicism is not really a religion, but more of a social group? No. The word *religion* has a plain meaning, and courts apply its commonsense definition.

- *Legislative History and Intent.* If the language is unclear, the court must look deeper. Section 703(a)(2) prohibits classifying employees in ways that are discriminatory. Does that section prevent an employer from requiring high school diplomas, as Duke Power did? The explicit language of the statute does not answer the question. The court will look at the law's history to determine the intent of the legislature. The court will examine committee hearings, reports, and the floor debates that we have seen.

- *Public Policy.* If the legislative history is unclear, courts will rely on general public policies, such as reducing crime, creating equal opportunity, and so forth. They may include in this examination some of their own prior decisions. Courts assume that the legislature is aware of prior judicial decisions, and if the legislature did not change those decisions, the statute will be interpreted to incorporate them.

Here is how the Supreme Court interpreted the 1964 Civil Rights Act.

GRIGGS V. DUKE POWER CO.

401 U.S. 424, 91 S. Ct. 849, 1971 U.S. LEXIS 134
United States Supreme Court, 1971

Excerpts from Mr. Chief Justice Burger's Decision: The objective of Congress in the enactment of Title VII is plain from the language of the statute. It was to achieve equality of employment opportunities and remove barriers that have operated in the past to favor an identifiable group of white employees over other employees. Under the ▼

Act, practices, procedures, or tests neutral on their face, and even neutral in terms of intent, cannot be maintained if they operate to "freeze" the status quo of prior discriminatory employment practices.

The Act proscribes not only overt discrimination but also practices that are fair in form, but discriminatory in operation. The touchstone is business necessity. If an employment practice which operates to exclude Negroes cannot be shown to be related to job performance, the practice is prohibited.

On the record before us, neither the high school completion requirement nor the general intelligence test is shown to bear a demonstrable relationship to successful performance of the jobs for which it was used.

Senator Tower offered an amendment which was adopted verbatim and is now the testing provision of section 703(h). Speaking for the supporters of Title VII, Senator Humphrey endorsed the amendment, stating: "Senators on both sides of the aisle who were deeply interested in Title VII have examined the text of this amendment and have found it to be in accord with the intent and purpose of that title." The amendment was then adopted. From the sum of the legislative history relevant in this case, the conclusion is inescapable that the . . . requirement that employment tests be job related comports with congressional intent. ■

And so the highest Court ruled that if a job requirement had a discriminatory impact, the employer could use that requirement only if it was related to job performance. Many more cases arose. For almost two decades courts held that, once workers showed that a job requirement had a discriminatory effect, the employer had the burden to prove that the requirement was necessary for the business. The requirement had to be essential to achieve an important goal. If there was any way to achieve that goal without discriminatory impact, the employer had to use it.

Changing Times

But things changed. In 1989 a more conservative Supreme Court decided *Wards Cove Packing Co. v. Atonio.*[11] The plaintiffs were nonwhite workers in salmon canneries in Alaska. The canneries had two types of jobs, skilled and unskilled. Nonwhites (Filipinos and native Alaskans) invariably worked as low-paid, unskilled workers, canning the fish. The higher paid, skilled positions were filled almost entirely with white workers, who were hired during the off-season in Washington and Oregon.

There was no overt discrimination. But plaintiffs claimed that various practices led to the racial imbalances. The practices included failing to promote from within the company, hiring through separate channels (cannery jobs were done through a union hall, skilled positions were filled out of state), nepotism, and an English language requirement. Once again the case reached the Supreme Court, where Justice White wrote the Court's opinion.

If the plaintiffs succeeded in showing that the job requirements led to racial imbalance, said the Court, the employer now only had to demonstrate that the requirement or practice "serves, in a significant way, the legitimate employment goals of the employer. . . . [T]here is no requirement that the challenged practice be 'essential' or 'indispensable' to the employer's business." In other words, the Court removed the "business necessity" requirement of *Griggs* and replaced it with "legitimate employment goals."

---

[11] 490 U.S. 642, 109 S. Ct. 2115, 1989 U.S. LEXIS 2794 (1989).

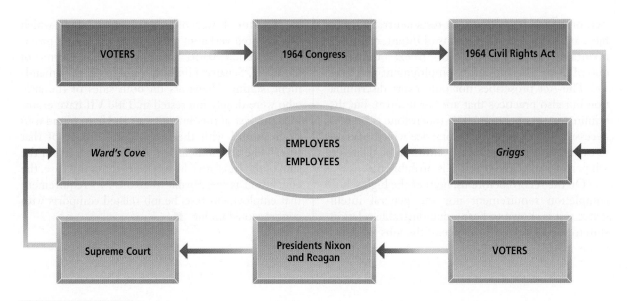

Exhibit 4.2
Statutory interpretation can be just as volatile as the common law, because voters, politicians, and courts all change over time.

Voters' Role

The response to *Wards Cove* was quick. Liberals decried it; conservatives hailed it. Everyone agreed that it was a major change that would make it substantially harder for plaintiffs to bring successful discrimination cases. Why had the Court changed its interpretation? Because the *Court* was different. The Court of the 1980s was more conservative, with a majority of justices appointed by Presidents Nixon and Reagan. And so the voters' political preference had affected the high Court, which in turn changed the interpretation of a statute passed in response to voter concerns of the 1960s. (See Exhibit 4.2.)

Democrats introduced bills to reverse the interpretation of *Wards Cove*. President George H. W. Bush strongly opposed any new bill. He said it would lead to "quotas"— that is, that employers would feel obligated to hire a certain percentage of workers from all racial categories to protect themselves from suits. This was the issue that Congressman Johansen had raised in the original House debate in 1964, but it had not been mentioned since.

Both houses passed bills restoring the "business necessity" holding of *Griggs*. Again there were differences, and a Conference Committee resolved them. After acrimonious debate, both houses passed the compromise bill in October 1990. Was it therefore law? No. President Bush immediately vetoed the bill. He said it would compel employers to adopt quotas.

Congressional Override

When the president vetoes a bill, Congress has one last chance to make it law: an override. If both houses repass the bill, each by a two-thirds margin, it becomes law over the president's veto. Congress attempted to pass the 1990 Civil Rights bill over the Bush veto, but it fell short in the Senate by one vote.

Civil rights advocates tried again in January 1991, introducing a new bill to reverse the *Wards Cove* rule. Again both houses debated and bargained. The new bill stated that once an employee proves that a particular employment practice causes a discriminatory impact, the employer must "demonstrate that the challenged practice is job related for the position in question and consistent with business necessity."

Now the two sides fought over the exact meanings of two terms: "job related" and "business necessity." Each side offered definitions, but they could not reach agreement. It appeared that the entire bill would founder over those terms. So Congress did what it often does when faced with a problem of definition: it dropped the issue. Liberals and conservatives agreed not to define the troublesome terms. They would leave that task to courts to perform through statutory interpretation.

With the definitions left out, the new bill passed both houses. In November 1991, President Bush signed the bill into law. The president stated that the new bill had been improved and no longer threatened to create racial quotas. His opponents charged he had reversed course for political reasons, anticipating the 1992 presidential election.

And so the Congress restored the "business necessity" interpretation to its own 1964 Civil Rights Act. No one would say, however, that it had been a simple process.

The Other Player: Money

No description of the legislative process would be complete, or even realistic, without mentioning money. Campaign contributions and spending have aroused controversy for decades. In 1971, Congress passed the Federal Election Campaign Act (FECA), which limited how much of his own money a federal candidate could spend. Three years later the statute was amended to place two more limitations on federal campaigns: how much a campaign as a whole could spend, and how much anyone else could spend to promote a candidate. One goal was to reduce the power and influence of donors, who gave money expecting favors in return; another purpose was to permit candidates of modest means to compete with millionaire office seekers.

In 1976 the Supreme Court unsettled things in *Buckley v. Valeo*,[12] by ruling that mandatory *spending* limits violate the First Amendment. The Court permitted Congress to limit campaign *contributions*, from individuals and groups, but not to cap the amount that a candidate could spend. This decision was a windfall for wealthy candidates, who could now spend as much of their own money as they chose. It is no coincidence that most members of Congress are very rich.

In 1979, Congress amended the FECA to permit unlimited donations to *political parties* for use in "party building." Initially, party building meant only minor activities like get-out-the-vote drives and distribution of bumper stickers and buttons. Both parties, however, eventually discovered that it was easy to use party-building money in ways that would directly benefit candidates. These funds came to be known as *soft money*. Because the law placed no limit on soft money, the parties went after it feverishly, raising and spending hundreds of millions of dollars every election, effectively destroying any distinction between party building and campaigning.

*up*date

In 2002, Congress passed legislation designed to curtail the influence of campaign donations by eliminating soft money and regulating campaign advertising. However, it is already apparent that the legislation did not eliminate soft money. During the 2004 election cycle, both parties exploited a new device, so-called 527 committees. These are tax-exempt groups, named after section 527 of the Internal Revenue Code, that raise enormous sums attempting to influence elections. Generally speaking they may

---

[12] 424 U.S. 1, 96 S. Ct. 612, 1976 U.S. LEXIS 16 (1976).

not advocate for or against a federal candidate. Instead, they spend their money advocating positions on volatile topics, criticizing selected candidates on those same issues, and mobilizing voters they deem sympathetic to their cause. The 2004 presidential election was the most expensive in history, and 527s raised a total of $434 million, with the two largest groups spending more than $70 million each. Soft money is proving hard to uproot.

Senators John McCain and Russ Feingold, authors of the original effort to reduce influence peddling, have already sponsored new legislation to clamp down on 527s. The nonprofit Center for Public Integrity has brought to light many money scandals in Washington. To see what a sharp spotlight will reveal, glance at the center's Web page, http://www. publicintegrity.org. Common Cause, which you can visit at http://www.commoncause. org, works hard for campaign finance reform. The Center for Responsive Politics, at http:// www.crp.org/, includes in its Website a dollar-by-dollar description of recent elections, demonstrating which candidates took how much from whom. ◆

ECONOMICS & the LAW

When a contributor gives money to a congressman or senator, what is she hoping to accomplish? Does she merely want to assist an incumbent whose views match her own, in the hope of securing his reelection? Or is she attempting to influence the office holder's position on a particular issue? Economists agree that this is an important question but disagree on the answer. One study concluded that campaign donors do hope to influence votes on particular issues. This economist charted the timing of donations. He discovered that disproportionate sums were donated, not during election campaigns but during legislative sessions, as important bills were coming up for vote. The donors tended to be those directly affected by the proposed legislation. The author of the study concluded that a substantial number of campaign donors attempt to influence a legislator's vote on a particular bill—regardless of whether they succeed.[13]

A second study reached a different conclusion. The authors compared how a legislator voted after he had announced his retirement (but still held office) with his voting pattern while he was an incumbent seeking reelection. These economists reasoned that if campaign donations influence a politician's views, then once the office holder announces his retirement and stops fund raising, his votes should shift back to his own, honest positions. But they discovered no such voting shift. The authors concluded that most politicians vote their conscience.[14] Which study do you find more persuasive? ◆

ADMINISTRATIVE LAW

Before beginning this section, please return your seat to its upright position. Stow the tray firmly in the seatback in front of you. Turn off any radios, CD players, or other electronic equipment. Sound familiar? Administrative agencies affect each of us every day in hundreds of ways. They have become the fourth branch of government. Supporters believe that they provide unique expertise in complex areas; detractors regard them as unelected government run amok.

Many administrative agencies are familiar. The Federal Aviation Agency, which requires all airlines to ensure that your seats are upright before takeoff and landing, is an administrative agency. The Internal Revenue Service haunts us every April 15.

---

[13] Stratman, "The Market for Congressional Votes: Is Timing of Contributions Everything?" *Journal of Law and Economics*, 1998, vol. 41, p. 85.

[14] Bronars and Lott, "Campaign Donations," *Journal of Law and Economics*, 1997, vol. 40, p. 317.

The Environmental Protection Agency regulates the water quality of the river in your town. The Federal Trade Commission oversees the commercials that shout at you from your television set.

Other agencies are less familiar. You may never have heard of the Bureau of Land Management, but if you go into the oil and gas industry, you will learn that this powerful agency has more control over your land than you do. If you develop real estate in Palos Hills, Illinois, you will tremble every time the Appearance Commission of the City of Palos Hills speaks, because you cannot construct a new building without its approval. If your software corporation wants to hire an Argentine expert on databases, you will get to know the complex workings of the U.S. Citizenship and Immigration Services: no one lawfully enters this country without its nod of approval.

Background

By the 1880s, the amazing iron horse crisscrossed America. But this technological miracle became an economic headache. Congress worried that the railroads' economic muscle enabled a few powerful corporations to reap unfair profits. The railroad industry needed closer regulation. Who would do it? Courts decide individual cases; they do not regulate industries. Congress itself passes statutes, but it has no personnel to oversee the day-to-day working of a huge industry. For example, Congress lacks the expertise to establish rates for freight passing from Kansas City to Chicago, and it has no personnel to enforce rates once they are set.

A new entity was needed. Congress passed the Interstate Commerce Act, creating the Interstate Commerce Commission (ICC), the first administrative agency. The ICC began regulating freight and passenger transportation over the growing rail system and continued to do so for more than 100 years. Congress gave the ICC power to regulate rates and investigate harmful practices, hold hearings, issue orders, and punish railroads that did not comply.

The ICC was able to hire and develop a staff that was expert in the issues that Congress wanted controlled. The agency had enough flexibility to deal with the problems in a variety of ways: by regulating, investigating, and punishing. And that is what has made administrative agencies an attractive solution for Congress: One entity, focusing on one industry, can combine expertise and flexibility. However, the ICC also developed great power, which voters could not reach, and thereby started the great and lasting conflict over the role of agencies.

During the Great Depression of the 1930s, the Roosevelt administration and Congress created dozens of new agencies. Many were based on social demands, such as the need of the elderly population for a secure income. Political and social conditions dominated again in the 1960s, as Congress created agencies, such as the Equal Employment Opportunity Commission, to combat discrimination.

Then during the 1980s the Reagan administration made an effort to decrease the number and strength of the agencies. For several years some agencies declined in influence, though others did not. As we begin a new millennium, there is still controversy about how much power agencies should have, but there is no doubt that administrative agencies are a permanent part of our society.

Classification of Agencies

Agencies exist at the federal, state, and local level. We will focus on federal agencies because they have national impact and great power. Most of the principles discussed apply to state and local agencies as well. Virtually any business or profession you choose to work in will be regulated by at least one administrative agency, and it may be regulated by several.

Executive-Independent

Some federal agencies are part of the executive branch, whereas others are independent agencies. This is a major distinction. The president has much greater control of executive agencies for the simple reason that he can fire the agency head at any time. An executive agency will seldom diverge far from the president's preferred policies. Some familiar executive agencies are the Internal Revenue Service (part of the Treasury Department); the Federal Bureau of Investigation (Department of Justice); the Food and Drug Administration (Department of Health and Human Services); and the Nuclear Regulatory Commission (Department of Energy).

The president has no such removal power over independent agencies. The Federal Communications Commission (FCC) is an independent agency. For many corporations involved in broadcasting, the FCC has more day-to-day influence on their business than Congress, the courts, and the president combined. Other powerful independent agencies are the Federal Trade Commission, the Securities and Exchange Commission, the National Labor Relations Board, and the Environmental Protection Agency.

Enabling Legislation

Congress creates a federal agency by passing **enabling legislation.** The Interstate Commerce Act was the enabling legislation that established the ICC. Typically, the enabling legislation describes the problems that Congress believes need regulation, establishes an agency to do it, and defines the agency's powers.

Critics argue that Congress is delegating to another body powers that only the legislature or courts are supposed to exercise. This puts administrative agencies above the voters. But legal attacks on administrative agencies invariably fail. Courts acknowledge that agencies have become an integral part of a complex economy. As long as there are some limits on an agency's discretion, a court will uphold its powers.

The Administrative Procedure Act

The Administrative Procedure Act (APA) is a major limitation on how agencies do their work. Congress passed the APA in 1946 in an effort to bring uniformity and control to the many federal agencies. The APA regulates how federal agencies make rules, conduct investigations, hold meetings and hearings, reach decisions, and obtain and release information. How much power should agencies have? How much control should we impose on them? These are two of the major questions that businesses and courts face as we enter a new century.

Power of Agencies

Administrative agencies use three kinds of power to do the work assigned to them: They make rules, they investigate, and they adjudicate.

Rulemaking

One of the most important functions of an administrative agency is to make rules. In doing this, the agency attempts, prospectively, to establish fair and uniform behavior for all businesses in the affected area. **To create a new rule is to promulgate it.** Agencies promulgate two types of rules: legislative and interpretive.

Legislative Rules. These are the most important agency rules, and they are much like statutes. Here, an agency creates law by requiring businesses or private citizens to act in a certain way. Suppose you operate a Website for young shoppers, aged 10 to 18. Like most online merchants, you consider yourself free to collect as much data as possible about consumers. Wrong. The Federal Trade Commission, a federal agency, has promulgated detailed rules governing any site directed to young children. Before obtaining private data from these immature consumers, you must let them know exactly who you are, how to contact site operators, precisely what you are seeking, and how it will be used. You must also obtain verifiable parental consent before collecting, using, or disclosing any personal information. Failure to follow the rules can result in a substantial civil penalty. This modest legislative rule, in short, will be more important to your business than most statutes passed by Congress.

Interpretive Rules.   These rules do not change the law. They are the agency's interpretation of what the law already requires. But they can still affect all of us.

In 1977, Congress passed the Clean Air Act in an attempt to reduce pollution from factories. The act required the Environmental Protection Agency (EPA) to impose emission standards on "stationary sources" of pollution. But what did "stationary source" mean? It was the EPA's job to define that term. Obscure work, to be sure, yet the results could be seen and even smelled, because the EPA's definition would determine the quality of air entering our lungs every time we breathe. Environmentalists wanted the term defined to include every smokestack in a factory so that the EPA could regulate each one. The EPA, however, developed the "bubble concept," ruling that "stationary source" meant an entire factory, but not the individual smokestacks. As a result, polluters could shift emission among smokestacks in a single factory to avoid EPA regulation. Environmentalists howled that this gutted the purpose of the statute, but to no avail. The agency had spoken, merely by interpreting a statute.[15]

How Rules Are Made.   Corporations fight many a court battle over whether an agency has the right to issue a particular rule and whether it was promulgated properly. The critical issue is this: How much participation is the public entitled to before an agency issues a rule? There are two basic methods of rulemaking.[16]

Informal Rulemaking.   On many issues, agencies may use a simple "notice and comment" method of rulemaking. The agency must publish a proposed rule in advance and permit the public a comment period. During this period, the public may submit any objections and arguments, with supporting data. The agency will make its decision and publish the final rule.

For example, the Department of Transportation may use the informal rulemaking procedure to require safety features for all new automobiles. The agency must listen to objections from interested parties, notably car manufacturers, and it must give a written response to the objections. The agency is required to have rational reasons for the final choices it makes. However, it is not obligated to satisfy all parties or do their bidding.

Formal Rulemaking.   In the enabling legislation, Congress may require that an agency hold a hearing before promulgating rules. Congress does this to make the agency more accountable to the public. After the agency publishes its proposed rule, it must hold a public hearing. Opponents of the rule, typically affected businesses, may cross-examine the agency experts about the need for the rule and may testify against it. When the agency makes its final decision about the rule, it must prepare a formal, written response to everything that occurred at the hearing.

When used responsibly, these hearings give the public access to the agency and can help formulate sound policy. When used irresponsibly, hearings can be manipulated to stymie needed regulation. The most famous example concerns peanut butter. The Food and Drug Administration (FDA) began investigating peanut butter content in 1958.

---

[15] An agency's interpretation can be challenged in court, and this one was.

[16] Certain rules may be made with no public participation at all. For example, an agency's internal business affairs and procedures can be regulated without public comment, as can its general policy statements. None of these directly affect the public, and the public has no right to participate.

It found, for example, that Jif peanut butter, made by Procter & Gamble, had only 75 percent peanuts and 20 percent of a Crisco-type base. P&G fought the investigation, and any changes, for years. Finally, in 1965 the FDA proposed a minimum of 90 percent peanuts in peanut butter; P&G wanted 87 percent. The FDA wanted no more than 3 percent hydrogenated vegetable oil; P&G wanted no limit.

The hearings dragged on for months. One day, the P&G lawyer objected to the hearing going forward because he needed to vote that day. Another time, when an FDA official testified that consumer letters indicated the public wanted to know what was really in peanut butter, the P&G attorney demanded that the official bring in and identify the letters—all 20,000 of them. Finally, in 1968, a decade after beginning its investigation, the FDA promulgated final rules requiring 90 percent peanuts but eliminating the 3 percent cap on vegetable oil.[17]

Hybrid Rulemaking.   In an effort to avoid the agency paralysis made famous in the peanut butter case, some agencies use hybrid rulemaking, following the informal model but adding a few elements of the formal. The agency may give notice and a comment period, deny the right to a full hearing, but allow limited cross-examination on one or two key issues.

Investigation

Agencies do an infinite variety of work, but they all need broad factual knowledge of the field they govern. Some companies cooperate with an agency, furnishing information and even voluntarily accepting agency recommendations. For example, the U.S. Consumer Product Safety Commission investigates hundreds of consumer products every year and often urges companies to recall goods that the agency considers defective. Many firms comply. (For an up-to-the-minute report on dangerous products and company compliance, proceed carefully to http://www.cpsc.gov/index.html.)

Other companies, however, jealously guard information, often because corporate officers believe that disclosure would lead to adverse rules. To force disclosure, agencies use *subpoenas* and *searches.*

Subpoenas.   A **subpoena** is an order to appear at a particular time and place to provide evidence. A **subpoena** *duces tecum* requires the person to appear and bring specified documents. Businesses and other organizations intensely dislike subpoenas and resent government agents plowing through records and questioning employees. What are the limits on an agency's investigation? The information sought:

- Must be *relevant* to a lawful agency investigation. The FCC is clearly empowered to investigate the safety of broadcasting towers, and any documents about tower construction are obviously relevant. Documents about employee racial statistics might indicate discrimination, but the FCC lacks jurisdiction on that issue and thus may not demand such documents.

- Must not be *unreasonably burdensome.* A court will compare the agency's need for the information with the intrusion on the corporation.

- Must not be *privileged.* The Fifth Amendment privilege against self-incrimination means that a corporate officer accused of criminal securities violations may not be compelled to testify about his behavior.

In the following case, an agency's subpoena power conflicted with an important right of confidentiality.

---

[17] For an excellent account of this high-fat hearing, see Mark J. Green, *The Other Government* (New York: W. W. Norton & Co., 1978), pp. 136–150.

DOE V. MARYLAND BOARD OF SOCIAL WORKERS

384 Md. 161, 862 A.2d 996
Maryland Court of Appeals, 2004

Facts: "Ms. F." was a licensed social worker in Maryland. One of her clients, "John Doe," was convicted of child abuse and sex offenses involving his minor granddaughter. The Board of Social Work Examiners, an administrative agency, learned that Ms. F. had likely violated the law by failing to report the abuse. The agency began an investigation and issued a subpoena *duces tecum* to Ms. F., demanding all treatment records for John Doe and his wife, "Jane Doe," for the year in which the abuse occurred.

The Does ("Petitioners") sued, asking the court to quash the subpoena, that is, to nullify it. They claimed that a social worker–client privilege prohibited disclosure of their records. The intermediate court of appeals declared the subpoena valid. The Does appealed to the state's highest court.

Issue: Was the subpoena valid?

Excerpts from Judge Cathell's Decision: [A state statute] affords social workers and their clients similar protections that have long been applicable to other relationships where privacy issues and the need for open communication are of paramount importance, e.g., marital privilege, attorney–client privilege, psychiatrist/psychologist–patient privilege, clergyman–communicant privilege, etc. We consider the information contained in those treatment records to be both confidential *and* privileged. Therefore, we must examine the Board's claim that its subpoena power and obligation to oversee the conduct of the licensed social workers of this State provides an exception to petitioners' privilege and confidentiality rights as provided by law.

We agree with the intermediate appellate court that the Board's interests in obtaining Ms. F.'s treatment records of petitioners are clearly compelling. Of great importance is the fact that the Board itself was established by the Legislature "to protect the public by: (1) Setting minimum qualification, education, training, and experience standards for the licensing of individuals to practice social work; and (2) Promoting and maintaining high professional standards for the practice of social work." As the Court of Special Appeals stated in this regard: "To deny the Board access to patient files is to deny it the ability to carry out its legislative mandate. If the Social Worker Board receives a complaint that a social worker failed to notify the appropriate agency of his/her reason to believe that a child had been subjected to abuse, a lack of access to the worker's records would effectively foreclose any meaningful investigation into that conduct and any basis for disciplinary action."

We hold that neither the social worker–client privilege nor any claim concerning petitioners' constitutional right to privacy automatically prevents the Board from subpoenaing petitioners' treatment records. While the Board is required by law to protect the petitioners' treatment records from further disclosure, the Board must be allowed to have access to those treatment records in order to fulfill its statutory mandate to protect the public by conducting a full investigation and, where appropriate, disciplining those licensed social workers who are found to be in violation of the [law]. This mandate cannot be carried out if clients are automatically allowed, after claiming either a social worker–client privilege or a constitutional privacy right, to block from disclosure records that the Board determines are necessary to its investigations. Affirmed. ∎

Public Policy

The court is comparing two important public policy concerns. What are they? How does the court attempt to limit the intrusion into confidential records? What would happen if the administrative agency, reviewing the treatment notes, discovered evidence that the Does had committed additional crimes—or were planning to do so? Could the agency act on its knowledge? ◆

Search and Seizure. At times an agency will want to conduct a surprise **search** of an enterprise and **seize** any evidence of wrongdoing. May an agency do that? Yes, although there are limitations. When a particular industry is *comprehensively regulated,* courts will assume that companies know they are subject to periodic, unannounced inspections. In those industries, an administrative agency may conduct a search without a warrant and seize evidence of violations. For example, the mining industry is minutely regulated, with strict rules covering equipment, mining depths, transport and safety structures, air quality, and countless other things. Mining executives know that they are closely watched, and for good reason: mine safety is a matter of life and death, and surprise is an essential element of effective inspection. Accordingly, the Bureau of Mines may make unannounced, warrantless searches to ensure safety.[18] Today it is a rare case that finds a warrantless search by an administrative agency to have been illegal.

Adjudication

To **adjudicate** a case is to hold a hearing about an issue and then decide it. Agencies adjudicate countless cases. The FCC adjudicates which applicant for a new television license is best qualified. The Occupational Safety and Health Administration (OSHA) holds adversarial hearings to determine whether a manufacturing plant is dangerous.

Most adjudications begin with a hearing before an **administrative law judge** (ALJ). There is no jury. An ALJ is an employee of the agency but is expected to be impartial in her rulings. All parties are represented by counsel. The rules of evidence are informal, and an ALJ may receive any testimony or documents that will help resolve the dispute.

After all evidence is taken, the ALJ makes a decision. The losing party has a right to appeal to an appellate board within the agency. The appellate board has the power to make a *de novo* **decision,** meaning it may ignore the ALJ's decision. A party unhappy with that decision may appeal to federal court.

LIMITS ON AGENCY POWER

There are four primary methods of reining in these powerful creatures: statutory, political, judicial, and informational.

Statutory Control

As discussed, the enabling legislation of an agency provides some limits. It may require that the agency use formal rulemaking or investigate only certain issues. The APA imposes additional controls by requiring basic fairness in areas not regulated by the enabling legislation.

Political Control

The president's influence is greatest with executive agencies. Congress, though, controls the purse. No agency, executive or independent, can spend money it does not have. An agency that angers Congress risks having a particular program defunded or its entire budget cut. Further, Congress may decide to defund an agency as a cost-cutting measure. In its effort to balance the budget, Congress abolished the Interstate Commerce Commission, transferring its functions to the Transportation Department.

Congress has additional control because it must approve presidential nominees to head agencies. Before approving a nominee, Congress will attempt to determine her

---

[18] Donovan v. Dewey, 452 U.S. 594, 101 S. Ct. 2534, 1980 U.S. LEXIS 58 (1981).

intentions. And, finally, Congress may amend an agency's enabling legislation, limiting its power.

Judicial Review

An individual or corporation directly harmed by an administrative rule, investigation, or adjudication may generally have that action reviewed in federal court.[19] The party seeking review, for example, a corporation, must have suffered direct harm; the courts will not listen to theoretical complaints about an agency action.[20] And that party must first have taken all possible appeals within the agency itself.[21]

Standard on Review

Suppose OSHA promulgates a new rule limiting the noise level within steel mills. Certain mill operators are furious because they will have to retool their mills in order to comply. After exhausting their administrative appeals, they file suit seeking to force OSHA to withdraw the new rule. How does a court decide the case? Or, in legal terms, what standard does a court use in reviewing the case? Does it simply substitute its own opinion for that of the agency? No, it does not. The standard a court uses must take into account:

Facts.   Courts generally defer to an agency's factfinding. If OSHA finds that human hearing starts to suffer when decibels reach a particular level, a court will probably accept that as final. The agency is presumed to have expertise on such subjects. As long as there is *substantial evidence* to support the fact decision, it will be respected.

Law.   Courts often—but not always—defer to an agency's interpretation of the law. This is due in part to the enormous range of subjects that administrative agencies monitor. Consider the following examples. "Chicken catchers" work in large poultry operations, entering coops, manually capturing broilers, loading them into cages, and driving them to a processing plant where they . . . well, never mind. On one farm, the catchers wanted to organize a union, but the company objected, pointing out that *agricultural* workers had no right to do so. Were chicken catchers agricultural workers? The National Labor Relations Board, an administrative agency, declared that chicken catchers were in fact *ordinary* workers, entitled to organize. The Supreme Court ruled that courts were obligated to give deference to the agency's decision about chicken catchers. If the agency's interpretation was *reasonable*, it was binding, even if the court itself might not have made the same analysis. The workers were permitted to form a union—though the chickens were not.

The killer whales (Orcas) who live in Puget Sound are a threatened group. But are they a *separate population* from those that live in the ocean? If so, that would make

---

[19] In two narrow groups of cases, a court may not review an agency action. In a few cases, courts hold that a decision is "committed to agency discretion," a formal way of saying that courts will keep hands off. This happens only with politically sensitive issues, such as international air routes. In some cases the enabling legislation makes it absolutely clear that Congress wanted no court to review certain decisions. Courts will honor that.

[20] The law describes this requirement by saying that a party must have standing to bring a case. A college student who has a theoretical belief that the EPA should not interfere with the timber industry has no standing to challenge an EPA rule that prohibits logging in a national forest. A lumber company that was ready to log that area has suffered a direct economic injury: it has standing to sue.

[21] This is the doctrine of exhaustion of remedies. A lumber company may not go into court the day after the EPA publishes a proposed ban on logging. It must first exhaust its administrative remedies by participating in the administrative hearing and then pursuing appeals within the agency before venturing into court.

them an *endangered species*, entitled to major protections from the federal government. The National Marine Fisheries Services (NMFS), an administrative agency, ruled that the Puget Sound whales were not a separate population and therefore not endangered. However, a reviewing court disagreed and refused to defer to the NMFS decision. The agency, said the court, reached its conclusion without using the best available scientific data. The judge ordered the NMFS to reconsider differences between the various whales, this time taking into account the animals' language (clicks, calls, and whistles), rituals, and culture. The Puget Sound Orcas may still obtain protected status.

In the case that follows, the agency determination is again very technical—but of profound significance to one frightened man.

AMADOR-PALOMARES V. ASHCROFT

382 F.3d 864
United States Court of Appeals for the Eighth Circuit, 2004

Facts: Abelardo Amador-Palomares illegally entered the United States from Mexico as a 13-year-old boy, along with his family. He lived in this country continuously for about 20 years except for one four-month period when he returned to his native country. He had a young son, a United States citizen who suffered from tuberculosis and asthma.

The Citizenship and Immigration Services (USCIS), an administrative agency, began deportation proceedings against Amador-Palomares, who admitted he was in the country illegally but requested a discretionary form of relief called "suspension of deportation." Under the Immigration and Naturalization Act (INA), suspension is potentially available to those (1) who have been in the nation at least seven years, (2) who are of good moral character, and (3) whose deportation would result in extreme hardship.

The Board of Immigration Appeals (BIA), part of the USCIS, rejected his claim for suspension, finding that he was not of good moral character. While awaiting a decision on his claim of suspension, Amador-Palomares was convicted of soliciting a prostitute and fined $350. The BIA noted that a different section of the INA, section 1182(a)(2)(D), prohibited admission into the United States of anyone who

> ii) directly or indirectly procures or attempts to procure or to import, prostitutes or persons for the purpose of prostitution, or receives the proceeds of prostitution.

The BIA interpreted this section of the law to mean that anyone convicted of soliciting a prostitute could not be a person of good moral character for purposes of suspension of deportation. Amador-Palomares appealed.

Issue: Did the BIA improperly interpret immigration law and wrongfully deny suspension of deportation to Amador-Palomares?

Excerpts from Judge Melloy's Decision: If congressional intent is clear from the plain meaning of the statute, our inquiry ends. However, if we conclude that congressional intent is not obvious from the plain meaning, we must defer to the Board's interpretation of the statute, provided its construction is reasonable. Because the BIA is charged with administering the INA, its interpretation of the INA's provisions must be granted deference. We need not conclude that the agency construction was the only one it permissibly could have adopted to uphold the construction, or even the reading the court would have reached if the question initially had arisen in a judicial proceeding.

The [BIA] found that Mr. Amador-Palomares's single conviction for attempting to solicit for immoral purposes was a crime falling within the scope of §212(a)(2)(D). The petitioner may well be correct that Congress did not foresee the consequences that would attach to a single conviction of solicitation, but the Board's interpretation of the INA is entitled to deference, and we cannot say its interpretation was unreasonable. Therefore, we affirm the Board's decision and deny Mr. Amador-Palomares's petition for review. ■

Devil's
Advocate

Why bow down to an agency decision that is harsh and poorly reasoned? The statutory section focuses on people who attempt to run a prostitution ring, not those caught soliciting. Surely a man who has lived in this country for 20 years should not be thrown out for one moral slip. ◆

Informational Control and the Public

We started this section describing the pervasiveness of administrative agencies. We should end it by noting one way in which all of us have some direct control over these ubiquitous authorities: information.

> A popular government, without popular information, or the means of acquiring it, is but a Prologue to a Farce or a Tragedy—or perhaps both. Knowledge will forever govern ignorance, and a people who mean to be their own Governors must arm themselves with the power which knowledge gives.
>
> James Madison, President, 1809–1817

Two federal statutes arm us with the power of knowledge.

Freedom of Information Act

Congress passed the Freedom of Information Act (known as "FOIA"), a landmark statute, in 1966. It is designed to give all of us, citizens, businesses, and organizations alike, access to the information that federal agencies are using. The idea is to avoid government by secrecy.

Any citizen or executive may make an "FOIA request" to any federal government agency. It is simply a written request that the agency furnish whatever information it has on the subject specified. Two types of data are available under FOIA. Anyone is entitled to information about how the agency operates, how it spends its money, and what statistics and other information it has collected on a given subject. People routinely obtain records about agency policies, environmental hazards, consumer product safety, taxes and spending, purchasing decisions, and agency forays into foreign affairs. A corporation that believes that OSHA is making more inspections of its textile mills than it makes of the competition could demand all relevant information, including OSHA's documents on the mill itself, comparative statistics on different inspections, OSHA's policies on choosing inspection sites, and so forth.

Second, all citizens are entitled to any records the government has *about them*. You are entitled to information that the Internal Revenue Service, or the Federal Bureau of Investigation, has collected about you.

FOIA does not apply to Congress, the federal courts, or the executive staff at the White House. Note also that because FOIA applies to federal government agencies, you may not use it to obtain information from state or local governments or private businesses. For a step-by-step guide explaining how to make an FOIA request, see http:// www.aclu.org/library/foia.html. For dramatic proof of FOIA's power, see http://www. gwu.edu and search for "FOIA." This Website is devoted to government documents that have been declassified as a result of FOIA requests.

Exemptions.   An agency officially has 10 days to respond to the request. In reality, most agencies are unable to meet the deadline but are obligated to make good faith efforts. FOIA exempts altogether nine categories from disclosure. The most important exemptions permit an agency to keep confidential information that relates to national security, criminal investigations, internal agency matters such as personnel or policy discussions, trade secrets or financial institutions, or an individual's private life.

Privacy Act

The Privacy Act of 1974 prohibits federal agencies from giving information about an individual to other agencies or organizations without written consent. There are exceptions, but overall this act has reduced the government's exchange of information about us "behind our back."

Chapter Conclusion

"Why can't they just fix the law?" They can, and sometimes they do—but it is a difficult and complex task. "They" includes a great many people and forces, from common law courts to members of Congress to campaign donors to administrative agencies. The courts have made the bystander rule slightly more humane, but it has been a long and bumpy road. Congress managed to restore the legal interpretation of its own 1964 Civil Rights Act, but it took months of debate and compromising. The FDA squeezed more peanuts into a jar of Jif, but it took nearly a decade to get the lid on.

A study of law is certain to create some frustrations. This chapter cannot prevent them all. However, an understanding of how law is made is the first step toward controlling that law.

Chapter Review

1. *Stare decisis* means "let the decision stand" and indicates that once a court has decided a particular issue, it will generally apply the same rule in future cases.

2. The common law evolves in awkward fits and starts because courts attempt to achieve two contradictory purposes: predictability and flexibility.

3. The common law bystander rule holds that, generally, no one has a duty to assist someone in peril unless the bystander himself created the danger. Courts have carved some exceptions during the last 100 years, but the basic rule still stands.

4. Bills originate in congressional committees and go from there to the full House of Representatives or Senate. If both houses pass the bill, the legislation normally must go to a Conference Committee to resolve differences between the two versions. The compromise version then goes from the Conference Committee back to both houses, and if passed by both, to the President. If the President signs the bill, it becomes a statute; if he vetoes it, Congress can pass it over his veto with a two-thirds majority in each house.

5. Courts interpret a statute by using the plain meaning rule; then, if necessary, legislative history and intent; and finally, if necessary, public policy.

6. Campaign contributions and spending are largely uncontrolled.

7. Congress creates federal administrative agencies with enabling legislation. The Administrative Procedure Act controls how agencies do their work.

8. Agencies may promulgate legislative rules, which generally have the effect of statutes, or interpretive rules, which merely interpret existing statutes.

9. Agencies have broad investigatory powers and may use subpoenas and, in some cases, warrantless searches to obtain information.

10. Agencies adjudicate cases, meaning that they hold hearings and decide issues. Adjudication generally begins with a hearing before an administrative law judge and may involve an appeal to the full agency or ultimately to federal court.

11. The four most important limitations on the power of federal agencies are statutory control in the enabling legislation and the APA; political control by Congress and the president; judicial review; and the informational control created by the Freedom of Information Act and the Privacy Act.

Practice Test

1. **ETHICS** Suppose you were on a state supreme court and faced with a restaurant-choking case. Should you require restaurant employees to know and employ the Heimlich maneuver to assist a choking victim? If they do a bad job, they could cause additional injury. Should you permit them to do nothing at all? Is there a compromise position? What social policies are most important?

2. **YOU BE THE JUDGE** WRITING PROBLEM An off-duty, out-of-uniform police officer and his son purchased some food from a 7-Eleven store and were still in the parking lot when a carload of teenagers became rowdy. The officer went to speak to them and the teenagers assaulted him. The officer shouted to his son to get the 7-Eleven clerk to call for help. The son entered the store, told the clerk that a police officer needed help, and told the clerk to call the police. He returned 30 seconds later and repeated the request, urging the clerk to say it was a Code 13. The son claimed that the clerk laughed at him and refused to do it. The policeman sued the store. **Argument for the Store:** We sympathize with the policeman and his family, but the store has no liability. A bystander is not obligated to come to the aid of anyone in distress unless the bystander created the peril, and obviously the store did not do so. The policeman should prosecute *and* sue those who attacked him. **Argument for the Police Officer:** We agree that in general a bystander has no obligation to come to the aid of one in distress. However, when a business that is open to the public receives an urgent request to call the police, the business should either make the call or permit someone else to do it.

3. You sign a two-year lease with a landlord for an apartment. The rent will be $1,000 per month. A clause in the lease requires payment on the first of every month. The clause states that the landlord has the right to evict you if you are even one day late with the payment. You forget to pay on time and deliver your check to the landlord on the third day of the month. He starts an eviction case against you. Who should win? If we enforce the contract, what social result does that have? If we ignore the clause, what effect does that have on contract law?

4. Federal antitrust statutes are complex, but the basic goal is straightforward: to prevent a major industry from being so dominated by a small group of corporations that they destroy competition and injure consumers. Does Major League Baseball violate the antitrust laws? Many observers say that it does. A small group of owners not only dominate the industry but actually *own* it, controlling the entry of new owners into the game. This issue went to the United States Supreme Court in 1922. Justice Holmes ruled, perhaps surprisingly, that baseball is exempt from the antitrust laws, holding that baseball is not "trade or commerce." Suppose that a congressman dislikes this ruling and dislikes the current condition of baseball. What could he do?

5. Until recently, every state had a statute outlawing the burning of American flags. But in *Texas v. Johnson*,[22] the Supreme Court declared such statutes unconstitutional, saying that flag burning is symbolic speech, protected by the First Amendment. Does Congress have the power to overrule the Court's decision?

6. Whitfield, who was black, worked for Ohio Edison. Edison fired him, but then later offered to rehire him. At about that time, another employee, representing Whitfield, argued that Edison's original termination of Whitfield had been race discrimination. Edison rescinded its offer to rehire Whitfield. Whitfield sued Edison, claiming that the rescission of the offer to rehire was in retaliation for the other employee's opposition to discrimination. Edison defended by saying that Title VII of the 1964 Civil Rights Act did not protect in such cases. Title VII prohibits, among other things, an employer from retaliating against *an employee who has opposed* illegal discrimination. But it does not explicitly prohibit an employer from retaliating against one employee based on *another employee's* opposition to discrimination. Edison argued that the statute did not protect Whitfield. Outcome?

---

[22] 491 U.S. 397, 109 S. Ct. 2533, 1989 U.S. LEXIS 3115 (1989).

Background for Questions 7 through 9. The following three questions begin with a deadly explosion. In 1988, terrorists bombed Pan Am Flight 103 over Lockerbie, Scotland, killing all passengers on board. Congress sought to remedy security shortcomings by passing the Aviation Security Improvement Act of 1990, which, among other things, ordered the Federal Aviation Administration (FAA) to prescribe minimum training requirements and minimum staffing levels for airport security. The FAA promulgated rules according to the informal rulemaking process. However, the FAA refused to disclose certain rules concerning training at specific airports. *Public Citizen, Inc. v. FAA.*[23]

7. Explain what "promulgated rules according to the informal rulemaking process" means.

8. A public interest group called Public Citizen, Inc., along with family members of those who had died at Lockerbie, wanted to know the details of airport security. What steps should they take to obtain the information? Are they entitled to obtain it?

9. The Aviation Security Improvement Act (ASIA) states that the FAA can refuse to divulge information about airport security. The FAA interprets this to mean that it can withhold the data in spite of FOIA. Public Citizen and the Lockerbie family members interpret FOIA as being the controlling statute, requiring disclosure. Is the FAA interpretation binding?

10. Hiller Systems, Inc., was performing a safety inspection on board the M/V *Cape Diamond*, an ocean-going vessel, when an accident occurred involving the fire extinguishing equipment. Two men were killed. The Occupational Safety and Health Administration (OSHA), a federal agency, attempted to investigate, but Hiller refused to permit any of its employees to speak to OSHA investigators. What could OSHA do to pursue the investigation? What limits were there on what OSHA could do?

11. **ROLE REVERSAL** Draft a multiple-choice question that highlights the path of legislation from the first congressional committee to the president's desk.

Internet Research Problem

Research some pending legislation in Congress. Go to **academic.cengage.com/blaw/beatty** and click on "bills." Choose some key words that interest you, and see what your government is doing. Read the summary of the bill, if one is provided, or go to the text of the bill, and scan the introduction. What do the sponsors of this bill hope to accomplish? Do you agree or disagree with their goals?

> You can find further practice problems at **academic.cengage.com/blaw/beatty.**

---

[23] 988 F.2d 186, 1993 U.S. App. LEXIS 6024 (D.C. Cir. 1993).

Constitutional Law

5

© PHILIP COBLENTZ/PHOTODISC/GETTY IMAGES

Suppose you want to dance naked in front of 75 strangers. Do you have the right to do it? May the police interrupt your show and insist that you don a few garments? You may consider these odd questions, as relatively few business law students contemplate a career as a nude dancer. Yet the answers to these questions will affect you every day of your life, even if you choose a more prosaic line such as investments or retailing (it is good to have a backup plan).

Consider a very different—yet related—question. A state government wants to reduce the number of children who get hooked on tobacco. The government prohibits most advertising aimed at youngsters, although the effect is to eliminate many ads that reach adults. The regulations are well intended, but are they fair? May a state forbid any conduct that it regards as harmful to its citizens? What if the same state passes a law preventing new construction along the coastline? This measure will protect the environment, but in the process it may render some very expensive beachfront property worthless. Whose interest is more important, that of the public or the property owners?

These seemingly unrelated questions all involve the same critical issue: power. Does your state have the power to prohibit nude dancing? If so, does that mean it could outlaw a campaign poster on your front lawn? Prohibit political protest? Is the state entitled to abolish tobacco ads, for a well-intended purpose? Outlaw beachfront development?

Questions about regulating nude dancing affect all of us because the answers reveal how much control the government may exercise. Constitutional law is a series of variations on one vital theme: government power. ∎

GOVERNMENT POWER

One in a Million

The Constitution of the United States is the greatest legal document ever written. No other written constitution has lasted so long, governed so many, or withstood such challenge. This amazing work was drafted in 1787, when two weeks were needed to make the horseback ride from Boston to Philadelphia, a pair of young cities in a weak and disorganized nation. Yet today, when that trip requires less than two hours by jet, the same Constitution successfully governs the most powerful country on earth. This longevity is a tribute to the wisdom and idealism of the Founding Fathers.

The Constitution is not perfect. The original document contained provisions that were racist.[1] Other sections were unclear, and some needed early amendment. Overall, however, the Constitution has worked astonishingly well and has become the model for many constitutions around the world.

The Constitution is short and relatively easy to read. This brevity is potent. The Founding Fathers, also called the **Framers,** wanted it to last for centuries, and they understood that would happen only if the document permitted interpretation and "fleshing out" by later generations. The Constitution's versatility is striking, as we can see from the fact that the document can be used to resolve the crazy quilt of questions posed earlier. The *First Amendment* governs the two issues of nude dancing and tobacco advertising. Courts will use the *Takings Clause* to decide when a state's efforts to protect the environment have unfairly injured property owners.

This chapter is organized around the issue of power. The first part provides an overview of the Constitution, discussing how it came to be and how it is organized. The second part describes the power given to the three branches of government. The third part is the flip side of power, explaining what individual rights the Constitution guarantees to citizens.

OVERVIEW

Thirteen American colonies gained independence from Great Britain in 1783. The new status was exhilarating. This was the first nation in modern history founded on the idea that the people could govern themselves, democratically. The idea was daring, brilliant, and fraught with difficulties. The states were governing themselves under the Articles of Confederation, but these articles gave the central government no real power. The government could not tax any state or its citizens and had no way to raise money. A government without the ability to raise money does not govern, it panhandles. The national government also lacked the power to regulate commerce between the states or between foreign nations and any state. This was disastrous. States began to impose taxes on goods entering from other states. The young "nation" was a collection of poor relations, threatening to squabble themselves to death.

---

[1] Two provisions explicitly endorsed slavery, belying the proposition that all people are created equal. The "Three-Fifths Clause," in Article I, section 2, required that for purposes of taxation and representation, a slave must be counted as three fifths of a person. Article I, section 9, ensured that southern states would be permitted to continue importing slaves into the country at least until 1808.

By 1787 the articles were largely deemed a failure, and the states sent a group of 55 delegates to Philadelphia to amend them. These delegates—the Framers of our Constitution—were not a true cross section of the populace. There were no women or blacks, artisans or small farmers. Most were wealthy; all were powerful within their states.

Rather than amend the old document, the Framers set out to draft a new one, to create a government that had never existed before. It was hard going. What structure should the government have? How much power? Representatives like Alexander Hamilton urged a strong central government. They were the *federalists.* The new government must be able to tax and spend, regulate commerce, control the borders, and do all things that national governments routinely do. But Patrick Henry and other *anti-federalists* feared a powerful central government. They had fought a bitter war precisely to get rid of autocratic rulers; they had seen the evil that a distant government could inflict. The anti-federalists insisted that the states retain maximum authority, keeping political control closer to home.

Another critical question was how much power the *people* should have. Most of the aristocratic delegates had little love for the common people and feared that extending this idea of democracy too far would lead to mob rule. Anti-federalists again disagreed. The British had been thrown out, they insisted, to guarantee individual liberty and a chance to participate in the government. Power corrupted. It must be dispersed amongst the people to avoid its abuse.

How to settle these basic differences? By compromise, of course. **The Constitution is a series of compromises about power.** We will see many provisions granting power to one branch of the government while at the same time restraining the authority given.

Separation of Powers

One method of limiting power was to create a national government divided into three branches, each independent and equal. Each branch would act as a check on the power of the other two, avoiding the despotic rule that had come from London. Article I of the Constitution created a Congress, which was to have legislative power. Article II created the office of president, defining the scope of executive power. Article III established judicial power by creating the Supreme Court and permitting additional federal courts.

Consider how the three separate powers balance one another: Congress was given the power to pass statutes, a major grant of power. But the president was permitted to veto legislation, a nearly equal grant. Congress, in turn, had the right to override the veto, ensuring that the president would not become a dictator. The president was allowed to appoint federal judges and members of his cabinet, but only with a consenting vote from the Senate.

Federalism

The national government was indeed to have considerable power, but it would still be *limited power.* Article I, section 8, enumerates those issues on which Congress may pass statutes. If an issue is not on the list, Congress has no power to legislate. Thus Congress may create and regulate a post office because postal service is on the list. But Congress may not pass statutes regulating child custody in a divorce: that issue is not on the list. Only the states may legislate child custody issues.

Individual Rights

The original Constitution was silent about the rights of citizens. This alarmed many who feared that the new federal government would have unlimited power over their lives. So in 1791 the first 10 amendments, known as the **Bill of Rights,** were added to the Constitution, guaranteeing many liberties directly to individual citizens.

In the next two sections, we look in more detail at the two sides of the great series of compromises: power granted and rights protected.

POWER GRANTED

Congressional Power

Article I of the Constitution creates the Congress with its two houses. Representation in the House of Representatives is proportionate with a state's population, but each state elects two senators. The article establishes who is qualified to serve in Congress, setting only three requirements: age, citizenship, and residence.

Congress may perform any of the functions enumerated in Article I, section 8, such as imposing taxes, spending money, creating copyrights, supporting the military, declaring war, and so forth. None of these rights is more important than the authority to raise and spend money (the *power of the purse*), because every branch of government is dependent upon Congress for its money. One of the most important items on this list of congressional powers concerns trade.

Interstate Commerce

"The Congress shall have power to regulate commerce with foreign nations, and among the several states." This is the **Commerce Clause.** With it, the Framers were accomplishing several things in response to the commercial chaos that existed under the Articles of Confederation:

1. *International Commerce—Exclusive Power.* As to international commerce, the Commerce Clause is clear: Only the federal government may regulate it. The federal government must speak with one voice when regulating commercial relations with foreign governments.[2]

2. *Domestic Commerce—Concurrent Power.* As to domestic commerce, the clause gives *concurrent power*, meaning that both Congress and the states may regulate it. Congress is authorized to regulate trade between states; each state regulates business within its own borders. Conflicts are inevitable, and they are important to all of us: *How* business is regulated depends upon *who* does it.

   - *Positive Aspect: Congressional Power.* The Framers wanted to give power to Congress to bring coordination and fairness to trade between the states. This is the positive aspect of the Commerce Clause: **Congress is authorized to regulate interstate commerce.**

   - *Negative or Dormant Aspect: A Limit on the States.* The Framers also wanted to stop the states from imposing the taxes and regulations that were wrecking the nation's domestic trade. This is the negative, or dormant, aspect of the Commerce Clause: **The power of the states to regulate interstate commerce is severely restricted.**

---

2 *Michelin Tire Corp. v. Wages, Tax Commissioner,* 423 U.S. 276, 96 S. Ct. 535, 1976 U.S. LEXIS 120 (1976).

Substantial Effect Rule

An early test of the Commerce Clause's positive aspect came in the depression years of the 1930s, in *Wickard v. Filburn*.[3] The price of wheat and other grains had fluctuated wildly, severely harming farmers and the national food market. Congress sought to stabilize prices by limiting the bushels per acre that a farmer could grow. Filburn grew more wheat than federal law allowed and was fined. In defense, he claimed that Congress had no right to regulate him. None of his wheat went into interstate commerce. He sold some locally and used the rest on his own farm as food for livestock and as seed. The Commerce Clause, Filburn claimed, gave Congress no authority to limit what he could do.

The Supreme Court disagreed and held that **Congress may regulate any activity that has a substantial economic effect on interstate commerce.** Filburn's wheat affected interstate commerce because the more he grew for use on his own farm, the less he would need to buy in the open market of interstate commerce. Congress could regulate his farm. Since this ruling, most federal statutes based on the Commerce Clause have been upheld. Congress has used the Commerce Clause to regulate such diverse issues as the working conditions in a factory, discrimination in a motel, and the environmental aspects of coal mining.[4] Each of these has substantial effect on interstate commerce.

In *United States v. Lopez*,[5] however, the Supreme Court ruled that Congress had exceeded its power under the Commerce Clause. Congress had passed a criminal statute called the Gun-Free School Zones Act, which forbade any individual from possessing a firearm in a school zone. The goal of the statute was obvious: to keep schools safe. Lopez was convicted of violating the act and appealed his conviction all the way to the high Court, claiming that Congress had no power to pass such a law. The government argued that the Commerce Clause gave it the power to pass the law, but the Supreme Court was unpersuaded.

> The possession of a gun in a local school zone is in no sense an economic activity that might, through repetition elsewhere, substantially affect any sort of interstate commerce. [Lopez] was a local student at a local school; there is no indication that he had recently moved in interstate commerce, and there is no requirement that his possession of the firearm have any concrete tie to interstate commerce. To uphold the Government's contentions here, we would have to pile inference upon inference in a manner that would bid fair to convert congressional authority under the Commerce Clause to a general police power of the sort retained by the States. [The statute was unconstitutional and void.]

Congress's power is great—but still limited.

State Legislative Power

The "dormant" or "negative" aspect of the Commerce Clause governs state efforts to regulate interstate commerce. **The dormant aspect holds that a state statute that discriminates against interstate commerce is invariably unconstitutional.** The following case looks at interstate wine sales, so please do not read it if you plan to drive later today.

---

[3] 317 U.S. 111, 63 S. Ct. 82, 1942 U.S. LEXIS 1046 (1942).

[4] *Maryland v. Wirts*, 392 U.S. 183, 88 S. Ct. 2017, 1968 U.S. LEXIS 2981 (1968); *Heart of Atlanta Motel v. United States*, 379 U.S. 241, 85 S. Ct. 348, 1964 U.S. LEXIS 2187 (1964); *Hodel v. Indiana*, 452 U.S. 314, 101 S. Ct. 2376, 1981 U.S. LEXIS 34 (1981).

[5] 514 U.S. 549, 115 S. Ct. 1624, 1995 U.S. LEXIS 3039 (1995).

GRANHOLM V. HEALD

2005 WL 1130571
United States Supreme Court, 2005

Facts: Michigan and New York permitted in-state wineries to sell directly to consumers. They both denied this privilege to out-of-state producers, who were required to sell to wholesalers, who offered the wine to retailers, who sold to consumers. This created an impossible barrier for many small vineyards, which did not produce enough wine to attract wholesalers.

Local residents and out-of-state wineries sued, claiming that the state regulations violated the dormant Commerce Clause. The Sixth Circuit Court of Appeals found that the regulations violated the Commerce Clause, but the Second Circuit declared the statutes valid. Because of this "split in the circuits," the Supreme Court accepted the case.

Issue: Did the direct-sales regulations violate the dormant Commerce Clause?

Excerpts from Justice Kennedy's Decision: Time and again this Court has held that, in all but the narrowest circumstances, state laws violate the Commerce Clause if they mandate differential treatment of in-state and out-of-state economic interests that benefits the former and burdens the latter. This rule is essential to the foundations of the Union. The mere fact of nonresidence should not foreclose a producer in one State from access to markets in other States. States may not enact laws that burden out-of-state producers or shippers simply to give a competitive advantage to in-state businesses. This mandate reflects a central concern of the Framers that was an immediate reason for calling the Constitutional Convention: the conviction that in order to succeed, the new Union would have to avoid the tendencies toward economic Balkanization that had plagued relations among the Colonies and later among the States under the Articles of Confederation.

The discriminatory character of the Michigan system is obvious. The differential treatment requires all out-of-state wine, but not all in-state wine, to pass through an in-state wholesaler and retailer before reaching consumers. These two extra layers of overhead increase the cost of out-of-state wines to Michigan consumers. The cost differential, and in some cases the inability to secure a wholesaler for small shipments, can effectively bar small wineries from the Michigan market.

We have no difficulty concluding that [the laws of both states discriminate] against interstate commerce through direct-shipping laws.

We still must consider whether either State regime advances a legitimate local purpose that cannot be adequately served by reasonable nondiscriminatory alternatives. The States claim that allowing direct shipment from out-of-state wineries undermines their ability to police underage drinking. Minors, the States argue, have easy access to credit cards and the Internet and are likely to take advantage of direct wine shipments as a means of obtaining alcohol illegally.

The States provide little evidence that the purchase of wine over the Internet by minors is a problem. Indeed, there is some evidence to the contrary. A recent study by the staff of the FTC found that the 26 States currently allowing direct shipments report no problems with minors' increased access to wine. This is not surprising. Minors are less likely to consume wine, as opposed to beer, wine coolers, and hard liquor. Minors who decide to disobey the law have more direct means of doing so. [Finally,] minors want instant gratification. Without concrete evidence that direct shipping of wine is likely to increase alcohol consumption by minors, we are left with the States' unsupported assertions. This is not enough.

[The Court struck down the regulations, leaving it to lower courts to fashion an appropriate remedy.] ■

Devil's **Advocate**	Underage drinking is a serious problem. The Court should allow states wide leeway in their efforts to limit the harm. Even if the regulations are imperfect, they may help reduce the damage. ◆

Supremacy Clause

What happens when both the federal and state governments pass regulations that are permissible but conflicting? For example, Congress passed the federal Occupational Safety and Health Act (OSHA) establishing many job safety standards, including those for training workers who handle hazardous waste. Congress had the power to do so under the Commerce Clause. Later, Illinois passed its own hazardous waste statutes, seeking to protect both the general public and workers. The state statute did not violate the Commerce Clause because it imposed no restriction on interstate commerce.

Each statute specified worker training and employer licensing. But the requirements differed. Which statute did Illinois corporations have to obey? Article VI of the Constitution contains the answer. **The Supremacy Clause states that the Constitution, and federal statutes and treaties, shall be the supreme law of the land.**

- If there is a conflict between federal and state statutes, the federal law **preempts** the field, meaning it controls the issue. The state law is void.

- Even in cases where there is no conflict, if Congress demonstrates that it intends to exercise exclusive control over an issue, federal law preempts.

Thus state law controls only when there is no conflicting federal law *and* Congress has not intended to dominate the issue. In the Illinois case, the Supreme Court concluded that Congress intended to regulate the issue exclusively. Federal law therefore preempted the field, and local employers were obligated to obey only the federal regulations.

Executive Power

Article II of the Constitution defines the executive power. Once again the Constitution gives powers in general terms. The basic job of the president is to enforce the nation's laws. Three of his key powers concern appointment, legislation, and foreign policy.

Appointment

Administrative agencies play a powerful role in business regulation, and the president nominates the heads of most of them. These choices dramatically influence what issues the agencies choose to pursue and how aggressively they do it. For example, a president who believes that it is vital to protect our natural resources may appoint a forceful environmentalist to run the Environmental Protection Agency, whereas a president who dislikes federal regulations will choose a more passive agency head.[6]

Legislation

The president and his advisers propose bills to Congress. During the last 50 years, a vast number of newly proposed bills have come from the executive branch. Some

---

[6] For a discussion of administrative agency power, see Chapter 4, on administrative law.

argue that *too many* proposals come from the president and that Congress has become overly passive. When a president proposes controversial legislation on a major issue, such as Social Security reform, the bill can dominate the news—and Congress—for months or even years. The president, of course, also has the power to veto bills.[7]

Foreign Policy

The president conducts the nation's foreign affairs, coordinating international efforts, negotiating treaties, and so forth. The president is also the commander in chief of the armed forces, meaning that he heads the military. But Article II does not give him the right to declare war—only the Senate may do that. Thus a continuing tension between president and Congress has resulted from the president's use of troops overseas *without* a formal declaration of war. Once again, the Founding Fathers' desire to create a balanced government leads to uncertain application of the law.

Judicial Power

Article III of the Constitution creates the Supreme Court and permits Congress to establish lower courts within the federal court system.[8] Federal courts have two key functions: adjudication and judicial review.

Adjudicating Cases

The federal court system hears criminal and civil cases. All prosecutions of federal crimes begin in United States District Court. That same court has limited jurisdiction to hear civil lawsuits, a subject discussed in Chapter 3 on dispute resolution.

Judicial Review

One of the greatest "constitutional" powers appears nowhere in the Constitution. In 1803 the Supreme Court decided *Marbury v. Madison.*[9] Congress had passed a relatively minor statute that gave certain powers to the Supreme Court, and Marbury wanted the Court to use those powers. The Court refused. In an opinion written by Chief Justice John Marshall, the Court held that the statute violated the Constitution because Article III of the Constitution did not grant the Court those powers. The details of the case were insignificant, but the ruling was profound: because the statute violated the Constitution, said the Court, it was void. **Judicial review refers to the power of federal courts to declare a statute or governmental action unconstitutional and void.**

This formidable grab of power has produced two centuries of controversy. The Court was declaring that it alone had the right to evaluate acts of the other two branches of government—the Congress and the executive—and to decide which were valid and which void. The Constitution nowhere grants this power. Undaunted, Marshall declared that "[I]t is emphatically the province and duty of the judicial department to say what the law is." In later cases, the Supreme Court expanded on the idea, holding that it could also nullify state statutes, rulings by state courts, and actions by federal and state officials. In this chapter we have already encountered an example

---

[7] For a discussion of the president's veto power and Congress's power to override a veto, see Chapter 4, on statutory law.

[8] For a discussion of the federal court system, see Chapter 3, on dispute resolution.

[9] 5 U.S. (1 Cranch) 137 (1803).

of judicial review, for example, in the *Lopez* case, where the justices declared that Congress lacked the power to pass local gun regulations.

Is judicial review good for the nation? Those who oppose it argue that federal court judges are all appointed, not elected, and that we should not permit judges to nullify a statute passed by elected officials because that diminishes the people's role in their government. Those who favor judicial review insist that there must be one cohesive interpretation of the Constitution and the judicial branch is the logical one to provide it. This dispute about power simmers continuously beneath the surface and occasionally comes to the boil.

YOUNGSTOWN SHEET & TUBE CO. V. SAWYER

343 U.S. 579, 72 S. Ct. 863, 1952 U.S. LEXIS 2625
United States Supreme Court, 1952

Facts: During the Korean War, steel companies and the unions were unable to reach a contract. The union notified the companies that they would strike, beginning April 9, 1952. President Truman declared steel essential to the war effort and ordered his Secretary of Commerce, Sawyer, to take control of the steel mills and keep them running. Sawyer immediately ordered the presidents of the various companies to serve as operating managers for the United States.

On April 30, the federal district court issued an injunction to stop Sawyer from running the mills. That same day the United States Court of Appeals "stayed" the injunction—that is, it permitted Sawyer to keep operating the mills. The Supreme Court quickly granted *certiorari*, heard argument, May 12, and issued its decision June 2 (at least five years faster than most cases reach final decision).

Issue: Did President Truman have the constitutional power to seize the steel mills?

Excerpts from Justice Black's Decision: It is clear that if the President had authority to issue the order he did, it must be found in some provision of the Constitution. And it is not claimed that express constitutional language grants this power to the President. The contention is that presidential power should be implied from the aggregate of his powers under the Constitution [including the clauses stating that "the executive power shall be vested in a President," that "he shall take care that the laws be faithfully executed," and that he "shall be Commander in Chief"].

The order cannot properly be sustained as an exercise of the President's military power as Commander in Chief. We cannot with faithfulness to our constitutional system hold that the Commander in Chief has the ultimate power as such to take possession of private property in order to keep labor disputes from stopping production. This is a job for the Nation's lawmakers, not for its military authorities.

Nor can the seizure order be sustained because of the several constitutional provisions that grant executive power to the President. In the framework of our Constitution, the President's power to see that the laws are faithfully executed refutes the idea that he is to be a lawmaker. The Constitution limits his functions in the lawmaking process to the recommending of laws he thinks wise and the vetoing of laws he thinks bad. And the Constitution is neither silent nor equivocal about who shall make laws which the President is to execute. The first section of the first article says that "All legislative powers herein granted shall be vested in a Congress of the United States." The Constitution did not subject this lawmaking power of Congress to presidential or military supervision or control.

The Founders of this Nation entrusted the lawmaking power to the Congress alone in both good and bad times. It would do no good to recall the historical events, the fears of power and the hopes for freedom that lay behind their choice. Such a review would but confirm our holding that this seizure order cannot stand.

[The district court's injunction is *affirmed.*] ■

President Truman disliked anyone telling him what to do, and he disliked even more having the Supreme Court limit his powers during wartime. But he obeyed the Court's order.

Judicial Activism/Judicial Restraint.   The power of judicial review is potentially dictatorial. The Supreme Court nullifies statutes passed by Congress (*Marbury v. Madison, United States v. Lopez*) and executive actions (*Youngstown Sheet & Tube*). May it strike down any law it dislikes? In theory, no. The Court should nullify only laws that violate the Constitution. But of course that is circular, because it is the Court that will tell us which laws are violative.

Judicial activism refers to a court's willingness, or even eagerness, to become involved in major issues and to decide cases on constitutional grounds. **Judicial restraint** is the opposite, an attitude that courts should leave lawmaking to legislators and nullify a law only when it unquestionably violates the Constitution.

From the 1950s through the 1970s, the Supreme Court took an active role, deciding many major social issues on constitutional grounds. The landmark 1954 decision in *Brown v. Board of Education*[10] ordered an end to racial segregation in public schools, not only changing the nation's educational systems but altering forever its expectations about race. The Court also struck down many state laws that denied minorities the right to vote. Beginning with *Miranda v. Arizona*,[11] the Court began a sweeping reappraisal of the police power of the state and the rights of criminal suspects during searches, interrogations, trials, and appeals. And in *Roe v. Wade*[12] the Supreme Court established certain rights to abortion, most of which remain after 30 years of continuous litigation and violence.

Beginning in the late 1970s, and lasting to the present, the Court has pulled back from its activism. Some justices believe that the Founding Fathers never intended the judicial branch to take so prominent a role in sculpting the nation's laws and its social vision. Simple numbers tell part of the story of a changing Court. Every year roughly 8,000 requests for review are made to the Court. In the early 1970s the Supreme Court accepted almost 200 of these cases, but by the new millennium it was taking fewer than 100. The Court's practice of judicial restraint means that major social issues will increasingly be left to state legislatures and Congress. For a look at the current justices, the full text of famous cases, and a calendar of pending cases, see http://supct.law.cornell.edu/supct/. You can tour the Court itself and even hear some of the justices read their opinions at http://www.oyez.org.

Exhibit 5.1 illustrates the balance among Congress, the President, and the Court.

uPdate

Find an article that describes a recent Supreme Court decision declaring a statute unconstitutional. What was the purpose of the statute? Why did the justices nullify the law? Do you agree with the Court's decision? ◆

PROTECTED RIGHTS

The amendments to the Constitution protect the people of this nation from the power of state and federal government. The First Amendment guarantees rights of free speech, free press, and religion; the Fourth Amendment protects against illegal searches; the Fifth Amendment ensures due process; the Sixth Amendment demands

---

[10] 347 U.S. 483, 74 S. Ct. 686, 1954 U.S. LEXIS 2094 (1954).

[11] 384 U.S. 436, 86 S. Ct. 1602, 1966 U.S. LEXIS 2817 (1966).

[12] 410 U.S. 113, 93 S. Ct. 705, 1973 U.S. LEXIS 159 (1973).

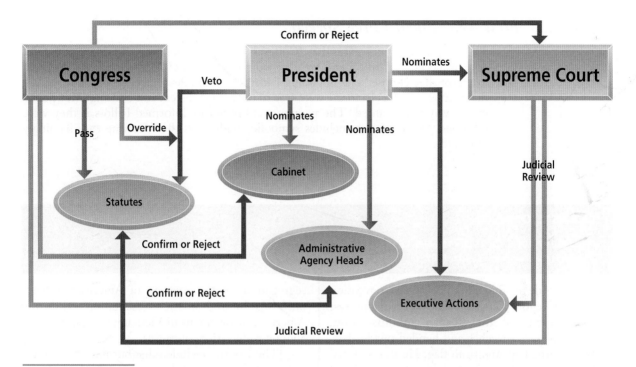

Exhibit 5.1
The Constitution established a federal government of checks and balances. Congress may pass statutes; the President may veto them; and Congress may override the veto. The President nominates cabinet officers, administrative heads, and Supreme Court justices, but the Senate must confirm his nominees. Finally, the Supreme Court (and lower federal courts) exercise judicial review over statutes and executive actions. Unlike the other checks and balances, judicial review is not provided for in the Constitution, but is a creation of the Court itself in *Marbury v. Madison.*

fair treatment for defendants in criminal prosecutions; and the Fourteenth Amendment guarantees equal protection of the law. We consider the First, Fifth, and Fourteenth Amendments in this chapter and the Fourth, Fifth, and Sixth Amendments in Chapter 8, on crime.

The "people" who are protected include citizens and, for most purposes, corporations. Corporations are considered persons and receive most of the same protections. The great majority of these rights also extend to citizens of other countries who are in the United States.

Constitutional rights generally protect only against governmental acts. The Constitution generally does not protect us from the conduct of private parties, such as corporations or other citizens.

Incorporation

Constitutional protections apply to federal, state, and local governments. Yet that is not what the Bill of Rights explicitly states. The First Amendment declares that *Congress* shall not abridge the right of free speech. The Fourteenth Amendment explicitly limits the power only of *state* governments. But a series of Supreme Court cases has extended virtually all the important constitutional protections to all levels of national, state, and local government. This process is called **incorporation** because rights explicitly guaranteed at one level are incorporated into rights that apply at other levels.

First Amendment: Free Speech

The First Amendment states that "Congress shall make no law . . . abridging the freedom of speech. . . ." In general, we expect our government to let people speak and hear whatever they choose. The Founding Fathers believed democracy would only work if the members of the electorate were free to talk, argue, listen, and exchange viewpoints in any way they wanted. The people could only cast informed ballots if they were informed. "Speech" also includes symbolic conduct, as the following case flamingly illustrates.

TEXAS V. JOHNSON

491 U.S. 397, 109 S. Ct. 2533, 1989 U.S. LEXIS 3115
United States Supreme Court, 1989

Facts: Outside the Republican National Convention in Dallas, Gregory Johnson participated in a protest against policies of the Reagan administration. Participants gave speeches and handed out leaflets. Johnson burned an American flag. He was arrested and convicted under a Texas statute that prohibited desecrating the flag, but the Texas Court of Criminal Appeals reversed on the grounds that the conviction violated the First Amendment. Texas appealed to the United States Supreme Court.

Issue: Does the First Amendment protect flag burning?

Excerpts from Justice Brennan's Decision: The First Amendment literally forbids the abridgment only of "speech," but we have long recognized that its protection does not end at the spoken or written word. While we have rejected the view that an apparently limitless variety of conduct can be labeled "speech," we have acknowledged that conduct may be sufficiently imbued with elements of communication to fall within the scope of the First and Fourteenth Amendments.

In deciding whether particular conduct possesses sufficient communicative elements to bring the First Amendment into play, we have asked whether an intent to convey a particularized message was present, and [whether] the likelihood was great that the message would be understood by those who viewed it. Hence, we have recognized the expressive nature of students' wearing of black armbands to protest American military involvement in Vietnam; of a sit-in by blacks in a "whites only" area to protest segregation; of the wearing of American military uniforms in a dramatic presentation criticizing American involvement in Vietnam; and of picketing about a wide variety of causes.

[The Court concluded that burning the flag was in fact symbolic speech.]

It remains to consider whether the State's interest in reserving the flag as a symbol of nationhood and national unity justifies Johnson's conviction. Johnson was prosecuted because he knew that his politically charged expression would cause "serious offense."

If there is a bedrock principle underlying the First Amendment, it is that the Government may not prohibit the expression of an idea simply because society finds the idea itself offensive or disagreeable. Nothing in our precedents suggests that a State may foster its own view of the flag by prohibiting expressive conduct relating to it.

Could the Government, on this theory, prohibit the burning of state flags? Of copies of the Presidential seal? Of the Constitution? In evaluating these choices under the First Amendment, how would we decide which symbols were sufficiently special to warrant this unique status? To do so, we would be forced to consult our own political preferences, and impose them on the citizenry, in the very way that the First Amendment forbids us to do.

The way to preserve the flag's special role is not to punish those who feel differently about these matters. It is to persuade them that they are wrong. We can imagine no more appropriate response to burning a flag than waving one's own, no better way to counter a flagburner's message than by saluting the

▼

flag that burns, no surer means of preserving the dignity even of the flag that burned than by—as one witness here did—according its remains a respectful burial. We do not consecrate the flag by punishing its desecration, for in doing so we dilute the freedom that this cherished emblem represents.

The judgment of the Texas Court of Criminal Appeals is therefore *affirmed.* ■

Flag burning is an issue that will not go away. For additional thoughts on the subject, ignite http://www.esquilax.com (click on "The Flag-Burning Page"), an irreverent page that strongly supports the rights of free speech. To read an anti–flag burning Web page, extinguish all matches and go to http://www.cfa-inc.org/.

Political Speech

Because the Framers were primarily concerned with enabling democracy to function, political speech has been given an especially high degree of protection. Such speech may not be barred even when it is offensive or outrageous. A speaker, for example, could accuse a U.S. senator of being insane and could use crude, violent language to describe him. The speech is still protected. The speech lacks protection only if it is *intended and likely to create imminent lawless action.*[13] For example, suppose the speaker said, "The senator is inside that restaurant. Let's get some matches and burn the place down." Speech of this sort is not protected. The speaker could be arrested for attempted arson or attempted murder.

Time, Place, and Manner

Even when speech is protected, the government may regulate the *time, place,* and *manner* of such speech. A town may require a group to apply for a permit before using a public park for a political demonstration. The town may insist that the demonstration take place during daylight hours and that there be adequate police supervision and sanitation provided. However, the town may not prohibit such demonstrations outright.

The Supreme Court is often called upon to balance the rights of the general public with the rights of those seeking to publicize their causes. In *Madsen v. Women's Health Center, Inc.,*[14] the Court ruled that a local judge could limit protesters' access to a family planning clinic. The protesters, opposed to abortion, had repeatedly blocked access to the clinic, harassed patients and doctors at the clinic and at their homes, and paraded with graphic signs and bullhorns. The Court upheld the order prohibiting the protesters from coming within 36 feet of the clinic and also the order that prohibited excessive noise. But the Court overturned a part of the order that had forbidden protesters from displaying graphic images that could be seen inside the clinic. The Court said that the proper remedy was for the clinic to close its curtains.

Morality and Obscenity

The regulation of morality and obscenity presents additional problems. Obscenity has never received constitutional protection. The Supreme Court has consistently held that it does not play a valued role in our society and has refused to give protection to obscene works. That is well and good, but it merely forces the question: What is obscene? (For a list of books that have been—and in some cases still are—banned by

---

[13] *Brandenburg v. Ohio*, 395 U.S. 444, 89 S. Ct. 1827, 1969 U.S. LEXIS 1367 (1969).
[14] 511 U.S. 1016, 114 S. Ct. 1395, 1994 U.S. LEXIS 2671 (1994).

local, state, or foreign governments, go to http://onlinebooks.library.upenn.edu and click on "Banned Books."

In *Miller v. California*,[15] the Court created a three-part test to determine if a creative work is obscene. The basic guidelines for the factfinder are:

- Whether the average person, applying contemporary community standards, would find that the work, taken as a whole, appeals to the prurient interest;

- Whether the work depicts or describes, in a patently offensive way, sexual conduct specifically defined by the applicable state law; and

- Whether the work, taken as a whole, lacks serious literary, artistic, political, or scientific value.

If the trial court finds that the answer to all three of those questions is "yes," it may judge the material obscene; the state may then prohibit the work. If the state fails to prove any one of the three criteria, though, the work is not obscene.[16] A United States District Court ruled that "As Nasty As They Wanna Be," recorded by 2 Live Crew, was obscene. The appeals court, however, reversed, finding that the state had failed to prove lack of artistic merit.[17]

What if sexual conduct is not obscene? Let's go back to the chapter's starting point, nude dancing.

YOU BE THE JUDGE

BARNES V. GLEN THEATRE, INC.

501 U.S. 560, 111 S. Ct. 2456, 1991 U.S. LEXIS 3633 United States Supreme Court, 1991

Facts: Indiana's public indecency statute prohibits any person from appearing nude in a public place. State courts have interpreted this to mean that a dancer in a theater or bar must wear pasties and a G-string. A nightclub called the Kitty Kat Lounge and several dancers who wished to perform nude filed suit, seeking an order that the statute was unconstitutional. The United States District Court ruled that the dancing was not expressive conduct and therefore was not entitled to First Amendment protection. The Court of Appeals reversed, declaring that it was nonobscene expressive conduct and thus protected by the First Amendment.

Indiana did not argue that the dancing was obscene. (If that were the issue, the *Miller* test would have determined the outcome.) Instead, Indiana claimed that its general police powers, including the power to protect social order, allowed it to enforce such a statute.

You Be the Judge: Does Indiana's public indecency statute violate the First Amendment?

Argument for Indiana: Your honors, the State of Indiana has no wish to suppress ideas or censor speech. We are not trying to outlaw eroticism or any other legitimate form of expression. We are simply prohibiting nudity in public. We have outlawed all public nudity, not just nightclub performances.

▼

---

15 413 U.S. 15, 93 S. Ct. 2607, 1973 U.S. LEXIS 149 (1973).

16 *Penthouse Intern Ltd. v. McAuliffe*, 610 F.2d 1353 (5th Cir. 1980).

17 *Luke Records, Inc. v. Navarro*, 960 F.2d 134, 1992 U.S. App. LEXIS 9592 (11th Cir. 1992).

Nudity on the beach, in the park, or anywhere in public is prohibited.

We do this to protect societal order, to foster a stable morality. It is well established that the police power of the state includes the right to regulate the public health, safety, and morals. Our citizens disapprove of people appearing in the nude in public places. The citizens of virtually all states feel the same. Decent dress has been a part of good society since time immemorial. Our voting public is entitled to have that standard upheld.

We also enforce this statute because experience has shown that nightclubs such as these are often associated with criminal behavior. Prostitution, illegal drugs, and violence appear too frequently in the vicinity. It is a reasonable step for the State to maintain control over the performances and the people they will attract.

Argument for Kitty Kat: It is apparent beyond debate that dance is expressive conduct. As an art form it has existed for at least several thousand years. Eroticism, also, is not exactly news. Erotic dance is clearly expressive conduct. Indeed, the present dancing derives its strength from its eroticism. If the

State did not consider it erotic, doubtless it would have left the dancers alone. This dancing is expressive conduct and deserves the full protection of the First Amendment.

Indiana is choosing a certain type of expression and outlawing it. The state has not outlawed all nudity, since quite obviously nudity in private is beyond the State's reach. Nor has it prohibited all nude performances. Testimony of police at trial indicated that no arrests have ever been made for nudity as part of a play or ballet. Nudity is no longer anything novel in musicals, ballets, stage plays, or film. Indiana permits nudity in all of them and enforces its moralizing law only against nightclubs.

This is an obvious value judgment on the part of the State. The State is saying that if you can afford to pay for a Broadway show that happens to have nudity, you are free to enjoy it; if your taste or pocketbook leads you to the Kitty Kat Lounge, we deny your right to witness nudity. If the State is allowed to make that appraisal, then it is free to censor any expression—artistic, political, or any other—that it finds inferior. It was *precisely* to prevent states from outlawing unpopular expression that the Founding Fathers added the First Amendment. ●

cyberLaw

Concerned that pornography on the Internet was easily available to minors, Congress passed the Communications Decency Act (CDA), making it illegal for any person or company to send "obscene or indecent" communications to anyone under 18. Various plaintiffs, including library associations, booksellers, Internet service providers, and others, filed suit, claiming that the law would diminish the extraordinary opportunities for research and education that the Internet provides. The Supreme Court agreed, striking down the law as a violation of the First Amendment. The justices declared that the law failed to define "indecent." The CDA ignored the obscenity standard provided in *Miller v. California* and outlawed material that *did* have socially redeeming value. The Court noted that the law would deny adults access to a vast amount of material that they were legally entitled to obtain. Finally, the Court pointed out that concerned parents could purchase software to screen out objectionable items, avoiding the need for such far-reaching censorship.[18]

Congress has made additional attempts to protect minors from online pornography, but thus far each effort has been struck down as an overly broad restriction on free speech. ◆

Commercial Speech

This refers to speech that has a **dominant theme to propose a commercial transaction.** For example, most advertisements on television and in the newspapers are commercial speech. This sort of speech is protected by the First Amendment, but the

---

[18] *Reno v. American Civil Liberties Union,* 521 U.S. 844, 117 S. Ct. 2329, 1997 U.S. LEXIS 4037 (1997).

government is permitted to regulate it more closely than other forms of speech. **Commercial speech that is false or misleading may be outlawed altogether.** However, regulations on commercial speech must be reasonable and directed to a legitimate goal, as the following case shows.

LORILLARD TOBACCO CO. V. REILLY

533 U.S. 525, 121 S. Ct. 2404, 150 L. Ed. 2d 532
United States Supreme Court, 2001

Facts: The Massachusetts government was convinced that advertising caused ever greater numbers of children to use tobacco products. The state crafted four regulations, which:

1. restricted most cigarette advertising;

2. prohibited outdoor advertising of smokeless tobacco and cigars within 1,000 feet of schools or playgrounds;

3. prohibited indoor, point-of-sale advertising of smokeless tobacco and cigars placed less than five feet from the retailer's floor; and

4. required retailers to put all tobacco products behind a counter.

Tobacco manufacturers and sellers sued, and the case reached the United States Supreme Court.

The Supreme Court ruled that the first restriction violated the Supremacy Clause. Congress had passed a statute regulating cigarette warnings and advertising, and the federal law clearly stated that no states could pass any additional requirements. Congress had *preempted* the field and the Massachusetts regulation was void.

The plaintiffs next argued that the other three regulations violated their free speech rights.

Issue: Did the three Massachusetts regulations violate the First Amendment?

Excerpts from Justice O'Connor's Decision: We must determine whether the regulation directly advances the governmental interest asserted, and whether it is not more extensive than is necessary to serve that interest.

[The court acknowledged that advertising played a major role in a child's decision to use tobacco.] For instance, children smoke fewer brands of cigarettes than adults, and those choices directly track the most heavily advertised brands, unlike adult choices, which are more dispersed and related to pricing. Another

study revealed that 72% of 6-year-olds and 52% of children ages 3 to 6 recognized "Joe Camel," the cartoon anthropomorphic symbol of R. J. Reynolds' Camel brand cigarettes. The FDA also made specific findings with respect to smokeless tobacco. The FDA concluded that "[t]he recent and very large increase in the use of smokeless tobacco products by young people and the addictive nature of these products has persuaded the agency that these products must be included in any regulatory approach that is designed to help prevent future generations of young people from becoming addicted to nicotine-containing tobacco products."

Whatever the strength of the Attorney General's evidence to justify the outdoor advertising regulations, however, we conclude that the regulations [are not] a reasonable fit between the means and ends of the regulatory scheme.

The outdoor advertising regulations prohibit any smokeless tobacco or cigar advertising within 1,000 feet of schools or playgrounds. In the District Court, petitioners maintained that this prohibition would prevent advertising in 87% to 91% of Boston, Worcester, and Springfield, Massachusetts. In some geographical areas, these regulations would constitute nearly a complete ban on the communication of truthful information about smokeless tobacco and cigars to adult consumers.

The State's interest in preventing underage tobacco use is substantial, and even compelling, but it is no less true that the sale and use of tobacco products by adults is a legal activity. We must consider that tobacco retailers and manufacturers have an interest in conveying truthful information about their products to adults, and adults have a corresponding interest in receiving truthful information about tobacco products.

A regulation cannot be sustained if it provides only ineffective or remote support for the government's purpose, or if there is "little chance" that the restriction

▼

will advance the State's goal. As outlined above, the State's goal is to prevent minors from using tobacco products and to curb demand for that activity by limiting youth exposure to advertising. The 5-foot rule does not seem to advance that goal. Not all children are less than 5 feet tall, and those who are certainly have the ability to look up and take in their surroundings.

[The court struck down the restrictions on outdoor advertising and the "five-foot" rule. The justices upheld the regulation that required all tobacco products to be placed behind a counter, declaring that the rule was a sensible way to stop youngsters from using unmonitored vending machines and that the restriction had no effect on free speech.] ■

<table><tr><td>*Devil's Advocate*</td><td>If 72 percent of six year olds know who Joe Camel is, something is wrong. Which is more important, the health of our children or the "right" of tobacco manufacturers to pander their goods to youngsters? The court made the wrong choice. ◆</td></tr></table>

Fifth Amendment: Due Process and the Takings Clause

You are a third-year student in a combined business/law program at a major state university. You feel great about a difficult securities exam you took in Professor Watson's class. The Dean's Office sends for you, and you enter curiously, wondering if your exam was so good that the dean is awarding you a prize. Not quite. The exam proctor has accused you of cheating. Based on the accusation, Watson has flunked you. You protest that you are innocent and demand to know what the accusation is. The dean says that you will learn the details at a hearing, if you wish to have one. She reminds you that if you lose the hearing you will be expelled from the university. Three years of work and your entire career are suddenly on the line.

The hearing is run by Professor Holmes, who will make the final decision. Holmes is a junior faculty member in Watson's department. (Next year, Watson will decide Holmes's tenure application.) At the hearing the proctor accuses you of copying from a student sitting in front of you. Both Watson and Holmes have already compared the two papers and concluded that they are strongly similar. Holmes tells you that you must convince him the charge is wrong. You examine the papers, acknowledge that there are similarities, but plead as best you can that you never copied. Holmes doesn't buy it. The university expels you, placing on your transcript a notation of cheating.

Have you received fair treatment? To answer that, we must look to the Fifth Amendment, which provides several vital protections. We will consider two related provisions, the Due Process Clause and the Takings Clause. Together, they state: "No person shall be . . . deprived of life, liberty, or property without due process of law; nor shall private property be taken for public use, without just compensation." These clauses prevent the government from arbitrarily taking the most valuable possessions of a citizen or corporation. We will discuss the civil law aspects of these clauses, but due process also applies to criminal law. The reference to "life" refers to capital punishment. The criminal law issues of this subject are discussed in Chapter 7, on crime.

In civil law proceedings, the government does have the right to take a person's liberty or property. But there are three important limitations:

- *Procedural Due Process.* Before depriving anyone of liberty or property, the government must go through certain procedures to ensure that the result is fair.

- *The Takings Clause.* When the government takes property for public use, such as to build a new highway, it has to pay a fair price.

- *Substantive Due Process.* Some rights are so fundamental that the government may not take them from us at all.

Procedural Due Process

The government deprives citizens or corporations of their property in a variety of ways. The Internal Revenue Service may fine a corporation for late payment of taxes. The Customs Service may seize goods at the border. As to liberty, the government may take it by confining someone in a mental institution or by taking a child out of the home because of parental neglect. **The purpose of procedural due process is to ensure that before the government takes liberty or property, the affected person has a fair chance to oppose the action.**

There are two steps in analyzing a procedural due process case:

- Is the government attempting to take liberty or property?

- If so, how much process is due? (If the government is *not* attempting to take liberty or property, there is no due process issue.)

Is the Government Attempting to Take Liberty or Property?   Liberty interests are generally easy to spot: confining someone in a mental institution and taking a child from her home are both deprivations of liberty. A property interest may be obvious. Suppose that, during a civil lawsuit, the court **attaches** a defendant's house, meaning it bars the defendant from selling the property at least until the case is decided. This way, if the plaintiff wins, the defendant will have assets to pay the judgment. The court has clearly deprived the defendant of an important interest in his house, and the defendant is entitled to due process. However, a property interest may be subtler than that. A woman holding a job with a government agency has a "property interest" in that job, because her employer has agreed not to fire her without cause, and she can rely on it for income. If the government does fire her, it is taking away that property interest, and she is entitled to due process. A student attending any public school has a property interest in that education. If a public university suspends a law/business student, as described earlier, it is taking her property, and she, too, should receive due process.

How Much Process Is Due?   Assuming that a liberty or property interest is affected, a court must decide how much process is due. Does the person get a formal trial, or an informal hearing, or merely a chance to reply in writing to the charges against her? If she gets a hearing, must it be held before the government deprives her of her property, or is it enough that she can be heard shortly thereafter? **What sort of hearing the government must offer depends upon how important the property or liberty interest is and on whether the government has a competing need for efficiency.** The more important the interest, the more formal the procedures must be.

Neutral Factfinder.   Regardless of how formal the hearing, one requirement is constant: the factfinder must be neutral. Whether it is a superior court judge deciding a multimillion dollar contract suit or an employment supervisor deciding the fate of a government employee, the factfinder must have no personal interest in the outcome. In *Ward v. Monroeville*,[19] the plaintiff was a motorist who had been stopped for traffic offenses in a small town. He protested his innocence and received a judicial hearing. But the "judge" at the hearing was the town mayor. Traffic fines were a significant part of the town's budget. The motorist argued that the town was depriving him of procedural due process because the mayor had a financial interest in the outcome of the case. The United States Supreme Court agreed and reversed his conviction.

---

[19] 409 U.S. 57, 93 S. Ct. 80, 1972 U.S. LEXIS 11 (1972).

Attachment of Property.   As described earlier, a plaintiff in a civil lawsuit often seeks to *attach* the defendant's property. This protects the plaintiff, but it may also harm the defendant if, for example, he is about to close a profitable real estate deal. Attachments used to be routine. In *Connecticut v. Doehr*, the Supreme Court required more caution.[20] Based on *Doehr*, when a plaintiff seeks to attach at the beginning of the trial, a court must look at the plaintiff's likelihood of winning. Generally, the court must grant the defendant a hearing *before* attaching the property. The defendant, represented by a lawyer, may offer evidence regarding how attachment would harm him and why it should be denied.

Government Employment.   A government employee must receive due process before being fired. Generally, this means some kind of hearing, but not necessarily a formal court hearing. The employee is entitled to know the charges against him, to hear the employer's evidence, and to have an opportunity to tell his side of the story. He is not entitled to have a lawyer present. The hearing "officer" need only be a neutral employee. Further, in an emergency, where the employee is a danger to the public or the organization, the government may suspend with pay, before holding a hearing. It then must provide a hearing before the decision becomes final.

Academic Suspension.   There is still a property interest here, but it is the least important of those discussed. When a public school concludes that a student has failed to meet its normal academic standards, such as by failing too many courses, it may dismiss him without a hearing. Due process is served if the student receives notice of the reason and has some opportunity to respond, such as by writing a letter contradicting the school's claims.

In cases of disciplinary suspension or expulsion, courts generally require schools to provide a higher level of due process. In the hypothetical at the beginning of this section, the university has failed to provide adequate due process.[21] The school has accused the student of a serious infraction. The school must promptly provide details of the charge and cannot wait until the hearing to do so. The student should see the two papers and have a chance to rebut the charge. Moreover, Professor Holmes has demonstrated bias. He appears to have made up his mind in advance. He has placed the burden on the student to disprove the charges. And he probably feels obligated to support Watson's original conclusion, because Watson will be deciding his tenure case next year.

The Takings Clause

Florence Dolan ran a plumbing store in Tigard, Oregon. She and her husband wanted to enlarge it on land they already owned. But the city government said that they could expand only if they dedicated some of their own land for use as a public bicycle path and for other public use. Does the city have the right to make them do that? For an answer we must look to a different part of the Fifth Amendment.

The Takings Clause is closely related to the Due Process Clause. **The Takings Clause prohibits a state from taking private property for public use without just compensation.** A town wishing to build a new football field may boot you out of your house. But the town must compensate you. The government takes your land through the power of **eminent domain.** Officials must notify you of their intentions and give you an opportunity to oppose the project and to challenge the amount the town offers to pay. But when the hearings are done, the town may write you a check and grind your house into goalposts, whether you like it or not.

---

[20] 501 U.S. 1, 111 S. Ct. 2105, 1991 U.S. LEXIS 3317 (1991).

[21] See, e.g., *University of Texas Medical School at Houston v. Than*, 901 S.W.2d 926, 1995 Tex. LEXIS 105 (Tex. 1995).

More controversial issues arise when a local government does not physically take the property but passes regulations that restrict its use. Tigard is a city of 30,000 in Oregon. The city developed a comprehensive land use plan for its downtown area in order to preserve green space, to encourage transportation other than autos, and to reduce its flooding problems. Under the plan, when a property owner sought permission to build in the downtown section, the city could require some of her land to be used for public purposes. This has become a standard method of land use planning throughout the nation. States have used it to preserve coastline, urban green belts, and many environmental features.

When Florence Dolan applied for permission to expand, the city required that she dedicate a 15-foot strip of her property to the city as a bicycle pathway and that she preserve, as greenway, a portion of her land within a floodplain. She sued, and though she lost in the Oregon courts, she won in the United States Supreme Court. The Court held that Tigard City's method of routinely forcing all owners to dedicate land to public use violated the Takings Clause. The city was taking the land, even though title never changed hands.[22]

The Court did not outlaw all such requirements. What it required was that, **before a government may require an owner to dedicate land to a public use, it must show that this owner's proposed building requires this dedication of land.** In other words, it is not enough for Tigard to have a general plan, such as a bicycle pathway, and to make all owners participate in it. Tigard must show that it needs *Dolan's* land *specifically for a bike path and greenway.* This will be much harder for local governments to demonstrate than merely showing a city-wide plan. Some observers consider the decision a major advance for the interests of private property. They say that now the government cannot so easily demand that you give up land for public use. Property you have purchased with hard-earned money should truly be yours. Others decry the Court's ruling. In their view it harms our nation's effort to preserve the environment and gives a freer hand to those who value short-term profit over long-term planning.

In the following case, state regulations prohibited commercial development of a large waterfront property. However, the owner knew about the regulations when he obtained the land. Does his awareness of the regulations prevent him from raising the Takings Clause? Has he lost the entire value of his property?

PALAZZOLO V. RHODE ISLAND

533 U.S. 606, 121 S. Ct. 2448, 150 L. Ed. 2d 592, 2001 U.S. LEXIS 4910, 69 U.S.L.W. 4605
Supreme Court of the United States, 2001

Facts: In 1959, Shore Gardens, Inc. (SGI), bought a large parcel of waterfront property in Westerly, Rhode Island, a popular vacation area. The land was almost entirely salt marsh, subject to tidal flooding. SGI failed in its early efforts to develop the parcel. In the 1970s, Rhode Island created a Coastal Resources Management Council, to protect the state's extensive shoreline. The council published regulations that sharply limited development of coastal wetlands such as SGI's property. Later, SGI transferred the property to Anthony Palazzolo. In the 1980s the new owner proposed a 74-lot residential subdivision and private beach club.

The council rejected his plan, and Palazzolo filed suit, claiming a violation of the Takings Clause. He sought $3,150,000, the value of the parcel if it were developed. The Rhode Island Supreme Court held that he could not even raise such claims, because when he took the property he had notice of the restrictive regulations. The state court also held that Palazzolo had not been deprived of the land's ▼

---

22 *Dolan v. City of Tigard*, 512 U.S. 374, 114 S. Ct. 2309, 1994 U.S. LEXIS 4826 (1994).

use, because he was permitted to build a large, single-family house on an upland portion of the property worth about $200,000. Palazzolo appealed.

Issues: Was Palazzolo barred from making the claim because he took the property with notice of the development regulations? Was he entirely deprived of the use of his property?

Excerpts from Justice Kennedy's Decision: The Takings Clause of the Fifth Amendment prohibits the government from taking private property for public use without just compensation. The clearest sort of taking occurs when the government encroaches upon or occupies private land for its own proposed use. In [a 1922 case] the Court recognized that there will be instances when government actions do not encroach upon or occupy the property yet still affect and limit its use to such an extent that a taking occurs. In Justice Holmes' well-known, if less than self-defining, formulation, "while property may be regulated to a certain extent, if a regulation goes too far it will be recognized as a taking."

Since [then], we have given some, but not too specific, guidance to courts confronted with deciding whether a particular government action goes too far and effects a regulatory taking. First, we have observed that a regulation which "denies all economically beneficial or productive use of land" will require compensation under the Takings Clause. Where a regulation places limitations on land that fall short of eliminating all economically beneficial use, a taking nonetheless may have occurred, depending on a complex of factors including the regulation's economic effect on the landowner, the extent to which the regulation interferes with reasonable investment-backed expectations, and the character of the government action. [This is known as the "Penn Central" analysis, based on a case of that name.]

The state court held the postregulation acquisition of title was fatal to the claim for deprivation of all economic use, and to the Penn Central claim. Were we to accept the State's rule, the postenactment transfer of title would absolve the State of its obligation to defend any action restricting land use, no matter how extreme or unreasonable. A State would be allowed, in effect, to put an expiration date on the Takings Clause. This ought not to be the rule. Future generations, too, have a right to challenge unreasonable limitations on the use and value of land.

[The Rhode Island Supreme Court held] that all economically beneficial use was not deprived because the uplands portion of the property can still be improved. On this point, we agree with the court's decision. Petitioner accepts the Council's contention and the state trial court's finding that his parcel retains $200,000 in development value under the State's wetlands regulations. He asserts, nonetheless, that he has suffered a total taking and contends the Council cannot sidestep [earlier cases] by the simple expedient of leaving a landowner a few crumbs of value.

Assuming a taking is otherwise established, a State may not evade the duty to compensate on the premise that the landowner is left with a token interest. This is not the situation of the landowner in this case, however. A regulation permitting a landowner to build a substantial residence on an 18-acre parcel does not leave the property "economically idle."

The court did not err in finding that petitioner failed to establish a deprivation of all economic value, for it is undisputed that the parcel retains significant worth for construction of a residence. The claims under the Penn Central analysis were not examined, and for this purpose the case should be remanded. The judgment of the Rhode Island Supreme Court is affirmed in part and reversed in part, and the case is remanded for further proceedings not inconsistent with this opinion. ■

Substantive Due Process

This doctrine is part of the Due Process Clause, but it is entirely different from procedural due process and from government taking. During the first third of the twentieth century, the Supreme Court often nullified state and federal laws, asserting that they interfered with basic rights. For example, in a famous 1905 case, *Lochner v. New York*,[23] the Supreme Court invalidated a New York statute that had limited the number of hours that bakers could work in a week. New York had passed the law to protect

---

[23] 198 U.S. 45, 25 S. Ct. 539, 1905 U.S. LEXIS 1153 (1905).

employee health. But the Court declared that private parties had a basic constitutional right to contract. In this case the statute interfered with the rights of the employer and the baker to make any bargain they wished. Over the next three decades, the Court struck down dozens of state and federal laws that were aimed at working conditions, union rights, and social welfare generally. This was called **substantive due process** because the Court was looking at the substantive rights being affected, such as the right to contract, not at any procedures.

Critics complained that the Court was interfering with the desires of the voting public by nullifying laws that the justices personally disliked (judicial activism). During the Great Depression, however, things changed. Beginning in 1934, the Court completely reversed itself and began to uphold the types of laws it earlier had struck down. How does the Court now regard substantive due process issues? It treats economic and social regulations differently from cases involving fundamental rights.

Economic and Social Regulations.   Generally speaking, the Court will now *presume valid* any statute that regulates economic or social conditions. If the *Lochner* case were heard today, the legislation would be upheld. State or federal laws regulating wages, working conditions, discrimination, union rights, and any similar topics are presumed valid. The Court will invalidate such a law only if it is *arbitrary or irrational*. Almost all statutes have some minimal rationality, and most are now upheld.

Fundamental Rights.   The standard of review is different for laws that affect **fundamental rights.** The Constitution expressly provides some of these rights, such as the right of free speech, the right to vote, and the right to travel. Other rights do not explicitly appear in the Constitution, but the Supreme Court has determined that they are implied. One of the most important of these is the right to privacy. The Court has decided that the Bill of Rights, taken together, implies a right of privacy for all persons. This includes the right to contraception, to marriage, and, most controversially, to abortion.

Any law that infringes upon a fundamental right is presumed invalid and will be struck down unless it is necessary to a compelling government interest. For example, because it is a fundamental right, no state may outlaw abortion altogether. But the state may require a minor to obtain the consent of a parent or a judge. Although this infringes upon a fundamental right, the government has a compelling interest in regulating the welfare of minors, and this regulation is necessary to achieve that goal.

Fourteenth Amendment: Equal Protection Clause

Shannon Faulkner wanted to attend The Citadel, a state-supported military college in South Carolina. She was a fine student who met every admission requirement that The Citadel set except one: she was not a male. The Citadel argued that its long and distinguished history demanded that it remain all male. The state government claimed that Ms. Faulkner had no need to attend this particular school. Faulkner responded that she was a citizen of the state and ought to receive the benefits that others got, including the right to a military education. Could the school exclude her on the basis of gender?

The Fourteenth Amendment provides that "No State shall . . . deny to any person within its jurisdiction the equal protection of the laws." This is the **Equal Protection Clause,** and it means that, generally speaking, **governments must treat people equally.** Unfair classifications among people or corporations will not be permitted. A notorious example of unfair classification would be race discrimination: permitting only white children to attend a public school violates the Equal Protection Clause.

Yet clearly, governments do make classifications every day. Rich people pay a higher tax rate than poor people; some corporations are permitted to deal in securities, others are not. To determine which classifications are constitutionally permissible, we need to know what is being classified. There are three major groups of classifications. The outcome of a case can generally be predicted by knowing which group it is in.

- *Minimal Scrutiny: Economic and Social Relations.* Government actions that classify people or corporations on these bases are almost always upheld.
- *Intermediate Scrutiny: Gender.* Government classifications are sometimes upheld.
- *Strict Scrutiny: Race, Ethnicity, and Fundamental Rights.* Classifications based on any of these are almost never upheld.

Minimal Scrutiny: Economic and Social Regulation

Just as with the Due Process Clause, laws that regulate economic or social issues are presumed valid. They will be upheld if they are *rationally related to a legitimate goal.* This means a statute may classify corporations and/or people and the classifications will be upheld if they make any sense at all. The New York City Transit Authority excluded all methadone users from any employment. The United States District Court concluded that this violated the Equal Protection Clause by unfairly excluding all those who were on methadone. The court noted that even those who tested free of any illegal drugs and were seeking non–safety-sensitive jobs, such as clerks, were turned away. That, said the district court, was irrational.

Not so, said the United States Supreme Court. The Court admitted that the policy might not be the wisest. It would probably make more sense to test individually for illegal drugs rather than automatically exclude methadone users. But, said the Court, it was not up to the justices to choose the best policy. They were only to decide if the policy was rational. Excluding methadone users related rationally to the safety of public transport and therefore did not violate the Equal Protection Clause.[24]

Intermediate Scrutiny: Gender

Classifications based on sex must meet a tougher test than those resulting from economic or social regulation. Such laws must *substantially relate to important government objectives.* Courts have increasingly nullified government sex classifications as societal concern with gender equality has grown.

At about the same time Shannon Faulkner began her campaign to enter The Citadel, another woman sought admission to the Virginia Military Institute (VMI), an all-male state school. The Supreme Court held that Virginia had violated the Equal Protection Clause by excluding women from VMI. The Court ruled that gender-based government discrimination requires an "exceedingly persuasive justification," and that Virginia had failed that standard of proof. The Citadel promptly opened its doors to women.[25]

Today more than 800 high school girls wrestle competitively. Some join female clubs but others have no such opportunity and compete with boys—or seek to. Some schools allow girls to join the boys' wrestling team, but others refuse, citing moral reasons, concern for the girls' safety, and the possibility of sexual harassment. If a particular school has no female team, should girls be permitted to wrestle boys? Do they have an equal protection right to do so?

---

24 *New York City Transit Authority v. Beazer,* 440 U.S. 568, 99 S. Ct. 1355, 1979 U.S. LEXIS 77 (1979).
25 *United States v. Virginia,* 518 U.S. 515, 116 S. Ct. 2264, 1996 U.S. LEXIS 4259 (1996).

Strict Scrutiny: Race, Ethnicity, and Fundamental Rights

Any government action that intentionally discriminates against racial or ethnic minorities, or interferes with a fundamental right, is presumed invalid. In such cases, courts will look at the statute or policy with *strict scrutiny;* that is, courts will examine it very closely to determine whether there is compelling justification for it. The law will be upheld only if it is *necessary to promote a compelling state interest.* Very few meet that test.

- *Racial and Ethnic Minorities.* Any government action that intentionally discriminates on the basis of race or ethnicity is presumed invalid. For example, in *Palmore v. Sidoti,*[26] the state had refused to give child custody to a mother because her new spouse was racially different from the child. The practice was declared unconstitutional. The state had made a racial classification, it was presumed invalid, and the government had no *compelling need* to make such a ruling.

- *Fundamental Rights.* A government action interfering with a fundamental right also receives strict scrutiny and will likely be declared void. For example, New York State gave an employment preference to any veteran who had been a state resident when he entered the military. Newcomers who were veterans were less likely to get jobs, and therefore this statute interfered with the right to travel, a fundamental right. The Supreme Court declared the law invalid.[27]

Private Regulations

All the rights discussed thus far offer protection only from government action, not from the conduct of private citizens or corporations. Suppose it is Sunday morning. You are happily reading the newspaper, sipping coffee, while your nine-year-old niece, visiting for the weekend, plays hopscotch on your front walk. There is a knock at the front door. The Neighborhood Association has arrived with a stern message: "Get the kid out of the neighborhood; she's not allowed." Astonished and enraged, you call your lawyer. But her answer leaves you dazed: You may not have children in your house. "But this is America!" you shout. "The Constitution," she replies, "does not apply."

Like 50 million other Americans, you live in a *common interest development (CID).* Yours happens to be a gated community of single-family homes, all of which were built by a developer. When you bought the house, you automatically joined the Neighborhood Association. Other CIDs take different forms: condominiums, co-ops, or retirement or vacation communities. They are increasingly common, and some observers predict that soon about 25 percent of all Americans will live in one.

Some CIDs ban children from living in the development or even visiting. Some prohibit signs on the lawns or windows; others outlaw pets, certain flowers, laundry drying in the sun, day-care centers, or pickup trucks. But various features make CIDs attractive to prospective residents. CIDs are often gated or locked in other ways, so they may be safer than surrounding neighborhoods. The community collects its own fees and operates many services, such as water and sewer, road maintenance, garbage collection, and other work traditionally done by towns and cities. Because they are privately managed by boards elected by the residents, CIDs often do this work more promptly and efficiently than public agencies.

However, the price residents pay is more than cash: they do indeed forfeit constitutional rights. The Constitution protects citizens from government action, and the

---

[26] 466 U.S. 429, 104 S. Ct. 1879, 1984 U.S. LEXIS 69 (1984).

[27] *Attorney General of New York v. Soto-Lopez,* 476 U.S. 898, 106 S. Ct. 2317, 1986 U.S. LEXIS 59 (1986).

local CID is not a government. As the law currently stands, you are probably giving up constitutional protections when you enter a CID. If the Neighborhood Association demands that your niece leave, you will probably have to drive her home. Suppose the nasty Neighborhood Association official also notices that your cat looks heavy. "No cats over 20 pounds," he snarls. "Read the rules." The pet-weight rule is also probably enforceable: get that cat off the sofa and onto a treadmill, fast.

Chapter Conclusion

The legal battle over power never stops. The obligation of a state to provide equal educational opportunity for both genders relates to whether Tigard, Oregon, may demand some of Ms. Dolan's store lot for public use. Both issues are governed by one amazing document. That same Constitution determines what tax preferences are permissible, and even whether a state may require you to wear clothing. As social mores change in step with broad cultural developments, as the membership of the Supreme Court changes, the balance of power between federal government, state government, and citizens will continue to evolve. There are no easy answers to these constitutional questions because there has never been a democracy so large, so diverse, or so powerful.

Chapter Review

1. The Constitution is a series of compromises about power.

2. Article I of the Constitution creates the Congress and grants all legislative power to it. Article II establishes the office of President and defines executive powers. Article III creates the Supreme Court and permits lower federal courts; the article also outlines the powers of the federal judiciary.

3. Under the Commerce Clause, Congress may regulate any activity that has a substantial effect on interstate commerce.

4. A state may not regulate commerce in any way that will interfere with interstate commerce.

5. Under the Supremacy Clause, if there is a conflict between federal and state statutes, the federal law preempts the field. Even without a conflict, federal law preempts if Congress intended to exercise exclusive control.

6. The President's key powers include making agency appointments, proposing legislation, conducting foreign policy, and acting as Commander in Chief of the armed forces.

7. The federal courts adjudicate cases and also exercise judicial review, which is the right to declare a statute or governmental action unconstitutional and void.

8. Freedom of speech includes symbolic acts. Political speech is protected unless it is intended and likely to create imminent lawless action.

9. The government may regulate the time, place, and manner of speech.

10. Obscene speech is not protected.

11. Commercial speech that is false or misleading may be outlawed; otherwise, regulations on this speech must be reasonable and directed to a legitimate goal.

12. Procedural due process is required whenever the government attempts to take liberty or property. The amount of process that is due depends upon the importance of the liberty or property threatened.

13. The Takings Clause prohibits a state from taking private property for public use without just compensation.

14. A substantive due process analysis presumes that any economic or social regulation is valid and presumes invalid any law that infringes upon a fundamental right.

15. The Equal Protection Clause generally requires the government to treat people equally. Courts apply strict scrutiny in any equal protection case involving race, ethnicity, or fundamental rights; intermediate scrutiny to any case involving gender; and minimal scrutiny to an economic or social regulation.

16. Generally, constitutional rights protect citizens only from the action of the government, not from actions of private organizations such as common interest developments.

Practice Test

1. Michigan's Solid Waste Management Act (SWMA) generally prohibited Michigan counties from accepting for disposal solid waste that had been generated outside that county. Fort Gratiot operated a sanitary landfill in St. Clair County, Michigan. The county denied Fort Gratiot permission to bring in solid waste from out of state, and Fort Gratiot sued. This case involves the negative, or dormant, aspect of the Commerce Clause. What is the difference between that aspect and the positive aspect? What is the evil that the dormant aspect is designed to avoid? How would you rule in this case?

2. *YOU BE THE JUDGE* WRITING PROBLEM Scott Fane was a certified public accountant (CPA) licensed to practice in New Jersey and Florida. He built his New Jersey practice by making unsolicited phone calls to executives. When he moved to Florida, the Board of Accountancy there prohibited him (and all CPAs) from personally soliciting new business. Fane sued. Does the First Amendment force Florida to forgo foreclosing Fane's phoning? **Argument for Fane:** The Florida regulation violates the First Amendment, which protects commercial speech. Fane was not saying anything false or misleading, but was just trying to secure business. This is an unreasonable regulation, designed to keep newcomers out of the marketplace and maintain steady business and high prices for established CPAs. **Argument for the Florida Board of Accountancy:** Commercial speech deserves—and gets—a lower level of protection than other speech. This regulation is a reasonable method of ensuring that the level of CPA work in our state remains high. CPAs who personally solicit clients are obviously in need of business. They are more likely to bend legal and ethical rules to obtain clients and keep them happy and will lower the standards throughout the state.

3. Dairy farming in Massachusetts became more expensive than in other states. In order to help its dairy farmers, the state began taxing all milk sales in the state, whether the milk was produced in state or out of state. The money went into a fund that was then distributed among Massachusetts milk producers as a subsidy for their milk. Discuss.

4. President George H. W. Bush insisted that he had the power to send American troops into combat in the Middle East without congressional assent. Yet before authorizing force in Operation Desert Storm, he secured congressional authorization. President Clinton stated that he was prepared to invade Haiti without a congressional vote. Yet he bargained hard to avoid an invasion, and ultimately American troops entered without the use of force. Why the seeming double talk by both presidents?

5. In the early 1970s, President Nixon became embroiled in the Watergate dispute. He was accused of covering up a criminal break-in at the national headquarters of the Democratic Party. Nixon denied any wrongdoing. A United States District Court judge ordered the President to produce tapes of conversations held in his office. Nixon knew that complying with the order would produce damaging evidence, probably destroying his presidency. He refused, claiming executive privilege. The case went to the Supreme Court. Nixon strongly implied that even if the Supreme Court ordered him to produce the tapes, he would refuse. What major constitutional issue did this raise?

6. *ETHICS* In the landmark 1965 case of *Griswold v. Connecticut*, the Supreme Court examined a Connecticut statute that made it a crime for any person to use contraception. The majority declared the law an unconstitutional violation of the right of privacy. Justice Black dissented, saying, "I do not to any extent whatever base my view that this Connecticut law is constitutional on a belief that the law is wise or that its policy is a good one. [It] is every bit as offensive to me as it is to the majority. [There is no criticism by the majority of this law] to which I cannot subscribe—except their conclusion that the evil qualities they see in the law make it unconstitutional." What legal doctrines are involved here? Why did Justice Black distinguish between his personal views on the statute and the power of the Court to overturn it? Should a federal court act as a "superlegislature," nullifying statutes with which it disagrees? If a court aggressively takes on social issues, what dangers—and what advantages—does that present to society?

7. You begin work at Everhappy Corp. at the beginning of November. On your second day at work, you wear a political button on your overcoat, supporting your choice for governor in the upcoming election. Your boss glances at it and says, "Get that stupid thing out of this office or you're history, chump." You protest that his statement (a) violates your constitutional rights and (b) uses a boring cliché. Are you right?

8. Gilleo opposed American participation in the war in the Persian Gulf. She displayed a large sign on her front lawn that read, "Say No to War in the Persian Gulf, Call Congress Now." The city of Ladue prohibited signs on front lawns and Gilleo sued. The city claimed that it was regulating "time, place, and manner." Explain that statement, and decide who should win.

9. A federal statute prohibits the broadcasting of lottery advertisements, except by stations that broadcast in states permitting lotteries. The purpose of the statute is to support efforts of states that outlaw lotteries. Edge Broadcasting operated a radio station in North Carolina (a nonlottery state) but broadcast primarily in Virginia (a lottery state). Edge wanted to advertise Virginia's lottery but was barred by the statute. Did the federal statute violate Edge's constitutional rights?

10. Fox's Fine Furs claims that Ermine owes $68,000 for a mink coat on which she has stopped making payments. Fox goes to court, files a complaint, and also asks the clerk to *garnishee* Ermine's wages. A garnishment is a court order to an employer to hold an employee's wages, or a portion of them, and pay the money into court so that there will be money for the plaintiff, if she wins. What constitutional issue does Fox's request for garnishment raise?

11. David Lucas paid $975,000 for two residential lots on the Isle of Palms near Charleston, South Carolina. He intended to build houses on them. Two years later the South Carolina legislature passed a statute that prohibited building seaward of a certain line, and Lucas's property fell in the prohibited zone. Lucas claimed that his land was now useless and that South Carolina owed him its value. Explain his claim. Should he win?

12. This case concerns unequal taxes on property. In Pennsylvania, a county tax commissioner appraises land, meaning that he sets a value for the land, and the owner then pays real estate taxes based on that value. A commissioner valued land at its sales price, whenever it was sold. If land did not sell for many years, he made little or no adjustment in its appraised value. As a result, some property was assessed at 35 times as much as neighboring land. A corporate landowner sued. What constitutional issue is raised? What should the outcome be?

13. **ROLE REVERSAL** Write an exam question that distinguishes between these three important Fifth Amendment protections: procedural due process, the Takings Clause, and substantive due process.

Internet Research Problem

Visit academic.cengage.com/blaw/beatty. Find a book that was formerly censored. Find another volume that is currently banned, either in the United States or elsewhere. How have changing mores affected censorship? Will the book that is currently outlawed someday be legal?

You can find further practice problems at academic.cengage.com/blaw/beatty.

6 Torts

© SPIKE MAFFORD/PHOTODISC/GETTY IMAGES

In a small Louisiana town, Don Mashburn ran a restaurant called Maison de Mashburn. The New Orleans States-Item newspaper reviewed his eatery, and here is what the article said:

"'Tain't Creole, 'tain't Cajun, 'tain't French, 'tain't country American, 'tain't good. I don't know how much real talent in cooking is hidden under the mélange of hideous sauces which make this food and the menu a travesty of pretentious amateurism but I find it all quite depressing. Put a yellow flour sauce on top of the duck, flame it for drama and serve it with some horrible multi-flavored rice in hollowed-out fruit and what have you got? A well-cooked duck with an ugly sauce that tastes too sweet and thick and makes you want to scrape off the glop to eat the plain duck. [The stuffed eggplant was prepared by emptying] a shaker full (more or less) of paprika on top of it. [One sauce created] trout à la green plague [while another should have been called] yellow death on duck."

Mashburn sued, claiming that the newspaper had committed libel, damaging his reputation and hurting his business.[1] Trout à la green plague will be the first course on our menu of tort law. ■

---

1 *Mashburn v. Collins*, 355 So. 2d 879 (La. 1977).

This odd word *tort* is borrowed from the French, meaning "wrong." **A tort is a violation of a duty imposed by the civil law.** When a person breaks one of those duties and injures another, it is a tort. The injury could be to a person or her property. Libel is one example of a tort, in which, for example, a newspaper columnist falsely accuses someone of being an alcoholic. A surgeon who removes the wrong kidney from a patient commits a different kind of tort, called negligence. A con artist who tricks you out of money with a phony offer to sell you a boat commits fraud, yet another tort.

Because tort law is so broad, it takes awhile to understand its boundaries. To start with, we must distinguish torts from two other areas of law: criminal law and contract law.

It is a crime to steal a car, to embezzle money from a bank, to sell cocaine. As discussed in Chapter 1, society considers such behavior so threatening that the government itself will prosecute the wrongdoer, whether or not the car owner or bank president wants the case to go forward.

In a tort case, it is up to the injured party, the plaintiff, to seek compensation. She must hire her own lawyer, who will file a lawsuit. Her lawyer must convince the court that the defendant breached some legal duty and ought to pay money damages to the plaintiff. The plaintiff has no power to send the defendant to jail. Bear in mind that a defendant's action might be both a crime and a tort. The con artist who tricks you out of money with a fake offer to sell you a boat has committed the tort of fraud. You may file a civil suit against him and will collect money damages if you can prove your case. The con artist has also committed the crime of fraud. The state will prosecute, seeking to imprison and fine him.

Differences between Contract, Tort, and Criminal Law			
Type of Obligation	**Contract**	**Tort**	**Criminal Law**
How the obligation is created	The parties agree on a contract, which creates duties for both.	The civil law imposes duties of conduct on all persons.	The criminal law prohibits certain conduct.
How the obligation is enforced	Suit by plaintiff.	Suit by plaintiff.	Prosecution by government.
Possible result	Money damages for plaintiff.	Money damages for plaintiff.	Punishment for defendant, including prison and/or fine.
Example	Raul contracts to sell Deirdre 5,000 pairs of sneakers at $50 per pair but fails to deliver them. Deirdre buys the sneakers elsewhere for $60 per pair and receives $50,000, her extra expense.	A newspaper falsely accuses a private citizen of being an alcoholic. The plaintiff sues and wins money damages to compensate for her injured reputation.	Leo steals Kelly's car. The government prosecutes Leo for grand theft, and the judge sentences him to two years in prison. Kelly gets nothing.

A tort is also different from a contract dispute. A contract case is based on an agreement two people have already made. For example, Deirdre claims that Raul promised to sell her 10,000 pairs of sneakers at a good price but has failed to deliver them. She files a contract lawsuit. In a tort case, there is usually no "deal" between the parties. Don Mashburn had never met the restaurant critic who attacked his restaurant and obviously had never made any kind of contract. The plaintiff in a tort case claims that the law itself creates obligations that the defendant has breached.

Tort law itself is divided into categories. We begin by considering intentional torts—that is, harm caused by a deliberate action. Then we will examine negligence and strict liability, which are injuries caused by neglect.

INTENTIONAL TORTS

Defamation

Defamation refers to false statements that harm someone's reputation. Defamatory statements can be written or spoken. Written defamation is libel. Suppose a newspaper accuses a local retail store of programming its cash registers to overcharge customers, when the store has never done so. That is libel. Oral defamation is **slander.** If Professor Wisdom, in class, refers to Sally Student as a drug dealer, and Sally has never sold anything stronger than Arm & Hammer, he has slandered her.

There are four elements to a defamation case. **An element is a fact that a plaintiff must prove to win a lawsuit.** In *any* kind of lawsuit, the plaintiff must prove *all* of the elements to prevail. The elements in a defamation case are:

- *Defamatory Statement.* These are words likely to harm another person's reputation. When Professor Wisdom accuses Sally of dealing drugs, that will clearly harm her reputation.

- *Falseness.* The statement must be false. If Sally Student actually sold marijuana to a classmate, then Professor Wisdom has a defense to slander.

- *Communicated.* The statement must be communicated to at least one person other than the plaintiff. If Wisdom speaks only to Sally and accuses her of dealing drugs, there is no slander.

- *Injury.* In slander cases, the plaintiff generally must show some injury. Sally's injury would be a lower reputation in the school, embarrassment, and humiliation. But in libel cases, the law is willing to assume injury. Because libel is written and more permanent, courts award damages even without proof of injury.[2]

Opinion

Opinion is generally a valid defense in a defamation suit because it cannot be proven true or false. Suppose that a television commentator says, "Frank Landlord

---

[2] When defamation by radio and television became possible, the courts chose to consider it libel, analogizing it to newspapers because of the vast audience. This means that in broadcasting cases, a plaintiff generally does not have to prove damages.

certainly does less than many rich people do for our community." Is that defamation? Probably not. Who are the "rich people"? How much do they do? How do we define "does less"? These vague assertions indicate the statement is one of opinion. Even if Frank works hard feeding homeless families, he will probably lose a defamation case.

A related defense involves cases in which a supposed statement of fact should not be taken literally. "Reverend Wilson's sermons go on so long, many parishioners suffer brain death before receiving communion." Brain death is a tragic fact of medical science, but this author obviously exaggerates to express her opinion. No defamation.

Mr. Mashburn, who opened the chapter suing over his restaurant review, lost his case. The court held that a reasonable reader would have understood the statements to be opinion only. "A shaker full of paprika" and "yellow death on duck" were not to be taken literally but were merely the author's expression of his personal dislike.

The following case features a word that is shocking to many but humorous to some. Is it defamatory?

You Be the Judge

KNIEVEL V. ESPN

393 F.3d 1068 Ninth Circuit Court of Appeals, 2005

Facts: Evel Knievel was a motorcycle stuntman who had built an international reputation through decades of daredevil feats. He rode through fire walls, flew over rattlesnakes, set world records for blasting over 14 parked buses, and spent 30 days in a coma when his 151-foot jump over the fountains of Caesar's Palace hotel came up a few feet short. The Smithsonian Institute honored his deeds, and he built a solid reputation as a community activist and advocate for young people, using his fame to promote anti-drug programs and motorcycle safety.

ESPN held an awards program honoring winners in extreme sports (skateboarding, surfing, and motorcycle racing) and photographed many attending celebrities. On its Website, www.EXPN.com, the network featured photos from the event, including one that depicted Knievel with his right arm around his wife, Krystal, and his left arm around a young woman. The caption read, "Evel Knievel proves that you're never too old to be a pimp."

The Knievels sued for defamation, claiming that the word "pimp" subjected them to hatred, contempt and ridicule and caused several of Evel's former clients to stop working with them. The District Court dismissed the case without a jury trial, ruling that the photo and caption could not be defamatory because no reasonable viewer would have taken the phrase in its literal, criminal sense. The Knievels appealed.

Issue: **Should a jury have decided whether the photo and caption were defamatory?**

Argument for the Knievels: The issue is whether reasonable viewers (and reasonable jurors) might consider the material defamatory. Of course they could. A pimp is a criminal, and a particularly disgusting one at that. We can easily prove that Evel Knievel has never had anything to do with such revolting conduct. Let the Knievels make their case to a jury. If a dozen fair-minded people find the phrase funny, we will accept the verdict. We suspect they will conclude that an arrogant sports network has gone too far with insulting language and injured a hardworking man who has spent a lifetime building a marvelous reputation.

Argument for ESPN: Lighten up. This is a Website for young, hip people who watch extreme sports, use contemporary language, and possess what is known as a sense of humor. In the series of photographs on

▼

this site, one showed two men grasping hands; the caption read, "Colin McKay and Cary Hart share the love." Another shows a woman in a black dress, captioned, "Tara Dakides lookin' sexy, even though we all know she is hardcore."

The term "pimp" was not intended as a criminal accusation, nor would any reasonable viewer take it literally. Other photo captions, such as "hardcore," "scooping," "hottie of the year," and "throwing down a pose," indicate that all the descriptions were loose, figurative, and humorous.

The Knievels' Rebuttal: Is broadcast vocabulary to be nothing more than a race to the gutter? And even if it is, who appointed ESPN as the referee in that ugly contest? Journalists owe us a higher standard.

ESPN's Rebuttal: If the Knievels want to take part in extreme events, and enjoy the attendant publicity, they have to be willing to take a joke. Everyone else does. ●

Public Policy

What standards do we want in journalism? A college paper published a photograph of a staff member, an assistant to the vice-president of student affairs, who helped students apply for—and frequently win—fellowships. Under the picture the paper gave her name and described her as "Director of Butt Licking," because of her high success rate in placing students. She sued for libel. The paper defended, as ESPN did, claiming the phrase was a joke that no one would take seriously. Who should win? ◆

Public Personalities

The rules of the game change for those who play in public. Public officials and public figures receive less protection from defamation. An example of a **public official** is a police chief. A **public figure** is a movie star, for example, or a multimillionaire playboy constantly in the news. In the landmark case *New York Times Co. v. Sullivan,*[3] the Supreme Court ruled that the free exchange of information is vital in a democracy and is protected by the First Amendment to the Constitution. A public official or public figure can win a defamation case only by proving actual malice by the defendant. **Actual malice means that the defendant knew the statement was false or acted with reckless disregard of the truth.** If the plaintiff merely shows that the defendant newspaper printed incorrect statements, even very damaging ones, he loses. In the *New York Times* case, the police chief of Birmingham, Alabama, claimed that the *Times* falsely accused him of racial violence in his job. He lost the suit because he could not prove that the *Times* had acted with actual malice. If he had demonstrated that the *Times* knew its accusation was false, he would have won.

cyberLaw

Kenneth Zeran awoke one day to learn he had become notorious. An unidentified person had posted a message on an AOL bulletin board advertising "Naughty Oklahoma T-Shirts." The shirts featured deeply offensive slogans relating to the 1995 bombing of a federal building in Oklahoma City, in which hundreds of innocent people died. Those interested in purchasing such a T-shirt were instructed to call "Ken" at Zeran's home telephone number. Zeran had nothing to do with the posting or the T-shirts. He was quickly inundated with phone messages from furious callers, some of whom made death threats.

Zeran could not change his number because he ran his business from his home. A radio station in Oklahoma City learned of the alleged offer and angrily urged its listeners to call

---

[3] 376 U.S. 254, 84 S. Ct. 710, 1964 U.S. LEXIS 1655 (1964).

Zeran, which they did. Over the next few days, additional similar messages were posted, and before long Zeran was receiving an abusive call every two minutes. Zeran phoned AOL on the first day. The company promised to remove the messages immediately but did not promptly delete the postings or close the responsible account. Zeran sued AOL for defamation—and lost.

The court held that AOL was immune from a defamation suit based on a third-party posting, based on the Communications Decency Act (CDA). Section 230 of the CDA creates this immunity for any Internet service provider. The court held that it would be impossible for a service provider to screen each of its millions of postings and that was why Congress prohibited suits such as Zeran's. ◆

Privilege

Defendants receive additional protection from defamation cases when it is important for them to speak freely. **Absolute privilege** exists in courtrooms and legislative hearings. Anyone speaking there, such as a witness in a trial, can say anything at all and never be sued for defamation. Courts extend an absolute privilege in those few instances when candor is essential to a functioning democracy.[4]

Qualified privilege exists when two people have a legitimate need to exchange information. Suppose Trisha Tenant lives in a housing project. She honestly believes that her neighbor is selling guns illegally. She reports this to the manager of the project, who investigates and discovers the guns were toys, being sold legally. Trisha is not liable for slander because she had a good faith reason to report this and the manager needed to hear it. As long as Trisha acts in good faith and talks only to someone who ought to know about the activity, she is protected by qualified privilege.

False Imprisonment

False imprisonment is the intentional restraint of another person without reasonable cause and without consent. A bank teller became seriously ill and wanted to go to the doctor, but the bank forbade her to leave until she made a final tally of her accounts. Officials barred her from leaving the bank. That was false imprisonment. The restraint was unreasonable because her accounts could have been verified later.[5]

False imprisonment cases most commonly arise in retail stores, which sometimes detain employees or customers for suspected theft. Most states now have statutes governing the detention of suspected shoplifters. **Generally, a store may detain a customer or worker for alleged shoplifting provided there is a reasonable basis for the suspicion and the detention is done reasonably.** To detain a customer in the manager's office for 20 minutes and question him about where he got an item is lawful. To chain that customer to a display counter for three hours and humiliate him in front of other customers is unreasonable, and false imprisonment.

Intentional Infliction of Emotional Distress

What should happen when a defendant's conduct hurts a plaintiff emotionally but not physically? Most courts allow a plaintiff to recover for emotional injury that a defendant intentionally caused.

---

[4] A witness who lies is guilty of perjury but not liable for slander.

[5] *Kanner v. First National Bank of South Miami,* 287 So. 2d 715, 1974 Fla. App. LEXIS 8989 (Fla. Dist. Ct. App. 1974).

The intentional infliction of emotional distress results from extreme and outrageous conduct that causes serious emotional harm. A credit officer was struggling vainly to locate Sheehan, who owed money on his car. The officer phoned Sheehan's mother, falsely identified herself as a hospital employee, and said she needed to find Sheehan because his children had been in a serious auto accident. The mother provided Sheehan's whereabouts, which enabled the company to seize his car. But Sheehan spent seven hours frantically trying to locate his supposedly injured children, who in fact were fine. The credit company was liable for the intentional infliction of emotional distress.[6]

By contrast, a muffler shop, trying to collect a debt from a customer, made six phone calls over three months, using abusive language. The customer testified that this caused her to be upset, to cry, and to have difficulty sleeping. The court ruled that the muffler shop's conduct was neither extreme nor outrageous and sent the customer home for another sleepless night.[7]

The following case arose in a setting that guarantees controversy: an abortion clinic.

JANE DOE AND NANCY ROE V. LYNN MILLS

212 Mich. App. 73, 536 N.W. 2d 824, 1995 Mich. App. LEXIS 313
Michigan Court of Appeals, 1995

Facts: Late one night, an anti-abortion protestor named Robert Thomas climbed into a dumpster located behind an abortion clinic. He found documents indicating that Doe and Roe (not their real names) were soon to have abortions at the clinic. Thomas gave the information to Lynn Mills. She and another woman created signs, using the women's names, indicating that they were about to undergo abortions and urging them not to "kill their babies." Doe and Roe sued, claiming intentional infliction of emotional distress. The trial court gave summary judgment for the defendants, stating that they had a right to express their views on abortion. The plaintiffs appealed.

Issue: Have the plaintiffs made a valid claim of intentional infliction of emotional distress?

Excerpts from the Court's *Per Curiam*[8] Decision: Liability for the intentional infliction of emotional distress has been found only where the conduct complained of has been so outrageous in character, and so extreme in degree, as to go beyond all possible bounds of decency. Liability does not extend to mere insults, indignities, threats, annoyances, petty oppressions, or other trivialities, [but to cases where] an average member of the community would exclaim "Outrageous!"

The trial court observed that defendants have a constitutional right to "protest peaceably against abortion." However, the objectionable aspect of defendants' conduct does not relate to their views on abortion but, rather, to the fact that defendants gave unreasonable or unnecessary publicity to purely private matters involving plaintiffs.

We believe this is the type of case that might cause an average member of the community, upon learning of defendants' conduct, to exclaim, "Outrageous!" Because reasonable men may differ with regard to whether defendants' conduct may be considered sufficiently outrageous and extreme so as to subject them to liability for intentional infliction of emotional distress, this matter should be determined by the trier of fact. [Summary judgment for the defendants is reversed, and the case is remanded for trial.] ∎

---

[6] *Ford Motor Credit Co. v. Sheehan,* 373 So. 2d 956, 1979 Fla. App. LEXIS 15416 (Fla. Dist. Ct. App. 1979).

[7] *Midas Muffler Shop v. Ellison,* 133 Ariz. 194, 650 P.2d 496, 1982 Ariz. App. LEXIS 488 (Ariz. Ct. App. 1982).

[8] A *per curiam* decision is one made by the entire court but not attributed to a specific justice.

Additional Intentional Torts

Battery is an intentional touching of another person in a way that is unwanted or offensive. There need be no intention to *hurt* the plaintiff. If the defendant intended to do the physical act, and a reasonable plaintiff would be offended by it, battery has occurred.

Suppose an irate parent throws a chair at a referee during his daughter's basketball game, breaking the man's jaw. It is irrelevant that the father did not intend to injure the referee. But a parent who cheerfully slaps the winning coach on the back has not committed battery, because a reasonable coach would not be offended.

Assault occurs when a defendant does some act that makes a plaintiff fear an imminent battery. It is assault even though the battery never occurs. Suppose Ms. Wilson shouts "Think fast!" at her husband and hurls a toaster at him. He turns and sees it flying at him. His fear of being struck is enough to win a case of assault, even if the toaster misses.

Fraud is injuring another person by deliberate deception. It is fraud to sell real estate knowing that there is a large toxic waste deposit underground of which the buyer is ignorant. Later in this chapter, a plaintiff claims that for many years, a cigarette manufacturer fraudulently suggested its product was safe, knowing its assurances were deadly lies. Fraud is a tort that typically occurs during contract negotiation, and it is discussed in detail in Chapter 9, on contracts.

DAMAGES

Compensatory Damages

Mitchel Bien, who is deaf, enters the George Grubbs Nissan dealership, where folks sell cars aggressively—*very* aggressively. Maturelli, a salesman, and Bien communicate by writing messages back and forth. Maturelli takes Bien's own car keys, and the two then test drive a 300ZX. Bien says he does not want the car, but Maturelli escorts him back inside and fills out a sales sheet. Bien repeatedly asks for his keys, but Maturelli only laughs, pressuring him to buy the new car. Minutes pass. Hours pass. Bien becomes frantic, writing a dozen notes, begging to leave, threatening to call the police. Maturelli mocks Bien and his physical disabilities. Finally, after four hours, the customer escapes.

Bien sues for the intentional infliction of emotional distress. Two former salesmen from Grubbs testify they have witnessed customers cry, yell, and curse as a result of the aggressive tactics. Doctors state that the incident has traumatized Bien, dramatically reducing his confidence and self-esteem and preventing his return to work even three years later.

The jury awards Bien damages. But how does a jury calculate the money? For that matter, why should a jury even try? Money can never erase pain or undo a permanent injury. The answer is simple: money, however inexact and ineffective, is the only thing a court has to give.

A successful plaintiff generally receives **compensatory damages,** meaning an amount of money that the court believes will restore him to the position he was in before the defendant's conduct caused an injury. Here is how compensatory damages are calculated.

First, a plaintiff receives money for medical expenses that he has proven by producing bills from doctors, hospitals, physical therapists, and psychotherapists. Bien receives all the money he has paid. If a doctor testifies that Bien needs future treatment, he will offer evidence of how much that will cost. **The single-recovery principle requires a court to settle the matter once and for all, by awarding a lump sum for past and future expenses.** A plaintiff may not return in a year and say, "Oh, by the way, there are some new bills."

Second, the defendants are liable for lost wages. The court takes the number of days or months that Bien missed work and multiplies that times his salary. If Bien is currently unable to work, a doctor estimates how many more months he will miss work, and the court adds that to his damages.

Third, a plaintiff is paid for pain and suffering. Bien testifies about how traumatic the four hours were and how the experience has affected his life. He may state that he now fears shopping, suffers nightmares, and seldom socializes. To bolster the case, a plaintiff uses expert testimony, such as the psychiatrists who testified for Bien. Awards for pain and suffering vary enormously, from a few dollars to many millions, depending on the injury and depending on the jury. In some lawsuits, physical and psychological pain are momentary and insignificant; in other cases, the pain is the biggest part of the verdict. In Bien's case, the jury returns with its verdict: $573,815, calculated as in the table that follows.[9]

Past medical	$ 70.00
Future medical	$ 6,000.00
Past rehabilitation	$ 3,205.00
Past lost earning capacity	$112,910.00
Future lost earning capacity	$ 34,650.00
Past physical symptoms and discomfort	$ 50,000.00
Future physical symptoms and discomfort	$ 50,000.00
Past emotional injury and mental anguish	$101,980.00
Future emotional injury and mental anguish	$200,000.00
Past loss of society and reduced ability to socially interact with family, former fiancée, and friends and hearing (i.e., nondeaf) people in general	$ 10,000.00
Future loss of society and reduced ability to socially interact with family, former fiancée, and friends and hearing people	$ 5,000.00
TOTAL	$573,815.00

---

[9] The compensatory damages are described in *George Grubbs Enterprises v. Bien*, 881 S.W.2d 843, 1994 Tex. App. LEXIS 1870 (Tex. Ct. App. 1994). In addition to the compensatory damages described, the jury awarded $5 million in punitive damages. The Texas Supreme Court reversed the award of punitive damages, but not the compensatory. Id., 900 S.W.2d 337, 1995 Tex. LEXIS 91 (Tex. 1995). The high court did not dispute the appropriateness of punitive damages, but reversed because the trial court failed to instruct the jury properly as to how it should determine the assets actually under the defendants' control, an issue essential to punitive damages but not compensatory.

Punitive Damages

Here we look at a different kind of award, one that is more controversial and potentially more powerful: punitive damages. The purpose is not to compensate the plaintiff for harm, because compensatory damages will have done that. Punitive damages are intended to punish the defendant for conduct that is extreme and outrageous. Courts award these damages in relatively few cases. When an award of punitive damages is made, it is generally in a case of intentional tort, although they occasionally appear in negligence suits.

The idea behind punitive damages is that certain behavior is so unacceptable that society must make an example of it. A large award of money should deter the defendant from repeating the mistake and others from ever making it. This is social engineering in an extreme form. Predictably, some believe punitive damages represent the law at its most avaricious,[10] while others attribute to them great social benefit. Large verdicts make headlines, but in fact punitive damages are rare and generally modest.

When plaintiffs suffer serious personal injuries, high awards may occur. However, when a plaintiff has suffered only economic harm and no personal injury, a court will not permit such a high award.

The United States Supreme Court has declared that in awarding punitive damages, a court must consider three "guideposts":

- The reprehensibility of the defendant's conduct;
- The ratio between the harm suffered and the award; and
- The difference between the punitive award and any civil penalties used in similar cases.[11]

The Court has refused to provide a definitive ratio between compensatory and punitive damages but has given additional guidance to lower courts:

- The trial court generally should not permit a punitive award more than nine times higher than the compensatory damages.
- The trial court may not use the defendant's wealth as an excuse to award an unreasonably high award.

Despite the Supreme Court guidelines, dramatic cases may still lead to very large awards, as the following case illustrates.

WILLIAMS V. PHILIP MORRIS INCORPORATED

93 Or.App.527, 92 P.3d 126
Court of Appeals of Oregon, 2004

Facts: Jesse Williams smoked three packs of Marlboros a day—and died of lung cancer. Philip Morris sold Marlboros and controlled about half the cigarette market in the United States. Mayola Williams, Jesse's widow, sued the tobacco company, claiming fraud. She argued that for decades Philip Morris knew its cigarettes were addictive and knew ▼

---

[10] Lawyers normally take personal injury cases on a contingency basis, meaning that they receive no money upfront from their client. Their fee will be a percentage of the plaintiff's judgment if she wins. Lawyers often take about one third of the award. But if the defendant wins, the plaintiff's lawyer will have worked several years for no pay.

[11] *BMW of North America, Inc. v. Gore,* 517 U.S. 559, 116 S. Ct. 1589, 1996 U.S. LEXIS 3390 (1996).

they caused illness and death but deceived the public to boost its profits. The jury awarded her $21,485 in economic damages, $800,000 in pain and suffering—and $79.5 million in punitive damages. Then the Supreme Court established the guidelines described earlier, and the case was sent back to the Oregon appellate court for reconsideration.

Issue: Was the punitive damage award excessive?

Excerpts from Judge Edmonds' Decision: [Jesse Williams] was highly addicted to tobacco, both physiologically and psychologically. Although, at the urging of his wife and children, he made several attempts to stop smoking, each time he failed, in part because of his addiction. When his family told him that cigarettes were dangerous to his health, he replied that the cigarette companies would not sell them if they were as dangerous as his family claimed. He died about six months after his diagnosis.

The jury could have found the following facts from the evidence before it. Defendant sold a product that it knew would cause death or serious injury to its customers when they used it as defendant intended them to use it. Despite that knowledge, defendant, together with the rest of the tobacco industry, engaged in an extensive campaign to convince smokers that the issue of cigarette safety was unresolved. It insisted that more research was necessary at the very time that it was carefully avoiding doing the very research for which it called, although it had an extensive program of research into other issues. Rather, it used its research to determine the optimum dose of nicotine in each cigarette, knowing of, but publicly denying, nicotine's highly addictive properties.

We are mindful that the [Supreme Court has declared] that "few awards exceeding a single-digit ratio will satisfy due process." But even if the $79 million award is deemed to exceed a single-digit ratio, it is difficult to conceive of more reprehensible misconduct for a longer duration of time on the part of a supplier of consumer products to the Oregon public than what occurred in this case. We think the unique facts in this case, when compared to the circumstances considered by the Supreme Court and this court in other cases, would justify more than a single-digit award under the Due Process Clause.

We conclude that an award of punitive damages in the amount of $79.5 million does not violate the Due Process Clause under the [Supreme Court] guidelines because the amount of the award is reasonable and proportionate to the wrong inflicted on decedent and the public of this state. We reinstate the award of punitive damages as originally found by the jury. ∎

Tort Reform

Some people believe that jury awards are excessive and need statutory reform. For example, critics claim that large medical malpractice awards can drive doctors out of business. In medical cases and others, they argue, unrestrained juries harm hospitals, corporations, and communities with massive verdicts. About half the states have passed some limits on tort awards. The laws vary, but many work this way: A jury is permitted to award whatever it considers fair for *economic* damages, meaning lost wages and medical expenses. However, *noneconomic* damages (pain and suffering), together with any punitive award, may not exceed a prescribed limit, such as three times the economic damages, or sometimes a flat cap, such as $250,000 total. These restrictions can drastically lower the total verdict. Congress has proposed and debated similar bills, but thus far none of these federal revisions have been enacted into law.

Opponents consider tort reform misplaced. They offer evidence that medical malpractice costs account for less than 2 percent of our astronomical health care costs. A report of 720 malpractice suits in two allegedly litigious counties showed only 6 verdicts for plaintiffs, and only one that would have been affected by a cap. Other studies indicate that punitive damages in general are rare and generally modest. One showed, for example, that courts award them in about 6 percent of those cases that plaintiffs win. When compensatory damages are $10,000, punitive damages (when given) average $10,000; when the compensatory award is $100,000, the punitive award, if any, averages $66,000.

Is tort reform a necessary step to control runaway juries or is it a gift to large corporations that do not wish to pay for the harm they cause?

BUSINESS TORTS

In this section we look at intentional torts that occur in a commercial setting: interference with a contract, interference with a prospective advantage, and the rights to privacy and publicity. Patents, copyrights, and trademarks are discussed in Chapter 22, on intellectual property, as are Lanham Act violations.

Tortious Interference with Business Relations

Competition is the essence of business. Successful corporations compete aggressively, and the law permits and expects them to. But there are times when healthy competition becomes illegal interference. This is called tortious interference with business relations. It can take one of two closely related forms: interference with a contract or interference with a prospective advantage.

Tortious Interference with a Contract

Tortious interference with a contract exists only if the plaintiff can establish the following four elements:

- There was a contract between the plaintiff and a third party;
- The defendant knew of the contract;
- The defendant improperly induced the third party to breach the contract or made performance of the contract impossible; and
- There was injury to the plaintiff.

There is nothing wrong with two companies bidding against each other to buy a parcel of land, and nothing wrong with one corporation doing everything possible to convince the seller to ignore all competitors. But once a company has signed a contract to buy the land, it is improper to induce the seller to break the deal. The most commonly disputed issues in these cases concern elements one and three: Was there a contract between the plaintiff and another party? Did the defendant *improperly* induce a party to breach it?

Texaco v. Pennzoil. One of the largest verdicts in the history of American law came in a case of contract interference. Pennzoil made an unsolicited bid to buy 20 percent of Getty Oil at $112.50 per share, and the Getty board approved the agreement. Before the lawyers for both sides could complete the paperwork, Texaco appeared and offered Getty stockholders $128 per share for the entire company. Getty officers turned their attention to Texaco, but Pennzoil sued, claiming tortious interference. Texaco replied that it had not interfered because there was no binding contract.

The jury bought Pennzoil's argument, and they bought it big: $7.53 billion in actual damages, and $3 billion more in punitive damages. After appeals and frantic negotiations, the two parties reached a settlement. Texaco agreed to pay Pennzoil $3 billion as settlement for having wrongfully interfered with Pennzoil's agreement to buy Getty.

Tortious Interference with a Prospective Advantage

Interference with a prospective advantage is an awkward name for a tort that is simply a variation on interference with a contract. The difference is that, for this tort, there need be no contract; the plaintiff is claiming outside interference with an expected economic relationship. Obviously, the plaintiff must show more than just the hope of a profit. **A plaintiff who has a definite and reasonable expectation of obtaining an**

economic advantage may sue a corporation that maliciously interferes and prevents the relationship from developing.

Suppose that Jump Co. and Block Co. both hope to purchase a professional basketball team. The team's owners reject the offer from Block. They informally agree to a price with Jump but refuse to make a binding deal until Jump leases a stadium. Block owns the only stadium in town and refuses to lease to Jump, meaning that Jump cannot buy the team. Block has interfered with Jump's prospective advantage.[12]

Privacy and Publicity

We live in a world of dazzling technology, and it is easier than ever—and more profitable—to spy on someone. For example, the Web page http://www.thesmokinggun.com specializes in publishing revealing data about celebrities. Does the law protect us? What power do we have to limit the intrusion of others into our lives and to prohibit them from commercially exploiting information about us? Privacy and publicity law involves four main issues: intrusion, disclosure, false information, and commercial exploitation.

Intrusion

Intrusion into someone's private life is a tort if a reasonable person would find it offensive. Peeping through someone's windows or wiretapping his telephone are obvious examples of intrusion. In a famous case involving a "paparazzo" photographer and Jacqueline Kennedy Onassis, the court found that the photographer had invaded her privacy by making a career out of photographing her. He had bribed doormen to gain access to hotels and restaurants she visited, had jumped out of bushes to photograph her young children, and had driven power boats dangerously close to her. The court ordered him to stop.[13] Nine years later the paparazzo was found in contempt of court for again taking photographs too close to Ms. Onassis. He agreed to stop once and for all—in exchange for a suspended contempt sentence.

Commercial Exploitation

This right prohibits the use of someone's likeness or voice for commercial purposes. For example, it would be illegal to run a magazine ad showing actress Gwyneth Paltrow holding a can of soda without her permission. The ad would imply that she endorses the product. Someone's identity is her own, and it cannot be exploited unless she permits it.

NEGLIGENCE

Party time! A fraternity at the University of Arizona welcomed new members, and the alcohol flowed freely. Several hundred people danced and shrieked and drank, and no one checked for proof of age. A common occurrence—but one that ended tragically. A minor student drove away, intoxicated, and slammed into another car. The other driver, utterly innocent of wrongdoing, was gravely injured.

The drunken student was obviously liable, but his insurance did not cover the huge medical bills. The injured man also sued the fraternity. Should that organization

---

12 Or, to rephrase it, Jump, having courted the owners, must now jump into court and block Block's attempt to bounce Jump off its court. For a case with similar facts, see *Fishman v. Estate* of Wirtz, 807 F.2d 520 (7th Cir. 1986).

13 *Galella v. Onassis*, 487 F.2d 986, 1973 U.S. App. LEXIS 7901 (2d Cir. 1973).

be legally responsible? The question leads to other similar issues. Should a restaurant that serves an intoxicated adult be liable for resulting harm? If *you* give a party, should you be responsible for any damage caused by your guests?

These are moral questions—but very practical ones, as well. They are typical issues of negligence law. In this contentious area, courts continually face one question: *When someone is injured, how far should responsibility extend?*

We might call negligence the "unintentional" tort because it concerns harm that arises by accident. A person, or perhaps an organization, does some act, neither intending nor expecting to hurt anyone, yet someone is harmed. Should a court impose liability? The fraternity members who gave the party never wanted—or thought—that an innocent man would suffer terrible damage. But he did. Is it in society's interest to hold the fraternity responsible?

Before we can answer this question, we need some background knowledge. Things go wrong all the time, and society needs a means of analyzing negligence cases consistently and fairly.

To win a negligence case, the plaintiff must prove five elements:

- *Duty of Due Care.* The defendant had a duty of due care to this plaintiff.
- *Breach.* The defendant breached her duty.
- *Factual Cause.* The defendant's conduct actually caused the injury.
- *Foreseeable Harm.* It was foreseeable that conduct like the defendant's might cause this type of harm.
- *Injury.* The plaintiff has actually been hurt.

Duty of Due Care

The first issue may be the most difficult in all of tort law: Did the defendant have a duty of due care *to the injured person?* The test is generally "foreseeability." **If the defendant could have foreseen injury to a particular person, she has a duty to him.** If she could not have foreseen the harm, there is usually no duty. Let us apply this principle to the fraternity case.

HERNANDEZ V. ARIZONA BOARD OF REGENTS

177 Ariz. 244, 866 P.2d 1330, 1994 Ariz. LEXIS 6
Arizona Supreme Court, 1994

Facts: At the University of Arizona, the Epsilon Epsilon chapter of Delta Tau Delta fraternity gave a welcoming party for new members. The fraternity's officers knew that the majority of its members were under the legal drinking age, but permitted everyone to consume alcohol. John Rayner, who was under 21 years of age, left the party. He drove negligently and caused a collision with an auto driven by Ruben Hernandez. At the time of the accident, Rayner's blood alcohol level was 0.15, exceeding the legal limit. The crash left Hernandez blind, severely brain damaged, and quadriplegic.

Hernandez sued Rayner, who settled the case, based on the amount of his insurance coverage. The

victim also sued the fraternity, its officers and national organization, all fraternity members who contributed money to buy alcohol, the university, and others. The trial court granted summary judgment for all defendants, and the court of appeals affirmed. Hernandez appealed to the Arizona Supreme Court.

Issue: Did the fraternity and the other defendants have a duty of due care to Hernandez?

Excerpts from Judge Feldman's Decision: Before 1983, this court arguably recognized the common-law rule of non-liability for tavern owners and,

▼

presumably, for social hosts. Traditional authority held that when "an able-bodied man" caused harm because of his intoxication, the act from which liability arose was the consuming not the furnishing of alcohol. However, the common law also provides that:

> One who supplies [a thing] for the use of another whom the supplier knows or has reason to know to be likely because of his youth, inexperience, or otherwise to use it in a manner involving unreasonable risk of physical harm to himself and others is subject to liability for physical harm resulting to them.

We perceive little difference in principle between liability for giving a car to an intoxicated youth and liability for giving drinks to a youth with a car. A growing number of cases have recognized that one of the very hazards that makes it negligent to furnish liquor to a minor is the foreseeable prospect that the [youthful] patron will become drunk and injure himself or others. Accordingly, modern authority has increasingly recognized that one who furnishes liquor to a minor breaches a common law duty owed to innocent third parties who may be injured.

Furnishing alcohol to underaged drinkers violates numerous statutes. The conduct in question violates well-established common-law principles that recognize a duty to avoid furnishing dangerous items to those known to have diminished capacity to use them safely. We join the majority of other states and conclude that as to Plaintiffs and the public in general, Defendants had a duty of care to avoid furnishing alcohol to underage consumers.

Arizona courts, therefore, will entertain an action for damages against [one] who negligently furnishes alcohol to those under the legal drinking age when that act is a cause of injury to a third person. [Reversed and remanded.] ■

Ethics

Let us move the liability question away from the fraternity house. Should a *social* host (home owner) be liable for serving alcohol to a guest who then causes an accident? Many states do hold a social host liable for serving a *minor*. New Jersey is one of the few states to go further, and hold a home owner liable even for serving an *adult*. Finally, many states now have some type of **dram act,** making liquor stores, bars, and restaurants liable for serving drinks to intoxicated customers who later cause harm. Which of these rules do you find persuasive? ◆

Economics & the Law

Economists often analyze legal issues by looking at **externalities: costs or benefits of one person's activity that affect someone else.** For example, a factory that pollutes the air imposes *negative externalities,* because the sullied atmosphere makes life unpleasant and unhealthy for those who live nearby. By contrast, a corporation that landscapes its headquarters to include a duck pond with waterfall creates *positive externalities,* by making the neighborhood more attractive for local residents.

Bars and restaurants can generate negative externalities because innocent people may be injured or killed by drivers who become intoxicated in those establishments. **Dram shop laws** are a response. These acts make liquor stores, bars, and restaurants liable for serving drinks to intoxicated customers who later cause harm. (Historically, a dram was a small serving of alcohol.) These statutes force a financial dilemma on such firms. The more a tavern or café encourages its customers to drink, the greater its revenue—but also the larger its risk of a liability lawsuit. The goal of dram shop laws is to force businesses serving liquor to consider these externalities. In states without a dram shop statute, the threat of a lawsuit is removed and the establishment has an incentive to maximize alcohol consumption, despite the external costs.

Do dram shop acts work? Yes, answer the authors of one economic study. In states with such statutes, bars monitor underage drinking more aggressively, refuse drinks earlier to an intoxicated customer, check the references of their own employees more carefully, and prohibit their workers from drinking on the job. These economists conclude that dram shop laws are a promising way to reduce drunk driving accidents.[14] ◆

---

14 Sloan, Liang, Stout, and Whetten-Goldstein, "Liability, Risk Perceptions, and Precautions at Bars," *Journal of Law and Economics,* 2000, vol. 43, p. 473.

Crime and Tort: Landowner's Liability

Regrettably, a major concern of tort law today is how to respond to injury caused by criminals. If a criminal assaults and robs a pedestrian in a shopping mall, that act is a crime and may be prosecuted by the state. But prosecution leaves the victim uncompensated. The assault is also an intentional tort, and the victim could file a civil lawsuit against the criminal. But most violent criminals have no assets. Given this economic frustration and the flexibility of the common law, it is inevitable that victims of violence look elsewhere for compensation, as they did in the following tragic case.

WIENER V. SOUTHCOAST CHILDCARE CENTERS, INC.

32 Ca.4th 1138, 88 P.3d. 517, 12 Cal. Rptr.3d. 615
Supreme Court of California, 2004

Facts: Southcoast operated a child-care facility on a busy street corner property that it leased from First Baptist Church. A four-foot-high chain link fence enclosed the playground located adjacent to the sidewalk and street. Steven Abrams intentionally drove his large Cadillac through the fence, onto the playground and into a group of children, causing horrific carnage. He killed two children and injured many others. Abrams was convicted of first-degree murder.

Parents of killed and injured youngsters sued Southcoast and the church, alleging that the defendants knew the fence was inadequate to protect the children. The trial judge granted summary judgment for the defendants, ruling that Southcoast and the others owed no duty to prevent such harm. The appellate court reversed, and Southcoast appealed to the state's highest panel.

Issue: Did Southcoast have a duty to the plaintiffs to prevent this kind of harm?

Excerpts from Justice Chin's Decision: [Plaintiffs alleged] that defendants were aware the chain link fence in front of the property provided inadequate protection, and that Shirley Hawkinson, owner of Southcoast, had previously requested the Church provide funds to erect a higher fence. In the past, before Southcoast operated the child care center, a few non-injury traffic accidents happened near the property next to the sidewalk.

One freak accident [had] occurred, of which Hawkinson testified she had no knowledge. According to a neighbor, [a mail truck driver had fallen out of his truck]. The truck took off and bounced over the curb and went through the fence before coming to a stop at a tree inside the yard. No one was injured in the incident. Neighbors testified that other traffic incidents occurred near the premises involving vehicles that hit the curb.

Plaintiffs argued that it did not matter whether the driver of the vehicle that killed the children acted negligently or with criminal intent, because the risk of harm from an unsafe fence was the same, and that defendants owed a duty to make the fence stronger.

[Our cases] analyze third party criminal acts differently from ordinary negligence, and require us to apply a heightened sense of foreseeability before we can hold a defendant liable for the criminal acts of third parties. There are two reasons for this: first, it is difficult if not impossible in today's society to predict when a criminal might strike. Also, if a criminal decides on a particular goal or victim, it is extremely difficult to remove his every means for achieving that goal. A criminal can commit a crime anywhere. The burden of requiring a landlord to protect against crime everywhere has been considered too great in comparison with the foreseeability of crime occurring at a particular location to justify imposing an omnibus duty on landowners to control crime.

We conclude defendants owed no duty to plaintiffs because Abrams's brutal criminal act was unforeseeable. No evidence indicated defendants' child care facility had ever been the target of violence in the past and no hint existed that either defendants or any other similar business establishment had ever been the target of any criminal acts. Indeed, here, the foreseeability of a perpetrator's committing premeditated murder against the children was impossible to anticipate, and the particular criminal conduct so outrageous and bizarre, that it could not have been anticipated under any circumstances.

[Reversed. Summary judgment for the defendants.] ∎

Devil's
Advocate

This decision is bad public policy. The court is giving the day care center (and everyone who cares for children) one free pass. Do nothing to make the premises safer because, even if you foresee the harm, you cannot be sued. Then, after the first tragedy, get busy and improve the place. We ought to use the law to protect our children. ◆

Breach of Duty

The second element of a plaintiff's negligence case is **breach of duty.** Courts apply the reasonable person standard: **a defendant breaches his duty of due care by failing to behave the way a reasonable person would under similar circumstances.** Reasonable "person" means someone of the defendant's occupation. A taxi driver must drive as a reasonable taxi driver would. A heart surgeon must perform bypass surgery with the care of a trained specialist in that field.

Two medical cases illustrate the reasonable person standard. A doctor prescribes a powerful drug without asking his 21-year-old patient about other medicines she is currently taking. The patient suffers a serious drug reaction from the combined medications. The physician is liable for the harm. A reasonable doctor always checks current medicines before prescribing new ones.

On the other hand, assume that an 84-year-old patient dies on the operating table in an emergency room. While the surgeon was repairing heart damage, the man had a fatal stroke. If the physician followed normal medical procedures and acted with reasonable speed, he is not liable. A doctor must do a reasonable professional job but cannot guarantee a happy outcome.

Crime and Tort: Negligent Hiring

In a recent one-year period, more than 1,000 homicides and two million attacks occurred in the workplace. Companies must beware because they can be liable for hiring or retaining violent employees. A mailroom clerk with a previous rape and robbery conviction followed a secretary home after work and fatally assaulted her. Even though the murder took place off the company premises, the court held that the defendant would be liable if it knew or should have known of the mail clerk's criminal history.[15] In other cases, companies have been found liable for failing to check an applicant's driving record, to contact personal references, and to search criminal records.

at **R!SK**

What can an employer do to diminish the likelihood of workplace violence? Many things.

- Evaluate the workplace for unsafe physical features. Install adequate lighting in parking lots and common areas, hire security guards if necessary, and use closed-circuit television and identification cards.

- Ensure that the company uses thorough prehire screening, contacts all former employers, and checks all references and criminal records. Nursing homes have paid huge sums for negligently hiring convicted assailants who later attack elderly residents.

- Respond quickly to dangerous behavior. In many cases of workplace violence, the perpetrator had demonstrated repeated bizarre, threatening, or obsessive behavior on the job, but his supervisors had not taken it seriously. ◆

---

[15] *Gaines v. Monsanto*, 655 S.W.2d 568, 1983 Mo. LEXIS 3439 (Mo. Ct. App. 1983).

Negligence Per Se

In certain areas of life, courts are not free to decide what a "reasonable" person would have done, because the state legislature has made the decision for them. **When a legislature sets a minimum standard of care for a particular activity, in order to protect a certain group of people, and a violation of the statute injures a member of that group, the defendant has committed negligence per se.** A plaintiff who can show negligence per se need not prove breach of duty.

In Minnesota, the state legislature became alarmed about children sniffing glue and passed a statute prohibiting the sale to a minor of any glue containing toluene. About one month later, 14-year-old Steven Zerby purchased glue containing toluene from a store in his hometown. Steven inhaled the glue and died from injury to his central nervous system. A reasonable person might have made the same error, but that is irrelevant: the clerk violated the statute, and the store was liable.[16]

Factual Cause and Foreseeable Harm

A plaintiff must also show that the defendant's breach of duty caused the plaintiff's harm. Courts look at two issues to settle causation: Was the defendant's behavior the *factual cause* of the harm? Was *this type of harm foreseeable?*[17]

Factual Cause

Nothing mysterious here. **If the defendant's breach physically led to the ultimate harm, it is the factual cause.** Suppose that Dom's Brake Shop tells Customer his brakes are now working fine, even though Dom knows that is false. Customer drives out of the shop, cannot stop at a red light, and hits Bicyclist crossing at the intersection. Dom is liable to Bicyclist. Dom's unreasonable behavior was the factual cause of the harm. Think of it as a row of dominoes. The first domino (Dom's behavior) knocked over the next one (failing brakes), which toppled the last one (the cyclist's injury).

Suppose, alternatively, that just as Customer is exiting the repair shop, Bicyclist hits a pothole and tumbles off her cycle, avoiding Customer's auto. Bicyclist's injuries stem from her fall, not from the auto. Customer's brakes still fail, and Dom has breached his duty to Customer, but Dom is not liable to Bicyclist. She would have been hurt anyway. This is a row of dominoes that veers off to the side, leaving the last domino (cyclist's injury) untouched. No factual causation.

Foreseeable Type of Harm

For the defendant to be liable, the *type of harm* must have been reasonably foreseeable. In the case just discussed, Dom could easily foresee that bad brakes would cause an automobile accident. He need not have foreseen exactly what happened. He did not know there would be a cyclist nearby. What he could foresee was this general type of harm involving defective brakes.

By contrast, assume the collision of car and bicycle produces a loud crash. Two blocks away, a pet pig, asleep on the window ledge of a twelfth-story apartment, is startled by the noise, awakens with a start, and plunges to the sidewalk, killing a veterinarian who was making a house call. If the vet's family sues Dom, should it win? Dom's negligence was the factual cause: it led to the collision, which startled the pig, which

---

[16] *Zerby v. Warren*, 297 Minn. 134, 210 N.W.2d 58 (1973).

[17] Courts often refer to these two elements, grouped together, as *proximate cause* or *legal cause*. But, as many judges acknowledge, those terms have created confusion, so we use *factual cause* and *foreseeable type of harm*, the issues on which most decisions ultimately focus.

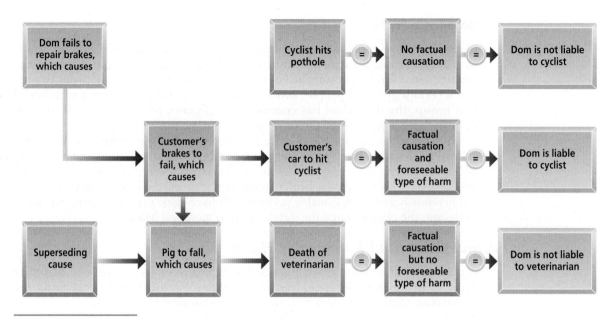

Exhibit 6.1

flattened the vet. Most courts would rule, though, that Dom is not liable. The type of harm is too bizarre. Dom could not reasonably foresee such an extraordinary chain of events, and it would be unfair to make him pay for it. (See Exhibit 6.1.)

Another way of stating that Dom is not liable to the vet's family is by calling the falling pig a *superseding cause*. When one of the "dominoes" in the row is entirely unforeseeable, courts will consider it a superseding cause, letting the defendant off the hook. Negligence cases often revolve around whether the chain of events leading from the defendant's conduct to the injury was broken by a superseding cause.

Public Policy

Enos asked Hebert to water his flowers while he was on vacation. For three days, the agreeable neighbor did this without incident, but on the fourth day, when Hebert touched the outside faucet, he received a violent electric shock that shot him through the air, melted his sneakers and glasses, set his clothes on fire, and left him seriously injured. Hebert sued, claiming that Enos had caused the damage when he negligently repaired a second-floor toilet. Water from the steady leak had flooded through the walls, soaking wires and eventually causing the faucet to become electrified. As a matter of public policy, who should win?

The defendant, Enos, prevailed. The court declared, "Although we can envision a variety of foreseeable injuries arising out of a defective toilet, the electric shock to a neighbor when he touches a faucet outside the house is well beyond the range of reasonable apprehension and therefore not foreseeable. Hebert's severe and unfortunate injuries were the consequence of the type of unforeseeable accident for which we do not hold the defendant responsible in tort."[18] From society's perspective, was this a wise ruling? ◆

Res Ipsa Loquitur

Normally, a plaintiff must prove factual cause and foreseeable type of harm in order to establish negligence. But in a few cases, a court may *infer* that the defendant caused the harm, under the doctrine of ***res ipsa loquitur*** ("the thing speaks for itself"). Suppose a pedestrian is walking along a sidewalk when an air-conditioning unit falls

---

[18] *Hebert v. Enos*, 60 Mass. App. Ct. 817, 806 N.E.2d 452 (Mass. App., 2004).

on his head from a third-story window. The defendant, who owns the third-story apartment, denies any wrongdoing, and it may be difficult or impossible for the plaintiff to prove why the air conditioner fell. In such cases, many courts will apply *res ipsa loquitur* and declare that the **facts imply that the defendant's negligence caused the accident.** If a court uses this doctrine, then the defendant must come forward with evidence establishing that it did not cause the harm.

Because *res ipsa loquitur* dramatically shifts the burden of proof from plaintiff to defendant, it applies only when (1) the defendant had exclusive control of the thing that caused the harm, (2) the harm normally would not have occurred without negligence, and (3) the plaintiff had no role in causing the harm. In the air conditioner example, most states would apply the doctrine and force the defendant to prove she did nothing wrong.

Injury

Finally, a plaintiff must prove that he has been injured. In some cases, injury is obvious. For example, Ruben Hernandez, struck by the intoxicated fraternity member, obviously suffered grievous harm. In other cases, though, injury is unclear. **The plaintiff must persuade the court that he has suffered a harm that is genuine, not speculative.**

Among the most vexing are suits involving future harm. Exposure to toxins or trauma may lead to serious medical problems down the road—or it may not. A woman's knee is damaged in an auto accident, causing severe pain for two years. She is clearly entitled to compensation for her suffering. After two years, all of her troubles may cease. Yet there is a chance that in 15 years the trauma will lead to painful arthritis. A court must decide today the full extent of present and *future* damages.

The following lawsuit concerns a couple's fear of developing AIDS. This worry can be overwhelming. A court must still decide, however, whether the cause of the unhappiness is genuine injury or speculation.

COLE V. QUIRK

2001 Mass.App.Div. 139, 2001 WL 705730
Massachusetts Appellate Division, 2001

Facts: The Coles bought a used car from a dealership owned by Quirk. The dealer agreed to thoroughly clean the interior before delivery. Dissatisfied with the car's appearance, Timothy Cole began to clean the interior. As he reached into the pocket behind the driver's seat, a pair of surgical tweezers cut his finger, drawing blood. Cole feverishly washed his hands and phoned his doctor, who told him he was at risk of contracting hepatitis B and human immunodeficiency virus (HIV). The Coles found medical prescriptions in the car and learned that its former owner was a doctor. Terrified that Timothy might have contracted hepatitis B or HIV, the Coles abstained from sex for more than a year and then practiced safe sex. Mr. Cole suffered from diarrhea, nausea, and vomiting based on this fear of HIV. He never tested positive for the disease. The tweezers were never tested.

The Coles sued Quirk. At the close of the Coles' case, the trial judge directed a verdict for Quirk. The Coles appealed.

Issue: Have the Coles demonstrated an injury?

Excerpts from Judge Winslow's Decision: Claims for HIV/AIDS-phobia have been described as an "uneasy class of cases in which bad news is worse than no news at all." Courts in other states have expressed two competing views regarding the proof of causation necessary to establish a claim for HIV/AIDS-phobia: (1) Actual Exposure: in order to maintain a cause of action for damages due to the fear of contracting HIV/AIDS, the plaintiff, who has not tested seropositive, must offer proof of actual exposure, meaning

▼

proof of both a scientifically accepted method of transmission of the virus *and* that the source of the allegedly transmitted blood or fluid was in fact HIV-positive; and (2) Reasonable Fear: the plaintiff, not tested seropositive, must prove a specific incident of potential exposure sufficient to create a reasonable fear of having contracted the AIDS virus, even in the absence of a proven source and channel of exposure.

We adopt the objective Actual Exposure standard of causation in reviewing the directed verdict in this action. Today, although much more is known about how HIV in fact is spread than was known at the beginning of the epidemic, many lay persons continue to believe that HIV can be transmitted through food, silverware, handshakes, and toilet seats. Should a person be compensated for fears which, although entirely unrealistic from a scientific perspective, in fact affect the person very significantly? A person who truly believes HIV may be communicated through a handshake may suffer significant physical and emotional trauma as a result of shaking hands with a person whom he subsequently learns was HIV-infected.

We agree that the widespread ignorance about the nature of this disease and the accompanying prejudices against persons suffering from it or, as here, merely alleged to suffer from it, pose dangers to the accuracy and fairness of the legal process in many ways. To prove their claim for HIV/AIDS-phobia, the Coles were required to prove both a scientifically accepted method of transmission of the virus *and* that the source of the allegedly transmitted blood or fluid was in fact HIV-positive. They did not meet this burden at trial. [Affirmed.] ■

Damages

The plaintiff's damages in a negligence case are generally compensatory damages. In unusual cases, a court may award punitive damages—that is, money intended not to compensate the plaintiff but to punish the defendant. We discussed both forms of damages earlier in this chapter.

Defenses

Contributory and Comparative Negligence

Joe is a mental patient in a hospital. The hospital knows he is dangerous to himself and others, but it permits him to wander around unattended. Joe leaves the hospital and steals a gun. Shawn drives by Joe, and Joe waves the gun at him. Shawn notices a police officer a block away. But instead of informing the cop, Shawn leans out his window and shouts, "Hey, knucklehead, what are you doing pointing guns at people?" Joe shoots and kills Shawn.

Shawn's widow sues the hospital for negligently permitting Joe to leave. But the hospital, in defense, claims that Shawn's foolishness got him killed. Who wins? It depends on whether the state in which the suit is heard uses a legal theory called **contributory negligence.** This used to be the law throughout the nation, but it remains in effect in only a few states. It means that, even assuming the defendant is negligent, **if the plaintiff is even** *slightly* **negligent himself, he recovers nothing.** So if Shawn's homicide occurs in a contributory negligence state, the hospital is not liable regardless of how negligent it was.

Critics attacked the rule as unreasonable. A plaintiff who was 1 percent negligent could not recover from a defendant who was 99 percent negligent. So most states threw out the contributory negligence rule, replacing it with comparative negligence. **In a comparative negligence state, a plaintiff may generally recover even if she is partially negligent.** A jury will be asked to assess the relative negligence of plaintiff and defendant.

Suppose we are in a comparative negligence state, and the jury believes the hospital was 80 percent responsible for Shawn's death, and Shawn himself was 20 percent responsible. It might conclude that the total damages for Shawn's widow are $2 million, based on Shawn's pain in dying and the widow's loss of his income. If so, the hospital would owe $1.6 million, or 80 percent of the damages. (See Exhibit 6.2.)

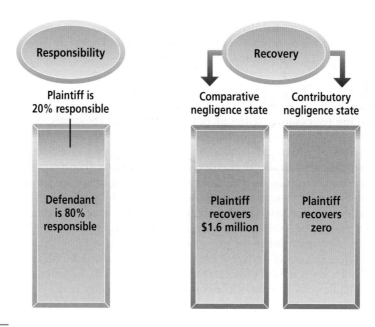

Exhibit 6.2
Defendant's negligence injures plaintiff, who suffers $2 million in damages.

Today, most states have adopted some form of comparative negligence. Critics of comparative negligence claim that it rewards a plaintiff for being careless. Suppose, they say, a driver speeds to beat an approaching train, and the railroad's mechanical arm fails to operate. Why should we reward the driver for his foolishness? In response to this complaint, some comparative negligence states do not permit a plaintiff to recover anything if he was more than 50 percent responsible for his injury.

Assumption of the Risk

Quick, duck! That was a close call—the baseball nearly knocked your ear off. If it had, the team would owe you . . . nothing. Here at the ballpark, there is always a slight chance of injury, and you are expected to realize it. Wherever there is an obvious hazard, a special rule applies. **Assumption of the risk: A person who voluntarily enters a situation that has an obvious danger cannot complain if she is injured.** If you are not willing to tolerate the risk of being hurt by a batted ball, stay home and watch the game on television. And while you are here—pay attention, will you?

Suppose that Good Guys, a restaurant, holds an ice-fishing contest on a frozen lake, to raise money for accident victims. Margie grabs a can full of worms and strolls to the middle of the lake to try her luck but slips on the ice and suffers a concussion. When she returns to consciousness, Margie should not bother filing suit—she assumed the risk.

STRICT LIABILITY

Some activities are so naturally dangerous that the law places an especially high burden on anyone who engages in them. A corporation that produces toxic waste can foresee dire consequences from its business that a stationery store cannot. This higher burden is **strict liability.** There are two main areas of business that incur strict liability: *ultrahazardous activity* and *defective products*. Defective products are discussed in Chapter 12, on products liability.

Ultrahazardous Activity

Ultrahazardous activities include using harmful chemicals, operating explosives, keeping wild animals, bringing dangerous substances onto property, and a few similar activities where the danger to the general public is especially great. **A defendant engaging in an ultrahazardous activity is virtually always liable for any harm that results.** Plaintiffs do not have to prove duty or breach or foreseeable harm. Recall the deliberately bizarre case we posed earlier of the pig falling from a window ledge and killing a veterinarian. Dom, the mechanic whose negligence caused the car crash, could not be liable for the veterinarian's death because the plunging pig was a superseding cause. But if the pig was jolted off the window ledge by Sam's Blasting Co., which was doing perfectly lawful blasting for a new building down the street, Sam is liable. Even if Sam took extraordinary care, it will do him no good at trial. The "reasonable person" rule is irrelevant in a strict liability case.

Chapter Conclusion

This chapter has been a potpourri of sin, a bubbling cauldron of conduct best avoided. Although tortious acts and their consequences are diverse, two generalities apply. First, the boundaries of torts are imprecise, the outcome of a particular case depending to a considerable extent upon the factfinder who analyzes it. Second, the thoughtful executive and the careful citizen, aware of the shifting standards and potentially vast liability, will strive to ensure that his or her conduct never provides that factfinder an opportunity to give judgment.

Chapter Review

1. A tort is a violation of a duty imposed by the civil law.

2. Defamation involves a false statement, likely to harm another's reputation, which is uttered to a third person and causes an injury. Opinion and privilege are valid defenses. Public personalities can win a defamation suit only by proving actual malice.

3. False imprisonment is the intentional restraint of another person without reasonable cause and without consent.

4. The intentional infliction of emotional distress involves extreme and outrageous conduct that causes serious emotional harm.

5. Battery is an intentional touching of another person in a way that is offensive. Assault involves an act that makes the plaintiff fear an imminent battery.

6. Compensatory damages are the normal remedy in a tort case. In unusual cases, the court may award punitive damages to punish the defendant.

7. Tortious interference with business relations involves the defendant harming an existing contract or a prospective relationship that has a definite expectation of success.

8. The related torts of privacy and publicity involve unreasonable intrusion into someone's private life or unfair commercial exploitation by using someone's name, likeness, or voice without permission.

9. The five elements of negligence are duty of due care, breach, factual causation, foreseeable type of harm, and injury.

10. If the defendant could foresee that misconduct would injure a particular person, he probably has a duty to her.

11. A defendant breaches his duty of due care by failing to behave the way a reasonable person would under similar conditions.

12. Employers may be liable for negligent hiring.

13. If a legislature sets a minimum standard of care for a particular activity in order to protect a certain group of people, and a violation of the statute injures a member of that group, the defendant has committed negligence per se.

14. If an event physically leads to the ultimate harm, it is the factual cause.

15. For the defendant to be liable, th[...] must have been reasonably fores[...]

16. The plaintiff must persuade the court that he has suffered a harm that is genuine, not speculative.

17. In a contributory negligence state, a plaintiff who is even slightly responsible for his own injury recovers nothing; in a comparative negligence state, the jury may apportion liability between plaintiff and defendant.

18. A defendant is strictly liable for harm caused by an ultrahazardous activity or a defective product. Strict liability means that if the defendant's conduct led to the harm, the defendant is liable, even if she exercised extraordinary care.

Practice Test

1. Benzaquin had a radio talk show in Boston. On the program, he complained about an incident earlier in the day, in which state trooper Fleming had stopped his car, apparently for lack of a proper license plate and safety sticker. Even though Benzaquin explained that the license plate had been stolen and the sticker had fallen onto the dashboard, Fleming refused to let him drive the car away, and Benzaquin and his daughter and two young grandsons had to find other transportation. On the show, Benzaquin angrily recounted the incident, then made the following statements about Fleming and troopers generally: "arrogants wearing troopers' uniforms like tights"; "little monkey, you wind him up and he does his thing"; "we're not paying them to be dictators and Nazis"; "this man is an absolute barbarian, a lunkhead, a meathead." Fleming sued Benzaquin for defamation. Comment.

2. Caldwell, carrying a large purse, was shopping in a K-Mart store. A security guard observed her look at various small items such as stain, hinges, and antenna wire. On occasion she bent down out of sight of the guard. The guard thought he saw Caldwell put something in her purse. Caldwell removed her glasses from her purse and returned them a few times. After she left, the guard approached her in the parking lot and said that he believed she had store merchandise in her purse but was unable to say what he thought was put there. Caldwell opened the purse, and the guard testified he saw no K-Mart merchandise in it. The guard then told Caldwell to return to the store with him. They walked around the store for approximately 15 minutes, while the guard said six or seven times that he saw her put something in her purse. Caldwell left the store after another store employee indicated she could go. Caldwell sued. What kind of suit did she file, and what should the outcome be?

3. Fifteen-year-old Terri Stubblefield was riding in the back seat of a Ford Mustang II when the car was hit from behind. The Mustang was engulfed in a ball of fire, and Terri was severely burned. She died. Terri's family sued Ford, alleging that the car was badly designed—and that Ford knew it. At trial, Terri's family introduced evidence that Ford knew the fuel tank was dangerous and that it could have taken measures to make the tank safe. There was evidence that Ford consciously decided not to remedy the fuel tanks in order to save money. The family sought two different kinds of damages from Ford. What were they?

4. **ETHICS** In the *Stubblefield* case in Question 3, the jury awarded $8 million in punitive damages to the family. Ford appealed. Should the punitive damages be affirmed? What are the obligations of a corporation when it knows one of its products may be dangerous? Is an automobile company ethically obligated to make a *totally safe* car? Should we require a manufacturer to improve the safety of its cars if doing so will make them too expensive for many drivers? What would you do if you were a mid-level executive and saw evidence that your company was endangering the lives of consumers to save money? What would you do if you were on a *jury* and saw such evidence?

5. Caudle worked at Betts Lincoln-Mercury dealer. During an office party, many of the employees, including President Betts, were playing with an electric auto condenser, which gave a slight electric shock when touched. Some employees played catch with the condenser. Betts shocked Caudle on the back of his neck and then chased him around, holding the condenser. The shock later caused Caudle to suffer headaches, to pass out, and eventually to require surgery on a nerve in his neck. Even after surgery, Caudle had a slight numbness on one side of his head. He sued Betts for battery. Betts defended by saying that it was all horseplay and that he had intended no injury. Please rule.

6. **YOU BE THE JUDGE** WRITING PROBLEM Johnny Carson was for many years the star of a well-known television program, *The Tonight Show*. For about 20 years, he was introduced nightly on the show with the phrase, "Here's Johnny!" A large segment of the television watching public associated the phrase with Carson. A Michigan corporation was in the business of renting and selling portable toilets. The company chose the name "Here's Johnny Portable Toilets," and coupled the company name with the marketing phrase, "The World's Foremost Commodian." Carson sued, claiming that the company's name and slogan violated his right to commercial exploitation. Who should win? **Argument for Carson:** The toilet company is deliberately taking advantage of Johnny Carson's good name. He worked hard for decades to build a brilliant career and earn a reputation as a creative, funny, likable performer. No company has the right to use his name, his picture, or anything else closely identified with him, such as the phrase "Here's Johnny." The pun is personally offensive and commercially unfair. **Argument for Here's Johnny Portable Toilets:** Johnny Carson doesn't own his first name. It is available for anyone to use for any purpose. Further, the popular term

john, meaning toilet, has been around much longer than Carson or even television. We are entitled to make any use of it we want. Our corporate name is amusing to customers who have never heard of Carson, and we are entitled to profit from our brand recognition.

7. Jason Jacque was riding as a passenger in a car driven by his sister, who was drunk and driving 19 mph over the speed limit. She failed to negotiate a curve, skidded off the road, and collided with a wooden utility pole erected by the Public Service Company of Colorado (PSC). Jacque suffered severe brain injury. He sued PSC for negligently installing the pole too close to the highway at a dangerous curve where an accident was likely to happen. The trial court gave summary judgment for PSC, ruling that PSC owed no duty to Jacque. He appealed. Please rule.

8. Ryder leased a truck to Florida Food Service; Powers, an employee, drove it to make deliveries. He noticed that the door strap used to close the rear door was frayed, and he asked Ryder to fix it. Ryder failed to do so in spite of numerous requests. The strap broke, and Powers replaced it with a nylon rope. Later, when Powers was attempting to close the rear door, the nylon rope broke and he fell, sustaining severe injuries to his neck and back. He sued Ryder. The trial court found that Powers's attachment of the replacement rope was a superseding cause, relieving Ryder of any liability, and granted summary judgment for Ryder. Powers appealed. How should the appellate court rule?

9. A new truck, manufactured by General Motors Corp. (GMC), stalled in rush hour traffic on a busy interstate highway because of a defective alternator, which caused a complete failure of the truck's electrical system. The driver stood nearby and waved traffic around his stalled truck. A panel truck approached the GMC truck, and immediately behind the panel truck, Davis was driving a Volkswagen fastback. Because of the panel truck, Davis was unable to see the stalled GMC truck. The panel truck swerved out of the way of the GMC truck, and Davis drove straight into it. The accident killed him. Davis's widow sued GMC. GMC moved for summary judgment, alleging (1) no duty to Davis, (2) no factual causation, and (3) no foreseeable harm. Comment.

10. A prison inmate bit a hospital employee. The employee sued the state for negligence and lack

of supervision, claiming a fear of AIDS. The plaintiff had tested negative for HIV three times, and there was no proof that the inmate was HIV positive. Comment on the probable outcome.

11. ***ETHICS*** Swimming pools in private homes often have diving boards, but those in public parks, hotels, and clubs rarely do. Why is that? Is it good or bad?

12. There is a collision between cars driven by Candy and Zeke, and both drivers are partly at fault. The evidence is that Candy is about 25 percent responsible, for failing to stop quickly enough, and Zeke about 75 percent responsible, for making a dangerous turn. Candy is most likely to win:

    a. A lawsuit for battery;

    b. A lawsuit for negligence, in a comparative negligence state;

    c. A lawsuit for negligence, in a contributory negligence state;

    d. A lawsuit for strict liability; or

    e. A lawsuit for assault.

13. Van Houten owned a cat and allowed it to roam freely outside. In the three years he had owned it, it had never bitten anyone. The cat entered Pritchard's garage. Pritchard attempted to move it outside his garage, and the cat bit him. As a direct result of the bite, Pritchard underwent four surgeries, was fitted with a plastic finger joint, and spent more than $39,000 in medical bills. He sued Van Houten, claiming both strict liability and ordinary negligence. Evaluate his claims.

14. ***ROLE REVERSAL*** Write a multiple-choice question about defamation in which one and only one element is missing from the plaintiff's case. Choose a set of answers that forces the student to isolate the missing element.

Internet Research Problem

Take a look at http://response.restoration.noaa.gov/. What are some of the long-term problems associated with oil spills? View some of the photos in the "gallery." Are punitive damages for oil spills appropriate or excessive?

You can find further practice problems at academic.cengage.com/blaw/beatty.

7 Crime

© IMAGE 100/GETTY IMAGES

Crime can take us by surprise. Stacey tucks her nine-year-old daughter, Beth, into bed. Promising her husband, Mark, that she will be home by 11:00 PM, she jumps into her car and heads back to Be Patient, Inc. She puts a compact disc in the player of her $85,000 sedan and tries to relax. Be Patient is a health care organization that owns five geriatric hospitals. Most of its patients use Medicare, and Stacey supervises all billing to their largest client, the federal government.

She parks in a well-lighted spot on the street and walks to her building, failing to notice two men, collars turned up, watching from a parked truck. Once in her office she goes straight to her computer and works on billing issues. Tonight's work goes more quickly than she expected, thanks to new software she helped develop. At 10:30 she emerges from the building with a quick step and a light heart, walks to her car—and finds it missing.

A major crime has occurred during the 90 minutes Stacey was at her desk, but she will never report it to the police. It is a crime that costs Americans countless dollars each year, yet Stacey will not even mention it to friends or family. Stacey is the criminal. ■

When we think of crime, we imagine the drug dealers and bank robbers endlessly portrayed on television. We do not picture corporate executives sitting at polished desks. "Street crimes" are indeed serious threats to our security and happiness. They deservedly receive the attention of the public and the law. (For a look at the FBI's 10 most wanted list, see http://www.fbi.gov.) But when measured only in dollars, street crime takes second place to white-collar crime, which costs society *tens of billions* of dollars annually.

The hypothetical about Stacey is based on many real cases and is used to illustrate that crime does not always dress the way we expect. Her car was never stolen; it was simply towed. Two parking bureau employees, watching from their truck, saw Stacey park illegally and did their job. It is Stacey who committed a crime—Medicare fraud. Stacey has learned the simple but useful lesson that company profits rise when she charges the government for work Be Patient has never done. For months she billed the government for imaginary patients. Then she hired a computer hacker to worm into the Medicare computer system and plant a "Trojan horse," a program that seemed useful to Medicare employees but actually contained a series of codes opening the computer to Stacey. Stacey simply entered the Medicare system and altered the calculations for payments owed to Be Patient. Every month, the government paid Be Patient about $10 million for imaginary work. Stacey's scheme was quick and profitable—and a distressingly common crime.

What do we do about cases like these? These questions involve multifarious fact issues and important philosophical values. In this chapter, we look first at the big picture of criminal law and then focus on that part of it that most affects business—white-collar crime. We examine four major issues:

- *Crime, Society, and Law.* What makes conduct criminal? We enumerate the basic elements that the prosecution must establish to prove that a crime has been committed, and also some of the most common defenses.

- *Crimes That Harm Business.* We look at specific crimes, such as fraud and embezzlement, that cost businesses enormous sums every year.

- *Crimes Committed by Business.* We analyze "white-collar crimes," which are generally committed by businesspeople and may be directed at consumers, other businesses, or the government.

- *Criminal Process and Constitutional Protections.* We examine how the Bill of Rights protects citizens subjected to search, interrogation, and trial. And we pay a final visit to Stacey.

CRIME, SOCIETY, AND LAW

Civil Law/Criminal Law

Most of this book concerns the civil law—the rights and liabilities that exist between private parties. As we have seen, if one person claims that another has caused her a civil injury, she must file a lawsuit and convince a court of her damages.

Criminal law is different. Conduct is **criminal** when society outlaws it. When a state legislature or Congress concludes that certain behavior threatens the population generally, it passes a statute forbidding that behavior—in other words, declaring it criminal. Medicare fraud, which Stacey committed, is a crime because Congress has outlawed it. Money laundering is a crime because Congress concluded it was a fundamental part of the drug trade and prohibited it.

Prosecution

Suppose the police arrest Roger and accuse him of breaking into a video store and stealing 25 video cameras, videos, and other equipment. The owner of the video store is the one harmed, but **it is the government that prosecutes crimes.** The local prosecutor will decide whether or not to charge Roger and bring him to trial.

Jury Right

The facts of the case will be decided by a judge or jury. A criminal defendant has a right to a trial by jury for any charge that could result in a sentence of six months or longer. The defendant may demand a jury trial or may waive that right, in which case the judge will be the factfinder.

Punishment

In a civil lawsuit, the plaintiff seeks a verdict that the defendant is liable for harm caused to her. But in a criminal case, the government asks the court to find the defendant **guilty** of the crime. The government wants the court to **punish** the defendant. If the judge or jury finds the defendant guilty, the court will punish him with a fine and/or a prison sentence. The fine is paid to the government, not to the injured person (although the court will sometimes order **restitution,** meaning that the defendant must reimburse the victim for harm suffered). It is almost always the judge who imposes the sentence. If the jury is not persuaded of the defendant's guilt, it will **acquit** him—that is, find him not guilty.

Felony/Misdemeanor

A **felony** is a serious crime, for which a defendant can be sentenced to one year or more in prison. Murder, robbery, rape, drug dealing, money laundering, wire fraud, and embezzlement are felonies. A **misdemeanor** is a less serious crime, often punishable by a year or less in a county jail. Public drunkenness, driving without a license, and simple possession of one marijuana cigarette are considered misdemeanors in most states.

Punishment

Why punish a defendant? Sometimes the answer is obvious. If a defendant has committed armed robbery, we want that person locked up. Other cases are not so apparent.

You are the judge in charge of sentencing Jason. He is a 61-year-old minister who has devoted 40 years to serving his community, leading his church, and helping to rehabilitate schools. Fifteen years ago he founded a children's hospital and has raised enormous sums to maintain it. He has labored with local government to rebuild abandoned housing and has established a center for battered women. Jason suffers from a terminal illness and will die in three to four years. But the jury has just found that in his zeal to get housing built, Jason took kickbacks from construction firms run by gangsters. The construction companies padded their bills, some of which were paid with state and city money. They kicked back a small amount of this illegal profit to Jason, who gave the money to his charities. Jason thought of himself as Robin Hood, but the law regards him as a felon. You can fine Jason and/or sentence him to prison for a maximum of five years.

A flood of letters urges you to allow Jason to continue raising money and helping others. You need to understand the rationale of punishment. Over the past several centuries, philosophers in many countries—and judges in this country—have proposed various reasons for punishing the guilty.

Restraint

A violent criminal who appears likely to commit more crimes must be physically restrained. Here there is no pretense of prison being anything but a cage to protect the rest of society. (An online group that sees little good and much evil in our system of incarceration gives examples of perceived abuses at **http://www.prisonactivist.org.**) In Jason's case, there is clearly no reason to restrain him.

Deterrence

Imprisonment may deter future crimes in two ways. **Specific deterrence** is intended to teach *this defendant* that crime carries a heavy price tag, in the hope that he will never do it again. **General deterrence** is the goal of demonstrating to *society generally* that crime must be shunned. Notice that both ideas of deterrence are utilitarian; that is, they are a means to an end. Specific and general deterrence both assume that by imprisoning someone, the law achieves a greater good for everyone. Jason almost certainly requires no specific deterrence. Is general deterrence a reason to imprison him?

Retribution

The German philosopher Immanuel Kant (1724–1804) rejected the idea of deterrence. He argued that human beings were supremely important and as a result must always be treated as ends in themselves, *never as a means to an end*. Kant would argue that, if deterrence were legitimate, then it would be all right to torture prisoners—even innocent prisoners—if this deterred massive amounts of crime.

For Kant, there is only one valid reason to punish: the prisoner deserves it. This is the idea of **retribution**—giving back to the criminal precisely what he deserves. A moral world, said Kant, requires that the government administer to all prisoners a punishment exactly equal to the crime they committed. A murderer must be put to death (even if he is dying from an illness and would live only a few days); an executive who bribes a government official must suffer a punishment equal to the harm he caused. To Kant, all of Jason's good deeds would be irrelevant, as would his terminal illness. If three years is the appropriate imprisonment for the crime of fraud, then he must serve three years, even if he dies in prison, even if it stops him from raising $10 million for charity.

Related to the idea of retribution is **vengeance.** When a serious crime has occurred, society wants the perpetrator to suffer. If we punish no one, people lose faith in the power and effectiveness of government and may take the law into their own hands.

Rehabilitation

To rehabilitate someone is to provide training so that he may return to a normal life. Most criminal justice experts believe that little or no rehabilitation occurs in a prison, though other forms of punishment may achieve this worthy goal.

Jason's Case.   What is your decision? Restraint and specific deterrence are unnecessary. You may imprison him for general deterrence or for retribution. Should you let him go free so that he can raise more money for good causes? In a similar case, a federal court judge decided that general deterrence was essential. To allow someone to go free, he said, would be to send a message that certain people can get away with crime.

The judge sentenced the defendant to a prison term, though he shortened the sentence based on the defendant's age and ill health.[1]

The Prosecution's Case

In all criminal cases, the prosecution faces several basic issues.

Conduct Outlawed

Virtually all crimes are created by statute. The prosecution must demonstrate to the court that the defendant's alleged conduct is indeed outlawed by a statute. Returning to Roger, the alleged video thief, the state charges that he stole video cameras from a store, a crime clearly defined by statute as burglary.

Burden of Proof

In a civil case, the plaintiff must prove her case by a preponderance of the evidence.[2] But in a criminal case, the government must prove its case **beyond a reasonable doubt.** This is because the potential harm to a criminal defendant is far greater. Roger, the video thief, can be fined and/or sent to prison. The stigma of a criminal conviction will stay with him, making it more difficult to obtain work and housing. Therefore, in all criminal cases, if the jury has any significant doubt at all that Roger stole the video cameras, it *must* acquit him. This high standard of proof in a criminal case reflects a very old belief, inherited from English law, that it is better to set 10 guilty people free than to convict a single innocent one. We will see that our law offers many protections for the accused.

Actus Reus

Actus reus means the "guilty act." **The prosecution must prove that the defendant voluntarily committed a prohibited act.** Suppose Mary Jo files an insurance claim for a stolen car, knowing that her car was not stolen. That is insurance fraud, and mail fraud if she sent documents through the Post Office. Filing the claim is the *actus reus:* Mary Jo voluntarily filled out the insurance claim and mailed it. At a bar, Mary Jo describes the claim to her friend, Chi Ling, who laughs and replies, "That's great. It'll serve the company right." Has Chi Ling committed a crime? No. There is no *actus reus,* because Chi Ling has done nothing illegal. Her cynical attitude may contribute to higher premiums for all of us, but criminal law punishes acts, not thoughts or omissions.

Mens Rea

The prosecution must also show *mens rea,* a "guilty state of mind," on the defendant's part. This is harder to prove than *actus reus*—it requires convincing evidence about something that is essentially psychological. Precisely what "state of mind" the prosecution must prove varies, depending on the crime. We will discuss the exact *mens rea* requirement for various crimes later in the chapter. In general, however, there are four mental states that a prosecutor may be required to prove, depending on the crime:

General Intent.   Most crimes require a showing of general intent, meaning that the defendant intended to do the prohibited physical action (the *actus reus*). Suppose Miller, a customer in a bar, picks up a bottle and smashes it over the head of Bud. In a trial for criminal assault, the *mens rea* would simply be the intention to hit Bud. The prosecution need not show that Miller intended serious harm, only that he intended the blow.

---

1 *United States v. Bergman,* 416 F. Supp. 496, 1976 U.S. Dist. LEXIS 14577 (S.D.N.Y. 1976).
2 See the earlier discussion in Chapter 3 on dispute resolution.

How will a prosecutor prove what was in Miller's mind? By circumstantial evidence: a witness will describe how Miller picked up the bottle and what he did with it. A jury is free to conclude that Miller intended physical contact because there would be no other reason for his action.

Specific Intent.   Some crimes require the prosecution to prove that the defendant willfully intended to do something beyond the physical act. For example, burglary requires proof that the defendant entered a building at night and intended to commit a felony inside, such as stealing property.

Reckless or Negligent Conduct.   For a few crimes, the prosecution is concerned more with the defendant's irresponsible conduct than with what the defendant was thinking. **Criminal recklessness** means consciously disregarding a substantial risk of injury. A pedestrian who jokingly points a gun at another commits criminal recklessness. The danger of the gun going off is obvious, and the defendant is guilty even if no shot is fired. A slightly lesser crime, **criminal negligence,** refers to gross deviations from reasonable conduct. A hunter who sees movement and shoots at it without bothering to determine whether the target is a turkey or a professor commits criminal negligence.

Strict Liability.   In strict liability cases, the prosecution must only prove *actus reus*. If the defendant committed the act, he is guilty, regardless of mental state or irresponsibility. For example, in an effort to improve the environment, many states now hold corporate defendants strictly liable for discharging certain pollutants into the air. If an oil refinery discharges toxic fumes, it is strictly liable, regardless of what efforts it may have taken to control emissions. Thus, strict liability crimes are the easiest for a prosecutor to prove and potentially the most dangerous to corporations.

Defenses

A criminal defendant will often dispute the facts that link her to the crime. For example, she might claim mistaken identity (that she merely resembles the real criminal) or offer an alibi (that she can prove she was elsewhere when the crime was committed). In addition, a defendant may offer **legal defenses.** Many of these are controversial, as we will see.

Insanity

A defendant who can prove that he was **insane** at the time of the criminal act will be declared not guilty. This reflects the moral basis of our criminal law. Insane people, though capable of great harm, historically have not been considered responsible for their acts. A defendant found to be insane will generally be committed to a mental institution. If and when that hospital determines he is no longer a danger to society, he will, in theory, be released. Some people applaud this as deeply humane, whereas others see it as muddled thinking that allows guilty people to walk free. The most common test for insanity is the M'Naghten Rule.

M'Naghten Rule.   The defendant must show (1) that he suffered a serious, identifiable mental disease and that because of it (2) he did not understand the nature of his act or did not know that it was wrong. Suppose Jerry, a homeless man, stabs Phil. At trial, a psychiatrist testifies that Jerry suffers from chronic schizophrenia, that he does not know where he is or what he is doing, and that when he stabbed Phil he believed he was sponging down his pet giraffe. If the jury believes the psychiatrist, it may find Jerry not guilty by reason of insanity.

What if the alleged mental defect is a result of the defendant's own behavior? You be the judge.

YOU BE THE JUDGE

BIEBER V. PEOPLE

856 P.2d 811, 1993 Colo. LEXIS 630
Supreme Court of Colorado, 1993

Facts: Donald Bieber walked up to a truck in which William Ellis was sitting and shot Ellis, whom he did not know, in the back of his head. He threw Ellis's body from the truck and drove away. Shortly before and after the killing, Bieber encountered various people in different places. He sang "God Bless America" and the "Marine Hymn" to them and told them he was a prisoner of war and was being followed by communists. He told people he had killed a communist on "War Memorial Highway." The police arrested him.

Bieber had a long history of drug abuse. As a teenager, he began using drugs, including amphetamines. As an adult, he continued his heavy drug use while making money selling drugs. Several years before the homicide, Bieber voluntarily sought treatment for mental impairment, entering a hospital and saying he thought he was going to hurt someone. He was later released into a long-term drug program.

Bieber was charged with first-degree murder. He pleaded not guilty by reason of insanity. An expert witness testified that he was insane, suffering from "amphetamine delusional disorder" (ADD), a recognized psychiatric illness resulting from long-term use of amphetamines and characterized by delusions. At trial, Bieber's attorney argued that he was not intoxicated at the time of the crime but that he was insane due to ADD. The trial court refused to instruct that Bieber could be legally insane due to ADD, and the jury found Bieber guilty of first-degree murder. He appealed.

You Be the Judge: **May a jury find that a defendant with ADD is legally insane?**

Argument for Bieber: Your honors, Mr. Bieber acknowledges the rule that someone who becomes voluntarily intoxicated and commits an offense is liable for the crime. That rule is irrelevant here, since Mr. Bieber was not intoxicated at the time of this homicide. He was insane.

The state of Colorado has long held that insanity is a valid defense to a criminal charge. It is morally and legally proper to distinguish between people who commit a crime out of viciousness and those who suffer serious mental illness. Mr. Bieber suffered from amphetamine delusional disorder, a serious psychotic illness recognized by the American Psychiatric Association. There was overwhelming evidence that he was out of control and did not know what he was doing at the time of the homicide.

The fact that ADD is brought about by years of amphetamine use should make no difference in an insanity case. This man's reason was destroyed by a serious illness. He should not be treated the same as a cold-blooded killer.

Argument for the State: Your honors, there is no qualitative difference between a person who drinks or takes drugs knowing that he or she will be momentarily "mentally defective" as an immediate result and one who drinks or takes drugs knowing that he or she may be "mentally defective" as an eventual, long-term result. In both cases, the person is aware of the possible consequences of his or her actions. We do not believe that in the latter case, such knowledge should be excused simply because the resulting affliction is more severe.

It is a matter of common knowledge that the excessive use of liquor or drugs impairs the perceptual, judgmental, and volitional faculties of the user. Also, because the intoxication must be "self-induced," the defendant necessarily must have had the conscious ability to prevent this temporary incapacity from coming into being at all. Self-induced intoxication by its very nature involves culpability.

As a matter of public policy, therefore, we must not excuse a defendant's actions, which endanger others, based upon a mental disturbance or illness that he or she actively and voluntarily contracted. There is no principled basis to distinguish between the short-term and long-term effects of voluntary intoxication by punishing the first and excusing the second. If anything, the moral blameworthiness would seem to be even greater with respect to the long-term effects of many, repeated instances of voluntary intoxication occurring over an extended period of time. We ask that you affirm. ●

Jury Role.   The insanity defense creates fear and confusion in the public, but most experts believe the concern is unwarranted. A Connecticut study showed that the defense was invoked in only one tenth of 1 percent of criminal prosecutions in that state, and that in more than 90 percent of *those* cases it still failed. Juries are reluctant to acquit based on insanity, probably fearing that the defendant will soon be back on the streets. But just the opposite is true. Most defendants acquitted by reason of insanity spend more time in a mental hospital than convicts spend in prison for the same act.

Entrapment

You go to a fraternity party where you meet a friendly new frat member, Joey. After a drink or two, Joey asks if you can get him some marijuana. You tell him you never use drugs. A week later you accidentally meet Joey in the cafeteria and he repeats the question, promising a very large profit if you will supply him with an ounce. You again say "no thanks." About once a week Joey bumps into you, in the school hallways, in the bookstore, at parties. He continues to ask you to "get him some stuff," and his offers grow more lucrative. Finally, after six requests, you speak to someone who is reputed to deal in drugs. You buy an ounce, then offer it to Joey at a large markup. Joey gratefully hands over the money, takes your package—and flashes his badge in your face, identifying himself as an undercover agent of the state police. You are speechless, which is fine, because Joey informs you that you have the right to remain silent.

Drugs are a deadly serious problem in our society, involved directly or indirectly in more than half of all street crime. We need creative police efforts. Has this one gone too far? The issue is entrapment. **When the government induces the defendant to break the law, the prosecution must prove beyond a reasonable doubt that the defendant was predisposed to commit the crime.**

If the government cannot prove predisposition, the defendant is not guilty. In other words, the goal is to separate the cases where the defendant was innocent before the government tempted him from those where the defendant was only too eager to break the law.

Most courts would agree that the state police officer entrapped the student. The seller said no five times. Unless the government has other evidence that the defendant was involved in dealing drugs, there appears to be no predisposition, and the entrapment defense is valid.

Duress

A defendant may plead duress if she can show that a threat by a third person caused her fear of imminent serious physical harm. The threatened harm must be physical. If Roger, the video thief, could show that a drug addict threatened to kill him if he did not steal the videos, he would have a valid duress defense.

By contrast, assume that Roger, a former accountant, stole the videos because he had been out of work for 14 months. A bank foreclosed his suburban home, and he had exhausted his savings during his job search. He and his two children were subsisting in an abandoned station wagon as his wife lay in a sanatorium, weak with tuberculosis. Roger was desperate for money to make a deposit on an apartment. His claim—and all claims—of *economic* duress will fail because there is no imminent physical harm.

CRIMES THAT HARM BUSINESS

Three major crimes involve taking money from businesses: larceny, fraud, and embezzlement. In each case the criminal ends up with money or property that belongs to someone else.

Larceny

It is holiday season at the mall, the period of greatest profits—and the most crime. At the Foot Forum, a teenager limps in wearing ragged sneakers and sneaks out wearing Super Rags, valued at $145. Down the aisle at a home furnishing store, a man is so taken by a $375 power saw that he takes it. Sweethearts swipe sweaters, pensioners pocket produce. All are committing larceny.

Larceny is the trespassory taking of personal property with the intent to steal it. "Trespassory taking" means that someone else originally has the property. The Super Rags are personal property (not real estate), they were in the possession of the Foot Forum, and the teenager deliberately left without paying, intending never to return the goods. That is larceny. By contrast, suppose Fast Eddie leaves Bloomingdale's in New York, descends to the subway system, and jumps over a turnstile without paying. Larceny? No. He has "taken" a service—the train ride—but not personal property.

Every day in the United States, more than $25 million in merchandise is stolen from retail stores. Economists estimate that *12 cents out of every dollar* spent in retail stores covers the cost of shoplifting. Some criminal experts believe that drug addicts commit more than half of all shoplifting to support their habits. Stores have added electronic surveillance, security patrols, and magnetic antitheft devices, but the problem will not disappear. We revisit this issue later, in the Ewing case, where we examine the heavy penalty one state has imposed on repeat offenders.

Fraud

Robert Dorsey owned Bob's Chrysler in Highland, Illinois. He ordered cars from the manufacturer, the First National Bank of Highland paid Chrysler, and Dorsey—supposedly—repaid the loans as he sold autos. Dorsey, though, began to suffer financial problems, and the bank suspected he was selling cars without repaying his loans. A state investigator notified Dorsey that he planned to review all dealership records. One week later a fire engulfed the dealership. An arson investigator discovered that an electric iron, connected to a timer, had been placed on a pile of financial papers doused with accelerant.

The saddest part of this true story is that it is only too common. Some experts suggest that 1 percent of corporate revenues are wasted on fraud alone. Dorsey was convicted and imprisoned for committing two crimes that cost business billions of dollars annually—fraud and arson.[3]

Fraud refers to various crimes, all of which have a common element: **the deception of another person for the purpose of obtaining money or property from him.** Robert Dorsey's precise violation was bank fraud, a federal crime. It is bank fraud to use deceit to obtain money, assets, securities, or other property under the control of any financial institution. The maximum penalty is a fine of $1 million and/or a prison term of 30 years.[4]

Wire fraud and **mail fraud** are additional federal crimes, involving the use of interstate mail, telegram, telephone, radio, or television to obtain property by deceit.[5] For example, if Marsha makes an interstate phone call to sell land that she does not own, that is wire fraud.

Insurance fraud is another common crime. A Ford suddenly swerves in front of a Toyota, causing it to brake hard. A Mercedes, unable to stop, slams into the Toyota, as the Ford races away. Regrettable accident? No: a "swoop and squat" fraud scheme.

---

[3] *United States v. Dorsey*, 27 F.3d 285, 1994 U.S. App. LEXIS 15010 (7th Cir. 1994).

[4] 18 U.S.C. §1344.

[5] 18 U.S.C. §§1341–1346.

The Ford and Toyota drivers were working together, hoping for an accident. The "injured" Toyota driver now goes to a third member of the fraud team—a dishonest doctor—who diagnoses serious back and neck injuries and predicts long-term pain and disability. The driver files a claim against the Mercedes's driver, whose insurer may be forced to pay tens or even hundreds of thousands of dollars for an accident that was no accident. Insurance companies investigate countless cases like this each year, trying to distinguish the honest victim from the criminal.

Finally, Stacey, the hospital executive described in the chapter's introduction, committed a fourth type of fraud. **Medicare fraud** includes using false statements, bribes, or kickbacks to obtain Medicare payments from the federal or state government.[6]

Find a current news article describing a case of *wire, mail,* or *insurance fraud.* What did the perpetrator do? Was the scheme subtly crafted or crudely executed? How did authorities discover the crime? What was the outcome of the case? Were there steps that a concerned businessperson or insurance executive should have taken to avoid the problem? Now be fiendishly clever: If you were a criminal, how would you "improve" on this scheme to avoid detection? What should a business executive learn from your scheming?

Arson

Robert Dorsey, the Chrysler dealer, committed a second serious crime. **Arson** is the malicious use of fire or explosives to damage or destroy any real estate or personal property. It is both a federal and a state crime. Dorsey used arson to conceal his bank fraud. Most arsonists hope to collect on insurance policies. Every year thousands of buildings burn, particularly in economically depressed neighborhoods, as owners try to make a quick kill or extricate themselves from financial difficulties. We involuntarily subsidize their immorality by paying higher insurance premiums.

Embezzlement

This crime also involves illegally obtaining property, but with one big difference: the culprit begins with legal possession. **Embezzlement is the fraudulent conversion of property already in the defendant's possession.**

Professor Beach, in North Dakota, asks his work-study student, Sandy, to drive his car to the repair shop. Sandy drives halfway and then hears on the car radio a forecast of snow. "I don't like snow," she thinks. Sandy turns south and never stops until she reaches Key West, Florida. "This is nicer," she murmurs. Sandy is innocent of larceny because she took the car keys with Beach's permission but guilty of embezzlement because she converted the auto to her own use.

Wherever money abounds, embezzlement tempts. Banks are prime targets. A loan officer embezzled money simply by creating false loans and taking the money for himself. He paid off earlier loans by taking out new ones and managed to stay ahead of the game until he had embezzled more than $5 million. He was eventually caught by a suspicious teller.[7]

Computer Crime

A 29-year-old computer whiz stole a car—using his keyboard. The man infiltrated a telephone company network and rigged a radio station's call-in promotion, winning himself a splendid new Porsche. He also damaged court-ordered wiretaps of alleged

---

[6] 18 U.S.C. §§1320 et seq. (1994).

[7] *Peoples State Bank v. American Casualty Co. of Reading, Mich.,* No. Ed-8425-11, *Lawyers Weekly,* May 17, 1993, p. 6A.

gangsters and may even have jammed the phones on an *Unsolved Mysteries* television episode in which *he was the featured fugitive!* In another case, a teenage boy crippled the airport control tower in Worcester, Massachusetts, by breaking into a telephone network and causing a computer crash that eliminated all power at the airport.

The ascent of the Internet inevitably brings with it new forms of crime. Various federal statutes criminalize this behavior.

- The **Computer Fraud and Abuse Act** prohibits using a computer to commit theft, espionage, trespass, fraud, and damage to another computer.[8] This statute is the focal point of the case on pp. 168–169.

- The **Access Device Fraud Act** outlaws the fraudulent use of cards, codes, account numbers, and other devices to obtain money, goods, or services.[9] For example, it is a violation of this act to reprogram a cellular telephone so that calls are charged to an improper account.

- The **Identity Theft and Assumption Deterrence Act** bars the use of false identification to commit fraud or other crime.[10] A waiter who uses stolen credit card numbers to buy airline tickets has violated this act. The Federal Trade Commission receives about 100,000 complaints of identity theft every year, so you should guard identifying data carefully.

- The **Wire and Electronic Communications Interception Act** makes it a crime to intercept most wire, oral, and electronic communications.[11] (This law does not prohibit recording your own conversations.) We *warned* you not to tape your roommate's conversations!

Identity Theft

Identity theft is growing explosively. How do thieves get personal information?

- Steal records at work by hacking into company files or bribing coworkers
- Rummage through trash or mailboxes
- Pose as a landlord or employer with a valid interest in your credit
- "Skim," which means to use an electronic device to record your personal information when you are using a credit card for a proper purpose, such as paying at a retail store
- "Phish," which means to contact you by phone or e-mail, posing as a legitimate company attempting to correct a problem with your account

What do thieves do with private data?

- Open new credit card accounts and purchase "big ticket" items
- Open a new bank account and write bad checks
- Use credit cards and checks to drain your bank account
- Give your name to police during an investigation, meaning that when the thieves fail to appear in court, a warrant will be issued for *your* arrest

How should an identity theft victim respond?

---

[8] 18 U.S.C. §1030.
[9] 18 U.S.C. §1029.
[10] 18 U.S.C. §1028.
[11] 18 U.S.C. §2511.

- Place a fraud alert on your credit reports, by phoning one of three credit companies (Equifax, 800-525-6285; Experian, 888-397-3742; TransUnion, 800-680-7289).

- Close any account that is potentially affected.

- Notify the local police.

- File a complaint with the Federal Trade Commission. You may do this online, at http://www.consumer.gov. Click on "ID Theft: What It's All About."

The following case illustrates the type of simple scam that can blight the credit rating of innocent victims.

UNITED STATES V. AMURE

83 Fed. Appx. 52, 2003 WL 22905306
Sixth Circuit Court of Appeals, 2003

Facts: Femi Amure was convicted of identity theft in the sale of automobiles. He was sentenced to 26 months incarceration and two years of supervised release and ordered to pay restitution of $73,817. Amure appealed, claiming that there was no credible evidence he had committed this crime.

Issue: Was there sufficient evidence that Amure committed identity theft?

Excerpts from the Court's *Per Curiam* Decision: Amure's sole argument on appeal centers on the purported lack of credibility of Anthony Davis ("Davis"). As a cooperating co-defendant, Davis testified at trial, describing how he obtained the credit histories and social security numbers of various individuals using credit software, then used—or had others use—the information to buy vehicles at several dealerships in Tennessee and Mississippi.

Davis explained that he wanted to help a friend, Kevin Walsh ("Walsh"), buy a Lexus automobile. Walsh contacted the Herrin-Gear Lexus dealership in Jackson and asked that a credit application be faxed to Davis's office. When Davis received the fax from the Jackson dealership, he called the salesman who had sent the fax. That salesman was Amure. According to Davis, Amure was told about, and agreed to go along with, Davis's scheme. Davis and Walsh thereafter traveled to Herrin-Gear where they purchased a 1998 Lexus LS400 using the identifying information of a person who, unlike Walsh, had a good credit history.

Davis next explained that he helped Winfred Boyd ("Boyd") buy a 2001 Lexus GS430 from Amure. The car was intended for someone to whom Boyd owed money. According to Davis, Amure was paid $1,000.00 for his part in the Boyd sale.

Davis also testified that Amure processed the sale of a 2001 Chevrolet Tahoe for a "Sean Kearney." "Sean Kearney" was, in fact, Sylvester Kearney ("Kearney"), a co-defendant in this case. Because Kearney did not have insurance, Davis made up an insurance certificate for Kearney that he faxed to Amure. Kearney (who pleaded guilty in the case) testified that he paid Amure $1,000.00 when Amure delivered the car to him.

Davis finally testified that he purchased from Amure a 1998 Chevrolet Corvette for a friend of his, Deadrick Clayborn ("Clayborn"). Davis negotiated the deal in the name of John C. Davis, using a Social Security number that he obtained using his credit software. The car was delivered by Amure to Davis and Clayborn at an exit ramp on the expressway outside of Jackson.

Amure contends that, if the jurors had been rational, they would have disbelieved Davis and acquitted him on all counts. The jurors, however, observed Davis on the witness stand; they heard defense counsel's attacks on Davis's credibility during cross-examination and closing arguments; they were instructed as to their role in assessing witness credibility; and they chose to believe at least part of what Davis said. It is not our role to question the jury's assessment of Davis's credibility.

We affirm. ∎

CRIMES COMMITTED BY BUSINESS

A corporation can be found guilty of a crime based on the conduct of any of its **agents,** who include anyone undertaking work on behalf of the corporation. An agent can be a corporate officer, an accountant hired to audit a statement, a sales clerk, or almost any other person performing a job at the company's request.

If an agent commits a criminal act within the scope of his employment and with the intent to benefit the corporation, the company is liable.[12] This means that the agent himself must first be guilty. The normal requirements of *actus reus* and *mens rea* apply. If the agent is guilty, the corporation is, too.

Critics believe that the criminal law has gone too far. It is unfair, they argue, to impose *criminal* liability on a corporation, and thus penalize the shareholders, unless high-ranking officers were directly involved in the illegal conduct. The following case concerns a corporation's responsibility for an employee's death.

WISCONSIN V. KNUTSON, INC.

196 Wis. 2d 86, 537 N.W.2d 420, 1995 Wis. App. LEXIS 1223
Wisconsin Court of Appeals, 1995

Facts: Richard Knutson, Inc. (RKI) was constructing a sanitary sewer line for the city of Oconomowoc. An RKI crew attempted to place a section of corrugated metal pipe in a trench in order to remove groundwater. The backhoe operator misjudged the distance from the backhoe's boom to the overhead power lines and failed to realize he had placed the boom in contact with the wires. A crew member attempted to attach a chain to the backhoe's bucket and was instantly electrocuted.

The state charged RKI with negligent vehicular homicide under a statute that says: "Whoever causes the death of another human being by the negligent operation or handling of a vehicle is guilty of a Class E felony." The jury convicted, and RKI appealed, claiming that a corporation could not be held guilty under the statute.

Issue: May a corporation be guilty of vehicular homicide under the statute?

Excerpts from Judge Anderson's Decision: Here, the statute does not provide a definition of "whoever." We will thus employ extrinsic aids to uncover the legislature's intent.

LaFave and Scott [authors of a leading treatise] summarize the persuasive policy considerations supporting corporate criminal liability. Among those considerations is the factor that the corporate business entity has become a way of life in this country and the imposition of criminal liability is an essential part of the regulatory process. Another consideration centers on the premise that it would be unjust to single out one or more persons for criminal punishment when it is the corporate culture that is the origin of the criminal behavior. Also, the size of many corporations makes it impossible to adequately allocate responsibility to individuals.

An additional consideration is the indirect economic benefits that may accrue to the corporation through crimes against the person. To get these economic benefits, corporate management may shortcut expensive safety precautions, respond forcibly to strikes, or engage in criminal anticompetitive behavior. It has also been suggested that the free market system cannot be depended upon to guide corporate decisions in socially acceptable ways, and the threat of imposition of criminal liability is needed to deter inappropriate (criminal) corporate behavior. We ▼

---

12 *New York Central & Hudson River R.R. Co. v. United States,* 212 U.S. 481, 29 S. Ct. 304, 1909 U.S. LEXIS 1832 (1909). And note that what counts is the intention to benefit, not actual benefit. A corporation will not escape liability by showing that the scheme failed.

agree that if a penal statute is intended to inhibit an act, a corporation is included within the class of perpetrators if to do so is within the spirit and purpose of the act. [The court concluded that a corporation may be guilty of vehicular homicide.]

Sufficiency of the Evidence: Homicide by negligent use of a vehicle has three elements: (1) that the defendant cause death (2) by criminal negligence (3) in the operation of a vehicle. Criminal negligence differs from ordinary negligence in two respects. First, the risk is more serious—death or great bodily harm as opposed to simple harm. Second, the risk must be more than an unreasonable risk—it must also be substantial.

RKI's management took no action to have the power lines de-energized or barriers erected; rather,

management elected to merely warn employees about the overhead lines.

The evidence supports the conclusion that if RKI had enforced the written safety regulations of OSHA, had abided by its own written safety program and had complied with the contract requirements for construction on Wisconsin Electric's property, the electrocution death would likely not have happened. The finder of fact was justified in concluding that RKI operated vehicles in close proximity to the overhead power lines without recognizing the potential hazard to its employees in the vicinity of the vehicles. The jury could reasonably find that RKI's failure to take elementary precautions for the safety of its employees was a substantial cause of the electrocution death.

Judgment *affirmed.* ∎

Punishing a Corporation

Fines

The most common punishment for a corporation is a fine. This makes sense in that the purpose of a business is to earn a profit, and a fine, theoretically, hurts. But most fines are modest by the present standards of corporate wealth.

Odwalla, Inc., sold fruit juices and nutritional shakes throughout much of the United States. A batch of its apple juice, which contained the highly toxic *E. coli* bacteria, killed a 16-month-old girl and seriously harmed 70 other people. Federal officials prosecuted, charging the company with violating food safety laws. Eventually, the company pleaded guilty, agreed to pay a $1.5 million fine, and submitted to a court-supervised probation for five years. Some public interest law groups applauded the punishment. Critics, though, complained that a million-dollar fine is petty change for a large corporation and may have no deterrent effect on other companies. Odwalla has also paid millions of dollars to settle civil lawsuits brought by the injured consumers.

Compliance Programs

The **Federal Sentencing Guidelines** are the detailed rules that judges must follow when sentencing defendants convicted of crimes in federal court. The guidelines instruct judges to determine whether, at the time of the crime, the corporation had in place a serious **compliance program**—that is, a plan to prevent and detect criminal conduct at all levels of the company. A company that can point to a detailed, functioning compliance program may benefit from a dramatic reduction in the fine or other punishment meted out. Indeed, a tough compliance program may even convince federal investigators to curtail an investigation and to limit any prosecution to those directly involved, rather than attempting to get a conviction against high-ranking officers or the company itself.

at **RISK**

To persuade prosecutors or judges that it seriously intended to follow the law, a company must demonstrate a thorough and effective compliance plan:

- The program must be reasonably capable of reducing the prospect of criminal conduct.
- Specific, high-level officers must be responsible for overseeing the program.

- The company must not place in charge any officers it knows or should have known, from past experience, who are likely to engage in illegal conduct.
- The company must effectively communicate the program to all employees and agents.
- The company must ensure compliance by monitoring employees in a position to cheat and by promptly disciplining any who break the law. ◆

Selected Crimes Committed by Business

Workplace Crimes

The workplace can be dangerous. Working on an assembly line exposes factory employees to fast-moving machinery. For a roofer, the first slip may be the last. The invisible radiation in a nuclear power plant can be deadlier than a bullet. The most important statute regulating the workplace is the federal **Occupational Safety and Health Act of 1970 (OSHA),**[13] which sets safety standards for many industries.[14] May a state government go beyond standards set by OSHA and use the criminal law to punish dangerous conditions? In *People v. O'Neill,*[15] the courts of Illinois answered that question with a potent "yes," permitting a *murder prosecution* against corporate executives. Notice that whereas Wisconsin prosecuted RKI *Corporation* for vehicular homicide, Illinois brought this case against the corporate executives themselves.

NEWS*worthy*

Film Recovery Systems was an Illinois corporation in business to extract silver from used X-ray film and then resell it. Steven O'Neill was president of Film Recovery, Charles Kirschbaum was its plant manager, and Daniel Rodriguez the foreman. To extract the silver, workers at Film Recovery soaked the X-ray film in large, open, bubbling vats that contained sodium cyanide.

A worker named Stefan Golab became faint. He left the production area and walked to the lunchroom, where workers found him trembling and foaming at the mouth. He lost consciousness. Paramedics were unable to revive him. They rushed him to a hospital where he was pronounced dead on arrival. The Cook County medical examiner determined that Golab died from acute cyanide poisoning caused by inhalation of cyanide fumes in the plant.

Illinois indicted Film Recovery and several of its managers for murder. The indictment charged that O'Neill and Kirschbaum committed murder by failing to disclose to Golab that he was working with cyanide and other potentially lethal substances and by failing to provide him with appropriate and necessary safety equipment.

The case was tried to a judge without a jury. Workers testified that O'Neill, Kirschbaum, and other managers never told them they were using cyanide or that the fumes they inhaled could be harmful; that management made no effort to ventilate the factory; that Film Recovery gave the workers no goggles or protective clothing; that the chemicals they worked with burned their skin; that breathing was difficult in the plant because of strong, foul orders; and that workers suffered frequent dizziness, nausea, and vomiting.

The trial judge found O'Neill, Kirschbaum, and others guilty of murder. Illinois defines murder as performing an act that the defendant *knows will create a strong probability of death* in the victim, and the judge found they had done that. He found Film Recovery guilty of involuntary manslaughter. Involuntary manslaughter is *recklessly* performing an act that causes death. He sentenced O'Neill, Kirschbaum, and Rodriguez to 25 years in prison.

---

[13] 29 U.S.C. §§651 et seq. (1982).

[14] See Chapter 15, on employment law.

[15] 194 Ill. App. 3d 79, 550 N.E.2d 1090, 1990 Ill. App. LEXIS 65 (Ill. App. Ct. 1990).

The defendants appealed, contending that the verdicts were inconsistent. They argued, and the Illinois Court of Appeals agreed, that the judge had made contradictory findings. Murder required the specific intent of *knowing there was a strong probability of death,* whereas the manslaughter conviction required *reckless* conduct. The appeals court reversed the convictions and remanded for a new trial.

Moments before the new trial was to start, O'Neill, Kirschbaum, and Rodriguez all pleaded guilty to involuntary manslaughter. They received sentences of three years, two years, and four months, respectively. ◆

RICO

The **Racketeer Influenced and Corrupt Organizations Act (RICO)**[16] is one of the most powerful and controversial statutes ever written. Congress passed the law primarily to prevent gangsters from taking money they earned illegally and investing it in legitimate businesses. But RICO has expanded far beyond the original intentions of Congress and is now used more often against ordinary businesses than against organized criminals. Some regard this wide application as a tremendous advance in law enforcement, but others view it as an oppressive weapon used to club ethical companies into settlements they should never have to make.

RICO creates both criminal and civil law liabilities. The government may prosecute both individuals and organizations for violating RICO. For example, the government may prosecute a mobster, claiming that he has run a heroin ring for years. It may also prosecute an accounting firm, claiming that it lied about corporate assets in a stock sale to make the shares appear more valuable than they really were. If the government proves its case, the defendant can be hit with large fines and a prison sentence of up to 20 years. RICO also permits the government to seek forfeiture of the defendant's property. A court may order a convicted defendant to hand over any property or money used in the criminal acts or derived from them.

RICO creates civil liability as well. The government, organizations, and individuals all have the right to file civil lawsuits, seeking damages and, if necessary, injunctions. For example, shareholders claiming that they were harmed by the accounting firm's lies could sue the firm for money lost in buying and selling the stock. RICO is powerful (and for defendants, frightening) in part because a civil plaintiff can recover **treble damages**—that is, a judgment for three times the harm actually suffered—and can also recover attorney's fees.

What is a violation of this law? **RICO prohibits using two or more racketeering acts to accomplish any of these goals: (1) investing in or acquiring legitimate businesses with criminal money; (2) maintaining or acquiring businesses through criminal activity; or (3) operating businesses through criminal activity.**

What does that mean in English? It is a two-step process to prove that a person or an organization has violated RICO. We will assume that this is a criminal prosecution, though the steps are similar in a civil lawsuit.

- The prosecutor must show that the defendant committed two or more **racketeering acts,** which are any of a long list of specified crimes: embezzlement, arson, mail fraud, wire fraud, and so forth. Thus, if a gangster ordered a building torched in January and then burned a second building in October, that would be two racketeering acts. If a stockbroker told two customers that Bronx Gold Mines was a promising stock when she knew that it was worthless, that would be two racketeering acts.

---

[16] 18 U.S.C. §§1961–1968.

- The prosecutor must show that the defendant used these racketeering acts to accomplish one of the three *purposes* listed earlier. If the gangster committed two arsons and then used the insurance payments to buy a dry cleaning business, that would violate RICO. If the stockbroker gave fraudulent advice and used the commissions to buy advertising for her firm, that would violate RICO.

Money Laundering

Money laundering consists of taking the proceeds of certain criminal acts and either (1) using the money to promote crime, or (2) attempting to conceal the source of the money.[17]

Money laundering is an important part of major criminal enterprises. Successful criminals earn enormous sums, and they strive to filter their profits back into the flow of commerce so that their crimes go undetected. Laundering is an essential part of the corrosive traffic in drugs. Profits, all in cash, mount so swiftly that the most difficult step for a successful dealer can be to use the money without attracting the government's attention. However, as the following case illustrates, it is not only drug dealers who seek to launder their wrongfully obtained cash. Why don't you stop by the clinic and let us have a look at that knee?

UNITED STATES V. BIEGANOWSKI

313 F.3d 264
Fifth Circuit Court of Appeals, 2002

Facts: Dr. Arthur Bieganowski operated five health clinics in El Paso, Texas. Richard Goldberg was his accountant. The government charged the pair with mail fraud and money laundering in a three-part conspiracy. First, the defendants used a telemarketer, Richard Griego, to solicit patients, mostly auto-accident victims. Second, the pair submitted false invoices to insurance companies, billing for services that were unnecessary or never performed. Third, the two laundered the proceeds. Their billing service, called Servicio de Facturacion (Servicio) and located in Ciudad Juarez, Mexico, mailed invoices, then deposited insurance company reimbursements in clinic accounts at Bank of the West, in El Paso. From there the money was transferred to a Servicio account at the same bank, then to an account called UTM Professional Management (same bank), then to a different UTM account at Barclays Bank in New York, and finally to a Barclays bank in the Cayman Islands.

Both Bieganowski and Goldberg were convicted of mail fraud and money laundering. In this part of the case, Goldberg appeals his conviction and eight-year sentence, claiming there was insufficient evidence.

Issue: Was there sufficient evidence to convict Goldberg of mail fraud and money laundering?

Excerpts from Judge Garwood's Decision:

Mail Fraud
Goldberg's affiliation with Dr. Bieganowski's practice far exceeded the limits of an ordinary professional relationship, and involved him in nearly every aspect of the operation of the clinics. He spent almost every afternoon at Dr. Bieganowski's clinic and attended multiple meetings with the clinic staff, including meetings addressing such mundane administrative matters as employee dress codes.

The record also indicates that Goldberg was closely involved with Dr. Bieganowski's solicitation efforts. He not only attended meetings with Robert Griego, Bieganowski's telemarketer, but also reviewed the script that Griego used to solicit new patients. Goldberg knew that Griego told reluctant patients that they could increase their automobile insurance settlements by generating higher medical bills, and he ▼

---

[17] 18 U.S.C. §§1956 et seq.

knew that Griego advised patients to obtain medical examinations even when those same patients told Griego that they were not injured.

Further, Goldberg's extensive efforts in setting up and overseeing an elaborate virtual labyrinth of bank accounts for Dr. Bieganowski's clinics, which concealed both the clinics' and Dr. Bieganowski's relationship to the accounts and the ultimate disposition of the funds, is plainly suggestive of guilty knowledge. Goldberg correctly points out that each piece of evidence against him, viewed separately, may admit of an innocent explanation. That, however, is not determinative. The cumulative effect of this evidence is sufficient to support the inference that Goldberg was aware of the fraudulent billing practices.

Money Laundering

Agent Hivic of the IRS testified that over $6 million of insurance company reimbursements were deposited in the various clinics' accounts. All of that $6 million dollars was then transferred from the clinics' accounts at the Bank of the West to the Servicio account, also located at the Bank of the West. Of that $6 million dollars, a little over $2 million was eventually transferred to the Cayman Islands.

Goldberg's argument proceeds from the premise that the Government failed to prove that *all* of Dr. Bieganowski's billings were fraudulent. If *some* billings were legitimate, then at least *some* of the money that was deposited into the clinic accounts at the Bank of the West and then consolidated in the Servicio account was also legitimate.

The entire $6 million dollars deposited into the clinics' accounts was thereafter transferred to the Servicio account. Therefore, even assuming that the Government only proved that a portion of those $6 million dollars represented the proceeds of fraudulent activity, the prosecution nevertheless satisfied its burden of demonstrating that the transfer involved the proceeds of specified unlawful activity.

There is also little doubt that the transfers from the clinics' accounts to the Servicio account were designed to conceal the source of the unlawful funds. A casual observer would not have immediately linked the contents of the Servicio account to Bieganowski, as neither Dr. Bieganowski nor Goldberg were listed as shareholders (or officers or directors or authorized agents or account signatories) of Servicio.

[Affirmed as to mail fraud and money laundering convictions.] ■

Public Policy

Some people describe financial scams as "victimless crimes." Clearly this court, by imposing an eight-year sentence on Goldberg, sees the harm as real. Who is hurt by an insurance scheme like this? Was the punishment appropriate? ◆

Other Crimes

Many additional crimes affect business. An increasing number of federal and state statutes are designed to punish those who harm the environment. (See Chapter 25 on environmental law.) Antitrust violations, in which a corporation establishes a monopoly, can lead to criminal prosecutions. Securities fraud is a crime and can lead to severe prison sentences. (See Chapter 19 on securities regulation.)

ECONOMICS
& the LAW

Reputational Penalty. Businesses convicted of criminal conduct often pay more than just a fine. Many economists have concluded that companies suffer significant reputational penalties as well. Studies indicate that several negative consequences generally follow a criminal conviction.

First, stock prices fall significantly, reducing shareholder wealth. The angry shareholders may seek compensation from the executives who committed the crime. Second, executives are often forced out of the offending company.

Finally, business relationships often suffer, especially for crimes such as fraud or overcharging in a contract. Suppose that Integrity Motors promises to sell to PlaneMaker 1,000 aircraft engines that have been tested for quality control. When too many of the engines fail, the state government convicts Integrity of falsifying test results. PlaneMaker will never buy another engine from Integrity, and other aircraft manufacturers may also turn away from the convicted company. One study concluded that these reputational penalties are much more likely to occur when the crime is committed against customers, as in the fraud case, rather than against the general public, as in a case of environmental damage.[18] ◆

CONSTITUTIONAL PROTECTIONS

The police arrest Jake and charge him with armed robbery and rape. They claim that he entered a convenience store, took all the money from the cash register, robbed the clerk of her wristwatch, and then raped her. Jake refuses to talk, but the police are absolutely certain he is guilty. The community is outraged and wants a conviction. Should the police be allowed to question Jake for hours without stopping? May they lock him in a walk-in freezer? Beat him? After 5 hours of interrogation, followed by 10 hours in a freezer and a severe beating, Jake confesses. He tells the police where to find the money and the clerk's watch. Does his guilt render the police conduct acceptable?

These are issues of **criminal procedure.** We are no longer looking at the elements of particular crimes, as we have thus far, but at the *process of investigating, interrogating, and trying* a criminal defendant. The first 10 amendments to the United States Constitution, known as the Bill of Rights, control the behavior of all law enforcement officers.[19] In this section we look at some of the protections these amendments offer.

The Criminal Process

In order to understand constitutional safeguards, we need to know how the police do their work. The exact steps will vary from case to case, but the summary in Exhibit 7.1 highlights the important steps.

Informant

Yasmin is a secretary to Stacey, the Be Patient executive who opened this chapter. On her lunch break, Yasmin gets up the courage to telephone an FBI office and speaks to Moe, an agent. She reports that Stacey routinely charges the government for patients who do not exist. Moe arranges to interview Yasmin at her apartment that evening. He tape-records everything she says, including her own job history, her duties at Be Patient, and how she knows about the fraud. Yasmin has not only seen the false bills, she has entered some of them on computers. The next day, Moe prepares an **affidavit** for Yasmin to sign, detailing everything she told him. An affidavit is simply a written statement signed under oath.

Warrant

Moe takes Yasmin's affidavit to a United States magistrate, an employee of the federal courts who is similar to a judge. Moe asks the magistrate to issue search warrants for Be Patient's patient records. A search warrant is written permission from a neutral official, such as the magistrate, to conduct a search. **A warrant must specify with reasonable**

---

18 Alexander, "On the Nature of the Reputational Penalty for Corporate Crime: Evidence," *Journal of Law and Economics*, 1999, vol. 42, p. 489.

19 As discussed in Chapter 5 on constitutional law, most of the protections as written apply only to state government or the federal government. But through the process of incorporation, almost all important criminal procedure rights have been expanded to apply to federal, state, and local governments.

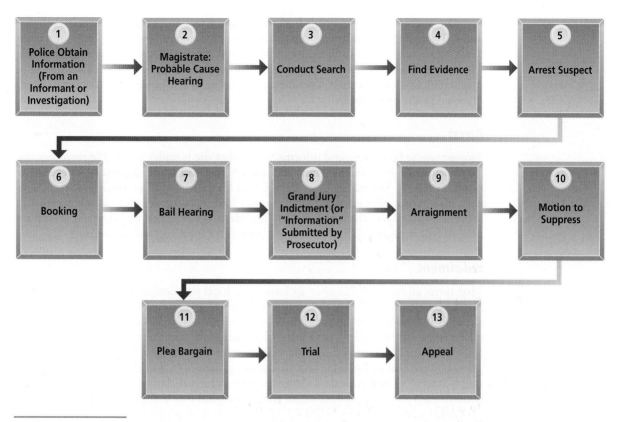

Exhibit 7.1

certainty the place to be searched and the items to be seized. This warrant application names all five of Be Patient's hospitals and asks to look through their admission notes, surgery and doctor reports, and discharge data. It states that the records will be copied so that they can be compared with the bills the government has received.

Probable Cause

The magistrate will issue a warrant only if there is probable cause. **Probable cause** means that based on all the information presented, **it is likely that evidence of crime will be found in the place mentioned.** The magistrate will look at Yasmin's affidavit to determine (1) whether the informant (Yasmin) is reliable and (2) whether she has a sound basis for the information. If Yasmin is a five-time drug offender whose information has proven wrong in the past, the warrant should not issue. Here, Yasmin's career record is good, she has no apparent motive to lie, and she is in an excellent position to know what she is talking about. The magistrate issues the warrant, specifying exactly what records may be examined.

Search and Seizure

Armed with the warrants, Moe and other agents arrive at the various hospitals, show the warrants, and take away the appropriate records. The **search** may not exceed what is described in the warrant. Even if Moe suspects that Dr. Narkem is illegally drugging certain patients, he may not seize test tube samples from the lab. He may take only the records described in the warrant.

The agents cart the records back to headquarters and enter the data on a computer. The computer compares the records of actual patients with the bills submitted to the government and indicates that 10 percent of all bills are for fictional patients. Moe summarizes the new data on additional affidavits and presents the affidavits to the magistrate, who issues **arrest warrants,** authorizing the FBI to arrest Stacey and others involved in the overbilling.

Arrest

Moe arrives at Be Patient and informs Stacey that she is under arrest. He reads her the *Miranda* warnings, discussed later. He drives Stacey to FBI headquarters, where she is **booked;** that is, her name, photograph, and fingerprints are entered in a log, along with the charges. She is entitled to a prompt **bail hearing.** A judge or magistrate will set an amount of bail that she must pay in order to go free pending the trial. The purpose of bail is to ensure that Stacey will appear for all future court hearings.

Indictment

Moe turns all his evidence over to Larry, the local prosecutor for the United States. Larry presents the evidence to a **grand jury,** which is a group of ordinary citizens, like a trial jury. But the grand jury holds hearings for several weeks at a time, on many different cases. It is the grand jury's job to determine whether there is probable cause that this defendant committed the crime with which she is charged. Larry shows the computer comparison of the bills with the actual patient lists, and the grand jury votes to indict Stacey. An **indictment** is the government's formal charge that the defendant has committed a crime and must stand trial. The grand jury is persuaded that there is probable cause that Stacey billed for 1,550 nonexistent patients, charging the government for $290 million worth of services that were never performed. The grand jury indicts her for (1) Medicare fraud, (2) mail fraud, (3) several computer crimes, and (4) RICO violations.[20] It also indicts Be Patient, Inc., and other employees.

Arraignment

Stacey is ordered back to court. A clerk reads her the formal charges of the indictment. The judge asks whether Stacey has a lawyer, and of course she does. If she did not, the judge would urge her to get one quickly. If a defendant cannot afford a lawyer, the court will appoint one to represent her free of charge. The judge now asks the lawyer how Stacey pleads to the charges. Her lawyer answers that she pleads not guilty to all charges.

Discovery

During the months before trial, both prosecution and defense will prepare the most effective case possible. There is less formal discovery than in civil trials. The prosecution is obligated to hand over any evidence favorable to the defense that the defense attorney requests. The defense has a more limited obligation to inform the prosecution. In most states, for example, if the defense will be based on an alibi, counsel must explain the alibi to the government before trial. In Stacey's case most of the evidence is data that both sides already possess.

---

20 In federal court, when the defendant is charged with a felony, formal charges may be made only by indictment. In many state court cases, the prosecutor is not required to seek an indictment. Instead, she may file an **information,** which is simply a formal written accusation. In state courts, most cases now begin by information.

Motion to Suppress

If the defense claims that the prosecution obtained evidence illegally, it will move to suppress it. A **motion to suppress** is a request that the court exclude certain evidence because it was obtained in violation of the Constitution. We look at those violations later.

Plea Bargaining

Sometime before trial the two attorneys will meet to consider a plea bargain. A **plea bargain** is an agreement between prosecution and defense that the defendant will plead guilty to a reduced charge, and the prosecution will recommend to the judge a relatively lenient sentence. Based on the RICO violations alone, Stacey faces a possible 20-year prison sentence, along with a large fine and a devastating forfeiture order. The government makes this offer: Stacey will plead guilty to 100 counts of mail fraud; Be Patient will repay all $290 million and an additional $150 million in fines; the government will drop the RICO and computer crime charges and recommend to the judge that Stacey be fined only $1 million and sentenced to three years in prison. In the federal court system, about 75 percent of all prosecutions end in a plea bargain. In state court systems the number is often higher.

Stacey agrees to the government's offer. The judge accepts the plea, and Stacey is fined and sentenced accordingly. A judge need not accept the bargain but usually does.

Trial and Appeal

When there is no plea bargain, the case must go to trial. The mechanics of a criminal trial are similar to those for a civil trial, described in Chapter 3, on dispute resolution. It is the prosecution's job to convince the jury beyond a reasonable doubt that the defendant committed every element of the crime charged. The defense counsel will do everything possible to win an acquittal. In federal courts, prosecutors obtain a conviction in about 80 percent of cases; in state courts, the percentage is slightly lower. Convicted defendants have a right to appeal, and again, the appellate process is similar to that described in Chapter 3.

The Fourth Amendment

The Fourth Amendment prohibits the government from making illegal searches and seizures. This amendment protects individuals, corporations, partnerships, and other organizations.

In general, the police must obtain a warrant before conducting a search. There are six exceptions to this rule, in which the police may **search without a warrant:**

- *Plain View.* Police may search if they see a machine gun, for example, sticking out from under the front seat of a parked car.
- *Stop and Frisk.* If police have an articulable reason for suspecting that someone may be armed and dangerous, they may pat him down.
- *Emergencies.* If police pursue a store robber and catch him, they may search.
- *Automobiles.* If police have lawfully stopped a car and observe evidence of other crimes in the car, such as burglary tools, they may search.
- *Lawful Arrest.* Police may always search a suspect they have arrested.
- *Consent.* If someone in lawful occupancy of a home gives consent to a search, the police may do so.

Apart from those six cases, a warrant is required. If the police search without one, they have violated the Fourth Amendment. Even a search conducted with a warrant can violate the amendment. **A search with a warrant violates the Fourth Amendment if:**

- There was no probable cause to issue the warrant;
- The warrant does not specify the place to be searched and the things sought; or
- The search extends beyond what is specified in the warrant.

Exclusionary Rule

Under the exclusionary rule, evidence obtained illegally may not be used at trial against the victim of the search. If the police conduct a warrantless search that is not one of the six exceptions, any evidence they find will be excluded from the trial.

Suppose when Yasmin called the FBI, Moe simply drove straight to one of Be Patient's hospitals and grabbed patient records. Moe lacked a warrant, and his search would be illegal. Stacey's lawyer would file a **motion to suppress** the evidence. Before the trial starts, the judge would hold a hearing. If he agreed that the search was illegal, he would **exclude** the evidence—that is, refuse to allow it in trial. The government could go forward with the prosecution only if it had other evidence.[21]

Is the exclusionary rule a good idea? The Supreme Court created the exclusionary rule to ensure that police conduct legal searches. The theory is simple: if police know in advance that illegally obtained evidence cannot be used in court, they will not be tempted to make improper searches.

Opponents of the rule argue that a guilty person may go free because one police officer bungled. They are outraged by cases like *Coolidge v. New Hampshire*.[22] Pamela Mason, a 14-year-old babysitter, was brutally murdered. Citizens of New Hampshire were furious, and the state's attorney general personally led the investigation. Police found strong evidence that Edward Coolidge had done it. They took the evidence to the attorney general, who personally issued a search warrant. The search of Coolidge's car uncovered incriminating evidence, and he was found guilty of murder and sentenced to life in prison. But the United States Supreme Court reversed the conviction. The warrant had not been issued by a neutral magistrate. A law officer may not lead an investigation and simultaneously decide what searches are permissible.

After the Supreme Court reversed Coolidge's conviction, New Hampshire scheduled a new trial, attempting to convict him with evidence lawfully obtained. Before the trial began, Coolidge pleaded guilty to second-degree murder. He was sentenced and remained in prison until his release 27 years later.

---

[21] There are two important exceptions to the exclusionary rule:

Inevitable Discovery Exception. Suppose that Moe's search of Be Patient is declared illegal. But then officials in the Medicare office testify that they were already aware of Be Patient's fraud, had already obtained some proof, and were about to seek a search warrant for the same records that Moe took. If the court believes the testimony, it will allow the evidence to be used. The inevitable discovery exception permits the use of evidence that would inevitably have been discovered even without the illegal search.

Good Faith Exception. Suppose the police use a search warrant believing it to be proper, but it later proves to have been defective. Is the search therefore illegal? No, said the Supreme Court in *United States v. Leon,* 468 U.S. 897, 104 S. Ct. 3405, 1984 U.S. LEXIS 153 (1984). As long as the police reasonably believed the warrant was valid, the search is legal. It would violate the Fourth Amendment if, for example, it was later shown that the police knew the affidavit used to obtain the warrant was filled with lies. In such a case, the search would be illegal and the evidence obtained would be excluded.

[22] 403 U.S. 443, 91 S. Ct. 2022, 1971 U.S. LEXIS 25 (1971).

In fact, very few people do go free because of the exclusionary rule. For example, a study by the General Accounting Office showed that suppression motions were filed in 10.5 percent of all federal prosecutions. But in 80 to 90 percent of those motions, the judge declared that the search was legal. Evidence was actually excluded in only 1.3 percent of all prosecutions. And in about one half of *those* cases, the court convicted the defendant on other evidence. Only in 0.7 percent of all prosecutions did the defendant go free after the evidence was suppressed. Other studies reveal similar results.[23]

The Patriot Act of 2001

In response to the devastating attacks of September 11, 2001, Congress passed a sweeping anti-terrorist law known as the Patriot Act. The statute was designed to give law enforcement officials greater power to investigate and prevent potential terrorist assaults. The bill raced through Congress nearly unopposed. Proponents hailed it as a vital weapon for use against continuing lethal threats. Opponents argued that the law was passed in haste and threatened the liberties of the very people it purported to shield. They urged that the statute gave law officers too much power, permitting them to conduct searches, intercept private Internet communications, and examine financial and academic records—all with little or no judicial oversight. Supporters of the law responded that its most controversial sections were scheduled to expire in four years. In the meantime, they said, constitutional protections governed the law as they did all others.

As this book goes to press, it is difficult to assess the full impact of the Patriot Act. In an early legal test, a federal judge permitted the government to use secret evidence in its effort to freeze the assets of Global Relief Foundation, a religious organization suspected of terrorist activity. The group, which claimed to be purely humanitarian, asserted that it could hardly defend itself against unseen evidence. Finding "acute national security concerns," the judge allowed the government to introduce the evidence in private, without the foundation ever seeing it.

However, a different court struck down a controversial provision of the Patriot Act. The statute permits the FBI to issue a **national security letter** (NSL) to communications firms such as Internet service providers and telephone companies. An NSL typically demands that the recipient furnish to the government its customer records and that the recipient never divulge to anyone what it has done. Under the Patriot Act, the FBI may issue an NSL, without court approval, anytime it believes the records are relevant to a terrorist investigation. A federal judge declared this section of the Patriot Act unconstitutional, because it authorized "coercive searches effectively immune from any judicial process, in violation of the Fourth Amendment." The court also declared that the section's nondisclosure requirement violated the free speech protections of the First Amendment.[24]

Public Policy	Terrorism is frightening. Freedom is vital. These competing dynamics shape the debate over the Patriot Act. In your view, where does the proper balance lie? ◆

The Fifth Amendment

The Fifth Amendment includes three important protections for criminal defendants: due process, double jeopardy, and self-incrimination.

---

23 See the discussion in *United States v. Leon* (Justice Brennan, dissenting), cited at footnote 21.
24 *Doe v. Ashcroft,* 334 F. Supp. 2d 471 (S.D.N.Y. 2004).

Due Process

Due process requires fundamental fairness at all stages of the case. The basic elements of due process are discussed in Chapter 5 on constitutional law. In the context of criminal law, due process sets additional limits. The requirement that the prosecution disclose evidence favorable to the defendant is a due process rule. Similarly, if a witness says that a tall white male robbed the liquor store, it would violate due process for the police to place the male suspect in a lineup with four short women and two rabbits.

Double Jeopardy

The prohibition against **double jeopardy** means that a criminal defendant may be prosecuted only once for a particular criminal offense. The purpose is to guarantee that the government may not destroy the lives of innocent citizens with repetitive prosecutions. Assume that Roger, the video thief, goes to trial. But the police officer cannot remember what the suspect looked like, and the jury acquits. Later, the prosecutor learns that a second witness actually *videotaped* Roger hauling VCRs from the store. Too late. The Double Jeopardy Clause prohibits the state from retrying Roger for the same offense.

Self-Incrimination

The Fifth Amendment bars the government from forcing any person to testify against himself. In other words, the police may not use mental or physical coercion to force a confession out of someone. (This clause applies only to people; corporations and other organizations are not protected.) Society does not want a government that engages in torture. Such abuse might occasionally catch a criminal, but it would grievously injure innocent people and make all citizens fearful of the government that is supposed to represent them. Also, confessions that are forced out of someone are inherently unreliable. The defendant may confess simply to end the torture. So Jake, the rape-robbery suspect who confessed at the beginning of this section, will never hear his confession used against him in court. Unless the police have other evidence, he will walk free.

When the FBI arrests Stacey for Medicare fraud, she may refuse to answer any questions. The privilege against self-incrimination covers any statement that might help to prosecute her. So, if the FBI agent asks Stacey, "Did you commit Medicare fraud?" she will refuse to answer. If the agent asks, "What are your duties here?" she will also remain silent.

Miranda

In *Miranda v. Arizona*,[25] the Supreme Court ruled that a confession obtained from a custodial interrogation may not be used against a defendant unless he was first warned of his Fifth Amendment rights. A "custodial interrogation" means that the police have prevented the defendant from leaving (usually by arresting him) and are asking him questions. If they do that, and obtain a confession from the defendant, they may use that confession in court only if they first warned him of his Fifth Amendment rights. He must be told that:

- He has the right to remain silent;
- Anything he says can be used against him at trial;
- He has the right to a lawyer; and
- If he cannot afford a lawyer, the court will appoint one for him.

---

[25] 384 U.S. 436, 86 S. Ct. 1602, 1966 U.S. LEXIS 2817 (1966).

Exclusionary Rule (Again).   If the police fail to give these warnings before inter-rogating a defendant, the exclusionary rule prohibits the prosecution from using any confession. The rationale is the same as for Fourth Amendment searches: suppressing the evidence means that the police will not attempt to get it illegally. But remember that the confession is void only if it results from custodial questioning. Suppose a policeman, investigating a bank robbery, asks a pedestrian if he noticed anything peculiar. The pedestrian says, "You mean after I robbed the bank?" Result? No custodial questioning, and the confession *may* be used against him.

The Sixth Amendment

The Sixth Amendment guarantees the **right to a lawyer** at all important stages of the criminal process. Stacey, the hospital administrator, is entitled to have her lawyer present during custodial questioning and all court hearings. Because of this right, the government must **appoint a lawyer** to represent, free of charge, any defendant who cannot afford one.

The Eighth Amendment

The Eighth Amendment prohibits cruel and unusual punishment. The most dra-matic issue litigated under this clause is the death penalty. The Supreme Court has ruled that capital punishment is not inherently unconstitutional. Most state statutes bifurcate a capital case, so that the jury first considers only guilt or innocence, and then, if the defendant is found guilty, deliberates on the death penalty. As part of that final decision, the jury must consider aggravating and mitigating circumstances that may make the ultimate penalty more or less appropriate.[26] However, other "cruel and unusual" issues are now coming to the forefront.

EWING V. CALIFORNIA

538 U.S. 11, 123 S. Ct. 1179, 155 L. Ed. 2d 108
United States Supreme Court, 2003

Facts: California passed a "three strikes" law, dra-matically increasing sentences for repeat offenders. A defendant with two or more serious convictions, who was convicted of a third felony, had to receive an indeterminate sentence of life imprisonment. Such a sentence required the defendant to actually serve a minimum of 25 years, and in some cases much more.

Gary Ewing, on parole from a nine-year prison term, stole three golf clubs worth $399 each, and was prosecuted. Because he had prior convictions, the crime, normally a misdemeanor, was treated as a felony. Ewing was convicted and sentenced to 25 years to life. He appealed, claiming that the sentence vio-lated the Eighth Amendment.

Issue: Did Ewing's sentence violate the Eighth Amendment?

Excerpts from Justice O'Connor's Decision: When the California Legislature enacted the three strikes law, it made a judgment that protecting the public safety requires incapacitating criminals who have already been convicted of at least one serious or violent crime. Nothing in the Eighth Amendment prohibits California from making that choice. To the contrary, our cases establish that States have a valid interest in deterring and segregating habitual criminals.

California's justification is no pretext. Recidivism is a serious public safety concern in California and throughout the Nation. According to a recent report, approximately 67 percent of former inmates released from state prisons were charged with at least one "seri-ous" new crime within three years of their release. In

▼

---

[26] *Gregg v. Georgia*, 428 U.S. 153, 96 S. Ct. 2909, 1976 U.S. LEXIS 82 (1976).

particular, released property offenders like Ewing had higher recidivism rates than those released after committing violent, drug, or public-order offenses.

To be sure, California's three strikes law has sparked controversy. Critics have doubted the law's wisdom, cost-efficiency, and effectiveness in reaching its goals. This criticism is appropriately directed at the legislature, which has primary responsibility for making the difficult policy choices that underlie any criminal sentencing scheme. We do not sit as a "superlegislature" to second-guess these policy choices.

In imposing a three strikes sentence, the State's interest is not merely punishing the offense of conviction, or the "triggering" offense: It is in addition the interest in dealing in a harsher manner with those who by repeated criminal acts have shown that they are simply incapable of conforming to the norms of society as established by its criminal law.

Ewing's sentence is justified by the State's public-safety interest in incapacitating and deterring recidivist felons, and amply supported by his own long, serious criminal record. Ewing has been convicted of numerous misdemeanor and felony offenses, served nine separate terms of incarceration, and committed most of his crimes while on probation or parole. His prior "strikes" were serious felonies including robbery and three residential burglaries. To be sure, Ewing's sentence is a long one. But it reflects a rational legislative judgment, entitled to deference, that offenders who have committed serious or violent felonies and who continue to commit felonies must be incapacitated. The State of California was entitled to place upon Ewing the onus of one who is simply unable to bring his conduct within the social norms prescribed by the criminal law of the State.

We hold that Ewing's sentence of 25 years to life in prison, imposed for the offense of felony grand theft under the three strikes law, is not grossly disproportionate and therefore does not violate the Eighth Amendment's prohibition on cruel and unusual punishments. ∎

Devil's Advocate

Are we really going to send Ewing to prison for a minimum of 25 years—for *shoplifting?* It is true that Ewing is a recidivist, and undoubtedly a state is entitled to punish chronic troublemakers more harshly than first-time offenders. However, this still seems excessive. In California, a first-time offense of "arson causing *great bodily injury*" incurs a maximum nine-year sentence. A first-time offender convicted of voluntary manslaughter receives a sentence of no more than 11 years. Only a first-time murderer receives a penalty equal to Ewing's—25 years to life. It is unfair to Ewing to equate his property crimes with a homicide and foolish for society to spend this much money locking him up. ◆

The Eighth Amendment also outlaws excessive fines. Forfeiture is the most controversial topic under this clause. **Forfeiture** is a *civil* law proceeding that is permitted by many different *criminal* statutes. Once a court has convicted a defendant under certain criminal statutes—such as RICO or a controlled substance law—the government may seek forfeiture of property associated with the criminal act. *How much* property can the government take? To determine if forfeiture was fair, courts generally look at three factors: whether the property was used in committing the crime, whether it was purchased with proceeds from illegal acts, and whether the punishment is disproportionate to the defendant's wrongdoing. Neal Brunk pleaded guilty to selling 2.5 ounces of marijuana, and the government promptly sought forfeiture of his house on 90 acres, worth about $99,000. The court found forfeiture was legitimate, because Brunk had used drug money to buy the land, and then sold narcotics from the property.[27] By contrast, Hosep Bajakajian attempted to leave the United States without reporting $375,000 cash to customs officials as the law requires. The government demanded forfeiture of the full sum, but the Supreme Court ruled that seizure of the entire amount would be grossly disproportionate to the minor crime of failing to report cash movement.[28]

---

[27] *U.S. v. Brunk,* 2001 U.S. App. LEXIS 7566 (4th Cir. 2001).

[28] *U.S. v. Bajakajian,* 524 U.S. 321, 118 S. Ct. 2028, 1998 U.S. LEXIS 4172 (1998).

Chapter Conclusion

Business crime appears in unexpected places, with surprising suspects. A corporate executive aware of its protean nature is in the best position to prevent it. Classic fraud and embezzlement schemes are often foiled with commonsense preventive measures. Federal sentencing guidelines make it eminently worthwhile for corporations to establish aggressive compliance programs. Sophisticated computer and money laundering crimes can be thwarted only with determination and the cooperation of citizens and police agencies. We can defeat business crime if we have the knowledge and the will.

Chapter Review

1. The rationales for punishment include restraint, deterrence, retribution, and rehabilitation.

2. In all prosecutions, the government must establish that the defendant's conduct was outlawed, that the defendant committed the *actus reus*, and that he had the necessary *mens rea*.

3. In addition to factual defenses, such as mistaken identity or alibi, a defendant may offer various legal defenses, including insanity, entrapment, and duress.

4. Larceny is the trespassory taking of personal property with the intent to steal.

5. Fraud refers to a variety of crimes, all of which involve the deception of another person for the purpose of obtaining money or property.

6. Arson is the malicious use of fire or explosives to damage or destroy real estate or personal property.

7. Embezzlement is the fraudulent conversion of property already in the defendant's possession.

8. Computer crime statutes prohibit computer trespass and fraud; wrongful use of cards, codes, and identification; and most intercepting or taping of conversations.

9. If a company's agent commits a criminal act within the scope of her employment and with the intent to benefit the corporation, the company is liable.

10. RICO prohibits using two or more racketeering acts to invest in legitimate business or carry on certain other criminal acts. RICO permits civil lawsuits as well as criminal prosecutions.

11. Money laundering consists of taking profits from a criminal act and either using them to promote crime or attempting to conceal their source.

12. The Fourth Amendment prohibits the government from making illegal searches and seizures.

13. The Fifth Amendment requires due process in all criminal procedures and prohibits double jeopardy and self-incrimination.

14. The Sixth Amendment guarantees criminal defendants the right to a lawyer.

15. Information obtained in violation of the Fourth, Fifth, or Sixth Amendment is generally excluded from trial.

16. The Eighth Amendment prohibits excessive fines and cruel and unusual punishments.

Practice Test

1. Arnie owns a two-family house in a poor section of the city. A fire breaks out, destroying the building and causing $150,000 of damage to an adjacent store. The state charges Arnie with arson. Simultaneously, Vickie, the store owner, sues Arnie for the damage to her property. Both cases are tried to juries, and the two juries hear identical evidence of Arnie's actions. But the criminal jury acquits Arnie, while the civil jury awards Vickie $150,000. How did that happen?

2. **YOU BE THE JUDGE** WRITING PROBLEM An undercover drug informant learned from a mutual friend that Philip Friedman "knew where

to get marijuana." The informant asked Friedman three times to get him some marijuana, and Friedman agreed after the third request. Shortly thereafter Friedman sold the informant a small amount of the drug. The informant later offered to sell Friedman three pounds of marijuana. They negotiated the price and then made the sale. Friedman was tried for trafficking in drugs. He argued entrapment. Was Friedman entrapped? **Argument for Friedman:** The undercover agent had to ask three times before Friedman sold him a small amount of drugs. A real drug dealer, predisposed to commit the crime, leaps at an opportunity to sell. If the government spends time and money luring innocent people into the commission of crimes, all of us are the losers. **Argument for the Government:** Government officials suspected Friedman of being a sophisticated drug dealer, and they were right. When he had a chance to buy three pounds, a quantity only a dealer would purchase, he not only did so but bargained with skill, showing a working knowledge of the business. Friedman was not entrapped—he was caught.

3. **ETHICS** Nineteen-year-old David Lee Nagel viciously murdered his grandparents, stabbing them repeatedly and slitting their throats, all because they denied him use of the family car. He was tried for murder and found not guilty by reason of insanity. He has lived ever since in mental hospitals. In 1994 he applied for release. The two psychiatrists who examined him stated that he was no longer mentally ill and was a danger neither to society nor to himself. Yet the Georgia Supreme Court refused to release him, seemingly because of the brutality of the killings. Comment on the court's ruling. What is the rationale for treating an insane defendant differently than others? Do you find the theory persuasive? If you do, what result must logically follow when psychiatrists testify that the defendant is no longer a danger? Should the brutality of the crime be a factor in deciding whether to prolong the detention? If you do not accept the rationale for treating such defendants differently, explain why not.

4. National Medical Enterprises (NME) is a large for-profit hospital and health corporation. One of its hospitals, Los Altos Hospital, in Long Beach, California, paid one doctor $219,275, allegedly for consulting work. In fact, the government claimed, the payment was in exchange for the doctor's referring to the hospital a large number of Medicare patients. Other NME hospitals engaged in similar practices, said the government. What crime is the government accusing NME of committing?

5. Kathy Hathcoat was a teller at a Pendleton, Indiana, bank. In 1990 she began taking home money that belonged in her cash drawer. Her branch manager, Mary Jane Cooper, caught her. But rather than reporting Hathcoat, Cooper joined in. The two helped cover for each other by verifying that their cash drawers were in balance. They took nearly $200,000 before bank officials found them out. What criminal charge did the government bring against Hathcoat?

6. Federal law requires that all banks file reports with the IRS any time a customer engages in a cash transaction in an amount over $10,000. It is a crime for a bank to "structure" a cash transaction—that is, to break up a single transaction of more than $10,000 into two or more smaller transactions (and thus avoid the filing requirement). In *Ratzlaf v. United States*, 510 U.S. 135, 114 S. Ct. 655, 1994 U.S. LEXIS 936 (1994), the Supreme Court held that in order to find a defendant guilty of structuring, the government must prove that he specifically intended to break the law—that is, that he knew what he was doing was a crime and meant to commit it. Congress promptly passed a law "undoing" *Ratzlaf*. A bank official can now be convicted on evidence that he structured a payment, even with no evidence that he knew it was a crime. The penalties are harsh. (1) Why is structuring so serious? (2) Why did Congress change the law about the defendant's intent?

7. Conley owned video poker machines. They are outlawed in Pennsylvania, but he placed them in bars and clubs. He used profits from the machines to buy more machines. Is he guilty of money laundering?

8. Northwest Telco Corp. (Telco) provides long-distance telephone service. Customers dial a general access number, then enter a six-digit access code and then the phone number they want to call. A computer places the call and charges the account. On January 10, 1990, Cal Edwards, a Telco engineer, noticed that Telco's general access number was being dialed exactly every 40 seconds. After

each dialing, a different six-digit number was entered, followed by a particular long-distance number. This continued from 10 PM to 6 AM. Why was Edwards concerned?

9. Under a new British law, a police officer must now say the following to a suspect placed under arrest: "You do not have to say anything. But if you do not mention now something which you later use in your defense, the court may decide that your failure to mention it now strengthens the case against you. A record will be made of anything you say and it may be given in evidence if you are brought to trial." What does a police officer in the United States have to say, and what difference does it make at the time of an arrest?

10. After graduating from college, you work hard for 15 years, saving money to buy your dream property. Finally, you spend all your savings to buy a 300-acre farm with a splendid house and pool. Happy, an old college friend, stops by. She is saving her money to make a down payment on a coffee shop in town. You let her have a nice room in your big house for a few months, until she has the funds to make her down payment. But odd acquaintances stop by almost daily for short visits, and you realize that Happy is saving money from marijuana sales. You are unhappy with this, but out of loyalty you permit it to go on for a month. Why is that a big mistake?

11. **ROLE REVERSAL** Write a short-answer question that focuses on the elements of a RICO violation.

Internet Research Problem

Go to academic.cengage.com/blaw/beatty to find a Website devoted to Internet crime. Find a current crime that might victimize you. What steps should you take to avoid harm?

You can find further practice problems at academic.cengage.com/blaw/beatty.

8 International Law

© PHOTOLINK/GETTY IMAGES

The day after Anfernee graduates from business school, he opens a shop specializing in sports caps and funky hats. Sales are brisk, but Anfernee is making little profit because his American-made caps are expensive. Then an Asian company offers to sell him identical merchandise for 45 percent less than the American suppliers charge. Anfernee is elated but quickly begins to wonder. Why is the new price so low? Are the foreign workers paid a living wage? Could the Asian company be using child labor? The sales representative expects Anfernee to sell no caps except his. Is that legal? He also requests a $50,000 cash "commission" to smooth the export process in his country. That sounds suspicious. The questions multiply without end. Will the contract be written in English or a foreign language? Must Anfernee pay in dollars or some other currency? The foreign company wants a letter of credit. What does that mean? What law will govern the agreement? If the caps are defective, how will disputes be resolved—and where?

Anfernee should put this lesson under his cap: the world is now one vast economy, and negotiations quickly cross borders. Transnational business grows with breathtaking speed. The United States now exports more than $800 billion worth of goods each year and an additional $330 billion worth of services. Leading exports include industrial machinery, computers, aircraft and other transportation equipment, electronic equipment, and chemicals.

Here are the nations that trade the most goods with the United States:

Rank	Country	Total Trade in Goods (Exports plus Imports), 2004, in Billions of Dollars
1	Canada	446
2	Mexico	267
3	China	231
4	Japan	184

Rank	Country	Total Trade in Goods (Exports plus Imports), 2004, in Billions of Dollars
5	Federal Republic of Germany	109
6	United Kingdom	82
7	South Korea	73
8	Taiwan	56
9	France	53
10	Malaysia	39
11	Italy	39
12	Netherlands	37
13	Ireland	36
14	Brazil	35
15	Singapore	35

Source: United States Census Bureau, http://census.gov.

The end is nowhere in sight. By 2010, a dozen developing countries with a total population 10 times that of the United States will account for 40 percent of all export opportunities. In China alone roughly 300 million people are entering the economic middle class— and the rank of potential consumers.

*Who are the people who do all this trading? Anfernee's modest sports cap concern is at one end of the spectrum. At the other are **multinational enterprises (MNEs)**—that is, companies doing business in several countries simultaneously.* ■

MNEs and Power

An MNE can take various forms. It may be an Italian corporation with a wholly owned American subsidiary that manufactures electrical components in Alabama and sells them in Brazil. Or it could be a Japanese company that licenses a software company in India to manufacture computer programs for sale throughout Europe. One thing is constant: the power of these huge enterprises. Each of the top 10 MNEs earns annual revenue greater than the gross domestic product of *two thirds of the world's nations*. More than 200 MNEs have annual sales exceeding $1 billion and more cash available at any one time than the majority of countries do. Money means power. This corporate might can be used to create jobs, train workers, and build lifesaving medical equipment. Such power can also be used to corrupt government officials, rip up the environment, and exploit already impoverished workers. International law is vital.

TRADE REGULATION

Nations regulate international trade in many ways. In this section we look at export and import controls that affect trade out of and into the United States. **Exporting** is shipping goods or services out of a country. The United States, with its huge farms, is the world's largest exporter of agricultural products. **Importing** is shipping goods and services into a country. The United States suffers trade deficits every year because the value of its imports exceeds that of its exports, as the following table demonstrates.

U.S. International Trade in Goods and Services (in Millions of Dollars)

	BALANCE			EXPORTS			IMPORTS		
Year	Total	Goods	Services	Total	Goods	Services	Total	Goods	Services
1980	−19,407	−25,500	6,093	271,834	224,250	47,584	291,241	249,750	41,491
1990	−80,864	−111,037	30,173	535,233	387,401	147,832	616,097	498,438	117,659
2000	−378,344	−452,414	74,070	1,070,980	771,994	298,986	1,449,324	1,224,408	224,916
2004	−617,725	−666,183	48,458	1,146,137	807,584	338,553	1,763,863	1,473,768	290,095

Source: United States Census Bureau, http://census.gov.

Export Controls

You and a friend open an electronics business, intending to purchase goods in this country for sale abroad. A representative of Interlex stops in to see you. Interlex is a Latin American electronics company, and the firm wants you to obtain for it a certain kind of infrared dome. The representative explains that this electronic miracle helps helicopters identify nearby aircraft. You find a Pennsylvania company that manufactures the domes, and you realize that you can buy and sell them to Interlex for a handsome profit. Any reason not to? As a matter of fact, there is.

All nations limit what may be exported. In the United States, several statutes do this. **Export Administration Act of 1985**[1] is one. This statute balances the need for free trade, which is essential in a capitalist society, with important requirements of national security. The statute permits the federal government to restrict exports if they endanger national security, harm foreign policy goals, or drain scarce materials.

The Secretary of Commerce makes a **Controlled Commodities List** of those items that meet any of these criteria. No one may export any commodity on the list without a license, and the license may well be denied. A second major limitation comes from the **Arms Export Control Act.**[2] This statute permits the president to create a second list of controlled goods, all related to military weaponry. Again, no person may export any listed item without a license.

The Arms Export Control Act (AECA) will prohibit you from exporting the infrared domes to the overseas company. They are used in the guidance system of one of the most sophisticated weapons in the American defense arsenal. Foreign governments have attempted to obtain the equipment through official channels, but the American government has placed the domes on the list of restricted military items. When a U.S. citizen did send such goods overseas, he was convicted and imprisoned.[3]

---

[1] 50 U.S.C. §2402 (1994).

[2] 22 U.S.C. §2778 (1994).

[3] *United States v. Tsai,* 954 F.2d 155, 1992 U.S. App. LEXIS 601 (3d Cir. 1992).

Import Controls

Tariffs

Tariffs are the most widespread method of limiting what may be imported into a nation. **A tariff is a duty (a tax) imposed on goods when they enter a country.** Nations use tariffs primarily to protect their domestic industries. Because the company importing the goods must pay this duty, the importer's costs increase, making the merchandise more expensive for consumers. This renders domestic products more attractive. High tariffs unquestionably help local industry, but they proportionately harm local buyers. Consumers benefit from zero tariffs, because the unfettered competition drives down prices.

Tariffs change frequently and vary widely from one country to another. Even within one nation, tariffs may be low on some products and high on others, as the following table demonstrates.

Country	AVERAGE TARIFFS IMPOSED ON . . .		
	Manufactured Goods	**Clothing**	**Agricultural Produce**
Brazil	16.8%	22.9%	25–49%
China	9.6%	16.1%	100–200%
European Union	4.4%	11.4%	25–49%
Egypt	22.3%	39.7%	50–99%
India	34.1%	40%	50–99%
Japan	2.9%	11%	25–49%
Sub-Saharan Africa	16.8%	34.5%	50–200%
Turkey	5.9%	11.8%	25–49%
United States	4%	11.4%	0–24%

Sources: Economic Research Service, USDA; UNCTAD; the World Bank.

As we will see later in the chapter, regional trade treaties have changed the tariff landscape. Two thirds of all U.S. products entering Mexico are duty free. Almost all trade between Canada and the United States is done with zero tariffs, which is partly why the two nations do more bilateral commerce than any others in the world.

Classification. The U.S. Customs Service imposes tariffs at the point of entry into the United States. A customs official inspects the merchandise as it arrives and **classifies** it—in other words, decides precisely what the goods are. This decision is critical because the tariff will vary depending on the classification.

Disputes at this stage typically involve an importer claiming that the Customs Service has imposed the wrong classification. The company seeks a different classification and lower tariff. The following case involves an unusual twist: The company argues that the tariff is *too low*. Now why would a sensible merchant do that?

RUBIE'S COSTUME COMPANY V. UNITED STATES

337 F.3d 1350
United States Court of Appeals for the Federal Circuit, 2003

Facts: The Customs Service examined five Halloween costumes, including "Witch of the Webs," "Pirate Boy," and "Cute and Cuddly Clown." The Service declared that "Cute and Cuddly Clown" was a baby's *garment*, with a duty rate of 16 percent; it ruled that all the other outfits were *festive articles* permitted to enter duty free.

Rubie's Costume Company filed suit, asking for a declaration that the costumes were *fancy dress*, which, under Customs regulations, are garments. Why? Because, of course, Rubie's was the largest *domestic* manufacturer of costumes in the United States. It was a different company that wanted to import the costumes. Rubie's hoped to cause two major problems for importers. First, if the costumes were garments, they would be subject to *quotas*, beyond which a company could bring in none at all. Second, each costume that did enter would cost an importer an additional 16 percent, a potentially fatal price difference in the cut-throat world of holiday fun.

The Court of International Trade ruled that the costumes were fancy-dress garments, subject to the quotas and duties. The government and various importers appealed.

Issue: Were the costumes taxable fancy-dress garments or duty-free festive articles?

Excerpts from Judge Bryson's Decision: Wearing apparel refers to clothes or coverings for the human body worn for decency or comfort. Cognizant of these definitions, Customs' classification ruling is supported by a logical and well-reasoned explanation. [The Service] presents the correct classification as "festive articles" of flimsy, non-durable costumes having utility and used as well for festive occasions, based on functional or structural deficiencies as compared with the standard counterpart articles (e.g., wearing apparel). Customs focused on the texture and quality of the materials as "flimsy and non-durable textile costumes whose principal intended use is for a one time festive occasion [which] are distinct from 'wearing apparel' which the courts have

held to be used for decency, comfort, adornment or protection." Customs reasons that the texture and quality of the materials is to be determined by such factors as the extent of styling features such as zippers, inset panels, darts or hoops, and whether the edges of the materials had been left raw or finished.

While the imports may simulate the structural features of wearing apparel, and have some incidents of clothes or coverings for the human body worn for decency or comfort, they are not practical articles which are ordinarily worn. Rather, the Halloween costumes for consumers have enormous "make believe" or festive value during appropriate occasions such as Halloween and incidentally afford the element of covering for decency or comfort. To the extent that such elements have any characteristics similar to "wearing apparel" to consumers of Halloween costumes, such features are clearly secondary to the costumes' festive value.

In addition to the festive value fostered by the imports' features of styling, and of course, the simulation of fictitious characters, the subject merchandise such as the "one-size-fits-all" Scream Robe Costume has accessories such as a hood, belt, and "ghost-face" mask that further serve to enhance the festive value of imitating a character during Halloween or at a costume party. While an adult or child might wear a "one-size-fits-all" costume with its attendant accessories for decency or comfort, such benefits are incidental and the imports are primarily created for Halloween fun, strongly promoting festive value rather than cognitive association as wearing apparel. Such costumes are generally recognized as not being normal articles of apparel.

Mindful of Customs' specialized expertise in classifying imported articles, we conclude that textile costumes of a flimsy nature and construction, lacking in durability, and generally recognized as not being normal articles of apparel are classifiable as "festive articles." The decision of the Court of International Trade holding that the subject merchandise be classified as "wearing apparel" is reversed. ∎

Valuation.   After classifying the imported goods, customs officials impose the appropriate duty *ad valorem,* meaning "according to the value of the goods." In other words, the service must determine the value of the merchandise before it can tax a percentage of that value. This step can be equally contentious, because goods will have different prices at each stage of manufacturing and delivery. The question is supposed to be settled by the **transaction value** of the goods, meaning the price actually paid for the merchandise when sold for export to the United States (plus shipping and other minor costs). But there is often room for debate, so importers use customs agents to help negotiate the most favorable valuation.

Duties for Dumping and Subsidizing

Dumping means selling merchandise at one price in the domestic market and at a cheaper, unfair price in an international market. Suppose a Singapore company, CelMaker, makes cellular telephones for $20 per unit and sells them in the United States for $12 each, vastly undercutting domestic American competitors. CelMaker may be willing to suffer short-term losses in order to drive out competitors for the American market. Once it has gained control of that market, it will raise its prices, more than compensating for its initial losses. And CelMaker may get help from its home government. Suppose the Singapore government prohibits foreign cellular phones from entering Singapore. CelMaker may sell its phones for $75 at home, earning such high profits that it can afford the temporary losses in America.

In the United States, the Commerce Department investigates suspected dumping. If the Department concludes that the foreign company is selling items at **less than fair value,** and that this harms an American industry, it will impose a **dumping duty** sufficiently high to put the foreign goods back on fair footing with domestic products.

Subsidized goods are also unfair. Suppose the Singapore government permits CelMaker to pay no taxes for 10 years. This enormous benefit will enable the company to produce cheap phones and undersell competitors. Again, the United States imposes a tariff on subsidized goods, called **countervailing duties.** If CelMaker sells phones for $15 that would cost an unsubsidized competitor $21 to make, it will pay a $6 countervailing duty on every phone entering the United States.

Nontariff Barriers

All countries use additional methods to limit imports. A **quota** is a limit on the quantity of a particular good that may enter a nation. For example, the United States, like most importing nations, has agreements with many developing nations, placing a quota on imported textiles. In some cases, textile imports from a particular country may grow by only a small percentage each year. Without such a limit, textile imports from the developing world would increase explosively because costs are so much lower there. As part of the GATT treaty (discussed later), the wealthier nations pledged to increase textile imports from the developing countries, but whether that has occurred is open to dispute.

An **import ban** means that particular goods are flatly prohibited. Some nations prohibit alcohol imports for religious reasons. The United States bars the importation of narcotic drugs. Virtually all countries from time to time halt certain goods for political purposes, for example, to protest the behavior of the exporting country. The United States has increasingly used economic sanctions in an effort to advance its foreign policy goals. During one three-year period, it threatened or imposed sanctions 60 times, against 35 nations. Sanctions were aimed at Colombia for permitting drug trafficking; the Netherlands, Switzerland, and other European nations for trading with Cuba; and Taiwan for environmental violations. Proponents of such sanctions consider them essential components of an ethical foreign policy. Opponents regard them as hypocritical attempts at moral superiority.

Money and politics are a volatile mix, as demonstrated by all recorded history from 3000 B.C.E. to the present. As long as nations have existed, they have engaged in disputes about quotas and import bans. And that is why more than 100 countries negotiated and signed the GATT treaty, the subject of the next section.

General Agreement on Tariffs and Trade (GATT)

What is GATT? The greatest boon to American commerce in a century. The worst assault on the American economy in 200 years. It depends on whom you ask. Let's start where everyone agrees.

GATT is the General Agreement on Tariffs and Trade. This massive international treaty has been negotiated on and off since the 1940s to eliminate trade barriers and bolster commerce. GATT has already had considerable effect. In 1947 the worldwide average tariff on industrial goods was about 40 percent. Now it is about 4 percent (although agricultural duties still average more than 40 percent). The world's economies have exploded over that half century. Proponents of GATT applaud the agreement. Opponents scoff that both lower duties and higher trade would have arrived without GATT.

The most recent round of bargaining took seven hard years. Finally, in 1994, the United States and 125 other countries signed the treaty. A **signatory** (i.e., a nation that signs a treaty) is still not bound by the agreement until it is **ratified**—that is, until the nation's legislature votes to honor it. In the United States, Congress voted to ratify GATT. If the latest round of cuts is fully implemented, average duties in all signatories should drop to about 3.7 percent. Further, nearly half of all trade in industrial goods will be duty free, at least in developed countries. That must be good—or is it?

Trade

Leading supporters of GATT suggest that its lower tariffs vastly increase world trade. The United States is one of the biggest beneficiaries because for decades this country has imposed lower duties than most other nations. American companies for once compete on equal footing. A typical American family's annual income has increased due to the more vigorous domestic economy, and at the same time many goods are less expensive because they enter with low duties.

But opponents claim that the United States now competes against nations with unlimited pools of exploited labor. These countries dominate labor-intensive industries such as textiles, clothing, and manufacturing and are steadily taking jobs from millions of American workers. It is unfair for U.S. companies to struggle against competitors in countries with no labor standards and dirt-cheap pay. Because domestic job losses come in low-end employment, those put out of work are precisely those least able to find a new job. The chasm between rich and poor is widening, leaving us all the losers.

World Trade Organization and the Environment

GATT created the **World Trade Organization (WTO)** to stimulate international commerce and resolve trade disputes. The WTO is empowered to hear arguments from any signatory nation about tariff violations or nontariff barriers. This international "court" may order compliance from any nation violating GATT and may penalize countries by imposing trade sanctions. Proponents say that it is high time to have one international body to resolve complex issues impartially and create an international body of trade law that corporations can rely on when planning business.

Here is how the WTO decides a trade dispute. Suppose that the United States believes that Brazil is unfairly restricting trade. The United States uses the WTO offices to request a consultation with Brazil's trade representative. In the majority of cases, these discussions lead to a satisfactory settlement. If the consultation does not resolve the problem, the United States asks the WTO's Dispute Settlement Body (DSB) to form a panel, which consists of three nations uninvolved in the dispute. After the panel hears testimony and arguments from both countries, it releases its report. The DSB generally approves the report, unless either nation appeals. If there is an appeal, the WTO Appellate Body hears the dispute and generally makes the final decision, subject to approval by the entire WTO. No single nation has the power to block final decisions. If a country refuses to comply with the WTO's ruling, affected nations may retaliate by imposing punitive tariffs. (The official Web site of the WTO, http://www.wto.org/, includes libraries on all sorts of international trade topics, from goods and services to dispute settlement and legal texts.)

The following case forced the WTO to weigh the merits of two important, competing goals: environmental protection and trade growth.

UNITED STATES—IMPORT PROHIBITION OF CERTAIN SHRIMP AND SHRIMP PRODUCTS

WT/DS58/R15
WTO Panel, 1998

Facts: Sea turtles are migratory animals that live throughout the world. The United States recognizes the animals as an endangered species. Studies showed that the greatest threat to the turtles, around the world, came from shrimp fishermen inadvertently catching the animals in their nets. The federal government responded by requiring any importers to certify that shrimp had been caught using Turtle Excluder Devices (TEDs), which keep the animals out of the nets.

India, Pakistan, Malaysia, and Thailand filed complaints with the WTO, claiming that the United States had no right to impose its environmental concerns on world trade. The United States argued that Article XX of the WTO Agreement permitted trade restrictions based on environmental concerns. Article XX states in part:

> Nothing in this Agreement shall be construed to prevent the adoption or enforcement by any Member of measures:
> (b) necessary to protect human, animal or plant life or health;
> (g) relating to the conservation of exhaustible natural resources if such measures are made effective in conjunction with restrictions on domestic production or consumption.

The Dispute Settlement Body appointed a panel to hear the dispute and make recommendations.

Issue: Did Article XX permit the United States to impose environmental restrictions on shrimp importers?

Excerpts from the Panel's Report: The WTO Agreement acknowledges that the optimal use of the world's resources must be pursued "in accordance with the objective of sustainable development, seeking both to protect and preserve the environment and to enhance the means of doing so in a manner consistent with [Members'] respective needs and concerns at different levels of economic development." On the other hand, [different sections of the Agreement] refer to "entering into reciprocal and mutually advantageous arrangements directed to the substantial reduction of tariffs and other barriers to trade and to the elimination of discriminatory treatment" in international trade relations. The central focus of that agreement remains the promotion of economic development through trade.

If one WTO Member were allowed to adopt such measures [as the shrimp regulation], then other Members would also have the right to adopt similar measures on the same subject but with differing, or even conflicting, requirements. If that happened, it would be impossible for exporting Members to

▼

comply at the same time with multiple conflicting policy requirements.

The United States claims that sea turtles are a shared global resource and that, therefore, it has an interest and a right to impose the measures at issue. Even assuming that sea turtles were a shared global resource, we consider that the notion of "shared" resource implies a common interest in the resource concerned. If such a common interest exists, it would be better addressed through the negotiation of international agreements than by measures taken by one Member conditioning access to its market to the adoption by other Members of certain conservation policies.

The Panel recommends that the Dispute Settlement Body request the United States to bring this measure into conformity with its obligations under the WTO Agreement. ■

The United States appealed the panel's decision to the WTO's Appellate Body.

UNITED STATES—IMPORT PROHIBITION OF CERTAIN SHRIMP AND SHRIMP PRODUCTS

AB-1998-4
WTO Appellate Body, 1998

Excerpts from the Appellate Body's Report:
The [shrimp policy] requires other WTO Members to adopt a regulatory program that is not merely comparable, but rather essentially the same, as that applied to the United States shrimp trawl vessels. The effect is to establish a rigid and unbending standard by which United States officials determine whether or not countries will be certified, thus granting or refusing other countries the right to export shrimp to the United States.

The United States requires the use of approved TEDs at all times by domestic, commercial shrimp trawl vessels. It may be quite acceptable for a government to adopt a single standard applicable to all its citizens throughout that country. However, it is not acceptable, in international trade relations, for one WTO Member to use an economic embargo to require other Members to adopt essentially the same comprehensive regulatory program, without taking into consideration different conditions which may occur in the territories of those other Members.

The United States [failed] to engage other Members exporting shrimp to the United States, in serious, across-the-board negotiations with the objective of concluding bilateral or multilateral agreements for the protection and conservation of sea turtles.

We have not decided that the protection and preservation of the environment is of no significance to the Members of the WTO. Clearly, it is. We have not decided that the sovereign nations that are Members of the WTO cannot adopt effective measures to protect endangered species, such as sea turtles. Clearly, they can and should.

What we have decided in this appeal is simply this: although the measure of the United States in dispute in this appeal serves an environmental objective that is recognized as legitimate, this measure has been applied by the United States in a manner which constitutes arbitrary and unjustifiable discrimination between Members of the WTO. ■

Public Policy

Environmental groups attacked the ruling, declaring that the WTO paid lip service to the environment but ensured further killing of an important endangered species. Trade supporters applauded it. In addition to the trade versus environment tension, there is a second conflict: rich versus poor. Critics of the shrimp regulations claim that it is unseemly for a wealthy nation to punish subsistence fishermen because of environmental concerns. Their opponents argue that we all share this planet, and long-term growth for each of us depends upon living in harmony with limited resources and fragile ecosystems. Which of the competing goals is more important to you? ◆

Child labor is an even more wrenching issue. The practice exists to some degree in all countries and is common throughout the developing world. The International Labor Organization, an affiliate of the United Nations, estimates that 120 million children between the ages of 5 and 14 work full time, and 130 million more labor part time. As the world generally becomes more prosperous, this ugly problem has actually increased. Children in developing countries typically work in agriculture and domestic work, but many toil in mines and others in factories, making rugs, glass, clothing, and other goods.

The rug industry illustrates the international nature of this tragedy. In the 1970s, the Shah of Iran banned child labor in rug factories, but many manufacturers simply packed up and moved to southern Asia. Today in India and Pakistan, tens of millions of children, some as young as four, toil in rug workrooms, seven days a week, 12 hours a day. Many, shackled to the looms they operate, are essentially slaves, working for pennies a day or, in some cases, for no money at all.

Ethics

Child labor raises compelling moral questions—and economic ones as well. No American company can compete with an industry that uses slave labor. As discussed earlier, the United States is relatively quick to impose trade sanctions in response to moral issues. In 1997, Congress passed a statute prohibiting the import of goods created by forced or indentured child labor. The first suit under the new law targeted the carpet factories of southern Asia and sought an outright ban on most rugs from that area. Is this statute humane legislation or cultural imperialism dressed as a nontariff barrier? Should the voters of this country or the WTO decide the issue? In answering such difficult questions, we must bear in mind that child labor is truly universal. The United Farm Workers union estimates that 800,000 underage children help their migrant parents harvest U.S. crops—work that few Americans are willing to do.

Our response to such a troubling moral issue need not take the form of a statute or lawsuit. Duke University is one of the most popular names in sports apparel, and the school annually sells about $20 million worth of T-shirts, sweatshirts, jackets, caps, and other sportswear bearing its logo. To produce its clothing, the university licenses about 700 companies in the United States and 10 foreign countries. In response to the troubling issue of child labor, Duke adopted a code of conduct that prohibits its manufacturers from using forced or child labor and requires all of the firms to pay a minimum wage, permit union organizing, and maintain a safe workplace. The university plans to monitor the companies producing its apparel and terminate the contract for any firm that violates its rules. ◆

Intellectual Property

Some foreign countries, particularly developing nations, have long ignored U.S. copyrights and patents. GATT changes things. It allows this country to halt duty-free imports from, and assess tariffs against, a nation that refuses to honor American copyrights or patents.

WTO Summary

It will be many years before we can fairly evaluate GATT and the WTO. In all likelihood, some of the most extreme claims will prove false, and the agreement's effects will evolve somewhere in the middle. Unquestionably, some industries will suffer, forcing workers into unemployment. Others will discover and exploit lucrative opportunities. Perhaps the final cost/benefit analysis of the WTO will be decided not by the letter of its rulings but by the spirit and goodwill of those who implement them.

Regional Agreements

Many regional agreements also regulate international trade. We will briefly describe some that affect the United States.

The EU (European Union) Countries)

The European Union

The **European Union (EU)** used to be known as the Common Market. The original six members—Belgium, France, Luxembourg, the Netherlands, West Germany, and Italy—have been joined by nineteen additional countries. See the map on this page.

The EU is one of the world's most powerful associations, with a prosperous population of more than 460 million. Its sophisticated legal system sets Union-wide standards for tariffs, dumping, subsidies, antitrust, transportation, and many other issues. The first goals of the EU were to eliminate trade barriers between member nations, establish common tariffs with respect to external countries, permit the free movement of citizens across its borders, and coordinate its agricultural and fishing policies for the collective good. The EU has largely achieved these goals. Most but not all of the EU countries have adopted a common currency, the euro. During the next decade the union will focus on further economic integration and effective coordination of foreign policy.

NAFTA

In 1993, the United States, Canada, and Mexico signed the **North American Free Trade Agreement (NAFTA).** The principal goal was to eliminate almost all trade barriers, tariff and nontariff, between the three nations. Like GATT, this trilateral (three-nation) compact has been controversial, and there will probably never be agreement on NAFTA's value because the treaty has enriched some while impoverishing others. Unquestionably, trade between the three nations has increased enormously. Mexico now exports more goods to the United States than do Germany, Britain, and Korea combined. Opponents of the treaty argue that NAFTA costs the United States jobs and lowers the living standards of American workers by forcing them to compete with low-paid labor. For example, Swingline Staplers closed a factory in Queens, New York, after 75 years of operation and moved to Mexico. Instead of paying its American workers $11.58 per hour, Swingline will pay Mexican workers 50 cents an hour to do the same job. Proponents contend that although some jobs are lost, many others are gained, especially in fields with a future, such as high technology. They claim that as new jobs invigorate the Mexican economy, consumers there will be able to afford American goods for the first time, providing an enormous new market. Both Canadian and Mexican laws are available online at http://www.lawsource.com by clicking on "Canada" and "Mexico."

ASEAN

The Association of Southeast Asian Nations consists of 10 countries: Brunei Darussalam, Cambodia, Indonesia, Laos, Malaysia, Myanmar, the Philippines, Singapore, Thailand, and Vietnam. The group's population of about 500 million produces a combined gross domestic product of $737 billion and total trade of $720 billion. ASEAN seeks to eliminate tariffs, accelerate economic growth, and promote peace and stability in the region.

Mercosur

Brazil, Argentina, Uruguay, and Paraguay formed Mercosur to improve commerce among the four South American nations. The organization represents the fourth largest economic entity in the world, after the EU, the United States, and Japan. The Mercosur nations have a combined population of more than 200 million and a GDP of more than $1 trillion. Almost all trade barriers between the nations have been eliminated, and the organization has established a broad social agenda focusing on education, labor, culture, the environment, justice, and consumer protection.

INTERNATIONAL SALES AGREEMENTS

Cowboy boots are hot in France. Big Heel, Inc., your small company in Tucson, Arizona, makes superb boots with exquisite detailing, and you realize that France could be a bonanza. Your first decision is how to produce and sell the boots in France. For our purposes, Big Heel has three choices:

- *Direct Sales.* You can continue to manufacture the boots in Tucson and sell them directly to French retailers.
- *Indirect Sales.* You can manufacture the boots in Tucson and use a French distributor to wholesale them to French stores.
- *Licensing.* You can license a French manufacturer to make Big Heel boots in France and wholesale them.

Direct Sales

You decide to sell the boots directly. Le Pied D'Or, a new, fast-growing French chain of shoe stores, is interested in buying 10,000 pairs of your boots, at about $300 per pair. You must focus on two principal issues: the sales contract and letters of credit. You are wise enough to know that you must have a written contract—$3 million is a lot of money for Big Heel.

This is a contract for the sale of goods. **Goods** are things that can be moved, such as boots, airplanes, pencils, and computers. A sale of goods is governed by different law than the sale of real estate (e.g., a house), securities (e.g., a share of stock), or services (e.g., accounting).

What Law Governs the Sale of Goods?

Potentially, three conflicting laws could govern your boot contract: Arizona law, French law, and an international treaty. Each is different, and it is therefore essential to negotiate which law will control.

Because this contract is for the sale of goods, your local law is the Arizona **Uniform Commercial Code (UCC).** The UCC is discussed throughout Units 2 and 3 on contracts and commercial transactions. This statute has taken the common law principles of contract and modified them to meet the needs of contemporary business. Article 2 of the UCC governs the sale of goods. American business lawyers are familiar with the UCC and will generally prefer that it govern. French law is based on **Roman law** and the **Napoleonic Code** and is obviously different. French lawyers and business executives are naturally partial to it. How to compromise? Perhaps by using a neutral law.

The **United Nations Convention on Contracts for the International Sale of Goods (CISG)** is the result of 50 years of work by various international groups, all seeking to create a uniform, international law on this important subject. Finally, in 1980, a United Nations conference adopted the CISG, though it became the law in individual nations only if and when they adopted it. The United States and most of its principal trading partners have adopted this important treaty.

The CISG applies automatically to any contract for the sale of goods between two parties, from different countries, each of which is a signatory. France and the United States have both signed. Thus the CISG automatically applies to the Big Heel–Pied D'Or deal unless the parties *specifically opt out*. If the parties want to be governed by other law, they must state very clearly that they exclude the CISG and elect, for example, the UCC.

at RISK

Should the parties allow the CISG to govern? They can make an intelligent choice by first understanding how the CISG differs from other law. Here are a few key differences between the CISG and the UCC:

- **Must the contract be written?** Under the UCC, a contract for the sale of goods valued at more than $500 generally must be written to be enforceable. But the CISG does not require a writing for any contract. Be advised that discussions you consider informal or preliminary might create a contract under the CISG.

- **When is an offer irrevocable?** The UCC declares that an offer is irrevocable only if it is in writing and states that it will be held open for a fixed period. But the CISG makes some offers irrevocable even if unwritten.

- **What if an acceptance includes new terms?** Under the UCC, an acceptance generally creates a contract, even if it uses new terms. But the CISG insists on an acceptance that is a "mirror image" of the offer. Almost anything else constitutes a rejection.

- **What remedies are available?** The UCC entitles a plaintiff only to money damages for breach of a sales contract. But the CISG permits many plaintiffs to seek specific performance of the contract—that is, to force the other party to perform the contract. ◆

Choice of Forum

The parties must decide not only what law governs, but where disagreements will be resolved. The French and American legal systems are dramatically different. In a French civil lawsuit, generally neither side is entitled to depose the other or to obtain interrogatories or even documents, in sharp contrast to the American system where such discovery methods dominate litigation. American lawyers, accustomed to discovery to prepare a case and advance settlement talks, are unnerved by the French system. Similarly, French lawyers are dismayed at the idea of spending two years taking depositions, exchanging paper, and arguing motions, all at great expense. At trial, the contrasts grow. In a French civil trial, there is generally no right to a jury. The rules of evidence are more flexible (and unpredictable), neither side employs its own expert witnesses, and the parties themselves never appear as witnesses.

Choice of Language and Currency

The parties must select a language for the contract and a currency for payment. Language counts because legal terms seldom translate literally. Currency is vital because the exchange rate may alter between the signing and payment. Suppose the Argentine peso falls 30 percent against the dollar in one week. An Argentine company that contracted on Monday to pay $1 million for U.S. aircraft engines will suddenly have to pay 30 percent more in pesos to meet its contractual obligations. To avoid such calamities, companies engaged in international commerce often purchase from currency dealers a guarantee to obtain the needed currency at a future date for a guaranteed price. Assuming that Big Heel insists on being paid in U.S. dollars, Pied D'Or could obtain a quote from a currency dealer as to the present cost of obtaining $3 million at the time the boots are to be delivered. Pied D'Or might pay a 5 percent premium for this guarantee, but it will have insured itself against disastrous currency changes.

Choices Made.   The parties agree that the contract price will be paid in U.S. dollars. Pied D'Or is unfamiliar with the UCC and absolutely refuses to make a deal unless either French law or the CISG governs. Your lawyer, Susan Fisher, recommends accepting the CISG, provided that the contract is written in English and that any disputes will be resolved in Arizona courts. Pied D'Or balks at this, but Fisher presses hard, and ultimately those are the terms agreed upon. Fisher is delighted with the arrangement, pointing out that the CISG provisions can all be taken into account as the contract is written, and that by using Arizona courts to settle any dispute, Big Heel has an advantage in terms of familiarity and location.

Letter of Credit

Because Pied D'Or is new and fast growing, you are not sure it will be able to foot the bill. Pied D'Or provides a letter of reference from its bank, La Banque Bouffon, but this is a small bank in Pleasanterie, France, unfamiliar to you. You need greater assurance of payment, and Fisher recommends that payment be made by **letter of credit.** Here is how the letter will work.

Big Heel demands that the contract include a provision requiring payment by confirmed, irrevocable letter of credit. Le Pied D'Or agrees. The French company now contacts its bank, La Banque Bouffon, and instructs Bouffon to issue a letter of credit to Big Heel. The letter of credit is a promise *by the bank itself* to pay Big Heel, if Big Heel presents certain documents. Banque Bouffon, of course, expects to be repaid by Pied D'Or. The bank is in a good position to assess Pied D'Or's creditworthiness because it is local and can do any investigating it wants before issuing the credit. It may also insist that Pied D'Or give Bouffon a mortgage on property or that Pied D'Or deposit money in a separate Bouffon account. Pied D'Or is the **account party** on the letter of credit, and Big Heel is the **beneficiary.**

But at Big Heel you are still not entirely satisfied about getting paid because you don't know anything about Bouffon. That is why you have required a *confirmed* letter of credit. Bouffon will forward its letter of credit to Big Heel's own bank, the Bandito Trust Company of Tucson. Bandito examines the letter and then *confirms* the letter. This is *Bandito's own guarantee* that it will pay Big Heel. Bandito will do this only if it knows, through international banking contacts, that Bouffon is a sound bank. The risk has now been spread to two banks, and at Big Heel you are confident of payment.

You get busy, make excellent boots, and pack them. When they are ready, you truck them to Galveston, where they are taken alongside a ship, *Le Fond de la Mer.* Your agent presents the goods to the ship's officials, along with customs documents that describe the goods. *Le Fond de la Mer*'s officer in turn issues your agent a **negotiable bill of lading.** This document describes *exactly* the goods received—their quantity, color, quality, and anything else important.

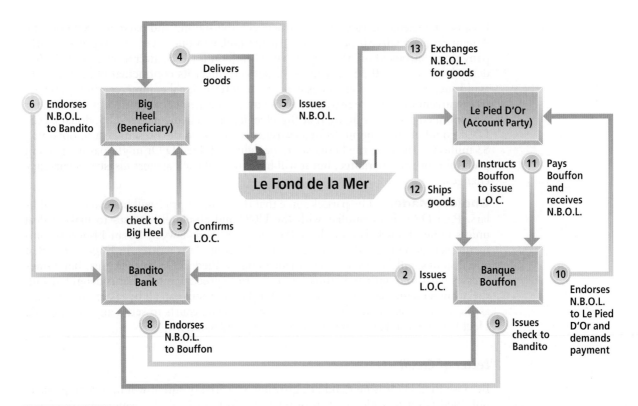

Exhibit 8.1

You now take the negotiable bill of lading to Bandito Trust. You also present to Bandito a **draft,** which is simply a formal order to Bandito to pay, based on the letter of credit. Bandito will look closely at the bill of lading, which must specify *precisely* the goods described in the letter of credit. Why so nitpicky? Because the bank is dealing only in paper. It never sees the boots. Bandito is exchanging $3 million of its own money based on instructions in the letter of credit. The bank should pay only if the bill of lading indicates that *Le Fond de la Mer* received exactly what is described in the letter of credit. Bandito will decide whether the bill of lading is *conforming* or *nonconforming.* If the terms of both documents are identical, the bill of lading is conforming and Bandito must pay. If the terms vary, the bill of lading is nonconforming and Bandito will deny payment. Thus, if the bill of lading indicated 9,000 pairs of boots and 1,000 pairs of sneakers, it is nonconforming and Big Heel would get no money.

Bandito concludes that the documents are conforming, so it issues a check to Big Heel for $3 million. In return, you endorse the bill of lading and other documents over to the Bandito Bank, which endorses the same documents and sends them to Banque Bouffon. Bouffon makes the same minute inspection and then writes a check to Bandito. Bouffon then demands payment from Le Pied D'Or. Pied D'Or pays its bank, receiving in exchange the bill of lading and customs documents. Note that payment in all stages is now complete, though the boots are still rolling on the high seas. Finally, when the boots arrive in Le Havre, Pied D'Or trucks roll up to the wharf and, using the bill of lading and customs documents, collect the boots. (See Exhibit 8.1.)

Good news: They fit! Not all customers walk away in such comfort, as the following case indicates.

CENTRIFUGAL CASTING MACHINE CO., INC. V. AMERICAN BANK & TRUST CO.

966 F.2d 1348, 1992 U.S. App. LEXIS 13089
Tenth Circuit Court of Appeals, 1992

Facts: Centrifugal Casting Machine Co. (CCM) entered into a contract with the State Machinery Trading Co. (SMTC), an agency of the Iraqi government. CCM agreed to manufacture cast iron pipe plant equipment for a total price of $27 million. The contract specified payment of the full amount by confirmed irrevocable letter of credit. The Central Bank of Iraq then issued the letter, on behalf of SMTC (the "account party") to be paid to CCM (the "beneficiary"). The Banca Nazionale del Lavorov (BNL) confirmed the letter.

Following Iraq's invasion of Kuwait on August 2, 1990, President George H.W. Bush issued two executive orders blocking the transfer of property in the United States in which Iraq held any interest. In other words, no one could use, buy, or sell any Iraqi property or cash. When CCM attempted to draw upon the letter of credit, the United States government intervened. The government claimed that like all Iraqi money in the United States, this money was frozen by the executive order. The United States District Court rejected the government's claim, and the government appealed.

Issue: Is CCM entitled to be paid pursuant to the letter of credit?

Excerpts from Judge Sentelle's Decision: The United States contends on appeal that the freeze of Iraq's assets furthers national policy to punish Iraq by preventing it from obtaining economic benefits from transactions with American citizens, and by preserving such assets both for use as a bargaining chip in resolving this country's differences with Iraq and as a source of compensation for claims Americans may have against Iraq. We agree that these policy considerations are compelling and that we are therefore required to construe Iraqi property interests broadly. However, we are not persuaded these policies would be furthered by [creating] a property interest on behalf of Iraq that would not otherwise be cognizable under governing legal principles.

Two interrelated features of the letter of credit provide it with its unique value in the marketplace and are of critical importance in our consideration of the United States' claim here. First, the simple result [of a letter of credit] is that the issuer [i.e., the bank] substitutes its credit, preferred by the beneficiary, for that of the account party. Second, the issuer's obligation to pay on a letter of credit is completely independent from the underlying commercial transaction between the beneficiary and the account party. Significantly, the issuer must honor a proper demand even though the beneficiary has breached the underlying contract; even though the insolvency of the account party renders reimbursement impossible; and notwithstanding supervening illegality, impossibility, war or insurrection. This principle of independence is universally viewed as essential to the proper functioning of a letter of credit and to its particular value, i.e., its certainty of payment.

This assurance of payment gives letters of credit a central role in commercial dealings, and gives them a particular value in international transactions, in which sophisticated investors knowingly undertake such risks as political upheaval or contractual breach in return for the benefits to be reaped from international trade. Law affecting such an essential instrument of the economy must be shaped with sensitivity to its special characteristics. Accordingly, courts have concluded that the whole purpose of a letter of credit would be defeated by examining the merits of the underlying contract dispute to determine whether the letter should be paid.

Because of the nature of a letter of credit, we conclude that Iraq does not have a property interest in the money CCM received under the letter. The United States contends in essence that Iraq has a property interest in this money because it was allegedly a contract payment made by Iraq, which Iraq should recover because CCM breached the contract. In so arguing, the United States makes a breach of contract claim on behalf of Iraq that Iraq has never made, creates a remedy for the contracting parties in derogation of the remedy they themselves provided and, most importantly, disregards the controlling legal principles with respect to letters of credit.

Affirmed. ∎

Indirect Sales through a Distributor

You might also have decided that Big Heel would be better off doing business through a French shoe distributor, on the theory that the local company would have superior market knowledge and easier access to valuable retailers. The questions you face regarding choice of law, forum, and method of payment are identical to those you face in direct sales; they must be worked out in advance. But there is one additional problem that deserves close attention.

Suppose you choose Voleurs Freres, a French fashion distributor, to do all of Big Heel's work in France. Voleurs Freres will be an **exclusive dealer,** meaning that it will take on no other accounts of cowboy boots. In return you will give it an **exclusive distributorship,** indicating that no other French distributors will get a chance at Big Heel boots. This is a common method of working. Voleurs Freres benefits because no one else in France may distribute the valuable boots. Big Heel in turn need not worry that Voleurs Freres will devote more energy to a competing boot. It is a tidy relationship, but does it violate antitrust laws?

Antitrust laws make it illegal to destroy competition and capture an entire market. The United States and the EU both have strong antitrust laws that can potentially be applied domestically and in foreign countries.

EU Antitrust Law

The European Union law is found in Articles 85 and 86 of the Treaty of Rome. From the American point of view, the former is more important. **Article 85 outlaws any agreement, contract, or discussion that distorts competition within EU countries.** In other words, any attempt to gain a market edge by *avoiding* competition is going to be suspect. Suppose three Italian cosmetic firms agree to act in unison to increase earnings. They set common prices for makeup and agree that none will undersell the others. This greatly reduces competition, leaving the consumer with fewer options and more expensive products. Their deal violates Article 85.

Will Big Heel's contract with Voleurs Freres violate Article 85? There is no quick answer. You will need to do a careful market analysis and consult with French lawyers, who undoubtedly will have many questions. How popular are Big Heel boots in Europe? How many competitors would like to distribute them? How many other boot companies want Voleurs Freres to sell *their* products? Does the exclusive arrangement between Big Heel and Voleurs Freres diminish competition? Will consumers pay more because of the contract? These questions are a nuisance and an expense, but it is easier and cheaper to make the inquiry now than to face years of antitrust litigation.

American Antitrust Law

In the United States, the primary antitrust law is the **Sherman Act.**[4] This statute controls anticompetitive conduct that harms the American market. It will probably not affect the Big Heel–Voleurs Freres contract, because that deal is likely to have consequences only in Europe. But it is important to understand the Sherman Act when facing foreign competition. In effect, this statute is the American counterpart to Article 85. Any conduct that eliminates competition in the United States and enables one company, or group of companies, to control a market probably violates this law. And "any conduct" means that anticompetitive acts taking place in a foreign country may still violate the Sherman Act. A company doing business in the United States **may sue a competitor based on its conduct in a foreign country,** provided the local

---

[4] See Chapter 20, on antitrust law.

firm can show (1) that the foreign competitor *intends* to affect the U.S. market, and (2) that the foreign conduct has a *direct and substantial effect* on the U.S. market.

Let's look again at the Italian cosmetics makers. Suppose they decide to act in unison in the United States. They set common prices and agree not to compete with each other. That agreement is illegal. It violates the Sherman Act *even if all arrangements were made in Milan.* The companies intend to affect the U.S. market. When an American cosmetics firm demonstrates that the agreement caused it direct and substantial harm, the company may file suit in the United States against all three Italian corporations and expect to recover large damages.

International Comity

But what if the foreign corporation is doing business in a way that is entirely legal in its native country? May U.S. antitrust law still penalize the company's conduct if it harms American business? That was the question presented in the following case, which raises the issue of **international comity.** The word "comity" in this context means "concomitant jurisdiction," meaning that two courts have the right to hear a particular case. When those two courts are in different nations, the laws of the two countries may conflict. **In the event of a conflict, international comity requires one court to respect the other legal system and decline to hear a suit if it would more logically be resolved in the foreign country.** Does that principle govern the following case? The plaintiffs wanted the case heard in the United States under the Sherman Act, while the defendants wanted any dispute settled in Britain, where they believed British law would find them innocent of any wrongdoing.

You Be the Judge

HARTFORD FIRE INSURANCE CO. V. CALIFORNIA

509 U.S. 764, 113 S. Ct. 2891, 1993
U.S. LEXIS 4404
United States Supreme Court, 1993

Facts: Nineteen states and many private plaintiffs sued various insurance companies, alleging Sherman Act violations. The conspiracies related to commercial general liability (CGL) insurance, which covers the insured against accident and damage claims by customers, other companies, or the general public. The defendants were "reinsurance" companies. When a primary insurer issues a CGL policy to a corporation, it usually obtains for itself insurance to cover at least a portion of the risk it is assuming.

Lloyd's of London is a major reinsurance center. Various English syndicates, working through Lloyd's, provide reinsurance for companies throughout the world. The plaintiffs alleged that reinsurers at Lloyd's forced American primary insurers to change the terms of their standard CGL insurance. These changes shortened the time during which a customer could file a claim under its policy and eliminated certain claims altogether. These changes made CGL less valuable to the insured and more profitable to the reinsurers. The reinsurers were able to impose these changes because (1) there are only a few reinsurers worldwide and (2) all the reinsurers worked in collusion to limit the coverage.

The United States District Court concluded that because the reinsurers' conduct was legal in Britain, international comity prevented an American court from hearing the claims. The court dismissed the case. The Court of Appeals reversed, and the London reinsurers appealed to the United States Supreme Court.

You Be the Judge: **Does the principle of international comity prevent an American court from**

▼

hearing these antitrust claims against London reinsurers?

Argument for the London Reinsurers: Lloyd's of London has been one of the world's most respected insurance organizations since 1688. Beginning in 1879, Parliament has directly regulated Lloyd's, and continues to control it today, pursuant to the Insurance Companies Act of 1982 and appropriate regulations. Under British law, insurance companies and reinsurance companies are *expressly exempt* from antitrust regulation. Everything that the defendants are alleged to have done in this case is *entirely legal* in Britain. It is an extraordinarily dangerous idea to permit the courts of one nation to subject foreign nationals to phenomenally expensive litigation for alleged conduct that was absolutely legal and proper where it was done.

Further, even though plaintiffs allege that the defendants' conduct technically violated American laws, there can be no suggestion that any of the reinsurers intended to harm any American corporation or citizen. This is not some shady conspiracy forged on a foggy night in an abandoned shack. The London reinsurers simply attempted to limit their own liability. They chose a lawful means to do it. They were doing, in other words, precisely what the plaintiffs in this case do when they buy insurance!

Argument for the Plaintiffs: Your honors, the defendants all engaged in conduct that they knew violated American antitrust laws. They did it for one reason: to increase their profits. That, of course, is why any corporation attempts to control a market. Here, by fixing deals with other major reinsurers, the Lloyd's syndicates were able to dictate the terms of American primary insurance and reduce coverage to the plaintiffs.

The defendants argue that they have obeyed British law, and that a so-called conflict in the laws requires American courts to stay away. But there is in fact no conflict between American and British law. It may be true that the reinsurers' monopolistic practices do not *violate* British law. But that does not mean that British law *requires* them to behave this way. It is black letter law that American antitrust laws may be applied against conduct that is lawful in a foreign nation. There would be a conflict only if British insurance law *required* Lloyd's firms to act collusively and attempt to control the American market. Obviously, it does not. The Lloyd's reinsurers are free to obey American law and British law, and that is what they ought to have done. They didn't, and we ask a chance to prove that in court.

These reinsurers are some of the most sophisticated business people in the world. They entered the American insurance market to make a profit and have stayed here many decades because they *are* earning money. They can't have it both ways. If they enter this market, they must be governed by its laws the same as anyone else. ●

Licensing a Foreign Manufacturer

Big Heel has a third option when selling abroad, which is to license a French manufacturer to produce Big Heel boots. It should do this only if it is convinced the manufacturer will maintain sufficiently high standards. Even so, there are two major issues.

First, Big Heel must ensure that all its patents and trademarks are protected. In fact, France will honor both forms of American intellectual property, and there should be no problems. But some nations may ignore American intellectual property rights, and no company should establish a licensing arrangement without investigating. As mentioned earlier, the WTO should increase respect worldwide for the intellectual property rights created by all nations.

Second, if Big Heel grants an exclusive license to any French manufacturer, it could encounter exactly the same antitrust problems as those discussed earlier. It must analyze both EU and American antitrust law before taking the risk.

INVESTING ABROAD

Foreign investment is another major source of international commerce. Assume that Ambux is an American communications corporation that decides to invest in a growing overseas market. The president of Ambux is particularly interested in building telephone systems in the former republics of the Soviet Union, reasoning that these economies offer great opportunity for growth. She wants you to report to her on the most important issues concerning possible investment in Uzbekistan and other former Soviet republics. You quickly realize that such an investment presents several related issues:

- Repatriation of profits
- Expropriation
- Sovereign immunity
- Act of State doctrine
- Foreign corrupt practices

Repatriation of Profits

Repatriation of profits occurs when an investing company pulls its earnings out of a foreign country and takes them back home. If Ambux builds a telephone system in Uzbekistan, it will plan to make money and then repatriate the profit to its headquarters in the United States. But Ambux must not assume an automatic right to do so. Many countries impose a much higher tax on repatriated profits than on normal income in order to keep the money in domestic commerce. Others bar repatriation altogether. Developing countries in particular want the money for further growth, and they tend to regard repatriation of rapidly earned profit as a close relative of exploitation. Thus, before Ambux invests anywhere, it must ensure that it can repatriate profits or be prepared to live with any limitations the foreign country might impose.

Fortunately, investing in Uzbekistan is relatively secure. Uzbekistan and the United States have signed a trade treaty guaranteeing unlimited repatriation for American investors. This treaty should suffice. But Ambux might still feel cautious. Uzbekistan is a new nation, and the mechanisms for actually getting the money out of Uzbekistan banks may be slow or faulty. The solution is to get a written agreement from the Minister of Commerce explicitly permitting Ambux to repatriate all profits and providing a clear mechanism to do it through the local banks.

Expropriation

Many nations, both developed and developing, **nationalize** property, meaning that they declare the national government to be the new owner. For example, during the 1940s and 1950s, Great Britain nationalized its coal, steel, and other heavy industries. The state assumed ownership and paid compensation to the previous owners. In the United States, nationalization is rare, but local governments often take land by eminent domain, to be used for roads or other public works. The United States Constitution requires that the owners be fairly compensated.

When a government takes property owned by foreign investors, it is called **expropriation.** Again, this practice is common and legal, provided there is adequate compensation. The U.S. government historically has acknowledged that the expropriation of American interests is legal, provided the host government pays the owners *promptly and fully, in dollars.* But if compensation is inadequate or long delayed, or made in a local currency that is hard to exchange, the taking is **confiscation.**

The courts of almost all nations concede that confiscation is illegal. But it can be difficult or impossible to prevent because courts of the host country may be partial to their own government. And any attempt to obtain compensation in an American court will encounter two separate problems: sovereign immunity and the Act of State doctrine.

Sovereign Immunity

Sovereign immunity holds that the courts of one nation lack the jurisdiction (power) to hear suits against foreign governments. Most nations respect this principle. In the United States, the **Foreign Sovereign Immunities Act (FSIA)** states that American courts generally cannot entertain suits against foreign governments. This is a difficult hurdle for a company to overcome when seeking compensation for foreign expropriation. There are three exceptions.

Waiver.   A lawsuit is permitted against a foreign country that waives its immunity—that is, voluntarily gives up this protection. Suppose the Czech government wishes to buy fighter planes from an American manufacturer. The manufacturer might insist on a waiver in the sales contract, and the Czech Republic might be willing to grant one to get the weapons it desires. If the planes land safely but the checks bounce, the manufacturer may sue.

Commercial Activity.   A plaintiff in the United States can sue a foreign country engaged in commercial activity, as opposed to political. Suppose the government of Iceland hires an American ecology-consulting firm to help its fishermen replenish depleted fishing grounds. Because fishing is a for-profit activity, the contract is commercial, and if Iceland refuses to pay, the company may sue in American courts.

Violation of International Law.   A plaintiff in this country may sue a foreign government that has confiscated property in violation of international law, provided that the property either ends up in the United States or is involved in commercial activity that affects someone in the United States. Suppose a foreign government confiscates a visiting American ship, with no claim of right, and begins to use it for shipping goods for profit. Later, the ship carries some American produce. The taking was illegal, and it now affects American commerce. The original owner may sue.

Act of State Doctrine

A second doctrine, annoyingly similar to sovereign immunity, could also affect Ambux or any company whose property is confiscated. The **Act of State doctrine** requires an American court to **abstain from any case in which a court order would interfere with the ability of the president or Congress to conduct foreign affairs.**

In the 1960s, Cuba expropriated American sugar interests, providing little or no compensation to the previous owners. The American owners sued, but in *Banco Nacional de Cuba v. Sabbatino,*[5] the United States Supreme Court refused to permit such suits in American courts. The Court ruled that even where there was strong evidence that the expropriation was illegal, American courts should not be involved because the executive and legislative branches must be free to conduct our foreign policy.

---

5 376 U.S. 398, 84 S. Ct. 923, 1964 U.S. LEXIS 2252 (1964).

Investment Insurance

Companies eager to do business abroad but anxious about expropriation should consider publicly funded insurance. In 1971, Congress established the **Overseas Private Investment Corporation (OPIC)** to insure U.S. investors against overseas losses due to political violence and expropriation. OPIC insurance is available to investors at relatively low rates for investment in almost any country. The agency has had remarkable success at no cost to the U.S. government. Every, OPIC participates in overseas ventures worth many billions of dollars, earning insurance fees that have paid the agency's entire budget and left a substantial surplus.

Should Ambux investigate OPIC insurance before investing in Uzbekistan? Absolutely. Although the Uzbekistan government has the best of intentions with respect to foreign investment, the nation is young and the government has no track record. A government can change course as quickly as a gnat, and often with less planning. Why take unnecessary risks?

Foreign Corrupt Practices Act

The Foreign Corrupt Practices Act (FCPA)[6] makes it illegal for an American businessperson to give "anything of value" to any foreign official in order to influence an official decision. It is sad but true that in many countries bribery is routine and widely accepted. When Congress investigated foreign bribes to see how common they were, more than 300 U.S. companies admitted paying hundreds of millions of dollars in bribes to foreign officials. Legislators concluded that such massive payments distorted competition between American companies for foreign contracts, interfered with the free market system, and undermined confidence everywhere in our way of doing business. The statutory response was simple: foreign bribery is illegal, plain and simple. The FCPA has two principal requirements:

- **Bribes.** The statute makes it illegal for U.S. companies and citizens to bribe foreign officials to influence a governmental decision. The statute prohibits giving anything of value and also bars using third parties as a conduit for such payments.
- **Record Keeping.** All publicly traded companies—whether they engage in international trade or not—must keep detailed records that prevent hiding or disguising bribes. These records must be available for U.S. government officials to inspect.

Not all payments violate the FCPA. A **grease** or **facilitating payment is legal,** provided the company is paying a foreign official only to expedite performance of a routine function. Grease payments are common in many foreign countries to obtain a permit, process governmental papers, or obtain utility service. For example, the cost of a permit to occupy an office building might be $100, but the government clerk suggests that you will receive the permit faster (within this lifetime) if you pay $150, one third of which he will pocket. Such small payments are legal. Further, a payment **does not violate the FCPA if it was legal under the written laws** of the country in which it was made. Because few countries establish written codes *permitting* officials to receive bribes, this defense is unlikely to help many Americans who hand out gifts.

The following case is a classic example of bribery. Not much loyalty within Owl Securities. Why is that? What does it teach us?

---

[6] 15 U.S.C. §§78 et seq.

UNITED STATES V. KING

354 F.3d 859
Eighth Circuit Court of Appeals, 2004

Facts: Owl Securities and Investments, Ltd., hoped to develop a large port in Limon, Costa Rica. The project included docks, housing, recreational facilities, an airport, and more. Richard King was one of Owl's largest investors, and Stephen Kingsley its CEO. The government charged King with attempting to bribe Costa Rican officials to obtain land and other concessions needed for their project. At trial, several of Owl's officers, including Kingsley, Richard Halford, and Albert Reitz, testified against King. A jury convicted King of violating the FCPA. He received a 30-month sentence and a fine of $60,000. He appealed.

Issue: Was there sufficient evidence that King had violated the FCPA?

Excerpts from Judge Beam's Decision: Viewing the evidence in the light most favorable to the verdict, there was ample evidence in the record to support the jury's convictions. The tape recordings, alone, support the jury's verdict. There was sufficient evidence to prove King's knowledge of the proposed payment long before Kingsley became an informant for the government.

For example, the following exchanges are just a small sample of what the jury heard:

Kingsley: Well you've always known about the closing cost fees and that.
King: I've known what?
Kingsley: You've known about the closing costs.
King: The one million dollars?
Kingsley: Yeah.
King: I've known about that for five years, yeah, . . .
[A later tape recording:]
Kingsley: Yeah, what, um, what Pablo had said, was why just pay, pay off the current politicians. Pay off the future ones.
King: That's right. Because we're gonna have to work with them anyway.

Kingsley: And so what he was saying was double, you know, give them more money. Buy the opposition. If you buy the current party and the opposition, then it doesn't matter who's in because there's only two parties.
King: The thing that really worries me is that, uh, if the Justice Department gets a hold of. Finds out how many people we've been paying off down there. Uh, or even if they don't. Are we gonna have to spend the rest of our lives paying off these petty politicians to keep them out of our hair? I can just see us, every, every day some politician on our doorstep down there wanting a hand out for this or that. . . . Think we could pay the top people enough, that the rest of the people won't bother us any. That's what I'm hoping this million and a half dollars does. I'm hoping it pays enough top people . . .
[A later recording:]
Kingsley: Now Pablo's continued to talk to the politicians. They know about the toll, closing costs call it what you will.
King: Does everybody agree to what we talked about recently?
Kingsley: Yeah, a million into escrow for the toll.
King: And then we get the property and then we do the (unintelligible)?
Kingsley: Um hum. Yeah now let me I'll, I'll, I'll come on to that because I'll explain how we work through that. Uh, essentially once the politicians see the money in escrow, they'll move. That's what it comes down to [clears throat]. Pablo's gonna send a list, an e-mail with a list of politicians already paid off and the ones he's gonna pay off.
King: Isn't that awfully dangerous?
Kingsley: No, e-mail's probably the most secure form of communication.
King: From what I read it's not, number one, and number two, there's got to be a better way.

We affirm the judgment of the district court. ■

Transparency International, a nonprofit agency based in Germany, publishes a "Corruption Perception Index," gauging how much dishonesty businesspeople and scholars encounter in different nations. In 2004 the agency listed 145 nations on its index. The highest-ranking countries (perceived *least* corrupt) were Finland, New Zealand, Denmark, Iceland, Singapore, Sweden, Switzerland, Norway, Australia, and the United Kingdom. The agency listed the United States as the seventeenth least corrupt. The countries ranking lowest (perceived *most* corrupt) were Cote d'Ivoire, Georgia, Indonesia, Tajikstan, Turkmenistan, Azerbaijan, Paraguay, Chad, Myanmar, Nigeria, Bangladesh, and Haiti. The full index is available from Transparency International at http://www.transparency.org.

But corruption is a two-sided coin. Of the more than 200 nations in the world, very few aggressively prevent their nationals from bribing foreign officials. Further, in some countries, a bribe paid to a foreign official may be treated as a tax deduction!

American executives have long complained that the FCPA puts their companies at a competitive disadvantage, and political leaders have lobbied for an international agreement. Finally, the efforts are reaching fruition. The Organization for Economic Cooperation and Development (OECD) produced a "Convention of Combating Bribery of Foreign Public Officials in International Business Transactions." About 36 of the world's largest trading nations have ratified the Convention.

The Convention requires signatories to enact criminal penalties for offering or giving bribes to foreign officials. The Convention also compels signatories to enact record-keeping laws that will prevent companies from disguising bribes. The Convention has various weaknesses, and it remains to be seen whether signatories will implement it aggressively, but the agreement is clearly a bold step on an ethical path.

Chapter Conclusion

Overseas investment, like sales abroad, offers potentially great rewards but significant pitfalls. A working knowledge of international law is essential to any entrepreneur or executive seriously considering foreign commerce. Issues such as choice of law, currency protection, antitrust statutes, and expropriation can mean the difference between profit and loss. As the WTO lowers barriers, international trade will increase, and your awareness of these principles will grow still more valuable.

Chapter Review

1. Several statutes restrict exports from the United States that would harm national security, foreign policy, or certain other goals.

2. A tariff is a duty (tax) imposed on goods when they enter a country. The U.S. Customs Service classifies goods when they enter the United States and imposes appropriate tariffs.

3. Most countries, including the United States, impose duties for goods that have been dumped (sold at an unfairly low price in the international market) and for subsidized goods (those benefiting from government financial assistance in the country of origin).

4. The General Agreement on Tariffs and Trade (GATT) is lowering the average duties worldwide. Proponents see it as a boon to trade; opponents see it as a threat to workers and the environment.

5. GATT created the World Trade Organization (WTO), which resolves disputes between signatories to the treaty.

6. A sales agreement between an American company and a foreign company may be governed by the UCC, by the law of the foreign country, or by the United Nations Convention on Contracts for the International Sale of Goods (CISG). The CISG differs from the UCC in several important respects.

7. A confirmed, irrevocable letter of credit is an important means of facilitating international sales contracts because the seller is assured of payment by a local bank as long as it delivers the specified goods.

8. Antitrust laws exist in the United States, the European Union (EU), and other countries.

International merchants must be careful not to make agreements that would distort competition.

9. International comity requires a local court to respect the legal system of a foreign country and dismiss a lawsuit if the dispute would more logically be resolved in the other nation.

10. A foreign government may restrict repatriation of profits.

11. Expropriation refers to a government taking property owned by foreign investors. U.S. courts regard this as lawful, provided the country pays the American owner promptly and fully, in dollars.

12. Sovereign immunity means that, in general, American courts lack jurisdiction to hear suits against foreign governments unless the foreign nation has waived immunity, is engaging in commercial activity, or has violated international law.

13. The Act of State doctrine requires an American court to abstain from any case in which a court order would interfere with the ability of the President or Congress to conduct foreign affairs.

14. The Foreign Corrupt Practices Act (FCPA) makes it illegal for an American businessperson to bribe foreign officials.

Practice Test

1. Arnold Mandel exported certain high-technology electronic equipment. Later, he was in court arguing that the equipment he shipped should not have been on the Department of Commerce's Commodity Control List. What items may be on that list, and why does Mandel care?

2. Sports Graphics, Inc., imports consumer goods, including "Chill" brand coolers, which come from Taiwan. Chill coolers have an outer shell of vinyl, with handles and pockets, and an inner layer of insulation. In a recent federal lawsuit, the issue was whether "Chill" coolers were technically "luggage" or "articles used for preparing, serving or storing food or beverages." Who were the parties to this dispute likely to be, and why did they care about such a technical description of these coolers?

3. **ETHICS** Hector works in Zoey's importing firm. Zoey overhears Hector on the phone say, "O.K., 30,000 ski parkas at $80 per parka. You've got yourself a deal. Thanks a lot." When Hector hangs up, Zoey is furious, yelling, "I told you not to make a deal on those Italian ski parkas without my permission! I think I can get a better price elsewhere." "Relax, Zoey," replies Hector. "I wanted to lock them in, to be sure we had some in case your deal fell through. It's just an oral contract, so we can always back out if we need to." Is that ethical? How far can a company go to protect its interests? Does it matter that another

business might make serious financial plans based on the discussion? Apart from the ethics, is Hector's idea smart?

4. **YOU BE THE JUDGE WRITING PROBLEM** Continental Illinois National Bank issued an irrevocable letter of credit on behalf of Bill's Coal Co. for $805,000, with the Allied Fidelity Insurance Co. as beneficiary. Bill's Coal Co. then went bankrupt. Allied then presented to Continental documents that were complete and conformed to the letter of credit. Continental refused to pay. Because Bill's Coal was bankrupt, there was no way Continental would collect once it had paid on the letter. Allied filed suit. Who should win? **Argument for Allied Fidelity:** An irrevocable letter of credit serves one purpose: to assure the seller that it will be paid if it performs the contract. Allied has met its obligation. The company furnished documents demonstrating compliance with the agreement. Continental *must* pay. Continental's duty to pay is an independent obligation, unrelated to the status of Bill's Coal. The bank issued this letter knowing the rules of the game and expecting to make a profit. It is time for Continental to honor its word. **Argument for Continental Bank:** In this transaction, the bank was merely a middleman, helping to facilitate payment of a contract. Allied has fulfilled its obligations under the contract, and we understand the company's desire to be paid. Regrettably, Bill's

Coal is bankrupt. No one is going to be paid on this deal. Allied should have researched Bill's financial status more thoroughly before entering into the agreement. While we sympathize with Allied's dilemma, it has only itself to blame and cannot expect the bank to act as some sort of insurance company for a deal gone awry.

5. Jean-François, a French wine exporter, sues Bob Joe, a Texas importer, claiming that Bob Joe owes him $2 million for wine. Jean-François takes the witness stand to describe how the contract was created. Where is the trial taking place?

6. Zenith and other American manufacturers of television sets sued Matsushita and 20 other Japanese competitors, claiming that the Japanese companies had conspired to drive Zenith and the Americans out of the American market. Supposedly, the Japanese companies agreed to maintain artificially high prices in Japan and artificially low prices in the United States. The goal of the low prices in the United States was to destroy American competition, and the goal of the high prices in Japan was to earn sufficient profits at home so that the companies could tolerate the temporary losses in the United States. Is the conduct of Matsushita in Japan subject to the Sherman Act?

7. The Kyrgyz Republic is another of the new nations that broke away from the old Soviet Union. In September 1994, the government of Kyrgyzstan made two independent announcements: (1) it was abolishing all taxes on repatriation; (2) the government was resigning and would shortly be replaced. Explain the significance of these announcements for an American company considering a major investment in Kyrgyzstan.

8. The Instituto de Auxilios y Viviendas is a government agency of the Dominican Republic. Dr. Marion Fernandez, the general administrator of the Instituto and Secretary of the Republic, sought a loan for the Instituto. She requested that Charles Meadows, an American citizen, secure the Instituto a bank loan of $12 million. If he obtained a loan on favorable terms, he would receive a fee of $240,000. Meadows secured a loan on satisfactory terms, which the Instituto accepted. He then sought his fee, but the Instituto and the Dominican government refused to pay. He sued the government in United States District Court. The Dominican government claimed immunity. Comment.

9. Environmental Tectonics Corp. and W. S. Kirkpatrick & Co. were both competing for a valuable contract with the Nigerian government. Kirkpatrick got it. Tectonics then sued Kirkpatrick in the United States, claiming that Kirkpatrick got the contract only because it bribed Nigerian officials. Kirkpatrick acknowledged that the district court had jurisdiction but argued that it should abstain from hearing the case. What doctrine does Kirkpatrick rely on, and what should the trial court do?

10. Blondek and Tull were two employees of an American company called Eagle Bus. They hoped that the Saskatchewan provincial government would award Eagle a contract for buses. To bolster their chances, they went to Saskatchewan and paid $50,000 to two government employees. Back in the United States, they were arrested and charged with a crime. Suppose they argue that even if they did something illegal, it occurred in Canada, and that is the only nation that can prosecute them. Comment on the defense.

11. Richard Johnson, an American citizen, was a highly trained electrical engineer who had worked for Hughes Aircraft and Norcroft Corp. He strongly believed in the cause of the Provisional Irish Republican Army (PIRA), which at the time was attacking British civilian and military targets in Northern Ireland and England. Johnson researched and developed explosives to be exported to Ireland and used by the PIRA. Christina Reid, an electrical engineer, worked with Johnson on IRA projects. She served as a courier of electronic components for remote-control bombs that the two sent to Northern Ireland. What legal problems did they risk by engaging in these transactions?

12. ***ROLE REVERSAL*** Draft an essay or short-answer question that involves a dispute brought to the WTO on one of these issues: dumping, nontariff barriers, or intellectual property.

Internet Research Problem

At academic.cengage.com/blaw/beatty read about the worldwide problem of sweatshops. Is this a serious problem? If so, what role should the law play in its resolution? What can one student do about it?

You can find further practice problems at academic.cengage.com/blaw/beatty.

CONTRACTS &
THE UCC

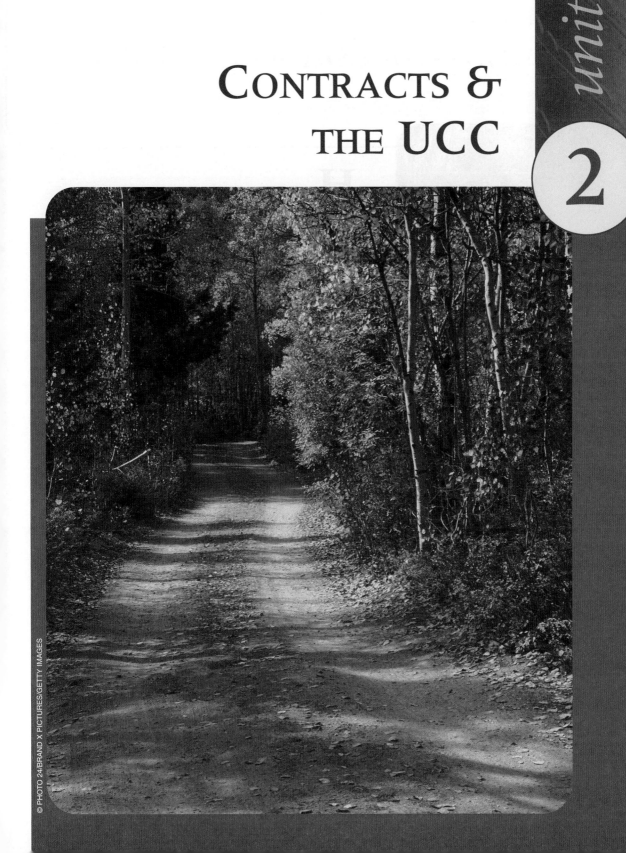

© PHOTO 24/BRAND X PICTURES/GETTY IMAGES

Introduction to Contracts

© MICHAEL BUSSELLE/DIGITAL VISION/GETTY IMAGES

Have a seat. Great to see you. Here, grab a menu. Yes, you're right: the tables at this café are jammed together. In fact, that's why I chose the spot. Listen to the conversations around us. Oh, go on, don't worry—eavesdropping is acceptable for academic purposes. To our right, a famous director is chatting with Katrina, the glamorous actress. He is trying to sign her up for a new film, Body Work, but she seems hesitant.

KATRINA (doubtful): I'm intrigued with the character, Bob, and I'd love to work with you. I am concerned about the nude scenes. The one on the toboggan run was okay. But that scene in the poultry factory—very explicit. I don't work fully nude.

BOB: We'll solve it—what am I, a sleaze? This is fine art; don't give it another thought. We're talking $2.5 million, Katrina. $600,000 up front, the rest deferred, the usual percentages.

KATRINA: As you know, my fee is $3 million. I should talk with my agent. I'd need something in writing about the nudity, the percentages, all of it.

BOB: I have to settle this fast. Julia is seriously considering the role.

KATRINA (worried): Julia! Are you kidding? Bob, I said I'm interested.

Oh my, look at that. Katrina hesitates; Bob nods encouragingly, then sticks out his hand and . . . Katrina shakes! It's a wrap—I guess. Now bend your ear toward the table on our left. The man wants to quit his job and accept a position with a competing company, but the woman, his boss, is insisting he stay.

EMILY: I taught you everything you know about computer encryption, Jake, and you're not taking that sophisticated training to my number one competitor.

JAKE: Emily, their offer is just too good to turn down. I deserve a chance to expand my horizons. Come on, be human!

EMILY (waving a document): Look here, my friend. Page four of your employment contract: "I agree that if I leave the company for any reason, I will not work for a competing firm anywhere in the United States for a period of three years." And here is your lovely, rounded signature. You work for me, Jake, or you go flip burgers.

Gee, that Emily is tough. I guess poor Jake is stuck in his present job. We need something cheerier. Listen to the two women behind you. While I was waiting, they have been bargaining over a vacation condo.

Li-Li: *I don't think I can go lower than 485.*

Maria: *Well . . . $450,000. I guess.*

Li-Li: *Maria, it has the best ocean view in the whole complex. And you would be on the top floor!*

Maria: *460.*

Li-Li: *475. My final offer. Do you happen to have the time?*

Maria: *The time? What's the hurry? Oh . . . okay, 475. Shake, partner.*

Li-Li: *It's a deal. That's great. I'm so happy for you. You're going to love it. Do we need to put this in writing?*

Maria: *Are you kidding? How long have we known each other, since we were six?*

Li-Li: *Five and a half! You're right, why spend the money on lawyers and boring documents? Let's spend it on champagne. Waiter!*

The café is a hotbed of contract negotiations—but then, so is our society. These three conversations demonstrate why it is important to understand contract law. Bob and Katrina think they have an agreement, but in fact they do not, *because the parties have not achieved a meeting of the minds. Jake, if he reads the next chapter, will be delighted to learn that* he is free to change jobs: *a court will not enforce Emily's noncompetition agreement. Finally, Li-Li should skip the champagne and instead scratch a simple contract onto a napkin. Without Maria's signature, Li-Li* cannot enforce her friend's promise *to pay.* ■

THE PURPOSE OF A CONTRACT

Parties enter into contracts attempting to control their future. **Contracts exist to make business matters more predictable.** Most contracts work out precisely as the parties intended because the parties fulfill their obligations. Most—but not all. We will study contracts that have gone wrong. We look at these errant deals to learn how to avoid the problems they manifest.

Judicial Activism versus Judicial Restraint

In most contract cases, judges do their best simply to enforce whatever terms the parties agreed to. Even if the contract results in serious harm to one party, a court will generally enforce it. This is **judicial restraint.** On the other hand, some courts practice **judicial activism.** In contract law, this means that a court will ignore certain provisions of a contract, or an entire agreement, if the judge believes that enforcing the deal would be unjust. A court may even be willing to create a contract where none existed if it appears necessary to avoid injustice. Judicial activism makes the law **more flexible but less predictable.**

Issues (and Answers)

The three contract negotiations described earlier illustrate several basic principles, and we will consider each. A contract has four elements:

1. **Agreement.** One party must make a valid offer, and the other party must accept it. (Bob failed to make a clear offer to Katrina.)
2. **Consideration.** There has to be bargaining that leads to an exchange between the parties.
3. **Legality.** The contract must be for a lawful purpose. (Emily's noncompetition agreement is probably illegal.)
4. **Capacity.** The parties must be adults of sound mind.

Contract cases often raise several other important issues, which we examine throughout the next three chapters:

- **Consent.** Neither party may trick or force the other into the agreement.
- **Written Contracts.** Some contracts must be in writing to be enforceable. (Neither Li-Li nor Maria may enforce the condo contract unless there is a signed agreement.)
- **Third-Party Interests.** Some contracts affect people other than the parties themselves.
- **Performance and Discharge.** If a party fully accomplishes what the contract requires, his duties are discharged.
- **Remedies.** A court will award money or other relief to a party injured by a breach of contract.

Contracts Defined

A contract is a promise that the law will enforce. As we look more closely at the elements of contract law, we will encounter some intricate issues, but remember that we are usually interested in answering three basic questions of common sense, all relating to promises:

- Is it certain that the defendant promised to do something?
- If she did promise, is it fair to make her honor her word?
- If she did not promise, are there unusual reasons to hold her liable anyway?

TYPES OF CONTRACTS

Bilateral and Unilateral Contracts

In a bilateral contract, both parties make a promise. Suppose a producer says to Gloria, "I'll pay you $2 million to star in my new romantic comedy, *A Promise for a Promise*, which we are shooting three months from now in Santa Fe." Gloria says, "It's a deal." That is a bilateral contract. Each party has made a promise to do something. The producer is now bound to pay Gloria $2 million, and Gloria is obligated to show up on time and act in the movie. The vast majority of contracts are bilateral contracts.

In a unilateral contract, one party makes a promise that the other party can accept only by *doing* something. These contracts are less common. Suppose the movie producer says to Leo, "I'll give you a hundred bucks if you mow my lawn this weekend." Leo is not promising to do it. If he mows the lawn, he has accepted the offer and is entitled to his hundred dollars. If he spends the weekend at the beach, neither he nor the producer owes anything.

Express and Implied Contracts

In an express contract, the two parties explicitly state all important terms of their agreement. *The great majority* of binding agreements are express contracts. The contract between the producer and Gloria is an express contract, because the parties explicitly state what Gloria will do, where and when she will do it, and how much she will be paid. Some express contracts are oral, as that one was, and some are written.

In an implied contract, the words and conduct of the parties indicate that they intended an agreement. Suppose every Friday, for two months, the producer asks Leo to mow his lawn, and loyal Leo does so each weekend. Then for three more weekends, Leo simply shows up without the producer asking, and the producer continues to pay for the work done. But on the twelfth weekend, when Leo rings the doorbell to collect, the producer suddenly says, "I never asked you to mow it. Scram." The producer is correct that there was no express contract, because the parties had not spoken for several weeks. But a court will probably rule that the conduct of the parties has *implied* a contract. Not only did Leo mow the lawn every weekend, but the producer even paid on three weekends when they had not spoken. It was reasonable for Leo to assume that he had a weekly deal to mow and be paid. Naturally, there is no implied contract thereafter.

Today, the hottest disputes about implied contracts often arise in the employment setting. Many employees have "at-will" agreements. This means that the employees are free to quit at any time and the company has the right to fire them at any time, for virtually any reason. Courts routinely enforce at-will contracts. But often a company provides its workers with personnel manuals that guarantee certain rights. The company may assure all workers that they will have a hearing and a chance to present evidence on their behalf before being fired. The legal issue is whether the handbook implies a contract guaranteeing the specified rights.

You Be the Judge

DEMASSE V. ITT CORPORATION

194 Ariz.500, 984 P.2d 1138
Supreme Court of Arizona, 1999

Facts: Roger DeMasse and five others were employees-at-will at ITT Corporation, where they started working at various times between 1960 and 1979. Each was paid an hourly wage. ITT issued an employee handbook that it revised four times over two decades. The first four editions of the handbook stated that within each job classification, any layoffs would be made in reverse order of seniority. The fifth handbook made two important changes. First, the document stated that "nothing contained herein shall be construed as a guarantee of continued employment. ITT does not guarantee continued employment to employees and retains the right to terminate or layoff employees."

Second, the handbook stated that "ITT reserves the right to amend, modify or cancel this handbook, as well as any or all of the various policies [or rules] outlined in it."

▼

Four years later, ITT notified its hourly employees that layoff guidelines for hourly employees would not be based on seniority but on ability and performance. About ten days later, the six employees were laid off, though employees with less seniority kept their jobs. The six employees sued.

You Be the Judge: **Did ITT have the right to unilaterally change the layoff policy?**

Argument for the Workers: It is true that all the plaintiffs were originally employees-at-will, subject to termination at the company's whim. However, things changed when the company issued the first handbook. ITT chose to include a promise that layoffs would be based on seniority. Long-term workers and new employees all understood the promise and relied on it. The company put it there to attract and retain good workers. The policy worked. Responsible employees understood that the longer they remained at ITT, the safer their job was. Company and employees worked together for many years with a common understanding, and that is a textbook definition of an implied contract.

Once a contract is formed, whether express or implied, it is binding on both sides. That is the whole point of a contract. If one side could simply change the terms of an agreement on its own, what value would any contract have? The company's legal argument is a perfect symbol of its arrogance: It believes that because these workers are mere hourly workers, they have no rights, even under contract law. The company is mistaken. Implied contracts are binding, and ITT should not make promises it does not intend to keep.

Argument for ITT: Once an at-will employee, always one. ITT had the right to fire any of its employees at any time—just as the workers had the right to quit whenever they wished. That never changed, and in case any workers forgot it, the company reiterated the point in its most recent handbook. If the plaintiffs thought they had a guaranteed lifetime job, that is their error, not ours.

All workers were bound by the terms of whichever handbook was then in place. For many years, the company had made a seniority-layoff promise. Had we fired a senior worker during that period, he or she would have had a legitimate complaint—and that is why we did not do it. Instead, we gave everyone four years' notice that things had changed. Any workers unhappy with the new policies should have left to find more congenial work.

Why should an employee be allowed to say, "I prefer to rely on the old, outdated handbooks, not the new one"? The plaintiffs' position would mean that no company is ever free to change its general work policies and rules. Since when does an at-will employee have the right to dictate company policy? That would be disastrous for the whole economy— but fortunately it is not the law. ●

Executory and Executed Contracts

A contract is **executory** when one or more parties have not fulfilled their obligations. Recall Gloria, who agrees to act in the producer's film beginning in three months. The moment Gloria and the producer strike their bargain, they have an executory bilateral express contract. A contract is **executed** when all parties have fulfilled their obligations. When Gloria finishes acting in the movie and the producer pays her final fee, their contract will be fully executed.

Valid, Unenforceable, Voidable, and Void Agreements

A **valid contract** is one that satisfies all the law's requirements. A court will therefore enforce it. The contract between Gloria and the producer is a valid contract, and if the producer fails to pay Gloria, she will win a lawsuit to collect the unpaid fee.

An **unenforceable agreement** occurs when the parties intend to form a valid bargain but a court declares that some rule of law prevents enforcing it. Suppose Gloria and the producer orally agree that she will star in his movie, which he will start filming in 18 months. The statute of frauds requires that this contract be in writing, because it cannot be completed within one year. If the producer signs up another actress two months later, Gloria has no claim against him.

A **voidable contract** occurs when the law permits one party to terminate the agreement. This happens, for example, when the other party has committed fraud or misrepresentation. Suppose that Klene Corp. induces Smart to purchase 1,000 acres of Klene land by telling Smart that there is no underground toxic waste, even though Klene knows that just under the topsoil lies an ocean of bubbling purple sludge. Klene is committing fraud. Smart may void the contract—that is, terminate it and owe nothing.

A **void agreement** is one that neither party can enforce, usually because the purpose of the deal is illegal or because one of the parties had no legal authority to make a contract.

REMEDIES CREATED BY JUDICIAL ACTIVISM

Now we turn away from true contracts and consider two remedies created by judicial activism: promissory estoppel and quasi-contract. Each of these remedies has grown in importance over the last 100 years. In each case, a sympathetic plaintiff can demonstrate an injury. But the crux of the matter is this: there is no contract. The plaintiff must hope for more "creative" relief. The two remedies can be confusingly similar. The best way to distinguish them is this:

- In **promissory estoppel** cases, the defendant made a promise that the plaintiff relied on.

- In **quasi-contract** cases, the defendant did not make any promise, but did receive a benefit from the plaintiff.

Promissory Estoppel

A fierce fire swept through Dana and Derek Andreason's house in Utah, seriously damaging it. The good news was that agents for Aetna Casualty promptly visited the Andreasons and helped them through the crisis. The agents reassured the couple that all the damage was covered by their insurance, instructed them on which things to throw out and replace, and helped them choose materials for repairing other items. The bad news was that the agents were wrong: the Andreasons' policy had expired six weeks before the fire. When Derek Andreason presented a bill for $41,957 worth of meticulously itemized work that he had done under the agents' supervision, Aetna refused to pay.

The Andreasons sued—but not for breach of contract, because the insurance agreement had expired. They sued Aetna under the legal theory of promissory estoppel: **Even when there is no contract, a plaintiff may use promissory estoppel to enforce the defendant's promise if he can show that:**

- The defendant made a promise knowing that the plaintiff would likely rely on it;

- The plaintiff did rely on the promise; and

- The only way to avoid injustice is to enforce the promise.

Aetna made a promise to the Andreasons, namely, its assurance that all the damage was covered by insurance. The company knew that the Andreasons would rely on that promise, which they did by ripping up a floor that might have been salvaged, throwing out some furniture, and buying materials to repair the house. Is enforcing the promise the only way to avoid injustice? Yes, ruled the Utah Court of Appeals.[1] The Andreasons' conduct was reasonable, based on what the Aetna agent said. Under promissory estoppel, the Andreasons received virtually the same amount they would have obtained had the insurance contract been valid.

Quasi-Contract

Don Easterwood leased more than 5,000 acres of farmland in Jackson County, Texas, from PIC Realty for one year. The next year he obtained a second one-year lease. During each year, Easterwood farmed the land, harvested the crops, and prepared the land for the following year's planting. Toward the end of the second lease, after Easterwood had harvested his crop, he and PIC began discussing the terms of another lease. As they negotiated, Easterwood prepared the land for the following year, cutting, plowing, and disking the soil. But the negotiations for a new lease failed, and Easterwood moved off the land. He sued PIC Realty for the value of his work preparing the soil.

Easterwood had neither an express nor an implied contract for the value of his work. How could he make any legal claim? By relying on the legal theory of a quasi-contract: **Even when there is no contract, a court may use quasi-contract to compensate a plaintiff who can show that:**

- The plaintiff gave some benefit to the defendant;
- The plaintiff reasonably expected to be paid for the benefit and the defendant knew this; and
- The defendant would be unjustly enriched if he did not pay.

If a court finds all these elements present, it will generally award the value of the goods or services that the plaintiff has conferred. The damages awarded are called *quantum meruit,* meaning that the plaintiff gets "as much as he deserved." The court is awarding money that it believes the plaintiff *morally ought to have,* even though there was no valid contract entitling her to it. This is judicial activism. The purpose is justice; the term is contradictory.

Don Easterwood testified that in Jackson County, it was common for a tenant farmer to prepare the soil for the following year but then move. In those cases, he claimed, the landowner compensated the farmer for the work done. Other witnesses agreed. The court ruled that indeed there was no contract but that all elements of quasi-contract had been satisfied. Easterwood gave a benefit to PIC because the land was ready for planting. Easterwood reasonably assumed he would be paid, and PIC Realty knew it. Finally, said the court, it would be unjust to let PIC benefit without paying anything. The court ordered PIC to pay the fair market value of Easterwood's labors.

SOURCES OF CONTRACT LAW

Common Law

Express and implied contracts, promissory estoppel, and quasi-contract were all crafted, over centuries, by appellate courts deciding one contract lawsuit at a time. In

---

[1] *Andreason v. Aetna Casualty & Surety Co.*, 848 P.2d 171, 1993 Utah App. LEXIS 26 (Utah App. 1993).

this country, the basic principles are similar from one state to another, but there have been significant differences concerning most important contract doctrines. In part because of these differences, the twentieth century saw the rise of two major new sources of contract law: the **Uniform Commercial Code** and the **Restatement of Contracts.**

Uniform Commercial Code

Business methods changed quickly during the first half of the last century. Executives used new forms of communication, such as telephone and wire, to make deals. Transportation speeded up. Corporations routinely conducted business across state borders and around the world. Executives, lawyers, and judges wanted a body of law for commercial transactions that reflected modern business methods and provided uniformity throughout the United States. That desire gave birth to the Uniform Commercial Code (UCC), created in 1952. The drafters intended the UCC to facilitate the easy formation and enforcement of contracts in a fast-paced world. The Code governs many aspects of commerce, including the sale and leasing of goods, negotiable instruments, bank deposits, letters of credit, investment securities, secured transactions, and other commercial matters. Every state has adopted at least part of the UCC to govern commercial transactions within that state. For our purposes in studying contract, the most important part of the Code is Article 2. The entire UCC is available online at http://www.law.cornell.edu. Click on "Constitutions and Codes," then "Uniform Commercial Code."

UCC Article 2 governs the sale of goods. "Goods" means anything movable, except for money, securities, and certain legal rights. Goods include pencils, commercial aircraft, books, and Christmas trees. Goods do not include land or a house, because neither is movable, nor do they include a stock certificate. A contract for the sale of 10,000 sneakers is governed by the UCC; a contract for the sale of a condominium in Los Angeles is governed by the California common law and its statute of frauds. Thus, when analyzing any contract problem as a student or business executive, you must note whether the agreement concerns the sale of goods.

Article 2 Alert. For more than a decade, the drafters of the UCC analyzed and debated significant revisions to Article 2 (and other articles). In 2003, they completed their work on Article 2, and the new version has many significant changes. However, the proposed changes will not become law until state legislatures choose to adopt them. As this book goes to press, no state has adopted the recommended changes. All references in this text are to the existing Article 2.

Restatement (Second) of Contracts

In 1932, the American Law Institute (ALI), a group of lawyers, scholars, and judges, drafted the Restatement of Contracts, attempting to codify what its members regarded as the best rulings of contract law. In 1979, the ALI issued a new version, the Restatement (Second) of Contracts. Like its predecessor, the Restatement (Second) is not the law anywhere, and in this respect it differs from the common law and the UCC. However, judges often refer to the Restatement (Second) when they decide cases, so we too will seek its counsel from time to time.

AGREEMENT

Meeting of the Minds

Two parties can form a contract only if they have had a meeting of the minds. This requires that they (1) understood each other and (2) intended to reach an agreement. Recall the café conversation between Katrina and Bob, concerning the new film. Was there a meeting of the minds? Judges make an objective assessment of each party's intent. A court will not try to get inside Katrina's head and decide what she was thinking as she shook hands. It will look at the handshake objectively, deciding how a reasonable person would interpret the words and conduct. Katrina may honestly have meant to conclude a deal for $3 million with no nude scenes, while Bob might in good faith have believed he was committing himself to $2.5 million and absolute control of the script. Neither belief will control the outcome. A reasonable person observing their discussion would not have known what terms they agreed to, and hence there is no agreement.

Offer

Bargaining begins with an offer. An offer is a serious matter because it permits the other party to create a contract by accepting. An offer is an act or a statement that proposes definite terms and permits the other party to create a contract by accepting those terms.

The person who makes an offer is the **offeror.** The person to whom he makes that offer is the **offeree.** The terms are annoying but inescapable because, like handcuffs, all courts use them. In most contract negotiations, two parties bargain back and forth, maybe for minutes, perhaps for months. Each may make several offers, revoke some proposals, suggest counteroffers, and so forth. For our purposes, the offeror remains the one who made the first offer.

Two questions determine whether a statement is an offer:

- Did the offeror intend to make a bargain?
- Are the terms of the offer definite?

Problems with Intent

Zachary says to Sharon, "Come work in my English language center as a teacher. I'll pay you $500 per week for a 35-hour week, for six months starting Monday." This is a valid offer. Zachary intends to make a bargain and his offer is definite. If Sharon accepts, the parties have a contract that either one can enforce. By contrast, we will consider several categories of statements that are generally not valid offers.

Invitations to Bargain.   An invitation to bargain is not an offer. Suppose Martha telephones Joe and leaves a message on his answering machine, asking if Joe would consider selling his vacation condo on Lake Michigan. Joe faxes a signed letter to Martha saying, "There is no way I could sell the condo for less than $150,000." Martha promptly sends Joe a cashier's check for that amount. Does she own the condo? No. Joe's fax is not an offer. It is merely an invitation to bargain. Joe is indicating that he would be happy to receive an offer from Martha. He is not promising to sell the condo for $150,000 or for any amount.

Letters of Intent. In complex business negotiations, the parties may spend months bargaining over dozens of interrelated issues. Because each party wants to protect itself during the discussions, ensuring that the other side is serious without binding itself to premature commitments, it may make sense during the negotiations to draft a **letter of intent.** The letter can help summarize the progress made thus far and assist the parties in securing necessary financing. But a letter of intent contains a built-in danger: one party may regard it as less than binding. Yet if it is not binding, what is it?

at RISK

Jones Brothers Construction was the general contractor on a job to expand American Airlines' facilities at O'Hare International Airport. The company invited bids from subcontractors. Quake Construction bid on part of the project, and Jones Brothers orally informed the company that it had won the bid and would soon receive a contract. Jones Brothers wanted the license numbers of the subcontractors that Quake would be using, but Quake could not furnish those numbers until it had assured its subcontractors that they had the job. Quake did not want to give that assurance until it was certain of obtaining the work. So Jones Brothers sent a letter of intent stating that:

- Jones was awarding the contract to Quake;
- Quake would begin the specified work immediately;
- Jones would pay a lump sum price of $1,060,568;
- A contract agreement with detailed terms would be prepared shortly; and
- Jones reserved the right to cancel the letter of intent if the parties could not reach a final agreement.

The parties never signed the full contract, and ultimately Jones Brothers hired another company. Quake sued, seeking to recover the money it had spent in preparation and its loss of anticipated profit. The legal issue: Was the letter of intent a valid offer?

The Illinois Supreme Court declared that the letter was ambiguous and sent the case back to the trial court. The document contained many phrases that made it seem like a firm contract. The letter awarded the work to Quake and authorized the work to begin quickly. On the other hand, the document referred to a future, formal contract, indicating that the parties did not yet consider themselves bound, and it permitted Jones to cancel the letter of intent.[2]

So after several years of litigation, Jones Brothers and Quake had to go back to the trial court to establish whether they intended the letter to be binding. Every year there are countless cases just like *Quake*. The problem is that both sides permit ambiguity and vagueness to enter their negotiations. Sometimes parties do this accidentally, by paying too little attention to what they are saying. The solution is simple: think carefully before offering or responding.

At other times, with sophisticated businesspeople, ambiguity may not be so accidental, as one party is trying to get a commitment from the other side without obligating itself. A party may feel *almost* ready to commit, yet still have reservations. It wants the other party to make a commitment so that planning can go forward. This is understandable but dangerous.

If you were negotiating for Jones Brothers and wanted to clarify negotiations without committing your company, how could you do it? From Quake's point of view, how should you proceed? ◆

Advertisements. **An advertisement is generally not an offer.** An advertisement is merely a request for offers. The consumer makes the offer by selecting merchandise in a store and taking it to the cashier. The seller is free to reject the offer.

---

2 *Quake Construction v. American Airlines*, 141 Ill. 2d 281, 565 N.E.2d 990, 1990 Ill. LEXIS 151 (Ill. 1990).

However, although the common law regards advertisements as mere solicitations, consumers do have protection from those shopkeepers intent upon deceit. Every state has some form of **consumer protection statute.** These statutes outlaw false advertising. For example, an automobile dealer who advertises a remarkably low price but then has only one automobile at that price has probably violated a consumer protection statute because the ad was published in bad faith, to trick consumers into coming to the dealership.

Problems with Definiteness

It is not enough that the offeror intends to enter into an agreement. **The terms of the offer must be definite.** If they are vague, then even if the offeree "accepts" the deal, a court does not have enough information to enforce it and there is no contract.

You want a friend to work in your store for the holiday season. This is a definite offer: "I offer you a job as a salesclerk in the store from November 1 through December 29, 40 hours per week at $10 per hour." But suppose, by contrast, you say: "I offer you a job as a salesclerk in the store from November 1 through December 29, 40 hours per week. We will work out a fair wage once we see how busy things get." Your friend replies, "That's fine with me." This offer is indefinite. What is a fair wage? $5 per hour? $15 per hour? How will the determination be made? There is no binding agreement.

The following case presents a problem with definiteness, concerning a famous television show. You want to know what happened? Go to the place. See the guy. No, not the one in hospitality. Our friend in waste management. Don't say nothing. Then get out.

BAER V. CHASE

392 F.3d 609
Third Circuit Court of Appeals, 2004

Facts: David Chase was a television writer-producer with many credits, including a detective series called *The Rockford Files.* He became interested in a new program, set in New Jersey, about a "mob boss in therapy," a concept he eventually developed into *The Sopranos.* Robert Baer was a prosecutor in New Jersey who wanted to write for television. He submitted a *Rockford Files* script to Chase, who agreed to meet with Baer.

When they met, Baer pitched a different idea, concerning "a film or television series about the New Jersey Mafia." He did not realize Chase was already working on such an idea. Later that year, Chase visited New Jersey. Baer arranged meetings for Chase with local detectives and prosecutors, who provided the producer with information, material, and personal stories about their experiences with organized crime. Detective Thomas Koczur drove Chase and Baer to various New Jersey locations and introduced Chase to Tony Spirito. Spirito shared stories about

loan sharking, power struggles between family members connected with the mob, and two colorful individuals known as Big Pussy and Little Pussy, both of whom later became characters on the show.

Back in Los Angeles, Chase wrote and sent to Baer a draft of the first *Sopranos* teleplay. Baer called Chase and commented on the script. The two spoke at least four times that year, and Baer sent Chase a letter about the script.

When the Sopranos became a hit television show, Baer sued Chase. He alleged that on three separate occasions Chase had agreed that if the program succeeded, Chase would "take care of" Baer, and would "remunerate Baer in a manner commensurate to the true value of his services." This happened twice on the phone, Baer claimed, and once during Chase's visit to New Jersey. The understanding was that if the show failed, Chase would owe nothing. Chase never paid Baer anything.

▼

The District Court dismissed the case, holding that the alleged promises were too vague to be enforced. Baer appealed.

Issue: Was Chase's promise definite enough to be enforced?

Excerpts from Judge Greenberg's Decision: A contract arises from offer and acceptance, and must be sufficiently definite so that the performance to be rendered by each party can be ascertained with reasonable certainty. Therefore parties create an enforceable contract when they agree on its essential terms and manifest an intent that the terms bind them. If parties to an agreement do not agree on one or more essential terms of the purported agreement courts generally hold it to be unenforceable.

New Jersey law deems the price term, *i.e.*, the amount of compensation, an essential term of any contract. An agreement lacking definiteness of price, however, is not unenforceable if the parties specify a practicable method by which they can determine the amount. However, in the absence of an agreement as to the manner or method of determining compensation the purported agreement is invalid. Additionally, the duration of the contract is deemed an essential term and therefore any agreement must be sufficiently definitive to allow a court to determine the agreed upon length of the contractual relationship.

Baer premises his argument on his view that New Jersey should disregard the well-established requirement of definiteness in its contract law when the subject-matter of the contract is an "idea submission." [However,] New Jersey precedent does not support Baer's attempt to carve out an exception to traditional principles of contract law for submission-of-idea cases. The New Jersey courts have not provided even the slightest indication that they intend to depart from their well-established requirement that enforceability of a contract requires definiteness with respect to the essential terms of that contract.

Nothing in the record indicates that the parties agreed on how, how much, where, or for what period Chase would compensate Baer. The parties did not discuss who would determine the "true value" of Baer's services, when the "true value" would be calculated, or what variables would go into such a calculation. There was no discussion or agreement as to the meaning of "success" of *The Sopranos*. There was no discussion how "profits" were to be defined. There was no contemplation of dates of commencement or termination of the contract. And again, nothing in Baer's or Chase's conduct, or the surrounding circumstances of the relationship, shed light on, or answers, any of these questions.

Affirmed. ■

Ethics | Was it fair for Chase to use Baer's services without compensation? Did Baer really *expect* to get paid, or was he simply hoping that his work would land him a job? Has either party violated the *Golden Rule?* What are the most important *values* involved? ◆

Termination of Offers

As we have seen, the great power that an offeree has is to form a contract by accepting an offer. But this power is lost when the offer is terminated, which can happen in several ways:

Revocation.   In general, the offeror may revoke the offer any time before it has been accepted. Revocation is effective as soon as the offeree receives it.

Rejection.   If an offeree rejects an offer, the rejection immediately terminates the offer. Suppose a major accounting firm telephones you and offers a job, starting at $80,000. You respond, "Nah. I'm gonna work on my surfing for a year or two." The next day you come to your senses and write the firm, accepting its offer. No contract. Your rejection terminated the offer and ended your power to accept.

Counteroffer.   Frederick faxes Kim, offering to sell a 50 percent interest in the Fab Hotel in New York for only $135 million. Kim faxes back, offering to pay $115 million.

Moments later, Kim's business partner convinces her that Frederick's offer was a bargain, and she faxes an acceptance of his $135 million offer. Does Kim have a binding deal? No. A counteroffer is a rejection. The parties have no contract at any price.

Expiration. When an offer specifies a time limit for acceptance, that period is binding. If the offer specifies no time limit, the offeree has a reasonable period in which to accept.

Destruction of the Subject Matter. A used car dealer offers to sell you a rare 1938 Bugatti for $75,000 if you bring cash the next day. You arrive, suitcase stuffed with century notes, just in time to see the dealer fall out of a blimp, dropping 3,000 feet through the air and crushing the Bugatti. The dealer's offer terminated.

Acceptance

As we have seen, when there is a valid offer outstanding, the offeree can create a contract by accepting. **The offeree must say or do something to accept.** Silence, though golden, is not acceptance. Marge telephones Vick and leaves a message on his answering machine: "I'll pay $75 for your law textbook from last semester. I'm desperate to get a copy, so I will assume you agree unless I hear from you by 6:00 tonight." Marge hears nothing by the deadline and assumes she has a deal. She is mistaken. Vick neither said nor did anything to indicate that he accepted.

When the offer is for a bilateral contract, the offeree generally must accept by making a promise. An employer calls you and says, "If you're able to start work two weeks from today, we can pay you $5,000 per month. Can you do it?" That is an offer for a bilateral contract. You must accept by promising to start in two weeks.

When the offer is for a unilateral contract, the offeree must accept by performing. A newspaper telephones you: "If you write us a 5,000-word article on iguanas that can play bridge, and get it to us by Friday at noon, we'll pay you $750." The newspaper does not want a promise, it wants the article. If—and only if—your work is ready on time, you get paid.

Mirror Image Rule

If only he had known! A splendid university, an excellent position as department chair—gone. And all because of the mirror image rule. The Ohio State University wrote to Philip Foster offering him an appointment as a professor and chair of the art history department. His position was to begin July 1, and he had until June 2 to accept the job. On June 2, Foster telephoned the Dean and left a message accepting the position, **effective July 15.** Later, Foster thought better of it and wrote the university, accepting the school's starting date of July 1. Too late! Professor Foster never did occupy that chair at Ohio State. The court held that since his acceptance varied the starting date, it was a counteroffer. And a counteroffer, as we know, is a rejection.[3]

The common law mirror image rule requires that acceptance be on precisely the same terms as the offer. If the acceptance contains terms that add to or contradict the offer, even in minor ways, courts generally consider it a counteroffer. The rule worked reasonably well in the nineteenth century, when parties would write an original contract and exchange it, penciling in any changes. But now that businesses use standardized forms to purchase most goods and services, the rule creates enormous difficulties. Sellers use forms they have prepared, with all conditions stated to

---

[3] *Foster v. Ohio State University,* 41 Ohio App. 3d 86, 534 N.E.2d 1220, 1987 Ohio App. LEXIS 10761 (Ohio Ct. App. 1987).

their advantage, and buyers employ their own forms, with terms they prefer. The forms are exchanged in the mail (or electronically), with neither side clearly agreeing to the other party's terms.

The problem is known as the "battle of forms." Once again, the UCC has entered the fray, attempting to provide flexibility and common sense for those contracts involving the sale of goods. But for contracts governed by the common law, such as Professor Foster's, the mirror image rule is still the law.

UCC and the Battle of Forms

UCC §2-207 dramatically modifies the mirror image rule for the sale of goods. Under this provision, an acceptance that adds additional or different terms **will often create a contract.** The rule is intricate, but may be summarized this way:

> For the sale of goods, the most important factor is whether the parties believe they have a binding agreement. If their conduct indicates that they have a deal, they probably do.
>
> If the offeree *adds new* terms to the offer, acceptance by the offeror generally creates a binding agreement.
>
> If the offeree *changes* the terms of the offer, a court will probably rely on general principles of the UCC to create a fair contract.
>
> If a party wants a contract on its terms only, with no changes, it must clearly indicate that.

Suppose Wholesaler writes to Manufacturer, offering to buy "10,000 wheelbarrows at $50 per unit. Payable on delivery, 30 days from today's date." Manufacturer writes back, "We accept your offer of 10,000 wheelbarrows at $50 per unit, payable on delivery. Interest at normal trade rates for unpaid balances." Manufacturer clearly intends to form a contract. The company has added a new term, but there is still a valid agreement.

cyberLaw

Clickwraps and Shrinkwraps. You want to purchase Attila brand software and download it to your computer. You type in your credit card number and other information, agreeing to pay $99. Attila also requires that you "read and agree to" all of the company's terms. You click "I agree," without having read one word of the terms. Three frustrating weeks later, tired of trying to operate defective Attilaware, you demand a refund and threaten to sue. The company breezily replies that you are barred from suing, because the terms you agreed to included an arbitration clause. To resolve any disputes, you must travel to Attila's hometown, halfway across the nation, use an arbitrator that the company chooses, pay half the arbitrator's fee, and also pay Attila's legal bills if you should lose. The agreement makes it financially impossible for you to get your money back. Is that contract enforceable?

You have entered into a "clickwrap" agreement. Similar agreements, called "shrinkwraps," are packaged inside many electronic products. A shrinkwrap notice might require that before inserting a purchased CD into you computer, you must read and agree to all terms in the brochure. Clickwraps and shrinkwraps often include arbitration clauses. They frequently limit the seller's liability if anything goes wrong, saying that the manufacturer's maximum responsibility is to refund the purchase price (even if the software destroys your hard drive).

Many of the courts that have analyzed these issues have ruled that clickwrap and shrinkwrap agreements are indeed binding, even against consumers. Some of the judges have relied on §2-207 to reach that conclusion (holding that any additional terms did not materially alter the agreement) and others have used different UCC provisions. The courts have emphasized that sellers are entitled to offer a product on any terms they wish, and that shrinkwrap and clickwrap are the most efficient methods of including complicated terms in a small space.[4] However, some courts have refused to enforce such contracts against a consumer, stating that the buyer never understood or agreed to the shrinkwrapped terms. Did the court in the following case strike the right balance? ◆

SPECHT V. NETSCAPE COMMUNICATIONS CORPORATION

306 F.3d 17
Second Circuit Court of Appeals, 2002

Facts: A group of plaintiffs sued Netscape, claiming that two of the company's products illegally captured private information about files that they downloaded from the Internet. The plaintiffs alleged that this was electronic eavesdropping, in violation of federal statutes.

From Netscape's Web page, the plaintiffs had downloaded SmartDownload, a software plug-in that enabled them to download the company's Communicator software. The Web page advertised the benefits of SmartDownload, and near the bottom of the screen was a tinted button labeled "Download." The plaintiffs clicked to download. If, instead of downloading, they had scrolled farther down, they would have seen an invitation to "review and agree to the terms of the Netscape SmartDownload software license agreement." By clicking the appropriate button, they would have been sent to a series of linked pages, and finally arrived at a license agreement. Among the terms was an agreement to arbitrate any dispute. However, the plaintiffs never reviewed the license terms.

Netscape moved to dismiss the case and compel arbitration, but the District Court ruled that the plaintiffs had not agreed to the terms of the license. Netscape appealed.

Issue: Had the plaintiffs agreed to arbitrate their claims?

Excerpts from Judge Sotomayor's Decision: Defendants argue that plaintiffs must be held to a standard of reasonable prudence and that, because notice of the existence of SmartDownload license terms was on the next scrollable screen, plaintiffs were on "inquiry notice" of those terms. We disagree that a reasonably prudent offeree in plaintiffs' position would necessarily have known or learned of the license agreement prior to acting.

Receipt of a physical document containing contract terms or notice thereof is frequently deemed, in the world of paper transactions, a sufficient circumstance to place the offeree on inquiry notice of those terms. These principles apply equally to the emergent world of online product delivery, pop-up screens, hyperlinked pages, clickwrap licensing, scrollable documents, and urgent admonitions to "Download Now!". What plaintiffs saw when they were being invited by defendants to download this fast, free plug-in called SmartDownload was a screen containing praise for the product and, at the very bottom of the screen, a "Download" button. Defendants argue that a fair and prudent person using ordinary care would have been on inquiry notice of SmartDownload's license terms.

We are not persuaded that a reasonably prudent offeree in these circumstances would have known of the existence of license terms. Plaintiffs were responding to an offer that did not carry an immediately visible notice of the existence of license terms or require unambiguous manifestation of assent to those terms. Moreover, the fact that, given the position of the scroll bar on their computer screens, plaintiffs may have been aware that an unexplored portion of the Netscape webpage remained below the download button does not mean that they reasonably should have concluded that this portion contained a notice of license terms.

We affirm the district court's denial of defendants' motion to compel arbitration and to stay court proceedings. ■

---

[4] *ProCD, Inc. v Zeidenberg,* 86 F.3d 1447 (7th Cir. 1996) is the leading case to enforce shrinkwrap agreements (and by extension, clickwraps). *Klocek v. Gateway,* 104 F. Supp. 1332 (D. Kan. 2000) is one of the few cases to reject such contracts. Klocek, however, was later dismissed for failure to reach the federal court's $75,000 jurisdictional level.

CONSIDERATION

We have all made promises that we soon regretted. Mercifully, the law does not hold us accountable for everything we say. Yet some promises must be enforced. Which ones? The doctrine of consideration exists for one purpose: to distinguish promises that are binding from those that are not.

Consideration is a required element of any contract. **Consideration means that there must be bargaining that leads to an exchange between the parties.** (See Exhibit 9.1.) *Bargaining* indicates that each side is obligating itself in some way to *induce the other side to agree.* Generally, a court will enforce one party's promise only if the other party did something or promised something in exchange.

If one party makes a promise without some kind of bargaining, there is generally no contract. Carol Kelsoe had worked at International Wood Products for many years. One day, her supervisor surprised her by promising her 5 percent of the company's stock. Unfortunately, he never gave her those shares. Heartbroken, Kelsoe sued—and lost.[5] Kelsoe had given nothing in exchange for her supervisor's words. There was no consideration on her part, and she could not enforce his promise. If Kelsoe had assured him that she would remain at International Wood for three extra years (or three extra days) in exchange for the stock, that would have been consideration, and she would have collected her shares.

The thing bargained for can be another promise or action. Usually one party bargains for another promise. Jennifer says to Ben, "I'm supposed to fly to Chicago in a week, to give a speech. Will you do it for me? I'll give you $15,000." "Sure," Ben responds, "I'll do that for $15,000." The very next day Jennifer changes her mind. Too late. Ben's *promise* to go to Chicago was consideration. The parties have a deal that either one can enforce.

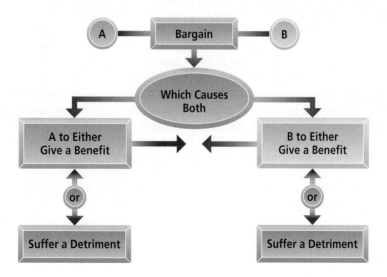

Exhibit 9.1
There is consideration to support a contract when **A** and **B** bargain, and their bargaining causes both **A** and **B** either to give a benefit to the other or to suffer a detriment.

---

[5] *Kelsoe v. International Wood Products, Inc.,* 588 So. 2d 877, 1991 Ala. LEXIS 1014 (Supreme Court of Alabama, 1991).

The thing bargained for can be action, rather than a promise. Manny tells Sandra, "I need someone to hook up my cable TV by tonight at 8:00. If you get it done, I'll give you $200." Manny seeks action, not a promise. If Sandra connects the television on time, her work is consideration and the parties have a binding deal.

The thing bargained for can be a promise to do something or a promise to refrain from doing something. Megan promises to deliver 1,000 canoes in two months if Casey agrees to pay $300 per canoe. Megan's promise to act is consideration. The most famous of all consideration lawsuits involved a promise to refrain. The case began in 1869, when a well-meaning uncle made a promise to his nephew. Ever since the nephew responded, generations of American law students have dutifully inhaled the facts and sworn by its wisdom; now you, too, may drink it in.

HAMER V. SIDWAY

124 N.Y.538, 27 N.E.256, 1891 N.Y. LEXIS 1396
New York Court of Appeals, 1891

Facts: This is a story with two Storys. William Story wanted his nephew to grow up healthy and prosperous. He promised the 15-year-old boy (also William Story) $5,000 if the lad would refrain from drinking liquor, using tobacco, swearing, and playing cards or billiards for money until his twenty-first birthday. (In that wild era—can you believe it?—the nephew had a legal right to do all those things.) The nephew agreed and, what is more, he kept his word. When he reached his twenty-first birthday, the nephew notified his uncle that he had honored the agreement. The uncle congratulated the young man and promised to give him the money, but said he would wait a few more years before handing over the cash, until the nephew was mature enough to handle such a large sum. The uncle died in 1887 without having paid, and his estate refused to honor the promise. Because the nephew had transferred his rights in the money, it was a man named Hamer who eventually sought to collect from the uncle's estate. The estate argued that because the nephew had given no consideration for the uncle's promise, there was no enforceable contract. The trial court found for the plaintiff, and the uncle's estate appealed.

Issue: Did the nephew give consideration for the uncle's promise?

Excerpts from Justice Parker's Decision: The defendant contends that the contract was without consideration to support it, and therefore invalid. He asserts that the promisee, by refraining from the use of liquor and tobacco, was not harmed, but benefited; that that which he did was best for him to do, independently of his uncle's promise, and insists that it follows that, unless the promisor was benefited, the contract was without consideration, a contention which, if well founded, would seem to leave open for controversy in many cases whether that which the promisee did or omitted to do was in fact of such benefit to him as to leave no consideration to support the enforcement of the promisor's agreement. Such a rule could not be tolerated, and is without foundation in the law. Courts will not ask whether the thing which forms the consideration does in fact benefit the promisee or a third party, or is of any substantial value to any one. It is enough that something is promised, done, forborne, or suffered by the party to whom the promise is made as consideration for the promise made to him.

Now applying this rule to the facts before us, the promisee used tobacco, occasionally drank liquor, and he had a legal right to do so. That right he abandoned for a period of years upon the strength of the promise of the testator [that is, the uncle] that for such forbearance he would give him $5,000. We need not speculate on the effort which may have been required to give up the use of those stimulants. It is sufficient that he restricted his lawful freedom of action within certain prescribed limits upon the faith of his uncle's agreement, and now, having fully performed the conditions imposed, it is of no moment whether such performance actually proved a benefit to the promisor, and the court will not inquire into it. ■

Illusory Promise

Annabel calls Jim and says, "I'll sell you my bicycle for 325 bucks. Interested?" Jim says, "I'll look at it tonight in the bike rack. If I like what I see, I'll pay you three and a quarter in the morning." At sunrise, Jim shows up with the $325 but Annabel refuses to sell. Can Jim enforce their deal? No. He said he would buy the bicycle *if he liked it*, keeping for himself the power to get out of the agreement for any reason at all. He is not committing himself to do anything, and the law considers his promise illusory, that is, not really a promise at all. **An illusory promise is not consideration.** Because he has given no consideration, there is no contract and *neither party* can enforce the deal.

Chapter Conclusion

Contracts govern countless areas of our lives, from intimate family issues to multibillion dollar corporate deals. Understanding contract principles is essential for a successful business or a professional career and is invaluable in private life. Courts no longer rubber-stamp any agreement that two parties have made. If we know the issues that courts scrutinize, the agreement we draft is likelier to be enforced. We thus achieve greater control over our affairs—the very purpose of a contract.

Chapter Review

1. A contract is a promise that the law will enforce. Contracts are intended to make business matters more predictable.

2. The common law governs contracts for services, employment, and real estate. The Uniform Commercial Code (UCC), Article 2, governs contracts for the sale of goods.

3. In an express contract, the two parties explicitly state all important terms of their agreement. In an implied contract, the words and conduct of the parties indicate that they intended an agreement.

4. A claim of promissory estoppel requires that the defendant made a promise knowing that the plaintiff would likely rely, the plaintiff did rely, and it would be wrong to deny recovery.

5. A claim of quasi-contract requires that the defendant received a benefit, knowing that the

plaintiff would expect compensation, and it would be unjust not to grant it.

6. The parties can form a contract only if they have a meeting of the minds.

7. An offer is an act or a statement that proposes definite terms and permits the other party to create a contract by accepting. The terms of the offer must be definite.

8. The offeree must say or do something to accept. The common law mirror image rule requires acceptance on precisely the same terms as the offer.

9. A promise is normally binding only if it is supported by consideration, which requires a bargaining and exchange between the parties.

Practice Test

1. Interactive Data Corp. hired Daniel Foley as an assistant product manager at a starting salary of $18,500. Over the next six years, Interactive

steadily promoted Foley until he became Los Angeles branch manager at a salary of $56,116. Interactive's officers repeatedly told Foley that he would have his job as long as his performance was adequate. In addition, Interactive distributed an employee handbook that specified "termination guidelines," including a mandatory seven-step pretermination procedure. Two years later, Foley learned that his recently hired supervisor, Robert Kuhne, was under investigation by the FBI for embezzlement at his previous job. Foley reported this to Interactive officers. Shortly thereafter, Interactive fired Foley. He sued, claiming that Interactive could only fire him for good cause, after the seven-step procedure. What kind of a claim is he making? Should he succeed?

2. The Hoffmans owned and operated a successful small bakery and grocery store. They spoke with Lukowitz, an agent of Red Owl Stores, who told them that for $18,000 Red Owl would build a store and fully stock it for them. The Hoffmans sold their bakery and grocery store and purchased a lot on which Red Owl was to build the store. Lukowitz then told Hoffman that the price had gone up to $26,000. The Hoffmans borrowed the extra money from relatives, but then Lukowitz informed them that the cost would be $34,000. Negotiations broke off and the Hoffmans sued. The court determined that there was no contract because too many details had not been worked out—the size of the store, its design, and the cost of constructing it. Can the Hoffmans recover any money?

3. Academy Chicago Publishers (Academy) approached the widow of author John Cheever about printing some of his unpublished stories. She signed a contract, which stated:

> The Author will deliver to the Publisher on a mutually agreeable date one copy of the manuscript of the Work as finally arranged by the editor and satisfactory to the Publisher in form and content. . . .
>
> Within a reasonable time and a mutually agreeable date after delivery of the final revised manuscript, the Publisher will publish the Work at its own expense, in such style and manner and at such price as it deems best, and will keep the Work in print as long as it deems it expedient.

Within a year, Academy located and delivered to Mrs. Cheever more than 60 unpublished stories. She refused to go ahead with the project. Academy sued for the right to publish. The trial court ruled that the agreement was valid; the appeals court affirmed; and the case went to the Illinois Supreme Court. Was the contract enforceable?

4. Rebecca, in Honolulu, faxes a job offer to Spike, in Pittsburgh, saying, "We can pay you $55,000 per year, starting June 1." Spike faxes a reply, saying, "Thank you! I accept your generous offer, though I will also need $3,000 in relocation money. See you June 1. Can't wait!" On June 1, Spike arrives, to find that his position is filled by Gus. He sues Rebecca.

   a. Spike wins $55,000.

   b. Spike wins $58,000.

   c. Spike wins $3,000.

   d. Spike wins restitution.

   e. Spike wins nothing.

5. An aunt saw her eight-year-old nephew enter the room, remarked what a nice boy he was, and said, "I would like to take care of him now." She promptly wrote a note, promising to pay the boy $3,000 upon her death. Her estate refused to pay. Is it obligated to do so?

6. Explain the difference between judicial restraint activism and judicial activism in contract law.

7. **YOU BE THE JUDGE** WRITING PROBLEM John Stevens owned a dilapidated apartment that he rented to James and Cora Chesney for a low rent. Over a four-year period, the Chesneys installed two new bathrooms, carpeted the floors, installed new septic and heating systems, and rewired, replumbed, and painted. Stevens periodically stopped by and saw the work in progress. Three years after their work was done, Stevens served the Chesneys with an eviction notice. The Chesneys counterclaimed, seeking the value of the work they had done. Are they entitled to it? **Argument for Stevens:** Mr. Stevens is willing to pay the Chesneys exactly the amount he agreed to pay: nothing. The Chesneys are making the absurd argument that anyone who chooses to perform certain work, without ever discussing it with another party, can charge it to the other person.

Argument for the Chesneys: The Chesneys have given an enormous benefit to Stevens by transforming the apartment and enabling him to rent it at greater profit. If Stevens never intended to pay the fair value of the work, he should have stopped the couple or notified them that there would be no compensation.

8. Describe the role each of the following plays in contract law: the common law, the UCC, and the Restatement (Second) of Contracts.

9. Which of these might be valid consideration?

   a. A promise to do something.

   b. A promise to refrain from doing something.

   c. An action.

   d. All of the above.

10. *ROLE REVERSAL* Write a multiple-choice question that distinguishes express, implied, and quasi-contracts.

Internet Research Problem

Visit http://www.law.cornell.edu. Click on "Constitutions and Codes," then "Other Uniform Laws." Select a state. Then click on "Judicial Opinions." Search for a case concerning "quasi-contract." What are the details of the quasi-contract dispute? Who won and why?

You can find further practice problems at academic.cengage.com/blaw/beatty.

CHAPTER 10

Legality, Consent, and Writing

Soheil Sadri, a California resident, did some serious gambling at Caesar's Tahoe casino in Nevada. And lost. To keep gambling, he wrote checks to Caesar's and then signed two memoranda pledging to repay money advanced. After two days, with his losses totaling more than $22,000, he went home. Back in California, Sadri stopped payment on the checks and refused to pay any of the money he owed Caesar's. The casino sued and recovered . . . nothing. Sadri relied on an important legal principle to defeat the suit: **A contract that is illegal is void and unenforceable.** We will examine a variety of contracts that may be void.

Gambling is one of America's fastest growing businesses, but a controversial one. Because our citizens—and our states— are divided over the ethics of wagering, conflicts such as the dispute between Sadri and Caesar's are inevitable. The basic rule, however, is clear: **A gambling** contract **is illegal unless it is specifically authorized by state statute.** In California, as in many states, gambling on credit is not allowed. In other words, it is illegal to lend money to help someone wager. However, in Nevada, gambling on credit is legal and debt memoranda such as Sadri's are enforceable contracts. Caesar's sued Sadri in California (where he lived). The court admitted that California's attitude toward gambling had changed and that bingo, poker clubs, and lotteries were common. Nonetheless, the court denied that the new tolerance extended to wagering on credit, stating: "The judiciary cannot protect pathological gamblers from themselves, but we can refuse to participate in their financial ruin."[1]

Caesar's lost, and Sadri kept his money. The dispute is a useful starting place from which to examine contract legality because it illustrates two important themes. First, morality is a

© DAVID PAPAZIAN PHOTOGRAPHY INC/BRAND X PICTURES/GETTY IMAGES

---

[1] *Metropolitan Creditors Service of Sacramento v. Sadri*, 15 Cal. App. 4th 1821, 1993 Cal App. LEXIS 559, 19 Cal. Rptr. 2d 646 (Cal. Ct. App. 1993).

*significant part of contract legality. In refusing to enforce an obligation that Sadri undeniably had made, the California court relied on the human and social consequences of gambling and on the ethics of judicial enforcement of gambling debts. Second, "void" really means just that: **a court will not assist either party to an illegal agreement,** even if its refusal leaves one party obviously shortchanged.*   ■

LEGALITY

Restraint of Trade

Free trade is the basis of the American economy, and any bargain that restricts it is suspect. Most restraint of free trade is barred by antitrust law. But it is the common law that still regulates one restriction on trade: agreements to refrain from competition. Some of these agreements are legal, some void. They are *very* common. Many readers of this book will find such a clause in their own employment contracts.

To be valid, an agreement not to compete must be ancillary to a legitimate bargain. "Ancillary" means that the noncompetition agreement must be part of a larger agreement. Suppose Cliff sells his gasoline station to Mina and the two agree that Cliff will not open a competing gas station within five miles anytime during the next two years. Cliff's agreement not to compete is ancillary to the sale of his service station. His noncompetition promise is enforceable. But suppose that Cliff and Mina already had the only two gas stations within 35 miles. They agree between themselves not to hire each other's workers. Their agreement might be profitable to them, because each could now keep wages artificially low. But their deal is ancillary to no legitimate bargain, and it is therefore void.

The two most common settings for legitimate noncompetition agreements are the *sale of a business* and an *employment relationship*.

Sale of a Business

Kory has operated a real estate office, Hearth Attack, in a small city for 35 years, building an excellent reputation and many ties with the community. She offers to sell you the business and its goodwill for $300,000. But you need assurance that Kory will not take your money and promptly open a competing office across the street. With her reputation and connections, she would ruin your chances of success. You insist on a noncompete clause in the sale contract. In this clause, Kory promises that for one year she will not open a new real estate office or go to work for a competing company within a 10-mile radius of Hearth Attack. Suppose, six months after selling you the business, Kory goes to work for a competing realtor, two blocks away. You seek an injunction (a court order) to prevent her from working. Who wins?

When a noncompete agreement is ancillary to the sale of a business, it is enforceable if reasonable in time, geographic area, and scope of activity. In other words, a court will not enforce a noncompete agreement that lasts an unreasonably long time, covers an unfairly large area, or prohibits the seller of the business from doing a type of work that she never had done before. Measured by this test, Kory is almost certainly bound by her agreement. One year is a reasonable time to allow you to get your new business started. A 10-mile radius is probably about the area that Hearth Attack covers, and realty is obviously a fair business from which to prohibit Kory. A court will grant the injunction, barring Kory from her new job.

If, on the other hand, the noncompetition agreement had prevented Kory from working anywhere within 200 miles of Hearth Attack, and she started working 50 miles away, a court would refuse to enforce the contract.

Employment

When you sign an employment contract, the document may well contain a noncompete clause. Employers have legitimate worries that employees might go to a competitor and take with them trade secrets or other proprietary information. Some employers, though, attempt to place harsh restrictions on their employees, perhaps demanding a blanket agreement that the employee will never go to work for a competitor. Once again, courts look at the reasonableness of restrictions placed on an employee's future work. Because the agreement now involves the very livelihood of the worker, a court scrutinizes the agreement more closely.

A noncompete clause in an employment contract is generally reasonable— and enforceable—only to the extent necessary to protect (1) trade secrets, (2) confidential information, or (3) customer lists developed over an extended period. In general, other restrictions on future employment are unenforceable.[2] Suppose that Gina, an engineer, goes to work for Fission Chips, a silicon chip manufacturer that specializes in defense work. She signs a noncompete agreement promising never to work for a competitor. Over a period of three years, Gina learns some of Fission's proprietary methods of etching information onto the chips. She acquires a great deal of new expertise about chips generally. And she periodically deals with Fission Chips' customers, all of whom are well-known software and hardware manufacturers.

Gina accepts an offer from WriteSmall, a competitor. Fission Chips races into court, seeking an injunction to block Gina from working for WriteSmall. This injunction threatens Gina's career. If she cannot work for a competitor, or use her general engineering skills, what will she do? And for exactly that reason, no court will grant such a broad order. The court will allow Gina to work for competitors, including WriteSmall. It will order her not to use or reveal any trade secrets belonging to Fission. She will, however, be permitted to use the general expertise she has acquired, and she may contact former customers because anyone could get their names from the yellow pages.

Was the noncompete in the following case styled fairly, or was the employee clipped?

KING V. HEAD START FAMILY HAIR SALONS, INC.

886 So.2d 769
Supreme Court of Alabama, 2004

Facts: Kathy King was a single mother supporting a college-aged daughter. For 25 years she had worked as a hair stylist. For the most recent 16 years, she worked at Head Start, which provided hair cuts, coloring, and styling for men and women. King was primarily a stylist, although she had also managed one of the Head Start facilities.

King quit Head Start and began working as manager of a Sports Clips shop, located in the same mall as the store she just left. Sports Clip offered only hair cuts and primarily served men and boys. Head Start filed suit, claiming that King was violating a noncompetition agreement that she had in ▼

---

[2] If the agreement restricts the employee from *starting a new business,* a court may apply the more lenient standard used for the sale of a business; the noncompete clause will be enforced if reasonable in time, geography, and scope of activity.

fact signed. The agreement prohibited King from working at a competing business within a two-mile radius of any Head Start facility for 12 months after leaving the company. The trial court issued an injunction enforcing the noncompete. King appealed.

Issue: *Was the noncompetition agreement valid?*

Excerpts from Justice Lyons's Decision: King's most persuasive argument is that the geographic restriction contained in the noncompetition agreement imposes an undue hardship on her. King has been in the hair-care industry for 25 years, and that it is the only industry in which she is skilled and the only industry in which she can find employment. Head Start has 30 locations throughout the Jefferson County and Shelby County area, making it virtually impossible for her to find employment in the hair-care industry at a facility that does not violate the terms of the noncompetition agreement. According to King, the geographic restriction constitutes a blanket prohibition on practicing her trade.

It cannot reasonably be argued that King, at the age of 40 and having spent more than half of her life as a hair stylist, can learn a new job skill that would allow her to be gainfully employed and meet her needs and the needs of her daughter. Under the circumstances presented here, enforcement of the noncompetition agreement works an undue hardship upon King. The noncompetition agreement cannot so burden King that it would result in her impoverishment.

Head Start is nevertheless entitled to some of the protection it sought in the noncompetition agreement. Head Start has a valid concern that King would be able to attract many of her former Head Start customers if she is allowed to provide hair-care services unencumbered by any limitations. To prevent an undue burden on King and to afford some protection to Head Start, the trial court should enforce a more reasonable geographic restriction—such as one prohibiting King from providing hair-care services within a two-mile radius of the location of the Head Start facility at which she was formerly employed or imposing some other limitation that does not unreasonably interfere with King's right to gainful employment while, at the same time, protecting Head Start's interest in preventing King from unreasonably competing with it during the one-year period following her resignation.

Reversed and remanded. ∎

The following chart summarizes the factors that courts look at in noncompete agreements.

The Legality of Noncompete Clauses		
Type of Noncompete Agreement	**When Enforceable**	
Not ancillary to a sale of business or employment	Never	
Ancillary to a sale of business	If reasonable in time, geography, and scope of activity	
Ancillary to employment	Contract is more likely to be enforced when it: • Involves trade secrets or confidential information: These are almost always protected • Includes customer lists developed over an extended period and carefully protected • Encompasses limited time and geographical scope • Is vital to protect the employer's business	Contract is less likely to be enforced when it: • Involves an employee who already had the skills when he arrived, or merely developed general skills on the job • Includes customer lists that can be derived from public sources • Encompasses excessive time or geographical scope • Is unduly harsh on the employee or contrary to public interest

Exculpatory Clauses

You decide to capitalize on your expert ability as a skier and open a ski school in Colorado, "Pike's Pique." But you realize that skiing sometimes causes injuries, so you require anyone signing up for lessons to sign this form:

> I agree to hold Pike's Pique and its employees entirely harmless in the event that I am injured in any way or for any reason or cause, including but not limited to any acts, whether negligent or otherwise, of Pike's Pique or any employee or agent thereof.

The day your school opens, Sara Beth, an instructor, deliberately pushes Toby over a cliff because Toby criticizes her color combinations. Eddie, a beginning student, "blows out" his knee attempting an advanced racing turn. And Maureen, another student, reaches the bottom of a steep run and slams into a snowmobile that Sara Beth parked there. Maureen, Eddie, and Toby's families all sue Pike's Pique. You defend based on the form you had them sign. Does it save the day?

The form on which you are relying is an **exculpatory clause,** that is, one that attempts to release you from liability in the event of injury to another party. Exculpatory clauses are common. Ski schools use them, and so do parking lots, landlords, warehouses, and daycare centers. All manner of businesses hope to avoid large tort judgments by requiring their customers to give up any right to recover. Is such a clause valid? Sometimes. Courts often—but not always—ignore exculpatory clauses, finding that one party was forcing the other party to give up legal rights that no one should be forced to surrender.

An exculpatory clause is generally unenforceable when it attempts to exclude an intentional tort or gross negligence. When Sara Beth pushes Toby over a cliff, that is the intentional tort of battery. A court will not enforce the exculpatory clause. Sara Beth is clearly liable.[3] As to the snowmobile at the bottom of the run, if a court determines that was gross negligence (carelessness far greater than ordinary negligence), then the exculpatory clause will again be ignored. If, however, it was ordinary negligence, then we must continue the analysis.

An exculpatory clause is generally unenforceable when the affected activity is in the public interest, such as medical care, public transportation, or some essential service. What about Eddie's suit against Pike's Pique? Eddie claims that he should never have been allowed to attempt an advanced maneuver. His suit is for ordinary negligence, and the exculpatory clause probably does bar him from recovery. Skiing is a recreational activity. No one is obligated to do it, and there is no strong public interest in ensuring that we have access to ski slopes.

An exculpatory clause is generally unenforceable when the parties have greatly unequal bargaining power. When Maureen flies to Colorado, suppose that the airline requires her to sign a form contract with an exculpatory clause. Because the airline almost certainly has much greater bargaining power, it can afford to offer a "take it or leave it" contract. But because the bargaining power is so unequal, the clause is probably unenforceable.

An exculpatory clause is generally unenforceable unless the clause is clearly written and readily visible. Thus, if Pike's Pique gave all ski students an eight-page contract, and the exculpatory clause was at the bottom of page seven in small print, the average customer would never notice it. The clause would be void. In the following case, the court examined the issues of public interest and unequal bargaining power, focusing on the public policy concerns of exculpatory clauses used in a very common setting.

---

[3] Note that Pike's Pique is probably not liable under agency law principles that preclude an employer's liability for an employee's intentional tort.

RANSBURG V. RICHARDS

770 N.E.2d 393
Indiana Court of Appeals, 2002

Facts: Barbara Richards leased an apartment at Twin Lakes, a complex owned by Lenna Ransburg. The written lease declared that:

- Twin Lakes would "gratuitously" maintain the common areas.

- Richards's use of the facilities would be "at her own risk."

- Twin Lakes was not responsible for any harm to the tenant or her guests, anywhere on the property (including the parking lot), even if the damage was caused by Twin Lakes' negligence.

It snowed. As Richards walked across the parking lot to her car, she slipped and fell on snow-covered ice. Richards sued Ransburg, who moved for summary judgment based on the exculpatory clause. The trial court denied Ransburg's motion and she appealed.

Issue: *Was the exculpatory clause valid?*

Excerpts from Judge Barnes's Decision: Resolving the question of whether this lease provision is void as against public policy turns on fairly balancing the parties' freedom to contract against the policy of promoting responsibility for damages caused by one's own negligent acts. We recognize a very strong presumption of enforceability of contracts that represent the freely bargained agreement of the parties. However, in certain circumstances a court may declare an otherwise valid contract unenforceable if it contravenes the public policy of Indiana.

[Some courts have found that the most important principle in these cases is freedom to contract, meaning that the exculpatory clauses are valid. But other courts disagree. One judge declared:]

> A tenant must live somewhere. The tenant has no meaningful choices. He can accept this landlord or go to another landlord who charges the same rent and asks the tenant to sign the same standard form lease. But is there any principle which is more familiar or

more firmly embedded in the history of Anglo-American law than the basic doctrine that the courts will not permit themselves to be used as instruments of inequity and injustice? The law is not so primitive that it sanctions every injustice except brute force and downright fraud.

A lease is no longer an isolated contract between one landlord and one tenant. The size of the rental industry is so great that construction of an exculpatory clause has an impact on thousands of citizens. Furthermore, the public has an interest in the quality of housing offered for rent to all members of the public.

With these thoughts in mind, we conclude that [several] factors weigh in favor of not enforcing this type of clause in residential leases. Given the vast number of people clauses like these affect, the inequality of bargaining power caused by the need for housing, the fact that people who are not parties to the contracts could suffer as a result of such clauses, and the desire to promote responsible maintenance by landlords to avoid personal injuries by tenants and third parties, we find that the factors weigh in favor of public policy. We conclude that the exculpatory clause in this residential lease is contrary to public policy insofar as it seeks to immunize Ransburg against damages caused by her negligence, if any, in maintaining common areas.

Affirmed.

Excerpts from Judge Najam's Dissent: The majority opinion nullifies a valid private agreement, rewrites the lease, and reallocates the exchange of costs and benefits between the parties. The majority ignores the plain meaning of the exculpatory clause and violates the well-settled common law right of the parties to make such a provision and to have it enforced according to its terms. In so doing, the majority has unilaterally altered the economic equation in countless residential leases across the state. ■

ECONOMICS
& the LAW

Judicial rejection of exculpatory clauses may have a hidden cost. Presumably, the landlord and tenant each attempted to negotiate the most favorable rent possible. The landlord may have offered a lower rent because of the exculpatory clause, assuming she could never be liable for damages. When the court threw the clause out the window, it notified landlords across the state that they had better fix up their rental property. Landlords passed on the increased costs in the form of higher rent. The court's decision is likely to result in rental units that are safer but more expensive. A judicial ruling that is essentially pro-consumer could leave some families out in the cold. ◆

Unconscionable Contracts

Gail Waters was young, naive, and insecure. A serious injury when she was 12 years old left her with an annuity, that is, a guaranteed annual payment for many years. When Gail was 21, she became involved with Thomas Beauchemin, an ex-convict, who introduced her to drugs. Beauchemin suggested that Gail sell her annuity to some friends of his, and she agreed. Beauchemin arranged for a lawyer to draw up a contract, and Gail signed it. She received one $50,000 payment for her annuity, which at that time had a cash value of $189,000 and was worth, over its remaining 25 years, $694,000. Gail later decided this was not an excellent bargain. Was the contract enforceable? That depends on the law of unconscionability.

An unconscionable contract is one that a court refuses to enforce because of fundamental unfairness. Historically, a contract was considered unconscionable if it was "such as no man in his senses and not under delusion would make on the one hand, and as no honest and fair man would accept on the other."[4] The two factors that most often lead a court to find unconscionability are (1) **oppression,** meaning that one party used its superior power to force a contract on the weaker party, and (2) **surprise,** meaning that the weaker party did not fully understand the consequences of its agreement.

Gail Waters won her case. The Massachusetts high court ruled:

> Beauchemin introduced the plaintiff to drugs, exhausted her credit card accounts, unduly influenced her, suggested that the plaintiff sell her annuity contract, initiated the contract negotiations, was the agent of the defendants, and benefited from the contract between the plaintiff and the defendants. The defendants were represented by legal counsel; the plaintiff was not. The cash value of the annuity policy at the time the contract was executed was approximately four times greater than the price to be paid by the defendants. For payment of not more than $50,000 the defendants were to receive an asset that could be immediately exchanged for $189,000, or they could elect to hold it for its guaranteed term and receive $694,000.
>
> The disparity of interests in this contract is so gross that the court cannot resist the inference that it was improperly obtained and is unconscionable.[5]

CAPACITY AND CONSENT

For Kevin Green, it was love at first sight. She was sleek, as quick as a cat, and a beautiful deep blue. He paid $4,600 cash for the used Camaro. The car soon blew a gasket, and Kevin demanded his money back. But the Camaro came with no guarantee, and

---

[4] *Hume v. United States,* 132 U.S. 406, 411, 10 S. Ct. 134, 1889 U.S. LEXIS 1888 (1889), quoting *Earl of Chesterfield v. Janssen,* 38 Eng. Rep. 82, 100 (Ch. 1750).

[5] *Waters v. Min Ltd.,* 412 Mass. 64, 587 N.E.2d 231, 1992 Mass. LEXIS 66 (1992).

Star Chevrolet, the dealer, refused. Kevin repaired the car himself. Next, some unpleasantness on the highway left the car a worthless wreck. Kevin received the full value of the car from his insurance company. Then he sued the dealer, seeking a refund of his purchase price. The dealer pointed out that it was not responsible for the accident, and that the car had no warranty of any kind. Yet the court awarded Kevin the full value of his car. How can this be?

The automobile dealer ignored *legal capacity*. Kevin Green was only 16 years old when he bought the car, and a minor, said the court, has the right to cancel any agreement he made, for any reason. Capacity concerns the legal ability of a party to enter a contract. Someone may lack capacity because of his young age or mental infirmity. Consent refers to whether a contracting party truly understood what he was getting into and whether he made the agreement voluntarily. Consent issues arise most often in cases of fraud and mistake.

Capacity

Capacity is the legal ability to enter into a contract. An adult of sound mind has the legal capacity to contract. Generally, any deal she enters into will be enforced if all elements we have seen—agreement, consideration, and so forth—are present. But two groups of people usually lack legal capacity: minors and those with a mental impairment.

Minors

A minor is someone under the age of 18. Because a minor lacks legal capacity, she normally can create only a voidable contract. **A voidable contract may be canceled by the party who lacks capacity.** Notice that *only the party lacking capacity* may cancel the agreement. So a minor who enters into a contract generally may choose between enforcing the agreement or negating it. The other party, however, has no such right.

Disaffirmance

A minor who wishes to escape from a contract generally may **disaffirm** it; that is, he may notify the other party that he refuses to be bound by the agreement. Because Kevin was 16 when he signed, the deal was voidable. When the Camaro blew a gasket and the lad informed Star Chevrolet that he wanted his money back, he was disaffirming the contract, which he could do for any reason at all. Kevin was entitled to his money back. If Star Chevrolet had understood the law of capacity, it would have towed the Camaro away and returned the young man's $4,600. At least the dealership would have had a repairable automobile.

Restitution

A minor who disaffirms a contract must return the consideration he has received, to the extent he is able. Restoring the other party to its original position is called **restitution**. The consideration that Kevin Green received in the contract was, of course, the Camaro. If Star Chevrolet had delivered a check for $4,600, Kevin would have been obligated to return the car.

What happens if the minor is not able to return the consideration because he no longer has it or it has been destroyed? Most states hold that the minor is still entitled to his money back. Kevin Green got his money and Star Chevrolet received a fine lesson.

Mentally Impaired Persons

A person suffers from a mental impairment if by reason of mental illness or defect he is unable to understand the nature and consequences of the transaction.[6] The mental impairment can be insanity that has been formally declared by a court or mental illness that has never been ruled on but is now evident. The impairment may also be due to some other mental illness, such as schizophrenia, or to mental retardation, brain injury, senility, or any other cause that renders the person unable to understand the nature and consequences of the contract.

A party suffering a mental impairment generally creates only a voidable contract. The impaired person has the right to disaffirm the contract just as a minor does. But again, the contract is voidable, not void. The mentally impaired party generally has the right to full performance if she wishes. Similar rules apply in cases of drug or alcohol **intoxication.** When one party is so intoxicated that he cannot understand the nature and consequences of the transaction, the contract is voidable.

Reality of Consent

Smiley offers to sell you his house for $300,000, and you agree in writing to buy. After you move in, you discover that the house is sinking into the earth at the rate of six inches per week. In 12 months, your only access to the house will be through the chimney. You sue, asking to **rescind, which means to cancel the agreement.** You argue that when you signed the contract you did not truly consent because you lacked essential information. In this section, we look at issues of misrepresentation, fraud, and mistake.

Misrepresentation and Fraud

Misrepresentation occurs when a party to a contract says something that is factually wrong. "This house has no termites," says a homeowner to a prospective buyer. If the house is swarming with the nasty pests, the statement is a misrepresentation. The misrepresentation might be innocent or fraudulent. If the owner believes the statement to be true and has a good reason for that belief, he has made an **innocent misrepresentation.** If the owner knows that it is false, the statement is **fraudulent misrepresentation.** To explain these concepts, we will assume that two people are discussing a possible deal. One is the "maker"—that is, the person who makes the statement that is later disputed. The other is the "injured person," the one who eventually claims to have been injured by the statement. In order to rescind the contract, the injured person must show that the maker's statement was either fraudulent or a material misrepresentation. She does not have to show both. Innocent misrepresentation and fraud each make a contract voidable. **To rescind a contract based on misrepresentation or fraud, a party must show three things: (1) there was a false statement of fact; (2) the statement was fraudulent or material; and (3) the injured person justifiably relied on the statement.**

Element One: False Statement of Fact.   The injured party must show a false statement of fact. Notice that this does not mean the statement was a lie. If a homeowner says that the famous architect Stanford White designed his house, but Bozo Loco actually did the work, it is a false statement. The owner might have a good reason for the error. Perhaps a local history book identifies the house as a Stanford White. Or the owner's words might be an intentional lie. In either case, it is a false statement of fact.

---

[6] Restatement (Second) of Contracts §15.

An **opinion,** though, is not a statement of fact. A realtor says, "I think land values around here will be going up 20 or 30 percent for the foreseeable future." That statement is pretty enticing to a buyer, but it is not a false statement of fact. The maker is clearly stating her own opinion, and the buyer who relies on it does so at his peril. A close relative of opinion is something called puffery. A statement is **puffery** when a reasonable person would realize that it is a sales pitch, representing the exaggerated opinion of the seller. Puffery is not a statement of fact and is never a basis for rescission.

Element Two: Fraud or Materiality.

This is the heart of the case. The injured party must demonstrate that the statement was fraudulent or material:

- The statement was fraudulent if the maker intended to induce the other party to contract, either knowing that her words were false or uncertain that they were true.

- The statement was material if the maker expected the other party to rely on her words in reaching an agreement.

So the injured party can win by showing either of two very different things. Fraud indicates a bad faith statement, whereas material misrepresentation signifies that the words were inaccurate—and effective.

Consider the examples in the following chart.

Statement: In each case, the words are false	Owner's Belief	Legal Result	Explanation
1. "The heating system is perfect."	Owner knows this is false.	Fraud.	Owner knew the statement was false and intended to induce the buyer to enter into a contract.
2. "The house is built on solid bedrock."	Owner has no idea what is under the surface.	Fraud.	Owner was not certain the statement was true and intended to induce the buyer to enter into a contract.
3. "The roof is only six years old."	Owner believes the statement is accurate, because when he bought the house six years ago, he was told the roof was new.	Material misrepresentation.	Owner acted in good faith, but the statement is material because owner expects the buyer to rely on it.
4. "The pool is 30 feet long."	Owner believes the statement is accurate because he measured the pool himself, though in fact it is only 29 feet	Not a material misrepresentation.	Although this is a misrepresentation, it is not material, because a reasonable buyer would not make a decision based on a one-foot error in the pool length.

Element Three: Justifiable Reliance.   The injured party must also show that she actually did rely on the false statement and that her reliance was reasonable. Suppose the seller of a gas station lies through his teeth about the structural soundness of the building. The buyer believes what he hears but does not much care, because he plans to demolish the building and construct a daycare center. There was fraud but no reliance, and the buyer may not rescind.

Plaintiff's Remedy for Misrepresentation or Fraud.   Both innocent and fraudulent misrepresentation permit the injured party to rescind the contract. In other words, the injured party who proves all three elements will get her money back. She will, of course, have to make restitution to the other party. If she bought land and now wants to rescind, she must return the property to the seller.

But the injured party is not forced to rescind the deal if it makes financial sense to go forward with it. After signing a contract to buy a new house, Nancy learns that the building has a terrible heating system. A new one will cost $12,000. If the seller told her the system was "like new," Nancy may rescind the deal. But it may be economically harmful for her to do so. She might have sold her old house, hired a mover, taken a new job, and so forth. She has the option of fully performing the contract and moving into the new house. What are her other remedies? That will depend on whether the misstatement ("the system is like new") was fraudulent or simply a material misrepresentation.

If the maker's statement is fraudulent, the injured party generally has a choice of rescinding the contract or suing for damages. If the seller's mistake was fraudulent, Nancy will generally be allowed to carry out the contract and sue for damages. She could move into the new house and sue for the difference between what she got and what was promised, which is probably about $12,000, the cost of replacing the heating system. But if the seller's mistake was innocent, and Nancy can prove only material misrepresentation, she has no remedy other than rescission. If she goes forward with the contract, she must accept the house as she finds it.

Special Problem: Silence.   We know that a party negotiating a contract may not misrepresent a material fact. But what about silence? Suppose the seller knows the roof is in dreadful condition (since she sleeps under an umbrella), but the buyer never asks. Must the seller disclose what she knows?

This is perhaps the hottest topic today in the law of misrepresentation. A seller who knows something that the buyer does not know is often required to divulge it. The Restatement (Second) of Contracts offers guidance:

Nondisclosure of a fact amounts to misrepresentation when:

- Disclosure is necessary to correct a previous assertion. During the course of negotiations, one party's perception of the facts may change. When an earlier statement later appears inaccurate, the change generally must be reported.

- Disclosure would correct a basic mistaken assumption that the other party is relying on. When one party knows that the other is negotiating with a mistaken assumption about an important fact, the party who knows of the error must correct it. Most courts require a property seller to disclose hidden defects. The judge in the following case states the rule somewhat differently, but the reasoning and outcome are the same.

FIMBEL V. DECLARK

695 N.E.2d 125
Indiana Court of Appeals, 1998

Facts: Ronald and Patricia Fimbel bought two lakefront lots on Lake Latonka in Indiana, intending to build a summer cottage. However, they discovered that the soil was not suitable for a septic system. They would have to hire an engineer at a substantial expense to determine if it was even possible to construct an alternative system. They decided to sell the land.

The Fimbels met with several interested buyers, including Thomas and Joan DeClark. The Fimbels said nothing about the septic problems. The DeClarks bought the property and, one week later, learned that the property was unbuildable. They sued, and the trial court granted them rescission. The Fimbels appealed.

Issue: *Did the Fimbels have a duty to disclose the septic problems?*

Excerpts from Judge Staton's Decision: Initially, the Fimbels contend that they cannot be held liable in fraud for failing to disclose the soil condition of the lots since they were under no duty to do so. Ordinarily a seller is not bound to disclose any material facts unless there exists a relationship for which the law imposes a duty of disclosure. Courts have found such a relationship, and therefore a duty to disclose, where the buyer makes inquiries about a condition on, the qualities of, or the characteristics of the property.

The evidence supports the conclusion that the DeClarks and Fimbels had conversations which imposed a duty upon the Fimbels to disclose the unsuitability of the lots for home construction. Mr. DeClark testified that, while viewing the lots, he asked Mr. Fimbel if he had ever intended to build a home on them. Mr. Fimbel stated that he was going to build, but he ultimately decided that he preferred some property he owned in Minnesota, noting its peacefulness and that he had a friend that lives there. Mr. DeClark told Mr. Fimbel that he wanted to build a home on the lots. The above inquiry and statement sufficiently introduced the issue of home construction into the parties' transaction such that a duty was imposed on the Fimbels to disclose the information they had regarding the suitability of the lots for residential construction.

The Fimbels also contend that they made no misrepresentation of fact as to whether a home could be constructed on the lots. True, the Fimbels never expressly stated whether or not a home could be constructed on the lots. However, this does not insulate the Fimbels from a judgment in fraud. If a seller undertakes to disclose facts within his knowledge, he must disclose the whole truth without concealing material facts and without doing anything to prevent the other party from making a thorough inspection. In this case, Mr. Fimbel told Mr. DeClark that the reason he never built on the lots was that he preferred other property. The preference for the other property is, at best, only one reason for not building on Lake Latonka: the other being the inability to place a septic system on the land. One cannot be allowed, under the law, to partially disclose the facts as he knows them to be, yet create a false impression in the mind of the hearer by failing to fully reveal the true state of affairs. The statement by Mr. DeClark at closing that he intended to build on the lots appears to have been met with silence. Given the circumstances, this silence can also support a judgment for fraud. Silence accompanied by deceptive conduct, results in active concealment, and is actionable.

Affirmed. ■

Ethics

There are various disclosure rules that a state could adopt:

- Caveat emptor—let the buyer beware.
- Seller has a duty to disclose only if asked.
- Seller has a duty to disclose regardless of whether asked.
- Seller's only duty is to notify buyer of important considerations that buyer may wish to investigate (soil condition, building laws, problems with neighboring property, etc.).

Which rule do you prefer, and why? As you answer this question, apply these concepts from the Chapter 2 ethics checklist: What are the alternatives? What outcome does the Golden Rule require? ◆

Mistake

Most contract principles come from appellate courts, but in the area of "legal mistake" a cow wrote much of the law. The cow was Rose 2d of Aberlone, a gentle animal that lived in Michigan in 1886. Rose's owner, Hiram Walker & Sons, had bought her for $850. After a few years, the company concluded that Rose could have no calves. As a barren cow she was worth much less, so Walker contracted to sell her to T. C. Sherwood for $80. But when Sherwood came to collect Rose, the parties realized she was pregnant. Walker refused to part with the happy mother, and Sherwood sued. Walker defended, claiming that both parties had made a mistake and that the contract was voidable.

Bilateral Mistake.   A **bilateral mistake** occurs when both parties negotiate based on the same factual error. Sherwood and Walker both thought Rose was barren, both negotiated accordingly, and both were wrong. The Michigan Supreme Court gave judgment for Walker, the seller, permitting him to rescind the contract because the parties were both wrong about the essence of what they were bargaining for.

If the parties contract based on an important factual error, the contract is voidable by the injured party. Sherwood and Walker were both wrong about Rose's reproductive ability, and the error was basic enough to cause a tenfold difference in price. Walker, the injured party, was entitled to rescind the contract. Note that the error must be *factual*. Suppose Walker sold Rose thinking that the price of beef was going to drop, when in fact the price rose 60 percent in five months. He made a mistake, but it was simply a business prediction that proved wrong. Walker would have no right to rescind.

Conscious Uncertainty.   No rescission is permitted where one of the parties knows he is taking on a risk—that is, he realizes there is uncertainty about the quality of the thing being exchanged. Rufus offers 10 acres of mountainous land to Priscilla. "I can't promise you anything about this land," he says, "but they've found gold on every adjoining parcel." Priscilla, panting with gold lust, buys the land, digs long and hard and discovers—mud. She may not rescind the contract. She understood her risk, and there was no mutual mistake.

Unilateral Mistake.   Sometimes only one party enters a contract under a mistaken assumption, a situation called **unilateral mistake.** In these cases, it is more difficult for the injured party to rescind a contract. To rescind for unilateral mistake, a party must demonstrate that she entered the contract because of a basic factual error and that either (1) enforcing the contract would be unconscionable or (2) the nonmistaken party knew of the error.

Contracts in Writing

Oliver and Perry were college roommates, two sophomores with contrasting personalities. They were sitting in the cafeteria with some friends, Oliver chatting away, Perry slumped on a plastic bench. Oliver suggested that they buy a lottery ticket, as the prize for that week's drawing was $3 million. Perry muttered, "Nah. You never win if you buy just one ticket." Oliver bubbled up, "OK, we'll buy a ticket every week.

We'll keep buying them from now until we graduate. Come on, it'll be fun. This month, I'll buy the tickets. Next month, you will, and so on." Other students urged Perry to do it and, finally, grudgingly, he agreed. The two friends carefully reviewed their deal. Each party was providing consideration, namely, the responsibility for purchasing tickets during his month. The amount of each purchase was clearly defined at one dollar. They would start that week and continue until graduation day, two and a half years down the road. Finally, they would share equally any money won. As three witnesses looked on, they shook hands on the bargain. That month, Oliver bought a ticket every week, randomly choosing numbers, and won nothing. The next month, Perry bought a ticket with equally random numbers—and won $52 million. Perry moved out of their dorm room into a suite at the Ritz and refused to give Oliver one red cent. Oliver sued, seeking $26 million and the return of an Eric Clapton CD that he had loaned to Perry.

If the former friends had read this chapter, they would never have slid into such a mess. In the last chapter, we covered the basics of contract law, and now we put the icing on the cake. We will examine which contracts must be in writing, when third parties have rights or obligations under an agreement, what problems arise in the performance of contracts, and the remedies available when a deal goes awry. Oliver and Perry's case involves the statute of frauds, which tells us which contracts must be written.

Written Contracts

The rule we examine in this chapter is not exactly news. Parliament passed the original statute of frauds in 1677. The purpose was to prevent lying (fraud) in civil lawsuits. The statute required that in several types of cases, a contract would be enforced only if it was in writing. Almost all states in our own country later passed their own statutes making the same requirements. It is important to remember, as we examine the rules and exceptions, that Parliament and the state legislatures all had a commendable, straightforward purpose in passing their respective statutes of fraud: *to provide a court with the best possible evidence of whether the parties intended to make a contract.*

The statute of frauds: A plaintiff may not enforce any of the following agreements, unless the agreement, or some memorandum of it, is in writing and signed by the defendant. The agreements that must be in writing are those:

- For any interest in **land;**
- That **cannot be performed within one year;**
- To pay the **debt of another;**
- Made by an **executor of an estate;**
- Made in **consideration of marriage;** and
- For the **sale of goods worth $500 or more.**

Unenforceable (Sorry, Oliver.)

In other words, when two parties make an agreement covered by any one of these six topics, it must be in writing to be enforceable. Oliver and Perry made a definite agreement to purchase lottery tickets during alternate months and share the proceeds of any winning ticket. But their agreement was to last two and one-half years. As the second item on the list indicates, a contract must be in writing if it cannot be performed within one year. The good news is that Oliver gets back his Eric Clapton CD.

The bad news is that he gets none of the lottery money. Even though three witnesses saw the deal made, it is unlikely to be enforced in any state. Perry the pessimist will probably walk away with all $52 million.[7]

Contracts That Must Be in Writing

Agreements for an Interest in Land

A contract for the sale of any interest in land must be in writing to be enforceable. Notice the phrase "interest in land." This means any legal right regarding land. A house on a lot is an interest in land. A mortgage, an easement, and a leased apartment are all interests in land. As a general rule, leases must therefore be in writing, although many states have created an exception for short-term leases of a year or less.

Exception: Full Performance by the Seller.   If the seller completely performs her side of a contract for an interest in land, a court is likely to enforce the agreement even if it was oral. Adam orally agrees to sell his condominium to Maggie for $150,000. Adam delivers the deed to Maggie and expects his money a week later, but Maggie fails to pay. Most courts will allow Adam to enforce the oral contract and collect the full purchase price from Maggie.

Exception: Part Performance by the Buyer.   The buyer of land may be able to enforce an oral contract if she paid part of the purchase price and either entered upon the land or made improvements to it. Suppose that Eloise sues Grover to enforce an alleged oral contract to sell a lot in Happydale. She claims they struck a bargain in January. Grover defends based on the statute of frauds, saying that even if the two did reach an oral agreement, it is unenforceable. Eloise proves that she paid 10 percent of the purchase price and that in February she began excavating on the lot to build a house, and that Grover knew of the work. Eloise has established part performance and will be allowed to enforce her contract.

In the following case, the defendant seems to have acknowledged *in court* that she agreed to sell her property. Does that satisfy the statute of frauds?

BAKER V. DAVES

83 Ark. App. 145, 119 S.W.3d 53
Court of Appeals of Arkansas, 2003

Facts: Tommy and Eleanor Daves had a daughter, Lisa Baker. The Daves gave Lisa a deed to a two-acre property with a house on it, keeping for themselves a *life interest* in the parcel. In other words, the Daves both had interest in the land for the rest of their ▼

---

[7] Perry might also raise *illegality* as a defense, claiming that a contract for gambling is illegal. That defense is likely to fail. Courts appear to distinguish between the simple purchase of a legal lottery ticket, which friends often share, and the more traditional—and socially dangerous—gambling contracts involving horse racing or casino betting. See, for example, *Pando v. Fernandez*, 118 A.D.2d 474, 499 N.Y.S.2d 950, 1986 N.Y. App. Div. LEXIS 54345 (N.Y. App. Div. 1986), finding no illegality in an agreement to purchase a lottery ticket, even where the purchaser was a minor! Because an illegality defense would probably fail Perry, it is all the more unfortunate that Oliver did not jot down their agreement in writing.

lives; they could live in the house and use the land any way they wished. When they died, the property returned to their daughter.

Tommy and Eleanor divorced and settled their affairs amicably. In court, with Lisa watching from the second row, their lawyers informed the court of an agreement that all three parties had allegedly made to sell the two-acre property. Lisa would be reimbursed for taxes and insurance she had paid during the two years she owned the property, and the Daves would split the rest of the money.

After the agreement was announced, Lisa put the property on the market but then withdrew it and refused to sell. Tommy Daves sued his daughter. Lisa defended based on the statute of frauds, saying she had never agreed in court to the deal and never signed any contract to sell. The trial court found that the courtroom statements proved the parties had formed a binding contract. The judge ordered Lisa to sell the house, and she appealed.

Issue: *Was Lisa obligated to sell the house?*

Excerpts from Judge Stroud's Opinion: The record of the divorce proceedings [includes these statements in the trial court]:

> [Attorney for Eleanor Daves]: The parties have a joint life estate in 2.2 acres of property and a house on Vimy Ridge Road in Alexander, Arkansas. The parties have agreed to sell the house and 2.2 acres and split the proceeds. They have agreed that Mr. Daves will contact a real estate agency.
>
> [Attorney for Mr. Daves, *appellee*]: They have a life estate. It was placed in her daughter's name and the daughter is the title owner. She is going to cooperate in listing the property for sale. They are actually selling the property not just the life estate.

> [Attorney for Eleanor Daves]: The daughter has agreed to sell her interest in the property as well as the life estate of the two parties.

Appellant contends that she never agreed to sell the property, and that "even if some of the parties thought there was an agreement to sell the land, it cannot be enforced since it was not in writing."

The record does not reveal any writing signed by appellant, or by any other person properly authorized by her, to sell the property in question. The fact that appellant was present in the courtroom when the property-settlement agreement was read into the record during the Daves's divorce proceedings is of no benefit to appellee under these circumstances.

It is not disputed that the agreement at issue here involves the sale of real property, that appellant was not a party to the original divorce action, that she was not represented by counsel during the divorce proceedings before the trial court, and that she was not asked by the court as part of the record of the divorce proceedings if she heard the agreement and agreed to its terms. Consequently, we hold that the trial court erred in concluding that she was bound by the terms of the agreement.

Reversed and remanded.

Excerpts from Judge Crabtree's Dissent: Appellant admitted that she was present in the hallway with her mother at the time of the divorce hearing when the agreement was being discussed, but she denied taking part in or having any knowledge of the negotiations. She admitted that she was in the courtroom when the agreement was being read into the record, but she denied that she was able to hear what the attorneys were saying. Appellant also admitted that she listed the property for sale pursuant to the agreement. Her conduct unequivocally demonstrates her assent to the agreement. [I would affirm the trial court's decision.] ∎

Agreements That Cannot be Performed Within One Year

Contracts that cannot be performed within one year are unenforceable unless they are in writing. This one-year period begins on the date the parties make the agreement. The critical phrase here is "cannot be performed within one year." If a contract could be completed within one year, it need not be in writing. Betty gets a job at Burger Brain, throwing fries in oil. Her boss tells her she can have Fridays off for as long as she works there. That oral contract is enforceable, whether Betty stays one week or 57 years.

It could have been performed within one year if, say, Betty quit the job after six months. Therefore it does not need to be in writing.[8]

If the agreement will necessarily take longer than one year to finish, it must be in writing to be enforceable. If Betty is hired for three years as manager of Burger Brain, the agreement is unenforceable unless put in writing. She cannot perform three years of work in one year.

Type of Agreement	Enforceability
Cannot be performed within one year. *Example:* An offer of employment for three years.	Must be in writing to be enforceable.
Might be performed within one year, although could take many years to perform. *Example:* "As long as you work here at Burger Brain you may have Fridays off."	Enforceable whether it is oral or written, because the employee might quit working a month later.

Promise to Pay the Debt of Another

When one person agrees to pay the debt of another as a favor to that debtor, it is called a collateral promise, and it must be in writing to be enforceable. A student applies for a $10,000 loan to help pay for college, and her father agrees to repay the bank if the student defaults. The bank will insist that the father's promise be in writing because his oral promise alone is unenforceable.

Promise Made by an Executor of an Estate

An executor is the person who is in charge of an estate after someone dies. The executor's job is to pay debts of the deceased, obtain money owed to him, and disburse the assets according to the will. In most cases, the executor will use only the estate's assets to pay those debts, but occasionally she might offer her own money. An executor's promise to use her own funds to pay a debt of the deceased must be in writing to be enforceable.

Promise Made in Consideration of Marriage

Barney is a multimillionaire with the integrity of a gangster and the charm of a tax collector. He proposes to Li-Tsing, who promptly rejects him. Barney then pleads that if Li-Tsing will be his bride, he will give her an island he owns off the coast of California. Li-Tsing begins to see his good qualities and accepts. After they are married, Barney refuses to deliver the deed. Li-Tsing will get nothing from a court either, because a promise made in consideration of marriage must be in writing to be enforceable.

What the Writing Must Contain

Each of the five types of contract described earlier must be in writing in order to be enforceable. What must the writing contain? It may be a carefully typed contract,

---

[8] This is the majority rule. In most states, if a company hires an employee "for life," the contract need not be in writing because the employee could die within one year. "Contracts of uncertain duration are simply excluded [from the statute of frauds]; the provision covers only those contracts whose performance cannot possibly be completed within a year." Restatement (Second) of Contracts §130, Comment a, at 328 (1981). However, a few states disagree. The Illinois Supreme Court ruled that a contract for lifetime employment is enforceable only if written. *McInerney v. Charter Golf, Inc.*, 176 Ill. 2d 482, 680 N.E.2d 1347, 1997 Ill. LEXIS 56 (Ill. 1997).

using precise legal terminology, or an informal memorandum scrawled on the back of a paper napkin at a business lunch. The writing may consist of more than one document, written at different times, with each document making a piece of the puzzle. However, there are some general requirements. The contract or memorandum:

- Must be signed by the defendant, and
- Must state with reasonable certainty the name of each party, the subject matter of the agreement, and all the essential terms and promises.[9]

Signature

A statute of frauds typically states that the writing must be "signed by the party to be charged therewith," in other words, the defendant. Judges define "signature" very broadly. Using a pen to write one's name, though sufficient, is not required. A secretary who stamps an executive's signature on a letter fulfills this requirement. Any other mark or logo placed on a document to indicate acceptance, even an "X," will likely satisfy the statute of frauds. Electronic commerce creates new methods of signing—and new controversies, discussed in the Cyberlaw feature later in this chapter.

Reasonable Certainty

Suppose Garfield and Hayes are having lunch, discussing the sale of Garfield's vacation condominium. They agree on a price and want to make some notation of the agreement even before their lawyers work out a detailed purchase and sales agreement. A perfectly adequate memorandum might say, "Garfield agrees to sell Hayes his condominium at 234 Baron Boulevard, apartment 18, for $350,000 cash, payable on June 18, 2004, and Hayes promises to pay the sum on that day." They should make two copies of their agreement and sign both.

Sale of Goods

The UCC requires a writing for the sale of goods worth $500 or more. This is the sixth and final contract that must be written, although the Code's requirements are easier to meet than those of the common law. In some cases, the Code dispenses altogether with the writing requirement. To read the UCC online, go to **http://www.law.cornell.edu** and click on "Contracts and Codes," then "Uniform Commercial Code." The basic statute of frauds rule is Section 2-201(1). Important exceptions are found at Section 2-201 (2) and (3).

The basic UCC rule: A contract for the sale of goods worth $500 or more is not enforceable unless there is some writing, signed by the defendant, indicating that the parties reached an agreement. The key difference between the common-law rule and the UCC rule is that the Code does not require all the terms of the agreement to be in writing. The Code demands only an indication that the parties reached an agreement. The two things that are essential are the signature of the defendant and the quantity of goods being sold. The quantity of goods is required because this is the one term for which there will be no objective evidence. Suppose a short memorandum between textile dealers indicates that Seller will sell to Buyer "grade AA 100% cotton, white athletic socks." If the writing does not state the price, the parties can testify at court about what the market price was at the time of the deal. But how many socks were to be delivered? One hundred pairs or 100,000? The quantity must be written. (A basic sale of goods contract appears at **http://www.lectlaw.com/**. Click on "Legal Forms," then "General Business Forms.")

---

[9] Restatement (Second) of Contracts §131.

Electronic Contracts and Signatures.   E-commerce has grown at a dazzling rate, and U.S. enterprises buy and sell tens of billions of dollars worth of goods and services over the Internet. What happens to the writing requirement, though, when there is no paper? The present statute of frauds requires some sort of "signing" to ensure that the defendant committed to the deal. Today, an "electronic signature" could mean a name typed (or automatically included) at the bottom of an e-mail message, a retinal or vocal scan, or a name signed by electronic pen on a writing tablet, among others.

Are electronic signatures valid? Yes. State legislatures and Congress are struggling to craft a cohesive law, and the job is incomplete, but here are the rules so far:

- **The Uniform Electronic Transaction Act (UETA).** This law was drafted by the National Conference of Commissioners on Uniform State Laws, who also draft the UCC. As this book goes to press, UETA is the law in 48 states and territories. **UETA declares that a contract or signature may not be denied enforceability simply because it is in electronic form.** In other words, the normal rules of contract law apply, but one party may not avoid such a deal merely because it originated in cyberspace.

- **The Electronic Signatures in Global and National Commerce Act (E-Sign).** This federal statute, which applies in any state that has not adopted UETA, also declares that contracts will not be denied enforcement simply because they are in electronic form, or signed electronically.

With cyberlaw in its early stages, how can an executive take advantage of the Internet's commercial opportunities while protecting his company against losses unique to the field?

First, acknowledge the risks, which include lost or intercepted communications, fraudulently altered documents, and difficulties authenticating the source of an offer or acceptance. Second, be cautious about "electronic signatures." Assume that any commitments you make electronically can be enforced against you. Paradoxically, if the contract is important, do not assume that the other party's promises, if made electronically, are enforceable. Get a hard copy, signed in ink. ◆

Parol Evidence

Tyrone agrees to buy Martha's house for $800,000. The contract obligates Tyrone to make a 10 percent down payment immediately and pay the remaining $720,000 in 45 days. As the two parties sign the deal, Tyrone discusses his need for financing. Unfortunately, at the end of 45 days, he has been unable to get a mortgage for the full amount. He claims that the parties orally agreed that he would get his deposit back if he could not obtain financing. But the written agreement says no such thing, and Martha disputes the claim. Who will win? Probably Martha, because of the parol evidence rule. To understand this rule, you need to know two terms. **Parol evidence** refers to anything (apart from the written contract itself) that was said, done, or written before the parties signed the agreement or as they signed it. Martha's conversation with Tyrone about financing the house was parol evidence because it occurred as they were signing the contract. The other important term is **integrated contract,** which means a writing that the parties intend as the final, complete expression of their agreement. Now for the rule.

The parol evidence rule: When two parties make an integrated contract, neither one may use parol evidence to contradict, vary, or add to its terms. Negotiations may last for hours, weeks, or even months. Almost no contract includes everything that the parties said. When parties consider their agreement integrated, any statements they made before or while signing are irrelevant. If a court determines that Martha and Tyrone intended their agreement to be integrated, it will prohibit testimony about Martha's oral promises.

Chapter Conclusion

It is not enough to bargain effectively and obtain a contract that gives you exactly what you want. Bargaining a contract with a noncompete or exculpatory clause that is too one-sided may lead a court to ignore it. Both parties must be adults of sound mind and must give genuine consent. Misrepresentation and mistakes indicate that at least one party did not truly consent. Some contracts must be in writing to be enforceable, and the writing must be clear and unambiguous.

Chapter Review

1. Illegal contracts are void and unenforceable. Claims of illegality often arise concerning noncompete clauses, exculpatory clauses, and unconscionable clauses.

2. Minors and mentally impaired persons generally may disaffirm contracts.

3. Fraud and material misrepresentation are grounds for disaffirming a contract. The injured party must prove a false statement of fact, fraud or materiality, and justifiable reliance.

4. In a bilateral mistake, either party may rescind the contract. In a case of unilateral mistake, the injured party may rescind only in limited circumstances. of unilateral mistake, the injured party may rescind only in limited circumstances.

5. Contracts that must be in writing to be enforceable concern:
   - The sale of any interest in land;
   - Agreements that cannot be performed within one year;
   - Promises to pay the debt of another;
   - Promises made by an executor of an estate;
   - Promises made in consideration of marriage; and
   - The sale of goods worth $500 or more.

6. The writing must be signed by the defendant and must state the name of all parties, the subject matter of the agreement, and all essential terms and promises.

Practice Test

1. Brockwell left his boat to be repaired at Lake Gaston Sales. The boat contained electronic equipment and other personal items. Brockwell signed a form stating that Lake Gaston had no responsibility for any loss to any property in or on the boat. Brockwell's electronic equipment was stolen and other personal items were damaged, and he sued. Is the exculpatory clause enforceable?

2. Guyan Machinery, a West Virginia manufacturing corporation, hired Albert Voorhees as a salesman and required him to sign a contract stating that if he left Guyan he would not work for a competing corporation anywhere within 250 miles of West Virginia for a two-year period. Later, Voorhees left Guyan and began working at Polydeck Corp., another West Virginia manufacturer. The only product Polydeck made was urethane screens, which comprised half of 1 percent of Guyan's business. Is Guyan entitled to enforce its noncompete clause?

3. **ETHICS** Richard and Michelle Kommit traveled to New Jersey to have fun in the casinos. While in Atlantic City, they used their MasterCard to withdraw cash from an ATM conveniently located in the "pit," which is the gambling area of a casino. They ran up debts of $5,500 on the credit card and did not pay. The Connecticut National Bank sued for the money. What argument should the Kommits make? Which party, if any, has the moral high ground here? Should a casino offer ATM services in the gambling pit? If a credit card company allows customers to withdraw cash in a casino, is it encouraging

them to lose money? Do the Kommits have any ethical right to use the ATM, attempt to win money by gambling, and then seek to avoid liability?

4. The McAllisters had several serious problems with their house, including leaks in the ceiling, a buckling wall, and dampness throughout. They repaired the buckling wall by installing I-beams to support it. They never resolved the leaks and the dampness. When they decided to sell the house, they said nothing to prospective buyers about the problems. They stated that the I-beams had been added for reinforcement. The Silvas bought the house for $60,000. Soon afterward, they began to have problems with leaks, mildew, and dampness. Are the Silvas entitled to any money damages? Why or why not?

5. **YOU BE THE JUDGE** WRITING PROBLEM Susan Gould was appointed to a three-year probationary position as a teacher at Sewanhaka High School. Normally, after three years, the school board either grants tenure or dismisses the teacher. The Sewanhaka school board notified Gould that she would not be rehired. To keep the termination out of her file, Gould agreed to resign. In fact, because Gould had previously taught at a different New York school, state law required that she be given a tenure decision after only two years. If the board failed to do that, the teacher was automatically tenured. When she learned this, Gould sued to rescind her agreement to resign. Is Gould entitled to rescind the contract (i.e., her agreement to resign)? **Argument for Gould:** Both parties assumed that Gould was on probation and could be dismissed after three years. Neither party understood that after three years, Gould actually had tenure under New York State law. Gould would never have resigned had she understood she was entitled to tenure. The misunderstanding goes to the essence of the resignation agreement, and she should be permitted to rescind. **Argument for the School Board:** The school board has done nothing wrong here. It is unfair to penalize the school system for an honest mistake. If Gould is serious about her career, she should understand the tenure process and should take the trouble to inform the board about unusual rules that pertain to her case. She failed to do that, causing

both parties to negotiate under a misperception, and she must bear the loss.

6. Ron buys from Karen 1,000 "Smudgy Dolls" for his toy store. Karen knows the dolls' heads are not properly attached but says nothing. Ron sells all the dolls quickly and then has 1,000 unhappy customers with headless dolls. Ron sues to rescind the contract with Karen and also seeks punitive damages. What is the likely outcome?

   a. Ron will be able to rescind, based on fraudulent nondisclosure, but he may not get punitive damages as well.

   b. Ron will be able to rescind, based on fraudulent nondisclosure, and may also obtain punitive damages.

   c. Ron will lose unless he can show that Karen intended to harm Ron's business.

   d. Ron will win only if he can show that both parties were mistaken about a basic assumption.

7. **ETHICS** Sixteen-year-old Travis Mitchell brought his 19-year-old Pontiac GTO into M&M Precision Body and Paint for body work and a paint job. M&M did the work and charged $1,900, which Travis paid. Travis later complained about the quality of the work and M&M did some touching up, but Travis was still dissatisfied. Travis demanded his $1,900 back, but M&M refused to give it back because all the work was "in" the car and Travis could not return it to the shop. The state of Nebraska, where this occurred, follows the majority rule on this issue. Does Travis get his money? What is the common-law rule? Who ought to win? Is the common-law rule fair? What is the rationale for the rule?

8. Lonnie Hippen moved to Long Island, Kansas, to work at an insurance company owned by Griffiths. After he moved there, Griffiths offered to sell Hippen a house he owned and Hippen agreed in writing to buy it. He did buy the house and moved in, but two years later Hippen left the insurance company. He then claimed that at the time of the sale, Griffiths had orally promised to buy back his house at the selling price if Hippen should happen to leave the company. Griffiths defended based on the statute of frauds. Hippen argued that the statute of frauds did not apply because the repurchase of the house

was essentially part of his employment with Griffiths. Comment.

9. Landlord owned a clothing store and agreed in writing to lease the store's basement to another retailer. The written lease, which both parties signed, (1) described the premises exactly, (2) identified the parties, and (3) stated the monthly rent clearly. But an appeals court held that the lease did not satisfy the statute of frauds. Why not?

10. **ROLE REVERSAL** Write one multiple-choice question with two noncompete clauses, one of which is valid and the other void.

You can find further practice problems at

academic.cengage.com/blaw/beatty.

11 Conclusion to Contracts

© PHOTODISC COLLECTION/GETTY IMAGES

During television's formative days, Howdy Doody was one of the medium's biggest stars. His acting was wooden—as were his head and body—but for 13 years Howdy and an assorted group of puppets starred in one of the most popular children's programs of all time. Rufus Rose maintained and repaired the puppets. When Howdy took his last double-jointed bow (to a chorus of toddler wails), NBC permitted Rose to keep the various puppets temporarily. Six years later, NBC became concerned that Rose was inadequately maintaining them. The network wanted Howdy and friends moved to a safe, public location. Rose claimed the puppets were in good shape and wanted payment for the maintenance he had provided. The two parties agreed in writing that Rose would give Howdy and the other stars of the show (including Dilly Dally and Flub-A-Dub) to a puppet museum at the Detroit Institute of Arts (DIA). NBC agreed to pay the puppeteer for his work. The company permitted Rose to keep some of the minor puppets from the program, provided they were not used for commercial purposes.

When Rose died, his son Christopher took possession of the famous puppet. At about that time, a copy of Howdy sold at auction for $113,000. Christopher then claimed ownership of Howdy Doody and refused to give him to the museum. The DIA wanted its famous puppet, but the museum had never been a party to the agreement between NBC and Rose. Did the DIA have any rights to Howdy? The museum filed suit, making a third party claim.

The basic pattern in third party law is quite simple. Two parties make a contract, and their rights and obligations are subject to the rules that we have already studied: offer and acceptance, consideration, legality, and so forth. However, sometimes their contract affects a third party, one who had no role in forming the agreement itself. The two contracting parties may intend to benefit a third person. Those are cases of third party beneficiary. In other cases, one of the contracting parties may actually transfer his rights or responsibilities to a third party, raising issues of assignment or delegation. We consider the issues one at a time. Then we examine issues of contract performance and remedies. ■

THIRD PARTY BENEFICIARY

The two parties who make a contract always intend to benefit themselves. Oftentimes their bargain will also benefit someone else. **A third party beneficiary is someone who was not a party to the contract but stands to benefit from it.** Many contracts create third party beneficiaries. In the chapter's introduction, NBC and Rufus Rose contracted to give Howdy Doody to the Detroit Institute of Arts. The museum stood to benefit from this agreement.

As another example, suppose a city contracts to purchase from Seller 20 acres of an abandoned industrial site in a rundown neighborhood to be used for a new domed stadium. The owner of a pizza parlor on the edge of Seller's land might benefit enormously. A once marginal operation could become a gold mine of cheese and pepperoni.

When the two contracting parties fulfill their obligations and the third party receives her benefit, there is no dispute to analyze. If Christopher Rose had walked Howdy Doody into the puppet museum, and if the city completed the stadium, there would be no unhappy third parties. Problems arise when one of the parties fails to perform the contract as expected. The issue is this: *May the third party beneficiary enforce the contract?* The museum had no contract with the Rose family. Is the museum entitled to the puppet? The pizza parlor owner was not a party to the contract for the sale of the stadium land. If the city breaks its agreement to buy the property, should the owner recover profits for unsold sausage and green pepper?

The outcome in cases like these depends upon the intentions of the two contracting parties. If they intended to benefit the third party, she will probably be permitted to enforce their contract. If they did not intend to benefit her, she probably has no power to enforce the agreement. The Restatement uses a bit more detail to analyze these cases. We must first recall the terms "promisor" and "promisee." The **promisor** is the one who makes the promise that the third party beneficiary is seeking to enforce. Parts of the contract may not interest her, so the Restatement looks only at the relevant promise, not at the entire contract. The **promisee** is the other party to the contract.

According to the **Restatement (Second) of Contracts §302: A beneficiary of a promise is an intended beneficiary and may enforce a contract if the parties** *intended* **her to benefit** *and if either* (a) enforcing the promise will satisfy a duty of the promisee to the beneficiary, or (b) the promisee intended to make a gift to the beneficiary.

Any beneficiary who is not an intended beneficiary is an **incidental beneficiary** and may not enforce the contract. In other words, a third party beneficiary must show two things in order to enforce a contract that two other people created. First, she must show that the two contracting parties were aware of her situation and knew that she would receive something of value from their deal. Second, she must show that the promisee wanted to benefit her for one of two reasons: either to satisfy some duty owed or to make her a gift.

If the promisee is fulfilling some duty, the third party beneficiary is called a creditor beneficiary. Most often, the "duty" that a promisee will be fulfilling is a debt already owed to the beneficiary. If the promisee is making a gift, the third party is a donee beneficiary.[1] As long as the third party is either a creditor or a donee beneficiary, she may enforce the contract. If she is only an incidental beneficiary, she may not. We will apply this rule to the dispute over Howdy Doody. Like most contracts, the deal between NBC and Rufus Rose had two promises: Rose's agreement to give the

---

[1] **Donee** comes from the word **donate,** meaning to give.

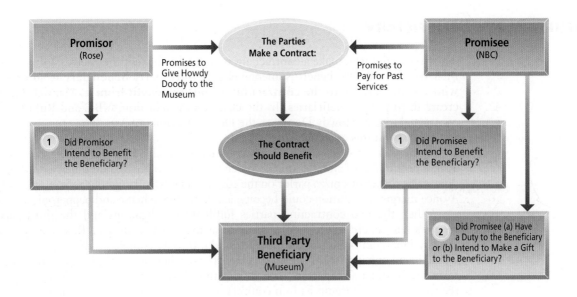

puppet to the museum, and NBC's promise to pay for the work done on Howdy. The promise that interests us is the one concerning Howdy's destination in Detroit. Rose was the promisor and NBC was the promisee.

Did the two parties intend to benefit the museum? Yes, they did. NBC wanted Howdy to be displayed to the general public, and in a noncommercial venue. Rose, who wanted payment for work already done, was happy to go along with the network's wishes. Did NBC owe a duty to the museum? No. Did the network intend to make a gift to the museum? Yes. The museum wins! The Detroit Institute of Arts was an intended third party beneficiary and is entitled to Howdy Doody.[2]

By contrast, the pizza parlor owner will surely lose. A stadium is a multimillion dollar investment, and it is most unlikely that the city and the seller of the land were even aware of the owner's existence, let alone that they intended to benefit him. He probably cannot prove either the first element or the second element, and certainly not both.

In the following case, a dazzling diamond loses its luster. Who is entitled to sue?

SCHAUER V. MANDARIN GEMS OF CALIFORNIA, INC.

2005 WL 57301
Court of Appeal of California, 2005

Facts: Sarah Schauer and her fiancé, Darin Erstad, went shopping for an engagement ring, first at Tiffany's and Cartier's, then at Mandarin Gems, where they were captivated by a 3.01 carat diamond with a clarity grading of "S11." Erstad bought the ring the same day for $43,121. Later, Mandarin

supplied Erstad with a written appraisal, again rating the ring as an S11, and valuing it at $45,500. Paul Lam, a certified gemologist, signed the appraisal.

Diamonds may last forever, but this marriage was short lived. The divorce decree gave each party ▼

---

2 **The Detroit Institute of Arts Founders Society v. Rose,** 127 F. Supp.2d 117 (D.Conn.2001).

the right to keep whatever personal property they currently held, meaning that Schauer could keep the ring. She had the ring appraised by the "Gem Trade Laboratory," which gave it a poorer clarity rating and a value of $20,000.

Schauer sued Mandarin for misrepresentation and breach of contract, but the jeweler defended by saying that it had never contracted with her and that she was not a third party beneficiary of the company's agreement with Erstad. The trial court dismissed Schauer's suit, and she appealed.

Issue: Does Schauer have any right to sue for breach of contract?

Excerpts from Judge Ikola's Decision: A contract, made expressly for the benefit of a third person, may be enforced by him or her at any time before the parties rescind it. A person seeking to enforce a contract as a third party beneficiary must plead a contract which was made expressly for his or her benefit and one in which it clearly appears that he or she was a beneficiary.

Although persons only incidentally or remotely benefited by the contract are not entitled to enforce it, it does not mean both of the contracting parties must intend to benefit the third party: Rather, it means the promisor—in this case, defendant jeweler—must have understood that the promisee (Erstad) had such intent.

We conclude the pleading here meets the test of demonstrating plaintiff's standing as a third party beneficiary to enforce the contract between Erstad and defendant. The couple went shopping for an engagement ring. They were together when plaintiff chose the ring she wanted or, as alleged in the complaint, she caused the ring to be purchased for her. Erstad allegedly bought the ring for the sole and *stated* purpose of giving the ring to plaintiff. Under the alleged facts, the jeweler *must* have understood Erstad's intent to enter the sales contract for plaintiff's benefit. Thus, plaintiff has adequately pleaded her status as a third party beneficiary, and she is entitled to proceed with her contract claim against defendant. ■

ASSIGNMENT AND DELEGATION

A contracting party may transfer his rights under the contract, which is called an **assignment of rights.** Or a contracting party may transfer her duties pursuant to the contract, which is a **delegation of duties.** Frequently, a party will do both simultaneously.

For our purposes, the Restatement serves as a good summary of common-law provisions. The UCC rules are generally similar. Our first example is a sale of goods case, governed by the UCC, but the outcome would be the same under the Restatement.

Lydia needs 500 bottles of champagne. Bruno agrees to sell them to her for $10,000, payable 30 days after delivery. He transports the wine to her. Bruno happens to owe Doug $8,000 from a previous deal, so he says to Doug, "I don't have the money, but I'll give you my claim to Lydia's $10,000." Doug agrees. Bruno then *assigns* to Doug *his rights* to Lydia's money, and in exchange Doug gives up his claim for $8,000. Bruno is the **assignor, the one making an assignment, and Doug is the assignee, the one receiving an assignment.**

Why would Bruno offer $10,000 when he owed Doug only $8,000? Because all he has is a *claim* to Lydia's money. Cash in hand is often more valuable. Doug, however, is willing to assume some risk for a potential $2,000 gain.

Bruno notifies Lydia of the assignment. Lydia, who owes the money, is called the **obligor,**—that is, the one obligated to do something. At the end of 30 days, Doug arrives at Lydia's doorstep, asks for his money, and gets it, because Lydia is obligated to him.

Lydia bought the champagne because she knew she could sell it at a profit. She promptly agrees to sell and deliver the 500 bottles to Coretta, at a mountaintop wilderness camp. Lydia has no four-wheel drive cars, so she finds Keith, who is willing to deliver the bottles for $1,000. Lydia *delegates her duty* to Keith to deliver the bottles to

Coretta. Keith is now obligated to deliver the bottles to Coretta, the **obligee**—that is, the one who has the obligation coming to her. Lydia also remains obligated to Coretta, the obligee, to ensure that the bottles are delivered.

Assignment and delegation can each create problems. We will examine the most common ones.

Assignment

What Rights Are Assignable?

Any contractual right may be assigned unless assignment

(a) would substantially change the obligor's rights or duties under the contract, or

(b) is forbidden by law or public policy, or

(c) is validly precluded by the contract itself.[3]

Substantial Change.   Assignment is prohibited if it would substantially change the obligor's situation. For example, Bruno may assign to Doug the payment from Lydia because it makes no difference to Lydia whether she writes a check to one or the other. But suppose Erica, who lives on a quarter-acre lot in Hardscrabble, hires Keith to mow her lawn once per week for the summer, for a total fee of $700. Erica pays up front before she leaves for the summer. May she assign her right to weekly lawn care to Lloyd, who enjoys a three-acre estate in Halcyon, 60 miles distant? No. The extra travel and far larger yard would dramatically change Keith's obligations.

Public Policy.   Some assignments are prohibited by public policy. For example, someone who has suffered a personal injury in an automobile accident may not assign her claim to a third person.

Contract Prohibition.   Finally, one of the contracting parties may try to prohibit assignment in the agreement itself. Most landlords include in the written lease a clause prohibiting the tenant from assigning the tenancy without the landlord's written permission. Such clauses are generally, but not always, enforced by a court.

How Rights Are Assigned

An assignment may be written or oral, and no particular formalities are required. However, when someone wants to assign rights governed by the statute of frauds, she must do it in writing. Suppose City contracts with Seller to buy Seller's land for a domed stadium and then brings in Investor to complete the project. If City wants to assign to Investor its rights to the land, it must do so in writing.

Rights of the Parties After Assignment

Once the assignment is made and the obligor notified, the assignee may enforce her contractual rights against the obligor. If Lydia fails to pay Doug for the champagne she gets from Bruno, Doug may sue to enforce the agreement. The law will treat Doug as though he had entered into the contract with Lydia.

But the reverse is also true. **The obligor may generally raise all defenses against the assignee that she could have raised against the assignor.** Suppose

---

[3] Restatement (Second) of Contracts §317(2). And note that UCC §2-210(2) is, for our purposes, nearly identical.

Lydia opens the first bottle of champagne—silently. "Where's the pop?" she wonders. All 500 bottles have gone flat. Bruno has failed to perform his part of the contract, and Lydia may use Bruno's nonperformance as a defense against Doug. If the champagne was indeed worthless, Lydia owes Doug nothing.

Delegation of Duties

Garret has always dreamed of racing stock cars. He borrows $250,000 from his sister, Maybelle, in order to buy a car and begin racing. He signs a promissory note in that amount, guaranteeing that he will repay Maybelle the full amount, plus interest, on a monthly basis over 10 years. Regrettably, during his first race, on a Saturday night, Garret discovers that he has a speed phobia. He finally finishes the race at noon on Sunday and quits the business. Garret transfers the car and equipment to Brady, who agrees in writing to pay all money owed to Maybelle. For a few months Brady sends a check, but he is killed while watching bumper cars at a local carnival. Maybelle sues Garret, who defends based on the transfer to Brady. Will his defense work?

Most duties are delegable. But delegation does not by itself relieve the delegator of his own liability to perform the contract.

Garret was the **delegator** and Brady was the **delegatee.** Garret has legally delegated to Brady his duty to repay Maybelle. However, Garret remains personally obligated. When Maybelle sues, she will win. Garret, like many debtors, would have preferred to wash his hands of his debt, but the law is not so obliging.

Garret's delegation to Brady was typical in that it included an assignment at the same time. If he had merely transferred ownership, that would have been only an assignment. If he had convinced Brady to pay off the loan without getting the car, that would have been merely a delegation. He did both at once.

What Duties Are Delegable

The rules concerning what duties may be delegated mirror those about the assignment of rights.

An obligor may delegate his duties unless

1. delegation would violate public policy, or

2. the contract prohibits delegation, or

3. the obligee has a substantial interest in personal performance by the obligor.[4]

Public Policy. Delegation may violate public policy, for example, in a public works contract. If City hires Builder to construct a subway system, state law may prohibit Builder from delegating his duties to Subcontractor. A public agency should not have to work with parties that it never agreed to hire.

Contract Prohibition. The parties may forbid almost any delegation, and the courts will enforce the agreement. Hammer, a contractor, is building a house and hires Spot as his painter, including in his contract a clause prohibiting delegation. Just before the house is ready for painting, Spot gets a better job elsewhere and wants to delegate his duties to Brush. Hammer may refuse the delegation even if Brush is equally qualified.

Substantial Interest in Personal Performance. Suppose Hammer had omitted the "nondelegation" clause from his contract with Spot. Could Hammer still refuse the delegation on the grounds that he has a substantial interest in having Spot

---

[4] Restatement (Second) of Contracts §318. And see UCC §2-210, establishing similar limits.

do the work? No. Most duties are delegable. There is nothing so special about painting a house that one particular painter is required to do it. But some kinds of work do require personal performance, and obligors may not delegate these tasks. The services of lawyers, doctors, dentists, artists, and performers are considered too personal to be delegated. There is no single test that will perfectly define this group, but generally when the work will test *the character, skill, discretion, and good faith* of the obligor, she *may not* delegate her job.

Novation

As we have seen, a delegator does not get rid of his duties merely by delegating them. But there is one way a delegator can do so. **A novation is a three-way agreement in which the obligor transfers all rights and duties to a third party. The obligee agrees to look *only* to that third party for performance.**

Recall Garret, the forlorn race car driver. When he wanted to get out of his obligations to Maybelle, he should have proposed a novation. He would assign all rights and delegate all duties to Brady, and Maybelle would agree that only Brady was obligated by the promissory note, releasing Garret from his responsibility to repay. Why would Maybelle do this? She might conclude that Brady was a financially better bet than Garret, who, in turn, might refuse to bring Brady into the deal until Maybelle permits a novation. In the example given, Garret failed to obtain a novation, and hence he and Brady (or Brady's estate) were both liable on the promissory note.

Because a novation has the critical effect of releasing the obligor from liability, you will not be surprised to learn that two parties to a contract sometimes fight over whether some event was a simple delegation of duties or a novation. Here is one such contest. Would you like it in a cone or cup?

You Be the Judge

ROSENBERG V. SON, INC.

491 N.W.2d 71, 1992 N.D. LEXIS 202
Supreme Court of North Dakota, 1992

You Be the Judge: **Did Pratt obtain a novation relieving her of her duties under the original sales contract?**

Facts: The Rosenbergs owned a Dairy Queen in Grand Forks, North Dakota. They agreed in writing to sell the Dairy Queen to Mary Pratt. The contract required her to pay $10,000 down and $52,000 over 15 years, at 10 percent interest. Two years later, Pratt assigned her rights and delegated her duties under the sales contract to Son, Inc. The agreement between Pratt and Son contained a "Consent to Assignment" clause that the Rosenbergs signed. Pratt then moved to Arizona and had nothing further to do with the Dairy Queen. The Rosenbergs never received full payment for the Dairy Queen. They sued Mary Pratt.

The trial court gave summary judgment for Pratt, finding that she was no longer obligated on the original contract. The Rosenbergs appealed.

Argument for the Rosenbergs: Your honors, a party cannot escape contract liability merely by assigning its rights and delegating its duties to a third party. It is evident from the express language of the agreement between Pratt and Son, Inc. that the parties only intended an assignment, not a novation. The agreement made no mention of discharging Pratt from liability. It would be odd to write a novation and make no mention of discharge, which happens to be the primary point of a true novation. It is true that the Rosenbergs signed a consent to the assignment, but merely by permitting Son, Inc. to become involved they did not discharge their principal obligor—Pratt.

▼

Argument for Ms. Pratt: Your honors, it is obvious from the contract that Ms. Pratt intended to rid herself entirely of this business. She planned to move out of state, and wanted to terminate all rights and responsibilities in the business. Why would she go to the trouble of assigning rights and delegating duties if she still expected to be involved in the business? If that weren't enough, she went one step further, by asking the Rosenbergs to acknowledge the new arrangement—which the Rosenbergs did. If Son, Inc. failed to keep its end of the bargain, then the Rosenbergs should sue that company—not an innocent woman who is long out of the business. ●

PERFORMANCE AND DISCHARGE

A party is discharged when she has no more duties under a contract. Most contracts are discharged by full performance. In other words, the parties generally do what they promise. Sally agrees to sell Arthur 300 tulip-shaped wine glasses for his new restaurant. Right on schedule, Sally delivers the correct glasses and Arthur pays in full. Contract, full performance, discharge, end of case.

Sometimes the parties discharge a contract by agreement. For example, the parties may agree to **rescind** their contract, meaning that they terminate it by mutual agreement. At times, a court may discharge a party who has not performed. When things have gone amiss, a judge must interpret the contract and issues of public policy to determine who in fairness should suffer the loss. We will analyze the most common issues of performance and discharge.

Performance

Caitlin has an architect draw up plans for a monumental new house, and Daniel agrees to build it by September 1. Caitlin promises to pay $900,000 on that date. The house is ready on time but Caitlin has some complaints. The living room ceiling was supposed to be 18 feet high but it is only 17 feet; the pool was to be azure yet it is aquamarine; the maid's room was not supposed to be wired for cable television but it is. Caitlin refuses to pay anything for the house. Is she justified? Of course not; it would be absurd to give her a magnificent house for free when it has only tiny defects. And that is how a court would decide the case. But in this easy answer lurks a danger. How much leeway will a court permit? Suppose the living room is only 14 feet high, or 12 feet, or 5 feet? What if Daniel finishes the house a month late? Six months late? Three years late? At some point, a court will conclude that Daniel has so thoroughly botched the job that he deserves little or no money. Where is that point? That is a question that businesses—and judges—face every day.

Strict Performance and Substantial Performance

Strict Performance. Courts dislike strict performance because it enables one party to benefit without paying and sends the other one home empty-handed. **A party is generally not required to render strict performance unless the contract expressly demands it and such a demand is reasonable.** Caitlin's contract never suggested that Daniel would forfeit all payment if there were minor problems. Even if Caitlin had insisted on such a clause, a court would be unlikely to enforce it, because the requirement is unreasonable.

In some cases, strict performance does make sense. Marshall agrees to deliver 500 sweaters to Leo's store, and Leo promises to pay $20,000 cash on delivery. If Leo has only $19,000 cash and a promissory note for $1,000, he has failed to perform, and Marshall need not give him the sweaters. Leo's payment represents 95 percent of what he promised, but there is a big difference between cash and a promissory note.

Substantial Performance.   Daniel, the house builder, won his case against Caitlin because he fulfilled most of his obligations, even though he did an imperfect job. Courts often rely on the substantial performance doctrine, especially in cases involving services as opposed to those concerning the sale of goods or land. **In a contract for services, a party that substantially performs its obligations will receive the full contract price, minus the value of any defects.** Daniel receives $900,000, the contract price, minus the value of a ceiling that is one foot too low, a pool the wrong color, and so forth. It will be for the trial court to decide how much those defects are worth. If the court decides the low ceiling is a $10,000 damage, the pool color worth $5,000, and the cable television worth $500, then Daniel receives $884,500.

On the other hand, a party that fails to perform substantially receives nothing on the contract itself and will only recover the value of the work if any. If the foundation cracks in Caitlin's house and the walls collapse, Daniel will not receive his $900,000. In such a case, he collects only the market value of the work he has done, which is probably zero.

When is performance substantial? There is no perfect test, but courts look at these issues:

- How much benefit has the promisee received?
- If it is a construction contract, can the owner use the thing for its intended purpose?
- Can the promisee be compensated with money damages for any defects?
- Did the promisor act in good faith?

Personal Satisfaction Contracts

Sujata, president of a public relations firm, hires Ben to design a huge multimedia project for her company, involving computer software, music, and live actors, all designed to sell frozen bologna sandwiches to supermarkets. His contract guarantees him two years' employment, provided all his work "is acceptable in the sole judgment of Sujata." Ben's immediate supervisor is delighted with his work, and his colleagues are impressed—all but Sujata. Three months later she fires him, claiming that his work is "uninspired." Does she have the right to do that?

This is a **personal satisfaction contract, in which the promisee makes a personal, subjective evaluation of the promisor's performance.** In resolving disputes like Ben and Sujata's, judges must decide: When is it fair for the promisee to claim that she is not satisfied? May she make that decision for any reason at all, even on a whim?

A court applies a subjective standard only if assessing the work involves personal feelings, taste, or judgment *and* the contract explicitly demands personal satisfaction. A "subjective standard" means that the promisee's personal views will greatly influence her judgment, even if her decision is foolish and unfair. Artistic or creative work, or highly specialized tasks designed for a particular employer, may involve subtle issues of quality and personal preference. Ben's work combines several media and revolves around his judgment. Accordingly, the law applies a subjective standard to Sujata's decision. Because she concludes that his work is uninspired, she may legally fire him, even if her decision is irrational.

In all other cases, a court applies an objective standard to the promisee's decision. An objective standard means that the promisee's judgment of the work must be reasonable.

Good Faith

The parties to a contract must carry out their obligations in good faith. The Restatement (Second) of Contracts §205 states: **"Every contract imposes upon each party a duty of good faith and fair dealing in its performance and its enforcement."** The UCC establishes a similar requirement for all contracts governed by the Code.[5] How far must one side go to meet its good faith burden? The Restatement emphasizes that the parties must remain faithful to the "agreed common purpose and justified expectations of the other party."

In the following case, one party to a contract played its cards very close to its chest. Too close?

BRUNSWICK HILLS RACQUET CLUB INC. V. ROUTE 18 SHOPPING CENTER ASSOCIATES

182 N.J. 210, 864 A.2d 387
Supreme Court of New Jersey, 2005

Facts: Brunswick Hills Racquet Club (Brunswick) owned a tennis club on property that it leased from Route 18 Shopping Center Associates (Route 18). The lease ran for 25 years, and Brunswick had spent about $1 million in capital improvements. The lease expired March 30, 2002. Brunswick had the option of either buying the property or purchasing a 99-year lease, both on very favorable terms. To exercise its option, Brunswick had to notify Route 18 no later than September 30, 2001, and had to pay the option price of $150,000. If Brunswick failed to exercise its options, the existing lease automatically renewed as of September 30, for 25 more years, but at more than triple the current rent.

In February 2000—19 months before the option deadline—Brunswick's lawyer, Gabriel Spector, wrote to Rosen Associates, the company that managed Route 18, stating that Brunswick intended to exercise the option for a 99-year lease. He requested that the lease be sent well in advance so that he could review it. He did not make the required payment of $150,000.

In March, Rosen replied that it had forwarded Spector's letter to its attorney, who would be in touch. In April, Spector again wrote, asking for a reply from Rosen or its lawyer.

Over the next six months, Spector continually asked for a copy of the lease, or information, but neither Route 18's lawyer nor anyone else provided any data. In January 2001, Spector renewed his requests for a copy of the lease. Route 18's lawyer never replied. Sadly, in May 2001, after a long illness, Spector died. In August 2001, Spector's law partner, Arnold Levin, wrote to Rosen, again stating Brunswick's intention to buy the 99-year lease and requesting a copy of all relevant information. He received no reply, and the September deadline passed.

In February 2002, Route 18's lawyer dropped the hammer, notifying Levin that Brunswick could not exercise its option to lease because it had failed to pay the $150,000 by September 30, 2001.

Brunswick sued, claiming that Route 18 had breached its duty of good faith and fair dealing. The trial court found that Route 18 had no duty to notify Brunswick of impending deadlines and gave summary judgment for Route 18. The appellate court affirmed, and Brunswick appealed to the state supreme court.

Issue: Did Route 18 breach its duty of good faith and fair dealing?

Excerpts from Justice Albin's Decision: Courts generally should not tinker with a finely drawn and precise contract entered into by experienced business people that regulates their financial affairs. ▼

---

5 UCC §1-203.

[However,] every party to a contract is bound by a duty of good faith and fair dealing in both the performance and enforcement of the contract. Good faith is a concept that defies precise definition. Good faith conduct is conduct that does not violate community standards of decency, fairness or reasonableness. The covenant of good faith and fair dealing calls for parties to a contract to refrain from doing anything which will have the effect of destroying or injuring the right of the other party to receive the benefits of the contract.

Our review of the undisputed facts of this case leads us to the inescapable conclusion that defendant breached the covenant of good faith and fair dealing. Nineteen months in advance of the option deadline, plaintiff notified defendant in writing of its intent to exercise the option to purchase the ninety-nine-year lease. Plaintiff mistakenly believed that the purchase price was not due until the time of closing.

During a nineteen-month period, defendant, through its agents, engaged in a pattern of evasion, sidestepping every request by plaintiff to discuss the option and ignoring plaintiff's repeated written and verbal entreaties to move forward on closing the ninety-nine-year lease. After Spector's death,

defendant's attorney continued to play possum despite the impending option deadline and obvious potential harm to plaintiff.

Defendant never requested the purchase price of the lease. Indeed, as defendant's attorney candidly admitted at oral argument, defendant did not want the purchase price because the successful exercise of the option was not in defendant's economic interest.

Ordinarily, we are content to let experienced commercial parties fend for themselves and do not seek to introduce intolerable uncertainty into a carefully structured contractual relationship by balancing equities. But there are ethical norms that apply even to the harsh and sometimes cutthroat world of commercial transactions. We do not expect a landlord or even an attorney to act as his brother's keeper in a commercial transaction. We do expect, however, that they will act in good faith and deal fairly with an opposing party. Plaintiff's repeated letters and telephone calls to defendant concerning the exercise of the option and the closing of the ninety-nine-year lease obliged defendant to respond, and to respond truthfully.

[Plaintiff is entitled to exercise the 99-year lease.] ■

Public Policy

It is hard to argue against good faith. But how far does this approach go? Suppose Buyer holds a six-month option to purchase land for a shopping mall. With three months remaining, Seller learns through a well-connected friend that the state is likely to construct a new highway interchange one mile from the property. The land will double or triple in value. Is Seller obligated to give Buyer the good news? Or this: Suppose Owner, selling her home, knows that a convicted pedophile has moved into a house on the same block. Must she inform prospective buyers? Is there a difference between these two hypothetical situations? ◆

Time of the Essence Clauses

> Go, sir, gallop, and don't forget that the world was made in six days. You can ask me for anything you like, except time.

> —Napoleon, to an aide, 1803

A time of the essence clause will generally make contract dates strictly enforceable. Jackie owns the Starburst Hotel. She agrees in writing to sell it to Eduardo, provided that he demonstrates to her by July 2 that he has obtained all financing. Jackie includes a clause stating that "Owner considers that time is of the essence in the performance of this contract." On July 1, Eduardo asks for a one-month extension to obtain financing, and Jackie promptly sells the hotel elsewhere. Eduardo is out of luck. The time of the essence clause notified him that he must be prompt, and such a clause is reasonable in a real estate agreement. Notice that without the clause, Jackie would be legally obligated to allow Eduardo a reasonable extension.

Breach

When one party *materially* breaches a contract, the other party is discharged. A material breach is one that substantially harms the innocent party. The discharged party has no obligation to perform and may sue for damages. Edwin promises that on July 1 he will deliver 20 tuxedos, tailored to fit male chimpanzees, to Bubba's circus for $300 per suit. After weeks of delay, Edwin concedes he hasn't a cummerbund to his name. This is a material breach and Bubba is discharged. Notice that a trivial breach, such as a one-day delay in delivering the tuxedos, would not have discharged Bubba.

Anticipatory Breach

Sally will receive her bachelor's degree in May and already has a job lined up for September—a two-year contract as window display designer for Surebet Department Store. The morning of graduation she reads in the paper that Surebet is going out of business that very day. Sally need not wait until September to learn her fate. Surebet has committed an anticipatory breach by making it unmistakably clear that it will not honor the contract. Sally is discharged and may immediately seek other work. She is also entitled to file suit for breach of contract.

Statute of Limitations

A party injured by a breach of contract should act promptly. **A statute of limitations begins to run at the time of injury and will limit the time within which the injured party may file suit.** Statutes of limitation vary widely. In some states, for example, an injured party must sue on oral contracts within three years, on a sale of goods contract within four years, and on some written contracts within five years. Failure to file suit within the time-limits discharges the breaching party.

Impossibility

"Your honor, my client wanted to honor the contract. He just couldn't. Honest." Does the argument work? It depends. A court will discharge an agreement if performing a contract was truly impossible but not if honoring the deal merely imposed a financial burden.

True Impossibility

These cases are easy—and rare. **True impossibility means that something has happened making it utterly impossible to do what the promisor said he would do.** Francoise owns a vineyard that produces Beaujolais Nouveau wine. She agrees to ship 1,000 cases of her wine to Tyrone, a New York importer, as soon as this year's vintage is ready. Tyrone will pay $50 per case. But a fungus wipes out her entire vineyard. Francoise is discharged. It is theoretically impossible for Francoise to deliver wine from her vineyard, and she owes Tyrone nothing.

True impossibility is generally limited to these three causes:

- *Destruction of the Subject Matter.* This happened with Francoise's vineyard.

- *Death of the Promisor in a Personal Services Contract.* When the promisor agrees personally to render a service that cannot be transferred to someone else, her death discharges the contract.

- *Illegality.* If the purpose of a contract becomes illegal, that change discharges the contract.

Commercial Impracticability and Frustration of Purpose

It is rare for contract performance to be truly impossible but common for it to become a financial burden to one party. Suppose Bradshaw Steel in Pittsburgh agrees to deliver 1,000 tons of steel beams to Rice Construction in Saudi Arabia at a given price, but a week later the cost of raw ore increases 30 percent. A contract once lucrative to the manufacturer is suddenly a major liability. Does that change discharge Bradshaw? Absolutely not. Rice signed the deal *precisely to protect itself against price increases.* The whole purpose of contracts is to enable the parties to control their futures.

Yet there may be times when a change in circumstances is so extreme that it would be unfair to enforce a deal. What if a strike made it impossible for Bradshaw to ship the steel to Saudi Arabia, and the only way to deliver would be by air, at five times the sea cost? Must Bradshaw fulfill its deal? What if war in the Middle East meant that any ships or planes delivering the goods might be fired upon? Other changes could make the contract undesirable for Rice. Suppose the builder wanted steel for a major public building in Riyadh, but the Saudi government decided not to go forward with the construction. The steel would then be worthless to Rice. Must the company still accept it?

None of these hypothetical situations involves true impossibility. It is physically possible for Bradshaw to deliver the goods and for Rice to receive. But in some cases it may be so dangerous or costly to enforce a bargain that a court will discharge it instead. Courts use the related doctrines of commercial impracticability and frustration of purpose to decide when a change in circumstances should permit one side to escape its duties.

Commercial impracticability means some event has occurred that neither party anticipated and *fulfilling the contract would now be extraordinarily difficult and unfair to one party.* If a shipping strike forces Bradshaw to ship by air, the company will argue that neither side expected the strike and that Bradshaw should not suffer a fivefold increase in shipping costs. Bradshaw will probably win the argument.

Frustration of purpose means some event has occurred that neither party anticipated and *the contract now has no value for one party.* If Rice's building project is canceled, Rice will argue that the steel now is useless to the company. Frustration cases are hard to predict. Some states would agree with Rice, but others would hold that it was Rice's obligation to protect itself with a government guarantee that the project would be completed. Courts consider the following factors in deciding impracticability and frustration claims:

- Mere financial difficulties will never suffice to discharge a contract.

- The event must have been truly unexpected.

- If the promisor must use a different means to accomplish her task, at a greatly increased cost, she probably does have a valid claim of impracticability.

- The UCC, like the common law, permits discharge only for major, unforeseen disruptions.

REMEDIES

A remedy is the method a court uses to compensate an injured party. The most common remedy, used in the great majority of lawsuits, is money damages.

The first step that a court takes in choosing a remedy is to decide what interest it is trying to protect. An **interest** is a legal right in something. Someone can have an interest in property, for example, by owning it, or renting it to a tenant, or lending money so someone else may buy it. He can have an interest in a *contract* if the agreement gives him some benefit. There are four principal contract interests that a court may seek to protect:

- *Expectation Interest.* This refers to what the injured party reasonably thought she would get from the contract.
- *Reliance Interest.* The injured party may be unable to demonstrate expectation damages but may still prove that he expended money in reliance on the agreement.
- *Restitution Interest.* An injured party may only be able to demonstrate that she has conferred a benefit on the other party. Here, the objective is to restore to the injured party the benefit she has provided.
- *Equitable Interest.* In some cases, something more than money is needed, such as an order to transfer property to the injured party (specific performance) or an order forcing one party to stop doing something (an injunction).

We will look at all four interests. The first two, expectation and reliance, create what are known as *legal* remedies, because they developed in English courts of *law*. The other interests lead to what are termed *equitable* remedies. Historically, when law courts were unable to help a plaintiff, the injured party would sometimes appeal to the Chancellor in London, who had more flexible authority. The Chancellor's powers became known as equitable remedies, a term still used today.

Expectation Interest

This is the most common remedy. **The expectation interest is designed to put the injured party in the position she would have been in had both sides fully performed their obligations.** A court tries to give the injured party the money she would have made from the contract. If accurately computed, this should take into account all the gains she reasonably expected and all the expenses and losses she would have incurred. The injured party should not end up better off than she would have been under the agreement, nor should she suffer serious loss.

William Colby was a former director of the CIA. He wanted to write a book about his 15 years in Vietnam. He paid James McCarger $5,000 for help in writing an early draft and promised McCarger another $5,000 if the book was published. Then he hired Alexander Burnham to co-write the book. Colby's agent secured a contract with Contemporary Books, which included a $100,000 advance. But Burnham was hopelessly late with the manuscript, and Colby missed his publication date. Colby fired Burnham and finished the book without him. Contemporary published *Lost Victory* several years late, and the book flopped, earning no significant revenue. Because the book was so late, Contemporary paid Colby a total of only $17,000. Colby sued Burnham for his lost expectation interest. The court awarded him $23,000, calculated as follows:

	$	100,000	advance, the only money Colby was promised
	–	10,000	agent's fee
	=	90,000	fee for the two authors, combined
divided by 2	=	45,000	Colby's fee
	–	5,000	owed to McCarger under the earlier agreement
	=	40,000	Colby's expectation interest
	–	17,000	fee Colby received from Contemporary
	=	23,000	Colby's expectation damages—that is, the amount he would have received had Burnham finished on time[6]

---

[6] **Colby v. Burnham,** 31 Conn. App. 707, 627 A.2d 457, 1993 Conn. App LEXIS 299 (Conn. App. Ct. 1993).

The *Colby* case presented an easy calculation of damages. Other contracts are complex. Courts typically divide the expectation damages into three parts: (1) compensatory (or "direct") damages, which represent harm that flowed directly from the contract's breach; (2) consequential (or "special") damages, which represent harm caused by the injured party's unique situation; and (3) incidental damages, which are minor costs such as storing or returning defective goods, advertising for alternative goods, and so forth. The first two—compensatory and consequential—are the important ones.

Compensatory Damages

Compensatory damages are the most common monetary awards for the expectation interest. Courts also refer to these as "direct damages." **Compensatory damages are those that flow directly from the contract.** In other words, these are the damages that inevitably result from the breach. Suppose Ace Productions hires Reina to star in its new movie, *Inside Straight*. Ace promises Reina $3 million, providing she shows up June 1 and works until the film is finished. But in late May, Joker Entertainment offers Reina $6 million to star in its new feature, and on June 1 Reina informs Ace that she will not appear. Reina has breached her contract, and Ace should recover compensatory damages.

What are the damages that flow directly from the contract? Ace obviously has to replace Reina. If Ace hires Kween as its star and pays her a fee of $4 million, Ace is entitled to the difference between what it expected to pay ($3 million) and what the breach forced it to pay ($4 million), or $1 million in compensatory damages. Suppose the rest of the cast and crew are idle for two weeks because of the delay in hiring a substitute, and the lost time costs the producers an extra $2.5 million. Reina is also liable for those expenses. Both the new actress and the delay are inevitable.

Reasonable Certainty. The injured party must prove the breach of contract caused damages that can be quantified with reasonable certainty. What if *Inside Straight*, now starring Kween, bombs at the box office. Ace proves that each of Reina's last three movies grossed over $60 million, but *Inside Straight* grossed only $28 million. Is Reina liable for the lost profits? No. Ace cannot prove that it was Reina's absence that caused the film to fare poorly. The script may have been mediocre, or Kween's co-stars dull, or the publicity efforts inadequate. Mere "speculative damages" are worth nothing.

Consequential Damages

In addition to compensatory damages, the injured party may seek consequential damages or, as they are also known, "special damages." **Consequential damages are those resulting from the unique circumstances of this *injured party*.** The rule concerning this remedy comes from a famous 1854 case, *Hadley v. Baxendale*, which all American law students read. Now it is your turn.

HADLEY V. BAXENDALE

9 Ex. 341, 156 Eng. Rep. 145
Court of Exchequer, 1854

Facts: The Hadleys operated a flour mill in Gloucester. The crankshaft broke, causing the mill to grind to a halt. The Hadleys employed Baxendale to cart the damaged part to a foundry in Greenwich, where a new one could be manufactured. Baxendale promised to make the delivery in one day, but he was late transporting the shaft, and as a result the

▼

Hadleys' mill was shut for five extra days. They sued, and the jury awarded damages based in part on their lost profits. Baxendale appealed.

Issue: Should the defendant be liable for profits lost because of his delay in delivering the shaft?

Excerpts from Judge Alderson's Decision: Where two parties have made a contract which one of them has broken, the damages which the other party ought to receive in respect of such breach of contract should be such as may fairly and reasonably be considered either arising naturally, i.e., according to the usual course of things, from such breach of contract itself, or such as may reasonably be supposed to have been in the contemplation of both parties, at the time they made the contract, as the probable result of the breach of it. Now, if the special circumstances under which the contract was actually made were communicated by the plaintiffs to the defendants, and thus known to both parties, the damages resulting from the breach of such a contract, which they would reasonably contemplate, would be the amount of injury which would ordinarily follow from a breach of contract under these special circumstances so known and communicated. But, on the other hand, if these special circumstances were wholly unknown to the party breaking the contract, he, at the most, could only be supposed

to have had in his contemplation the amount of injury which would arise generally, and in the great multitude of cases not affected by any special circumstances, from such a breach of contract.

Now, in the present case, if we are to apply the principles above laid down, we find that the only circumstances here communicated by the plaintiffs to the defendants at the time the contract was made, were, that the article to be carried was the broken shaft of a mill, and that the plaintiffs were the millers of that mill. But how do these circumstances shew [sic] reasonably that the profits of the mill must be stopped by an unreasonable delay in the delivery of the broken shaft by the carrier to the third person? Suppose the plaintiffs had another shaft in their possession put up or putting up at the time, and that they only wished to send back the broken shaft to the engineer who made it; it is clear that this would be quite consistent with the above circumstances, and yet the unreasonable delay in the delivery would have no effect upon the intermediate profits of the mill. It follows, therefore, that the loss of profits here cannot reasonably be considered such a consequence of the breach of contract as could have been fairly and reasonably contemplated by both the parties when they made this contract.

[The court ordered a new trial, in which the jury would not be allowed to consider the plaintiffs' lost profits.] ∎

The rule from *Hadley v. Baxendale* has been unchanged ever since: **the injured party may recover consequential damages only if the breaching party should have foreseen them when the two sides formed the contract.**

Let us return briefly to *Inside Straight*. Suppose that, long before shooting began, Ace had sold the film's soundtrack rights to Spinem Sound for $2 million. Spinem believed it would make a profit only if Reina appeared in the film, so it demanded the right to discharge the agreement if Reina dropped out. When Reina quit, Spinem terminated the contract. Now, when Ace sues Reina, it will also seek $2 million in consequential damages for the lost music revenue. If Reina knew about Ace's contract with Spinem when she signed to do the film, she is liable for $2 million. If she never realized she was an essential part of the music contract, she owes nothing for the lost profits.

Incidental Damages

Incidental damages are the relatively minor costs that the injured party suffers when responding to the breach. When Reina, the actress, breaches the film contract, the producers may have to leave the set and fly back to Los Angeles to hire a new actress. The cost of travel, renting a room for auditions, and other related expenses are incidental damages.

Reliance Interest

George plans to manufacture and sell silk scarves during the holiday season. In the summer, he contracts with Cecily, the owner of a shopping mall, to rent a high-visibility stall for $100 per day. George then buys hundreds of yards of costly silk and gets to work cutting and sewing. Then in September, Cecily refuses to honor the contract. George sues and easily proves Cecily breached a valid contract. But what is his remedy?

George cannot establish an expectation interest in his scarf business. He hoped to sell each scarf for a $40 gross profit and wanted to make $2,000 per day. But how much would he actually have earned? Enough to retire on—or enough to buy a salami sandwich for lunch? A court cannot give him an expectation interest, so George will ask for *reliance damages*. **The reliance interest is designed to put the injured party in the position he would have been in had the parties never entered into a contract.** This remedy focuses on the time and money the injured party spent performing his part of the agreement.

Assuming he is unable to sell the scarves to a retail store (which is probable because retailers will have made purchases long ago), George should be able to recover the cost of the silk fabric he bought and perhaps something for the hours of labor he spent cutting and sewing. However, reliance damages can be difficult to win because *they are harder to quantify.* Judges dislike vague calculations. How much was George's time worth in making the scarves? How good was his work? How likely were the scarves to sell? If George has a track record in the industry, he will be able to show a market price for his services. Without such a record, his reliance claim becomes a tough battle.

In one type of case, courts use reliance damages exclusively. Recall the doctrine of promissory estoppel, which sometimes permits a plaintiff to recover damages even without a valid contract. The plaintiff must show that the defendant made a promise knowing that the plaintiff would likely rely on it, that the plaintiff did rely, and that the only way to avoid injustice is to enforce the promise. In promissory estoppel cases, a court will generally award *only* reliance damages. It would be unfair to give expectation damages for the full benefit of the bargain when, legally, there has been no bargain. Lou says to Costas, who lives in Philadelphia, "You're a great chef. Come out to Los Angeles. My new restaurant needs you, and I can double your salary if not more." Costas quits his job and travels west, but Lou has no job for him. There is no binding contract, because the terms were too vague; however, the chef will *probably* obtain some reliance damages based on lost income and moving costs.

at RISK   Costas's reliance damages are uncertain. How should he have protected himself? ◆

Restitution Interest

Jim and Bonnie Hyler bought an expensive recreational vehicle (RV) from Autorama. The salesman promised the Hylers that a manufacturer's warranty covered the entire vehicle for a year. The Hylers had a succession of major problems with their RV, including windows that wouldn't shut, a door that fell off, a loose windshield, and defective walls. Then they learned that the manufacturer had gone bankrupt. In fact, the Autorama salesman knew of the bankruptcy when he made the sales pitch.

The Hylers returned the RV to Autorama and demanded their money back. They wanted restitution.

The restitution interest is designed to return to the injured party a benefit that he has conferred on the other party, which it would be unjust to leave with that person.

Restitution is a common remedy in contracts involving fraud, misrepresentation, mistake, and duress. In these cases, restitution often goes hand-in-hand with **rescission,** which means to "undo" a contract and put the parties where they were before they made the agreement. The court declared that Autorama had misrepresented the manufacturer's warranty by omitting the small fact that the manufacturer itself no longer existed. Autorama was forced to return to the Hylers the full purchase price plus the value of the automobile they had traded. The dealer, of course, was allowed to keep the defective RV and stare out the ill-fitting windows.[7]

Courts also award restitution in cases of quasi-contract, which we examined in Chapter 9. In quasi-contract cases, the parties never made a contract, but one side did benefit the other. A court may choose to award restitution where one party has conferred a benefit on another and it would be unjust for the other party to retain the benefit. Suppose Owner asks Supplier to install a new furnace in her home. Supplier forgets to ask Owner to sign a contract. If the furnace works properly, it would be unfair to let Owner keep it for free, and a court might order full payment as restitution, even though there was no valid contract.

Other Equitable Interests

In addition to restitution, the other three equitable powers that concern us are specific performance, injunction, and reformation.

Specific Performance

Leona Claussen owned Iowa farmland. She sold some of it to her sister-in-law, Evelyn Claussen, and, along with the land, granted Evelyn an option to buy additional property at $800 per acre. Evelyn could exercise her option anytime during Leona's lifetime or within six months of Leona's death. When Leona died, Evelyn informed the estate's executor that she was exercising her option. But other relatives wanted the property, and the executor refused to sell. Evelyn sued and asked for *specific performance*. She did not want an award of damages; she wanted the land itself. The remedy of specific performance forces the two parties to perform their contract.

A court will award specific performance, ordering the parties to perform the contract, only in cases involving the sale of land or some other asset that is unique. Courts use this equitable remedy when money damages would be inadequate to compensate the injured party. If the subject is unique and irreplaceable, money damages will not put the injured party in the same position she would have been in had the agreement been kept. So a court will order the seller to convey the rare object and the buyer to pay for it.

Historically, every parcel of land has been regarded as unique, and therefore specific performance is always available in real estate contracts. Evelyn Claussen won specific performance. The Iowa Supreme Court ordered Leona's estate to convey the land to Evelyn, for $800 per acre.[8] Generally speaking, either the seller or the buyer may be granted specific performance.

Other unique items, for which a court will order specific performance, include such things as rare works of art, secret formulas, patents, and shares in a closely held corporation. By contrast, a contract for a new Jeep Grand Cherokee is not enforceable by specific performance. An injured buyer can use money damages to purchase a virtually identical auto.

---

[7] **Hyler v. Garner,** 548 N.W.2d 864, 1996 Iowa Sup. LEXIS 322 (Iowa, 1966).

[8] In re **Estate of Claussen,** 482 N.W.2d 381, 1992 Iowa Sup. LEXIS 52 (Iowa 1992).

Injunction

You move into your new suburban house on two acres of land, and the fresh air is exhilarating. But the wind shifts to the west, and you find yourself thinking of farm animals, especially pigs. Your next-door neighbor just started an organic bacon ranch, and the first 15 porkers have checked in. You check out the town's zoning code, discover that it is illegal to raise livestock in the neighborhood, and sue. Money damages will not suffice, because you want the bouquet to disappear. You seek the equitable remedy of injunction. **An injunction is a court order that requires someone to do something or refrain from doing something.**

The court will order your neighbor immediately to cease and desist raising any pigs or other farm animals on his land. "Cease" means to stop, and "desist" means to refrain from doing it in the future. The injunction will not get you any money, but it will move the pigs out of town, and that was your goal.

In the increasingly litigious world of professional sports, injunctions are commonplace. In the following basketball case, the trial court issued a preliminary injunction—that is, an order issued early in a lawsuit prohibiting a party from doing something during the course of the lawsuit. The court attempts to protect the interests of the plaintiff immediately. If, after trial, it appears that the plaintiff has been injured and is entitled to an injunction, the trial court will make its order a permanent injunction. If it appears that the preliminary injunction should never have been issued, the court will terminate the order.

MILICIC V. BASKETBALL MARKETING COMPANY, INC.

2004 PA Super 333, 857 A.2d 689
Superior Court of Pennsylvania, 2004

Facts: The Basketball Marketing Company (BMC) markets, distributes, and sells basketball apparel and related products. BMC signed a long-term endorsement contract with a 16-year-old Serbian player, Darko Milicic, who was virtually unknown in the United States. Two years later, Milicic became the second pick in the National Basketball Association's draft, making him an immensely marketable young man.

Four days after his eighteenth birthday, Milicic made a buyout offer to BMC, seeking release from his contract so that he could arrange a more lucrative one elsewhere. BMC refused to release him. Six days later, Milicic notified BMC in writing that he was disaffirming the contract, and returned all money and goods he had received from the company. BMC again refused to release Milicic.

Believing that Milicic was negotiating an endorsement deal with either Reebok or Adidas,

BMC sent both companies letters informing them it had an enforceable endorsement deal with Milicic that was valid for several more years. Because of BMC's letter, Adidas ceased negotiating with Milicic just short of signing a contract. Milicic sued BMC, seeking a preliminary injunction that would prohibit BMC from sending such letters to competitors. The trial court granted the preliminary injunction and BMC appealed.

Issue: Was Milicic entitled to a preliminary injunction?

Excerpts from Judge McCaffery's Decision[9]: BMC argues that the trial court erred by concluding that Milicic had proven the four essential prerequisites necessary for injunctive relief. However, Milicic did meet these four requirements.

▼

---

[9] Because we are unwilling to assume, as the court apparently does, that this decision will be read only by robots, the authors have substituted "BMC" for "appellant" and "Milicic" for "appellee."

(1) Milicic had a strong likelihood of success on the merits.

Pennsylvania law recognizes, except as to necessities, the contract of a minor is voidable if the minor disaffirms it at any reasonable time after the minor attains majority. Just eleven days after his 18th birthday, Milicic sent BMC a letter withdrawing from the agreement. This letter was sent within a reasonable time after Milicic's reaching the age of majority and stated his unequivocal revocation and voidance of the agreement. There exists more than a reasonable probability that Milicic will succeed in [nullifying the contract with BMC].

(2) Injunctive relief was necessary to prevent immediate and irreparable harm that could not be adequately compensated by the awarding of monetary damages. Top N.B.A. draft picks generally solicit, negotiate and secure endorsement contracts within a short time after the draft to take advantage of the publicity, excitement and attendant marketability associated with the promotion. BMC blocked Milicic's efforts to enter into such an endorsement agreement. After being contacted by BMC, advanced negotiations between Milicic and Adidas were suspended. These business opportunity and market advantage losses may aptly be characterized as irreparable injury for purposes of equitable relief.

(3) Greater injury would have occurred from denying the injunction than from granting the injunction.

BMC's refusal to acknowledge Milicic's ability to disaffirm the contract is at odds with public policy. Because infants are not competent to contract, the ability to disaffirm protects them from their own immaturity and lack of discretion. It is established practice in Pennsylvania to petition the court to appoint a guardian for the child, to protect the interests of both parties. It confounds the Court that BMC, a corporation of great magnitude, whose business may be said to be based in contract law, failed to have a guardian appointed for Milicic.

Harm to the public is an additional consideration. The public policy consideration underlying the rule which allows a child to disaffirm a contract within a reasonable time after reaching the age of majority is that minors should not be bound by mistakes resulting from their immaturity or the overbearance of unscrupulous adults.

(4) The preliminary injunction restored the parties to the *status quo* that existed prior to the wrongful conduct.

Enjoining BMC from further interfering with Milicic's ability to contract will place the parties where they were prior to BMC's wrongful conduct. As all four of the essential prerequisites have been satisfied in this case, the Court properly granted injunctive relief.

Order affirmed. ∎

Reformation

The final remedy, and perhaps the least common, is **reformation,** in which a court will partially "rewrite" a contract. Courts seldom do this, because the whole point of a contract is to enable the parties to control their own futures. However, a court may reform a contract if it believes a written agreement includes a simple mistake. Suppose that Roger orally agrees to sell 35 acres to Hannah for $600,000. The parties then draw up a written agreement, accidentally stating the price as $60,000. Most courts would reform the agreement and enforce it.

Special Issues of Damages

Mitigation of Damages

Note one limitation on *all* contract remedies: **A party injured by a breach of contract may not recover for damages that he could have avoided with reasonable efforts.** In other words, when one party perceives that the other has breached or will breach the contract, the injured party must try to prevent unnecessary loss. A party is expected to **mitigate** his damages—that is, to keep damages as low as he reasonably can.

Liquidated Damages

John Carney reserved a spot in the fourth grade class at Lake Ridge Academy for his son, Michael. He paid a $630 deposit and agreed in writing to pay the balance of the tuition, $5,610, later that year. The contract permitted Carney to cancel the agreement with no further obligation provided he did so before August 1. Otherwise, he became liable for the full tuition. Carney wrote a letter notifying Lake Ridge that Michael would not attend. He dated the letter August 1, mailed it August 7, and the school received it August 14. Lake Ridge demanded its full tuition. Must Carney pay?

It can be difficult or even impossible to prove how much damage the injured party has suffered. So lawyers and executives negotiating a deal may include in the contract **a liquidated damages clause, a provision stating in advance how much a party must pay if it breaches.** Is that fair? The answer depends on two factors: **a court will generally enforce a liquidated damages clause if (1) at the time of creating the contract it was very difficult to estimate actual damages *and* (2) the liquidated amount is reasonable.** In any other case, the liquidated damage will be considered a penalty and will prove unenforceable.

In the tuition case, the court held the following:

> Lake Ridge goes through a long budgeting process that begins each year in January and ends in the fall. The tuition money paid by students is pooled and goes toward staff salaries and benefits, department budgets, student materials, maintenance, improvements, and utilities. The school budget process is an uncertain science; Lake Ridge would be unable to calculate and prove the damages caused by the loss of one student's tuition.
>
> Nor is the contract as a whole unreasonable. Carney had almost five months after he signed the contract to decide whether to cancel it. [We affirm liquidated damages of full tuition.][10]

Chapter Conclusion

A moment's caution! Often that is the only thing needed to avoid years of litigation. Yes, the broad powers of a court may enable it to compensate an injured party, but problems of proof and the uncertainty of remedies demonstrate that the best solution is a carefully drafted contract and socially responsible behavior.

Chapter Review

1. A third party beneficiary is an intended beneficiary and may enforce a contract only if the parties intended her to benefit from the agreement and (1) enforcing the promise will satisfy a debt of the promisee to the beneficiary or (2) the promisee intended to make a gift to the beneficiary.

2. An assignment transfers the assignor's contract rights to the assignee. A delegation transfers the delegator's duties to the delegatee.

3. A party generally may assign contract rights unless doing so would substantially change the

---

[10] **Lake Ridge Academy v. Carney,** 66 Ohio St. 3d 376, 613 N.E.2d 183, 1993 Ohio LEXIS 1210 (Ohio, 1993).

obligor's rights or duties; is forbidden by law; or is validly precluded by the contract.

4. Duties are delegable unless delegation would violate public policy; the contract prohibits delegation; or the obligee has a substantial interest in personal performance by the obligor.

5. Unless the obligee agrees otherwise, delegation does not discharge the delegator's duty to perform.

6. Strict performance, which requires one party to fulfill its duties perfectly, is unusual. In construction and service contracts, substantial performance is generally sufficient to entitle the promisor to the contract price, minus the cost of defects.

7. Good faith performance is required in all contracts.

8. True impossibility means that some event has made it impossible to perform an agreement. Commercial impracticability means that some unexpected event has made it extraordinarily difficult and unfair for one party to perform its obligations.

9. A remedy is the method a court uses to compensate an injured party.

10. The expectation interest puts the injured party in the position she would have been in had both sides fully performed. It has three components: compensatory, consequential, and incidental damages.

11. The reliance interest puts the injured party in the position he would have been in had the parties never entered into a contract.

12. The restitution interest returns to the injured party a benefit that she has conferred on the other party, which it would be unjust to leave with that person.

13. Specific performance, ordered only in cases of a unique asset, requires both parties to perform the contract.

14. An injunction is a court order that requires someone to do something or refrain from doing something.

Practice Test

1. Intercontinental Metals Corp. (IMC) contracted with the accounting firm of Cherry, Bekaert & Holland to perform an audit. Cherry issued its opinion about IMC, giving all copies of its report directly to the company. IMC later permitted Dun & Bradstreet to examine the statements, and Raritan River Steel Company saw a report published by Dun & Bradstreet. Relying on the audit, Raritan sold IMC $2.2 million worth of steel on credit, but IMC promptly went bankrupt. Raritan sued Cherry, claiming that IMC was not as sound as Cherry had reported and that the accounting firm had breached its contract with IMC. Comment on Raritan's suit.

2. Nationwide Discount Furniture hired Rampart Security to install an alarm in its warehouse. A fire would set off an alarm in Rampart's office, and the security company was then supposed to notify Nationwide immediately. A fire did break out, but Rampart allegedly failed to notify Nationwide, causing the fire to spread next door and damage a building owned by Gasket Materials Corp. Gasket sued Rampart for breach of contract, and Rampart moved for summary judgment. Comment.

3. Pizza of Gaithersburg, Maryland, owned five pizza shops. Pizza arranged with Virginia Coffee Service to install soft-drink machines in each of its stores and maintain them. The contract made no mention of the rights of either party to delegate. Virginia Coffee delegated its duties to the Macke Co., leading to litigation between Pizza and Macke. Pizza claimed that Virginia Coffee was barred from delegating because Pizza had a close working relationship with the president of Virginia Coffee, who personally kept the machines in working order. Was the delegation legal?

4. Evans built a house for Sandra Dyer, but the house had some problems. The garage ceiling was too low. Load-bearing beams in the "great room" cracked and appeared to be steadily weakening. The patio did not drain properly.

Pipes froze. Evans wanted the money promised for the job, but Dyer refused to pay. Comment.

5. Omega Concrete had a gravel pit and factory. Access was difficult, so Omega contracted with Union Pacific Railroad (UP) for the right to use a private road that crossed UP property and tracks. The contract stated that use of the road was solely for Omega employees and that Omega would be responsible for closing a gate that UP planned to build where the private road joined a public highway. In fact, UP never constructed the gate. Omega had no authority to construct the gate. Mathew Rogers, an Omega employee, was killed by a train while using the private road to reach Omega. Rogers's family sued Omega, claiming, among other things, that Omega failed to keep the gate closed as the contract required. Is Omega liable based on that failure?

6. ***YOU BE THE JUDGE*** WRITING PROBLEM Kuhn Farm Machinery, a European company, signed an agreement with Scottsdale Plaza Resort, of Arizona, to rent 190 guest rooms for its North American dealers' convention during March 1991. Kuhn invited its top 225 dealers and employees from around the world, although it never mentioned those plans to Scottsdale.

On August 2, 1990, Iraq invaded Kuwait, and on January 16, 1991, the United States and allied forces were at war with Iraq. Iraqi leaders threatened terrorist acts against the United States and its allies. Kuhn became concerned about the safety of international employees traveling to Arizona, especially those coming from Europe. By mid-February, 11 of the top 50 dealers with expense-paid trips had either canceled their plans to attend or failed to sign up. Kuhn postponed the convention. The resort sued. Did commercial impracticability or frustration of purpose discharge the contract? **Argument for Scottsdale Plaza Resort:** The resort did not know that Kuhn expected to bring executives from Europe, or that if anything interfered with their travel, the convention would become pointless. Most of the dealers could have attended the convention. **Argument for Kuhn:** The parties never anticipated the threat of terrorism. Kuhn wanted this convention so that its European executives, among others, could meet top North American dealers. That is now impossible. As a result, the contract has no value at all to Kuhn, and its obligations should be discharged by law.

7. Racicky was in the process of buying 320 acres of ranch land. While that sale was being negotiated, Racicky signed a contract to sell the land to Simon. Simon paid $144,000, the full price of the land. But Racicky then went bankrupt, before he could complete the purchase of the land, let alone its sale. Which of these remedies should Simon seek: expectation, restitution, or specific performance?

8. ***ETHICS*** The National Football League owns the copyright to the broadcasts of its games. It licenses local television stations to telecast certain games and maintains a "blackout rule," which prohibits stations from broadcasting home games that are not sold-out 72 hours before the game starts. Certain home games of the Cleveland team were not sold out, and the NFL blocked local broadcast. But several bars in the Cleveland area were able to pick up the game's signal by using special antennas. The NFL wanted the bars to stop showing the games. What did it do? Was it unethical of the bars to broadcast the games that they were able to pick up? Apart from the NFL's legal rights, do you think it had the moral right to stop the bars from broadcasting the games?

9. ***ROLE REVERSAL*** Write a short-answer question that highlights the difference between an assignment and a novation.

Internet Research Problem

You represent a group of neighborhood residents in a large city who are protesting construction of a skyscraper that will violate building height limitations. Draft a complaint, requesting an appropriate injunction. You may use the sample injunction complaint found at http://www.kinseylaw.com. Click on "Free Stuff," "Complaints," and "Injunction."

You can find further practice problems at
academic.cengage.com/blaw/beatty.

Sales, Product Liability, and Negotiable Instruments

He Sued, She Sued. Harold and Maude made a great couple because both were compulsive entrepreneurs. One evening they sat on their penthouse roof deck, overlooking the twinkling Chicago skyline. Harold sipped a decaf coffee while negotiating, over the phone, with a real estate developer in San Antonio. Maude puffed a cigar as she bargained on a different line with a toy manufacturer in Cleveland. They hung up at the same time. "I did it!" shrieked Maude, "I made an incredible deal for the robots—five bucks each!" "No, I did it!" triumphed Harold, "I sold the 50 acres in Texas for $300,000 more than it's worth." They dashed indoors.

Maude quickly scrawled a handwritten memo, which read, "Confirming our deal—100,000 Psychopath Robots—you deliver Chicago—end of summer." She didn't mention a price, or an exact delivery date, or when payment would be made. She signed her

memo and faxed it to the toy manufacturer. Harold took more time. He typed a thorough contract, describing precisely the land he was selling, the $2.3 million price, how and when each payment would be made, and what the deed conveyed. He signed the contract and faxed it, along with a plot plan showing the surveyed land. Then the happy couple grabbed a bottle of champagne, returned to the deck—and placed a side bet on whose contract would prove more profitable. The loser would have to cook and serve dinner for six months.

Neither Harold nor Maude ever heard again from the other parties. The toy manufacturer sold the robots to another retailer at a higher price. Maude was forced to buy comparable toys elsewhere for $9 each. She sued. And the Texas property buyer changed his mind, deciding to develop a Club Med in Greenland and refusing to pay Harold for his land. He sued. Only one of the two plaintiffs succeeded. Which one? ■

© PHOTO 24/BRAND X PICTURES/GETTY IMAGES

SALES

The adventures of Harold and Maude illustrate the Uniform Commercial Code (UCC) in action. The Code is the single most important source of law for people engaged in commerce and controls the vast majority of contracts made every day in every state. The Code is old in origin, contemporary in usage, admirable in purpose, and flawed in application. "Yeah, yeah, that's fascinating," snaps Harold, "but who wins the bet?" Relax, Harold, we'll tell you in a minute.

Development of the UCC

Throughout the first half of the twentieth century, commercial transactions changed dramatically in this country, as advances in transportation and communication revolutionized negotiation and trade. The nation needed a modernized business law to give nationwide uniformity and predictability in a new and faster world. In 1942, two groups of scholars, the American Law Institute (ALI) and the National Conference of Commissioners on Uniform State Laws (NCCUSL), began the effort to draft a modern, national law of commerce. The scholars debated and formulated for nearly a decade. Finally, in 1952, the lawyers published their work—the Uniform Commercial Code. The entire Code is available online at http://www.law.cornell.edu by clicking on "Constitutions and Codes," then "Uniform Commercial Code."

The ALI and the NCCUSL have revised the Code several times since then, with important changes coming as recently as 2003. Remember, though, that the UCC is the creation of scholars. No section of the Code has any legal effect until a state legislature adopts it. In fact, all 50 states and the District of Columbia have adopted the UCC, but not all have used identical versions.

This book discusses and applies provisions of the Code that have been widely adopted. The commissioners completely rewrote Article 9, on secured transactions, at the turn of the millennium, and this text reflects those changes because every state has adopted them. The commissioners have also revised Article 1, which provides definitions and general guidance, and Article 2, on sales. However, as this book goes to press, very few states have adopted revised Article 1, and none have adopted revised Article 2. We focus on existing law, not the proposed changes to Articles 1 and 2.

This chapter is designed to:

- illustrate key elements of the Code *that have changed the common law rules* of contracts;
- survey the leading doctrines of product liability; and
- highlight important features of negotiable instruments.

Article 1: General Provisions	The purpose of the Code, general guidance in applying it, and definitions.
Article 2: Sale of Goods	The sale of *goods*, such as a new car, 20,000 pairs of gloves, or 101 Dalmatians. This is one of the two most important articles in the UCC.
Article 2A: Leases	A temporary exchange of goods for money, such as renting a car.
Article 3: Negotiable Instruments	The use of checks, promissory notes, and other negotiable instruments.

Article 4: Bank Deposits and Collections	The rights and obligations of banks and their customers.
Article 4A: Funds Transfers	An instruction, given by a bank customer, to credit a sum of money to another's account.
Article 5: Letters of Credit	The use of credit, extended by two or more banks, to facilitate a contract between two parties who do not know each other and require guarantees by banks they trust.
Article 6: Bulk Transfers	The sale of a major part of a company's inventory or equipment.
Article 7: Warehouse Receipts, Bills of Lading, and Other Documents of Title	Documents proving ownership of goods that are being transported or stored.
Article 8: Investment Securities	Rights and liabilities concerning shares of stock or other ownership of an enterprise.
Article 9: Secured Transaction	A sale of goods in which the seller keeps a financial stake in the goods he has sold, such as a car dealer who may repossess the car if the buyer fails to make payments. This is one of the two most important articles in the Code.

Harold and Maude, Revisited

Harold and Maude each negotiated what they believed was an enforceable agreement, and both filed suit: Harold for the sale of his land, Maude for the purchase of toy robots. Only one prevailed. The difference in outcome demonstrates why everyone in business needs a working knowledge of the Code. As we revisit the happy couple, Harold is clearing the dinner dishes. Maude sits back in her chair, lights a cigar, and compliments her husband on the apple tart.

Harold's contract was for the sale of land and was governed by the common law of contracts, which requires any agreement for the sale of land to be in writing and *signed by the defendant*, in this case the buyer in Texas. Harold signed it, but the buyer never did, so Harold's meticulously detailed document was worth less than a five-cent cigar.

Maude's quickly scribbled memorandum, concerning robot toys, was for the sale of goods and was governed by Article 2 of the UCC. The Code requires less detail and formality in a writing. Because Maude and the seller were both merchants, the document she scribbled could be enforced *even against the defendant*, who had never signed anything. The fact that Maude left out the price and other significant terms was not fatal to a contract under the UCC, though under the common law such omissions would have made the bargain unenforceable.

Scope of Article 2

Because the UCC changes the common law, it is essential to know whether the Code applies in a given case. Negotiations may lead to an enforceable agreement when the UCC applies, even though the same bargaining would create no contract under the common law.

UCC §2-102: Article 2 applies to the sale of goods.[1] Goods are things that are movable, other than money and investment securities. Hats are goods, and so are railroad cars, lumber, books, and bottles of wine. Land is not a good, nor is a house. Article 2 regulates sales, which means that one party transfers title to the other in exchange for money. If you sell your motorcycle to a friend, that is a sale of goods.[2]

Merchants

The UCC evolved to provide merchants with rules that would meet their unique business needs. However, while the UCC offers a contract law that is more flexible than the common law, it also requires a higher level of responsibility from the merchants it serves. Those who make a living by crafting agreements are expected to understand the legal consequences of their words and deeds. Thus, many sections of the Code offer two rules: one for "merchants" and one for everybody else.

UCC §2-104: A merchant is someone who routinely deals in the particular goods involved, or who appears to have special knowledge or skill in those goods, or who uses agents with special knowledge or skill in those goods. A used car dealer is a "merchant" when it comes to selling autos, because he routinely deals in them. He is not a merchant when he goes to a furniture store and purchases a new sofa.

The UCC frequently holds a merchant to a higher standard of conduct than a non-merchant. For example, a merchant may be held to an oral contract if she received written confirmation of it, even though the merchant herself never signed the confirmation. That same confirmation memo, arriving at the house of a non-merchant, would not create a binding deal.

Contract Formation

The common law expected the parties to form a contract in a fairly predictable and traditional way: the offeror made a clear offer that included all important terms, and the offeree agreed to all terms. Nothing was left open. The drafters of the UCC recognized that businesspeople frequently do not think or work that way and that the law should reflect business reality.

Formation Basics: Section 2-204

UCC §2-204 provides three important rules that enable parties to make a contract quickly and informally:

1. *Any Manner That Shows Agreement.* The parties may make a contract in any manner sufficient to show that they reached an agreement. They may show the agreement with words, writings, or even their conduct. Lisa negotiates with Ed to buy 300 barbecue grills. The parties agree on a price, but other business prevents them from finishing the deal. Then six months later Lisa writes, "Remember our deal for 300 grills? I still want to do it if you do." Ed does not respond, but a week

---

[1] Officially, Article 2 tells us that it applies to *transactions* in goods, which is a slightly broader category than sale of goods. But most sections of Article 2, and most court decisions, focus exclusively on sales, and so shall we.

[2] Because leasing is so important, the drafters of the Code added Article 2A to cover the subject. Article 2A is similar to Article 2, but there are important differences, and anyone engaging in a significant amount of commercial leasing must become familiar with Article 2A. For our purposes, leasing law is a variation on the theme of Article 2, and we will concentrate on the principal melody of sales.

later a truck shows up at Lisa's store with the 300 grills, and Lisa accepts them. The combination of their original discussion, Lisa's subsequent letter, Ed's delivery, and her acceptance all adds up to show that they reached an agreement. The court will enforce their deal, and Lisa must pay the agreed-upon price.

2. *Moment of Making Is Not Critical.* The UCC will enforce a deal even though it is difficult, in common-law terms, to say exactly when it was formed. Was Lisa's deal formed when they orally agreed? When he delivered? She accepted? The Code's answer: it does not matter. The contract is enforceable.

3. *One or More Terms May Be Left Open.* The common law insisted that the parties clearly agree on all important terms. The Code changes that. **Under the UCC, a court may enforce a bargain even though one or more terms were left open.** Lisa's letter never said when she required delivery of the barbecue grills or when she would pay. Under the UCC, the omission is not fatal. As long as there is some certain basis for giving damages to the injured party, the court will do just that. If Lisa refused to pay, a court would rule that the parties assumed she would pay within a commercially reasonable time, such as 30 days.

Statute of Frauds

UCC §2-201 requires a writing for any sale of goods worth $500 or more. However, under the UCC, the writing need not completely summarize the agreement. The Code only requires a writing *sufficient to indicate* that the parties made a contract. In other words, the writing need not be a contract. A simple memo is enough, or a letter or informal note, mentioning that the two sides reached an agreement.

In general, the writing must be signed by the defendant—that is, whichever party is claiming there was no deal. Dick signs and sends to Shirley a letter saying, "This is to acknowledge your agreement to buy all 650 books in my rare book collection for $188,000." Shirley signs nothing. A day later, Louis offers Dick $250,000. Is Dick free to sell? No. He signed the memo, it indicates a contract, and Shirley can enforce it against him.

Now reverse the problem. Suppose that after Shirley receives Dick's letter, she decides against rare books in favor of original scripts from the *South Park* television show. Dick sues. Shirley wins because she signed nothing.

Enforceable Only to Quantity Stated. Because the writing only has to indicate that the parties agreed, it need not state every term of their deal. But one term is essential: quantity. **The Code will enforce the contract only up to the quantity of goods stated in the writing.** This is logical, since a court can surmise other terms, such as price, based on market conditions. Buyer agrees to purchase pencils from Seller. The market value of the pencils is easy to determine, but a court would have no way of knowing whether Buyer meant to purchase 1,000 pencils or 100,000; the quantity must be stated.

Merchant Exception. This is a major change from the common law. **When two merchants make an oral contract, and one sends a confirming memo to the other within a reasonable time, and the memo is sufficiently definite that it could be enforced against the sender herself, then the memo is also valid against the merchant who receives it, unless he objects within 10 days.** Laura, a tire wholesaler, signs and sends a memo to Scott, a retailer, saying, "Confm yr order today—500 tires cat #886—cat price." Scott realizes he can get the tires cheaper elsewhere and ignores the memo. Big mistake. Both parties are merchants, and Laura's memo is sufficient to bind her. So it also satisfies the statute of frauds against Scott, unless he objects within 10 days.

The following case illustrates the merchant exception in action.

Code Provisions Discussed in this Case	
Issue	**Relevant Code Section**
1. Was there a writing sufficient to indicate a contract?	UCC §2-201 requires a writing for any sale of goods worth $500 or more.
2. Did the purchase orders satisfy the merchant exception?	UCC §2-201(2), the "merchant exception." When two merchants make an oral contract, and one sends a confirming memo to the other within a reasonable time, and the memo is sufficiently definite that it could be enforced against the sender herself, then the memo is also valid against the merchant who receives it, unless he objects within ten days.

RAPOCA ENERGY COMPANY, L.P. V. AMCI EXPORT CORPORATION

2001 WL 401424
United States District Court for the Western District of Virginia, 2001

Facts: Robert Moir, an AMCI executive, met with Rapoca's officer, Gary Chilcot, at O'Charley's Restaurant and discussed buying a large quantity of coal from Rapoca. According to Moir, the two agreed that Rapoca would sell 140,000 tons of coal. AMCI confirmed this in two purchase orders (P.O.s), which it sent to Rapoca. Chilcot's version was very different. He stated that the parties never reached an oral agreement, that the P.O.s were inconsistent as to the quantity of coal, and that the price was too low for a reasonable seller to have agreed. What is clear is that Rapoca did not respond in writing to the P.O.s for several months.

Rapoca filed suit, seeking a declaration from the court that it had no contractual obligation to AMCI. The company argued that there had been no agreement, and that even if the parties had orally agreed, the P.O.s did not satisfy the statute of frauds. AMCI counterclaimed, seeking damages for its costs in buying coal elsewhere. The judge first ruled that the parties had in fact reached an oral agreement. That left one important issue remaining.

Issues: Did the purchase orders satisfy the statute of frauds?

Excerpts from Judge Jones's Decision: The next question that I must resolve is whether the oral contracts are barred by the statute of frauds. It is clear that there is no writing signed by Rapoca in this case sufficient to indicate that the contracts in question were made. However, there is an exception to § 2-201. [The court describes the "merchant exception."]

There is no question but that the parties were merchants within the meaning of this exception. Under the circumstances, I find that the two weeks in which these purchase orders were received by Rapoca was a reasonable time after the oral agreement between Moir and Chilcot. It is unlikely that memories would fade or that Rapoca would be unduly burdened by such a short period of time. The closer question is whether the purchase orders, which were not objected to in writing within ten days, were writings in confirmation of the contracts.

On the one side, the purchase orders here appear to require the recipient to take some affirmative action, by virtue of the printed form language that states, "This order must be acknowledged by the return of the signed second copy" and because the purchase order contains a place for the recipient to sign below the words, "Accepted and Agreed." In addition, the purchase orders contain printed form language that states that delivery of coal after the date of the purchase order constitutes acceptance of the order.

▼

Some courts have held that a purchase order, particularly with language like this, is more akin to an offer for a contract, rather than a confirmation of an existing agreement. Moreover, there is no reference in these purchase orders to any specific antecedent oral agreement, and some courts have found that the absence of such confirming language precludes the use of the writing as a confirmation.

However, I find from the undisputed evidence in this case, that the clear trade practice was to use purchase orders such as these to confirm oral agreements. Gary Chilcot's testimony supports this finding:

THE COURT: And why do you think you get a purchase order? What's the . . . reason for that?
WITNESS: Well, it's, it's a reconfirmation of what was verbally agreed to.
THE COURT: So that in your experience there normally is an agreement as to the sale which is typically oral?

WITNESS: Typically.
THE COURT: And that . . . is followed by the purchaser sending you or your company a purchase order which confirms the terms?
WITNESS: Correct.

In this business, at the time, purchase orders were rarely if ever signed and returned, which is further evidence that they were simply used as confirmations. The practice was not to use them as offers, and they were not offers in this case, but rather confirmations of the prior oral agreement. Thus, the fact that the purchase orders had the acceptance language does not preclude them, under the circumstances of this case, from being writings in confirmation within the meaning of the statute of frauds.

Thus, I find that the contracts in questions are valid and enforceable. ■

Added Terms: Section 2-207

Under the common law's mirror image rule, when one party makes an offer, the offeree must accept those exact terms. If the offeree adds or alters any terms, the acceptance is ineffective, and the offeree's response becomes a counteroffer. In one of its most significant modifications of contract law, the UCC changes that outcome. **Under §2-207, an acceptance that adds or alters terms will often create a contract.** The Code has made this change in response to the *battles of the form*. Every day, corporations buy and sell millions of dollars of goods using preprinted forms. The vast majority of all contracts involve such documents. Typically, the buyer places an order by using a preprinted form, and the seller acknowledges with its own preprinted acceptance form. Because each form contains language favorable to the party sending it, the two documents rarely agree. The Code's drafters concluded that the law must cope with real practices.

Intention. The parties must still *intend* to create a contract. Section 2-207 is full of exceptions, but there is no change in this basic requirement of contract law. If the differing forms indicate that the parties never reached agreement, there is no contract.

Additional or Different Terms. An offeree may include a new term in his acceptance and still create a binding deal. Suppose Breeder writes to Pet Shop, offering to sell 100 guinea pigs at $2 each. Pet Shop faxes a memo saying, "We agree to buy 100 g.p. We receive normal industry credit for any unhealthy pig." Pet Shop has added a new term, concerning unhealthy pigs, but the parties have created a binding contract because the writings show they intended an agreement. Now the court must decide what the terms of the contract are because there is some discrepancy. The first step is to decide whether the new language is an *additional term* or a *different term*.

Additional terms are those that raise issues not covered in the offer. The "unhealthy pig" issue is an additional term because the offer said nothing about it. **When both parties are *merchants*, additional terms generally become part of the**

bargain.[3] Both Pet Shop and Breeder are merchants, and the additional term about credit for unhealthy animals does become part of their agreement.

Different terms *contradict* those in the offer. Suppose Brilliant Corp. orders 1,500 cell phones from Makem Co., for use by Brilliant's sales force. Brilliant places the order by using a preprinted form stating that the product is fully warranted for normal use and that seller is liable for compensatory *and consequential* damages. This means, for example, that Makem could be liable for lost profits if a salesperson's phone fails during a lucrative sales pitch. Makem responds with its own memo stating that in the event of defective phones, Makem is liable only to repair or replace, and *is not liable for consequential damages, lost profits, or any other damages.*

Makem's acceptance has included a different term because its language contradicts the offer. **Different terms cancel each other out. The Code then supplies its own terms, called gap-fillers,** which cover prices, delivery dates and places, warranties, and other subjects. The Code's gap-filler about warranties does permit recovery of compensatory and consequential damages. Therefore, Makem would be liable for lost profits.

Performance and Remedies

The Code's practical, flexible approach also shapes its rules about contract performance and remedy. Once again, our goal in this chapter is to highlight doctrines that demonstrate a *change or an evolution in common-law principles.*

Buyer's Remedies

A seller is expected to deliver what the buyer ordered. **Conforming goods satisfy the contract terms.** Nonconforming goods do not.[4] Frame Shop orders from Wholesaler a large quantity of walnut wood, due on March 15, to be used for picture frames. If Wholesaler delivers, on March 8, high-quality *cherry* wood, it has shipped nonconforming goods.

A buyer has the right to **inspect the goods** before paying or accepting[5] and may **reject nonconforming goods** by notifying the seller within a reasonable time.[6] Frame Shop may lawfully open Wholesaler's shipping crates before paying and is entitled to refuse the cherry wood. However, when the buyer rejects nonconforming goods, **the seller has the right to cure,** by delivering conforming goods before the contract deadline.[7] If Wholesaler delivers walnut wood by March 15, Frame Shop must pay in full. The Code even permits the seller to cure *after* the delivery date if doing so is reasonable. Notice the UCC's eminently pragmatic goal: to make contracts work.

Cover. **If the seller breaches, the buyer may *cover* by reasonably obtaining substitute goods; it may then obtain the difference between the contract price and its cover price, plus incidental and consequential damages, minus expenses saved.**[8] Retailer orders 10,000 pairs of ballet shoes from Shoemaker, at $55 per pair,

---

3 There are three circumstances in which additional terms do *not* become part of the agreement: when the original offer *insisted on its own terms;* when the additional term *materially alters* the offer— that is, makes a dramatic change in the proposal; and when the offeror *promptly objects* to the new terms.

4 UCC §2-106(2).

5 UCC §2-513.

6 UCC §§2-601, 602.

7 UCC §2-508.

8 UCC §2-712.

to be delivered August 1. When no shoes dance through the door, Shoemaker explains that its workers in Europe are on strike and no delivery date can be guaranteed. Retailer purchases comparable shoes elsewhere for $70 and files suit. Retailer will win $150,000, representing the increased cost of $15 per pair.

Incidental and Consequential Damages. **An injured buyer is generally entitled to incidental and consequential damages.** Incidental damages cover such costs as advertising for replacements, sending buyers to obtain new goods, and shipping the replacement goods. Consequential damages are those resulting from the unique circumstances of *this injured party.* They can be much more extensive and may include lost profits. **A buyer expecting to resell goods may obtain the loss of profit caused by the seller's failure to deliver.** In the ballet shoes case, suppose Retailer has contracts to resell the goods to ballet companies at an average profit of $10 per pair. Retailer is also entitled to those lost profits.

Seller's Remedies

Of course, a seller has rights, too. Sometimes a buyer breaches before the seller has delivered the goods, for example, by failing to make a payment due under the contract. If that happens, **the seller may refuse to deliver the goods.**[9]

If a buyer unjustly refuses to accept or pay for goods, the injured seller may resell them. **If the resale is commercially reasonable, the seller may recover the difference between the resale price and contract price, plus incidental damages, minus expenses saved.**[10] Incidental damages are expenses the seller incurs in holding the goods and reselling them, costs such as storage, shipping, and advertising for resale. The seller must deduct expenses saved by the breach. For example, if the contract required the seller to ship heavy machinery from Detroit to San Diego, and the buyer's breach enables the seller to market its goods profitably in Detroit, the seller must deduct from its claimed losses the transportation costs that it saved.

Finally, the seller may simply sue **for the contract price** if the buyer has accepted the goods *or if* the goods are conforming and resale is impossible.[11] If the goods were manufactured to the buyer's unique specifications, there might be no other market for them, and the seller should receive the contract price.

WARRANTIES AND PRODUCT LIABILITY

You are sitting in a fast-food restaurant in Washington, D.C. Your friend Harley, who works for a member of Congress, is eating with one hand and gesturing with the other. "We want product liability reform and we want it now," he proclaims, stabbing the air with his free hand. "It's absurd, these multimillion dollar verdicts, just because something has a *slight defect.*" He waves angrily at the absurdity, takes a ferocious bite from his burger—and with a loud CRACK breaks a tooth. Harley howls in pain and throws down the bun, revealing a large piece of bone in the meat. As he tips back in misery, his defectively manufactured chair collapses, and Harley slams into the tile, knocking himself unconscious. Hours later, when he revives in the hospital, he refuses to speak to you until he talks with his lawyer. They will discuss **product liability,** which refers to goods that have caused an injury. The harm may be physical, as it was in Harley's case,

---

[9] UCC §2-705.
[10] UCC §2-706.
[11] UCC §2-709.

Or it can be purely economic, as when a corporation buys a computer so defective it must be replaced, costing the buyer lost time and profits. The injured party may have a choice of possible remedies, including:

- *Warranty*, which is an assurance provided in a sales contract;
- *Negligence*, which refers to unreasonable conduct by the defendant; and
- *Strict liability*, which prohibits defective products whether the defendant acted reasonably or not.

We discuss each of these remedies in this chapter. What all product liability cases have in common is that a person or business has been hurt by goods. We begin with warranties.

Express Warranties

A warranty is a contractual assurance that goods will meet certain standards. It is normally a manufacturer or a seller who gives a warranty, and a buyer who relies on it. A warranty might be explicit and written: "The manufacturer warrants that the lightbulbs in this package will provide 100 watts of power for 2,000 hours." Or a warranty could be oral: "Don't worry, this machine can harvest any size of wheat crop ever planted in the state."

An express warranty is one that the seller creates with his words or actions.[12] Whenever a seller *clearly indicates* to a buyer that the goods being sold will meet certain standards, she has created an express warranty. For example, if the salesclerk for a paint store tells a professional house painter that "this exterior paint will not fade for three years, even in direct sunlight," that is an express warranty and the store is bound by it. The store is also bound by express warranty if the clerk gives the painter a brochure making the same promise or a sample that indicates the same thing.

The seller may **disclaim** a warranty. **A disclaimer is a statement that a particular warranty *does not* apply.** The seller may disclaim an oral express warranty by including in the sales contract a statement such as "sold as is," or "any oral promises are disclaimed." Written express warranties generally *cannot* be disclaimed.

Implied Warranties

Emily sells Sam a new jukebox for his restaurant, but the machine is so defective it never plays a note. When Sam demands a refund, Emily scoffs that she never made any promises. She is correct that she made no express warranties but is liable nonetheless. Many sales are covered by implied warranties.

Implied warranties are those created by the Code itself, not by any act or statement of the seller.

Implied Warranty of Merchantability

This is the most important warranty in the Code. **Unless excluded or modified, a warranty that the goods shall be merchantable is implied in a contract for their sale if the seller is a merchant with respect to goods of that kind.** *Merchantable* means that the goods are fit for the ordinary purposes for which they are used.[13] This rule contains several important principles:

---

12 UCC §2-313.
13 UCC §2-314(1).

- *Unless excluded or modified* means that the seller does have a chance to escape this warranty. A seller may disclaim this warranty provided he actually mentions the word "merchantability." A seller also has the option to disclaim *all* warranties, by stating that the goods are sold "as is" or "with all faults."

- *Merchantability* requires that goods be fit for their normal purposes. A ladder, to be merchantable, must be able to rest securely against a building and support someone who is climbing it. The ladder need not be serviceable as a boat ramp.

- *Implied* means that the law itself imposes this liability on the seller.

- *A merchant with respect to goods of that kind* means that the seller is someone who routinely deals in these goods or holds himself out as having special knowledge about these goods.

Dacor Corp. manufactured and sold scuba diving equipment. Dacor ordered air hoses from Sierra Precision, specifying the exact size and couplings so that the hose would fit safely into Dacor's oxygen units. Within a year, customers returned a dozen Dacor units, complaining that the hose connections had cracked and were unusable. Dacor recalled 16,000 units and refit them at a cost of $136,000. Dacor sued Sierra and won its full costs. Sierra was a merchant with respect to scuba hoses because it routinely manufactured and sold them. The defects were life-threatening to scuba divers, and the hoses could not be used for normal purposes.[14]

The scuba equipment was not merchantable, because a properly made scuba hose should never crack under normal use. What if the product being sold is food, and the food contains something that is harmful—yet quite normal?

GOODMAN V. WENCO FOODS, INC.

333 N.C. 1, 423 S.E.2d 444, 1992 N.C.LEXIS 671
Supreme Court of North Carolina, 1992

Facts: Fred Goodman and a friend stopped for lunch at a Wendy's restaurant in Hillsborough, North Carolina. Goodman had eaten about half of his double hamburger when he bit down and suddenly felt terrible pain in his lower jaw. He took from his mouth a triangular piece of cow bone, about one-sixteenth to one-quarter inch thick and one-half inch long, along with several pieces of his teeth. Goodman's pain was intense and his dental repairs took months.

The restaurant purchased all its meat from Greensboro Meat Supply Company (GMSC). Wendy's required its meat to be chopped and "free from bone or cartilage in excess of 1/8 inch in any dimension." GMSC beef was inspected continuously by state regulators and was certified by the United States Department of Agriculture (USDA). The

USDA considered any bone fragment less than three-quarters of an inch long to be "insignificant."

Goodman sued, claiming a breach of the implied warranty of merchantability. The trial court dismissed the claim, ruling that the bone was natural to the food and that the hamburger was therefore fit for its ordinary purpose. The appeals court reversed this, holding that a hamburger could be unfit even if the bone occurred naturally. Wendy's appealed to the state's highest court.

Issue: Was the hamburger unfit for its ordinary purpose because it contained a harmful but natural bone?

Excerpts from Judge Exum's Decision: We hold that when a substance in food causes injury to a ▼

---

[14] *Dacor Corp. v. Sierra Precision,* 1993 U.S. Dist. LEXIS 8009 (N.D. Ill. 1993).

consumer of the food, it is not a bar to recovery against the seller that the substance was "natural" to the food, provided the substance is of such a size, quality or quantity that the substance's presence should not reasonably have been anticipated by the consumer.

A triangular, one-half-inch, inflexible bone shaving is indubitably "inherent" in or "natural" to a cut of beef, but whether it is so "natural" to hamburger as to put a consumer on his guard—whether it "is to be reasonably expected by the consumer"— is, in most cases, a question for the jury. We are not requiring that the respondent's hamburgers be perfect, only that they be fit for their intended purpose. It is difficult to conceive of how a consumer might guard against the type of injury present here, short of removing the hamburger from its bun, breaking it apart and inspecting its small components.

Wendy's argues that the evidence supported its contention that its hamburger complied with [federal and state] standards. Wendy's reasons that [state and federal regulators permit] some bone fragments in meat and that its hamburgers are therefore merchantable as a matter of law. The court of appeals rejected this argument, noting that compliance "with all state and federal regulations is only some evidence which the jury may consider in determining whether the product was merchantable." We agree.

We thus conclude, as did the court of appeals majority, that a jury could reasonably determine the meat to be of such a nature, i.e., hamburger, and the bone in the meat of such a size that a consumer of the meat should not reasonably have anticipated the bone's presence. The court of appeals therefore properly reversed the directed verdict for Wendy's on plaintiff's implied warranty of merchantability claim. ■

Implied Warranty of Fitness for a Particular Purpose

The other warranty that the law imposes on sellers is the implied warranty of fitness for a particular purpose. This cumbersome name is often shortened to the *warranty of fitness*. **Where the seller at the time of contracting knows about a particular purpose for which the buyer wants the goods, and knows that the buyer is relying on the seller's skill or judgment, there is (unless excluded or modified) an implied warranty that the goods shall be fit for such purpose.**[15]

Notice that the seller must know about some special use the buyer intends and realize that the buyer is relying on the seller's judgment. Suppose a lumber sales clerk knows that a buyer is relying on his advice to choose the best wood for a house being built in a swamp. The Code implies a warranty that the wood sold will withstand those special conditions.

Once again, a seller may disclaim this warranty if she clearly states "as is" or "sold with all faults," or some similar language.

Consumer Sales

The Code often provides stronger protection for consumers than for businesses. Many states prohibit a seller from disclaiming implied warranties in the sale of consumer goods. In these states, if a home furnishings store sells a bunk bed to a consumer and the top bunk tips out the window on the first night, the seller is liable. If the sales contract clearly stated "no warranties of merchantability or fitness," the court would reject the clause and find that the seller breached the implied warranty of merchantability.

---

[15] UCC §2-315.

Negligence

A buyer of goods may have remedies other than warranty claims. One is negligence. Here we focus on how this law applies to the sale of goods. Negligence is notably different from contract law. In a contract case, the two parties have reached an agreement, and the terms of their bargain will usually determine how to settle any dispute. If the parties agreed that the seller disclaimed all warranties, then the buyer may be out of luck. But in a negligence case, there has been no bargaining between the parties, who may never have met. A consumer injured by an exploding cola bottle is unlikely to have bargained for her beverage with the CEO of the cola company. Instead, the law *imposes* a standard of conduct on everyone in society, corporation and individual alike. The two key elements of this standard, for present purposes, are *duty* and *breach*. A plaintiff injured by goods she bought must show that the defendant, usually a manufacturer or seller of a product, had a duty to her and breached that duty. A defendant has a duty of due care to anyone who could foreseeably be injured by its misconduct. Generally, it is the duty to act as *a reasonable person* would in like circumstances; a defendant who acts unreasonably has breached his duty.

In negligence cases concerning the sale of goods, plaintiffs most often raise one or more of these claims:

- *Negligent Design.* The buyer claims that the product injured her because the manufacturer designed it poorly. Negligence law requires a manufacturer to design a product free of *unreasonable* risks. The product does not have to be absolutely safe. An automobile that guaranteed a driver's safety could be made but would be prohibitively expensive. Reasonable safety features must be built in if they can be included at a tolerable cost.

- *Negligent Manufacture.* The buyer claims that the design was adequate but that failure to inspect or some other sloppy conduct caused a dangerous product to leave the plant.

- *Failure to Warn.* A manufacturer is liable for failing to warn the purchaser or users about the dangers of normal use and also foreseeable misuse. However, there is no duty to warn about obvious dangers, a point evidently lost on some manufacturers. A Batman costume unnecessarily included this statement: "For play only: Mask and chest plate are not protective; cape does not enable user to fly."

Ethics

Ibrahim Boumelhem, age four, began playing with a Bic disposable lighter that his parents had bought. He started a fire that burned his legs and severely burned his six-month-old brother over 85 percent of his body. Ibrahim's father sued Bic, claiming that the lighter was negligently designed because it could have been child-proof. He also claimed failure to warn, because the lighter did not clearly warn of the danger to children.

The *Boumelhem* court considered evidence and analyses from several other cases against Bic. The court noted that consumers use more than 500 million disposable lighters annually in the United States. Each lighter provides 1,000 to 2,000 lights. During one three-year period, children playing with disposable lighters started 8,100 fires annually, causing an average of 180 people to die every year, of whom 140 were children under five. Another 990 people were injured. The average annual cost of deaths, injuries, and property damage from child-play fires was estimated at $310 to $375 million, or 60 to 75 cents per lighter sold. Bic had acknowledged in earlier litigation that it was foreseeable that lighters would get into children's hands and injure them. Bic had also agreed that it was feasible to make a more child-resistant lighter.

How should the court rule? Does this case present an irresponsible parent launching a frivolous lawsuit or a callous corporation disregarding children's safety to make a few extra dollars? ◆

Strict Liability

The other tort claim that an injured person can bring against the manufacturer or seller of a product is strict liability. Like negligence, strict liability is a burden created by the law rather than by the parties. And, as with all torts, strict liability concerns claims of physical harm. But there is a key distinction between negligence and strict liability: in a negligence case, the injured buyer must demonstrate that the seller's conduct was unreasonable. Not so in strict liability.

In strict liability, the injured person need not prove that the defendant's conduct was unreasonable. The injured person must show only that the defendant manufactured or sold a product that was defective and that the defect caused harm. Almost all states permit such lawsuits, and most adopted the summary of strict liability provided by the Restatement (Second) of Torts §402A. Because §402A is the most frequently cited section in all of tort law, we quote it in full:

1. One who sells any product in a defective condition unreasonably dangerous to the user or consumer or to his property is subject to liability for physical harm thereby caused to the ultimate user or consumer, or to his property, if

   a. the seller is engaged in the business of selling such a product, and

   b. it is expected to and does reach the user or consumer without substantial change in the condition in which it is sold.

2. The rule stated in Subsection (1) applies although

   a. the seller has exercised all possible care in the preparation and sale of his product, and

   b. the user or consumer has not bought the product from or entered into any contractual relation with the seller.

These are the key terms in subsection (1):

- *Defective condition unreasonably dangerous to the user.* The defendant is liable only if the product is defective when it leaves his hands. There must be something wrong with the goods. If they are reasonably safe and the buyer's mishandling of the goods causes the harm, there is no strict liability. If you attempt to open a soda bottle by knocking the cap against a counter, and the glass shatters and cuts you, the manufacturer owes nothing.

  The article sold must be *more dangerous* than the ordinary consumer would expect. A carving knife can produce a lethal wound, but everyone knows that, and a sharp knife is not unreasonably dangerous. On the other hand, prescription drugs may harm in ways that neither a layperson nor a doctor would anticipate. The manufacturer *must provide adequate warnings* of any dangers that are not apparent.

- *In the business of selling.* The seller is liable only if she normally sells this kind of product. Suppose your roommate makes you a peanut butter sandwich and, while eating it, you cut your mouth on a sliver of glass that was in the jar. The peanut butter manufacturer faces strict liability, as does the grocery store where your roommate bought the goods. But your roommate is not strictly liable because he does not serve sandwiches as a business.

- *Reaches the user without substantial change.* Obviously, if your roommate put the glass in the peanut butter thinking it was funny, neither the manufacturer nor the store is liable.

And here are the important phrases in subsection (2):

- *Has exercised all possible care.* This is the heart of strict liability, which makes it a potent claim for consumers. *It is no defense that the seller used reasonable care.*

If the product is dangerously defective and injures the user, the seller is liable even if it took every precaution to design and manufacture the product safely. Suppose the peanut butter jar did in fact contain a glass sliver when it left the factory. The manufacturer proves that it uses extraordinary care in keeping foreign particles out of the jars and thoroughly inspects each container before it is shipped. The evidence is irrelevant. The manufacturer has shown that it was not negligent in packaging the food, but reasonable care is irrelevant in strict liability.

- *No contractual relation.* This means that the injured party need not have bought the goods directly from the party responsible for the defect. Suppose the manufacturer that made the peanut butter sold it to a distributor, which sold it to a wholesaler, which sold it to a grocery store, which sold it to your roommate. You may sue the manufacturer, distributor, wholesaler, and store, even though you never contracted with any of them.

Restatement (Third) and Contemporary Trends.   We saw that under traditional negligence law, a company could be found liable based on design, manufacture, or failure to warn. The same three activities can give rise to a claim of strict liability. It will normally be easier for a plaintiff to win a claim of strict liability, because she does not need to demonstrate that the manufacturer's conduct was unreasonable.

If the steering wheel on a brand new car falls off, and the driver is injured, that is a clear case of defective manufacturing, and the company will be strictly liable. Those are the easy cases. As courts have applied §402A, defective design cases have been more contentious. Suppose a vaccine that prevents serious childhood illnesses inevitably causes brain damage in a very small number of children, because of the nature of the drug. Is the manufacturer liable? What if a racing sailboat, designed only for speed, is dangerously unstable in the hands of a less experienced sailor? Is the boat's maker responsible for fatalities? Suppose an automobile made of lightweight metal uses less fuel but exposes its occupants to more serious injuries in an accident. How is a court to decide whether the design was defective? Often, these design cases also involve issues of warnings: Did drug designer diligently detail dangers to doctors? Should sailboat seller sell speedy sailboat solely to seasoned sailors?

Over the years, most courts have adopted one of two tests for design and warning cases. The first is consumer expectation. Here, a court finds the manufacturer liable for defective design if the product is less safe than a reasonable consumer would expect. If a smoke detector has a 3 percent failure rate, and the average consumer has no way of anticipating that danger, effective cautions must be included, though the design may be defective anyway. Many states have moved away from that test and now use a *risk-utility test*. Here, a court must weigh the benefits for society against the dangers that the product poses. Principal factors in the risk-utility test include:

- The *value* of the product;
- The *gravity* of the danger (how bad will the harm be);
- The *likelihood* that such danger will occur (the odds);
- The mechanical feasibility of a *safer alternative design*; and
- The *adverse consequences* of an alternative design (greater cost, different risks created).

Because of the conflicting court decisions, the American Law Institute drafted the Restatement (Third) of Torts: Product Liability, in an attempt to harmonize judicial opinions about product liability generally and design defects in particular. The new

Restatement treats manufacturing cases differently from those involving design defects and failure to warn.

- In manufacturing cases, a product is defective whenever it departs from its intended design, regardless of how much care was taken. This is the traditional standard.

- In design and warnings cases, a product is defective only when the *foreseeable* risks of harm could have been reduced by using a reasonable alternative design or warning. So-called strict liability in these cases is beginning to resemble plain old negligence. If courts adopt this new approach, it will become more difficult for plaintiffs to win a design or warning case because they will need to prove that the manufacturer should have foreseen the danger and could have done something about it.

There is no strong trend in how judges examine these cases: courts tend to pick and choose the analytic tools they use. Most still regard §402A as the basic law for all strict liability lawsuits. In design cases, many courts use the risk-utility test, quite a few still examine consumer expectation, and some permit both analyses. Most states consider the availability of alternative designs to be important, and some consider it essential. And finally, as the following case indicates, some courts employ elements of the Restatement (Third)—with plenty of disagreement.

UNIROYAL GOODRICH TIRE COMPANY V. MARTINEZ

977 S.W.2d 328
Texas Supreme Court, 1998

Facts: When Roberto Martinez, a mechanic, attempted to mount a 16-inch tire on a 16.5-inch rim (wheel), the tire exploded, causing him serious, permanent injuries. He sued Goodrich, the tire manufacturer; the Budd Company, which made the rim; and Ford Motor Company, which designed it. Budd and Ford settled out of court, and the case proceeded against Goodrich.

The tire had a conspicuous label, advising users never to mount a 16-inch tire on a 16.5-inch rim, warning of the danger of severe injury or death, and including a picture of a worker thrown into the air by an explosion. The label also urged the user never to lean or reach over the assembly while working. Martinez ignored the warnings.

Martinez admitted that the warnings were adequate but claimed that Goodrich was strictly liable for failing to use a safer "bead" design. The bead, a rubber-encased steel wire, encircles the tire and holds it to the rim. Martinez's expert testified that an alternative design, used by other tire manufacturers, would have prevented his injury. The trial court gave judgment for Martinez in the amount of $10,308,792.45, the Court of Appeals affirmed, and Goodrich appealed to the state's highest court.

Issue: When warnings are adequate, is a manufacturer still obligated to use a safer alternative design?

Excerpts from Chief Justice Phillips' Decision: This Court has adopted the products liability standard set forth in section 402A of the Restatement (Second) of Torts. A product may be unreasonably dangerous because of a defect in manufacturing, design, or marketing. To prove a design defect, a claimant must establish, among other things, that the defendant could have provided a safer alternative design. [If] there are no safer alternatives, a product is not unreasonably dangerous as a matter of law.

The newly released Restatement (Third) of Torts: Product Liability carries forward this focus on reasonable alternative design:

A broad range of factors may be considered in determining whether an alternative design is reasonable and whether its omission renders a product not reasonably safe. The factors include, among others, the magnitude and probability of the foreseeable risks of harm, the instructions and warnings accompanying

▼

the product, and the nature and strength of consumer expectations regarding the product, including expectations arising from product portrayal and marketing.

Goodrich urges this Court to depart from this standard by following certain language from Comment j of the Restatement (Second) of Torts. Comment j provides in part: "Where warning is given, the seller may reasonably assume that it will be read and heeded; and a product bearing such a warning, which is safe for use if it is followed, is not in defective condition, nor is it unreasonably dangerous." The new Restatement, however, expressly rejects the Comment j approach [and we refuse to adopt it].

The dissenting justices argue that Goodrich's warning was clear and that it could have been followed, and consequently Martinez was injured only by "[i]gnoring . . . his own good sense." Even if this were true, it is precisely because it is not at all unusual for a person to fail to follow basic warnings and instructions, that we have rejected the superseded Comment j. The jury heard firsthand how an accident can occur despite the warning label, and how a redesigned tire would have prevented that accident. The jury also heard evidence that Goodrich's competitors had incorporated the single strand programmed bead by the early 1980s, and that Goodrich itself adopted this design in 1991, a year after manufacturing the tire that injured Martinez.

The Martinezes offered evidence that their alternative design would have prevented the injury to Martinez. It is undisputed that the single strand programmed bead is more resistant to breaking in mismatch situations. Goodrich expert Tom Conner testified that in a mismatch situation the tape bead may break at 60 psi, while a single strand bead will not break until at least 130 psi. Goodrich representative Stanley Lew testified that if the tire inflated by Martinez had a single strand bead it would not have exploded. Both Conner and Lew testified that they would prefer a tire inflated by their loved one to have a single strand bead.

For the foregoing reasons, we affirm the judgment of the court of appeals. [Affirmed]

Excerpts from the Dissenting Opinion of Justice Hecht: The Uniroyal Goodrich Tire Company, which made the tire Martinez was using, chose to put a prominent, pictographic label on it, which Martinez actually saw but did not heed. Had he done so, he would not have been injured. In fact, according to the record, only one other person has ever claimed to have been injured attempting to mount a 160 tire with a warning label like Goodrich's on a 16.50 wheel, although thousands of labeled tires and more than thirty million 16.5 wheels have been manufactured in the past two decades.

[The] Court holds that a product can be found to be defective whenever it could be more safely designed without substantially impairing its utility. This is not, and should not be, the law. As the *Restatement (Third) of Torts: Product Liability* advises, a "broad range of factors" besides the utility of a reasonable alternate design should be considered in determining whether its use is necessary to keep the product reasonably safe, including "the magnitude and probability of the foreseeable risks of harm [and] the instructions and warnings accompanying the product." When the undisputed evidence is that the magnitude and probability of a risk are low, an alternative design could reduce but not eliminate that risk, and the instructions and warnings given do eliminate the risk, the product should be determined not to be defective as a matter of law. ∎

ECONOMICS *& the* LAW	Smoking is expensive. In fact, virtually all state governments concluded that tobacco use causes lung cancer, emphysema, heart disease, and other illnesses, and that these ailments are very expensive to treat. The states filed suit against the tobacco industry, which settled most of the cases for a total of about $206 *billion*, to be paid gradually between the years 2000 and 2025. That is a lot of money, even for a profitable industry. (To find out how much your state will receive, go to http://tobaccowars.com; click first on "Legal," and then on "Tobacco Index.") Ironically, one economist claims that the settlements make little money sense, because cigarettes are self-financing. This expert concedes that tobacco use causes expensive illnesses,

yet argues that the increased costs are offset by savings due to earlier mortality! Because smokers die younger than others, states pay less money for nursing homes and pensions. These savings more than offset the increased medical costs of smoking.

If that is correct, then why would the tobacco industry agree to the pricey settlements? This economist suggests that a tobacco industry defense based on earlier mortality would be very risky to make in court. Jurors might find the argument so offensive that they would impose even higher punitive damages.[16] ◆

NEGOTIABLE INSTRUMENTS

The first part of this chapter has covered Articles 2 and 2A of the UCC, dealing with contracts and product liability. Articles 3 and 4 of the Code regulate negotiable instruments.[17] The second half of the chapter focuses on this important topic.

Commercial Paper

In early human history, people lived on whatever they could hunt, grow, or make for themselves. Over time, people improved their standard of living by bartering for goods and services they could not make themselves. But traders needed a method for keeping account of who owed how much to whom. The first currencies—gold and silver—had two disadvantages: they were easy to steal and heavy to carry. Paper currency solved the weight problem but was even easier to steal than gold. As a result, money had to be kept in a safe place, and banks developed to meet that need. However, money in a vault is not very useful unless it can be readily spent. Society needed a system for transferring paper funds easily. Commercial paper is that system. The UCC's goal is to facilitate commerce by transforming these pieces of paper into something almost as easily transferable and reliable as money. (For more on the history of money, see http://www.ex.ac.uk/~RDavies/arian/llyfr.html.)

Types of Negotiable Instruments

There are two kinds of commercial paper: negotiable and non-negotiable instruments. Article 3 of the Code covers only negotiable instruments; non-negotiable instruments are governed by ordinary contract law. There are also two categories of negotiable instruments: notes and drafts.

A **note** (also called a **promissory note**) is your promise that you will pay money. A promissory note is used in virtually every loan transaction, whether the borrower is buying a multimillion dollar company or a TV set. For example, when you borrow money from Aunt Leila to buy a car, you will sign a note promising to repay the money. You are the **maker** because you are the one who has made the promise. Aunt Leila is the **payee** because she expects to be paid. (The Web site http://www.legaldocs.com/ provides a sample promissory note with fill-in blanks.)

A **draft** is an order directing someone else to pay money for you. A **check** is the most common form of a draft—it is an order telling a bank to pay money. In a draft,

---

[16] W. Kip Viscusi, "The Governmental Composition of the Insurance Costs of Smoking," *Journal of Law and Economics*, 1999, vol. 42, p. 575.

[17] In 2002, the Uniform Law Commissioners approved a revision of Articles 3 and 4 that deals with changing technology for checks and other paper instruments. So far, only five states have passed this new version. Therefore, this chapter is based on the older version. (A list of states that have passed the new version is available at http://www.nccusl.org.)

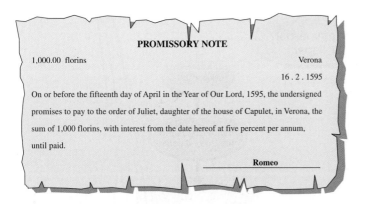

PROMISSORY NOTE

1,000.00 florins
Verona
16 . 2 . 1595

On or before the fifteenth day of April in the Year of Our Lord, 1595, the undersigned promises to pay to the order of Juliet, daughter of the house of Capulet, in Verona, the sum of 1,000 florins, with interest from the date hereof at five percent per annum, until paid.

Romeo

In this note, Romeo is the maker and Juliet is the payee.

three people are involved: the **drawer** orders the **drawee** to pay money to the **payee.** Now before you slam the book shut in despair, let us sort out the players. Suppose that Maria Sharapova wins the River Oaks Club Open. River Oaks writes her a check for $500,000. This check is simply an order by River Oaks (the drawer) to its bank (the drawee) to pay money to Sharapova (the payee). The terms make sense if you remember that, when you take money out of your account, you *draw* it out. Therefore, when you write a check, you are the draw*er* and the bank is the draw*ee*. The person to whom you make out the check is being paid, so she is called the pay*ee*.

The following table illustrates the difference between notes and drafts. Even courts sometimes confuse the terms *drawer* (the person who signs a check) and *maker* (someone who signs a promissory note). *Issuer* is an all-purpose term that means both maker and drawer.

	Who Pays	Who Plays
Note	You make a promise that you will pay.	Two people are involved: maker and payee.
Draft	You order someone else to pay.	Three people are involved: drawer, drawee, and payee.

The Fundamental "Rule" of Commercial Paper

The possessor of a piece of commercial paper has an unconditional right to be paid, as long as (1) the paper is *negotiable;* (2) it has been *negotiated* to the possessor; (3) the possessor is a *holder in due course;* and (4) the issuer cannot claim a valid defense.

Negotiability

To work as a substitute for money, commercial paper must be freely transferable in the marketplace, just as money is. In other words, it must be *negotiable*.

The possessor of *non*-negotiable commercial paper has the same rights— no more, no less—as the person who made the original contract. With non-negotiable commercial paper, the transferee's rights are *conditional* because they depend upon the rights of the original party to the contract. If, for some reason, the original party loses his right to be paid, so does the transferee. The value of non-negotiable commercial paper is greatly reduced because the transferee cannot be absolutely sure what his rights are or whether he will be paid at all.

Suppose that Krystal buys a used car from the Trustie Car Lot for her business, Krystal Rocks. She cannot afford to pay the full $15,000 right now, but she is willing to sign a note promising to pay later. As long as Trustie keeps the note, Krystal's obligation to pay is contingent upon the validity of the underlying contract. If, for example, the car is defective, then Krystal might not be liable to Trustie for the full amount of the note. Trustie, however, does not want to keep the note. He needs the cash *now*

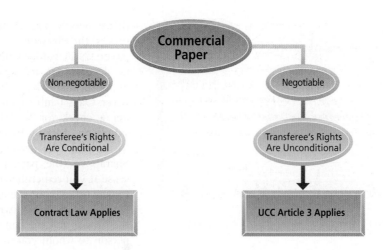

Exhibit 12.1

so that he can buy more cars to sell to other customers. Reggie's Finance Co. is happy to buy Krystal's promissory note from Trustie, but the price Reggie is willing to pay depends upon whether her note is negotiable.

If Krystal's promissory note is non-negotiable, Reggie gets exactly the same rights that Trustie had. As the saying goes, he steps into Trustie's shoes. Suppose that Trustie tampered with the odometer and, as a result, Krystal's car is worth only $12,000. If, under contract law, she owes Trustie only $12,000, then that is all she has to pay Reggie, even though the note *says* $15,000.

The possessor of *negotiable* commercial paper has *more* rights than the person who made the original contract. With negotiable commercial paper, the transferee's rights are *unconditional*. He is entitled to be paid the full amount of the note, regardless of the relationship between the original parties. If Krystal's promissory note is a negotiable instrument, she must pay the full amount to whoever has possession of it, no matter what complaints she might have against Trustie.

Exhibit 12.1 illustrates the difference between negotiable and non-negotiable commercial paper.

Because negotiable instruments are more valuable than non-negotiable ones, it is important for buyers and sellers to be able to tell, easily and accurately, if an instrument is indeed negotiable. To be negotiable:

1. **The instrument must be in *writing*.**

2. **The instrument must be *signed* by the maker or drawer.**

3. **The instrument must contain an *unconditional promise* or *order to pay*.** If Krystal's promissory note says, "I will pay $15,000 as long as the car is still in working order," it is not negotiable because it is making a conditional promise. The instrument must also contain a promise or order to pay. It is not enough simply to say, "Krystal owes Trustie $15,000." She has to indicate that she owes the money and also that she intends to pay it. "Krystal promises to pay Trustie $15,000" would work.

4. **The instrument must state a *definite amount* of money.** "I promise to pay Trustie one-third of my profits this year" would not work, because the amount is unclear. If Krystal's note says, "I promise to pay $15,000 worth of diamonds," it is not negotiable because it does not state a definite amount of *money*.

5. **The instrument must be payable on *demand* or at a *definite time*.** A demand instrument is one that must be paid whenever the holder requests payment. If an instrument is undated, it is treated as a demand instrument and is negotiable. An instrument can be negotiable even if it will not be paid until some time in the future, provided that the payment date can be determined when the document is made. A graduate of a well-known prep school wrote a generous check to his alma mater, but for payment date he put, "The day the headmaster is fired." This check is not negotiable because it is neither payable on demand nor at a definite time.

6. **The instrument must be payable to *order* or to *bearer*. Order paper** must include the words "Pay to the order of" someone. By including the word "order," the maker is indicating that the instrument is not limited to only one person. "Pay to the order of Trustie Car Lot" means that the money will be paid to Trustie *or to anyone Trustie designates*. If the note is made out "To bearer," it is **bearer paper** and can be redeemed by *any* holder in due course.

The rules for checks are different from other negotiable instruments. All checks are, by definition, negotiable. Most checks are preprinted with the words "Pay to the order of," but sometimes people inadvertently cross out "order of." Even so, the check is still negotiable. Checks are frequently received by consumers who, sadly, have not completed a course on business law. The drafters of the UCC did not think it fair to penalize them when the drawer of the check was the one who made the mistake.

cyberLaw

An instrument must be *signed* by the maker or drawer. This sounds straightforward, but what does it mean to sign a note or draft? Many people, for example, pay bills online. How do they sign an online check? How does their bank know the signature is valid? Many states now grant digital signatures the same legal status under the UCC as a traditional paper signature (which is called a "wet" signature).[18] A computer signature does not look like handwriting; instead, it is a unique series of letters and numbers in code. A digital signature can actually be safer than the traditional wet signature. If the digital document is dishonestly altered, the sender and recipient can tell. ◆

In the following case, the *intent* of the parties is clear. But is the note enforceable? You be the judge.

YOU BE THE JUDGE

YYY CORPORATION V. GAZDA

145 N.H. 53; 761 A.2d 395; 2000 N.H. LEXIS 17
Supreme Court of New Hampshire, 2000

Facts: Craig Krisel and William Volante borrowed $1,360,000 from United Federal Bank to buy two apartment buildings in Rochester, New York. They gave the bank a promissory note in this amount.

Krisel and Volante then sold the apartment buildings to Richard and Everette Gazda. The Gazdas agreed to assume liability on the note. The Gazdas executed the following agreement with the bank:

Witness that: [That is the way lawyers sometimes write agreements.]

▼

---

[18] The federal Electronic Signatures in Global and National Commerce Act expanded the definition of electronic signature to include "biometric" identifications such as fingerprints, retina scans, and voiceprints. However, the federal statute does not apply to UCC Articles 3 and 4.

WHEREAS, the Bank loaned to Krisel and Volante the sum of $1,360,000.00; and

WHEREAS, by mutual agreement the Gazdas and Bank wish to revise the terms of payment of the note signed by Krisel and Volante,

NOW IT IS HEREBY AGREED THAT;

(1) the rate of interest on the unpaid balance shall be 10.00 percent per annum.

(2) The Gazdas agree to make and the Bank agrees to accept principal and interest payments in the amount of $12,217.91. The Gazdas agree that on March 1, 2012, the entire balance due under the note shall be due and payable at the option of the Bank.

This agreement shall not otherwise waive any of the terms of the original note signed by Krisel and Volante.

United Federal sold the note to another bank. Ultimately, the note ended up in the hands of the YYY Corporation. When the Gazdas failed to pay the sums due under the note, YYY sued to enforce it.

You Be the Judge: **Was the note that the Gazdas signed a negotiable instrument?**

Argument for the Gazdas: To be a negotiable instrument, a note must

- Contain an unconditional promise or order to pay; and
- Be payable to order or bearer.

This note is not a negotiable instrument because it does not contain an unconditional promise to pay. The words "we promise to pay" are never stated. Nor is the note payable to order or bearer.

Argument for YYY: The note provides that the "Gazdas agree to make and the Bank agrees to accept principal and interest payments in the amount of $12,217.91. The Gazdas agree that on March 1, 2012 the entire balance due under the note shall be due and payable. . . ." That is an unconditional promise to pay. What else could those words mean?

The agreement also provided that it did not "waive any of the terms of the original note." That note was payable to order or bearer and therefore so is this note.

The Gazdas borrowed this money and now they do not want to repay it. A finding for the Gazdas would be a serious miscarriage of justice. ●

Public Policy

If the system of negotiable instruments is to work, buyers and sellers must be able to tell, easily and accurately, whether an instrument is indeed negotiable. It is also essential—and fair—that lenders be repaid what they are owed. Both these interests are important to commerce. In this case, which interest is most crucial? ◆

Negotiation

Negotiation means that an instrument has been transferred to the holder by someone *other than the issuer*. If the issuer has transferred the instrument to the holder, then it has not been negotiated and the issuer can refuse to pay the holder if there was some flaw in the underlying contract. Thus, if Jake gives Madison a promissory note for $2,000 in payment for a new computer, but the computer crashes and burns the first week, Jake has the right to refuse to pay the note. Jake was the issuer and the note was not negotiated. But if, before the computer self-destructs, Madison indorses and transfers the note to Kayla, then Jake is liable to Kayla for the full amount of the note, regardless of his claims against Madison.

To be negotiated, order paper must first be *indorsed* and then *delivered* to the transferee. Bearer paper must simply be *delivered* to the transferee; no indorsement is required.[19]

---

[19] The UCC spells the word "indorsed." Outside the UCC, the word is more commonly spelled "endorsed."

An indorsement is the signature of the payee. Tess writes a rent check for $475 to her landlord, Larnell. If Larnell signs the back of the check and delivers it to Patty, he has met the two requirements for negotiating order paper: indorsement and delivery. If Larnell delivers the check to Patty but forgets to sign it, the check has not been indorsed and therefore cannot be negotiated—it has no value to Patty.

Holder in Due Course

A holder in due course has an automatic right to receive payment for a negotiable instrument (unless the issuer can claim a valid defense). If the possessor of an instrument is not a holder in due course, then his right to payment depends upon the relationship between the issuer and payee. He inherits whatever claims and defenses arise out of that contract. Clearly, then, holder in due course status dramatically increases the value of an instrument because it enhances the probability of being paid.

Requirements for Being a Holder in Due Course. Under §3-302 of the UCC, a holder in due course is a *holder* who has given value for the instrument, in *good faith, without notice* of outstanding claims or other defects.

Holder. For order paper, a **holder** is anyone in possession of the instrument if it is payable to or indorsed to her. For bearer paper, a **holder** is anyone in possession. Tristesse gives Felix a check payable to him. Because Felix owes his mother money, he indorses the check and delivers it to her. This is a valid negotiation because Felix has both indorsed the check (which is order paper) and delivered it. Therefore, Felix's mother is a holder.

Value. A holder in due course must give value for an instrument. **Value** means that the holder has *already* done something in exchange for the instrument. Felix's mother has already loaned him money, so she has given value.

Good Faith. There are two tests to determine if a holder acquired an instrument in good faith. The holder must meet *both* these tests:

- **Subjective Test.** Did the holder *believe* the transaction was honest in fact?

- **Objective Test.** Did the transaction *appear* to be commercially reasonable?

Felix persuades his elderly neighbor, Faith, that he has invented a fabulous beauty cream guaranteed to remove wrinkles. She gives him a $10,000 promissory note, payable in 90 days, in return for exclusive sales rights in Pittsburgh. Felix sells the note to his old friend Griffin for $2,000. Felix never delivers the sales samples to Faith. When Griffin presents the note to Faith, she refuses to pay on the grounds that Griffin is not a holder in due course. She contends that he did not buy the note in good faith.

Griffin fails both tests. Any friend of Felix knows he is not trustworthy, especially when presenting a promissory note signed by an elderly neighbor. Griffin did not believe the transaction was honest in fact. Also, $10,000 notes are not usually discounted to $2,000; $9,000 would be more normal. This transaction is not commercially reasonable, and Griffin should have realized immediately that Felix was up to no good.

Notice of Outstanding Claims or Other Defects. In certain circumstances, a holder is on notice that an instrument has an outstanding claim or other defect:

1. **The instrument is overdue.** An instrument is overdue the day after its due date. At that point, the recipient ought to wonder why no one has bothered to collect the money owed. A check is overdue 90 days after its date. Any other demand instrument is overdue (1) the day after a request for payment is made or (2) a reasonable time after the instrument was issued.

2. **The instrument is dishonored.** To dishonor an instrument is to refuse to pay it. For example, once a check has been stamped "Insufficient Funds" by the bank, it has been dishonored, and no one who obtains it afterward can be a holder in due course.

3. **The instrument is altered, forged, or incomplete.** Anyone who knows that an instrument has been altered or forged cannot be a holder in due course. Suppose Joe wrote a check to Tony for $200. While showing the check to Liza, Tony cackles to himself and says, "Can you believe what that goof did? Look, he left the line blank after the words 'two hundred.'" Taking his pen out with a flourish, Tony changes the zeroes to nines and adds the words "ninety-nine." He then indorses the check over to Liza, who is definitely not a holder in due course.

4. **The holder has notice of certain claims or disputes.** No one can qualify as a holder in due course if she is on notice that (1) someone else has a claim to the instrument or (2) there is a dispute between the original parties to the instrument. Matt hires Sheila to put aluminum siding on his house. In payment, he gives her a $15,000 promissory note with the due date left blank. They agree that the note will not be due until 60 days after completion of the work. Despite the agreement, Sheila fills in the date immediately and sells the note to Rupert at American Finance Corp., who has bought many similar notes from Sheila. Rupert knows that the note is not supposed to be due until after the work is finished. Usually, before he buys a note from her, he demands a signed document from the home owner certifying that the work is complete. Also, he lives near Matt and can see that Matt's house is only half finished. Rupert is not a holder in due course because he has reason to suspect there is a dispute between Sheila and Matt.

Defenses against a Holder in Due Course. Negotiable instruments are meant to be a close substitute for money, and, as a general rule, holders expect to be paid. **However, the issuer of a negotiable instrument is not required to pay if:**

1. His signature on the instrument was forged.

2. After signing the instrument, his debts were discharged in bankruptcy.

3. He was a minor at the time he signed the instrument.

4. The amount of the instrument was altered after he signed it. (Although, if he left the instrument blank, he is liable for any amounts later filled in.)

5. He signed the instrument under duress, while mentally incapacitated, or as part of an illegal transaction.

6. He was tricked into signing the instrument without knowing what it was and without any reasonable way to find out.

Consumer Exception

In the eighteenth and nineteenth centuries, negotiable instruments often circulated through several hands. The business community treated them as money. The concept of holder in due course was essential because the instruments had little use if they could not be transferred for value. In the modern banking system, however, instruments are much less likely to circulate. Currently, the most common use for negotiable instruments is in consumer transactions. A consumer pays for a refrigerator by giving the store a promissory note. The store promptly sells the note to a finance company. Even if the refrigerator is defective, under Article 3 the consumer must pay full value on the note because the finance company is a holder in due course.

Some commentators have argued that the concept of holder in due course no longer serves a useful purpose and that it should be eliminated once and for all (and with it Article 3 of the UCC). No state has yet taken such a dramatic step. Instead,

```
            PROMISSORY NOTE


$500.00                    September 5, 1950


On or before 60 days after date, I promise to pay $500 to

the order of Soames for value received.


                           Irene
    _____
```

The holder of this note should realize that there may be a problem.

some states require promissory notes given by a consumer to carry the words "consumer paper." Notes with this legend are non-negotiable.

Meanwhile, the Federal Trade Commission (FTC) has special rules for consumer credit contracts. A consumer credit contract is one in which a consumer borrows money from a lender to purchase goods and services from a seller who is affiliated with the lender. If Sears loans money to Gerald to buy a big-screen TV at Sears, that is a consumer credit contract. It is not a consumer credit contract if Gerald borrows money from his cousin Vinnie to buy the TV from Sears. The FTC requires all promissory notes in consumer credit contracts to contain the following language:

NOTICE
ANY HOLDER OF THIS CONSUMER CREDIT CONTRACT IS SUBJECT TO ALL CLAIMS AND DEFENSES WHICH THE DEBTOR COULD ASSERT AGAINST THE SELLER OF GOODS OR SERVICES OBTAINED WITH THE PROCEEDS HEREOF.

Under §3-106(d) of the UCC, no one can be a holder in due course of an instrument with this language. If the language is omitted from a consumer note, it is possible to be a holder in due course, but the seller can be punished by a fine of up to $10,000.

In the following case, the plaintiff borrowed money from Sterling to pay Mayflower. The FTC rule applied because the two companies were "affiliated."

SCOTT V. MAYFLOWER HOME IMPROVEMENT CORP.

363 N.J. Super. 145; 831 A.2d 564; 2001 N.J. Super. LEXIS 524
Superior Court of New Jersey, 2001

Facts: Mary Johnson signed a contract with Mayflower Home Improvement Corporation for repair work on her home. The contract specified a fee of $25,900. Later, Mayflower arranged for Johnson to pay for this work by borrowing money from Sterling Resources. In the note she signed with Sterling, the price was unconscionably high—$50,108.60—and so was the interest rate—17.98 percent.

Johnson alleges that Mayflower was running a scam. It hired unlicensed salespeople who targeted minority neighborhoods. The contracts prepared by the salespeople specified the work in general terms but omitted the name, make, quality, and model of the products and materials to be used. The contracts did not specify the interest rate or the total cost. The contractor's work was done in a shoddy or incomplete manner often using poor-quality materials.

Sterling routinely loaned money to Mayflower customers. The interest rates on these loans were between 15 percent and 19 percent. Sterling then ▼

sold the loans to banks and other financial institutions (the Lender). BankAtlantic purchased from Sterling more than $60 million worth of consumer loans in a three-year period.

When Johnson failed to make the payments due on the note, the Lender sued her. It moved for summary judgment against Johnson on the grounds that, as a holder in due course, it was entitled to enforce the note regardless of her claims against Mayflower or Sterling. She responded that, under the FTC consumer exception rule, the Lender was not a holder in due course. Therefore, the Lender was subject to whatever defenses she had against Sterling or Mayflower.

Issue: Was the Lender a holder in due course?

Excerpts from Justice Humphrey's Decision:
The assignees argue that they are holders in due course of negotiable instruments and therefore immune from the claims of the [defendant]. In recent years a large body of law has developed restricting the use of the holder in due course doctrine in consumer transactions. The FTC spearheaded that new body of law some 25 years ago by adopting the FTC Holder Rule.

[T]he FTC concluded that unethical merchants and their financiers were using the venerable Holder in Due Course doctrine from the law of negotiable instruments to victimize thousands of innocent consumers. Inner-city stores were selling shoddy furniture, fly-by-night contractors were promising to install aluminum siding that never appeared, the proverbial used-car dealers were hawking lemons, and countless other shady characters were operating in similar fashion in scores of different fields. In each of these cases, the defrauded consumer was saddled with the bill when a holder in due course demanded payment.

The note [that Sterling assigned had] the FTC Holder notice conspicuously printed thereon. Consequently, the assignees were on notice that the FTC Holder Rule was applicable to the notes that they were purchasing from Sterling. The FTC Holder Rule, is therefore, applicable to the consumer obligations here. The Holder in Due Course doctrine will not immunize the financial institutions from the claims of the [plaintiff].

The FTC Holder Rule is designed to require the assignee of a consumer contract to step into the shoes of the seller with respect to the claims and defenses of the consumer. If the seller's shoes are too tight a fit, then the assignee need not purchase the consumer contract. The creditor faced with the loss of the holder in due course defense against the victimized consumer has a variety of acceptable options, e.g., buy the commercial paper with some type of recourse, or protect against losses by raising the interest rate or purchase insurance.

[Summary judgment is denied for the plaintiff, but granted for the defendant.] ■

Public Policy

Someone—either the plaintiff or the defendant—will lose money in this case. Although one could argue that the buyer should beware, that Mary Johnson should not have signed such an unfair contract, the court decided that the Lender was in a better position to protect itself than she was. What does the court suggest that the Lender should have done? Is it reasonable to expect the Lender to take such steps? Why is it important to protect Mary Johnson? ◆

Chapter Conclusion

The development of the UCC was an enormous and ambitious undertaking. Its goal was to facilitate the free flow of commerce across this large nation. By any measure, the UCC has been a success. Each and every day, thousands of businesspeople comply with the UCC as they sign contracts, write checks, and deliver promissory notes. It is worth remembering, however, that the terms of the UCC are precise and that failure to comply with these exacting provisions can lead to unfortunate consequences. In some ways, the UCC is like a marine drill instructor: rigid, but predictable if you follow the rules.

Chapter Review

1. The Code is designed to modernize commercial law and make it uniform throughout the country. Article 2 applies to the sale of goods.

2. A merchant is someone who routinely deals in the particular goods involved, or who appears to have special knowledge or skill in those goods, or who uses agents with special knowledge or skill.

3. UCC §2-204 permits the parties to form a contract in any manner that shows agreement.

4. For the sale of goods worth $500 or more, UCC §2-201 requires some writing that indicates an agreement.

5. A merchant who receives a signed memo confirming an oral contract may become liable if he fails to object within 10 days.

6. UCC §2-207 governs an acceptance that does not "mirror" the offer. *Additional* terms usually become part of the contract. *Different* terms contradict the offer, and are generally replaced by the Code's own gap-filler terms.

7. An injured seller may resell the goods and obtain the difference between the contract and resale prices. An injured buyer may buy substitute goods and obtain the difference between the contract and cover prices.

8. Product liability may arise in various ways:

   - A party may create an express warranty with words or actions. The Code may *imply* a warranty of merchantability or fitness for a particular purpose.

   - A seller will be liable if her conduct is not that of a reasonable person.

   - A seller may be strictly liable for a defective product that reaches the user without substantial change.

9. The possessor of non-negotiable commercial paper has the same rights—no more, no less—as the person who made the original contract. The possessor of negotiable commercial paper has more rights than the person who made the original contract.

10. The possessor of a piece of commercial paper has an unconditional right to be paid, as long as:

    - The paper is negotiable;

    - It has been negotiated to the possessor;

    - The possessor is a holder in due course; and

    - The issuer cannot claim a valid defense.

11. To be negotiable, an instrument must:

    - Be in writing;

    - Be signed by the maker or drawer;

    - Contain an unconditional promise or order to pay;

    - State a definite amount of money;

    - Be payable on demand or at a definite time; and

    - Be payable to order or to bearer.

12. To be negotiated, order paper must first be indorsed and then delivered to the transferee. Bearer paper must simply be delivered to the transferee; no indorsement is required.

13. A holder in due course is a holder who has given value for the instrument, in good faith, without notice of outstanding claims or other defects.

14. The Federal Trade Commission (FTC) requires all promissory notes in consumer credit contracts to contain language preventing any subsequent holder from being a holder in due course.

Practice Test

1. Nina owns a used car lot. She signs and sends a fax to Seth, a used car wholesaler who has a huge lot of cars in the same city. The fax says, "Confirming our agrmt—I pick any 15 cars fr yr lot—30% below blue book." Seth reads the fax, laughs, and throws it away. Two weeks later, Nina arrives and demands to purchase 15 of Seth's cars. Is he obligated to sell?

2. **YOU BE THE JUDGE** WRITING PROBLEM
United Technologies advertised a used Beechcraft Baron airplane for sale in an aviation journal. Attorney Thompson Comerford spoke with a United agent who described the plane as "excellently maintained" and said it had been operated "under §135 flight regulations," meaning the plane had been subject to airworthiness inspections every 100 hours. Comerford arrived at a Dallas airport to pick up the plane, where he paid $80,000 for it. He signed a sales agreement stating that the plane was sold "as is" and that there were "no representations or warranties, express or implied, including the condition of the aircraft, its merchantability or its fitness for any particular purpose." Comerford attempted to fly the plane home but immediately experienced problems with its brakes, steering, ability to climb, and performance while cruising. (Otherwise it was fine.) He sued, claiming breach of express and implied warranties. Did United Technologies breach express or implied warranties? **Argument for Comerford:** United described the airplane as "excellently maintained," knowing that Mr. Comerford would rely. The company should not be allowed to say one thing and put the opposite in writing. **Argument for United Technologies:** Comerford is a lawyer, and we assume he can read. The contract clearly stated that the plane was sold as is. There were no warranties.

3. To satisfy the UCC statute of frauds regarding the sale of goods, which of the following must generally be in writing?

   a. Designation of the parties as buyer and seller

   b. Delivery terms

   c. Quantity of the goods

   d. Warranties to be made

4. **ETHICS** Texaco, Inc., and other oil companies sold mineral spirits in bulk to distributors, which then resold to retailers. Mineral spirits are used for cleaning and are harmful or fatal if swallowed. Texaco allegedly knew that the retailers, such as hardware stores, frequently packaged the mineral spirits (illegally) in used half-gallon milk containers and sold them to consumers, often with no warnings on the packages. David Hunnings, age 21 months, found a milk container in his home, swallowed the mineral spirits, and died. The Hunningses sued Texaco in negligence. The trial court dismissed the complaint, and the Hunningses appealed. What is the legal standard in a negligence case? Have the plaintiffs made out a valid case of negligence? Assume that Texaco knew about the repackaging and the grave risk but continued to sell in bulk because doing so was profitable. (If the plaintiffs cannot prove those facts, they will lose even if they do get to a jury.) Would that make you angry? Should the case go to a jury? Or did the fault still lie with the retailer and/or the parents?

5. **CPA QUESTION** Which of the following factors is least important in determining whether a manufacturer is strictly liable in tort for a defective product?

   a. The negligence of the manufacturer

   b. The contributory negligence of the plaintiff

   c. Modifications to the product by the wholesaler

   d. Whether the product caused injuries

6. Lewis River Golf, Inc., grew and sold sod. It bought seed from defendant, O. M. Scott & Sons, under an express warranty. But the sod grown from the Scott seeds developed weeds, a breach of Scott's warranty. Several of Lewis River's customers sued, unhappy with the weeds in their grass. Lewis River lost most of its customers, cut back its production from 275 acres to 45 acres, and destroyed all remaining sod grown from Scott's seeds. Eventually, Lewis River sold its business at a large loss. A jury awarded Lewis River $1,026,800, largely for lost profits and loss of goodwill. Scott appealed, claiming that a plaintiff may not recover for lost profits and goodwill. Comment.

7. Gary Culver, a farmer in Missouri, was having financial problems. He agreed to let Nasib Ed Kalliel assume control of the farm's finances. After a few months, Culver urgently asked Kalliel for money. One week later, $30,000 was wire-transferred to Culver from the Rexford State Bank. Culver thought that Kalliel would be responsible for repaying this sum. A man who worked for Kalliel stopped Culver on the street and asked him to sign a receipt for the $30,000. Culver signed without intending to commit himself to repaying the money. In fact, the document

Culver signed was a blank promissory note, payable to Rexford. Someone later filled in the blanks, putting in $50,000 instead of $30,000. Kalliel had received $50,000 before transferring $30,000 to Culver. Is Culver liable on the note?

8. **CPA QUESTION** In order to negotiate bearer paper, one must:

   a. Indorse the paper

   b. Indorse and deliver the paper with consideration

   c. Deliver the paper

   d. Deliver and indorse the paper

9. Gina and Douglas Felde purchased a Dodge Daytona with a 70,000-mile warranty. (Dodge is a division of Chrysler.) They signed a loan contract with the dealer to pay for the car in 48 monthly installments of $250. The dealer sold the contract to the Chrysler Credit Corp. Soon, the Feldes complained that the car had developed a tendency to accelerate abruptly and without warning. Neither of two Dodge dealers was able to correct the problem. The Feldes filed suit against Chrysler Credit Corp., but the company refused to rescind the loan contract. The company argued that, as a holder in due course on the note, it was entitled to be paid regardless of any defects in the car. How would you decide this case if you were the judge?

10. **ETHICS** S. J. Littlegreen owned the Lookout Mountain Hotel. In financial trouble, he put the hotel on the market at a price of $850,000. C. Abbott Gardner was his real estate agent. To obtain more time to sell, Littlegreen decided to refinance his debt. Mr. Rupe agreed to lend Littlegreen $300,000. When this loan was ready for closing, Gardner informed Littlegreen that he expected a commission of 5 percent of the amount of the loan, or $15,000. Gardner threatened to block the loan if his demands were not met. Littlegreen needed the proceeds of the loan badly, so he agreed to give Gardner $4,000 in cash and a promissory note for $11,000. On what grounds might Littlegreen claim that the note is invalid? Would this be a valid defense? Even if Gardner was in the right legally, was he in the right ethically? Would he like everyone in town to know that he had squeezed Littlegreen in this way? How would he have felt if he had been in Littlegreen's position? Does might make right?

11. Catherine Wagner suffered serious physical injuries in an automobile accident and became acutely depressed as a result. One morning, she received a check for $17,400 in settlement of her claims arising out of the accident. She indorsed the check and placed it on the kitchen table. She then called Robert Scherer, her long-time roommate, to tell him the check had arrived. That afternoon, she jumped from the roof of her apartment building, killing herself. The police found the check and a note from her, stating that she was giving it to Scherer. Had Wagner negotiated the check to Scherer?

12. **ROLE REVERSAL** Write a multiple-choice question that contrasts the common-law rules of contract formation with those of UCC §2-204.

13. **ROLE REVERSAL** Write a multiple-choice question that concerns a holder in due course.

Internet Research Problem

Look at http://www.insure.com/auto/. Which cars are safer than average? Less safe? How important is auto safety to you? Are you willing to pay more for a safe car? Who should be the final judge of auto safety: auto companies, insurance companies, juries, government regulators, or consumers?

Go to http://www.legaldocs.com and fill in the blanks of a promissory note. Who is the maker, and who is the payee of your note? Did you create a demand note?

You can find further practice problems at academic.cengage.com/blaw/beatty.

Secured Transactions and Bankruptcy

© JAMES GRITZ/PHOTODISC/GETTY IMAGES

Dear Help-for-All:

Somebody must be crazy. When I got out of school, I paid $18,000 for a used Lexus. I made every payment for over two years. I shelled out over 9,000 bucks for that car. Then I got laid off through no fault of my own. I missed a few payments, and the bank repossessed the car. They auctioned off the Lexus. Now the bank's lawyer phones and says I'm still liable for over $5,000. I owe money for a car I can't drive anymore? If they say I really have to pay all that money, I'm heading straight for bankruptcy court.

Signed,

Still Sane, I Hope

Dear Still Sane,

I am sympathetic, but unfortunately the bank is entitled to its money. When you bought the car, you signed two documents: a note, in which you promised to pay the full balance owed, and a security agreement, which said that if you stopped making payments, the bank could repossess the vehicle and sell it.

There are two problems. First, even after two years of writing checks, you might still have owed about $10,000 (because of interest). Second, cars depreciate quickly. Your $18,000 vehicle probably had a market value of about $8,000 30 months later. The security agreement allowed the bank to sell the Lexus at auction, where prices are still lower. Your car evidently fetched about $5,000. That leaves a deficiency of $5,000—for which you are legally responsible, regardless of who is driving the car. Bankruptcy law can indeed provide important relief, though the process is not so easy nor the results so absolute as many people think.

Sorry,

Help-for-Almost-All ∎

SECURED TRANSACTIONS AND BANKRUPTCY: INTRODUCTION[1]

We can sympathize with "Still Sane," but the bank is entitled to its money. The buyer and the bank had entered into a secured transaction, meaning that one party gave credit to another, insisting on full repayment *and* the right to seize certain property if the debt went unpaid.

It is essential to understand the basics of this law because we live and work in a world economy based solidly—or shakily—on credit. An equally important and closely related topic is bankruptcy law. A debtor unable to pay his bills may end up in bankruptcy court, along with a host of creditors clamoring to be paid. We will examine major issues of bankruptcy law in the second half of this chapter, but we begin by looking at secured transactions.

Article 9 of the Uniform Commercial Code (UCC) governs secured transactions in personal property. Article 9 employs terms not used elsewhere, so we must lead off with some definitions:

- **Fixtures** are goods that have become attached to real estate. For example, heating ducts are *goods* when a company manufactures them, but they become *fixtures* when installed in a house.

- **Security interest** means an interest in personal property or fixtures that secure the performance of some *obligation*. If an automobile dealer sells you a new car on credit and retains a security interest, it means she is keeping legal rights *in your car*, including the right to drive it away if you fall behind in your payments. Usually, the obligation is to pay money, such the money due on the new car, though occasionally the obligation is to perform some other action.

- **Secured party** is the person or company that holds the security interest. The automobile dealer who sells you a car on credit is the secured party.

- **Collateral** is the property subject to a security interest. When a dealer sells you a new car and keeps a security interest, the vehicle is the collateral.

- **Debtor and obligor.** For our purposes, **debtor** refers to a person who has some original ownership interest in the collateral. If Alice borrows money from a bank and uses her Mercedes as collateral, she is the debtor because she owns the car. **Obligor** means a person who must repay money or perform some other task.

  The obligor and debtor are generally the same person but not always. When Alice borrows money from a bank and uses her Mercedes as collateral, she is the obligor, because she must repay the loan; as we know, Alice is also the debtor. However, suppose that Toby borrows money from a bank and provides no collateral; Jake co-signs the loan as a favor to Toby, using his Steinway piano as collateral. Jake is the only debtor, because he owns the piano. *Both parties* are obligors, because both have agreed to repay the loan.

- **Security agreement** is the contract in which the debtor gives a security interest to the secured party. This agreement protects the secured party's rights in the collateral.

- **Default** occurs when the debtor fails to pay money that is due, for example, on a loan or for a purchase made on credit. Default also includes other failures by the debtor, such as failing to keep the collateral insured.

---

[1] In this chapter we use more footnotes than usual, for two reasons. First, Article 9 is a challenging series of interlocking provisions, and many readers will want to peruse the actual Code (in the Appendix) to reinforce the myriad concepts. Second, the revised Article 9 is substantially rewritten and entirely renumbered; experienced practitioners may appreciate guidelines as they encounter new rules and discover familiar concepts in unexpected places.

- **Repossession** occurs when the secured party takes back collateral because the debtor has defaulted.
- **Perfection** is a series of steps the secured party must take to protect its rights in the collateral against people other than the debtor.
- **Financing statement** is a record intended to notify the general public that the secured party has a security interest in the collateral.
- **Record** refers to information written on paper or stored in an electronic or other medium.
- **Authenticate** means to sign a document or to use any symbol or encryption method that identifies the person and clearly indicates she is adopting the record as her own. You authenticate a security agreement when you sign the papers at an auto dealership. A corporation electronically authenticates a loan agreement by using the Internet to transmit a public-key signature. (See the Cyberlaw feature in Chapter 10 for a discussion of electronic signatures.)

Here is an example using the terms just discussed. A medical equipment company manufactures a CT scanner and sells it to a clinic for $2 million, taking $500,000 cash and the clinic's promise to pay the rest over five years. The clinic simultaneously authenticates a security agreement, giving the manufacturer a security interest in the CT scanner. The manufacturer then electronically files a financing statement in an appropriate state agency. This perfects the manufacturer's rights, meaning that its security interest in the CT scanner is now valid against all the world. Exhibit 13.1 illustrates this transaction.

If the clinic goes bankrupt and many creditors try to seize its assets, the manufacturer has first claim to the CT scanner. The clinic's bankruptcy is of great importance. When a debtor has money to pay all its debts, there are no concerns about security

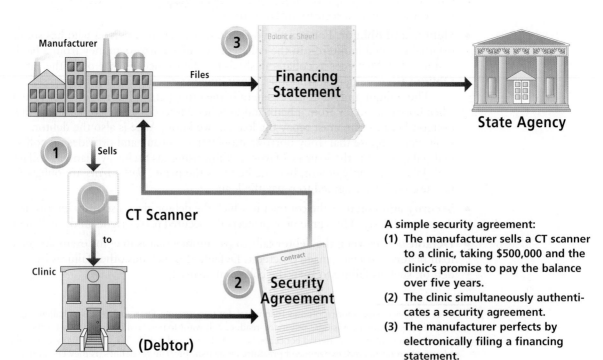

A simple security agreement:
(1) The manufacturer sells a CT scanner to a clinic, taking $500,000 and the clinic's promise to pay the balance over five years.
(2) The clinic simultaneously authenticates a security agreement.
(3) The manufacturer perfects by electronically filing a financing statement.

Exhibit 13.1

interests. A creditor insists on a security interest to protect itself in the event the debtor cannot pay all its debts. The secured party intends (1) to give itself a legal interest in specific property of the debtor and (2) to establish a priority claim in that property ahead of other creditors.

Article 9 Revisions

The American Law Institute and the National Conference of Commissioners on Uniform State Laws have rewritten Article 9, and the proposed revisions are now the law in all states. **All citations in this chapter are to the 2000 Revision of Article 9.** The Uniform Commercial Code is available online at http://www.law.cornell.edu.[2] Click on "Constitutions and Codes," then "Uniform Commercial Code." For the actual statutory versions of Article 9 that have been adopted state-by-state, go to http://www.law.cornell.edu. Click on "Constitutions and Codes," then "Uniform Commercial Code," then click the link provided to see each state's enactment of Article 9.

Scope of Revised Article 9

Article 9 applies to any transaction intended to create a security interest in personal property or fixtures. The personal property that may be used as collateral includes:

- **Goods,** which are things that are movable.
- **Inventory,** meaning goods held by someone for sale or lease, such as all the beds and chairs in a furniture store.
- **Instruments,** such as drafts, checks, certificates of deposit, and notes.
- **Investment property,** which refers primarily to securities and related rights.
- **Documents of title,** which are the proof of ownership retained by someone who ships or stores goods.
- **Accounts,** meaning the right to receive payment for goods sold or leased.
- **Deposit accounts,** which refer to money placed in banks.
- **General intangibles,** a residual category that includes collateral such as copyrights, patents, trademarks, goodwill, and the right to payment of some loans.
- **Chattel paper,** which is a record that indicates two things: (1) an obligor owes money, and (2) a secured party has a security interest in specific goods. Chattel paper most commonly occurs in a consumer sale on credit. If a dealer sells an air conditioner to a customer, who agrees in writing to make monthly payments and also agrees that the dealer has a security interest in the air conditioner, that agreement is chattel paper. The confusing point is that the same chattel paper may be collateral for a second security interest. The dealer who sells the air conditioner could use the chattel paper to obtain a loan. If the dealer gives the chattel paper to a bank as collateral for the loan, the bank has a security interest in the chattel paper, while the dealer continues to have a security interest in the air conditioner. **Electronic chattel paper** is the same thing except that it is an electronic record rather than a writing.

---

2 When researching any article of the Code online, be certain that you are reading the most recent revision.

cyberLaw

Software.   Article 9 takes into account the increasingly important role that computer software plays in all business. The Code distinguishes *software* from *goods*, and this becomes important when competing creditors are fighting over both a computer system and the software inside it. A program embedded in a computer is goods *if* it is customarily considered part of those goods *or if* by purchasing the goods the owner acquires the right to use the program. A program that does not meet those criteria is termed *software* and will be treated differently for some purposes. ◆

In sum, Article 9 applies anytime the parties intended to create a security interest in any of the items listed earlier.

ATTACHMENT OF A SECURITY INTEREST

Attachment is a vital step in a secured transaction. This means that the secured party has taken three steps to create an enforceable security interest:

- The two parties made a security agreement *and either* the debtor has *authenticated a security agreement* describing the collateral *or* the secured party has obtained possession or control;
- The secured party has given value to obtain the security agreement; and
- The debtor has rights in the collateral.[3]

Agreement

Without an agreement there can be no security interest. Generally, the agreement either must be written on paper and signed by the debtor or electronically recorded and authenticated by the debtor. The agreement must reasonably identify the collateral. For example, a security agreement may properly describe the collateral as "all equipment in the store at 123 Periwinkle Street."[4]

A security agreement at a minimum might:

- State that Happy Homes, Inc. and Martha agree that Martha is buying an Arctic Co. refrigerator and identify the exact unit by its serial number;
- Give the price, the down payment, the monthly payments, and the interest rate;
- State that because Happy Homes is selling Martha the refrigerator on credit, it has a security interest in the refrigerator; and
- Provide that if Martha defaults on her payments, Happy Homes is entitled to repossess the refrigerator.

An actual security agreement will add many details, such as Martha's obligation to keep the refrigerator in good condition and to deliver it to the store if she defaults; a precise definition of "default"; and how Happy Homes may go about repossessing the goods if Martha defaults.

---

[3] UCC §9-203.

[4] A security agreement may not use a **super-generic term** such as "all of Smith's personal property." We will see later that, by contrast, such a super-generic description is legally adequate in a *financing statement*.

Control and Possession

In certain cases, the security agreement need not be in writing if the parties have an oral agreement and the secured party has either **control** or **possession.** For many kinds of collateral it is safer for the secured party actually to take the item than to rely upon a security agreement.

For deposit accounts, electronic chattel paper, and certain other collateral, the security interest attaches if the secured party has *control.* Generally speaking, *control means that the secured party has certain exclusive rights to dispose of the collateral.* If Peter deposits $250,000 in Smiley Bank and instructs the bank to dispose of the money as instructed by Wendy, then Wendy has control of the money.

For most other forms of collateral, a security interest attaches if the secured party has *possession.* For example, if you loan your neighbor $175,000 and he gives you a Winslow Homer watercolor as collateral, you have an attached security interest in the painting once it is in your possession.

The court decided the following case based on former Article 9, but the outcome would be the same under the revised Code.

IN RE CFLC, INC.

209 B.R. 508, 1997 Bankr. LEXIS 821
United States Bankruptcy Appellate Panel of the Ninth Circuit, 1997

Facts: Expeditors was a freight company that supervised importing and exporting for Everex Systems, Inc. Expeditors negotiated rates and services for its client and often had possession of Everex's goods. During a 17-month period, Expeditors sent more than 300 invoices to Everex. Each invoice stated that the customer either had to accept all the invoice's terms or to pay cash, receiving no work on credit. One of those terms gave Expeditors a security interest in all the customer's property in its possession. In other words, if the customer failed to pay a bill, Expeditors asserted a right to keep the goods.

Everex filed for bankruptcy, and Expeditors claimed the right to sell Everex's goods, worth about $81,000. The trial judge rejected the claim, ruling that Expeditors lacked a valid security interest. Expeditors appealed.

Issue: Did Expeditors have a security interest in Everex's goods?

Excerpts from Judge Ollason's Decision: Under the common law, silence in the face of an offer is not an acceptance, unless there is a relationship between the parties or a previous course of dealing pursuant to which silence would be understood as acceptance.

In this case, Expeditors and Everex had been doing business for about one and one-half years. They had never discussed the terms of the invoice nor negotiated for a security interest. Everex had never expressly acknowledged the invoice terms by accepting or objecting to them, nor did it take actions which acknowledged Expeditors' alleged general lien on the goods. Its only pertinent acts were its payment of the invoices and silence as to the added terms.

The evidence consisting of Everex's receipt and payment of invoices containing terms for a general lien in the goods in favor of Expeditors did not amount to an agreement for such a security interest, pursuant to [revised section 9-102]. As a matter of law, the repetitive sending by Expeditors to Everex of terms which Expeditors wished to be made part of the oral contract was not evidence of course of dealing because an agreement did not exist as to the security interest which could be supplemented by such evidence.

Affirmed. ■

Value

For the security interest to attach, the secured party must give value. Usually, the value will be apparent. If a bank loans $400 million to an airline, that money is the value, and the bank may therefore obtain a security interest in the planes that the airline is buying. The parties may also agree that some of the value will be given in the future. For example, a finance company might extend a $5 million line of credit to a retail store even though the store initially takes only $1 million of the money. The Code considers the entire $5 million line of credit to be value.[5]

Debtor Rights in the Collateral

The debtor can only grant a security interest in goods if he has some legal right to those goods himself. Typically, the debtor owns the goods. But a debtor may also give a security interest if he is leasing the goods or even if he is a bailee, meaning that he is lawfully holding them for someone else.

Result

Once the security interest has attached to the collateral, the secured party is protected against the debtor. If the debtor fails to pay, the secured party may repossess the collateral.

Attachment to Future Property

The security agreement may specify that the security interest attaches to personal property that the debtor does not yet possess but might obtain in the future.

After-Acquired Property

After-acquired property refers to items that the debtor obtains after the parties have made their security agreement. **The parties may agree that the security interest attaches to after-acquired property.**[6] Basil is starting a catering business but owns only a beat-up car. He borrows $55,000 from the Pesto Bank, which takes a security interest in the car. But Pesto also insists on an after-acquired clause. When Basil purchases a commercial stove, cooking equipment, and freezer, Pesto's security interest attaches to each item as Basil acquires it.

Proceeds

Proceeds are whatever is obtained by a debtor who sells the collateral or otherwise disposes of it. **The secured party *automatically* obtains a security interest in the proceeds of the collateral.**[7] Suppose the Pesto Bank obtains a security interest in Basil's $4,000 freezer. Basil then decides he needs a larger model and sells the original freezer to his neighbor for $3,000. The $3,000 cash is proceeds, in which Pesto automatically obtains a security interest.

---

[5] UCC §9-204(c).
[6] UCC §9-204(a).
[7] UCC §9-203(f).

PERFECTION

Nothing Less Than Perfection

Once the security interest has attached to the collateral, the secured party is protected *against the debtor*. Pesto Bank loaned money to Basil and has a security interest in all his property. If Basil defaults on his loan, Pesto may insist he deliver the goods to the bank. If he fails to do that, the bank can seize the collateral. But Pesto's security interest is valid only against Basil; if a third person claims some interest in the goods, the bank may never get them. For example, Basil might have taken out *another* loan, from his friend Olive, and used the same property as collateral. Olive knew nothing about the bank's original loan. To protect itself against Olive, and all other parties, the bank must *perfect* its interest.

There are several kinds of perfection:

- Perfection by filing
- Perfection by possession or control
- Perfection of consumer goods
- Perfection of movable collateral and fixtures

In some cases the secured party will have a choice of which method to use; in other cases only one method works.

Perfection by Filing

The most common way to perfect is by filing a financing statement with the appropriate state agency. A **financing statement** gives the names of all parties, describes the collateral, and outlines the security interest, enabling any interested person to learn about it. Suppose the Pesto Bank obtains a security interest in Basil's catering equipment and then perfects by filing with the Secretary of State in the state capital. When Basil asks his friend Olive for a loan, she will check the records to see if anyone has a security interest in the catering equipment. Olive's search uncovers Basil's previous security agreement, and she realizes it would be unwise to make the loan. If Basil were to default, the collateral would go straight to Pesto Bank, leaving Olive empty-handed. (See Exhibit 13.2.)

Article 9 prescribes one form, to be used nationwide for financing statements.[8] The financing form is available online at http://www.ss.ca.gov. Click on "Business Filings," "Forms," "Uniform Commercial Code," and "National Financing Statement." Remember that the filing may be done on paper or electronically.

The most common problems that arise in filing cases are (1) whether the financing statement contained enough information to put other people on notice of the security interest, and (2) whether the secured party filed the papers in the right place.

Contents of the Financing Statement

A financing statement is sufficient if it provides the name of the debtor, the name of the secured party, and an indication of the collateral.[9]

---

[8] UCC §9-521.
[9] UCC §9-502(a).

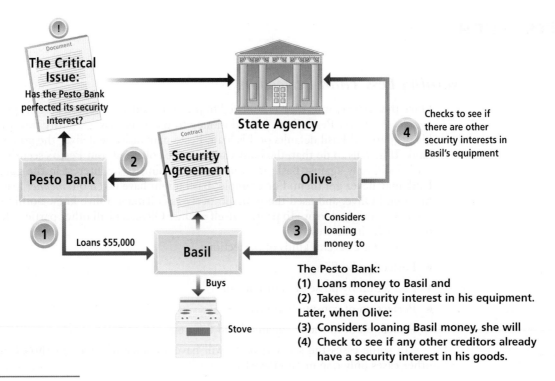

Exhibit 13.2

The name of the debtor is critical because that is what an interested person will use to search among the millions of other financing statements on file. If the debtor is a "registered organization," such as a corporation, limited partnership, or limited liability company, the official, registered name of the company is the only one acceptable. If the debtor is a person or an unregistered organization (such as a club), then the correct name is required. Trade names are not sufficient.

The collateral must be described reasonably so that another party contemplating a loan to the debtor will understand which property is already secured. A financing statement could properly state that it applies to "all inventory in the debtor's Houston warehouse." If the debtor has given a security interest in everything he owns, then it is sufficient to state simply that the financing statement covers "all assets" or "all personal property."

Place and Duration of Filing

Article 9 specifies *where* a secured party must file. These provisions may vary from state to state, so it is essential to check local law: a misfiled record accomplishes nothing. Generally speaking, a party must file in a central filing office located in the state where an individual debtor lives or where an organization has its executive office.[10]

Once a financing statement has been filed, it is effective for five years (except for a manufactured home, where it lasts 30 years). After five years the statement will expire and leave the secured party unprotected, unless she files a continuation statement within six months prior to expiration. The continuation statement is valid for an additional five years, and a secured party may file one periodically, forever.[11]

---

[10] UCC §9-307.
[11] UCC §9-515.

Perfection by Possession or Control

For most types of collateral, in addition to filing, a secured party generally may perfect by possession or control (described earlier). So if the collateral is a diamond brooch or 1,000 shares of stock, a bank may perfect its security interest by holding the items until the loan is paid off.

Perfection by possession has some advantages. Notice to other parties is very clear, and if the debtor defaults, a secured party obviously has no difficulties repossessing. **However, both possession and control impose one important duty: a secured party must use reasonable care in the custody and preservation of collateral in her possession or control.**[12] What does "reasonable care" mean when the collateral is something as volatile as shares of stock? The following case is an early response under the revised article.

LAYNE V. BANK ONE

395 F.3d 271
United States Court of Appeals for the Sixth Circuit, 2005

Facts: Charles E. Johnson was the founder and C.E.O. of PurchasePro.com, Inc., and Geoff Layne was its marketing director. When their Internet stock went public, both officers suddenly owned shares worth millions of dollars. To increase his liquidity, Johnson took out a loan for $2.8 million from Bank One, and Layne borrowed $3.25 million. Each secured the loan with shares of PurchasePro stock.

The loan agreement required a loan-to-value (LTV) ratio of 50%, meaning that the value of the shares had to be at least double the outstanding loan balance. If the value of the shares sank below the required level, the two men could either pay off some of the loan or offer additional security. If the two borrowers failed to remedy the problem, the Bank was entitled (but not obligated) to sell the shares. Johnson secured his loan with $6.9 million worth of PurchasePro stock.

In February, Internet stocks suddenly plummeted and both loans immediately exceeded their LTV ratio. Johnson and Layne spoke with the Bank several times, stating that they would offer additional collateral. During March and April, more calls went back and forth, with the debtors occasionally suggesting that the collateral be sold, while at other times agreeing to provide more security. Finally, in

July, over a four-day period, the Bank sold Johnson's PurchasePro shares for $524,757, more than 90% below its original worth.

Johnson and Layne both filed suit against the Bank, claiming that it failed to exercise reasonable care of the collateral. The trial court gave judgment for the Bank, and the plaintiffs appealed.

Issue: Did the Bank exercise reasonable care of the shares?

Excerpts from Judge Moore's Decision: We first consider Johnson's argument that Bank One violated a duty under Kentucky law to preserve the value of the collateral held in its possession. With respect to the regulation of secured transactions, Kentucky has adopted the Uniform Commercial Code ("U.C.C."), which states that "a secured party shall use reasonable care in the custody and preservation of collateral in the secured party's possession. In the case of chattel paper or an instrument, reasonable care includes taking necessary steps to preserve rights against prior parties unless otherwise agreed."

The comment to §9-207 states that the provision "imposes a duty of care, similar to that imposed ▼

---

on a pledgee at common law, on a secured party in possession of collateral," and cites to [a different treatise, called the Restatement of Security. The explanatory comment in that Restatement says,] "The pledgee is not liable *for a decline in the value* of pledged instruments, even if timely action could have prevented such decline." In the context of pledged stock, courts have used this language from the Restatement to hold that "a bank has no duty to its borrower to sell collateral stock of declining value."

As [another court] stated, "It is the borrower who makes the investment decision to purchase stock. A lender in these situations merely accepts the stock as collateral, and does not thereby itself invest in the issuing firm. Given the volatility of the stock market, a requirement that a secured party sell shares held as collateral, at a particular time, would be to shift the investment risk from the borrower to the lender."

We conclude that under Kentucky law a lender has no obligation to sell pledged stock held as collateral merely because of a market decline. If the borrower is concerned with the decline in the share value, it is his responsibility, rather than that of the lender, to take appropriate remedial steps, such as paying off the loan in return for the collateral, substituting the pledged stock with other equally valued assets, or selling the pledged stock himself and paying off the loan. ■

Devil's Advocate	Although a bank cannot be expected to do a perfect job anticipating stock price changes, it must perform reasonably, as we would expect from an experienced financial institution. Bank One failed. The bank should either have sold the stock quickly or decided to wait and give the shares a chance to rebound. Instead, it foolishly split the difference, dithering while PurchasePro lost more than 90% of its value and *then* selling when the shares were nearly worthless. We would get a more prudent hold/sell strategy from a chimpanzee flipping coins. Bank One is liable. ◆

Perfection of Consumer Goods

The Code gives special treatment to security interests in most consumer goods. Merchants cannot file a financing statement for every bed, television, and stereo for which a consumer owes money. To understand the UCC's treatment of these transactions, we need to know two terms. The first is *consumer goods*, which are those used primarily for personal, family, or household purposes. The second term is *purchase money security interest.*

A purchase money security interest (PMSI) is one taken by the person who sells the collateral or by the person who advances money so the debtor can buy the collateral.[13] Assume the Gobroke Home Center sells Marion a $5,000 stereo system. The sales document requires a payment of $500 down and $50 per month for the next 300 years and gives Gobroke a security interest in the system. Because the security interest was "taken by the seller," the document is a PMSI. It would also be a PMSI if a bank had loaned Marion the money to buy the system and the document gave the bank a security interest. (See Exhibit 13.3.)

But aren't all security interests PMSIs? No, many are not. Suppose a bank loans a retail company $800,000 and takes a security interest in the store's present inventory. That is not a PMSI because the store did not use the money to purchase the collateral.

What must Gobroke Home Center do to perfect its security interest? Nothing. **A PMSI in consumer goods perfects automatically, without filing.**[14] Marion's new

---

[13] UCC §9-103.
[14] UCC §9-309(1).

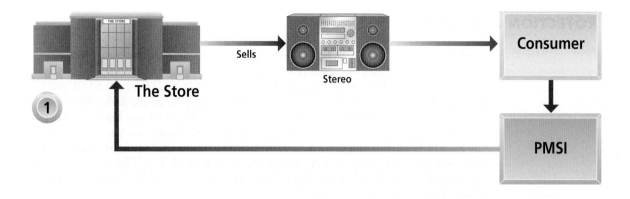

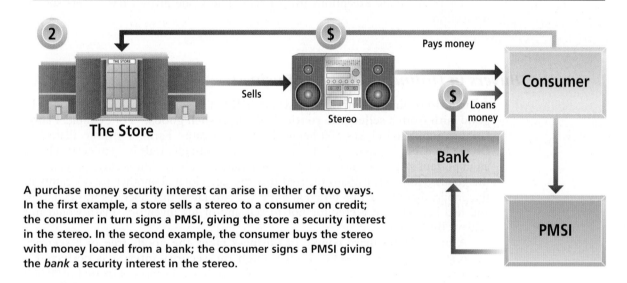

A purchase money security interest can arise in either of two ways. In the first example, a store sells a stereo to a consumer on credit; the consumer in turn signs a PMSI, giving the store a security interest in the stereo. In the second example, the consumer buys the stereo with money loaned from a bank; the consumer signs a PMSI giving the *bank* a security interest in the stereo.

Exhibit 13.3

stereo is clearly consumer goods, because she will use it only in her home. Gobroke's security interest is a PMSI, so the interest has perfected automatically.

The Code provisions about perfecting generally do not apply to motor vehicles, trailers, mobile homes, boats, or farm tractors.[15] These types of secured interests are governed by state law, which often requires a security interest to be noted directly on the vehicle's certificate of title.

A PMSI may be created only in goods, fixtures, or software.[16] No other types of collateral are allowed. Recall that for Article 9 purposes, *software* is defined to mean a computer program that is not embedded in hardware. A seller may obtain a PMSI in software if the debtor is buying the program to run hardware purchased in the same transaction and if the secured party also has a PMSI in that hardware. Merry Bank advances $250,000 to Ben's Books to enable Ben to purchase a new computer system and some separate software to run the computer. Merry may acquire a PMSI in the software, provided it is obtaining a PMSI in the computer as well.

cyberLaw

---

[15] UCC §9-311(a)(2).
[16] UCC §9-103(b)(c).

PROTECTION OF BUYERS

Generally, once a security interest is perfected, it remains effective regardless of whether the collateral is sold, exchanged, or transferred in some other way. Bubba's Bus Co. needs money to meet its payroll, so it borrows $150,000 from Francine's Finance Co., which takes a security interest in Bubba's 180 buses and perfects its interest. Bubba, still short of cash, sells 30 of his buses to Antelope Transit. But even that money is not enough to keep Bubba solvent: he defaults on his loan to Francine and goes into bankruptcy. Francine pounces on Bubba's buses. May she repossess the 30 that *Antelope* now operates? Yes. The security interest continued in the buses even after Antelope purchased them, and Francine can whisk them away.

There are some exceptions to this rule. The Code gives a few buyers special protection.

Buyers in Ordinary Course of Business

A buyer in ordinary course of business (BIOC) is someone who buys goods in good faith from a seller who routinely deals in such goods.[17] For example, Plato's Garden Supply purchases 500 hemlocks from Socrates' Farm, a grower. Plato is a BIOC: he is buying in good faith, and Socrates routinely deals in hemlocks. This is an important status, because a BIOC is generally not affected by security interests in the goods. However, if Plato realized that the sale violated another party's rights in the goods, there would be no good faith. If Plato knew that Socrates was bankrupt and had agreed with a creditor not to sell any of his inventory, Plato would not achieve BIOC status.

A buyer in ordinary course of business takes the goods free of a security interest created by his seller even though the security interest is perfected.[18] Suppose that, a month before Plato made his purchase, Socrates borrowed $200,000 from the Athenian Bank. Athenian took a security interest in all of Socrates' trees and perfected by filing. Then Plato purchased his 500 hemlocks. If Socrates defaults on the loan, Athenian will have *no right* to repossess the 500 trees that are now at the Garden Supply. Plato took them free and clear. (Of course, Athenian can still attempt to repossess other trees from Socrates.) The BIOC exception is designed to encourage ordinary commerce. A buyer making routine purchases should not be forced to perform a financing check before buying. Because the BIOC exception undercuts the basic protection given to a secured party, the courts interpret it narrowly, an issue raised in the following case.

---

[17] UCC §1-201(9).

[18] UCC §9-320(a). In fact, the buyer takes free of the security interest *even if the buyer knew of it.* Yet a BIOC, by definition, must be acting in good faith. Is this a contradiction? No. Plato might know that a third party has a security interest in Socrates' crops, yet not realize that his purchase violates the third party's rights. Generally, for example, a security interest will permit a retailer to sell consumer goods, the presumption being that part of the proceeds will go to the secured party. A BIOC cannot be expected to determine what a retailer plans to do with the money he is paid.

You Be the Judge

CONSECO FINANCE SERVICING CORP. V. LEE

2004 WL 1243417
Court of Appeals of Texas, 2004

Facts: Lila Williams purchased a new Roadtrek 200 motor home from New World R.V. Inc. She paid about $14,000 down and financed $63,000, giving a security interest to New World. The RV company assigned its security interest to Conseco Finance, which perfected. Two years later, Williams returned the vehicle to New World (the record does not indicate why) and New World sold the RV to Robert and Ann Lee for $42,800. A year later, Williams defaulted on her payments to Conseco.

The Lees sued Conseco, claiming to be BIOCs and asking for a court declaration that they had sole title to the Roadtrek. Conseco counterclaimed, seeking title based on its perfected security interest. The trial court ruled that the Lees were BIOCs, with full rights to the vehicle (along with $8,500 in attorney's fees). Conseco appealed.

You Be the Judge: **Were the Lees BIOCs?**

Conseco's Argument: Under UCC §9-319, a buyer in ordinary course takes free of a security interest *created by the buyer's seller*. The buyers were the Lees. The seller was New World. New World did not create the security interest—Lila Williams did. There is no security interest created by New World. The security interest held by Conseco was created

by someone else (Williams) and is not affected by the Lees' status as BIOC. The law is clear and Conseco is entitled to the Roadtrek.

The Lees' Argument: Conseco weaves a clever argument, but let's remove the mumbo-jumbo and look at what they are saying. Two honest buyers, acting in perfect good faith, can walk into an RV dealership, spend $42,000 for a used vehicle, and end up with—nothing. Conseco claims it is entitled to an RV that the Lees paid for because someone that the Lees have never dealt with, never even heard of, gave *to this RV seller* a security interest which the seller, years earlier, passed on to a finance company. Conseco's argument defies common sense and the goals of Article 9.

Conseco's Rebuttal: A reasonable buyer is careful to do business with conscientious, ethical sellers. New World, which knew that Williams financed the RV and knew who held the security interest, never bothered to check on the status of the payments. If the Lees have suffered wrongdoing, it is at the hands of an irresponsible seller.

The Lees' Rebuttal: Conseco's suggestion would demolish the used car industry. What buyers will ever pay serious money—*any* money—for a used vehicle, knowing that thousands of dollars later the car might be towed out of their driveway by a finance company they have never heard of? ●

Buyers of Chattel Paper, Instruments, and Documents

We have seen that debtors often use chattel paper and instruments as collateral. Because each of these is so easily transferred, the Code gives buyers special protection. **A buyer who purchases chattel paper or instruments in good faith in the ordinary course of her business and then obtains *possession or control*, generally takes free of any security interest.**[19]

---

[19] UCC §9-330(a)(b)(d).

PRIORITIES AMONG CREDITORS

What happens when two creditors have a security interest in the same collateral? The party who has **priority** in the collateral gets it. Typically, the debtor lacks assets to pay everyone, so all creditors struggle to be the first in line. After the first creditor has repossessed the collateral, sold it, and taken enough of the proceeds to pay off his debt, there may be nothing left for anyone else. (There may not even be enough to pay the first creditor all that he is due, in which case that creditor will sue for the deficiency.) Who gets priority? There are three principal rules.

The first rule is easy: **a party with a perfected security interest takes priority over a party with an unperfected interest.**[20] This is the whole point of perfecting: to ensure that your security interest gets priority over everyone else's. On August 15 Meredith's Market, an antique store, borrows $100,000 from the Happy Bank, which takes a security interest in all of Meredith's inventory. Happy Bank does not perfect. On September 15 Meredith uses the same collateral to borrow $50,000 from the Suspicion Bank, which files a financing statement the same day. On October 15, as if on cue, Meredith files for bankruptcy and stops paying both creditors. Suspicion wins because it holds a perfected interest, whereas Happy Bank holds merely an unperfected interest.

The second rule: **if neither secured party has perfected, the first interest to attach gets priority.**[21] Suppose that Suspicion Bank and Happy Bank had both failed to perfect. In that case, Happy Bank would have the first claim to Meredith's inventory because Happy's interest *attached* first.

And the third rule follows logically: **between perfected security interests, the first to file *or* perfect wins.**[22] Diminishing Perspective, a railroad, borrows $75 million from the First Bank, which takes a security interest in Diminishing's rolling stock (railroad cars) and immediately perfects by filing. Two months later, Diminishing borrows $100 million from Second Bank, which takes a security interest in the same collateral and also files. When Diminishing arrives, on schedule, in Bankruptcy Court, both banks will race to seize the rolling stock. First Bank gets the railcars because it perfected first.

March 1:	April 2:	May 3:	The Winner:
First Bank loans money and perfects its security interest by filing a financing statement.	Second Bank loans money and perfects its security interest by filing a financing statement.	Diminishing goes bankrupt, and both banks attempt to take the rolling stock.	First Bank, because it perfected first.

The general rules of priority are quite straightforward. However, you will not be surprised to learn that there are some exceptions.

Priority Exceptions

You may recall that a purchase money security interest (PMSI) is a security interest taken by the seller of the collateral or by a lender whose loan enables the debtor to buy the collateral. A PMSI can be created only in goods, fixtures, and software. **A PMSI**

---

[20] UCC §9-322(a)(2).
[21] UCC §9-322(a)(3).
[22] UCC §9-322(a)(1).

that is promptly perfected generally takes priority over a conflicting perfected security interest (even one perfected earlier). The holder of the PMSI is sometimes required to notify other secured parties of the new PMSI and generally must perfect before the goods are sold or shortly thereafter, depending on what type of collateral is involved.

On February 1, Tool Shop borrows $100,000 from the Gargoyle Bank, giving Gargoyle a security interest in after-acquired property. Then on November 1, Manufacturer sells a specially built lathe to Tool Shop for $80,000, taking a PMSI in the machine. When the lathe arrives at the Tool Shop, Gargoyle's earlier security interest attaches to the same collateral. Who wins? Manufacturer, provided it promptly perfects its PMSI.

Another significant exception involves perfection by possession or control. **A party that uses possession or control to perfect its interest in deposit accounts, investment property, letter-of-credit rights, or instruments generally obtains priority over a party that perfected earlier by filing.**

DEFAULT AND TERMINATION

We have reached the end of the line. Either the debtor has defaulted, or it has performed its obligations and may terminate the security agreement.

Default

The parties define "default" in their security agreement. **Generally, a debtor defaults when he fails to make payments due or enters bankruptcy proceedings.** The parties can agree that other acts will constitute default, such as the debtor's failure to maintain insurance on the collateral. When a debtor defaults, the secured party has two principal options: (1) it may take possession of the collateral, or (2) it may file suit against the debtor for the money owed. The secured party does not have to choose between these two remedies; it may try one after the other, or both simultaneously.[23]

Taking Possession of the Collateral

When the debtor defaults, the secured party may take possession of the collateral.[24] The secured party may act on its own, without any court order, and simply take the collateral, provided this can be done *without a breach of the peace*. Otherwise, the secured party must file suit against the debtor and request that the court *order* the debtor to deliver the collateral.

Disposition of the Collateral

Once the secured party has obtained possession of the collateral, it has two choices. The secured party may (1) dispose of the collateral or (2) retain the collateral as full satisfaction of the debt. Notice that until the secured party disposes of the collateral, the debtor has the right to *redeem* it—that is, to pay the full value of the debt and retrieve her property.[25]

---

[23] UCC §9-601(a)(b)(c).
[24] UCC §9-609.
[25] UCC §9-623.

Disposal of the Collateral.   A secured party may sell, lease, or otherwise dispose of the collateral in any commercially reasonable manner.[26] Typically, the secured party will sell the collateral in either a private or a public sale. First, however, the debtor must receive *reasonable notice* of the time and place of the sale, so that she may bid on the collateral. The higher the price that the secured party gets for the collateral, the lower the balance still owed by the debtor. Giving the debtor notice of the sale and a chance to bid ensures that the collateral will not be sold for an unreasonably low price.

Suppose Bank loans $65,000 to Farmer to purchase a tractor. While still owing $40,000, Farmer defaults. Bank takes possession of the tractor and then notifies Farmer that it intends to sell the tractor at an auction. Farmer has the right to attend and bid on the tractor.

When the secured party has sold the collateral, it applies the proceeds of the sale: first, to its expenses in repossessing and selling the collateral, and second, to the debt.[27] Assume Bank sold the tractor for $35,000, and that the process of repossessing and selling the tractor cost $5,000. Bank applies the remaining $30,000 to the debt.

Deficiency or Surplus.   The sale of the tractor yielded $30,000 to be applied to the debt, which was $40,000. The disposition has left a **deficiency**—that is, insufficient funds to pay off the debt. **The debtor is liable for any deficiency.** So the bank will sue the farmer for the remaining $10,000. On the other hand, sometimes the sale of the collateral yields a **surplus**—that is, a sum greater than the debt. In that case, the secured party must pay the surplus to the debtor.[28] Finally, when a secured party disposes of collateral in a *commercially unreasonable* manner, it will be liable to the debtor for the shortfall.

Acceptance of the Collateral.   In many cases, the secured party has the option to satisfy the debt simply by keeping the collateral. *Acceptance* **refers to a secured party's retention of the collateral as full or partial satisfaction of the debt.** *Partial satisfaction* means that the debtor will still owe some deficiency to the secured party.[29] Generally speaking, a secured party may accept the collateral as full satisfaction unless the debtor objects.

A secured party who wishes to accept the collateral must notify the debtor. If the debtor agrees in an authenticated record, then the secured party may keep the collateral as full *or* partial satisfaction of the debt. If the debtor does not respond within 20 days, the secured party may still accept the collateral as *full* satisfaction but not as partial satisfaction. In other words, the debtor's silence does not give the secured party the right to keep the goods and still sue for more money.

Occasionally, the secured party will prefer to ignore its rights in the collateral and simply sue the debtor. **A secured party may sue the debtor for the full debt.**[30]

Termination

Finally, we need to look at what happens when a debtor does not default, but pays the full debt. (You are forgiven if you lost track of the fact that things sometimes work out smoothly.) Once that happens, the secured party must complete a **termination**

---

26 UCC §9-610.
27 UCC §9-615(a).
28 UCC §9-615(d).
29 UCC §9-620.
30 UCC §9-601(a).

statement, a document indicating that it no longer claims a security interest in the collateral.[31]

OVERVIEW OF BANKRUPTCY

As you may have noticed in the first half of this chapter, many of the cases involving secured transactions are decided in bankruptcy court as part of an overall sorting out of a debtor's financial problems. The U.S. Bankruptcy Code (Code) has three primary goals:

- To preserve as much of the debtor's property as possible.
- To divide the debtor's assets fairly between the debtor and creditors.
- To divide the debtor's assets fairly among creditors.

The following options are available under the Bankruptcy Code:

Number	Topic	Description
Chapter 7	Liquidation	The bankrupt's assets are sold to pay creditors. If the debtor owns a business, it terminates. The creditors have no right to the debtor's future earnings.
Chapter 9	Municipal bankruptcies	This chapter is not covered in this book.
Chapter 11	Reorganization	This chapter is designed for businesses and wealthy individuals. Businesses continue in operation, and creditors receive a portion of both current assets and future earnings.
Chapter 12	Family farmers	This chapter is not covered in this book.
Chapter 13	Consumer reorganizations	Chapter 13 offers reorganizations for the typical consumer. Creditors usually receive a portion of the individual's current assets and future earnings.

All the Code's chapters have one of two objectives—rehabilitation or liquidation. Chapters 11 and 13, for example, focus on rehabilitation. Many debtors can return to financial health provided they have the time and breathing space to work out their problems. These chapters hold creditors at bay while the debtor develops a payment plan. In return for retaining some of their assets, debtors typically promise to pay creditors a portion of their future earnings. However, when debtors are unable to develop a feasible plan for rehabilitation under Chapter 11 or 13, Chapter 7 provides for liquidation (also known as a **straight bankruptcy**). Most of the debtor's assets are distributed to creditors, but the debtor has no obligation to share future earnings.

Debtors are sometimes eligible to file under more than one chapter. No choice is irrevocable because both debtors and creditors have the right to ask the court to convert a case from one chapter to another at any time during the proceedings.

---

[31] UCC §9-513.

Public Policy

In response to intense lobbying by the credit card industry, Congress passed the Bankruptcy Abuse Prevention and Consumer Protection Act of 2005 (the BAPCPA), which makes the bankruptcy process more difficult. Before filing, individual debtors must now submit to credit counseling—an expensive process that does not necessarily reduce bankruptcy filings. Moreover, if debtors earn more than their state's median income, the new amendment requires them to pay back some of their debt. Those in favor of this amendment argued that all consumers would benefit from lower prices if fewer people were allowed to avoid their debts by going bankrupt. In the prior decade the number of bankruptcies had doubled—perhaps in part because people no longer felt ashamed of bankruptcy. Critics of the statute countered that credit card companies were to blame for the high rate of bankruptcy. These companies issued credit cards willy-nilly without adequate credit checks and then charged high (and sometimes misleading) late fees. Most bankrupts are in the middle class but have suffered a misfortune shortly before filing—unemployment, illness, or divorce. As you read this chapter, formulate your own view on this debate. ◆

CHAPTER 7 LIQUIDATION

All bankruptcy cases proceed in a roughly similar pattern, regardless of chapter. We use Chapter 7 as a template to illustrate common features of all bankruptcy cases. Later on, the discussions of the other chapters will indicate how they differ from Chapter 7. The latest news on bankruptcy is available at http://www.abiworld.org.

Filing a Petition

Any individual, partnership, corporation, or other business organization that lives, conducts business, or owns property in the United States can file under the Code. (Chapter 13, however, is available only to individuals.) The traditional term for someone who could not pay his debts was **bankrupt,** but the Code uses the term **debtor** instead. We use both terms interchangeably.

A case begins with the filing of a bankruptcy petition in federal district court. Debtors may go willingly into the bankruptcy process by filing a **voluntary petition,** or they may be dragged into court by creditors who file an **involuntary petition.** The district court typically refers bankruptcy cases to a specialized bankruptcy judge. Either party can appeal the decision of the bankruptcy judge back to the district court and, from there, to the federal appeals court.

Voluntary Petition

Any debtor may file for bankruptcy. It is not necessary that the debtor's liabilities exceed assets. Debtors sometimes file a bankruptcy petition because cash flow is so tight they cannot pay their debts, even though they are not technically insolvent. Under the BAPCPA, however, there are two new criteria for a bankruptcy filing:

- Within 180 days before filing, individual debtors must undergo credit counseling with an approved agency.

- Debtors may file under Chapter 7 if they earn less than the median income in their state *or* they cannot afford to pay back at least $6,000 over five years.[32]

---

[32] In some circumstances, debtors with income higher than $6,000 may still be eligible to file under Chapter 7, but the formula is highly complex and more than most readers want to know. The formula is available at 11 USC §707(b)(2)(A).

Generally, all other debtors must file under Chapters 11 or 13. (These Chapters require the bankrupt to repay some debt.) To determine the median income in your state, click on http://www.census.gov, then "State Median Incomes."

The voluntary petition must include the following documents:

Document	Description
Petition	Begins the case. Easy to fill out, it requires checking a few boxes and typing in little more than name, address, and Social Security number.
List of Creditors	The names and addresses of all creditors.
Schedule of Assets and Liabilities	A list of the debtor's assets and debts.
Claim of Exemptions	A list of all assets that the debtor is entitled to keep.
Schedule of Income and Expenditures	The debtor's job, income, and expenses.
Statement of Financial Affairs	A summary of the debtor's financial history and current financial condition. In particular, the debtor must list any recent payments to creditors and any other property held by someone else for the debtor.

Involuntary Petition

Creditors may force a debtor into bankruptcy by filing an involuntary petition. The creditors' goal is to preserve as much of the debtor's assets as possible and to ensure that all creditors receive a fair share. Naturally, the Code sets strict limits—debtors cannot be forced into bankruptcy every time they miss a credit card payment. **An involuntary petition must meet all of the following requirements:**

- The debtor must owe at least $12,300 in unsecured claims to the creditors who file.
- If the debtor has at least 12 creditors, three or more must sign the petition. If the debtor has fewer than 12 creditors, any one of them can file a petition.
- The creditors must allege either that a custodian for the debtor's property has been appointed in the prior 120 days or that the debtor has generally not been paying debts that are due.

What does "a custodian for the debtor's property" mean? *State* laws sometimes permit the appointment of a custodian to protect a debtor's assets. The Code allows creditors to pull a case out from under state law and into federal bankruptcy court by filing an involuntary petition. Creditors also have the right to file an involuntary petition if they can show that the debtor is not paying debts. In the event that a debtor objects to an involuntary petition, the bankruptcy court must hold a trial to determine whether the creditors have met the Code's requirements.

Once a voluntary petition is filed or an involuntary petition approved, the bankruptcy court issues an **order for relief.** This order is an official acknowledgment that the debtor is under the jurisdiction of the court, and it is, in a sense, the start of the whole bankruptcy process. An involuntary debtor must now make all the filings that accompany a voluntary petition. Official bankruptcy forms are available at http://www.uscourts.gov. Click on "Bankruptcy Courts," then "Bankruptcy Forms."

Trustee

The trustee is responsible for gathering the bankrupt's assets and dividing them among creditors. Creditors have the right to elect the trustee, but often they do not bother. In this case, the **U.S. Trustee** makes the selection. The U.S. Attorney General appoints a U.S. Trustee for each region of the country to administer the bankruptcy law. More information about the U.S. Trustee program is available at http://www.usdoj.gov. Click on "DOJ Agencies," "U.S. Trustee Program," and "About Bankruptcy & the United States Trustee Program."

Creditors

After the court enters an order for relief, the U.S. Trustee calls a meeting of creditors. At the meeting the bankrupt must answer (under oath) any question the creditors pose about his financial situation. If the creditors want to elect a trustee, they do so at this meeting.

After a meeting of creditors, unsecured creditors must submit a *proof of claim* within 90 days after the meeting of creditors. The proof of claim is a simple form stating the name of the creditor and the amount of the claim. **Secured creditors do not file proofs of claim unless the claim exceeds the value of their collateral.** In this case, they are unsecured creditors for the excess amount and must file a proof of claim for it. Suppose that Deborah borrows $750,000 from Morton in return for a mortgage on her house. If she does not repay the debt, he can foreclose. Unfortunately, property values plummet, and by the time Deborah files a voluntary petition in bankruptcy, the house is worth only $500,000. Morton is a secured creditor for $500,000 and need file no proof of claim for that amount. But he is an unsecured creditor for $250,000 and will lose his right to this excess amount unless he files a proof of claim for it.

Automatic Stay

A fox chased by hounds has no time to make rational long-term decisions. What that fox needs is a safe burrow. Similarly, it is difficult for debtors to make sound financial decisions when hounded night and day by creditors shouting, "Pay me! Pay me!" The Code is designed to give debtors enough breathing space to sort out their affairs sensibly. An automatic stay is a safe burrow for the bankrupt. It goes into effect as soon as the petition is filed. An automatic stay prohibits creditors from collecting debts that the bankrupt incurred before the petition was filed. Creditors may not sue a bankrupt to obtain payment nor may they take other steps, outside of court, to pressure the debtor for payment. The following case illustrates how persistent creditors can be.

JACKSON V. HOLIDAY FURNITURE

309 B.R. 33; 2004 Bankr. LEXIS 548
United States Bankruptcy Court for the Western District of Missouri, 2004

Facts: Chris Wilcoxon and her mother, Alice Bokonich, owned Dan Holiday Furniture. Wilcoxon's sister, Judith Bokonich, was an employee. In April, Cora and Frank Jackson purchased a recliner chair on credit from the store. They made payments until November. That month, they filed for protection under the Bankruptcy Code. Dan Holiday ▼

received a notice of the bankruptcy. This notice stated that the store must stop all efforts to collect on the Jacksons's debt.

Despite this notice, a Dan Holiday collector telephoned the Jacksons's house ten times between November 15 and December 1 and left a card in their door threatening repossession of the chair. On December 1, Frank—without Cora's knowledge—went to Dan Holiday to pay the $230.00 owed for November and December. He told Wilcoxon about the bankruptcy filing but allegedly added that he and his wife wanted to continue making payments directly to Dan Holiday.

In early January, employees at Dan Holiday learned that Frank had died the month before. Nevertheless, after Cora failed to make the payment for the month of January, a collector telephoned her house 26 times between January 14 and February 19. One of the taped messages from her answering machine stated:

> Hello. This is Judy over at Dan Holiday Furniture. And this is the last time I am going to call you. If you do not call me I will be at your house. And I expect you to call me today. If there is a problem I need to speak to you about it. You need to call me. We need to get this thing going. You are a January and February payment behind. And if you think you are going to get away with it, you've got another thing coming.

Judith Bokonich admitted that she had made this call.

When Cora returned home on February 18, she found seven bright yellow slips of paper in her door jamb stating that a Dan Holiday truck had stopped by to repossess her furniture. The cards read:

> "OUR TRUCK was here to **REPOSSESS** Your furniture [sic]. 241-6933. Dan Holiday Furn. & Appl. Co."

The threat to send a truck was merely a ruse designed to frighten Cora into paying. Wilcoxon testified that Dan Holiday does not typically send a truck and that they do not want the furniture back. What they want is to talk directly to the customer about making payments.

Also on February 18, Dan Holiday sent Cora a letter stating that she had 24 hours to bring her account current or else **"Repossession Will Be Made and Legal Action Will Be Taken."** That same day, Cora's bankruptcy attorney contacted Dan Holiday. Thereafter all collection activity ceased.

Issues: Did Dan Holiday violate the automatic stay provisions of the Bankruptcy Code? What is the penalty for a violation?

Excerpts from Judge Venters's Decision[33]: The automatic stay prohibits the commencement or continuation of any action against the debtor that arose before the commencement of the bankruptcy case and forbids any act by a pre-petition creditor to obtain possession of property of the bankruptcy estate. An individual injured by a creditor's violation of the automatic stay shall recover actual damages, including costs and attorneys' fees, and in appropriate circumstances, may recover punitive damages.

In this case, there is no question that Dan Holiday repeatedly violated the automatic stay. [T]he Court finds that the Jacksons suffered financial damages in the amount of $230.00, which represents the coerced payments that Dan Holiday received from Frank Jackson on December 1.

The Court finds that punitive damages are warranted in this case based on Dan Holiday's egregious, intentional violations of the automatic stay. Dan Holiday's conduct was remarkably bad in that, after it had actual knowledge of the Jacksons' bankruptcy, and after coercing payments from the Jacksons covering the months of November and December, it made no less than twenty-six telephone calls to the Jacksons' household in January and February. Dan Holiday's continued collection efforts were in flagrant violation of the protections Congress afforded to debtors under the automatic stay.

In this matter the Court is somewhat hampered in assessing punitive damages by the lack of evidence concerning the ability of Dan Holiday to pay. Wilcoxon testified that Dan Holiday was a family-owned business that has been in existence for 52 years, and the Court assumes that it is a relatively

▼

---

33 For readability's sake, we refer to the plaintiffs as "the Jacksons," not "debtors" as the court did.

small business. Under the circumstances of this case, the Court believes that an appropriate penalty would be $100.00 for each illegal contact with the Jacksons after December 1, when it is crystal clear that Dan Holiday had actual knowledge of the Jacksons' bankruptcy filing, for a total of $2,800.00. The Court believes that this penalty will be sufficient to sting the pocketbook of Dan Holiday and impress upon Dan Holiday and its owners and employees the importance of debtor protections under the Bankruptcy Code, as well as to deter further transgressions.

The Court also will award the Jacksons their attorneys' fees and costs in the amount of $1,142.42, an amount the Court considers eminently fair and reasonable under the circumstances of this case. ∎

Bankruptcy Estate

The filing of the bankruptcy petition creates a new legal entity separate from the debtor—the **bankruptcy estate.** All the bankrupt's assets pass to the estate, except exempt property and new property that the debtor acquires after the petition is filed.

Exempt Property

The Code permits *individual* debtors (but not organizations) to keep some property for themselves. This exempt property saves the debtor from destitution during the bankruptcy process and provides the foundation for a new life once the process is over.

In this one area of bankruptcy law, the Code defers to state law. Although the Code lists various types of exempt property, it permits states to opt out of the federal system and define a different set of exemptions. A majority of states have indeed opted out of the Code, and for their residents the Code exemptions are irrelevant.

Under the *federal* Code, a debtor is allowed to exempt only $18,450 of the value of her home. If the home is worth more than that, the trustee sells it and returns $18,450 of the proceeds to the debtor. Most *states* exempt items such as the debtor's home, household goods, cars, work tools, disability and pension benefits, alimony, and health aids. Indeed, some states set no limit on the value of exempt property. Both Florida and Texas, for example, permit debtors to keep homes of unlimited value and a certain amount of land. Not surprisingly, these generous exemptions sometimes lead to abuses. Therefore, under the BAPCPA, debtors can take advantage of state exemptions only if they have lived in that state for two years prior to the bankruptcy. And they can exempt only $125,000 of any house that was acquired during the 40 months before the bankruptcy.

Voidable Preferences

A major goal of the bankruptcy system is to divide the debtor's assets fairly among creditors. It would not be fair, or in keeping with this goal, if debtors were permitted to pay off some of their creditors immediately before filing a bankruptcy petition. Such a payment is called a **preference** because it gives unfair preferential treatment to a creditor. **The trustee can void any transfer to a creditor that took place in the 90-day period before the filing of a petition if the creditor received more from the transfer than she would have received during the bankruptcy process.**

Fraudulent Transfers

Suppose that a debtor sees bankruptcy inexorably approaching across the horizon like a tornado. He knows that, once the storm hits and he files a petition, everything he owns except a few items of exempt property will become part of the bankruptcy estate.

Before that happens, he may be tempted to give some of his property to friends or family to shelter it from the tornado. If he succumbs to temptation, however, he is committing a fraudulent transfer.

A transfer is fraudulent if it is made within the year before a petition is filed and its purpose is to hinder, delay, or defraud creditors. The trustee can void any fraudulent transfer. Fraudulent transfers sound similar to voidable preferences, but there is an important distinction: voidable preferences pay legitimate debts, while fraudulent transfers protect the debtor's assets from legitimate creditors. For example, Lawrence Williams and his wife, Diana, enjoyed a luxurious lifestyle while his investment bank flourished. But when the bank failed, Lawrence was faced with debts of $6 million. On the eve of the bankruptcy filing, Diana suddenly announced that she wanted a divorce. In what had to be the most amicable breakup ever, Lawrence willingly transferred all of his assets to her. The court found that the transfer had been fraudulent.[34]

Payment of Claims

Imagine a crowded delicatessen on Saturday evening. People are pushing and shoving because they know there is not enough food for everyone; some customers will go home hungry. The delicatessen could simply serve whoever pushes to the front of the line, or it could establish a number system to ensure that the most deserving customers are served first. The Code has, in essence, adopted a number system to prevent a free-for-all fight over the bankrupt's assets. Indeed, one of the Code's primary goals is to ensure that creditors are paid in the proper order, not according to who pushes to the front of the line.

All claims are placed in one of three classes: (1) secured claims, (2) priority claims, and (3) unsecured claims. **The trustee pays the bankruptcy estate to the various classes of claims in order of rank.** A higher class is paid in full before the next class receives any payment at all. The debtor is entitled to any funds remaining after all claims have been paid. The payment order is shown in Exhibit 13.4.

Secured Claims

Creditors whose loans are secured by specific collateral are paid first. Secured claims are fundamentally different from all other claims because they are paid by selling a specific asset, not out of the general funds of the estate.

Exhibit 13.4

---

[34] *In re Williams,* 159 B.R. 648, 1993 Bankr. LEXIS 1482 (Bankr. D.R.I. 1993), *remanded,* 190 B.R. 728, 1996 U.S. Dist. LEXIS 539.

Priority Claims

Each category of priority claims is paid in order, with the first group receiving full payment before the next group receives anything. Priority claims include:

- Alimony and child support.
- Administrative expenses (such as fees to the trustee, lawyers, and accountants).
- Back wages to the debtor's employees for work performed during the 180 days prior to the date of the petition.
- Income and property taxes.
- Claims of anyone injured by a bankrupt who was driving a vehicle while drunk or on drugs.

Unsecured Claims

Last, and often very much least, unsecured creditors have now reached the delicatessen counter. They can only hope that some food remains.

Discharge

Filing a bankruptcy petition is embarrassing, time-consuming, and disruptive. It can affect the debtor's credit rating for years, making the simplest car loan a challenge. To add to the pain, the BAPCPA requires debtors to complete an approved course on financial management before receiving a discharge. But to encourage debtors to file for bankruptcy despite the pain involved, the Code offers a powerful incentive: the **fresh start.** Once a bankruptcy estate has been distributed to creditors, they cannot make a claim against the debtor for money owed before the filing, *whether or not they actually received any payment.* These pre-petition debts are **discharged.** All is forgiven, if not forgotten.

Discharge is an essential part of bankruptcy law. Without it, debtors would have little incentive to take part. To avoid abuses, however, the Code limits both the type of debts that can be discharged and the circumstances under which discharge can take place.

Debts That Cannot Be Discharged

The following debts are among those that can never be discharged. The debtor remains liable in full until they are paid:

- Recent income and property taxes.
- Money obtained by fraud.
- Cash advances on a credit card totaling more that $750 that an individual debtor takes out within 70 days before the order of relief.
- Debts omitted from the Schedule of Assets and Liabilities that the debtor filed with the petition if the creditor did not know about the bankruptcy and therefore did not file a proof of claim.
- Money owed for alimony or child support.
- Debts stemming from intentional and malicious injury.
- Debts stemming from a violation of securities laws.
- Student loans made or guaranteed by the government. These loans can only be discharged if repayment would cause undue hardship. As the following case illustrates, proving undue hardship is difficult.

IN RE STERN

288 B.R. 36; 2002 Bankr. LEXIS 1609
United States Bankruptcy Court for the Northern District of New York, 2002

Facts: James Stern took out student loans to attend Bates College and Syracuse College of Law. Afterward, he had difficulty finding a job as a lawyer, so he opened his own practice. His annual income averaged $17,000, and his wife's earnings averaged $18,000.

After Stern was sued (unsuccessfully) for malpractice, he could no longer afford malpractice insurance. Believing that his debt and the default on his student loans made him unemployable as a lawyer, he moved with his wife to her native country, France. Unfortunately, he did not speak French and, therefore, could not obtain a job. His wife's total income over six months in France was $2,200. Even more unfortunately, their expenses in France were higher than in the United States.

After paying back $27,000, Stern still owed $147,000 in student loans: $56,000 in principal and $91,000 in interest. He asked the court to discharge these loans on grounds of undue hardship.

Issue: **Is Stern entitled to a discharge of his student loans on grounds of undue hardship?**

Excerpts from Judge Gerling's Decision[35]: Congress, in enacting the [student loan provision of the Bankruptcy] statute, was cognizant of the fact that educational loans are different from most loans. They are made without business considerations, without security, without cosigners, and rely for repayment solely on the debtor's future increased income resulting from the education. In this sense, the loan is viewed as a mortgage on the debtor's future.

[To obtain a discharge] Stern must prove more than his present inability to pay his student loan obligations. He must also establish that his current financial hardship is likely to be long-term. In this case, Stern possesses both a bachelor's degree and a Juris Doctorate. Stern apparently has decided that he no longer wishes to pursue a legal career. He is certainly well within his rights to make such a choice.

Nevertheless, [b]orrowers under the various guaranteed student loan programs are obligated to repay their loans even if they are unable to obtain employment in their chosen field of study.

The Court finds disturbing Stern's failure to maximize his income and minimize his expenses. He and his wife have elected to relocate to France where Stern admitted that the cost of living is higher. Nor is there any evidence that he ever made any effort to obtain employment in the United States in order to enhance his earnings, whether it be in business, government, or in a private law firm in Syracuse or elsewhere. Instead, he opted to move to a country where he acknowledges he cannot even get a job as a street sweeper because of his inability to speak the language.

Obviously, Stern would prefer to be in a position that would allow him to allocate those monies [he owes] to a mortgage on a home or to the raising of children. Those are certainly commendable goals; however, but the fact that they may not be attainable at this time because of the student loans and Stern's, as well as his wife's, current employment situation, does not meet the fundamental standard from which "undue hardship" is measured and does not provide a basis for granting Stern [even] a partial discharge at this time.

While Stern and his wife have experienced some "bumps in the road," the direction they take in the future appears very much in their control based on their age, health, and education. Indeed, it is the very education that he obtained as a result of the student loans at both the undergraduate and graduate levels, which, arguably, should ultimately allow him to pursue employment opportunities not available to others who were unable to pursue higher education for whatever reason. While Stern testified that he no longer wishes to continue in the legal profession, certainly, there are other career opportunities available to him by virtue of his education, training, and experience. ∎

---

[35] Although the court refers to Stern as "Debtor," we use his surname.

Circumstances that Prevent Debts from Being Discharged

The Code also prohibits the discharge of debts under the following circumstances:

- *Business Organizations.* Under Chapter 7 (but *not* the other chapters), only the debts of individuals can be discharged, not those of business organizations. Once its assets have been distributed, the organization must cease operation. If the company resumes business again, it becomes responsible for all its pre-filing debts.

- *Repeated Filings for Bankruptcy.* Congress feared that some debtors, attracted by the lure of a fresh start, would make a habit of bankruptcy. Therefore, a debtor who has received a discharge under Chapter 7 or 11 cannot receive another discharge under Chapter 7 for at least eight years after the prior filing.

- *Revocation.* A court can revoke a discharge within one year if it discovers the debtor engaged in fraud or concealment.

- *Dishonesty or Bad Faith Behavior.* The court may deny discharge altogether if the debtor has made fraudulent transfers, hidden assets, falsified records, or otherwise acted in bad faith.

Reaffirmation

Sometimes debtors are willing to reaffirm a debt, meaning they promise to pay even after discharge. They may want to reaffirm a secured debt to avoid losing the collateral. For example, a debtor who has taken out a loan secured by a car may reaffirm that debt so that the finance company will agree not to repossess it. Sometimes debtors reaffirm because they feel guilty, or they want to maintain a good relationship with the creditor. They may have borrowed from a family member or an important supplier. Because discharge is a fundamental pillar of the bankruptcy process, courts look closely at each reaffirmation to ensure that the creditor has not unfairly pressured the bankrupt. To be valid, either the court must determine that the reaffirmation is in the debtor's best interest and does not impose undue hardship or the attorney representing the debtor must file an affidavit in court stating that the debtor's consent was informed and voluntary and the agreement does not create a hardship.

CHAPTER 11 REORGANIZATION

For a business, the goal of a Chapter 7 bankruptcy is euthanasia—putting it out of its misery by shutting it down and distributing its assets to creditors. Chapter 11 has a much more complicated and ambitious goal—resuscitating a business so that it can ultimately emerge as a viable economic concern.

Both individuals and businesses can use Chapter 11. Businesses usually prefer Chapter 11 over Chapter 7 because Chapter 11 does not require them to dissolve at the end as Chapter 7 does. The threat of death creates a powerful incentive to try rehabilitation under Chapter 11. Individuals, however, tend to prefer Chapter 13 because it is specifically designed for them.

A Chapter 11 proceeding follows many of the same steps as Chapter 7: a petition (either voluntary or involuntary), an order for relief, a meeting of creditors, proofs of claim, and an automatic stay. There are, however, some significant differences.

Debtor in Possession

Chapter 11 does not require a trustee. The bankrupt is called the **debtor in possession** and, in essence, serves as trustee. The debtor in possession has two jobs: to operate the business and to develop a plan of reorganization. A trustee is chosen only if the debtor is incompetent or uncooperative. In that case, the creditors can elect the trustee, but if they do not choose to do so, the U.S. Trustee appoints one.

Creditors' Committee

In a Chapter 11 case, the creditors' committee plays a particularly important role because typically there is no neutral trustee to watch over their interests. The committee has the right to help develop the plan of reorganization and to participate in any other way necessary to protect the interests of its constituency. Moreover, the BAPCPA requires the committee to communicate diligently with all creditors. The U.S. Trustee typically appoints the seven largest unsecured creditors to the committee. However, under the BAPCPA, the court may require the U.S. Trustee to appoint some small business creditors to the committee. Secured creditors do not serve because their interests require less protection. If the debtor is a corporation, the U.S. Trustee may also appoint a committee of shareholders.

Plan of Reorganization

Once the bankruptcy petition is filed, an automatic stay goes into effect to provide the debtor with temporary relief from creditors. The next stage is to develop a plan of reorganization that provides for the payment of debts and the continuation of the business. For the first 120 days after the order for relief, the debtor has the exclusive right to propose a plan. If the shareholders and creditors accept it, then the bankruptcy case terminates. If the creditors or shareholders reject the debtor's plan, they may file their own version. The debtor has a strong incentive to develop a fair plan the first time because the creditors' proposals are likely to be less favorable.

Confirmation of the Plan

All the creditors and shareholders have the right to vote on the plan of reorganization. In preparation for the vote, each creditor and shareholder is assigned to a class. Chapter 11 classifies claims in the same way as Chapter 7: (1) secured claims, (2) priority claims, and (3) unsecured claims. Each secured claim is usually in its own class because each one is secured by different collateral. Shareholders are also divided into classes, depending upon their interests. For example, holders of preferred stock are in a different class from common shareholders.

The bankruptcy court will approve a plan if a majority of *each class* votes in favor of it. Even if some classes vote against the plan, the court can still confirm it under what is called a **cramdown** (as in "the plan is crammed down the creditors' throats"). The court will only impose a cramdown if, in its view, the plan is feasible and fair. If the court rejects the plan of reorganization, the creditors must develop a new one.

Discharge

A confirmed plan of reorganization is binding on the debtor, creditors, and shareholders. **The debtor now owns the assets in the bankrupt estate, free of all obligations except those listed in the plan.** Under a typical plan of reorganization, the debtor gives some current assets to creditors and also promises to pay them a portion of future earnings. In contrast, the Chapter 7 debtor typically relinquishes all assets (except exempt property) to creditors but then has no obligation to turn over future income. Exhibit 13.5 illustrates the steps in a Chapter 11 bankruptcy.

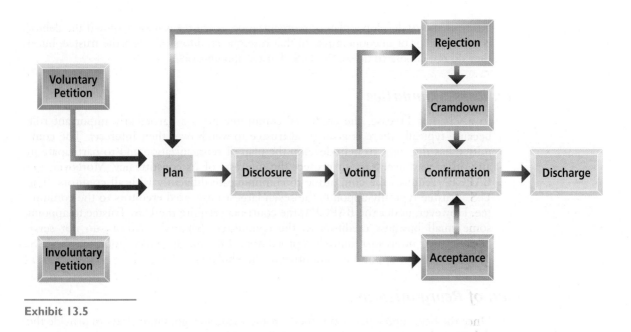

Exhibit 13.5

Small Business Bankruptcy

Out of concern that the lengthy procedure in Chapter 11 was harming the creditors of small businesses, Congress included provisions in the BAPCPA designed to speed up the process for businesses with less than $2 million in debt. After the order of relief, the bankrupt has the exclusive right to file a plan for 180 days. Both a plan and a disclosure statement must be filed within 300 days. The court must confirm or reject the plan within 45 days after its filing. If these deadlines are not met, the case can be converted to Chapter 7 or dismissed. This amendment may well cause more small companies to go out of business.

CHAPTER 13 CONSUMER REORGANIZATIONS

The purpose of Chapter 13 is to rehabilitate an individual debtor. It is not available at all to businesses or to individuals with more than $307,675 in unsecured debts or $922,975 in secured debts. Under Chapter 13, the bankrupt consumer typically keeps most of her assets in exchange for a promise to repay some of her debts using future income. Therefore, to be eligible, the debtor must have a regular source of income. Individuals usually choose this chapter because it is easier and cheaper than Chapters 7 and 11. Consequently, more money is retained for both creditors and debtor.

A bankruptcy under Chapter 13 generally follows the same course as Chapter 11: the debtor files a petition, creditors submit proofs of claim, the court imposes an automatic stay, the debtor files a plan, and the court confirms the plan. But there are some differences.

Beginning a Chapter 13 Case

To initiate a Chapter 13 case, the debtor must file a voluntary petition. **Creditors cannot use an involuntary petition to force a debtor into Chapter 13.** In all

Chapter 13 cases, the U.S. Trustee appoints a trustee to supervise the debtor although the debtor remains in possession of the bankruptcy estate. The trustee also serves as a central clearinghouse for the debtor's payments to creditors. The debtor pays the trustee who, in turn, transmits these funds to creditors. For this service the trustee is allowed to keep 10 percent of the payments.

Plan of Payment

The debtor must file a plan of payment within 15 days after filing the voluntary petition. Only the debtor can file a plan; the creditors have no right to file their own version. Under the plan, the debtor must (1) commit some future earnings to pay off debts, (2) promise to pay all secured and priority claims in full, and (3) treat all remaining classes equally. If the plan does not provide for the debtor to pay off creditors in full, then all of the debtor's disposable income for the next five years must go to creditors.

Within 30 days after filing the plan of payment, the debtor must begin making payments to the trustee under the plan. The trustee holds these payments until the plan is confirmed and then transmits them to creditors. The debtor continues to make payments to the trustee until the plan has been fully implemented. If the plan is rejected, the trustee returns the payments to the debtor.

Only the bankruptcy court has the authority to confirm or reject a plan of payment. Creditors have no right to vote on it. However, to confirm a plan, the court must ensure that:

- All of the unsecured creditors receive at least as much as they would have under Chapter 7;

- The plan is feasible and the bankrupt will be able to make the promised payments;

- The plan does not extend beyond three years without good reason and in no event lasts longer than five years; and

- The debtor is acting in good faith, making a reasonable effort to pay obligations.

In the following case, a creditor argued that the debtor's plan was not made in good faith.

IN RE LEMAIRE

898 F.2d 1346, 1990 U.S. App. LEXIS 4374
United States Court of Appeals for the Eighth Circuit, 1990

Facts: As Paul Handeen got out of his car one Sunday morning, Gregory LeMaire shot at him nine times with a bolt action rifle. Bullets struck Handeen in the mouth, neck, spine, arm, knee, and ankle. LeMaire pleaded guilty to a charge of aggravated assault and served 27 months in prison. After his release he earned a doctorate from the University of Minnesota.

Handeen received a judgment of $50,000 against LeMaire. To avoid paying this judgment, LeMaire filed a bankruptcy petition under Chapter 13. He proposed a plan under which he would pay his creditors 42 percent of their claims. The bankruptcy court confirmed the plan over Handeen's objection. Handeen appealed to the district court, arguing that LeMaire had not filed his plan in good faith. The district court affirmed and, upon appeal, the appeals court also affirmed. Handeen then asked for a rehearing. This time, the appeals court granted a rehearing *en banc*. (Usually, only three judges hear an appeal. "*En banc*" means that all the judges on the court hear it.)

▼

Issues: Is a judgment awarded to the victim of an intentional shooting dischargeable under Chapter 13? Did LeMaire file his plan in good faith?

Excerpts from Judge Gibson's Decision: In evaluating LeMaire's motivation and sincerity, the bankruptcy court balanced Handeen's desire to be compensated for his injuries against LeMaire's desire to have a fresh start and found the latter to outweigh the former in importance. The court noted that, while LeMaire had been unable to pay his debt to his victim, he had paid his debt to society by serving a prison sentence and had attempted to reorder his life and make a fresh start. The court found that forcing LeMaire to be burdened the rest of his life with a judgment which would continue to accrue interest, result in endless garnishments, and prevent him from accumulating property would be inimical to such a fresh start. The court concluded that LeMaire had made a wholehearted attempt to pay Handeen as much as possible, and that LeMaire's motivation was proper and his sincerity real.

We do not believe that LeMaire has fulfilled the good faith requirement of Chapter 13. The record here very clearly indicates that LeMaire intended to kill Handeen, and he nearly succeeded in his intention. While pre-filing conduct is not determinative of the good faith issue, it is nevertheless relevant. When we consider the pre-filing conduct here, including the maliciousness of the injury which LeMaire inflicted upon Handeen, in light of the lack of other factors sufficient to establish good faith, we are persuaded that the bankruptcy court clearly erred in finding that LeMaire proposed his plan in good faith.

We remand this case to the district court with instructions to remand, in turn, to the bankruptcy court for further proceedings consistent with this opinion. ■

Discharge

Once confirmed, a plan is binding on all creditors, whether they like it or not. **The debtor is washed clean of all pre-petition debts except those provided for in the plan, but, unlike Chapter 7, the debts are not** *permanently* **discharged.** If the debtor violates the plan, all of the debts are revived and the creditors have a right to recover them under Chapter 7. The debts become permanently discharged only when the bankrupt fully complies with the plan.

If the debtor's circumstances change, the debtor, the trustee, or unsecured creditors can ask the court to modify the plan. Most such requests come from debtors whose income has declined. However, if the debtor's income rises, the creditors or the trustee can ask that payments increase, too.

Chapter Conclusion

Borrowed money is the lubricant that keeps a modern economy motoring smoothly. Without it many consumers would never own a home or a car and many businesses would be unable to grow. But unless these debts are repaid, the economy will falter. Secured transactions are one method for ensuring that creditors are paid.

Bankruptcy law is the safety net that catches those who are not able to meet their financial obligations. Bankruptcy laws cannot create assets where there are none (or not enough), but they can ensure that the debtor's assets, however limited, are fairly divided between the debtor and creditors. Any bankruptcy system that accomplishes this goal must be deemed a success.

Chapter Review

1. Article 9 applies to any transaction intended to create a security interest in personal property or fixtures.

2. Attachment means that (1) the two parties made a security agreement and either the debtor has authenticated a security agreement describing the collateral or the secured party has obtained possession or control; and (2) the secured party gave value in order to get the security agreement; and (3) the debtor has rights in the collateral.

3. Attachment protects against the debtor. Perfection of a security interest protects the secured party against parties other than the debtor.

4. Filing is the most common way to perfect. For many forms of collateral, the secured party may also perfect by obtaining either possession or control.

5. A purchase money security interest (PMSI) is one taken by the person who sells the collateral or advances money so the debtor can buy the collateral.

6. A buyer in ordinary course of business (BIOC) takes the goods free of a security interest created by his seller even though the security interest is perfected.

7. Priority among secured parties is generally as follows:

   a. A party with a perfected security interest takes priority over a party with an unperfected interest.

   b. If neither secured party has perfected, the first interest to attach gets priority.

   c. Between perfected security interests, the first to file or perfect wins.

8. When the debtor defaults, the secured party may take possession of the collateral on its own, without a court order, if it can do so without a breach of the peace.

9. A secured party may sell, lease, or otherwise dispose of the collateral in any commercially reasonable way, or it may ignore the collateral and sue the debtor for the full debt.

10. When the debtor pays the full debt, the secured party must complete a termination statement, notifying the public that it no longer claims a security interest in the collateral.

The following chart sets out the important elements of each bankruptcy chapter.

	Chapter 7	Chapter 11	Chapter 13
Objective	Liquidation	Reorganization	Consumer reorganization
Who May Use It	Individual or organization	Individual or organization	Individual
Type of Petition	Voluntary or involuntary	Voluntary or involuntary	Only voluntary
Administration of Bankruptcy Estate	Trustee	Debtor in possession (trustee selected only if debtor is unable to serve)	Trustee
Selection of Trustee	Creditors have right to elect trustee; otherwise, U.S. Trustee makes appointment	Usually no trustee	Appointed by U.S. Trustee

(Continued)

(Continued)

	Chapter 7	Chapter 11	Chapter 13
Participation in Formulation of Plan	No plan is filed	Both creditors and debtor can propose plans	Only debtor can propose a plan
Creditor Approval of Plan	Creditors do not vote	Creditors vote on plan, but court may approve plan without the creditors support	Creditors do not vote on plan
Impact on Debtors Post-petition Income	Not affected; debtor keeps all future earnings	Must contribute toward payment of pre-petition debts	Must contribute toward payment of pre-petition debts

Practice Test

Note to the student: The following cases and problems were decided under the former Article 9. In each instance, the outcome would be the same under the revised laws.

1. CPA QUESTION Under the UCC Secured Transactions Article, perfection of a security interest by a creditor provides added protection against other parties in the event the debtor does not pay its debts. Which of the following parties is not affected by perfection of a security interest?

a. Other prospective creditors of the debtor

b. The trustee in a bankruptcy case

c. A buyer in the ordinary course of business

d. A subsequent personal injury judgment creditor

2. Eugene Ables ran an excavation company. He borrowed $500,000 from the Highland Park State Bank. Ables signed a note promising to repay the money and an agreement giving Highland a security interest in all of his equipment, including after-acquired equipment. Several years later, Ables agreed with Patricia Myers to purchase a Bantam Backhoe from her for $16,000, which he would repay at the rate of $100 per month, while he used the machine. Ables later defaulted on his note to Highland, and the bank attempted to take the backhoe. Myers and Ables contended that the bank had

no right to take the backhoe. Was the backhoe covered by Highland's security interest? Did Ables have sufficient rights in the backhoe for the bank's security interest to attach?

3. Jerry Payne owed the First State Bank of Pflugerville $342,000. The loan was secured by a 9.25-carat diamond ring. The bank claimed a default on the loan and, without notifying Payne, sold the ring. But the proceeds did not pay off the full debt, and the bank sued Payne for the deficiency. Is Payne liable for the deficiency?

4. John and Clara Lockovich bought a 22-foot Chaparrel Villian II boat from Greene County Yacht Club for $32,500. They paid $6,000 cash and borrowed the rest of the purchase money from Gallatin National Bank, which took a security interest in the boat. Gallatin filed a financing statement in *Greene* County, Pennsylvania, where the bank was located. But Pennsylvania law at that time required financing statements to be filed in the county of the debtor's residence, and the Lockoviches lived in Allegheny County. The Lockoviches soon washed up in Bankruptcy Court. Other creditors demanded that the boat be sold, claiming that Gallatin's security interest had been filed in the wrong place. Who wins? (Please be advised: this is a trick question.)

5. McMann Golf Ball Co. manufactured, as you might suppose, golf balls. Barwell, Inc., sold McMann a "preformer," a machine that makes golf balls, for $55,000. Barwell delivered the machine on February 20. McMann paid $3,000 down, the remainder to be paid over several years, and signed an agreement giving Barwell a security interest in the preformer. Barwell did not perfect its interest. On March 1, McMann borrowed $350,000 from First of America Bank, giving the bank a security interest in McMann's present and after-acquired property. First of America perfected by filing on March 2. McMann, of course, became insolvent, and both Barwell and the bank attempted to repossess the preformer. Who gets it?

6. **ETHICS** On November 5, The Fred Hawes Organization, Inc., a small subcontractor, opened an account with Basic Distribution Corp., a supplier of construction materials. Hawes promised to pay its bills within 30 days of purchase. Although Hawes purchased a substantial quantity of goods on credit from Basic, it made few payments on the accounts until the following March when it paid Basic more than $21,000. On May 14, Hawes filed a voluntary petition under Chapter 7. Does the bankruptcy trustee have a right to recover this payment? Is it fair to Hawes's other creditors if Basic is allowed to keep the $21,000 payment?

7. Mark Milbank built custom furniture in Port Chester, New York. His business was unsuccessful, and he repeatedly borrowed money from his wife and her father. He promised that the loans would enable him to spend more time with his family. Instead, he spent more time in bed with his next-door neighbor. After the divorce, his ex-wife and her father demanded repayment of the loans. When Milbank filed under Chapter 13, his ex-wife and her father asked the court not to discharge Milbank's debts on the grounds that he had acted in bad faith toward them. Should the bankruptcy court discharge Milbank's loans?

8. **CPA QUESTION** Decal Corp. incurred substantial operating losses for the past three years. Unable to meet its current obligations, Decal filed a petition of reorganization under Chapter 11 of the federal Bankruptcy Code. Which of the following statements is correct?

a. A creditors' committee, if appointed, will consist of unsecured creditors.

b. The court must appoint a trustee to manage Decal's affairs.

c. Decal may continue in business only with the approval of a trustee.

d. The creditors' committee must select a trustee to manage Decal's affairs.

9. **CPA QUESTION** A voluntary petition filed under the liquidation provisions of Chapter 7 of the federal Bankruptcy Code:

a. Is not available to a corporation unless it has previously filed a petition under the reorganization provisions of Chapter 11 of the Code

b. Automatically stays collection actions against the debtor except by secured creditors

c. Will be dismissed unless the debtor has 12 or more unsecured creditors whose claims total at least $5,000

d. Does not require the debtor to show that the debtor's liabilities exceed the fair market value of assets

10. **YOU BE THE JUDGE** WRITING PROBLEM Lydia D'Ettore received a degree in computer programming at DeVry Institute of Technology, with a grade-point average of 2.51. To finance her education, she borrowed $20,516.52 from a federal student loan program. After graduation she could not find a job in her field, so she went to work as a clerk at a salary of $12,500. D'Ettore and her daughter lived with her parents free of charge. After setting aside $50 a month in savings and paying bills that included $233 for a new car (a Suzuki Samurai) and $50 for jewelry from Zales, her disposable income was $125 per month. D'Ettore asked the bankruptcy court to discharge the debts she owed DeVry. Under the Code these student loans cannot be discharged unless they impose an "undue hardship" on the debtor. Did the debts to DeVry Institute impose an undue hardship on D'Ettore? **Argument for D'Ettore:** Lydia D'Ettore lives at home with her parents. Even so, her disposable income is a meager $125 a month. She would have to spend every single penny of her disposable income for nearly 15 years to pay back her $20,000 debt to DeVry. That would be an undue hardship. **Argument for the Creditors:** The U.S. government guaranteed D'Ettore's loan. Therefore, if the court discharges it, the American taxpayer will have to pay the bill. Why should taxpayers subsidize an irresponsible student? D'Ettore must also stop

buying new cars and jewelry. And why should the government pay her debts while she saves money every month?

Internet Research Problem

Write a security agreement in which your friend gives you a security interest in her $20,000 home entertainment system, in exchange for a loan of $12,000. Because the collateral is something that she uses daily, what special concerns do you have? How will you protect yourself? Next, find the UCC1 financing form at **http://www.intercountyclearance. com/ra9/ra9ucc1.pdf**. Print the form, then complete it. In what office of your state should you file in order to perfect?

What are your state's exemption rules? You can find them at **http://www.bankruptcyaction.com/**

11. ROLE REVERSAL Write a multiple-choice question that highlights the difference between Chapters 7 and 11.

bankruptcyexemptions.htm or elsewhere on the Web. Compared with other jurisdictions, is your state generous or stingy with exemptions? In considering a new bankruptcy statute, Congress struggled mightily over this issue. What do you think is a fair exemption?

You can find further practice problems at **academic.cengage.com/blaw/beatty.**

AGENCY & EMPLOYMENT

© ADAM CROWLEY/PHOTODISC/GETTY IMAGES

© PHOTO 24/BRAND X PICTURES/GETTY IMAGES

As Leo Tolstoy observed, "Happy families are all alike; every unhappy family is unhappy in its own way."[1] The Gagnon family of Massachusetts found its own way to be unhappy. Eighty-five year old Francis Gagnon and his wife lived on a 184-acre farm in Shelburne. They also owned a smaller parcel of land in Hillsborough, New Hampshire. Their daughter, Joan Coombs, resided twenty miles from Shelburne while their son, Frank, lived in a trailer on a far corner of the farm.

Because of their advancing age, Joan suggested that her parents sign powers of attorney appointing her as their agent. In this way, if they became ill she would have the legal authority to take care of them and their property. In theory, this was a sensible step that estate lawyers often recommend. But in this family sensible took a backseat to jealous and resentful. No one told Frank about the power of attorney.

The next year, Mrs. Gagnon went into a nursing home. In the process of admitting her, Frank learned of Joan's power of attorney. He was not exactly pleased. After moving from his trailer into the main house, Frank prevailed upon his father to revoke the power of attorney. Naturally, neither Frank nor Francis told Joan this interesting fact. (At trial the siblings pointed fingers at each other with accusations of undue influence on their father, but the judge concluded that Francis was mentally competent during this entire episode.)

Two months later, Mrs. Gagnon died and Francis decided to sell the Shelburne farm. Shortly thereafter, he signed a purchase and sale agreement on the property at a price of $750,000. He then gave the property in New Hampshire to Frank.

When Francis told Joan about the sale of the land and his intention to move to New Hampshire to live with Frank, she crafted her own plan. Not realizing that her power of

---

[1] Leo Tolstoy, *Anna Karenina*, Barnes & Noble Books, p. 1.

attorney had been revoked, she used it to transfer the Shelburne property to a trust that she had created and that she controlled. When Joan wrote Frank to tell him about these developments, he was furious. This unhappy family was now reduced to communicating through their attorneys. Francis's lawyer wrote to Joan demanding that she return the Shelburne property to him. She refused, setting the family on the path to court.

Although this case undoubtedly raises issues that could keep a family therapist employed for some time, it is the questions of agency law that concern us. Was Joan an agent for her father? As an agent, did she have the right to convey his property to her trust? Later in this chapter, the case of Gagnon v. Coombs lays out the arguments for both sides. ■

Thus far, this book has primarily dealt with issues of individual responsibility: What happens if *you* knock someone down or *you* sign an agreement? Agency law, on the other hand, is concerned with your responsibility for the actions of others. What happens if your agent assaults someone or enters into an agreement? Agency law presents a significant trade-off: if you do everything yourself, you have control over the result. But the size and scope of your business (and your life) will be severely limited. Once you hire other people, you can accomplish a great deal more, but your risk of legal liability increases immensely. Though it might be safer to do everything yourself, that is not a practical decision for most business owners (or most people). The alternative is to hire carefully and to limit the risks as much as possible by understanding the law of agency.

CREATING AN AGENCY RELATIONSHIP

Principals have substantial liability for the actions of their agents.[2] Therefore, disputes about whether an agency relationship exists are not mere legal quibbles but important issues with potentially profound financial consequences. According to the Restatement of Agency:

> Agency is the fiduciary relation which results from the manifestation of consent by one person to another that the other shall act on his behalf and subject to his control, and consent by the other so to act.[3]

In other words, in an agency relationship, someone (the agent) agrees to perform a task for, and under the control of, someone else (the principal). To create an agency relationship, there must be:

- A **principal** and
- An **agent**
- Who mutually **consent** that the agent will act on behalf of the principal and
- Be subject to the principal's **control**
- Thereby creating a **fiduciary** relationship.

---

[2] The word "principal" is always used when referring to a person. It is not to be confused with the word "principle," which refers to a fundamental idea.

[3] Section 1 of the Restatement (Second) of Agency (1958), prepared by the American Law Institute.

Consent

To establish consent, the principal must ask the agent to do something, and the agent must agree. In the most straightforward example, Francis Gagnon asked his daughter to act as his agent and she agreed. Matters were more complicated, however, when Steven James met some friends one evening at a restaurant. During the two hours he was there, he drank four to six beers. (It is probably a bad sign that he cannot remember how many.) From then on, one misfortune piled upon another. After leaving the restaurant at about 7:00 p.m., James sped down a highway and crashed into a car that had stalled on the roadway, thereby killing the driver. James told the police at the scene that he had not seen the parked car (another bad sign). Evidently, James's lawyer was not as perceptive as the police in recognizing drunkenness. In a misguided attempt to help his client, James's lawyer took him to the local hospital for a blood test. Unfortunately, the test confirmed that James had indeed been drunk at the time of the accident.

The attorney knew that if this evidence was admitted at trial, his client would soon be receiving free room and board from the Massachusetts Department of Corrections. So at trial the lawyer argued that the blood test was protected by the client-attorney privilege because the hospital had been his agent and therefore a member of the defense team. The court disagreed, however, holding that the hospital employees were not agents for the lawyer because they had not consented to act in the role.

The court upheld James's conviction of murder in the first degree by reason of extreme atrocity or cruelty.[4]

Control

Principals are liable for the acts of their agents because they exercise control over the agents. If principals direct their agents to commit an act, it seems fair to hold the principal liable when that act causes harm. In the following example, did Northwest Airlines exercise control over Kuwait Air?

NEWSworthy

The horse-drawn caisson wound slowly through Arlington National Cemetery and stopped in front of lot number 59, the section reserved for victims of terrorist acts. The flag-draped casket of William L. Stanford, one of the two Agency for International Development auditors killed by plane hijackers in Iran, was carried to the gravesite amid full military honors. Three volleys of rifle fire pierced the unusually warm December air as scores of family, friends, and colleagues lowered their heads and wept. Stanford, 52, was killed as he was traveling to join his wife and 13-year-old daughter in Karachi, Pakistan, where he intended to spend the holidays.[5] ◆

The hijacked plane—with William Stanford aboard—was a Kuwait Airways (KA) flight from Kuwait to Pakistan. Stanford had originally purchased a ticket on Northwest Airlines but had traded in his Northwest ticket for a seat on the KA flight. Stanford's widow sued Northwest on the theory that KA was Northwest's agent. The airlines had an agreement permitting passengers to exchange tickets from one to another. In this case, however, the court found that no agency relationship existed because Northwest had no *control* over KA.[6] Northwest did not tell KA how to fly

---

4 Commonwealth v. James, 427 Mass. 312, 693 N.E.2d 148, 1998 Mass. LEXIS 175.

5 Mary Jordan, "Terrorists' Victim Is Buried," The Washington Post, Dec. 18, 1984, p. A14.

6 Stanford v. Kuwait Airways Corp., 648 F. Supp. 1158, 1986 U.S. Dist. LEXIS 18880 (S.D.N.Y. 1986).

planes or handle terrorists; therefore it should not be liable when KA made fatal errors. An agent and principal must not only *consent* to an agency relationship, but the principal must also have *control* over the agent.

Fiduciary Relationship

A fiduciary relationship is a special relationship, with high standards. The beneficiary places special confidence in the fiduciary who, in turn, is obligated to act in good faith and candor, putting his own needs second. The purpose of a fiduciary relationship is for one person to benefit another. **Agents have a fiduciary duty to their principals.**

All three elements—consent, control, and a fiduciary duty—are necessary to create an agency relationship. In some relationships, for example, there might be a *fiduciary duty* but no *control*. A trustee of a trust must act for the benefit of the beneficiaries, but the beneficiaries have no right to control the trustee. Therefore, a trustee is not an agent of the beneficiaries. *Consent* is present in every contractual relationship, but that does not necessarily mean that the two parties are agent and principal. If Horace sells his car to Lily, they both expect to benefit under the contract, but neither has a *fiduciary duty* to the other and neither *controls* the other, so there is no agency relationship.

Elements Not Required for an Agency Relationship

Consent, control, and a fiduciary relationship are necessary to establish an agency relationship. The following elements are **not** required:

- *A Written Agreement.* In most cases an agency agreement does not have to be in writing. An oral understanding is valid, except in one circumstance—the **equal dignities rule.** According to this rule, if an agent is empowered to enter into a contract that must be in writing, then the appointment of the agent must also be written. For example, under the statute of frauds, a contract for the sale of land is unenforceable unless in writing, so the agency agreement to sell land must also be *in writing.*

- *A Formal Agreement.* The principal and agent need not agree formally that they have an agency relationship. They do not even have to think the word "agent." As long as they act like an agent and a principal, the law will treat them as such.

- *Consideration.* An agency relationship need not meet all the standards of contract law. For example, a contract is not valid without consideration, but an agency agreement is valid *even if the agent is not paid.*

In the following case, a Boston University basketball player injured an opposing player. Was he the university's agent?

KAVANAGH V. TRUSTEES OF BOSTON UNIVERSITY

440 Mass. 195; 795 N.E.2d 1170; 2003 Mass. LEXIS 643
SUPREME JUDICIAL COURT OF MASSACHUSETTS, 2003

Facts: The Boston University men's basketball team played a game against Manhattan College. Following a contested rebound, the referee blew his whistle to signal a foul. Some of the players began to push and elbow each other. Kenneth Kavanagh, a Manhattan College player, intervened to break up a developing scuffle. Levar Folk, a Boston University player, ▼

punched him in the nose. Folk was immediately ejected from the game. Kavanagh was treated for what turned out to be a broken nose and returned to play later in the same game.

Folk was at the university on a full athletic scholarship. Kavanagh contends that Folk's status as a scholarship athlete made him an agent of the university and that the university is therefore liable for any torts committed by Folk while playing for the basketball team.

The trial court granted summary judgment to the university. Kavanagh appealed.

Issue: Is a basketball player on scholarship an agent of the university team for which he plays?

Excerpts from Justice Sosman's Decision: A student's status as student does not, by itself, make the student an "employee" of the school the student attends. Neither party understands the student's relationship with the school to be one of employment. Students attend school to serve their own interests, not the interests of the school. The student is a buyer of education rather than an agent. A student retains the benefit of that education for himself rather than for the university.

While schools may benefit in various ways from the presence of a particular student, or may benefit in the future from a former student's later success, the student does not attend school to do the school's bidding.

While scholarships may introduce some element of "payment" into the relationship, scholarships are not wages. Nor does a scholarship student "work for" the school in exchange for that scholarship. The benefits that may accrue to a school from the attendance of particularly talented athletes is conceptually no different from the benefits that schools obtain from the attendance of other forms of talented and successful students—both as undergraduates and later as alumni, such students enhance the school's reputation, draw favorable attention to the school, and may increase the school's ability to raise funds.

It is undeniable that a successful athletic program, particularly in popular sports like basketball, can garner substantial revenues for colleges and universities, both directly from the sporting activities themselves (e.g., gate receipts, sale of broadcasting rights) and indirectly from the attention those activities attract (e.g., increased alumni giving). In recent years, the enormity of the revenues at stake in collegiate sports has prompted some to recommend that colleges and universities be allowed to compensate student athletes for their "services" and thereby transform them into employees. It is recognized, however, that the current relationship of a player to a school remains that of scholarship student, not employee.

Kavanagh argues that scholarship athletes should nevertheless be treated as "agents" of their schools because it is said that they "represent" their schools. When one speaks of an athlete, or any other student, as a "representative" of his or her school, the term is not being used in its legal sense. Rather, it connotes only that a student's performance will reflect on the school and will be seen as indicative of the school's quality. Students do not "represent" their schools in the sense of being able to bind their schools to agreements, or to act on behalf of their schools.

Judgment affirmed. ■

DUTIES OF AGENTS TO PRINCIPALS

Agents owe a fiduciary duty to their principals. In the following example, employees of Steinberg, Moorad & Dunn (SMD) were agents of the firm—they had agreed to act on behalf of SMD and be subject to its control. Did they violate their duty?

NEWS*worthy*

Sports agent Leigh Steinberg, whose story inspired the Tom Cruise film *Jerry Maguire,* is caught up in a legal battle with his former partner that echoes moments from the movie. Steinberg's firm, SMD, has sued David Dunn, claiming Dunn was planning to form his own stable of sports stars while working for SMD. Dunn and agents at his new firm, Athletes First, have said that as many as 80 percent of SMD's clients plan to switch management firms or already have.

SMD plans to ask Los Angeles Superior Court Judge Marilyn Hoffman to order Dunn to stop representing athletes he knew through SMD. "Earlier this year, Dunn orchestrated a despicable raid on [SMD] and its clientele," SMD says in court papers for its suit. Dunn counters that SMD "neglected and lost clients it now accuses Athletes First of stealing."

Overall, about one-third of SMD's former 30-person staff in Newport Beach, California, has since joined Dunn at Athletes First. Steinberg claims that Dunn and his recruits downloaded lists of clients and their specific contract terms and needs, as well as information on prospective clients, while still at SMD.[7] ◆

^{uP}*date*

Search on the Internet for further information about the dispute between Leigh Steinberg and David Dunn. If Dunn won, what were the important factors in the court's decision? If Steinberg was victorious, what penalties were imposed on Dunn? ◆

Duty of Loyalty

The agent must act solely for the benefit of the principal in all matters connected with the agency.[8] The agent has an obligation to put the principal first, to strive to accomplish the principal's goals. If Dunn and his colleagues stole client information from SMD in preparation for their departure to Athletes First, they were violating their duty of loyalty to their principal because they were acting in their own interest, not that of their principal.

An agent is bound by the duty of loyalty *whether or not the agent and principal have consciously agreed to it.* The agent should know his obligations. However, a principal and agent can change this rule by agreement. SMD, for example, could have given Dunn permission to download the client lists, in which case Dunn would not have been liable, at least for that activity. The various components of the duty of loyalty follow.

Outside Benefits

An agent may not receive profits unless the principal knows and approves. Suppose that Hope is an employee of the agency Big Egos and Talents, Inc. (BEAT). She has been representing Will Smith in his latest movie negotiations.[9] Smith often drives her to meetings in his new Maybach. He is so thrilled that she has arranged for him to star in the new movie *Little Men* that he buys her a Maybach. Can Hope keep this generous gift? Only with BEAT's permission. She must tell BEAT about the Maybach; the company may then take the vehicle itself or allow her to keep it.

Confidential Information

The ability to keep secrets is important in any relationship, but especially a fiduciary relationship. Agents can neither disclose nor use for their own benefit any confidential information they acquire during their agency. As the following case shows, this duty continues even after the agency relationship ends.

---

[7] Joyzelle Davis, "Real-Life Breakup of 'Jerry Maguire' Agency Mirrors Movie," The Houston Chronicle, Aug. 12, 2001, Sports, p. 2.

[8] Restatement (Second) of Agency §387.

[9] Do not be confused by the fact that Hope works as an agent for movie stars. As an employee of BEAT, her duty is to the company. She is an agent of BEAT and BEAT works for the celebrities.

ABKCO MUSIC, INC. V. HARRISONGS MUSIC, LTD.

722 F.2d 988, 1983 U.S. App. LEXIS 15562
United States Court of Appeals for the Second Circuit, 1983

Facts: Bright Tunes Music Corp. (Bright Tunes) owned the copyright to the song "He's So Fine." The company sued George Harrison, a Beatle, alleging that the Harrison composition "My Sweet Lord" copied "He's So Fine." At the time the suit was filed, Allen B. Klein handled the business affairs of the Beatles.

Klein (representing Harrison) met with the president of Bright Tunes to discuss possible settlement of the copyright lawsuit. Klein suggested that Harrison might be interested in purchasing the copyright to "He's So Fine." Shortly thereafter, Klein's management contract with the Beatles expired. Without telling Harrison, Klein began negotiating with Bright Tunes to purchase the copyright to "He's So Fine" for himself. To advance these negotiations, Klein gave Bright Tunes information about royalty income for "My Sweet Lord"—information that he had gained as Harrison's agent.

The trial judge in the copyright case ultimately found that Harrison had infringed the copyright on "He's So Fine" and assessed damages of $1,599,987. After the trial Klein purchased the "He's So Fine" copyright from Bright Tunes and with it, the right to recover from Harrison for the breach of copyright.

Issue: Did Klein violate his fiduciary duty to Harrison by using confidential information after the agency relationship terminated?

Excerpts from Judge Pierce's Decision: There is no doubt that the relationship between Harrison and [Klein] prior to the termination of the management agreement was that of principal and agent, and that the relationship was fiduciary in nature. [A]n agent has a duty not to use confidential knowledge acquired in his employment in competition with his principal. This duty exists as well after the employment is terminated as during its continuance. On the other hand, use of information based on general business knowledge or gleaned from general business experience is not covered by the rule, and the former agent is permitted to compete with his former principal in reliance on such general publicly available information. The evidence presented herein is not at all convincing that the information imparted to Bright Tunes by Klein was publicly available.

While the initial attempt to purchase [the copyright to "He's So Fine"] was several years removed from the eventual purchase on [Klein]'s own account, we are not of the view that such a fact rendered [Klein] unfettered in the later negotiations. Taking all of these circumstances together, we agree that [Klein's] conduct did not meet the standard required of him as a former fiduciary. ■

Ethics

Klein was angry that the Beatles had failed to renew his management contract. Was it reasonable for him to think that he owed no duty to the principal who had fired him? Should his sense of ethics have told him that his behavior was wrong? Would the ethics checklist in Chapter 2 have helped Klein to make a better decision? Why would George Harrison prefer to owe money to Bright Tunes than to Klein? ◆

Competition with the Principal

Agents are not allowed to compete with their principal in any matter within the scope of the agency business. If Allen Klein had purchased the "He's So Fine" copyright while he was George Harrison's agent, he would have committed an additional sin against the agency relationship. Owning song rights was clearly part of the agency business, so Klein could not make such purchases without Harrison's consent. Once the agency relationship ends, however, so does the rule against competition. Klein was entitled to buy the "He's So Fine" copyright after the agency relationship ended (as long as he did not use confidential information).

Conflict of Interest between Two Principals

Unless otherwise agreed, an agent may not act for two principals whose interests conflict. Suppose Travis represents both director Steven Spielberg and actor Julia Roberts. Spielberg is casting the title role in his new movie, *Nancy Drew: Girl Detective*, a role that Roberts covets. Travis cannot represent these two clients when they are negotiating with each other, unless they both know about the conflict and agree to ignore it. The following article illustrates the dangers of acting for two principals at once.

NEWS*worthy*

Faced with growing health care and retirement costs, the Sisters of Charity decided to sell a 207-acre property that they owned in New Jersey. The order of nuns soon found, however, that the world is not always a charitable place. They agreed to sell the land to Linpro for nearly $10 million. But before the deal closed, Linpro signed a contract to resell the property to Sammis for $34 million. So, you say, the sisters made a bad deal. There is no law against that. But it turned out that the nuns' lawyer, Peter Berkley, also represented Sammis. He knew about the deal between Sammis and Linpro, but never told the sisters. Was that the charitable—or legal—thing to do? For ideas on how Berkley should have handled this delicate situation, look at the discussion on dual agency at http://www.thbuyers.com by clicking on "News," then the link under the "Watch Out!" head. ◆

Secretly Dealing with the Principal

If a principal hires an agent to arrange a transaction, the agent may not become a party to the transaction without the principal's permission. Matt Damon became an overnight sensation after starring in the movie *Good Will Hunting*. Suppose that he hired Trang to read scripts for him. Unbeknownst to Damon, Trang had written her own script, which she thought would be ideal for him. She may not sell it to him without revealing that she wrote it herself. Damon may be perfectly happy to buy Trang's script, but he has the right, as her principal, to know that she is the person selling it.

Appropriate Behavior

An agent may not engage in inappropriate behavior that reflects badly on the principal. This rule applies even to *off-duty* conduct. For example, two of the flight attendants featured in the following article were fired for inappropriate off-duty behavior; the third was given a warning letter.

NEWS*worthy*

The guests at a hotel bar in London were stunned when British Airways flight attendant Shirlie Johns raised her shirt so that colleague Stefania Lanza could caress her breasts while kissing her on the mouth. Johns then lowered her trousers, revealing her underwear. Meanwhile, crew member Matthew Swadling took off his shirt and poured wine down his trousers. All three rubbed up against each other provocatively while downing beer, vodka, and wine. It was, bystanders agreed, a huge embarrassment for British Airways. ◆

Other Duties of an Agent

Before Taylor left for a five-week trip to England, he hired Angie to rent his vacation house. Angie never got around to listing his house on the regional rental list used by all the area brokers, but when the Fords contacted her looking for rental housing, she did show them Taylor's place. They offered to rent it for $750 per month.

Angie called Taylor in England to tell him. He responded that he would not accept less than $850 a month, which Angie thought the Fords would be willing to pay. He told Angie to call back if there was any problem. The Fords decided that they would go no higher than $800 a month. Instead of calling Taylor in England, Angie left a message on his home answering machine. When the Fords pressed her for an answer, she said she could not get in touch with Taylor. Not until Taylor returned home did he learn that the Fords had rented another house. Did Angie violate any of the duties that agents owe to their principals?

Duty to Obey Instructions

An agent must obey her principal's instructions unless the principal directs her to behave illegally or unethically. Taylor instructed Angie to call him if the Fords rejected the offer. When Angie failed to do so, she violated her duty to obey instructions. If, however, Taylor had asked her to say that the house's basement was dry, when in fact it looked like a rice paddy every spring, Angie would be under no obligation to follow those illegal instructions.

Duty of Care

An agent has a duty to act with reasonable care. In other words, an agent must act as a reasonable person would, under the circumstances. A reasonable person would not have left a message on Taylor's home answering machine when she knew he was in Europe.

Under some circumstances, an agent is held to a higher—or lower—standard than usual. **An agent with special skills is held to a higher standard because she is expected to use those skills.** A trained real estate agent should know enough to use the regional rental list.

But suppose Taylor had asked his neighbor, Jed, to help him sell the house. Jed is not a trained real estate agent, and he is not being paid, which makes him a *gratuitous agent*. A gratuitous agent is held to a lower standard because he is doing his principal a favor and, as the old saying goes, you get what you pay for—up to a point. **Gratuitous agents are liable if they commit *gross* negligence, but not *ordinary* negligence.** If Jed, as a gratuitous agent, left Taylor an important message on his answering machine because he forgot about the trip to England, he would not be liable to them for that ordinary negligence. But if the answering machine had a message that *warned* him Taylor was away and would not be picking up messages, he would be liable for gross negligence and a violation of his duty.

Duty to Provide Information

An agent has a duty to provide the principal with all information in her possession that she has reason to believe the principal wants to know. She also has a duty to provide accurate information. For example, Oma Grigsby signed up with O.K. Travel for a tour of Israel. O.K. purchased the tour from Trinity Tours. Under state law, tour promoters were required to register and post a financial bond. Although Trinity had not done so, O.K. never warned Grigsby. Matters were far from OK when Grigsby learned a week before her trip that Trinity had gone out of business. In the end, however, she was able to obtain a refund from O.K. because it had violated its duty to tell her that Trinity was unregistered and unbonded.[10] Did Angie violate her duty to provide information to Taylor?

Principal's Remedies when the Agent Breaches a Duty

A principal has three potential remedies when an agent breaches her duty:

- The principal can recover from the agent any **damages** the breach has caused. Thus, if Taylor can only rent his house for $600 a month instead of the $800 the Fords offered, Angie would be liable for $2,400—$200 a month for one year.

- If an agent breaches the duty of loyalty, he must turn over to the principal any **profits** he has earned as a result of his wrongdoing. Thus, after Klein violated his duty of loyalty to Harrison, he forfeited profits he would have earned from the copyright of "He's So Fine."

- If the agent has violated her duty of loyalty, the principal may **rescind** the transaction. When Trang sold a script to her principal, Matt Damon, without telling him that she was the author, she violated her duty of loyalty. Damon could rescind the contract to buy the script.[11]

DUTIES OF PRINCIPALS TO AGENTS

In a typical agency relationship, the agent agrees to perform tasks for the principal, and the principal agrees to pay the agent. The range of tasks undertaken by an agent is limited only by the imagination of the principal. Because the agent's job can be so varied, the law has needed to define an agent's duties carefully. The role of the principal, on the other hand, is typically less complicated—often little more than writing a check to pay the agent. Thus the law enumerates fewer duties for the principal. Primarily, the principal must reimburse the agent for reasonable expenses and cooperate with the agent in performing agency tasks. The respective duties of agents and principals can be summarized as follows:

Duties of Agents to Principals	Duty of Principals to Agents
Duty of loyalty	Duty to reimburse
Duty to obey instructions	Duty to cooperate
Duty of care	
Duty to provide information	
Duty to reimburse the agent	

---

10 Grigsby v. O.K. Travel, 118 Ohio App. 3d 671, 693 N.E.2d 1142,1997 Ohio App. LEXIS 875 (1997).

11 A principal can rescind his contract with an agent who has violated her duty, but, as we shall see later in the chapter, the principal might not be able to rescind a contract with a third party when the agent misbehaves.

As a general rule, the principal must indemnify (i.e., reimburse) the agent for any expenses she has reasonably incurred. These reimbursable expenses fall into three categories:

- **A principal must indemnify an agent for any expenses or damages reasonably incurred in carrying out his agency responsibilities.** For example, Peace Baptist Church of Birmingham, Alabama, asked its pastor to buy land for a new church. He paid part of the purchase price out of his own pocket, but the church refused to reimburse him. Although the pastor lost in church, he won in court.[12]

- **A principal must indemnify an agent for tort claims brought by a third party if the principal authorized the agent's behavior and the agent did not realize he was committing a tort.** Marisa owns all the apartment buildings on Elm Street, except one. She hires Rajiv to manage the units and tells him that, under the terms of the leases, she has the right to ask guests to leave if a party becomes too rowdy. But she forgets to tell Rajiv that she does not own one of the buildings, which happens to house a college sorority. One night, when the sorority is having a rambunctious party, Rajiv hustles over and starts ejecting the noisy guests. The sorority is furious and sues Rajiv for trespass. If the sorority wins its suit against Rajiv, Marisa would have to pay the judgment, plus Rajiv's attorney's fees, because she had told him to quell noisy parties, and he did not realize he was trespassing.

- **The principal must indemnify the agent for any liability she incurs from third parties as a result of entering into a contract on the principal's behalf, including attorney's fees and reasonable settlements.** An agent signed a contract to buy cucumbers for Vlasic Food Products Co. to use in making pickles. When the first shipment of cucumbers arrived, Vlasic inspectors found them unsuitable and directed the agent to refuse the shipment. The agent found himself in a pickle when the cucumber farmer sued. The agent notified Vlasic, but the company refused to defend him. He settled the claim himself and, in turn, sued Vlasic. The court ordered Vlasic to reimburse the agent because he had notified them of the suit and had acted reasonably and in good faith.[13]

Duty to Cooperate

Principals have a duty to cooperate with their agent:

- **The principal must furnish the agent with the opportunity to work.** If Lewis agrees to serve as Ida's real estate agent, Ida must allow Lewis access to the house. It is unlikely that Lewis will be able to sell the house without taking anyone inside.

- **The principal cannot unreasonably interfere with the agent's ability to accomplish his task.** Ida allows Lewis to show the house, but she refuses to clean it and then makes disparaging comments to prospective purchasers. "I really get tired of living in such a dank, dreary house," she says. "And the neighborhood children are vicious juvenile delinquents." This behavior would constitute unreasonable interference with an agent.

- **The principal must perform her part of the contract.** Once the agent has successfully completed the task, the principal must pay him, even if the principal has

---

12 Lauderdale v. Peace Baptist Church of Birmingham, 246 Ala. 178, 19 So. 2d 538, 1944 Ala. LEXIS 508 (1944).

13 Long v. Vlasic Food Products Co., 439 F.2d 229, 1971 U.S. App. LEXIS 11455 (4th Cir. 1971).

changed her mind and no longer wants the agent to perform. Ida is a 78-year-old widow who has lived alone for many years in a house that she loves. Her asking price is outrageously high. But lo and behold, Lewis finds a couple happy to pay Ida's price. There is only one problem. Ida does not really want to sell. She put her house on the market because she enjoys showing it to all the folks who move to town. She rejects the offer. Now there is a second problem. The contract provided that Lewis would find a willing buyer at the asking price. Because he has done so, Ida must pay his real estate commission, even if she does not want to sell her house.

TERMINATING AN AGENCY RELATIONSHIP

Either the agent or the principal can terminate the agency relationship at any time. In addition, the relationship terminates automatically if the principal or agent can no longer perform their required duties or a change in circumstances renders the agency relationship pointless.

Termination by Agent or Principal

The two parties—principal and agent—have five choices in terminating their relationship:

- *Term Agreement.* The principal and agent can agree in advance how long their relationship will last. Alexandra hires Boris to help her purchase exquisite enameled Easter eggs made for the Russian czars by Fabergé. If they agree that the relationship will last five years, they have a term agreement.

- *Achieving a Purpose.* The principal and agent can agree that the agency relationship will terminate when the principal's goals have been achieved. Alexandra and Boris might agree that their relationship will end when Alexandra has purchased 10 eggs.

- *Mutual Agreement.* No matter what the principal and agent agree at the start, they can always change their minds later on, as long as the change is mutual. If Boris and Alexandra originally agree to a five-year term, but after only three years Boris decides he wants to go back to business school and Alexandra runs out of money, they can decide together to terminate the agency.

- *Agency at Will.* If they make no agreement in advance about the term of the agreement, either principal or agent can terminate at any time.

- *Wrongful Termination.* An agency relationship is a personal relationship. Hiring an agent is not like buying a book. You might not care which copy of the book you buy, but you do care which agent you hire. If an agency relationship is not working out, the courts will not force the agent and principal to stay together. **Either party always has the *power* to walk out. They may not, however, have the *right*.** If one party's departure from the agency relationship violates the agreement and causes harm to the other party, the wrongful party must pay damages. He will nonetheless be permitted to leave. If Boris has agreed to work for Alexandra for five years but he wants to leave after three, he can leave, provided he pays Alexandra the cost of hiring and training a replacement.

  If the agent is a **gratuitous** agent (i.e., is not being paid), he has both the power and the right to quit any time he wants, regardless of the agency agreement. If Boris is doing this job for Alexandra as a favor, he will not owe her damages when he stops work.

Principal or Agent Can No Longer Perform Required Duties

If the principal or the agent is unable to perform the duties required under the agency agreement, the agreement terminates.

- **If either the agent or the principal fails to obtain (or keep) a license necessary to perform duties under the agency agreement, the agreement ends.** Caleb hires Allegra to represent him in a lawsuit. If she is disbarred, their agency agreement terminates because the agent is no longer allowed in court. Alternatively, if Emil hires Bess to work in his gun shop, their agency relationship terminates when he loses his license to sell firearms.

- **The bankruptcy of the agent or the principal terminates an agency relationship only if it affects their ability to perform.** Bankruptcy rarely interferes with an agent's responsibilities. After all, there is generally no reason why an agent cannot continue to act for the principal whether the agent is rich or poor. If Lewis, the real estate agent, becomes bankrupt, he can continue to represent Ida or anyone else who wants to sell a house. The bankruptcy of a principal is different, however, because after filing for bankruptcy, the principal loses control of his assets. A bankrupt principal may be unable to pay the agent or honor contracts that the agent enters into on his behalf. Therefore, the bankruptcy of a principal is more likely to terminate an agency relationship.

- **An agency relationship terminates upon the death or incapacity of either the principal or the agent.** Agency is a personal relationship, and when the principal dies, the agent cannot act on behalf of a nonexistent person.[14] Of course, a nonexistent person cannot act either, so the relationship also terminates when the agent dies. Incapacity has the same legal effect because either the principal or the agent is at least temporarily unable to act.

- **If the agent violates her duty of loyalty, the agency agreement automatically terminates.** Agents are appointed to represent the principal's interest; if they fail to do so, there is no point to the relationship. Sam is negotiating a military procurement contract on behalf of his employer, Missiles R Us, Inc. In the midst of these negotiations, he becomes very friendly with Louisa, the government negotiator. One night over drinks, he tells Louisa what Missiles' real costs are on the project and the lowest bid it could possibly make. By passing on this confidential information, Sam has violated his duty of loyalty, and his agency relationship terminates.

Change in Circumstances

After the agency agreement is negotiated, circumstances may change. If these changes are significant enough to undermine the purpose of the agreement, the relationship ends automatically. Andrew hires Melissa to sell his country farm for $100,000. Shortly thereafter, the largest oil reserve in North America is discovered nearby. The farm is now worth 10 times Andrew's asking price. Melissa's authority terminates automatically. Other changes in circumstance that affect an agency agreement are:

- *Change of Law.* If the agent's responsibilities become illegal, the agency agreement terminates. Oscar has hired Marta to ship him succulent avocados from

---

[14] Restatement (Second) of Agency §120, Comment a.

California's Imperial Valley. Before she sends the shipment, Mediterranean fruit flies are discovered, and all fruits and vegetables in California are quarantined. The agency agreement terminates because it is now illegal to ship the California avocados.

- *Loss or Destruction of Subject Matter.* Andrew hired Damian to sell his Palm Beach condominium, but before Damian could even measure the living room, Andrew's creditors attached the condo. Damian is no longer authorized to sell the real estate because Andrew has "lost" the subject matter of his agency agreement with Damian.

The following case not only deals with the issue of loss or destruction of subject matter, it provides a useful review of other agency issues in this chapter.

YOU BE THE JUDGE

GAGNON V. COOMBS

39 Mass. App. Ct. 144; 654 N.E. 2d 54; 1995
Mass. App. LEXIS 545
APPEALS COURT OF MASSACHUSETTS, 1995

Facts: The facts of this case are set out in the scenario at the beginning of the chapter. The trial court found that Joan had the authority under the power of attorney to convey the Shelburne property to the trust. Francis appealed.

You Be the Judge: Did Joan have the right to convey the Shelburne farm to a trust that she had established? Does the property belong to the trust or to Francis?

Argument for Joan: Francis had the right to terminate the agency agreement with Joan, but he had to *tell* her that he had done so. Joan cannot read minds. When she transferred the property to the trust she was, as far as she knew, an authorized agent. Now the land has been transferred; it is a done deal. The land belongs to the trust.

Francis did indeed sign a purchase & sale agreement (P&S) to sell the Shelburne farm. That document indicated his *intent* to sell the property. But at that point, he still owned the land. He had not yet "lost" it, for purposes of agency law and would not until he actually sold it.

Everything Joan did was designed to protect Francis. He was eighty-five years old and clearly not

as strong as he had once been. For years, he and Frank had barely spoken but now suddenly he was doing whatever Frank told him to do. Without the protection of the trust, he might end up with no assets at all.

Argument for Francis: Admittedly, Francis never told Joan that he had terminated her agency, but she should have been able to figure it out when she discovered that he was planning to sell the property. She must have known then that he no longer wanted her to act for him. Her job as an agent was to further his desires, not thwart them. Likewise, when Francis's lawyer wrote demanding that she return the land, her duty as an agent was to comply with his request.

Joan's authority ended when Francis signed the P&S for the farm. At that point, he had "lost" the property. He no longer had the right to dispose of it because he had legally promised it to someone else. If it was no longer his, she could not act for him in transferring it to the trust.

As an agent, Joan had an obligation to inform Francis of any material facts. Certainly her transfer of the property to the trust was material. By failing to tell him, she violated her duty of loyalty. Once an agent violates her duty of loyalty, the agency agreement automatically terminates.

Joan also violated her duty of loyalty by self-dealing. She was the person who primarily benefited from her transfer of the land to the trust, not Francis. ●

Effect of Termination

Once an agency relationship ends, the agent no longer has the authority to act for the principal. If she continues to act, she is liable to the principal for any damages he incurs as a result. The Mediterranean fruit fly quarantine ended Marta's agency. If she sends Oscar the avocados anyway and he is fined for possession of a fruit fly, Marta must pay the fine.

The agent loses her authority to act, but some of the duties of both the principal and agent continue even after the relationship ends:

- *Principal's Duty to Indemnify Agent.* Oscar must reimburse Marta for expenses she incurred before the agency ended. If Marta accumulated mileage on her car during her search for the perfect avocado, Oscar must pay her for gasoline and depreciation. But he owes her nothing for her expenses after the agency relationship ends.

- *Confidential Information.* Remember the "He's So Fine" case earlier in the chapter. George Harrison's agent used confidential information to negotiate on his own behalf the purchase of the "He's So Fine" copyright. An agent is not entitled to use confidential information even after the agency relationship terminates.

LIABILITY

Thus far, this chapter has dealt with the relationship between principals and agents. Although an agent can dramatically increase his principal's ability to accomplish her goals, an agency relationship also dramatically increases the risk of legal liability to third parties. A principal may be liable in contract for agreements that the agent signs and also liable in tort for harm the agent causes. Indeed, once a principal hires an agent, she may be liable to third parties for his acts, even if he disobeys instructions. Agents may also find themselves liable to third parties.

Principal's Liability for Contracts

Many agents are hired for the primary purpose of entering into contracts on behalf of their principals. Salespeople, for example, may do little other than sign on the dotted line. Most of the time, the principal is delighted to be bound by these contracts. But even if the principal is unhappy (because, say, the agent has disobeyed orders), the principal generally cannot rescind contracts entered into by the agent. After all, if someone is going to be penalized, it should be the principal who hired the disobedient agent, not the innocent third party.

The principal is bound by the acts of an agent if (1) the agent had *authority*, or (2) the principal, for reasons of fairness, is *estopped* from denying that the agent had authority, or (3) the principal *ratifies* the acts of the agent.

To say that the principal is "bound by the acts" of the agent means that the principal is as liable as if he had performed the acts himself. It also means that the principal is liable for statements the agent makes to a third party. Thus, when a lawyer lied on an application for malpractice insurance, the insurance company was allowed to void the policy for the entire law firm. It was as if the firm had lied. In addition, the principal is deemed to know any information that the agent knows or should know.

Authority

A principal is bound by the acts of an agent if the agent has authority. There are three types of authority: express, implied, and apparent. Express and implied authority are categories of actual authority because the agent is truly authorized to act for the principal. In apparent authority the principal is liable for the agent's actions even though the agent was *not* authorized.

Express Authority. The principal grants **express authority** by words or conduct that, reasonably interpreted, cause the agent to believe the principal desires her to act on the principal's account.[15] In other words, the principal asks the agent to do something and the agent does it. Craig calls his stockbroker, Alice, and asks her to buy 100 shares of Banshee Corp. for his account. She has *express authority* to carry out this transaction.

Implied Authority. **Unless otherwise agreed, authority to conduct a transaction includes authority to do acts that are reasonably necessary to accomplish it.**[16] David has recently inherited a house from his grandmother. He hires Nell to auction off the house and its contents. She hires an auctioneer, advertises the event, rents a tent, and generally does everything necessary to conduct a successful auction. After withholding her expenses, she sends the tidy balance to David. Totally outraged, he calls her on the phone, "How dare you hire an auctioneer and rent a tent? I never gave you permission! I absolutely *refuse* to pay these expenses!"

David is wrong. A principal almost never gives an agent absolutely complete instructions. Unless some authority was implied, David would have had to say, "Open the car door, get in, put the key in the ignition, drive to the store, buy stickers, mark an auction number on each sticker . . ." and so forth. To solve this problem, the law assumes that the agent has authority to do anything that is reasonably necessary to accomplish her task.

Apparent Authority. **A principal can be liable for the acts of an agent who is not, in fact, acting with authority if the principal's conduct causes a third party reasonably to believe that the agent is authorized.** In the case of *express* and *implied* authority, the principal has authorized the agent to act. Apparent authority is different: the principal has *not* authorized the agent, but has done something to make an innocent third party *believe* the agent is authorized. As a result, the principal is every bit as liable to the third party as if the agent did have authority.

For example, Zbigniew Lambo and Scott Kennedy were brokers at Paulson Investment Co., a stock brokerage firm in Oregon. The two men violated securities laws by selling unregistered stock, which ultimately proved to be worthless. Kennedy and Lambo were liable, but they were unable to repay the money. Either Paulson or its customers would end up bearing the loss. What is the fair result? The law takes the view that the principal is liable, not the third party, because the principal, by word or deed, allowed the third party to believe that the agent was acting on the principal's behalf. The principal could have prevented the third party from losing money.

Although the two brokers did not have *actual* or *implied* authority to sell the stock (Paulson had not authorized them to break the law), the company was nonetheless liable on the grounds that the brokers had *apparent* authority. Paulson had sent letters to its customers notifying them when it hired Kennedy. The two brokers made sales presentations at Paulson's offices. The company had never told customers that the two men were not authorized to sell this worthless stock.[17] Thus the agents *appeared* to have authority, even though they did not. Of course, Paulson had the right to recover from Kennedy and Lambo if it could ever compel them to pay.

---

[15] Restatement (Second) of Agency §26.
[16] Restatement (Second) of Agency §35.
[17] Badger v. Paulson Investment Co., 311 Ore. 14, 803 P.2d 1178, 1991 Ore. LEXIS 7 (S.Ct. OR 1991).

Remember that the issue in apparent authority is always what the *principal* has done to make the *third party* believe that the *agent* has authority. Suppose that Kennedy and Lambo never worked for Paulson but, on their own, printed up Paulson stationery. The company would not be liable for the stock the two men sold because it had never done or said anything that would reasonably make a third party believe that the men were its agents.

Ratification

If a person accepts the benefit of an unauthorized transaction or fails to repudiate it, then he is as bound by the act as if he had originally authorized it. He has *ratified* the act.[18] Many of the cases in agency law involve instances in which one person acts *without* authority for another. To avoid liability, the alleged principal shows that he had not authorized the task at issue. But sometimes after the fact, the principal decides that he approves of what the agent has done even though it was not authorized at the time. The law would be perverse if it did not permit the principal, under those circumstances, to agree to the deal the agent has made. The law is not perverse, but it is careful. Even if an agent acts without authority, the principal can decide later to be bound by her actions as long as these requirements are met:

- The "agent" indicates to the third party that she is acting for a principal.
- The "principal" knows all the material facts of the transaction.
- The "principal" accepts the benefit of the whole transaction, not just part.
- The third party does not withdraw from the contract before ratification.

A night clerk at the St. Regis Hotel in Detroit, Michigan, was brutally murdered in the course of a robbery. A few days later, the *Detroit News* reported that the St. Regis management had offered a $1,000 reward for any information leading to the arrest and conviction of the killer. Two days after the article appeared, Robert Jackson turned in the man who was subsequently convicted of the crime. But then it was Jackson's turn to be robbed—the hotel refused to pay the reward on the grounds that the manager who had made the offer had no authority. Jackson still had one weapon left: he convinced the court that the hotel had ratified the offer. One of the hotel's owners admitted he read the *Detroit News*. The court concluded that if someone reads a newspaper, he is sure to read any articles about a business he owns; therefore, the owner must have been aware of the offer. He accepted the benefit of the reward by failing to revoke it publicly. This failure to revoke constituted a ratification, and the hotel was liable.[19]

Subagents

Many of the examples in this chapter involve a single agent acting for a principal. Real life is often more complex. Daniel, the owner of a restaurant, hires Michaela to manage it. She in turn hires chefs, waiters, and dishwashers. Daniel has never even met the restaurant help, yet they are also his agents, albeit a special category called **subagent.** Michaela is called an **intermediary agent**—someone who hires subagents for the principal.

---

18 Restatement (Second) of Agency §82.

19 Jackson v. Goodman, 69 Mich. App. 225, 244 N.W.2d 423, 1976 Mich. App. LEXIS 741 (Mich. Ct. App. 1976).

As a general rule, an agent has no authority to delegate her tasks to another unless the principal authorizes her to do so. But when an agent is authorized to hire a subagent, the principal is as liable for the acts of the subagent as he is for the acts of a regular agent. Daniel authorizes Michaela to hire a restaurant staff. She hires Lydia to serve as produce buyer. When Lydia buys food for the restaurant, Daniel must pay the bill.

Agent's Liability for Contracts

The agent's liability on a contract depends upon how much the third party knows about the principal. Disclosure is the agent's best protection against liability.

Fully Disclosed Principal

An agent is not liable for any contracts she makes on behalf of a *fully* disclosed principal. A principal is fully disclosed if the third party knows of his *existence* and his *identity*. Augusta acts as agent for Parker when he buys Tracey's prize-winning show horse. Augusta and Tracey both grew up in posh Grosse Pointe, Michigan, where they attended the same elite schools. Tracey does not know Parker, but she figures any friend of Augusta's must be OK. She figures wrong—Parker is a charming deadbeat. He injures Tracey's horse, fails to pay the full contract price, and promptly disappears. Tracey angrily demands that Augusta make good on Parker's debt. Unfortunately for Tracey, Parker was a fully disclosed principal—Tracey knew of his *existence* and his *identity*. Although Tracey partly relied on Augusta's good character when contracting with Parker, Augusta is not liable because Tracey knew who the principal was and could have (should have) investigated him. Augusta did not promise anything herself, and Tracey's only recourse is against the principal, Parker (wherever he may be).

at RISK To avoid liability when signing a contract on behalf of a principal, an agent must clearly state that she is an agent and must also identify the principal. Augusta should sign a contract on behalf of her principal, Parker, as follows: "Augusta, as agent for Parker" or "Parker, by Augusta, Agent." ◆

Partially Disclosed Principal

In the case of a *partially* disclosed principal, the third party can recover from either the agent or the principal. A principal is partially disclosed if the third party knew of his *existence* but not his *identity*. Suppose that, when approaching Tracey about the horse, Augusta simply says, "I have a friend who is interested in buying your champion." Any friend of Augusta's is a friend of Tracey's—or so Tracey thinks. Parker is a partially disclosed principal because Tracey knows only that he exists, not who he is. She cannot investigate his creditworthiness because she does not know his name. Tracey relies solely on what she is able to learn from the agent, Augusta. Both Augusta and Parker are liable to Tracey. (They are jointly and severally liable, which means that Tracey can recover from either or both of them. She cannot, however, recover more than the total that she is owed: if her damages are $100,000, she can recover that amount from either Augusta or Parker, or partial amounts from both, but in no event more than $100,000.)

Undisclosed Principal

In the case of an *undisclosed* principal, the third party can recover from either the agent or the principal. A principal is undisclosed if the third party did not know

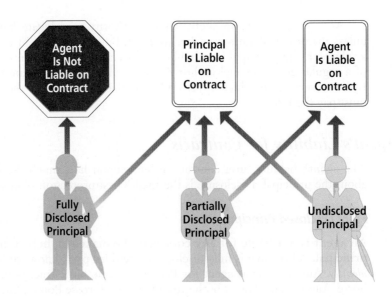

Exhibit 14.1

of his existence. Suppose that Augusta simply asks to buy the horse herself, without mentioning that she is purchasing it for Parker. In this case Parker is an undisclosed principal because Tracey does not know that Augusta is acting for someone else. Both Parker and Augusta are jointly and severally liable. As Exhibit 14.1 illustrates, the principal is always liable, but the agent is not unless the principal's identity is a mystery.

In some ways the concept of an undisclosed principal violates principles of contract law. If Tracey does not even know that Parker exists, how can they have an agreement or a meeting of the minds? Is such an arrangement fair to Tracey? No matter, a contract with an undisclosed principal is binding. The following incident illustrates why.

William Zeckendorf was a man with a plan. For years he had been eyeing a six-block tract of land along New York's East River. It was a wasteland of slums and slaughterhouses, but he could see its potential. The meat packers had refused to sell to him, however, because they knew they would never be permitted to build slaughterhouses in Manhattan again. Finally, in 1946 he got the phone call he had been waiting for. The companies were willing to sell—at $17 a square foot, when surrounding land cost less than $5. Undeterred, Zeckendorf immediately put down a $1 million deposit. But to make his investment worthwhile, he needed to buy the neighboring property—once the slaughterhouses were gone, the other land would be much more valuable. Zeckendorf was well-known as a wealthy developer; he had begun his business career managing the Astor family's real estate holdings. If he personally tried to negotiate the purchase of the surrounding land, word would soon get out that he wanted to put together a large parcel. Prices would skyrocket and the project would become too costly. So he hired agents to purchase the land for him. To further conceal his involvement, he went to South America for a month. When he returned, his agents had completed 75 different purchases, and he owned 18 acres of land.

Shortly afterwards, the United Nations began seeking a site for its headquarters. President Truman favored Boston, Philadelphia, or a location in the Midwest. The UN committee suggested Greenwich or Stamford, Connecticut. But John D. Rockefeller settled the question once and for all. He purchased Zeckendorf's land for

$8.5 million and donated it to the UN (netting Zeckendorf a profit of $2 million). Without the cooperation of agency law, the UN headquarters would not be in New York today. The law permits the concept of an undisclosed principal out of commercial necessity. The following article suggests that Harvard behaved unethically when it purchased land secretly. Do you agree?

NEWS*worthy*

Harvard University has bought 52 acres during the past nine years in a secret buying spree that increases the school's land in Allston (across the river from its Cambridge headquarters) by more than a third. Working through the Beal Cos., a prominent real estate development company, Harvard spent $88 million to buy 14 separate parcels. Harvard officials said the university made the purchases without revealing its identity to the sellers, residents, local politicians, or city officials because property owners would have drastically inflated the prices if they knew Harvard was the buyer. "We were really driven by the need to get these properties at fair market value" and avoid "overly inflated acquisition costs," said James H. Rowe, vice president for public affairs at Harvard. But those who were left in the dark—including Mayor Thomas M. Menino—weren't buying it. "That's absurd," Menino scoffed. "Without informing anyone or telling anybody? That's total arrogance." Menino was so incensed that he adopted a mocking singsong tone to express his view of Harvard's attitude, saying: "We're from Harvard, and we're going to do what we want."

"As far as I'm concerned, they practiced a deception," said Ray Mellone, chairman of a neighborhood task force. "There are a lot of people who are going to say we can't trust them. We have to make the process work, and that means making the neighborhood involved, not having deals made in a back room and then coming to us and saying: 'Take it or leave it.'"[20] ◆

Because of concerns about fair play, there are some exceptions to the rule on undisclosed principals. **A third party is not bound to the contract with an undisclosed principal if (1) the contract specifically provides that the third party is not bound to anyone other than the agent, or (2) the agent lies about the principal because she knows the third party would refuse to contract with him.** A cagey property owner, when approached by one of Harvard's agents, could have asked for a clause in the contract providing that the agent was not representing someone else. If the agent told the truth, the owner could have demanded a higher price. If the agent lied, then the owner could have rescinded the contract when the truth emerged.

Unauthorized Agent

Thus far in this section, we have been discussing an agent's liability to a third party for a transaction that was authorized by the principal. Sometimes, however, agents act without the authority of a principal. **If the agent has no authority (express, implied, or apparent), the principal is not liable to the third party and the agent is.** Suppose that Augusta agrees to sell Parker's horse to Tracey. Unfortunately, Parker has never met Augusta and has certainly not authorized this transaction. Augusta is hoping that she can persuade him to sell, but Parker refuses. Augusta, but not Parker, is liable to Tracey for breach of contract.

---

20 Tina Cassidy and Dan Aucoin, "Harvard Reveals Secret Purchases of 52 Acres Worth $88M in Allston," The Boston Globe, June 10, 1997, p. A1. Republished with permission of The Boston Globe; permission conveyed through the Copyright Clearance Center, Inc.

Principal's Liability for Torts

A master is liable for physical harm caused by the negligent conduct of servants within the scope of employment.[21] This principle of liability is called ***respondeat superior,*** which is a Latin phrase that means "let the master answer." Under the theory of *respondeat superior,* the master (i.e., the principal) is liable for the agent's misbehavior whether or not the principal was at fault. Indeed, the principal is liable even if he forbade or tried to prevent the agent from misbehaving. This sounds like a harsh rule. The logic is that because the principal controls the agent, he should be able to *prevent* misbehavior. If he cannot prevent it, at least he can *insure* against the risks. Furthermore, the principal may have deeper pockets than the agent or the injured third party and thus be better able to *afford* the cost of the agent's misbehavior.

To apply the principle of *respondeat superior,* it is important to understand each of the following terms: *master and servant, scope of employment, negligent and intentional torts,* and *physical harm.*

Master and Servant

There are two kinds of agents: (1) *servants* and (2) *independent contractors.* **A principal *may be* liable for the torts of a servant but generally is *not* liable for the torts of an independent contractor.** Because of this rule, the distinction between a servant and an independent contractor is important.

Servant or Independent Contractor? The more control the principal has over an agent, the more likely that the agent will be considered a servant. Therefore, when determining if agents are servants or independent contractors, courts consider whether:

- The principal controls details of the work.
- The principal supplies the tools and place of work.
- The agents work full-time for the principal.
- The agents are paid by time, not by the job.
- The work is part of the regular business of the principal.
- The principal and agents believe they have an employer-employee relationship.
- The principal is in business.[22]

Do not be misled by the term *servant.* A servant does not mean Jeeves, the butler, or Maisie, the maid. In fact, if Mrs. Dillworth hires Jeeves and Maisie for the evening from a catering firm, they are *not* her servants, they are independent contractors. On the other hand, the president of General Motors is a servant of that corporation.

Negligent Hiring. Principals prefer agents to be considered independent contractors not servants because, as a general rule, principals are not liable for the torts of an independent contractor. There is, however, one exception to this rule: **The principal is liable for the physical torts of an independent contractor *only if* the principal has been negligent in hiring or supervising her.** Remember that, under *respondeat superior,* the principal is liable *without fault* for the physical torts of servants. The case of independent contractors is different: the principal is liable only if he was *at fault* by being careless in his hiring or supervising. Was the supermarket at fault in the following case?

---

[21] Restatement (Second) of Agency §243.
[22] Restatement (Second) of Agency §220(2).

DURAN V. FURR'S SUPERMARKETS, INC.

921 S.W.2d 778, 1996 Tex. App. LEXIS 1345
Court of Appeals of Texas, 1996

Facts: Steve Romero was an off-duty police officer working as a security guard for Furr's Supermarkets. He approached a car parked in the supermarket's fire lane and began yelling at a passenger to move it. The passenger, Graciela Duran, asked Romero for his name. He opened the car door and tried to pull her out, all the while threatening to arrest her. Duran ultimately required surgery to repair the injury that Romero's tugs and twists caused to her left arm.

Duran filed suit against Furr's. The supermarket filed a motion for summary judgment on the grounds that it was not responsible for Romero's conduct because he was an independent contractor. Duran argued that Furr's had been negligent in hiring Romero. The trial court granted the motion for summary judgment.

Issues: Did the trial court properly grant Furr's motion for summary judgment? Is Duran entitled to a trial?

Excerpts from Judge McClure's Decision: The basis of responsibility under the doctrine of negligent hiring is the master's own negligence in hiring or retaining in his employ an incompetent servant whom the master knows or by the exercise of reasonable care should have known was incompetent or unfit and thereby creating an unreasonable risk of harm to others. The evidence showed that Furr's did not require Romero to complete a job application and otherwise made no inquiry into his background as a police officer. Furr's never interviewed Romero or spoke with him before he began working at the store. If Furr's had conducted an investigation of Romero's performance as a police officer, it would have learned that Romero had a prior complaint for using vulgar and abusive language towards a member of the public while on duty as a police officer.

Duran argues that this complaint demonstrates Romero's propensity for aggressive behavior so that Furr's could have reasonably anticipated that Romero might verbally and physically abuse a patron of the store. On the other hand, Furr's argues that even if it had discovered the prior complaint, the information would not have caused Furr's to reasonably anticipate his physical assault upon Duran. In attempting to distinguish between the prior verbal abuse complaint and the physical assault upon Duran, Furr's ignores the evidence showing that Romero first verbally abused Duran during this incident. According to Duran, the verbal abuse escalated into the physical assault. We find that a fact question is raised whether knowledge of this abusive language complaint would put a reasonable person on notice that Romero might verbally abuse a store patron, and that such conduct might escalate into a physical assault. Because of the existence of this fact issue, summary judgment on this ground is improper. ∎

Exhibit 14.2 on the following page illustrates the difference in liability between a servant and an independent contractor.

Scope of Employment

Principals are only liable for torts that a servant commits within the *scope of employment*. If an employee leaves a pool of water on the floor of a store and a customer slips and falls, the employer is liable. But if the same employee leaves water on his own kitchen floor and a friend falls, the employer is not liable because the employee is not acting within the scope of employment. A servant is acting within the scope of employment if the act:

- Is one that servants are generally responsible for
- Takes place during hours that the servant is generally employed

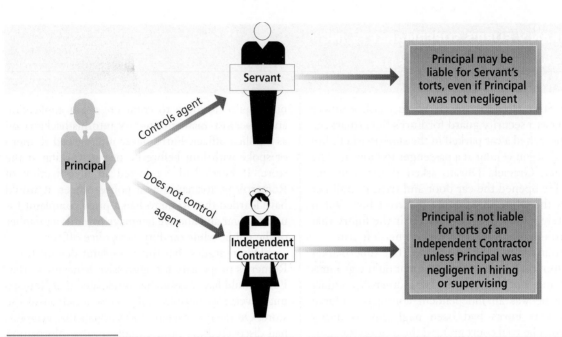

Exhibit 14.2

- Is part of the principal's business
- Is similar to the one the principal authorized
- Is one for which the principal supplied the tools; and
- Is not seriously criminal.

Scope of employment cases raise two major issues: authorization and abandonment.

Authorization. In authorization cases the agent is clearly working for the principal but commits an act that the principal has not authorized. Although Jane has often told the driver of her delivery van not to speed, Hank ignores her instructions and plows into Bernadette. At the time of the accident, he is working for Jane, delivering flowers for her shop, but his act is not authorized. **An act is within the scope of employment, even if expressly forbidden, if it is of the same general nature as that authorized or if it is incidental to the conduct authorized.**[23] Hank was authorized to drive the van but not to speed. However, his speeding was of the same general nature as the authorized act, so Jane is liable to Bernadette.

Abandonment. The second major issue in a *scope of employment* case involves abandonment. **The master is liable for the actions of the servant that occur while the servant is at work, but not for actions that occur after the servant has abandoned the master's business.** Although the rule sounds straightforward, the

---

[23] Restatement (Second) of Agency §229(1).

difficulty lies in determining whether the employee has in fact abandoned the master's business. The employer is liable if the employee is simply on a *detour* from company business, but the employer is not liable if the employee is off on a *frolic of his own*. Suppose that Hank, the delivery van driver, speeds during his afternoon commute home. A servant is generally not acting within the scope of his employment when he commutes to and from work, so his master, Jane, is not liable. Or suppose that, while on the way to a delivery, he stops to view his favorite movie classic, *Dead on Arrival*. Unable to see in the darkened theater, he knocks Anna down, causing grave harm. Jane is not liable because Hank's visit to the movies is outside the scope of his employment. On the other hand, if Hank stops at the Burger Box drive-in window en route to making a delivery, Jane is liable when he crashes into Anna on the way out of the parking lot because this time he is simply making a detour.

Negligent and Intentional Torts

The master is liable if the servant commits a negligent tort that causes physical harm to a person or property. When Hank crashes into Anna, he is committing a negligent tort, and Jane is liable if all the other requirements for *respondeat superior* are met.

A master is *not* liable for the *intentional* torts of the servant unless the servant was motivated, at least in part, by a desire to serve the master, or the conduct was reasonably foreseeable. During an NBA basketball game, Kobe pushes Shaq into some chairs under the basket to prevent him from scoring a breakaway lay-up. Kobe's team is liable for his actions because he was motivated, at least in part, by a desire to help his team. But if Kobe hits Shaq in the parking lot after the playoffs are over, Kobe's team is not liable because he is no longer motivated by a desire to help the team. His motivation now is personal revenge or frustration.

The courts (of law, not basketball) are generally expansive in their definition of behavior that is intended to serve the master. In one case, a police trainee shot a fellow officer while practicing his quick draw technique. In another, a drunken sailor knocked a shipmate out of bed with the admonition, "Get up, you big son of a bitch, and turn to," after which the two men fought. The courts ruled that both the police trainee and the sailor were motivated by a desire to serve their master and, therefore, the master was liable for their intentional torts.[24]

Physical Harm

In the case of *physical* torts, a master is liable for the negligent conduct of a servant that occurs within the scope of employment. The rule for *nonphysical* torts (i.e., torts that harm only reputation, feelings, or wallet) is different. **Nonphysical torts are treated more like a contract claim, and the principal is liable only if the servant acted with actual, implied, or apparent authority.** For example, the Small Business Administration (SBA) granted Midwest Knitting Mills, Inc. more than $2 million in loans, but the SBA employee in charge of the case never told Midwest. (He was allegedly

---

[24] Nelson v. American-West African Line, Inc., 86 F.2d 730, 1936 U.S. App. LEXIS 3841 (2d Cir. 1936), and Thompson v. United States, 504 F. Supp. 1087, 1980 U.S. Dist. LEXIS 15834 (D.S.D. 1980).

a drug addict.) The company sued the SBA for the negligence of its employee. Although the conduct had occurred within the scope of employment, it was a non-physical tort. Since the employee had not acted with actual, implied, or apparent authority, the SBA was not liable.[25]

Misrepresentation and defamation are, however, treated differently from other nonphysical torts.

Misrepresentation

A principal is liable if:

- The agent makes a misrepresentation
- The agent has express, implied, or apparent authority
- The third party relies on the misrepresentation; and
- The third party suffers harm.

This rule applies to any agent, not just a servant. If the agent is authorized to make a *truthful* statement, the principal is liable for any related *false* statement.

Althea hires Morris, a real estate agent, to sell a piece of land. Morris knows that part of the land floods every spring, but when Helen inquires about flooding, Morris lies. He is not authorized to make the false statement, but he is authorized to make statements about the land. Althea is liable to Helen for any harm caused by Morris's misrepresentation, even though Morris is an independent contractor.

Defamation

A principal is liable if:

- The agent makes a defamatory statement
- The agent has express, implied, or apparent authority; and
- The third party is harmed by the statement.

Again, this rule applies to all agents, not simply to servants. If the agent is authorized to make a *truthful* statement, the principal is liable for any related *defamatory* statements.

A newspaper reporter writes an untrue story alleging that the mayor has been taking kickbacks from contractors who work for the city. The reporter has defamed the mayor, and the newspaper is liable because the reporter is an agent authorized to write the article, even though he is not authorized to write false statements.

---

cyberLaw

Electronic communication has created new risks for employers. They fear that their employees may commit libel by sending flaming e-mails or violate intellectual property laws by downloading copyrighted software from the Internet. Is the company liable in these circumstances? What if an employee posts defamatory information on an Internet bulletin board? Even if the employee is not authorized, she may have *apparent* authority—especially if the posting appears with a company e-mail address. For this reason companies increasingly monitor their employees' e-mail content and Internet usage. Some companies also require employees, when posting on a bulletin board, to include a disclaimer that they do not speak for their company. ◆

---

[25] Midwest Knitting Mills, Inc. v. United States, 741 F. Supp. 1345, 1990 U.S. Dist. LEXIS 8663 (E.D. Wis. 1990).

Agent's Liability for Torts

The focus of this section has been on the *principal's* liability for the agent's torts. But it is important to remember that **agents are always liable for their own torts.** Agents who commit torts are personally responsible whether or not their principal is also liable. Even if the tort was committed to benefit the principal, the agent is still liable. So the sailor who got into a fistfight while rousting a shipmate from bed is liable even though he thought he was acting for the benefit of his principal.

This rule makes obvious sense. If the agent were not liable, he would have little incentive to be careful. Imagine Hank driving his delivery van for Jane. If he were not personally liable for his own torts, he might think, "If I drive fast enough, I can make it through that light even though it just turned red. And if I don't, what the heck, it'll be Jane's problem, not mine." Agents, as a rule, may have fewer assets than their principal, but it is important that their personal assets be at risk in the event of their negligent behavior.

If the agent and principal are *both* liable, which does the injured third party sue? The principal and the agent are *jointly and severally liable*, which means, as we have seen, that the injured third party can sue either one or both, as she chooses. If she recovers from the principal, he can sue the agent.

Chapter Conclusion

When students enroll in a business law course, they fully expect to learn about torts and contracts, corporations and partnerships. They probably do not think much about agency law; many of them have not even heard the term before. Yet it is an area of the law that affects us all because each of us has been and will continue to be both an agent and a principal many times in our lives.

Chapter Review

1. In an agency relationship, a principal and an agent mutually consent that the agent will act on behalf of the principal and be subject to the principal's control, thereby creating a fiduciary relationship.

2. An agent owes these duties to the principal: duty of loyalty, duty to obey instructions, duty of care, and duty to provide information.

3. The principal has three potential remedies when the agent breaches her duty: recovery of damages the breach has caused, recovery of any profits earned by the agent from the breach, and rescission of any transaction with the agent.

4. The principal has two duties to the agent: to reimburse legitimate expenses, and to cooperate with the agent.

5. Both the agent and the principal have the power to terminate an agency relationship, but they may not have the right. If the termination violates the agency agreement and causes harm to the other party, the wrongful party must pay damages.

6. An agency relationship automatically terminates if the principal or agent can no longer perform the required duties or if a change in circumstances renders the agency relationship pointless.

7. A principal is bound by the contracts of the agent if the agent has express, implied, or apparent authority.

8. The principal grants express authority by words or conduct that, reasonably interpreted, cause the agent to believe that the principal desires her to act on the principal's account.

9. Implied authority includes authority to do acts that are incidental to a transaction, usually accompany it, or are reasonably necessary to accomplish it.

10. Apparent authority means that a principal is liable for the acts of an agent who is not, in fact, acting with authority if the principal's conduct causes a third party reasonably to believe that the agent is authorized.

11. An agent is not liable for any contract she makes on behalf of a fully disclosed principal. The principal is liable. In the case of a partially disclosed or undisclosed principal, both the agent and the principal are liable on the contract.

12. Under *respondeat superior,* a master is liable when a servant acting within the scope of employment commits a negligent tort that causes physical harm to a person or property. Under some limited circumstances, a master is also liable for a servant's intentional torts.

13. The principal is only liable for the physical torts of an independent contractor if the principal has been negligent in hiring or supervising him.

14. A principal is liable for nonphysical torts only if the servant acts with actual, implied, or apparent authority.

15. Agents are always liable for their own torts.

Practice Test

1. The German-American Vocational League was formed in New York during World War II to serve as a propaganda agency for the German Reich. Under U.S. law all foreign agents were required to register. Neither the Vocational League nor its officers registered. When they were charged with violating U.S. law, they argued that they were not agents of the German government because they had no formal agency agreement. Their one written agreement with the German Reich said nothing about being a propaganda agency. Is a formal contract necessary to establish an agency relationship?

2. **ETHICS** Radio TV Reports (RTV) was in the business of recording, transcribing, and monitoring radio and video programming for its clients. The Department of Defense (DOD) in Washington, D.C., was one of RTV's major clients. Paul Ingersoll worked for RTV until August 31. In July the DOD solicited bids for a new contract for the following year. During this same month, Ingersoll formed his own media monitoring business, Transmedia. RTV and Transmedia were the only two bidders on the DOD contract, which was awarded to Transmedia. Did Ingersoll violate his fiduciary duty to RTV? Aside from his legal obligations, did Ingersoll behave ethically? How does his behavior look in the light of day? Was it right?

3. David and Fiona Rookard purchased tickets for a trip through Mexico from a Mexicoach office in San Diego. Mexicoach told them that the trip would be safe. It did not tell them, however, that their tickets had disclaimers written in Spanish warning that, under Mexican law, a bus company is not liable for any harm that befalls its passengers. The Rookards did not read Spanish. They were injured in a bus accident caused by gross negligence on the part of the driver. Did Mexicoach violate its duty to the Rookards?

4. Penny Wilson went to Arlington Chrysler-Plymouth-Dodge to buy an automobile. Penny told Arlington that, as a minor, she could not buy the car unless she obtained credit life insurance that would pay the balance of any loan owing if her mother died. She also disclosed that her mother had cancer. Arlington was an agent for Western Pioneer Life Insurance Co. Western Pioneer reported that a credit insurance policy would be invalid if Mrs. Wilson died within six months. In fact, the policy was invalid if Mrs. Wilson died of cancer within one year. Seven months later, Mrs. Wilson died, and Western Pioneer refused to pay. Penny Wilson sued Western Pioneer and Arlington. The trial court found Western Pioneer liable, but not Arlington. Was Western Pioneer liable for Arlington's legal expenses?

5. One Friday afternoon a custodian at the Lazear Elementary School in Oakland, California, raped an 11-year-old student in his office on the school premises. The student sued the school district on

a theory of *respondeat superior.* Is the school district liable for this intentional tort by its employee?

6. This article appeared in The New York *Times:*

> A week after criminal charges were announced in the death of tennis star Vitas Gerulaitis, his mother filed suit yesterday against eight defendants, including the owner of the Long Island estate where Mr. Gerulaitis died of carbon monoxide poisoning last fall. Prosecutors have charged that a new swimming pool heater, installed at a cost of $8,000, was improperly vented and sent deadly fumes into a pool house where Mr. Gerulaitis was taking a nap. The lawsuit accuses the companies that manufactured, installed and maintained the pool heater, and the mechanic who installed it, with negligence and reckless disregard for human life. It makes similar charges against the owners of the oceanfront estate, Beatrice Raynes and her son Martin, a real-estate executive.[26]

Why would the owners of the estate be liable?

7. **CPA QUESTION** A principal will not be liable to a third party for a tort committed by an agent:

   a. Unless the principal instructed the agent to commit the tort

   b. Unless the tort was committed within the scope of the agency relationship

   c. If the agency agreement limits the principal's liability for the agent's tort

   d. If the tort is also regarded as a criminal act

8. A. B. Rains worked as a broker for the Joseph Denunzio Fruit Co. Raymond Crane offered to sell Rains nine carloads of emperor grapes. Rains accepted the offer on behalf of Denunzio. Later, Rains and Denunzio discovered that Crane was an agent for John Kazanjian. Who is liable on this contract?

9. Roy Watson bought vacuum cleaners from T & F Distributing Co. and then resold them door-to-door. He was an independent contractor. Before hiring Watson, the president of T & F checked with two former employers but could not remember if he called Watson's two references. Watson had an extensive criminal record, primarily under the alias Leroy Turner, but he was listed in FBI records under both Leroy Turner and Roy Watson. T & F granted Watson sales territory that included Neptune City, New Jersey. This city required that all "peddlers" such as Watson be licensed. Applicants for this license were routinely fingerprinted. T & F never insisted that Watson apply for such a license. Watson attacked Miriam Bennett after selling a vacuum cleaner to her at her home in Neptune City. Is T & F liable to Bennett?

10. **YOU BE THE JUDGE** WRITING PROBLEM Sara Kearns went to an auction at Christie's to bid on a tapestry for her employer, Nardin Fine Arts Gallery. The good news is that she purchased a Dufy tapestry for $77,000. The bad news is that it was not the one her employer had told her to buy. In the excitement of the auction, she forgot her instructions. Nardin refused to pay, and Christie's filed suit. Is Nardin liable for the unauthorized act of its agent? **Argument for Christie's:** Kearns executed a bidder form as agent for Nardin. This is a common practice for many purchasers. Christie's cannot possibly ascertain in each case the exact nature of the bidder's authority. Whether or not Kearns had actual authority, she certainly had apparent authority and Nardin is liable. **Argument for Nardin:** Kearns was not authorized to purchase the Dufy tapestry, and therefore Christie's must recover from her, not Nardin.

11. Jack and Rita Powers purchased 312 head of cattle at an auction conducted by Coffeyville Livestock Sales Co. They did not know who owned the cattle they bought. The Powers, in turn, sold 159 of this lot to Leonard Hoefling. He sued the Powers, alleging the cattle were diseased and dying in large numbers, and recovered $38,360. Are the Powers entitled to reimbursement from Coffeyville?

12. **ROLE REVERSAL** Write a multiple choice question that deals with the liability of principals for the acts of their servants.

---

[26] Vivian S. Toy, "Gerulaitis's Mother Files Suit in Son's Carbon Monoxide Death," The New York Times, June 1, 1995, p. B5.

Internet Research Problem

Acting as an undisclosed principal, William Zeck-endorf employed agents to purchase the land in New York on which the United Nations headquarters was ultimately built. Can you find any other examples on the Internet of business dealings in which agents made purchases for an undisclosed principal? Were these business arrangements ethical? What risks did the agents face?

You can find further practice problems at
academic.cengage.com/blaw/beatty.

Employment Law

"**O**n the killing beds you were apt to be covered with blood, and it would freeze solid; if you leaned against a pillar, you would freeze to that, and if you put your hand upon the blade of your knife, you would run a chance of leaving your skin on it. The men would tie up their feet in newspapers and old sacks, and these would be soaked in blood and frozen, and then soaked again, and so on, until by nighttime a man would be walking on great lumps the size of the feet of an elephant. Now and then, when the bosses were not looking, you would see them plunging their feet and ankles into the steaming hot carcass of the steer. . . . The cruelest thing of all was that nearly all of them—all of those who used knives—were unable to wear gloves, and their arms would be white with frost and their hands would grow numb, and then of course there would be accidents."[1] ■

---

[1] Upton Sinclair, *The Jungle* (New York: Bantam Books, 1981), p. 80, a 1906 novel about the meatpacking industry.

© PHOTO 24/BRAND X PICTURES/GETTY IMAGES

INTRODUCTION

For most of history, the concept of career planning was unknown. By and large, people were born into their jobs. Whatever their parents had been—landowner, soldier, farmer, servant, merchant, or beggar—they became, too. People not only knew their place, they also understood the rights and obligations inherent in each position. The landowner had the right to receive labor from his tenants, but he also cared for them if they fell ill. Certainly there were abuses, but at a time when people held religious convictions about their position in life and workers had few expectations that their lives would be better than their parents', the role of law was limited. The primary English law of employment simply established that, in the absence of a contract, an employee was hired for a year at a time. This rule was designed to prevent injustice in an agrarian society. If an employee worked through harvest time, the landowner could not fire him in the unproductive winter. Conversely, a worker could not stay the winter and then leave for greener pastures in the spring.

In the eighteenth and nineteenth centuries, the Industrial Revolution profoundly altered the employment relationship. Many workers left the farms and villages for large factories in the city. Bosses no longer knew their workers personally, so they felt little responsibility toward them. The old laws that had suited an agrarian economy with stable relationships did not fit the new employment conditions. Instead of duties and responsibilities, courts emphasized the freedom to contract. Because employees could quit their factory jobs whenever they wanted, it was only fair for employers to have the same freedom to fire a worker. That was indeed the rule adopted by the courts: unless workers had an explicit employment contract, they were employees at will. **An *employee at will* could be fired for a good reason, a bad reason, or no reason at all.** For nearly a century, this was the basic common law rule of employment. A court explained the rule this way:

> Precisely as may the employee cease labor at his whim or pleasure, and, whatever be his reason, good, bad, or indifferent, leave no one a legal right to complain; so, upon the other hand, may the employer discharge, and, whatever be his reason, good, bad, or indifferent, no one has suffered a legal wrong.[2]

However evenhanded this common law rule of employment may have sounded in theory, in practice it could lead to harsh results. The lives of factory workers were grim.[3] It was not as if they could simply pack up and leave; conditions were no better elsewhere. For the worker, freedom to contract often meant little more than freedom to starve. Courts and legislatures gradually began to recognize that individual workers were generally unable to negotiate fair contracts with powerful employers. Since the beginning of the twentieth century, employment law has changed dramatically. Now the employment relationship is more strictly regulated by statutes and by the common law. No longer can a boss discharge an employee for any reason whatsoever.

Note that many of the statutes discussed in this chapter were passed by Congress and therefore apply nationally. The common law, however, comes from state courts and only applies locally. We will look at a sampling of cases that illustrates national trends, even though the law may not be the same in every state.

This chapter covers four topics in employment law: (1) employment security, (2) safety and privacy in the workplace, (3) financial protection, and (4) employment discrimination.

---

2 *Union Labor Hospital Assn. v. Vance Redwood Lumber Co.,* 112 P.886, 888, 1910 Cal. LEXIS 417 (Cal. 1910).
3 For examples of some truly grim modern jobs, work your way over to http://www.worstjob.com.

EMPLOYMENT SECURITY

National Labor Relations Act

Without unions to represent employee interests, employers could simply fire any troublemaking workers who complained about conditions in factories or mines. By joining together, workers could bargain with their employers on more equal terms. Naturally, the owners fought against the unions, firing organizers and even hiring goons to beat them up. Distressed by anti-union violence, Congress passed the **National Labor Relations Act** in 1935. Known as the **NLRA** or the **Wagner Act,** this statute:

- Created the National Labor Relations Board to enforce labor laws;
- Prohibits employers from penalizing workers who engage in union activity; (e.g., joining a preexisting union or forming a new one); and
- Requires employers to "bargain in good faith" with unions.

  Labor law is covered at greater length in Chapter 16.

Family and Medical Leave Act

In 1993, Congress passed the Family and Medical Leave Act (FMLA), which guarantees both men and women up to 12 weeks of *unpaid* leave each year for childbirth, adoption, or medical emergencies for themselves or a family member. An employee who takes a leave must be allowed to return to the same or an equivalent job with the same pay and benefits. The FMLA applies only to companies with at least 50 workers and to employees who have been with the company full-time for at least a year; this is about 60 percent of all employees. The Labor Department answers questions about the FMLA at http://www.dol.gov (click on "Family and Medical Leave Act," then "Frequently Asked Questions").

When Randy Seale's wife went into premature labor with triplets, he stayed home from his job as a truck driver with Associated Milk Producers, Inc. in Roswell, New Mexico. However, the milk of human kindness did not flow in this company's veins: it promptly fired the expectant father. Because Seale was an employee at will, the company's action would have been perfectly legal without the FMLA. But after the U.S. Department of Labor filed suit, the company agreed to pay Seale $10,000.

COBRA

Many companies provide health insurance for their employees. The problem with this system used to be that losing your job meant losing your health insurance on the spot. Then Congress passed the Consolidated Omnibus Budget Reconciliation Act (COBRA). This statute provides that former employees must be allowed to continue their health insurance for 18 months after leaving their job. The catch is that employees must pay for it themselves, up to 102 percent of the cost. (The extra 2 percent covers administrative expenses.)

COBRA applies to any company with 20 or more workers. Both employees and their families are covered. So, for example, if the child of a worker graduates from college and is no longer eligible under her parent's health insurance plan, she can elect to continue her coverage by paying for it herself.

Wrongful Discharge

Olga Monge was a schoolteacher in her native Costa Rica. After moving to New Hampshire, she attended college in the evenings to earn U.S. teaching credentials. At night, she worked at the Beebe Rubber Co. During the day, she cared for her husband and three children. When she applied for a better job at her plant, the foreman offered to promote her if she would be "nice" and go out on a date with him. When she refused, he assigned her to a lower wage job, took away her overtime, made her clean the washrooms, and generally ridiculed her. Finally, she collapsed at work and he fired her.[4]

Imagine that you are one of the judges who decided this case. Olga Monge has been treated abominably, but she was an employee at will and, as you well know, could be fired for any reason. But how can you let the foreman get away with this despicable behavior? The New Hampshire Supreme Court decided that even an employee at will has rights:

> We hold that a termination by the employer of a contract of employment at will which is motivated by bad faith or malice or based on retaliation is not in the best interest of the economic system or the public good and constitutes a breach of the employment contract.[5]

The employment at will doctrine was created by the courts. Because that rule has sometimes led to absurdly unfair results, the courts have now created a major exception to the rule—**wrongful discharge**. The *Monge* case illustrates this concept. *Wrongful discharge* **prohibits an employer from firing a worker for a *bad reason*.** There are three categories of wrongful discharge claims: public policy, contract law, and tort law.

Public Policy

The *Monge* case is an example of the **public policy rule.** Unfortunately, naming the rule is easier than defining it, because its definition and application vary from state to state. **In essence, the public policy rule prohibits an employer from firing a worker for a reason that violates basic social rights, duties, or responsibilities.** Almost every employee who has ever been fired feels that a horrible injustice has been done. The difficulty, from the courts' perspective, is to distinguish those cases of dismissal that are offensive enough to affront the community at large from those that outrage only the employee. The courts have primarily applied the public policy rule when an employee refuses to violate the law or insists upon exercising a legal right or performing a legal duty.

Refusing to Violate the Law. Larry Downs went to Duke Hospital for surgery on his cleft palate. When he came out of the operating room, the doctor instructed a nurse, Marie Sides, to give Downs enough anesthetic to immobilize him. Sides refused because she thought the anesthetic was wrong for this patient. The doctor angrily administered the anesthetic himself. Shortly thereafter, Downs stopped breathing. Before the doctors could resuscitate him, he suffered permanent brain damage. When Downs's family sued the hospital, Sides was called to testify. A number of Duke doctors told her that she would be "in trouble" if she testified. She did

---

[4] *Monge v. Beebe*, 114 N.H. 130, 316 A.2d 549, 1974 N.H. LEXIS 223 (1974).
[5] *Id.* at 133.

testify and, after three months of harassment, was fired. When she sued Duke University, the court held:

> It would be obnoxious to the interests of the state and contrary to public policy and sound morality to allow an employer to discharge any employee, whether the employment be for a designated or unspecified duration, on the ground that the employee declined to commit perjury, an act specifically enjoined by statute. To hold otherwise would be without reason and contrary to the spirit of the law.[6]

As a general rule, employees may not be discharged for refusing to break the law. For example, courts have protected employees who refused to participate in an illegal price-fixing scheme, falsify pollution control records required by state law, pollute navigable waters in violation of federal law, or assist a supervisor in stealing from customers.[7]

Exercising a Legal Right. **As a general rule, an employer may not discharge a worker for exercising a legal right if that right supports public policy.** Dorothy Frampton injured her arm while working at the Central Indiana Gas Co. Her employer (and its insurance company) paid her medical expenses and her salary during the four months she was unable to work. When she discovered that she also qualified for benefits under the state's workers' compensation plan, she filed a claim and received payment. One month later, the company fired her without giving a reason. In her suit against the gas company, the court held:

> The [Workers' Compensation] Act creates a duty in the employer to compensate employees for work-related injuries and a right in the employee to receive such compensation. If employers are permitted to penalize employees for filing workmen's compensation claims, a most important public policy will be undermined. Employees will not file claims for justly deserved compensation—opting, instead, to continue their employment without incident. The end result, of course, is that the employer is effectively relieved of his obligation.[8]

Performing a Legal Duty. **Courts have consistently held that an employee may not be fired for serving on a jury.** Employers sometimes have difficulty replacing employees who are called up for jury duty and, therefore, prefer that their workers find some excuse for not serving. But jury duty is an important civic obligation that employers are not permitted to undermine.

What about an employee who performs a good deed that is not legally required? Kevin Gardner had just parked his armored truck in front of a bank in Spokane, Washington, when he saw a man with a knife chase the manager out of the bank. While running past the truck, the manager looked directly at Gardner and yelled, "Help me, help me." Gardner got out of his truck and locked the door. By then, the suspect had grabbed another woman, put his knife to her throat, and dragged her into the bank. Gardner followed them in, tackled the suspect, and disarmed him. The rescued woman hailed Gardner as a hero, but his employer fired him for violating a "fundamental"

---

[6] *Sides v. Duke University*, 74 N.C. App. 331, 328 S.E.2d 818, 1985 N.C. App. LEXIS 3501 (N.C. Ct. App. 1985).

[7] *Tameny v. Atlantic Richfield Co.*, 27 Cal. 3d 167, 610 P.2d 1330, 1980 Cal. LEXIS 171 (1980); *Trombetta v. Detroit, T. & I. R.*, 81 Mich. App. 489, 265 N.W.2d 385, 1978 Mich. App. LEXIS 2153 (Mich. Ct. App. 1978); *Sabine Pilot Service, Inc. v. Hauck*, 28 Tex. Sup. J. 339, 687 S.W.2d 733, 1985 Tex. LEXIS 755 (1985); *Vermillion v. AAA Pro Moving & Storage*, 146 Ariz. 215, 704 P.2d 1360, 1985 Ariz. App. LEXIS 592 (Ariz. Ct. App. 1985).

[8] *Frampton v. Central Indiana Gas Co.*, 260 Ind. 249, 297 N.E.2d 425, 1973 Ind. LEXIS 522 (1973).

company rule that prohibited drivers from leaving their armored trucks unattended. However, the court held for Gardner on the grounds that, although there is no affirmative legal duty to intervene in such a situation, society values and encourages voluntary rescuers when a life is in danger.[9]

In the following case, the court adopts an expansive view of the public policy rule.

WELLS V. ORMET CORP.

1999 Ohio App. LEXIS 1087
Court of Appeals of Ohio, 1999

Facts: Mark Wells had worked for the Ormet Corporation for 19 years and was foreman of one of its plants. One evening, he had to cancel an overtime shift when five workers failed to show up. Wells and Lee Smith, one of the company's labor relations specialists, met with union officials to determine if the employees had legitimate excuses for not working or if they had collaborated to shut the plant down.

After the meeting, Wells and Smith concluded that the employees had had good excuses for their absences and that they had not been part of an organized effort to cause trouble. However, Dunlap, the general manager of the plant, disagreed and suspended the five employees. The union requested a formal hearing. At the hearing, a union official asked Wells if he believed that the absences were part of a concerted plan. After Smith gave Wells permission to answer, Wells responded that he did not believe the employees had collaborated.

Three days later, Dunlap had Wells fired. Wells sued the company, alleging wrongful discharge under the public policy exception to the employment-at-will doctrine. Ormet filed a motion to dismiss, which the trial court granted.

Issue: Does the public policy doctrine protect an employee from being fired for disagreeing with his boss at a hearing?

Excerpts from Judge Vukovich's Decision: [T]he issue before this court is whether there exists a sufficiently clear public policy against the corporate firing of a member of management for answering a question in a way that favors the laborers' position at a grievance hearing. Due to the fact that appellant was a nineteen-year veteran worker at the corporation and the fact that he was only answering the question in a manner that he believed was being directed by the corporation's labor relations specialist, we hold that, as limited to the facts alleged in the complaint, a sufficiently clear public policy was violated by appellant's discharge.

The public policy in the case consists of various established interests of society as a whole. These broad societal interests include a fair workplace, truthful grievance proceedings, job stability for long-term employees, and economic productivity. There is a clear public policy supporting the aforementioned interests, the violation of which is of similar import to the violation of a statute. The adoption of such a policy exception to employment-at-will adequately inures to the benefit of the general public. ■

Whistleblowing. No one likes to be accused of wrongdoing even if (or perhaps, especially if) the accusations are true. **This is exactly what whistleblowers do: they are employees who disclose illegal behavior on the part of their employer.** Not surprisingly, many companies, when faced with such an accusation by an employee, prefer to shoot the messenger. Here is the story of Henry Boisvert.

---

[9] *Gardner v. Loomis Armored, Inc.*, 913 P.2d 377, 1996 Wash. LEXIS 109 (1996).

NEWSworthy

FMC Corp. sold 9,000 Bradley Fighting Vehicles to the U.S. Army for as much as $1.5 million each. But the Bradley was controversial from the moment it began rolling off FMC's manufacturing lines. Designed to carry soldiers around battlefields in Eastern Europe, its ability to "swim" across rivers and lakes was an important part of its job description. But Henry Boisvert, a testing supervisor for FMC, charged that the Bradley swam like a rock. Boisvert said he first encountered problems with the Bradley in the early days of the Army procurement process. He had one driven into a test pond and watched it quickly fill with water. FMC welders who worked on Bradleys claimed they weren't given enough time to do their work properly and so would simply fill gaps with putty. FMC quashed Boisvert's report on the Bradley and fired him when he refused to sign a falsified version. FMC disputes his account, but a jury ultimately agreed with him.[10] ◆

The law on whistleblowers varies across the country. As a general rule, however, whistleblowers are protected in the following situations:

- *The False Claims Act.* Henry Boisvert refused to sign his name to a report he thought was inaccurate. As a result, he earned the right to sign a check from FMC for about $20 million. Boisvert recovered under the federal False Claims Act, a statute that permits anyone to bring suit against a "person" (including a company) who defrauds the government. The Act also prohibits employers from firing workers who file suit under the statute. A successful whistleblower receives between 15 and 30 percent of any damages awarded to the government.

- *Constitutional Protection for Government Employees.* Employees of federal, state, and local governments have a right to free speech under the United States Constitution. Therefore, the government cannot retaliate against public employees who blow the whistle as long as the employee is speaking out on a matter of public concern. For example, a New York City child welfare agency received numerous reports that six-year-old Elisa Izquierdo was being abused. After Elisa was beaten to death by her mother, ABC News broadcast an interview with a social worker from the agency. She stated on air that "The workers who are considered the best workers are the ones who seem to be able to move cases out quickly. . . . There are lots of fatalities the press doesn't know anything about." By giving this interview, the social worker violated New York City rules prohibiting employees from disclosing information about families supervised by city agencies. The city suspended the social worker from her job, and she sued. The court acknowledged that the government has the right to prohibit some employee speech. However, if the employee speaks on matters of public concern, the government bears the burden of justifying any retaliation. In this case, the court held for the social worker. The city reinstated her and gave her back pay.[11]

- *Statutory Protection for Federal Employees.* Congress passed the Civil Service Reform Act in 1978 and the Whistleblower Protection Act in 1989. These two statutes prevent retaliation against federal employees who report wrongdoing. They also permit the award of back pay and attorney's fees to the whistleblower. This statute was used to prevent the National Park Service from disciplining two managers who wrote a report expressing concern over development in Yellowstone National Park.

---

[10] *Lee Gomes,* "A Whistle-Blower Finds Jackpot at the End of His Quest," *The Wall Street Journal,* April 27, 1998, p. B1.

[11] *Harman v. City of New York,* 140 F.3d 111, 1998 U.S. App. LEXIS 5567 (2d Cir. 1998).

- *Employees of Publicly Traded Companies.* In response to a series of corporate financial scandals, Congress passed the Sarbanes-Oxley Act of 2002. Among other provisions, this Act protects employees of publicly traded companies who provide evidence of fraud to investigators (whether in or outside the company). A successful plaintiff is entitled to reinstatement, back pay, and attorney's fees. The Web page http://www.oalj.dol.gov provides a summary of some recent whistleblower complaints filed under Sarbanes-Oxley. Click on "Whistleblower," then "Federal Court Decisions."

- *State Statutes.* The good news is that all 50 states have statutes that protect whistleblowers from retaliation by their employers. The bad news is that the scope of this protection varies greatly from state to state. For example, in some states, protection only extends to public employees, while in other states, all employees are covered.

- *Common Law.* Most courts will prohibit the discharge of employees who report illegal activity that relates to their own jobs. For example, a Connecticut court held a company liable when it fired a quality control director for reporting to his boss that some products had failed the quality tests.[12] Sometimes, however, courts have held that employees do not have a right to report wrongdoing if it does not relate to their own job functions. For example, Donald Smith's boss told him to ignore the fact that 73,000 pounds of caustic soda had spilled into the river next to a company warehouse. When Smith instead reported the spill to corporate headquarters, he was fired. The court held that because Smith had no responsibility for reporting spills, the public's interest "in harmony and productivity in the workplace must prevail over the public's interest in encouraging an employee in Smith's position to express his 'informed view.'"[13]

Public Policy	Which public interest is greater—harmony in the workplace or protection of the environment? Why should it matter that Donald Smith was not responsible for reporting spills? If you were living downstream from 73,000 pounds of caustic soda, would you want Smith to report that spill? ◆

Contract Law

Traditionally, many employers (and employees) thought that only a formal, signed document qualified as an employment contract. Increasingly, however, courts have been willing to enforce an employer's more casual promises, whether written or oral. Sometimes courts have also been willing to *imply* contract terms in the absence of an *express* agreement.

Truth in Hiring. **Oral promises made during the hiring process can be enforceable, even if not approved by the company's top executives.** When the Tanana Valley Medical-Surgical Group, Inc. hired James Eales as a physician's assistant, it promised him that as long as he did his job, he could stay there until retirement age. Six years later the company fired him without cause. The Alaska Supreme Court held that the clinic's promise was enforceable.[14]

---

[12] *Sheets v. Teddy's Frosted Foods, Inc.,* 179 Conn. 471, 427 A.2d 385, 1980 Conn. LEXIS 690 (1980).

[13] *Smith v. Calgon Carbon Corp.,* 917 F.2d 1338, 1990 U.S. App. LEXIS 19193 (3rd Cir. 1990).

[14] *Eales v. Tanana Valley Medical-Surgical Group, Inc.,* 663 P.2d 958, 1983 Alas. LEXIS 430 (Alaska 1983).

In the following case, an insurance company was tackled for a big loss when it failed to disclose information during the hiring process.

NEWS*worthy*

While a player with the New York Giants football team, Phil McConkey was used to rough treatment. He expected life in the insurance business to be more civilized. But shortly after Alexander & Alexander hired him, it was acquired by Aon Corp. and the new company sacked him immediately. McConkey filed suit, alleging that Alexander & Alexander should have told him during the hiring process that it was engaged in merger talks (even though those discussions were, at that point, secret). A jury agreed, awarding the downed player $10 million. ◆

Employee Handbooks.   The employee handbook at Blue Cross & Blue Shield stated that employees could be fired only for just cause and then only after warnings, notice, a hearing, and other procedures. Charles Toussaint was fired summarily five years after he joined the company. Although this decision was ultimately reviewed by the personnel department, company president, and chairman of the board of trustees, Toussaint was not given the benefit of all the procedures in the handbook. The court held that **an employee handbook creates a contract.**[15]

at **RISK**

Employers are now taking steps to protect themselves from liability for implied contracts. Some employers require new hires to sign a document acknowledging that (1) they are employees at will, (2) they can be terminated at any time for any reason, and (3) no one at the company has made any oral representations concerning the terms of employment. These employers caution interviewers not to make promises. Their employee handbooks now feature stern legal warnings, rather than friendly welcomes. And some companies have dispensed with handbooks altogether. ◆

Covenant of Good Faith and Fair Dealing.   A covenant of good faith and fair dealing prohibits one party to a contract from interfering with the other's right to benefit under the contract. All parties are expected to behave in a fair, decent, and reasonable manner. **In some cases, courts will imply a covenant of good faith and fair dealing in an at-will employment relationship.**

When Forrest Fleming went to work for Parametric Technology Corp., the company promised him valuable stock options if he met his sales goals. He would not be able to *exercise* the options (i.e., purchase the stock), however, until several years after they were granted and then only if he was still employed by the company. During his four years with Parametric, Fleming received options to purchase about 18,000 shares for a price as low as 25 cents each. The shares ultimately traded in the market for as much as $50. Although Fleming exercised some options, the company fired him three months before he became eligible to purchase an additional 1,000 shares. The jury awarded him $1.6 million in damages. Although Parametric had not violated the explicit terms of the option agreement, the jury believed it had violated the covenant of good faith and fair dealing by firing Fleming to prevent him from exercising his remaining options.[16]

Tort Law

Workers have successfully sued their employers under the following tort theories.

---

[15] *Toussaint v. Blue Cross & Blue Shield,* 408 Mich. 579, 292 N.W.2d 880, 1980 Mich. LEXIS 227 (1980).
[16] *Fleming v. Parametric Tech. Corp.,* 1999 U.S. App. LEXIS 14864.

Defamation. **Employers may be liable for defamation when they give false and unfavorable references about a former employee.** John R. Glennon, Jr., was the branch manager of Dean Witter's Nashville office. Dean Witter fired him and filed a termination notice with the National Association of Securities Dealers saying that Glennon "was under internal review for violating investment-related statutes." This statement was untrue, and Witter had to pay $1.5 million in damages for defamation.

More than half the states, however, recognize a qualified privilege for employers who give references about former employees. A qualified privilege means that employers are liable only for false statements that they know to be false or that are primarily motivated by ill will. After Becky Chambers left her job at American Trans Air, Inc., she discovered that her former boss was telling anyone who called for a reference that Chambers "does not work good with other people," is a "trouble-maker," and "would not be a good person to rehire." Chambers was unable, however, to present compelling evidence that her boss had been primarily motivated by ill will. Neither Trans Air nor the boss was held liable for these statements because they were protected by the qualified privilege.[17]

Even if the employer wins, a trial is an expensive and time-consuming undertaking. Not surprisingly, companies are leery about offering any references for former employees. The company gains little benefit from giving an honest evaluation and may suffer substantial liability. As a matter of policy, many companies instruct their managers to reveal only a person's salary and dates of employment and not to offer an opinion on job performance. According to one survey, only 55 percent of former employers are totally honest when they give references.

NEWS*worthy*

Human resources managers have been drilled for years by their lawyers to provide only the most limited job references on former employees. Now they have even more reason to be cautious. Growing numbers of job applicants are hiring companies to find out what their former employers are saying about them. Job seekers can use information from these companies to confront former employers or even to bolster legal action they may take after being let go. Companies like References etc., Documented Reference Check, and Allison & Taylor Inc. will provide a reference-check report for a fee between $50 and $90.

The reference-checking companies are adding to the difficulty that employers have long had in providing references on former employees. A company that gives a glowing reference on an employee fired with cause could soon be defending a wrongful termination case. A company that fails to mention negative information about a former employee with known dangerous tendencies could be sued by a future employer for failing to disclose the damaging information.[18] ◆

Employers are afraid of liability if they give a negative reference, but this article suggests that they are liable if they tell less than the whole truth. **Generally, courts have held that employers do not have a legal obligation to disclose information about former employees.** For example, while Jeffrey St. Clair worked at the St. Joseph Nursing Home, he was disciplined 24 times for actions ranging from extreme violence to drug and alcohol use. When he applied for a job with Maintenance Management Corp. (MMC), St. Joseph refused to give any information other than

---

17 *Chambers v. American Trans Air, Inc.*, 577 N.E.2d 612, 1991 Ind. App. LEXIS 1413 (Ind. Ct. App. 1991).

18 Marci Alboher Nusbaum, "When a Reference Is Not What It Seems," *The New York Times*, Oct. 19, 2003, p. C12.

St. Clair's dates of employment. After he savagely murdered a security guard at his new job, the guard's family sued, but the court dismissed the case.[19]

In some recent cases, however, courts have held that, when a former worker is potentially dangerous, employers do have an obligation to disclose this information. For example, officials from two junior high schools gave Robert Gadams glowing letters of recommendation without mentioning that he had been fired for inappropriate sexual conduct with students. While an assistant principal at a new school, he molested a 13 year old. Her parents sued the former employers. The court held that the writer of a letter of recommendation owes to third parties (in this case, the student) "a duty not to misrepresent the facts in describing the qualifications and character of a former employee, if making these misrepresentations would present a substantial, foreseeable risk of physical injury to the third persons."[20] As a result of cases such as this, it makes sense to disclose past violent behavior.

To assist employers who are asked for references, Lehigh economist Robert Thornton has written "The Lexicon of Intentional Ambiguous Recommendations" (LIAR). For a candidate with interpersonal problems, he suggests saying, "I am pleased to say that this person is a former colleague of mine." For the lazy worker, "In my opinion, you will be very fortunate to get this person to work for you." For the criminal, he suggests, "He's a man of many convictions" and "I'm sorry we let her get away." For the untrustworthy candidate, "Her true ability is deceiving."[21]

Ethics

All joking aside, what if someone calls you to check references on a former employee who had a drinking problem? The job is driving a van for junior high school sports teams. What is the manager's ethical obligation in this situation? Many managers say that, in the case of a serious problem such as alcoholism, sexual harassment, or drug use, they will find a way to communicate that an employee is unsuitable. What if the ex-employee says she is reformed? Aren't people entitled to a second chance? Is it right to risk a defamation suit against your company to protect others from harm? What solutions does the Ethics Checklist in Chapter 2 suggest? Would it be just to reveal private information about a former employee? Is the process fair if you provide information that the job applicant has no opportunity to rebut because it is kept secret? ◆

Intentional Infliction of Emotional Distress. **Employers who condone cruel treatment of their workers face liability under the tort of intentional infliction of emotional distress.** For example:

- When a 57-year-old social-work manager at Yale–New Haven Hospital was fired, she was forced to place her personal belongings in a plastic bag and was escorted out the door by security guards in full view of gaping co-workers. A supervisor told her that she would be arrested for trespassing if she returned. A jury awarded her $105,000.

- An employee swore at a co-worker and threatened her with a knife because she rejected his sexual advances. Her superiors fired her for complaining about the incident. A court held that the employer had inflicted emotional distress.[22]

---

[19] *Moore v. St. Joseph Nursing Home, Inc.,* 184 Mich. App. 766, 459 N.W.2d 100, 1990 Mich. App. LEXIS 285 (Mich. Ct. App. 1990).

[20] *Randi W. v. Muroc Joint Unified School District,* 14 Cal. 4th 1066, 929 P.2d 582, 1997 Cal. LEXIS 10 (1997), modified, 14 Cal. 4th 1282c, 97 Cal. Daily Op. Service 1439.

[21] *Wall Street Journal,* March 22, 1994, p. 1.

[22] *Hogan v. Forsyth Country Club Co.,* 79 N.C. App. 483, 340 S.E.2d 116, 1986 N.C. App. LEXIS 2098 (N.C. Ct. App. 1986).

- On the other hand, another court held that an employee who was fired for dating a co-worker did not have a valid claim for infliction of emotional distress.[23]

Safety and Privacy in the Workplace

Workplace Safety

In 1970, Congress passed the Occupational Safety and Health Act (OSHA) to ensure safe working conditions. Under OSHA:

- Employers must comply with specific health and safety standards. For example, health care personnel who work with blood are not permitted to eat or drink in areas where the blood is kept and must not put their mouths on any instruments used to store blood. Protective clothing—gloves, gowns, and laboratory coats—must be impermeable to blood.

- Employers are under a general obligation to keep their workplace "free from recognized hazards that are causing or are likely to cause death or serious physical harm" to employees.

- Employers must keep records of all workplace injuries and accidents.

- OSHA may inspect workplaces to ensure that they are safe. OSHA may assess fines for violations and order employers to correct unsafe conditions.

OSHA has done a lot to make the American workplace safer. In 1900, roughly 35,000 workers died and 350,000 were injured at work. One hundred years later, the workforce had grown five times larger but the number of annual deaths had fallen to 5,100. You can report hazards at your worksite to OSHA online at http://www.osha.gov by clicking on "Worker" and then "Complain."

Employee Privacy

Upon opening the country's first moving assembly line in the early 1900s, Henry Ford issued a booklet, "Helpful Hints and Advice to Employees," that warned against drinking, gambling, borrowing money, taking in boarders, and practicing poor hygiene. Ford also created a department of 100 investigators for door-to-door checks on his employees' drinking habits, sexual practices, and housekeeping skills. It sounds outrageous, but in modern times employees have been fired or disciplined for such extracurricular activities as playing dangerous sports, dating co-workers, or even having high cholesterol.

The right to hire, fire, and make an honest profit is enshrined in American tradition. But so is the right to privacy. Justice Louis D. Brandeis called it the "right to be let alone—the most comprehensive of rights and the right most valued by civilized men." What protection do workers have against intrusive employers?

Off-Duty Conduct

In an era of rapidly expanding health care costs, employers are concerned about the health of their workers. Some companies have banned off-duty smoking and have even fired employees who show traces of nicotine in their blood. In response, more than

---

[23] *Patton v. J. C. Penney Co.,* 301 Or. 117, 719 P.2d 854, 1986 Ore. LEXIS 1144 (1986).

half the states have passed laws that protect the right of employees to smoke cigarettes while off-duty. Some of these statutes permit *any* lawful activity when off-duty, including drinking socially, having high cholesterol, being overweight, or engaging in dangerous hobbies—bungee jumping or rollerblading, for instance.

Alcohol and Drug Testing

Government employees can be tested for drug and alcohol use only if they show signs of use or if they are in a job where this type of abuse endangers the public. Most states permit private employers to administer alcohol and drug tests. According to one survey, more than 80 percent of large firms test employees for drugs.

Lie Detector Tests

Under the Employee Polygraph Protection Act of 1988, employers may not require, or even *suggest*, that an employee or job candidate submit to a lie detector test except as part of an "ongoing investigation" into crimes that have occurred.

Electronic Monitoring of the Workplace

Technological advances in communications have raised a host of new privacy issues.

cyberLaw

Many companies monitor employee use of electronic equipment in the workplace: telephone calls, voice mail, e-mail, and Internet usage. **The Electronic Communications Privacy Act of 1986 (ECPA) permits employers to monitor workers' telephone calls and e-mail messages if (1) the employee consents, (2) the monitoring occurs in the ordinary course of business, or (3) in the case of e-mail, the employer provides the e-mail system.** However, bosses may not disclose any private information revealed by the monitoring.

Although workers may feel that their e-mail should be private, employers argue that this monitoring improves employee productivity and protects the company from lawsuits. For example, a West Coast company fired a woman "because of a tough economy." When she sued, her attorneys demanded access to the company's e-mail system as part of the discovery process. They found a message from the woman's supervisor saying, "Get that bitch out of here as fast as you can. I don't care what it takes. Just do it." The supervisor had long since erased the message from his computer, but it had remained buried in the system. A few hours after the message was revealed in court, the company settled for $250,000.

When companies monitor employee use of the Internet, they are concerned not only about lawsuits but also that workers may be wasting time. During one month, employees at IBM, Apple Computer, and AT&T logged on to *Penthouse* magazine's Website 12,823 times, using the equivalent of more than 347 workdays. One company discovered that some of its employees were using their company computers to buy and sell child pornography. Employers fear that even legal logging on to sexually explicit sites may give rise to sexual harassment claims. ◆

FINANCIAL PROTECTION

Congress and the states have enacted laws that provide employees with a measure of financial security. All the laws in this section were created by statute, not by the courts.

Fair Labor Standards Act

Passed in 1938, the Fair Labor Standards Act (FLSA) regulates wages and limits child labor. The wage provisions do not apply to managerial, administrative, or professional staff, which means that accounting, consulting, and law firms (among others) are free to require as many hours a week as their employees can humanly perform without having to pay overtime or the minimum wage.

Minimum Wage

The current federal minimum wage is $5.15 per hour, although Congressional leaders have pledged to raise it. Also, some states have set a higher minimum. To find the minimum wage in your state, check in at http://www.dol.gov and click on "ESA," "Minimum Wage," and "Minimum Wage in the States." Employers can pay students and apprentices under age 20 a training wage of $4.25 per hour. The Department of Labor Website lists any changes in the minimum wage and also answers related questions: http://www.dol.gov. Click on "Wages."

Overtime Pay

The FLSA does not limit the number of hours a week that an employee can work, but it does specify that workers must be paid time and a half for any hours over 40 in one week.

Child Labor

The FLSA prohibits "oppressive child labor," which means that children under 14 may work only in agriculture and entertainment. Fourteen and fifteen year olds are permitted to work *limited* hours after school in nonhazardous jobs. Sixteen and seventeen year olds may work *unlimited* hours in nonhazardous jobs.

Workers' Compensation

Workers' compensation statutes ensure that employees receive payment for injuries incurred at work. Before workers' comp, injured employees could recover damages only if they sued their employer. It is the brave (or carefree) worker who is willing to risk a suit against his own boss. Lawsuits poison the atmosphere at work. Moreover, employers frequently won these suits by claiming that (1) the injured worker was contributorily negligent, (2) a fellow employee had caused the accident, or (3) the injured worker had assumed the risk of injury. As a result, seriously injured workers (or their families) often had no recourse against the employer.

Workers' comp statutes provide a fixed, certain recovery to the injured employee, no matter who was at fault for the accident. In return, employees are not permitted to sue their employers for negligence. The amounts allowed (for medical expenses and lost wages) under workers' comp statutes are often less than a worker might recover in court, but the injured employee trades the certainty of some recovery for the higher risk of rolling the dice at trial. Payments are approved by an administrative board that conducts an informal hearing into each claim. These payments are funded either through the purchase of private insurance or by a tax on employers—a tax that is based on how many injuries their employees have suffered. Thus, employers have an incentive to maintain a safe working environment.

Social Security

The federal Social Security system began in 1935, during the depths of the Great Depression, to provide a basic safety net for the elderly, ill, and unemployed. **Currently,**

the Social Security system pays benefits to workers who are retired, disabled, or temporarily unemployed and to the spouses and children of disabled or deceased workers. It also provides medical insurance to the retired and disabled. The Social Security program is financed through a tax on wages that is paid by employers, employees, and the self-employed.

Although the Social Security system has done much to reduce poverty among the elderly, many worry that it cannot survive in its current form. When workers pay taxes, the proceeds do not go into a savings account for their retirement, but instead are used to pay benefits to current retirees. In 1940, there were 40 workers for each retiree; currently, there are 3.3. By 2030, when the last baby boomers retire, there will be only 2 workers to support each retiree—a prohibitive burden. No wonder baby boomers are often cautioned not to count on Social Security when making their retirement plans.

The Federal Unemployment Tax Act (FUTA) is the part of the Social Security system that provides support to the unemployed. FUTA establishes some national standards, but states are free to set their own benefit levels and payment schedules. These payments are funded by a tax on employers. A worker who quits voluntarily or is fired for just cause is ineligible for benefits. While receiving payments, she must make a good faith effort to look for other employment.

Pension Benefits

In 1974, Congress passed the Employee Retirement Income Security Act (ERISA) to protect workers covered by private pension plans. Under ERISA, employers are not required to establish pension plans, but if they do, they must follow these federal rules. The law was aimed, in particular, at protecting benefits of retired workers if their companies subsequently go bankrupt. The statute also prohibits risky investments by pension plans. In addition, the statute sets rules on the vesting of benefits. (An employer cannot cancel *vested* benefits; *nonvested* benefits are forfeited when the employee leaves.) Before ERISA, retirement benefits at some companies did not vest until the employee retired—if he quit or was fired before retirement, even after years of service, he lost his pension. Under current law, employee benefits vest after five years of employment.

Employment Discrimination

In the last five decades, Congress has enacted important legislation to prevent discrimination in the workplace.

Equal Pay Act of 1963

Under the Equal Pay Act, an employee may not be paid at a lesser rate than employees of the opposite sex for equal work. "Equal work" means tasks that require equal skill, effort, and responsibility under similar working conditions. If the employee proves that she is not being paid equally, the employer will be found liable unless the pay difference is based on merit, productivity, seniority, or some factor other than sex. A "factor other than sex" includes prior wages, training, profitability, performance in an interview, and value to the company. For example, female agents sued Allstate Insurance Co. because its salary for new agents was based, in part, on prior salary. The women argued that this system was unfair because it perpetuated the historic wage differences between men and women. The court, however, held for Allstate.[24]

---

[24] *Kouba v. Allstate Insurance Co.*, 691 F.2d 873, 1982 U.S. App. LEXIS 24479 (9th Cir. 1982).

To find out how much less women earn than men, in spite of the Equal Pay Act, click on **http://www.aflcio.org,** then "Issues," "Working Women," and "Equal Pay."

Title VII

Title VII of the Civil Rights Act of 1964 prohibits employers from discriminating on the basis of race, color, religion, sex, or national origin. More specifically, it prohibits (1) discrimination in the workplace, (2) sexual harassment, and (3) discrimination because of pregnancy. It also permits employers to develop affirmative action plans. The following article reveals what life was like before Title VII.

NEWS*worthy*

Fresh out of college in 1963, I got my first job at *Newsweek* magazine. In those days, women were hired as researchers and men were hired as writers . . . and that was that. It was, as we used to say, a good job for a woman. If we groused about working for the men we studied with in college, we did it privately. It was the way things were.

I don't share my garden-variety piece of personal history as a lament or gripe. Woe isn't me. Nor am I one to regale the younger generation with memories of the bad old days when I walked 4 miles in the snow to school. They already know that women were treated as second-class citizens. But what they don't know, I have found, is that this was legal.

It was legal to have segregated ads that read "male wanted" and "female wanted." It was legal to fire a flight attendant if she got married. It was legal to get rid of a teacher when she became pregnant. If a boss paid a woman less because she was a woman, he was unapologetic. If he didn't want to hire a woman for a "man's job," he just didn't.

When President Johnson signed the Civil Rights Act of 1964, it became illegal for the first time to discriminate in employment on the grounds of sex. What had seemed to many like a "natural" way of treating men and women differently because of their roles in the family and society became what the courts now call "invidious."

In the first Title VII case, the Supreme Court ruled that it was illegal to refuse to hire a woman because she had small children. Under pressure, newspapers stopped segregating their employment pages. Women tiptoed into some "male jobs" and took hold in others.[25] ◆

Proof of Discrimination

Discrimination under Title VII means firing, refusing to hire, failing to promote, or otherwise reducing a person's employment opportunities because of race, color, religion, sex, or national origin. This protection applies to every stage of the employment process from job ads to postemployment references and includes placement, wages, benefits, and working conditions.

Plaintiffs in Title VII cases can prove discrimination two different ways: disparate treatment and disparate impact.

Disparate Treatment.   To prove a disparate treatment case, the plaintiff must show that she was *treated* differently because of her sex, race, color, religion, or national origin. The required steps in a disparate treatment case are:

---

[25] Ellen Goodman, "The Next Step for Women," *The Boston Globe,* June 27, 2004, p. D11.

> **Step 1** The plaintiff presents evidence that the defendant has discriminated against her because of a protected trait. This is called a **prima facie case.** The plaintiff is not required to prove discrimination; she need only create a *presumption* that discrimination occurred.
>
> Suppose that Louisa applies for a job coaching a boys' high school ice hockey team. She was an All-American hockey star in college. Although Louisa is obviously qualified for the job, Harry, the school principal, rejects her and continues to interview other people. This is not proof of discrimination, because Harry may have a perfectly good, nondiscriminatory explanation. However, his behavior *could have been* motivated by discrimination.
>
> **Step 2** The defendant must present evidence that its decision was based on *legitimate, nondiscriminatory* reasons. Harry might say, for example, that he wanted someone with prior coaching experience. Although Louisa is clearly a great player, she has never coached before.
>
> **Step 3** To win, the plaintiff must now prove that the employer discriminated. She may do so by showing that the reasons offered were simply a *pretext*. Louisa might show that Harry had recently hired a male tennis coach who had no prior coaching experience. Or Harry's assistant might testify that Harry said, "No way I'm going to put a woman on the ice with those guys." If she can present evidence such as this, Louisa wins.

In the following case, was the bartender treated differently because of her sex? You be the judge.

YOU BE THE JUDGE

JESPERSEN V. HARRAH'S
444 F.3d 1104, 2006 U.S. App. LEXIS 9307
United States Court of Appeals for the Ninth Circuit, 2006

Facts: Darlene Jespersen was a bartender at the sports bar in Harrah's Casino in Reno, Nevada. She was an outstanding employee. Her supervisors commented that she was "highly effective," her attitude was "very positive," and she made a "positive impression" on Harrah's guests. Harrah's customers repeatedly praised Jespersen on employee feedback forms, writing that Jespersen's excellent service and good attitude enhanced their experience at the sports bar and encouraged them to come back.

When Jespersen first went to work for Harrah's, the casino encouraged, but did not require, its female beverage servers to wear makeup. Jespersen tried for a short time but found that it made her feel sick, degraded, exposed, and violated. Moreover, wearing makeup interfered with her ability to deal with unruly

intoxicated guests because it "took away [her] credibility as an individual and as a person."

After Jespersen had been at Harrah's for almost 20 years, the casino implemented a program whose goal was to create a "brand standard of excellence." The program required beverage servers to be "well groomed, appealing to the eye, be firm and body toned, and be comfortable with maintaining this look while wearing the specified uniform." More explicitly, the rules for men were:

- Hair must not extend below top of shirt collar. Ponytails are prohibited.
- Hands and fingernails must be clean and nails neatly trimmed at all times.
- No colored polish is permitted.
- Eye and facial makeup is not permitted.
- Shoes will be solid black leather or leather type with rubber (non-skid) soles.

▼

The rules for women were:

- Hair must be teased, curled, or styled every day you work. Hair must be worn down at all times, no exceptions.

- Stockings are to be of nude or natural color consistent with employee's skin tone. No runs.

- Nail polish can be clear, white, pink, or red color only. No exotic nail art or length.

- Shoes will be solid black leather or leather type with rubber (non-skid) soles.

- Makeup (foundation/concealer and/or face powder, as well as blush and mascara) must be worn and applied neatly in complimentary colors, and lip color must be worn at all times.

An expert was brought in to show the employees how to dress. The workers (both male and female) were then photographed and told that they must look like the photographs every day at work.

Jespersen refused to wear makeup. She was told either to comply or to apply for a position that did not require makeup. When she did neither, Harrah's fired her. Jespersen sued under Title VII. The district court granted Harrah's motion for summary judgment. Jespersen appealed.

You Be the Judge: **Did Harrah's requirement that women wear makeup violate Title VII?**

Argument for Jespersen: Jespersen refused to wear makeup to work because the cost—in time, money, and personal dignity—was too high. Despite the fact that she did not wear makeup, numerous customers and supervisors consistently gave her glowing recommendations. Nonetheless, Harrah's fired her.

Employers are free to adopt different appearance standards for each sex, but these standards may not impose a greater burden on one sex than the other. Men were not required to wear makeup; women were. That difference meant a savings for men of hundreds of dollars and hours of time. Harrah's did not have the right to fire Jespersen for violating a rule that applies only to women, with no equivalent for men.

Argument for Harrah's: Employers are permitted to impose different appearance rules on men than on women as long as the overall burden on employees is the same. For example, it is not discriminatory to require men to wear their hair short. When looking at all of Harrah's rules, on balance the burden on men was no heavier than on women. ●

Disparate Impact.   Disparate impact becomes an issue if the employer has a rule that, *on its face*, is not discriminatory but *in practice* excludes too many people in a protected group. The steps in a disparate impact case are:

Step 1 The plaintiff must present a *prima facie* case. The plaintiff is not required to prove discrimination; he need only show a disparate impact—that the employment practice in question excludes a disproportionate number of people in a protected group (e.g., women and minorities).

Suppose that Harry will only hire teachers who are at least 5 feet 10 inches tall and weigh 170 pounds. He says he is afraid that students will literally push around anyone smaller. When Chou Ping, an Asian male, applies for a job, he cannot meet Harry's physical requirements. Chou Ping must show that Harry's rule, *in fact*, eliminates more women or minorities than white males. He might offer evidence that 50 percent of all white males can meet Harry's standard, but only 20 percent of white women and Asian males qualify.

Step 2 The defendant must offer some evidence that the employment practice was a *job-related business necessity*. Harry might produce evidence that teachers are

> regularly expected to wrestle students into their classroom seats. Further, he might cite studies showing that his standards are essential for this task.
>
> **Step 3** To win, the plaintiff must now prove either that the employer's reason is a *pretext* or that other, *less discriminatory* rules would achieve the same results. Chou Ping might suggest that all teachers could take a self-defense course or engage in martial arts training.

Note that the mere existence of a disparate impact does not *necessarily* mean that an employment practice violates the law. When the Illinois Law Enforcement Officers Training Board created an exam to test aspiring police officers, a higher percentage of minority applicants than white candidates failed the test. Some of the unsuccessful aspirants filed suit, alleging that the exam was illegal because it had a disparate impact. In response, the board presented evidence that the exam had been very carefully prepared by a consulting company that specialized in creating such exams. The court held that the exam was legal because it was "demonstrably a reasonable measure of job performance."[26]

Color

Title VII prohibits discrimination based on both race and color. Many people assume that these are essentially the same issue. Not so, as the following article demonstrates:

NEWS*worthy*

Dwight Burch says the insults began soon after he started working as a waiter at an Applebee's restaurant in Jonesboro, GA. His boss called him a "black monkey" and "tar baby" and suggested he bleach his skin, he says, and then co-workers began taunting him, too. "You name it, any dark-skinned, monstrous name you can think of, they called me it—porch monkey, jig-a-boo, blackie," Mr. Burch recalls. "I was the brunt of every joke . . . from the moment I got there until I left."

A case of racial discrimination? No, the alleged abuse came from fellow African-Americans. But Mr. Burch sued anyway, becoming one of an increasing number of workers publicly complaining about "color discrimination" at the hands of fellow minority-group members. Mr. Burch has very dark skin, and his alleged tormentors were lighter-skinned.[27] ◆

Title VII prohibits the type of treatment that Dwight Burch allegedly suffered. While denying any wrongdoing, Applebee's settled the case by paying Burch $40,000 and agreeing to conduct antidiscrimination training.

Religion

Employers must make *reasonable accommodation* for a worker's religious beliefs unless the request would cause *undue hardship* for the business. Scott Hamby told his manager at Wal-Mart that he could never work on Sunday because that was his Sabbath. It also happened to be one of the store's busiest days. When the manager forced Hamby to quit, he promptly sued on the grounds of religious discrimination. Lawsuits such as his are on the rise as more businesses remain open on Sundays. Wal-Mart denied wrongdoing but settled the case with a cash payment of

---

[26] *Bew v. Chicago,* 252 F.3d 891, 2001 U.S. App. LEXIS 9247 (7th Cir. 2001).

[27] Marjorie Valbrun, "EEOC Sees Rise in Intrarace Complaints of Color Bias," *Wall Street Journal,* Aug. 7, 2003, p. B1.

undisclosed amount. It also established a company-wide training program on religious accommodation.

Defenses to Charges of Discrimination

Under Title VII, the defendant has three possible defenses.

Merit.   A defendant is not liable if he shows that the person he favored was the most qualified. Test results, education, or productivity can all be used to demonstrate merit, provided they relate to the job in question. Harry can show that he hired Bruce instead of Louisa because Bruce has a master's degree in physical education and seven years of coaching experience. On the other hand, the fact that Bruce scored higher on the National Latin Exam in the eighth grade is not a good reason to hire him over Louisa.

ECONOMICS
& the LAW

It is easy to say that the most qualified person should be hired or promoted. But how do you measure merit? Take the case of Santa Clara, California, for example. No woman had ever held the job of radio dispatcher there. Although Paul Johnson scored higher on the dispatcher exam than Diane Joyce, the county hired Joyce.[28] This case ultimately reached the U.S. Supreme Court on the issue of whether a less qualified woman could be promoted over a more qualified man. (The court ruled that she could.)

So do we feel sorry for Paul Johnson? Of course, we feel sorry for anyone who does not get the job of his dreams. It turns out, however, that his score on the dispatcher exam had been 75 out of 100; hers was 73. This two-point difference is simply not persuasive evidence that Johnson would be a better radio dispatcher than Joyce. Indeed, employment tests are typically not very good predictors of on-the-job performance. They are at best blunt instruments. Moreover, a 2-point differential on a 100-point test is meaningless. As an affirmative action case, *Johnson* was unusual only in that the court actually reported the test scores. Typically, in such cases the actual difference in scores is rarely reported or discussed.

The moral of the story? Before concluding that a less qualified applicant has been promoted over a more qualified competitor, it is wise to ask about the validity of the test and the significance of the difference in scores.[29] ◆

Seniority.   A legitimate seniority system is legal, even if it perpetuates past discrimination. Suppose that Harry has always chosen the most senior assistant coach to take over as head coach when a vacancy occurs. Because the majority of the senior assistant coaches are male, most of the head coaches are, too. Such a system does not violate Title VII.

Bona Fide Occupational Qualification.   An employer is permitted to establish discriminatory job requirements if they are *essential* to the position in question. Such a requirement is called a **bona fide occupational qualification (BFOQ).** Catholic schools may, if they choose, refuse to hire non-Catholic teachers; mail order companies may refuse to hire men to model women's clothing. Generally, however, courts are not sympathetic to claims of BFOQ. They have, for example, almost always rejected BFOQ claims that are based on customer preference. Thus, airlines could not refuse to hire male flight attendants even though travelers prefer female attendants.[30] The major

---

[28] *Johnson v. Transportation Agency,* 489 U.S. 616, 1987 U.S. LEXIS 1387 (1987).

[29] Michael Selmi, "Testing for Equality: Merit, Efficiency, and the Affirmative Action Debate," *UCLA Law Review,* June 1995, vol. 42, p. 1251.

[30] *Diaz v. Pan American World Airways, Inc.,* 442 F.2d 385, 1971 U.S. App. LEXIS 10920 (5th Cir. 1971).

exception to this customer preference rule is sexual privacy: an employer may refuse to hire women to work in a men's bathroom and vice versa.

Affirmative Action

Affirmative action has become a hot political issue: white males protest that such programs are reverse discrimination against them; political candidates campaign on anti–affirmative action platforms.

Affirmative action is not required by Title VII, nor is it prohibited. Affirmative action programs have three different sources:

- *Litigation.* Courts have the power under Title VII to order affirmative action to remedy the effects of past discrimination.

- *Voluntary Action.* Employers can voluntarily introduce an affirmative action plan to remedy the effects of past practices or to achieve equitable representation of minorities and women.

- *Government Contracts.* In 1965, President Johnson signed Executive Order 11246, which prohibits discrimination by federal contractors. This order had a profound impact on the American workplace because one third of all workers are employed by companies that do business with the federal government. If an employer found that women or minorities were underrepresented in its workplace, it was required to establish goals and timetables to correct the deficiency.

In 1995, however, the Supreme Court dramatically limited the extent to which the government can require contractors to establish affirmative action programs. The Court ruled that these programs are permissible only if they serve a "compelling national interest" and are "narrowly tailored" so that they minimize the harm to white males. The government must be able to show that (1) the programs are needed to overcome specific past discrimination, (2) they have time limits, and (3) nondiscriminatory alternatives are not available.[31] This case led to a sharp decrease in the number of federal contracts awarded to companies owned by women and minorities.

Sexual Harassment

When Professor Anita Hill accused Supreme Court nominee Clarence Thomas of sexually harassing her, people across the country were glued to their televisions, watching the Senate hearings on her charges. Thomas was ultimately confirmed to the Supreme Court, but "sexual harassment" became a household phrase. The number of cases—and the size of the damage awards—skyrocketed.

Everyone has heard of sexual harassment, but few people know exactly what it is. Men fear that a casual comment or glance will be met with career-ruining charges; women claim that men "just don't get it." So what is sexual harassment anyway? **Sexual harassment involves unwelcome sexual advances, requests for sexual favors, and other verbal or physical conduct of a sexual nature.** There are two major categories of sexual harassment: (1) *quid pro quo* and (2) hostile work environment.

Quid Pro Quo. From a Latin phrase that means "this for that," *quid pro quo* harassment occurs if any aspect of a job is made contingent upon sexual activity. In other words, when a banker says to a secretary, "You can be promoted to teller if you sleep with me," that is *quid pro quo* sexual harassment.

---

31 *Adarand Constructors, Inc. v. Pena*, 515 U.S. 200, 115 S. Ct. 2097, 1995 U.S. LEXIS 4037 (1995).

Hostile Work Environment.   This is a more subtle claim and the one that managers worry about most. An employee has a valid claim of sexual harassment if sexual talk and innuendo are so pervasive that they interfere with her (or his) ability to work. Courts have found that offensive jokes, comments about clothes or body parts, and public displays of pornographic pictures create a hostile environment. In the following case, the company president repeatedly insulted and demeaned his female employees.

TERESA HARRIS V. FORKLIFT SYSTEMS, INC.

510 U.S. 17, 114 S. Ct. 367, 1993 U.S. LEXIS 7155
United States Supreme Court, 1993

Facts: Teresa Harris was a manager at Forklift Systems; Charles Hardy was its president. Hardy frequently made inappropriate sexual comments to Harris and other women at the company. For example, he said to Harris, in the presence of others, "You're a woman, what do you know?" and "We need a man as the rental manager." He called her "a dumb ass woman" and suggested that the two of them "go to the Holiday Inn to negotiate her raise." He also asked Harris and other female employees to get coins from his front pants pocket. He insisted that Harris and other women pick up objects he had thrown on the ground. When Harris complained to Hardy, he apologized and claimed he was only joking. A month later, while Harris was arranging a deal with one of Forklift's customers, he asked her, in front of other employees, "What did you do, promise the guy some sex Saturday night?"

Harris sued Forklift, claiming that Hardy had created an abusive work environment. The federal trial court ruled against Harris on the grounds that Hardy's comments might offend a reasonable woman, but they were not severe enough to have a serious impact on Harris's psychological well-being. The appeals court confirmed, and the Supreme Court granted *certiorari*.

Issue: To be a violation of Title VII, must sexual harassment seriously affect the employee's psychological well-being?

Excerpts from Justice O'Connor's Decision: Title VII of the Civil Rights Act of 1964 makes it "an unlawful employment practice for an employer to discriminate against any individual with respect to

his compensation, terms, conditions, or privileges of employment, because of such individual's race, color, religion, sex, or national origin." [T]his language is not limited to economic or tangible discrimination. The phrase "terms, conditions, or privileges of employment" evinces a congressional intent to strike at the entire spectrum of disparate treatment of men and women in employment, which includes requiring people to work in a discriminatorily hostile or abusive environment. When the workplace is permeated with discriminatory intimidation, ridicule, and insult, that is sufficiently severe or pervasive to alter the conditions of the victim's employment and create an abusive working environment, Title VII is violated.

This standard takes a middle path between making actionable any conduct that is merely offensive and requiring the conduct to cause a tangible psychological injury. [M]ere utterance of an epithet which engenders offensive feelings in an employee does not sufficiently affect the conditions of employment to implicate Title VII. Conduct that is not severe or pervasive enough to create an objectively hostile or abusive work environment—an environment that a reasonable person would find hostile or abusive—is beyond Title VII's purview. Likewise, if the victim does not subjectively perceive the environment to be abusive, the conduct has not actually altered the conditions of the victim's employment, and there is no Title VII violation.

But Title VII comes into play before the harassing conduct leads to a nervous breakdown. A discriminatorily abusive work environment, even one that does not seriously affect employees' psychological well-being, can and often will detract from

▼

employees' job performance, discourage employees from remaining on the job, or keep them from advancing in their careers. Moreover, even without regard to these tangible effects, the very fact that the discriminatory conduct was so severe or pervasive that it created a work environment abusive to employees because of their race, gender, religion, or national origin offends Title VII's broad rule of workplace equality.

We therefore believe the [trial court] erred in relying on whether the conduct "seriously affected plaintiff's psychological well-being" or led her to "suffer injury." So long as the environment would reasonably be perceived, and is perceived, as hostile or abusive there is no need for it also to be psychologically injurious. ■

Employees who commit sexual harassment are liable for their own misdeeds. But is their company also liable? The Supreme Court has held that:

- If the victimized employee has suffered a "tangible employment action" such as firing, demotion, or reassignment, the company is liable to her for sexual harassment by a supervisor.
- If the victimized employee has not suffered a tangible employment action, the company is not liable if it can prove that (1) it used reasonable care to prevent and correct sexually harassing behavior, and (2) the employee unreasonably failed to take advantage of the complaint procedure or other preventive opportunities provided by the company.[32]

at RISK

Corning Consumer Products Co. asks its employees to apply four tests in determining whether their behavior constitutes sexual harassment:

- Would you say or do this in front of your spouse or parents?
- What about in front of a colleague of the opposite sex?
- Would you like your behavior reported in your local newspaper?
- Does it need to be said or done at all? ◆

Procedures and Remedies

Before a plaintiff in a Title VII case brings suit, she must first file a complaint with a federal agency, the Equal Employment Opportunity Commission (EEOC). The EEOC then has the right to sue on behalf of the plaintiff. This arrangement is favorable for the plaintiff because the government pays the legal bill. If the EEOC decides *not* to bring the case, or does not make a decision within six months, it issues a **right to sue letter,** and the plaintiff may proceed on her own in court. Many states also have their own version of the EEOC, but these state commissions are often understaffed.

Remedies available to the successful plaintiff include hiring, reinstatement, retroactive seniority, back pay, reasonable attorney's fees, and damages of up to $300,000. Two recent trends, however, have reduced employees' chances of taking home substantial damages. Concerned about a rise in discrimination lawsuits, employers now often require new hires to agree in advance to arbitrate, not litigate, any future

---

[32] *Burlington Industries, Inc. v. Ellerth,* 524 U.S. 742, 118 S. Ct. 2257, 1998 U.S. LEXIS 4217 (1998); *Faragher v. Boca Raton,* 524 U.S. 775, 118 S. Ct. 2275, 1998 U.S. LEXIS 4216 (1998).

employment claims. The Supreme Court has upheld the employers' right to do so.[33] Typically, employees receive worse results in the arbitrator's office than in the courtroom, largely because arbitrators tend to favor repeat customers (such as management) over one-time users (such as employees). But even if a case does go to trial, plaintiffs in job discrimination cases have a much worse track record than other types of plaintiffs. About 43 percent of all plaintiffs in federal district court win their cases; for discrimination plaintiffs, the win rate is only about 30 percent. Even if discrimination plaintiffs win at trial, they have a 44 percent probability of losing on appeal. Victorious plaintiffs in other types of cases are overturned only 33 percent of the time.

Pregnancy

Under the Pregnancy Discrimination Act of 1978, an employer may not fire, refuse to hire, or fail to promote a woman because she is pregnant. An employer must also treat pregnancy as any other temporary disability. If, for example, employees are allowed time off from work for other medical disabilities, women must also be allowed a maternity leave. The United States and Australia are the only industrialized nations that do not require employers to provide paid maternity leave.

Age Discrimination

The Age Discrimination in Employment Act (ADEA) of 1967 prohibits age discrimination against employees or job applicants who are at least 40 years old. An employer may not fire, refuse to hire, fail to promote, or otherwise reduce a person's employment opportunities because he is 40 or older. Under this statute, an employer may not require a worker to retire at any age. These retirement rules do not apply to police and top-level corporate executives, who may indeed be forced to retire at a certain age.

The procedure for an age-bias claim is similar to that under Title VII—plaintiffs must first file a charge with the EEOC. If the EEOC does not take action, they can file suit themselves.

During tight economic times, companies often feel great pressure to lower costs. They are sometimes tempted to replace older, higher paid workers with younger, less expensive employees. Courts traditionally held that replacing expensive, older workers with cheaper, younger ones was illegal discrimination under the ADEA. In some recent cases, however, courts have held that an employer is entitled to prefer *lower paid* workers even if that preference results in the company also choosing *younger* workers. As the court put it in one case, "An action based on price differentials represents the very quintessence of a legitimate business decision."[34]

As we have seen, Title VII permits employees to prove discrimination two ways: *disparate treatment* and *disparate impact*. Although the courts had always agreed that disparate treatment was a violation of the ADEA, they were divided on the illegality of disparate impact. In the following case, the plaintiffs convinced the Supreme Court that disparate impact is a violation of the law, but they still lost their case. Recall when reading this case that the opinion was written by the court's oldest member, 84-year-old Justice Stevens.

---

[33] *Circuit City Stores, Inc. v. Adams,* 532 U.S. 105, 2001 U.S. LEXIS 2459 (2001).
[34] *Marks v. Loral Corp.,* 57 Cal. App. 4th 30, 1997 Cal. App. LEXIS 611 (Cal. Ct. App. 1997).

SMITH V. CITY OF JACKSON

2005 U.S. LEXIS 2931
Supreme Court of the United States, 2005

Facts: The city of Jackson, Mississippi (the City), granted pay raises to everyone on its police force. One of the City's goals in granting these increases was to attract new recruits. Under this plan, officers with less than five years of service received proportionately greater raises than their more senior colleagues. Senior officers tended to be older. Some of these older officers filed suit under the ADEA claiming a disparate impact: that they were adversely affected by the plan because of their age. The District Court granted summary judgment to the City. The Court of Appeals affirmed.

Issues: Is disparate impact a violation of the ADEA? Were these police officers adversely affected because of their age?

Excerpts from Justice Steven's Decision[35]: Except for substitution of the word "age" for the words "race, color, religion, sex, or national origin," the language of that provision in the ADEA is identical to that found in Title VII. Unlike Title VII, however, the ADEA contains language that significantly narrows its coverage by permitting any "otherwise prohibited" action "where the differentiation is based on reasonable factors other than age" (RFOA provision).

In determining whether the ADEA authorizes disparate-impact claims, we begin with the premise that when Congress uses the same language in two statutes having similar purposes, particularly when one is enacted shortly after the other, it is appropriate to presume that Congress intended that text to have the same meaning in both statutes. We [have already] held that Title VII did not require a showing of discriminatory intent. Finally, we note that both the Department of Labor, which initially drafted the legislation, and the EEOC, which is the agency charged by Congress with responsibility for implementing the statute, have consistently interpreted the ADEA to authorize relief on a disparate-impact theory.

[But] the scope of disparate-impact liability under ADEA is narrower than under Title VII. Congress' decision to limit the coverage of the ADEA by including the RFOA provision is consistent with the fact that age, unlike race or other classifications protected by Title VII, not uncommonly has relevance to an individual's capacity to engage in certain types of employment. Thus, it is not surprising that certain employment criteria that are routinely used may be reasonable despite their adverse impact on older workers as a group. Moreover, intentional discrimination on the basis of age has not occurred at the same levels as discrimination against those protected by Title VII. While the ADEA reflects Congress' intent to give older workers employment opportunities whenever possible, the RFOA provision reflects this historical difference.

Turning to the case before us, we initially note that plaintiffs have done little more than point out that the pay plan at issue is relatively less generous to older workers than to younger workers. They have not identified any specific test, requirement, or practice within the pay plan that has an adverse impact on older workers. [I]t is not enough to simply allege that there is a disparate impact on workers, or point to a generalized policy that leads to such an impact. Rather, the employee is responsible for isolating and identifying the *specific* employment practices that are allegedly responsible for any observed statistical disparities. Plaintiffs have failed to do so. Their failure to identify the specific practice being challenged is the sort of omission that could result in employers being potentially liable for the myriad of innocent causes that may lead to statistical imbalances. In this case not only did plaintiffs thus err by failing to identify the relevant practice, but it is also clear from the record that the City's plan was based on reasonable factors other than age.

Plaintiffs' evidence established two principal facts: First, almost two-thirds (66.2 percent) of the officers under 40 received raises of more than 10 percent while

▼

---

[35] For clarity, we have substituted the word "plaintiffs" for "petitioners."

less than half (45.3 percent) of those over 40 did. Second, the average percentage increase for the entire class of officers with less than five years of tenure was somewhat higher than the percentage for those with more seniority. The basic explanation for the differential was the City's perceived need to raise the salaries of junior officers to make them competitive with comparable positions in the market. Reliance on seniority and rank is unquestionably reasonable given the City's goal of raising employees' salaries to match those in surrounding communities.

While there may have been other reasonable ways for the City to achieve its goals, the one selected was not unreasonable. Accordingly, while we do not agree with the Court of Appeals' holding that the disparate-impact theory of recovery is never available under the ADEA, we affirm its judgment.

It is so ordered. ■

Devil's Advocate

The court says that the plaintiffs needed to show a "specific test, requirement, or practice within the pay plan that has an adverse impact on older workers." Otherwise, an employer might be liable for the "myriad of innocent causes that may lead to statistical imbalances." The City gave larger raises to junior officers than their more senior colleagues. The senior officers were older. What could be more specific than that? This plan was hardly an "innocent cause" that led to a "statistical imbalance." ◆

Americans with Disabilities Act

Passed in 1990, the Americans with Disabilities Act (ADA) prohibits employers from discriminating on the basis of disability. (The Justice Department's ADA home page is http://www.usdoj.gov/crt/ada.) As with Title VII, a plaintiff under the ADA must first file a charge with the EEOC. If the EEOC decides not to file suit, the individual may do so himself.

A disabled person is someone with a physical or mental impairment that substantially limits a major life activity, or someone who is regarded as having such an impairment. This definition includes people with mental illness, visual impairment, epilepsy, dyslexia, and AIDS, or who are *recovered* drug addicts and alcoholics. It does not cover people with sexual disorders, pyromania, exhibitionism, or compulsive gambling.

An employer may not disqualify an employee or job applicant because of disability as long as she can, with *reasonable accommodation*, perform the *essential functions* of the job. An accommodation is not reasonable if it would create *undue hardship* for the employer. In one case, a court held that a welder who could perform 88 percent of a job was doing the essential functions. Reasonable accommodation includes buying necessary equipment, providing readers or interpreters, or permitting a part-time schedule. In determining undue hardship, *relative* cost, not *absolute* cost, is the issue. Even an expensive accommodation—such as hiring a full-time reader—is not considered an undue hardship unless it imposes a significant burden on the overall finances of the company.

An employer may not ask about disabilities before making a job offer. The interviewer may ask only whether an applicant can perform the work. Nor can an employer require applicants to take a medical exam unless the exam is (1) job-related and (2) required of all applicants for similar jobs. However, drug testing is permitted.

After a job offer has been made, an employer may require a medical test, but it must be related to the *essential functions* of the job. For example, an employer could not test the cholesterol of someone applying for an accounting job because high cholesterol is no impediment to good accounting.

An employer may not discriminate against someone because of his *relationship* with a disabled person. For example, an employer cannot refuse to hire an applicant because he has a child with Down's syndrome or a spouse with cancer.

In 1997, the EEOC issued rules on the treatment of mental disabilities. These rules were based on an assumption of parity—that physical and mental disabilities should be treated the same. The difficulty is that physical ailments such as diabetes and deafness may be easy to diagnose, but what does a supervisor do when an employee is chronically late, rude, or impulsive? Does this mean the worker is mentally disabled or just a lazy, irresponsible jerk? Among other accommodations, the EEOC rules indicated that employers should be willing to put up barriers to isolate people who have difficulty concentrating, provide detailed day-to-day feedback to those who need greater structure in performing their jobs, or allow workers on antidepressants to come to work later if they are groggy in the morning.

It appears that courts may not be as accommodating of mental illness as the EEOC. In one case, for example, an engineer had been criticized for his "negative attitude." Later his supervisor warned him that he might be terminated if his behavior did not improve. He then told the company that the warning had caused him to be depressed, which, in turn, affected his ability to interact with other people. He asked, as a special accommodation, to be assigned to clerical work that did not require him to run meetings. The company fired him. Although EEOC guidelines state that interacting with others is a major life activity, the court held that it is not. Therefore the engineer was not disabled for purposes of the ADA.[36]

While lauding the ADA's objectives, many managers have been apprehensive about its impact on the workplace. Most acknowledge, however, that society is clearly better off if every member has the opportunity to work. And as advocates for the disabled point out, we are all, at best, only temporarily able-bodied. Even with the ADA, only 29 percent of the disabled population who are of working age are actually employed, while 79 percent of able-bodied people have jobs.

When cases go to litigation, employers win more than 93 percent of the time. Workers are caught in something of a legal Catch-22: they must prove that they can perform the essential functions of the job, but they must also show that their disability limits a major life activity. In the following case, the Supreme Court takes a close look at the definition of "major life activity."

TOYOTA V. WILLIAMS

534 U.S. 184, 122 S. Ct. 681, 2002 U.S. LEXIS 400
United States Supreme Court, 2002

Facts: Ella Williams worked in a Toyota manufacturing plant in Georgetown, Kentucky. Her job required her to use pneumatic tools. When her arms and hands began to hurt, she went to see a doctor who diagnosed her with carpal tunnel syndrome. He advised her to avoid using pneumatic tools or lifting more than 20 pounds. Toyota transferred Williams to a position in Quality Control Inspection Operations (QCIO). Employees in this department typically performed four different jobs, but Williams was initially assigned only two tasks. Toyota then ▼

---

36 *Soileau v. Guildford of Maine*, 105 F.3d 12, 1997 U.S. App. LEXIS 1171 (1st Cir. 1997).

changed its policy and required QCIO employees to rotate through all four jobs.

Williams began to perform the "shell body audit." After applying oil to the outside of cars, she visually inspected each car for flaws. To perform this task, she had to hold her hands and arms up around shoulder height for several hours at a time.

A short while after beginning this job, she began to experience pain in her neck and shoulders. She asked permission to perform only the two tasks that she could do without difficulty. Williams claimed that Toyota refused this request. Toyota said that Williams simply began missing work regularly. Ultimately, Williams's doctor told her she should not do any work of any kind. Toyota fired her.

When Williams sued Toyota, alleging that the company had violated the Americans with Disabilities Act, the district court granted summary judgment to Toyota on the grounds that Williams's impairments did not substantially limit any of her major life activities. The Court of Appeals for the Sixth Circuit reversed, finding that the impairments substantially limited Williams in the major life activity of performing manual tasks. The Supreme Court granted *certiorari*.

Issues: Was Williams disabled, within the terms of the Americans with Disabilities Act? Did Toyota violate the ADA?

Excerpts from Justice O'Connor's Decision, Writing for a Unanimous Court: When it enacted the ADA in 1990, Congress found that some 43,000,000 Americans have one or more physical or mental disabilities. If Congress intended everyone with a physical impairment that precluded the performance of some isolated, unimportant, or particularly difficult manual task to qualify as disabled, the number of disabled Americans would surely have been much higher. We therefore hold that to be substantially limited in performing manual tasks, an individual must have an impairment that prevents or severely restricts the individual from doing activities that are of central importance to most people's daily

lives. The impairment's impact must also be permanent or long-term.

When addressing the major life activity of performing manual tasks, the central inquiry must be whether the claimant is unable to perform the variety of tasks central to most people's daily lives, not whether the claimant is unable to perform the tasks associated with her specific job. In this case, "repetitive work with hands and arms extended at or above shoulder levels for extended periods of time" is not an important part of most people's daily lives. The court, therefore, should not have considered respondent's inability to do such manual work in her specialized assembly line job as sufficient proof that she was substantially limited in performing manual tasks.

[T]he Court of Appeals treated as irrelevant the fact that respondent can tend to her personal hygiene and carry out personal or household chores. Yet household chores, bathing, and brushing one's teeth are among the types of manual tasks of central importance to people's daily lives, and should have been part of the assessment of whether respondent was substantially limited in performing manual tasks.

The District Court noted that at the time respondent sought an accommodation from petitioner, she admitted that she was able to do the manual tasks required by her original two jobs in QCIO. In addition, even after her condition worsened, she could still brush her teeth, wash her face, bathe, tend her flower garden, fix breakfast, do laundry, and pick up around the house. The record also indicates that her medical conditions caused her to avoid sweeping, to quit dancing, to occasionally seek help dressing, and to reduce how often she plays with her children, gardens, and drives long distances. But these changes in her life did not amount to such severe restrictions in the activities that are of central importance to most people's daily lives that they establish a manual-task disability as a matter of law.

Accordingly, we reverse the Court of Appeals' judgment granting summary judgment to respondent and remand the case for further proceedings consistent with this opinion.

So ordered. ■

at **R**i**SK**

Every applicant feels slightly apprehensive before a job interview, but now the interviewer may be even more nervous—fearing that every question is a potential land mine of liability. Most interviewers (and students who have read this chapter) would know better than Delta Airlines interviewers who allegedly asked applicants about their sexual preference, birth control methods, and abortion history. The following list provides guidelines for interviewers.

Don't Even Consider Asking	Go Ahead and Ask
Can you perform this function with or without reasonable accommodation?	Would you need reasonable accommodation in this job?
How many days were you sick last year?	How many days were you absent from work last year?
What medications are you currently taking?	Are you currently using drugs illegally?
Where were you born? Are you a United States citizen?	Are you authorized to work in the United States?
How old are you?	What work experience have you had?
How tall are you? How much do you weigh?	Could you carry a 100-pound weight, as required by this job?
When did you graduate from college?	Where did you go to college?
How did you learn this language?	What languages do you speak and write fluently?
Have you ever been arrested?	Have you ever been convicted of a crime that would affect the performance of this job?
Do you plan to have children? How old are your children? What method of birth control do you use?	Can you work weekends? Travel extensively? Would you be willing to relocate?
What is your corrected vision?	Do you have 20/20 corrected vision?
Are you a man or a woman? Are you single or married? What does your spouse do? What will happen if your spouse is transferred? What clubs, societies, or lodges do you belong to?	Leave well enough alone!

The most common gaffe on the part of interviewers? Asking women about their child-care arrangements. That question assumes the woman is responsible for child care. ◆

Chapter Conclusion

Although managers sometimes feel overwhelmed by the long list of laws that protect workers, the United States guarantees its workers fewer rights than virtually any other industrialized nation. For instance, Japan, Great Britain, France, Germany, and Canada all require employers to show just cause before terminating workers. Although American employers are no longer insulated from minimum standards of fairness, reasonable behavior, and compliance with important policies, they still have great freedom to manage their employees.

Chapter Review

1. The traditional common-law rule of employment provided that an employee at will could be fired for a good reason, a bad reason, or no reason at all.

2. The National Labor Relations Act prohibits employers from penalizing workers for union activity.

3. The Family and Medical Leave Act guarantees workers up to 12 weeks of unpaid leave each year for childbirth, adoption, or medical emergencies for themselves or a family member.

4. An employer who fires a worker for a bad reason is liable under a theory of wrongful discharge.

5. Generally, an employee may not be fired for refusing to break the law, exercising a legal right, or performing a legal duty.

6. Whistleblowers receive some protection under both federal and state laws.

7. Oral promises made during the hiring process may be enforceable, even if not approved by the company's top executives. An employee handbook may create a contract.

8. Employers may be liable for defamation if they give false and unfavorable references.

9. The goal of the Occupational Safety and Health Act is to ensure safe conditions in the workplace.

10. Employees have a limited right to privacy in the workplace.

11. The Fair Labor Standards Act regulates minimum and overtime wages. It also limits child labor.

12. Workers' compensation statutes ensure that employees receive payment for injuries incurred at work.

13. The Social Security system pays benefits to workers who are retired, disabled, or temporarily unemployed and to the spouses and children of disabled or deceased workers.

14. The Employee Retirement Income Security Act regulates private pension plans.

15. Under the Equal Pay Act, an employee may not be paid at a lesser rate than employees of the opposite sex for equal work.

16. Title VII of the Civil Rights Act of 1964 prohibits employers from discriminating on the basis of race, color, religion, sex, or national origin.

17. The Age Discrimination in Employment Act prohibits age discrimination against employees or job applicants who are age 40 or older.

18. The Americans with Disabilities Act prohibits employers from discriminating on the basis of disability.

Practice Test

1. When Theodore Staats went to his company's "Council of Honor Convention," he was accompanied by a woman who was not his wife, although he told everyone she was. The company fired him. Staats alleged that his termination violated public policy because it infringed upon his freedom of association. He also alleged that he had been fired because he was too successful—his commissions were so high, he out-earned even the highest paid officer of the company. Has Staats's employer violated public policy?

2. This article appeared in *The Wall Street Journal*:

> When Michelle Lawrence discovered she was pregnant, she avoided telling Ron Rogers, the owner of the Los Angeles public relations agency where she worked as manager of media relations. "I had heard he wasn't crazy about pregnant women," she says. Instead, she asked her immediate supervisor to pass along the news. Mr. Rogers didn't speak to her for a week. His first comment was, "Congratulations on your pregnancy. My sister vomited for months." A few weeks later, Ms. Lawrence was fired. Mr. Rogers told her the business was shifting away from her area of expertise.[37]

Does Lawrence have a valid claim against Rogers? Under what law?

3. Reginald Delaney managed a Taco Time restaurant in Portland, Oregon. Some of his customers told Mr. Ledbetter, the district manager,

---

[37] Sue Shellenbarger, "As More Pregnant Women Work, Bias Complaints Rise," *Wall Street Journal*, Dec. 6, 1993, p. B1.

that they would not be eating there so often because there were too many black employees. Ledbetter told Delaney to fire Ms. White, who was black. Delaney did as he was told. Ledbetter's report on the incident said: "My notes show that Delaney told me that White asked him to sleep with her and that when he would not that she started causing dissension within the crew. She asked him to come over to her house and that he declined." Delaney refused to sign the report because it was untrue, so Ledbetter fired him. What claim might Delaney make against his former employer?

4. When Walton Weiner interviewed for a job with McGraw-Hill, Inc., he was assured that the company would not terminate an employee without "just cause." Weiner also signed a contract specifying that his employment would be subject to the provisions of McGraw-Hill's handbook. The handbook said, "[The] company will resort to dismissal for just and sufficient cause only, and only after all practical steps toward rehabilitation or salvage of the employee have been taken and failed. However, if the welfare of the company indicates that dismissal is necessary, then that decision is arrived at and is carried out forthrightly." After eight years, Weiner was fired suddenly for "lack of application." Does Weiner have a valid claim against McGraw-Hill?

5. ***ETHICS*** John Mundorf hired three women to work for Gus Construction Co. as traffic controllers at road construction sites in Iowa. Male members of the construction crew incessantly referred to the women as "f—king flag girls." They repeatedly asked the women if they "wanted to f—k" or engage in oral sex. One crew member held a woman up to the cab window so other men could touch her. Another male employee exposed himself to the women. Male employees also urinated in a woman's water bottle and the gas tank of her car. Mundorf, the supervisor, was present during some of these incidents. He talked to crew members about their conduct, but the abuse continued until the women quit. What claim might the women make against their co-workers? Is Gus Construction Co. liable for the acts of its employees? What procedure must the women follow to pursue their claim? Why do you think these men behaved this way? Why did they want to humiliate their co-workers?

What should the supervisor have done when he observed these incidents? What would you have done if you were the supervisor? A fellow employee?

6. ***CPA QUESTION*** An unemployed CPA generally would receive unemployment compensation benefits if the CPA:

a. Was fired as a result of the employer's business reversals

b. Refused to accept a job as an accountant while receiving extended benefits

c. Was fired for embezzling from a client

d. Left work voluntarily without good cause

7. Debra Agis worked in a Ground Round restaurant. The manager, Roger Dionne, informed the waitresses that "there was some stealing going on." Until he found out who was doing it, he intended to fire all the waitresses in alphabetical order, starting with the letter "A." Dionne then fired Agis. Does she have a valid claim against her employer?

8. The Duke Power Co. refused to transfer any employees at its generating plant to better jobs unless they had a high school diploma or could pass an intelligence test. The company was willing to pay two thirds of the tuition for an employee's high school training. Neither a high school education nor the intelligence test was significantly related to successful job performance. Both requirements disqualified African Americans at a substantially higher rate than white applicants. Is the company in violation of Title VII?

9. The Lillie Rubin boutique in Phoenix would not permit Dick Kovacic to apply for a job as a salesperson. It only hired women to work in sales because fittings and alterations took place in the dressing room or immediately outside. The customers were buying expensive clothes and demanded a male-free dressing area. Has the Lillie Rubin store violated Title VII? What would its defense be?

10. ***YOU BE THE JUDGE*** WRITING PROBLEM Nationwide Insurance Co. circulated a memorandum asking all employees to lobby in favor of a bill that had been introduced in the Pennsylvania House of Representatives. By limiting the damages that an injured motorist could

recover from a person who caused an accident, this bill would have saved Nationwide significant money. Not only did John Novosel refuse to lobby, but he privately criticized the bill for harming consumers. Nationwide was definitely not on his side—it fired him. Novosel filed suit, alleging that his discharge had violated public policy by infringing his right to free speech. Did Nationwide violate public policy by firing Novosel? **Argument for Novosel:** The United States Constitution and the Pennsylvania Constitution both guarantee the right to free speech. Nationwide has violated an important public policy by firing Novosel for expressing his opinions. **Argument for Nationwide:** For all the high-flown talk about the Constitution, what we have here is an employee who refused to carry out company policy. If the employee prevails in this case, where will it all end? What if an employee for a tobacco company refuses to market cigarettes because he does not approve of smoking? How can businesses operate without loyalty from their employees?

11. When Thomas Lussier filled out a Postal Service employment application, he did not admit that he had twice pleaded guilty to charges of disorderly conduct. Lussier suffered from post-traumatic stress disorder (PTSD) acquired during military service in Vietnam. Because of this disorder, he sometimes had panic attacks that required him to leave meetings. He

was also a recovered alcoholic and drug user. During his stint with the Postal Service, he had some personality conflicts with other employees. Once another employee hit him. He also had one episode of "erratic emotional behavior and verbal outburst." In the meantime, a postal employee in Ridgewood, New Jersey, killed four colleagues. The Postmaster General encouraged all supervisors to identify workers who had dangerous propensities. Lussier's boss discovered that he had lied on his employment application about the disorderly conduct charges and fired him. Is the Postal Service in violation of the law?

12. The following question appeared in *The Wall Street Journal.* How would you answer it?

Q: Imagine an employer and a male job candidate discussing employment. The candidate discloses that his wife is pregnant, and the employer is turned off, thinking the candidate will need time off during a busy time. The employer may even ask the candidate if he's planning to take family leave after the birth. If the candidate says yes, the employer might not hire him because of that. Would this be discriminatory?[38]

13. **ROLE REVERSAL** Prepare a short-answer question in which an employee alleges that his discharge violated public policy, but you think a court would not agree.

Internet Research Problem

At http://www.usdoj.gov/crt/ada/workta.htm, the federal government provides a guide for people with disabilities. Employers sometimes complain that the EEOA unfairly favors workers. What do you think of this guide? Does it adequately balance the rights of workers and employees?

You can find further practice problems at academic.cengage.com/blaw/beatty.

---

[38] Sue Shellenbarger, "Work and Family Mailbox," *The Wall Street Journal,* March 10, 2005, p. D4.

Labor Law

A strike! For five weeks the union workers have been walking picket lines at JMJ, a manufacturer of small electrical engines. An entire town of 70,000 citizens, most of them blue-collar workers, is sharply divided, right down to the McNally kitchen table. Buddy, age 48, has worked on the assembly lines at JMJ for more than 25 years. Now he's sipping coffee in the house where he grew up. His sister Kristina, age 46, is a vice-president for personnel at JMJ. The two have always been close. In high school, Kristina idolized her older brother, the football and track star. Buddy was immensely proud of his kid sister's academic triumphs, boasting to the world that she would "be the first lady president." Today, though, conversation is halting.

"It's time to get back together, Buddy," Kristina murmurs. "The strike is hurting the whole company—and the town."

"Not the whole town, Kristina," he tries to quip lightly. "Your management pals still have fat incomes and nice houses."

"Oh yeah?" she attempts to joke, "you haven't seen our porch lately."

"Go talk to Tony Falcione," Buddy replies. "He can't pay his rent."

"Talk to the Ericksons," Kristina snaps back, "they don't even work for JMJ. Their sandwich shop is going under because none of you guys stop in for lunch. Come back to work."

"Not with that clause on the table."

That *clause* is management's proposal for the new union contract—one that Kristina helped draft. The company officers want the right to subcontract work—that is, to send it out for other companies to perform.

"Buddy, we need the flexibility. K-Ball is underselling us by 35 percent. If we can't compete, there won't be any jobs or any contract!"

"The way to save money is not by sending our jobs overseas, where a bunch of foreigners will work for 50 bucks a month."

"Okay, fine. Tell me how we should save money."

© PHOTO 24/BRAND X PICTURES/GETTY IMAGES

"Kristina, I really do not know how you can sit at this table and say these things—in this household. You never would have gotten a fancy college degree if Dad hadn't made union wages."

"If we can't sell motors to Latin America, we're out of business. Then what's your union going to do for you? All we're asking is the right to subcontract some of the smallest components. Everything else gets built here."

"This is just the start. Next it'll be the wiring, then the batteries, then you'll assemble the whole thing over there—and that'll be it for me. You take that clause off the table, we'll be back in 15 minutes."

"Never."

Buddy stands up. They stare silently, sadly, at each other, and then Kristina says, in a barely audible voice, "I have to tell you this. My boss is starting to talk about hiring replacement workers." Buddy walks out. ■

Some Americans revere unions, believing that organized labor has pulled the working class up from poverty and shielded it from exploitative management. Others loathe organized labor, convinced that unions foment mindless conflicts, decrease productivity, increase costs, and generally harm corporations and the economy. Why do unions exist?

UNIONS DEVELOP . . . AND THE LAW RESPONDS

During the nineteenth century, as industrialization spread across America, workers found employment conditions increasingly unbearable and wages inadequate. Here is a contemporary account of mining in the American West:

> View their work! Descending from the surface in the shaft-cages, they enter narrow galleries where the air is scarce respirable. By the dim light of their lanterns a dingy rock surface, braced by rotting props, is visible. The stenches of decaying vegetable matter, hot foul water, and human excretions intensify the effects of the heat. The men throw off their clothes at once. Only a light breech-cloth covers their hips, and thick-soled shoes protect their feet from the scorching rocks and steaming rills of water that trickle over the floor. Except for these coverings they toil naked, with heavy drops of sweat starting from every pore.[1]

Temperatures in the mines were well over 100 degrees. Miners drank more than three gallons of water every day. Some suddenly collapsed, with swollen veins, purple faces, and glazed eyes. Within minutes they were dead, but even before they died, their places in the mine were taken by other workers desperate for pay.

---

[1] Eliot Lord, *Comstock Mining and Miners* (Washington: G.P.O., 1883), p. 386, *quoted in* Richard E. Lingenfelter, *The Hardrock Miners* (Berkeley: University of California Press, 1974), p. 13.

Conditions were equally oppressive in the new factories back east. Workers, often women and sometimes children, worked 60 to 70 hours per week and sometimes more, standing at assembly lines in suffocating, dimly lit factories, performing monotonous yet dangerous work with heavy machinery. A visitor to a factory in Lowell, Massachusetts, in 1855 was shocked by the degrading conditions and the exhausting hours required of all workers.

> I inquired of the agent of a principal factory whether it was the custom of the manufacturers to do anything for the physical, intellectual, and moral welfare of their work-people. "We never do," he said. "As for myself, I regard my work-people just as I regard my machinery. So long as they can do my work for what I choose to pay them, I keep them, getting out of them all I can. What they do or how they fare outside my walls I don't know, nor do I consider it my business to know. When my machines get old and useless, I reject them and get new, and these people are part of my machinery."[2]

Because of the intolerable conditions and impoverishing wages, workers began to band together into unions. But early in the nineteenth century, American courts regarded any coordinated effort by workers as a criminal conspiracy. Courts convicted workers merely for the *act of joining together*, even if no strike took place. In 1842 the Massachusetts high court became the first to reject this use of the criminal law. The court ruled that workers could join together for legitimate economic goals; their efforts would become criminal only if the workers used illegal means to achieve them.[3] Other courts came to agree, and so management resorted to the civil law to curtail unions.

In 1890, Congress passed the Sherman Act to outlaw monopolies.[4] For the next 40 years, courts relied on this statute to issue anti-strike injunctions, declaring that strikes illegally restrained trade. A company could usually obtain an immediate injunction merely by alleging that a strike *might* cause harm. Courts were so quick to issue injunctions that most companies became immune to union efforts. But with the economic collapse of 1929 and the vast suffering of the Great Depression, public sympathy shifted to the workers. Congress responded with the first of several landmark statutes.

In 1932, Congress passed the **Norris-LaGuardia Act,** which prohibited federal court injunctions in nonviolent labor disputes. No longer could management obtain an injunction merely by mentioning the word "strike." By taking away the injunction remedy, Congress was declaring that workers should be permitted to organize unions and to use their collective power to achieve legitimate economic ends. The statute led to explosive growth in union membership.

In 1935, Congress passed the Wagner Act, generally known as the **National Labor Relations Act (NLRA).** This is the most important of all labor laws. A fundamental aim of the NLRA is the establishment and maintenance of industrial peace to preserve the flow of commerce. The NLRA ensures the right of workers to form unions and encourages management and unions to bargain collectively and productively. For our purposes, §§7 and 8 of the NLRA are the most important.

Section 7 guarantees employees the right to organize and join unions, bargain collectively through representatives of their own choosing, and engage in other concerted activities. This is the cornerstone of union power. With the

---

[2] Massachusetts Senate Dock. no. 21, 1868, p. 23, *quoted in* Norman Ware, *The Industrial Worker* (Chicago: Quadrangle Books, 1964), p. 77.

[3] *Commonwealth v. Hunt,* 45 Mass. 111, 4 Met. 111 (1842).

[4] See Chapter 20 on antitrust law.

enactment of the NLRA, Congress put an end to any notion that unions were criminal or inherently illegal by explicitly recognizing that workers could join together and bargain as a group, using their collective power to seek better conditions. Section 8 reinforces these rights by outlawing *unfair labor practices.*

Section 8(a) makes it an unfair labor practice (ULP) for an employer:

- To interfere with union organizing efforts;
- To dominate or interfere with any union;
- To discriminate against a union member; or
- To refuse to bargain collectively with a union.

The NLRA also established the **National Labor Relations Board (NLRB)** to administer and interpret the statute and to adjudicate labor cases. For example, when a union charges that an employer has committed an unfair labor practice—say, by refusing to bargain—the ULP charge goes first to the NLRB.

The NLRB has two primary tasks:

- *Representation.* The Board decides whether a particular union is entitled to represent a group of employees.
- *Unfair Labor Practices.* The Board adjudicates claims by either the employer or workers that the other side has committed a ULP.

To accomplish these tasks, the NLRB has several divisions. Although the agency is headquartered in Washington, it performs the greatest volume of its work in local offices. **Regional offices,** each headed by a regional director, are located throughout the country. These local offices handle most ULP claims. The General Counsel, a staff of lawyers, investigates such claims. If the General Counsel's office believes that a party has committed a ULP, it prosecutes the case before an administrative law judge (ALJ).

The **Board** itself, which sits in Washington, has five members, all appointed by the president. The Board makes final agency decisions about representation and ULP cases. But note that the Board has no power to *enforce* its orders. If it is evident that the losing party will not comply, the Board must petition a federal appeals court to enforce the order. Typically, the steps resulting in an appeal follow this pattern: the Board issues a decision, for example, finding that a company has unfairly refused to bargain with a union. The Board orders the company to bargain. The Board then appeals to the United States Court of Appeals to enforce its order, and the company *cross-appeals,* requesting the court *not* to enforce the Board's order. (The NLRB describes its mission and methods at http://www.nlrb.gov/.)

Throughout the 1930s and 1940s, unions grew in size and power. As strikes became more common, employers complained loudly of union abuse. Unions coerced unwilling workers to join and engaged in *secondary boycotts*, picketing an innocent company to stop it from doing business with an employer the union was fighting. In 1947, Congress responded with the Taft-Hartley Act, also known as the **Labor-Management Relations Act,** designed to curb union abuses. The statute amended §8 of the NLRA to outlaw certain unfair labor practices *by unions.*

Section 8(b) makes it an unfair labor practice for a union:

- To interfere with employees who are exercising their labor rights under §7;
- To encourage an employer to discriminate against a particular employee because of a union dispute;
- To refuse to bargain collectively; or
- To engage in an illegal strike or boycott, particularly secondary boycotts.

Finally, in the 1950s the public became aware that certain labor leaders were corrupt. Some officers stole money from large union treasuries, rigged union elections, and stifled opposition within the organization. In response, in 1959 Congress passed the Landrum-Griffin Act, generally called the **Labor-Management Reporting and Disclosure Act (LMRDA).** The LMRDA requires union leadership to make certain financial disclosures and guarantees free speech and fair elections within a union.

These landmark federal labor laws are outlined below:

Four Key Labor Statutes	
Norris-LaGuardia Act (1932)	Prohibits federal court injunctions in peaceful strikes.
National Labor Relations Act (1935)	Guarantees workers' right to organize unions and bargain collectively. Prohibits an employer from interfering with union organizing or discriminating against union members. Requires an employer to bargain collectively.
Labor-Management Relations Act (1947)	Prohibits union abuses such as coercing employees to join. Outlaws secondary boycotts.
Labor-Management Reporting and Disclosure Act (1959)	Requires financial disclosures by union leadership. Guarantees union members free speech and fair elections.

NEWS*worthy*

Today, labor abuses are less visible—but as ugly as ever. From New York City to Los Angeles, desperately poor, frightened immigrants cut and sew about half of all the garments this country produces, often working in appalling sweatshops where conditions are little better than in nineteenth-century factories. Often the employees are undocumented immigrants who speak no English, know nothing of their rights, and fear that any complaints they make will lead to deportation. Exploitative owners force the workers to toil 50 to 60 hours a week with few breaks in cramped rooms with weak lighting, no ventilation, and inadequate sanitation. Pay is below the minimum wage—and vicious bosses often steal the small amounts they promised. For a report on sweatshops in the United States, see http://www.sweatshopwatch.org. ◆

State Labor Law

All states have labor statutes. Some are comprehensive, while others focus on narrow issues. For example, certain states prohibit particular kinds of picketing, while many states outlaw strikes by public employees. A court enforces a state statute when no federal law applies. In general, when a federal law such as the NLRA does apply, it controls the outcome. This is the doctrine of *preemption*, discussed in Chapter 5 on constitutional law. *Preemption* **means that states have no jurisdiction to regulate any labor issue that is governed by federal law.**

In this chapter, we look principally at federal law because it is uniform and because it controls the most fundamental issues of labor policy.

Labor Unions Today

Organized labor is shrinking in the United States. In the 1950s about 25 percent of the workforce belonged to a union. Today, only about 13.5 percent of all workers are union members. Employers point to this figure with satisfaction and claim that it shows that unions have failed their memberships. In an increasingly high-tech, service-oriented economy, employers argue, there is no place for organized labor. Union supporters respond that although the country has shed many old factories, workers have not benefited. Throughout the last 20 years, they assert, compensation for executives has soared into the stratosphere, with many CEOs earning several *million* dollars per year, while wages for the average worker, in real dollars, have fallen for two decades.

Whether organized labor is disappearing from the United States or is only retreating temporarily, labor law still affects many. About 16 million workers are union members. The largest unions are national in scope, with hundreds of affiliated **locals** throughout the country. A local is the regional union, which represents workers at a particular company. For example, more than 2.2 million teachers belong to the National Education Association, with thousands of locals spread throughout the nation. Here are some current labor numbers[5]:

Who Are Union Workers?

- Government employees—36.4 percent are in unions
- Private sector—7.9 percent are in unions

Which Occupational Groups Have Higher Membership?

- Education—37.6 percent unionized
- Police and fire—37.3 percent unionized

Which Private Industries Have the Highest Percentages of Union Workers?

- Transportation and utilities—24.9 percent
- Construction—14.7 percent
- Information industries—14.2 percent
- Manufacturing—12.9 percent

Where Do Union Workers Live?

- Union membership is highest in the Northeast, North Central, and Pacific states.
- Half of all union workers live in just six states: California, New York, Illinois, Michigan, Ohio, and Pennsylvania.
- Union membership is lowest in the South.
- In four states, union membership is below five percent: North Carolina, South Carolina, Arkansas, and Mississippi.

How Does Union/Nonunion Pay Compare? (Wage and Salary Workers)

- Union members average $781 per week
- Nonunion members average $612 per week

ORGANIZING A UNION

Exclusivity

It is difficult to organize a union. When a worker starts to talk about collective action, or when an organizer appears from a national union, many employees are suspicious or fearful; some may be hostile. Management will generally be opposed—sometimes

---

[5] All statistics from the Bureau of Labor Statistics Website at http://bls.gov/.

fiercely opposed—to any union organizing effort. The fight can become ugly, and all because of one principle: *exclusivity.*

Under §9 of the NLRA, a validly recognized union is the *exclusive* representative of the employees. This means that the union will represent all the designated employees, regardless of whether a particular worker *wants* to be represented. The company may not bargain directly with any employee in the group, nor with any other organization representing the designated employees.

A collective bargaining unit is the precisely defined group of employees who will be represented by a particular union. Suppose a hotel workers' union attempts to organize the Excelsior Hotel. The union will seek to represent some of Excelsior's employees, but not all. The union may represent, for example, all maids, busboys, and bellhops. Those employees are in the collective bargaining unit. Many other people who work for the hotel will *not* be in the collective bargaining unit. Managers who run the hotel, reservation agents who work in other cities, launderers who work in separate facilities for a different employer—all these people are *outside* the collective bargaining unit and will be unaffected by the union's bargaining.

It is the union's *exclusive* right to bargain for the unit that gives the organization its power. But some employees may be unhappy with the way a union exercises this power. In the following case, workers believed the union was failing to represent them on a vital issue. Should they be allowed to bargain on their own behalf? You be the judge.

You Be the Judge

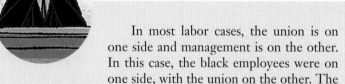

EMPORIUM CAPWELL CO. V. WESTERN ADDITIONAL COMMUNITY ORGANIZATION

420 U.S. 50, 95 S. Ct. 977, 1975 U.S. LEXIS 134
United States Supreme Court, 1975

Facts: Emporium Capwell operated a department store in San Francisco. The Department Store Employees Union represented all stock workers. Several black union members complained to the union about racial discrimination in promotions, asserting that highly qualified black workers were routinely passed over in favor of less qualified whites. The union promised to pursue the issue with management, but the black employees were not satisfied with the union's effort. The unhappy workers demanded to speak with top management of the store and then, without the union's permission, picketed the store and handed out leaflets accusing the company of discrimination. Emporium Capwell fired the picketing employees. The resulting case went all the way to the Supreme Court.

In most labor cases, the union is on one side and management is on the other. In this case, the black employees were on one side, with the union on the other. The union argued that exclusivity prohibited any group of workers from demanding to meet separately with management. It claimed that the disgruntled workers violated the NLRA by insisting on separate bargaining and that it was proper for the company to fire the workers. In other words, the union placed a higher value on exclusivity than on maintaining the jobs of those employees. The black workers, on the other hand, argued that eliminating discrimination was more important than union exclusivity. They insisted that management had no right to fire them and that they were entitled to get their jobs back and to bargain independently.

You Be the Judge: **Did the picketing employees violate the NLRA by demanding to bargain directly with management?**

▼

Argument for the Union: Your honors, exclusivity is the core of a union's strength. If management is free to talk with employees individually—or if it can be *compelled* to talk with them—the union has no leverage. An astute manager will quickly use worker conflicts as a tool to divide the union and destroy it. By cutting deals with favored employees, management could demonstrate to all workers that affiliation with the union is a losing tactic, and that the smart worker bargains for himself—and then does what management tells him to do.

Racial discrimination is a terrible evil. It must be eradicated from the workplace. This union is committed to fighting prejudice. But the union must do it *collectively*. If an exception to the principle of exclusivity can be carved out for one important issue, such as race discrimination, then an exception can be carved out for other important issues, such as gender bias, age discrimination, language differences, retirement pay, health benefits . . . and on and on. To allow this group of picketers to pursue a worthy goal with separate bargaining would be to destroy the union—and ensure that *no* valuable goals are obtained.

Argument for the Picketing Workers: Congress granted employees the right to organize *for their mutual benefit*, not to advance the cause of unions. A labor organization is a means to an end, not an end in itself. When a union fails to support its members on a vital issue, employees must be free to fend for themselves. Race discrimination is not a simple bargaining issue like retirement benefits; it is a vital matter of human dignity. This union failed to act promptly and vigorously to protect its black members and end discrimination. Why should those employees now be shackled to an organization that has failed them?

It makes no difference *why* the union failed to protect its members. Weak-kneed, docile union leadership can be just as devastating to the cause of racial equality as bad faith. We are not asking that union members be free to pursue every petty complaint directly with management. To equate racial justice with retirement benefits is to ignore the singular evil of discrimination. We merely ask that, when a union fails to protect its members concerning a profound issue such as this, the injured employees be allowed to speak for themselves. ●

Organizing

A union organizing effort generally involves the following pattern.

Campaign

Union organizers talk with employees—or attempt to talk—and interest them in forming a union. The organizers may be employees of the company who simply chat with fellow workers about unsatisfactory conditions. Or a union may send nonemployees of the company to hand out union leaflets to workers as they arrive and depart from the factory.

Authorization Cards

Union organizers ask workers to sign authorization cards, which state that the particular worker requests the specified union to act as her sole bargaining representative.

Recognition

If a union obtains authorization cards from a sizable percentage of workers, it seeks **recognition** as the exclusive representative for the bargaining unit. The union may ask the employer to recognize it as the bargaining representative, but most of the time employers refuse to recognize the union voluntarily. The NLRA permits an employer to refuse recognition.

Petition

Assuming that the employer does not voluntarily recognize a union, the union generally petitions the NLRB for an election. It must submit to the NLRB regional office authorization cards signed by at least 30 percent of the workers. The regional office verifies whether there are enough valid cards to warrant an election and looks closely at the proposed bargaining unit to make sure that it is appropriate. If the regional director determines that the union has identified an appropriate bargaining unit and has enough valid cards, it orders an election.

Election

The NLRB closely supervises the election to ensure fairness. All members of the proposed bargaining unit vote on whether they want the union to represent them. If more than 50 percent of the workers vote for the union, the NLRB designates that union as the exclusive representative of all members of the bargaining unit. When unions hold representation elections in private corporations, they win about half the time. Labor organizations claim that management typically uses paid company time to campaign against the union. Employers respond that labor loses elections because workers fear that a union will hurt them, not help. Among public employers, unions generally do much better, winning about 85 percent of representation campaigns. Public employers often do not campaign against the union.

These are some of the issues that most commonly arise during an organizing effort: (1) What may a union do during its organizing campaign? (2) What may the employer do to defeat the campaign? (3) What is an appropriate bargaining unit?

What Workers May Do

The NLRA guarantees employees the right to talk among themselves about forming a union, to hand out literature, and ultimately to join a union.[6] Workers may urge other employees to sign authorization cards and may vigorously push their cause. When employees hand out leaflets, the employer generally may not limit the content. In one case a union distributed leaflets urging workers to vote against political candidates who opposed minimum wage laws. The employer objected to the union using company property to distribute the information, but the Supreme Court upheld the union's right. Even though the content of the writing was not directly related to the union, the connection was close enough that the NLRA protected the union's activity.[7]

There are, of course, limits to what union organizers may do. The statute permits an employer to restrict organizing discussions if they interfere with discipline or production. A worker on a moving assembly line has no right to walk away from his task to talk with other employees about organizing a union; the employer may insist that the worker stay at his job and leave discussions until lunch or some other break.[8]

---

[6] NLRA §7.

[7] *Eastex, Inc. v. NLRB*, 434 U.S. 1045, 98 S. Ct. 888, 1978 U.S. LEXIS 547 (1978).

[8] *NLRB v. Babcock & Wilcox Co.*, 351 U.S. 105, 76 S. Ct. 679, 1956 U.S. LEXIS 1721 (1956).

What Employers May Do

As mentioned earlier, an employer may prohibit employees from organizing if the efforts interfere with the company's work. In a retail store, for example, management may prohibit union discussions in the presence of customers, because the discussions could harm business.

May the employer speak out against a union organizing drive? Yes. Management is entitled to communicate to the employees why it believes a union will be harmful to the company. But the employer's efforts must be limited to explanation and advocacy. **The employer may vigorously present anti-union views to its employees but may not use either threats or promises of benefits to defeat a union drive.**[9] Notice that the employer is prohibited not only from threatening reprisals, such as firing a worker who favors the union, but also from offering benefits designed to defeat the union. A company that has vigorously rejected employee demands for higher wages may not suddenly grant a 10 percent pay increase in the midst of a union campaign.

It is an unfair labor practice for an employer to interfere with a union organizing effort. Normally, a union claiming such interference will file a ULP charge. If the Board upholds the union's claim, it will order the employer to stop its interference and permit a fair election. In some cases, though, management's interference is so pervasive and intrusive that the Board may conclude an election would be pointless. **When an employer outrageously interferes with a union organizing campaign, the NLRB may forgo the normal election, certify the union as the exclusive representative, and order the company to bargain.** This *bargaining order* is an extreme measure, and the Board uses it only when an employer has shown extreme anti-union animus. In the following case, the union contended that the employer had done just that.

GARVEY MARINE, INC. V. NATIONAL LABOR RELATIONS BOARD

245 F.3d 819
United States District Court of Appeals for the District of Columbia Circuit, 2001

Facts: Garvey Marine operated a fleet of tugboats. Each boat had two or more pilots and various deckhands, assigned by a company dispatcher. The International Longshoremen's Association, Local 2038, AFL-CIO, sought to represent the deckhands. When the Union lost the representation vote, it filed a complaint with the NLRB, stating that Garvey had intimidated the deckhands. The ALJ found numerous ULPs. He declared that Garvey made its pilots promise deckhands pay increases if the union were defeated but wage reductions and a strike if it won. He found that Garvey instituted a stricter disciplinary policy and used it to fire deckhand Steven Bradley. The NLRB affirmed the findings and ordered Garvey to bargain with the union, without another election. Garvey appealed.

Issues: Had Garvey committed ULPs? Did the NLRB properly issue an order to bargain?

Excerpts from Judge Ginsburg's Decision: According to Garvey, the deckhands could not reasonably have believed that the pilots who made promises and threats to union adherents were acting on the Company's behalf. Garvey points out that its vice president, Hudson, made repeated written and oral statements disclaiming any promises or threats and assuring deckhands there would be no reprisals taken for their union activity. The Board took the opposite position. Garvey required its pilots to sign a policy that they would support the Company in the Union campaign—and the deckhands knew it. ▼

---

[9] *NLRB v. Gissel Packing Co.*, 395 U.S. 575, 89 S. Ct. 1918, 1969 U.S. LEXIS 3172 (1969).

A reasonable deckhand, therefore, would not necessarily have assumed that a pilot's statement in contravention of Garvey's official policies was unauthorized; he would as likely have concluded that Garvey's public statements were primarily for show while the pilot's private warnings reflected management's actual position.

The Board was justified in concluding that Bradley's dismissal was motivated in part by his union advocacy: Garvey's dispatcher told him so. The Board also relied upon Garvey's elaborate choreography of Bradley's initial suspension, which preceded his formal dismissal by a few days: Garvey sent Bradley's boat back to the dock midshift, where Bradley—observed by the crews of three boats that had been held at the dock, presumably so they could witness the event—was met by a sheriff's officer who escorted him off the premises. This procedure suggests that Garvey at the least wanted to make an example of Bradley; it had staged no such spectacle when, on an earlier occasion, it delayed until shift's end the dismissal of a deckhand who had threatened a pilot with a knife.

Garvey objects to several features of the Board's analysis. First, the Company points out that the threats cited by the Board in support of its order were made during one-on-one encounters between pilots and a relatively small number of deckhands. Moreover, those most seriously threatened—[Bradley and others]—were undeterred in their union advocacy and, according to Garvey, there was no evidence that the many deckhands who were not personally threatened ever learned of the threats. Garvey also marshals the ALJ's point that the threats were less serious because they came only from pilots and were at odds with the official statements made by Vice President Hudson.

These arguments do not show that the Board acted unreasonably. The Board acknowledged that relatively few deckhands were threatened in person, but it balanced that fact against the small size of the unit, which had only 22 voters; the frequency of the threats, of which there were more than 30 during the two-month union campaign; and the nature of those threats, several of which menaced union adherents with physical harm. The Board believed that Bradley's suspension alone, having been "carried out in a manner that would ensure a dramatic and lasting impression on other employees . . . obviates any argument that other employees would not have been aware of the unlawful conduct and its import."

The Board was also reasonable in hypothesizing that a "rough and ready" threat made by an immediate supervisor "may be far more credible and influential so far as the ordinary worker is concerned than a necessarily more formal, structured, and purposeful statement of a high-ranking executive."

We grant the Board's application for enforcement. ■

Public Policy | Is the court being overly protective of the workers? These are deckhands on tugboats. Are they so easily intimidated? The order to bargain means that the union "wins" without an election. Is that right? ◆

Unlike the company in the *Garvey* case, the employer in the following dispute admitted a glaring violation of labor law, yet claimed it should pay no damages because the injured worker was in the country illegally.

HOFFMAN PLASTIC COMPOUNDS, INC. V. NATIONAL LABOR RELATIONS BOARD

122 S. Ct. 1275, 152 L. Ed. 2d 271
United States Supreme Court, 2002

Facts: The United Rubber, Cork, Linoleum and Plastic Workers of America began an organizing campaign at Hoffman Plastic Compounds, Inc. (Hoffman). Jose Castro and others supported this effort and, in retaliation, Hoffman fired them. Several years later (labor cases move very slowly), during hearings concerning his termination, Castro ▼

revealed for the first time that he was illegally in the United States. He had used false documents to obtain the job at Hoffman. Despite his illegal status, the NLRB found that Hoffman's retaliatory firing violated the NLRA and ordered the company to pay Castro $66,951, representing back pay from the date of firing until the employer learned that he was ineligible to work. The company appealed, and the issue reached the United States Supreme Court.

Issue: May an employer who has fired a worker for union organizing be ordered to pay back wages when the employee was illegally in the country?

Excerpts from Chief Justice Rehnquist's Decision: Under the [Immigration Reform and Control Act (IRCA), which regulates immigration into the United States], it is impossible for an undocumented alien to obtain employment in the United States without some party directly contravening explicit congressional policies. Either the undocumented alien tenders fraudulent identification, which subverts the cornerstone of IRCA's enforcement mechanism, or the employer knowingly hires the undocumented alien in direct contradiction of its IRCA obligations. The Board asks that we overlook this fact and allow it to award backpay to an illegal alien for years of work not performed, for wages that could not lawfully have been earned, and for a job obtained in the first instance by a criminal fraud. We find, however, that awarding backpay to illegal aliens runs counter to policies underlying IRCA, policies the Board has no authority to enforce or administer. Therefore, as we have consistently held in like circumstances, the award lies beyond the bounds of the Board's remedial discretion.

The Board contends that awarding limited backpay to Castro "reasonably accommodates" IRCA, because, in the Board's view, such an award is not "inconsistent" with IRCA. The Board argues that because the backpay period was closed as of the date Hoffman learned of Castro's illegal status, Hoffman could have employed Castro during the backpay period without violating IRCA. The Board further argues that while IRCA criminalized the misuse of documents, "it did not make violators ineligible for backpay awards or other compensation flowing from

employment secured by the misuse of such documents." This latter statement, of course, proves little. What matters here, and what sinks both of the Board's claims, is that Congress has expressly made it criminally punishable for an alien to obtain employment with false documents. There is no reason to think that Congress nonetheless intended to permit backpay where but for an employer's unfair labor practices, an alien-employee would have remained in the United States illegally, and continued to work illegally, all the while successfully evading apprehension by immigration authorities. Far from "accommodating" IRCA, the Board's position, recognizing employer misconduct but discounting the misconduct of illegal alien employees, subverts it.

[The NLRB's ruling is reversed.]

Excerpts from Justice Breyer's Dissent: The Court does not deny that the employer in this case dismissed an employee for trying to organize a union—a crude and obvious violation of the labor laws. And it cannot deny that the Board has especially broad discretion in choosing an appropriate remedy for addressing such violations. Nor can it deny that in such circumstances backpay awards serve critically important remedial purposes. Those purposes involve more than victim compensation; they also include deterrence, *i.e.*, discouraging employers from violating the Nation's labor laws.

[Denying backpay] lowers the cost to the employer of an initial labor law violation (provided, of course, that the only victims are illegal aliens). It thereby increases the employer's incentive to find and to hire illegal-alien employees. Were the Board forbidden to assess backpay against a *knowing* employer—a circumstance not before us today—this perverse economic incentive, which runs directly contrary to the immigration statute's basic objective, would be obvious and serious. But even if limited to cases where the employer did not know of the employee's status, the incentive may prove significant—for, as the Board has told us, the Court's rule offers employers immunity in borderline cases, thereby encouraging them to take risks, *i.e.*, to hire with a wink and a nod those potentially unlawful aliens whose unlawful employment (given the Court's views) ultimately will lower the costs of labor law violations. ∎

Appropriate Bargaining Unit

When a union petitions the NLRB for an election, the Board determines whether the proposed bargaining unit is appropriate. **The Board generally certifies a proposed bargaining unit if and only if the employees share a community of interest.** Employers frequently assert that the bargaining unit is inappropriate. If the Board agrees with the employer and rejects the proposed bargaining unit, it dismisses the union's request for an election. The Board pays particular attention to two kinds of employees: managerial and confidential.

Managerial employees must be excluded from the bargaining unit.[10] An employee is managerial if she is so closely aligned with management that her membership in the bargaining unit would create a conflict of interest between her union membership and her actual work. Courts generally find such a conflict only if *the employee is substantially involved in the employer's labor policy.*

For example, a factory worker who spends one third of his time performing assembly work but two thirds of his time supervising a dozen other workers is so closely aligned with management that he could not fairly be part of the bargaining unit. There would be constant tension between his supervisory work and his advocacy on behalf of the union. By contrast, an engineer who analyzes production methods and merely reports her findings to management may not be closely aligned with the employer. Unless the engineer has actual control over personnel decisions, she can probably be included in a bargaining unit of other engineers.[11]

Confidential employees are generally excluded from the bargaining unit.[12] A confidential employee is one who works so closely with executives or other management employees that there would be a conflict of interest if the employee were in the bargaining unit. An executive secretary may be so intimately acquainted with her boss's ideas, plans, and other confidential information that it would be unfair to allow her to join a bargaining unit of other secretaries.

Once the Board has excluded managerial and confidential employees, it looks at various criteria to decide whether the remaining employees should logically be grouped in one bargaining unit—that is, whether they share a **community of interest.** The Board looks for:

- Rough equality of pay and benefits, and methods of computing both;

- Similar total hours per week and type of work;

- Similar skills and training; and

- Previous bargaining history and the number of authorization cards from any different groups within the unit.

Having applied these criteria to all members of the proposed unit, the Board either certifies the bargaining unit or rejects the unit and dismisses the union's petition. Suppose the employees in a public high school decide to organize. The Board will probably find that an appropriate bargaining unit includes all academic teachers and physical education teachers because they do roughly similar work and are paid similarly. The principal and vice-principal will not be included in the unit because their work is supervisory and administrative and they are paid on a separate scale.

---

10 *NLRB v. Bell Aerospace Co., Div. of Textron, Inc.,* 416 U.S. 267, 94 S. Ct. 1757, 1974 U.S. LEXIS 35 (1974).

11 See, e.g., *NLRB v. Case Corp.,* 995 F.2d 700, 1993 U.S. App. LEXIS 13246 (7th Cir. 1993).

12 Ibid.

COLLECTIVE BARGAINING

The goal of bargaining is a contract, which is called a **collective bargaining agreement (CBA).** As mentioned, Congress passed the NLRA to foster industrial peace, and a CBA is designed to do that. But problems arise as union and employer advocate their respective positions. Three of the most common conflicts are (1) whether an issue is a mandatory subject of bargaining, (2) whether the parties are bargaining in good faith, and (3) how to enforce the agreement. For a Web page devoted to articles and reports on collective bargaining, see http://www.ilr.cornell.edu and search for "Collective Bargaining."

Subjects of Bargaining

The NLRA *permits* the parties to bargain almost any subject they wish but *requires* them to bargain certain issues. **Mandatory subjects include wages, hours, and other terms and conditions of employment.** Either side may propose to bargain *other* subjects, but neither side may insist upon bargaining them.

Management and unions often disagree as to whether a particular topic is mandatory or not. Typically, unions attempt to expand the number of mandatory subjects, seeking more input into a greater number of issues, while the company argues that subjects are not mandatory and are none of the union's business. In general, a court is likely to find a given issue mandatory when it *directly relates* to individual workers; when a subject only indirectly affects employees, it is likely to be found not mandatory. In passing the NLRA, Congress never intended a union negotiator to become an equal partner in running the business.

Courts generally find these subjects to be mandatory: pay, benefits, order of layoffs and recalls, production quotas, work rules (such as safety practices), retirement benefits, and in-plant food service and prices (e.g., cafeteria food). Courts usually consider these subjects to be nonmandatory: product type and design, advertising, sales, financing, corporate organization, and location of plants.

Today, some of the angriest disputes between management and labor arise from a company's desire to subcontract work and/or to move plants to areas with cheaper costs. **Subcontracting** means that a manufacturer, rather than producing all parts of a product and then assembling them, contracts for other companies, frequently overseas, to make some of the parts. Is a business free to subcontract work? That depends on management's motive. **A company that subcontracts in order to maintain its economic viability is probably *not* required to bargain first; however, bargaining *is* mandatory if the subcontracting is designed to replace union workers with cheaper labor.**

Dorsey Trailers manufactured dump trucks. During a period of heavy sales, Dorsey subcontracted some of its production work to Bankhead Enterprises, which agreed to manufacture two trucks per week and split the profits. The union filed a ULP charge, claiming that subcontracting was a mandatory subject of bargaining and that Dorsey had no right to make the deal before negotiating with the union.

The court noted that Dorsey was losing business because it could not fill orders fast enough. The dump truck industry was cyclical, and in a period of strong demand, the company had to be able to manufacture its goods quickly. Dorsey had been unable to hire enough welders and other skilled workers to keep up with demand. The court stated that Dorsey could not survive without the subcontracting. Further, the company had not reduced union jobs; it had simply failed to add more union workers—through no fault of its own. Dorsey was free to subcontract without bargaining the issue.[13]

Plant closings, which can result in hundreds or thousands of lost jobs, are also a volatile issue. Although the job losses are potentially greater than those that result from subcontracting, management is not obligated to bargain such a decision. **An employer is not required to bargain over the closing of a plant, only the *effects* of the closing.**[14]

The reasoning behind this rule is basic: the company that opened a plant ought to be able to close it. The competing interest of the employees—the need for work—is obviously strong but not strong enough to mandate bargaining. Further, having concluded that the employer has the right to shut down a facility, courts also allow the employer to do so fairly quickly. Management may need speed and flexibility in effecting such major business changes. In contrast, the union will want to slow down or prevent the closing. The two sides will have few things to discuss, and mandated bargaining will gain little for employees while potentially costing the company time and money. When a plant closing will cost jobs, management must bargain such things as the order of layoffs, but it need not bargain the closing itself.

Employer and Union Security

Both the employer and the union will seek clauses making their positions more secure. Management, above all, wants to be sure that there will be no strikes during the course of the agreement. For its part, the union tries to ensure that its members cannot be turned away from work during the CBA's term and that all newly hired workers will affiliate with the union. We look at several union security issues.

No Strike/No Lockout.   Most agreements include some form of no-strike clause, meaning that the union promises not to strike during the term of the contract. In turn, unions insist on a no-lockout clause, meaning that in the event of a labor dispute, management will not prevent union members from working. **No-strike and no-lockout clauses are both legal.**

Closed Shop.   A closed shop means the employer must hire only union members. Though obviously very attractive to a union, effectively giving it veto power over new hires, a closed shop is not possible. **A closed shop is illegal.** Indeed, for a union to bargain for a closed shop violates the NLRA.

Union and Agency Shops.   In a union shop, membership in the union becomes compulsory *after* the employee has been hired. Thus management retains an unfettered right to hire whom it pleases, but all new employees who fit into the bargaining unit must affiliate with the union. **A union shop is generally legal.** There are two limitations, however. First, new members need not join the union for 30 days. Second, the new members, after joining the union, can only be required to pay initiation fees and union dues. If the new hire decides he does not want to participate in the union, the union may not compel him to do so, and management may not terminate him (pursuant to a CBA) for his refusal. This is a compromise, designed to protect workers from having to play an active role in a union while ensuring that the union receives normal dues from all employees, whether they participate in union affairs or not. If employees could avoid dues, they would be "free riders," benefiting from the union's bargaining without paying for it.

---

13 *Dorsey Trailers, Inc. Northumberland PA Plant v. NLRB,* 134 F.3d 125, 1998 U.S. App. LEXIS 764 (3rd. Cir. 1998).
14 *First National Maintenance Corp. v. NLRB,* 452 U.S. 666, 101 S. Ct. 2573, 1981 U.S. LEXIS 117 (1981).

An **agency shop** is similar to a union shop. Here, the new hire must pay union fees but need not actually join the organization. In both a union shop and an agency shop, the worker may insist on paying only the percentage of dues that is devoted to collective bargaining, contract administration, and grievances. An employee may refuse to pay, for example, the percentage of union dues devoted to organizing other companies.[15]

Some states have passed so-called **right to work** laws, which restrict or even outlaw union shop and agency shop agreements. These statutes typically prohibit a labor organization from demanding that all employees join the union or pay dues. Right to work laws prompt an intense response from both supporters and opponents of organized labor, and the Internet offers plenty of evidence. At http://www.nrtw.org/, the National Right to Work Legal Defense Foundation explains these statutes and counsels employees about their rights to reject union membership and avoid paying dues. The organization also discusses what it considers to be union abuses. Meanwhile the AFL-CIO, the nation's largest labor organization, offers statistics demonstrating that union workers earn higher pay than their nonunion counterparts in virtually all jobs and professions and that wages are lower in right to work states than elsewhere in the country. See its Website at http://www.aflcio.org/.

Hot Cargo Clause.   A hot cargo clause would prohibit an employer from doing business with a specified company. A union might like such a clause to put pressure on the *other* company, where the union already has a dispute. But the effort must fail: **hot cargo clauses are illegal.**

Duty to Bargain

Both the union and the employer must bargain in good faith with an open mind. However, they are *not* obligated to reach an agreement. This means that the two sides must meet and make a reasonable effort to reach a contract. The goal is good faith bargaining, with the hope that it will lead to a contract and labor peace. Each side must listen to the other's proposals and consider possible compromises. But the NLRA does not require agreement. Suppose a union proposes a 15 percent pay increase, and management offers a 1 percent raise. Each side is required to attend bargaining sessions, listen to the other side's proposal, and consider its supporting argument. But neither side has to agree. Management need not raise its offer to 2 percent, nor must the union drop its demand. However, **if an employer states that it is financially unable to meet the union's demands, the union is entitled to see records that support the claim.** It is an unfair labor practice for an employer to say, "We can't afford a pay raise now," and then refuse to supply its financial data. An employer could easily destroy good faith bargaining if it were allowed to claim financial impossibility without demonstrating it. Similarly, if an employer argues that it must subcontract work to save money, it must furnish the documents it is relying on in making its proposal.

Sometimes an employer will attempt to make changes without bargaining the issues at all. However, **management may not unilaterally change wages, hours, or terms and conditions of employment without bargaining the issues to impasse.** "Bargaining to impasse" means that both parties must continue to meet and bargain in good faith until it is clear that they cannot reach an agreement. The goal in requiring collective bargaining is to bring the parties together, to reach an agreement that

---

[15] *Communications Workers of America v. Beck*, 487 U.S. 735, 108 S. Ct. 2641, 1988 U.S. LEXIS 3030 (1988).

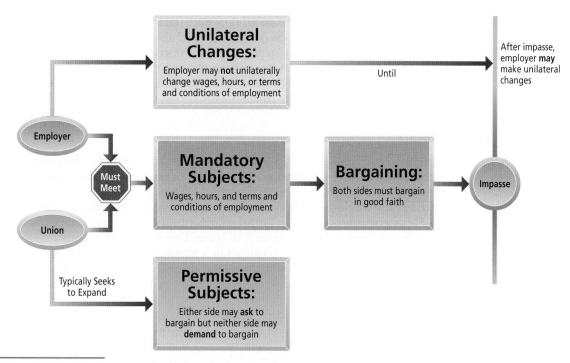

Exhibit 16.1
The **NLRA** requires that the employer and the union meet. They *must* bargain mandatory subjects and may bargain permissive subjects. The employer may not make any unilateral change concerning a mandatory subject until bargaining has reached an impasse.

brings labor peace. In one case, the union won an election, but before bargaining could begin, management changed the schedule from five 8-hour days to four 10-hour days a week. The company also changed its layoff policy from one of strict seniority to one based on ability and began laying off employees based on alleged poor performance. The court held that each of these acts violated the company's duty to bargain. The employer ultimately might be allowed to make every one of these changes, but first it had to bargain the issues to impasse.[16]

For the same reasons, though the employer may implement new policies after impasse, it may *implement only what it has proposed at the table*. Again, it would defeat the purpose of the NLRA if a company were free to implement a business decision that it had never proposed; the two sides *could not* have discussed plans that were never offered at the table. Exhibit 16.1 outlines the respective bargaining rights and responsibilities between employers and unions.

Illegal implementation put major league baseball players back on the field after the longest strike in sports history. The CBA had expired, and the players' union bargained with team owners throughout the spring and summer. The two sides could not agree, primarily because the owners demanded a salary cap, which would give all teams equal payrolls. In August the players struck, ending the season without a World Series for the first time in more than 100 years. The two sides continued talking until

---

[16] *Adair Standish Corp. v. NLRB*, 912 F.2d 854, 1990 U.S. App. LEXIS 14670 (6th Cir. 1990).

December, when the owners announced they were implementing their salary cap proposal and changing various aspects of "free agency," the policy that allows a player to seek the highest salary from any team. A federal district court judge ruled that the owners had violated the NLRA by unilaterally imposing new rules concerning a mandatory subject (free agency) that they had never bargained. The judge ordered the owners back to the table, and the parties finally agreed to a new CBA.

Enforcement

Virtually all collective bargaining agreements provide for their own enforcement, typically through **grievance-arbitration.** Suppose a company transfers an employee from the day shift to the night shift, and the worker believes the contract prohibits such a transfer for any employee with her seniority. The employee complains to the union, which files a **grievance**—that is, a formal complaint with the company, notifying management that the union claims a contract violation. Generally, the CBA establishes some kind of informal hearing, usually conducted by a member of management, at which the employee, represented by the union, may state her case and respond to the company's assertions. The manager has a limited period—say, seven days—to decide the grievance.

If, after the manager's decision, the employee is still dissatisfied, the union normally has the right to appeal to some kind of formal hearing, perhaps before a top company executive or committee. This appeal hearing is slightly more formal. If this hearing still fails to satisfy the employee, the union typically may file for **arbitration**—that is, a formal hearing before a neutral arbitrator. In the arbitration hearing, each side is represented by its lawyer. The arbitrator is required to decide the case based on the CBA. An arbitrator finds either for the employee, and orders the company to take certain corrective action, or for the employer, and dismisses the grievance. (The American Arbitration Association offers its rules, procedures, and forms at http://www.adr.org/.)

A CBA also permits the company to file a grievance. Its complaint normally goes directly to arbitration. In the vast majority of grievances, the arbitrator's decision is final. In a limited number of cases, however, the losing party attempts to convince a federal court that the arbitration award is unjust. Usually, such an appeal is futile. **Courts generally do not examine the merits of an arbitrator's decision.** The idea of all contracts, including CBAs, is to give the parties a chance to control their own destiny. When a CBA states that grievances should be settled by arbitration, courts seldom undercut the contract by reviewing the arbitrator's award. Of course, a rule would hardly be a rule without an exception. **A court may refuse to enforce an arbitrator's award that is contrary to public policy.** So if an arbitrator's decision encourages either party to violate the law or engage in clearly immoral conduct, a court will probably nullify the award. The following case demonstrates how reluctant courts are to interfere with an arbitrator's decision.

BRENTWOOD MEDICAL ASSOCIATES V. UNITED MINE WORKERS OF AMERICA

396 F. 3d 237
United States Court of Appeals for the Third Circuit, 2005

Facts: Brentwood Medical Associates operated a hospital. The United Mine Workers of America represented one unit of employees, which included Denise Cope, a phlebotomist (someone who draws blood). Exercising her seniority rights, Cope changed jobs to Charge Entry Associate. A year and a half later, BMA announced it was terminating the position. Cope asked to return to her old job. This would have required "bumping" the least senior ▼

phlebotomist out of a job. BMA refused, claiming that bumping was not allowed under the collective bargaining agreement (CBA). Cope filed a grievance, which an arbitrator heard.

The arbitrator ruled in Cope's favor. In his decision, he asked rhetorically why, if the CBA disallowed bumping, did it include the following language:

> . . . employees who exercise seniority rights and bump must have the skill to perform all of the work [in the new job].

The problem with the quoted language was that it did not in fact exist anywhere in the CBA. BMA filed suit, asking a federal court to overturn the arbitration decision. The trial court upheld the award and BMA appealed.

Issue: Should the arbitration award be affirmed even though the arbitrator relied on language that cannot be found in the CBA?

Excerpts from Judge Van Antwerpen's Decision: The narrow issue before us is whether the arbitrator's conclusion is supported, in any way, by a rational interpretation of the collective bargaining agreement. We ask merely whether the parties to the collective bargaining agreement got what they bargained for, namely an arbitrator who would first provide an interpretation of the contract that was rationally based on the language of the agreement, and second would produce a rational award. BMA contends that the arbitrator's reference to the language not found in the collective bargaining agreement fatally taints the award, because this reference is essential to the arbitrator's ultimate conclusion and is inseparable from the remainder of the award. As such, our focus must be on whether the arbitrator's

discussion can still support the award if we excise the anomalous language.

In additional support for his conclusion, the arbitrator cited several provisions of the agreement. For example, Section 1 defines seniority as "bargaining unit-wide" and not within classification. Section 2 provides that the principle of seniority is a factor in layoffs, recalls, and certain types of promotional opportunities provided the employee is fully qualified. Section 5 specifies that in filling vacancies when the qualifications of two or more applicants are relatively equal, preference will be based on seniority.

After reviewing the totality of the arbitrator's decision, we are confident that his award does not rest solely upon the aberrant language added by the arbitrator. Faced with what he perceived as an incongruity between BMA's position and the bargaining unit-wide seniority rights of employees, the arbitrator attempted to construe together, and then give effect to, all provisions of the agreement. While BMA may take issue with his contractual interpretation, this is not sufficient to justify [overturning] the award.

Full-blown judicial review of the arbitrator's decision would annul the bargain between BMA and UMWA for an arbitrator's construction of their agreement and replace it with a judicial interpretation that was not bargained for. Only where there is manifest disregard for the agreement can we override an arbitrator. Because the remainder of the justification for the award offered by the arbitrator was capable of separation from the aberrant language, his decision reflects an interpretation of the contract that is at least minimally rooted in the collective bargaining agreement, and not his own brand of industrial justice.

For the foregoing reasons, we affirm the decision of the District Court. ∎

| *Devil's* *Advocate* | It is one thing to respect an arbitrator's award and presume it final; it is quite another to rubber-stamp a decision. This arbitrator based his opinion in large part on alleged "CBA language" that in fact came out of thin air. The court blithely suggests that the imaginary language was not of overriding importance—but the *arbitrator* thought so! This is the rare, even bizarre case in which a court should say, "Not good enough. We are taking over." ◆ |

CONCERTED ACTION

Concerted action refers to any tactics union members take in unison to gain some bargaining advantage. It is this power that gives a union strength. **The NLRA guarantees the right of employees to engage in concerted action for mutual**

aid or protection.[17] The most common forms of concerted action are strikes and picketing.

Strikes

The NLRA guarantees employees the right to strike, but with some limitations.[18] A union has a guaranteed right to call a strike if the parties are unable to reach a collective bargaining agreement. A union may call a strike to exert economic pressure on management, to protest an unfair labor practice, or to preserve work that the employer is considering sending elsewhere. Note that the right to strike can be waived. Management will generally insist that the CBA include a **no-strike clause,** which prohibits the union from striking while the CBA is in force. A strike is illegal in several other situations as well; here we mention the most important.

Cooling Off Period

Once the union agrees to a CBA, it may not strike to terminate the agreement, or modify it, without giving management 60 days' notice. Suppose a union contract expires July 1. The two sides attempt to bargain a new contract, but progress is slow. The union may strike as an economic weapon but must notify management of its intention to do so *and then must wait 60 days.* This cooling off period is designed to give both sides a chance to reassess negotiations and to decide whether some additional compromise would be wiser than enduring a strike.

Statutory Prohibition

Many states have outlawed strikes by public employees. In some states, the prohibition applies to selected employees, such as firefighters or teachers. In other states, all public employees are barred from striking, whether or not they have a contract. The purpose of these statutes is to ensure that unions do not use the public health or welfare as a weapon to secure an unfair bargaining advantage. However, even employees subject to such a rule may find other tactics to press their cause.

Ethics

Jen has worked hard throughout high school, achieving a 3.8 GPA and high test scores, and now she is ready to apply to some of the best colleges in the country. All her teachers think she is an extraordinary student—yet no one will write her a letter of recommendation.

The teacher's union has been bargaining a new contract for a year and a half. The teachers seek a 4 percent raise; the school board has offered 1 percent. The struggle has grown increasingly bitter. There will be no strike—state law prohibits that—but the teachers have decided they will "work to rule," meaning that they will do only what their (expired) contract requires: teach classes, issue grades, and so forth. No teacher will write a letter of recommendation, coach a team, supervise detention, or offer extra help to a student.

"This stinks," wails Jen. "I've never asked for extra assistance. I've tried to be helpful in class, and a lot of times, I've tutored other kids. This is the one time in my life I really need my teachers to be there for me, and they're turning their backs."

"My heart goes out to Jen," responds her American history teacher, "but our problem is simple: as long as we quietly ask for decent pay, no one listens. Students and parents notice us only when they suffer inconvenience."

---

[17] NLRA §7.
[18] NLRA §13.

"This is a moral outrage!" shouts Jen's father. "These so-called teachers have no right to hurt my child over their pay disputes. If they were serious about their profession, they would do everything they could to help the children who are entrusted to them. Our high school normally sends 95 percent of its students to good colleges, and now the teachers are sabotaging everything."

"If the parents were serious about education," the history teacher retorts, "or truly concerned about their children's welfare, they would demand that the town pay respectable salaries. They prefer lower taxes so they can spend more on fancy cars."

Who is right? From the Chapter 2 Ethics Checklist: What are the alternatives? What are the consequences of each? ◆

Violent Strikes

The NLRA prohibits violent strikes. Violence does sometimes occur on the picket line, when union members attempt to prevent other workers from entering the job site. Or a union may stage a **sit-down strike,** in which members stop working but remain at their job posts, physically blocking replacement workers from taking their places. Any such violence is illegal.

Partial Strikes

A partial strike occurs when employees stop working temporarily, then resume, then stop again, and so forth. This tactic is particularly disruptive because management cannot bring in replacement workers. A union may either walk off the job or stay on it, but it may not alternate.

Replacement Workers

When employees go on strike, management generally wants to replace them to keep the company operating. When replacement workers begin to cross a union picket line, tempers are certain to explode and entire communities may feel the repercussions. Are replacement workers legal? Yes. **Management has the right to hire replacement workers during a strike.** May the employer offer the replacement workers *permanent* jobs, or must the company give union members their jobs back when the strike is over? It depends on the type of strike.

After an *economic strike*, an employer may not discriminate against a striker, but the employer is *not* obligated to lay off a replacement worker to give a striker his job back. An economic strike is one intended to gain wages or benefits. When a union bargains for a pay raise but fails to get it and walks off the job, that is an economic strike. During such a strike, an employer may hire permanent replacement workers. When the strike is over, the company has no obligation to lay off the replacement workers to make room for the strikers. However, if the company does hire more workers, it may not discriminate against the strikers.

After a *ULP strike*, a union member is entitled to her job back, even if that means the employer must lay off a replacement worker. Suppose management refuses to bargain in good faith, by claiming poverty without producing records to substantiate its claim. The union strikes. Management's refusal to bargain was an unfair labor practice, and the strike is a ULP strike. When it ends, the striking workers must get their jobs back. The following case raises the pivotal distinction concerning a strike: Was this one sparked by a ULP—or by money?

CITIZENS PUBLISHING AND PRINTING COMPANY V. NATIONAL LABOR RELATIONS BOARD

263 F.3d 224
United States Court of Appeals for the Third Circuit, 2001

Facts: Citizens Publishing was a family-owned corporation that published the *Ellwood City Ledger* and another local newspaper. Bud Dimeo had been the company's sole photographer for more than 35 years. When the needs for daytime photography declined, Citizens began requiring Dimeo to work at night and on weekends as well. Citizens also occasionally employed stringers, meaning freelance photographers who were paid per photo.

Teamsters Local No. 261 was certified as the representative for certain Citizens' employees, including photographers but excluding stringers. While the company and union were negotiating a contract, Dimeo retired and Citizens assigned most of the night/weekend photography to stringers. The union filed a ULP charge with the NLRB, claiming that Citizens had unilaterally changed the terms and conditions of employment without bargaining, by giving to stringers work previously done by Dimeo, a bargaining unit member.

On July 23, fully 18 months after contract negotiations had started, the union met with employees and informed them that the NLRB intended to issue a complaint based on Citizens' use of stringers. The members voted to strike, and walked out on July 24. The paper continued to publish, using family members, supervisors, and nonstriking employees. The following February, six months into the strike, Citizens reassured the union that none of the replacement workers were considered permanent; the strikers could return if they wished.

The parties met to bargain on March 14. The union representative indicated the union was prepared to return to work. Company representatives took a break to caucus; when they returned, they informed the union that all replacements were permanent. In other words, the strikers had lost their jobs. The next day, Citizens informed the replacement workers they were permanent. The NLRB found that the union's job action was a ULP strike and ordered Citizens to offer the union members their jobs back. Citizens appealed.

Issue: Was the job action a ULP strike?

Excerpts from Judge Fuentes's Decision: An employer violates § 8(a)(5) if, without bargaining to impasse, it effects a unilateral change of an existing term or condition of employment. By unilaterally changing the employees' terms and conditions of employment, an employer minimizes the influence of organized bargaining and emphasizes to the employees that there is no necessity for a collective bargaining agent.

Here, substantial evidence supports the Board's finding that Citizens Publishing's night/weekend work became an integral part of the regular full-time photographer's work, and thus, became bargaining unit work. When Citizens Publishing assigned the night/weekend work to Dimeo, that work became a necessary and integral part of the full-time photographer's position. Additionally, Dimeo did not receive any additional remuneration for his night/weekend work. Thus, at the time of the Union's certification, the status quo included a full-time photographer's position with night/weekend work. Accordingly, substantial evidence supports the determination that Citizens Publishing violated the Act when it unilaterally subcontracted the bargaining unit work during the negotiations over the initial collective-bargaining agreement.

We next address whether the strike was an "unfair labor practice strike," as opposed to a mere economic strike. Unfair labor practice strikers are entitled to immediate reinstatement upon their unconditional offers to return to work; any replacements hired during the strike must be dismissed, if necessary, to effect reinstatement of the strikers.

Here, substantial evidence supports the Board's finding that the strike was an unfair labor practice strike. The Union convened a meeting of bargaining unit members on the day before the strike began. After learning of Citizens Publishing's action, numerous employees indicated their desire to go on strike, and the membership held a strike vote. These facts support the Board's finding that its decision to issue a complaint galvanized the bargaining unit members' belief that an unfair labor practice had

▼

been committed and served as the flashpoint for discussion about calling a strike.

Moreover, even if Citizens Publishing's subcontracting of night/weekend work did not constitute an unfair labor practice, its discharge of the striking employees on March 14 converted the strike into an unfair labor practice strike because it prolonged the strike. Citizens Publishing's false declaration that it had permanently replaced the strikers prolonged the strike by thwarting the Union's attempt to make an unconditional offer to return to work that day. Indeed, the Union informed Citizens Publishing at the March 14 bargaining session of its intent to make an unconditional offer to return to work. Before the Union could make its offer, however, Citizens Publishing preemptively notified the Union that it had permanently replaced the strikers, thereby effectively informing the Union that any unconditional offer to return to work would be futile.

We will enforce the Board's order in its entirety. ■

Find a thorough description of a current strike. What issues caused the union to walk out? Is this an economic or a ULP strike? In your opinion, which side is making the stronger case, and why? ◆

Picketing

Picketing the employer's workplace in support of a strike is generally lawful. Striking workers are permitted to establish picket lines at the employer's job site and to urge all others—employees, replacement workers, and customers—not to cross the line. But the picketers are not permitted to use physical force to *prevent* anyone from crossing the line. The NLRA does not authorize or protect violence on the picket line. The company may terminate violent picketers and permanently replace them, regardless of the nature of the strike.

Secondary boycotts are generally illegal. A secondary boycott is a picket line established, not at the employer's premises, but at the workplace of a *different* company that does business with the union's employer. Such a boycott is designed to put pressure on the union's employer by forcing other companies to stop doing business with it. Suppose Union is on strike against Truck Co. Union is free to picket Truck Co.'s office or terminal. If Truck Co. hires replacement workers, the trucks will be back on the road, making deliveries. Now Union wants to put additional pressure on Truck Co., so it sets up picket lines at a *supermarket* where Truck Co. delivers. Union attempts to persuade customers not to shop at the store and other workers, including delivery drivers, not to enter the premises. If allowed, the picketing might result in the supermarket demanding that Truck Co. compromise with Union. But this is a secondary boycott, so it is illegal. Truck Co. and the supermarket will obtain an injunction, prohibiting the secondary boycott. See Exhibit 16.2.

Lockouts

The workers have bargained with management for weeks, and discussions have turned belligerent. It is 6:00 AM, the start of another day at the factory. But as 150 employees arrive for work, they are amazed to find the company's gate locked and armed guards standing on the other side. What is this? A lockout.

The power of a union comes ultimately from its potential to strike. But management, too, has weapons. In a lockout, management prohibits workers from entering the premises, denying the employees work and a chance to earn a paycheck. Most, but not all, lockouts are legal.

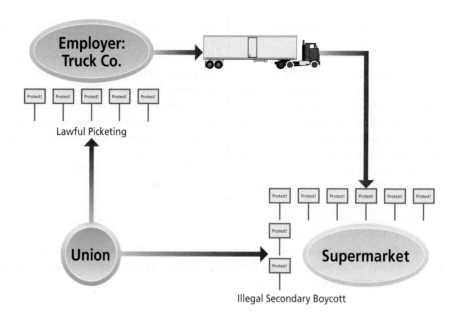

Exhibit 16.2

A union striking against Truck Co. may lawfully picket the employer, using peaceful means to urge all others to stay away. But if the union attempts to put indirect pressure on Truck Co. by picketing one of the company's customers, it is engaging in an illegal secondary boycott.

A defensive lockout is almost always legal. It is one way management can respond to union pressure such as a sit-down strike or a **whipsaw strike,** which may occur when a union is simultaneously bargaining with various employers. Suppose a machinists' union is simultaneously bargaining a contract with three engine manufacturers, attempting to obtain an identical contract from all the companies. To pressure the companies, the union might choose to strike against only *one* of the manufacturers. This is a whipsaw strike, and it can be very effective because the struck company, losing money while the others profit, will push strongly for a compromise. But management of all three companies may respond by locking out the workers from *all* factories, even those where no strike is under way. That is a defensive lockout, and it is legal.

An offensive lockout is legal if the parties have reached a bargaining impasse. Management, bargaining a new CBA with a union, may wish to use a lockout to advance its position. It is allowed to do so *provided the parties have reached an impasse.* If there is no impasse, a lockout will *probably* be illegal. Most courts consider that a lockout before impasse indicates hostility to the union. That kind of general antagonism to a union is illegal because the NLRA guarantees employees the right to organize. In addition, management usually *must notify the union before locking it out.* Again, the purpose of the NLRA is to bring the parties together through bargaining. A lockout is a legitimate method to pressure a union into compromise, but it can have that effect only if the union is warned and given a chance to bargain.

REGULATING UNION AFFAIRS

Along with a union's exclusive bargaining power goes a duty of fairness to all of its members. The union's *duty of fair representation* was created by the NLRA and the Labor-Management Reporting and Disclosure Act. **The duty of fair representation**

requires that a union represent all members fairly, impartially, and in good faith. A union is not entitled to favor some members over others. No union may discriminate against a member based on impermissible characteristics such as race or sex. A union is allowed to discipline a member for certain acts, such as engaging in an illegal strike or working for wages below union scale. But the union may *not* discipline a member for criticizing union leadership or attempting to replace the leadership through a proper election.

Unions must make reasonable decisions about whether to pursue an employee's grievance. A member may sue his union, claiming that the organization violated its duty of fair representation by deciding not to pursue a grievance on his behalf. But courts generally allow unions a *wide range of latitude* in deciding whether to pursue a grievance. **A union's decision not to file a grievance is illegal only if it was arbitrary, discriminatory, or in bad faith.**

Most employees fail when claiming that a union violated its duty of fair representation. Ramon Hayes worked at the Peoples Gas, Light and Coke Co. Peoples Gas fired him for theft, and the union filed a grievance. Before the grievance could be arbitrated, Hayes was convicted on drug charges. The union, mistakenly believing Hayes had been convicted on the *theft* accusation, withdrew its grievance. Later, the union learned of its error but refused to pursue the grievance because Peoples Gas had added the drug charge as a reason for the dismissal. A court ruled that the union had probably been inept and negligent in dismissing the original grievance but had shown no *bad faith* in its belief that the grievance was futile. The union had not violated its duty of fair representation.[19]

Chapter Conclusion

Workers first attempted to organize unions in this country about 200 years ago in response to appalling working conditions. These conditions are *generally* better today, and contemporary clashes between union and management are less likely to stem from sweltering temperatures in a mine than from a management decision to subcontract work or from a teacher's refusal to write college recommendations. But although the flash points have changed, labor law is still dominated by issues of organizing, collective bargaining, and concerted action.

Chapter Review

1. Section 7 of the National Labor Relations Act (NLRA) guarantees employees the right to organize and join unions, bargain collectively, and engage in other concerted activities.

2. Section 8(a) of the NLRA makes it an unfair labor practice for an employer to interfere with union organizing, discriminate against a union member, or refuse to bargain collectively.

3. Section 8(b) of the NLRA makes it an unfair labor practice for a union to interfere with employees who are exercising their rights under §7, to encourage an employer to discriminate against an employee because of a labor dispute, to refuse to bargain collectively, or to engage in an illegal strike or boycott.

---

[19] *Hayes v. People's Gas, Light and Coke Co.*, 1992 U.S. App. LEXIS 30592 (7th Cir. 1992).

4. Section 9 of the NLRA makes a validly recognized union the *exclusive* representative of the employees.

5. During a union organizing campaign, an employer may vigorously present anti-union views to its employees, but it may not use threats or promises of benefits to defeat the union effort.

6. The National Labor Relations Board (NLRB) will certify a proposed bargaining unit only if the employees share a community of interest.

7. The employer and the union *must* bargain over wages, hours, and other terms and conditions of employment. They *may* bargain other subjects, but neither side may insist on doing so.

8. The union and the employer must bargain in good faith, but they are not obligated to reach an agreement. Management may not unilaterally change wages, hours, or terms and conditions of employment without bargaining to impasse.

9. The NLRA guarantees employees the right to strike, with some limitations.

10. After an *economic* strike, an employer is not obligated to lay off replacement workers to give a striker her job back, but he may not discriminate against a striker. After a *ULP* strike, the striking worker must get her job back.

11. Picketing the employer's workplace in support of a strike is generally lawful; a secondary boycott is generally illegal.

12. An employer may lock out workers, but only after giving them notice.

13. Multi-employer bargaining and implementation do not violate antitrust laws.

14. The duty of fair representation requires that a union represent all members fairly, impartially, and in good faith.

Practice Test

1. Power, Inc., operated a surface coal mine in central Pennsylvania. Financial losses led it to lay off a number of employees. After that, several employees contacted the United Mine Workers of America (UMWA), which began an organizing drive at the company. Power's general manager and foreman both warned the miners that if the company was unionized, it would be shut down. An office manager told one of the miners that the company would get rid of union supporters. Shortly before the election was to take place, Power laid off 13 employees, all of whom had signed union cards. One employee, who had not signed a union card, had low seniority but was not laid off. Later, one of Power's lawyers told several miners that anyone caught helping the 13 laid-off workers by contributing to a union hardship fund would "be out there looking for help from somebody else." Comment.

2. Triec, Inc., is a small electrical contracting company in Springfield, Ohio, owned by its executives Yeazell, Jones, and Heaton. Employees contacted the International Brotherhood of Electrical Workers, which began an organizing drive. Six of the 11 employees in the bargaining unit signed authorization cards. The company declined to recognize the union, which petitioned the NLRB to schedule an election. The company then granted several new benefits for all workers, including higher wages, paid vacations, and other measures. When the election was held, only 2 of the 11 bargaining unit members voted for the union. Did the company violate the NLRA?

3. Q-1 Motor Express was an interstate trucking company. When a union attempted to organize Q-1's drivers, it met heavy resistance. A supervisor told one driver that if he knew what was good for him, he would stay away from the union organizer. The company president told another employee that he had the right to fire everybody, close the company, and then rehire new drivers after 72 hours. He made numerous other threats to workers and their families. Based on the extreme nature of the company's opposition, what exceptional remedy did the union seek before the NLRB?

4. Douglas Kuroda worked for the Hertz Corp. He and his supervisor had a heated argument in which Kuroda told his boss, "You may have a

master's degree but you don't know shit." The supervisor instructed Kuroda to punch out for the day, but Kuroda refused to leave until security officers escorted him off the premises. Hertz fired him, and Kuroda filed a grievance. The union represented Kuroda at an arbitration hearing. During the hearing, the union made no objection to certain evidence that the company offered to demonstrate why it fired Kuroda. The arbitrator ruled in favor of the company. Kuroda sued his union (and also Hertz). What kind of claim is he making against the union? Is he likely to win his claim?

5. Gibson Greetings, Inc., had a plant in Berea, Kentucky, where the workers belonged to the International Brotherhood of Firemen & Oilers. The old CBA expired, and the parties negotiated a new one but were unable to reach an agreement on economic issues. The union struck. At the next bargaining session, the company claimed that the strike violated the *old* CBA, which had a no-strike clause and which stated that the terms of the old CBA would continue in force as long as the parties were bargaining a *new* CBA. The company refused to bargain until the union at least agreed that by bargaining, the company was not giving up its claim of an illegal strike. The two sides returned to bargaining, but meanwhile the company hired replacement workers. Eventually, the striking workers offered to return to work, but Gibson refused to rehire many of them. In court, the union claimed that the company had committed a ULP by (1) insisting the strike was illegal and (2) refusing to bargain until the union acknowledged the company's position. Why is it very important to the union to establish the company's act as a ULP? *Was* it a ULP?

6. **YOU BE THE JUDGE** WRITING PROBLEM
Plainville Ready Mix Concrete Co. was bargaining a CBA with the drivers' union. Negotiations went forward, on and off, over many months, with wages the major source of disagreement. Plainville made its final offer of $9.50 per hour, with step increases of $.25 per hour in a year and another $.25 per hour the following year. The plan also included certain incentive pay. The union refused to accept the offer, and the two sides reached an impasse. Plainville then announced it was implementing its plans. It established a wage rate of $9.50 per

hour but eliminated the step increases and incentive pay. Was the company's implementation of the wage increase legal? **Argument for Plainville:** The NLRA only requires the company to bargain in good faith, which we did. The law does not obligate us to agree to anything. Once the parties reached an impasse, Plainville could implement any plan it wanted. **Argument for the Union:** When the parties reach an impasse, the employer is permitted to implement whatever it proposed at the bargaining table. It would defeat the purpose of collective bargaining if a company could implement plans it had never proposed.

7. Eads Transfer, Inc., was a moving and storage company with a small workforce represented by the General Teamsters, Chauffeurs and Helpers Union. When the CBA expired, the parties failed to reach agreement on a new one, and the union struck. As negotiations continued, Eads hired temporary replacement workers. After 10 months of the strike, some union workers offered to return to work, but Eads made no response to the offer. Two months later, more workers offered to return to work, but Eads would not accept any of the offers. Eventually, Eads notified all workers that they would not be allowed back to work until a new CBA had been signed. The union filed ULP claims against the company. Please rule.

8. Olivetti Office U.S.A., Inc., was located in Newington, Connecticut, and its workers were represented by the United Automobile, Aerospace and Agriculture Implement Workers of America. The company's president reported to the union that Olivetti was losing money. He insisted that unless the union renegotiated certain wage increases in the current CBA, Olivetti would subcontract work to cheaper parts of the country to save money. The union requested to bargain over the proposed subcontracting, and Olivetti agreed. But when the sides met, the company would not permit the union to see the financial data that supported its arguments. After several meetings, the company declared an impasse, implemented its subcontracting proposal, and laid off workers in Connecticut. The union claimed this was a ULP. Was it?

9. Fred Schipul taught English at the Thomaston (Connecticut) High School for 18 years. When the position of English Department chairperson

became vacant, Schipul applied, but the Board of Education appointed a less senior teacher. Schipul filed a grievance, based on a CBA provision that required the Board to promote the most senior teacher where two or more applicants were equal in qualification. Before the arbitrator ruled on the grievance, the Board eliminated all department chairpersons. The arbitrator ruled in Schipul's favor. The Board then reinstated all department chairs—all but the English Department. Comment.

10. Labor Day is a national holiday originally intended to celebrate the contributions of working men and women. But for most people today it simply means a day off from work—or the day before school begins. What are some reasons that unions have declined in membership and power? Are there are any reasons to think that organized labor may rebound and increase its strength?

11. *ETHICS* The chapter refers in several places to the contentious issue of subcontracting. Make an argument for management in favor of a company's ethical right to subcontract, and one for unions in opposition.

12. *ROLE REVERSAL* Write an essay question involving a union organizing campaign and a management response that includes both permissible advocacy and illegal conduct.

Internet Research Problem

Find a Website that is campaigning against sweatshops. What are sweatshops? Do they exist in the United States? Describe a current campaign about this issue. Do you agree or disagree with what is being done? Why?

You can find further practice problems at

http://academic.cengage.com/westbuslaw/beatty

BUSINESS ORGANIZATIONS

© PHOTODISC COLLECTION/GETTY IMAGES

unit

4

17 Starting a Business

© PHOTO 24/BRAND X PICTURES/GETTY IMAGES

James Parker founded Factory Connections, Inc. (FCI) to sell franchises of automotive parts. First, a distributor would purchase a territory (which cost $30,000 to $250,000, depending on the size). Then an FCI sales team would set up accounts at garages in that area, stocking each garage with various FCI car parts. The distributor paid for this initial supply but was reimbursed by the garage after the parts were used. To resupply the garages, the distributors would purchase parts from FCI.

Unfortunately for all involved, nothing went according to plan. Parker promised in the sales brochures that FCI products were of the highest quality. That was not the case: among other problems, the brakes squealed and then quickly disintegrated. When distributors complained to Parker, he told them that the products had worked fine for everyone else and the mechanics must have ruined them during installation. These accusations soured relationships between the distributors and their garages. Parker also promised that the FCI sales staff would set up accounts at high-quality garages. Instead, the customers were oftentimes not garages at all, but were dump sites for the salesperson's inventory, such as bait shops and junk yards. To entice garage owners to accept an FCI account, salespeople would tell the owners that they need not use the products but could keep them on hand for emergencies.

FCI promotional materials included wildly optimistic profitability estimates. Although Parker knew that profitability was declining, he predicted a 10% annual increase in sales and profits. He told potential investors that FCI distributorships were 100% successful, but that was not true. FCI advertised that, according to an independent survey, it was "Number 1." No survey had ever been conducted. ■

Legal issues can have as profound an impact on the success of a company as any business decision. The goal of the law is to balance the rights, obligations and liabilities of entrepreneurs, managers, investors and customers. Wise (and successful) entrepreneurs know how to use the law to their advantage. Because James Parker was not wise, he soon found himself on the wrong end of the law. Parker violated the Federal Trade Commission (FTC) rules on franchises and, as a result, was sentenced to prison for fraud.[1]

To begin, entrepreneurs must select a form of organization. The correct choice can reduce taxes, liability, and conflict while facilitating outside investment. If entrepreneurs do not make a choice for themselves, the law will automatically select a (potentially undesirable) default option. Numerous alternatives are available: sole proprietorship, general partnership, limited partnership, corporation, limited liability company, limited liability partnership, joint venture, business trust, or cooperative. At http://www.onlinewbc.gov/docs/starting/test.html, the U.S. Small Business Administration offers advice about starting a business and includes an entrepreneurial test to help you assess your potential as an entrepreneur.

SOLE PROPRIETORSHIPS

A sole proprietorship is an unincorporated business owned by a single person. It is the most common form of business organization. For example, Linda runs ExSciTe (which stands for Excellence in Science Teaching), a company that helps teachers prepare hands-on science experiments in the classroom, using such basic items as vinegar, lemon juice, and red cabbage.

Sole proprietorships are easy and inexpensive to create and operate. There is no need to hire a lawyer or register with the government. The company is not even required to file a separate tax return—all profits and losses are reported on the owner's personal return. A very few states and some cities and towns require sole proprietors to obtain a business license. And states generally require sole proprietors to register their business name if it is different from their own. Linda, for example, would file a "d/b/a" or "doing business as" certificate for "ExSciTe."

Sole proprietorships also have some serious disadvantages. First, the owner of the business is responsible for all the business's debts. If ExSciTe cannot pay its suppliers or if a student is injured by an exploding cabbage, Linda is personally liable. She may have to sell her house and car to pay the debt. Second, the owner of a sole proprietorship has limited options for financing her business. Debt is generally her only source of working capital because she has no stock or memberships to sell. If someone else brings in capital and helps with the management of the business, then it is a partnership, not a sole proprietorship. For this reason sole proprietorships work best for small businesses without large capital needs.

No form of organization is right—or wrong—for everyone. Consider these very different experiences of two small-business owners.

Judith Gross felt that the fees and taxes imposed on her young corporation were a major factor in its failure:

> It seemed like a dream come true. I always thought I had the right instincts to publish a newsletter. When 500 people packed a seminar on a controversial new technology sweeping my industry, dollar signs danced in my head. I was on my way. Now, two and a

---

[1] *United States of America v. Parker*, 364 F.3d 934; 2004 U.S. App. LEXIS 7549 (2004).

half years later, I realize that what I was on my way to was becoming one of those small-business owners who list failure on their resumes.

Incorporating my business was a major mistake because the expenses were more than I could afford. I did not find out until later that 76 percent of all small businesses operate as sole proprietorships. Although being a corporation protected me in case of a lawsuit, I got a shock when my accountant pointed out the disadvantages of incorporation in the heavily taxed, heavily regulated nation's capital. Now I realize that incorporating is good for a company when raising capital is an essential part of the ongoing business. Real estate and construction are two examples that come to mind. But a service business, which relies mostly on money put up by the people involved, would be better operated as a sole proprietorship or partnership.

For Beth and Drexel Wright, however, a sole proprietorship was disastrous. Mr. Wright was the founder and sole proprietor of Quaker Siding Co., a construction and remodeling business in Millville, Pennsylvania. Within a year of their marriage, the Wrights went into bankruptcy proceedings. Because the company was a sole proprietorship, the court liquidated many of their personal assets—farm equipment, cattle, vehicles, rental properties—to pay creditors. For a time, they were afraid they might even lose their home. Four years later, the Wrights reached an agreement with their creditors and were allowed out of bankruptcy. They immediately incorporated their business as Quaker Construction Services, Inc.

GENERAL PARTNERSHIPS

A partnership has an important advantage over a sole proprietorship—partners. Sole proprietors are on their own; partners have colleagues to help them and, equally important, to supply capital for the business. Sole proprietorships often turn into partnerships for exactly this reason.

Traditionally, partnerships were regulated by common law, but a lack of consistency among the states became troublesome as interstate commerce grew. To solve this problem, the National Conference of Commissioners on Uniform State Laws proposed the Uniform Partnership Act (UPA) in 1914. Since then there have been several revisions, the most recent in 1997. A majority of states have now passed the latest revisions, so we include them in our discussion of partnership law.

Partnerships have two important advantages: they do not pay taxes, and they are easy to form. Partnerships, however, also have some major disadvantages:

- *Liability.* Each partner is personally liable for the debts of the enterprise whether or not she caused them.

- *Funding.* Financing a partnership may be difficult because the firm cannot sell shares as a corporation does. The capital needs of the partnership must be provided by contributions from partners or by borrowing.

- *Management.* Managing a partnership can also be difficult because, in the absence of an agreement to the contrary, all partners have an equal say in running the business.

- *Transferability.* A partner only has the right to transfer the value of her partnership interest, not the interest itself. Thus, a mother who is a partner in a law firm can pass on to her son the value of her partnership interest, not the right to be a partner in the firm (or even the right to work there).

Formation

A partnership is an association of two or more co-owners who carry on a business for profit.[2] Each co-owner is called a **general partner.** Like sole proprietorships, partnerships are easy to form. Although, practically speaking, a partnership should have a written agreement, the UPA does not require anything in the way of forms or filings or agreements. If people act like partners—by sharing management and profits—the law will treat them as such, and if they do not act like partners, then nothing they say or write will make them a partnership. (For examples of a partnership agreement, go to http://www.lectlaw.com/formb.htm or http://www.toolkit.cch.com.)

For example, Kevin and Brenda formed an electrical contracting business. The business did so well that Kevin's first wife, Cynthia, asked the court to increase his child support payments. Kevin argued that, because he and Brenda were partners, he was entitled to only half of the business's profits. Therefore, his child support should not be increased.

Cynthia claimed that Kevin and Brenda were not partners because Kevin had reported all the income from the business on his personal tax return while Brenda had reported none. Kevin had even put "sole proprietorship" in bold letters on the top of his return. No written partnership agreement existed. Kevin and Brenda never informed their accountant that they were a partnership. When Kevin answered interrogatories for Cynthia's lawsuit, he stated that he was sole owner and that Brenda worked for him. Nonetheless, the court held that Brenda and Kevin were partners because Brenda helped manage the business and shared in its profits.[3]

Partnership by Estoppel

Brenda and Kevin wanted to be partners so that they could share the **profits** of their business. In *partnership by estoppel*, non-nonpartners are treated as if they were actually partners and are forced to share *liability*. **Partnership by estoppel applies if:**

- **Participants tell other people that they are partners (even though they are not), or they allow other people to say, without contradiction, that they are partners;**
- **A third party relies on this assertion; and**
- **The third party suffers harm.**

Dr. William Martin was held liable under a theory of partnership by estoppel because: he told a patient that he and Dr. John Maceluch were partners (although they were not); the patient relied on this statement and made appointments to see Dr. Maceluch; and she was harmed by Dr. Maceluch's malpractice. He refused to come to the hospital when she was in labor and, as a result, her child was born with brain damage. Although Dr. Martin was out of the country at the time, he was as liable as if he had committed the malpractice himself.[4]

Taxes

A partnership is not a taxable entity, which means it does not pay taxes itself. All income and losses are passed through to the partners and reported on their personal income tax returns. Corporations, by contrast, are taxable entities and pay income tax

---

[2] UPA §101 (6).
[3] *In Re Marriage of Cynthia Hassiepen,* 269 Ill. App. 3d 559, 646 N.E.2d 1348, 1995 Ill. App. LEXIS 101.
[4] *Haught v. Maceluch,* 681 F.2d 290, 1982 U.S. App. LEXIS 17123 (5th Cir. 1982).

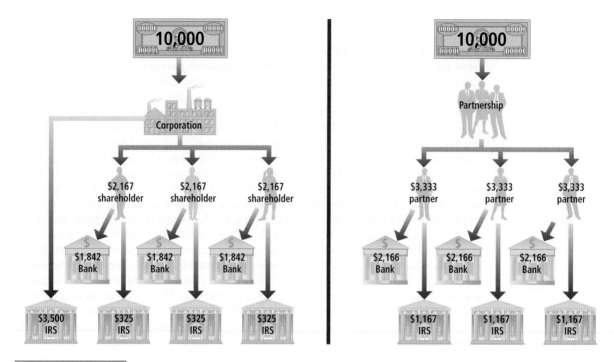

Exhibit 17.1

on their profits. Shareholders must then pay tax on dividends from the corporation. Thus, a dollar is taxed only once before it ends up in a partner's bank account, but twice before it is deposited by a shareholder.

Exhibit 17.1 compares the single taxation of partnerships with the double taxation of corporations. Suppose, as shown in the exhibit, that a corporation and a partnership each receive $10,000 in additional income. The corporation pays tax at a top rate of 35 percent.[5] Thus, the corporation pays $3,500 of the $10,000 in tax. The corporation pays out the remaining $6,500 as a dividend of $2,167 to each of its three shareholders. Then the shareholders are taxed at the special dividend rate of 15 percent, which means they each pay a tax of $325. They are each left with $1,842. Of the initial $10,000, almost 45 percent ($4,475) has gone to the Internal Revenue Service (IRS).

Compare the corporation with a partnership. The partnership itself pays no taxes, so it can pass on $3,333 to each of its partners. At a 35 percent individual rate, they will each pay an income tax of $1,167. As partners, they pocket $2,166, which is $324 more than they could keep as shareholders. Of the partnership's initial $10,000, 35 percent ($3,501) has gone to the IRS—compared with the corporation's 45 percent.

Liability

Under the UPA, **every partner is an agent of the partnership.** Thus, the entire partnership is liable for the act of one partner in, say, signing a contract. **A partnership is also liable for any torts that a partner commits in the ordinary course of the partnership's business.** Thus, if one partner wields a careless calculator, the whole partnership is liable.

---

[5] This is the federal tax rate; most states also levy a corporate tax.

It gets worse. **If a partnership does not have enough assets to pay its debts, creditors may go after the personal property of individual partners, whether or not they were in any way responsible for the debt.** Because partners have *joint and several liability*, creditors can sue the partnership and the partners together or in separate lawsuits or in any combination. The partnership and the partners are all individually liable for the full amount of the debt, but obviously the creditor cannot keep collecting after he has already received the total amount owed. Also note that, even if creditors have a judgment against an individual partner, they cannot go after that partner's assets until all the partnership's assets are exhausted.[6]

Letitia, one of the world's wealthiest people, enters into a partnership with penniless Harry to drill for oil on her estate. While driving on partnership business, Harry crashes into Gus, seriously injuring him. Gus can sue any combination of the partnership, Letitia, and Harry for the full amount, even though Letitia was 2,000 miles away on her Caribbean island when the accident occurred and she had many times cautioned Harry to drive carefully. Even if Gus obtains a judgment against Letitia, however, he cannot recover against her while the partnership still has assets. So, for all practical purposes, he must try to collect first against the partnership. If the partnership is bankrupt and he manages to collect the full amount from Letitia, he cannot then try to recover against Harry.

Management

The management of a partnership can be a significant challenge.

Management Rights

Unless the partnership agrees otherwise, partners share both profits and losses equally, and each partner has an equal right to manage the business.[7] In a large partnership, with hundreds of partners, too many cooks can definitely spoil the firm's profitability. That is why large partnerships are almost always run by one or a few partners who are designated as **managing partners** or **members of the executive committee.** Some firms are run almost dictatorially by the partner who brings in the most business (called a "rainmaker"). Nonetheless, even in relatively autocratic firms, the atmosphere tends to be less hierarchical than in a corporation, where employees are accustomed to the concept of having a boss. Whatever the reality, partners by and large like to think of themselves as being the equal of every other partner.

Management Duties

Partners have a *fiduciary duty* to the partnership. This duty means that:

- *Partners are liable to the partnership for gross negligence or intentional misconduct.*

- *Partners cannot compete with the partnership.* Each partner must turn over to the partnership all earnings from any activity that is related to the partnership's business. Thus, law firms would typically expect a partner to turn over any fees he earned as a director of a company, but he could keep royalties from his novel on scuba diving.

- **A partner may not take an opportunity away from the partnership unless the other partners consent.** If the partnership wants to buy a private plane and

---

[6] UPA §307.

[7] Partnerships have the right to change internal management rules, but they cannot alter the rules governing their relationship with outsiders (such as the rules on liability).

a partner hears of one for sale, she must give the partnership an opportunity to buy it before she purchases it herself.

- **If a partner engages in a conflict of interest, he must turn over to the partnership any profits he earned from that activity.** In the following case, one partner bought partnership property secretly. Is that a conflict of interest?

MARSH V. GENTRY

642 S.W.2d 574, 1982 Ky. LEXIS 315
Supreme Court of Kentucky, 1982

Facts: Tom Gentry and John Marsh were partners in a business that bought and sold racehorses. The partnership paid $155,000 for Champagne Woman, who subsequently had a foal named Excitable Lady. The partners decided to sell Champagne Woman at the annual Keeneland auction, the world's premier thoroughbred horse auction. On the day of the auction, Gentry decided to bid on the horse personally, without telling Marsh. Gentry bought Champagne Woman for $135,000. Later, he told Marsh that someone from California had approached him about buying Excitable Lady. Marsh agreed to the sale. Although he repeatedly asked Gentry the name of the purchaser, Gentry refused to tell him. Not until 11 months later, when Excitable Lady won a race at Churchill Downs, did Marsh learn that Gentry had been the purchaser. Marsh became the Excitable Man.

Issue: Did Gentry violate his fiduciary duty when he bought partnership property without telling his partner?

Excerpts from Justice O'Hara's Decision: Admittedly, at an auction sale, the specific identity of a purchaser cannot be ascertained before the sale, but [Kentucky partnership law] required a full disclosure by Gentry to Marsh that he would be a prospective purchaser. As to the private sale of Excitable Lady, Marsh consented to a sale from the partnership, at a specified price, to the prospective purchaser in California. Even though Marsh obtained the stipulated purchase price, a partner has an absolute right to know when his partner is the purchaser. Partners scrutinize buy-outs by their partners in an entirely different light than an ordinary third party sale. This distinction is vividly made without contradiction when Marsh later indicated that he would not have consented to either sale had he known that Gentry was the purchaser. Under these facts, it is obvious that Gentry failed to disclose all that he knew concerning the sales, including his desire to purchase partnership property.

[P]artners, in their relations with other partners, [must] maintain a higher degree of good faith due to the partnership agreement. The requirement of full disclosure among partners as to partnership business cannot be escaped. Had Gentry made a full disclosure to his partner of his intentions to purchase the partnership property, Marsh would not later be heard to complain of the transaction.

Finally, Gentry maintains that it is an accepted practice at auction sales of thoroughbreds for one partner to secretly bid on partnership stock to accomplish a buy-out. We would emphatically state, however, for the benefit of those engaged in such practices, that where an "accepted business practice" conflicts with existing law, the law, whether statutory or court ordered, is controlling. To hold otherwise would be chaotic. ∎

Terminating a Partnership

A partnership begins with an association of two or more people. Appropriately, the end of a partnership begins with a dissociation. A dissociation occurs when a partner quits.

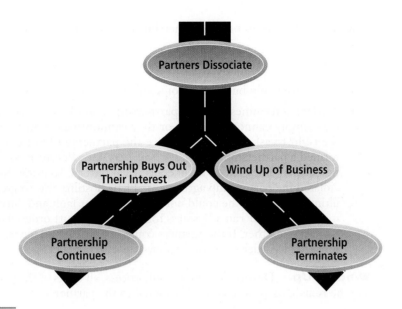

Exhibit 17.2

Dissociation

A partnership is a personal relationship built on trust. All partners are agents for the partnership, and each partner is personally liable for its debts. Under these circumstances, courts will not force someone to remain in a partnership, no matter what the partnership agreement says. **A partner always has the *power* to leave a partnership but may not have the *right*.** In other words, a partner can always dissociate, but she may have to pay damages for any harm that her departure causes.

A dissociation is a fork in the road: **the partnership can either buy out the departing partner(s) and continue in business or wind up the business and terminate the partnership.** Exhibit 17.2 illustrates the dissociation process under the UPA. Most large firms provide in their partnership agreement that, upon dissociation, the business continues. If, however, the partnership chooses to terminate the business, it must follow three steps: dissolution, winding up, and termination.

Three Steps to Termination

Dissolution.   The rules on dissolution depend, in part, on the type of partnership. If the partners have agreed in advance how long the partnership will last, it is a **term partnership.** At the end of the specified term, the partnership automatically ends. Otherwise, it is a **partnership at will,** which means that any of the partners can leave at any time, for any reason.

The UPA provides certain circumstances under which a partnership automatically dissolves (although partners can always overrule the UPA and decide by unanimous vote to continue the partnership). According to the UPA, a partnership dissolves:

- In a partnership at will, when a partner withdraws.
- In a term partnership when:
  - A partner is dissociated and half the remaining partners vote to wind up the partnership business.
  - All the partners agree to dissolve.

- The term expires or the partnership achieves its goal.
- In any partnership when:
  - An event occurs that the partners had agreed would cause dissolution.
  - The partnership business becomes illegal.
  - A court determines that the partnership is unlikely to succeed. If the partners simply cannot get along or they cannot make a profit, any partner has the right to ask a court to dissolve the partnership. For example, two men formed a partnership to buy *The San Juan Star*, Puerto Rico's English-language newspaper. They ended up in court, each bitterly accusing the other of having violated the partnership agreement. Their hostility was so great that the judge ultimately decided he could not tell who was at fault and, furthermore, the two men could never run a business together. The court ordered one partner to buy out the other. If the partners could not agree on a buyout, the judge was prepared to order a sale of the newspaper to outsiders.[8]

Winding Up. During the winding up process, all debts of the partnership are paid, and the remaining proceeds are distributed to the partners.

Termination. After the sometimes lengthy and complex winding up, the actual termination of a partnership is anticlimactic. Termination happens automatically once the winding up is finished. The partnership is not required to do anything official; it can go out of the world even more quietly and simply than it came in.

LIMITED LIABILITY PARTNERSHIPS

A limited liability partnership (LLP) is a type of general partnership that most states now permit. There is a very important distinction, however, between these two forms of organization: **in an LLP, the partners are not liable for the debts of the partnership.**[9] To form an LLP, the partners must file a statement of qualification with state officials. LLPs must also file annual reports. The other attributes of a partnership remain the same. Thus, an LLP is not a taxable entity, and it has the right to choose its duration (i.e., it can, but does not have to, survive the dissociation of a member).

Although an LLP can be much more advantageous for partners than a general partnership, the following case provides an important warning: it is essential to comply with all the technicalities of the LLP statute.

APCAR V. GAUS

2005 Tex. App. LEXIS 379
Court of Appeals of Texas, 2005

Facts: Smith & West, LLP had two partners: Michael L. Gaus and John C. West. The partnership registered in Texas as a limited liability partnership. The Texas statute requires LLPs to renew their registrations each year, but Smith & West never did so. Four years after its initial registration, the partnership entered into a lease with MF Partners ▼

---

[8] *Nemazee Capital Corp. v. Angulo Capital Corp.*, 1996 U.S. Dist. LEXIS 10750 (S. Dist. NY, 1996).
[9] UPA §306(c).

(which subsequently assigned the lease to Apcar). Three years into the lease, Smith & West stopped paying rent and abandoned the premises. Apcar filed suit against the two partners individually and against the partnership. Gaus, West, and Apcar each filed a motion for summary judgment. The trial court granted Gaus and West's motions while denying Apcar's.

Issue: Were Gaus and West personally liable for payments due under Smith & West's lease?

Excerpts from Justice McCall's Decision: [The Texas Limited Liability Partnership statute] provides:

> An initial application filed under this subsection and registered by the secretary of state expires one year after the date of registration or later effective date unless earlier withdrawn or revoked or unless renewed.

Smith & West did not file a renewal application before the expiration date. Therefore, its status as a registered limited liability partnership expired [one year after the initial filing]. Smith & West entered into the lease three years after its status as a registered limited liability partnership expired.

Smith & West was not a registered limited liability partnership when it incurred the lease obligations. Thus, the clear language [of the statute] supports Apcar's position that Gaus and West are not protected from individual liability for the lease obligations.

Gaus and West argue that a limited liability partnership is not required to strictly comply with the registration requirements for its partners to be protected from individual liability. [But the statute] does not contain a "substantial compliance" section, nor does it contain a grace period for filing a renewal application. We hold that a partnership must be in compliance with the registration requirements for its partners to receive protection from individual liability. Smith & West was not a registered limited liability partnership when it incurred the lease obligations; therefore, Gaus and West are not protected from individual liability for the lease obligations.

The judgment of the trial court is reversed, and this cause is remanded for further proceedings consistent with this opinion. ■

PROFESSIONAL CORPORATIONS

Most states now allow professionals to incorporate, but in a special way. These organizations are called "professional corporations" or "PCs." **In many states, PCs provide more liability protection than a partnership.** If a member of a PC commits malpractice, the corporation's assets are at risk, but not the personal assets of the innocent members. If Drs. Sharp, Payne, and Graves form a *partnership*, all the partners will be personally liable when Dr. Payne accidentally leaves her scalpel inside a patient. If the three doctors have formed a *PC* instead, Dr. Payne's Aspen condo and the assets of the PC will be at risk, but not the personal assets of the two other doctors.

Generally, the shareholders of a PC are not personally liable for the contract debts of the organization, such as leases or bank loans. Thus, if Sharp, Payne & Graves, P.C. is unable to pay its rent, the landlord cannot recover from the personal assets of any of the doctors. As partners, the doctors would be personally liable.

PCs have some limitations. First, all shareholders of the corporation must be members of the same profession. For Sharp, Payne & Graves, P.C., that means all shareholders must be licensed physicians. Other valued employees cannot own stock. Second, like other corporations, the required legal technicalities for forming and maintaining a PC are expensive and time-consuming. Third, tax issues can be complicated. A PC is a separate taxable entity, like any other corporation. It must pay tax on its profits, and then its shareholders pay tax on any dividends they receive. *Salaries*, however, are deductible from firm profits. Thus, the PC can avoid taxes on its profits by paying out all profits as salary. But any profits remaining in firm coffers *at the end of the year* are taxable. To avoid tax, PCs must be careful to calculate their profits accurately and pay them out before year's end. This chore can be time-consuming, and any error may cause unnecessary tax liability.

LIMITED PARTNERSHIPS AND LIMITED LIABILITY LIMITED PARTNERSHIPS

The owners of the Montreal Expos asked investment banker Jacques Menard to find a buyer for the baseball team. Instead, he found 11 other people to help him buy the team. They formed a limited partnership, and each purchaser invested between $1 million and $7 million. During their first year of ownership, the Expos lost nearly $5 million and their final 14 home games, finishing in the cellar of their division. Given this dismal showing, management had no choice but to fire the popular team manager. Then a concrete beam in the team's stadium collapsed.

Fortunately, the owners had formed a limited partnership. Limited partnerships and general partnerships have similar names but, like many siblings, they operate very differently. Here are the major differences between these two types of organizations.

Structure

General partnerships have only *general* partners. Limited partnerships have two types of partners—*limited* partners and *general* partners. A limited partnership must have at least one of each.

Liability

All the partners in a general partnership are *personally* liable for the debts of the partnership. **In a limited partnership, however, the limited partners are not *personally* liable.** The limited partners are like corporate shareholders—they risk only their investment in the partnership (which is called their "capital contribution"). No matter how much money the Expos lost, creditors could not take the personal property of the limited partners.

General partners are personally liable for the debts of a limited partnership. To avoid this liability, most general partners are, in fact, corporations. Thus, Claude Brochu, the Expos' general manager, could form a corporation—Brochu, Inc.—to serve as general partner. Then, only the assets of the corporation, not Brochu's personal assets, would be at risk.

The revised version of the Uniform Limited Partnership Act, however, permits a limited partnership, in its certificate of formation, simply to declare itself a *limited liability* limited partnership.[10] **In a limited liability limited partnership, the general partner is not personally liable for the debts of the partnership.** This provision effectively removes the major disadvantage of limited partnerships. Although, at this writing, fewer than 10 states have actually passed the revised version of the Uniform Limited Partnership Act, this revision would seem to indicate the trend for the future.

Taxes

Limited partnerships, like general partnerships, are not taxable entities. Income is taxed only once before landing in a partner's pocket.

---

[10] ULPA §102(9).

Formation

General partnerships can be formed very casually, sometimes without the partners even being aware of it. Not so for limited partnerships: the general partners must file a **certificate of limited partnership** with their Secretary of State. Although most limited partnerships do have a partnership agreement, it is not required. (A sample limited partnership agreement is available at http://www.worldlawdirect.com/builddoc.php by clicking on "Build a Document.")

Management

General partners have the right to manage a limited partnership. Limited partners are essentially passive investors with few management rights beyond the right to be informed about the partnership business. Limited partnership agreements can, however, expand the rights of limited partners. These agreements, for example, often permit a substantial majority (e.g., two-thirds) of the limited partners to remove a general partner. In any event, when general partnerships grow large, management becomes difficult. But because limited partners are not allowed to manage, a limited partnership can handle a very large number of partners.

Transfer of Ownership

As is the case with a general partnership, limited partners always have the right to transfer the value of their partnership interest, but they can only sell or give away the interest itself if the partnership agreement permits. Thus, if Sadie is a limited partner in the Expos but decides to invest in basketball instead, she does not have the automatic right to sell her limited partnership interest to Pedro. Although she could sell Pedro the right to receive profit distributions from the Expos, he would not be a limited partner, with the right to vote in meetings.

Duration

Unless the partnership agreement provides otherwise, limited partnerships enjoy perpetual existence—they continue even as partners come and go.

Although a limited partnership structure protected the Expos's owners from liability, it did not solve the team's problems on the ball field or at the bank. Perhaps the team's move to Washington, D.C. (and its transformation into the Washington Nationals) will bring athletic and financial success.

CORPORATIONS

Although the concept of a corporation is very old—it began with the Greeks and spread from them through the Romans into English law—corporations were traditionally viewed with deep suspicion. What were shareholders doing that they needed limited liability? Why did they have to cower behind a corporate shield? For this reason, shareholders originally had to obtain special permission to form a corporation. In England, corporations could be created only by special charter from the king or,

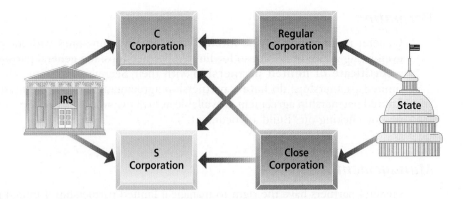

Exhibit 17.3
Both a regular and a close corporation can be either a C or an S corporation.

later, from Parliament. But with the advent of the Industrial Revolution, large-scale manufacturing enterprises needed huge amounts of capital from investors who were not involved in management and did not want to be personally liable for the debts of an organization that they were not managing. In 1811, New York became the first jurisdiction in the United States to permit routine incorporation.[11]

State laws regulate corporations, but federal statutes determine their tax status. Many states treat small corporations differently and even give them a different name: close corporations. The federal tax code also provides more favorable tax treatment to some small corporations and calls them S corporations. But the two sets of statutes are completely independent. Thus, a close corporation or a regular (nonclose) corporation may or may not be an S corporation. Exhibit 17.3 illustrates the difference between state and IRS regulation of corporations.

Corporations in General

When Judy George was a young child, her parents started a plating business using a process her father had invented. Like many entrepreneurs, her parents devoted so much time and energy to this new project that they were rarely at home. Feeling abandoned by her parents, George became obsessed with her surroundings. If she could make her room just the way she wanted it, she would feel safe. As she put it, "Design was a way of fulfilling my own personal fantasy." She also vowed that one day she would start her own business to make money and create beautiful designs. George realized her dream when she started Domain, an upscale, European-style chain of furniture stores.

George's lawyer suggested that she incorporate Domain. He explained that a corporation would offer the protection of limited liability. If Domain flopped and could not pay its bills, George and her backers would lose their investment in the company but not their other assets.

---

[11] *An Act Relative to Incorporation for Manufacturing Purpose,* 1811 N.Y. Laws ch. 67, §111.

He also explained that limited liability does not protect against all debts. Individuals are always responsible for their own acts. If a Domain employee was in an accident while driving a company van, Domain would be liable for any harm to the other driver, but its shareholders would not be personally liable. If George herself crashed the van, Domain would be liable and *so would George*. If Domain did not pay the judgment, George would have to, from her personal assets if necessary. A corporation protects managers and investors from personal liability for the debts of the corporation and the actions of others but not against personal negligence (or other torts and crimes).

Corporations have other advantages besides limited liability. They provide flexibility for enterprises small (with one owner) and large (thousands of shareholders). For example, partnership interests are not transferable without the permission of the other partners, whereas corporate stock can be easily bought and sold. Further, when a sole proprietor dies, legally so does the business. But corporations have perpetual existence: they can continue without their founders.

There are two major disadvantages of a corporation: logistics and taxes. Corporations require substantial expense and effort to create and operate. Because corporations are taxable entities, they must pay taxes and file returns. The cost of establishing a corporation may exceed $1,000 in legal and filing fees, not to mention the cost of the annual filings that states require. Corporations must also hold annual meetings for both shareholders and directors. Minutes of these meetings must be kept indefinitely in the company minute book.

Judy George knew that she needed at least $3 million to get Domain up and running. She could not borrow that much money, so she needed to sell stock. She chose the corporate form of organization because, at the time she formed Domain, limited liability companies (LLCs) were not as well known or as well understood by potential investors as they are now. (LLCs are discussed later in this chapter.)

Close Corporations

Although most entrepreneurs would now choose to form an LLC rather than a close corporation, it is important to understand the legal contours of close corporations simply because so many still exist. Originally, the terms "close corporation" and "closely held corporation" referred simply to a company whose stock was not publicly traded on a stock exchange (in other words, a "privately held" company). Most close corporations are small, although some privately held corporations, such as Hallmark Cards, Inc., and Mars, Inc. (maker of Mars candy bars), are huge. Beginning in New York in 1948, some states have amended their corporation statutes to make special provisions for entrepreneurs. In some cases, a corporation must affirmatively elect to be treated as a close corporation; in others, any corporation can take advantage of these special provisions. Now when lawyers refer to close corporations, they usually mean not merely a privately held company, but one that has taken advantage of the close corporation provisions of its state code.

Although the provisions of close corporation statutes vary from state to state, they tend to have certain common themes:

- **Protection of Minority Shareholders.** As there is no public market for the stock of a close corporation, a minority shareholder who is being mistreated by the majority cannot simply sell his shares and depart. Therefore, close corporation statutes often provide some protection for minority shareholders. For example, the charter of a close corporation could require a unanimous vote of all shareholders to choose officers, set salaries, or pay dividends. It could grant each shareholder veto power over all important corporate decisions.

- **Transfer Restrictions.** The shareholders of a close corporation often need to work closely together in the management of the company. Therefore, statutes often typically permit the corporation to require that a shareholder first offer shares to the other owners before selling them to an outsider. In that way, the remaining shareholders have some control over who their new co-owners will be.

- **Flexibility.** Close corporations can typically operate without a board of directors, a formal set of bylaws, or annual shareholder meetings.

- **Dispute Resolution.** The shareholders are allowed to agree in advance that any one of them can dissolve the corporation if some particular event occurs or, if they choose, for any reason at all. If the shareholders are in a stalemate, the problem can be solved by dissolving the corporation. Even without such an agreement, a shareholder can ask a court to dissolve a close corporation if the other owners behave "oppressively" or "unfairly."

S CORPORATIONS

Although entrepreneurs are often optimistic about the likely success of their new enterprise, in truth, the majority of new businesses lose money in their early years. Congress created S corporations (aka "S corps") to encourage entrepreneurship by offering tax breaks. The name "S corporation" comes from the provision of the Internal Revenue Code that created this form of organization.[12] **Shareholders of S corps have both the limited liability of a corporation and the tax status of a partnership.** Like a partnership, an S corp is not a taxable entity—all the company's profits and losses pass through to the shareholders, who pay tax at their individual rates. It avoids the double taxation of a regular corporation (called a "C corporation"). If, as is often the case, the startup loses money, investors can deduct these losses against their other income.

S corps do face some major restrictions:

- There can be only one class of stock (although voting rights can vary within the class).

- There can be only 100 shareholders.

- Shareholders must be individuals, estates, charities, pension funds, or trusts, not partnerships or corporations.

- Shareholders must be citizens or residents of the United States, not nonresident aliens.

- All shareholders must agree that the company should be an S corporation.

Although *most* states follow the federal lead on S corporations, a small number treat an S corp like a regular C corporation. In these states, the companies must pay state corporate tax.

These rules governing S corps can be burdensome. Therefore, most companies do not remain S corps forever, and many entrepreneurs choose an LLC over an S corp. However, S corps do have some advantages. The rules governing LLCs are not

---

[12] 26 U.S.C. §1361.

as established as those for S corps. Thus, the process of organizing an LLC is less standardized and more expensive. Also, LLC statutes have changed rapidly and can vary dramatically from state to state. It is perhaps for these reasons that S corps are the single most popular choice of corporate entity. There are 3.2 million of them, with total assets that exceed $2 trillion. In contrast, there are only about 1 million LLCs.

LIMITED LIABILITY COMPANIES

You may be thinking that there are already as many different forms of organization as any entrepreneur could possibly need, but, as you have seen, none of them is perfect. In a continuing search for earthly perfection, states now permit limited liability companies (LLCs). **An LLC offers the limited liability of a corporation and the tax status of a partnership without the disadvantages of an S corporation.**

An LLC is an extremely useful form of organization increasingly favored by entrepreneurs. It is not, however, as simple as it perhaps should be. Owing to a complex history that involves painful interaction between IRS regulations and state laws (the details of which we will spare you), the specific provisions of state laws vary greatly. To add to the difficulty, there are few court decisions interpreting LLC statutes and these few cases sometimes disagree. An effort to remedy this confusion—the Uniform Limited Liability Company Act—has not at this point been widely accepted and, in fact, has been heavily criticized. Thus, we can only discuss general trends in state laws. Before forming an LLC, you should carefully review the laws in your particular state.

Formation

To organize an LLC, you generally need two documents: a charter and an operating agreement. The charter is short, containing basic information such as name and address. It must be filed with the secretary of state in your jurisdiction. An operating agreement sets out the rights and obligations of the owners, called members. If an LLC does not adopt its own operating agreement, most LLC statutes provide a default option. However, these standardized provisions are usually not what members would choose if they thought about it. Therefore, it is often better for an LLC to prepare its own personalized operating agreement. Although some states do not require an operating agreement, lawyers recommend them as a way to avoid disputes. A sample agreement sample is shown at http://www.tannedfeet.com by clicking on "Legal Forms" and "Limited Liability Company Operating Agreement."

Limited Liability

As in a corporation, members are not personally liable for debts of the company. They risk only their investment, just as they would if they were shareholders of a corporation. Are the members of an LLC liable in the following case? You be the judge.

You Be the Judge

RIDGAWAY V. SILK

2004 Conn. Super. LEXIS 548
Superior Court of Connecticut, 2004

Facts: Norman Costello and Joseph Ruggiero were members of Silk, LLC, the owner of Silk Stockings and Cafe Del Mar, which was a bar and adult entertainment nightclub in Groton, Connecticut. Anthony Sulls went drinking there one night—drinking heavily. Although he was obviously drunk, employees at Silk Stockings continued to serve him. Giordano and Costello were working there that night. They both greeted customers (who numbered in the hundreds), supervised employees, and performed "other PR work." When Sulls left the nightclub at 1:45 AM with two friends, he drove off the highway at high speed, killing himself and one of his passengers, William Ridgaway, Jr.

Ridgaway's estate sued Costello and Giordano personally. The defendants filed a motion for summary judgment seeking dismissal of the complaint.

You Be the Judge: **Are Costello and Giordano personally liable to Ridgaway's estate?**

Argument for Costello and Giordano: The defendants did not own Silk Stockings, they were simply members of an LLC that owned the nightclub. The whole point of an LLC is to protect members against personal liability. The assets of Silk, LLC are at risk, but not the personal assets of Costello and Giordano.

Argument for Ridgaway's estate: The defendants are not liable for being *members* of Silk, LLC, they are liable for their own misdeeds as *employees* of the LLC. They were both present at Silk Stockings on the night in question, meeting and greeting customers and supervising employees. It is possible that they might actually have served drinks to Sulls, but in any event they did not adequately supervise and train their employees so as to prevent them from serving alcohol to someone who was clearly drunk. The world would be an intolerable place to live if employees were free to be as careless as they wished, knowing that they were not liable because they were members of an LLC. ●

Tax Status

As in a partnership, income flows through the company to the individual members, avoiding the double taxation of a corporation.

Flexibility

Unlike S corporations, LLCs can have members that are corporations, partnerships, or nonresident aliens. LLCs can also have different classes of stock. Unlike corporations, LLCs are not required to hold annual meetings or maintain a minute book.

Standard Forms

Corporations are so familiar that the standard documents (such as a charter, bylaws, and shareholder agreement) are well established and widely available. Lawyers can form a corporation easily, and the Internet offers a host of free forms. This is not the case with LLCs. As yet, there are no standard forms to make the formation of an LLC both easy and inexpensive. With state laws varying so widely, standard forms may even be dangerous.

Transferability of Interests

In corporations, shareholders can generally sell or give their shares to whomever they want. In partnerships, partners generally must obtain the unanimous approval of the other partners before transferring their partnership. In keeping with the flexible approach of LLCs, the members have a choice. If they want, the operating agreement can give them the right to transfer their interests freely to anyone. However, if the operating agreement is silent on this issue, then typically the members of the LLC must obtain the unanimous permission of the remaining members before transferring their ownership rights.

Duration

It used to be that LLCs automatically dissolved upon the withdrawal of a member (owing to, for example, death, resignation, or bankruptcy). The current trend in state laws, however, is to permit an LLC to continue in operation even after a member withdraws. Unless the operating agreement provides otherwise, the LLC must usually pay the departing member the value of her interest.

Going Public

Once an LLC goes public, it loses its favorable tax status and is taxed as a corporation, not a partnership.[13] Thus, there is no real advantage to using the LLC form of organization for a publicly traded company. And there are some disadvantages: unlike corporations, LLCs do not enjoy a well-established set of statutory and case law that is relatively consistent across the many states. For this reason, it may well turn out that most privately held companies begin as LLCs but change to corporations when they go public.

Changing Forms

Some companies that are now corporations might prefer to be LLCs. However, the IRS would consider this change to be a sale of the corporate assets and would levy a tax on the value of these assets. For this reason, few corporations have made the change. However, switching from a partnership to an LLC or from an LLC to a corporation is not considered a sale and does not have the same adverse tax impact.

JOINT VENTURES

NEWS*worthy* Ckrush Entertainment, Inc. announced today that it has entered into a joint venture with Identity Films, LLC. Ckrush and Identity formed "Identity Films & Company, LLC" for the purpose of, among other things, developing, financing, and producing feature films. Ckrush is obligated to contribute overhead financing to the joint venture and it is anticipated that Identity will contribute approximately twelve film properties in various stages of development. Lisa Fielding and Anthony Mastromauro, of Identity Films, will be responsible for the

---

13 26 U.S.C. §7704.

day-to-day management of the joint venture. Jeremy Dallow and Jim DiLorenzo of Ckrush Entertainment will serve as officers of the joint venture along with Fielding and Mastromauro.

"We believe that the joint venture and the formation of Identity Films & Company is a real milestone for Ckrush Entertainment, Inc. We feel that this joint venture gives Ckrush Entertainment the opportunity to participate in a number of quality film projects along-side Lisa Fielding and Anthony Mastromauro. It is our position that the slate of properties currently in development and production are outstanding. We further feel that the joint venture is positioned to execute on these properties and can result in the growth of Identity Films & Company in the film business," said Jim DiLorenzo, President of Ckrush Entertainment.

"We are thrilled beyond our expectations to be in business with Ckrush. We have the opportunity to not only work with people we respect but to truly grow our company into a presence in the film business. We're coming into this joint venture knowing that pro-ducing award-winning films will be the first item on our agenda. Fortune has smiled on Identity Films," said Lisa Fielding of Identity Films, LLC.[14] ◆

This newspaper article refers to a joint venture between Identity Films and Ckrush Entertainment. **What is the difference in meaning? A joint venture is a partner-ship for a limited purpose.** Ckrush and Identity are not merging; they are simply working together on some movies. Each organization retains its own identity (so to speak). If they had joined in a full-scale partnership, both parties would be bound by contracts that either of them signed. In a joint venture, only contracts relating to the limited purpose are binding on both. If Ckrush Entertainment signed a contract with Chris Rock to make a boxing movie, Identity Films would not be liable on that con-tract. But if the joint venture enters into a contract with Jennifer Aniston to star in a movie, both Ckrush and Identity would be liable. Nonprofit enterprises do not qualify as joint ventures—the purpose, however limited, must include making a profit.

OTHER FORMS OF ORGANIZATION

When starting a business, most entrepreneurs choose one of the forms of organization that we have discussed. There are, however, an assortment of other, less common forms that we must briefly cover—not so much because you are likely to use one of them yourself, but so that you will know what they are if you come across them in your business life or in reading the newspaper.

Business Trusts

A business trust is an unincorporated association run by trustees for the benefit of investors (who are called "beneficiaries"). This arrangement sounds like an unfavor-able one for investors. They buy certificates in the trust, just as shareholders buy stock in a corporation, but they have fewer rights than shareholders. They do not elect the trustees; if a trustee resigns or dies, the other trustees choose a replacement. The trustees can take almost any action without approval of the investors and can issue an

---

14 "Ckrush Entertainment, Inc. Closes on Joint Venture with Identity Films," *Business Wire,* July 5, 2005.

unlimited number of shares. The beneficiaries are not liable for the debts of the trust. Theoretically, the trustees are liable, but the trust agreement usually protects them from liability.

Ordinary businesses usually do not consider this form of organization, but it does make sense for mutual funds and other investment management companies. Investors buy shares or certificates in the trust. The trustees, who are investment experts, invest the funds, paying out any returns to the investors, minus management fees. If investors are unhappy with a fund's performance, they do not have the right to vote out the trustees, but they can sell their shares and take their money elsewhere. It would be difficult to run an investment company if the beneficiaries were always changing trustees and investment style. A mutual fund is the one type of investment where it makes sense that investors cannot replace trustees.

Cooperatives

Cooperatives are groups of individuals or businesses that join together to gain the advantages of volume purchases or sales. Profits are distributed to members using whatever formula they choose. Unincorporated cooperatives are generally subject to partnership law; incorporated cooperatives are governed by corporation law.

For example, the Harvard Cooperative Society is the oldest retail cooperative in the country. Founded in 1882 by Harvard students aiming to undercut price-gouging local merchants, the Coop (rhymes with "hoop") originally sold just textbooks and firewood. It has long since outgrown its first location—a five-foot shelf in a local tobacco store. Now the Coop is a landmark in Harvard Square, selling textbooks, clothing, and dorm supplies. Owned by its members, who are primarily students and alumni of Harvard and MIT, its sales exceed $40 million a year.

Franchises

This chapter has presented an overview of the various forms of organization. Franchises are not, strictly speaking, a separate form of organization. They are included here because they represent an important option for entrepreneurs. In the United States, 1 in 12 small businesses is a franchise. Franchises generate sales of close to $1 trillion each year and provide jobs for more than eight million people. Well-known franchises include Dunkin' Donuts, Midas Muffler, McDonald's, and Mail Boxes, Etc. Most franchisors and franchisees are corporations, although they could legally choose to be any of the forms discussed in this chapter.

Buying a franchise is a compromise between starting one's own business as an entrepreneur and working for someone else as an employee. Franchisees are free to choose which franchise to buy, where to locate it, and how to staff it. But they are not completely on their own. They are buying an established business with all the kinks worked out. In case the owner has never boiled water before, the McDonald's operations manual explains everything from how to set the temperature controls on the stove, to the number of seconds that fries must cook, to the length of time they can be held in the rack before being discarded. And a well-known name like McDonald's or Mrs. Fields ought, by itself, to bring customers through the door.

There is, however, a fine line between being helpful and being oppressive. Franchisees sometimes complain that franchisor control is too tight—tips on cooking fries might be appreciated, but rules on how often to sweep the floor are not. Sometimes franchisors, in their zeal to maintain standards, prohibit innovation that appeals to regional tastes. Just because spicy biscuits are not popular in New England does not mean they should be banned in the South.

Franchises can be very costly to acquire, anywhere from several thousand dollars to several million. That fee is usually payable up front, whether or not a cookie or burger is ever sold. On top of the up-front fee, franchisees also pay an annual fee that is a percentage of *gross sales revenues,* not *profit.* Sometimes the fee seems to eat up all the profits. Franchisees also complain when they are forced to buy supplies from headquarters. In theory, the franchisors can purchase hamburger meat and paper plates more cheaply in bulk. On the other hand, the franchisees are a captive audience, and they sometimes allege that headquarters has little incentive to keep prices low. Franchisees also grumble when they are forced to contribute to expensive "co-op advertising" that benefits all the outlets in the region. The following article illustrates the good news—and bad—about buying a franchise.

NEWS*worthy*

Bellingham, Mass. Stephen Gurwitz is proud that his Hilltop Farms convenience store has long been a fixture here in this small town on the Rhode Island border. His grandfather, Milton Gurwitz, opened the little roadside building in 1955 as a place to sell milk and eggs from his farm. His father, Gary Gurwitz, added a deli counter. Four years ago, Stephen converted half the store to a Subway fast-food franchise.

Mr. Gurwitz, 32, said he felt no shame at trading in the old deli counter for a nationally promoted name and formulaic sandwiches that taste the same as their Subway counterparts around the world. For Mr. Gurwitz, joining Subway was a welcome respite from the myriad decisions he has to make in running the convenience store. "They give you the operations manual, which is as thick as the New York City telephone book, and it tells you within a millimeter how thick to slice the onions," said Mr. Gurwitz.

Indeed, Mr. Gurwitz discovered that many issues were no longer his sole responsibility. "Someone stubs his toe in the store, you call the Subway legal department," he said. "How many convenience stores have a legal department?" Research and development, pricing and menus—all are handled for him. The Subway brand also brings name recognition. Mr. Gurwitz credits it with increasing the traffic in his store by about 1,000 customers a week—roughly a 10 percent gain—more than making up for the 11.5 percent of revenues from the sandwich operation he pays to headquarters.

It seems enticing, but Susan P. Kezios learned to be wary of such a deal. She put all her money into a franchise operation of VR Business Brokers in Chicago Heights, Illinois. Although she managed to keep the doors open, she struggled with what she calls "the flaws in the system." They began with the contract, which usually imposes an iron-clad form with no exceptions for a franchisee's particular needs.

"These franchise contracts are often legal works of art with franchisor attorneys determining every possible scenario during the entire length of time you'll own the franchise, to the franchisor's benefit—not yours," she said. When the contract comes up for renewal, the terms often change. "If they were taking a 5 percent royalty, they might change it to 8 percent," she said. Some franchisors force their licensees to purchase from certain vendors at inflated prices. They can open franchise units close by, intensifying competition. Franchisees often find it difficult to sell their businesses if they want out, or to open another business in the same industry because of "noncompete" agreements.

Although Subway allowed Mr. Gurwitz to stray from the standard menu by offering Willow Tree Farms chicken salad, a popular local brand, he has few other opportunities to personalize the business. Still, he said, that is all the sovereignty he needs. "If you're a free-spirited person and want to do it your own way," he advised, "you don't buy a franchise."[15] ◆

---

[15] Julie Flaherty, "By the Book: Individuality vs. Franchising; Trading Spark of Creativity for the Safety of Numbers," *The New York Times,* Feb. 17, 2001, sec. C, p. 1. Copyright (c) 2001 by The New York Times Co. Reprinted by permission.

Although franchises were once relatively unregulated, the states and the federal government have dramatically increased their supervision and regulation of these businesses. The FTC requires that, at least 10 business days prior to the sale, franchisors must give prospective franchisees an **offering circular.** This circular must comply either with FTC rules or with the provisions of the Uniform Franchise Offering Circular (UFOC) Guidelines of the North American Securities Administrators' Association (available at http://www.nasaa.org/). Most franchisors choose to comply with the UFOC guidelines, because they are accepted by more states than the FTC rules. The circular must include the following information:

- Any litigation against the company
- Whether it has gone through bankruptcy proceedings in the prior 10 years
- All fees
- Estimates of the required initial investment
- What goods must be purchased from the franchisor
- The number of franchisees in operation
- How many franchisees have gone out of business in the prior three years

The offering circular must also contain audited financial statements and a sample set of the contracts that a franchisee is expected to sign.

The purpose of the offering circular is to ensure that the franchisor discloses all relevant facts. It is not a guarantee of quality. Under UFOC guidelines, the following statement must appear on the cover page of the offering circular:

> Registration of this franchise by a state does not mean that the state recommends it or has verified the information in this offering circular. If you learn that anything in the offering circular is untrue, contact the Federal Trade Commission and (State or Provincial authority).

Suppose you obtain an offering circular for "Shrinking Cats," a franchise that offers psychiatric services for neurotic felines. The company has lost money on all the outlets it operates itself; it has sold only three franchises, two of which have gone out of business; and all the required contracts are ridiculously favorable to the franchisor. Nevertheless, the FTC will still permit sales as long as the franchisor discloses all the information required in the offering circular. Nor will the FTC investigate to make sure that the information is accurate. After the fact, if the FTC discovers the franchisor has violated the rules, it may sue on your behalf. (You do not have the right to bring suit personally against someone who violates the FTC franchise rules.)

As we have seen, some states also regulate the sale of franchises. They often require franchisors to register and to provide offering circulars, but the franchisor can use the UFOC guidelines to meet the requirements of both the state and the FTC. The states that do regulate franchisors are often stricter than the FTC. Some states, for instance, require franchisors to file all advertisements ahead of time and meet minimum capital requirements. State laws may also prohibit unfair terms in the franchising contract. Unlike FTC rules, some states permit franchisees themselves to sue for damages or rescission anyone who violates franchise laws.

In the following case, a franchisee filed suit under the Illinois Franchise Disclosure Act.

BIXBY'S FOOD SYSTEMS, INC. V. MCKAY

193 F. Supp. 2d 1053, 2002 U.S. Dist. LEXIS 5243
United States District Court for the Northern District of Illinois, 2002

Fact: Phillip McKay was a dentist, and his wife, Jan, worked for Ameritech. They were looking for a business to buy when a friend told them about Bixby's, a franchisor of bagel restaurants. This same friend introduced them to Ken Miyamoto, Bixby's president.

Miyamoto gave the McKays a franchise offering circular (FOC), which stated that the initial investment for a franchise, including the initial franchise fee, would be between $143,000 and $198,000. It also stated that, with a store space of between 1,400 and 2,200 square feet, each franchise would have annual sales of $625,000 and would earn an annual profit of $139,450. Miyamoto told the McKays that the FOC figures were conservative, that "existing bagel stores were doing annual sales in excess of $1 million," and that "Bixby's franchises would exceed these revenue figures."

The McKays purchased the right to own a Bixby's franchise. They found a 2,000-square-foot space for lease, but Miyamoto urged them repeatedly to lease an additional space next door, for a total of more than 3,000 square feet. Miyamoto assured them that the site would bring in annual revenues in excess of $1 million. No other Bixby's restaurant nationwide was as large as 3,000 square feet.

At a reception that the McKays attended for existing and prospective Bixby's franchisees, Miyamoto told the guests that the company had 340 franchise agreements. In fact, the company had no more than 15 such agreements. Miyamoto was also quoted in a company newsletter as stating that Bixby's had 340 signed and paid-for agreements, which represented "a $68 million vote of confidence."

The McKays executed a lease for the 3,000-square-foot space and proceeded to renovate the property. Their initial investment was more than $400,000, significantly higher than the estimated investment of between $143,000 and $198,000 in the FOC. Miyamoto assured them that the FOC was accurate, that their costs were normal, and that their sales would cover their costs. Miyamoto knew that these statements were false.

After the McKays opened their store, monthly sales ranged from $25,000 to $30,000, far less than Miyamoto had predicted. Because the McKays fell behind on their payments, Bixby's terminated their franchise agreement after only eight months.

Bixby's sued the McKays for violating the franchise agreement. The McKays counter-claimed against Bixby's, alleging that the company had violated the Illinois Franchise Disclosure Act (IFDA). They then filed a motion for summary judgment.

Issue: Did Bixby's violate the Illinois Franchise Disclosure Act?

Excerpts from Judge Nolan's Decision: The McKays claim that Miyamoto violated the IFDA by providing false information with respect to the franchise sale. The McKays relied on these representations when they executed their franchise agreement.

To be actionable under the IFDA, the misrepresentation must be an untrue statement of a material fact. A material fact is one in which a buyer would have acted differently knowing the information. In other words, the fact must be essential to the transaction between the parties.

A statement expressing an opinion or that relates to future or contingent events rather than to present facts, however, ordinarily does not constitute an actionable misrepresentation under Illinois law. For example, predictions of future sales or profitability are not considered representations of preexisting material facts.

The McKays have not shown that, contrary to the general rule, Miyamoto's statements about future events, costs, and profitability are actionable misrepresentations under the IFDA, so summary judgment cannot be granted based upon those statements.

The McKays have, however, conclusively shown that Miyamoto falsely claimed that Bixby's had 340 signed and paid-for agreements when no more than fifteen agreements had in fact been executed. Miyamoto's untrue statement was material to the McKays' decision to execute the Bixby's franchise agreement a week later. [T]herefore summary judgment should be granted as to the McKays' claim under the IFDA. ■

Chapter Conclusion

The process of starting a business is immensely time-consuming. Eighteen-hour days are the norm. Not surprisingly, entrepreneurs are sometimes reluctant to spend their valuable time on legal issues that, after all, do not contribute directly to the bottom line. No customer buys more biscuits because the franchise is a limited liability company instead of a corporation. Wise entrepreneurs know, however, that careful attention to legal issues is an essential component of success. The form of organization affects everything from taxes to liability to management control. The idea for the business may come first, but legal considerations occupy a close second place.

Chapter Review

	Separate Taxable Entity	Personal Liability for Owners	Ease of Formation	Transferable Interests (Easily Bought and Sold)	Perpetual Existence	Other Features
Sole Proprietorship	No	Yes	Very easy	No, can only sell entire business	No	
General Partnership	No	Yes	Easy	No	Depends on the partnership agreement	Management can be difficult.
Limited Liability Partnership	No	No	Difficult	No	Depends on the partnership agreement	
Professional Corporation	Yes	No	Difficult	Shareholders must all be members of same profession	Yes, as long as it has shareholders	Complex tax issues.
Limited Partnership	No	Yes, for general partner No, for limited partners	Difficult	Yes (for limited partners), if partnership agreement permits	Yes	
Limited Liability Limited Partnership	No	No	Difficult	Yes (for limited partners), if partnership agreement permits	Yes	
Corporation	Yes	No	Difficult	Yes	Yes	

(Continued)

(Continued)

	Separate Taxable Entity	Personal Liability for Owners	Ease of Formation	Transferable Interests (Easily Bought and Sold)	Perpetual Existence	Other Features
Close Corporation	Yes, for C corporation No, for S corporation	No	Difficult	Transfer restrictions	Yes	Protection of minority shareholders. No board of directors required.
S Corporation	No	No	Difficult	Transfer restrictions	Yes	Only 100 shareholders. Only one class of stock. Shareholders must be individuals, estates, trusts, charities, or pension funds and be citizens or residents of the United States. All shareholders must agree to S status.
Limited Liability Company	No	No	Difficult	Yes, if the operating agreement permits	Varies by state, but generally, yes	No limit on the number of shareholders, the number of classes of stock, or the type of shareholder.
Joint Venture	No	Yes	Easy	No	No	Partnership for a limited purpose.
Business Trust	Yes	No	Difficult	Yes	Yes	Most commonly used by mutual funds and other investment companies.
Cooperative	All these issues depend on the form of organization chosen by participants.					Groups of individuals or businesses that join together to gain the advantages of volume purchases or sales.
Franchise	All these issues depend on the form of organization chosen by participants.					Established business. Name recognition. Management assistance. Loss of control. Fees may be high.

Practice Test

1. *ETHICS* McNeely told Hardee's officials that he was interested in purchasing multiple restaurants in Arkansas. A Hardee's officer assured him that any of the company-owned stores in Arkansas would be available for purchase. However, the company urged him to open a new store in Maumelle and sent him a letter estimating first-year sales at around $800,000. McNeely built the Maumelle restaurant, but gross sales the first year were only $508,000. When McNeely asked to buy an existing restaurant, a Hardee's officer refused, informing him that Hardee's rarely sold company-owned restaurants. The franchise offering circular contained no misstatements, but McNeely brought suit alleging fraud in the sale of the Maumelle franchise. Does McNeely have a valid claim against Hardee's? Apart from the legal issues, did Hardee's officers behave ethically? Would they want their behavior to be publicized? Would they like to be treated this way themselves? Is all fair in love, war, and franchising?

2. *CPA QUESTION* Assuming all other requirements are met, a corporation may elect to be treated as an S corporation under the Internal Revenue Code if it has:

a. Both common and preferred stockholders

b. A partnership as a stockholder

c. One hundred or fewer stockholders

d. The consent of a majority of the stockholders

3. Under Delaware law, a corporation cannot appear in court without a lawyer, but a partnership can. Fox Hollow Ventures, Ltd., was a limited liability company. One of its employees, who was not a lawyer, appeared in court to represent the company. Does an LLC more closely resemble a partnership, which may represent itself in court, or a corporation, which requires representation by a lawyer?

4. Glenleigh Falls Development Co. was a limited liability company that hired architects John and Marion Zaugg to design a residential golf course. The Zauggs were to receive partial payment for their services plus part ownership in the LLC. Although the articles of organization had been filed with the Secretary of State in Ohio, the operating agreement had not yet been signed by the members. The Zauggs signed the agreement, but two of the original four members did not. The agreement provided that no member could voluntarily withdraw. When the LLC refused to pay the Zauggs' bill for architectural services, they withdrew from the LLC and filed suit, seeking payment of their bill. The LLC counter-claimed, alleging that the Zauggs had wrongfully withdrawn. Did the Zauggs have the right to withdraw?

5. Alan Dershowitz, a law professor famous for his wealthy clients (O. J. Simpson, Claus von Bulow, Leona Helmsley), joined with other lawyers to open a kosher delicatessen, Maven's Court. Dershowitz met with greater success at the bar than in the kitchen—the deli failed after barely a year in business. One supplier sued for overdue bills. What form of organization would have been the best choice for Maven's Court?

6. *CPA QUESTION* A joint venture is a(n):

a. Association limited to no more than two persons in business for profit

b. Enterprise of numerous co-owners in a non-profit undertaking

c. Corporate enterprise for a single undertaking of limited duration

d. Association of persons engaged as co-owners in a single undertaking for profit

7. Mrs. Meadows opened a biscuit shop called The Biscuit Bakery. The business was not incorporated. Whenever she ordered supplies, she was careful to sign the contract in the name of the business, not personally: The Biscuit Bakery by Daisy Meadows. Unfortunately, she had no money to pay her flour bill. When the vendor threatened to sue her, Mrs. Meadows told him that he could only sue the business, because all the contracts were in the business's name. Will Mrs. Meadows lose her dough?

8. *YOU BE THE JUDGE* WRITING PROBLEM Cellwave was a limited partnership that applied to the Federal Communications Commission (FCC) for a license to operate cellular telephone systems. After the FCC awarded the license it discovered that, although all the limited partners had signed the limited partnership agreement, Cellwave had never filed its limited partnership certificate with the Secretary of State in Delaware. The FCC dismissed Cellwave's application on the grounds that the partnership did not exist when the application was filed. Did the FCC have the right to dismiss Cellwave's application? **Argument for Cellwave:** The limited partnership was effectively in existence as soon as the limited partners signed the agreement. The Secretary of State could not refuse to accept the certificate for filing; that was a mere formality. **Argument for the FCC:** When Cellwave applied for a license, it did not exist legally. Formalities matter.

9. Arnold and Judith Germain bought two franchises from My Pie International, Inc. They did not receive the franchise disclosure statement from My Pie until two years after the purchase. Did My Pie violate franchise law?

10. Leonard C. Blum, an attorney, was negligent in his representation of Louis Anthony, Sr. In settlement of Anthony's claim against him, Blum signed a promissory note for $10,400 on behalf of his law firm, an LLC. When the law firm did not pay, Anthony filed suit against Blum personally for payment of the note. Is a member personally liable for the debt of an LLC that was caused by his own negligence?

11. *ROLE REVERSAL* Draft a multiple-choice question that focuses on the difference between an LLC and an S corporation.

Internet Research Problem

At http://ftc.gov/ the Federal Trade Commission provides information on enforcement cases it has brought against franchisors who violate FTC rules. Do you see a pattern? Are some violations more common than others? How can you avoid falling prey to an unsuitable franchise offering?

You can find further practice problems at academic.cengage.com/blaw/beatty.

CHAPTER 18

Corporations

Becker Interiors, Inc. was overseeing a major renovation of a house in McLean, Virginia. The company hired Stephen Brooks as a subcontractor on the project. When the corporation refused to pay him, Brooks sued.

Ronald Becker was the sole shareholder, officer, and director of Becker Interiors. Becker and his companion, Robert LaPointe, used approximately $300,000 of Becker Interiors's funds to renovate their residence, pay their personal credit card bills and invest in another company of which Becker was president and a shareholder. Becker also sold a corporate car for $73,700 and deposited those funds into his personal account, along with the corporation's income tax refund check of $12,850.

Brooks won his lawsuit against Becker Interiors, and the court ordered the company to pay him $54,597.09. But when Brooks tried to collect the judgment, he discovered that Becker Interiors had no assets.

Can Brooks recover what Becker Interiors owes him? Is Ronald Becker personally liable for the corporation's debts? Are shareholders ever liable for the debts of their corporation? Later in this chapter, the case of Brooks v. Becker *will reveal all.* ■

© PHILIP COBLENTZ/BRAND X PICTURES/GETTY IMAGES

In this chapter, you will learn how to form a corporation. You will also learn about the rights and responsibilities of corporate managers and shareholders.

PROMOTER'S LIABILITY

Someone who organizes a corporation is called a **promoter. A promoter is personally liable on any contract he signs before the corporation is formed.** After formation, the corporation can **adopt** the contract, in which case, both it and the promoter are liable. The promoter can get off the hook personally only if the landlord agrees to a **novation**—that is, a new contract with the corporation alone.

In the following case, the entrepreneur did not understand the rules of promoter liability.

HARDY V. SOUTHWESTERN BELL YELLOW PAGES, INC.

2001 Tex. App. LEXIS 587
Court of Appeals of Texas, 2001

Bruce Hardy signed a contract on behalf of A-Z Business Products, Inc. agreeing to pay Southwestern Bell $23,240.00 for an advertisement in its Yellow Pages. The contract was in the name of A-Z Business Products, Inc. Next to Hardy's signature on the contract was a line marked "Title:" where Hardy wrote "Pres."

At the time, A-Z Business Products, Inc. had not yet been formed. After Hardy failed to make any payments on the contract, Southwestern Bell sued him individually, d/b/a A-Z Business Products. Hardy argued that only A-Z Business Products, Inc. was liable. The trial court found for Southwestern Bell, and Hardy appealed.

Issue: Is Hardy personally liable on the contract with Southwestern Bell?

Excerpts from Justice Kinkeade's Decision: Hardy contends that the contract was between Southwestern Bell and A-Z Business Products, Inc., and that he signed the document in his capacity as president of A-Z. Southwestern Bell argues, and we agree, that even assuming he signed the contract as the president of A-Z, he is still personally liable because A-Z was not yet formed as a corporation at the time of the contract.

Although Hardy asserts that he acted as an agent for the corporation, he admitted at trial that the corporation was not in existence at the time he signed the contract. Further, the corporate charter showing the date of incorporation, several months after the contract was signed, was admitted into evidence. Hardy could not have acted as an agent for a nonexistent corporation, because a nonexistent corporation can have no agent. He could only have acted as a promoter in contemplation of the formation of a corporation.

A promoter who enters a contract on behalf of an unformed corporation is personally liable on the contract unless (1) there is an agreement with the contracting party that the promoter is not liable, (2) the contract is made in the name and on the credit of the proposed corporation and the contracting party knows that the corporation does not yet exist, or (3) the corporation adopts the agreement after its incorporation.

The only evidence Hardy offered was his own testimony that when he signed the contract, he advised Southwestern Bell that he had applied for, but not yet received, the corporate charter number. Absent proof that A-Z adopted the agreement after its incorporation or that the agreement was in A-Z's name and that Southwestern Bell agreed at the time of contracting that it would look only to A-Z's credit, Hardy is bound individually.

We hold the evidence is legally and factually sufficient to support the trial court's verdict that Hardy is personally liable on the contract. ■

INCORPORATION PROCESS

The mechanics of incorporation are easy: simply fill out the form online or mail or fax it to the Secretary of State for your state. But do not let this easy process fool you; the incorporation document needs to be completed with some care. The corporate charter defines the corporation, including everything from the company's name to the number of shares it will issue. States use different terms to refer to a charter; some call it the "articles of incorporation," others use "articles of organization," and still others say "certificate" instead of "articles." All these terms mean the same thing. Similarly, some states use the term "shareholders," and others use "stockholders"; they are both the same.

There is no federal corporation code, which means that a company can incorporate only under state, not federal, law. No matter where a company actually does business, it may incorporate in any state. This decision is important because the organization must live by the laws of whichever state it chooses for incorporation. To encourage similarity among state corporation statutes, the American Bar Association drafted the Model Business Corporation Act (the Model Act) as a guide. Many states do use the Model Act as a guide, although Delaware does not. Therefore, in this chapter we will give examples from both the Model Act and specific states, such as Delaware. Why Delaware? Despite its small size, it has a disproportionate influence on corporate law. Although only one third of 1 percent of the U.S. population lives in Delaware, more than half of all public companies have incorporated there, including 58 percent of Fortune 500 companies.

Where To Incorporate?

A company is called a **domestic corporation** in the state where it incorporates and a **foreign corporation** everywhere else. Companies generally incorporate either in the state where they do most of their business or in Delaware. They typically must pay filing fees and franchise taxes in their state of incorporation, as well as in any state in which they do business. To avoid this double set of fees, a business that will be operating primarily in one state would probably select that state for incorporation rather than Delaware. But if a company is going to do business in several states, it might consider choosing Delaware (or, perhaps, Ohio, Pennsylvania, Nevada, or one of the other states with sophisticated corporate laws). More information about Delaware law is available at http://www.state.de.us by searching for "Corporations." Or browse http://www.findlaw.com by clicking on "State Laws" and "Corporations" for links to all state corporation Websites.

Delaware offers corporations several advantages:

- *Laws that Favor Management.* For example, if the shareholders want to take a vote in writing instead of holding a meeting, many other states require the vote to be unanimous; Delaware requires only a majority to agree. The Delaware legislature also tries to keep up-to-date by changing its code to reflect new developments in corporate law.

- *An Efficient Court System.* Delaware has a special court (called "Chancery Court") that hears nothing but business cases and has judges who are experts in corporate law.

- *An Established Body of Precedent.* Because so many businesses incorporate in the state, its courts hear a vast number of corporate cases, creating a large body of precedent. Thus, lawyers feel they can more easily predict the outcome of a case in Delaware than in a state where few corporate disputes are tried each year.

The Charter

Once a company has decided *where* to incorporate, the next step is to prepare and file the charter. The charter must always be filed with the Secretary of State; some jurisdictions also require that it be filed in a county office. Sample articles of incorporation for Delaware are available at http://www.state.de.us/corp.

Name

The Model Act imposes two requirements in selecting a name. First, all corporations must use one of the following words in their name: "corporation," "incorporated," "company," or "limited." Delaware also accepts some additional terms, such as "association" or "institute." Second, under both the Model Act and Delaware law, a new corporate name must be different from that of any corporation, limited liability company, or limited partnership that already exists in that state. If your name is Freddy Dupont, you cannot name your corporation "Freddy Dupont, Inc.," because Delaware already has a company named E. I. Dupont de Nemours & Co. It does not matter that Freddy Dupont is your real name or that the existing company is a large chemical business, whereas you want to open a video arcade. The names are too similar.

Address and Registered Agent

A company must have an official address in the state in which it is incorporated so that the Secretary of State knows where to contact it and so that anyone who wants to sue the corporation can serve the complaint in-state. Because most companies incorporated in Delaware do not actually have an office there, they hire a registered agent to serve as their official presence in the state. Agents typically charge about $100 annually for this service.

Incorporator

The incorporator signs the charter and delivers it to the Secretary of State for filing. Incorporators are not required to buy stock, nor do they necessarily have any future relationship with the company. Typically, the lawyer who forms the corporation serves as its incorporator.

Purpose

The corporation is required to give its purpose for existence. Most companies use a very broad purpose clause such as:

> The nature of the business or purposes to be conducted or promoted is to engage in any lawful act or activity for which corporations may be organized under the General Corporation Law of Delaware.

Stock

The charter must provide three items of information about the company's stock.

Par Value.   The concept of par value was designed to protect investors. Originally, par value was supposed to be close to market price. A company could not issue stock at a price less than par, which meant that it could not sell to insiders at a sweetheart price well below market value. (Once the stock was issued, it could be traded at any price.) In modern times, par value does not relate to market value; it is usually some nominal figure such as 1¢ or $1 per share. Companies may even issue stock with no par value.

Number of Shares. Before stock can be sold, it must first be authorized in the charter. The corporation can authorize as many shares as the incorporators choose, but the more shares, the higher the filing fee. In Delaware, the basic filing fee for a certificate of incorporation is $89. That fee includes 1500 shares at no par value. The filing fee is higher if the corporation wants more shares or shares with par value. After incorporation, a company can add authorized shares by simply amending its charter and paying the additional fee.

Stock that has been authorized but not yet sold is called **authorized and unissued.** Stock that has been sold is termed **authorized and issued** or **outstanding.** Stock that the company has sold but later bought back is **treasury stock.**

Classes and Series. Different shareholders often make different contributions to a company. Some may be involved in management, whereas others may simply contribute financially. Early investors may feel that they are entitled to more control than those who come along later (and who perhaps take less risk). Corporate structure can be infinitely flexible in defining the rights of these various shareholders. Stock can be divided into categories called **classes,** and these classes can be further divided into subcategories called **series.** All stock in a series has the same rights, and all series in a class are fundamentally the same, except for minor distinctions. For example, in a class of preferred stock, all shareholders may be entitled to a dividend, but the amount of the dividend may vary by series. Different classes of stock, however, may have very different rights—a class of preferred stock is different from a class of common stock. Exhibit 18.1 illustrates the concept of class and series.

Defining the rights of a class or series of stock is like baking a cake—the stock can contain virtually any combination of the following ingredients (although the result may not be to everyone's taste):

- *Dividend Rights.* The charter establishes whether the shareholder is entitled to dividends and, if so, in what amount.

- *Voting Rights.* Shareholders are usually entitled to elect directors and vote on charter amendments, among other issues, but these rights can vary among different series and classes of stock. When Ford Motor Co. went public in 1956, it issued Class B common stock to members of the Ford family. This class of stock holds about 40 percent of the voting power and, thereby, effectively controls

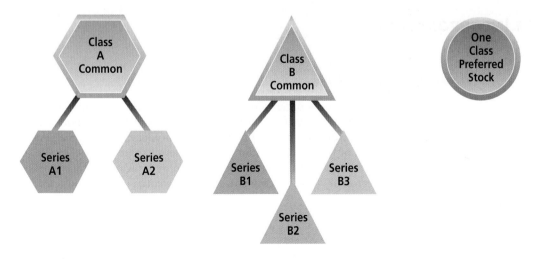

Exhibit 18.1

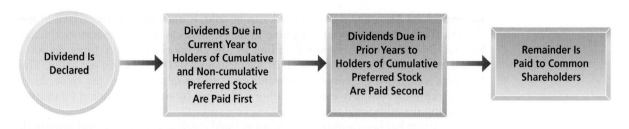

Exhibit 18.2

the company. Not surprisingly, the chairman of the company is often named "Ford."

- *Liquidation Rights.* The charter specifies the order in which classes of stockholders will be paid upon dissolution of the company.

These are the ingredients for any class or series of stock. Some stock comes prepackaged like a cake mix. "Preferred" and "common" stock are two classic types. The Model Act does not use these terms, but many states still do.

Owners of *preferred stock* have preference on dividends and also, typically, in liquidation. If a class of preferred stock is entitled to dividends, then it must receive its dividends before common stockholders are paid theirs. If holders of ***cumulative* preferred stock** miss their dividend one year, common shareholders cannot receive a dividend until the cumulative preferred shareholders have been paid, no matter how long that takes. Alternatively, holders of ***non* cumulative preferred stock** lose an annual dividend for good if the company cannot afford it in the year it is due. When a company dissolves, preferred stockholders typically have the right to receive their share of corporate assets before common shareholders. Exhibit 18.2 illustrates the order of payment for dividends.

***Common* stock is last in line for any corporate payouts, including dividends and liquidation payments.** If the company is liquidated, creditors of the company and preferred shareholders are paid before common shareholders.

AFTER INCORPORATION

Directors and Officers

Once the corporation is organized, the incorporators elect the first set of directors. Thereafter, shareholders elect directors. Under the Model Act, a corporation is required to have at least one director, unless (1) all the shareholders sign an agreement that eliminates the board, or (2) the corporation has 50 or fewer shareholders. To elect directors, the shareholders may hold a meeting, or, in the more typical case for a small company, they elect directors by **written consent.** A typical written consent looks like this:

Classic American Novels, Inc.

Written Consent

The undersigned shareholders of Classic American Novels, Inc., a corporation organized and existing under the General Corporation Law of the State of Wherever, hereby agree that the following action shall be taken with full force and effect as if voted at a validly called and held meeting of the shareholders of the corporation:

> Agreed: That the following people are elected to serve as directors for one year or until their successors have been duly elected and qualified:

Herman Melville

Louisa May Alcott

Mark Twain

Dated: _____   Signed: _____
                                            Willa Cather

Dated: _____   Signed: _____
                                       Nathaniel Hawthorne

Dated: _____   Signed: _____
                                       Harriet Beecher Stowe

Once the incorporators or shareholders have chosen the directors, the directors must elect the officers of the corporation. They can use a consent form if they wish. The Model Act is flexible. It simply requires a corporation to have whatever officers are described in the bylaws. The same person can hold more than one office.

The written consents and any records of actual meetings are kept in a **minute book,** which is the official record of the corporation. Entrepreneurs sometimes feel they are too busy to bother with all these details, but if a corporation is ever sold, the lawyers for the buyers will *insist* on a well-organized and complete minute book. In one case, a company that was seeking a $100,000 bank loan could not find all its minutes. Many of its early shareholders and directors were not available to re-authorize prior deeds. In the end, the company had to merge itself into a newly created corporation so it could start fresh with a new set of corporate records. The company spent $10,000 on this task, a large chunk out of the $100,000 loan.

Bylaws

The **bylaws** list all the "housekeeping" details for the corporation. For example, bylaws set the date of the annual shareholders' meeting, define what a quorum is (i.e., what percentage of stock must be represented for a meeting to count), indicate how many directors there will be, give titles to officers, and establish the fiscal (i.e., tax) year of the corporation. A sample set of bylaws is available at http://www.lectlaw.com (search for "Bylaws") and http://www.tannedfeet.com (click on "Legal Forms," then "By-laws for a Business Corporation").

Issuing Debt

Most startup companies begin with some combination of equity and debt. Equity (i.e., stock) is described in the charter; debt is not. Authorizing debt is often one of the first steps a new company takes. There are several types of debt:

- **Bonds** are long-term debt secured by company assets. If the company is unable to pay the debt, creditors have a right to specific assets, such as accounts receivable or inventory.

- **Debentures** are long-term *unsecured* debt. If the company cannot meet its obligations, the debenture holders are paid after bondholders but before stockholders.

- **Notes** are short-term debt, typically payable within five years. They may be either secured or unsecured.

DEATH OF THE CORPORATION

Sometimes, business ideas are not successful and the corporation fails. This death can be voluntary (the shareholders elect to terminate the corporation) or forced (by court order). Sometimes, a court takes a step that is much more damaging to shareholders than simply dissolving the corporation—it removes the shareholders' limited liability.

Piercing the Corporate Veil

One of the major purposes of a corporation is to protect its owners—the shareholders—from personal liability for the debts of the organization. Sometimes, however, a court will **pierce the corporate veil;** that is, the court will hold shareholders personally liable for the debts of the corporation. Courts generally pierce a corporate veil in four circumstances:

- *Failure to Observe Formalities.* If an organization does not act like a corporation, it will not be treated like one. It must, for example, hold required shareholders' and directors' meetings (or sign consents), keep a minute book as a record of these meetings, and make all the required state filings. In addition, officers must be careful to sign all corporate documents with a corporate title, not as an individual. An officer should sign like this:

  Classic American Novels, Inc.

  By: *Stephen Crane*

  Stephen Crane, President

- *Commingling of Assets.* Nothing makes a court more willing to pierce a corporate veil than evidence that shareholders have mixed their assets with those of the corporation. Sometimes, for example, shareholders may use corporate assets to pay their personal debts. If shareholders commingle assets, it is genuinely difficult for creditors to determine which assets belong to whom. This confusion is generally resolved in favor of the creditors—all assets are deemed to belong to the corporation.

- *Inadequate Capitalization.* If the founders of a corporation do not raise enough capital (either through debt or equity) to give the business a fighting chance of paying its debts, courts may require shareholders to pay corporate obligations. Therefore, if the corporation does not have sufficient capital, it needs to buy insurance, particularly to protect against tort liability. Judges are likelier to hold shareholders liable if the alternative is to send an injured tort victim away empty-handed. For example, Oriental Fireworks Co. had hundreds of thousands of dollars in annual sales, but only $13,000 in assets. The company did not bother to obtain any liability insurance, keep a minute book, or defend lawsuits. There was no need because the company had no money. But then a court pierced the corporate veil and found the owner of the company personally liable.[1]

---

[1] *Rice v. Oriental Fireworks Co.*, 75 Or. App. 627, 707 P.2d 1250, 1985 Ore. App. LEXIS 3928.

- *Fraud.* If fraud is committed in the name of a corporation, victims can make a claim against the personal assets of the shareholders who profited from the fraud.

The following case is a good example of when a court should pierce the corporate veil.

BROOKS V. BECKER

2005 Va. Cir. LEXIS 13
Circuit Court of Fairfax County, Virginia, 2005

Facts: The facts are set out in the opening scenario. Brooks sued Becker in an attempt to pierce the corporate veil and hold Becker personally liable for the debts of the corporation.

Issues: Can Brooks pierce the corporate veil? Is Becker personally liable for the debts of the corporation?

Excerpts from Judge Roush's Decision: The decision to ignore the separate existence of a corporate entity and impose personal liability upon shareholders for debts of the corporation is an extraordinary act to be taken only when necessary to promote justice. Disregarding the corporate entity is usually warranted only under the extraordinary circumstances where: the shareholder sought to be held personally liable has controlled or used the corporation to evade a personal obligation, to perpetrate fraud or a crime, to commit an injustice, or to gain an unfair advantage. Piercing the corporate veil is justified when the unity of interest and ownership is such that the separate personalities of the corporation and the individual no longer exist and to adhere to that separateness would work an injustice.

In this case, the evidence convinces the court that the extraordinary remedy of piercing the corporate veil should be granted. Becker knowingly violated his duties as an officer, director and shareholder of Becker Interiors and treated the corporation's funds as his personal piggy bank. His testimony that the corporate expenditures on his personal residence were a legitimate business expense because he wanted to use the residence as a showcase of his work was simply not credible. Nor did the court believe Becker's testimony that he commingled his personal funds with the corporation's funds on the advice of his accountant. The court found more credible Becker's later testimony that his accountant was "mystified" by his commingling of funds between his personal and corporate accounts.

Accordingly, the court will enter judgment against Becker in the amount of $54,597.09. ∎

Termination

Terminating a corporation is a three-step process:

- *Vote.* The directors recommend to the shareholders that the corporation be dissolved, and a majority of the shareholders agree.
- *Filing.* The corporation files "Articles of Dissolution" with the Secretary of State.
- *Winding Up.* The officers of the corporation pay its debts and distribute the remaining property to shareholders. When the winding up is completed, the corporation ceases to exist.

The Secretary of State may dissolve a corporation that violates state law by, for example, failing to pay the required annual fees. Indeed, many corporations, particularly small ones, do not bother with the formal dissolution process. They simply cease paying their required annual fees and let the Secretary of State act. A court may dissolve a corporation if it is insolvent or if its directors and shareholders cannot resolve conflict over how the corporation should be managed. The court will then appoint a receiver to oversee the winding up.

THE ROLE OF CORPORATE MANAGEMENT

Now you know how to avoid some of the legal pitfalls that can ensnare the unwary entrepreneur when organizing a corporation. But what happens as the business grows? In the beginning, many entrepreneurs fund their startup themselves (with the aid of credit cards), but most expect that the business will ultimately attract outside investors. This concept of outside investors is, in historical terms, relatively new. Before the Industrial Revolution in the eighteenth and nineteenth centuries, a business owner typically supplied both capital and management. However, the capital needs of the great manufacturing enterprises spawned by the Industrial Revolution were larger than any small group of individuals could supply. To find capital, firms sought outside investors, who often had neither the knowledge nor the desire to manage the enterprise. Investors without management skills complemented managers without capital. ("Manager" includes both directors and officers.)

Modern businesses still have the same vast need for capital and the same division between managers and investors. As businesses grow, shareholders are too numerous and too uninformed to manage the enterprises they own. Therefore, they elect directors to manage for them. The directors set policy and then appoint officers to implement corporate goals. The Model Act describes the directors' role thus: "All corporate powers shall be exercised by or under the authority of, and the business and affairs of the corporation managed by or under the direction of, its board of directors. . . ."

Directors have the authority to manage the corporate business, but they also have important responsibilities to shareholders and perhaps to other stakeholders who are affected by corporate decisions, such as employees, customers, creditors, suppliers, and neighbors. The interests of these various stakeholders often conflict. What are the rights—and responsibilities—of directors and officers to manage these conflicts?

Managers have a fiduciary duty to act in the best interests of the corporation's shareholders. Because shareholders are primarily concerned about their return on investment, managers must *maximize shareholder value*, which means providing shareholders with the highest possible financial return from dividends and stock price. However, reality is more complicated than this simple rule indicates. It is often difficult to determine which strategy will best maximize shareholder value. And what about stakeholders? A number of states have adopted statutes that permit directors to take into account the interests of stakeholders as well as stockholders. The Indiana Code, for example, permits directors to consider "both the short term and long term best interests of the corporation, taking into account, and weighing as the directors deem appropriate, the effects thereof on the corporation's shareholders and the other corporate constituent groups. . . ."[2] The next section looks more closely at directors' responsibilities to their various constituencies.

---

2 Indiana Code §23-1-35-1.

THE BUSINESS JUDGMENT RULE

Officers and directors have a fiduciary duty to act in the best interests of their stockholders, but under the **business judgment rule,** the courts allow managers great leeway in carrying out this responsibility. The business judgment rule is a common law concept that virtually every court in the country recognizes. In addition, some states have enacted statutes that codify the business judgment rule. To be protected by the business judgment rule, managers must act in good faith:

Duty of Loyalty	1. Without a conflict of interest
Duty of Care	2. With the care that an ordinarily prudent person would take in a similar situation, and
	3. In a manner they reasonably believe to be in the best interests of the corporation

The business judgment rule is two shields in one: it protects both the manager and her decision. If a manager has complied with the rule, a court will not hold her personally liable for any harm her decision has caused the company, nor will the court rescind her decision. If the manager violates the business judgment rule, then she has the burden of proving that her decision was fair to the shareholders. If it was not fair, she may be held personally liable, and the decision can be rescinded.

The business judgment rule accomplishes three goals:

- *It permits directors to do their job.* If directors were afraid they would be liable for every decision that led to a loss, they would never make a decision, or at least not a risky one.

- *It keeps judges out of corporate management.* Without the business judgment rule, judges would be tempted, if not required, to second-guess managers' decisions.

- *It encourages directors to serve.* No one in his right mind would serve as a director if he knew that every decision was open to attack in the courtroom.

Analysis of the business judgment rule is divided into two parts. The obligation of a manager to act without a conflict of interest is called the **duty of loyalty.** The requirements that a manager act with care and in the best interests of the corporation are referred to as the **duty of care.**

Duty of Loyalty

The duty of loyalty prohibits managers from making a decision that benefits them at the expense of the corporation.

Self-Dealing

Self-dealing means that a manager makes a decision benefiting either himself or another company with which he has a relationship. While working at the Blue Moon restaurant, Zeke signs a contract on behalf of the restaurant to purchase bread from Rising Sun Bakery. Unbeknownst to anyone at Blue Moon, he is a part owner of Rising Sun. Zeke has engaged in self-dealing, which is a violation of the duty of loyalty.

Once a manager engages in self-dealing, the business judgment rule no longer applies. This does not mean the manager is automatically liable to the corporation

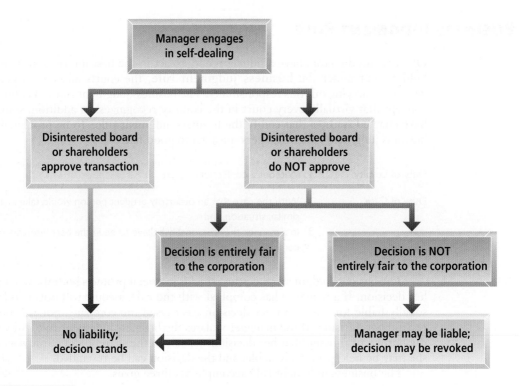

Exhibit 18.3

or that his decision is automatically void. All it means is that the court will no longer presume that the transaction was acceptable. Instead, the court will scrutinize the deal more carefully. A self-dealing transaction is valid in any one of the following situations:

- **The disinterested members of the board of directors approve the transaction.** Disinterested directors are those who do not themselves benefit from the transaction.

- **The disinterested shareholders approve it.** The transaction is valid if the shareholders who do not benefit from it are willing to approve it.

- **The transaction was entirely fair to the corporation.** In determining fairness, the courts will consider the impact of the transaction on the corporation and whether the price was reasonable.

Exhibit 18.3 illustrates the rules on self-dealing.

Corporate Opportunity

The self-dealing rules prevent managers from forcing their companies into unfair deals. The corporate opportunity doctrine is the reverse—it prohibits managers from excluding their company from favorable deals. **Managers are in violation of the corporate opportunity doctrine if they compete against the corporation without its consent.**

Charles Guth was president of Loft, Inc., which operated a chain of candy stores. These stores sold Coca-Cola. Guth purchased the Pepsi-Cola Co. personally, without offering the opportunity to Loft. The Delaware court found that Guth had violated the corporate opportunity doctrine and ordered him to transfer all his shares in Pepsi to Loft.[3] That was in 1939, and Pepsi-Cola was bankrupt; today, PepsiCo, Inc. is worth $96 billion.

Duty of Care

In addition to the *duty of loyalty*, managers also owe a *duty of care*. **The duty of care requires officers and directors to act in the best interests of the corporation and to use the same care that an ordinarily prudent person would in the management of her own assets.**

Rational Business Purpose

Courts generally agree in principle that directors and officers are liable for decisions that have no rational business purpose. In practice, however, these same courts have been extremely supportive of managerial decisions, looking hard to find some justification. For decades, the Chicago Cubs baseball team refused to install lights in Wrigley Field. Cubs' fans could only take themselves out to the ball game during the day. A shareholder sued on the grounds that the Cubs' revenues were peanuts and crackerjack compared with those generated by other teams that played at night. The Cubs defended their decision on the grounds that a large night crowd would cause the neighborhood to deteriorate, depressing the value of Wrigley Field (which was not owned by the Cubs). The court rooted for the home team and found that the Cubs' excuse was a "rational purpose" and a legitimate exercise of the business judgment rule.[4]

Legality

Courts are generally unsympathetic to managers who engage in illegal behavior, even if their goal is to help the company. For example, the managing director of an amusement park in New York State used corporate funds to purchase the silence of people who threatened to complain that the park was illegally operating on Sunday. The court ordered the director to repay the money he had spent on bribes, even though the company had earned large profits on Sundays.[5]

Informed Decision

Generally, courts will protect managers who make an *informed* decision, even if the decision ultimately harms the company. Making an informed decision means carefully investigating the facts. However, even if the decision is uninformed, the directors will not be held liable if the decision was entirely fair to the shareholders.

Exhibit 18.4 provides an overview of the duty of care.

---

3 *Guth v. Loft*, 5 A.2d 503, 23 Del. Ch. 255, 1939 Del. LEXIS 13 (Del. 1939).

4 *Shlensky v. Wrigley*, 95 Ill. App. 2d 173, 237 N.E.2d 776, 1968 Ill. App. LEXIS 1107 (Ill. App. Ct. 1968).

5 *Roth v. Robertson*, 64 Misc. 343, 118 N.Y.S. 351, 1909 N.Y. Misc. LEXIS 279 (N.Y. 1909).

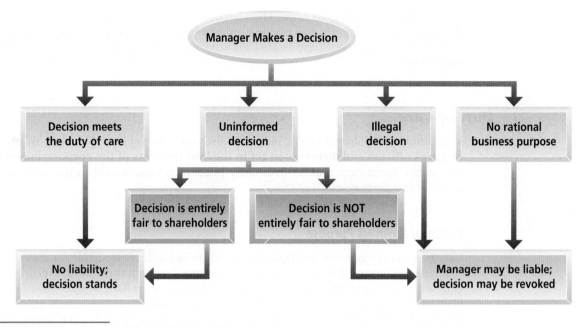

Exhibit 18.4

In the following case, shareholders sued the board of directors for accepting a purchase price that they felt was too low. Did the directors violate their duty of care? You be the judge.

YOU BE THE JUDGE

SMITH V. VAN GORKOM

488 A.2d 858, 1985 Del. LEXIS 421
Supreme Court of Delaware, 1985

Facts: Trans Union was a publicly traded company in the railcar leasing business. Jerome Van Gorkom had been its chief executive officer for more than 17 years. He was nearing the mandatory retirement age of 65 and was concerned about maximizing the value of his 75,000 shares of Trans Union stock. In the preceding five years, Trans Union's stock had traded at a high of $39.50 and a low of $24.25 per share. The price was now about $37.

Although Trans Union had hundreds of millions of dollars in annual cash flow, it did not have enough income to take advantage of large investment tax credits (ITCs). Van Gorkom fretted that competi-

tors who could efficiently use their ITCs would be able to cut their lease prices and take business away from Trans Union. He believed that Trans Union would be more profitable if it was bought by a company that could use the credits.

On September 13, Van Gorkom met with Jay Pritzker, a well-known corporate takeover specialist, to discuss the potential market for Trans Union. Van Gorkom suggested to Pritzker that a leveraged buyout (LBO) could be done at $55 per share. (In an LBO, the acquiring company buys the target company's stock, using a loan secured by the target's assets.) On Thursday, September 18, Pritzker offered to buy all of Trans Union's stock for $55 per share. The offer expired three days later, on Sunday evening.   ▼

On Saturday, Van Gorkom met separately with senior managers and later with the board of directors. Salomon Brothers, the company's investment banker, was not invited to attend. At both meetings, Van Gorkom disclosed the offer and described its terms but furnished no copies of the proposed agreement. At the first meeting with senior management, the managers' reaction to the Pritzker proposal was completely negative—they feared losing their jobs, they did not like Pritzker, and they thought the price was too low. Nevertheless, Van Gorkom proceeded to the board meeting.

The board was composed of five inside and five outside directors. Of the outside directors, four were corporate CEOs and one was the former dean of the University of Chicago Business School. None was an investment banker or trained financial analyst. All members of the board were familiar with the company's financial condition and the ITC problem. They had all recently reviewed the company's five-year forecast as well as a comprehensive 18-month study by a well-known consulting firm.

Van Gorkom explained that the issue was not whether $55 per share was the highest price the company could obtain, but whether it was a fair price that the stockholders should be given the opportunity to accept or reject. He also explained that the company had the right to accept a higher offer if one was made. Van Gorkom did not disclose to the board that he had proposed the $55 price in his negotiations with Pritzker. The company's attorney advised the directors that they might be sued if they failed to accept the offer. The company's chief financial officer said that $55 was "in the range of a fair price" for an LBO, but "at the beginning of the range." The board approved the sale.

Van Gorkom executed the agreement at a formal social event that he hosted for the opening of the Chicago Lyric Opera. Neither he nor any other director read the agreement before signing it. The company issued a press release announcing that Trans Union had entered into a "definitive" agreement with Pritzker. At the same time, it hired Salomon Brothers to solicit other offers. No one else made a firm offer, perhaps because other bidders believed the company was already committed to Pritzker. On February 10, 69 percent of the stockholders of Trans Union voted in favor of the Pritzker proposal.

The plaintiff, Alden Smith, objected to the sale because he did not want to pay tax on the huge profits he realized.

You Be the Judge: **Did the directors of Trans Union violate their duty of care to the corporation by making an uninformed decision? Did the shareholders consent to the board's decision?**

Argument for the Shareholders: The whole procedure for this sale was shockingly casual. Van Gorkom signed the final agreement at a social function. When the directors voted to sell the company, they had not (1) tried to negotiate a higher price with Pritzker, (2) read the agreement, (3) consulted their investment bankers, or (4) determined the intrinsic value of the company. The stock price simply represents the value of a minority stake (one share); a controlling share is worth more, but the board did not know how much more.

The board did not know this important information and neither did the shareholders when they approved the sale. For that reason, the shareholder consent is invalid.

Argument for the Board of Directors: Pritzker paid a fair price for the Trans Union stock. It represented a premium of (1) 62 percent over the average of the high and low price in the prior year, (2) 48 percent over the last closing price, and (3) 39 percent over the highest price at which the stock had ever traded. The plaintiffs suggest that the "intrinsic value" of the company was higher. The board hired Salomon Brothers to look for better offers and agreed to pay them millions of dollars in fees if they were successful, but they could not find a buyer willing to pay more than Pritzker.

Jerome Van Gorkom served the company for 24 years, and he knew $55 was a favorable price. He also had an enormous incentive to obtain the highest price available because he personally owned 75,000 shares. The five inside directors had collectively worked for the company for 116 years. The outside directors knew the company well, and they were experienced business people; four of them were CEOs of their own large companies. The board was ▼

forced to make a decision quickly because Pritzker's offer expired in three days. What could an expert have discovered in three days that the board did not already know? The Trans Union lawyer warned the directors that if they refused the offer, they would be sued.

Alden Smith's tax problems are not a legitimate reason to hold the board liable. The business judgment rule is meant to protect a board that makes a good faith decision. This board did what it thought best for all of the company's shareholders, not for Alden Smith alone. ●

Remember that managers are only liable if they make an uninformed decision and the transaction is unfair to the shareholders. If the appeals court in the Trans Union case determined that the directors had violated their duty of care, it would remand the case to the lower court to determine if $55 was a fair price.

Some states have modified their business judgment rule to increase protection for directors. These states either limit liability by statute or permit corporations to include charter provisions that shield directors from personal liability.[6]

TAKEOVERS

The business judgment rule is an important guideline for officers and directors in the routine management of corporations. It also plays a crucial role in the regulation of hostile takeovers. In addition, both Congress and many state legislatures have passed statutes that define the roles of the various combatants in takeovers.

There are three ways to acquire control of a company:

- *Buy the company's assets.* Such a sale must be approved by both the shareholders and the board of directors of the acquired company.

- *Merge with the company.* In a merger, one company absorbs another. The acquired company ceases to exist. A merger must also be approved by the shareholders and the board of directors of the target company. If the current directors object, an acquiring company could buy enough stock to replace the board, but these battles are difficult and often end in defeat for the acquirer.

- *Buy stock from the shareholders.* This method is called a tender offer because the acquirer asks shareholders to "tender," or offer their stock for sale. Unlike the other methods of obtaining control, approval from the board of directors of the target company is not strictly necessary. As long as shareholders tender enough stock, the acquirer gains control. A tender offer is called a hostile takeover if the board of the target resists.

As a shareholder, would you prefer for the law to favor the target or the bidder? Economic research suggests an answer.

---

[6] For example, the Delaware code permits a corporation to include in its charter a provision limiting a director's personal liability except in certain cases such as intentional misconduct. 8 Del. C. §102(b)(7).

ECONOMICS
& *the* LAW

Suppose you are thinking about buying stock in two companies. The directors and officers of Bright Future, Inc., own 25 percent of the company, whereas the managers of Dim Bulb Co. own virtually none. You might think that it would be better to invest in a company in which the managers own substantial amounts of stock. In such a case, managers have the same incentives as shareholders—you both benefit from higher stock prices. Moreover, you assume that managers who own lots of stock must have reason to believe that their company's future is promising. Because managers are likely to know more about the inner workings of a company than an ordinary shareholder would, you might legitimately conclude that Bright Future has, well, the brighter future.

It turns out that reality is more complex. If managers own so much stock that they can defeat takeovers, then they tend to become complacent and care less about shareholder value. This phenomenon is called the "entrenchment effect." According to some estimates, the entrenchment effect is most pronounced in companies in which managers own between 5 and 25 percent of the stock.[7] Investors might be wise to investigate such companies carefully. Dim Bulb could be a better choice than Bright Future. ◆

Federal Regulation of Tender Offers: The Williams Act

The Williams Act applies only if the target company's stock is publicly traded. Under the Williams Act:

- Any individual or group who together acquire more than 5 percent of a company's stock must file a public disclosure document (called a "Schedule 13D") with the Securities and Exchange Commission (SEC);

- On the day a tender offer begins, a bidder must file a disclosure statement with the SEC;

- A bidder must keep a tender offer open for at least 20 business days initially and for at least 10 business days after any substantial change in the terms of the offer;

- Any shareholder may withdraw acceptance of the tender offer at any time while the offer is still open;

- If the bidder raises the price offered, all selling shareholders must be paid the higher price, regardless of when they tendered; and

- If the stockholders tender more shares than the bidder wants to buy, the bidder must purchase shares pro rata (i.e., it must buy the same proportion from everyone, not first come, first served).

State Regulation of Takeovers

Common Law of Takeovers

To protect themselves from hostile takeovers, companies adopt defensive measures known as **anti-takeover devices** or **shark repellents.** (The acquiring shareholder in a hostile takeover is sometimes referred to as a "shark.") **Shareholder rights plans**

---

[7] R. Morck, A. Schleifer, and R.W. Vishny, "Management Ownership and Market Valuation: An Empirical Analysis," Working Paper No. 23, Institute for Financial Research, Faculty of Business, University of Alberta, quoted in P.-O. Bjuggren, "Ownership and Efficiency in Companies Listed on Stockholm Stock Exchange 1985," in M. Faure and R. Van den Bergh, *Essays in Law and Economics* (MAKLU, Antwerp, 1985).

(aka poison pills) are among the most common anti-takeover devices. A target company will, for example, amend its charter to permit it to issue one share of preferred stock to each of its shareholders. If a shark purchases more than 20 percent of the target's stock and subsequently merges with the target, the preferred stock is convertible into 10 shares of the shark. This device makes a takeover much more expensive for the acquiring company.

Conventional wisdom views antitakeover devices as a mixed blessing—beneficial if used to ensure that shareholders receive the highest possible price for their stock in the event of a sale but harmful to shareholders if used only to protect management from being fired. However, recent research indicates that the stock prices of companies with few shark repellents significantly outperform those of companies that provide more protection to their managers.[8]

When establishing takeover defenses, shareholder welfare must be the board's primary concern. The directors may institute shark repellents, but they must do so to ensure that bids are high, not to protect their own jobs.

State Anti-takeover Statutes

When fighting takeover battles, companies have also found support in state governments. Legislators may not care if a group of directors is thrown into the unemployment line, but they do fear the impact on the local economy if a major employer leaves. When the Belzberg family threatened a hostile takeover of auto parts manufacturer Arvin Industries, the second largest employer in Columbus, Indiana, the state legislature quickly passed a tough anti-takeover bill that had been drafted by Arvin's own lawyers. Arvin and the Belzbergs quickly settled.

Most states have now passed laws to deter hostile takeovers. Among the common varieties:

- *Statutes that Automatically Impede Hostile Takeovers.* These statutes, for example, might ban hostile (but not friendly) mergers for five years after the acquirer buys 10 percent of a company.

- *Statutes that Authorize Companies to Fight Off Hostile Takeovers.* These statutes typically permit management, when responding to a hostile takeover, to consider the welfare of company stakeholders, such as the community, customers, suppliers, and employees. Some even go so far as to allow management to consider the regional or national economy.

Most of these statutes do not totally eliminate hostile takeovers. A determined, well-financed bidder can still be successful. But these state statutes do tip the playing field in favor of management. In the process they prevent some takeovers that shareholders might want, but they also ensure that shareholders receive a high price in those takeovers that are successful.

Ethics

Supporters of these state statutes argue that large, publicly traded corporations owe a duty to all their constituencies. The loss of a large corporate presence can be immensely disruptive to a community. Perhaps a state should have the right to prevent economic upheaval within its borders.

Opponents contend that shareholders own the company, and their interests ought to be paramount. Anti-takeover legislation entrenches management and prevents shareholders

[8] P.A. Gompers, J. Ishii, A. Metrick, "Corporate Governance and Equity Prices," *Quarterly Journal of Economics*, 118(1), Feb. 2003.

from obtaining the premium that accompanies a takeover. Opponents also argue that, if other stakeholders are so concerned with the well-being of the company, let them put their money where their mouths are and buy stock. And if current managers cannot offer shareholders as high a stock price as an outside raider, they ought to be replaced.

Delaware companies can choose not to accept the protection of the anti-takeover statute. Is that the ethical choice for directors? What guidance does the Chapter 2 Ethics Checklist offer? Who are the stakeholders? What values are important to a company director? If a director owned stock in another company, how would she wish the directors of that company to respond to a takeover? ◆

THE ROLE OF SHAREHOLDERS

As we have seen, *directors,* **not** *shareholders,* **have the right to manage the corporate business.** At one time corporate stock was primarily owned by individuals, but now institutional investors—pension plans, mutual funds, insurance companies, banks, foundations, and university endowments—own more than 50 percent of all shares publicly traded in the United States. Traditionally, unhappy shareholders did little more than the "Wall Street walk"—they sold their shares. The next section of this chapter explores the rights of shareholders. Corporate governance is of such interest to investors that many Websites contain discussions of these issues. Take a look, for example, at http://www.corpgov.net.

Rights of Shareholders

Shareholders have neither the right nor the obligation to manage the day-to-day business of the enterprise. If you own stock in Starbucks Corp., your share of stock plus $4.45 entitles you to a cup of mocha Valencia, the same as everyone else. By the same token, if the pipes freeze and the local Starbucks store floods, the manager has no right to call you, as a shareholder, to help clean up the mess. What rights do shareholders have?

Right to Information

Under the Model Act, shareholders acting in good faith and with a proper purpose have the right to inspect and copy the corporation's minute book, accounting records, and shareholder lists. A proper purpose is one that aids the shareholder in managing and protecting her investment. If, for example, Celeste is convinced that the directors of Devil Desserts, Inc., are mismanaging the company, she might demand a list of other shareholders so that she can ask them to join her in a lawsuit. This purpose is proper—although the company may not like it—and the company is required to give her the list. If, however, Celeste wants to use the shareholder list as a potential source for her new mail-order catalog featuring exercise equipment, the company could legitimately turn her down.

Right to Vote

A corporation must have at least one class of stock with voting rights.

Proxies

Shareholders who do not wish to attend a shareholders' meeting may appoint someone else to vote for them. Confusingly, both this person and the document the shareholder signs to appoint the substitute voter are called a **proxy.** Under SEC rules, companies are not required to solicit proxies. However, a meeting is invalid without a certain percentage of shareholders in attendance, either in person or by proxy. This attendance requirement is referred to as a **quorum.** As a practical matter, if a public company with thousands of investors does not solicit proxies, it will not obtain a quorum. Therefore, virtually all public companies do solicit proxies. Along with the proxy, the company must also give shareholders a **proxy statement** and an **annual report.** The proxy statement provides information on everything from management compensation to a list of directors who miss too many meetings. The annual report contains detailed financial data.

---

cyberLaw

Under SEC rules, companies can offer (but not require) electronic delivery of proxy statements and annual reports. Intel Corp. was one of the first companies to make its proxy statements and annual reports available on its Website. See http://www.intel.com and click on "Investor Relations." You can also read about Intel's policies on corporate governance at http://www.intel.com by clicking on "Investor Relations" and "Corporate Overview." ◆

Typically, only the company itself solicits proxies for a shareholder meeting. But sometimes shareholders who disapprove of company policies try to convince other shareholders to appoint them as proxy instead of management. These dissident shareholders must also prepare a proxy statement that discloses, among other information, who they are, how they are financing their opposition, and how many other proxy contests they have participated in. If enough shareholders give their proxies to the dissidents, then the dissidents can elect themselves or their representatives to replace the board of directors.

Shareholder Proposals

Some shareholders who oppose a company policy may not aspire to a board seat or perhaps cannot afford to send material individually to other investors. Such shareholders may use an alternative method, provided by the SEC, for communicating with fellow shareholders. **Under SEC rules, any shareholder who has continuously owned for one year at least 1 percent of the company or $2,000 of stock can require that one proposal be placed in the company's proxy statement to be voted on at the shareholder meeting.** In practice, many of these resolutions have a political agenda: save the environment, withdraw from Myanmar, ban genetically modified ingredients. Others relate to corporate-governance issues: reduce executive compensation and permit secret ballots. Over the last three years, public companies voted on 370 shareholder proposals. Prior to 1985, only two proposals had been approved—ever. Currently, about a quarter of all shareholder proposals receive a majority vote each year, a definite improvement (or deterioration, depending on your perspective). If a company refuses to include a shareholder proposal in its proxy material, shareholders can appeal to the SEC.

Despite the long history of shareholder proposals, an essential question remains unanswered: Are shareholder proposals binding on the company? The SEC recommends that proposals be couched in the form of a request or recommendation because state laws sometimes prohibit binding resolutions. Although shareholders traditionally followed this advice, many activists have been angered by companies that refuse to implement proposals that receive a majority vote from shareholders. In response, an increasing number of shareholders have begun to propose binding resolutions. The Supreme Court of Oklahoma provided ammunition when it ruled that a shareholder vote on takeover defenses could be binding.[9]

Ironically, companies sometimes implement shareholder proposals that have not received support from a majority of the shareholders. The pressure of shareholder proposals is credited with inducing many American companies to withdraw from South Africa in protest against its apartheid regime. Other companies implement shareholder proposals without even putting them up for a vote. Indeed, nearly half of all shareholder proposals are now withdrawn before a vote because the company capitulates. Many companies feel they have little choice but to negotiate, particularly with institutional investors over issues of corporate governance. For example, Colgate-Palmolive Co. agreed to a proposal by institutional investors to permit secret ballots at shareholder meetings. The following article illustrates the influence of even "unsuccessful" proposals.

NEWS*worthy*

Decades ago, during the Vietnam war, many churches were at the forefront of antiwar efforts. A band of Catholic nuns has remained true to the cause of peace—though today's activism takes them to corporate boardrooms and shareholders' meetings. At the moment, nuns from dozens of orders are completing a series of resolutions to be introduced at shareholder meetings this spring. The shareholder proposals to be offered by the nuns are making military executives squirm. At the top of their agenda is limiting military sales in countries where the arms can fall into the hands of child soldiers or perpetuate long-running wars. The nuns are also promoting a code of conduct that holds arms makers accountable for the effect of their business on the environment, and on the political and social stability of countries where they operate.

Last year, shareholder proposals from religious orders gained 11 percent of the vote at Textron, nearly 9 percent at Raytheon and 5 percent at General Dynamics. Religious groups say this compares with 2 percent to 3 percent of the vote in years past.

Nicholas D. Chabraja, the chief executive of General Dynamics, said he had given serious thought to some of the issues raised by the nuns, especially in the area of foreign military sales. While he said he was comfortable with selling arms to foreign countries at the request of the United States government, in the smaller number of cases where the United States government was not party to the transaction, the words of the nuns gave him pause.

Judging the success of the nuns' activism by the shareholder ballot box may be short-sighted, according to Nell Minnow, editor at the Corporate Library, an online organization that promotes corporate governance. Ms. Minnow said that while the nuns' campaign might be seen as "quixotic," such efforts "often turn out to be the leading edge of a cultural phenomenon." Ms. Minnow pointed to early antitobacco shareholders and environmental activists who raised issues at corporate annual meetings long before they caught on with the public at large.[10] ◆

Shareholder Meetings

Annual shareholder meetings are the norm for publicly traded companies. (Although technically not all states require public companies to hold an annual meeting of shareholders, the New York Stock Exchange [NYSE] does.) Companies whose

9 *International Bhd. of Teamsters Gen. Fund v. Fleming Cos.*, 1999 OK 3, 975 P.2d 907, 1999 Okla. LEXIS 3 (OK, 1999).

10 Leslie Wayne, "Shareholders Who Answer to a Higher C.E.O.," *The New York Times*, Feb. 1, 2005, p. 1.

stock is not publicly traded can either hold an annual meeting or use written consents from their shareholders. Everyone who owns stock on the **record date** must be sent notice of a meeting.

cyberLaw

Delaware law has entered cyberspace. It now permits companies to send official notices to their shareholders electronically and allows shareholders to vote electronically both before and during a meeting. Shareholder meetings can be held in cyberspace as long as shareholders have a reasonable opportunity to participate in and vote at the meeting. Many corporations now provide a live webcast of their annual meetings in real time and permit shareholders to send in email questions. So far, though, very few companies have held an annual meeting that is exclusively online. ◆

Election and Removal of Directors

The process of electing directors of a publicly traded company is different from what most people think. The nominating committee of the board of directors produces a slate of directors, with one name per opening. This slate is then sent to shareholders whose only choice is to vote in favor of a nominee or to withhold their vote (i.e., not vote at all). If a large number of shareholders withhold their votes, the nominee may be embarrassed a little, but the reality is that as long as he receives at least one vote (which can be his own), he is elected. If shareholders want to have a choice, they have to nominate their own slate, prepare and distribute a proxy statement to shareholders, and then communicate with shareholders why their slate is superior. This process is complex and expensive. Not surprisingly, each year only about one or two shareholder groups in the country undertake this effort. As this book goes to press, however, the SEC is considering a proposal to allow shareholders to include their own nominees on the company's ballot.

The voting process would be fairer if the nominating committee of the board was independent. Although the NYSE does not permit the CEO of a listed company to serve on the board's nominating committee, these committees rarely, if ever, nominate someone to whom the CEO is opposed.

What are unhappy shareholders to do? In the waning years of Michael Eisner's rule at the Walt Disney Company, shareholders withheld 43 percent of their votes from him. But that vote of no confidence did not cause the board to fire him, nor did he resign, at least not immediately. To oust Eisner, the shareholders would have had to nominate their own slate, pay for the preparation and distribution of their own proxy statement, and then compete against the company's almost unlimited budget to per- suade other shareholders to vote for the rebel slate.[11] Although shareholders theoreti- cally elect directors who then choose the officers, the reality is that officers (particularly the CEO) choose the directors.

Compensation for Officers and Directors

Given the control that the CEO has over the selection process for the board of direc- tors, it is not surprising that when the board sets the CEO's compensation, the results can sometimes appear to unfairly favor the CEO over the shareholders whose money is being used to compensate her.

---

[11] Ultimately, the Disney board did change its rules to require any directors receiving less than a majority of the votes cast to tender their resignation from the board. The board would then have the option of accepting or rejecting the resignation. Even under this new rule, Eisner would not have been forced to resign.

For many children *Pat the Bunny* is their first book. It contains few words but much interaction. "Readers" can pat the bunny, sniff the flowers, and play peekaboo with the blanket. After *Pat the Bunny,* many children graduate to *The Poky Little Puppy* and *Richard Scarry's Busy, Busy Town,* all published by Golden Books Family Entertainment, Inc.

Despite its portfolio of classics, Golden Books was having financial difficulties. The company hired Richard Snyder, an experienced publishing executive, to solve its distribution and sales problems. Such experience does not come cheap. At Golden Books he was the third highest paid executive in the publishing industry. But an executive does not live by pay alone. Snyder relocated the company to posh new quarters, hired a private chef, and used the corporate jet for his vacations. He also hired other executives (including his wife) at salaries two to three times the industry average. In return investors expected the stock price to zoom. They just did not expect it to zoom *down.* Not only did the stock price plummet 80 percent, but the company was put up for sale. In the midst of this turmoil, the board doubled Snyder's salary and paid him a $500,000 signing bonus for extending his contract two years. The company's stock price promptly plummeted again. Golden Books ended up filing for bankruptcy protection, not once, but twice, under Snyder's leadership. Ultimately, it was bought out and Snyder received close to $8 million in severance pay for a job well done. This sum was about 11 percent of the total purchase price for the company. ◆

To many investors, sky-high executive salaries have become the symbol of all that is wrong with corporate governance. It is difficult to justify CEO compensation that runs as high as $872 million in one year. In many companies, salaries are the least of the compensation. Executives also receive stock options, retirement plans, and lavish perks. Executives have long received perks such as country club memberships and cars, but the roster of options has expanded to include private school tuition for children and million dollar birthday parties for spouses. One company spent $8 million to buy the personal papers of Franklin Roosevelt for an executive who was writing a biography of the former president.

As we saw with Golden Books, even failure is well rewarded. When AT&T fired John Walter after less than one year, the board of directors offered him $26 million in severance pay. Indeed, many CEO employment contracts provide that the employee is entitled to severance pay unless fired for committing a particular type of felony. Incompetence or job failure does not disqualify the CEO from receiving a massive reward at the end. The chief of J.C. Penney would lose his severance pay only for "theft or moral turpitude" (and signing this contract does not count).

How much more does a CEO earn than an average worker? In 1975, the answer for the top 100 CEOs was 39 times as much. By 2005, that ratio had risen to more than 1000. To make matters even worse for shareholders, lavish compensation does not appear to improve the business's success. A study of the 58 companies that were most generous to their CEOs found that, on average, these companies significantly underperformed both the market generally and their industry in particular. No wonder that executive compensation has become a hot topic for shareholder proposals. And no surprise that, so far, these shareholder efforts have had little impact. More information about CEO compensation is available at **http://www.thecorporatelibrary.com/.**

As the following case demonstrates, however, shareholders' efforts to challenge executive compensation have met with little success. An officer's salary is presumed to be reasonable unless she voted for it as a director of the company. To be successful in challenging an executive's compensation, shareholders must prove that the board was grossly uninformed or that the amount was so high that it had no relation to the value of the services performed and was really a gift. As the following case indicates, the courts tend to be unsympathetic to this line of argument.

IN RE THE WALT DISNEY COMPANY DERIVATIVE LITIGATION

2006 Del. LEXIS 307
Supreme Court of Delaware, 2006

Facts: Michael Ovitz founded Creative Artists Agency (CAA), the premier talent agency in Hollywood. As a partner at this agency, he earned between $20 and $25 million per year. He was also a longtime friend of Michael Eisner, Chairman and CEO of the Walt Disney Company. Ovitz lacked experience managing a diversified public company, but Disney hired him to be its president with the hope that he could improve the company's talent relationships and increase foreign revenues. Upon the advice of Graef Crystal, a compensation consultant, the board approved Ovitz's contract.

After 14 months, all parties agreed that the experiment had failed, so Ovitz left Disney—but not empty-handed. Under his contract, he was entitled to $130 million in severance pay.[12]

Shareholders of Disney sued the board, alleging that its members had violated the business judgment rule and that such a large payout was a waste of corporate assets. The trial court held for Disney and the shareholders appealed.

Issues: Did Disney directors have the right to pay $130 million to an employee who had worked at the company unsuccessfully and for only 14 months?

Excerpts from Justice Jacobs's Decision: [T]he compensation committee [of the Board of Directors] was informed of the material facts relating to the payout. If measured in terms of the documentation that would have been generated if "best practices" had been followed, that record leaves much to be desired. [But, the] committee reasonably believed that the analysis of the terms of the [contract] was within Crystal's professional or expert competence, and the committee relied on the information, opinions, reports and statements made by Crystal. Furthermore, Crystal appears to have been selected with reasonable care, especially in light of his previous engagements with the company.

[The purpose of the business judgment rule] is to protect directors who rely in good faith upon information presented to them from various sources, including any other person as to matters the member reasonably believes are within such person's professional or expert competence and who has been selected with reasonable care by and on behalf of the corporation. For these reasons, we uphold the Chancellor's [i.e., the trial court's] determination that the compensation committee members did not breach their fiduciary duty of care.

The shareholders claim the payment of the severance amount to Ovitz constituted waste. To recover on a claim of corporate waste, the plaintiffs must shoulder the burden of proving that the exchange was so one sided that no business person of ordinary, sound judgment could conclude that the corporation has received adequate consideration. A claim of waste will arise only in the rare, unconscionable case where directors irrationally squander or give away corporate assets.

[The shareholders] claim that provisions of the [contract] were wasteful because they incentivized Ovitz to perform poorly in order to obtain payment. The approval of the [contract] had a rational business purpose: to induce Ovitz to leave CAA, at what would otherwise be a considerable cost to him, in order to join Disney. The Chancellor found that the evidence does not support any notion that the [contract] irrationally incentivized Ovitz to get himself fired. To suggest that at the time he entered into the [contract] Ovitz would engineer an early departure, at the cost of his extraordinary reputation in the entertainment industry and his historical friendship with Eisner, is not only fanciful but also without proof in the record.

For the reasons stated above, the judgment of the Chancellor is affirmed. ■

---

12 As Ira Gershwin put it, "Nice work if you can get it, and if you get it—won't you tell me how?"

Directors not only set the salaries of company officers, they also determine their own compensation (unless the charter or bylaws provide otherwise). Directors of Fortune 200 companies are paid on average $152,000 annually, while directors of Fortune 1000 companies earn on average $116,000.

Fundamental Corporate Changes

A corporation must seek shareholder approval before undergoing any of the following fundamental changes: a merger, a sale of major assets, dissolution of the corporation, or an amendment to the charter or bylaws.

Right to Dissent

If a private corporation (i.e., one whose stock is not publicly traded) decides to undertake a fundamental change, the Model Act and many state laws require the company to buy back the stock of any shareholders who object. This process is referred to as dissenters' rights, and the company must pay "fair value" for the stock. Fundamental changes include a merger or a sale of most of the company's assets.

Right to Protection from Other Shareholders

Anyone who owns enough stock to control a corporation has a fiduciary duty to minority shareholders. (Minority shareholders are those with less than a controlling interest.) The courts have long recognized that minority shareholders are entitled to extra protection because it is easy (perhaps even natural) for controlling shareholders to take advantage of them. For example:

- The Sinclair Oil Company owned 97 percent of Sinven Co. Sinclair violated its fiduciary duty to Sinven's minority shareholders when it forced Sinven to pay dividends large enough to bankrupt the company.[13]

- A court refused to allow one brother, who was a majority shareholder of the family company, to force the other to sell his shares. According to the court, a minority shareholder can be ejected only for a reason that is fair or has a business purpose.[14]

Corporate Governance in Publicly Traded Companies: Sarbanes-Oxley and Stock Exchange Rules

A recent spate of corporate scandals, involving such high-flying companies as Enron Corp., revealed that some boards of directors have not provided adequate oversight of their companies. In response, Congress passed the Sarbanes-Oxley Act of 2002 (SOX). This statute applies to public companies as well as to all foreign companies listed on a U.S. stock exchange. Under SOX:

- Rule 404 requires each company to adopt effective financial controls.

- CEOs and CFOs must personally certify their company's financial statements. They are subject to criminal penalties for violations.

- All members of a board's audit committee must be independent.

---

13 *Sinclair Oil Corp. v. Levien*, 280 A.2d 717, 1971 Del. LEXIS 225 (Del. 1971).
14 *Lerner v. Lerner*, 306 Md. 771, 511 A.2d 501, 1986 Md. LEXIS 264 (Md. 1986).

- A company cannot make personal loans to its directors or officers.
- If a company has to restate its earnings, its chief executive officer and chief financial officer must reimburse the company for any bonus or profits they have received from selling company stock within a year of the release of the flawed financials.
- Each company must disclose if it has an ethics code and, if it does not, why not.
- It is a felony to interfere with a federal investigation into fraud.
- Whistleblowing employees are protected.
- A new Public Accounting Oversight Board has been established to oversee the auditing of public companies.

    The text of the statute is available at http://sarbanes-oxley.com.

    The NYSE and NASDAQ have also established a new role for independent directors at listed companies:

- Independent directors must comprise a majority of the board.
- They must meet regularly on their own without inside directors.
- Only independent directors can serve on compensation or nominating committees.
- Audit committees must have at least three independent directors who are financially literate.

Public Policy

The goal of these reforms was to prevent corporate abuses and restore investor confidence. Have the goals been achieved? Were they worth the cost? For large companies (with annual revenues that exceeded $5 billion), the cost of compliance with Rule 404 averaged $4.6 million in the first year of the act. These firms also required on average 70,000 hours of their employees' time to comply. Some smaller companies have spent a substantial portion of their total revenue on SOX. Indeed, 20 percent of public companies have considered going private simply to avoid this heavy compliance expense. Some foreign companies decided not to be listed in the United States because of this statute.

It is difficult to quantify the benefit that investors gain from a reduction in accounting fraud and an increase in confidence in the stock market. Only time will reveal whether SOX has given the boot to corporate scandals. ◆

ENFORCING SHAREHOLDER RIGHTS

Shareholders in serious conflict with management have three different mechanisms for enforcing their rights: a derivative lawsuit, a direct lawsuit, or a class action.

Derivative Lawsuits

A derivative lawsuit is brought by *shareholders* to remedy a wrong to the *corporation.* The suit is brought in the name of the corporation, and all proceeds of the litigation go to the corporation. As we have seen, the shareholders of Disney were upset when the board of directors approved a $130 million severance package for Michael Ovitz. Because they felt that that decision had harmed the company, they wanted to sue the directors. But they had no right to sue on their own behalf, because the company had been harmed, not they themselves. Only the corporation could sue. And who would authorize a suit by the corporation against the directors? The directors have to authorize any such litigation. Because the directors are unlikely to file suit against themselves, shareholders are permitted to bring a derivative action, in the name of the corporation, against managers who have violated their duty to the corporation.

There is a complication, however: **Before bringing a suit in the name of the corporation, shareholders must *make demand* on the board of directors of the corporation asking it to bring the lawsuit, unless demand would *clearly be futile*.** Boards almost always reject this request because they do not want to sue themselves. **The shareholders' only real hope is to convince a court that demand would clearly be futile either because the directors had a conflict of interest or because their decision violated the business judgment rule.** As we have seen, the court in the *Disney* case decided that the decision to pay Michael Ovitz $130 million did not violate the business judgment rule, hence the shareholder suit ended.

If shareholders are permitted to proceed with their derivative action, all damages go to the corporation; the individual shareholders benefit only to the extent that the settlement causes their stock to rise in value. Litigation is tremendously expensive. How can shareholders afford to sue if they are not entitled to damages? A corporation that loses a derivative suit must pay the legal fees of the victorious shareholders. Most derivative lawsuits are brought by lawyers seeking to earn these fees. (Losing shareholders are generally not required to pay the corporation's legal fees.)

Direct Lawsuits

Shareholders are permitted to sue the corporation directly only if their own rights have been harmed. If, for example, the corporation denies shareholders the right to inspect its books and records or to hold a shareholder meeting, they may sue in their own names and keep any damages awarded. The corporation is not required to pay the shareholders' legal fees; winning shareholders can use part of any damage award for this purpose.

Class Action Lawsuits

If a group of shareholders all have the same claim, they can join together and file suit as a class action, rather than suing separately. By joining forces, they can share the expense and effort of litigation. It is also far more efficient for the judicial system for one court to try one case than for tens or hundreds of courts all over the country to try the same issue. For obvious reasons, companies tend to resist class actions. In such suits, management is assailed by many small shareholders who otherwise could not afford to (or would not bother to) sue individually.

Chapter Conclusion

Corporations first became prominent in the eighteenth and nineteenth centuries as a means for businesses to raise the outside capital needed for large-scale manufacturing. Shareholders without management skills complemented managers without capital. Although this separation between management and owners makes great economic sense and has contributed significantly to the rise of the American economy, it also creates complex legal issues. How can shareholders ensure that the corporation will operate in their best interest? How can managers make tough decisions without being second-guessed by shareholders? Balancing the interests of managers and shareholders is a complex problem the law has struggled to resolve, without completely satisfying either side.

Chapter Review

1. Promoters are personally liable for contracts they sign before the corporation is formed unless the corporation and the third party agree to a novation.

2. Companies generally incorporate in the state in which they will be doing business. However, if they intend to operate in several states, they may choose to incorporate in a jurisdiction known for its favorable corporate laws, such as Delaware or Nevada.

3. A corporate charter must generally include the company's name, address, registered agent, purpose, and a description of its stock.

4. A court may, under certain circumstances, pierce the corporate veil and hold shareholders personally liable for the debts of the corporation.

5. Termination of a corporation is a three-step process requiring a shareholder vote, the filing of "Articles of Dissolution," and the winding up of the enterprise's business.

6. Officers and directors have a fiduciary duty to act in the best interests of the shareholders of the corporation.

7. The business judgment rule protects managers from liability for their decisions as long as the managers observe the duty of care and the duty of loyalty.

8. Under the duty of loyalty, managers may not enter into an agreement on behalf of their corporation that benefits them personally, unless the board of directors or the shareholders have first approved it. If the manager does not seek the necessary approval, the business judgment rule no longer applies, and the manager will be liable unless the transaction was entirely fair to the corporation.

9. Under the duty of loyalty, managers may not take advantage of an opportunity that rightfully belongs to the corporation.

10. Under the duty of care, managers must make honest, informed decisions that have a rational business purpose.

11. The Williams Act regulates the activities of a bidder in a tender offer for stock in a publicly traded corporation.

12. Virtually all publicly held companies solicit proxies from their shareholders. A proxy authorizes someone else to vote in place of the shareholder.

13. Under certain circumstances public companies must include shareholder proposals in the proxy statement.

14. A shareholder of a privately held company who objects to a fundamental change in the corporation can insist that her shares be bought out at fair value. This protection is referred to as "dissenters' rights."

15. Controlling shareholders have a fiduciary duty to minority shareholders.

16. Congress, the NYSE, and NASDAQ have all taken steps to prevent management abuses. These new regulations require that companies adopt effective financial controls. They also require more independent directors on the board as a whole and on important subcommittees.

17. A derivative lawsuit is brought by shareholders to remedy a wrong to the corporation. The suit is brought in the name of the corporation, and all proceeds of the litigation go to the corporation.

18. If a group of shareholders all have the same claim against the corporation, they can join together and file a class action, rather than suing separately.

Practice Test

1. Michael Ferns incorporated Erin Homes, Inc., to manufacture mobile homes. He issued himself a stock certificate for 100 shares for which he made no payment. He and his wife served as officers and directors of the organization, but, during the eight years of its existence, the corporation held only one meeting. Erin always had its own checking account, and all proceeds from the sales of mobile homes were deposited there. It filed federal income tax returns each year, using its own federal identification number. John and Thelma Laya paid $17,500 to purchase a mobile home

from Erin, but the company never delivered it to them. The Layas sued Erin Homes and Michael Ferns, individually. Should the court "pierce the corporate veil" and hold Ferns personally liable?

2. **CPA QUESTION** A corporate stockholder is entitled to which of the following rights?

   a. Elect officers

   b. Receive annual dividends

   c. Approve dissolution

   d. Prevent corporate borrowing

3. An appraiser valued a subsidiary of Signal Co. at between $230 million and $260 million. Six months later, Burmah Oil offered to buy the subsidiary at $480 million, giving Signal only three days to respond. The board of directors accepted the offer without obtaining an updated evaluation of the subsidiary or determining if other companies would offer a higher price. Members of the board were sophisticated, with a great deal of experience in the oil industry. A Signal Co. shareholder sued to prevent the sale. Is the Signal board protected by the business judgment rule?

4. **YOU BE THE JUDGE** WRITING PROBLEM Asher Hyman and Stephen Stahl formed a corporation named Ampersand to produce plays. Both men were employed by the corporation. After producing one play, Stahl decided to write *Philly's Beat*, focusing on the history of rock and roll in Philadelphia. As the play went into production, however, the two men quarreled over Hyman's repeated absences from work and the company's serious financial difficulties. Stahl resigned from Ampersand and formed another corporation to produce the play. Did the opportunity to produce *Philly's Beat* belong to Ampersand? **Argument for Stahl:** Ampersand was formed for the purpose of producing plays, not writing them. When Stahl wrote *Philly's Beat*, he was not competing against Ampersand. **Argument for Hyman:** Ampersand was in the business of producing plays, and it wanted *Philly's Beat.*

5. Davis Ajouelo signed an employment contract with William Wilkerson. The contract stated: "whatever company, partnership, or corporation that Wilkerson may form for the purpose of manufacturing shall succeed Wilkerson and exercise the rights and assume all of Wilkerson's

obligations as fixed by this contract." Two months later, Wilkerson formed Auto-Soler Company. Ajouelo entered into a new contract with Auto-Soler providing that the company was liable for Wilkerson's obligations under the old contract. Neither Wilkerson nor the company ever paid Ajouelo the sums owed him under the contracts. Ajouelo sued Wilkerson personally. Does Wilkerson have any obligations to Ajouelo?

6. **ETHICS** Edgar Bronfman, Jr., dropped out of high school to go to Hollywood and write songs and produce movies. Eventually, he left Hollywood to work in the family business—the Bronfmans owned 36 percent of Seagram Co., a liquor and beverage conglomerate. Promoted to president of the company at the age of 32, Bronfman seized a second chance to live his dream. Seagram received 70 percent of its earnings from its 24 percent ownership of DuPont Co. Bronfman sold this stock at less than market value to purchase (at an inflated price) 80 percent of MCA, a movie and music company that had been a financial disaster for its prior owners. Some observers thought Bronfman had gone Hollywood; others that he had gone crazy. After the deal was announced, the price of Seagram shares fell 18 percent. Was there anything Seagram shareholders could have done to prevent what to them was not a dream but a nightmare? Apart from legal issues, was Bronfman's decision ethical? What ethical obligations did he owe Seagram's shareholders?

7. Daniel Cowin was a minority shareholder of Bresler & Reiner, Inc., a public company that developed real estate in Washington, D.C. He alleged numerous instances of corporate mismanagement, fraud, self-dealing, and breach of fiduciary duty by the board of directors. He sought damages for the diminished value of his stock. Could Cowin bring this suit as a direct action, or must it be a derivative suit?

8. **CPA QUESTION** Generally, a corporation's articles of incorporation must include all of the following except the:

   a. Name of the corporation's registered agent.

   b. Name of each incorporator.

   c. Number of authorized shares.

   d. Quorum requirements.

9. Two shareholders of Bruce Company, Harry and Yolan Gilbert, were fighting management for control of the company. They asked for permission to inspect Bruce's stockholder list so that they could either solicit support for their slate of directors at the upcoming stockholders' meeting, or attempt to buy additional stock from other stockholders, or both. Bruce's board refused to allow the Gilberts to see the shareholder list on the grounds that the Gilberts owned another corporation that competed with Bruce. Do the Gilberts have the right to see Bruce's shareholder list?

10. *ROLE REVERSAL* Write a short-answer question that deals with the duty of care under the business judgment rule.

Internet Research Problem

Think of an idea for a new company and prepare a corporate charter for your business. You can find examples of Delaware charters at **http://contracts. corporate.findlaw.com.** For extra credit, find a sample charter for your own state.

Using the Internet, find information on a company's shareholder proposals in the last year. (You can, for example, type into Google: "shareholder proposals 2007.") What were these proposals about? What was the outcome of the shareholder vote? Can you find a proposal that shareholders supported?

You can find further practice problems at **academic.cengage.com/blaw/beatty.**

Securities Regulation

In 1926, America was gripped by a fever of stock market speculation. "Playing the market" became a national mania. The most engrossing news on any day's front page was the market. Up and up it soared. The cause of this psychological virus is uncertain, but the focus of the infection was the New York Stock Exchange. Between 1926 and 1929, annual volume leaped from 451 million to more than 1.1 billion shares. In one year alone, the price of AT&T went from $179.50 to $335.62.

Much of this feverish trading was done on margin. Customers put down only 10 or 20 percent of a stock's purchase price and then borrowed the rest from their broker. This easy-payment plan excited the gambling instinct of unwary amateurs and professional speculators alike. By September 1929, the volume of these margin loans was equal to about half the entire public debt of the United States.

On September 4, 1929, stock prices began to soften, and for the next month they slid gently. Over the weekend of October 19, brokers sent out thousands of margin calls, asking customers to pay down loans that now exceeded the value of their stock. If customers failed to pay, brokers dumped their stock on the market, causing prices to fall further and brokers to make more margin calls. Soon there was a mad scramble of selling as prices plunged in wild disorder. Tens of thousands of investors across the country were wiped out. On Tuesday, October 29, 1929, the speculative boom completely collapsed. That day, 4 million shares were traded, a record that stood for 30 years. From the peak of the bull market in September to the debacle of October 29, more than $32 billion of equity value simply vanished from the earth.

The stock market crash spawned the Great Depression—the most pervasive, persistent, and destructive economic crisis the nation has ever faced. Retail trade fell by one half, automobile production by two thirds, steel by three quarters. In 1933, more businesses failed than in any other year in history. Surviving businesses responded to the crisis by cutting dividends, reducing inventories, laying off workers, slashing wages, and canceling capital investments.

© ARTHUR S. AUBRY/PHOTODISC/GETTY IMAGES

Unemployment statistics were the most poignant of all. In 1932, one in every five people in the labor force was out of a job. Million of others were underemployed, working only two or three days a week for wages that could not support a family. Distress cut indiscriminately across all economic and social classes. Bankers, insurance agents, architects, and lawyers joined the throng of unemployed. Articles such as the following were common in newspapers across the land:

New York, Jan. 6, 1933 (AP)—After vainly trying to get a stay of dispossession until Jan. 15 from his apartment in Brooklyn, yesterday, Peter J. Cornell, 48 years old, a former roofing contractor out of work and penniless, fell dead in the arms of his wife. A doctor gave the cause of his death as heart disease, and the police said it had at least partly been caused by the bitter disappointment of a long day's fruitless attempt to prevent himself and his family being put out on the streets.[1] ■

INTRODUCTION

At the time of the great stock market crash, there was no federal securities law, only state law. Congress recognized that the country needed a national securities system if it was to avoid another such catastrophe. In 1933, Congress passed the Securities Act of 1933 (1933 Act) to regulate the issuance of new securities. The next year, it passed the Securities Exchange Act of 1934 (1934 Act) to regulate companies with publicly traded securities. The 1934 Act also established the Securities and Exchange Commission (SEC), the regulatory agency that oversees the securities industry.

The Securities and Exchange Commission

The SEC creates law in three different ways:

- **Rules.** The securities statutes are often little more than general guides. Through its rules, the SEC fills in the crucial details.
- **Releases.** These are informal pronouncements from the SEC on current issues. Releases often operate as two-way communication. When the SEC issues a release to announce a proposed change in the rules, it also asks for comments on the proposal.
- **No-Action Letters.** Anyone who is in doubt about whether a particular transaction complies with the securities laws can ask the SEC directly. The response is called a no-action letter because it states that "the staff will recommend that the Commission take no action" if the transaction is done in a specified manner.

In addition to creating laws, the SEC has the power to enforce them. It can bring **cease and desist orders** against those who violate the securities laws, and it can also levy fines or confiscate profits from illegal transactions. Those accused of wrongdoing

---

[1] The material in this section is adapted from Cabell Phillips, *From the Crash to the Blitz* (Toronto: Macmillan, 1969).

can appeal these sanctions to the courts. The SEC does not have the authority to bring a criminal action; it refers criminal cases to the Justice Department.

What Is a Security?

Both the 1933 and the 1934 Acts regulate securities. The official definition of a security includes a note, stock, treasury stock, bond, debenture, evidence of indebtedness, certificate of interest or participation in any profit-sharing agreement, and 17 other equivalents. Courts have interpreted this definition to mean that **a security is any transaction in which the buyer (1) invests money in a common enterprise and (2) expects to earn a profit predominantly from the efforts of others.**

This definition covers investments that are not necessarily called *securities*. For example, they may be called orange trees. W. J. Howey Co. owned large citrus groves in Florida. It sold these trees to investors, most of whom were from out of state and knew nothing about farming. Purchasers were expected to hire someone to take care of their trees. Someone like Howey-in-the-Hills, Inc., a related company that just happened to be in the service business. Customers were free to hire any service company, but 85 percent of the acreage was covered by service contracts with Howey-in-the-Hills. The court held that Howey was selling a security (no matter how orange or tart), because the purchaser was investing in a common enterprise (the orange grove) expecting to earn a profit from Howey's farm work.

Other courts have interpreted the term "security" to include animal breeding arrangements (chinchillas, silver foxes, or beavers, take your pick); condominium purchases in which the developer promises the owner a certain level of income from rentals; and even investments in whiskey.

SECURITIES ACT OF 1933

The 1933 Act requires that, before offering or selling securities, the issuer must register the securities with the SEC, unless the securities qualify for an exemption. An **issuer** is the company that issues the stock. Registering securities with the SEC in a public offering is a major undertaking, but the 1933 Act exempts some securities and also some particular types of securities transactions from the full-blown registration requirements of a public offering.

It is also important to remember that **when an issuer registers securities, the SEC does not investigate the quality of the offering.** Permission from the SEC to sell securities does not mean that the company has a good product or will be successful. SEC approval simply means that, on the surface, the company has answered all relevant questions about itself and its major products. The guiding principle of the federal securities laws is that investors can make a reasoned decision on whether to buy or sell securities if they have full and accurate information about a company and the security it is selling. For example, the Green Bay Packers football team sold an offering of stock to finance stadium improvements. The prospectus admitted:

> IT IS VIRTUALLY IMPOSSIBLE that any investor will ever make a profit on the stock purchase. The company will pay no dividends, and the shares cannot be sold.

This does not sound like a stock you want in your retirement fund; on the other hand, the SEC will not prevent Green Bay from selling it, or you from buying it, as long as you understand what the risks are.

One last point: **the 1933 Act prohibits fraud in *any* securities transaction.** Anyone who issues fraudulent securities is in violation of the 1933 Act, whether or not the securities are registered. Both the SEC and any purchasers of the stock can sue the issuer.

cyberLaw

Companies must deliver certain documents to investors and also file them with the SEC. Almost all filings with the SEC must be made electronically, using the EDGAR (Electronic Data Gathering, Analysis, and Retrieval) system. Once filed with the SEC, this information is available online (at http://www.sec.gov).

Companies file online with the SEC, but delivering documents to investors electronically is more difficult because computer literacy and availability among investors vary widely. The SEC does *permit* (but not require) issuers to communicate electronically with investors, provided that the following standards are met:

- *Consent.* Although many investors have computers, an issuer cannot assume that all do, or that all want to receive data this way. Therefore, an electronic document is valid only if the investor agrees to receive information in this form.

- *Notice.* A company cannot simply post information on its Internet Web site, because investors will not necessarily know it is there. The issuer must notify investors, via e-mail or snail mail, that information is available.

- *Access.* The recipients must have access to the information for a reasonable period and be able to download or print it. The investor can always request the paper version of a document, even after consenting to electronic delivery. ◆

General Exemption

Before offering securities for sale, the issuer must determine whether they are exempt from registration under the 1933 Act. Typically, exemptions are based on two factors: the type of security and the type of transaction. However, the National Securities Markets Improvement Act of 1996 gave the SEC new authority under both the 1933 and the 1934 Acts to grant exemptions that are "in the public interest" and "consistent with the protection of investors."

Exempt Securities

The 1933 Act exempts some types of securities from registration because they (1) are inherently low risk, (2) are regulated by other statutes, or (3) are not really investments. The following securities are exempt from registration:

- **Government securities,** which include any security issued or guaranteed by federal or state government

- **Bank securities,** which include any security issued or guaranteed by a bank

- **Short-term notes,** which are high-quality negotiable notes or drafts that are due within nine months of issuance and are not sold to the general public

- **Nonprofit issues,** which include any security issued by a nonprofit religious, educational, or charitable organization

- **Insurance policies and annuity contracts,** which are governed by insurance regulations

Exempt Transactions

Section 4(2) of the 1933 Act exempts from registration "transactions by an issuer not involving any public offering." These are simple words to define a complex problem. In effect, the 1933 Act says that an issuer is not required to register securities that are sold in a private offering—that is, an offering with only a few investors or a relatively small amount of money involved. In private offerings, the full-blown disclosure of a public offering is neither necessary nor appropriate. For instance, a group of sophisticated investors who know an industry well do not need full disclosure. Or, if the amount at stake is relatively small, it would not make economic sense for the issuer to incur the heavy expense of a public offering.

There is an important distinction between exempt *securities* and exempt *transactions*. Exempt *securities* are always exempt throughout their lives, no matter how many times they are sold. Stock sold in an exempt *transaction* is exempt only that one time, not necessarily in any subsequent sale. Suppose that County Bank sells stock to the public. Under the 1933 Act, the bank is never required to register these securities, no matter how many times they are sold. On the other hand, suppose that Tumbleweed, Inc., a quilt maker, sells $5 million worth of stock in a private offering that is exempt from registration. Shamika buys 100 shares of this stock. Seven years later, the company decides to sell stock in a public offering that must be registered. As part of this public offering, Shamika sells her 100 shares. This time, the shares must be registered because they are being sold in a *public offering*.

Most small companies use private, not public, offerings to raise capital. There are three different types of private offerings—intrastate, Regulation D, and Regulation A—each with its own set of rules.

Intrastate Offering Exemption

Under SEC Rule 147, an issuer is not required to register securities that are *offered* **and** *sold* **only to residents of the state in which the issuer is incorporated and does business.** This exemption was designed to provide local financing for local businesses. To qualify under Rule 147, 80 percent of the issuer's revenues and assets must be in-state, and it must also intend to spend 80 percent of the offering's proceeds in-state. Neither the issuer nor any purchaser can sell the securities outside the state for nine months after the offering.

Rule 147 is a **safe harbor**—if an issuer totally complies with it, the offering definitely qualifies as intrastate. But even if the issuer does not comply absolutely with the rule, the SEC or the courts may still consider the offering to be intrastate; however, the issuer cannot be sure in advance how the decision will come out. Sonic was a Utah corporation that sold stock to Utah residents. *Seven* months later, the company sold stock to an Illinois company. Although Sonic violated Rule 147 by making the second sale too early, the court held that the company had nonetheless qualified for an intrastate offering because it had not intended, at the time of the original offering, to sell stock outside Utah.[2] Although Sonic had not totally complied with Rule 147, it had come close enough to avoid liability. A safe harbor is less dangerous, but a voyage outside its boundaries does not necessarily end in disaster.

Regulation D

Three different types of private offerings can be made under Regulation D (often referred to as Reg D) under Rules 504, 505, and 506.

Rule 504. Under this rule (known as the "seed capital" rule), a company:

- May sell up to $1 million in securities during each 12-month period.
- May advertise the stock and solicit an unlimited number of investors if:
  - The transaction is registered under a state law with disclosure requirements, or

---

2 *Busch v. Carpenter*, 827 F.2d 653, 1987 U.S. App. LEXIS 11034 (10th Cir. 1987).

- Sales are limited to accredited investors. **Accredited investors** are institutions (such as banks and insurance companies) or wealthy individuals (with a net worth of more than $1 million or an annual income of more than $200,000).

If the securities are neither registered under state law nor sold exclusively to accredited investors, they are **restricted** stock, which means they must be purchased for investment purposes. As a general rule, the buyer cannot resell restricted securities, either publicly or privately, for one year.

Rule 505.   This rule permits a company to sell up to $5 million of stock during each 12-month period, subject to the following restrictions:

- The company may not advertise the stock publicly.
- The issuer can sell to as many accredited investors as it wants, but is limited to only 35 unaccredited investors.
- The company need not provide information to accredited investors but must make some disclosure to unaccredited investors. This requirement provides issuers with a serious incentive to avoid unaccredited investors because the disclosure requirements, although less demanding than for a public offering, are nonetheless burdensome.
- Stock purchased under this rule is restricted.

Rule 506.   This rule is similar to Rule 505. The differences are that:

- There is no limit on the amount of stock a company can sell.
- If an unaccredited purchaser is unsophisticated, he must have a **purchaser representative** to help him evaluate the investment. Is an *unsophisticated* investor someone who does not care for opera? No, it is someone who is unable to assess the risks of the offering himself.

The following table sets out the menu of choices under Reg D:

	Maximum Value of Securities Sold in a 12-Month Period	Maximum Number of Investors		Is Disclosure Required?	Is Public Advertising Permitted?	Are Securities Restricted?
Rule 504 Option 1:	$1 million	No limit on accredited investors	or	Disclosure under state law	Yes	No
Option 2:	$1 million	No limit	and	No	No	Yes
Rule 505	$5 million	No limit on accredited investors; no more than 35 unaccredited investors		Only for unaccredited investors	No	Yes
Rule 506	No limit	No limit on accredited investors; no more than 35 unaccredited investors, who must either be sophisticated or have a purchaser representative		Only for unaccredited investors	No	Yes

Regulation A

Although an offering under Regulation A is *called* a private offering, it really is a small public offering. **Reg A permits an issuer to sell $5 million of securities *publicly* in any 12-month period.** The issuer must give each purchaser an offering circular that provides the same disclosure required for unaccredited investors under Reg D. The following table compares a public offering, Reg A, and Reg D:

	Initial Public Offering	Regulation A	Regulation D
Maximum Value of Securities Sold	No limit	$5 million	$1 million, $5 million, or no limit, depending on the rule
Public Solicitation of Purchasers	Permitted	Permitted	Permitted only under Rule 504
Suitability Requirements for Purchasers	No requirements	No requirements	Must determine if investors are accredited or sophisticated
Disclosure Requirements	Elaborate registration statement, audited financials	Offering circular that is less detailed than a registration statement	Rule 504: may require disclosure under state law Rules 505 and 506: none for accredited investors, the same requirements as Reg A for unaccredited investors
Resale of Securities	Permitted	Permitted	Sometimes permitted under Rule 504, otherwise not permitted for one year
Number of Offerings in 2001	770	50	15,000
Number of Offerings in 2004	630	25	15,795

Direct Public Offerings

Traditionally, a small company either sold stock to people it knew well or hired an investment banker to place the securities with a wider public. But now, instead of going through Wall Street, many companies trying to raise capital for the first time sell stock to the public themselves through a direct public offering (DPO). In a DPO, the issuer typically sells shares to its stakeholders: customers, employees, suppliers, or the community. The issuer makes a DPO offering under Regulation A or Rule 504, because both permit public offerings without full-blown registration and disclosure requirements.

The advantages of a DPO are:

- It is much cheaper than a regular public offering done through an underwriter.

- It can be an effective marketing tool—shareholders tend to become even more loyal customers.

The downside:

- Each investor must receive written information about the company. The cost of this disclosure can be prohibitive when dealing with many small investors. Mailing a $10 disclosure document to hundreds of investors who only want to buy $50 worth of stock each may not be an efficient means of raising money.

- Although shareholders are warned that they should view their purchases as long-term investments, some will inevitably want to sell their shares. Setting up a system to permit these trades can be tricky and time consuming.

Although the companies featured in the following article found their DPOs worthwhile, the process consumed significant management time.

NEWS*worthy*

In 1995, Spring Street Brewery, a New York microbrewery, became the first company to conduct an offering on the Internet. It established a home page that allowed potential investors to examine and download its offering documents. In the end, it raised $1.6 million.

Thanksgiving Coffee Co. of Fort Bragg, California, used both cybertechnology and the old-fashioned face-to-face approach. It had originally planned simply to sell to its loyal customer base. "You think that everybody who knows about you will line up around the block to buy stock, but you have to put the offering in front of potential investors' faces seven times to get them to take action," says Thanksgiving general manager Rick Moon. He did just that. He put offering notices on coffee-bean bags; he hung announcements on bean dispensers. Vendors got the advertisements, as did mail-order customers. Information about the stock sale appeared on the company's Website, in its catalog, and in advertisements in targeted magazines. Anyone who called about the stock got regular updates on the offering. In the end, the huge effort paid off. By the time the offering closed, Thanksgiving Coffee had sold 20 percent of its stock for $1.25 million.[3] ◆

The "screen test" at http://www.dfdpo.com can help you gauge whether you and your company are ready for a DPO.

Public Offerings

When a company wishes to raise significant amounts of capital from a large number of people, it is time for a public offering. A company's first public sale of securities is called an **initial public offering** or an **IPO.** Here is one company's experience with an IPO.

Shortly after graduating from the Massachusetts Institute of Technology, Daniel Schwinn and Frank Slaughter founded Shiva Corp. (pronounced SHE-va) in Burlington, Massachusetts. The company made hardware and software that allowed personal computers to tie directly into a corporate network from outside the office. Although within a decade sales had reached $42 million and net income was $2.7 million, the company was constantly strapped for cash to fund expansion. Its two founders began thinking about a public offering.

Underwriting

As we have seen, companies can sell stock directly to the public themselves, but they primarily do so if the amounts involved are small. Shiva sought to raise more than $20 million, so it decided to hire an investment bank to serve as underwriter. In a **firm commitment** underwriting, the underwriter buys the stock from the issuer and resells

---

[3] Stephanie Gruner, "When Mom & Pop Go Public," *INC.,* Dec. 1996, p. 66. Republished with permission of INC. Magazine; permission conveyed through the Copyright Clearance Center, Inc.

it to the public. The underwriter bears the risk that the stock may sell at a lower price than expected. In a **best efforts** underwriting, the underwriter does not buy the stock but instead acts as the company's agent in selling it. If the stock sells at a low price, the company, not the underwriter, is the loser.

In underwriting, as in life, timing is everything. As it happened, just when Shiva hoped to complete its offering, Wall Street's interest in the high-tech sector suddenly cooled. Investment bankers offered the company only $6 a share for its stock. Shiva decided to wait. Within three months, the market in high-tech stocks picked up again. The company's president, Frank Ingari, and its chief financial officer, Cynthia Deysher, went to New York to sign on with the investment bank Goldman Sachs. Shiva agreed to sell Goldman 2.4 million shares at a tentative price of $12 per share.

Registration Statement

The **registration statement** has two purposes: to notify the SEC that a sale of securities is pending and to disclose information to prospective purchasers. The registration statement must include detailed information about the issuer and its business, a description of the stock, the proposed use of the proceeds from the offering, and audited balance sheets and income statements. Preparing a registration statement is neither quick—it typically takes two to three months—nor inexpensive. Shiva spent $900,000 on audits and other expenses.

Within a month of hiring an investment bank, Shiva filed its *preliminary* draft of the registration statement with the SEC. This preliminary draft is called a **red herring** because it contains a notice in red ink warning that the securities cannot yet be sold.[4] The SEC typically spends between 30 and 100 days reviewing this preliminary draft of the registration statement. Remember that the Commission does not assess the value of the stock or the merit of the investment. Its role is to ensure that the company has disclosed enough to enable investors to make an informed decision.

Prospectus

Typically, buyers never see the registration statement; they are given the **prospectus** instead. (The prospectus is also included in the registration statement that is sent to the SEC.) The prospectus includes all the important disclosures about the company, whereas the registration statement includes additional information that is of interest to the SEC but not to the typical investor, such as the names and addresses of the lawyers for the issuer and underwriter. All investors must receive a copy of the prospectus before purchasing the stock.

Sales Effort

The SEC closely regulates an issuer's sales effort.

Quiet Period. The quiet period begins when a company hires an underwriter and ends 25 days after the stock is first sold to the public. During this period, company officers must guard their words carefully to avoid any appearance of hyping the stock. For example, the SEC delayed an offering of stock by Saleforce.com after *The New York Times* published a profile of its CEO during the company's quiet period. A few months later, *Playboy* magazine printed an interview with the founders of Google and the SEC delayed its public offering. Although the SEC recently relaxed the rules for

---

[4] The term "red herring" is a bit of a joke because, outside securities offerings, it means a false clue.

the quiet period, it seems unlikely that even under the new standards the SEC will ignore interviews with *Playboy*.

Waiting Period.   This is the time after the registration statement has been filed but before the SEC has approved it. The underwriter can publish a **tombstone ad**—that is, a simple, unadorned announcement of the offering that includes the amount and type of security, the name of the underwriter, and the price of stock. You can see many of these ads in *The Wall Street Journal* and also on company Websites. During the waiting period, the underwriter may distribute the preliminary prospectus. It can also solicit offers but cannot make sales. The underwriter uses this period to estimate market demand for the stock. It **makes book,** meaning that it talks with traders to determine how many shares it can sell and at what price. It also takes **indications of interest** from traders but makes no sales.

Road Show.   During the waiting period, Goldman and Shiva began the **road show**—the cross-country road trip to convince traders that Shiva was a stock their clients should buy. Ingari and Schwinn spent a grueling two weeks visiting 16 cities. At each stop, they made the same impassioned pitch to influential traders. Sometimes road shows are broadcast on the Web so that they can be viewed by a larger group that includes wealthy individuals. "We felt like door-to-door salesmen," Ingari said. So strong was the response to Shiva that in the second week of the road show, Goldman suggested raising the price to $15 a share, from $12, and selling an additional 360,000 shares. When the road show ended, orders for the stock exceeded the number of shares by a factor of 30. That the IPO would be hot was certain. But how hot?

Going Effective

Once its review of the preliminary registration statement is complete, the SEC sends the issuer a **comment letter,** listing changes that must be made to the registration statement. An issuer almost always amends the registration statement at least once, and sometimes more than once. After the SEC has approved a final registration statement (which includes, of course, the final prospectus), the issuer then decides on a date to **go effective**—that is, to begin selling the stock. One last step remained: Goldman and Shiva had to agree on an opening price. They decided to raise the price from $12 to $15 per share. Shiva would sell to Goldman at $13.95 per share, and Goldman, in turn, would sell it on the market at $15.

The night before the sale, Shiva executives and the underwriters met for dinner and made bets about the next day's closing price and trading volume. No one guessed nearly high enough. As soon as Goldman sold at $15, the price zoomed to $30.50. The stock closed that day at $31.50 per share. At Goldman, there were hugs, tears of joy, and champagne toasts. But founders Schwinn and Slaughter, with their stock suddenly worth $30 million each, suffered chest pains. And Ingari, the president and chief executive, felt even worse. As the value of his stake in Shiva soared past $14 million, he fled to the men's room. "I was ready to throw up, I was sweating badly, and I could barely stand up. When I looked in the mirror, I had blood coming out of my nose."

In the end, Shiva raised $28 million that day, and its founders and other insiders, who sold about 700,000 shares, took home another $10 million. Goldman earned almost $3 million, or 7 percent of the proceeds. Did Goldman price the offering too low? Pricing an IPO is more art than science. Everyone would like the price to rise gently. At all cost, however, the underwriter wishes to avoid a disaster in which the stock price collapses, leaving it with a large loss. Of course, the underwriter looks bad if the company sells stock for a lot less than it is worth. Shares that Goldman sold in the morning for $15 were trading for twice that amount later in the day. Half the initial worth of Shiva's stock, or about $43 million, went into the pockets of early buyers who "flipped" the stock, selling it immediately to other investors. In hindsight, Goldman should have priced the stock higher, but it is not clear that it or anyone else could reasonably have predicted the market's reaction.

Frank Slaughter went home after the IPO and spent a day "scrubbing toilets—to retain some humility." He had come through one of the most unnerving, and quintessential, rites of passage of the American capitalist system. The company obtained money to develop new products and build factories. The public got a chance to buy in. And the company's founders, and other key insiders, found a way to cash out.[5]

So what happened to Shiva? Its stock continued an upward climb for two years, reaching a peak of $87 per share. But when the company failed to develop new products, both its business and its stock price faltered. Five years after the public offering, Intel Corp. acquired Shiva at a price of $6 per share.

In the following case, eToys sued its underwriter, Goldman Sachs (also Shiva's underwriter), for underpricing its stock offering. Should Goldman be liable? You be the judge.

YOU BE THE JUDGE

EBCI, INC. V. GOLDMAN SACHS & CO.

2005 N.Y. LEXIS 1178
Court of Appeals of New York, 2005

Facts: Goldman Sachs was the lead underwriter for eToys' initial public offering. eToys agreed to sell 8,320,000 shares of its stock to Goldman at a price of $18.65 per share, for resale to the public at $20. (Goldman had the option to buy an additional 1,248,000 shares at the same price.) The bank's potential profit was $1.35 per share, for a maximum of $12,916,800.

On the first day of the offering, the price of eToys' stock rose as high as $85 and closed at $76.56. Within a year, however, the price had fallen below $20. eToys ultimately filed for bankruptcy protection.

eToys alleged that Goldman made side deals with other clients allowing them to purchase shares in eToys' offering in exchange for kickbacks to Goldman of a portion of their profits on the stock. This arrangement would have created an incentive for Goldman to underprice the stock. eToys also alleged that Goldman had a fiduciary duty to eToys that it violated by not disclosing this conflict of interest.

Goldman filed a motion to dismiss denying that it had a fiduciary relationship to eToys.

You Be the Judge: **Did Goldman have a fiduciary duty to eToys? Did it violate this duty?**

Argument for eToys: A fiduciary relationship exists between two parties if one of them is under a duty to act for or to give advice for the benefit of the other. eToys hired Goldman for its expertise and paid handsomely for its advice about many aspects of going public. The company would never have relied on this advice had it known about the side deals with other clients—deals that could harm eToys.

eToys trusted Goldman, the bank betrayed that trust, and eToys suffered an enormous financial penalty as a result.

▼

---

5 The information about Shiva Corp. is from Glenn Rifkin, "Anatomy of a Highflying IPO, Nosebleeds and All," *The New York Times*, Feb. 19, 1995, p. F7. Copyright © 1995 by The New York Times Co. Reprinted by permission.

Argument for Goldman Sachs: This is a simple case: eToys sold stock, Goldman bought it. Goldman negotiated the best price it could. If eToys was unhappy with this deal, it had no one to blame but itself.

If eToys expected Goldman to act as a fiduciary, the agreement should have stated so explicitly. The company always knew that its interests were different from Goldman's. eToys sought the highest price; Goldman had to ensure that it could resell the shares at a profit. The lower the price to eToys, the lower the risk to Goldman. Goldman took a substantial risk buying this stock, and in this case the risk paid off. It does not always do so.

eToys was a sophisticated company with sophisticated advisors. Its stockholders included well-known venture-capital firms. Its largest single stockholder, Idealab, was an incubator for successful technology companies (see http://www.idealab.com). eToys' law firm—the Venture Law Group, P.C.—specialized in representing high-tech companies. During one year, this law firm was fourth on the list of firms that handled the most initial public offerings for technology companies.

In short, the offering price was not "set" by Goldman, it was negotiated by two sophisticated parties. ●

Sales of Restricted Securities

After the public offering, Shiva insiders still owned a substantial block of stock. Between them, Schwinn, Slaughter, and Ingari held stock or options for 2.8 million shares. With the stock trading as high as $87 per share, on paper they were worth $245 million, but they could not actually sell their stock, at least not right away. **Rule 144 limits the resale of two types of securities:** *control securities* **and** *restricted securities.*

A **control security** is stock held by any shareholder who owns more than 10 percent of a class of stock or by any officer or director. In any three-month period, such an insider can sell only an amount of stock equal to the average weekly trading volume for the prior four weeks or 1 percent of the number of shares outstanding, whichever is greater. Shiva had 9,589,000 shares outstanding and an (unusually high) average weekly trading volume of roughly 938,000. A Shiva insider could sell at most 938,000 shares during each three-month period. In a company with a more typical trading volume, the number might be a tenth of that. The purpose of this rule is to protect other investors from precipitous declines in stock price. If company insiders sold all their stock in one day, the price would plunge, causing losses to the other shareholders.

For owners of restricted securities, the rules are more complex. A **restricted security** is any stock purchased from the issuer in a private offering (such as Regulation D). These securities may not be sold within one year of the offering. After the first year, restricted securities can be sold as long as the sale does not exceed the limitations that apply to control stock: the greater of the average weekly trading volume for the prior four weeks or 1 percent of the number of shares outstanding. After two years, restricted securities can be sold freely, unless they are also control securities, in which case those restrictions still apply. Exhibit 19.1 illustrates the sale of restricted securities under Rule 144.

Liability

Liability for Unregistered Securities

Section 12(a)(1) of the 1933 Act imposes liability on anyone who sells a security that is not registered and not exempt. The purchaser of the security can demand

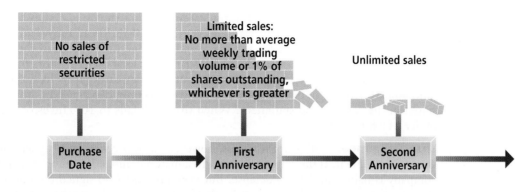

Exhibit 19.1
The sale of restricted securities under Rule 144.

rescission—a return of his money in exchange for the stock—or, if he no longer owns the stock, he can ask for damages.

Fraud

Under §12(a)(2) of the 1933 Act, the seller of a security is liable for making any material misstatement or omission, either oral or written, in connection with the offer or sale of a security. This provision applies to both *public* and *private* offerings if there is some use of interstate commerce, such as the mails, telephone (even for an *intra* state call), or check (which clears). It is difficult to imagine a securities transaction that does not involve interstate commerce. The SEC provides information on how to invest wisely and avoid securities fraud at http://www.sec.gov/investor.shtml. The North American Securities Administrators Association also offers advice on "how to spot a con artist" and popular securities scams (http://www.nasaa.org). You can obtain disciplinary reports on securities firms or individual brokers at http://www.nasdr.com. To report fraud, contact the SEC at its Complaint Center (http://www.sec.gov/complaint.shtml).

Criminal Liability

Under §24 of the 1933 Act, the Justice Department can prosecute anyone who willfully violates the Act.

Liability for the Registration Statement

Section 11 of the 1933 Act establishes the penalties for any errors in a registration statement. **If a final registration statement contains a material misstatement or omission, the purchaser of the security can recover from everyone who signed the registration statement.** This list of signatories includes the issuer, its directors, and chief officers; experts (such as auditors, engineers, or lawyers); and the underwriters. Everyone who signed the registration statement is jointly and severally liable for any error, except the experts, who are liable only for misstatements in the part of the registration statement for which they were responsible. Thus, an auditor is liable for misstatements in the financials but not, say, for omissions about the CEO's criminal past.

Damages. To prevail under §11, the plaintiff need only prove that there was a material misstatement or omission and that she lost money. **Material** means important enough to affect an investor's decision. The plaintiff does not have to prove that she relied on (or even *read*) the registration statement, that she bought the stock from the issuer, or that the defendant was negligent. The plaintiff can recover the difference between what she paid for the stock and its value on the date of the lawsuit. Suppose that Pet Detective, Inc., does an IPO. A week later, Ace Investora buys 1,000 shares at $10 a share. He knows nothing about the company, but he likes the name. This stock turns out to be a dog—Pet Detective has only two agencies, not the 200 stated in the registration statement. When the stock falls to 10¢, Investora can sue under §11 for $9,900.

Due Diligence.   All is not hopeless, however, for those who have signed the registration statement. If the statement contains a material misstatement or omission, the company is liable and has no defense. But everyone else who signed the registration statement can avoid liability by showing that he investigated the registration statement as thoroughly as a "prudent person in the management of his own property." This investigation is called **due diligence.** Its importance cannot be overstated. The SEC does not conduct its own investigation to ensure that the registration statement is accurate. It can only ensure that, on the surface, the issuer has supplied all relevant information. If an issuer chooses to lie, the SEC has no way of knowing. It is the job of the underwriters to check the accuracy of the filing. Thus, underwriters typically spend two or three weeks visiting the company, reading all its corporate documents (including minutes back to the beginning), and calling its bankers, customers, suppliers, and competitors to ensure that the registration statement is accurate and no skeletons have been overlooked.

When §11 was first passed, investment bankers were outraged. Some predicted that this liability provision would cause capital in America to dry up, that grass would grow on Wall Street. In fact, the first case under §11 arose 35 years and 27,000 registration statements later. In this case—*Escott v. Barchris Construction Corp.*—the registration statement was seriously flawed.[6] The underwriter failed to read the minutes of the executive committee meetings that revealed the company to be in serious financial condition. Much of the company's alleged backlog of orders was from nonexistent corporations. Proceeds of the offering were earmarked to pay off debt, not to buy new plant and equipment, as the registration statement had indicated. The company's directors, underwriters, and underwriters' counsel were held liable.

Although *Barchris* still strikes fear in the hearts of underwriters, some commentators now argue that underwriters do not take their due diligence obligations seriously enough. Was there adequate disclosure in the following case?

ROMBACH V. CHANG

355 F.3d 164, 2004 U.S. App. LEXIS 778
United States Court of Appeals for the Second Circuit, 2004

Facts: Family Golf Centers, Inc. was a public company that owned and operated 119 golf courses nationwide. To raise funds for the purchase of additional courses, it sold shares in a second public offering. During the year following that second offering, Family Golf had lower than expected earnings and its stock price plummeted by more than 43 percent. Within two years of the offering, the company filed for bankruptcy protection.

▼

---

6 283 F. Supp. 643, 1968 U.S. Dist. LEXIS 3853 (S.D.N.Y. 1968).

The plaintiffs purchased stock from the company in the second public offering. They filed suit against the company's officers and underwriters, alleging that the registration statement contained misrepresentations about Family Golf's financial performance and projected income. The district court granted defendants' motion to dismiss and the plaintiffs appealed.

Issue: Did the defendants violate §11 by issuing a false or misleading registration statement?

Excerpts from Judge Jacobs's Decision: Plaintiffs do not identify any materially false statements in the registration statement that were false or misleading when made. Plaintiffs, rather, simply allege generally that the registration statement "failed to disclose that the Offering was necessitated by pressure from the Company's lenders and its deteriorating cash position, and it failed to disclose that the integration of recently acquired sites was proceeding poorly and that the Company was experiencing operation problems associated with these acquired properties."

Such allegations, however, are undercut by the fact that the offering documents contained cautionary language and information about the financial risks, including:

- that the company experienced a net loss of $3.6 million for [the prior] fiscal year

- that some Family Golf facilities had experienced losses

- that no assurance could be given that additional facilities would be readily integrated into the Company's operating structure

- that the company had lower cash reserves [than it had the year before]

- that there existed a need to raise substantial additional capital for continued long-term expansion, and the caution that there was no assurance Family Golf would be able to raise enough

- that the company had a $180 million debt, coupled with the admonition that there was no assurance the company would be able to generate sufficient cash to service that debt; and

- that the company's past performance was "not necessarily indicative of future results."

While some of these cautionary statements were formulaic, we conclude that as a whole they provided a sobering picture of Family Golf's financial condition and future plans.

For the foregoing reasons, we affirm the decision of the district court. ∎

SECURITIES EXCHANGE ACT OF 1934

Most buyers do not purchase new securities from the issuer in an initial public offering. Rather they buy stock that is publicly traded in the open market. This stock is, in a sense, *secondhand* because others, perhaps many others, have already owned it. The purpose of the 1934 Act is to maintain the integrity of this secondary market.

General Provisions of the 1934 Act

Registration Requirements

As we have seen, the 1933 Act requires an issuer to register securities before selling them. That is a onetime effort for the company. The 1933 Act does not require the issuer to provide shareholders with any additional information in later years. Suppose that an automobile company registered and sold securities for the first time in 1946. Purchasers of those securities knew a lot about the firm—in 1946. But how can current investors assess the company? The 1934 Act plugs this hole. It requires issuers with publicly traded stock to continue to make information available to the public so that current—and potential—shareholders can evaluate the company. It is often said that the 1933 Act registers securities, and the 1934 Act registers companies.

Under the 1934 Act, an issuer must register with the SEC if (1) it completes a public offering under the 1933 Act, or (2) its securities are traded on a national exchange (such as the New York Stock Exchange), or (3) it has at least 500 shareholders and total assets that exceed $10 million. A company can *de*register if its number of shareholders falls below 300 or if it has fewer than 500 shareholders and assets of less than $10 million.

Disclosure Requirements—Section 13

Like the 1933 Act, the 1934 Act focuses on disclosure. The difference is that the 1933 Act requires onetime disclosure when a company sells stock to the public. The 1934 Act requires *ongoing*, regular disclosure for any company with a class of stock that is publicly traded. Companies that are required to register under the 1934 Act are called **reporting companies.**

Section 13 requires reporting companies to file the following documents:

- An initial, detailed information statement when the company first registers (similar to the filing required under the 1933 Act)
- Annual reports on Form 10-K, containing audited financial statements, a detailed analysis of the company's performance, and information about officers and directors
- Quarterly reports on Form 10-Q, which are less detailed than 10-Ks and contain unaudited financials
- Form 8-Ks to report any significant developments, such as bankruptcy, a change in control, a purchase or sale of significant assets, the resignation of a director as a result of a policy dispute, or a change in auditing firms

In response to corporate scandals involving Enron Corp. and other companies, Congress passed the Sarbanes-Oxley Act of 2002. It requires each company's CEO and CFO to certify that:

- The information in the quarterly and annual reports is true;
- The company has effective internal controls; and
- The officers have informed the company's audit committee and its auditors of any concerns that they have about the internal control system.

A reporting company must send its annual report to shareholders. All annual reports and other 1934 Act filings are available on the SEC Website (http://www.sec.gov). For particularly lively examples of this form of literature, check out the filings for Jack in the Box, Inc. The Website at http://www.sidcato.com provides an (often humorous) analysis of annual reports.

Proxy Requirements—Section 14

Most shareholders of public corporations do not attend annual shareholder meetings. Instead, the company solicits their proxies, permitting them to vote by mail rather than in person. If a company solicits proxies, it is required to supply shareholders with a proxy statement that is intended to give them enough information to make informed decisions about the company. The proxy statement contains detailed information about officers and directors, including their experience, relationship with the company, and compensation. (The annual report provides financial information.) Proxy statements must also be filed with the SEC. Proxy contests and shareholder proposals are discussed in Chapter 18.

Under SEC rules, a company is not *required* to solicit proxies from shareholders, but if it does not, it is unlikely to obtain the quorum needed for the meeting to be held. In any event, a company cannot avoid its responsibility to inform shareholders. Whether or not it solicits proxies, it is still required to furnish shareholders with an information statement that contains essentially the same material as a proxy statement.

Short-Swing Trading—Section 16

During congressional hearings after the 1929 stock market crash, witnesses testified that insiders had manipulated the stock market. For example, insiders would buy a large block of stock, announce a substantial dividend, and then divest before the dividend was reduced. Section 16 was designed to prevent corporate insiders—officers, directors, and shareholders who own more than 10 percent of the company—from taking unfair advantage of privileged information to manipulate the market.

Section 16 takes a two-pronged approach:

- First, insiders must **report** their trades within two business days. This report must also reveal their total stock holdings in the company. The filings must be made to the SEC electronically, and both the SEC and the company are required to post them on their respective Websites within one business day after they are made.

- Second, insiders must **turn over to the corporation** any profits they make from the purchase and sale or sale and purchase of company securities in a six-month period. Section 16 is a strict liability provision. It applies even if the insider did not actually take advantage of secret information or try to manipulate the market; if she bought and sold or sold and bought stock in a six-month period, she is liable.

Suppose that Manuela buys 20,000 shares of her company's stock in June at $10 a share. In September, her (uninsured) summer house in Florida is destroyed by a hurricane. To raise money for rebuilding, she sells the stock at $12 per share, making a profit of $40,000. Her house will have to remain in ruins because she has violated §16 and must turn over the profit to her company.

Liability

Section 18

Under §18, anyone who makes a false or misleading statement in a filing under the 1934 Act is liable to buyers or sellers who (1) acted in reliance on the statement and (2) can prove that the price at which they bought or sold was affected by the false filing. Section 18 applies to all filings under the 1934 Act, including proxy statements and annual reports.

Section 10(b)

Section 18 applies only to *filings* under the 1934 Act. What happens if a company executive makes a false public *statement* about the company? Or writes an untrue statement somewhere other than in a filing? In one case, a corporate officer bought up shares of his company's stock even as he made pessimistic public statements about the company. That is the type of behavior that §10(b) is designed to prevent. **Section 10(b) prohibits fraud in connection with the purchase and sale of any security, whether or not the security is registered under the 1934 Act.**

The SEC adopted Rule 10b-5 to clarify §10(b), but the rule is still a relatively vague, catch-all provision designed to fill any holes left by other sections of the securities laws.[7] Interpretation has largely been left to the courts, which generally have interpreted Rule 10b-5 to require:

- **A Misstatement or Omission of a Material Fact.** Anyone who fails to disclose material information, or makes incomplete or inaccurate disclosure, is liable. **Material** has the same meaning as under the 1933 Act: important enough to affect an investor's decision. For example, a company repeatedly and falsely denied that it was involved in merger negotiations. It was liable even though the negotiations had only been in a preliminary stage.[8]

- **Scienter.** This is a legal term meaning *willfully, knowingly,* or *recklessly.* To be liable under Rule 10b-5, the defendant must have (1) known (or been reckless in not knowing) that the statement was inaccurate and (2) intended for the plaintiff to rely on the statement. Negligence is not enough. A group of shareholders sued the accounting firm Ernst & Ernst because it had failed to discover, during the course of an audit, that a company's chief executive was stealing funds. According to the shareholders, the auditors should have discovered that the executive refused to allow anyone else to open his mail and, therefore, should have been suspicious of wrongdoing. The court found Ernst & Ernst not liable. Although it may have been negligent, it had not *intentionally* or even *recklessly* facilitated fraud.[9]

- **Purchase or Sale.** Rule 10b-5 covers both buyers and sellers. It does not include, however, someone who failed to purchase stock because of a material misstatement. In the case of the company executive who spread negative rumors about his company while he bought stock, those who sold because of his false rumors could sue under Rule 10b-5, but not those who simply failed to buy.

- **Reliance.** To bring suit, a plaintiff must show that she relied on the misstatement or omission. In the case of open-market trades, reliance is difficult to prove, so the courts are willing to assume it.

- **Economic Loss.** The plaintiffs must suffer a loss in the value of their investment. For example, a couple sold their pharmaceutical business to another company in exchange for stock of the purchaser. Some time later, they discovered that the purchaser had lied about its financial condition. However, the court held that the couple could not recover because, by the time they sold their stock in the purchaser, it was worth substantially more than when they acquired it. Thus, they had not suffered an economic loss.

- **Loss Causation.** The economic loss must have been caused by the misstatement of a material fact.

In the following case, the Supreme Court decided that the misrepresentation did not cause a loss.

---

[7] Rule 10b-5 prohibits any person, in connection with a purchase or sale of any security, from (1) employing any device, scheme, or artifice to defraud; (2) making any untrue statement of a material fact or omitting to state a material fact necessary in order to make the statements made, in light of the circumstances under which they were made, not misleading; or (3) engaging in any act, practice, or course of business that operates or would operate as a fraud or deceit upon any person.

[8] *Basic Inc. v. Levinson,* 485 U.S. 224, 108 S. Ct. 978, 1988 U.S. LEXIS 1197 (1988).

[9] *Ernst & Ernst v. Hochfelder,* 425 U.S. 185, 96 S. Ct. 1375, 1976 U.S. LEXIS 2 (1976).

DURA PHARMACEUTICALS, INC. V. BROUDO

125 S. Ct. 1627, 2005 U.S. LEXIS 3478
Supreme Court of the United States, 2005

Facts: Over the course of a year, plaintiffs bought stock in Dura Pharmaceuticals, Inc., a publicly traded company. They alleged that during this time Dura executives falsely stated that (1) company drug sales would be profitable and (2) the Food and Drug Administration (FDA) would approve its new asthma spray device.

The plaintiffs halted their purchases of Dura stock on the day the company announced that, owing to slow drug sales, its earnings would be lower than expected. After this announcement, Dura shares lost almost half their value. About eight months later, Dura announced that the FDA would not approve the new asthma spray device. The next day Dura's share price temporarily fell but almost fully recovered within one week.

The district court dismissed the plaintiff's complaint on the grounds they had not shown that the false statements caused the fall in stock price. The Court of Appeals for the Ninth Circuit reversed, holding that the defendants' false statements had indeed caused the plaintiffs' loss. The Ninth Circuit reasoned that if it had not been for the misrepresentations, the stock price would have been lower when the plaintiffs purchased it and then would not have fallen as far (or at all) when the truth came out. Dura appealed and the Supreme Court granted *certiorari*.

Issue: Did the defendants' false statements cause the plaintiffs' loss?

Excerpts from Justice Breyer's Decision: [T]he logical link between the inflated share purchase price and any later economic loss is not invariably strong. Shares are normally purchased with an eye toward a later sale. But if, say, the purchaser sells the shares quickly before the relevant truth begins to leak out, the misrepresentation will not have led to any loss. If the purchaser sells later after the truth makes its way into the market place, an initially inflated purchase price *might* mean a later loss. But that is far from inevitably so.

When the purchaser subsequently resells such shares, even at a lower price, that lower price may reflect, not the earlier misrepresentation, but changed economic circumstances, changed investor expectations, new industry-specific or firm-specific facts, conditions, or other events, which taken separately or together account for some or all of that lower price. Other things being equal, the longer the time between purchase and sale, the more likely that this is so, i.e., the more likely that other factors caused the loss.

Given the tangle of factors affecting price, the most logic alone permits us to say is that the higher purchase price will *sometimes* play a role in bringing about a future loss. It may prove to be a necessary condition of any such loss, and in that sense one might say that the inflated purchase price suggests that the misrepresentation (using language the Ninth Circuit used) "touches upon" a later economic loss. But, even if that is so, it is insufficient. To "touch upon" a loss is not to *cause* a loss, and it is the latter that the law requires. [A] plaintiff in such a case [must] show not only that had he known the truth he would not have acted but also that he suffered actual economic loss.

Finally, the Ninth Circuit's approach overlooks an important securities law objective. The securities statutes seek to maintain public confidence in the marketplace. They do so by deterring fraud, in part, through the availability of private securities fraud actions. But the statutes make these latter actions available, not to provide investors with broad insurance against market losses, but to protect them against those economic losses that misrepresentations actually cause. Allowing recovery in the face of affirmative evidence of nonreliance would effectively convert Rule 10b-5 into a scheme of investor's insurance. There is no support in the Securities Exchange Act for such a result.

For these reasons, we find the plaintiffs' complaint legally insufficient. We reverse the judgment of the Ninth Circuit. ■

Devil's Advocate

If the Dura stock price is inflated because of false claims made by company executives, it seems virtually inevitable that, once the truth comes out, shareholders will lose money. It may be difficult to estimate exactly what the stock was worth on the day the plaintiffs bought it, but courts are often called upon to make difficult decisions. Would it be better for the stock market if these defendants were held liable? ◆

The Private Securities Litigation Reform Act of 1995

The Private Securities Litigation Reform Act is an amendment to the 1934 Act intended to discourage fraud suits by shareholders. Under this amendment, companies are liable to shareholders for so-called forward-looking statements (i.e., financial projections or statements about future plans) *only if* (1) the company fails to include a warning that the predictions may not come to pass, *and* (2) the shareholders can show that company executives knew the predictions were false. Suppose a pharmaceutical company predicts that a new drug will generate billions in sales, but two years later the drug is a total failure. Before 1995, shareholders would have had a strong case, but now the company would not be liable as long as it had disclosed, at the time of making the prediction, reasons why the drug might not be a success. Even if the company failed to mention these reasons, it would be liable only if executives knew the prediction to be false when they made it.

Despite this statute, the number of securities fraud lawsuits and the cost of settling them has continued to increase each year. (Shareholders even sued Shiva, the company discussed earlier in the chapter, when its stock price fell.) For more information about these lawsuits, browse at http://securities.stanford.edu.

Insider Trading

Insider trading is immensely tempting. Anyone with reliable secret information can earn millions of dollars overnight. Costandi Nasser bought shares of Santa Fe International, Inc., after learning that Kuwait Petroleum Co. was set to acquire the company. His profit? $4.6 million in three weeks. The downside? Insider trading is a crime punishable by fines and imprisonment. The guilty party may also be forced to turn over to the SEC three times the profit made. Ivan Boesky paid $100 million and spent two years in prison. Dennis Levine suffered an $11.6 million penalty and three years in prison.

Why is insider trading a crime? Who is harmed? After all, if you buy or sell stock in a company, presumably you are reasonably content with the price or you would not have traded. Insider trading is illegal because:

- It offends our fundamental sense of fairness. No one wants to be in a poker game with marked cards.

- Investors will lose confidence in the market if they feel that insiders have an unfair advantage.

- Investment banks typically "make a market" in stocks, meaning that they hold extra shares so that orders can be filled smoothly. If an insider buys stock because she knows the company is about to sign an important contract, she earns the profit on that information at the expense of the marketmaker who sold her the stock. These marketmakers expect to earn a certain profit. If they do not earn it from normal stock appreciation, they simply raise the commission they charge for being a marketmaker. As a result, everyone who buys and sells stock pays a slightly higher price because insider trading skims off some of the profits.

In the following feature, economists argue that there is another reason insider trading is illegal.

ECONOMICS *& the* LAW	Although economists generally laud free markets, at times markets create inefficient results. The market for information is particularly subject to inefficiencies. Stock markets, for example, tend to create too much information. (And, as we will see in Chapter 22, intellectual property markets have the opposite problem.)

Although economists generally laud free markets, at times markets create inefficient results. The market for information is particularly subject to inefficiencies. Stock markets, for example, tend to create too much information. (And, as we will see in Chapter 22, intellectual property markets have the opposite problem.)

Generally, economists think that society benefits when financial information spreads widely and quickly. Investors are thereby able to make more informed decisions. However, insider trading is an exception to this rule. When someone trades on inside information, she can quickly earn vast profits—but she has effectively stolen these profits from uninformed shareholders. The benefit that society gains from having this hidden information indirectly revealed to the market (via her purchase or sale of stock) is less than the harm to the shareholders who trade in ignorance. True, everyone now knows that the stock is more or less valuable than the market thought, but they have learned this information at a high price. Thus, the government prohibits insider trading to prevent society from "paying too much" for this private information.

Recent research supports the view that insider trading harms securities markets. In comparing returns in all 103 stock markets in the world, two economists found that markets in those countries that enforced insider trading laws earned 5 percent higher returns than did markets in countries with no laws or with lax enforcement. Five percent of the world's stock market capitalization amounts to $1.75 trillion.[10] ◆

As noted, Rule 10b-5 is a vaguely worded rule that generally prohibits fraud. The language of the rule never explicitly mentions insider trading, but courts have interpreted it to prohibit this activity. Although the courts are nominally *interpreting* the rule, in fact, they are more or less fashioning this crime out of whole cloth. Insider trading has been described as "the judicial oak that has grown from little more than a legislative acorn." The current rules on insider trading are as follows:

- **Strangers.** The SEC has argued many times that anyone in possession of non-public material information must disclose it or refrain from trading. The courts, however, have definitively rejected this approach. The Supreme Court has held that **someone who trades on inside information is liable only if he has a fiduciary duty to the company whose stock he has traded.** Suppose that, while looking in a dumpster, Harry finds correspondence indicating that MediSearch, Inc., will shortly announce a major breakthrough in the treatment of AIDS. Harry buys the stock, which promptly quadruples in value. Harry will be dining at the Ritz, not in the dumpster, nor in federal prison, because he has no fiduciary duty to MediSearch.

- **Fiduciaries.** Anyone who works for a company is a fiduciary. **A fiduciary violates Rule 10b-5 if she trades stock of her company while in possession of nonpublic material information.** If the director of research for MediSearch learns of the promising new treatment for AIDS and buys stock in the company before the information is public, she has violated Rule 10b-5. This rule applies not only to employees who work for the company but also to **constructive insiders**—others who have an indirect employment relationship, such as employees of the company's auditors or law firm. Thus, if a lawyer who works at the

---

10 Hazem Daouk and Utpal Bhattacharya, "The World Price of Insider Trading," *Journal of Finance,* 2002, vol. 57, pp. 75–108. Discussed in *The Economist,* Jan. 22, 2000, p. 75.

firm that is patenting MediSearch's new discovery buys stock before the information is public, she has violated Rule 10b-5.

- *Possession* versus *use* **of information.** Suppose that an insider sells stock just after learning that her company is about to report lower earnings but before this information is public. When challenged by the SEC, she argues that she sold her stock for other reasons—say, to buy a new house, or set her son up in business. The appeals courts were divided on whether the SEC actually had to prove that the insider had traded because of the secret information and not for some other (legitimate) reason. To clarify this murky issue, the SEC issued Rule 10b5-1. **This rule provides that an insider violates Rule 10b-5 if she trades while in possession of material, nonpublic information, unless she has committed in advance to a plan to sell those securities.** Thus, if an insider knows that she will want to sell stock to pay college tuition, she can establish such a sales plan in advance. (And, then, despite any change in circumstances, she must sell according to the plan.) She will then not be liable for the sales, no matter what inside information she ultimately learns.

- **Tippers.** Now things become really complicated. **Insiders who pass on nonpublic, material information are liable under Rule 10b-5, even if they do not trade themselves, as long as (1) they know the information is confidential and (2) they expect some personal gain.** Personal gain is loosely defined. Essentially, any gift to a friend counts as personal gain. W. Paul Thayer was a corporate director, deputy secretary of defense, and former fighter pilot ace who gave stock tips to his girlfriend in lieu of paying her rent. That counted as personal gain, and he spent a year and a half in prison.

- **Tippees.** Those who receive tips—tippees—are liable for trading on inside information, even if they do not have a fiduciary relationship to the company, as long as (1) they know the information is confidential, (2) they know it came from an insider who was violating his fiduciary duty, and (3) the insider expected some personal gain.** Barry Switzer, then head football coach at the University of Oklahoma, went to a track meet to see his son compete. While sunbathing on the bleachers, he overheard someone talking about a company that was going to be acquired. Switzer bought the stock but was acquitted of insider trading charges, because the insider had not breached his fiduciary duty. He had not tipped anyone on purpose—he had simply been careless. Also, Switzer did not know that the insider was breaching a fiduciary duty, and the insider expected no personal gain.[11]

- **Takeovers.** Frustrated by its lack of success under Rule 10b-5, the SEC adopted Rule 14e-3. **This rule prohibits trading on inside information during a tender offer if the trader knows the information was obtained from either the bidder or the target company.** The trader or tipper need not have violated a fiduciary duty.

- **Misappropriation.** In an effort to tighten the insider trading noose further, the SEC developed a new theory—misappropriation. Under this theory, **a person is liable if he trades in securities (1) for personal profit, (2) using confidential information, and (3) in breach of a fiduciary duty to the source of the information.** This theory applies even if that source was not the company whose stock

---

11 *SEC v. Switzer*, 590 F. Supp. 756, 1984 U.S. Dist. LEXIS 15303 (W.D. Okla. 1984). After this case, some wags joked, "When Barry Switzer listens, people talk."

was traded. Foster Winans wrote a column for *The Wall Street Journal* titled "Heard on the Street" in which he reported rumors he had heard about companies. Often the stock of these companies would rise or fall in response to his story. He began leaking information about his columns in advance to Peter Brant, a stockbroker at Kidder, Peabody & Co. Brant would trade the stock and split the profits with Winans. After the first episode, the SEC noticed the abnormally large trade. When it called the company to find out who was buying, the officers said they could think of no explanation except that the company had been the subject of a "Heard on the Street" column. It was all over for Winans, though the SEC let him pass on information a few more times, to make sure.

But had Winans and Brant violated Rule 10b-5? Not according to traditional insider trading rules. Neither of them had a fiduciary relationship to the company whose stock was traded. When the case went to the Supreme Court, it split 4–4 on the issue of misappropriation (there were only eight justices because one had resigned and his successor had not yet been appointed). However, the Court did find 8–0 that Winans was guilty of mail and wire fraud for having violated *The Wall Street Journal's* rules about confidentiality.[12] Ten years later, the Supreme Court finally resolved the misappropriation issue.

UNITED STATES V. O'HAGAN

521 U.S. 642, 117 S. Ct. 2199, 1997 U.S. LEXIS 4033
United States Supreme Court, 1997

Facts: Grand Metropolitan PLC (Grand Met) hired the law firm of Dorsey & Whitney to represent it in a takeover of Pillsbury Co. James O'Hagan, a partner in Dorsey & Whitney, did not work for Grand Met, but he found out about the deal and purchased significant amounts of Pillsbury stock. After Grand Met publicly announced its takeover attempt, the price of Pillsbury stock rose dramatically. O'Hagan sold his stock at a profit of more than $4.3 million. A jury convicted O'Hagan of misappropriation in violation of §10(b), and he was sentenced to prison.[13] The appeals court reversed, ruling that misappropriation is not a violation of §10(b). The Supreme Court granted *certiorari*.

Issue: Is misappropriation a violation of §10(b)?

Excerpts from Justice Ginsburg's Decision: Under the "traditional" or "classical theory" of insider trading liability, §10(b) and Rule 10b-5 are violated when a corporate insider trades in the securities of his corporation on the basis of material, nonpublic information. The classical theory applies not only to officers, directors, and other permanent insiders of a corporation, but also to attorneys, accountants, consultants, and others who temporarily become fiduciaries of a corporation.

The "misappropriation theory" holds that a person commits fraud "in connection with" a securities transaction, and thereby violates §10(b) and Rule 10b-5, when he misappropriates confidential information for securities trading purposes, in breach of a duty owed to the source of the information. Under this theory, a fiduciary's undisclosed, self-serving use of a principal's information to purchase or sell securities, in breach of a duty of loyalty and confidentiality, defrauds the principal of the exclusive use of that information.

The two theories are complementary, each addressing efforts to capitalize on nonpublic information through the purchase or sale of securities.

▼

---

[12] *Carpenter v. United States*, 484 U.S. 19, 108 S. Ct. 316, 1987 U.S. LEXIS 4815 (1987).

[13] O'Hagan used the profits he gained through this trading to conceal his previous embezzlement of client funds. There is a moral here.

The classical theory targets a corporate insider's breach of duty to shareholders with whom the insider transacts; the misappropriation theory outlaws trading on the basis of nonpublic information by a corporate "outsider" in breach of a duty owed not to a trading party, but to the source of the information. The misappropriation theory is thus designed to protect the integrity of the securities markets against abuses by "outsiders" to a corporation who have access to confidential information that will affect the corporation's security price when revealed, but who owe no fiduciary or other duty to that corporation's shareholders.

A company's confidential information qualifies as property to which the company has a right of exclusive use. The undisclosed misappropriation of such information, in violation of a fiduciary duty constitutes fraud akin to embezzlement.

The theory is also well-tuned to an animating purpose of the Exchange Act: to insure honest securities markets and thereby promote investor confidence. Although informational disparity is inevitable in the securities markets, investors likely would hesitate to venture their capital in a market where trading based on misappropriated nonpublic information is unchecked by law. An investor's informational disadvantage vis-à-vis a misappropriator with material, nonpublic information stems from contrivance, not luck; it is a disadvantage that cannot be overcome with research or skill.

It makes scant sense to hold a lawyer like O'Hagan a §10(b) violator if he works for a law firm representing the target of a tender offer, but not if he works for a law firm representing the bidder. The text of the statute requires no such result. The misappropriation at issue here was properly made the subject of a §10(b) charge because it meets the statutory requirement that there be "deceptive" conduct "in connection with" securities transactions. ■

After the *O'Hagan* case established the principle of misappropriation, it was still not clear how this rule applied to family members. If a wife told her husband that her company was about to be taken over and he then sold company stock as a result, was he in violation of 10b-5? Did he have a fiduciary duty to her? Rule 10b-5-2 establishes that anyone who receives nonpublic, material information from a spouse, parent, child, or sibling has a fiduciary duty unless the trader can prove that he did not have a duty of trust or confidence to the family member in question.

| at RISK | If you learn confidential information about a company, what can you do? Of course, it is always safe *not* to trade. If you want to trade anyway, you should wait 24 to 48 hours after the information is disseminated through wire services or in the financial press. ◆ |

Foreign Corrupt Practices Act

In the 1970s, more than 450 major U.S. corporations paid millions of dollars in foreign bribes. The Japanese premier and the Italian president both resigned after it was revealed that Lockheed had paid them off. In the Netherlands, members of the royal family were implicated in the scandal. Many of these payments had been labeled "commissions" or other legitimate business expenses and then illegally deducted from the company's income tax. In response, Congress passed the Foreign Corrupt Practices Act as an amendment to the 1934 Act.

Under the Foreign Corrupt Practices Act, it is a crime for *any American company* (whether reporting under the 1934 Act or not) to make or promise to make payments or gifts to foreign officials, political candidates, or parties in order to influence a governmental decision, even if the payment is legal under local law. There is one exception: it is legal for a company to make payments to a foreign official to expedite a "routine governmental action." Anyone who violates the law is subject to fines and imprisonment. The Department of Justice reveals its enforcement guidelines at http://www.usdoj.gov. Search for "Foreign Corrupt Practices Act."

Congress believed that the ready availability of corporate "slush funds" had facilitated the payment of bribes. Therefore, it also tightened accounting standards for companies that report under the 1934 Act. It requires *reporting companies* to (1) keep books that accurately and fairly reflect the transactions of the issuer, and (2) maintain a system of internal controls that ensures transactions are executed only "in accordance with management's authorization."

For years, American companies complained that they were handicapped when competing against rivals who could bribe their way to success overseas. The U.S. government estimated that American companies lost contracts worth more than $15 billion a year to competitors who paid bribes. But in 1997, 34 developed countries signed a treaty in Paris outlawing bribery of foreign officials.

Ethics   What's wrong with bribery anyway? Many businesspeople think it is relatively harmless, just a cost of doing business, like New York City's high taxes or Germany's high labor costs. Corruption is not a victimless crime. Poor people in poor countries are the losers when officials are on the take: corruption means that good projects are squeezed out by bad ones. And corruption can reduce a country's entire administration to a state of decay. Honest officials give up. Bribes grow ever bigger and more ubiquitous. The trough becomes less well stocked; the snouts plunge deeper.[14] Worldwide about $400 billion is lost each year to corruption in government procurement. The anti-corruption czar in Mexico estimated that bribes reduce Mexico's gross domestic product (GDP) annually by 9.5 percent. This sum is twice the country's education budget. From the Chapter 2 Ethics Checklist: Who are the stakeholders? What are the consequences of corruption? ◆

Which countries are most corrupt? As rules of thumb:

- Poor countries are more corrupt than rich ones, although corruption can be found everywhere.

- Autocratic countries are more corrupt than democratic ones. Democratic institutions—an independent judiciary, a free press, and strong opposition parties—reduce corruption.

- Economies based on natural resources are more corrupt than those based on trade. Thus, for example, countries that produce oil tend to be more corrupt than traditional trading powers, such as Hong Kong, Singapore, and Chile.[15]

According to Transparency International, an international nonprofit agency, Cote d'Ivoire, Georgia, Indonesia, Tajikistan, Turkmenistan, Azerbaijan, Paraguay, Chad, Myanmar, Nigeria, Bangladesh, and Haiti lead the list of shame. The most honest? Finland, New Zealand, Denmark, Iceland, Singapore, Sweden, Switzerland, Norway, Australia, and the Netherlands. (The United States was seventeenth on the honest list.) A complete list is available at http://www.transparency.org.

---

14 "Who Will Listen to Mr. Clean?" *The Economist,* Aug. 2, 1997, p. 52.

15 Tina Rosenberg, "The Taint of the Greased Palm," *The New York Times,* Aug. 10, 2003, sec. 6, p. 28.

BLUE SKY LAWS

At the end of the nineteenth century, years before the great stock market crash, states had already begun to regulate the sale of securities. These statutes are called **blue sky laws** (because crooks were willing to sell naive investors a "piece of the great blue sky"). Currently, all states and the District of Columbia have blue sky laws.

Exemption from State Regulation

To make life easier for issuers of stock, Congress passed the **National Securities Markets Improvement Act** (NSMIA) **of 1996.** Essentially, states may no longer regulate offerings of securities that are:

- Traded on a national exchange;
- Exempt under Rule 506; or
- Sold to "qualified purchasers."

State Regulation

Any securities offerings not covered by the NSMIA must comply with state securities laws. Easier said than done. The 50 states have exhibited great creativity in crafting their securities laws and, as a result, have caused many headaches for issuers of securities. To begin, the 1933 Act is primarily concerned with disclosure, but many state statutes focus on the quality of the investment and require a so-called *merit review*. For example, in 1981 the Massachusetts securities commissioner refused to allow Apple Computer Co. to sell its initial public offering in Massachusetts because he believed the stock, selling at 92 times earnings, was too risky. He "protected" Massachusetts residents from this investment.

Typically, states take one of the following approaches to securities offerings:

- *Registration by notification.* Some states permit issuers with an established track record simply to file a notice before offering their securities.

- *Registration by coordination.* Some states permit issuers that have registered with the SEC simply to file copies of the federal registration statement (and perhaps some additional documents) with the state.

- *Registration by qualification.* Some states require issuers to undergo a full-blown registration, complete with a merit review.

Facilitating State Regulation

All is not bleak, however. There are three options that ease the process of complying with state securities requirements.

Coordinated Equity Review (CER)

For offerings over $5 million that are registered with the SEC, the issuer might be able to take advantage of the **Coordinated Equity Review** (CER) program. Under this program, the issuer deals with only one state, which takes responsibility for coordinating the comments from all other states. The process is simpler, but state officials still have the right to conduct a merit review.

Small Company Offering Registration (SCOR)

Most states permit a so-called **SCOR (small company offering registration)** for use in offerings of up to $1 million over any 12-month period. The issuer has the right to advertise publicly (even on the Internet) and can sell any amount of securities to any number of investors (as long as the total offering does not exceed $1 million). The relatively simple form (U-7) is in a question-and-answer format. It is designed to be filled out by company executives without the assistance of lawyers or accountants who are securities experts. Any company using a SCOR form can request a coordinated review from the states in which it has filed. Under this system, a designated lead state takes responsibility for coordinating the process with all other states. The result is a faster, simpler process. States do have the right to conduct a merit review, although it tends to be less burdensome than the usual merit examination. SCOR registration is designed to be used with

- Rule 147;
- Rule 504; and
- Regulation A.

Uniform Limited Offering Exemption

Under the **Uniform Limited Offering Exemption,** most states are largely exempt from registering any offerings under Rule 505.

The moral of the story? Securities offerings are exceedingly complex and require professional supervision. Do not attempt this at home!

Chapter Conclusion

The 1929 stock market crash and the Great Depression that followed were an economic catastrophe for the United States. The Securities Act of 1933 and the Securities Exchange Act of 1934 were designed to prevent such disasters from ever occurring again. This country has enjoyed years of prosperity that is based, at least in part, on a reliable and honest securities market. The securities laws deserve some of the credit for that stability.

Chapter Review

1. A security is any transaction in which the buyer invests money in a common enterprise and expects to earn a profit predominantly from the efforts of others.

2. Before any offer or sale, an issuer must register securities with the SEC, unless the securities qualify for an exemption.

3. These securities are exempt from the registration requirement: government securities, bank securities, short-term notes, nonprofit issues, insurance policies, and annuity contracts.

4. The following table compares the different types of securities offerings:

	Public Offering	Intrastate Offering	Regulation A	Regulation D: Rule 504	Regulation D: Rule 505	Regulation D: Rule 506
Maximum Value of Securities Sold	Unlimited	Unlimited	$5 million	$1 million	$5 million	Unlimited
Public Solicitation of Purchasers	Permitted	Permitted	Permitted	Sometimes permitted	Not permitted	Not permitted
Suitability Requirements for Purchasers	No requirements	Must reside in issuer's state	No requirements	May be limited to accredited investors	No limit on accredited investors; no more than 35 unaccredited investors	No limit on accredited investors; no more than 35 unaccredited investors who, if unsophisticated, must have a purchaser representative
Disclosure Requirements	Elaborate registration statement; audited financials	None	Offering circular that is less detailed than a registration statement	May be required under state law	Same requirements as Reg A for unaccredited investors; no disclosure to accredited investors	Same requirements as Reg A for unaccredited investors; no disclosure to accredited investors
Resale of Securities	Permitted	Permitted, but may not be made out of state for nine months	Permitted	Sometimes permitted	Not permitted for one year	Not permitted for one year

5. If a final registration statement contains a material misstatement or omission, the purchaser of a security offered under that statement can recover from everyone who signed it.

6. The 1934 Act requires public companies to make regular filings with the SEC.

7. Under §16, insiders who buy and sell or sell and buy company stock within a six-month period must turn over to the corporation any profits from the trades. They must also disclose any trades they make in company stock.

8. Section 10(b) prohibits fraud in connection with the purchase and sale of any security, whether or not the issuer is registered under the 1934 Act.

9. Section 10(b) also prohibits insider trading.

10. Under the Foreign Corrupt Practices Act, it is a crime for any U.S. company to make payments to foreign officials to influence a government decision. This statute also requires reporting companies to keep accurate records.

11. The NSMIA prohibits states from regulating securities offerings that are:

- Traded on a national exchange;
- Exempt under Rule 506; or
- Sold to "qualified purchasers."

12. Any securities offerings not covered by the NSMIA must comply with state securities laws, which are varied and complex.

Practice Test

1. Christopher Stenger bought 12 Impressionist paintings from R. H. Love Galleries for $1.5 million. Love told Stenger that art investment would produce a safe profit. The two men agreed that Stenger could exchange any painting within five years for any one or two other paintings with the same or greater value. When Stenger's paintings did not increase in value, he sued Love, arguing that the right to trade paintings made them securities. Is Stenger correct?

2. **CPA QUESTION** When a common stock offering requires registration under the Securities Act of 1933:

   a. The registration statement is automatically effective when filed with the SEC

   b. The issuer would act unlawfully if it were to sell the common stock without providing the investor with a prospectus

   c. The SEC will determine the investment value of the common stock before approving the offering

   d. The issuer may make sales 10 days after filing the registration statement

3. Fluor, an engineering and construction company, was awarded a $1 billion project to build a coal gasification plant in South Africa. Fluor signed an agreement with a South African client that prohibited them both from announcing the agreement until March 10. Accordingly, Fluor denied all rumors that a major transaction was pending. Between March 3 and March 6, the State Teachers Retirement Board pension fund sold 288,257 shares of Fluor stock. After the contract was announced, the stock price went up. Did Fluor violate Rule 10b-5?

4. **CPA QUESTION** Hamilton Corp. makes a $4.5 million securities offering under Rule 505 of Regulation D of the Securities Act of 1933. Under this regulation, Hamilton is:

   a. Required to provide full financial information to accredited investors only

   b. Allowed to make the offering through a general solicitation

   c. Limited to selling to no more than 35 nonaccredited investors

   d. Allowed to sell to an unlimited number of investors both accredited and nonaccredited

5. Does this excerpt from *The Boston Globe* reveal any potential securities law problems?

   Berkshire Ice Cream's down-home investment strategy is paying off for more than 100 people who last year put up $800 to $1,000 to "own" a company cow. Last month, the company sent out about $32,000 to investors who bought a total of 110 cows a year ago, with the expectation of a 20 percent annual return on their money. [I]nitially, there were 63 investors who agreed to finance the purchase of a cow—which the company then cares for—in return for a piece of the company's profits.[16]

6. **ETHICS** ETS Payphones, Inc., sold pay phones to the public. The company then leased back the pay phones from the purchaser, promising a fixed 14 percent annual return on their investment. Although ETS's marketing materials trumpeted the "incomparable pay phone" as "an exciting business opportunity," the pay phones did not generate enough revenue for ETS to make the required payments, so the company depended on funds from new investors to meet its obligations to its existing customers. After ETS filed for bankruptcy protection, the SEC sued, alleging that ETS had been selling unregistered securities. Were the pay phone contracts securities under the 1933 Act? ETS advertised this investment as low risk (offering a "guaranteed" fixed return). These sorts of advertisements are particularly attractive to individuals more vulnerable to investment fraud, including older and less sophisticated investors. Whether or not the pay phone contracts were securities, was it ethical to pitch what was, in fact, a high-risk investment to vulnerable investors who were unable to accurately assess the risks? Were these actions right? How would the CEO of

---

16 Ellen Labr, "Investors Milk Profits of Ice Cream Firm," *The Boston Globe,* July 30, 1995, p. 38. Republished with permission of The Boston Globe; permission conveyed through the Copyright Clearance Center, Inc.

ETS have felt if someone had sold such an investment to his poor, elderly mother?

7. **CPA QUESTION** Pace Corp. previously issued 300,000 shares of its common stock. The shares are now actively traded on a national securities exchange. The original offering was exempt from registration under the Securities Act of 1933. Pace has $2.5 million in assets and 425 shareholders. With regard to the Securities Exchange Act of 1934, Pace is:

   a. Required to file a registration statement because its assets exceed $2 million in value

   b. Required to file a registration statement even though it has fewer than 500 shareholders

   c. Not required to file a registration statement because the original offering of its stock was exempt from registration

   d. Not required to file a registration statement unless insiders own at least 5 percent of its outstanding shares of stock

8. **YOU BE THE JUDGE** WRITING PROBLEM World-Wide Coin Investments Ltd. sold rare coins, precious metals, camera equipment, and Coca-Cola collector items. Its stock was registered with the SEC under the 1934 Act. Joseph Hale was the controlling shareholder, chairman of the board, CEO, and president. World-Wide's independent auditor warned Hale that the company's faulty system of accounting procedures was causing problems with inventory control. Furthermore, the auditor could not document transactions, and it had found that the books and records of the company were inaccurate. Is World-Wide in violation of the Foreign Corrupt Practices Act? **Argument for the SEC:** Without exception, all reporting companies are required to maintain accurate books and records. **Argument for World-Wide:** This is a small company, and the cost of such an elaborate internal control system would bankrupt it.

9. Consider this scenario from the periodical *Investor's Business Daily, Inc.:*

   You're in line at the grocery store when you overhear a stranger say: "That new widget is going to make XYZ Co. a fortune. I can't wait until the product launches tomorrow."

   What do you do? (a) Nothing? (b) Call your broker and buy as much XYZ Co. stock as you possibly can?

10. Malaga Arabian Limited Partnership sold investments in the Spanish Arabian horse industry under Rule 506. James E. Mark, who purchased one of the partnership interests, alleged that the partnership violated Rule 506 because it never gave him any disclosure about the risks of the investment. He was not an accredited investor. At trial, the partnership said that it had surveyed investors to ensure that they were either accredited or sophisticated but had not actually read the surveys and did not have them available for the trial court. Is this offering exempt from registration under the 1933 Act?

11. CoolCom, Inc., sends notice to all its shareholders that its annual report and proxy soliciting materials are on its Internet Website. It provides investors with the Internet location and a telephone number that they may call to request a paper copy. Is CoolCom in compliance with SEC rules?

12. **ROLE REVERSAL** Prepare a multiple-choice question that focuses on an issue involving Rule 504, restricted securities, or insider trading.

Internet Research Problem

Choose a company, go to the EDGAR database at the SEC (http://www.sec.gov/edgar.shtml), and look at all filings this company has made during the last year. What filings has it made and why? Extra credit: Search EDGAR for a prospectus for an initial public offering.

You can find further practice problems at academic.cengage.com/blaw/beatty.

GOVERNMENT REGULATION AND PROPERTY

© TR IMAGE/BRAND X PICTURES/GETTY IMAGES

© MEL CURTIS/PHOTODISC/GETTY IMAGES

Mike Elliott was not looking for trouble when he brought an order form for Girl Scout cookies to work. Mr. Elliott, an employee at DaimlerChrysler's factory in Dearborn, Michigan, started asking co-workers to buy a few boxes on behalf of his girlfriend's eight-year-old daughter. "I worked for four or five hours, and suddenly this lady came up to me and said that a guy who worked 50 feet down the line from me was selling them cheaper," Mr. Elliott says. "The first thing that everyone thinks is, 'You're trying to rip me off.'"

In an increasingly competitive marketplace, price wars are breaking out over Thin Mints and Peanut Butter Patties. The 36,500-member Michigan Metro Council, citing rising costs and the need to subsidize inner city troops, reluctantly raised its price to $3 a box this year. The neighboring—but much smaller—Macomb County Girl Scout Council stayed at $2.50 a box, setting the stage for a marketing battle. However, most of the troops in this skirmish are not Scouts: they are grown-ups who peddle the cookies at work. Such scenarios have been repeated in other parts of the country, as many of the nation's 330 Girl Scout councils go through their annual pricing debate. Why don't the councils simply agree on one national price? Because antitrust laws prohibit price-fixing.[1] ■

---

[1] Rebecca Blumenstein, "Cookie Price War Sends Adult Troops into Marketing Battle," *The Wall Street Journal*, Mar. 8, 1996, p. A1. Republished with permission of The Wall Street Journal Co.; permission conveyed through the Copyright Clearance Center, Inc.

Competition is an essential element of the American economic system. Antitrust laws are the rules that govern that competition. As this chapter opening illustrates, these laws affect many aspects of our lives—both as consumers and as businesspeople.

IN THE BEGINNING

Throughout much of the nineteenth century, competition in America was largely a local affair. The country was so big and transportation so poor that companies primarily competed in small local markets. It was too costly to transport goods great distances. State laws rather than national statutes regulated competition.

By the second half of the nineteenth century, four railroad lines crossed the continent from coast to coast. For the first time, national markets were a real possibility. John D. Rockefeller saw the potential. In 1859, Edwin L. Drake, a retired railroad conductor, drilled the first commercially successful oil well in the United States. Three years later, when the 23-year-old Rockefeller entered the scene, the oil industry was full of producers too small to benefit from economies of scale. Production was inefficient, and prices varied dramatically in different parts of the country.

Rockefeller set out to reorganize the industry. He began by buying refineries, first in Cleveland and then in other cities. He and his partners spread into all segments of the oil industry—buying oil fields, building pipelines, and establishing an efficient marketing system. To unify the management of these companies, they transferred their stock to the Standard Oil Trust. By 1870, Rockefeller had achieved his goal—the Standard Oil Trust controlled virtually all the oil in the country, from producer to consumer. Rockefeller was the wealthiest person in the world.

Some of Rockefeller's tactics were controversial. When a competitor tried to build an oil pipeline, Rockefeller used every weapon short of violence to stop it. He planted stories in the press suggesting the pipes would leak and ruin nearby fields. He flooded local builders with orders for tank cars so no workers would be available to build the pipeline. When the pipeline was finished, he refused to allow his oil to flow through it. These tactics were frightening, especially in an industry as important as oil. What if Rockefeller decided to raise prices unfairly? Or cut off oil altogether? Newspapers began to attack him ferociously.

Sherman Act

With the coming of the railroads, it became clear that large companies might be able to control other industries as well. To prevent extreme concentrations of economic power, Congress passed the **Sherman Act** in 1890. It was one of the first national laws designed to regulate competition. Because this statute was aimed at the Standard Oil Trust and other similar organizations, it was termed **antitrust** legislation. In 1892, the Ohio Supreme Court dissolved the Standard Oil Trust, which was replaced by the Standard Oil Co. But the government was not satisfied until a spring day in 1911, when Supreme Court Chief Justice Edward White quietly read aloud his dramatic 20,000-word opinion ordering the breakup of Standard Oil.[2] The 33 companies that made up Standard Oil were forced to compete as separate businesses. Today, descendants of Standard Oil include Amoco, Atlantic Richfield, Chevron, ExxonMobil, and Pennzoil. Imagine what kind of giant they would be if still united.

For the first 70 or so years after the passage of the Sherman Act, most scholars and judges took the view that large concentrations of economic power were suspect, even

---

2 *Standard Oil Company of New Jersey v. United States,* 221 U.S. 1, 31 S. Ct. 502, 1911 U.S. LEXIS 1725 (1911).

if they had no obvious impact on competition itself. Big was bad. Big meant too much economic and political power. As Senator John Sherman, sponsor of the Sherman Act, put it, a nation that "would not submit to an emperor should not submit to an autocrat of trade." Fragmented, competitive markets were desirable in and of themselves. Standard Oil should not control the oil markets, even if the company was very efficient and had gained control by completely acceptable methods.

Chicago School

Beginning in the 1960s and 1970s, however, a group of influential economists and lawyers at the University of Chicago began to argue that the goal of antitrust enforcement should be *efficiency*. Let a company grow as large as it likes provided that this growth is based on a superior product or lower costs, not ruthless tactics. Insist on a clean fight, but do not handicap large successful companies to help weaker competitors. Some companies will thrive, others will die, but in either case, the consumer will come out ahead. Adherents of the **Chicago School** argued further that the market should decide the most efficient size for each industry. In some cases, such as automobiles or aircrafts, the most efficient size might be very large indeed. Under traditional antitrust analysis, courts often asked, "Has a competitor been harmed?" The Chicago School suggests that courts should ask instead, "Has *competition* been harmed?"

At the turn of the twentieth century, President Theodore Roosevelt personally plotted the breakup of Standard Oil. (As one of Rockefeller's compatriots said of Roosevelt, "We bought the son of a bitch, and then he didn't stay bought.") At the turn of the twenty-first century, two descendants of Standard Oil—Exxon and Mobil—announced their intention to merge. This time, not one politician so much as grabbed a microphone to object to the recombination. Where once size alone was cause for concern, now regulators believe that a certain bulk may be necessary if American companies are to compete in the intense global economy.

Antitrust policy, however, continues to evolve. Adherents of the so-called **Post Chicago School** are beginning to recognize that competition alone may not be enough to protect consumers. For example, an industry with a large number of competitors may foster collusion, not competition. Or activities that appear consumer friendly, such as giving a product away for free, may in the long run harm consumers. (Take, for example, Microsoft's decision to give away its Internet browser. Although consumers benefited in the short run, the Justice Department alleged that this giveaway harmed consumers by driving competitors out of business.) Now, when deciding whether to take action, federal trustbusters are beginning to focus directly on consumers, asking two questions: Will this action cause consumers to pay higher prices? Are the higher prices sustainable in the face of existing competition? As you read the cases in this chapter, think about which factors the court considered important: size, competition, or the impact on consumers.

It is worth noting that throughout the twentieth century, the United States had stricter antitrust laws than most other countries. Indeed, our markets are more competitive than most. No matter what standard of law the government has applied, it has managed to prevent the worst competitive abuses.

OVERVIEW OF ANTITRUST LAWS

The major provisions of the antitrust laws are:

- Section 1 of the Sherman Act prohibits all agreements "in restraint of trade."
- Section 2 of the Sherman Act bans "monopolization"—the wrongful acquisition of a monopoly.

- The Clayton Act prohibits anti-competitive mergers, tying arrangements, and exclusive dealing agreements.
- The Robinson-Patman Act bans price discrimination that reduces competition.

The full text of the antitrust statutes is available at **http://www.antitrustinstitute.org/** by clicking on "Links" and "Codes."

In 1914, Congress passed the **Clayton Act** in part because the courts were not enforcing the Sherman Act as strictly as it had intended. The purpose of the Clayton Act was to clarify the earlier statute. As a result, the two laws overlap significantly. The **Robinson-Patman Act** (passed in 1936) is an amendment to the Clayton Act. Rather than systematically reviewing the terms of each statute in order, this chapter focuses instead on the *kinds of behavior* that the antitrust laws regulate.

Violations of the antitrust laws are divided into two categories: ***per se*** and **rule of reason.** As the name implies, *per se* violations are automatic. Defendants charged with this type of violation cannot defend themselves by saying, "But the impact wasn't so bad" or "No one was hurt." The court will not listen to excuses, and the defendants are subject to both *criminal* and *civil* penalties. Typically, the Justice Department has sought criminal sanctions only against *per se* violators.

Rule of reason violations, on the other hand, are illegal only if they have an anti-competitive impact. To determine if an activity is an unreasonable restraint of trade, the courts consider its circumstances, intent, and impact. For example, if competitors join together and agree that they will not deal with a particular supplier, their action is illegal only if it harms competition. Although rule of reason violators may be subject to civil penalties or private lawsuits, traditionally the Justice Department has not sought criminal penalties against them.

Both the Justice Department and the Federal Trade Commission (FTC) have authority to enforce the antitrust laws. However, only the Justice Department can bring criminal proceedings; the FTC is limited to civil injunctions and other administrative remedies. In addition to the government, anyone injured by an antitrust violation has the right to sue for damages. The United States is unusual in this regard—in most other countries, only the government is able to sue antitrust violators. A successful plaintiff can recover treble (i.e., triple) damages from the defendant.

In developing a competitive strategy, managers typically consider two different approaches:

- Cooperative strategies that allow companies to work together to their mutual advantage
- Aggressive strategies, designed to create an advantage over competitors

COOPERATIVE STRATEGIES

Three types of cooperative strategies are potentially illegal:

- **Horizontal agreements** among competitors. An agreement between Levi Strauss and Wrangler—both manufacturers of denim jeans—would be a horizontal agreement.
- **Vertical agreements** among participants at different stages of the production process. An agreement between Levi Strauss and Macy's—one company makes jeans, the other sells them—would be a vertical agreement.
- **Mergers and joint ventures** among competitors. Here, companies go beyond simple agreements to combine forces more permanently.

The following table lists the cooperative strategies that will be discussed in this chapter:

Horizontal Strategies	Vertical Strategies	Mergers
Market division	Reciprocal dealing	Horizontal mergers
Price-fixing	Price discrimination	Vertical mergers
Bid-rigging		Joint ventures
Refusal to deal		

Horizontal Cooperative Strategies

Although the term "cooperative strategies" *sounds* benign, these tactics are often harmful to competition. Many horizontal cooperative strategies are *per se* violations of the law and can lead to prison terms, heavy fines, and expensive lawsuits with customers and competitors.

Market Division

Any effort by a group of competitors to divide its market is a *per se* violation of §1 of the Sherman Act. Illegal arrangements include agreements to allocate customers, territory, or products. For example, these business schools would be in violation if:

- Georgetown agreed to accept only men and, in return, George Washington would take only women[3];
- Stanford agreed to accept only students from west of the Mississippi, leaving the east to Yale; or
- Northwestern agreed not to provide courses in entrepreneurship, while the University of Chicago eliminated its international offerings.

Price-Fixing and Bid-Rigging

When competitors agree on the prices at which they will buy or sell products or services, their price-fixing is a *per se* violation of §1 of the Sherman Act. Bid-rigging is also a *per se* violation. In bid-rigging, competitors eliminate price competition by agreeing on who will submit the lowest bid. In an early case, the defendants argued that price-fixing was only wrong if the prices were *unfair*. The Supreme Court disagreed. In its view, prices should be set by markets, not by competitors—or judges. Moreover, "The reasonable price fixed today may through economic and business changes become the unreasonable price of tomorrow."[4]

For the better part of a century, price-fixing and bid-rigging have been illegal, yet they never seem to go away. Here are some examples:

- *Dairy Industry.* Using a computer to analyze the bids that schools received on their milk contracts, the Florida Attorney General uncovered a pervasive price-fixing scheme. By some estimates, price-fixing raised milk prices in Florida by 14 percent. Forty-three companies were convicted or pleaded guilty; two dozen individuals went to prison. Companies paid fines in excess of $90 million.

---

3 This, of course, does not mean that all single-sex schools are violating the antitrust laws. They are in violation only if their admissions policy results from an agreement with competitors.

4 *United States v. Trenton Potteries Co.*, 273 U.S. 392, 397, 1927 U.S. LEXIS 975 (1927).

- *College Athletics.* Colleges were concerned about the cost of their athletic programs. In particular, the cost of the coaching staffs seemed out of control. Some assistant coaches were being paid as much as $70,000 a year. In response, NCAA schools (i.e., members of the National Collegiate Athletic Association) agreed to cap the salaries of assistant coaches at (a very stingy) $12,000. But a court blew the whistle, finding that the NCAA had engaged in illegal price-fixing. A jury awarded the coaches $66 million.

The following article discusses the Justice Department's successful strategy for ensnaring price-fixers.

NEWS*worthy*

Meeting clandestinely at an airport hotel outside London, top executives from the leading makers of a crucial raw material for forging steel reached an agreement to fix global prices. The executives were from France, Germany, Japan, and the United States. But the cartel began to unravel after a steel maker complained to federal investigators about the lack of competition. The U.S. government filed suit and ultimately obtained corporate fines in the case of $437 million. Two executives pleaded guilty, paid large fines, and received prison sentences.

The antitrust division, once a small and sleepy backwater of the Justice Department, has become a power center against white-collar crime. All told, the antitrust division has won fines—corporate and individual—of more than $1.7 billion in the last four years. No one doubts that the global price-fixing collusions it has exposed affected every American consumer. These collusions have raised prices for gasoline, vitamins, soft drinks, and other food products.

The recent takeoff in investigations and prosecutions is a result of a new Justice Department policy that made amnesty automatic if the company came in before an investigation began and permitted broad amnesty afterward to the first company to offer assistance. It also covered all executives from that company who cooperated, a significant inducement because violations of the Sherman Act carry a potential prison sentence of three years for every count, in addition to virtually limitless fines. Almost immediately, the change could be seen in the quantity and quality of tips coming to prosecutors. Before the new rule, the division reported an average of one amnesty request a year. Since the change, it is one a month.[5] ◆

As this Newsworthy feature indicates, the Justice Department sometimes finds a smoking gun. But what if there is no obvious weapon, only circumstantial evidence? Suppose competitors just happen to charge the same prices. Is that practice illegal? The following case discusses the legality of so-called *conscious parallelism.*

FEARS V. WILHELMINA MODEL AGENCY, INC.

2004 U.S. Dist. LEXIS 5045
United States District Court for the Southern District of New York, 2004

Facts: A group of models sued some of the top agencies in New York, alleging that these firms had violated §1 of the Sherman Act by conspiring to fix the commissions that they charged the models for placing them. The agencies were all members of the International Model Managers Association, Inc. (IMMA).

Under New York law, *employment* agencies could not charge a commission of more than 10 percent,

▼

---

[5] Stephen Labaton, "The World Gets Tough on Fixing Prices," *The New York Times,* June 3, 2001, sec. 3, p. 1. Copyright © 2001 by The New York Times Co. Reprinted by permission.

but *management* agencies could. All agencies that were members of IMMA changed their state registration from employment agency to management agency and then raised their standard commission to 20 percent. Several of the agencies used identical language in their contracts, specifying that they were personal managers, not employment agencies. At IMMA meetings, executives at various agencies announced that they were raising their commissions to 20 percent. One executive stated, "We are all committing suicide, if we do not stick together."

During depositions, executives at the agencies admitted that they knew instantly every time an agency raised prices. One executive stated, "The more uniformity in the prices, the more I think it was—it was something that you could then compete on the quality of your models on the service, and not just on—on rates, you know. So we were always favorable to letting everyone know as much as possible about—about our pricing policies."

The models also presented memoranda from the agencies, stating:

- "IMMA should send out a letter stating that we plan on pursuing a $1\frac{1}{2}$ percent finance charge on clients who pay after 30 days in lieu of increasing our service charge."

- The commission would increase from 15 to 20 percent, and "all other agencies will go along with this increase. Please inform your clients accordingly so that there is no misunderstanding."

- "Pauline's agreed with me but as usual, Bill Weinberg cautioned me about price fixing . . . Ha! Ha! Ha! . . . the usual bulls-t! I warned him that by not sticking together, we would have to make 40 percent more volume in order to make the same figures as last year, but you know Bill, he always thinks he can get more if he acts that way."

IMMA minutes reported that members had adopted uniform schedules for the Christmas holiday. In addition, the agencies agreed to operate "ethically," by which they meant that they would not try to hire models from other agencies. A letter to all members of IMMA reported that one agency had broken this rule by hiring model Michele Weweje.

The agencies admitted that they had engaged in parallel behavior but they argued that these activities were not sufficient to support a charge of illegal price-fixing. The agencies moved for summary judgment.

Issues: Did the modeling agencies engage in illegal price-fixing? Is parallel behavior illegal?

Excerpts from Judge Baer's Decision: To be sure, business behavior is admissible circumstantial evidence from which the fact finder may infer agreement. But this Court has never held that proof of parallel business behavior conclusively establishes agreement or, phrased differently, that such behavior itself constitutes a Sherman Act offense. Because parallel activity may be equally suggestive of independent conduct, plaintiffs offering parallel conduct as evidence of an antitrust conspiracy must demonstrate additional circumstances, often referred to as "plus factors," which provide a supplemental basis to infer a conspiracy. Among recognized plus factors, two in particular have received significant exposure in case law, both of which have a strong presence in this case—a motive to conspire and a high level of inter-firm communication.

With regard to the first plus factor, there is no question that defendants possessed a common rational motive to conspire—the ability to raise models' commissions without suffering loss of business. While I agree with defendants that the majority of this evidence more directly demonstrates agreement on elements other than models' commissions, I do not agree that, as a result, such evidence is irrelevant. Rather, I find that the extensive evidence of agreements between IMMA members, on various components of their businesses, such as client service fees, holiday closing schedules, cancellation policies, and penalties borne by management companies who attract models from competitors, may reasonably be inferred to demonstrate an industry inundated with collusion.

Plaintiffs have established that all defendants who were members of IMMA, and therefore participated in or were privy to the conversations and agreements discussed above, had a unity of purpose or a common design and understanding, or a meeting of minds in an unlawful arrangement. [Therefore, the court denies the agencies' motion for summary judgment.] ■

Refusals to Deal

Every company generally has the right to decide with whom it will or will not do business. **However, a refusal to deal is a rule of reason violation of the Sherman Act, illegal if it harms competition.** In a **refusal to deal,** a group of competitors boycotts a buyer, supplier, or even another competitor. For example, a group of clothing manufacturers agreed that they would not sell apparel to retailers who also bought from style pirates—companies that copied the manufacturers' designs. The Supreme Court held that this was an illegal refusal to deal because it was harming competition.[6]

Vertical Cooperative Strategies

Vertical cooperative strategies are agreements among participants at different stages of the production process.

Reciprocal Dealing Agreements

Under a reciprocal dealing agreement, a buyer refuses to purchase goods from a supplier unless the supplier also purchases items from the buyer. Imagine that you are in the business of processing beets into sugar. During this process, it is easy to separate the seeds, which can then be used to grow more beets. Why not suggest to your beet suppliers that they buy their seeds from you? Why not further suggest that if *they* are not willing, you will find other suppliers who are?[7]

You are proposing a reciprocal dealing agreement. In the past, such arrangements were common. Many major corporations even kept computer records of purchases, sales, and "balance of trade" with other companies. Although these arrangements might have made *business* sense, the government took the view that they were also *rule of reason* violations of the Sherman Act; that is, they were illegal if they had an anticompetitive effect. The government brought suit against several companies, including a beet processor. It also halted a number of mergers that might have resulted in internal reciprocal arrangements. In recent years, however, the government has brought few of these cases. Reciprocal dealing agreements are likely to be a problem now only if they foreclose a *significant share* of the market and if the participants *agree* not to buy from others.

Price Discrimination

Under the Robinson-Patman Act, it is illegal to charge different prices to different purchasers if:

- The items are the same, and
- The price discrimination lessens competition.

However, it is legal to charge a lower price to a particular buyer if:

- The costs of serving this buyer are lower, or
- The seller is simply meeting competition.

Congress passed the Robinson-Patman Act (RPA) in 1936 to prevent large chains from driving small, local stores out of business. Owners of these "Ma and Pa stores" complained that the large chains could sell goods cheaper because suppliers charged

6 *Fashion Originators' Guild of America, Inc. v. Federal Trade Commission,* 312 U.S. 457, 61 S. Ct. 703, 1941 U.S. LEXIS 1318 (1941).

7 See *Betaseed, Inc. v. U & I, Inc.,* 681 F.2d 1203, 1982 U.S. App. LEXIS 17190 (9th Cir. 1982).

them lower prices. As a result of the RPA, managers who would otherwise like to develop different pricing strategies for specific customers or regions may hesitate to do so for fear of violating this statute. In reality, however, they have little to fear.

Under the RPA, a plaintiff must prove that price discrimination occurred and that it lessened competition. It is now perfectly permissible, for example, for a supplier to sell at a different price to its Texas and California distributors, or to its health care and educational distributors, as long as the distributors are not in competition with each other.

The RPA also expressly permits price variations that are based on differences in cost. Thus, Kosmo's Kitchen would be perfectly within its legal rights to sell its frozen cheese enchiladas to Giant at a lower price than to Corner Grocery if Kosmo's costs are lower to do so. Giant often buys shipments the size of railroad containers that cost less to deliver than smaller boxes.

During the last decade, the federal government has dramatically reduced its enforcement of the RPA. Some federal officials have even urged that the RPA be repealed to prevent it from interfering with the smooth operation of the market. This fadeout of government action has left enforcement in the hands of individual plaintiffs, but these cases are receiving little encouragement from the courts.

The Supreme Court has, for instance, made it much more difficult for plaintiffs to win damages in price discrimination cases. Chrysler Motors charged the J. Truett Payne dealership more than other car dealers in Birmingham, Alabama. Unable to compete, Payne went out of business. The accepted formula for determining damages in a Robinson-Patman Act case *had been* the difference between the two prices multiplied by the number of units purchased. These numbers were easy to calculate. However, in *Payne*, the Supreme Court held that it is not enough to prove that competitors are able to buy at a lower cost. The plaintiff must also show that these competitors passed their savings on to customers and, as a result, plaintiff lost profits.[8] These are difficult facts to prove. As a result of cases such as this, antitrust lawyers sometimes advise their clients not to worry too much about price discrimination suits because dissatisfied customers will usually not seek damages in court but will instead try to negotiate a better price.

Mergers and Joint Ventures

The Clayton Act prohibits mergers that are anticompetitive. Companies with substantial assets must notify the FTC *before* consummating a merger.[9] This notification gives the government an opportunity to prevent a merger ahead of time, rather than trying to untangle one after the fact.

Horizontal Mergers

A horizontal merger involves companies that compete in the same market. Traditionally, the government has aggressively sought to prevent horizontal mergers that could lead to a monopoly or even a highly concentrated industry. In the *Von's Grocery* case, decided in 1966, the Supreme Court upheld the Justice Department in its suit to prevent the merger of two grocery chains that represented only 7.5 percent of the grocery market in Los Angeles.[10] Compare that decision with the following case, decided almost 20 years later.

---

[8] *J. Truett Payne Co., Inc. v. Chrysler Motors Corp.*, 451 U.S. 557, 101 S. Ct. 1923, 1981 U.S. LEXIS 49 (1981).

[9] If, for example, the acquiring company is purchasing stock or assets of the acquired company that is worth more than $212 million (adjusted annually for inflation).

[10] *United States v. Von's Grocery Co.*, 384 U.S. 270, 86 S. Ct. 1478, 1966 U.S. LEXIS 2823 (1966).

UNITED STATES V. WASTE MANAGEMENT, INC.

743 F.2d 976, 1984 U.S. App. LEXIS 18843
United States Court of Appeals for the Second Circuit, 1984

Facts: Waste Management, Inc. (WMI), acquired Texas Industrial Disposal, Inc. (TIDI). Both companies were in the trash collection business. In Dallas, their combined market share was 48.8 percent. The trial court held that the merger was illegal and ordered WMI to divest itself of TIDI.

Issue: Did WMI violate the Clayton Act by acquiring TIDI?

Excerpts from Judge Winter's Decision: A post-merger market share of 48.8 percent is sufficient to establish *prima facie* illegality under *United States v. Philadelphia National Bank* and its progeny. That decision held that large market shares are a convenient proxy for appraising the danger of monopoly power resulting from a horizontal merger. Under its rationale, a merger resulting in a large market share is presumptively illegal, rebuttable only by a demonstration that the merger will not have anticompetitive effects.

[In the present case, the *Philadelphia National Bank*] presumption is rebutted by the fact that competitors can enter the Dallas waste hauling market with such ease. WMI argues that it is unable to raise prices over the competitive level because new firms would quickly enter the market and undercut them. A person wanting to start in the trash collection business can acquire a truck, a few containers, drive the truck himself, and operate out of his home. A great deal depends on the individual's personal initiative, and whether he has the desire and energy to perform a high quality of service. If he measures up well by these standards, he can compete successfully with any other company for a portion of the trade, even though a small portion. Over the last 10 years or so a number of companies have started in the commercial trash collection business.

We conclude that the 48.8 percent market share attributed to WMI does not accurately reflect future market power. Because that power is in fact insubstantial, the merger does not, therefore, substantially lessen competition in the relevant market and does not violate the [Clayton Act]. ■

Traditionally, market share was the most important factor in evaluating mergers. As *Waste Management* indicates, however, market share is no longer the sole issue in merger cases. The government and the courts now also consider how the merger will affect competition and consumers. Thus, the government cleared a merger between aircraft giants Boeing and McDonnell Douglas, which together had a virtual monopoly on the American aircraft business. But the aircraft market is global, and American companies faced severe competition from Europe's Airbus consortium. Therefore, the government believed that the merger would not harm competition.

Conversely, the FTC blocked the merger of office supply giants Staples, Inc., and Office Depot. Nationally, these two retailers controlled only 4 percent of the market for office supplies. Was the FTC harking back to the days of *Von's Grocery*? Not exactly. The office superstores' *national* market share was relatively low because they had no stores at all in many areas of the country. Rather than national market share, the FTC focused instead on their ability to control prices locally. The agency found that, when both stores operated in the same market, prices were significantly lower than when only one store was present. Thus a box of file folders cost $1.72 in Orlando, Florida (where both stores competed), and $4.17 in nearby Leesburg (where Office Depot had a monopoly). In the FTC's view, if the two stores combined, they would have had enough power in local markets to raise prices and harm consumers.

FTC merger guidelines are available at http://www.ftc.gov by searching for "Horizontal Merger Guidelines." As the following article illustrates, antitrust enforcement is a worldwide issue.

NEWS*worthy*

The United States has always felt perfectly comfortable enforcing its antitrust laws overseas, as long as the activity had some impact within its borders. (Remember the article earlier about the price-fixing charges against foreign companies.) Now the gavel is in the other hand: the European Union scuttled a proposed merger between General Electric and Honeywell International—a marriage between two American companies that had already been approved in Washington. More trouble may be ahead because Europe and the United States each applies a different standard when evaluating mergers. The European Commission considers whether a merger would create or strengthen a *dominant position*. The commission reasoned that since GE makes jet engines and Honeywell manufactures avionics equipment, this portfolio of products together might make them more dominant. To U.S. authorities, the important issue was whether the merger would reduce competition or harm consumers. ◆

Vertical Mergers

A vertical merger involves companies at different stages of the production process—for example, when a producer of a final good acquires a supplier or vice versa. Vertical mergers can also be anticompetitive, especially if they reduce entry into a market by locking up an important supplier or a top distributor. Consider the following example.

NEWS*worthy*

International Management Group (IMG) is a management conglomerate that dominates the tennis world. IMG operates tournaments, sets up exhibitions, holds broadcast rights, and manages the careers of more than 100 pros. IMG even acquired the Nick Bolletieri Tennis Academy, training ground for many of the sport's present and future stars. IMG's competitors questioned whether this acquisition violated the antitrust laws. Says the head coach of another tennis academy, "You name it, IMG owns it, owns tournaments, owns the players, owns the academy. It's impossible to compete at that level, so we don't even bother to try."[11] ◆

IMG's acquisition of the Nick Bolletieri Tennis Academy was a vertical merger—IMG acquired a source of supply for its management group. The Justice Department has not been overly concerned about vertical mergers. The department's guidelines provide that it will challenge vertical mergers only if they are likely to increase entry barriers in a concentrated market.

Joint Ventures

A joint venture is a partnership for a limited purpose—the companies do not combine permanently, they simply work together on a specific project. The government will usually permit a joint venture, even between competitors with significant market power. The FTC approved, over strenuous objections from competitors, a joint venture between General Motors and Toyota to produce cars.

AGGRESSIVE STRATEGIES

The goal of an aggressive strategy is to gain an unfair advantage over competitors.

Monopolization

Aggressive competition is beneficial for consumers—up until the moment a company develops enough power to control a market. One purpose of the Sherman Act is to prevent this type of control. **Under §2 of the act, it is illegal to monopolize or attempt**

---

[11] Robin Finn, "Mixed Doubles: Players as Business," *The New York Times,* Mar. 16, 1994, p. B17.

to **monopolize a market.** To monopolize means to acquire a monopoly in the wrong way. *Having* a monopoly is legal unless it is *gained* or *maintained* by using wrongful tactics.

ECONOMICS
& the LAW

What is so bad about a monopoly? Imagine, for example, that you owned the only movie theater in town. Although the price of movie tickets in other towns is $10, you are able to charge $20 or maybe even $30 (for *Star Wars,* Part XVII). Although fewer customers might buy tickets at this expensive price, your profits are still higher because you earn so much on each ticket. There are two things wrong with this picture: fewer people are able to afford the movies and, when they do attend, they have less choice about what to see. The owner of the only theater in town might not be in tune with the tastes of his audiences. Economists believe that it is harmful for the movie theater to have many buyers while the customers have only one seller. ◆

To determine if a defendant has illegally monopolized, we must ask three questions:

- **What is the market?** Without knowing the market, it is impossible to determine if someone is controlling it.

- **Does the company control the market?** Without control, there is no monopoly.

- **How did the company acquire or maintain its control?** Monopolization is illegal only if gained or kept in the wrong way.

What Is the Market?

This question is not as easy to answer as it sounds. Some people refer to the antitrust laws as the "Economists' Full-Employment Acts" because antitrust litigation requires detailed testimony from economic experts.

Imagine that your company sells soft drinks with unusual food flavors—steak and cheese, among others. For some reason, you are the only company that sells food-flavored soft drinks so, by definition, you control 100 percent of the market. But is that the *relevant* market? Perhaps the relevant market is flavored drinks or soft drinks or all beverages. The question economists ask is: **How high can your prices rise before your buyers will switch to a different product?** If a price rise from $1.00 to $1.05 a bottle causes many of your customers to desert to Snapple or Coke, it is clear you are part of a larger market. Moreover, if changes in the prices of other drinks affect *your* sales, your products and theirs are probably close competitors. However, if you could raise your price to $5.00 per bottle and still hold on to many of your customers, then you might well be in your own market.

The following case illustrates the importance of market definition in an antitrust case. What is the relevant market in this case?

CUPP V. ALBERTO-CULVER USA, INC.

310 F. Supp. 2d 963, 2004 U.S. Dist. LEXIS 5244
United States District Court for the Western District of Tennessee, 2004

Facts: Billy Cupp and his wife, Cathy R. Craig, owned and operated the Looks hair salon in Cordova, Tennessee, a suburb of Memphis. The salon used hair care products that were sold only to salons, not to consumers. It bought Paul Mitchell products from

Heil Beauty Systems (Heil) and Redken products from Arnold's, Inc. (Arnold's).

Beauty Systems Group, Inc. (BSG) purchased both Heil and Arnold's. Without warning, it stopped ▼

all product deliveries to Cupp and Craig unless they would agree to sign a distribution agreement. The agreement included restrictions on where the products could be used and how they could be resold. It also prohibited purchasers from changing product tracking codes. Cupp and Craig refused to sign the agreement, so BSG stopped supplying them. The salon lost customers as a result.

Cupp and Craig filed sued against BSG, alleging that it had monopolized the market in violation of §2 of the Sherman Act. The defendant filed a motion to dismiss.

Issue: Did BSG engage in illegal monopolization?

Excerpts from Judge Donald's Decision: A plaintiff must first define the relevant market in order to state a claim under the antitrust statutes. Determining the relevant market enables the court to assess whether the defendant has monopoly power in that market, what the area of competition is, and whether the allegedly unlawful acts have anticompetitive effects in that market. The relevant market analysis includes both a product market and a geographic market.

The essential test for ascertaining the relevant product market involves the identification of those products or services that are either (1) identical to or (2) available substitutes for the defendant's product or service. Reasonable interchangeability may be gauged by (1) the product uses; i.e., whether the substitute products or services can perform the same function, and/or (2) consumer response (cross-elasticity); that is, consumer sensitivity to price levels at which they elect substitutes for the defendant's product or service. Unless a product is completely unique or exceptional market conditions exist, one brand in a market of competing brands may not constitute the relevant market.

The court determines the geographic market by assessing the market area in which the seller operates and to which the buyer can practicably turn for supplies. Plaintiff neglects entirely to define a geographic market. In the complaint, Plaintiff simultaneously mentions, without elaboration, both Defendants' international reach and its own inability to obtain Redken and Paul Mitchell products in the Memphis, Tennessee, area. Similarly, Plaintiff states both that SBC [BSG's parent corporation] is the "largest marketer of professional beauty care products in the world" and that BSG sells beauty products in "exclusive geographic territories," which Plaintiff leaves unspecified. The disconnect between a strictly local or exclusive geographic area and Defendants' global reach leaves the Court without any ability to formulate a relevant geographic market.

Furthermore, Plaintiff's attempted definition of the relevant product market is insufficient and fatally vague. In the complaint, Plaintiff refers to the relevant product market as "exclusive salon hair care products . . . those sold exclusively through salons under the advice of professional hair stylists." First, Plaintiff offered no allegation of which hair care product brands are interchangeable with Defendants' products. From the face of the complaint, it is clear that many brands and suppliers of hair care products exist. Defendants themselves manufacture or distribute several product lines other than those purchased by Plaintiff or distributed by BSG. Plaintiff even names one other distributor of hair care products in the Memphis area, which carried Redken products. The Court would be skeptical of any claim that such other hair care products are not reasonably interchangeable with Defendants' products, given the conformity of uses among hair care products, or that other, unnamed distributors could not supply those other hair care products in suitable amounts for Plaintiff's use.

Without a more specific definition and accounting of the brands and suppliers to be included in the relevant market, the Court cannot determine the boundaries of the market. It is thus unable to assess Defendants' market power, which is one of the purposes of defining a relevant market.

Second, the Court is unsure why the product market should be limited only to those hair care products sold in salons. The interchangeability among retail and salon products of this type seems high, particularly given that the price of hair care products retailed directly to consumers is generally lower than those retailed through salons, thus providing readily available substitutes.

Third, the description "hair care products" is itself so vague that it leaves the Court at a loss as to what sorts of products to include. [T]hose products could include shampoos, cosmetics, hair rinses, styling aids, or something more. Each category considered could expand the relevant market further, and Plaintiff's allegations do not indicate how broad the category is.

The Court therefore *grants* Defendants' motion to dismiss. ∎

Does the Company Control the Market?

You have 100 percent of the food-flavored soft drink market (although only 1 percent of the overall soft drink market and an infinitesimal percentage of the total beverage market). Traditionally, courts considered a share anywhere between 70 and 90 percent to constitute a monopoly. However, under modern antitrust law, market share is not important if other competitors can enter the market anytime they want (or anytime you raise your prices or lower your quality). **No matter what your market share, you do not have a monopoly unless you can exclude competitors or control prices.** For example, the Justice Department sued a movie theater chain that possessed a 93 percent share of the box office in Las Vegas. But the court ruled against the Justice Department because the chain's market share decreased to 75 percent within three years. This decline indicated that the company did not control the market and that barriers to entry were low.[12]

How Did the Company Acquire or Maintain Its Control?

Possessing a monopoly is not necessarily illegal; using *"bad acts"* to acquire or maintain one is. If the law prohibited the mere possession of a monopoly, it might discourage companies from producing excellent products or offering low prices. Anyone who can produce a better product cheaper is entitled to a monopoly. In your case, you have very cleverly developed a secret method for adding flavors to carbonated water. You also have an efficient factory and highly trained workers, so you can sell your drinks for 5¢ a bottle less than your competitors. If, in fact, you do have a monopoly, it is for all the right reasons. You have demonstrated exactly the kind of innovative, efficient behavior that benefits consumers. If you were sued for a violation of the antitrust laws, you would win.

Some companies use ruthless tactics to acquire or maintain a monopoly. It is these "bad acts" that render a monopoly illegal. In the past, the definition of bad acts was broad, and any company with a monopoly could be in violation unless it showed that, despite its best efforts to duck, a monopoly had been *thrust upon* it. In 1945, a famous judge, with the appropriate name of Learned Hand, found that Alcoa's monopoly in the aluminum industry was illegal because the company had repeatedly expanded capacity to anticipate demand.[13] In his view, the company should have waited to expand until demand actually existed. Alcoa was in violation because it could have easily *avoided* a monopoly—the monopoly had not been thrust upon it.

Everyone makes mistakes. Although Learned Hand is generally considered one of the greatest judges of his era, most commentators now believe that Alcoa was wrongly decided. *Berkey Photo* is a more typical modern case.[14] Berkey accused Eastman Kodak Co. of repeatedly and unnecessarily changing the size of its cameras to confound competitors who manufactured film to fit them. Although Learned Hand most likely would have found such actions to be illegal, the *Berkey* court rejected the view that monopolies are acceptable only if *thrust upon* the defendant and instead held that aggressive competitive strategies are legal even if they have the effect of hindering competitors. In finding Kodak not liable, the court reasoned that the company would

---

12 *United States v. Syufy Enterprises*, 903 F.2d 659, 1990 U.S. App. LEXIS 7396 (9th Cir. 1990).

13 *United States v. Aluminum Co. of America*, 148 F.2d 416, 1945 U.S. App. LEXIS 4091 (2d Cir. 1945). Judge Hand's parents did not necessarily foresee his illustrious career when naming him. "Learned" was his mother's maiden name, and it was the tradition in his family to give the mother's name to one of the children.

14 *Berkey Photo, Inc. v. Eastman Kodak Co.*, 603 F.2d 263, 1979 U.S. App. LEXIS 13692 (2d Cir. 1979), cert. denied, 444 U.S. 1093, 1980 U.S. LEXIS 923 (1980).

not have repeatedly changed camera and film specifications if consumers had objected. The success or failure of Kodak's strategy ought to be determined in the market and not by the courts.

Predatory Pricing

Predatory pricing occurs when a company lowers its prices below cost to drive competitors out of business. Once the predator has the market to itself, it raises prices to make up lost profits—and more besides.

Recall that, under §2 of the Sherman Act, it is illegal "to monopolize" and also to "attempt to monopolize." Typically, the goal of a predatory pricing scheme is either to win control of a market or to maintain it. A ban on these schemes prevents monopolization and attempts to monopolize. To win a predatory pricing case, the plaintiff must prove three elements:

- The defendant is selling its products *below cost*.
- The defendant *intends* that the plaintiff go out of business.
- If the plaintiff does go out of business, the defendant will be able to earn sufficient profits to *recoup* its prior losses.

The classic example of predatory pricing is a large grocery store that comes into a small town offering exceptionally low prices subsidized by profits from its other branches. Once all the "Ma and Pa" corner groceries go out of business, MegaGrocery raises its prices to much higher levels.

Predatory pricing offers a good example of how attitudes toward antitrust laws have changed. Formerly, courts took predatory pricing very seriously. The term certainly *sounds* bad. But despite its name, courts generally are not as concerned about predatory pricing now as they used to be. For one thing, consumers benefit from price wars, at least in the short run. For another, the cases are hard to prove. Here is why:

- **The defendant is selling its products below cost.** This rule sounds sensible, but what does "cost" mean? As you know from your economics courses, there are many different kinds of costs—total, average variable, marginal, to name a few. Under current law, any price below *average variable cost* is generally presumed to be predatory.[15] The rule may be easy to state, but in real life, average variable cost is difficult to calculate. First, plaintiffs must obtain most of the data from the defendant. Even if a defendant has a good idea of what its average variable costs are, it will not willingly tell all in court. Moreover, many of the economic decisions about what items fit into which cost category are subjective. It is difficult for the plaintiff to prove that its subjective view is closer to the truth than the defendant's.

- **The defendant intends that the plaintiff go out of business.** Even if Ma and Pa can calculate MegaGrocery's average variable cost to the satisfaction of a court, they will not necessarily win their case. They must prove that MegaGrocery intended to put them out of business. That is a pretty tall order, short of finding some smoking gun like a strategic plan that explicitly says MegaGrocery wants Ma and Pa gone.

- **If the plaintiff does go out of business, the defendant will be able to earn sufficient profits to recoup its prior losses.** Until Ma and Pa go out of business, MegaGrocery will lose money—after all, it is selling food below cost. To win

---

[15] To calculate average variable cost, add all the firm's costs except its fixed costs and then divide by the total quantity of output.

their case, Ma and Pa must show that MegaGrocery will be able to make up all its lost profits once the corner grocery is out of the way. They need to prove, for example, that no other grocery chain will come to town. It is difficult to prove a negative proposition like that, especially in the grocery business where barriers to entry are low.

Recently, plaintiffs have not had much success with predatory pricing suits. For example, Liggett began selling generic cigarettes 30 percent below the price of branded cigarettes. Brown & Williamson retaliated by introducing its own generics at an even lower price. Liggett sued, claiming that Brown's prices were below cost. The Supreme Court agreed that Brown was not only selling below cost but also intended to harm Liggett. Brown still won the case, however, because there was no evidence that it would be able to recover its losses from the below-cost pricing. If Brown raised its prices, other competitors would come back into the market.[16]

Tying Arrangements

A tying arrangement is an agreement to sell a product on the condition that the buyer also purchases a different (or tied) product. A tying arrangement is illegal under §3 of the Clayton Act and §1 of the Sherman Act if:

- The two products are clearly separate;
- The seller requires the buyer to purchase the two products together;
- The seller has significant power in the market for the tying product; and
- The seller is shutting out a significant part of the market for the tied product.

Six movie distributors refused to sell individual films to television stations. Instead, they insisted that a station buy an entire package of movies. To obtain classics such as *Treasure of the Sierra Madre* and *Casablanca* (the **tying product**), the station also had to purchase such forgettable films as *Nancy Drew Troubleshooter*, *Gorilla Man*, and *Tugboat Annie Sails Again* (the **tied product**).[17] The distributors engaged in an illegal tying arrangement. These are the questions that the court asked:

- **Are the two products clearly separate?** A left and right shoe are not separate products, and a seller can legally require that they be purchased together. *Gorilla Man*, on the other hand, is a separate product from *Casablanca*.

- **Is the seller requiring the buyer to purchase the two products together?** Yes, that is the whole point of these "package deals."

- **Does the seller have significant power in the market for the tying product?** In this case, the tying products are the classic movies. Because they are copyrighted, no one else can show them without the distributor's permission. The six distributors controlled a great many classic movies. So, yes, they do have significant market power.

- **Is the seller shutting out a significant part of the market for the tied product?** In this case, the tied products are the undesirable films like *Tugboat Annie Sails Again*. Television stations forced to take the unwanted films did not buy "B" movies from other distributors. These other distributors were effectively foreclosed from a substantial part of the market.

16 *Brooke Group Ltd. v. Brown & Williamson Tobacco Corp.*, 509 U.S. 209, 113 S. Ct. 2578, 1993 U.S. LEXIS 4245 (1993).
17 *United States v. Loew's Inc.*, 371 U.S. 38, 83 S. Ct. 97, 1962 U.S. LEXIS 2332 (1962).

Controlling Distributors and Retailers

The goal of an aggressive strategy is to force competitors out of a market—by undercutting their prices or tying products together, for example. Controlling distributors and retailers is another method for excluding competitors. It is difficult to compete in a market if you are foreclosed from the best distribution channels.

Allocating Customers and Territory

As we saw earlier in this chapter, a *horizontal* agreement by *competitors* to allocate customers and territories is a *per se* violation of §1 of the Sherman Act. **However, a vertical allocation of customers or territory is illegal only if it adversely affects competition in the market as a whole.** It is a rule of reason, not a *per se*, violation.

Suppose that Hot Sound, Inc., produces expensive, high-quality speakers. It grants its distributors the exclusive right to sell in a particular territory or the exclusive right over a particular type of customer (consumers, corporate, automobiles). In return for these exclusive rights, Hot Sound requires the distributors to stock a wide range of inventory, hire highly trained (expensive) sales help, and advertise widely. Such requirements not only increase sales but also enhance distributor loyalty. The distributors have such a large investment in Hot Sound's products that they are reluctant to switch to another manufacturer. A change would mean unloading a large inventory, developing new advertisements, and retraining or laying off some of the sales force.

Hot Sound clearly has good business reasons for adopting such a plan. It is reducing intrabrand competition (among its dealers) but enhancing interbrand competition (between brands). With its committed dealer network, Hot Sound can compete more fiercely against other brands. Vertical allocation is a rule of reason violation, which means that the law will intervene only if Hot Sound's activities have an anticompetitive impact on the market as a whole. But because Hot Sound's plan increases interbrand competition, it is unlikely to have an anticompetitive impact.

Exclusive Dealing Agreements

An **exclusive dealing contract** is one in which a distributor or retailer agrees with a supplier not to carry the products of any other supplier. **Under §1 of the Sherman Act and §3 of the Clayton Act, exclusive dealing contracts are subject to a rule of reason and are illegal only if they have an anticompetitive effect.**

Consider the case of Ben & Jerry's. With more than $100 million in sales, it was a major player in the ice cream market. And some of its competitors alleged that it was playing hardball. Just ask Amy Miller. She started Amy's Ice Creams in a small storefront in Austin, Texas. Her ice cream was so popular that she decided to begin producing pints for sale in grocery stores. But when she tried to enter the Houston market, Sunbelt, the dominant distributor in the area, refused to carry her desserts. She thinks Sunbelt turned her down because Ben & Jerry's had forbidden it to carry other premium brands.

Ironically, the ice cream was once in the other bowl, so to speak. When Ben and Jerry were the new boys on the block, they discovered that Pillsbury (owner of Häagen-Dazs) included provisions in its contracts that prohibited distributors from carrying Ben & Jerry's brand. When Ben & Jerry's produced written contracts containing these exclusory clauses, Pillsbury backed down immediately. Thereafter, no one in the industry used written distribution contracts.

Amy Miller threatened to sue Ben & Jerry's for violating the antitrust laws with exclusive dealing contracts. In determining if these agreements had an anticompetitive impact on the market, a court would consider the following factors:

- **The number of other distributors available.** Amy said that no one but Sunbelt would do because only the best distributors were able to preserve her ice cream's quality.
- **The portion of the market foreclosed by the exclusive dealing agreements.** Without Sunbelt, Amy's Ice Creams could not penetrate the Houston market, so it had to shut down its pint production line.
- **The ease with which new distributors could enter the market.** Sunbelt had few, if any, competitors. Presumably, the market was a difficult one to enter.
- **The possibility that Amy could distribute the products herself.** Not likely. Amy's talents lay in *making* a good ice cream, not distributing it.
- **The legitimate business reasons that might have led the distributor to accept an exclusive contract.** Here is what Sunbelt's vice-president had to say: "We already had our table full with super premium pints. We felt Amy's was an underfinanced product and we would have had to replace a high-volume product to give it a shot. And we personally did not think the product was very good."[18]

Would an exclusive dealing agreement between Ben & Jerry's and Sunbelt be anti-competitive? If so, would their business reasons justify the contract?

Resale Price Maintenance

NEWS*worthy*

Peter Polites (pronounced po-LEE-tus), owner of a Nine West store in New Jersey, slashed the price of a popular, smart-looking women's shoe last winter, knowing he would attract many more customers—and still earn a smooth 60 percent on each pair. But Mr. Polites's sale irritated some managers at large department stores down the hall in the Mall at Short Hills. One Nordstrom manager, he said, walked into Mr. Polites's small store, picked some shoes off the shelf, looked at the prices, slammed them down, and left without a word.

Mr. Polites said the Nordstrom manager later explained that the flats Mr. Polites had reduced to $49.99 from $60 were included on a confidential list of styles—known as the "off-limits list"—whose prices Nine West Group, Inc., rarely, if ever, lets stores mark down. Mr. Polites's low prices also maddened executives at Nine West, the footwear giant that says it sells one out of every five pairs of shoes sold to women in the United States. Vincent Camuto, chief executive of Nine West, called Mr. Polites and demanded that he end his sale. When Mr. Polites refused, Mr. Camuto told him that in that case, "We can't ship you those shoes."[19] ◆

Is it legal for Nine West to cut off a retailer who refuses to raise his prices? This question is at the heart of an important antitrust conundrum—the validity of **resale price maintenance (RPM).** RPM means the manufacturer sets *minimum* prices that retailers may charge. In other words, it prevents retailers from discounting. Why does the manufacturer care? After all, once the retailer purchases the shoes, the manufacturer has made its profit. The only way the manufacturer makes more money is to raise its *wholesale* price, not the *retail* price. RPM guarantees a profit margin for the *retailer.*

Manufacturers argue that they ought to have the right to decide how and at what price their products are sold. They may, for instance, want to promote an upscale brand image, one that could be destroyed by discount prices. Or the manufacturer may expect its dealers to provide a higher level of service than discounters can afford.

---

18 Rickie Windle, "Ben & Jerry's Creams Amy's," *Austin Business Journal,* Oct. 4, 1993, vol. 13, no. 33, sec. 1, p. 1.

19 Melody Petersen, "Treading a Contentious Line," *The New York Times,* Jan. 13, 1999, p. C1. Copyright © 1999 by The New York Times Co. Reprinted by permission.

Consumer advocates contend, however, that manufacturers such as Nine West are simply protecting dealers from competition. Discounting may or may not harm products, but, they insist, RPM certainly hurts consumers.

To settle this controversy, the Supreme Court has spoken. Spray-Rite was an herbicide dealer selling products manufactured by Monsanto. Spray-Rite claimed that Monsanto terminated the dealership contract because other dealers had complained about Spray-Rite's discount prices. Monsanto countered that Spray-Rite had not spent enough money training its salespeople or promoting the products. The jury, however, found for Spray-Rite and awarded $3.5 million in damages, which were trebled to $10.5 million. Monsanto appealed to the Supreme Court.[20]

Many commentators expected the Supreme Court to decide that RPM was a rule of reason, not a *per se*, violation. The Court ruled unanimously, however, that **RPM is a *per se* violation of §1 of the Sherman Act. A manufacturer may not enter into an agreement with distributors to fix prices.** The Court did create a potential loophole by saying that an agreement cannot be inferred simply because a manufacturer cuts off one distributor after receiving complaints from another. Unilateral action by a manufacturer to set prices is legal; an agreement with distributors about prices is not.[21]

And what happened to Nine West? It agreed to end RPM and to pay a settlement of $34 million to be used for women's health, educational, and safety programs.

In the following case, a clothing manufacturer terminated its sales to a store. Was this illegal RPM or simply a change in business strategy?

You Be the Judge

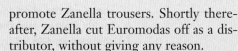

EUROMODAS, INC.

V. ZANELLA, LTD.

368 F.3d 11; 2004 U.S. App. LEXIS 9550
United States Court of Appeals for the First Circuit, 2004

Facts: Zanella, Ltd., was a manufacturer of men's clothing that distributed its products in Puerto Rico through the Clubman and Euromodas stores. Euromodas sold Zanella trousers at a much lower price than Clubman did. A Zanella executive told Euromodas that Clubman was unhappy about this price competition. Nonetheless, Zanella continued to sell to Euromodas. Clubman cancelled its Zanella order because Euromodas's discount pricing was undermining Clubman's image as an upscale clothing boutique.

The following year, Clubman proposed that it create "Zanella corners" in its stores to display and promote Zanella trousers. Shortly thereafter, Zanella cut Euromodas off as a distributor, without giving any reason.

Euromodas filed suit alleging that Zanella had violated §1 of the Sherman Act by committing resale price maintenance. Zanella filed a motion for summary judgment.

You Be the Judge: **Did Zanella engage in resale price maintenance?**

Argument for Euromodas: Section 1 of the Sherman Act prohibits a manufacturer from entering into an agreement with distributors to fix prices. Clubman complained to Zanella that Euromodas was discounting, then Zanella terminated Euromodas. Clearly, there was some sort of agreement, whether ▼

20 *Monsanto Co. v. Spray-Rite Corp.*, 465 U.S. 752, 104 S. Ct. 1464, 1984 U.S. LEXIS 39 (1984).

21 The court decided that Monsanto had engaged in RPM because it had terminated Spray-Rite as part of an agreement with other distributors.

implicit or explicit. Clubman did not want to compete against a discounter. As a reward for terminating Euromodas, Zanella was given a special corner in the Clubman stores.

The law on resale price maintenance is designed to protect consumers. Now consumers in Puerto Rico no longer have a low-cost option for buying Zanella trousers—they will be forced to pay Clubman's high prices.

Argument for Zanella: Clubman offered Zanella an exclusive deal to set up special displays of Zanella trousers. The decision to terminate Euromodas had nothing to do with pricing; the company simply wanted to sell more trousers and Clubman provided that opportunity. This choice was a perfectly legal business decision.

Yes, it is illegal for a manufacturer to agree with its distributors to fix prices. However, the simple decision to terminate a discounter—even in response to complaints from other distributors—does not in and of itself prove an illegal conspiracy. There must be some further evidence of an agreement. No such evidence is present in this case.

Vertical Maximum Price-Fixing

In *Spray-Rite*, the Supreme Court held that resale price maintenance is a *per se* violation of the Sherman Act. In that case, the manufacturer set the *minimum* prices its distributors could charge. **Vertical *maximum* price-fixing (when a manufacturer sets *maximum* prices), however, is a rule of *reason* violation of the Sherman Act.** The defendant is liable only if the price-fixing harms competition. (You remember, from earlier in this chapter, that all *horizontal* price-fixing is a *per se* violation.)

When State Oil Co. leased a gas station to Barkat Khan, it set a maximum price that Khan could charge for gas. Khan sued State Oil, but the Supreme Court ruled in favor of the oil company, on the grounds that cutting prices to increase business is the very essence of competition and, furthermore, low prices benefit consumers.[22]

Chapter Conclusion

The purpose of the antitrust laws in the United States is to keep businesses on a narrow road. On the one hand, they may not swerve to one side and work too closely with competitors. Nor may they swerve to the other side and attack competitors too aggressively. Although managers sometimes resent the constraints imposed on them by antitrust laws, it is these laws that ensure the fair and open competition necessary for a healthy economy. In the end, the antitrust laws benefit us all.

Chapter Review

1. There are two categories of antitrust violations: *per se* and rule of reason. *Per se* violations are automatic; courts do not consider mitigating circumstances. Rule of reason violations, on the other hand, are illegal only if they have an anticompetitive impact.

2. Any effort by a group of competitors to divide their market is a *per se* violation of the Sherman Act. Illegal arrangements include agreements to allocate customers, territory, or products.

---

22 *State Oil Co. v. Khan*, 522 U.S. 3, 118 S. Ct. 275, 1997 U.S. LEXIS 6705 (1997).

3. Price-fixing and bid-rigging are *per se* violations of the Sherman Act.

4. Every company generally has the right to decide with whom it will do business. However, the Sherman Act prohibits competitors from joining together in an agreement to exclude a particular supplier, buyer, or even another competitor if the agreement would hurt competition.

5. Under a reciprocal dealing agreement, a buyer refuses to purchase goods from a supplier unless the supplier also purchases items from the buyer. Reciprocal dealing agreements violate the Sherman Act if they foreclose competitors from a significant part of the market.

6. The Robinson-Patman Act prohibits companies from selling the same item at different prices if the sale lessens competition. However, a seller may charge different prices if these prices reflect different costs.

7. Under the Clayton Act, the federal government has the authority to prohibit anticompetitive mergers and joint ventures.

8. Possessing a monopoly need not be illegal; acquiring or maintaining it through "bad acts" is.

9. To determine if a company is guilty of monopolization, ask three questions:

   - What is the market?

   - Does the company control the market?

   - How did the company acquire its control?

10. To win a predatory pricing case, a plaintiff must prove three elements:

    - The defendant is selling its products below cost.

    - The defendant intends that the plaintiff go out of business.

    - If the plaintiff does go out of business, the defendant will be able to earn sufficient profit to recoup its prior losses.

11. A tying arrangement is illegal if:

    - The two products are clearly separate;

    - The seller requires that the buyer purchase the two products together;

    - The seller has significant power in the market for the tying product; and

    - The seller is shutting out a significant part of the market for the tied product.

12. Efforts by a manufacturer to allocate customers or territory among its distributors are subject to a rule of reason. These allocations are illegal only if they adversely affect competition in the market.

13. An exclusive dealing contract is one in which a distributor or retailer agrees with a supplier not to carry the products of any other supplier. Exclusive dealing contracts are subject to a rule of reason and are prohibited only if they have an anticompetitive effect.

14. When a manufacturer enters into an agreement with distributors or retailers to fix minimum prices, this arrangement is called resale price maintenance. RPM is a *per se* violation of the law.

15. Vertical maximum price-fixing is a rule of reason violation of the Sherman Act. It is illegal only if it has an adverse impact on competition.

Practice Test

1. Harcourt Brace Jovanovich (HBJ) granted BRG an exclusive license to market HBJ's bar review materials in Georgia and to use HBJ's trade name. HBJ agreed not to compete with BRG in Georgia, and BRG agreed not to compete with HBJ outside the state. HBJ was entitled to receive $100 per student enrolled by BRG and 40 percent of revenues over $350 per student. Did this agreement violate the antitrust laws?

2. Fifty bakeries in New York formed an association. They developed a system of distribution under which stores were only allowed to buy from a single baker. A store that wanted to shift to another baker had to consult the association and pay cash to the former baker. The association also decided to raise the retail price of bread from 75 to 85 cents. All the association's members printed the new price on their bread

sleeves. Are the bakeries in violation of the antitrust laws?

3. Fifty restaurants in Boston threatened to stop accepting the American Express card if the company refused to reduce the commission it charged on each purchase. Visa International, one of American Express's rivals, offered to pay the group's legal expenses. American Express then lowered its commission. For restaurants that processed more than $10 million in annual volume, American Express reduced charges from 3.25 percent to 2.75 percent. Rates for restaurants processing less than $10 million but more than $1 million a year fell to 3 percent. The company did not lower rates for restaurants with volume lower than $1 million a year. Have either the restaurants, Visa, or American Express potentially violated the antitrust laws?

4. Reserve Supply Corp., a cooperative of 379 lumber dealers, charged that Owens-Corning Fiberglass Corp. violated the Robinson-Patman Act by selling at lower prices to Reserve's competitors. Owens-Corning had granted lower prices to a number of Reserve's competitors to meet, but not beat, the prices of other insulation manufacturers. Is Owens-Corning in violation of the Robinson-Patman Act?

5. BAR/BRI is a company that prepares law students for bar exams. With branches in 45 states, it has the largest share of the bar review market in the country. Barpassers is a much smaller company located only in Arizona and California. BAR/BRI distributed pamphlets on campuses falsely suggesting Barpassers was near bankruptcy. Enrollments in Barpassers' courses dropped, and the company was forced to postpone plans for expansion. Does Barpassers have an antitrust claim against BAR/BRI?

6. **YOU BE THE JUDGE** WRITING PROBLEM American Academic Suppliers (AAS) and Beckley-Cardy (B-C) both sold educational supplies to schools. B-C's sales began to plummet, and it was rapidly losing market share. The company responded by reducing its catalog prices 5 to 12 percent. It also offered a discount of 25 to 40 percent in states in which AAS was making substantial gains. What claim might AAS make against B-C? Is it likely to prevail in court? **Argument for AAS:** B-C has

committed predatory pricing. The company is selling below cost for the purpose of driving us out of business. **Argument for B-C:** Even if we were to drive AAS out of business, we do not have enough market power to recoup our losses.

7. Two medical supply companies in the San Francisco area provide oxygen to homes of patients. The companies are owned by the doctors who prescribe the oxygen. These doctors make up 60 percent of the lung specialists in the area. Does this arrangement create an antitrust problem?

8. After acquiring the Schick brand name and electric shaver assets, North American Phillips controlled 55 percent of the electric shaver industry in the United States. Remington, a competitor, claimed that the acquisition of such a large market share was a violation of the law because the increased competition from Phillips would decrease Remington's profits. Does Remington have a valid claim?

9. Videos of *Jurassic Park* and *Snow White and the Seven Dwarfs* were due in stores the same month. The stores ought to have been delighted at the prospect of having two blockbusters to sell, but instead they were worried—how to price the videos? Both Disney (*Snow White*) and MCA/Universal (*Jurassic Park*) were longtime proponents of MAP-minimum advertised pricing. In other words, if retailers sold the videos at prices below $14.95, the studios would not subsidize their advertising budgets. Many retailers would have *liked* to sell the videos at $14.95, but they were afraid competitors would undercut them. To make matters even more complicated, they had all heard rumors that Disney planned to take other steps against retailers who ignored MAP, such as delaying shipment of the next hit—*The Lion King*. Is MAP legal? What if the studios take "other steps"?

10. **ETHICS** An 18-year-old woman with a mental disability and her mother (the Nelsons) brought a malpractice suit against one of the doctors at the Monroe Regional Medical Center. As a result, the Monroe Clinic notified the Nelsons that it would no longer treat them on a nonemergency basis. The patients then went to another local clinic, which was later acquired by

Monroe. The merged clinic refused to treat the Nelsons on a nonemergency basis, so the Nelsons were obliged to seek medical treatment in another town 40 miles away. Has Monroe violated the antitrust laws? Whether or not the Monroe clinic has violated the law, is it ethical to deny treatment to a patient?

11. ***ROLE REVERSAL*** Prepare a short-answer question based on an article you have found in the newspaper that involves an antitrust issue.

Internet Research Problem

Choose one of the cases featured at http://justice. gov/atr/cases.html. Read the Information (i.e., the complaint) in the case. Then see if you can find out how the case was ultimately resolved. You could try looking on WestLaw or LEXIS, in newspaper reports, at the company Website, or you could even call the Justice Department.

You can find further practice problems at academic.cengage.com/blaw/beatty.

Cyberlaw

CHAPTER 21

© PHOTODISC COLLECTION/GETTY IMAGES

Garrett always said that his computer was his best friend. He was online all the time, sending instant messages to his friends, listening to music, doing research for his courses, and, okay, maybe playing a few games now and again. Occasionally, the computer could be annoying. It would crash once in a while, trashing part of a paper he had forgotten to save. And there was the time that a copy of an e-mail he sent Lizzie complaining about Caroline somehow ended up in Caroline's mailbox. He was pretty irritated when the White Sox tickets he bought in an online auction turned out to be for a Little League team. And he was tired of all the spam advertising pornographic Websites. But these things happen, and despite the petty annoyances, his computer was an important part of his life.

Then one day, Garrett received a panicked instant message from a teammate on the college wrestling squad telling him to click on a certain Website pronto to see someone they knew. Garrett eagerly clicked on the Website and discovered, to his horror, that he was featured—in the nude. The Website was selling videos showing him and other members of the wrestling team in the locker room in various states of undress. Other videos, from other locker and shower rooms, were for sale, too, showing football players and wrestlers from dozens of universities. The videos had titles like "Straight Off the Mat" and "Voyeur Time." No longer trusting technology, Garrett pulled on his running shoes and dashed over to the office of his business law professor. ■

Computers and the Internet—cyberspace—together comprise one of the great technological developments of the twentieth century.[1] Inevitably, new technologies create the need for new law. In the thirteenth century, England was one of the first countries to develop passable roads. Like the Internet, these roadways greatly enhanced communication, creating social and business opportunities, but also enabled new crimes. Good roads meant that bad guys could sneak out of town without paying their bills. Parliament responded with laws to facilitate the collection of out-of-town debts. Similarly, although the Internet has opened up enormous opportunities in both our business and personal lives, it has also created the need for new laws, both to pave the way for these opportunities and to limit their dangers.

The process of lawmaking never stops. Judges sit and legislatures meet—all in an effort to create better rules and a better society. However, in an established area of law, such as contracts, the basic structure changes little. Cyberlaw is different because it is still very much in its infancy. Not only are new laws being created almost daily but whole areas of regulation are, as yet, unpaved roads. Although the process of rule making has progressed well, much debate still surrounds cyberspace law and much work remains to be done. This chapter focuses on the existing rules and also discusses the areas of regulation that are still incomplete and in debate.

Cyberlaw affects many areas of our lives. You will have noticed that this book contains numerous Cyberlaw features throughout. Chapter 10, for instance, discusses the validity of electronic contracts and signatures, Chapter 19 deals with cyber issues in securities law, and Chapter 22 contains a lengthy discussion of cyberlaw and intellectual property. This chapter, however, deals with issues that are unique to the cyberworld, such as online privacy, hacking, and spam. If some of the words confuse you, consult the glossary of Internet terms at **http://www.matisse.net.**

Before beginning the chapter in earnest, let's return briefly to Garrett, the wrestler. What recourse does Garrett have for his Internet injuries? The nude video incident happened at Illinois State University and seven other colleges. Approximately 30 athletes filed suit against GTE and PSINet for selling the videos online, but the two Web hosts were found not liable under the Communications Decency Act because they had not produced the videos themselves, they had simply permitted the sale of someone else's content. What about Garrett's other computer injuries? Lizzie was not being a good friend, but it was perfectly legal for her to forward Garrett's e-mail to Caroline. The seller of the White Sox tickets violated both federal and state fraud statutes. The federal CAN-SPAM Act prohibits spam—unsolicited commercial e-mail—but a lawsuit is a slow and awkward tool for killing such a flourishing weed. Thus far, the available legal tools have been relatively ineffectual (as you can tell from your e-mail inbox).

PRIVACY

The Internet has vastly increased our ability to communicate quickly and widely. There was a time when intraoffice memos were typed, photocopied, and then hand-delivered by messengers. Catalog orders were sent via regular mail, a comparatively slow, inefficient, and costly method.

---

[1] The term "Internet" means "the international computer network of both Federal and non-Federal interoperable packet switched data networks." 47 U.S. §230 (f)(1). It began in the 1960s as a project to link military contractors and universities. Now it is a giant network that connects smaller groups of linked computer networks. The World Wide Web was created in 1991 by Tim Berners-Lee as a subnetwork of the Internet. It is a decentralized collection of documents containing text, pictures, and sound. Users can move from document to document using links that form a "web" of information.

As wonderful as computerized communication can be, though, it is not without its dangers. Consumers enter the most personal data—credit card numbers, bank accounts, lists of friends, medical information, product preferences—on the Internet. Who will have access to this data? Who can see it, use it, sell it? Many people fear that the Internet is a very large window through which the government, employers, business, and criminals can find out more than they should about you and your money, habits, beliefs, and health. Even e-mail has its dangers: Who has not been embarrassed by an e-mail that ended up in the wrong mailbox?

Many commentators argue that, without significant changes in the law, our privacy will be obliterated. At the moment, however, privacy on the Internet is very much like the weather—everyone talks about it, but (so far) no one has done much about it.

Of Cookies and Caches

If you order a book from **Amazon.com,** you may notice that the next time you log on, you will be greeted with the message, "Hello, [Your Name]. We have <u>recommendations</u> for you." Click on the link and you may find that, because you previously bought a GMAT study guide, Amazon will entice you with other guides for standardized tests. However did Amazon know? Many Websites automatically place a cookie on the hard drive of your computer when you visit them. **A cookie is a small file that includes an identification number and may also include personal data such as your address, phone and credit card numbers, and searches you have made or advertisements you have clicked on.**[2]

Some cookies are designed to follow a user from site to site, along the entire Internet trail. Indeed, a whole industry of Internet marketing firms knows how to target Web banners to individual surfers. Thus, if you visit Websites for hotels in Togo you might, without your knowledge, be invisibly linked to an Internet marketing company that will automatically record this site visit in a cookie on your hard drive. Then, when you visit a travel site, in less time than it takes you to say "click," the marketing company can automatically retrieve your cookie, realize you are interested in Togo, and show you banner ads for travel there. You, meanwhile, are blissfully unaware that you have a dossier in cyberspace.

Other cookies can be used to authenticate who you are, storing such information as your name, address, and credit card number. **Amazon.com** has patented its so-called One-Click system that permits a shopper to buy an item by clicking once on the button. What could be easier than that? One-click buying would not be possible without cookies. No doubt, cookies are convenient. And not just for one-click shopping. Consumers benefit from targeted advertisements—for instance, long-distance runners see ads for running shoes, not cigarettes. Industry representatives also argue that, without the revenue from cookie-based ads, many Internet sites would not be free to consumers.

But there is no such thing as a free lunch, or even a free snack. Cookies raise privacy issues. When you traipse around the Internet, cookies create a dossier that could come back to haunt you. Although much of the information gathered is anonymous (i.e., the consumer is identified only by a computer identification number), this anonymous information can be linked to **personally identifiable information (PII),** such as name and address. One company now markets a databank with the names of

---

[2] Legend has it that the term "cookie" refers to the Hansel and Gretel fairy tale. An evil stepmother forced her husband to take his two young children out into the woods and lose them. Anticipating such a plan, the children left a trail of bread crumbs to follow home. Legend does not reveal why these files are called cookies rather than crumbs.

150 million registered voters. Anyone can buy a list of voters that is sliced and diced however they want—say, Republicans between the ages of 45 and 60 with Hispanic surnames and incomes greater than $50,000. This company can also transmit specially tailored banner ads to voters surfing the Web.[3]

If marketers can put together a databank of Hispanic Republican voters, they can also find out that you have visited a Website for recovering alcoholics or unrecovered gamblers or Nazi sympathizers. Do you want information about every Website you visit to be public?

Even without cookies, your computer creates a dossier about you. When you surf the Web, your computer stores a copy of the Web pages you visit in a cache file on your hard drive. Thus, anyone with access to your hard drive could get a good idea of your regular stopping places. Would you be concerned if your boss knew that you were visiting sites that specialized in job searches, cancer, or, for that matter, *any* non–job-related site? (For advice on how to protect your privacy, slip over to http://www.consumerprivacyguide.org.)

Self-Regulation of Online Privacy

Congress and the Federal Trade Commission (FTC) have been reluctant to establish laws that would regulate and protect consumer privacy on the Internet. They have instead favored self-regulation. In 2000, the commissioners of the FTC voted 3–2 to recommend that Congress enact Internet privacy legislation, but the next year a new FTC chair revoked that recommendation. Although the FTC promotes its Fair Information Practices (available at http://www.ftc.gov by clicking on "Reports"), which are voluntary standards, few businesses have elected to follow them. Privacy protection on the Internet is now an uncertain, piecemeal affair. There is not, for instance, any law requiring Websites to have or disclose a privacy policy, although if they do have one they are expected to abide by it. Consumers are largely unable to detect or prevent the collection and sharing of their personal information. Surfer beware!

Government Regulation of Online Privacy

Members of Congress have filed many bills to regulate online privacy. So intense, however, is the debate between industry and consumer advocates that no consensus—and little law—has emerged. There has, however, been some government regulation.

The FTC

As we will see in Chapter 24 on consumer law, **§5 of the FTC Act prohibits unfair and deceptive acts or practices.** The FTC applies this statute to online privacy policies: It does not require Websites to have a privacy policy, but if they do have one, they must follow it. For example, Gateway Learning Corporation sold *Hooked on Phonics* products online. The privacy policy on its Website sounded good: it promised that the company would not give PII to third parties without the customer's consent and would not change its privacy policy without first notifying customers. Wrong on both counts—the company changed its policy, gave PII to third parties, and never told its customers. Gateway admitted that it was in violation of the FTC Act and agreed to discontinue its illegal practices.

---

[3] For example, during the 2000 Republican presidential primaries, time was running short for John McCain to obtain enough voter signatures to get his name on the Virginia ballot. For $5,000, his campaign hired a company to send Internet advertisements to registered Republican voters in Virginia. When people in this database went online, they would see a McCain banner asking them to sign his petition.

Electronic Communications Privacy Act of 1986

The Electronic Communications Privacy Act of 1986 (ECPA) is a federal statute that prohibits unauthorized interception or disclosure of wire and electronic communications or unauthorized access to stored communications. The definition of electronic communication includes e-mail and transmissions from pagers and cellular phones. Violators are subject to both criminal and civil penalties. An action does not violate the ECPA if it is unintentional or if either party consents. Also, the USA PATRIOT Act, passed after the September 11 attacks, has broadened the *government's* right to monitor electronic communications.

Under the ECPA:

1. **Any intended recipient of an electronic communication has the right to disclose it.** Thus, if you sound off in an e-mail to a friend about your boss, the (erstwhile) friend may legally forward that e-mail to the boss or anyone else.

2. **Internet service providers (ISPs) are generally prohibited from disclosing electronic messages to anyone other than the addressee** unless this disclosure is necessary for the performance of their service or for the protection of their own rights or property.

3. **An employer has the right to monitor workers' electronic communications if (1) the employee consents, (2) the monitoring occurs in the ordinary course of business, or (3) the employer provides the computer system (in the case of e-mail).** Note that an employer has the right to monitor electronic communication even if it does not relate to work activities.

4. **The government has the right to access electronic communication if it first obtains a search warrant or court order.**

Two lessons from the ECPA: e-mail is not private, and it is dangerous. Sixty percent of employers monitor their employees' e-mail. In the event of litigation, the other party can access e-mail, even messages that have in theory been deleted. The following article illustrates some of the many dangers.

NEWS*worthy*

Let's be clear. Harry Stonecipher wasn't fired simply because he had an extramarital affair with an employee. Plenty of chief executives have done that in the past, and plenty more will do it in the future. It's a bad idea, it often violates company policies, but for the most part, it isn't a firing offense—yet.

No, the Boeing CEO was fired because, among other things, he had the bad judgment to detail his actions and desires in a series of very explicit e-mails to the woman in question. To borrow from one of my favorite country-music songs: We know what you were feeling, Harry. But what were you thinking?

E-mail, unlike love, is forever. You may think you've destroyed every last vestige of it, but it lives on, in some forgotten corner of some far-off server, waiting like Sleeping Beauty to be brought back to life by a zealous prosecutor or an overcompensated trial lawyer.

Has Mr. Stonecipher ever heard of Eliot Spitzer? The New York attorney general has built an awe-inspiring career on indiscreet e-mail, and now believes they are his e-ticket to the governor's mansion. Among his most prized discoveries were Henry Blodget's e-mail using the acronym POS (hint: the first two words are "piece" and "of") to refer to a tech stock that he was touting to the public on behalf of Merrill Lynch. Then there was Jack Grubman's e-mail boasting that Citigroup Chairman Sandy Weill had helped his children get into an exclusive Manhattan nursery school after he boosted his rating of AT&T stock.

> The lesson of all this couldn't be clearer. Don't ever put anything in an e-mail that you wouldn't want to read on the jumbotron at Times Square.[4] ◆

What about information that consumers provide online—is that private? In the following case, consumers discovered that their PII was being collected by pharmaceutical company Websites.

YOU BE THE JUDGE

IN RE PHARMATRAK, INC. PRIVACY LITIGATION

329 F.3d 9, 2003 U.S. App. LEXIS 8758
United States Court of Appeals for the First Circuit, 2003

Facts: Pharmatrak provided software that enabled pharmaceutical companies to compare traffic on different parts of their Websites with the same information from competitors' sites. This software, called NETcompare, recorded the time a viewer spent on each Web page, her IP address, and the Web page she viewed immediately before arriving at the client's site. NETcompare was not designed to collect personal information about individual visitors, and Pharmatrak promised potential clients that the software could not and did not collect PII. Some of the pharmaceutical clients explicitly conditioned their purchase of NETcompare on Pharmatrak's guarantees of visitor confidentiality.

Pharmatrak sent monthly reports to its clients covering topics such as the most important links to a site and its most heavily visited pages. The monthly reports did not contain any PII. It turned out, though, that by an accident of programming, NETcompare did collect some personal information on a small number of users. Some of these mistakes occurred because of an interaction between NETcompare and the computer code used by clients on their Web pages. Pharmatrak could have warned its clients not to use this particular type of code, but it did not. Other data were mistakenly collected because of a bug in a popular e-mail program. Pharmatrak never collated or used this information.

Plaintiffs were a group of Internet users whose personal data were collected by NETcompare. Although the company monitored approximately 18.7 million Website visitors, the computer expert hired by the plaintiffs was able to develop individual profiles for just 232 users. This information included name, address, telephone number, e-mail address, date of birth, gender, insurance status, education level, occupation, medical conditions, medications taken, and reasons for visiting the particular Website. Occasionally, NETcompare also recorded the subject, sender, and date of the Web-based e-mail message a user was reading immediately prior to visiting a Website.

Plaintiffs filed a class action complaint against Pharmatrak, alleging that the company had violated the Electronic Communications Privacy Act (ECPA). Both parties moved for summary judgment. The district court held for the defendants on the grounds that the pharmaceutical companies had consented to the placement of NETcompare on their Websites. Plaintiffs appealed.

You Be the Judge: Is Pharmatrak liable under the ECPA for having gathered PII about Website visitors? Did Pharmatrak act intentionally? Was there consent?

Argument for the Website Visitors: Pharmatrak promised that it would not collect PII, yet it did. The Website visitors did not consent. The pharmaceutical companies consented to the installation of NETcompare, but not to the collection of the ▼

---

4 Alan Murray, "Indiscreet E-Mail Claims a Fresh Casualty," *The Wall Street Journal,* Mar. 9, 2005, p. A2.

personal data. Pharmatrak had an obligation to live up to its promises. At a minimum, it should have warned its clients about the possible interaction between their software and NETcompare.

Argument for Pharmatrak: The ECPA only applies if there is intent and lack of consent.

Pharmatrak did not design NETcompare so that it would gather PII and it never used the information. This information could be gleaned only by a computer expert. Any violation by Pharmatrak was at worst inadvertent, not intentional. Also, the pharmaceutical companies had consented to the installation of this software. ●

Children's Online Privacy Protection Act of 1998

The Children's Online Privacy Protection Act of 1998 (COPPA) prohibits Internet operators from collecting information from children under 13 without parental permission. It also requires sites to disclose how they will use any information they acquire. The standard for obtaining parental consent is on a sliding scale—a higher standard applies if the information will be disclosed publicly. Enforcement is in the hands of the FTC. (An explanation of the statute is available at http://www.ftc.gov by clicking on "Privacy Initiatives," "Children's Online Privacy Protection Act," "Education & Guidance," and "How to Comply With The Children's Online Privacy Protection Rule.")

The Website for Mrs. Fields cookies offered birthday coupons for free cookies to children under 13. Although the company did not share information with outsiders, it did collect PII without parental consent from 84,000 children. This information included name, home address, and birth date. Mrs. Fields paid a penalty of $100,000 and agreed not to violate the law again.

Gramm-Leach-Bliley Privacy Act of 1999

The Gramm-Leach-Bliley Privacy Act of 1999 (GLB) requires banks and other financial institutions to disclose to consumers any non-public information they wish to reveal to third parties.[5] A financial institution cannot disclose this private information if the consumer opts out (i.e., denies permission). Advice on how to opt out is available at http://www.privacyrights.org by clicking on "Financial Privacy" and "Sample Opt-Out Letter from Fact Sheet 24(a)."

GLB also prohibits *pretexting*, a process by which so-called *information brokers* use deception to find out private financial information. Thus, an FTC investigator contacted a Website that was offering to sell private financial information. She offered to pay for information about her "fiancé's" bank balances. Someone working for the Website successfully obtained this information by calling the bank and pretending to be the fiancé. The Website settled with the FTC and agreed not to violate the GLB in the future.

State Regulation

A few states have passed their own online privacy statutes. For instance, the California Online Privacy Act of 2003 requires any Website that collects PII from California residents to post a privacy policy conspicuously and then abide by its terms.

---

[5] 15 U.S.C. §6801.

The European Directive

The European Union (EU) has established strict privacy rules for the collection of personal data. This directive could have far-reaching impact outside Europe because it prohibits the transfer of personal data to any countries that do not provide adequate privacy protection. Canada, South America, Australia, New Zealand, and parts of Asia have passed legislation to comply with the directive. Because the United States has not done so, the Department of Commerce reached agreement with the EU on so-called *safe harbor principles.* Any company that complies with the safe harbor rules will be permitted to receive data from European companies.

To be in compliance with the safe harbor principles, a company must:

1. Tell consumers how it intends to use their data and how they can limit its use.

2. Provide consumers with the opportunity to prevent disclosure of their personal data (in other words, to opt out). If the data are particularly sensitive (involving, for example, health or sex), then the data cannot be used unless the consumer opts in.

3. Provide adequate security for the data.

4. Provide customers with reasonable access to their data.

5. Establish a procedure for resolving disputes with customers.

To date, fewer than 500 U.S. companies are in compliance with the safe harbor principles. Most American companies have not complied because:

- The rules are cumbersome and require major changes in how companies manage customer data.

- European countries are not aggressively enforcing the rules, even against their own companies.

- If a U.S. company announces that it will comply with the safe harbor principles and then does not, the FTC has the authority to sanction the company. Therefore, companies may be better off complying with a weak policy rather than violating a strict one.

Spyware

Is your computer running sluggishly? Does it crash frequently? Has the home page on your Web browser suddenly changed without your consent? Is there a program in your systems tray that you do not recognize? You might have **spyware** on your computer. Spyware is a computer program that slips onto your computer without your permission—through e-mails, Internet downloads, or software installations. These programs monitor your activities, log your keystrokes, and can report e-mail addresses, passwords, and credit card numbers to outsiders. For more about spyware (and how to get rid of it), sneak over to http://getnetwise.org.

Congress has considered legislation to control spyware but has not taken final action. California has enacted the Consumer Protection Against Computer Spyware Act, which makes spyware illegal.

---

at RISK

What can you do to protect your privacy online? Here are some options:

- Use a fake name or provide false personal information when browsing Websites (without committing fraud, of course!).

- Use secondary e-mail addresses to disguise your identity.

- Remember, before you click, to look for a Website's privacy policy. If you cannot find one, or do not like what you find, you have the right to go elsewhere.
- Use privacy tools, such as those offered by The Electronic Privacy Information Center at http://www.epic.org. ◆

Your Hard Drive as Witness (Against You)

Many people confide their deepest secrets to their computers. Would you want everything you have ever typed into your computer to be revealed publicly? Monica Lewinsky certainly did not. Investigators in the President Clinton impeachment case discovered damaging evidence on the hard drive of Lewinsky's computer—evidence she clearly thought was private, including copies of deleted e-mails and drafts of letters she had never sent. What protection do you have for information stored on your computer?

Criminal Law

The Fourth Amendment to the Constitution prohibits unreasonable searches and seizures by the government. In enforcing this provision of the Constitution, the courts ask: Did the person being searched have a legitimate expectation of privacy in the place searched or the item seized? If yes, then the government must obtain a warrant from a court before conducting the search. (For more on this topic, investigate Chapter 7 on crime.) The Fourth Amendment applies to computers.

The architecture professor in the following case would have benefited from a course in business law and perhaps in computer science, too.

UNITED STATES OF AMERICA V. ANGEVINE

281 F.3d 1130, 2002 U.S. App. LEXIS 2746
United States Court of Appeals for the Tenth Circuit, 2002

Facts: Professor Eric Angevine taught architecture at Oklahoma State University. The university provided him with a computer that was linked to the university network, and through it to the Internet. Professor Angevine used this computer to download more than 3,000 pornographic images of young boys. After viewing the images and printing some of them, he deleted the files. Tipped off by Professor Angevine's wife, police officers seized the computer and turned it over to a police computer expert who retrieved the pornographic files that the professor had deleted.

The Oklahoma State University computer policy states that:

- The contents of all storage media owned or stored on university computing facilities are the property of the university.

- Employees cannot use university computers to access obscene material.

- The university reserves the right to view or scan any file or software stored on a computer or passing through the network and will do so periodically to audit the use of university resources. The university cannot guarantee confidentiality of stored data.

- System administrators keep logs of file names that may indicate why a particular data file is being erased, when it was erased, and what user identification has erased it.

The trial court held that federal agents did not need a warrant to search Professor Angevine's office computer because he had no expectation of privacy. He was sentenced to 51 months in prison for "knowing possession of child pornography." The professor appealed.

▼

Issue: Did Professor Angevine have a reasonable expectation of privacy in his office computer?

Excerpts from Judge Brorby's Decision: Oklahoma State University policies and procedures prevent its employees from reasonably expecting privacy in data downloaded from the Internet onto University computers. The University computer-use policy reserved the right to randomly audit Internet use and to monitor specific individuals suspected of misusing University computers. The policy explicitly cautions computer users that information flowing through the University network is not confidential either in transit or in storage on a University computer. These office practices and procedures should have warned reasonable employees not to access child pornography with University computers.

We are reluctant to find a reasonable expectation of privacy where the circumstances reveal a careless effort to maintain a privacy interest. Professor Angevine downloaded child pornography through a monitored University computer network. The policy explained network administrators actively audit network transmissions for such misuse. While Professor Angevine did attempt to erase the child pornography, the University computer policy warned system administrators kept file logs recording when and by whom files were deleted. Moreover, given his transmission of the pornographic data through a monitored University network, deleting the files alone was not sufficient to establish a reasonable expectation of privacy.

We hold Professor Angevine could not have an objectively reasonable expectation of privacy. ■

Civil Litigation

Increasingly, computers are fair game in civil litigation. Suppose that you sue your company for wrongful termination. The company counterclaims, alleging that you cheated on your expense account. During litigation, it might subpoena your computer to find support for its allegations. Or suppose that, in the midst of a bitter divorce, your spouse alleges that you have shown pornography to your children. Your computer—with its Web trail—could end up in court. The following article illustrates how fragile privacy is when hard drives become pawns in litigation.

NEWS*worthy*

Each day, Ted Reeve pours his life into his home computer. He spends hours reading news online, and dutifully records monthly payments for his Visa card and Toyota Camry, along with ATM withdrawals. He regularly types up notes from talks with his doctor. It never occurred to him that such personal data could be extracted and shared among strangers. But that's what happened when his computer's hard drive was copied by two investigators retained for his employer, Northwest Airlines. Working right in his living room with a program called EnCase, they excavated every last bit and byte from his desktop hard drive.

Northwest suspected that its flight-attendant union had used the Internet to run an illegal call-in-sick campaign to disrupt the airline. So the airline won a court order to search 20 or so hard drives at flight attendants' homes and union offices. As people commit an ever-growing pile of information to computers, their hard drives are becoming a digital mother lode for lawyers. More federal courts are approving searches of home PCs for evidence in civil cases.[6] ◆

---

[6] Michael J. McCarthy, "In Airline's Suit, PC Becomes Legal Pawn, Raising Privacy Issues," *The Wall Street Journal*, May 24, 2000, p. 1.

Spam

Spam is officially known as unsolicited commercial e-mail (UCE) or unsolicited bulk e-mail (UBE). Whatever it is called, it can be annoying as millions of these messages clog ISP computers and consumer mailboxes. As much as 80 percent of all e-mail is spam. It is estimated that roughly half of all spam is fraudulent—either in content (promoting a scam) or in packaging (the headers or return address are false). At a minimum, bulk e-mail adds to the cost of connecting to the Internet. ISPs must, for example, increase server capacity to handle the millions of spam e-mails. Moreover, both consumers and ISPs must endure the cost of outages caused by an overload of bulk e-mail. ISPs also argue that their reputations as service providers are harmed when consumers blame them for unsolicited advertisements. ISPs typically use filters to block this unwanted mail, but these programs are not foolproof and much spam sneaks through. The average worker spends 10 business days a year dealing with spam. This lost productivity costs business $50 billion worldwide.

The Controlling the Assault of Non-Solicited Pornography and Marketing Act (CAN-SPAM) is a federal statute regulating spam. This statute applies to virtually all promotional e-mails, whether or not the sender has a preexisting relationship with the recipient. E-mails covered by CAN-SPAM must:

- Provide an opt-out system that permits the recipient to unsubscribe.

- Clearly indicate that the e-mail is an advertisement.

- Provide a valid physical return address (not a post office box).

- Clearly indicate the nature of pornographic messages.

A company can avoid these requirements by obtaining advance permission from the recipients.

Although one can only applaud the effort, in truth, the CAN-SPAM Act has not noticeably decreased the amount of spam. Spammers operate in the netherworld of cyberspace where they are difficult to identify and locate. It may be, too, that the opt-out provision is having a perverse effect—instead of inspiring a spammer to remove e-mail addresses from his list, an opt-out request simply confirms to him that a live person is receiving his e-mails. But the statute does provide a new tool for fighting spam, and ISPs have filed hundreds of lawsuits against spammers. For the optimistic, SpamCop (**http://spamcop.net**) offers a service to which you can report spammers.

In the following case, Intel tried to prevent unsolicited bulk e-mail from a former employee. The company used a common law principle: trespass to chattels. Did the company have the right to prevent this ex-employee from getting inside Intel with e-mail?

INTEL CORPORATION V. HAMIDI

30 Cal. 4th 1342, 71 P.3d 296, 2003 Cal. LEXIS 4205
Supreme Court of California, 2003

Facts: Kourosh Kenneth Hamidi, a former Intel engineer, founded an organization named Former and Current Employees of Intel (FACE-Intel) to disseminate information critical of Intel's employment practices. In addition to maintaining a Website with critical information about Intel, FACE-Intel sent six mass e-mails to Intel employees. Each message was ▼

sent to as many as 35,000 addresses. These messages criticized Intel's employment practices, warned employees of the dangers those practices posed to their careers, suggested that employees consider moving to other companies, solicited employees' participation in FACE-Intel, and urged employees to inform themselves further by visiting FACE-Intel's Website.

If any recipient asked to be removed from FACE-Intel's mailing list, Hamidi complied. He did not breach any computer security barriers. Nor did his e-mails cause physical damage or functional disruption to the company's computers. Intel was not deprived of the use of its computers. Many employees did ask the company to stop the messages, and staff members spent time attempting to block further messages. Employees also spent time discussing the content of the messages.

Intel sought an injunction against Hamidi to prevent him from sending any more e-mails on the grounds that he was committing the tort of trespass to chattels. The trial court granted Intel's motion for summary judgment and enjoined Hamidi from any further mailings. The Court of Appeal affirmed. The Supreme Court of California agreed to hear the case.

Issue: Did Intel have the right to prevent Hamidi from sending e-mails to its employees?

Excerpts from Justice Werdegar's Decision:
[T]he tort of trespass to chattels allows recovery for interferences with possession of personal property. [T]he defendant's interference must, to be actionable, have caused some injury to the chattel or to the plaintiff's rights in it. The dispositive issue in this case, therefore, is whether the facts demonstrate Hamidi's actions caused or threatened to cause damage to Intel's computer system, or injury to its rights in that personal property.

[A] series of federal district court decisions held that sending UCE [spam] through an ISP's equipment may constitute trespass to the ISP's computer system. In each of these spamming cases, the plaintiff showed, or was prepared to show, some interference with the efficient functioning of its computer system. Intel has demonstrated neither any appreciable effect on the operation of its computer system from Hamidi's messages, nor any likelihood that Hamidi's actions will be replicated by others if found not to constitute a trespass. The functional burden on Intel's computers, or the cost in time to individual recipients, of receiving Hamidi's occasional advocacy messages cannot be compared to the burdens and costs caused ISPs and their customers by the ever-rising deluge of commercial e-mail.

Intel's workers were allegedly distracted from their work not because of the frequency or quantity of Hamidi's messages, but because of assertions and opinions the messages conveyed. Intel's complaint is thus about *the contents of the messages* rather than the functioning of the company's e-mail system. Intel's theory would expand the tort of trespass to chattels to cover virtually any unconsented-to communication that, solely because of its content, is unwelcome to the recipient or intermediate transmitter. Indeed, if a chattel's receipt of an electronic communication constitutes a trespass to that chattel, then unwelcome radio waves and television signals also constitute a trespass to chattel every time the viewer inadvertently sees or hears the unwanted program.

Nor, finally, can the fact Intel staff spent time attempting to block Hamidi's messages be bootstrapped into an injury to Intel's possessory interest in its computers. [I]t is circular to premise the damage element of a tort solely upon the steps taken to prevent the damage. Injury can only be established by the completed tort's consequences, not by the cost of the steps taken to avoid the injury and prevent the tort; otherwise, we can create injury for every supposed tort.

We conclude, therefore, that Intel has not presented undisputed facts demonstrating an injury to its personal property, or to its legal interest in that property, that support, under California tort law, an action for trespass to chattels. ■

Devil's Advocate Hamidi's goal was to undermine Intel. Why should the company be forced to allow him access to its e-mail system when his goal is to cause harm? ◆

Internet Service Providers and Web Hosts: Communications Decency Act of 1996

ISPs are companies, such as Earthlink, that provide connection to the Internet. Web hosts post Web pages on the Internet. Both play important roles in the Internet. As the legal structure that supports the Internet develops, so have legal issues involving these players.

The Internet is an enormously powerful tool for disseminating information. But what if some of this information happens to be false or in violation of our privacy rights? Is an ISP liable for transmitting it to the world? In 1995, a trial judge in New York held that an ISP, Prodigy Services Company, was potentially liable for defamatory statements that an unidentified person posted on one of its bulletin boards.[7] The message alleged that the president of an investment bank had committed "criminal and fraudulent acts." It was not only a false statement, it was posted on the most widely read financial computer bulletin board in the country. Although one can only feel sympathy for the target of this slur, the decision nonetheless alarmed many observers who argued that there was no way ISPs could review every piece of information that hurtles through their portals. The next year, Congress overruled the Prodigy case by passing the Communications Decency Act of 1996 (CDA).[8] **Under the CDA, ISPs and Web hosts are not liable for information that is provided by someone else. Only content providers are liable.** The following case lays out the arguments in favor of the CDA but also illustrates some of the costs of the statute (and of the Internet).

CARAFANO V. METROSPLASH.COM, INC.

339 F.3d 1119, 2003 U.S. App. LEXIS 16548
United States Court of Appeals for the Ninth Circuit, 2003

Facts: Matchmaker.com is an Internet dating service that permits members to post profiles of themselves and to view the profiles of other members. Matchmaker reviews photos for impropriety before posting them but does not examine the profiles themselves.

Christianne Carafano pursues a career as an actor under the stage name Chase Masterson. She has appeared in numerous films and television shows, such as *Star Trek: Deep Space Nine* and *General Hospital*. Without her knowledge or consent, someone in Berlin posted a profile of her in the Los Angeles section of Matchmaker. In answer to the question "Main source of current events?," the person posting the profile put *"Playboy Playgirl"* and for "Why did you call?" responded "Looking for a one-night stand." In addition, the essays indicated that she was looking for a "hard and dominant" man with "a strong sexual appetite" and that she "liked sort of being controlled by a man, in and out of bed." Pictures of the actor taken off the Internet were included with the profile. The profile also provided her home address and an e-mail address, which, when contacted, produced an automatic e-mail reply stating, "You think you are the right one? Proof it !!" [sic], and providing Carafano's home address and telephone number.

▼

---

[7] *Stratton Oakmont, Inc. v. Prodigy Services Company*, 1995 N.Y. Misc. LEXIS 229.

[8] 47 U.S.C. 230.

Unaware of the improper posting, Carafano began receiving sexually explicit messages on her home voice mail as well as a sexually explicit fax that threatened her and her son. She received numerous phone calls, letters, and e-mails from male fans, expressing concern that she had given out her address and phone number (but simultaneously indicating an interest in meeting her). Feeling unsafe, Carafano and her son stayed in hotels or away from Los Angeles for several months.

One Saturday a week or two after the profile was first posted, Carafano's assistant, Siouxzan Perry, learned of the false profile through a message from "Jeff." Acting on Carafano's instructions, Perry contacted Matchmaker, demanding that the profile be removed immediately. The Matchmaker employee did not remove it then because Perry herself had not posted it, but on Monday morning the company blocked the profile from public view and then deleted it the following day.

Carafano filed suit against Matchmaker alleging invasion of privacy, misappropriation of the right of publicity, defamation, and negligence. The district court rejected Matchmaker's argument for immunity under the CDA on the grounds that the company provided part of the profile content.

Issue: Does the CDA protect Matchmaker from liability?

Excerpts from Judge Thomas's Decision: Through [the CDA], Congress granted most Internet services immunity from liability for publishing false or defamatory material so long as the information was provided by another party. As a result, Internet publishers are treated differently from corresponding publishers in print, television, and radio. Congress enacted this provision for two basic policy reasons: to promote the free exchange of information and ideas over the Internet and to encourage voluntary monitoring for offensive or obscene material.

Interactive computer services have millions of users. It would be impossible for service providers to screen each of their millions of postings for possible problems. Faced with potential liability for each message republished by their services, interactive computer service providers might choose to severely restrict the number and type of messages posted. Congress considered the weight of the speech interests implicated and chose to immunize service providers to avoid any such restrictive effect. Under [the CDA], therefore, so long as a third party willingly provides the essential published content, the interactive service provider receives full immunity regardless of the specific editing or selection process.

The fact that some of the content [in Carafano's fake profile] was formulated in response to Matchmaker's questionnaire does not [make Matchmaker liable]. Doubtless, the questionnaire facilitated the expression of information by individual users. However, the selection of the content was left exclusively to the user. Matchmaker cannot be considered an "information content provider" under the statute because no profile has any content until a user actively creates it.

Further, even assuming Matchmaker could be considered an information content provider, the statute would still bar Carafano's claims unless Matchmaker created or developed the particular information at issue. In this case, critical information about Carafano's home address and the e-mail address that revealed her phone number were transmitted unaltered to profile viewers. Thus Matchmaker did not play a significant role in creating, developing, or "transforming" the relevant information.

Thus, despite the serious and utterly deplorable consequences that occurred in this case, we conclude that Congress intended that service providers such as Matchmaker be afforded immunity from suit. ■

Public Policy

As we saw in the case of the college athletes whose nude pictures were sold online, a great deal of harm can be done very quickly over the Internet. But Congress made a policy decision to protect open and free expression on the Internet without regard to the harm caused. The Carafano case discussed the reasons behind this policy. Do you agree with Congress' approach? If you were a legislator, what approach would you advocate? ◆

CRIME ON THE INTERNET

Despite its great benefits, the Internet has also opened new frontiers in crime for the dishonest and unscrupulous. For examples of recent cybercrimes, investigate http://computerworld.com (click on "Security," then "Cybercrime/Hacking").

Hacking

Gaining unauthorized access to a computer system is called *hacking.* The Pentagon reports that hackers make more than 250,000 attempts annually on its computers. The goal of hackers is varied; some do it for little more than the thrill of the challenge. The objective for other hackers may be industrial espionage, extortion, or theft of credit card information. Whatever the motive, hacking is a major crime. A survey of U.S. corporations, government agencies, and colleges revealed that 70 percent had experienced computer security breaches within the year. No surprise then that American companies spend more than $6 billion annually on computer security systems. The Federal Bureau of Investigation ranks cybercrime as its third highest priority, right behind terrorism and spying.

Hacking is illegal under the federal Computer Fraud and Abuse Act of 1986 (CFAA).[9] This statute applies to any computer attached to the Internet. **The CFAA prohibits:**

- Computer espionage;
- Theft of financial information;
- Theft of information from the U.S. government;
- Theft from a computer;
- Computer trespass;
- Computer fraud;
- Intentional, reckless, and negligent damage to a computer;
- Trafficking in computer passwords; and
- Computer extortion.

Some states have also adopted statutes prohibiting computer crime. A list of these statutes is available at http://www.cybercrimes.net (click on "States"). For advice on how to report a computer crime, visit http://cybercrimes.net (click on "Report a Crime").

There are two problems with the CFAA. First, although the statute prohibits the use of a virus to harm a computer, it does not ban the creation of viruses that someone else could use for hacking. Thus, it is legal for Websites such as American Eagle Publications (http://www.ameaglepubs.com) to sell source code for viruses—codes that even beginners can use destructively.

Second, the CFAA applies only to U.S. criminals. Because the Internet is truly international, cybercriminals do not always fall within the jurisdiction of American laws. For example, a computer virus called ILOVEYOU caused an estimated $7 billion worth of damage worldwide. Although the perpetrator would have been subject to prosecution under the CFAA in the United States, he lived in the Philippines, which did not have laws prohibiting cybercrime. Nor could the suspect be extradited automatically to the United States because the extradition treaty only applied if both nations had the same law. The Philippines ultimately dropped all charges against the suspect.

---

[9] 18 U.S.C. §1030.

Fraud

Fraud is a growth business on the Internet. The Internet's anonymity and speed facilitate fraud, and computers help criminals identify and contact victims. Common scams include the sale of merchandise that is either defective or nonexistent, the so-called Nigerian letter scam,[10] billing for services that are touted as "free," fraudulent stock offers, fake scholarship search services, business opportunity scams (for a small investment, you will get rich), and credit card scams (for a fee, you can get a credit card, even with a poor credit rating). To learn more about Internet fraud, steal over to http://fraud.org.

Fraud is the deception of another person for the purpose of obtaining money or property from him. It can be prosecuted under state law or the Computer Fraud and Abuse Act. In addition, federal mail and wire fraud statutes prohibit the use of mail or wire communication in furtherance of a fraudulent scheme.[11] The FTC can bring civil cases under §5 of the FTC act. (Chapter 7 on crime discusses fraud, and Chapter 24 on consumer law contains a detailed discussion of the FTC act.)

Auctions

Internet auctions are the number one source of consumer complaints about online fraud. Wrongdoers either sell goods they do not own, provide defective goods, or offer fakes. Fewer than 1 percent of online auctions involve fraud, but with upwards of $9 billion worth of goods being auctioned on the Internet each year, even 1 percent begins to add up.

Shilling is an increasingly popular online auction fraud. **Shilling means that a seller either bids on his own goods or agrees to cross-bid with a group of other sellers.** Shilling is prohibited because the owner drives up the price of his own item by bidding on it. Thus, for example, Kenneth Walton, a San Francisco lawyer, put up for auction on eBay an abstract painting purportedly by famous artist Richard Diebenkorn. A bidder offered $135,805 before eBay withdrew the item in response to charges that Walton had placed a bid on the painting himself and had also engaged in cross-bidding with a group of other eBay users. Although Walton claimed that he had placed the bids for friends, he ultimately pleaded guilty to charges of federal wire and mail fraud. He was sentenced to almost four years in prison and paid almost $100,000 in restitution to those who overpaid for the items he bid on.

To date, eBay has generally responded to shillers by suspending them for 30 days on the first offense and indefinitely on the second. Shillers are also subject to suit under general anti-fraud statutes. In addition, some states explicitly prohibit shilling.[12]

The FTC has initiated Project Safebid, under which it educates law enforcement officials and then maintains a national database of Internet auction fraud complaints so that it can refer cases to the appropriate law enforcement agencies. To file a fraud complaint, click on http://www.ifccfbi.gov.

---

[10] Victims receive an e-mail from someone alleging to be a Nigerian government official who has stolen money from the government. He needs some place safe to park the money for a short time. The official promises that, if the victim will permit her account to be used for this purpose, she will be allowed to keep a percentage of the stolen money. Instead, of course, once the "official" has the victim's bank information, he cleans out the account. The highest average dollar losses are reported in this Internet scam—$5,575 per victim.

[11] U.S.C. §§1341–1346.

[12] For example, New Mexico law provides that "It shall be unlawful to employ shills or puffers at any such auction sale or to offer or to make or to procure to be offered or made any false bid or offer any false bid to buy or pretend to buy any article sold or offered for sale." N.M. Stat. §61-16-14.

Identity Theft

Identity theft is one of the scariest crimes against property. Although it existed before computers, the Internet has made it much easier. For example, consumer activists were able to purchase the social security numbers of the director of the CIA, the Attorney General of the United States, and other top administration officials. The cost? $26 each. No surprise then that 10 million Americans are victims of this crime each year, at an estimated cost of $55 billion. The following article describes what it is like to be a victim of identity fraud.

NEWS*worthy*

I was working at Home Depot, where I'm a manager, when the Discover Card fraud unit called to find out why I'd requested an additional credit card. The Discover agent asked when I had moved to 1919 Madison Avenue, Norfolk, Va. My stomach turned inside out; I live on Long Island. I'd never even been to Virginia. The agent told me to notify the credit bureaus immediately.

A woman at one bureau told me someone had applied for eight cards in my name within the last month. My heart raced as I called each company to confirm my worst fear—they were all carrying large balances in my name. Even though I was able to cancel each card, I was freaking out. Two weeks later, I received more credit reports. He had opened 21 accounts overall. After two computers were delivered to his Norfolk address, I called the Norfolk police. They refused to arrest him. My wife had to stop me from going to sit in front of his house myself. In less than a month, this guy spent more than $40,000, a large chunk on stuff I'd never buy for myself, like Tommy Hilfiger and Nautica clothes and designer shoes.

I finally contacted the FBI, which discovered that the address he was using was fake and that the guy had a driver's license in my name. In the end, the FBI nabbed him in a stolen car. Turns out he conned 50 or 60 people out of more than $500,000. He plea-bargained and got six and a half years, but will probably get out earlier. This guy wrecked my credit history. What's worse is that he still knows my Social Security number. What would stop him from doing it again?[13] ◆

Although the owner of a credit card must generally pay only the first $50 that is stolen (as discussed in Chapter 24 on consumer law), the time and effort required to undo the damage can be substantial. And credit cards may be the least of it. Armed with data such as a Social Security number and mother's maiden name, thieves can obtain loans, acquire a passport and driver's license, or even commit (additional) crimes under their new identities. Meanwhile, the victim may find himself unable to obtain a credit card, loan, or job. One victim spent several nights in jail after he was arrested for a crime that his alter ego had committed.

Responding to these concerns, Congress passed the Identity Theft and Assumption Deterrence Act of 1998.[14] **This statute prohibits the use of false identification to commit fraud or other crime and it also permits the victim to seek restitution in court.**

A number of states have also passed identity theft statutes. California, for example, prohibits the use of Social Security numbers on ID cards or on bank statements or other documents sent by mail. Also, consumers can place a security freeze on their credit reports. When a freeze is in place, thieves cannot obtain a credit card or loan in

---

[13] Adam Ray, as told to Liz Welch, "Taken to the Bank," *The New York Times,* June 2, 2002, sec. 6, p. 106. Copyright © 2002 by The New York Times Co. Reprinted by permission.
[14] 18 U.S. §1028.

the consumer's name. California is the only state with a law requiring companies to notify consumers when their personal information has been stolen. Congress is considering similar legislation.

*ᵘᵖ*date

Has Congress passed legislation requiring companies to notify customers if their PII is stolen? ◆

at **RISK**

What can you do to prevent the theft of your identity?

1. Check your credit reports at least once a year. (Consumers are entitled by law to one free credit report every year from each of the three major reporting agencies. You can order these reports at https://www.annualcreditreport.com.)

2. Subscribe to a credit monitoring service that will notify you each week if there are any major changes to your credit reports.

3. If you suspect that your identity has been stolen, contact the FTC at 877-IDTHEFT, 877-438-4338, or http://www.consumer.gov/idtheft. Also, file a police report immediately and keep a copy to show creditors. Notify the three credit agencies.

For additional tips, visit http://www.ftc.gov (search for "Id Theft"). ◆

Phishing

Have you ever received an e-mail like this:

> We regret to inform you that your eBay account could be suspended if you don't re-update your account information. To resolve this problems [sic] please use the link below and re-enter your account information. If your problems could not be resolved your account will be suspended for a period of 24 hours; after this period your account will be terminated.

This e-mail is not from eBay, but rather from a fraudster hoping to lure the recipient into revealing her eBay account information, including credit card numbers and passwords. It is part of one of the most rapidly growing areas of Internet fraud: **phishing. In this crime, a fraudster sends an e-mail directing the recipient to enter personal information on a Website that is an illegal imitation of a legitimate site.** Prosecutors can bring criminal charges against phishers for fraud. The targeted companies have sued these criminals for fraud, trademark infringement, false advertising, and cybersquatting (discussed in Chapter 22 on intellectual property). No reputable company will ask customers to respond to an e-mail with personal information. When in doubt, close down the suspicious e-mail, re-launch your Web browser, and then go to the company's main Website. If the legitimate company needs information from you, it will so indicate on the site.

Chapter Conclusion

The Internet has changed our lives in ways that were inconceivable a generation ago, and the law is rushing to catch up. Old laws will be applied in new ways, other laws will need to change completely and, as legislators and courts learn from experience, new laws will be enacted.

Inevitably, the law of cyberspace will become increasingly international. What does Europe accomplish by regulating Internet privacy if its citizens spend a good portion of their time on American Websites? What will the FTC do if scam artists, or spammers, operate offshore? Leaders of e-commerce companies around the world have formed the Global Business Dialogue on Electronic Commerce to develop policies and advise governments on cyberspace issues. (To learn more about this organization, travel to http://www.gbd.org.) Effective regulation of cyberspace will require cooperation among nations and between government and industry.

Chapter Review

1. Section 5 of the FTC Act prohibits unfair and deceptive practices.

2. The Electronic Communications Privacy Act of 1986 is a federal statute that prohibits unauthorized interception or disclosure of wire and electronic communications or unauthorized access to stored communications.

3. The Children's Online Privacy Protection Act of 1998 prohibits Internet operators from collecting information from children under 13 without parental permission. It also requires sites to disclose how they will use any information they acquire.

4. The Gramm-Leach-Bliley Privacy Act of 1999 requires banks and other financial institutions to disclose to consumers any non-public information they wish to reveal to third parties.

5. The U.S. Department of Commerce and the European Union have established safe harbor principles for the collection of personal data. Any company that complies with the safe harbor rules will be permitted to receive data from European companies.

6. Spyware is a computer program that slips onto your computer without your permission—through e-mails, Internet downloads, or software installations. Congress has considered legislation to control spyware but has not taken final action. California has enacted the Consumer Protection Against Computer Spyware Act, which makes spyware illegal.

7. The Fourth Amendment to the Constitution prohibits unreasonable searches and seizures by government agents. This provision applies to computers.

8. Controlling the Assault of Non-Solicited Pornography and Marketing Act (CAN-SPAM) is a federal statute regulating spam. This statute applies to virtually all promotional e-mails, whether or not the sender has a preexisting relationship with the recipient. E-mails covered by CAN-SPAM must:

- Provide an opt-out system that permits the recipient to unsubscribe.

- Clearly indicate that the e-mail is an advertisement.

- Provide a valid physical return address (not a post office box).

- Clearly indicate the nature of pornographic messages.

9. Under the Communications Decency Act of 1996, ISPs and Web hosts are not liable for information that is provided by someone else.

10. Hacking is illegal under the federal Computer Fraud and Abuse Act of 1986. The CFAA prohibits:

- Computer espionage;

- Theft of financial information;

- Theft of information from the U.S. government;

- Theft from a computer;

- Computer trespass;

- Computer fraud;

- Intentional, reckless, and negligent damage to a computer;

- Trafficking in computer passwords; and

- Computer extortion.

11. Fraud is the deception of another person for the purpose of obtaining money or property from him.

12. The Identity Theft and Assumption Deterrence Act of 1998 prohibits the use of false identification to commit fraud or other crime.

Practice Test

1. Three travel agents used fictitious accounts to steal 61 million frequent flyer miles from American Airlines. They traded this mileage in for 546 free tickets, with a value of $1.3 million. As evidence in the criminal trial, prosecutors used electronic communications from the agents on SABRE, American's computerized travel reservations system. The agents alleged that this search was illegal under the Fourth Amendment to the Constitution. Do you agree?

2. ***ETHICS*** Matt Drudge published a report on his Website (http://www.drudgereport.com) that White House aide Sidney Blumenthal "has a spousal abuse past that has been effectively covered up. . . .There are court records of Blumenthal's violence against his wife." The Drudge Report is an electronic publication focusing on Hollywood and Washington gossip. AOL paid Drudge $3,000 a month to make the Drudge Report available to AOL subscribers. Drudge e-mailed his reports to AOL, which then posted them. Before posting, however, AOL had the right to edit content. Drudge ultimately retracted his allegations against Blumenthal, who sued AOL. He alleged that under the Communications Decency Act of 1996, AOL was a "content provider" because it paid Drudge and edited what he wrote. Do you agree? Putting liability aside, what moral obligation did AOL have to its members? To Blumenthal? Should AOL be liable for content it bought and provided to its members?

3. To demonstrate the inadequacies of existing computer security systems, Cornell student Robert Morris created a computer virus. His plan, however, went awry, as plans sometimes do. He thought his virus would be relatively harmless, but it ran amok, crashing scores of computers at universities, military sites, and medical research sites. Under what statute might Morris be charged? Has he committed a crime, or is he liable only for civil penalties? Does it matter that he did not intend to cause damage?

4. ***YOU BE THE JUDGE*** WRITING PROBLEM Jerome Schneider wrote several books on how to avoid taxes. These books were sold on Amazon.com. Amazon permits visitors to post comments about items for sale. Amazon's policy suggests that these comments should be civil (e.g., no profanity or spiteful remarks). The comments about Schneider's books were not so kind. One person alleged Schneider was a felon. When Schneider complained, an Amazon representative agreed that some of the postings violated its guidelines and promised that they would be removed within one to two business days. Two days later, the posting had not been removed. Schneider filed suit. **Argument for Schneider:** Amazon has editorial discretion over the posted comments: It both establishes guidelines and then monitors the comments to ensure that they comply with the guidelines. These activities make Amazon an information content provider, not protected by the Communications Decency Act. **Argument for Amazon:** The right to edit material is not the same thing as creating the material in the first place.

5. During the course of 10 months, Joseph Melle sent more than 60 million unsolicited e-mail advertisements to AOL members. What charges could be brought against him?

6. Anthony Davis operated a computer bulletin board system that permitted users to send and receive e-mail, access the Internet, and download software. Davis's system had one attribute that distinguished it from, say, AOL. It specialized in pornography. Alerted by an anonymous tip, the Oklahoma City Police Department obtained a warrant to search his premises for "equipment, order materials, papers, membership lists and other paraphernalia pertaining to the distribution or display of pornographic material." During their raid, the officers seized computer equipment that contained 150,000 e-mails in electronic storage, some of which had not been retrieved by the recipients. Alleging that the e-mails had not been included in the warrant, Davis filed suit against the police officers for violations of the Electronic Communications Privacy Act. Does Davis have a valid claim?

7. Ton Cremers was the director of security at Amsterdam's famous Rijksmuseum and the operator of the Museum Security Network ("the Network") Website. Robert Smith, a handyman working for Ellen Batzel in North Carolina, sent

an e-mail to the Network alleging that Batzel was the granddaughter of Heinrich Himmler (one of Hitler's henchman) and that she had art that Himmler had stolen. These allegations were completely untrue. Cremers posted Smith's e-mail on the Network's Website and sent it to the Network's subscribers. Cremers exercised some editorial discretion in choosing which e-mails to send to subscribers, generally omitting any that were unrelated to stolen art. Is Cremers liable to Batzel for the harm that this inaccurate information caused?

8. What can you do to protect your privacy online? Draw up a concrete list of steps that you might reasonably consider. Are there some actions that you would not be willing to take, either because they are not worth the effort or because they are too sneaky?

9. Craig Hare offered computers and related equipment for sale on various Internet auction Websites. He accepted payment but not responsibility—he never shipped the goods. Both the FTC and the U.S. attorney general in Florida (i.e., the prosecutor for the federal government) brought charges against him. What charges did they bring? Why would these two separate agencies of the federal government both bring suit?

10. *ROLE REVERSAL* Write a short-answer question that deals with an issue involving crime in cyberspace.

Internet Research Problem

The FTC offers advice to Website operators about how to comply with the Children's Online Privacy Protection Act at academic.cengage.com/blaw/beatty. Find a Website that does comply and one that does not.

The FTC provides an online brochure titled Site Seeing on the Internet (at academic.cengage.com/blaw/beatty) that offers suggestions for safe travel on the Internet. Have you ever violated the FTC's advice on how to protect yourself in cyberspace?

You can find further practice problems at academic.cengage.com/blaw/beatty.

22 Intellectual Property

© PHOTODISC COLLECTION/GETTY IMAGES

Jason, *a senior at the University of Maryland, ran one of the most popular Websites on campus out of his shoebox dorm room here. The site let his 8,500 fellow dorm residents search for music files, among other things, stored on one another's computers and copy them in seconds.*

Then came the news that the record industry had filed lawsuits against four students running similar sites at other universities, accusing them of enabling large-scale copyright infringement and asking for billions of dollars in damages. Within an hour, Jason, who insisted on anonymity for fear of being sued himself, had dismantled his site. "I don't think I was doing anything wrong," said Jason, a computer science major. "But who wants to face a $98 billion debt for the rest of their lives? I was scared."

These lawsuits are the most aggressive legal action the record industry has ever directed against college students, who in recent years have exercised an enduring predisposition to consume large quantities of music by copying it over the Internet without ever paying for it. College campuses, the record industry says, have become far and away the prime locus for online piracy.

Wary of alienating young customers who continue to generate a large chunk of their revenue, record companies until recently focused on prodding university administrators to discipline their students. But freshman orientation sessions on respect for intellectual property have had little effect. With CD sales in a tailspin that record executives attribute at least partly to the downloading frenzy in academia's hallowed halls, they said they needed to try another approach.

"We have decided to bring to the attention of universities just how much music piracy is going on college campuses and universities," said Cary Sherman, president of the Recording Industry Association of America, which brought the suits, "and we think that message has been received."

"It's been very difficult because students have grown up viewing the Internet as a place where you go to get lots of free access to things," said Graham Spanier, president of Pennsylvania State University. "As we have tried to educate our students, half of them understand it's like going into a store and putting a CD in your pocket and the other half just can't see it that way."[1] ∎

INTRODUCTION

For much of history, land was the most valuable form of property. It was the primary source of wealth and social status. Today, intellectual property is a major source of wealth. New ideas—for manufacturing processes, computer programs, medicines, books—bring both affluence and influence.

ECONOMICS & the LAW

Land and intellectual property, though both valuable assets, are fundamentally different. The value of land lies in the owner's right to exclude, to prevent others from entering or using it. Intellectual property, however, has little economic value unless it is used by many.

The crux of the economic problem is this: Intellectual property is typically expensive to *produce* but cheap to *reproduce and transmit.* Movies or computer software, for example, cost millions to make but can be copied or reproduced for virtually nothing. (How much does it cost to download software?) But if too much intellectual property is transmitted too freely, then those who create ideas will not be paid the full value of their efforts. Those who simply transmit ideas will tend to be overpaid. The resulting imbalance creates too many transmitters and not enough producers. So the next time you are tempted to copy a friend's CD or download music free from the Internet, remember that lost royalty payments to musicians may ultimately mean less music for you.

Because producers of intellectual property are likely to be underpaid in the free market, the government provides three remedies: It *protects* the property rights of producers (with patents and copyrights), *produces* information itself (such as weather reports), and *subsidizes* production by others (via government research grants).

Some commentators suggest that the United States has been a technological leader partly because its laws have provided strong protection for intellectual property since early in the country's history. Indeed, the Constitution provides for patent protection. In contrast, one of the oldest civilizations in the world, China, has been much slower in developing new technology. It did not institute a patent system until 1985 and its protection of patents is weak. ◆

The conflict between those who have intellectual property and those who want to use it has taken on a global dimension. Developing countries argue that American intellectual property laws increase the price of medicines, such as AIDS drugs and vaccines, that could save lives if only they were cheaper and, therefore, more readily available. "Patents kill" is their slogan. The United States responds that, without patent protection, there would be no innovation, no miracle drugs. In India, for example, biotech entrepreneurs hesitate to sell their new products at home where intellectual property laws offer little protection. Their inventions go overseas.

But even U.S. drug companies admit that patents can sometimes stifle innovation. The pharmaceutical company Bristol-Meyers Squibb says that it cannot conduct

---

[1] Amy Harmon, "Recording Industry Goes After Students Over Music Sharing," *The New York Times*, Apr. 23, 2003, Sec. A, p. 1.

research on many cancer-fighting drugs because of patents held by its competitors. Information technology firms make a similar complaint. In a study of the American semiconductor business, researchers found that more patents did not necessarily mean there was more innovation. Instead, some companies were simply more aggressive about patenting every possible aspect of their research. Nor was there any evidence that innovation increased as patent rights were enhanced.

The role of intellectual property law is to balance the rights of those who create intellectual property and those who would enjoy it. And as this chapter reveals, such a balancing act is no easy feat.

What about the four students in the opening scenario? They agreed to pay between $12,000 and $17,000 to settle the suits. The record industry expanded its legal action beyond students and ultimately sued thousands of people across the country who had illegally downloaded music from the Internet.

PATENTS

A patent is a grant by the government permitting the inventor exclusive use of an invention for 20 years (or 14 years in the case of design patents). During this period, no one may make, use, or sell the invention without permission. In return, the inventor publicly discloses information about the invention that anyone can use upon expiration of the patent.

Types of Patents

There are three types of patents: utility patents, design patents, and plant patents.

Utility Patent

Whenever people use the word "patent" by itself, they are referring to a utility patent. This type of patent is available to those who invent (or significantly improve) any of the following:

Type of Invention	Example
Mechanical invention	A hydraulic jack used to lift heavy aircraft
Electrical invention	A prewired, portable wall panel for use in large, open-plan offices
Chemical invention	The chemical 2-chloroethylphosphonic acid used as a plant growth regulator
Process	A method for applying a chemical compound to an established plant such as rice in order to inhibit the growth of weeds selectively; the application can be patented separately from the actual chemical
Machine	A device that enables a helicopter pilot to control all flight functions (pitch, roll, and heave) with one hand
Composition of matter	A sludge used as an explosive at construction sites; the patent specifies the water content, the density, and the types of solids contained in the mixture

A patent is not available solely for an idea, but only for its tangible application. Thus patents are not available for laws of nature, scientific principles, mathematical algorithms, or formulas such as $a^2 + b^2 = c^2$. In recent years, the status of computer software has been controversial: Is it an (unpatentable) mathematical formula or a (patentable) process or machine? The following case answers this question.

STATE STREET BANK & TRUST CO. V. SIGNATURE FINANCIAL GROUP, INC.

149 F.3d 1368, 1998 U.S. App. LEXIS 16869
United States Court of Appeals for the Federal Circuit,[2] 1998

Facts: Signature Financial Group, Inc., owns a patent on a computer software program that aids in the administration of mutual funds. The so-called Hub and Spoke System allows several mutual funds, or "Spokes," to pool their investment funds into a single portfolio, or "Hub." In this way, the funds can share administrative costs. Each Spoke sells shares to the public, and the cost of these shares depends upon the value of the assets pooled in the Hub. Therefore, each day within hours of the close of the stock market, each fund's administrator must know the value to the nearest penny of its pooled shares. The Signature software makes this calculation.

State Street Bank and Trust Co. negotiated with Signature for a license to use its software. When negotiations broke down, State Street brought suit alleging that the patent was invalid. The trial court granted State Street's motion for summary judgment.

Issue: Is data processing software patentable?

Excerpts from Judge Rich's Decision: [The Supreme] Court has held that mathematical algo-rithms are not patentable subject matter to the extent that they are merely abstract ideas. From a practical standpoint, this means that to be patentable an algorithm must be applied in a "useful" way.

Today, we hold that the transformation of data, representing discrete dollar amounts, by a machine through a series of mathematical calculations into a final share price, constitutes a practical application of a mathematical algorithm, formula, or calcula-tion, because it produces "a useful, concrete and tan-gible result"—a final share price momentarily fixed for recording and reporting purposes.

The question of whether a claim encompasses statutory subject matter should focus on the essential characteristics of the subject matter, in particular, its practical utility. For purpose of our analysis, [this] claim is directed to a machine programmed with the Hub and Spoke software and admittedly produces a "useful, concrete, and tangible result." This renders it statutory subject matter, even if the useful result is expressed in numbers, such as price, profit, percent-age, cost, or loss.

Reversed and remanded. ■

Public Policy

The *State Street* case could have a profound impact on e-commerce as companies rush to patent techniques for doing business over the Internet. For example, Amazon.com received a patent for its One-Click method of instant ordering. The company then obtained an injunction to prevent barnesandnoble.com from using its Express Lane ser-vice, which was similar to One-Click. The judge directed barnesandnoble.com to add an additional step to its ordering process.

Proponents of these patents argue that they permit innovators on the Internet to pro-tect their ideas. Otherwise, it is easy for copycats to open a rival Website overnight. Critics counter that these patents could stifle e-commerce by limiting the use of new ideas.

---

2 Recall from Chapter 3 that the Court of Appeals for the Federal Circuit is the thirteenth United States Court of Appeals. It hears appeals from specialized trial courts.

Companies have been forced to increase their patent applications simply to remain competitive—they fear that if they do not patent an idea, their rivals will. Apple developed a scroll wheel for the iPod, but Microsoft patented the idea first. The result is a dramatic increase in the number of patent applications. The Patent and Trademark Office (PTO) now receives about 350,000 applications a year and has a backlog of half a million. The process for accepting a patent is much simpler than for rejecting it, which gives patent examiners an incentive to accept even dubious applications. As many as 30 percent of patents make duplicate claims—an indication that too many are being accepted. ◆

Design Patent

A design patent protects the appearance, not the function, of an item. It is granted to anyone who invents a new, original, and ornamental design for an article. For example, Braun, Inc., patented the look of its handheld electric blenders. Design patents last only 14 years, not 20.

Plant Patent

Anyone who creates a new type of plant can patent it, *provided that* the inventor is able to reproduce it asexually—through grafting, for instance, not by planting its seeds. For example, one company patented its unique heather plant.

Requirements for a Patent

To obtain a patent, the inventor must show that her invention meets all the following tests:

- **Novel.** An invention is not patentable if it (1) is known or has already been used in this country, or (2) has been described in a publication here or overseas. For example, an inventor discovered a new use for existing chemical compounds but was not permitted to patent it because the compounds had already been described in prior publications, though the new uses had not.[3]

- **Nonobvious.** An invention is not patentable if it is obvious to a person with ordinary skill in that particular area. An inventor was not allowed to patent a water-flush system designed to remove cow manure from the floor of a barn because it was obvious.[4]

- **Useful.** To be patented, an invention must be useful. It need not necessarily be commercially valuable, but it must have some current use. Being merely of scientific interest is not enough. Thus, a company was denied a patent for a novel process for making steroids because they had no therapeutic value.[5]

A searchable database of all patents issued since 1976 is available at the Patent and Trademark Office's Website: http://www.uspto.gov. To find out just how creative inventors can be, check out the Wacky Patent of the Month at http://www.colitz.com.

Patent Application and Issuance

To obtain a patent, the inventor must file a complex application with the PTO Office in Washington, D.C. If a patent examiner determines that the application meets all

---

[3] *In re Schoenwald*, 964 F.2d 1122, 1992 U.S. App. LEXIS 10181 (Fed. Cir. 1992).

[4] *Sakraida v. Ag Pro, Inc.*, 425 U.S. 273, 96 S. Ct. 1532, 1976 U.S. LEXIS 146 (1976).

[5] *Brenner v. Manson*, 383 U.S. 519, 86 S. Ct. 1033, 1966 U.S. LEXIS 2907 (1966).

legal requirements, the PTO will issue the patent. If the examiner denies the patent application, the inventor can appeal that decision to the PTO Board of Appeals and from there to the Court of Appeals for the Federal Circuit in Washington. Alternatively, upon denial of the application, the inventor can file suit against the PTO in the federal district court in Washington.

Priority between Two Inventors

When two people invent the same product, who is entitled to a patent—the first to invent or the first to file an application? Generally, the person who invents and *puts the invention into practice* has priority over the first filer. Having the idea is not enough— the inventor must actually use the product.

Prior Sale

However, an inventor must apply for a patent within one year of selling the product commercially. The purpose of this rule is to encourage prompt disclosure of inventions. It prevents someone from inventing a product, selling it for years, and then obtaining a 20-year monopoly with a patent.

Provisional Patent Application

Investors who are unable to assess the market value of their ideas sometimes hesitate to file a patent application because the process is expensive and cumbersome. To solve this problem, the PTO now permits inventors to file a **provisional patent application (PPA).** The PPA is a simpler, shorter, cheaper application that gives inventors the opportunity to show their ideas to potential investors without incurring the full expense of a patent application. PPA protection lasts only one year. To maintain protection after that time, the inventor must file a regular patent application.

Duration of a Patent

Patents are valid for 20 years from the date of *filing* the application (except design patents, which are valid for 14 years from date of *issuance*). Currently, approval of a patent takes about 27 months from the date of filing, which means that patent holders effectively receive a little less than 18 years of protection (although in the case of exceptional delays, it is possible to request an extension).

Eighteen months after patents are filed, the PTO publishes them. This means that patent applications are often published before they have been approved. Although there is some concern that patent ideas are therefore easier to steal, publication also gives anyone with knowledge in the field an opportunity to provide the PTO with additional information about why the patent should or (more likely) should not be granted.

ECONOMICS & *the* LAW

How long should patents last? Holders enjoy a monopoly that protects them from competition and permits them to charge higher prices. But these monopoly profits are not all bad—they also provide inventors with the incentive to spend large sums hoping to develop new products. In theory, the duration of a patent should be individually tailored to each product. The goal is to ensure that a patent creates the right incentive for each product. Take, for example, a complex life-saving drug that costs $400 million to develop. No drug company would undertake such a project without assurance that it could recoup its costs. But if the company can make $300 million in the first year of sale, it needs only a short patent life to recoup its costs. On the other hand, if the company could only make $25 million a year, it should have at least a 16-year patent. Likewise, if a product has little value to society, its patent should be of short duration.

Of course, the PTO would be in chaos if examiners had to decide how much protection each individual patent deserved, but Germany has gone some distance along this path. It awards a standard patent for important inventions. Less important products receive a so-called *petty patent* that lasts only three years. Moreover, all patent owners pay an annual maintenance fee. At the beginning, this fee is low, but it increases so much each year that only 5 percent of German patents are maintained for a full term. Most owners abandon ship in less than eight years.[6]

Infringement

A patent holder has the exclusive right to use the invention during the term of the patent. A holder can prohibit others from using any product that is substantially the same, license the product to others for a fee, and recover damages from anyone who uses the product without permission.

International Patent Treaties

Suppose you have a great idea that you want to protect around the world. It used to be that filing an application in other countries was a logistical nightmare because almost every country had its own unique filing procedures and standards. Several treaties now facilitate this process, although it is still not the one-stop (or one-click) effort that inventors desire. These treaties were drafted by the World Intellectual Property Organization (WIPO) of the United Nations and are available on its Website at http://www.wipo.int.

The Paris Convention for the Protection of Industrial Property (Paris Convention) requires each member country to grant to citizens of other member countries the same rights under patent law as its own citizens enjoy. Thus, the patent office in each member country must accept and recognize all patent and trademark applications filed with it by anyone who lives in any member country. For example, the French patent office cannot refuse to accept an application from an American, as long as the American has complied with French law.

The Patent Law Treaty requires that countries use the same standards for the form and content of patent applications (whether submitted on paper or electronically). This treaty reduces the procedural conflicts over issues such as translations and fees. In short, it takes an important first step in standardizing the application *process*. Still to be worked out, however, is an international standard for the *substance* of patent laws. For instance, the U.S. "first to invent" rule conflicts with the "first to file" rule used in most other countries. Also countries often have very different definitions of what constitutes "novelty" under patent law.

In addition to these treaties, any country that joins the World Trade Organization must agree to TRIPS (trade-related aspects of intellectual property rights). This agreement does not create an international patent system, but it does require all participants to meet minimum standards for the protection of intellectual property. How individual countries achieve that goal is left to them.

---

[6] R. Cooter and T. Ulen, *Law and Economics*, 2nd ed. (Reading, Mass.: Addison-Wesley, 1997).

Copyrights

The holder of a copyright owns the *particular tangible expression* of an idea but not the underlying idea or method of operation. Abner Doubleday could copyright a book setting out his particular version of the rules of baseball, but he could not copyright the rules themselves nor could he require players to pay him a royalty. Similarly, the inventor of double-entry bookkeeping could copyright a pamphlet explaining his system but not the system itself.

Unlike patents, the ideas underlying copyrighted material need not be novel. Two movies that came out at the same time—*The Incredibles* and *Sky High*—were each about a family of superheroes. Neither violated the other's copyright because their *expressions* of the basic idea were different—indeed, one was a cartoon and the other a live action film.

The Copyright Act protects literature, music, drama, choreography, pictures, sculpture, movies, recordings, architectural works, and "computer data bases, and computer programs to the extent that they incorporate authorship in the programmer's expression of original ideas, as distinguished from the ideas themselves."

A copyright is valid until 70 years after the death of the work's only or last living author. In the case of works owned by a corporation—Mickey Mouse, for instance—the copyright lasts 95 years from publication or 120 years from creation. Once the copyright expires, anyone may use the material. Mark Twain died in 1910, so anyone may now publish *Tom Sawyer* without permission and without paying a copyright fee.

A work is automatically copyrighted once it is in tangible form. For example, once a songwriter puts notes on paper, the work is copyrighted without further ado. But if she whistles a happy tune without writing it down, the song is not copyrighted and anyone else can use it without permission. Registration with the Copyright Office of the Library of Congress is necessary only if the holder wishes to bring suit to enforce the copyright. Although authors still routinely place the copyright symbol (©) on their works, such a precaution is not necessary in the United States. However, some lawyers still recommend using the copyright symbol because other countries recognize it. Also, the penalties for intentional copyright infringement are heavier than for unintentional violations, and the presence of a copyright notice is evidence that the infringer's actions were intentional.

Infringement

Anyone who uses copyrighted material without permission is violating the Copyright Act. **To prove a violation, the plaintiff must present evidence that the work was original** and that either:

- The infringer actually copied the work, or
- The infringer had access to the original and the two works are substantially similar.

A court may (1) prohibit the infringer from committing further violations, (2) order destruction of the infringing material, and (3) require the infringer to pay damages, profits earned, and attorney's fees.

Fair Use

The purpose of copyright laws is to encourage creative work. A writer who can control, and profit from, artistic work will be inclined to produce more. If enforced oppressively, however, the copyright laws could stifle creativity by denying access to copyrighted work. **The doctrine of *fair use* permits limited use of copyrighted**

material without permission of the author for purposes such as criticism, comment, news reporting, scholarship, or research. Courts generally do not permit a use that will decrease revenues from the original work by, say, competing with it. A reviewer is permitted, for example, to quote from a book without the author's permission, but as we see later, online music companies cannot download entire versions of copyrighted songs.

Also under the fair use doctrine, faculty members are permitted to photocopy and distribute copyrighted materials to students, as long as the materials are brief and the teacher's action is spontaneous. If, over his breakfast coffee one morning, Professor Learned spots a terrific article in *Mad* Magazine that perfectly illustrates a point he intends to make in class that day, the fair use doctrine permits him to photocopy the page and distribute it to his class. However, under a misinterpretation of the fair use doctrine, some faculty had been in the habit of routinely preparing lengthy course packets of copyrighted material without permission of the authors. In *Basic Books, Inc. v. Kinko's Graphic Corp.,*[7] a federal court held that this practice violated the copyright laws because the material was more than one short passage and because it was sold to students. Now, when professors put together course packets, they (or the copy shop) must obtain permission and pay a royalty for the use of copyrighted material. Likewise, it is illegal for students to make photocopies of a classmate's course packet or textbook.

Parody

Parody has a long history in the United States—some of our most cherished songs have been the basis of parodies. Before Francis Scott Key wrote the words to "The Star-Spangled Banner," other lyrics that mocked colonial governors had been set to the same music. (The tune was well known as a drinking song.) During the Civil War, this parody of "*Battle Hymn of the Republic*" expressed anti-war sentiment:

> Tell Abe Lincoln of Antietam's bloody dell
> Tell Abe Lincoln where a thousand heroes fell
> Tell Abe Lincoln and his gang to go to hell
> And we'll go marching home.

The Capitol Steps, a singing group in Washington, wrote this version of Lee Greenwood's song "God Bless the USA," renamed "God Bless My SUV":

> But my Daddy wasn't fighting on Normandy that day
> For the right to drive a Hyundai, I refuse to live that way.
> And I'm proud to be an American, who gets just 5 mpg
> Though I live alone the car I own can seat one hundred three.

(For more parodies by the Capitol Steps, dance over to their Website at http://www.capsteps.com.) Have the Capitol Steps violated Greenwood's copyright? After all, they did use his music. What if the words or opinions expressed in a parody are ones with which the original creators (or whoever now owns the rights) do not agree? The Capitol Steps appear to be on safe ground. The United States has a long history of protecting the expression of unpopular ideas.

---

[7] 758 F. Supp. 1522, 1991 U.S. Dist. LEXIS 3804 (S.D.N.Y. 1991). A federal appeals court reached the same result in *Princeton University Press v. Michigan Document Services, Inc.,* 99 F.3d 1381, 1996 U.S. App. LEXIS 29132 (6th Cir. 1996).

The Supreme Court faced this issue in a case involving the rap group 2 Live Crew. The group wanted to record a parody of the song "Oh, Pretty Woman," but the copyright holder refused permission. Undaunted, 2 Live Crew went ahead anyway, and the group was sued, all the way to the Supreme Court. The following lyrics are excerpted from the Court's decision in this case:

Original:	Parody:
Pretty Woman, walking down the street,	Big hairy woman you need to shave that stuff
Pretty Woman, the kind I like to meet,	Big hairy woman you know I bet it's tough
Pretty Woman, I don't believe you, you're not the truth,	Big hairy woman all that hair it ain't legit
No one could look as good as you Mercy	'Cause you look like "Cousin It" Big hairy woman

The Court decided in favor of 2 Live Crew, holding that **parody is a fair use of copyrighted material as long as the use of the original is not excessive.** The parody may copy enough to remind the audience of the original work but not so much that the parody harms the market for the original. The Supreme Court remanded the case to the trial court to determine if the 2 Live Crew version had copied too much or harmed the market for a nonparody rap version of "Oh, Pretty Woman."[8] The two sides ultimately settled with 2 Live Crew agreeing to pay royalties.

Linking

A link is a connection between two files on the Web or between two parts of the same file. The ability to link is fundamental to the World Wide Web, but used improperly, linking violates copyright law.

Leslie Kelly was a photographer specializing in images of the American West. He posted some of his pictures on his Website. Arriba Soft Corp. operated an Internet search engine (at **http://www.ditto.com**) that searches for graphic images. It displays its results in the form of small pictures called *thumbnails.* By double-clicking on one of these thumbnails, a large version of that same picture is automatically copied from the originating Web page onto Arriba's site, complete with Arriba advertising. The user might think that the image was, in fact, on Arriba's Web site. Kelly alleged that Arriba was violating his copyright. Arriba claimed that its activities were protected by the fair use doctrine. The court ruled that, although the thumbnails were a fair use, the display of the larger image was a copyright violation. The thumbnails did not compete with Kelly's use of the works, but the full-size display did.[9]

The impact of this case is uncertain. Critics argue that it threatens the use of linking, not just for pictures but for text as well. If search engines are required to obtain the permission of every copyright holder before setting up a link, they will soon be out of business. Other commentators argue, however, that neither Arriba nor anyone else needs permission to create a link to Kelly's site; they are simply forbidden from competing with Kelly by offering his images in the same size and quality.

---

[8] *Campbell v. Acuff-Rose Music, Inc.,* 510 U.S. 569, 114 S. Ct. 1164, 1994 U.S. LEXIS 2052 (1994).

[9] *Kelly v. Arriba Soft Corporation,* 280 F.3d 934, 2002 U.S. App. LEXIS 1786, United States Court of Appeals (9th Cir. 2002).

Digital Music and Movies

Copyright protection is as old as the country itself, having been included in the Constitution. But intellectual property has changed dramatically in the last 250 years, and legal protections suitable for the eighteenth century do not work as well today. Now Congress and the courts are playing catch-up, trying to mend and patch the laws to cover the digital world.

One of the major challenges for legal institutions in regulating copyrights is simply that modern intellectual property is so easy to copy. Many consumers have been in the habit of violating the law by downloading copyrighted material—both music and movies—for free. The entertainment world used to turn a blind eye, but recording companies and movie studios have come to believe that illegal downloading is hurting profitability. For the first time, CD sales actually declined nationally. One study found that the decline was particularly sharp in areas around college campuses. Perhaps even more insidious, a whole generation has grown up believing that music and even movies were, and should be, free. Whereas an older sibling might have purchased a thousand CDs during her teens and twenties, her younger brother would buy none at all. Although at least one study seemed to indicate that downloading does not harm CD sales, the entertainment industry remained convinced that it does.[10] As the chapter opener illustrates, the Recording Industry Association of America (RIAA) has begun aggressively suing those who downloaded illegally. Then a coalition of entertainment businesses sued two companies that distributed the software used by many consumers to violate copyright law. So important was this issue that the Supreme Court waded into these murky waters.

METRO-GOLDWYN-MAYER STUDIOS INC. V. GROKSTER, LTD.

125 S. Ct. 2764, 2005 U.S. LEXIS 5212
Supreme Court of the United States, 2005

Facts: Grokster, Ltd., and StreamCast Networks, Inc., distributed free software that allowed computer users to share electronic files through peer-to-peer networks, so called because users' computers communicated directly with each other, not through central servers. The Grokster and StreamCast software could be used for legal purposes. Indeed, peer-to-peer networks were used by universities, government agencies, corporations, libraries, and individuals, among others. Even the briefs in this very case could be downloaded legally with the StreamCast software.

Nonetheless, nearly 90 percent of the files available for download through Grokster or StreamCast were copyrighted. Billions of files were shared each month—the probable scope of copyright infringement was staggering. The two companies encouraged the illegal uses of their software. For example, the chief technology officer of StreamCast said that "the goal is to get in trouble with the law and get sued. It's the best way to get in the news."

A group of copyright holders (MGM and others) sued Grokster and StreamCast alleging that they were violating the copyright law by knowingly and intentionally distributing their software to users who would reproduce and distribute copyrighted works illegally. Both parties moved for summary judgment. The trial court held for Grokster and

▼

---

10 Felix Oberholzer-Gee and Koleman Strumpf, "The Effect of File Sharing on Record Sales," 2004, available at http://www.unc.edu/~cigar/papers/FileSharing_March2004.pdf.

StreamCast; the appeals court affirmed. The Supreme Court granted *certiorari*.

Issue: Were Grokster and StreamCast violating copyright law?

Excerpts from Justice Souter's Decision: The more artistic protection is favored, the more technological innovation may be discouraged; the administration of copyright law is an exercise in managing the trade-off. [T]he indications are that the ease of copying songs or movies using software like Grokster's is fostering disdain for copyright protection. When a widely shared service or product is used to commit infringement, it may be impossible to enforce rights in the protected work effectively against all direct infringers, the only practical alternative being to go against the distributor of the copying device. We hold that one who distributes a device with the object of promoting its use to infringe copyright, as shown by clear expression or other affirmative steps taken to foster infringement, is liable for the resulting acts of infringement by third parties.

We are, of course, mindful of the need to keep from trenching on regular commerce or discouraging the development of technologies with lawful and unlawful potential. Accordingly, mere knowledge of infringing potential or of actual infringing uses would not be enough here to subject a distributor to liability. The inducement rule, instead, premises liability on purposeful, culpable expression and conduct, and thus does nothing to compromise legitimate commerce or discourage innovation having a lawful promise.

Grokster distributed an electronic newsletter containing links to articles promoting its software's ability to access popular copyrighted music. And both companies communicated a clear message by responding affirmatively to requests for help in locating and playing copyrighted materials. [N]either company attempted to develop filtering tools or other mechanisms to diminish the infringing activity using their software. It is useful to recall that StreamCast and Grokster make money by selling advertising space, by directing ads to the screens of computers employing their software. As the record shows, the more the software is used, the more ads are sent out and the greater the advertising revenue becomes. Since the extent of the software's use determines the gain to the distributors, the commercial sense of their enterprise turns on high-volume use, which the record shows is infringing. The unlawful objective is unmistakable.

In addition to intent to bring about infringement and distribution of a device suitable for infringing use, [MGM must show] evidence of actual infringement by recipients of the software. As the account of the facts indicates, there is evidence of infringement on a gigantic scale.

On remand, reconsideration of MGM's motion for summary judgment will be in order. ∎

Public Policy

The media industry argued that free downloads were killing profitability. Technology businesses countered that restrictions on downloading would hamper technology and that the media business model was simply out of date. Upstart (and illegal) companies like Grokster and its predecessor, Napster, created a whole industry around downloading music. It took years for legitimate businesses such as iTunes to follow this lead legally. But now iTunes is an enormous success. Without Napster, would iTunes even exist?

And perhaps the entertainment industry is unfairly aggressive over the copyright laws. The theory of copyright was that publishers and creative talent needed a brief period of monopoly to ensure that they could earn a fair return. Originally, copyright protection lasted only 28 years; now it can be as long as 95 years. The period of protection has tripled even as publication and distribution have become much cheaper and faster. In theory, publishers should need a shorter, not longer, monopoly. ◆

The No Electronic Theft Act

Enacted in 1997, the **No Electronic Theft Act** is intended to deter the downloading of copyrighted material. It provides for criminal penalties for the reproduction or distribution of copyrighted material that has a retail value greater than $1,000, even if the offender has no profit motive. Thus, for instance, if a student photocopied for ten of her friends a textbook that is worth $150, she could be subject to criminal penalties, including a prison term of one year. Originally, the Justice Department did not enforce this statute, but it has now begun to do so, particularly against those who set up networks to trade games, movies, and music.

The Family Entertainment and Copyright Act

Under the **Family Entertainment and Copyright Act** it is a criminal offense to use a camcorder to film a movie in the theater. This statute also establishes criminal penalties for willful copyright infringement that involves distributing software, music, or film on a computer network.

The Digital Millennium Copyright Act

The good news is that Mary Schmich wrote an influential article in the *Chicago Tribune.* The bad news is that people deleted her name, attributed the article to Kurt Vonnegut, and sent it around the world via e-mail. Tom Tomorrow's cartoon was syndicated to 100 newspapers, but, by the time the last papers received it, the cartoon had already gone zapping around cyberspace. Because his name had been deleted, some editors thought he had plagiarized it.

In response to such incidents, Congress passed the **Digital Millennium Copyright Act** (DMCA), which provides that:

- **It is illegal to delete copyright information, such as the name of the author or the title of the article.** It is also illegal to distribute false copyright information. Thus, anyone who e-mailed Schmich's article without her name on it, or who claimed it was his own work, would be violating the law.

- **It is illegal to circumvent encryption or scrambling devices that protect copyrighted works.** For example, some software programs are designed so that they can only be copied once. Anyone who overrides this protective device to make another copy is violating the law. (The statute does permit purchasers of copyrighted software to make one backup copy.) If you buy a Disney DVD that prevents you from fast-forwarding through commercials, you are violating the DMCA if you figure out how to do it anyway.

- **It is illegal to distribute tools and technologies used to circumvent encryption devices.** If you tell others how to fast-forward through the Disney commercials, you have violated the statute.

The DMCA has been controversial. Its goal was laudable: to protect legitimate businesses from copyright pirates. However, opponents allege that:

- The DMCA interferes with legal activities. For instance, copy-protected CDs prevent consumers from making copies for their own use. These copies are legal under the fair use doctrine.

- The DMCA interferes with legitimate scientific research. An organization called the Secure Digital Music Initiative (SDMI) developed a technology to encrypt digital music. It issued a public challenge to see if anyone could override the encryption. Edward Felten, a Princeton professor, did manage to circumvent the technology, but when he tried to present his results at an academic conference, the SDMI threatened him with suit for violating the DMCA. He ultimately was able to publish part of his research, but only after filing suit against SDMI.

International Copyright Treaties

The Berne Convention requires member countries to provide automatic copyright protection to any works created in another member country. The protection does not expire until 50 years after the death of the author.[11] The WIPO Copyright Treaty and the WIPO Performances and Phonograms Treaty add computer programs, movies, and music to the list of copyrightable materials.

In 2004, Congress enacted a law that permits the president to appoint a copyright law enforcement officer charged with the responsibility of stopping copyright infringement overseas. Also, for the first time, Congress funded the National Intellectual Property Law Enforcement Coordination Council, which was established to protect American intellectual property internationally.

TRADEMARKS

A trademark is any combination of words and symbols that a business uses to identify its products or services and distinguish them from others. Trademarks are important to both consumers and businesses. Consumers use trademarks to distinguish between competing products. People who feel that Nike shoes fit their feet best can rely on the Nike trademark to know they are buying the shoe they want. A business with a high-quality product can use a trademark to develop a loyal base of customers who are able to distinguish its product from another.

Types of Marks

There are four different types of marks:

- **Trademarks** are affixed to *goods* in interstate commerce.
- **Service marks** are used to identify services, not products. Fitness First, Burger King, and Weight Watchers are service marks. In this chapter, the terms "trademark" and "mark" are used to refer to both trademarks and service marks.
- **Certification marks** are words or symbols used by a person or organization to attest that products and services produced by others meet certain standards. The Good Housekeeping Seal of Approval means that the Good Housekeeping organization has determined that a product meets its standards.
- **Collective marks** are used to identify members of an organization. The Lions Club, the Girls Scouts of America, and the Masons are examples of collective marks.

Ownership and Registration

Under common law, the first person to use a mark in trade owns it. Registration with the federal government is not necessary. However, under the federal Lanham Act, the owner of a mark may register it on the Lanham Act Principal Register. A trademark

---

11 Under U.S. law, copyrights last 70 years. The United States must grant works created in other signatory countries a copyright that lasts either 50 years or the length of time granted in that country, whichever is longer, but in no case longer than 70 years.

owner may use the symbol ™ at any time, even before registering it, but not until the mark is registered can the symbol ® be placed next to it. Registration has several advantages:

- Even if a mark has been used in only one or two states, registration makes it valid nationally.
- Registration notifies the public that a mark is in use because anyone who applies for registration first searches the Public Register to ensure that no one else has rights to the mark.
- Five years after registration, a mark becomes virtually incontestable because most challenges are barred.
- The damages available under the Lanham Act are higher than under common law.
- The holder of a registered trademark generally has the right to use it as an Internet domain name.

Under the Lanham Act, the owner files an application with the PTO. The PTO will accept an application only if the owner has already used the mark attached to a product in interstate commerce or promises to use the mark within six months after the filing. In addition, the applicant must be the *first* to use the mark in interstate commerce. Initially, the trademark is valid for 10 years, but the owner can renew it for an unlimited number of 10-year terms as long as the mark is still in use. Trademark searches are free on PTO's Website: http://www.uspto.gov.

Valid Trademarks

Words (Reebok), symbols (Microsoft's flying window logo), phrases ("Just do it"), shapes (a Coca-Cola bottle), sounds (NBC's three chimes), colors (Owens Corning's pink insulation), and even scents (plumeria blossoms on sewing thread) can be trademarked. **To be valid, a trademark must be distinctive**—that is, the mark must clearly distinguish one product from another. There are five basic categories of distinctive marks:

- **Fanciful marks** are made-up words such as Converse or Saucony.
- **Arbitrary marks** use existing words that do *not* describe the product—Prince tennis racquets, for example. No one really thinks that these racquets are designed by or for royalty.
- **Suggestive marks** *indirectly* describe the product's function. Greyhound implies that the bus line is swift, and Coppertone suggests what customers will look like after applying the product.
- Marks with **secondary meaning** cannot, by themselves, be trademarked, unless they have been used so long that they are now associated with the product in the public's mind. When a film company released a movie called *Ape*, it used as an illustration a picture that looked like a scene from *King Kong*—a gigantic gorilla astride the World Trade Center in New York City. The court held that the movie posters of *King Kong* had acquired a secondary meaning in the mind of the public, so the *Ape* producers were forced to change their poster.[12]
- **Trade dress** is the image and overall appearance of a business or product. It may include size, shape, color, or texture. The Supreme Court held that a Mexican

---

12 *Paramount Pictures Corp. v. Worldwide Entertainment Corp.*, 2 Media L. Rep. 1311, 195 U.S.P.Q. (BNA) 539, 1977 U.S. Dist. LEXIS 17931 (S.D.N.Y. 1977).

restaurant was entitled to protection under the Lanham Act for the shape and general appearance of the exterior of its building as well as the decor, menu, servers' uniforms, and other features reflecting the total image of the restaurant.[13]

The following categories are not distinctive and *cannot* be trademarked:

- **Similar to an Existing Mark.** To avoid confusion, the PTO will not grant a trademark that is similar to one already in existence on a similar product. Once the PTO had granted a trademark for "Pledge" furniture polish, it refused to trademark "Promise" for the same product. "Chat noir" and "black cat" were also too similar because one is simply a translation of the other. Houghton-Mifflin Co. sued to prevent a punk rock band from calling itself Furious George because the name is too similar to Curious George, the star of a series of children's books.

- **Generic Trademarks.** No one is permitted to trademark an item's ordinary name—"shoe" or "book," for example. Sometimes, however, a word begins as a trademark and later becomes a generic name. Zipper, escalator, aspirin, linoleum, yo-yo, and nylon all started out as trademarks but became generic. Once a name is generic, the owner loses the trademark because the name can no longer be used to distinguish one product from another—all products are called the same thing. That is why, in advertisements for Sanka, people ask for "a cup of Sanka-brand decaffeinated coffee." And why Xerox Corp. encourages people to say, "I'll photo-copy this document," rather than "I'll xerox it." Jeep, Rollerblade, and TiVo are trademarks that seem destined for generic status.

- **Descriptive Marks.** Words cannot be trademarked if they simply describe the product—such as "low-fat," "green," or "crunchy." Descriptive words can, how-ever, be trademarked if they do *not* describe that particular product because they then become distinctive rather than descriptive. "Blue Diamond" is an acceptable trademark for nuts as long as the nuts are neither blue nor diamond shaped.

- **Names.** The PTO generally will not grant a trademark in a surname because other people are already using it and have the right to continue. No one could register "Jefferson" as a trademark. However, a surname can be used as part of a longer title—"Jefferson Home Tours," for instance. Similarly, no one can register a geographical name such as "Boston" unless it is also associated with another word, such as "Boston Ale."

- **Deceptive Marks.** The PTO will not register a mark that is deceptive. It refused to register a trademark with the words "National Collection and Credit Control" and an eagle superimposed on a map of the United States because this trademark gave the false impression that the organization was an official gov-ernment agency.

- **Scandalous or Immoral Trademarks.** The PTO refused to register a mark that featured a nude man and woman embracing. In upholding the PTO's decision, the court was unsympathetic to arguments that this was the perfect trademark for a newsletter on sex.[14]

Infringement

To win an infringement suit, the trademark owner must show that the defendant's trade-mark is likely to deceive customers about who has made the goods or provided the ser-vices. The rightful owner is entitled to (1) an injunction prohibiting further violations,

---

13 *Two Pesos, Inc. v. Taco Cabana, Inc.*, 505 U.S. 763, 112 S. Ct. 2753, 1992 U.S. LEXIS 4533 (1992).
14 *In re McGinley*, 660 F.2d 481, 211 U.S.P.Q. (BNA) 668, 1981 CCPA LEXIS 177 (C.C.P.A. 1981).

(2) destruction of the infringing material, (3) up to three times actual damages, (4) any profits the infringer earned on the product, and (5) attorney's fees.

What about a perfume for dogs? Would a reasonable consumer confuse Pucci with Gucci, Bono Sports with Ralph Lauren Polo Sports, or Miss Claybone for Liz Claiborne? None of these companies challenged the parody use of their names for a dog perfume. But Tommy Hilfiger Licensing, Inc. did not see the humor in the name Timmy Holedigger. The court, however, advised Hilfiger "to chill," pointing out that there was no evidence of actual confusion.[15]

cyberLaw	Many Websites give away free information and (try to) make money selling advertisements. To be successful, the sites must attract hordes of visitors. What can they do to lure cybersurfers? Some site operators embed words like "sex" and "nudity" in invisible coding, even if the sites have nothing to do with sex. Although visitors cannot see the words, search engines will still call up the site. Not content with these generic lures, Calvin Designer Label (no relation to Calvin Klein, the clothing designer) embedded the words "Playboy" and "Playmate" in machine-readable code on its Website. A federal court entered a restraining order preventing Calvin Designer from infringing on Playboy's trademarks.[16] ◆

Federal Trademark Dilution Act of 1995

Before Congress passed the Federal Trademark Dilution Act of 1995 (FTDA), a trademark owner could win an infringement lawsuit only by proving that consumers would be deceived about who had really made the product. **The new statute prevents others from using a trademark in a way that dilutes its value,** even though consumers are not confused about the origin of the product. For example, this statute would prohibit the use of Dupont shoes, Buick aspirin, or Kodak pianos.

In the following case, Victoria's Secret thought of itself as an upscale women's lingerie chain and Victor's Little Secret was, well, vulgar with its offerings of handcuffs and adult videos. Did Victor's Little Secret dilute the value of the Victoria's Secret trademark?

YOU BE THE JUDGE

VICTOR MOSELEY V. V SECRET CATALOGUE, INC.

537 U.S. 418, 123 S. Ct. 1115
United States Supreme Court, 2002

Facts: Victoria's Secret was a chain that sold women's lingerie, nightwear, caftans, kimonos, slippers, sachets,

lingerie bags, candles, soaps, cosmetic brushes, bath products, and fragrances. The company operated more than 750 stores and distributed 400 million copies of its catalog each year. Sales exceeded $1.5 billion annually. The name "Victoria's Secret" was trademarked.

▼

---

15 *Tommy Hilfiger Licensing, Inc. v. Nature Labs, LLC,* 221 F. Supp. 2d 410; 2002 U.S. Dist. LEXIS 14841 (2002).
16 *Playboy Enterprises, Inc. v. Calvin Designer Label,* 985 F. Supp. 1220, 1997 U.S. Dist. LEXIS 14345 (N.D. Cal. 1997).

Victor Moseley owned a store near the military base in Fort Knox, Kentucky, called "Victor's Little Secret." He sold clocks, patches, temporary tattoos, stuffed animals, coffee mugs, leather biker wallets, Zippo lighters, diet formula, jigsaw puzzles, handcuffs, hosiery, bubble machines, greeting cards, calendars, incense burners, car air fresheners, sunglasses, jewelry, candles, lava lamps, black lights, rock-and-roll prints, lingerie, pagers, candy, adult videotapes, and adult novelties. Women's lingerie represented only about 5 percent of his sales. Moseley placed an advertisement for his store in the military base's weekly newspaper.

An army colonel on the base was offended by what he considered to be an attempt to use a reputable company's trademark to promote the sale of unwholesome, tawdry merchandise. The colonel sent a copy of the ad to Victoria's Secret. The company filed suit under the FTDA alleging that Moseley's use of such a similar name was likely to blur the distinctiveness and tarnish the reputation of the Victoria's Secret trademark.

You Be the Judge: **Does the name Victor's Little Secret dilute the trademark of Victoria's Secret?**

Argument for Victoria's Secret: This case is a classic instance of dilution by tarnishing (associating the Victoria's Secret name with sex toys and lewd coffee mugs) and by blurring (linking the chain with a single, unauthorized store). While no consumer is likely to go to Moseley's store expecting to find Victoria's Secret's famed Miracle Bra, consumers who hear the name 'Victor's Little Secret' will automatically think of the more famous store and link it to Moseley's tawdrier shop. There is great potential for damage.

To prove that Victor's Little Secret had actually tarnished the name of Victoria's Secret would be difficult and expensive. This expense is unnecessary because it is obvious that a sleazy store using a very similar name will by its mere existence devalue the more upscale store.

Argument for Victor's Little Secret: The FTDA prohibits the use of a name that causes dilution of the famous mark. In other words, the law requires that there actually *be* dilution, not just that there be the *chance* of dilution. That does not mean that Victoria's Secret must prove an actual loss of sales or profits, but it must prove more than the mere fact that consumers mentally associate Victor's Little Secret with the more famous mark. The army officer who saw the advertisement in the base newspaper did associate Moseley's store with Victoria's Secret, but the ad did not change his perception of Victoria's Secret. It simply made him angry at Moseley.

It may be expensive to prove that dilution has taken place but that is not a reason to dispense with some reasonable standard of proof. It may also be expensive to show that someone has committed a murder, but we do not convict without it. ●

Domain Names

Roughly 50 million Internet addresses, known as domain names, have been registered, so it is often difficult to find a distinctive name for a new business. Domain names can be immensely valuable as they are an important component of doing business. Suppose you want to buy a new pair of jeans. Without thinking twice, you type in http://www.jcrew.com and there you are, ready to order. What if that address took you to a different site altogether, say, the personal site of one Jackie Crew? The store might lose out on a sale. Companies not only want to own their own domain name, they want to prevent complaint sites such as http://www.untied.com (about United Airlines), http://www.ihatestarbucks.com, or the always popular variation on the "sucks" theme, such as http://www.aolsucks.org. Generic domain names can be valuable, too. Shopping.com paid $750,000 to acquire its domain name from the previous (lucky) owner.

Who has the right to a domain name? In the beginning, the National Science Foundation, which maintained the Internet, granted Network Solutions, Inc. (NSI), a private company, the right to allocate domain names. NSI charged no fee for domain names and the rule was "first come, first served." Then so-called cybersquatters began to register domain names, not to use, but to sell to others. Someone, for example, tried to sell the name "Bill Gates" for $1 million.

In response to complaints, NSI began suspending any domain name that was challenged by the holder of a registered trademark. For instance, NSI would not allow Princeton Review to keep kaplan.com, which Princeton had acquired simply to inconvenience its arch-rival in the test preparation business. Congress then passed the **Anticybersquatting Consumer Protection Act, which permits both trademark owners and famous people to sue anyone who registers their name as a domain name in "bad faith."** The rightful owner of a trademark is entitled to damages of up to $100,000.

Although the goal of this statute was laudable, in practice it sometimes looked like a heavy club in the hands of corporations who used it to threaten innocent holders of domain names. The maker of Pokey toys threatened a boy who had registered his nickname, Pokey, and Archie Comics went after a girl named Veronica. The Chilling Effects Clearinghouse at http://www.chillingeffects.org provides a database of so-called cease and desist letters sent to holders of domain names.

As both the value and the number of domain names soared, the U.S. government transferred management of the Internet, including the allocation of names, to a private, nonprofit, international organization, the Internet Corporation for Assigned Names and Numbers (ICANN). Disputes over domain names can be decided by arbitration under ICANN's Uniform Domain Name Dispute Resolution Policy (UDRP) rather than by litigation under the Anticybersquatting Consumer Protection Act.

If a domain name is confusingly similar to a trademark, the owner has the right to bring a UDRP proceeding. To bring a case under the ICANN policy, the complainant (i.e., the plaintiff) must allege that:

- The domain name creates confusion because it is similar to a registered trademark.

- The respondent (i.e., the defendant) has no legitimate reason to use the domain name.

- The respondent registered the domain name in bad faith. If the respondent is a competitor of the complainant and has acquired the domain name to disrupt the complainant's business (à la Princeton Review), that is evidence of bad faith. So is an attempt by the respondent to sell the name to the complainant.

If the complainant wins, it is entitled either to take over the domain name or to cancel it.

For example, in a dispute over wal-martsucks.com, the WIPO arbitrator ordered that the name be transferred to Wal-Mart. The respondent had demonstrated his bad faith by attempting to sell the name for $530,000. In a similar case, however, the WIPO arbitrator found for a respondent who had registered Wallmartcanadasucks.com. In this case, the respondent had not tried to sell the name and was using the Website to criticize Wal-Mart. As the arbitrator stated in his opinion: "Posting defamatory material on a Web site would not justify revocation of a domain name. The Policy should not be used to shut down robust debate and criticism." (These cases, and others, are available at http://arbiter.wipo.int/.)

Critics have complained that WIPO arbitrators unfairly favor trademark holders, who win roughly 81 percent of the cases they bring. Either party has the option before or after an ICANN arbitration to litigate the issue in court. Of course, litigation is slower and more expensive.

Our discussion thus far has been about registering a trademark as a domain name. Sometimes businesses want to do the opposite—trademark a domain name. The PTO will issue such a trademark only for services offered via the Internet. Thus it trademarked "eBay" for "on-line trading services in which seller posts items to be auctioned and bidding is done electronically." The PTO will not trademark a domain name that is merely an address and does not identify the service provided.

International Trademark Treaties

Under the **Paris Convention,** if someone registers a trademark in one country, then he has a grace period of six months during which he can file in any other country using the same original filing date. Under the **Madrid Agreement,** any trademark registered with the international registry is valid in all signatory countries. (The United States is a signatory.) The **Trademark Law Treaty** simplifies and harmonizes the process of applying for trademarks around the world.

TRADE SECRETS

As the following news report indicates, trade secrets can be a company's most valuable asset.

NEWS*worthy*

At Slick 50, Inc., sneakiness is company policy. The handful of employees privy to the secret formula for the fancy engine treatment, which has nearly $80 million in annual sales, must swear a notarized oath of silence. Only those few who need to know are in possession of the combination to the fireproof vault with eight-inch-thick walls in which the sole printed copy of the Slick 50 recipe is housed. They alone are entrusted with the multiple passwords to the specially encoded database where the computer version is filed. When the company ships ingredients to hired blenders around the country, it dispatches them in odd allotments of containers identified only by numbered codes and mixing instructions. Masking chemicals are included in every batch so that chemical analysis to determine exactly what it takes to concoct the stuff is virtually impossible.

Despite the company's precautions, an employee at a Slick processing plant in the Cayman Islands was able to figure out the formula. He threatened to disclose it unless the company paid him $2.5 million. Fortunately for the company, when the extortionist faxed his demands, he included a cover page listing his mailbox address. The police arrested him immediately. As criminals go, he was not very slick.[17] ◆

Although a company can patent some types of trade secrets, it may be reluctant to do so because patent registration requires that the formula be disclosed publicly. In addition, patent protection expires after 20 years. Some types of trade secrets cannot be patented—customer lists, business plans, manufacturing processes, and marketing strategies.

It has been estimated that the theft of trade secrets costs U.S. businesses $100 billion a year. In response, the National Conference of Commissioners on Uniform State Laws drafted the Uniform Trade Secrets Act (UTSA), which most states have now adopted. **A trade secret is a formula, device, process, method, or compilation of information that, when used in business, gives the owner an advantage over competitors who do not know it.** In determining if information is a trade secret, courts consider:

- How difficult (and expensive) was the information to obtain? Was it readily available from other sources?

---

[17] Anne Reifenberg, "How Secret Formula for Coveted Slick 50 Fell into Bad Hands," *The Wall Street Journal,* Oct. 25, 1995, p. A1. Republished with permission of The Wall Street Journal; permission conveyed through the Copyright Clearance Center, Inc.

- Does the information create an important competitive advantage?
- Did the company make a reasonable effort to protect it?

Anyone who misappropriates a trade secret is liable to the owner for (1) actual damages, (2) unjust enrichment, or (3) a reasonable royalty. If the misappropriation was willful or malicious, the court may award attorney's fees and double damages. A jury recently awarded Avery Dennison Corp. $40 million in damages from a competitor that had misappropriated secret information about the adhesives used in self-stick stamps.

The following case deals with a typical issue: How much information can employees take with them when they start their own competing business?

POLLACK V. SKINSMART DERMATOLOGY AND AESTHETIC CENTER P.C.

2004 Pa. Dist. & Cnty. Dec. LEXIS 214, 68 Pa. D. & C.4th 417
Common Pleas Court of Philadelphia County, Pennsylvania, 2004

Facts: Dr. Andrew Pollack owned the Philadelphia Institute of Dermatology (PID), a dermatology practice. Drs. Toby Shawe and Samy Badawy worked for PID as independent contractors, receiving a certain percentage of the revenues from each patient they treated. Natalie Wilson was Dr. Pollack's medical assistant.

Pollack tentatively agreed to sell the practice to Shawe and Badawy. But instead of buying his practice, the two doctors decided to start their own, which they called Skinsmart. They executed a lease for the Skinsmart office space, offered Wilson a job, and instructed PID staff members to make copies of their appointment books and printouts of the patient list. Then they abruptly resigned from PID. Wilson called PID patients to reschedule procedures at Skinsmart. The two doctors also called patients and sent out a mailing to patients and referring physicians to tell them about Skinsmart.

Pollack filed suit, alleging that the two doctors had misappropriated trade secrets.

Issue: Did Shawe and Badawy misappropriate trade secrets from PID?

Excerpts from Judge Cohen's Decision: The right of a business person to be protected against unfair competition stemming from the usurpation of his or her trade secrets must be balanced against the right of an individual to the unhampered pursuit of the occupations and livelihoods for which he or she is best suited. For this reason, to qualify for protection, the information must be the particular secrets of the complaining employer, not general secrets of the trade in which he is engaged.

Against this backdrop, it is clear the patient list is a trade secret, worthy of protection. As conceded by defendants, the confidentiality of patient information ensures that it remain unknown to those outside the practice and makes the patient list valuable. Through the substantial efforts of plaintiff, the patient list was compiled over numerous years, and contained 20,000 names with related information. PID spent money for computers, software, and employees to keep and maintain the patient list. Within the offices of PID, the information was not universally known or accessible. Not every staff member, including the practicing physicians, could pull the records. Wilson did not have access to them and the doctors relied on other PID employees to access the patient list. These same factors demonstrate that plaintiff sought to protect the secrecy of the information.

The plaintiff must demonstrate that the trade secret has value and importance to him and his business. As noted above, defendants acknowledge the value of the patient list to PID's practice. In addition, plaintiff relied upon the patient list as the core component of his practice.

To have the rights to the use of the trade secret, the plaintiff needs to show he either discovered or owned the trade secret. Plaintiff compiled the patient list over numerous years. The patient list was maintained on PID's computers by PID's employees. Plaintiff's tax returns show that PID was owned solely by plaintiff. These facts establish plaintiff's ownership of the patient list.

Summary judgment is granted on the issue of liability against defendants Shawe, Badawy, and Wilson. ■

Only civil penalties are available under the Uniform Trade Secrets Act. To safeguard national security and maintain the nation's industrial and economic edge, Congress passed the **Economic Espionage Act of 1996, which makes it a *criminal* offense to steal (or attempt to steal) trade secrets for the benefit of someone other than the owner, including for the benefit of any foreign government.** Kai-Lo Hsu was charged under this statute for his alleged attempt to steal the formula for manufacturing Taxol, an anticancer drug produced by Bristol-Myers. His employer, Yuen Foong Paper Co. in Taiwan, had directed him to steal this information because it sought to diversify into biotechnology and obtain technology from other countries.[18]

Chapter Conclusion

Intellectual property takes many different forms. It can be an Internet domain name, a software program, a cartoon character, a formula for motor oil, or a process for making anticancer drugs. Because of its great variety, intellectual property is difficult to protect. Yet, for many individuals and companies, intellectual property is the most valuable asset they will ever own. As its economic value increases, so does the need to understand the rules of intellectual property law.

Chapter Review

	Patent Secrets	Copyright	Trademark	Trade Secrets
Protects:	Mechanical, electrical, chemical inventions; processes, machines; composition of matter; designs; plants	The tangible expression of an idea but not the idea itself	Words and symbols that a business uses to identify its products or services	A formula, device, process, method, or compilation of information that, when used in business, gives the owner an advantage over competitors who do not know it
Requirements for Legal Protection:	Application approved by PTO	An item is automatically copyrighted once it is in tangible form	Use is the only requirement; registration is not necessary but does offer some benefits	Must be kept confidential
Duration:	20 years after the application is filed (14 years from date of issuance for a design patent)	70 years after the death of the work's only or last living author or, for a corporation, 95 years from publication	Valid for 10 years, but the owner can renew for an unlimited number of terms as long as the mark is still being used	As long as it is kept confidential

---

[18] *United States v. Kai-Lo Hsu*, 155 F.3d 189, 1998 U.S. App. LEXIS 20810 (3rd Cir. 1998).

Practice Test

1. For many years, the jacket design for *Webster's Ninth New Collegiate Dictionary* featured a bright red background. The front was dominated by a "bull's-eye" logo. The center of the bull's-eye was white with the title of the book in blue. Merriam-Webster registered this logo as a trademark. Random House published a dictionary with a red dust jacket, the title in large black and white letters, and Random House's "house" logo—an angular drawing of a house—in white. What claim might Merriam-Webster make against Random House? Would it be successful?

2. "Hey, Paula," a pop hit that spent months on the music charts, was back on the radio 30 years later, but in a form the song's author never intended. Talk-show host Rush Limbaugh played a version with the same music as the original but with lyrics that poked fun at President Bill Clinton's alleged sexual misconduct with Paula Jones. Has Limbaugh violated the author's copyright?

3. From the following description of Jean-Pierre Foissey's activities one evening, can you guess what he is doing and why?

> Mr. Foissey waits until sundown. Then it is time to move. A friend whom he employs drops him off by car near the plum orchard, turning off the headlights as they approach. Mr. Foissey and another operative move quickly through adjacent cornfields and enter the orchard, careful not to leave footprints. Armed with a flashlight, his associate crawls through the orchard reading aloud the numbers on labels attached to the trees by the grower. Mr. Foissey picks leaves off the trees and marks the tree numbers on them. He takes those leaves back to an expert who will examine their size, shape, color, and texture and also test their DNA.[19]

4. Rebecca Reyher wrote (and copyrighted) a children's book titled *My Mother Is the Most Beautiful Woman in the World*. The story was based on a Russian folktale told to her by her own mother. Years later, the children's TV show *Sesame Street* televised a skit titled "The Most Beautiful Woman in the World." The *Sesame Street* version took place in a different locale and had fewer frills, but the sequence of events in both stories was identical. The author of the *Sesame Street* script denied he had ever seen Reyher's book but said his skit was based on a story told to his sister some 20 years before. Has *Sesame Street* infringed Reyher's copyright?

5. Roger Schlafly applied for a patent for two prime numbers. (A prime number cannot be evenly divided by any number other than itself and 1—2, 3, 5, 7, 11, 13, for example.) Schlafly's numbers are a bit longer—one is 150 digits, the other is 300. His numbers, when used together, can help perform the type of mathematical operation necessary for exchanging coded messages by computer. Should the PTO issue this patent?

6. DatagraphiX manufactured and sold computer graphics equipment that allowed users to transfer large volumes of information directly from computers to microfilm. Customers were required to keep maintenance documentation on-site for the DatagraphiX service personnel. The service manual carried this legend: "No other use, direct or indirect, of this document or of any information derived therefrom is authorized. No copies of any part of this document shall be made without written approval by DatagraphiX." Additionally, on every page of the maintenance manual the company placed warnings that the information was proprietary and not to be duplicated. Frederick J. Lennen left DatagraphiX to start his own company that serviced DatagraphiX equipment. Can DatagraphiX prevent Lennen from using its manuals?

7. A man asked a question of the advice columnist at his local newspaper. His wife had thought of a clever name for an automobile. He wanted to know if there was any way they could own or

---

19 Thomas Kamm, "Patented Plums Give French Fruit Sleuth His Raison D'être," *The Wall Street Journal*, Sep. 18, 1995, p. A1.

register the name so that no one else could use it. If you were the columnist, how would you respond?

8. Babe Ruth was one of the greatest baseball players of all time. After Ruth's death, his daughters registered the words "Babe Ruth" as a trademark. MacMillan, Inc., published a baseball calendar that contained three Babe Ruth photos. Ruth's daughters did not own the specific photographs, but they objected to the use of Ruth's likeness. As holders of the Babe Ruth trademark, do his daughters have the right to prevent others from publishing pictures of Ruth without their permission?

9. Harper & Row signed a contract with former President Gerald Ford to publish his memoirs. As part of the deal, the two agreed that *Time* magazine could print an excerpt from the memoirs shortly before the book was published. *Time* was to pay $25,000 for this right. Before *Time* published its version, *The Nation* magazine published an unauthorized excerpt. *Time* canceled its article and refused to pay the $25,000. Harper sued *The Nation* for copyright infringement. What was *The Nation*'s defense? Was it successful?

10. Frank B. McMahon wrote one of the first psychology textbooks to feature a light and easily readable style. He also included many colloquialisms and examples that appealed to a youthful student market. Charles G. Morris wrote a psychology textbook that copied McMahon's style. Has Morris infringed McMahon's copyright?

11. **ETHICS** After Edward Miller left his job as a salesperson at the New England Insurance Agency, Inc., he took some of his New England customers to his new employer. At New England, the customer lists had been kept in file cabinets. Although the company did not restrict access to these files, it claimed there was a "you do not peruse my files and I do not peruse yours" understanding. The lists were not marked "confidential" or "not to be disclosed." Did Miller steal New England's trade secrets? Whether or not he violated the law, was it ethical for him to use this information at his new job?

12. **YOU BE THE JUDGE** WRITING PROBLEM Three inventors developed a software program that generated a particularly clear screen display on a computer. The PTO refused to issue a patent for this software. Do the inventors have a right to a patent? **Argument for the PTO:** This software is merely a series of mathematical formulas that cannot be patented. **Argument for the inventors:** The program is not merely a mathematical concept or an abstract idea, but rather a specific machine to produce a useful, concrete, and tangible result.

13. **ROLE REVERSAL** Draft a multiple-choice question that focuses on an issue of copyright law.

Internet Research Problem

Think of a name for an interesting new product. Click on Search Trademarks at **http://www.uspto.gov/main/trademarks.htm** to see if this name is available as a trademark. Also look at **http://www.icann.org/registrars/accredited-list.html,** which provides a list of domain name registrars. See if your name is available as an Internet domain name.

You can find further practice problems at **academic.cengage.com/blaw/beatty.**

CHAPTER 23 Property

Charley lives in retirement in his modest bungalow, counting pennies to make his meager savings last. Then everything changes—or does it? He is playing bridge with three friends: a rabbi, a bishop, and a banker. As rain beats against the roof and everyone murmurs about possible flooding, the banker suddenly announces to the astonished group that he is obscenely rich and is going to give $100,000 to everyone at the table. "Meet me at the bank tomorrow at 10:00, and the money is yours." Shouts! Hugs! Tears!

That night, as rain continues to lash the house, Charley smiles in his sleep, dreaming that he is floating in a tropical paradise. He awakens to discover that he *is* floating. His bedroom is filled with water, and Charley's head is now pressing against the ceiling. To avoid a flooding catastrophe, the Power Company has released a nearby dam, inundating 150 acres. The flood level on Charley's property is 16 feet and rising. Charley squirms through a broken window and escapes from his uninsured house just as it disappears beneath roiling black water.

The next morning, Charley, sneezing, arrives at the bank, where the bishop and rabbi grimly announce that the banker died before he could sign the three cashier's checks. There is no money. Charley, dazed and distraught, sues the Power Company for the damage to his house compensation and recovers—nothing. The company was legally entitled to destroy his house! Desperate, he seeks his $100,000 from the bank. Read on for the result.

A bewildering two days for Charley, but instructive for us, as we have glimpsed two issues of property law. The Power Company was entitled to destroy his house if it chose, because it owned an easement. The banker's promise will be settled according to the law of gifts. Our survey will focus on three primary topics: real property, landlord-tenant law, and personal property. ▪

© AKIRA KAEDE/PHOTODISC/GETTY IMAGES

REAL PROPERTY

Nature of Real Property

We need to define a few terms. A **grantor** is an owner who conveys his property, or some interest in it, to someone else, called the **grantee.** If you sell your house to Veronica, you are the grantor and she is the grantee. Real property may be any of the following:

- **Land.** Land is the most common and important form of real property. In England, land was historically the greatest source of wealth and social status, far more important than industrial or commercial enterprises. As a result, the law of real property has been of paramount importance for nearly 1,000 years, developing very gradually to reflect changing conditions. Some real property terms sound medieval for the simple reason that they are medieval.

- **Buildings.** Buildings are real property. Houses, office buildings, and factories all fall (or stand) in this category.

- **Subsurface Rights.** In most states, the owner of the land also owns anything under the surface, down to the center of the earth. In some cases the subsurface rights may be worth far more than the surface land, for example, if there is oil or gold underfoot. Although the landowner generally owns these rights, she may sell them while retaining ownership of the surface land.

- **Air Rights.** The owner of land owns the air space above the land. Suppose you own an urban parking lot. The owner of an adjacent office building wishes to build a walkway across your parking lot to join her building with a neighboring skyscraper. The office owner needs your permission to build across the air space and will expect to pay you a handsome fee for the privilege.

- **Plant Life.** Plant life growing on land is real property, whether the plants are naturally occurring, such as trees, or cultivated crops.

- **Fixtures.** Fixtures are goods that have become attached to real property. A house (which is real property) contains many fixtures. The furnace and heating ducts were goods when they were manufactured and when they were sold to the builder, because they were movable. But when the builder attached them to the house, the items became fixtures. By contrast, neither the refrigerator nor the grand piano is a fixture.

When an owner sells real property, the buyer normally takes the fixtures, unless the parties specify otherwise. Sometimes it is difficult to determine whether something is a fixture. The general rule is this: **an object is a fixture if a reasonable person would consider the item to be a permanent part of the property.**

Estates in Real Property

Use and ownership of real estate can take many different legal forms. A person may own property outright, having the unrestricted use of the land and an unlimited right to sell it. However, someone may also own a lesser interest in real property. For example, you could inherit the use of a parcel of land during your lifetime, but have no power to leave the land to your heirs. Or you could retain ownership and possession of some land yet allow a corporation to explore for oil and drill wells. The different rights that someone can hold in real property are known as **estates** or **interests.** Both terms simply indicate specified rights in property.

Freehold Estates

The owner of a freehold estate has the present right to possess the property and to use it in any lawful way she wants. The three most important freehold estates are (1) fee simple absolute, (2) fee simple defeasible, and (3) life estate.

Fee Simple Absolute. **A fee simple absolute provides the owner with the greatest possible control of the property. This is the most common form of land ownership.** Suppose Cecily inherits a fee simple interest in a 30-acre vineyard. She may use the land for any purpose that the law allows. She may continue to raise grapes, or, if she hates wine, she may rip up the vines and build a condominium complex. Although zoning laws may regulate her use, nothing in Cecily's estate itself limits her use of the land. Cecily may pass on to her heirs her entire estate—that is, her full fee simple absolute.

Fee Simple Defeasible. Other estates contain more limited rights than the fee simple absolute. Wily establishes the Wily Church of Perfection. Upon his death, Wily leaves a 100-acre estate to the church for as long as it keeps the name "Wily Church of Perfection." Wily has included a significant limitation in the church's ownership. The church has a fee simple defeasible.

A fee simple defeasible may terminate upon the occurrence of some limiting event. If the congregation decides to rename itself the Happy Valley Church of Perfection, the church automatically loses its estate in the 100 acres. Ownership of the land then **reverts** to Wily's heirs, meaning title goes back to them. Because the heirs might someday inherit the land, they are said to have a *future interest* in the 100 acres. A landowner may create a fee simple defeasible to ensure that property is used in a particular way or is not used in a specified manner. In the following case, a California city was surprised to learn that this ancient doctrine still has plenty of life.

WALTON V. CITY OF RED BLUFF

2 Cal. App. 4th 117, 3 Cal. Rptr. 2d 275, 1991 Cal. App. LEXIS 1474
California Court of Appeal, 1991

Facts: In 1908 and 1916, Mrs. Elizabeth Kraft and her son, Edward Kraft, granted to the city of Red Bluff two adjoining properties, with buildings, for use as a public library. The grants from the Krafts required continuous use as a public library and stated that the property would return to the Kraft family if the city ever used it for other purposes.

In 1986, Red Bluff decided that the buildings were too small for its needs and moved all the books to a new building nearby. The city used the Kraft property for other civic purposes such as town meetings, social gatherings, and school tutoring. Herbert Kraft Walton, a descendant and heir, filed suit seeking to have the property reconveyed to him. The trial court found for Red Bluff, and Walton appealed.

Issue: Did Red Bluff violate the terms of the grants, so the property must now revert to Walton?

Excerpts from Judge Carr's Decision: The grants provide in part: "If the property herein conveyed shall cease to be used, for library purposes, by said Town, . . . or shall be put to [any] use other [than] the uses and purposes herein specifically referred to, . . . then the grant and conveyance herein made shall cease and terminate, and the title to the said property and all the improvements thereon shall at once revert to [the Kraft family].

Red Bluff admits all the books were removed from the library as of September 1986. The trial

▼

court framed the issue as one of abandonment. But the grantors specified that "if the said property shall cease to be used, for library purposes" the grants terminate.

Whether Red Bluff intended to "abandon" the use purpose of the property or not, it removed the books and stopped using the premises for library purposes. The grants defined library purposes broadly to include various educational endeavors, but there is no evidence any of these other activities took place. It stopped using the grant for library purposes and the property must go back to the Kraft heir. At oral argument Red Bluff focused on the "changed conditions" doctrine. The power of termination expires when it becomes "obsolete." In a leading case involving a covenant restricting the use of lots to residential purposes it was said that "where there has been a change in the uses to which the property in the neighborhood is being put, so that such property is no longer residence property, it would be unjust to give effect to the restrictions, if such change has resulted from causes other than their breach." In this case the alleged change in circumstance is that Red Bluff needs a bigger, modern library building, not that the present building cannot be used for the purposes of the grant or that the use of surrounding property makes operation of a library impracticable. In these circumstances there is nothing inequitable about enforcing the restriction in the grant.

The judgment is *reversed* with directions to the trial court to enter a judgment [granting title to] Walton. ■

Life Estate. A life estate is exactly what you would think: **an estate for the life of some named person.** For example, Aretha owns Respect Farm, and in her will she leaves it to Max, for his lifetime. Max is the **life tenant.** He is entitled to live on the property and work it as a normal farm during his lifetime, though he is obligated to maintain it properly. The moment Max dies, the farm reverts to Aretha or her heirs.

Concurrent Estates

When two or more people own real property at the same time, they have concurrent estates. In a **tenancy in common,** the owners have an equal interest in the entire property. Each co-tenant has the right to sell her interest to someone else, or to leave it to her heirs upon her death. A **joint tenancy** is similar, except that upon the death of one joint tenant (owner), his interest passes *to the surviving joint tenants,* not to his heirs.

To provide special rights for married couples, some states have created **tenancy by the entirety** and **community property.** These forms of ownership allow one spouse to protect some property from the other, and from the other's creditors.

Condominiums and **cooperatives** are most common in apartment buildings with multiple units, though they can be used in other settings, such as a cluster of houses on a single parcel of land. In a condominium, the owner of the apartment typically has a fee simple absolute in his particular unit. He is normally entitled to sell or lease the unit, must pay taxes on it, and may receive the normal tax deduction if he is carrying a mortgage. All unit owners belong to a condominium association, which manages the common areas. In a cooperative, the residents generally do not own their particular unit. Instead, they are shareholders in a corporation that owns the building and leases specified units to the shareholders.

Nonpossessory Interests

All the estates and interests that we have examined thus far focused on one thing: possession of the land. Now we look at interests that *never* involve possession. These interests may be very valuable, even though the holder never lives on the land.

Easements

The Alabama Power Co. drove a flatbed truck over land owned by Thomas Burgess, damaging the property. The power company did this to reach its power lines and wooden transmission poles. Burgess had never given Alabama Power permission to enter his land, and he sued for the damage that the heavy trucks caused. He recovered—nothing. Alabama Power had an easement to use Burgess's land.

An easement gives one person the right to enter land belonging to another and make a limited use of it, without taking anything away. Burgess had bought his land from a man named Denton, who years earlier had sold an easement to Alabama Power. The easement gave the power company the right to construct several transmission poles on one section of Denton's land and to use reasonable means to reach the poles. Alabama Power owned that easement forever, and when Burgess bought the land, he took it subject to the easement. Burgess is stuck with his uninvited guest as long as he owns the land.[1]

Property owners normally create easements in one of two ways. A **grant** occurs when a landowner expressly intends to convey an easement to someone else. This is how Alabama Power acquired its easement. A **reservation** occurs when an owner sells land but keeps some right to enter the property. A farmer might sell 40 acres to a developer but reserve an easement giving him the right to drive his equipment across a specified strip of the land.

In this chapter's opening scenario, the Power Company had a flood easement on Charley's property. If Charley had read the following case, he might not have bought the land.

CARVIN V. ARKANSAS POWER AND LIGHT

14 F.3d 399, 1993 U.S. App. LEXIS 33986
United States Court of Appeals for the Eighth Circuit, 1993

Facts: Between 1923 and 1947, Arkansas Power & Light (AP&L) constructed several dams on two Arkansas lakes, Hamilton and Catherine. The company then obtained "flood easements" on property adjoining the lakes. AP&L obtained some of the easements by grant and others by reservation, selling lakeside property and keeping the easement. These flood easements permitted AP&L to "clear of trees, brush and other obstructions and to submerge by water" certain acreage, which was described exactly. AP&L properly recorded the easements, and when the current landowners bought lakeside property, they were aware of the documents.

During one 12-hour period in May 1990, extraordinarily heavy rains fell in the Ouachita River Basin, including both lakes. In some areas, more than 10 inches of rain fell, causing the water to reach the highest levels ever recorded, even washing away the equipment designed to measure rainfall. To avoid flooding Lake Hamilton, AP&L opened the gates of a dam called Carpenter. This caused Lake Catherine to flood, with water in some places rising 25 feet. This flood caused massive damage to the plaintiffs' houses, with water in some cases rising to the roof level.

Several dozen landowners sued, claiming that AP&L was negligent in opening one dam without simultaneously opening another and also in failing to warn home owners of the intended action. The federal district court granted summary judgment for AP&L, based on the flood easements, and the landowners appealed.

▼

---

[1] *Burgess v. Alabama Power Co.,* 658 So. 2d 435, 1995 Ala. LEXIS 119 (Ala. 1995).

Issue: Did the easements relieve AP&L from liability for flooding?

Excerpts from Judge Gibson's Decision: This case involves a variety of easement forms, executed on different dates, but all with the same background. Some expressly reserved the right to "submerge" the land up to 307 feet and to "flood any part" of "said lands." Others conveyed the right to "flood any and all of said lands." Two of the three forms used, and the condemnation decree, specifically granted the right to flood the lands "by waters impounded by a dam." The language is plain and specific. The obvious purpose of the flood and flowage rights is to protect AP&L from liability from its management of the lake in circumstances such as occurred in the extremely heavy rainfall in the seven hours on May 19 and 20. When AP&L opened the flood gates during the heaviest rains experienced since the dam was built, with the resultant flooding on the property of the shores in Lake Catherine, it was exercising rights retained by it or granted to it in the documents creating the property interest of the landowners. We can only conclude that protection from liability for flooding of the plaintiffs' land was the very reason the dam owner purchased the easement.

The issues in this case are extremely close. The loss of property is most substantial and the result seems harsh. [However, in view of the property interest created by the documents involving each of the landholders, we cannot place liability on AP&L in such circumstances. Affirmed.] ∎

Profit

A *profit* **gives one person the right to enter land belonging to another and take something away.** You own 100 acres of vacation property, and suddenly a mining company informs you that the land contains valuable nickel deposits. You may choose to sell a profit to the mining company, allowing it to enter your land and take away the nickel. You receive cash up front, and the company earns money from the sale of the mineral.

License

A license gives the holder temporary permission to enter upon another's property. Unlike an easement or profit, a license is a *temporary* right. When you attend a basketball game by buying a ticket, the basketball club that sells you the ticket is the licensor and you are the licensee. You are entitled to enter the licensor's premises, namely the basketball arena, and to remain during the game, though the club can revoke the license if you behave unacceptably.

Mortgage

Generally, in order to buy a house, a prospective owner must borrow money. The bank or other lender will require security before it hands over its money, and the most common form of security for a real estate loan is a mortgage. **A mortgage is a security interest in real property.** The homeowner who borrows money is the **mortgagor,** because she is *giving* the mortgage to the lender. The lender, in turn, is the *mortgagee,* the party acquiring a security interest. The mortgagee in most cases obtains a **lien** on the house, meaning the right to foreclose on the property if the mortgagor fails to pay back the money borrowed.

Sale of Real Property

For most people, buying or selling a house is the biggest, most important financial transaction they will make. Here we consider several of the key issues that may arise.

Seller's Obligations Concerning the Property

Historically, the common law recognized the rule of caveat emptor in the sale of real property—that is, let the buyer beware. If a buyer walked into his new living room and fell through the floor into a lake of toxic waste, it was his tough luck. But the common law changes with the times, and today courts place an increasing burden of fairness on the sellers of real estate. Two of the most significant obligations are the implied warranty of habitability and the duty to disclose defects.

Implied Warranty of Habitability. **Most states now impose an implied warranty of habitability on a builder who sells a new home.** This means that, whether he wants to or not, the builder is guaranteeing that the new house contains **adequate materials and good workmanship.** The law implies this warranty because of the inherently unequal position of builder and buyer. Some defects might be obvious to a lay observer, such as a room with no roof or a front porch that sways whenever the neighbors sneeze. But only the builder will know if he made the frame with proper wood, if the heating system was second rate, the electrical work shabby, and so forth. Note that in most states the law implies this warranty to protect buyers of residential, but not commercial, property.

Duty to Disclose Defects. **The seller of a home must disclose facts that a buyer does not know and cannot readily observe if they materially affect the property's value.** Roy and Charlyne Terrell owned a house in the Florida Keys, where zoning codes required all living areas to be 15 feet above sea level. They knew that their house violated the code because a bedroom and bathroom were on the ground floor. They offered to sell the house to Robert Revitz, assuring him that the property complied with all codes and that flood insurance would cost about $350 per year. Revitz bought the house, moved in, and later learned that because of the code violations, flood insurance would be slightly more expensive—costing just over *$36,000 per year.* He sued and won. The court declared that the Terrells had a duty to disclose the code violations; it ordered a rescission of the contract, meaning that Revitz got his money back. The court mentioned that the duty to disclose was wide ranging and included leaking roofs, insect infestation, cracks in walls and foundations, and any other problems that a buyer might be unable to discern.[2]

Sales Contract and Title Examination

The statute of frauds requires that an agreement to sell real property must be in writing to be enforceable. A contract for the sale of a house is often several pages of dense legal reading, in which the lawyers for the buyer and seller attempt to allocate risks for every problem that might go wrong. However, the contract need not be so thorough. A written contract for the sale of land is generally valid if it includes the names of all parties, a precise description of the property being sold, the price, and signatures.

Once the parties have agreed to the terms and signed a contract, the buyer's lawyer performs a **title examination,** which means that she, or someone she hires, searches through the local land registry for all documents that relate to the property. The purpose is to ensure that the seller actually has valid title to this land, because it is dispiriting to give someone half a million dollars for property and then discover that he never owned it and neither do you. Even if the seller owns the land, his title may be subject to other claims, such as an easement or a mortgage.

---

[2] *Revitz v. Terrell,* 572 So. 2d 996, 1990 Fla. App. LEXIS 9655 (Fla. Dist. Ct. App. 1990).

Closing and Deeds

While the buyer is checking the seller's title, she also probably needs to arrange financing, as described earlier in the section on mortgages. When the title work is complete and the buyer has arranged financing, the parties arrange a **closing,** a meeting at which the property is actually sold. The seller brings to the closing a **deed,** which is the document proving ownership of the land. The seller signs the deed over to the buyer in exchange for the purchase price. The buyer pays the price either with a certified check and/or by having her lender pay. If a lender pays part or all of the price, the buyer executes a mortgage to the lender as part of the closing.

Recording

Recording the deed means filing it with the official state registry. The registry clerk places a photocopy of the deed in the agency's bound volumes and indexes the deed by the name of the grantor and the grantee. Recording is a critical step in the sale of land, because it puts all the world on notice that the grantor has sold the land. It has little effect between grantor and grantee: once the deed and money are exchanged, the sale is generally final between those two. But recording is vital to protect the general public.

Land Use Regulation

Zoning

Zoning statutes are state laws that permit local communities to regulate building and land use. The local communities, whether cities, towns, or counties, then pass zoning ordinances that control many aspects of land development. For example, a town's zoning ordinance may divide the community into an industrial zone where factories may be built, a commercial zone in which stores of a certain size are allowed, and several residential zones in which only houses may be constructed. Within the residential zones, there may be further divisions, for example, permitting two-family houses in certain areas and requiring larger lots in others.

An owner prohibited by an ordinance from erecting a certain kind of building, or adding on to his present building, may seek a **variance** from the zoning board, meaning an exception granted for special reasons unique to the property. Whether a board will grant a variance generally depends upon the type of the proposed building, the nature of the community, the reason the owner claims he is harmed by the ordinance, and the reaction of neighbors.

Eminent Domain

Eminent domain is the power of the government to take private property for public use. A government may need land to construct a highway, an airport, a university, or public housing. All levels of government—federal, state, and local—have this power. But the Fifth Amendment to the United States Constitution states: ". . . nor shall private property be taken for public use, without just compensation." The Supreme Court has held that this clause, the Takings Clause, applies not only to the federal government but also to state and local governments. So, although all levels of government have the power to take property, they must pay the owner a fair price.

A "fair price" generally means the reasonable market value of the land. Generally, if the property owner refuses the government's offer, the government will file suit seeking **condemnation** of the land—that is, a court order specifying what compensation is just and awarding title to the government.

LANDLORD-TENANT LAW

On a January morning in Studio City, California, Alpha Donchin took her small shih tzu for a walk. Suddenly, less than a block from her house, two large rottweilers attacked Donchin and her pet. The heavy animals mauled the 14-pound shih tzu, and when Donchin picked up her dog, the rottweilers knocked her down, breaking her hip and causing other serious injuries.

Ubaldo Guerrero, who lived in a rented house nearby, owned the two rottweilers, and Donchin sued him. But she also sued Guerrero's *landlord*, David Swift, who lived four blocks away from the rental property. Donchin claimed that the landlord was liable for her injuries, because he knew of the dogs' vicious nature and permitted them to escape from the property he rented to Guerrero. Should the landlord be liable for injuries caused by his tenant's dogs?

As is typical of many landlord-tenant issues, the law in this area is in flux. Under the common law, a landlord had no liability for injuries caused by animals belonging to a tenant, and many states adhere to that rule. But some states are expanding the landlord's liability for injuries caused on or near his property. The California court ruled that Donchin could maintain her suit against Swift. If Donchin could prove that Swift knew the dogs were dangerous and allowed them to escape through a defective fence, the landlord would be liable for her injuries.[3]

One reason for the erratic evolution of landlord-tenant law is that it is really a combination of three venerable areas of law: property, contract, and negligence. The confluence of these legal theories produces results that are unpredictable but interesting and important. We begin our examination of landlord-tenant law with an analysis of the different types of tenancy.

Recall that a freehold estate is the right to possess real property and use it in any lawful manner. **When an owner of a freehold estate allows another person temporary, exclusive possession of the property, the parties have created a landlord-tenant relationship.** The freehold owner is the **landlord,** and the person allowed to possess the property is the tenant. The landlord has conveyed a **leasehold** interest to the tenant, meaning the right to temporary possession. Courts also use the word "**tenancy**" to describe the tenant's right to possession. A leasehold may be commercial or residential.

Lease

The statute of frauds generally requires that a lease be in writing. Some states will enforce an oral lease if it is for a short term, such as one year or less, but even when an oral lease is permitted, it is wiser for the parties to put their agreement in writing, because a written lease avoids many misunderstandings. At a minimum, a lease must state the names of the parties, the premises being leased, the duration of the agreement, and the rent. But a well-drafted lease generally includes many provisions, called covenants. A **covenant** is simply a promise by either the landlord or the tenant to do something or refrain from doing something. For example, most leases include a covenant concerning the tenant's payment of a security deposit and the landlord's return of the deposit, a covenant describing how the tenant may use the premises, and several covenants about who must maintain and repair the property, who is liable for damage, and so forth. The parties should also agree about how the lease may be terminated and whether the parties have the right to renew it.

---

[3] *Donchin v. Guerrero*, 34 Cal. App. 4th 1832, 1995 Cal. App. LEXIS 462 (Cal. Ct. App. 1995).

Types of Tenancy

There are four types of tenancy: a tenancy for years, a periodic tenancy, a tenancy at will, and a tenancy at sufferance. The most important feature distinguishing one from the other is how each tenancy terminates. In some cases, a tenancy terminates automatically, while in others, one party must take certain steps to end the agreement.

Tenancy for Years

Any lease for a stated, fixed period is a tenancy for years. If a landlord rents a summer apartment for the months of June, July, and August of next year, that is a tenancy for years. A company that rents retail space in a mall beginning January 1, 2006, and ending December 31, 2009, also has a tenancy for years. A tenancy for years terminates automatically when the agreed period ends.

Periodic Tenancy

A periodic tenancy is created for a fixed period and then automatically continues for additional periods until either party notifies the other of termination. This is probably the most common variety of tenancy. Suppose a landlord agrees to rent you an apartment "from month to month, rent payable on the first." That is a periodic tenancy. The tenancy automatically renews itself every month, unless either party gives adequate notice to the other that she wishes to terminate. A periodic tenancy could also be for one-year periods—in which case it automatically renews for an additional year if neither party terminates—or for any other period.

Tenancy at Will

A tenancy at will has no fixed duration and may be terminated by either party at any time. Tenancies at will are unusual tenancies.[4] Typically, the agreement is vague, with no specified rental period and with payment, perhaps, to be made in kind. The parties might agree, for example, that a tenant farmer could use a portion of his crop as rent. Since either party can end the agreement at any time, it provides no security for either landlord or tenant.

Tenancy at Sufferance

A tenancy at sufferance occurs when a tenant remains on the premises, against the wishes of the landlord, after the expiration of a true tenancy. Thus, a tenancy at sufferance is not a true tenancy because the tenant is staying without the landlord's agreement. The landlord has the option of seeking to evict the tenant or of forcing the tenant to pay rent for a new rental period.

---

[4] The courts of some states, annoyingly, use the term "tenancy at will" for what are, in reality, periodic tenancies. They do this to bewilder law students and even lawyers, a goal at which they are quite successful. This text uses "tenancy at will" in its more widely known sense, meaning a tenancy terminable at any time.

LANDLORD'S DUTIES

Duty to Deliver Possession

The landlord's first important duty is to deliver possession of the premises at the beginning of the tenancy—that is, to make the rented space available to the tenant. In most cases, this presents no problems and the new tenant moves in. But what happens if the previous tenant has refused to leave when the new tenancy begins? In most states, the landlord is legally required to remove the previous tenant. In some states, it is up to the new tenant either to evict the existing occupant or begin charging him rent.

Quiet Enjoyment

All tenants are entitled to quiet enjoyment of the premises, meaning the right to use the property without the interference of the landlord. Most leases expressly state this covenant of quiet enjoyment. And if a lease includes no such covenant, the law implies the right of quiet enjoyment anyway, so all tenants are protected. If a landlord interferes with the tenant's quiet enjoyment, he has breached the lease, entitling the tenant to damages.

The most common interference with quiet enjoyment is an eviction, meaning some act that forces the tenant to abandon the premises. Of course, some evictions are legal, as when a tenant fails to pay the rent. But some evictions are illegal. There are two types of eviction: actual and constructive.

Actual Eviction. **If a landlord prevents the tenant from possessing the premises, he has actually evicted her.** Suppose a landlord decides that a group of students are "troublemakers." Without going through lawful eviction procedures in court, the landlord simply waits until the students are out of the apartment and changes the locks. By denying the students access to the premises, the landlord has actually evicted them and has breached their right of quiet enjoyment.

Constructive Eviction. **If a landlord substantially interferes with the tenant's use and enjoyment of the premises, he has constructively evicted her.** Courts construe certain behavior as the equivalent of an eviction. In these cases, the landlord has not actually prevented the tenant from possessing the premises but has instead interfered so greatly with her use and enjoyment that the law regards the landlord's actions as equivalent to an eviction. Suppose the heating system in an apartment house in Juneau, Alaska, fails during January. The landlord, an avid sled-dog racer, tells the tenants he is too busy to fix the problem. If the tenants move out, the landlord has constructively evicted them and is liable for all expenses they suffer.

To claim a constructive eviction, the tenant must vacate the premises. The tenant must also prove that the interference was sufficiently serious and lasted long enough that she was forced to move out. A lack of hot water for two days is not fatal, but lack of any water for two weeks creates a constructive eviction.

Duty to Maintain Premises

In most states, a landlord has a duty to deliver the premises in a habitable condition and a continuing duty to maintain the habitable condition. This duty overlaps with the quiet enjoyment obligation, but it is not identical. The tenant's right to quiet enjoyment focuses primarily on the tenant's *ability to use* the rented property. The landlord's duty to maintain the property focuses on whether the property *meets a particular legal standard.* The required standard may be stated in the lease, created by a state statute, or implied by law.

Lease. The lease itself generally obligates the landlord to maintain the exterior of any buildings and the common areas. If a lease does not do so, state law may imply the obligation.

Building Codes. Many state and local governments have passed building codes, which mandate minimum standards for commercial and/or residential property. The codes are likely to be stricter for residential property and may demand such things as minimum room size, sufficient hot water, secure locks, proper working kitchens and bathrooms, absence of insects and rodents, and other basics of decent housing. Generally, all rental property must comply with the building code, whether the lease mentions the code or not.

Implied Warranty of Habitability. Students Maria Ivanow, Thomas Tecza, and Kenneth Gearin rented a house from Les and Martha Vanlandingham. The monthly rent was $900. But the roommates failed to pay any rent for the final five months of the tenancy. After they moved out, the Vanlandinghams sued. How much did the landlords recover? Nothing. The landlords had breached the implied warranty of habitability.

The implied warranty of habitability requires that a landlord meet all standards set by the local building code, or that the premises be fit for human habitation. Most states, though not all, *imply* this warranty of habitability, meaning that the landlord must meet this standard whether the lease includes it or not.

The Vanlandinghams breached the implied warranty. The students had complained repeatedly about a variety of problems. The washer and dryer, which were included in the lease, frequently failed. A severe roof leak caused water damage in one of the bedrooms. Defective pipes flooded the bathroom. The refrigerator frequently malfunctioned, and the roommates repaired it several times. The basement often flooded, and when it was dry, rats and opossums lived in it. The heat sometimes failed.

In warranty of habitability cases, a court normally considers the severity of the problems and their duration. In the case of Maria Ivanow and friends, the court abated (reduced) the rent 50 percent. The students had already paid more than the abated rent to the landlord, so they owed nothing for the last five months.[5]

Tenant Remedies for Defective Conditions. Different states allow various remedies for defective conditions. For tenant rights in your state, see http://www. tenantsunion.org/tulist.html, which provides links to tenant organizations throughout the nation. Many states allow a tenant to withhold rent, representing the decreased value of the premises. In some states, if a tenant notifies the landlord of a serious defect and the landlord fails to remedy the problem, the tenant may deduct a reasonable amount of money from the rental payment and have the repair made himself. Also, a landlord who refuses to repair significant defects is breaching the lease and/or state law, and the tenant may simply sue for damages.

---

[5] *Vanlandingham v. Ivanow,* 246 Ill. App. 3d 348, 615 N.E.2d 1361, 1993 Ill. App. LEXIS 985 (Ill. Ct. App. 1993).

Duty to Return Security Deposit

Most landlords require tenants to pay a security deposit, in case the tenant damages the premises. In many states, a landlord must either return the security deposit soon after the tenant has moved out or notify the tenant of the damage and the cost of the repairs. A landlord who fails to do so may owe the tenant damages of two or even three times the deposit.

Your authors are always grateful when a litigant volunteers to illustrate half a dozen legal issues in one lawsuit. The landlord in the following case demonstrates problems of security deposit, quiet enjoyment, constructive eviction, and . . . well, see how many you can count.

HARRIS V. SOLEY

2000 Me. 150, 756 A. 2d 499
Supreme Judicial Court of Maine, 2000

Facts: Here is an apartment adventure that begins as a horror story but ends happily. The court will tell you what happened.

Issue: Are the tenants entitled to such large damages?

Excerpts from Justice Saufley's Decision: Near Labor Day, Andrea Harris, Kimberly Nightingale, Karen Simard, and Michelle Dussault moved into a large apartment that was located in the Old Port area of Portland and owned by Joseph Soley. Soley had promised the tenants that the apartment, which had previously been condemned by the City of Portland, would be repaired by the time they moved in. When they arrived, the condemnation notice was still on the door. Upon entering the apartment, they found it in an uninhabitable condition. They spoke to Soley's property manager who indicated that if the tenants were willing to clean the apartment themselves, she would credit them with $750 of their $1000 monthly rent for the month of September. They rented a steam cleaner, bought various cleaning supplies, and cleaned the apartment themselves. Soley's property manager also suggested that they buy a new refrigerator and deduct it from the rent because the one in the apartment did not work.

Despite their efforts to clean the apartment, the tenants continued to have problems with infestations of mice and cockroaches, as well as a persistent odor of cat urine. A dead cat was eventually found beneath the floorboards. The apartment had no heat during the month of October. One tenant slept with blankets over her head, not only because of the cold but also to keep bugs away from her. These problems persisted into November, and the tenants submitted to Soley a list of complaints including a broken skylight, a broken toilet, a broken garbage disposal, a leaking roof, and cockroach infestation. As winter arrived, snow would fall into the living room through the broken skylight. When Soley did not make the needed repairs, the tenants stopped paying rent. Soley telephoned them on several occasions regarding the rent and spoke to the tenants in a rude and abrasive manner. In February, the property manager told the tenants that Soley had begun eviction proceedings against them.

The tenants eventually found another place to live and had begun moving [when] Soley's agents broke into the apartment and took many of the tenants' remaining belongings. Upon confrontation with the returning tenants and police officers who had been called to the scene, Soley's agents indicated that Soley had directed their actions. Eventually, the officers and one of the tenants went to an apartment nearby and recovered some, but not all, of the missing property.

The tenants then sought out Soley to request that he return their remaining possessions. They located him at his restaurant, the Seamen's Club. According to one of the tenants, he replied that he would return their property only after they paid him $3000. He then ordered them to leave and threatened to call the police

▼

and have them forcibly removed. Soley told the tenants that he knew where they were moving and where their families lived, a statement that the tenants took as a threat.

The tenants brought suit against the defendants in a complaint that included claims for conversion [the wrongful taking of property], intentional infliction of emotional distress, punitive damages, breach of contract, wrongful eviction, and wrongful retention of a security deposit. [For months, Soley refused to respond to discovery requests and finally the trial court gave a default judgment for the plaintiffs. The judge instructed the jury that all the plaintiffs' allegations were deemed true and that their job was simply to award damages.]

The jury awarded each of the tenants $15,000 as damages for emotional distress. The evidence introduced at trial, including evidence of Soley's conduct and the tenants' testimony regarding their emotional responses, could support a determination that [each of] the tenants suffered comparable emotional distress.

Finally, Soley challenges the award of $1 million in punitive damages as excessive. Again, we begin with the facts of the complaint as conclusively established by the default judgment. Among other things, those facts included the following:

> Plaintiffs were shaken up, infuriated, violated, intimidated and in fear for their physical safety. . . . The conduct of Defendants, and each of them, was so extreme and outrageous as to exceed all possible bounds of decency. . . . Defendants acted intentionally, knowingly, willfully, wantonly and with malice.

There can be no question that the jury was justified in deciding that an award of punitive damages was warranted. The tenants had to endure the presence of insect and rodent infestations, dead animals, snow falling into the apartment, and a total lack of response from their landlord after repeated complaints. Soley's continued refusal to repair conditions that rendered the apartment unfit for human occupation, the violent removal of tenants' property before eviction proceedings had proceeded, the retention of property belonging to the tenants, the destruction of their property, and his threatening behavior combined to create a pattern of conduct that must be considered intolerable.

Judgment affirmed. ■

Tenant's Duties

Duty to Pay Rent

My landlord said he's gonna raise the rent. "Good," I said, " 'cause I can't raise it."

Slappy White, comedian, 1921–1995

Rent is the compensation the tenant pays the landlord for use of the premises, and paying the rent, despite Mr. White's wistful hope, is the tenant's foremost obligation. The lease normally specifies the amount of rent and when it must be paid. Typically, the landlord requires that rent be paid at the beginning of each rental period, whether that is monthly, annually, or otherwise.

If the tenant fails to pay rent on time, the landlord has several remedies. She is entitled to apply the security deposit to the unpaid rent. She may also sue the tenant for nonpayment of rent, demanding the unpaid sums, cost of collection, and interest. Finally, the landlord may evict a tenant who has failed to pay rent.

State statutes prescribe the steps a landlord must take to evict a tenant for nonpayment. Typically, the landlord must serve a termination notice on the tenant and wait for a court hearing. At the hearing, the landlord must prove that the tenant has failed to pay rent on time. If the tenant has no excuse for the nonpayment, the court grants an order evicting him. The order authorizes a sheriff to remove the tenant's goods and place them in storage, at the tenant's expense. However, if the tenant was withholding rent because of unlivable conditions, the court may refuse to evict.

Duty to Use Premises Properly

A lease normally lists what a tenant may do in the premises and prohibits other activities. For example, a residential lease allows the tenant to use the property for normal living purposes, but not for any retail, commercial, or industrial purpose.

A tenant is liable to the landlord for any significant damage he causes to the property. The tenant is not liable for normal wear and tear. If, however, he knocks a hole in a wall or damages the plumbing, the landlord may collect the cost of repairs, either by using the security deposit or by suing if necessary.

Injuries

Tenant's Liability

A tenant is generally liable for injuries occurring within the premises she is leasing, whether that is an apartment, a store, or otherwise. If a tenant permits grease to accumulate on a kitchen floor and a guest slips and falls, the tenant is liable. If a merchant negligently installs display shelving that tips onto a customer, the merchant pays for the harm. Generally, a tenant is not liable for injuries occurring in common areas over which she has no control, such as exterior walkways. If a tenant's dinner guest falls because the building's common stairway has loose steps, the landlord is probably liable.

Landlord's Liability

Historically, the common law held a landlord responsible only for injuries that occurred in the common areas or due to the landlord's negligent maintenance of the property. Increasingly, though, the law holds landlords liable under the normal rules of negligence law. **In many states, a landlord must use reasonable care to maintain safe premises and is liable for foreseeable harm.** For example, most states now have building codes that require a landlord to maintain structural elements in safe condition. States further imply a warranty of habitability, which mandates reasonably safe living conditions.

Crime.   Landlords may be liable in negligence to tenants or their guests for criminal attacks that occur on the premises. Courts have struggled with this issue and have reached opposing results in similar cases. The very prevalence of crime sharpens the debate. What must a landlord do to protect a tenant? Courts typically answer the question by looking at four factors.

- *Nature of the Crime.* How did the crime occur? Could the landlord have prevented it?
- *Reasonable Person Standard.* What would a reasonable landlord have done to prevent this type of crime? What did the landlord actually do?
- *Foreseeability.* Was it reasonably foreseeable that such a crime might occur? Were there earlier incidents or warnings?
- *Prevalence of Crime in the Area.* If the general area, or the particular premises, has a high crime rate, courts are more likely to hold that the crime was foreseeable and the landlord responsible.

The following case highlights some of the issues facing courts as they apply changing mores to a tragic loss.

DICKINSON ARMS-REO, L.P. V. CAMPBELL

4 S.W.3d 333
Texas Court of Appeals, 1999

Facts: About midnight, Joe Campbell and his girlfriend, Jenny Cady, left a club in separate cars, agreeing to meet at her apartment. Campbell parked his pickup truck in a space at the Dickinson Arms Apartments, where Cady lived.

Meanwhile, two sixteen-year-olds, Jeremy Gartrell and Donald Nichols, members of the Assassins, were visiting a fellow gang member who lived at the apartments. Gartrell approached Campbell, demanded the truck, and shot Campbell with a .22 caliber pistol, killing him. Gartrell was convicted of murder and sentenced to 50 years.

Campbell's parents sued the Dickinson Arms, claiming that the landlord's neglect of security had permitted the killing. Testimony indicated that over a three-year period, there had been 184 reported criminal offenses at the apartments. The property manager testified that no one told her gang members lived in the complex; company policy required her to check with police for possible preventive safety programs, but she had never done so; and she had never performed a security survey of the complex. The plaintiffs' expert witness testified that because of the high crime rates, the Dickinson Arms should have been protected with a perimeter fence, gates, and a security guard.

The jury found that the landlord failed to provide adequate security, and gave a judgment of $341,000 for the plaintiffs. The Dickinson Arms appealed.

Issue: Was the landlord liable for the murder?

Excerpts from Justice Mirabal's Decision: For a landowner to foresee criminal conduct on property, there must be evidence that other crimes have occurred on the property or in its immediate vicinity. Foreseeability also depends on how recently and how often criminal conduct has occurred in the past. The previous crimes must be sufficiently similar to the crime in question as to place the landowner on notice of the specific danger. However, the prior crimes need not be identical. The following evidence is relevant to similarity of other crimes: Out of the 184 crimes described in exhibit no. 38, there are included:

20 burglaries

13 auto thefts

11 assaults

8 thefts

These types of crimes could make the risk of other violent crimes, such as murder, foreseeable if there would be a confrontation.

Defendants argue that the shooter, Jeremy Gartrell, was an unstoppable and undeterrable individual whose conduct had no relation to defendant's alleged negligence. Defendants assert that the carjacking and shooting would have taken place even if defendants had used all reasonable care.

Defendants rely heavily on the testimony of their expert witness who testified that a security guard, perimeter fencing, and limited access gates would not have stopped an offender like Gartrell, who was an impulsive, explosive type individual—a time bomb just waiting to happen. Defendants also rely on the testimony of the former high school principal and Gartrell's peers regarding his violent nature, lack of respect for authority, and undeterrability.

Plaintiffs counter that the evidence shows Gartrell had wanted to do a car-jacking throughout much of the day and had ample opportunities to do so, but he was deterred by the surroundings. For example, before going to the Dickinson Arms Apartments, Gartrell and Nichols were at the nearby Taco Bell and Gartrell told Nichols he was going to car-jack a green Mustang that had pulled up. There were people present and Taco Bell was well-lit; Nichols said something like "Don't be stupid." Gartrell did not car-jack the green Mustang. Then Gartrell and Nichols walked to the next-door parking lot of Kroger's on the way to the apartments; the parking lot presented the opportunity to car-jack someone, but it was well-lit and Gartrell did not do so. Though he had spoken of car-jacking someone most of the day, it was not until Gartrell came to the Dickinson Arms Apartments—a place Nichols testified was dark and where they knew there was no security guard or access control gates—that he actually

▼

did a car-jacking. The evidence was conflicting regarding lighting in the parking lot the night of Campbell's murder: Charlotte Davis testified the lighting in the parking lot was good enough for her to see Campbell's body and truck from her apartment window; Nichols specifically testified it was dark in the parking lot that night and that there were no lights working in that area.

Plaintiffs' expert witness testified that if defendants had access control gates, a night security guard, and perimeter fencing, this offense, in all probability, would not have happened. Mindful that it is the role of the jury to resolve conflicts in the evidence, we conclude the evidence is legally and factually sufficient to support the jury's cause in fact determination.

We affirm the judgment. ■

Devil's Advocate	Gartrell was a lawful visitor to the apartments, as he would have been had there been more security. If there had been a guard, was he supposed to search all guests? All residents? Only suspected gang members? The court does not explain how the improved security would have prevented this crime. The decision imposes an unfair punishment on a low-rent apartment complex. The result will be greater expense to the owner, higher rents for tenants—and no guarantee of more security for anyone. ◆

PERSONAL PROPERTY

Personal property means all property other than real property. Real property, as we know, refers to land and things firmly attached to it. All other property is personal: a bus, a toothbrush, a share of stock. Most personal property is goods, meaning something that can be moved. We have already examined the purchase and sale of goods, which are governed by the Uniform Commercial Code (UCC). Now we look at two important aspects of personal property: gifts and bailments.

Gifts

A gift is a voluntary transfer of property from one person to another without any consideration. It is the lack of consideration that distinguishes a gift from a contract. Contracts usually consist of mutual promises to do something in the future. Each promise is consideration for the other one, and the mutual consideration makes each promise enforceable. But a gift is a one-way transaction, without consideration. The person who gives property away is the **donor** and the one who receives it is the **donee.**

A gift involves **three elements:**

- The donor intends to transfer ownership of the property to the donee immediately.
- The donor delivers the property to the donee.
- The donee accepts the property.

Intention to Transfer Ownership

The donor must intend to transfer ownership to the property right away, immediately giving up all control of the item. Notice the two important parts of this element. First, the donor's intention must be to transfer ownership—that is, to give title to the donee. Merely proving that the owner handed you property does not guarantee that you have received a gift; if the owner only intended that you use the item, there is no gift and she can demand it back.

Second, the donor must also intend the property to transfer *immediately.* A promise to make a gift in the future is unenforceable. Promises about future behavior are governed by contract law, and a contract is unenforceable without consideration. That is why poor Charley, at the beginning of this chapter, will never collect his $100,000 from the banker. If the banker had handed Charley the cash as he gushed his extravagant words, Charley could keep the money. However, the banker's promise to make the gift the next day is legally worthless. Nor does Charley have an enforceable contract, since there was no consideration for the banker's promise.

A *revocable gift* is a contradiction in terms, because it violates the rule just discussed. It is not a gift, and the donee keeps nothing.[6] Suppose Harold tells his daughter Faith, "The mule is yours from now on, but if you start acting stupid again, I'm taking her back." Harold has retained some control over the animal, which means he has not intended to transfer ownership. There is no gift, and Harold still owns the mule.

Delivery

Physical Delivery.   The donor must deliver the property to the donee. Generally, this involves physical delivery. If Anna hands Eddie a Rembrandt drawing, saying, "I want you to have this forever," she has satisfied the delivery requirement. This is the element missing from the banker's "gift" to Charley.

Constructive Delivery.   Physical delivery is the most common and the surest way to make a gift, but it is not always necessary. **A donor makes constructive delivery by transferring ownership without a physical delivery.** Most courts permit constructive delivery only when physical delivery is impossible or extremely inconvenient. Suppose Anna wants to give her niece Jen a blimp, which is parked in a hangar at the airport. The blimp will not fit through the doorway of Jen's dorm. Instead of flying the aircraft to the university, Anna may simply deliver to Jen the certificate of title and the keys to the blimp. When she has done that, Jen owns the aircraft.

Inter Vivos Gifts and Gifts Causa Mortis

A gift can be either *inter vivos* or *causa mortis*. **An *inter vivos* gift means a gift made during life—that is, when the donor is not under any fear of impending death.** The vast majority of gifts are *inter vivos*, involving a healthy donor and donee. Shirley, age 30 and in good health, gives her husband Terry an eraser for his birthday. This is an *inter vivos* gift, which is absolute. The gift becomes final upon delivery, and the donor may not revoke it. If Shirley and Terry have a fight the next day, Shirley has no power to erase her gift.

A gift *causa mortis* is one made in contemplation of approaching death. The gift is valid if the donor dies as expected but is revoked if he recovers. Suppose Lance's doctors have told him he will probably die of a liver ailment within a month. Lance calls Jane to his bedside and hands her a fistful of emeralds, saying, "I'm dying; these are yours." Jane sheds a tear, then sprints to the bank. If Lance dies of the liver ailment within a few weeks, Jane gets to keep the emeralds. The law permits the gift *causa mortis* to act as a substitute for a will because the donor's delivery of the property clearly indicates his intentions. But note that this kind of gift is revocable. Since a gift *causa mortis* is conditional (upon the donor's death), the donor has the right to revoke it at any time before he dies. If Lance telephones Jane the next day and says that he has changed his mind, he gets the jewels back. Further, if the donor recovers and does not die as expected, the gift is automatically revoked.

Acceptance

The donee must accept the gift. This rarely leads to disputes, but if a donee should refuse a gift and then change her mind, she is out of luck. Her repudiation of the donor's offer means there is no gift, and she has no rights in the property.

---

[6] The only exception to this rule is a gift *causa mortis,* discussed in a later section.

The following case offers a combination of love and anger, alcohol and diamonds—always a volatile mix.

YOU BE THE JUDGE

ALBINGER V. HARRIS

2002 Mont. 118, 2002 WL 1226858
Montana Supreme Court, 2002

Facts: Michelle Harris and Michael Albinger lived together, on and off, for three years. Their roller-coaster relationship was marred by alcohol abuse and violence. When they announced their engagement, Albinger gave Harris a $29,000 diamond ring, but the couple broke off their wedding plans because of emotional and physical turmoil. Harris returned the ring. Later, they reconciled and resumed their marriage plans, and Albinger gave his fiancee the ring again. This cycle repeated several times over the three years. Each time they broke off their relationship, Harris returned the ring to Albinger, and each time they made up, he gave it back to her.

On one occasion Albinger held a knife over Harris as she lay in bed, threatening to chop off her finger if she didn't remove the ring. He beat her and forcibly removed the ring. Criminal charges were brought but then dropped when, inevitably, the couple reconciled. Another time, Albinger told her to "take the car, the horse, the dog, and the ring and get the hell out." Finally, mercifully, they ended their stormy affair, and Harris moved to Kentucky—keeping the ring.

Albinger sued for the value of the ring. The trial court found that the ring was a conditional gift, made in contemplation of marriage, and ordered Harris to pay its full value. She appealed. The Montana Supreme Court had to decide, in a case of first impression, whether an engagement ring was given in contemplation of marriage. (In Montana and in many states, neither party to a broken engagement may sue for breach of contract, because it is impossible to determine who is responsible for ending the relationship.)

You Be the Judge: Who owns the ring?

Argument for Harris: The main problem with calling the ring a "conditional gift" is that there is no such thing. The elements of a gift are intent, delivery, and acceptance, and Harris has proven all three. A gift is not a contract, nor is it a loan. Once a gift has been accepted, the donor has no more rights in the property and may not demand its return. Hundreds of years of litigation have resulted in only one exception to this rule—a gift *causa mortis*—and despite some cynical claims to the contrary, marriage is not death. If this court carves a new exception to the long-standing rule, other unhappy donors will dream up more "conditions" that supposedly entitle them to their property. What is more, to create a special rule for engagement rings would be blatant gender bias, because the exception would only benefit men. This court should stick to settled law, and permit the recipient of a gift to keep it.

Argument for Albinger: The symbolism of an engagement ring is not exactly news. For decades, Americans have given rings—frequently diamond—in contemplation of marriage. All parties understand why the gift is made and what is expected if the engagement is called off: the ring must be returned. Albinger's intent, to focus on one element, was conditional—and Michelle Harris understood that. Each time the couple separated, she gave the ring back. She knew that she could wear this beautiful ring in anticipation of their marriage, but that custom and decency required its return if the wedding was off. She knew it, that is, until greed got the better of her and she fled to Kentucky, attempting to profit at the expense of Albinger's generosity. We are not asking for new law, but for confirmation of what everyone has known for generations: there is no wedding ring when there is no wedding. ●

The following chart distinguishes between a contract and a gift:

A Contract and a Gift Distinguished	
A Contract:	
Lou: I will pay you $2,000 to paint the house if you promise to finish by July 3.	Abby: I agreed to paint the house by July 3 for $2,000.
Lou and Abby have a contract. Each promise is consideration in support of the other promise. Lou and Abby can each enforce the other's promise.	
A Gift:	
Lou hands Phil two opera tickets, while saying:	
Lou: I want you to have these two tickets to *Rigoletto*.	Phil: Hey, thanks.
This is a valid *inter vivos* gift. Lou intended to transfer ownership immediately and deliver the property to Phil, who now owns the tickets.	
Neither Contract nor Gift:	
Lou: You're a great guy. Next week, I'm going to give you two tickets to *Rigoletto*.	Jason: Hey, thanks.
There is no gift because Lou did not intend to transfer ownership immediately, and he did not deliver the tickets. There is no contract because Jason has given no consideration to support Lou's promise.	

Bailment

A bailment is the rightful possession of goods by one who is not the owner. The one who delivers the goods is the **bailor** and the one in possession is the **bailee**. Bailments are common. Suppose you are going out of town for the weekend and loan your motorcycle to Stan. You are the bailor and your friend is the bailee. When you check your suitcase with the airline, you are again the bailor and the airline is the bailee. If you rent a car at your destination, you become the bailee while the rental agency is the bailor. In each case, someone other than the true owner has rightful, temporary possession of personal property.

The parties generally—but not always—create a bailment by agreement. In each of the examples, the parties agreed to the bailment. In two cases, the agreement included payment, which is common but not essential. When you buy your airline ticket, you pay for your ticket, and the price includes the airline's agreement, as bailee, to transport your suitcase. When you rent a car, you pay the bailor for the privilege of using it. By loaning your motorcycle, you engage in a bailment without either party paying compensation.

A bailment without any agreement is called a constructive, or involuntary, bailment. Suppose you find a wristwatch in your house that you know belongs to a friend. You are obligated to return the watch to the true owner, and until you do so, you are the bailee, liable for harm to the property. This is called a constructive bailment because, with no agreement between the parties, the law is *construing* a bailment.

Because the bailor is the one who delivers the goods to another, the bailor is typically the owner, but he need not be. Suppose that Stan, who borrowed your motorcycle, allows his girlfriend Sheila to try out the bike, and she takes it to a mall where she jumps over a row of six parked cars. Stan, the bailee from you, has become a bailor, and Sheila is his bailee.

Control

To create a bailment, the bailee must assume physical control with intent to possess. A bailee may be liable for loss or damage to the property. But it is not fair to hold him liable unless he has taken physical control of the goods, intending to possess them.

Disputes about whether someone has taken control often arise in parking lot cases. When a car is damaged or stolen, the lot's owner may try to avoid liability by claiming it lacked control of the parked auto and therefore was not a bailee. If the lot is a "park and lock" facility, where the car's owner retains the key and the lot owner exercises no control at all, then there may be no bailment, and no liability for damage. (For a sample automobile bailment form, see **http://www.gate.net/~legalsvc/autobail.html.**)

By contrast, when a driver leaves her keys with a parking attendant, the lot clearly is exercising control of the auto, and the parties have created a bailment. The lot is probably liable for loss or damage. What about cases in the middle, where the driver keeps her keys but the lot owner exercises *some other control?* There is no uniform rule, but the trend is probably toward liability for the lot owner.

Rights of the Bailee

The bailee's primary right is possession of the property. Anyone who interferes with the bailee's rightful possession is liable to her. **The bailee is typically, though not always, permitted to use the property.** Obviously, a customer is permitted to drive a car rented from an agency. When a farmer loans his tractor to a neighbor, the bailee is entitled to use the machine for normal farm purposes. But some bailees have no authority to use the goods. If you store your furniture in a warehouse, the storage company is your bailee, but it has no right to curl up in your bed. The bailee may or may not be entitled to compensation, depending on the parties' agreement.

Duties of the Bailee

The bailee is strictly liable to redeliver the goods on time to the bailor or to whomever the bailor designates. Strict liability means there are virtually no exceptions. Rudy stores his $6,000 drum set with Melissa's Warehouse while he is on vacation. Blake arrives at the warehouse and shows a forged letter, supposedly from Rudy, granting Blake permission to remove the drums. If Melissa permits Blake to take the drums, she will owe Rudy $6,000, even if the forgery was a high-quality job.

Due Care

The bailee is obligated to exercise due care. **The level of care required depends upon who receives the benefit of the bailment.** There are three possibilities.

- *Sole Benefit of Bailee.* If the bailment is for the sole benefit of the bailee, the bailee is required to use **extraordinary care** with the property. Generally, in these cases, the bailor loans something for free to the bailee. If your neighbor loans you a power lawn mower, the bailment is probably for your sole benefit. You are liable if you are even slightly inattentive in handling the lawn mower and can expect to pay for virtually any harm done.

- *Mutual Benefit.* When the bailment is for the mutual benefit of bailor and bailee, the bailee must use **ordinary care** with the property. Ordinary care is what a reasonably prudent person would use under the circumstances. When you rent a car, you benefit from the use of the car, and the agency profits from the fee you pay. Most bailments benefit both parties, and courts decide the majority of bailment disputes under this standard.

- *Sole Benefit of Bailor.* When the bailment benefits only the bailor, the bailee must use only **slight care.** This kind of bailment is called a **gratuitous bailment,** and the bailee is liable only for **gross negligence.** Sheila enters a greased-pig contest and asks you to hold her $140,000 diamond engagement ring while she competes. You put the ring in your pocket. Sheila wins the $20 first prize, but the ring has disappeared. This was a gratuitous bailment, and you are not liable to Sheila unless she can prove gross negligence on your part. If the ring dropped from your pocket or was stolen, you are not liable. If you used the ring to play catch with friends, you are liable.

Burden of Proof.   In an ordinary negligence case, the plaintiff has the burden of proof to demonstrate that the defendant was negligent and caused the alleged harm. In bailment cases, the burden of proof is reversed. **Once the bailor has proven the existence of a bailment and loss or harm to the goods, a presumption of negligence arises, and the burden shifts to the bailee to prove adequate care.** This is a major change from ordinary negligence cases. Georgina's car is struck by another auto. If Georgina sues for negligence, it is her burden to prove that the defendant was driving unreasonably and caused the harm. By comparison, assume that Georgina rents Sam her sailboat for a month. At the end of the month, Sam announces that the boat is at the bottom of Lake Michigan. If Georgina sues Sam, she only needs to demonstrate that the parties had a bailment and that he failed to return the boat. The burden then shifts to Sam to prove that the boat was lost through no fault of his own. If he cannot meet that burden, Georgina recovers the full value of the boat.

The parties may use a contract to specify whether they have created a bailment, hoping to protect their rights. But even then things do not always go smoothly, as the following case demonstrates.

MITCHELL V. BANK OF AMERICA NATIONAL ASSOCIATION

2002 WL 31139375
Court of Appeals of Texas, 2002

Facts: Donna and Timothy Mitchell rented a safe deposit box from a Dallas branch of the Bank of America. The lease agreement stated that the bank "had no possession or custody of, nor control over, the contents of the Box, and the Lessee [the couple] assumes all risks in connection with the depositing of such content." The lease also permitted the bank to remove the box's contents if the rental fee went unpaid.

Bank officers, believing the Mitchells were behind in their rental fees, drilled into the box and removed the contents, which they inventoried and sent to a central vault elsewhere. When the Mitchells learned of this, they were very upset and "loudly discussed the value of the contents" in the lobby of the Dallas branch.

A week later, the bank informed the Mitchells the contents were back at the Dallas branch. The couple placed the contents into a bag, which they put under the front seat of their car. Shortly after leaving the bank, the Mitchells had a flat tire. A stranger offered assistance. While they were all changing the tire, the bag disappeared.

▼

The Mitchells sued the bank, claiming that its negligence enabled bank employees to learn of the box's contents. In a well-prepared scam, an employee or his accomplice let the air out of the couple's tire, offered roadside assistance, and stole the bag.

The trial court gave summary judgment for the bank, finding that the contract language quoted above meant that there was no bailment and no possible negligence. The Mitchells appealed.

Issue: Was there a bailment?

Excerpts from Judge Farris's Decision: The Bank moved for summary judgment on the Mitchells' breach of bailment claim on the grounds the lease superseded any common law bailment claim. Generally, bailment relationships are governed by common law principles of negligence. However, the parties to the bailment can abrogate the law of bailment through an express written agreement that clearly varies the liability imposed by the law. To the extent the lease agreement clearly addressed the duties and liabilities of the Bank for the Mitchells' property, the lease agreement controls.

To establish a bailment, there must be a delivery of personal property from one person to another for a specific purpose. The lease clearly provides that so long as the contents of the box remained in the box, there was no delivery of the property to the Bank. Accordingly, no bailment occurred due to the deposit of the Mitchells' property into the box.

However, the lease authorized the Bank to remove the contents of the box for the non-payment of rent. The lease thus contemplated a delivery of the property to the Bank under certain circumstances and did not change the duties imposed by law once the Bank exercised its right to take control of the property. The trial court thus erred in granting summary judgment for the Bank on the grounds the Mitchells' common law cause of action for breach of bailment was superseded by the written contract. ■

Rights and Duties of the Bailor. The bailor's rights and duties are the reverse of the bailee's. The bailor is entitled to the return of his property on the agreed-upon date. He is also entitled to receive the property in good condition and to recover damages for harm to the property if the bailee failed to use adequate care.

Liability for Defects

Depending upon the type of bailment, the bailor is potentially liable for known or even unknown defects in the property. **If the bailment is for the sole benefit of the bailee, the bailor must notify the bailee of any known defects.** Suppose Megan lends her stepladder to Dave. The top rung is loose, and Megan knows it but forgets to tell Dave. The top rung crumbles and Dave falls onto his girlfriend's deck. Megan is liable to Dave and the girlfriend unless the defect in the ladder was obvious. Notice that Megan's liability is not only to the bailee but also to any others injured by the defects. Megan would not be liable if she had notified Dave of the defective rung.

In a mutual-benefit bailment, the bailor is liable not only for known defects but also for unknown defects that the bailor could have discovered with reasonable diligence. Suppose RentaLot rents a power sander to Dan. RentaLot does not realize that the sander has faulty wiring, but a reasonable inspection would have revealed the problem. When Dan suffers a serious shock from the defect, RentaLot is liable to him, even though it was unaware of the problem.

Chapter Conclusion

Real property law is ancient but forceful, as waterfront property owners discovered when a power company flooded their land and an old-fashioned easement deprived them of compensation. Had the families understood nonpossessory interests, they might have declined to buy the property. Landlord-tenant law, by contrast, is new and rapidly changing, especially as to liability for injuries. Personal property law affects most of us every day, as we leave goods with a repair shop or accept a diamond engagement ring. Understanding property law can be worth a lot of money, even if the wedding is cancelled.

Chapter Review

1. Real property includes land, buildings, air and subsurface rights, plant life, and fixtures. A fixture is any good that has become attached to other real property.

2. A fee simple absolute provides the owner with the greatest possible control of the property, including the right to make any lawful use of it and to sell it. A fee simple defeasible may terminate upon the occurrence of some limiting event. A life estate permits the owner to possess the property during her life but not to sell it or leave it to heirs.

3. An easement gives a person the right to enter land belonging to another and make a limited use of it, without taking anything away.

4. The implied warranty of habitability means that a builder selling a new home guarantees the adequacy of materials and workmanship.

5. The seller of a home must disclose facts that a buyer does not know and cannot readily observe if they materially affect the property's value.

6. When an owner of a freehold estate allows another person temporary, exclusive possession of the property, the parties have created a landlord-tenant relationship.

7. Any lease for a stated, fixed period is a tenancy for years. A periodic tenancy is created for a fixed period and then automatically continues for additional periods until either party notifies the other of termination. A tenancy at will has no fixed duration and may be terminated by either party at any time. A tenancy at sufferance occurs when a tenant remains, against the wishes of the landlord, after the expiration of a true tenancy.

8. A landlord may be liable for constructive eviction if he substantially interferes with the tenant's use and enjoyment of the premises.

9. The implied warranty of habitability requires that a landlord meet all standards set by the local building code and/or that the premises be fit for human habitation.

10. The tenant is obligated to pay the rent and must pay the landlord for any significant damage he causes to the property.

11. At common law, a landlord had very limited liability for injuries on the premises, but today many courts require a landlord to use reasonable care and hold her liable for foreseeable harm.

12. A gift is a voluntary transfer of property from one person to another without consideration. The elements of a gift are intention to transfer ownership immediately, delivery, and acceptance.

13. A bailment is the rightful possession of goods by one who is not the owner. The one who delivers the goods is the bailor and the one in possession is the bailee. To create a bailment, the bailee must assume physical control with intent to possess.

14. The bailee is obligated to exercise due care. The level of care required depends upon who receives the benefit of the bailment: if the bailee is the sole beneficiary, she must use extraordinary care; if the parties mutually benefit, the bailee must use ordinary care; and if the bailor is the sole beneficiary of the bailment, the bailee must use only slight care.

Practice Test

1. Paul and Shelly Higgins had two wood stoves in their home. Each rested on, but was not attached to, a built-in brick platform. The downstairs wood stove was connected to the chimney flue and was used as part of the main heating system for the house. The upstairs stove, in the master bedroom, was purely decorative. It had no stovepipe connecting it to the chimney. The Higginses sold their house to Jack Everitt, and neither party said anything about the two stoves. Is Everitt entitled to either stove? Both stoves?

2. In 1944, W. E. Collins conveyed land to the Church of God of Prophecy. The deed said: "This deed is made with the full understanding

that should the property fail to be used for the Church of God, it is to be null and void and property to revert to W. E. Collins or heirs." In the late 1980s, the church wished to move to another property and sought a judicial ruling that it had the right to sell the land. The trial court ruled that the church owned a fee simple absolute and had the right to sell the property. Comment.

3. *CPA QUESTION* On July 1, 1992, Quick, Onyx, and Nash were deeded a piece of land as tenants in common. The deed provided that Quick owned half the property and Onyx and Nash owned one quarter each. If Nash dies, the property will be owned as follows:

   a. Quick 1/2, Onyx 1/2

   b. Quick 5/8, Onyx 3/8

   c. Quick 1/3, Onyx 1/3, Nash's heirs 1/3

   d. Quick 1/2, Onyx 1/4, Nash's heirs 1/4

4. Summey Building Systems built a condominium project in Myrtle Beach, South Carolina. The project included an adjacent parking deck. Shortly after Summey relinquished control to the condominium association, the deck began to experience problems. Water and caustic materials leaked through the upper deck and dripped onto cars parked underneath. Cracks appeared, and an expert concluded that the bond between the top deck and the structural supports was insufficient. Repairs would cost about $205,000. Summey had never warranted that the deck would be free of all problems. Is the company liable for the repairs?

5. Kenmart Realty sued to evict Mr. and Ms. Alghalabio for nonpayment of rent and sought the unpaid monies, totaling several thousand dollars. In defense, the Alghalabios claimed that their apartment was infested with rats. They testified that there were numerous rat holes in the walls of the living room, bedroom, and kitchen, that there were rat droppings all over the apartment, and that on one occasion they saw their toddler holding a live rat. They testified that the landlord had refused numerous requests to exterminate. Please rule on the landlord's suit.

6. *YOU BE THE JUDGE* WRITING PROBLEM Dominion Bank owned a large office building in Washington, D.C. Because it planned to sell the building, the bank stopped leasing new space and

five of the 13 floors became vacant. Tenants complained to the bank that vagrants were using the empty spaces for drug deals and prostitution. Jane Doe, a secretary who worked in the building, was dragged to an empty, unlocked floor and raped. She sued the bank. A security expert testified that all vacant offices and floors should have been sealed off. Is the bank liable for Doe's injuries? **Argument for Jane Doe:** The bank created a dangerous situation by gradually abandoning a commercial building. The bank should be held to a "reasonable person" standard, one that it clearly failed to meet. **Argument for Dominion Bank:** The bank is not a police force. The bank's obligation was to keep the rented premises in good working order, which it did.

7. While in her second year at the Juilliard School of Music in New York City, Ann Rylands had a chance to borrow for one month a rare Guadagnini violin, made in 1768. She returned the violin to the owner in Philadelphia but telephoned her father to ask if he would buy it for her. He borrowed money from his pension fund and paid the owner. Ann traveled to Philadelphia to pick up the violin. She had exclusive possession of the violin for the next 20 years, using it in her professional career. Unfortunately, she became an alcoholic, and during one period when she was in a treatment center, she entrusted the violin to her mother for safekeeping. At about that time, her father died. When Ann was released from the center, she requested return of the violin, but her mother refused. Who owns the violin?

8. *ETHICS* Jane says to Cody, "If you will agree to work as my yard man, I'll pay you $1,000 per week for a normal work week. You can start on Monday, and I'll guarantee you eight months' work." Cody is elated at his good fortune and agrees to start work on Monday. Later that day, Cody, still rejoicing, says to Beth, his girlfriend, "You know those sapphire earrings in the jewelry store that you're wild about? At the end of next week I'm going to buy them for you." On Monday, Jane realizes what a foolish thing she said and refuses to hire Cody. Cody, in turn, refuses to buy the earrings for Beth. Cody sues Jane and wins; Beth sues Cody and loses. Why the opposite outcomes? What basic ideas of fairness underlie the two results?

9. Ronald Armstead worked for First American Bank as a courier. His duties included making

deliveries between the bank's branches in Washington, D.C. Armstead parked the bank's station wagon near the entrance of one branch in violation of a sign that read "No Parking Rush Hour Zone." In the rear luggage section of the station wagon were four locked bank dispatch bags containing checks and other valuable documents. Armstead had received tickets for illegal parking at this spot on five occasions. Shortly after Armstead entered the bank, a tow truck arrived and its operator prepared to tow the station wagon. Transportation Management, Inc., operated the towing service on behalf of the District of Columbia. Armstead ran out to the vehicle and told the tow truck operator that he was prepared to drive the vehicle away immediately. But the operator drove away with the station wagon in tow. One and one-half hours later, a bank employee paid for the car's release, but one dispatch bag, containing documents worth $107,000, was missing. First American sued Transportation Management and the District of Columbia. The defendants sought summary judgment, claiming they could not be liable. Were they correct?

10. ***YOU BE THE JUDGE*** WRITING PROBLEM Eileen Murphy often cared for her elderly neighbor, Thomas Kenney. He paid her $25 per day for her help and once gave her a bank certificate of deposit worth $25,000. Murphy alleged that shortly before his death, Kenney gave her a large block of shares in three corporations. He called his broker to instruct him to transfer the shares to Murphy's name, but the broker was unavailable. So Kenney told Murphy to write her name on the shares and keep them, which she did. Two weeks later Kenney died. When Murphy presented the shares to Kenney's broker to transfer ownership to her, the broker refused because Kenney had never signed them over to Murphy. Was Murphy entitled to the $25,000? To the shares? **Argument for Murphy:** The purpose of the law is to do what a donor intended, and it is obvious that Kenney intended Murphy to have the $25,000 and the shares. **Argument for the Estate:** Murphy is not entitled to the $25,000 because we have no way of knowing what Kenney's intentions were when he gave her the money. She is not entitled to the shares of stock because Kenney's failure to endorse them over to her meant he never delivered them.

11. ***ROLE REVERSAL*** Write a short-answer question focusing on one of the following: a fixture, an easement, or adverse possession.

12. ***ROLE REVERSAL*** Write a multiple-choice question highlighting the difference between any two of the following: a contract, an *inter vivos* gift, or a gift *causa mortis*.

Internet Research Problem

Go to http://www.tenantsunion.org/tulist.html, and search for the law of your state concerning a landlord's obligation to provide a habitable apartment. Now assume that you are living in a rental unit with serious defects. Write a letter to the landlord asking for prompt repairs. You may use the form letters provided at http://little.nhlink.net/nhlink/housing/cto/letters/letrs.htm as a guide.

You own a helicopter worth $250,000. A business associate wishes to use it for one week to show prospective clients around various islands in the Caribbean. You are willing to let him use it, for a fee of $15,000. Draft a bailment agreement. Use the form supplied at http://www.gate.net/~legalsvc/autobail.html as a model.

You can find further practice problems at academic.cengage.com/blaw/beatty.

24 Consumer Law

© PHOTODISC COLLECTION/GETTY IMAGES

Three women signed up for a lesson at the Arthur Murray dance studio in Washington, D.C. Expecting a session of decorous fun, they instead found themselves in a nightmare of humiliation and coercion:

- "First of all, I did not want the [additional] lesson, and I think it was unpleasant because I had three, maybe four, people, as I say, pressuring me to buy something by a certain time, and I do recall asking that I be let to think, let me think it over, and I was told that the contest would end at 6 o'clock or something to that effect and if I did not sign by a certain time it would be too late. I think we got under the deadline by maybe a minute or two. If I had been given time to think, I would not have signed that contract."

- "I tried to say no and get out of it and I got very, very upset because I got frightened at paying out all that money and having nothing to fall back on. I remember I started crying and couldn't stop crying. All I thought of was getting out of there. So finally after—I don't know how much time, Mr. Mara said, well, I could sign up for 250 hours, which was half the 500 Club, which would amount to $4,300. So I finally signed it. After that, I tried to raise the money from the bank and found I couldn't get a loan for that amount and I didn't have any savings and I had to get a bank loan to pay for it. That was when I went back and asked him to cancel that contract. But Mr. Mara said that he couldn't cancel it."

- "I did not join the carnival. I did not wish to join the carnival, and while it was only an additional $55, I had no desire to join. [My instructor] asked everyone in the room to sit down in a circle around me and he stood me up in that circle, in the middle of the circle, and said, 'Everybody, I want you to look at this woman here who is too cheap to join the carnival. I just want you to look at a woman like that. Isn't it awful?'"

Because of abuses such as these, the Federal Trade Commission (FTC) ordered the Arthur Murray dance studio to halt its high-pressure sales techniques, limit each contract to no more than $1,500 in dance lessons, and permit all contracts to be canceled within seven days.[1] ■

INTRODUCTION

Years ago consumers typically dealt with merchants they knew well. A dance instructor in a small town would not stay in business long if he tormented his elderly, vulnerable clients. As the population of this country grew and cities expanded, however, merchants became less and less subject to community pressure. The law has supplemented, if not replaced, these informal policing mechanisms. Both Congress and the states have passed statutes that protect consumers from the unscrupulous. But the legal system in America is generally too slow and expensive to handle small cases. The women who fell into the web of Arthur Murray had neither the wealth nor the energy to sue the studio themselves. To aid consumers such as these, Congress empowered federal agencies to enforce consumer laws. The FTC is the most important of these agencies.

Federal Trade Commission

Congress created the FTC in 1915 to regulate business. Although its original focus was on antitrust law, it now regulates a wide range of business activities that affect consumers, everything from advertising to consumer loans to warranties to debt collection practices.[2] It is, if you will, the consumer's best friend in Washington. The FTC has several options for enforcing the law:

- *Voluntary Compliance.* When the FTC determines that a business has violated the law, it first asks the offender to sign a voluntary compliance affidavit promising to stop the prohibited activity.

- *Administrative Hearings and Appeals.* If the company refuses to stop voluntarily, the FTC takes the case to an administrative law judge (ALJ) within the agency. The violator may settle the case at this point by signing a **consent order.** If the case proceeds to a hearing, the ALJ has the right to issue a **cease and desist order,** commanding the violator to stop the offending activity. The FTC issued a cease and desist order against the Arthur Murray dance studio. A defendant can appeal such an order to the five Commissioners of the FTC, from there to a federal appeals court, and ultimately to the United States Supreme Court. Both the Commissioners and the Fifth Circuit Court of Appeals confirmed the cease and desist order against Arthur Murray. The case never reached the Supreme Court.

- *Penalties.* The FTC can impose a fine for each violation of:
  - a voluntary compliance affidavit;
  - a consent order;
  - a cease and desist order;
  - an FTC rule; or
  - a cease and desist order issued against *someone else.*

---

[1] *In re Arthur Murray Studio of Washington, Inc.,* 78 F.T.C. 401, 1971 FTC LEXIS 75 (1971).
[2] Chapter 20 discusses the FTC's role in antitrust enforcement.

For example, the Arthur Murray studio could be liable for violating an FTC cease and desist order prohibiting high-pressure sales by the Fred Astaire studio. In addition, the FTC can file suit in federal court asking for damages on behalf of an injured consumer if (1) the defendant has violated FTC rules and (2) a reasonable person would have known under the circumstances that the conduct was dishonest or fraudulent.

SALES

Section 5 of the Federal Trade Commission Act (FTC Act) prohibits "unfair and deceptive acts or practices." You can report an unfair or deceptive practice to the FTC at its Website (**http://www.ftc.gov**).

Deceptive Acts or Practices

Many deceptive acts or practices involve advertisements. **Under the FTC Act, an advertisement is deceptive if it contains an important misrepresentation or omission that is likely to mislead a reasonable consumer.** A company advertised that a pain-relief ointment called "Aspercreme" provided "the strong relief of aspirin right where you hurt." From this ad and the name of the product, do you assume that the ointment contains aspirin? Are you a reasonable consumer? Consumers surveyed in a shopping mall believed the product contained aspirin. In fact, it does not. The FTC required the company to disclose that there is no aspirin in Aspercreme.[3]

Is there anything wrong with the following ads?

Do not believe a word of them, warns the FTC. It takes more than three minutes a day to get six-pack abs, no matter what equipment you use. As for the #1 Doctor Recommended Ensure, the doctors in the survey were asked which liquid meal they would choose, if they were going to recommend one to a patient. In fact, most doctors would not recommend Ensure to the healthy adults pictured in the advertisements. The half-price cars were for lease, not sale. By the end of the lease, owners would have paid only half the value of the cars, but they would also have to return the cars to the dealer. Was the company in the following case deceptive about its business opportunity?

---

[3] *In re Thompson Medical Co., Inc.*, 104 F.T.C. 648, 1984 FTC LEXIS 6 (1984).

YOU BE THE JUDGE

FEDERAL TRADE COMMISSION V. TASHMAN

318 F.3d 1273, 2003 U.S. App. LEXIS -1123
United States Court of Appeals for the Eleventh Circuit, 2003

Facts: Stephen Tashman owned Telecard Dispensing Corp. (TDC), which sold dispensing machines for phone cards (and the cards to go in them). To get the attention of passersby, these machines would call out, "Hi there! Get your long distance phone card and call anywhere, anytime, from any touchtone phone without a penny in your pocket and save up to 50 percent. Buy it here, buy it now."

TDC ran the following radio advertisement:

"Do you really want to make more money—an additional 25 to 35 thousand dollars a year or more, possibly a lot more, and only work three to five hours per week? Stop the excuses. You can do it. You can change your life."

Anyone who answered this ad was connected with a telemarketer, known as a "fronter," who claimed: (1) TDC's locators would put machines in public places with traffic flow of at least 500 people per day; (2) according to TDC's experience, 2 percent of passersby were likely to purchase phone cards from the machines; and (3) entrepreneurs could be expected to pay off their machines in about six months. Disclosure statements sent to prospective customers claimed that TDC had received 287 positive letters and only 20 negative ones from purchasers. TDC also encouraged prospective customers to speak to references who would give firsthand testimony about the profitability of this business. Some of these references had never owned phone card vending machines, and all of them were paid for their praise.

Most of TDC's claims were false. Locators put machines anyplace that was available, no matter what the foot traffic. The 2 percent figure was completely made up. In one TDC experiment, the machines made no sales whatsoever. Undaunted, TDC began reporting the usage rate from an unrelated business—vending machines in which people attempted to catch stuffed animals with a mechanical crane. Most of the customers who bought machines did not recoup their original investment. TDC received 20 to 30 calls per day complaining about sluggish phone card sales. The FTC presented 14 witnesses who claimed to have lost substantial sums as TDC customers. TDC presented only one witness who claimed to have made a profit, but half his machines were purchased from other sources and they had four times the capacity of the TDC machines. There was some evidence, however, that migrant workers purchased phone cards from dispensing machines.

The FTC filed suit against TDC. The trial court found for the company and the FTC appealed.

You Be the Judge: Did TDC violate §5 of the FTC Act?

Argument for the FTC: Many of TDC's claims were false. How could it claim that each machine had daily foot traffic of 500 and that 2 percent of the passersby would purchase phone cards? The company's only data were based upon an entirely different product.

Argument for TDC: The phone card business is new and unproven. That does not mean it is fraudulent. This business is potentially an important and viable one but it is also a high-risk entrepreneurial activity. Prospective customers bear the responsibility of weighing the risks and profit potential, and of following up their investment with the hard work and business savvy necessary to make the venture successful. Not every business venture will work for every person. Moreover, reasonable customers would have understood that they could not make tens of thousands of dollars while working only three to five hours per week. They cannot expect protection from sheer gullibility.

The FTC's Rebuttal: The FTC Act does not provide immunity for new businesses. Indeed, it is precisely in the context of a new venture that investors are most likely to need accurate data because they are unlikely to have any of their own. *Caveat emptor* is simply not the law. ●

Unfair Practices

The FTC Act also prohibits unfair acts or practices. **The Commission considers a practice to be *unfair* if it meets all of the following three tests:**

- *It causes a substantial consumer injury.* This can mean physical or financial injury. A furnace repair company that dismantled home furnaces for "inspection" and then refused to reassemble them until the consumers agreed to buy services or replacement parts had caused a substantial consumer injury.

- *The harm of the injury outweighs any countervailing benefit.* A pharmaceutical company sold a sunburn remedy without conducting adequate tests to ensure that it worked. The expense of these tests would have forced the company to raise the product's price. The company had demonstrated that the product was safe, and there was evidence in the medical literature that the ingredients when used in other products were effective. The FTC determined that, although the company was technically in violation of its rules, the benefit to consumers of a cheaper product more than outweighed the risk of injury to them.

- *The consumer could not reasonably avoid the injury.* The FTC is particularly vigilant in protecting susceptible consumers—such as the elderly or the ill—who are less able to avoid injury. For instance, the Commission looks especially carefully at those who offer a cure for cancer.

In addition, the FTC may decide that a practice is unfair simply because it violates public policy even if it does not meet these three tests. The Commission refused to allow a mail-order company to file collection suits in states far from where the defendants lived because the practice was unfair, whether or not it met the three tests.

What is the difference between *deceptive* and *unfair?* Consider this case: Audio Communications, Inc. (ACI) ran a telephone service for children. By dialing a 900 number, children could listen to recorded stories or games featuring characters such as Santa Claus and the Easter Bunny. ACI ran advertisements on children's TV shows and in children's magazines. The FTC held that the ads were *deceptive* because they did not reveal that the phone calls cost money. Moreover, the ads promised a free gift in return for one phone call. In reality, callers (who were, after all, young children) could not obtain a gift without following several complicated steps that were explained very rapidly. Often, more than one call was necessary to obtain the gift. This practice was also *unfair* because children often made the calls without parental permission. Parents (who paid the bill) had little control over children (who made the call). In its consent order, the FTC required ACI to include in all of its advertisements the following statement: "Kids, you must ask your mom or dad and get their permission before you call. This call costs money."[4]

Other Sales Practices

Bait and Switch

FTC rules prohibit bait and switch advertisements: a merchant may not advertise a product and then disparage it to consumers in an effort to sell a different item. In addition, merchants must have enough stock on hand to meet reasonable demand for any advertised product. Sears ran many advertisements like the one on page 617.

---

[4] F.T.C., 56 C.F.R. 22432 (May 15, 1991).

Portable Zig-Zag Sewing Machine

from SEARS

$58

Sews on buttons, sews buttonholes
Does zig-zag or straight stitching
monograms, appliqués, other fancy work
for household linens, gifts
Sews forward and reverse for her convenience

When eager customers went to buy this fabulous item, they were told that the machines were noisy, did not come with Sears's standard sewing machine guarantee, and could neither stitch in reverse nor do buttonholes. Also, the store was out of stock and would not be receiving any new machines for a long time.[5]

This is bait and switch advertising, and it violates FTC rules. The **bait** is an alluring offer that sounds almost too good to be true. Of course, it is. The advertiser does not wish to sell the advertised merchandise; it wants to **switch** consumers to another, higher priced product. The real purpose of the advertisement is simply to find customers who are interested in buying.

Mail or Telephone Order Merchandise

Many Americans rely on catalogs to buy everything from clothing to medicine to furnishings, so it is important that these merchants deliver as promised. **The FTC has established the following guidelines on mail or telephone order merchandise:**

- Mail-order companies must ship an item within the time stated or, if no time is given, within 30 days after receipt of the order.

- If a company cannot ship the product when promised, it must send the customer a notice with the new shipping date and an opportunity to cancel. If the new shipping date is within 30 days of the original one, and the customer does not cancel, the order is still on.

- If the company cannot ship within 30 days of the original date, it must send the customer another notice. This time, however, the company must cancel the order unless the customer returns the notice, indicating that he still wants the item.

For example, Dell Computer Corp. advertised that its Dimension computer came with the "Dell Software Suite." In fact, for several months the suite was not available. Instead of the software, Dell sent customers a coupon for the suite "when available." The FTC charged Dell with violations of the mail or telephone order rules because the company:

- Knew it could not ship the software within 30 days;

- Failed to offer buyers the opportunity to cancel their orders; and

- Did not cancel the orders automatically as it should have under the rules.[6]

Telemarketing

The telephone rings: "Could I speak with Alexander Johannson? This is Denise from Master Chimney Sweeps." It is 7:30 P.M.; you have just straggled in from work and are looking forward to a peaceful dinner of takeout cuisine. You are known as Sandy, your last name is pronounced Yohannson, and you live in a modern apartment without a chimney. A telemarketer has struck again! What can you do to protect your peace and quiet?

---

5 *In re Sears, Roebuck and Co.,* 89 F.T.C. 229, 1977 FTC LEXIS 225 (1977).
6 *United States v. Dell Computer Corp.,* 1998 FTC LEXIS 30 (1998).

The FTC prohibits telemarketers from calling any telephone number listed on its do-not-call registry. You can register your telephone numbers with the FTC online at http://www.donotcall.gov or by telephone at (888) 382-1222. FTC rules also prohibit telemarketers from blocking their names and telephone numbers on Caller ID systems.

Unordered Merchandise

Under §5 of the FTC Act, anyone who receives unordered merchandise in the mail can treat it as a gift. She can use it, throw it away, or do whatever else she wants with it.

There you are, watching an infomercial for Anushka products, guaranteed to fight that scourge of modern life—cellulite! Rushing to your phone, you place an order. The Anushka cosmetics arrive, but for some odd reason, the cellulite remains. A month later another bottle arrives, like magic, in the mail. The magic spell is broken, however, when you get your credit card bill and see that, without your authorization, the company has charged you for the new supply of Anushka. Is this a hot new marketing technique? Not exactly. The FTC ordered the company to cease and desist this unfair and deceptive practice. The company improperly billed its customers, said the FTC, and should have notified them that they were free to treat the unauthorized products as a gift, to use or throw out as they wished.[7]

Door-to-Door Sales

Consumers at home need special protection from unscrupulous salespeople. In a store, customers can simply walk out, but at home they may feel trapped. Also, it is difficult at home to compare products or prices offered by competitors. Under the FTC door-to-door rules, **a salesperson is required to notify the buyer that she has the right to cancel the transaction prior to midnight of the third business day thereafter.** This notice must be given both orally and in writing; the actual cancellation must be in writing. The seller must return the buyer's money within 10 days. The following news report illustrates an illegal method of selling magazine subscriptions.

NEWS*worthy*

A federal judge assessed a $50,000 civil penalty against a door-to-door magazine sales company. Customers who purchased magazine subscriptions from Tork & Associates were given (partial) receipts that misrepresented their right to cancel. The receipt indicated that a customer wishing to cancel was required to submit a copy of the complete receipt, the canceled check, the salesperson's name, the magazine name, the date of the transaction, and the total cost. Because the salesperson never gave the customer the complete receipt, it was difficult to comply. In two years, Tork generated $2 million in revenues.[8] ◆

Ethics

A vice-president of Grolier, the encyclopedia company, made the following statement:

> The proposition that a buyer should have the right to whimsically change his mind with respect to a transaction which has been formalized by an agreement containing all of the elements of a legally binding contract, is indeed, a revolutionary legal concept. This proposal represents an attack on the basic contractual concepts which are the foundation of the American economic system.[9]

---

[7] *In the Matter of Synchronal Corp.*, 116 F.T.C. 1189, 1993 FTC LEXIS 280 (1993).

[8] Nancy Stancill, "Door-to-Door Firm Hit with $50,000 Penalty," *Houston Chronicle,* Jan. 28, 1993, p. A17.

[9] Quoted in Douglas Whaley, *Problems and Materials on Consumer Law* (Boston: Little, Brown & Co., 1991), at p. 135.

Do you agree with this statement? From the Chapter 2 Ethics Checklist: What answer would the Golden Rule provide? If you were head of Grolier, would you support or resist the FTC door-to-door rule? ◆

CONSUMER CREDIT

Historically, the practice of charging interest on loans was banned by most countries and by three of the most prominent religions—Christianity, Islam, and Judaism. As the European economy developed, however, money lending became essential. To compromise, governments began to permit interest charges but limited the maximum rate to 6 percent. European settlers carried this concept to the United States, which soon adopted the 6 percent rule, too.

Even in modern times, most states limit the maximum interest rate a lender may charge. The penalty for violating usury statutes varies among the states. Depending upon the jurisdiction, the borrower may be allowed to keep (1) the interest above the usury limit, (2) all of the interest, or (3) all of the loan and the interest.

Before Congress passed the Truth in Lending Act (TILA), lenders found many creative methods to disguise the real interest rate and circumvent the law. For example, they would use a so-called add-on rate. That is, they would charge the permissible interest rate but would insist that the borrower begin to repay the loan in installments immediately. The borrower only had effective use of the money for half the term of the loan. Suppose that a car dealer loaned a customer $3,600 for three years, at 8 percent. The total interest would be $0.08 \times \$3,600 \times 3 = \$864$. If the borrower was required to repay $100 of the principal each month, she would be repaying half the loan within 18 months but would still pay the full $864 in interest. This customer's real interest rate was 16 percent, not 8 percent.

Truth in Lending Act

The problem with add-ons and other such devices designed to hide the real rate of interest from the authorities is that they also hide it from the borrower. Before TILA, many consumers had no idea what interest rate they were really paying. Congress passed the statute to ensure that consumers were adequately informed about credit terms before entering into a loan and could compare the cost of credit. TILA does not regulate interest rates or the terms of a loan; these are still set by state law. It simply requires lenders to *disclose* the terms of a loan in an understandable and complete manner. **TILA applies to a transaction only if all the following tests are met:**

- *It is a consumer loan.* That means a loan to an individual for personal, family, or household purposes but not a loan to a business. For example, TILA does not apply to a loan on a truck used to sell produce.

- *The loan has a finance charge or will be repaid in more than four installments.* Sometimes finance charges masquerade as installment plans. Boris can pay for his big-screen TV in six monthly installments of $200 each, or he can pay $900 cash up front. If he chooses the installment plan, he is effectively paying a finance charge of $300. That is why TILA applies to loans with more than four installments.

- *The loan is for less than $25,000 or secured by a mortgage on real estate.* If Boris borrows money to buy a $1 million house, TILA applies, but not if he buys a $50,000 yacht.

- *The loan is made by someone in the business of offering credit.* If Boris borrows $5,000 from his friend Ludmilla to buy a riding mower, TILA does not apply. If he borrows the money from Friendly Neighborhood Loan Depot, Inc., TILA does apply.

Required Disclosure

In all loans regulated by TILA:

- *The disclosure must be clear and in meaningful sequence.* A finance company violated TILA when it loaned money to Dorothy Allen. The company made all the required disclosures but scattered them throughout the loan document and inter-mixed them with confusing terms that were not required by TILA.[10] A TILA disclosure statement should not be a game of *Where's Waldo.*

- *The lender must disclose the finance charge.* The finance charge is the amount, in dollars, the consumer will pay in interest and fees over the life of the loan. It is important for consumers to know this amount because otherwise they may not understand the real cost of the loan. Of course, the longer the loan, the higher the finance charge. Someone who borrows $5 for 10 years at 10 percent annual interest will pay $.50 each year for 10 years, for a total finance charge of $5—equal to the principal borrowed. In 25-year mortgages, the finance charge will almost always exceed the amount of the principal.

- *The creditor must also disclose the annual percentage rate (APR).* This number is the actual rate of interest the consumer pays on an annual basis. Without this disclosure, it would be easy in a short-term loan to disguise a very high APR because the finance charge is low. Boris borrows $5 for lunch from his employer's credit union. Under the terms of the loan, he must repay $6 the following week. His finance charge is only $1, but his APR is astronomical—20 percent per week, which is more than 1,000 percent for a year.

All TILA loans must meet these three requirements. TILA requires additional disclosure for two types of loans: open-end credit and closed-end credit.

Open-End Credit.   This is a credit transaction in which the lender makes a *series* of loans that the consumer can repay at once or in installments. The typical VISA or MasterCard account is open-end credit—the cardholder has a choice of paying his balance in full each month or making only the required minimum payment.[11] In any advertisement or solicitation, the lender must disclose credit terms. If the lender is offering a *teaser rate*, it must clearly disclose that the rate is introductory, when it expires, and the permanent rate that will replace it. In addition, before beginning an open-end credit account, the lender must disclose to the consumer when a finance charge will be imposed and how the finance charge will be calculated (e.g., whether it will be based on the account balance at the beginning of the billing cycle, the end, or somewhere in between). **In each statement, the lender must disclose the following:** the amount owed at the beginning of the billing cycle (the previous balance); amounts and dates of all purchases, credits, and payments; finance charges and late fees; the date by which a bill must be paid to avoid these charges; and either the consequences of making the monthly minimum payment or a toll-free number at which to obtain such information. The Federal Reserve Board offers advice on choosing a credit card at http://www.federalreserve.gov/pubs/shop.

Closed-End Credit.   In a closed-end transaction, there is only one loan and the borrower knows the amount and the payment schedule in advance. Boris enters into a closed-end transaction when he buys a $30,000 car and agrees to make specified monthly payments over five years. Before a consumer enters into a closed-end transaction, the

---

[10] *Allen v. Beneficial Fin. Co. of Gary,* 531 F.2d 797, 1976 U.S. App. LEXIS 12935 (7th Cir. 1976).

[11] Open-end credit rules apply to all consumer credit cards, even those that require the balance to be paid each month.

lender must disclose the cash price; the total down payment; the amount financed; an itemized list of all other charges; the number, amount, and due dates of payments; the total amount of payments; late payment charges; penalties for prepaying the loan; and the lender's security interest in the item purchased.[12]

Other TILA Provisions

Home Equity Loans.   Scam artists sometimes prey upon the elderly, who are vulnerable to pressure, and upon the poor, who may not have access to conventional financing. These swindlers offer home equity loans, secured by a second mortgage, to finance fraudulent repairs. (There are, of course, many legitimate lenders in the home equity business.) The following news report shows scam artists at work.

NEWS*worthy*

Mack and Jacqueline Moon of East Baltimore hired a home improvement contractor to install a dropped ceiling, paneling, and cabinets in the unfinished basement of their rowhouse. The couple were determined not to put a second mortgage on their house, anticipating they would need backup money to pay medical expenses for their 10-year-old daughter, who had lupus. They signed the contract a few days later after a second salesman assured them, "We were able to work it out, and you don't have to worry about a mortgage." The Moons were never given copies of the loan documents nor told of the 17 percent interest rate. A year later, when they tried to use their home's equity to pay medical bills for their daughter, who had since died, they discovered they had given a second mortgage to the lender without knowing it.[13] ◆

In response to such scams, TILA was amended to provide additional consumer safeguards for home equity installment loans. If a home equity installment loan:

- Has an APR (interest rate) that is more than 10 percentage points higher than Treasury securities, or
- The consumer must pay fees and points at closing that are higher than 8 percent of the total loan amount, then
- At least three business days before the loan closing the lender must notify the consumer that (1) he does not have to go through with the loan (even if he has signed the loan agreement) and (2) he could lose his house if he fails to make payments, and
- Loans that are for less than five years may not contain balloon payments (i.e., a payment at the end that is more than twice the regular monthly payment).

Rescission.   This change in the law came too late to help the Moons, but they found relief in a different TILA provision. Under TILA, consumers have the right to rescind a mortgage for up to three business days after the signing (including Saturdays). If the lender does not comply with the disclosure provisions of TILA, the consumer can rescind for up to three years from the date of the mortgage.

The Moons were able to rescind the loan because the lender had not made adequate disclosure. This right of rescission does *not* apply to a *first* mortgage used to finance a house purchase or to any refinancing with the consumer's existing lender. (Note that some states have passed, and others are considering, predatory lending laws that more strictly regulate loans with high fees or interest rates.)

---

12 See Chapter 13, on secured transactions, for a discussion of security interests.

13 Lorraine Mirabella, "With Hopes of Improving Their Homes, Many Owners Fall Prey to Loan Scams," *The Baltimore Sun*, Sep. 4, 1994, p. 1K.

The table below summarizes the major provisions of TILA.

TILA applies to a transaction only if:	It is a consumer loan;
	The loan has a finance charge or will be repaid in more than four installments;
	The loan is for less than $25,000 or to secure a mortgage on real estate; and
	The loan is made by someone in the business of offering credit.
In all loans regulated by TILA:	The disclosure must be clear and in meaningful sequence; and
	The lender must disclose the finance charge and the annual percentage rate (APR).
Consumers have the right to rescind a mortgage:	For up to three business days after the signing; or
	For up to three years from the date of the mortgage if the lender does not comply with TILA disclosure provisions.
	This provision does not apply if the mortgage is a first mortgage used to finance a house purchase or a refinancing with the consumer's existing lender.

Advertising. TILA is meant to enable consumers to shop around and compare available financing alternatives. With this goal in mind, the statute requires lenders to advertise their rates accurately. A lender cannot **bait and switch;** that is, it cannot advertise rates unless they are generally available to anyone who applies. Moreover, if the lender advertises any credit terms, it must tell the whole story. For example, if it advertises "Nothing down, 12 months to pay," it must also disclose the APR and other terms of repayment.

Enforcement. The FTC generally has the right to enforce TILA. In addition, consumers who have been injured by any violation (except for the advertising provisions) have the right to file suit.

ECONOMICS & *the* LAW

What is the economic impact of TILA? This statute requires lenders to provide a service against their will: detailed information about loans. Although this information is important to consumers, it is relatively expensive for them to produce while being relatively easy for lenders. Without TILA, consumers could compile credit information only by spending hours on the phone, asking questions of each lender. With TILA, all this information to consumers is available more or less for free. (Although lenders do pass their costs on to consumers, this cost is low compared with the value of the information or the cost to consumers if they had to find out the information on their own.)

Economists believe in efficiency, which means, among other things, that a product should be produced as cheaply as possible. TILA is consistent with this goal: it ensures that loan information is produced cheaply (by lenders) rather than at great cost (by consumers).

Access to detailed loan information permits borrowers to compare competing offers. The ability to comparison shop enhances consumers' market power. Greater customer power leads to lower prices. In short, TILA not only protects consumers from entering into loans that are more expensive than they realized, it also lowers the cost of borrowing money. ◆

Special Credit Card Rules.   Your wallet is missing, and with it your cash, your driver's license, a photo of your dog, a coupon for a free DVD rental, and—oh no!—all your credit cards! It is a disaster, to be sure. But it could have been worse. There was a time when you would have been responsible for every charge the thief rang up. **Now, under TILA, you are liable only for the first $50 in charges the thief makes before you notify the credit card company.** If you call the company before any charges are made, you have no liability at all. But if, by the time you contact the company, the speedy robber has completely furnished her apartment on your card, you are still liable only for $50. Of course, if you carry a wallet full of cards, $50 for each one can add up to a sizable total. If the thief steals just your credit card number, but not the card itself, you are not liable for any unauthorized charges.

Suppose that a credit card company mails a card to you that you did not order and someone steals it out of your mailbox. You know nothing about the card until the bills arrive. If you did not request the card, and it is not a renewal or substitute for a card you already have, you are not liable, even for the $50.

You use your credit card to buy a new computer at ShadyComputers. When you arrive home and start to load software, you discover the hard disk is only 1 gigabyte, not the 80 that was advertised. The computer crashes six times the first day. In short, you have a major, $1,500 problem. But all is not lost. **In the event of a dispute between a customer and a merchant, the credit card company cannot bill the customer if** (1) she makes a good faith effort to resolve the dispute, (2) the dispute is for more than $50, and (3) the merchant is in the same state where she lives or is within 100 miles of her house.

What happens if the merchant and the consumer cannot resolve their dispute? Or if the merchant is not in the same state as the consumer? Clearly, credit card companies do not want to be caught in the middle between consumer and merchant. In practice, they now require all merchants to sign a contract specifying that, in the event of a dispute between the merchant and a customer, the credit card company has the right to charge back the merchant's account. If a customer seems to have a reasonable claim against a merchant, the credit card company will typically transfer the credit it has given the merchant back to the customer's account. Of course, the merchant can try to sue the customer for any money owed.

Debit Cards.   So your wallet is missing, and with it your debit card. No problem, right? It is just like a credit card. Wrong. Debit cards look and feel like credit cards, but legally they are a different plastic altogether. Debit cards work like checks (which is why they are also called **check cards**). When you use your debit card, the bank deducts money directly from your account, which means there is no bill to pay at the end of the month (and no interest charges on unpaid bills). That is the good news. The bad news is that your liability for a stolen debit card is much greater. If you report the loss before anyone uses your card, you are not liable for any unauthorized withdrawals. If you report the theft within two days of discovering it, the bank will make good on all losses above $50. If you wait until after two days, your bank will only replace stolen funds above $500. After 60 days of receipt of your bank statement, all losses are yours: the bank will not repay any stolen funds. If an unauthorized transfer takes place using just your number, not your card, then you are not liable at all as long as you report the loss within 60 days of receiving the bank statement showing the loss. After 60 days, however, you are liable for the full amount.

Fair Credit Billing Act

The Fair Credit Billing Act (FCBA) provides additional protection for credit card holders. Is there anyone in America who has not sometime or other discovered an error in a credit card bill? Before Congress passed the FCBA in 1975, a dispute with a credit card company often deteriorated into an avalanche of threatening form letters that ignored any response from the hapless cardholder. **Under the FCBA:**

- If, within 60 days of receipt of a bill, a consumer writes to a credit card company to complain about the bill, the company must acknowledge receipt of the complaint within 30 days.

- Within two billing cycles (but no more than 90 days) the credit card company must investigate the complaint and respond:

  - In the case of an error, by correcting the mistake and notifying the consumer.

  - If there is no error, by writing to the consumer with an explanation.

  - Whether or not there was a mistake, if the consumer requests it, the credit card company must supply documentary evidence to support its position—for example, copies of the bill signed by the consumer or evidence that the package actually arrived.

  - The credit card company cannot try to collect the disputed debt or close or suspend the account until it has responded to the consumer complaint.

  - The credit card company cannot report to credit agencies that the consumer has an unpaid bill until 10 days after the response. If the consumer still disputes the charge, the credit card company may report the amount to a credit agency but must disclose that it is disputed.

At **http://www.ftc.gov/bcp/conline/pubs/credit/fcb.htm** the FTC provides a sample form letter to send to a credit card company if you want to dispute a bill.

In the following case, American Express made a big mistake picking on a law professor. The court's opinion was written by Abner J. Mikva, a highly regarded judge on the federal appeals court. He was clearly exasperated by American Express's arguments and used strong language to reprimand the company—and the lower court. Because Judge Mikva had served in Congress, he could speak with some authority about Congress's approach to consumer legislation.

GRAY V. AMERICAN EXPRESS CO.

743 F.2d 10, 240 U.S. App. D.C. 10, 1984 U.S. App. LEXIS 19033
United States Court of Appeals for the District of Columbia Circuit, 1984

Facts: In December, Oscar Gray used his American Express credit card to buy airline tickets costing $9,312. American Express agreed that Gray could pay for the tickets in 12 monthly installments. In January, Gray paid $3,500 and then in February an additional $1,156. In March, American Express billed Gray by mistake for the entire remaining balance, which he did not pay. In April, Gray and his wife went out for dinner to celebrate their wedding anniversary. When he tried to pay with his American Express card, the restaurant told him that the credit card company had not only refused to accept the charges for the meal, but had instructed the restaurant to confiscate and destroy the card. While still at the restaurant, Gray spoke to an American Express employee on the telephone who informed him, "Your account is canceled as of now."

Gray wrote to American Express, pointing out the error. For more than a year, the company failed to respond to Gray or to investigate his claim. It then turned the bill over to a collection agency. Gray sued American Express for violating the Fair Credit Billing ▼

Act. The trial court granted summary judgment to American Express and dismissed the complaint on the grounds that Gray had waived his rights under the act.

Issue: Is American Express liable to Gray for violating the Fair Credit Billing Act?

Excerpts from Judge Mikva's Decision: The contract between Gray and American Express provides: "We can revoke your right to use [the card] at any time. We can do this with or without cause and without giving you notice." American Express concludes from this language that the cancellation was not of the kind prohibited by the Act, even though the Act regulates other aspects of the relationship between the cardholder and the card issuer.

[T]he Act states that, during the pendency of a disputed billing, the card issuer shall not cause the cardholder's account to be restricted or closed because of the failure of the obligor to pay the amount in dispute. American Express seems to argue that, despite that provision, it can exercise its right to cancellation for cause unrelated to the disputed

amount, or for no cause, thus bringing itself out from under the statute. At the very least, the argument is audacious. American Express would restrict the efficacy of the statute to those situations where the parties had not agreed to a "without cause, without notice" cancellation clause, or to those cases where the cardholder can prove that the sole reason for cancellation was the amount in dispute. We doubt that Congress painted with such a faint brush.

The effect of American Express's argument is to allow the equivalent of a "waiver" of coverage of the Act simply by allowing the parties to contract it away. Congress usually is not so tepid in its approach to consumer problems. The rationale of consumer protection legislation is to even out the inequalities that consumers normally bring to the bargain. To allow such protection to be waived by boiler plate language of the contract puts the legislative process to a foolish and unproductive task. A court ought not impute such nonsense to a Congress intent on correcting abuses in the market place.

The district court's order of summary judgment and dismissal is hereby *vacated*. ∎

Fair Credit Reporting Act

Gossip and rumor can cause great harm. Bad enough when whispered behind one's back, worse yet when placed in files and distributed to potential creditors. Most adults rely on credit—to acquire a house, credit cards, or overdraft privileges at the bank. A sullied credit report makes life immensely more difficult. The goal of the Fair Credit Reporting Act (FCRA) is to ensure that consumer credit reports are accurate.

The FCRA regulates **consumer reporting agencies.** These are businesses that supply consumer reports to third parties. If an insurance agency or bank conducts its own investigation to determine whether a consumer is creditworthy, the FCRA does not apply. A **consumer report** is any communication about a consumer's creditworthiness, character, general reputation, or lifestyle that is considered as a factor in establishing credit, obtaining insurance, securing a job, acquiring a government license, or for any other legitimate business need.

Under the FCRA:

- A consumer report can be used only for a legitimate business need, and a consumer reporting agency must be careful not to supply reports that will be used for any other purpose. A nosy neighbor does not have the right to order a report.

- A consumer reporting agency cannot report obsolete information. Ordinary credit information is obsolete after seven years, bankruptcies after 10 years. (But if a consumer is applying for more than $150,000 of credit or life insurance, or for a job that pays more than $75,000 a year, then there is no time limit.) **Investigative reports** that discuss character, reputation, or lifestyle become obsolete in three *months*. Some commentators argue that the type of information contained in investigative reports is not relevant and should not be used at all. Although the FCRA does not limit the kinds of information that can be collected and reported, it does specify that an investigative report cannot be ordered without first informing the consumer.

- A consumer reporting agency cannot report medical information without the consumer's permission.

- An employer cannot request a consumer report on any current or potential employee without the employee's permission. An employer cannot take action because of information in the consumer report without first giving the current or potential employee a copy of the report and a description of the employee's rights under this statute.

- Anyone who makes an adverse decision against a consumer because of a credit report must reveal the name and address of the reporting agency that supplied the information. An "adverse decision" includes denying credit or charging higher rates.

- Upon request from a consumer, a reporting agency must disclose all information in his file, the source of the information (except for investigative reports), the name of anyone to whom a report has been sent in the prior year (two years for employment purposes), and the name of anyone who has requested a report in the prior year.

- If a consumer tells an agency that some of the information in his file is incorrect, the agency must both investigate and forward the data to the information provider. The information provider must investigate and report the results to the agency. If the data are inaccurate, the information provider must so notify all national credit agencies. The consumer also has the right to give the agency a short report telling his side of the story. The agency must then include the consumer's statement with any credit reports it supplies and also, at the consumer's request, send the statement to anyone who has received a report within six months (or two years for employment purposes).

The following article illustrates the usefulness of the FCRA.

NEWS*worthy*

Kimberly Dorcik wanted a new job. An assistant manager at a Lechters housewares store, she applied for the manager's position at Ups 'N Downs, a women's clothing store a dozen doors away in Solano Mall, in Fairfield, California. But her hopes for the job, which paid a few thousand dollars more than she was earning, vanished, she said, when the staff member taking her application whispered: "We're not supposed to tell anybody, but we pull credit reports on people. Is that going to be a problem?"

Ms. Dorcik remembers mumbling a noncommittal response, but she knew that it was going to be a problem. Three years earlier, when she was 19, she had had emergency surgery resulting from complications from pregnancy. Because of what she calls a clerical error, $30,000 in medical bills were still unpaid and in dispute, tainting her credit history. Ms. Dorcik did not get the job, and she said she was almost certain that the deciding factor was her credit history. The FCRA now requires employers to tell applicants like Ms. Dorcik if credit histories are being used as part of hiring. Employers will also have to obtain written permission from applicants before even requesting a credit history. If someone is turned down for a job and a credit report was used in the decision, the applicant can presumably weed out wrong information in the report and reapply.[14] ◆

Fair and Accurate Credit Transactions Act

In identity theft, a fraudster steals his victim's personal information, such as social security number, credit card information, or mother's maiden name, and uses it to obtain credit or goods in the victim's name—in short, to wreak havoc in the victim's life. The goal of the Fair and Accurate Credit Transactions Act (FACTA) is to reduce identity theft.

---

[14] Anthony Ramirez, "Name, Resume, References. And How's Your Credit," *The New York Times,* Aug. 31, 1997, p. F8. Copyright © 1997 by The New York Times Co. Reprinted by permission.

FACTA provides that consumers are entitled by law to one free credit report every year from each of the three major reporting agencies: Equifax, Experian, and TransUnion. You can order these reports at **https://www.annualcreditreport.com.** Consumer advocates recommend that you do check your credit reports every year to make sure they are accurate and also that no one else has been obtaining credit in your name. If you find any errors, notify the agency in writing and warn it that failing to make corrections is a violation of the law. At **http://www.ftc.gov/bcp/conline/pubs/credit/crdtdis.htm,** the FTC offers advice on how to dispute credit report errors.

FACTA also created the National Fraud Alert System, which permits consumers who fear they may be the victims of identity theft to place an alert in their credit files, warning financial institutions to investigate carefully before issuing any new credit. It also requires credit bureaus to share information about identity theft.

Also, under the Gramm-Leach-Bliley Privacy Act of 1999, banks, other financial institutions, and consumer reporting agencies must notify a consumer (1) before disclosing any personal information to a third party or (2) if there has been unauthorized access to the consumer's sensitive personal information.[15] The company cannot disclose private information if the consumer *opts out* (i.e., denies permission).

Fair Debt Collection Practices Act

The introduction to the Fair Debt Collection Practices Act (FDCPA) states that "Abusive debt collection practices contribute to the number of personal bankruptcies, to marital instability, to the loss of jobs, and to invasions of individual privacy."[16] Debt collection practices can also disrupt Super Bowl Sunday. Debt collectors seek to catch their prey off guard, and what better time than when the entire nation is at home, glued to the television? If the phone rings, sports fans assume it is a friend calling to gab about the game.

Is that legal? It depends. **The FDCPA provides** that a collector must, within five days of contacting a debtor, send the debtor a written notice containing the amount of the debt, the name of the creditor to whom the debt is owed, and a statement that if the debtor disputes the debt (in writing), the collector will cease all collection efforts until it has sent evidence of the debt. **Also under the FDCPA, collectors may not:**

- Call or write a debtor who has notified the collector in writing that he wishes no further contact;
- Call or write a debtor who is represented by an attorney;
- Call a debtor before 8:00 A.M. or after 9:00 P.M.;
- Threaten a debtor or use obscene or abusive language;
- Call or visit the debtor at work if the consumer's employer prohibits such contact;
- Imply that they are attorneys or government representatives when they are not, or use a false name;
- Threaten to arrest consumers who do not pay their debts;
- Make other false or deceptive threats—that is, threats that would be illegal if carried out or which the collector has no intention of doing—such as suing the debtor or seizing property;

---

[15] 15 U.S.C. §6801.
[16] 15 U.S.C. §1692(a).

- Contact acquaintances of the debtor for any reason other than to locate the debtor (and then only once); or
- Tell acquaintances that the consumer is in debt.

Of course, these rules do not prevent the collector from filing suit against the debtor. In the event of a violation of the FDCPA, the debtor is entitled to damages, court costs, and attorney's fees. The FTC also has authority to enforce the Act.

The following case illustrates the types of abuses that the FDCPA was designed to prevent.

GRADISHER V. CHECK ENFORCEMENT UNIT, INC.

2002 U.S. Dist. LEXIS 6003
United States District Court for the Western District of Michigan, 2002

Facts: Check Enforcement Unit, Inc. (CEU), was in the business of helping merchants collect on bad checks. When a merchant received a dishonored check, it would forward the check directly to CEU, which would then send out a series of notices to the check writer, using the letterhead of the local Sheriff's Department. CEU had permission to use this letterhead, but the Sheriff's Department was not otherwise involved in the collection effort. Only after the three notices had been sent, and no payment received, would CEU notify the Sheriff's Department about a bad check. Even then, the check did not become a criminal matter until the Sheriff's Department assigned a complaint number.

After Sherri Gradisher bounced a check for $81.30 at Doug Born's Smokehouse, she received three notices from CEU. Gradisher filed suit alleging that CEU had violated the FDCPA.

Issue: Did CEU violate the FDCPA?

Excerpts from Judge Quist's Decision: CEU admits that the Notice did not contain the exact language required by the statute but contends that it did contain much of the information required, such as the amount of the debt, the name of the creditor, and a telephone number and address which Gradisher could use to contact CEU if she wished to dispute the debt. [But] the Notice does not state [as required by law] that the debtor may dispute the validity of the debt by notifying the debt collector in writing within thirty days after receipt of the Notice.

Gradisher contends that CEU violated [the statute] because CEU's use of the letterhead of the Office of the Sheriff gave the false and misleading impression that the notices were from the Sheriff's

Department when they were actually from CEU. In addition, Gradisher contends that CEU violated the FDCPA by failing to disclose its true name.

[The Notices] all conveyed the impression that they were authorized, created, and sent by the Sheriff's Department without any indication that CEU, an independent contractor of the County, was actually the entity that generated the notices. The fact that CEU had an "affiliation" with the Sheriff's Department is irrelevant because CEU's notices created the false impression that the notices were generated by the Sheriff's Department. Moreover, CEU's notices violated [the statute] because CEU used a name other than its own name.

Gradisher's next claim is that CEU violated the FDCPA by implying that Gradisher would be arrested or imprisoned if she failed to pay the debt. The back side of the Notice stated:

WARNING
Failure To Make Payment Can Result In A Warrant For Your Arrest

[Any] debtor would conclude after reading CEU's notices that the Sheriff's Department had determined that the debtor committed a crime and arrest or criminal prosecution was certain to occur if the debt was not paid. In fact, the Sheriff's Department had no involvement with the notices sent by CEU and never made any determination regarding violation of the law or arrest. Gradisher has shown that criminal prosecution occurs infrequently on files CEU sends to the Sheriff's Department. Thus, in any given case there is only a slight possibility of criminal prosecution. Under these circumstances, CEU's notices violated [the statute]. ■

at R**I**SK

If a debt collector calls you, what can you do? First of all, be sure to write down his name and the name of the agency for which he works. Tell the caller that you are recording the conversation and then do so. Send a letter to the agency, requesting that it not contact you. Report any violations to the FTC at http://www.ftc.gov/bcp/conline/pubs/credit/fdc.htm. ◆

Equal Credit Opportunity Act

The Equal Credit Opportunity Act (ECOA) prohibits any creditor from discriminating against a borrower because of race, color, religion, national origin, sex, marital status, age (as long as the borrower is old enough to enter into a legal contract), or because the borrower is receiving welfare. A lender must respond to a credit application within 30 days. If a lender rejects an application, it must either tell the applicant why or notify him that he has the right to a written explanation of the reasons for this *adverse action.* The following news report illustrates the types of abuses that the ECOA is designed to prevent.

NEWS*worthy*

Florence and Joe made an offer to buy a new home at the Meadowood housing development near Tampa. The developer accepted their offer, contingent upon their obtaining a mortgage. When the couple filed an application with Rancho Mortgage and Investment Corp., they were surprised by the hostility of Rancho's loan processor. She requested information they had already supplied and repeatedly questioned them about whether they intended to occupy the house, which was about 80 miles from their jobs. Florence and Joe insisted they wanted to live near their son and daughter-in-law and escape city crime. Rancho turned down their mortgage, refusing to give either an oral or a written explanation. The house was sold to another buyer.

Joe and Florence didn't get mad, they got even. They sued under the ECOA. Rancho was ordered to pay the African American couple $35,000.[17] ◆

As the following case illustrates, the ECOA protects against a broad range of wrongdoing.

TREADWAY V. GATEWAY CHEVROLET OLDSMOBILE INC.

362 F.3d 971, 2004 U.S. App. LEXIS 6325
United States Court of Appeals for the Seventh Circuit, 2004

Facts: Gateway Chevrolet Oldsmobile (GCO), a car dealership, sent an unsolicited letter to Tonja Treadway notifying her that she was "preapproved" for the financing to purchase a car. GCO did not provide financing itself; instead, it arranged loans through banks or finance companies.

Treadway called the dealer to say that she was interested in purchasing a used car. She divulged her social security number so that GCO could obtain her credit report. Based on this report, the dealer determined that Treadway was not eligible for financing. This was not surprising, given that GCO had purchased Treadway's name for the direct-mail solicitation from a list of people who had recently filed for bankruptcy.

Instead of applying for a loan on behalf of Treadway, GCO called her and invited her to come to the dealership. At the dealership, Gateway told her that it had found a bank that would finance her transaction, but only if she purchased a new car and provided a cosigner. Treadway agreed to purchase a   ▼

17 Robert J. Bruss, "Home Buyers Sue Mortgage Lender for Racial Discrimination," *Tampa Tribune,* Nov. 5, 1994, p. 3.

new car and came up with Pearlie Smith, her god-mother, to serve as a cosigner.

Concerned as it was with customer convenience, GCO had an agent deliver papers directly to Smith's house to be signed immediately. If Smith had read the papers before she signed them, she might have realized that she had committed herself to be the sole purchaser and owner of the car. But she had no idea that she was the owner until she began receiving bills on the car loan. After Treadway made the first payment on behalf of Smith, both women refused to pay more—Smith because she did not want a new car, Treadway because the car was not hers. The car was repossessed, but the financing company continued to demand payment.

On closer inspection, it appears that GCO was running a scam. It would lure desperate prospects off the bankruptcy rolls and into the showroom with promises of financing for a used car, and then sell a new car to their "co-signer" (who was, in fact, the sole signer). Instead of selling a used car to Tonja Treadway, GCO sold a new car to Pearlie Smith.

Treadway filed suit against GCO, alleging that it had violated the ECOA by not notifying her that it had taken an adverse action against her. The district court granted GCO's motion for summary judgment on the grounds that GCO had not committed an adverse action under the ECOA. This appeal followed.

Issue: Did Gateway violate the ECOA?

Excerpts from Judge Cudahy's Decision: The term "adverse action" is defined in relevant part by the ECOA as "a denial or revocation of credit." By unilaterally deciding not to send Treadway's application to *any* lender, Gateway effectively denied credit to Treadway. Whether it is the lender or the dealership that makes the decision, both the action and the outcome are the same. In both cases, the decision maker (1) reviews the applicant's credit report to determine whether she is creditworthy, (2) makes a determination adverse to the applicant (i.e., that she is not creditworthy), (3) decides not to proceed any further in arranging credit, and (4) as a result the applicant is not granted credit. There is no logical reason why these same steps would be considered an "adverse action" when taken by a lender but not when taken by a dealership, given that the result is the same in either case.

If an automobile dealership that decides against referring a particular applicant to any lender need not provide notice of this decision to the applicant, then it becomes significantly easier for it to discriminate. [I]f an applicant never receives notice, it will be difficult for her to ever determine that she was the victim of discrimination. This is particularly true because, as was the case here, without proper notice, the applicant may assume that her application *was* sent to lenders, and it was the lenders who did the rejecting. Car dealers could throw the credit report of every minority applicant in the "circular file" and none would be the wiser.

Therefore, based on the foregoing analysis, we find that Gateway's action constitutes an "adverse action" for purposes of the ECOA. ■

Consumer Leasing Act

If you, like many other consumers, lease a car rather than buy it, you are protected under the Consumer Leasing Act (CLA). The CLA does not apply to the rental of real property—that is, to house or apartment leases. **Before a lease is signed, a lessor must disclose the following in writing:**

- All required payments, including deposits, down payments, taxes, and license fees;
- The number and amount of each monthly payment and how payments are calculated;
- Balloon payments (i.e., payments due at the end of the lease);
- Required insurance payments;
- The total amount the consumer will have paid by the end of the lease;
- Available warranties;
- Maintenance requirements and a description of the lessor's wear and use standards;
- Penalties for late payments;

- The consumer's right to purchase the leased property and at what price;
- The consumer's right to terminate a lease early; and
- Any penalties for early termination.

The government brochure "Keys to Vehicle Leasing" is available at http://www. federalreserve.gov/pubs/leasing/. It lays out the lessor's rights and compares the advantages and disadvantages of leasing versus purchasing a car.

MAGNUSON-MOSS WARRANTY ACT

When Senator Frank E. Moss sponsored the Magnuson-Moss Warranty Act, this is how he explained the need for such a statute:

> [W]arranties have for many years confused, misled, and frequently angered American consumers. . . . Consumer anger is expected when purchasers of consumer products discover that their warranty may cover a 25-cent part but not the $100 labor charge or that there is full coverage on a piano so long as it is shipped at the purchaser's expense to the factory. . . . There is a growing need to generate consumer understanding by clearly and conspicuously disclosing the terms and conditions of the warranty and by telling the consumer what to do if his guaranteed product becomes defective or malfunctions.[18]

The Magnuson-Moss Warranty Act does not require manufacturers or sellers to provide a warranty on their products. **The Act does require any supplier that offers a written warranty on a consumer product that costs more than $15 to disclose the terms of the warranty in simple, understandable language** *before the sale*. This statute covers sales by catalog or on the Internet. Required disclosure includes the following:

- The name and address of the person the consumer should contact to obtain warranty service;
- The parts that are covered and those that are not;
- What services the warrantor will provide, at whose expense, and for what period; and
- A statement of what the consumer must do and what expenses he must pay.

Although suppliers are not required to offer a warranty, if they do offer one they must indicate whether it is *full* or *limited*. Under a **full warranty,** the warrantor must promise to fix a defective product for a reasonable time without charge. If, after a reasonable number of efforts to fix the defective product, it still does not work, the consumer must have the right to a refund or a replacement without charge; but the warrantor is not required to cover damage caused by the consumer's unreasonable use.

CONSUMER PRODUCT SAFETY

In 1969, the federal government estimated that consumer products caused 30,000 deaths, 110,000 disabling injuries, and 20 million trips to the doctor. Toys were among the worst offenders, injuring 700,000 children a year. Children were cut by Etch-a-Sketch glass

---

[18] Quoted in David G. Epstein and Steve H. Nickles, *Consumer Law* (Eagan, Minn.: West, 1981).

panels, choked by Zulu gun darts, and burned by Little Lady toy ovens. Although injured consumers had the right to seek damages under tort law, the goal of the Consumer Product Safety Act of 1972 (CPSA) was to prevent injuries in the first place. This act created the Consumer Product Safety Commission to evaluate consumer products and develop safety standards. The Commission can impose civil and criminal penalties on those who violate its standards. Individuals have the right to sue under the CPSA for damages, including attorney's fees, from anyone who knowingly violates a consumer product safety rule. You can find out about product recalls or file a report on an unsafe product at the Commission's Website (http://www.cpsc.gov).

Chapter Conclusion

Virtually no one will go through life without reading an advertisement, ordering from a catalog, borrowing money, needing a credit report, or using a consumer product. It is important to know your rights.

Chapter Review

1. The Federal Trade Commission (FTC) prohibits "unfair and deceptive acts or practices." A practice is unfair if it meets the following three tests:

- It causes a substantial consumer injury.

- The harm of the injury outweighs any countervailing benefit.

- The consumer could not reasonably avoid the injury.

2. The FTC considers an advertisement to be deceptive if it contains an important misrepresentation or omission that is likely to mislead a reasonable consumer.

3. FTC rules prohibit bait and switch advertisements. A merchant may not advertise a product and then disparage it to consumers in an effort to sell a different item.

4. The FTC prohibits telemarketers from calling telephone numbers listed on its do-not-call registry.

5. Consumers may keep as a gift any unordered merchandise that they receive in the mail.

6. Under the FTC door-to-door rules, a salesperson is required to notify the buyer that she has the right to cancel the transaction prior to midnight of the third business day thereafter.

7. In all loans regulated by the Truth in Lending Act (TILA), the disclosure must be clear and in meaningful sequence. The lender must disclose the finance charge and the annual percentage rate.

8. In the case of a high-rate home equity loan, the lender must notify the consumer at least three business days before the closing that (1) he does not have to go through with the loan (even if he has signed the loan agreement) and (2) he could lose his house if he fails to make payments. If the duration of a high-rate home equity loan is less than five years, it may not contain balloon payments.

9. Under TILA, consumers have the right to rescind a mortgage (other than a first mortgage) for three business days after the signing. If the lender does not comply with the disclosure provisions of TILA, the consumer may rescind for up to three years from the date of the mortgage.

10. Under TILA, a *credit* card holder is liable only for the first $50 in unauthorized charges made before the credit card company is notified that the card was stolen. If, however, you wait more than two days to report the loss of a *debit* card, your bank will only reimburse you for losses in excess of $500. If you fail to report the lost debit card within 60 days of receipt of your bank statement, the bank is not liable at all.

11. In the event of a dispute between a customer and a merchant, the credit card company cannot bill the customer if:

    - She makes a good faith effort to resolve the dispute;

    - The dispute is for more than $50; and

    - The merchant is in the same state where she lives or is within 100 miles of her house.

12. Under the Fair Credit Billing Act, a credit card company must promptly investigate and respond to any consumer complaints about a credit card bill.

13. Under the Fair Credit Reporting Act:

    - A consumer report can be used only for a legitimate business need;

    - A consumer reporting agency cannot report obsolete information;

    - An employer cannot request a consumer report on any current or potential employee without the employee's permission; and

    - Anyone who makes an adverse decision against a consumer because of a credit report must reveal the name and address of the reporting agency that supplied the negative information.

14. The Fair and Accurate Credit Transactions Act permits consumers to obtain one free credit report every year from each of the three major reporting agencies.

15. Under the Fair Debt Collection Practices Act, a debt collector may not harass or abuse debtors.

16. The Equal Credit Opportunity Act prohibits any creditor from discriminating against a borrower on the basis of race, color, religion, national origin, sex, marital status, age, or because the borrower is receiving welfare.

17. The Magnuson-Moss Warranty Act requires any supplier that offers a written warranty on a consumer product costing more than $15 to disclose the terms of the warranty in simple and readily understandable language before the sale.

18. The Consumer Product Safety Commission evaluates consumer products and develops safety standards.

Practice Test

1. In August, Dorothy Jenkins went to First American Mortgage and Loan Association of Virginia (the Bank) to sign a second mortgage on her home. Her first mortgage was with a different bank. She left the closing without a copy of the required Truth in Lending Act disclosure forms. Jenkins defaulted on her loan payments, and, the following May, the Bank began foreclosure proceedings on her house. In June, she notified the Bank that she wished to rescind the loan. Does Jenkins have a right to rescind the loan 10 months after it was made?

2. **YOU BE THE JUDGE** WRITING PROBLEM Process cheese food slices must contain at least 51 percent natural cheese. Imitation cheese slices, by contrast, contain little or no natural cheese and consist primarily of water, vegetable oil, flavoring, and fortifying agents. Kraft, Inc., makes Kraft Singles, which are individually wrapped process cheese food slices. When Kraft began losing market share to imitation slices that were advertised as both less expensive and equally nutritious as Singles, Kraft responded with a series of advertisements informing consumers that Kraft Singles cost more than imitation slices because they are made from five ounces of milk. Kraft does use five ounces of milk in making each Kraft Single, but 30 percent of the calcium contained in the milk is lost during processing. Imitation slices contain the same amount of calcium as Kraft Singles. Are the Kraft advertisements deceptive? **Argument for Kraft:** This statement is completely true— Kraft does use five ounces of milk in each Kraft Single. The FTC is assuming that the only value of milk is the calcium. In fact, people might prefer having milk rather than vegetable oil, regardless of the calcium. **Argument for the FTC:** It is deceptive to advertise more milk if the calcium is the same after all the processing.

3. Joel Curtis was two and his brother, Joshua, was three years old when their father left both children asleep in the rear seat of his automobile while visiting a friend. His cigarette lighter was on the dashboard of the car. After awaking, Joshua began playing with the lighter and set fire to Joel's diaper. Do the parents have a claim against the manufacturer of the lighter under the Consumer Product Safety Act?

4. Josephine Rutyna was a 60-year-old widow who suffered from high blood pressure and epilepsy. A bill collector from Collections Accounts Terminal, Inc., called her and demanded that she pay $56 she owed to Cabrini Hospital Medical Group. She told him that Medicare was supposed to pay the bill. Shortly thereafter, Rutyna received a letter from Collections that stated:

> You have shown that you are unwilling to work out a friendly settlement with us to clear the above debt. Our field investigator has now been instructed to make an investigation in your neighborhood and to personally call on your employer. The immediate payment of the full amount, or a personal visit to this office, will spare you this embarrassment.

Has Collections violated the law?

5. Thomas Pinner worked at a Sherwin-Williams paint store that was managed by James Schmidt. Pinner and Schmidt had a falling out when, according to Pinner, "a relationship began to bloom between Pinner and one of the young female employees, the one Schmidt was obsessed with." Pinner quit. Schmidt claimed that Pinner owed the company $121.71 for paint he had taken but not paid for. Sherwin-Williams reported this information to Chilton, who ran a credit reporting agency. Pinner's attorney sent a letter to Chilton notifying him that Pinner disputed the accuracy of the Sherwin-Williams charges. Chilton contacted Schmidt, who confirmed that Pinner's account remained delinquent. Chilton failed to note in Pinner's file that a dispute was pending. Thereafter, Pinner was denied credit cards at two stores. Have Schmidt and Chilton violated the Fair Credit Reporting Act?

6. Kathleen Carroll, a single woman, applied for an Exxon credit card. Exxon rejected her application without giving any specific reason and without providing the name of the credit bureau it had used. When Carroll asked for a reason for the rejection, she was told that the credit bureau did not have enough information about her to establish creditworthiness. In fact, Exxon had denied her credit application because she did not have a major credit card or a savings account, she had been employed for only one year, and she had no dependents. Did Exxon violate the law?

7. In October, Renie Guimond discovered that her credit report at TransUnion Credit Information Co. incorrectly stated that she was married, used the name "Ruth Guimond," and had a credit card from Saks Fifth Avenue. After she reported the errors, TransUnion wrote her in November to say that it had removed this information. However, in March, TransUnion again published the erroneous information. The following October, TransUnion finally removed the incorrect information from her file. Guimond was never denied credit because of these mistakes. Is TransUnion liable for violating the Fair Credit Reporting Act?

8. The National Coalition for Consumer Education and MasterCard International created the following quiz to help consumers find out how smart they are about buying on credit:

- What's the best way to correct a mistake on your credit card bill?

  a Call your credit card issuer immediately and explain the mistake.

  b Circle the mistake in red and return the bill to your card issuer.

  c Immediately write a letter to your credit card issuer and clearly describe the problem.

- How should you handle an unauthorized charge (a purchase that you didn't make) if you see one on your credit card statement?

  a Write a letter to the company that accepted your card for payment to absolve yourself of any liability.

  b Call your credit issuer immediately to alert them.

c Note the error on your credit card bill and refuse to pay it.[19]

9. Thomas Waldock purchased a 1983 BMW 320i from Universal Motors, Inc. It was warranted "to be free of defects in materials or workmanship for a period of three years or 36,000 miles, whichever occurs first." Within the warranty period, the car's engine failed and upon examination was found to be extensively damaged. Universal denied warranty coverage because it concluded that Waldock damaged the engine by over-revving it. Waldock vehemently disputed BMW's contention. He claimed that, while being driven at a low speed, the engine emitted a gear-crunching noise, ceased operation, and would not restart. Is Universal in violation of the law?

10. When customers called the number provided, New Rapids Carpet Center, Inc., sent salespeople to visit them at home to sell them carpet that was not as advertised—it was not continuous filament nylon pile broadloom, and the price was not $77. Has New Rapids violated a consumer law?

11. *ETHICS* After TNT Motor Express hired Joseph Bruce Drury as a truck driver, it ordered a background check from Robert Arden & Associates. TNT provided Drury's Social Security number and date of birth but not his middle name. Arden discovered that a Joseph *Thomas* Drury, who coincidentally had the same birth date as Joseph *Bruce* Drury, had served a prison sentence for drunk driving. Not knowing that it had the wrong Drury, Arden reported this information to TNT, which promptly fired Drury. When he asked why, the TNT executive merely stated, "We do not discuss these matters." Did TNT violate the law? Whether or not TNT was in violation, did its executives behave ethically? Who would have been harmed or helped if TNT managers had informed Drury of the Arden report?

12. Advertisements for Listerine mouthwash claimed that it was as effective as flossing in preventing tooth plaque and gum disease. This statement was true, but only if the flossing was done incorrectly. In fact, many consumers do floss incorrectly. However, if flossing is done right, it is more effective against plaque and gum disease than Listerine. Is this advertisement deceptive? Does it violate §5 of the FTC Act?

13. *ROLE REVERSAL* Prepare a short-answer question that focuses on deceptive advertisements. Include a sample ad in the question (either a real ad or one that you have made up).

Internet Research Problem

The Consumer Product Safety Commission (http://cpsc.gov) lists products that have been recalled and provides consumers with a telephone number for contacting the manufacturer. Choose a recalled product and telephone the manufacturer to find out how it is handling the problem. Also see if you can find the manufacturer's Website to learn if it has disclosed the recall there. What do you think of the manner in which the manufacturer has handled the recall? Is the manufacturer providing adequate protection to consumers?

You can find further practice problems at academic.cengage.com/blaw/beatty.

---

19 "Give Yourself Some Credit If You Pass This Quiz," *The Times-Picayune*, Apr. 7, 1994, p. E5. Permission granted by The Times-Picayune Publishing Corporation. All rights reserved. Reprinted with permission

25 Environmental Law

© PHOTODISC COLLECTION/GETTY IMAGES

"**W**hen my mother was left a widow almost 50 years ago, she taught school to support her family. A few years after my father's death, she took her savings and bought a small commercial building on a downtown lot in our little town in Oregon. The building, she said, would offer what my father couldn't—a source of support in her old age. In one half of the building was a children's clothing store, in the other a dry cleaners. The two stores served Main Street shoppers for years.

"Now the building that once represented security has produced a menace with the potential to bankrupt my mother. The discovery of contamination in city park well water triggered groundwater tests in the area. Waste products discarded by dry cleaners were identified as a likely source of contamination. Although a dry cleaner hasn't operated for 20 years on my mother's property, chemicals remain in the soil. Mother knew nothing of this hazard until a letter came from the Oregon Department of Environmental Quality. It said she should decide if she would oversee further testing and cleanup herself or if she would let the government handle it. In either case, my mother would pay the costs.

"The building is worth just under $70,000. Cleanup costs will be at least $200,000. At 84, my mother has enough savings to preserve her independence. She does not have enough money to bear the enormous costs of new community standards. The dry cleaner that operated in my mother's building disposed of chemicals the same way other dry cleaners did. None of these businesses was operated in a negligent fashion. They followed standards accepted by the community at the time. Now we are learning that we must live more carefully if we are to survive in a world that is safe and clean. My question is: Who will pay? Who will be responsible for cleaning up environmental messes made before we knew better?"[1] ■

---

1 Carolyn Scott Kortge, "Taken to the Cleaners," *Newsweek*, Oct. 23, 1995, p. 16. Reprinted with permission of the author.

INTRODUCTION

The environmental movement in the United States began in 1962 with the publication of Rachel Carson's book *Silent Spring*. She was the first to expose the deadly—and lingering—impact of DDT and other pesticides. These chemicals spread a wide web, poisoning not only the targeted insects but the entire food chain—fish, birds, and even humans. Since Carson first sounded the alarm, environmental issues have appeared regularly in the news—everything from acute disasters such as the *Exxon Valdez* tanker oil spill in Alaska to chronic concerns over pesticide residues in food. For more about Rachel Carson (and links to other environmental Websites), visit http://www.rachelcarson.org. To find out about environmental quality in your area, look at http://epa.gov.

The environmental movement began with the fervor of a moral crusade. How could anyone be against a clean environment? It has become clear, however, that the issue is more complex. It is not enough simply to say, "We are against pollution." As the opening vignette reveals, the question is: Who will pay? Who will pay for past damage inflicted before anyone understood the harm that pollutants cause? Who will pay for current changes necessary to prevent damage now and in the future? Are car owners willing to spend $100 or $1,000 more per car to prevent air pollution? Are easterners ready to ban oil drilling in the Arctic National Wildlife Refuge in Alaska if that means higher prices for heating oil? Will loggers in the West give up their jobs to protect endangered species? Are all consumers willing to pay more to insulate their homes? The first President George Bush, a Republican, said, "Beyond all the studies, the figures, and the debates, the environment is a moral issue." But Newt Gingrich, a Republican Speaker of the House of Representatives, called the Environmental Protection Agency "the biggest job-killing agency in inner-city America."[2]

The cost-benefit tradeoff is particularly complex in environmental issues because those who pay the cost often do not receive the benefit. If a company dumps toxic wastes into a stream, its shareholders benefit by avoiding the expense of safe disposal. Those who fish or drink the waters pay the real costs without receiving any of the benefit. Economists use the term **"externality"** to describe the situation in which people do not bear the full cost of their decisions. Externalities prevent the market system from achieving a clean environment on its own. Only government involvement can realign costs and benefits.

Environmental Protection Agency

Thirty-five years ago, environmental abuses were (ineffectively) governed by tort law and a smattering of local ordinances. Now, environmental law is a mammoth structure of federal and state regulation. In 1970, Congress created the Environmental Protection Agency (EPA) to consolidate environmental regulation under one roof. When Congress passes a new environmental law, the EPA issues regulations to implement it. The agency can bring administrative enforcement action against those who violate its regulations. An administrative law judge within the agency hears these actions. Either party can appeal this decision to a United States Court of Appeals and from there to the Supreme Court. Those who violate environmental laws are liable for civil damages. In addition, some statutes, such as the Clean Water Act, the Resource Conservation and Recovery Act, and the Endangered Species Act, provide for *criminal*

---

2 Both men are quoted in Robert V. Percival, Alan S. Miller, Christopher H. Schroeder, and James P. Leape, *Environmental Regulation* (Boston: Little, Brown & Co., 1992), p. 1, and 1995 supp. p. 2.

penalties, including imprisonment. The EPA is not shy about seeking criminal prosecutions of those who knowingly violate these statutes, and of those corporate officers who fail to prevent criminal negligence by their employees.

AIR POLLUTION

On October 26, 1948, almost half the 10,000 people in Donora, Pennsylvania, fell ill from air pollution. A weather inversion trapped industrial pollutants in the air, creating a lethal smog. Twenty residents ultimately died. Although air pollution rarely causes this type of acute illness, it can cause or increase the severity of diseases that are annoying, chronic, or even fatal—such as pneumonia, bronchitis, emphysema, and cancer. A rise in ozone levels is associated with an increase in deaths from heart and lung disease. Even apart from the health risks, air pollution can be irritating: it blocks visibility, damages car exteriors, and grimes windowsills. To find out the air quality today where you live, view http://www.epa.gov/airnow.

There are three major sources of air pollution: coal-burning utility plants, factories, and motor vehicles. Residential furnaces, farm operations, forest fires, and dust from mines and construction sites also contribute. Local regulation is ineffective in controlling air pollution. For instance, when cities limited pollution from factory smokestacks, plants simply built taller stacks that sent the pollution hundreds, or even thousands, of miles away. Local governments had little incentive to prevent this long-distance migration. Recognizing the national nature of the problem, Congress enacted three air pollution laws during the 1950s and 1960s. With little enforcement bite and no EPA to ensure implementation, these statutes had minimal impact.

Clean Air Act

Dissatisfied by this lack of progress, Congress passed the Clean Air Act of 1970. **The Clean Air Act has four major provisions:**

- **Primary Standards.** Congress directed the EPA to establish **national ambient air quality standards** (known as NAAQSs) for primary pollution—that is, pollution that harms the public health. The EPA's mandate was to set standards that protected public health and provided an adequate margin of safety *without regard to cost*. Pollution may not exceed these limits anyplace in the country. The EPA must regularly update the rules to reflect the latest scientific evidence.

- **Secondary Standards.** Congress also directed the EPA to establish NAAQSs for pollution that may not be a threat to health but has other unpleasant effects, such as obstructing visibility and harming plants or other materials.

- **State Implementation Plans (SIPs).** The Clean Air Act envisioned a partnership between the EPA and the states. After the EPA set primary and secondary standards, states would produce SIPs to meet the primary standards within three years and the secondary standards within a reasonable time. If a SIP was not acceptable, the EPA would produce its own plan for that state. In formulating their SIPs, states were required to identify the major sources of pollution. Each polluter would then be given a pollution limit to bring the area into compliance with national standards. The worse the pollution in a particular area, the tougher the regulations.

- **Citizen Suits.** The Clean Air Act (and many other environmental statutes) permits anyone to file suit against a polluter or against the EPA for failing to enforce the statute. Citizens have often been more assertive than the EPA in enforcing environmental statutes. For instance, the Arizona Center for Law in the Public Interest has sued the EPA more than a dozen times for failing to impose sufficiently strict air quality standards on Phoenix and Tucson.

Although air quality throughout the country improved dramatically, a 1990 EPA study revealed that, 20 years after passage of the Clean Air Act, virtually every American was still breathing unsafe levels of some pollutants. In 1990, Congress amended the Act, setting more realistic goals but also higher penalties for failure. For instance, the deadline for Los Angeles was extended, but the penalty for noncompliance was increased—a cutoff of federal highway funds (a serious blow indeed in Los Angeles) and the threat of even stricter controls. Already, everything in California from lawn mowers to bakeries to barbecue grills is subject to increasingly strict standards.

To find out about the general air quality in your community, feel your way over to http://www.scorecard.org.

In the following case, a power plant argued that the EPA had imposed a solution whose cost far outweighed its benefit. There is only one Grand Canyon. Should visibility there be preserved at any cost?

You Be the Judge

CENTRAL ARIZONA WATER CONSERVATION DISTRICT V. EPA

990 F.2d 1531, 1993 U.S. App. LEXIS 5881
United States Court of Appeals for the Ninth Circuit, 1993

Facts: In the Clean Air Act, Congress directed the EPA to issue regulations that would protect visibility at national landmarks. The Navaho Generating Station (NGS) is a power plant 12 miles from the Grand Canyon. In response to a citizen suit filed by the Environmental Defense Fund under the Clean Air Act, the EPA ordered NGS to reduce its sulfur dioxide emissions by 90 percent. To do so would cost NGS $430 million initially in capital expenditures and then $89.6 million annually. Average winter visibility in the Grand Canyon would be improved by at most 7 percent, but perhaps less. NGS sued to prevent implementation of the EPA's order. A court may nullify an EPA order if it determines that the agency action was arbitrary and capricious.

You Be the Judge: Did the EPA act arbitrarily and capriciously in requiring NGS to spend half a billion dollars to improve winter visibility at the Grand Canyon by at most 7 percent?

Argument for NGS: This case is a perfect example of environmentalism run amok. Half a billion dollars for the *chance* of increasing winter visibility at the Grand Canyon by 7 percent? No rational person would choose to spend his own money that way, but the EPA is happy to spend NGS's. Winter visitors to the Grand Canyon would undoubtedly prefer that NGS provide them with a free lunch rather than a 7 percent improvement in visibility. The EPA order is simply a waste of money.

Argument for the EPA: Under the Clean Air Act, Congress instructed the EPA to protect visibility at national landmarks such as the Grand Canyon. How can NGS, or anyone else, measure the benefit of protecting a national treasure like the Grand Canyon? Even people who never have and never will visit it during the winter sleep better at night knowing that the Canyon is protected. NGS has been causing harm to the Grand Canyon, and now it should remedy the damage.

Courts generally defer to federal agencies, whose experts deal with similar problems all the time. The EPA has greater expertise in these matters than either NGS or this court. ●

ECONOMICS
& the LAW

The Office of Management and Budget, the White House's research branch, calculated that over the past decade the benefit from environmental regulations has been five to seven times their cost. The benefits, which include fewer deaths, illnesses, and lost workdays, have been between $120 billion and $193 billion, whereas the costs have been from $23 billion to $26 billion. Of course, these types of calculations are by their very nature speculative. In any event, the Clean Air Act directs the EPA to set air quality standards without regard to cost. Should cost-benefit analysis matter? ◆

New Sources of Pollution

Some states had air so clean that they could have allowed air quality to decline and still have met EPA standards. However, the Clean Air Act declared that one of its purposes was to "protect and enhance" air quality. Using this phrase, the Sierra Club sued the EPA to prevent it from approving any SIPs that met EPA standards but nonetheless permitted a decline in air quality. As a result of this suit, the EPA developed a **prevention of significant deterioration (PSD)** program. **No one may undertake a building project that will cause a major increase in pollution without first obtaining a permit from the EPA.** The agency will grant permits only if an applicant can demonstrate that (1) its emissions will not cause an overall decline in air quality and (2) it has installed the **best available control technology** for every pollutant.

The PSD program prohibits any deterioration in current air quality, *regardless of health impact.* In essence, national policy values a clean environment for its own sake, apart from any health benefits.

Acid Rain

In some places, rain is now 10 times more acidic than it would naturally be. The results of acid rain are visible in the eastern United States and Canada—damaged forests, crops, and lakes. Acid is primarily created by sulfur emissions from large coal-burning utility plants in the Midwest. Many of these plants were built before the Clean Air Act, when the easiest way to meet state and local standards (while keeping electricity prices low) was to build tall stacks that would send the sulfur dioxide far away. Terrific for Ohio, not so wonderful for Maine.

The Clean Air Act banned the tall-stack solution, leaving coal plants, in theory, with two choices: install (expensive) scrubbers or buy (cheaper) low-sulfur western coal. Under pressure from members who represented states with high-sulfur coal, Congress compromised and required all power plants to install scrubbers regardless of the coal they burned. In this way, western coal would have no advantage.

In 1990, Congress amended the Clean Air Act to require power plants to cut their sulfur dioxide emissions by half. This time, however, Congress did not specify how the goal should be achieved and instead offered new methods for minimizing costs and maximizing economic efficiency. **Power plants have four options for meeting emissions standards: (1) installing scrubbers, (2) using low-sulfur coal, (3) switching to alternative fuels (such as natural gas), or (4) trading emissions allowances.** This last alternative requires some explanation. Each year, every utility receives an emissions allowance, meaning that it is allowed to emit a certain number of tons of pollutants. If a company does not need its entire allowance, because it uses cleaner fuels or has installed pollution control devices, it can sell the leftover allowance to other companies or stockpile the allowance for future use. Plants with high levels of pollution either buy more allowances or reduce their own emissions, depending on which alternative is cheaper. In effect, the government establishes the maximum amount of pollution, and then the market sets the price for meeting the national standard.

The market for sulfur dioxide emissions has become remarkably efficient and effective. Power plants now have a financial incentive to reduce pollution through innovation. In some years, pollution from sulfur dioxide has declined by as much as 25 percent, at a cost one tenth the original estimate. For more information on the emissions trading program, click on http://www.epa.gov and search for "emissions trading." This Website reveals who has bought allowances and at what cost. Note that sometimes the highest bidders are organizations such as the Birney Elementary School, which buys emissions allowances simply to keep polluters from using them.

There is, however, one catch to the emissions trading system: **new source review.** Originally, Congress had exempted the oldest power plants and factories from the Clean Air Act on the theory that they would be very expensive to upgrade and would be replaced soon enough anyway. As it turned out, many companies discovered it was easier to patch up the old plants than it was to replace them with new, clean operations. Congress amended the Act to impose the new source review system: companies are required to upgrade pollution devices anytime they renovate a plant (but not when they undertake routine maintenance). In the end, though, few plants have complied with the new source review requirements, at least in part because the EPA issued weak regulations to implement the law. For instance, the EPA defines routine maintenance as any activity that costs less than 20 percent of the value of the generating unit—which means a company could spend hundreds of millions of dollars on so-called routine maintenance and not be required to upgrade pollution facilities. The American Lung Association termed these rules "the most harmful and unlawful air-pollution initiative ever undertaken by the federal government."[3]

Automobile Pollution

The Clean Air Act of 1970 directed the EPA to reduce automobile pollution levels by 90 percent within six years. Although the technology to achieve this goal did not then exist, Congress believed that the auto industry could, if forced, be able to develop the necessary innovations. This approach has been referred to as **technology forcing,** in the sense that industry is forced to develop the technology. Indeed, by 1975, General Motors developed a catalytic converter that not only reduced harmful emissions but improved fuel economy.

Although new cars are 97 percent cleaner than 1970 models, motor vehicles are still a major source of air pollution, releasing more than 50 percent of the hazardous pollutants in the air. Each car may be cleaner, but Americans are driving more—and bigger—cars more miles on more trips. During 1970, Americans traveled one trillion miles, but by 2000 the annual total had increased to four trillion miles. In 2002, the auto industry fought off congressional efforts to increase automobile fuel efficiency requirements.

Plagued as it is by smog, California has been more aggressive than Congress in limiting automobile pollution. The state recently passed tough emission rules that, beginning with the 2016 model year, would require about a 30 percent decrease in emissions from cars and trucks sold in California. These regulations are now in limbo because automakers have challenged them in court. (To show support for these new rules, Governor Arnold Schwarzenegger traded in his fuel-guzzling Hummer for a specially designed version that runs on hydrogen.) Ten other states, including New York, Connecticut, Washington, and Oregon have also adopted California's tougher

---

3 Bruce Barcott, "Changing all the Rules," *The New York Times,* Apr. 4, 2004, sec. 6, p. 38.

car emission standards. Inhabitants of these states buy 29 percent of the cars purchased in America. This market power will presumably pressure the auto industry to produce more fuel-efficient cars.

Soot Particles

Produced primarily by power plants and diesel fuel, microscopic soot particles substantially increase the risk of premature death from lung cancer and other breathing and heart disorders. Because of these particles, residing in a city has the same impact on one's lungs as living with a smoker. The life expectancy of residents in cities with the cleanest air is on average two years longer than those in the dirtiest cities. In 1997, the EPA issued regulations limiting soot. However, a lawsuit by power plant operators and automobile manufacturers delayed the rules until 2001, when the Supreme Court ruled that the EPA had the right to impose these new regulations without conducting a cost-benefit analysis.[4]

Air Toxics

Some pollutants are so potent that even tiny amounts cause harm. For instance, the EPA has never been able to identify a safe level of exposure to asbestos. Each year, 2.7 billion pounds of toxics spew into the air in the United States, causing an estimated annual increase of 3,000 cancer deaths. Two thirds of Americans face an increased cancer risk from exposure to toxic chemicals in the air. Because the Clean Air Act directed the EPA to set safety standards that provided an adequate margin of safety without regard to cost, the agency in theory has no choice except an outright ban on some pollutants. Because such a ban would shut down the steel, chemical, and petroleum industries, among others, the EPA does not consider such a strategy to be politically viable.

The Environmental Defense Fund sued the EPA to force compliance with the law. Nevertheless, by 1990, the agency had proposed standards for only seven substances. Although these standards do not eliminate health risks, they are set at the lowest feasible level given existing technology, and the courts have upheld them.

In 1990 amendments to the Clean Air Act, Congress directed the EPA to set standards for each of 189 specific pollutants and any other toxics the EPA wanted to include. The EPA was permitted to base these standards initially on the **maximum achievable control technology (MACT).** Within eight years of developing MACT rules, the EPA was instructed to tighten the standards to a level at which the risk of cancer from these substances was no more than one in one million over a lifetime. This two-step process was meant to create an incentive for polluters to continue to develop better technology.

Global Warming

During the last 100 years, the average temperature worldwide has increased between 0.5° and 1.1° F. If current trends continue, the world's average temperature during the next 100 years will rise another 2° to 6° F, producing the warmest climate in the history of humankind. (By comparison, the planet is only 5° to 9° F warmer than during the last ice age.) The impact of this climate change is potentially catastrophic: a rise in sea level that would engulf coastal areas, a devastating decline in fishing stocks, the

---

4 *Whitman v. American Trucking Associations*, 531 U.S. 457; 2001 U.S. LEXIS 1952.

death of major forests, and a loss of farmland worldwide. It has been estimated that these changes could cost between 1 and 2.5 percent of global gross domestic product (GDP). For a long time, the scientific evidence underlying the theory of global warming was subject to doubt and debate. But today, most reasonable scientists accept that the burning of fossil fuels produces gases—carbon dioxide, methane, and nitrous oxide—that do indeed create a greenhouse effect by trapping heat in the earth's atmosphere.

Identifying the problem, however, does not illuminate the solution. Global warming is the most complex environmental problem of the new millennium because any solution requires international political cooperation coupled with major lifestyle changes. The Energy Department has estimated that, to fight global warming effectively, U.S. gasoline prices would have to rise by nearly $2 a gallon and electricity prices might have to increase by 86 percent.

The United States plays a particularly important role in finding a solution because with 5 percent of the world's population, it consumes 25 percent of the world's energy. Thus far, however, this country has largely elected to be part of the problem, not part of the solution. It is the only leading industrialized nation that refused to ratify the Kyoto Protocol. This treaty requires emissions to be reduced by the year 2012 to a level 5.2 percent below 1990 amounts.

In 2002, the American government sent the U.S. Climate Action Report to the United Nations. In this document, the United States acknowledged that the use of fossil fuels causes global warming. The report also conceded that global warming was likely to have a damaging impact on this country—causing severe heat waves, coastal flooding, and water shortages. However, the report also pointed out some potential benefits, such as a longer growing season, at least in the short run. Its proposed solution was not prevention but adaptation. It suggested, for example, that increased use of air conditioning could mitigate the impact of heat waves. The report stated that "In the real world, no one will forego meeting basic family needs to protect the global commons."

Although the United States has not ratified the Kyoto Protocol, there have been some grassroots efforts to comply voluntarily with some parts of it. As we have seen, California has become an important player in the global warming debate by tightening its fuel emission standards. Some business leaders have agreed to voluntary limits on the greenhouse gases that their companies produce. For example, the heads of seven electric-power companies volunteered to reduce their greenhouse gas emissions by 3 percent to 5 percent and General Motors has reduced its plant emissions in North America by 10 percent. It seems as if, by hook or by crook, bit by bit, we will all be affected by efforts to limit greenhouse gases.

WATER POLLUTION

One day, thousands of Milwaukeeans began to suffer nausea, cramps, and diarrhea. The suspected culprit? *Cryptosporidium*, a tiny protozoan that usually resides in the intestines of cattle and other animals. Ironically, the parasite may have entered Milwaukee's water supply at a purification plant on Lake Michigan. Officials suspect that infected runoff from dairy farms spilled into Lake Michigan near the plant's intake pipe. Doctors advised those with a damaged immune system (such as AIDS patients) to avoid drinking municipal water. Most Milwaukeeans were taking no chances—more than 800,000 switched to boiled or bottled water.

Polluted water can cause a number of loathsome diseases, such as typhus and dysentery. But by 1930, most American cities had dramatically reduced outbreaks of waterborne diseases by chlorinating their water. (The parasite that caused the Milwaukee outbreak is relatively immune to chlorine.) However, industrial discharges into the water supply have increased rapidly, with a significant impact on water quality. These industrial wastes may not induce acute illnesses like typhus, but they can cause serious diseases such as cancer. There is more at stake than health alone; clean water is valued for esthetics, recreation, and fishing.

Clean Water Act

In 1972, Congress passed a statute, now called the Clean Water Act (CWA), with two ambitious goals: (1) to make all navigable water suitable for swimming and fishing by 1983, and (2) to eliminate the discharge of pollutants into navigable water by 1985. Like the Clean Air Act, the CWA sets goals without regard to cost; leaves enforcement primarily to the states, with oversight by the EPA; and permits citizen suits. Also, like the Clean Air Act, the CWA's goals have not been met.

Industrial Discharges

The CWA prohibits any single producer from discharging pollution into water without a permit from the EPA. Before granting a permit, the EPA must set limits, by industry, on the amount of each type of pollution any single producer (called a **point source**) can discharge. These limits must be based on the **best available technology.** The EPA faces a gargantuan task in determining the best available technology that *each* industry can use to reduce pollution. Furthermore, standards become obsolete quickly as technology changes.

The CWA also requires the EPA to measure water quality broadly to determine if the permit system is working. Until clean water standards are met, every point source is held to the same standard, whether it is discharging into a clean ocean that can handle more pollution or a stagnant lake that cannot. Because determining the impact of a particular discharge may not be possible, especially when it is mingled with others, it is easier for the EPA to set the same standards for everyone. Easier and fairer—Congress did not want states to lure industry with promises of laxer pollution rules.

In the following case, the Supreme Court discusses the definition of "point source."

SOUTH FLORIDA WATER MANAGEMENT DISTRICT V. MICCOSUKEE TRIBE OF INDIANS

541 U.S. 95, 124 S. Ct. 1537, 2004 U.S. LEXIS 2376
Supreme Court of the United States, 2004

Facts: The land between south Florida's coastal hills and the Everglades was once part of the Everglades, and its surface and groundwater flowed south in a uniform and unchanneled sheet. Starting in the early 1900s, however, Florida began building canals to drain the Everglades and make parts of them suitable for cultivation. These canals proved to be trouble: they caused flooding, and they lowered the water table, allowing salt water into coastal wells.

In 1948, Congress instructed the United States Army Corps of Engineers to solve these problems.

In response, the Corps constructed the Central and South Florida Flood Control Project (Project): a vast array of levees, canals, pumps, and water storage areas. The Project fundamentally altered the hydrology of the Everglades, changing the natural sheet flow of the water. The South Florida Water Management District (District) operates the Project.

C-11 is a canal that collects groundwater and rainwater from a 104-square-mile area of Broward County that has a population of 136,000 people. ▼

When the water in C-11 rises too high, it is pumped into a wetland area (called WCA-3) that is a remnant of the original Everglades. Before entering C-11, the rainwater absorbs contaminants produced by human activities, including phosphorus from fertilizer used by farmers. When this phosphorus is pumped into WCA-3 (by a pump called S-9), it alters the balance of the WCA-3 ecosystem and stimulates the growth of algae and plants foreign to the Everglades.

A number of initiatives were underway to reduce these impacts and thereby restore the ecological integrity of the Everglades. The Miccosukee Tribe of Indians (the Tribe), impatient with the pace of this progress, brought suit under the Clean Water Act (the Act) to halt the pumping of water from C-11 into WCA-3. The Tribe alleged that C-11 was a point source and, therefore, could not discharge pollutants into WC-3 without a permit. The District argued that the canal was not a point source because it did not create the pollutants; it simply transported them. The Tribe filed a motion for summary judgment, which the trial court granted and the appellate court affirmed. The Supreme Court granted *certiorari*.

Issue: Is a canal a point source when it transmits pollutants that it did not create?

Excerpts from Justice O'Connor's Decision: Congress enacted the Act in 1972. Its stated objective was "to restore and maintain the chemical, physical, and biological integrity of the Nation's waters." To serve those ends, the Act prohibits the discharge of any pollutant by any person unless done in compliance with some provision of the Act. The provision relevant to this case requires dischargers to obtain permits that place limits on the type and quantity of pollutants that can be released into the Nation's waters. The Act defines the phrase "discharge of a pollutant" to mean "any addition of any pollutant to navigable waters from any point source." A "point source," in turn, is defined as "any discernible, confined and discrete conveyance," such as "a pipe, ditch, channel, or tunnel from which pollutants are or may be discharged."

The question is whether the operation of the S-9 pump constitutes the discharge of a pollutant within the meaning of the Act. The District argued that the [permit requirement] covers a point source only when a pollutant originates from the point source, and not when pollutants originating elsewhere merely pass through the point source.

A point source is, by definition, a "discernible, confined, and discrete *conveyance*." (emphasis added). That definition makes plain that a point source need not be the original source of the pollutant; it need only convey the pollutant to navigable waters, which are, in turn, defined as "the waters of the United States." Tellingly, the examples of "point sources" listed by the Act include pipes, ditches, tunnels, and conduits, objects that do not themselves generate pollutants but merely transport them. In addition, one of the Act's primary goals was to impose permitting requirements on municipal wastewater treatment plants. But under the District's interpretation of the Act, the [permit] program would not cover such plants, because they treat and discharge pollutants added to water by others. We therefore reject the District's proposed reading of the definition of "discharge of a pollutant." That definition includes within its reach point sources that do not themselves generate pollutants. ∎

Water Quality Standards

The CWA requires states to set EPA-approved water quality standards and develop plans to achieve them. The first step in developing a plan is to determine how each body of water is used. Standards may vary depending upon the designated use—higher for recreational lakes than for a river used to irrigate farmland. No matter what the water's designated use, standards may not be set at a level lower than its current condition. Congress is not in the business of permitting *more* pollution.

States are supposed to pay special attention to so-called **non-point sources**—that is, pollutants with no single source, such as water runoff from agricultural land or city streets. This runoff may contain gasoline, pesticides, or bacteria. Congress left non-point source pollution to the states because it is so difficult to regulate. This regulation also involves complex issues such as land use planning that are, in theory, better handled at the local level than by national fiat. However optimistic Congress may have been, to date the states have not successfully implemented this section of the CWA. They appear to lack both the political will and the technological know-how, for which they are not totally to blame. Determining the impact of individual pollutants on the overall quality of a body of water used for many different purposes is a complex problem. Land use planning requires a delicate and volatile mix of consensus and control.

As the ambitious goals set by the CWA have not been met, Congress has granted numerous extensions. At the same time, environmental advocates have filed citizen suits to force the EPA to toughen its enforcement.

Wetlands

Wetlands are the transition areas between land and open water. They may look like swamps, they may even be swamps, but their unattractive appearance should not disguise their vital role in the aquatic world. They are natural habitats for many fish and wildlife. They also serve as a filter for neighboring bodies of water, trapping chemicals and sediments. Moreover, they are an important aid in flood control because they can absorb a high level of water and then release it slowly after the emergency is past.

The CWA prohibits any discharge of dredge and fill material into wetlands without a permit. Although filling in wetlands requires a permit, many other activities that harm wetlands, such as draining them, originally did not. (However, many states require permits for draining wetlands.) After some particularly egregious abuses, the EPA issued regulations to limit the destruction of wetlands. These new regulations were, however, successfully challenged in the courts.[5] The EPA then rewrote the regulations to accomplish the same goal within the parameters set out by the courts. These new regulations will certainly be challenged, too.

Although, in theory, the government's official policy is no net loss of wetlands, the reality has been different. Since the country was settled, about half of the original 230 million acres of wetlands in the continental United States have been destroyed. In 2002, the Bush administration amended the "no net loss" rule so that it could issue waivers in some cases. The Web site **http://www.nwi.fws.gov** shows an inventory of wetlands in the United States.

Sewage

Plumbing drains must be attached to either a septic system or a sewer line. A septic system is, in effect, a freestanding waste treatment plant. A sewer line, on the other hand, feeds into a publicly owned wastewater treatment plant, also known as a municipal sewage plant. **Under the CWA, a municipality must obtain a permit for any discharge from a wastewater treatment plant.** To obtain a permit, the municipality must first treat the waste to reduce its toxicity. However, taxpayers have stubbornly resisted the large increases in taxes or fees necessary to fund required treatments. Because the fines imposed by the EPA are almost always less than the cost of treatment, some cities have been slow to comply. The following news report illustrates the complex tradeoffs between costs and benefits.

---

[5] *National Mining Ass'n v. U.S. Army Corps of Engineers*, 145 F.3d 1399 (D.C. Cir. 1998).

NEWS*worthy*

In the two years since Tom Cox took over as general manager of Constitution Marina, located in one of the sludgiest pockets of Boston's infamously sludgy Inner Harbor, he has seen an entire ecosystem reborn before his eyes. At the mouth of a now-sealed effluent pipe that once poured sewer waste directly into his anchorage, baby herring and krill shrimp feed. "This spring, for the first time in a decade, we even had porpoises in the Inner Harbor, and seals flopping onto my docks. Boston Harbor," Cox says, "is definitely back."[6]

Back? The Boston Harbor? The harbor that was gruesomely swamped with human waste during the disastrous crash of the old Deer Island treatment plant? The harbor that only a few years ago still reeked of 350 years of ill use?

The harbor has passed a vital milestone on its voyage from toilet bowl for 43 cities and towns to tourist attraction and recharging jobs engine. The new $183 million Deer Island sewage-treatment plant received a formal commission, and its predecessor, an obsolete and overburdened albatross that once channeled raw sewage directly in the bay, was bulldozed into dust.

This transformation has not come cheap. Sewer user charges for residents of the greater Boston area have risen more than 560 percent in the past decade, becoming among the highest in the country. These charges are expected to rise an additional 50 to 75 percent in the next few years. In protest, angry ratepayers dumped tea boxes full of sewer bills into the harbor. ◆

Other Water Pollution Statutes

The Safe Drinking Water Act of 1974:

- Requires the EPA to set national standards for contaminants potentially harmful to human health that are found in drinking water;

- Assigns enforcement responsibility to the states but permits the EPA to take enforcement action against states that do not adhere to the standards;

- Prohibits the use of lead in any pipes through which drinking water flows; and

- Requires community water systems to send every customer an annual *consumer confidence report* disclosing the level of contaminants in the drinking water. (One can only hope that consumers will remain confident after receiving the report.) To find out more about your drinking water, turn on http://www.epa.gov and click on "Where You Live."

The **Ocean Dumping Act of 1972** prohibits the dumping of wastes in ocean water without a permit from the EPA.

Congress passed the **Oil Pollution Act of 1990** in response to the mammoth 1989 *Exxon Valdez* tanker oil spill in Prince William Sound, Alaska. To prevent defective boats from leaking oil, this statute sets design standards for ships operating in U.S. waters. It also requires ship owners to pay for damage caused by oil discharged from their ships.

Although few would argue with the concept that those who spill ought to pay, there has been great controversy over how to measure damages. The U.S. government proposed that damages should be based on the subjective value that people assign to an injured area. Suppose that an oil spill prevents 1,000 people from using a beach. The government proposal would base the fine on the value that these people report (in a survey) that they place on a day of swimming or walking on the beach. If sea fowl are injured by the spill, nearby residents would be asked what they would be willing

---

[6] Tom Mashberg, "Harbor Cleans Up Its Act," *Boston Herald*, July 30, 1995, p. 1.

to pay to save a bird from death. Oil companies prefer to pay only the cost of fixing the damage. If 1,000 seagulls are killed by a spill, oil companies contend that the proper fine should equal the cost of cleaning up the area and increasing the number of seagulls. That might mean importing seagulls or augmenting their food supply.

WASTE DISPOSAL

The time is 1978. The place is 96th Street in Niagara Falls, New York. Six women are afflicted with breast cancer, one man has bladder cancer, another suffers from throat cancer. A seven-year-old boy suddenly goes into convulsions and dies of kidney failure. Other residents have chromosomal abnormalities, epilepsy, respiratory problems, and skin diseases. This street is three blocks away from Love Canal.

In 1945, Hooker Chemical Co. disposed of 21,800 tons of 82 different chemicals by dumping them into Love Canal or burying them nearby. An internal memorandum warned that this decision would lead to "potential future hazard" and be a "potential source of lawsuits." A year later, the company's lawyer wrote that "children in the neighborhood use portions of the water for swimming and, as a matter of fact, just before we left the site we saw several young children walking down the path with what appeared to be bathing costumes in hand." He suggested that Hooker build a fence around the canal, but the company never did. Instead, it sold the land to the local school board to build an elementary school. When the company's executive vice-president recommended against the sale, the company inserted a clause in the deed to eliminate the company's liability.

Schoolchildren tripped over drums of chemicals that worked their way up to the surface. Some children were burned playing with hot balls of chemical residue—what they called "fire stones"—that popped up through the ground. Homeowners noticed foul odors in their basements after heavy rains. Finally, a national health emergency was declared at Love Canal, and a joint federal-state program relocated 800 families. In 1994, Occidental Chemical Corp. (which had since bought Hooker) agreed to pay the state of New York $98 million to settle a lawsuit over Love Canal.[7] Two years later, the EPA settled its lawsuit with Occidental for $129 million. In the end, the cleanup cost almost $400 million and took 21 years to complete.

In its time, what Hooker did was not unusual. Companies historically dumped waste in waterways, landfills, or open dumps. Out of sight was out of mind. Waste disposal continues to be a major problem in the United States. It has been estimated that the cost of cleaning up existing waste products will exceed $1 *trillion*. At the same time, the country continues to produce more than six billion tons of agricultural, commercial, industrial, and domestic waste each year. Ironically, air and water pollution control devices have added to the problem because the pollutants they remove from the air and water become waste that must be discarded somewhere.

Two major statutes regulate wastes. The Resource Conservation and Recovery Act (RCRA) focuses on *preventing* future Love Canals by regulating the production and disposal of solid wastes, both toxic and otherwise. The Comprehensive Environmental Response, Compensation, and Liability Act (CERCLA), also referred to as **Superfund,** focuses on *cleaning up* existing hazardous waste sites.

---

7 William Glaberson, "Love Canal: Suit Focuses on Records from 1940s," *The New York Times,* Oct. 22, 1990, p. B1. Copyright © 1990 by The New York Times Co. Reprinted by permission.

Resource Conservation and Recovery Act

The RCRA establishes rules for treating both hazardous wastes and other forms of solid waste (such as ordinary garbage).

Solid Waste

Before 1895, the city of New York did not collect garbage. Residents simply piled it up in the streets, causing the streets to rise five feet in height over the century. At present, each American generates 4.5 pounds of solid waste a *day*, an increase of 60 percent since 1960 and more waste per capita than any other country.

But most Americans never gave much thought to their waste until the infamous case of the garbage barge. The trouble arose in 1983 when the New York legislature banned new landfills (garbage dumps) on Long Island. Three years later, the landfill began to fill up in Islip, a bedroom community outside New York City. Lowell Herrelson, an Alabama businessman, offered to put the Islip garbage on a barge and ship it to another state. But once he filled the barge, no other state would take the garbage. Loaded with 3,186 tons of waste, the barge traveled more than 6,000 miles in five months and was turned away by six states and three countries before returning to New York and anchoring near the Statue of Liberty. Its movements were reported daily in the newspapers and even became the subject of the *Tonight Show* monologue: "The only town to send its garbage on a 6,000 mile cruise." The garbage was ultimately burned in a Brooklyn incinerator, but not before Herrelson had lost $500,000 in the venture. Islip introduced recycling and built a $38 million garbage incinerator.

The disposal of nonhazardous solid waste has generally been left to the states, but they must follow guidelines set by the RCRA. **The RCRA:**

- Bans new open dumps;
- Requires that garbage be sent to sanitary landfills;
- Sets minimum standards for landfills;
- Requires landfills to monitor nearby groundwater;
- Requires states to develop a permit program for landfills; and
- Provides some financial assistance to aid states in waste management.

ECONOMICS *& the* LAW	The federal Office of Management and Budget (OMB) objected to the solid waste regulations that the EPA intended to issue under the RCRA because, according to the OMB's calculations, complying with the proposed regulations would have cost more than $19 billion for every life saved. Not worth it, said the OMB. As a result, the EPA's revised regulations are more flexible than the original version.

This dispute typifies the ongoing conflict in environmental law. On the one hand, the EPA argues that scientific data are uncertain and the health risks of pollutants may be much worse than we realize. The EPA's goal is to stop pollution virtually without regard to cost. The OMB, on the other hand, prefers to base decisions on a numerical cost-benefit analysis. The OMB believes that a clean-air-and-water-for-its-own-sake approach makes little economic sense. Is a human life worth $19 billion? Is your life? ◆

Ethics	Computers and other consumer electronic devices have created the most rapidly growing waste problem in the world. Containing chemicals such as lead and mercury, these products produce not only large volume but also dangerous toxicity. Industrialized nations have found a simple solution—between 50 and 80 percent of the "e-waste" collected for recycling is sent to countries such as China, India, and Pakistan.

Once the e-waste is in Asia, adults and children, working without any protective clothing or equipment, burn the plastic casings in the open air, dismantle toner cartridges by hand, and melt circuit boards. The ground, air, and water are polluted with the residue of these toxic components. Because this disposal method is so easy and cheap (for the industrialized nations), manufacturers have not attempted to reduce toxic components in electronic products, and governments have not forced them to take responsibility for safe disposal at the end of the product's life.[8]

What is the ethical obligation of developed nations to dispose of toxic e-waste? From the Chapter 2 Ethics Checklist: What would the Golden Rule suggest? What values are at stake?

What will you do with your old computer when you buy a new one? Hewlett Packard will safely recycle e-waste, whether or not HP made it, for a fee of $13 to $34 per item (see http://www.hp.com/go/recycle). Would you be willing to pay that sum? ◆

Underground Storage Tanks

Concerned that underground gasoline storage tanks were leaking into water supplies, Congress required the EPA to issue regulations for detecting and correcting leaks in existing tanks and establishing specifications for new receptacles. Anyone who owns property with an underground storage tank must notify the EPA and comply with regulations that require installation of leak detectors, periodic testing, and, in some cases, removal of old tanks.

Identifying Hazardous Wastes

The EPA must establish criteria for determining what is, and is not, hazardous waste. It must then prepare a list of wastes that qualify as hazardous.

Tracking Hazardous Wastes

Anyone who creates, transports, stores, treats, or disposes of more than a certain quantity of hazardous wastes must apply for an EPA permit. All hazardous wastes must be tracked from creation to final disposal. They must be disposed of at a certified facility. Any company that generates more than 100 kilograms of hazardous waste in any month (roughly 200,000 firms nationwide) must obtain an identification number for its wastes. When it ships this waste to a disposal facility, it must send along a multicopy manifest that identifies the waste, the transporter, and the destination. The company must notify the EPA if it does not receive a receipt from the disposal site indicating that the waste has been received.

Superfund

In the vignette that opened this chapter, an elderly woman faced financial ruin from the cost of cleaning up pollutants that her dry cleaner tenants had left. The RCRA was designed to ensure safe disposal of current hazardous wastes. In contrast, the goal of Superfund (also known as CERCLA) is to clean up hazardous wastes improperly dumped in the past.

The philosophy of Superfund is "the polluter pays." **Therefore, anyone who has ever owned or operated a site on which hazardous wastes are found, or who has**

---

[8] The Basel Action Networks, "Exporting Harm: The Techno-Trashing of Asia," Feb. 25, 2002, available at http://www.ban.org.

transported wastes to the site, or who has arranged for the disposal of wastes that were released at the site, is liable for (1) the cost of cleaning up the site, (2) any damage done to natural resources, and (3) any required health assessments.

In a "shovels first, lawyers later" approach, Congress established a $15.2 billion revolving trust fund for the EPA to use in cleaning up sites even before obtaining reimbursement from those responsible for the damage. Any reimbursements go into the trust fund to be used to repair other sites. The trust fund was initially financed by a tax on the oil and chemical industries, which produce the bulk of hazardous waste. In 1995, however, the taxes expired, and Congress refused to renew them, thereby threatening the viability of the statute. The EPA has identified 428 sites that need immediate cleanup, but the agency spends 52 percent of its annual $450 million Superfund budget on just nine of these sites. According to the EPA, there could be as many as 355,000 hazardous waste sites that would require up to $250 billion to restore.

Meanwhile, one in four Americans, including 10 million children below the age of 12, lives within four miles of a Superfund site. To find out about hazardous waste sites in your community, click on http://www.epa.gov/.

Property owners have complained, and litigated, bitterly because:

- Current and former owners are liable, even though they did nothing illegal at the time, and indeed even if they did nothing more than own property where someone else dumped hazardous wastes. In addition, officers or controlling shareholders in closely held corporations can be personally liable for operations of the company.

- Polluters have joint and several liability—each polluter is responsible for the entire cost of cleaning up a site, even if it contributed only a portion of the pollution. A polluter can reduce its liability only by proving that it caused a smaller percentage of the damage, but that proof is often impossible.

- The expense of a Superfund cleanup can be devastating—higher than $100 million on some sites. Property owners have often viewed litigation as a better investment. More than 50 percent of total Superfund spending has gone to administrative and legal expenses.

- Congress requires that land be returned to pristine condition. Owners point to scientific evidence indicating that this goal is often impossible to achieve, given existing knowledge. Once again, cost-benefit analysis enters the picture as property owners argue that the cost of perfection is higher than the benefit. To encourage redevelopment of contaminated land, the EPA has implemented a "Brownfields" program that bases the cleanup levels for some property on potential risk to human health. However, Superfund proponents counter that, to be safe, all hazardous wastes should be removed. They offer as Exhibit A the Forrest Glen real estate development in upstate New York. The developers knew they could buy the land cheap because it had been used as a hazardous waste dump. Instead of cleaning it up, they slapped on a bucolic name. Now chemicals ooze up on lawns.

at **RISK**   Virtually any commercial real estate is at risk for Superfund liability. Before purchasing land, it is important to investigate whether it has ever been used to dispose of hazardous wastes. Consider testing the soil and groundwater. It might also be a good idea to ask the seller for indemnification against Superfund liability or to purchase Superfund insurance. ◆

Unfortunately, as the following case illustrates, incentives under Superfund can sometimes be perverse.

COOPER INDUSTRIES, INC. V. AVIALL SERVICES, INC.

125 S. Ct. 577, 2004 U.S. LEXIS 8271
Supreme Court of the United States, 2004

Facts: Cooper Industries, Inc. owned and operated four aircraft engine maintenance sites in Texas. In 1981, it sold them to Aviall Services, Inc. During the time that Cooper owned the property and later when Aviall owned it, petroleum and other hazardous substances leaked into the ground and ground water from underground storage tanks. No one knew this, however, until Aviall owned the property. As soon as it discovered the contamination, Aviall notified the Texas Natural Resource Conservation Commission (Commission). The Commission directed Aviall to clean up the site, and threatened suit if it did not. Aviall cleaned up the property so neither the Commission nor the EPA needed to file suit. Aviall spent about $5 million in cleanup costs but was not yet finished.

Aviall filed a lawsuit against Cooper alleging that, as a former owner, it was also liable under CERCLA for the cleanup costs. Both parties moved for summary judgment. The trial court granted Cooper's motion on the grounds that Cooper did not have to contribute to the cleanup because Aviall had never been sued under CERCLA. A panel of the Court of Appeals for the Fifth Circuit affirmed, but on a rehearing *en banc* the Fifth Circuit reversed by a divided vote, holding for Aviall.[9] The Supreme Court granted *certiorari*.

Issue: If the owner of a contaminated site has not been sued under CERCLA but has paid cleanup costs, can it seek contribution from prior owners of the property?

Excerpts from Justice Thomas's Decision: The first sentence, the enabling clause that establishes the right of contribution, provides: "Any person *may* seek contribution . . . *during or following* any civil action under [CERCLA]." Aviall answers that "may" should be read permissively, such that "during or following" a civil action is one, but not the exclusive, instance in which a person may seek contribution. We disagree.

[If CERCLA] were read to authorize contribution actions at any time, regardless of the existence of a civil action, then Congress need not have included the explicit "during or following" condition. In other words, Aviall's reading would render part of the statute entirely superfluous, something we are loath to do. There is no reason why Congress would bother to specify conditions under which a person may bring a contribution claim, and at the same time allow contribution actions absent those conditions.

[CERCLA] authorizes contribution claims only "during or following" a civil action and it is undisputed that Aviall has never been subject to such an action. Aviall therefore has no claim. ∎

Public Policy	Aviall cooperated with the authorities in Texas and voluntarily cleaned up its contaminated site. If it had refused to clean up the site and forced Texas to sue, Aviall would have been entitled to some contribution from Cooper. As it is, Aviall got nothing and had to pay all the expenses itself. Does this result make sense? Is it in keeping with the goal of CERCLA: "shovels first, lawyers later"? Should Congress amend the statute? ◆
ECONOMICS *& the* LAW	In a perfect world, the EPA would make rational decisions based on sound science, using its limited resources to solve the most severe problems. Reality can be a bit different.
If you were head of the EPA, for instance, how would you decide which Superfund sites the EPA should address first? You might think that the environmental agency should focus on the most harmful sites. That may sound sensible, but it is not how the system works.

---

[9] Typically, a panel of three judges hears the appeal to a U.S. circuit court of appeals. However, sometimes the entire court will hear a case, and that is called sitting *en banc*.

A recent study reveals that the EPA's priorities are largely determined by two factors: the polluters and the local communities. An aggressive defendant can stave off EPA action, or an eager community can persuade the EPA to clean up their town first, even as a neighboring community with a more pressing problem finds itself moved down the waiting list.[10] Likewise, one would expect that decisions about which species to add to the endangered list (discussed later in the chapter) should perhaps be based solely on the rarity and importance of the species in question. In fact, public opinion (whether in favor or against) can dramatically affect the listing decision.[11]

Can you think of any way to render the decision-making process more effective? ◆

CHEMICALS

More than 70,000 chemicals are used in food, drugs, cosmetics, pesticides, and other products. Some of these chemicals are known to accumulate in human tissue and cause, among other harm, cancer, birth defects, and neurological damage. However, only 2 percent of these 70,000 chemicals have been adequately tested to determine their total health impact. Almost 70 percent have not been tested at all. Scientists know virtually nothing about their impact on the health of wildlife.

Several federal agencies share responsibility for regulating chemicals. The Food and Drug Administration (FDA) has control over foods, drugs, and cosmetics. The Occupational Safety and Health Administration (OSHA) is responsible for protecting workers from exposure to toxic chemicals. The Nuclear Regulatory Commission (NRC) regulates radioactive substances. The EPA regulates pesticides and other toxic chemicals.

Federal Insecticide, Fungicide, and Rodenticide Act

The Federal Insecticide, Fungicide, and Rodenticide Act (FIFRA) requires manufacturers to register all pesticides with the EPA. Before registering a pesticide, the EPA must ensure that its benefits exceed its (then-known) risks. However, many of the 50,000 pesticides currently registered with the EPA were approved at a time when little was known about their risks. In 1972, Congress directed the EPA to reevaluate all registered pesticides and cancel those whose risks exceed their benefits. This process has been very slow. Before the EPA cancels a registration, the manufacturer is entitled to a formal hearing, which may take several years. In the event of an emergency, the EPA may order an immediate suspension; otherwise the chemical stays on the market until the hearing. If a pesticide is banned, the EPA must reimburse end users of the chemicals for their useless inventory.

Federal Food, Drug, and Cosmetic Act

The Federal Food, Drug, and Cosmetic Act requires the EPA to set maximum levels for pesticide residue in raw or processed food. The Food and Drug Administration can confiscate food with pesticide levels that exceed the EPA standards.

---

10 Hilary Sigman, "The Pace of Progress at Superfund Sites: Policy Goals and Interest Group Influence," *Journal of Law and Economics*, April 2001, vol. 44, p. 315.

11 Amy Whritenour Ando, "Waiting to Be Protected Under the Endangered Species Act: The Political Economy of Regulatory Delay," *Journal of Law and Economics*, April 1999, vol. 42, p. 29.

Food Quality Protection Act of 1996

The Food Quality Protection Act requires the EPA to set pesticide standards at levels that are safe for children. If the data for children are unclear, the EPA must reduce levels to one tenth the amount now permitted in food. The EPA must also consider all sources of exposure. Thus, for example, in setting limits for pesticides on grapes, the EPA must factor in other sources of pesticides, such as drinking water.

This statute is highly controversial. The pesticide industry argues that the EPA could effectively ban many valuable chemicals for years while careful research into their impact on children is conducted. Environmental advocates, on the other hand, are dismayed that the EPA has not demanded more thorough research before setting standards for some pesticides.

Toxic Substances Control Act

The Toxic Substances Control Act (TSCA) regulates chemicals other than pesticides, foods, drugs, and cosmetics. For example, it regulates lead in gasoline and paints. **Before selling a new chemical (or an old chemical being used for a new purpose), the manufacturer must register it with the EPA.** As part of the registration process, the manufacturer must present evidence of the chemical's impact on health and the environment. The EPA may prohibit the manufacture, sale, or a particular use of any chemical that poses an unreasonable risk.

NATURAL RESOURCES

Thus far, this chapter has focused on the regulation of pollution. Congress has also passed statutes whose purpose is to preserve the country's natural resources.

National Environmental Policy Act

The National Environmental Policy Act of 1969 (NEPA) requires all *federal agencies* to prepare an *environmental impact statement* (EIS) for every major federal action significantly affecting the quality of the human environment. An EIS is a major undertaking—often hundreds, if not thousands, of pages long. It must discuss (1) environmental consequences of the proposed action; (2) available alternatives; (3) direct and indirect effects; (4) energy requirements; (5) impact on urban quality, historic, and cultural resources; and (6) means to mitigate adverse environmental impacts. Once a draft report is ready, the federal agency must hold a hearing to allow for outside comments.

The EIS requirement applies not only to actions *undertaken* by the federal government but also to activities *regulated* or *approved* by the government. For instance, the following projects required an EIS:

- Expanding the Snowmass ski area in Aspen, Colorado—because approval was required by the Forest Service;
- Killing a herd of wild goats that was causing damage at the Olympic National Park (outside Seattle);
- Closing a road to create a beachside pavilion in Redondo Beach, California;
- Creating a golf course outside Los Angeles—because the project required a government permit to build in wetlands.

The EIS process is controversial. If a project is likely to have an important impact, environmentalists almost always litigate the adequacy of the EIS. Industry advocates argue that environmentalists are simply using the EIS process to delay—or halt—any projects they oppose. In 1976, seven years after NEPA was passed, a dam on the Teton River in Idaho burst, killing 17 people and causing $1 billion in property damage. The Department of the Interior had built the dam in the face of allegations that its EIS was incomplete; it did not, for example, confirm that a large earth-filled dam resting on a riverbed was safe. To environmentalists, this tragedy graphically illustrated the need for a thorough EIS.

Researchers have found that the EIS process generally has a beneficial impact on the environment. The mere prospect of preparing an EIS tends to eliminate the worst projects. Litigation over the EIS eliminates the next weakest group. If an agency does a good faith EIS, honestly looking at the available alternatives, projects tend to be kinder to the environment, at little extra cost.

Endangered Species Act

The Endangered Species Act (ESA):

- Requires the Secretary of Commerce or the Secretary of the Interior to prepare a list of species that are in danger of becoming extinct;

- Requires the government to develop plans to revive these species;

- Requires all federal agencies to ensure that their actions will not jeopardize an endangered species;

- Prohibits any sale or transport of these species;

- Makes any taking of an endangered animal species unlawful—taking is defined as harassing, harming, killing, or capturing any endangered species or modifying its habitat in such a way that its population is likely to decline; and

- Prohibits the taking of any endangered plant species on federal property.

No environmental statute has been more controversial than the ESA. In theory, everyone is in favor of saving endangered species. There are currently 991 endangered species (392 animals and 599 plants) on the U.S. list, and species are becoming extinct at 100 to 1,000 times the rate one would expect to occur naturally. To quote the House of Representatives Report on the ESA:

> As we homogenize the habitats in which these plants and animals evolved . . . we threaten their—and our own—genetic heritage. . . . Who knows, or can say, what potential cures for cancer or other scourges, present or future, may lie locked up in the structures of plants which may yet be undiscovered, much less analyzed?

In practice, however, the cost of saving a species can be astronomical. One of the earliest ESA battles involved the snail darter—a three-inch fish that lived in the Little Tennessee River. The Supreme Court upheld a decision under the ESA to halt work on a dam that would have blocked the river, flooding 16,500 acres of farmland and destroying the snail darter's habitat. To the dam's supporters, this decision was ludicrous: stopping a dam (on which $100 million in taxpayer money had already been spent) to save a little fish that no one had ever even thought of before the dam (or damn) controversy. The real agenda, they argued, was simply to halt development. Environmental advocates argued, however, that the wanton destruction of whole species will ultimately and inevitably lead to disaster for humankind. In the end, Congress overruled the Supreme Court and authorized completion of the dam. It turned out that the snail darter has survived in other rivers.

The snail darter was the first in a long line of ESA controversies that have included the bighorn sheep, the spotted owl, the gnatcatcher, the island fox, and the pygmy rabbit, among others. Opponents argue that too much time and money have been spent on litigation to save too few species of too little importance. The following case, however, discusses the advantages of the ESA.

GIBBS V. BABBITT

214 F.3d 483, 2000 U.S. App. LEXIS 12280
United States Court of Appeals for the Fourth Circuit, 2000

Facts: The red wolf used to roam throughout the southeastern United States. Owing to wetlands drainage, dam construction, and hunting, this wolf is now on the endangered species list. The Fish and Wildlife Service (FWS) trapped the remaining red wolves, placed them in a captive breeding program, and then reintroduced them into the wild. Ultimately, the FWS reintroduced 75 wolves into the 120,000-acre Alligator River National Wildlife Refuge in eastern North Carolina and the Pocosin Lakes National Wildlife Refuge in Tennessee.

After reintroduction, about 41 red wolves wandered from federal refuges onto private property. Plaintiff Richard Lee Mann shot a red wolf that he feared might threaten his cattle. Mann pled guilty to violating a provision of the ESA that prohibits the taking of any endangered species without a permit.

Two individuals and two counties in North Carolina filed suit against the U.S. government, alleging that the anti-taking regulation as applied to the red wolves on private land exceeded Congress's power under the interstate Commerce Clause of the U.S. Constitution.

Issue: Is the anti-taking provision of the ESA constitutional?

Excerpts from Justice Wilkinson's Decision: Congress' commerce authority includes the power to regulate those activities having a substantial relation to interstate commerce. Although the connection to economic or commercial activity plays a central role in whether a regulation will be upheld under the Commerce Clause, economic activity must be understood in broad terms.

The red wolves are part of a $29.2 billion national wildlife-related recreational industry that involves tourism and interstate travel. Many tourists travel to North Carolina from throughout the country for "howling events"—evenings of listening to wolf howls accompanied by educational programs. According to a study conducted by Dr. William E. Rosen of Cornell University, the recovery of the red wolf and increased visitor activities could result in a significant regional economic impact. Rosen estimates that northeastern North Carolina could see an increase of between $39.61 and $183.65 million per year in tourism-related activities, and that the Great Smoky Mountains National Park could see an increase of between $132.09 and $354.50 million per year. This is hardly a trivial impact on interstate commerce.

Appellants argue that the tourism rationale relates only to howling events on national park land or wildlife refuges because people do not travel to private land. Yet this argument misses the mark. Indeed, wolves are known to be "great wanderers." Because so many members of this threatened species wander on private land, the regulation of takings on private land is essential to the entire program of reintroduction and eventual restoration of the species. Such regulation is necessary to conserve enough red wolves to sustain tourism.

The regulation of red wolf takings is also closely connected to a second interstate market—scientific research. Scientific research generates jobs. It also deepens our knowledge of the world in which we live. The red wolf reintroduction program has already generated numerous scientific studies. Scientists have studied how the red wolf affects small mammal populations and how the wolves interact with the ecosystem as a whole. Scientific research can also reveal other uses for animals—for instance, approximately 50 percent of all modern medicines are derived from wild plants or animals. ▼

The anti-taking regulation is also connected to a third market—the possibility of a renewed trade in fur pelts. Wolves have historically been hunted for their pelts. Congress had the renewal of trade in mind when it enacted the ESA. In such a case, businessmen may profit from the trading and marketing of that species for an indefinite number of years, where otherwise it would have been completely eliminated from commercial channels. The American alligator is a case in point. In 1975, the American alligator was nearing extinction and listed as endangered, but by 1987 conservation efforts restored the species. Now there is a vigorous trade in alligator hides.

Finally, the taking of red wolves is connected to interstate markets for agricultural products and livestock. For instance, appellant landowners find red wolves a menace because they threaten livestock and other animals of economic and commercial value. This effect on commerce, however, still qualifies as a legitimate subject for regulation. It is well-settled under Commerce Clause cases that a regulation can involve the promotion or the restriction of commercial enterprises and development.

It is anything but clear that red wolves harm farming enterprises. They may in fact help them, and in so doing confer additional benefits on commerce. For instance, red wolves prey on animals like raccoons, deer, and rabbits—helping farmers by killing the animals that destroy their crops.

[I]t is reasonable for Congress to decide that conservation of species will one day produce a substantial commercial benefit to this country and that failure to preserve a species will result in permanent, though unascertainable, commercial loss. If a species becomes extinct, we are left to speculate forever on what we might have learned or what we may have realized. If we conserve the species, it will be available for the study and benefit of future generations. We therefore hold that the anti-taking provision at issue here involves regulable economic and commercial activity as understood by current Commerce Clause jurisprudence. ■

The government has introduced the Habitat Conservation Plan (HCP) as a blueprint for compromise over the ESA. In an HCP, developers agree to conserve some land in return for developing other property as they want. These deals contain a "no surprises" clause, meaning that the government has no right to retrieve land once it has been approved for development, even if scientists later determine that a particular species needs that habitat for survival. Unfortunately, the natural world is full of surprises, and environmentalists worry about the ultimate impact of these HCPs. In the short run, however, the success has been striking. For example, to save the gnatcatcher, a songbird found near San Diego, federal and local governments agreed to set aside 82,000 acres that they owned. They bought an additional 27,000 acres, at a cost of $300 million, and developers donated 63,000 acres more. In return, the developers earned the right to build on their remaining land without limitation. More than 16 million acres, including 10 percent of timberland in the Pacific Northwest, are now designated HCPs.

In the long run, the real issue is not how much land developers will give up, but how each of us will change our lifestyle. The government recently announced that nine wild salmon species in the Pacific Northwest are threatened. The Columbia River was once home to 16 million salmon, but dozens of dams now block the river, interfering with the fish's annual migration. Fewer than a million salmon remain. The following article discusses some of the remedies that may be necessary to save the salmon.

NEWS*worthy*

With the salmon crisis, you step out the door and the rain that's running off your front lawn, awash in fertilizer, is a problem. You drive to work (alone) and you are adding to the oil and other chemicals that all eventually drain into the streams. You work for a company that wants to expand its offices into what is a salmon habitat, which describes just about every wetland within a day's drive of Seattle. At home, you turn on a light that is fed cheaply by the very dams that make it nearly impossible for salmon to swim upstream. For us to change this chain of events requires changing our lifestyles, which is something most Northwesterners have always seemed loath to do. We don't want anyone to tell us what to do with our lot size or with that instrument that is most integral to life here: the sport utility vehicle. All of a sudden being for the salmon means being against building a new home wherever you'd like, being for increased taxes, being prepared to change suburban life.

As this new debate begins, the phrase "putting salmon before people" will be heard over and over. Somehow the people need to line up behind the fish, knowing that the fish are like the canary in the coal mine. Now, the salmon are making us look not just at what we can do with the rivers but at what we can do with the way we commute and choose our homes and shop and live. The question is: Will it be too much of a hassle for us to look at ourselves?[12] ◆

Chapter Conclusion

Environmental laws have a pervasive impact on our lives. The cost has been great—whether it is the higher price for cars with pollution control devices or the time spent filling out environmental impact statements. Some argue that cost is irrelevant, that a clean environment has incalculable value for its own sake. Others insist on a more pragmatic approach and want to know if the benefits outweigh the costs.

What benefits has the country gained from environmental regulation? Since 1970, when Congress created the EPA, the record on common air pollutants, such as lead, has been extraordinarily successful. Total emissions of lead nationwide have declined by 96 percent. Before 1970, emissions of sulfur dioxide had been increasing rapidly. Since then, in spite of strong economic growth and an increase in population, these emissions have dropped. Despite this progress, however, many Americans live in areas that still do not meet EPA quality standards.

As for water, wetland acreage continues to decline at a rapid rate. However, the number of Americans whose sewage goes to wastewater treatment facilities has more than doubled. Two thirds of the nation's waters are safe for fishing and swimming, up from only one-third when the Clean Water Act was passed. Despite this progress, as a nation we still face many intractable problems. We have not developed a political consensus on global warming. The health effects of pesticides in our food supply are uncertain. Superfund and the Endangered Species Act are mired in a thorn bush of litigation.

In short, despite significant progress, much work remains to be done. In a study of worldwide environmental sustainability, which ranked countries on issues such as air quality, water quality, and biodiversity, the United States ranked forty-fifth out of 146 countries, behind Japan and all of Western Europe. Although many people, and many politicians, readily acknowledge the importance of the environment to both present and future generations, when the time comes to allocate resources, change lifestyles, make tough choices, the consensus too often breaks down, with the result that resources are spent on litigation instead of the environment.

---

12 Robert Sullivan, "And Now, the Salmon War," *The New York Times,* Mar. 20, 1999, p. A15.
Copyright © 1999 by The New York Times Co. Reprinted by permission.

Chapter Review

1. The following table provides a list of environmental statutes:

Air Pollution	Water Pollution	Waste Disposal	Chemicals	Natural Resources
Clean Air Act	Clean Water Act	Resource Conservation and Recovery Act	Federal Insecticide, Fungicide, and Rodenticide Act	National Environmental Policy Act
	Safe Drinking Water Act	Comprehensive Environmental Response, Compensation, and Liability Act (Superfund or CERCLA)	Federal Food, Drug, and Cosmetic Act	Endangered Species Act
	Ocean Dumping Act		Food Quality Protection Act	
	Oil Pollution Act		Toxic Substances Control Act	

2. Under the Clean Air Act of 1970, the Environmental Protection Agency must establish national ambient air quality standards for both primary and secondary pollution. States must produce implementation plans to meet the EPA standards.

3. Under the Clean Air Act, power plants may trade emission allowances.

4. The Clean Water Act prohibits the discharge of pollution into water without a permit from the EPA. States must set EPA-approved water quality standards and develop plans to achieve them. The Clean Water Act also prohibits any discharge of dredge and fill material into a wetland without a permit.

5. The Safe Drinking Water Act requires the EPA to set national standards for every contaminant potentially harmful to human health that is found in drinking water.

6. The Ocean Dumping Act prohibits the dumping of wastes in ocean water without a permit from the EPA.

7. The Oil Pollution Act of 1990 sets design standards for ships operating in U.S. waters and requires ship owners to pay for damage caused by oil discharged from their ships.

8. The Resource Conservation and Recovery Act establishes rules for treating hazardous wastes and other forms of solid waste.

9. Under Superfund (CERCLA), anyone who has ever owned or operated a site on which hazardous wastes are found, or who has transported wastes to the site, or who has arranged for the disposal of wastes that were released at the site, is liable for (1) the cost of cleaning up the site, (2) any damage done to natural resources, and (3) any required health assessments.

10. The Federal Insecticide, Fungicide, and Rodenticide Act requires manufacturers to register all pesticides with the EPA.

11. The Federal Food, Drug, and Cosmetic Act requires the EPA to set maximum levels for pesticide residue in raw or processed food. The Food Quality Protection Act requires the EPA to set pesticide standards at levels that are safe for children.

12. Under the Toxic Substances Control Act, manufacturers must register new chemicals with the EPA.

13. The National Environmental Policy Act requires all federal agencies to prepare an environmental impact statement for every major federal action significantly affecting the quality of the environment.

14. The Endangered Species Act prohibits activities that cause harm to endangered species.

Practice Test

1. Astro Circuit Corp. in Lowell, Massachusetts, manufactured printed circuit boards. David Boldt was in charge of the production line. In theory, the company pretreated its industrial waste to remove toxic metals, but, in practice, the factory was producing twice as much wastewater as the treatment facility could handle. The company often bypassed the treatment facility and dumped wastewater directly into the city sewer. Once, when caught by the city, Boldt wrote a letter implying that the violation was a temporary aberration. Boldt felt that he was caught "between the devil and the deep blue sea." It was his job to keep the production line moving, but he had no place to put the waste product. Has Boldt violated the law? What penalties might he face?

2. The U.S. Forest Service planned to build a road in the Nez Perce National Forest in Idaho to provide access to loggers. Is the Forest Service governed by any environmental statutes? Must it seek permission before building the road?

3. In 1963, FMC Corp. purchased a manufacturing plant in Virginia from American Viscose Corp., the owner of the plant since 1937. During World War II, the government's War Production Board had commissioned American Viscose to make rayon for airplanes and truck tires. In 1982, inspections revealed carbon disulfide, a chemical used to manufacture this rayon, in groundwater near the plant. American Viscose was out of business. Who is responsible for cleaning up the carbon disulfide? Under what statute?

4. Tariq Ahmad owned Shankman Laboratories. He decided to dispose of some of the lab's hazardous chemicals by shipping them to his home in Pakistan. He sent the chemicals to Castelazo & Associates (in the United States) to prepare the materials for shipment. Ahmad did not tell the driver who picked up the chemicals that they were hazardous. Nor did he give the driver any written documentation. Ahmad had packed the chemicals hurriedly in flimsy containers that were unsafe for transporting hazardous materials. He also grossly misrepresented to Castelazo the amount and type of hazardous material that he was shipping to Pakistan. Has Ahmad violated U.S. law? What penalties might he face?

5. Suppose that you are the manager of the General Motors Hummer plant in Mishawaka, Indiana. Hummers are the successor to the U.S. Army jeep and have become popular recreational vehicles among the rich and famous. Arnold Schwarzenegger has several. The Hummer requires special protective paint that, as it turns out, reacts with other chemicals during the application process to create ozone, a pollutant. You want to increase production of Hummers. Are there any legal requirements you must observe?

6. Alcan Aluminum Corp. manufactures aluminum sheet in Oswego, New York. It hired the Mahler Cos. to dispose of an emulsion used during the manufacturing process. This emulsion contained a variety of hazardous substances. Without Alcan's knowledge, Mahler dumped the emulsion into a borehole that connected to deep underground mines along the Susquehanna River in Pennsylvania. You can guess what happened next. Approximately 100,000 gallons of water contaminated with hazardous substances spilled from the borehole into the river. The EPA paid to clean up the river and then sued Alcan along with others who had hired Mahler for hazardous waste disposal. All other defendants settled. The court entered judgment against Alcan in the amount of $473,790.18, which was the difference between the full response costs the government had incurred in cleaning the river and the amount the government had recovered from the settling defendants. Is Alcan required to pay this amount?

7. In 1991, Illinois passed a statute requiring its four largest generating plants to install scrubbers so that they could continue using high-sulfur Illinois coal. What federal law was this Illinois statute designed to overcome? *Extra credit question:* On what grounds did a federal appeals court strike down the Illinois statute?

8. The marbled murrelet is a rare seabird that lives only in old-growth forests on the West Coast. Logging has destroyed so much of its habitat that its numbers in California have declined from 60,000 to between 2,000 and 5,000. Pacific Lumber Co. wanted to harvest trees from 137 acres of land it owned in the Owl Creek forest in California. It originally received approval to log, on the condition that it would cooperate

with regulators to protect the murrelet. But the company sneaked in one weekend and cut down trees before it met the condition. Caught in the act, it promised no more logging until it had a plan to protect the birds. This time it waited until the long weekend over Thanksgiving to take down some more trees. Finally, a federal court ordered a permanent halt to any further logging. There was no evidence that the company had harmed the murrelet. Had it violated the law?

9. *ETHICS* Geronimo Villegas owned a blood-testing lab in Brooklyn, New York. He threw vials of human blood from the lab into the Hudson River. A group of eighth graders on a field trip to Staten Island discovered 70 of these glass vials along the shore. Ten vials contained blood infected with the highly contagious hepatitis-B virus. Did Villegas violate the Clean Water Act? Why had Villegas disposed of the vials in this way? Whether or not he was in violation of the statute, was his behavior ethical? Did he violate any of the ethical tests from Chapter 2?

10. *YOU BE THE JUDGE* WRITING PROBLEM The Lordship Point Gun Club operated a trap and skeet shooting club in Stratford, Connecticut, for 70 years. During this time, customers deposited close to 5 million tons of lead shot and 11 million pounds of clay target fragments on land around the club and in Long Island Sound. Forty-five percent of sediment samples taken from the Sound exceeded the established limits for lead. Was the Gun Club in violation of the RCRA? **Argument for the Gun Club:** The Gun Club does not *dispose* of hazardous wastes, within the meaning of the RCRA. Congress meant the statute to apply only to companies in the business of manufacturing articles that produce hazardous waste. If the Gun Club happens to produce wastes, that is only *incidental* to the normal use of a product. **Argument for the plaintiff: Under the RCRA, lead shot is hazardous waste. The law applies to anyone who produces hazardous waste, no matter how.**

11. *ROLE REVERSAL* Write a short-answer question that poses an ethics or economics question under the environmental laws.

Internet Research Problem

Using the information provided at http://www.globalwarming.org and http://dels.nas.edu/ccgc, write an essay summarizing your views on global warming. What should our own government, and other governments, do? What should you do personally?

You can find further practice problems at academic.cengage.com/blaw/beatty.

Appendix A

The Constitution of the United States

Preamble We the People of the United States, in Order to form a more perfect Union, establish Justice, insure domestic Tranquility, provide for the common defense, promote the general Welfare, and secure the Blessings of Liberty to ourselves and our Posterity, do ordain and establish this Constitution for the United States of America.

ARTICLE I

Section 1.

All legislative Powers herein granted shall be vested in a Congress of the United States, which shall consist of a Senate and House of Representatives.

Section 2.

The House of Representatives shall be composed of Members chosen every second Year by the People of the several States, and the Electors in each State shall have the Qualifications requisite for Electors of the most numerous Branch of the State Legislature.

No Person shall be a Representative who shall not have attained to the Age of twenty five Years, and been seven Years a Citizen of the United States, and who shall not, when elected, be an Inhabitant of that State in which he shall be chosen.

Representatives and direct Taxes shall be apportioned among the several States which may be included within this Union, according to their respective Numbers, which shall be determined by adding to the whole Number of free Persons, including those bound to Service for a Term of Years, and excluding Indians not taxed, three fifths of all other Persons. The actual Enumeration shall be made within three Years after the first Meeting of the Congress of the United States, and within every subsequent Term of ten Years, in such Manner as they shall by Law direct. The number of Representatives shall not exceed one for every thirty Thousand, but each State shall have at Least one Representative; and until such enumeration shall be made, the State of New Hampshire shall be entitled to chuse three, Massachusetts eight, Rhode Island and Providence Plantations one, Connecticut five, New-York six, New Jersey four, Pennsylvania eight, Delaware one, Maryland six, Virginia ten, North Carolina five, South Carolina five, and Georgia three.

When vacancies happen in the Representation from any State, the Executive Authority thereof shall issue Writs of Election to fill such vacancies.

The House of Representatives shall chuse their Speaker and other Officers; and shall have the sole Power of Impeachment.

Section 3.

The Senate of the United States shall be composed of two Senators from each State, chosen by the Legislature thereof, for six Years; and each Senator shall have one Vote.

Immediately after they shall be assembled in Consequence of the first Election, they shall be divided as equally as may be into three Classes. The Seats of the Senators of the first Class shall be vacated at the Expiration of the second Year, of the second Class at the Expiration of the fourth Year, and of the third Class at the Expiration of the sixth Year, so that one third may be chosen every second Year; and if Vacancies happen by Resignation or otherwise, during the Recess of the Legislature of any State, the Executive thereof may make temporary Appointments until the next Meeting of the Legislature, which shall then fill such Vacancies.

No Person shall be a Senator who shall not have attained to the Age of thirty Years, and been nine Years a Citizen of the United States, and who shall not, when elected, be an Inhabitant of that State for which he shall be chosen.

The Vice President of the United States shall be President of the Senate, but shall have no Vote, unless they be equally divided.

The Senate shall chuse their other Officers, and also a President pro tempore, in the Absence of the Vice President, or when he shall exercise the Office of President of the United States.

The Senate shall have the sole power to try all Impeachments. When sitting for that Purpose, they shall be an Oath or Affirmation. When the President of the United States is tried, the Chief Justice shall preside: And no Person shall be convicted without the Concurrence of two thirds of the Members present.

Judgment in Cases of Impeachment shall not extend further than to removal from Office, and disqualification to hold and enjoy any Office of honor, Trust or Profit under the United States: but the Party convicted shall nevertheless be liable and subject to Indictment, Trial, Judgment and Punishment, according to Law.

Section 4.

The Times, Places and Manner of holding Elections for Senators and Representatives, shall be prescribed in each State by the Legislature thereof: but the Congress may at any time by Law make or alter such Regulations, except as to the Places of chusing Senators.

The Congress shall assemble at least once in every Year, and such Meeting shall be on the first Monday in December, unless they shall by Law appoint a different Day.

Section 5.

Each House shall be the Judge of the Elections, Returns and Qualifications of its own Members, and a Majority of each shall constitute a Quorum to do Business; but a smaller Number may adjourn from day to day, and may be authorized to compel the Attendance of absent Members, in such Manner, and under such Penalties as each House may provide.

Each House may determine the Rules of its Proceedings, punish its Members for disorderly Behaviour, and, with the Concurrence of two thirds, expel a Member.

Each House shall keep a Journal of its Proceedings, and from time to time publish the same, excepting such Parts as may in their Judgment require Secrecy; and the Yeas and Nays of the Members of either House on any question shall, at the Desire of one fifth of those Present, be entered on the Journal.

Neither House, during the Session of Congress, shall, without the Consent of the other, adjourn for more than three days, nor to any other Place than that in which the two Houses shall be sitting.

Section 6.

The Senators and Representatives shall receive a Compensation for their Services, to be ascertained by Law, and paid out of the Treasury of the United States. They shall in all Cases, except Treason, Felony and Breach of the Peace, be privileged from Arrest during their Attendance at the Session of their respective Houses, and in going to and returning from the same; and for any Speech or Debate in either House, they shall not be questioned in any other Place.

No Senator or Representative shall, during the Time for which he was elected, be appointed to any civil Office under the Authority of the United States, which shall have been created, or the Emoluments whereof shall have been encreased during such time; and no Person holding any Office under the United States, shall be a Member of either House during his Continuance in Office.

Section 7.

All Bills for raising Revenue shall originate in the House of Representatives; but the Senate may propose or concur with Amendments as on other Bills.

Every Bill which shall have passed the House of Representatives and the Senate, shall, before it become a Law, be presented to the President of the United States; If he approve he shall sign it, but if not he shall return it, with his Objections to that House in which it shall have originated, who shall enter the Objections at large on their Journal, and proceed to reconsider it. If after such Reconsideration two thirds of that House shall agree to pass the Bill, it shall be sent, together with the Objections, to the other House, by which it shall likewise be reconsidered, and if approved by two thirds of that House, it shall become a Law. But in all such Cases the Votes of both Houses shall be determined by Yeas and Nays, and the Names of the Persons voting for and against the Bill shall be entered on the Journal of each House respectively. If any Bill shall not be returned by the President within ten Days (Sundays excepted) after it shall have been presented to him, the Same shall be a Law, in like Manner as if he had signed it, unless the Congress by their Adjournment prevent its Return, in which Case it shall not be a Law.

Every Order, Resolution, or Vote to which the Concurrence of the Senate and House of Representatives may be necessary (except on a question of Adjournment) shall be presented to the President of the United States; and before the Same shall take Effect, shall be approved by him, or being disapproved by him, shall be repassed by two thirds of the Senate and House of Representatives, according to the Rules and Limitations prescribed in the Case of a Bill.

Section 8.

The Congress shall have Power to lay and collect Taxes, Duties, Imposts and Excises, to pay the Debts and provide for the common Defence and general Welfare of the United States; but all Duties, Imposts and Excises shall be uniform throughout the United States;

To borrow Money on the credit of the United States;

To regulate Commerce with foreign Nations, and among the several States, and with the Indian Tribes;

To establish an uniform Rule of Naturalization, and uniform Laws on the subject of Bankruptcies throughout the United States;

To coin Money, regulate the Value thereof, and of foreign Coin, and fix the Standard of Weights and Measures;

To provide for the Punishment of counterfeiting the Securities and current Coin of the United States;

To establish Post Offices and post Roads;

To promote the Progress of Science and useful Arts, by securing for limited Times to Authors and Inventors the exclusive Right to their respective Writings and Discoveries;

To constitute Tribunals inferior to the supreme Court;

To define and punish Piracies and Felonies committed on the high Seas, and Offenses against the Law of Nations;

To declare War, grant Letters of Marque and Reprisal, and make Rules concerning Captures on Land and Water;

To raise and support Armies, but no Appropriation of Money to that Use shall be for a longer Term than two Years;

To provide and maintain a Navy;

To make Rules for the Government and Regulation of the land and naval Forces;

To provide for calling forth the Militia to execute the Laws of the Union, suppress Insurrections and repel Invasions;

To provide for organizing, arming, and disciplining, the Militia, and for governing such Part of them as may be employed in the Service of the United States, reserving to the States respectively, the Appointment of the Officers, and the Authority of training the Militia according to the discipline described by Congress;

To exercise exclusive Legislation in all Cases whatsoever, over such District (not exceeding ten Miles square) as may, by Cession of particular States, and the Acceptance of Congress, become the Seat of the Government of the United States, and to exercise like Authority over all Places purchased by the Consent of the Legislature of the State in which the Same shall be, for the Erection of Forts, Magazines, Arsenals, dock-Yards, and other needful Buildings;—And

To make all Laws which shall be necessary and proper for carrying into Execution the foregoing Powers, and all other Powers vested by this Constitution in the Government of the United States, or in any Department or Officer thereof.

Section 9.

The Migration or Importation of such Persons as any of the States now existing shall think proper to admit, shall not be prohibited by the Congress prior to the Year one thousand eight hundred and eight, but a Tax or Duty may be imposed on such Importation, not exceeding ten dollars for each Person.

The Privilege of the Writ of Habeas Corpus shall not be suspended, unless when in Cases of Rebellion or Invasion the public Safety may require it.

No Bill of Attainder or ex post facto Law shall be passed.

No Capitation, or other direct, Tax shall be laid, unless in Proportion to the Census or Enumeration herein before directed to be taken.

No Tax or Duty shall be laid on Articles exported from any State.

No Preference shall be given by any Regulation of Commerce or Revenue to the Ports of one State over those of another; nor shall Vessels bound to, or from, one State, be obliged to enter, clear, or pay Duties in another.

No Money shall be drawn from the Treasury, but in Consequence of Appropriations made by Laws; and a regular Statement and Account of the Receipts and Expenditures of all public Money shall be published from time to time.

No Title of Nobility shall be granted by the United States: And no Person holding any Office of Profit or Trust under them, shall, without the Consent of the Congress, accept of any present, Emolument, Office, or Title, of any kind whatever, from any King, Prince, or foreign State.

Section 10.

No State shall enter into any Treaty, Alliance, or Confederation; grant Letters of Marque and Reprisal; coin Money; emit Bills of Credit; make any Thing but gold and silver Coin a Tender in Payment of Debts; pass any Bill of Attainder, ex post facto Law, or Law impairing the Obligation of Contracts, or grant any Title of Nobility.

No State shall, without the Consent of the Congress, lay any Imposts or Duties on Imports or Exports, except what may be absolutely necessary for executing its inspection Laws: and the net Produce of all Duties and Imposts, laid by any State on Imports or Exports, shall be for the Use of the Treasury of the United States; and all such Laws shall be subject to the Revision and Controul of the Congress.

No State shall, without the Consent of Congress, lay any Duty of Tonnage, keep Troops, or Ships of War in time of Peace, enter into any Agreement or Compact with another State, or with a foreign Power, or engage in War, unless actually invaded, or in such imminent Danger as will not admit of delay.

ARTICLE II

Section 1.

The executive Power shall be vested in a President of the United States of America. He shall hold his Office during the Term of four Years, and, together with the Vice President, chosen for the same Term, be elected, as follows:

Each State shall appoint, in such Manner as the Legislature thereof may direct, a Number of Electors, equal to the whole Number of Senators and Representatives to which the State may be entitled in the Congress: but no Senator or Representative, or Person holding an Office of Trust or Profit under the United States, shall be appointed an Elector.

The Electors shall meet in their respective States, and vote by Ballot for two Persons, of whom one at least shall not be an Inhabitant of the same State with themselves. And they shall make a list of all the Persons voted for, and of the Number of Votes for each; which List they shall sign and certify, and transmit sealed to the Seat of the Government of the United States, directed to the President of the Senate. The President of the Senate shall, in the presence of the Senate and House of Representatives, open all the Certificates, and the Votes shall be counted. The Person having the greatest Number of Votes shall be the President, if such Number be a Majority of the whole Number of Electors appointed; and if there be more than one who have such Majority, and have an equal Number of Votes, then the House of Representatives shall immediately chuse by Ballot one of them for President; and if no Person have a Majority, then from the five highest on the List the said House shall in like Manner chuse the President. But in chusing the President, the Votes shall be taken by States, the Representation from each State having one Vote; A quorum for this Purpose shall consist of a Member or Members from two thirds of the States, and a Majority of all the States shall be necessary to a Choice. In every Case, after the Choice of the President, the Person having the greatest Number of Votes of the Electors shall be the Vice President. But if there should remain two or more who have equal Votes, the Senate shall chuse from them by Ballot the Vice President.

The Congress may determine the Time of Chusing the Electors, and the Day on which they shall give their Votes; which Day shall be the same throughout the United States.

No Person except a natural born Citizen, or a Citizen of the United States, at the time of the Adoption of this Constitution, shall be eligible to the Office of President; neither shall any Person be eligible to that Office who shall not have attained to the Age of thirty five Years, and been fourteen Years a Resident within the United States.

In Case of the Removal of the President from Office, or of his Death, Resignation, or Inability to discharge the Powers and Duties of the said Office, the Same shall devolve on the Vice President, and the Congress may by Law provide for the Case of Removal, Death, Resignation or Inability, both of the President and Vice President, declaring what Officer shall then act as President, and such Officer shall act accordingly, until the Disability be removed, or a President shall be elected.

The President shall, at stated Times, receive for his Services, a Compensation, which shall neither be encreased nor diminished during the Period for which he shall have been elected, and he shall not receive within that Period any other Emolument from the United States, or any of them.

Before he enter on the Execution of his Office, he shall take the following Oath or Affirmation:—"I do solemnly swear (or affirm) that I will faithfully execute the Office of President of the United States, and will to the best of my Ability, preserve, protect and defend the Constitution of the United States."

Section 2.

The President shall be Commander in Chief of the Army and Navy of the United States, and of the Militia of the several States, when called into the actual Service of the United States; he may require the Opinion, in writing, of the principal Officer in each of the executive Departments, upon any Subject relating to the Duties of their respective Offices, and he shall have Power to grant Reprieves and Pardons for Offenses against the United States, except in Cases of Impeachment.

He shall have Power, by and with the Advice and Consent of the Senate, to make Treaties, providing two thirds of the Senators present concur; and he shall nominate, and by and with the Advice and Consent of the Senate, shall appoint Ambassadors, other public Ministers and Consuls, Judges of the supreme Court, and all other Officers of the United States, whose Appointments are not herein otherwise provided for, and which shall be established by Law: but the Congress may by Law vest the Appointment of such inferior Officers, as they think proper, in the President alone, in the Courts of Law, or in the Heads of Departments.

The President shall have Power to fill up all Vacancies that may happen during the Recess of the Senate, by granting Commissions which shall expire at the End of their next Session.

Section 3.

He shall from time to time give to the Congress Information of the State of the Union, and recommend to their Consideration such Measures as he shall judge necessary and expedient; he may, on extraordinary Occasions, convene both Houses, or either of them, and in Case of Disagreement between them, with Respect to the Time of Adjournment, he may adjourn them to such Time as he shall think proper, he shall receive Ambassadors and other public Ministers; he shall take Care that the Laws be faithfully executed, and shall Commission all the Offices of the United States.

Section 4.

The President, Vice President and all civil Officers of the United States, shall be removed from Office on Impeachment for, and Conviction of, Treason, Bribery, or other high Crimes and Misdemeanors.

ARTICLE III

Section I.

The judicial Power of the United States, shall be vested in one supreme Court, and in such inferior Courts as the Congress may from time to time ordain and establish. The Judges, both of the supreme and inferior Courts, shall hold their Offices during good Behaviour, and shall, at Times, receive for their Services, a Compensation, which shall not be diminished during their Continuance in Office.

Section 2.

The judicial Power shall extend to all Cases, in Law and Equity, arising under this Constitution, the Laws of the United States, and Treaties made, or which shall be made, under their Authority;—to all Cases affecting Ambassadors, other public Ministers and Consuls;—to all Cases of admiralty and maritime Jurisdiction;—to Controversies to which the United States shall be a Party;—to controversies between two or more States;—between a State and Citizens of another State;—between Citizens of different States;—between Citizens of the same State claiming Lands under Grants of different States; and between a State, or the Citizens thereof, and foreign States, Citizens or Subjects.

In all Cases affecting Ambassadors, other public Ministers and Consuls, and those in which a State shall be Party, the supreme Court shall have original Jurisdiction. In all the other Cases before mentioned, the supreme Court shall have appellate Jurisdiction, both as to Law and Fact, with such Exceptions, and under such Regulations as the Congress shall make.

The Trial of all Crimes, except in Cases of Impeachment, shall be by Jury; and such Trial shall be held in the State where the said Crimes shall have been committed; but when not committed within any State, the Trial shall be at such Place or Places as the Congress may by Law have directed.

Section 3.

Treason against the United States, shall consist only in levying War against them, or in adhering to their Enemies, giving them Aid and Comfort. No Person shall be convicted of Treason unless on the Testimony of two Witnesses to the same overt Act, or on Confession in open Court.

The Congress shall have Power to declare the Punishment of Treason, but no Attainder of Treason shall work Corruption of Blood, or Forfeiture except during the Life of the Person attainted.

ARTICLE IV

Section 1.

Full Faith and Credit shall be given in each State to the public Acts, Records, and judicial Proceedings of every other State. And the Congress may by general Laws prescribe the Manner in which such Acts, Records and Proceedings shall be proved, and the Effect thereof.

Section 2.

The Citizens of each State shall be entitled to all Privileges and Immunities of Citizens in the several States.

A Person charged in any State with Treason, Felony, or other Crime, who shall flee from Justice, and be found in another State, shall on Demand of the executive Authority of the State from which he fled, be delivered up, to be removed to the State having Jurisdiction of the Crime.

No Person held to Service or Labour in one State, under the Laws thereof, escaping into another, shall, in Consequence of any Law or Regulation therein, be discharged from such Service or Labour, but shall be delivered up on Claim of the Party to whom such Service or Labour may be due.

Section 3.

New States may be admitted by the Congress into this Union; but no new State shall be formed or erected within the Jurisdiction of any other State; nor any State be formed by the Junction of two or more States, or Parts of States, without the Consent of the Legislatures of the States concerned as well as the Congress.

The Congress shall have Power to dispose of and make all needful Rules and Regulations respecting the Territory or other Property belonging to the United States; and nothing in this Constitution shall be so construed as to Prejudice any Claims of the United States, or of any particular State.

Section 4.

The United States shall guarantee to every State in this Union a Republican Form of Government, and shall protect each of them against Invasion; and on Application of the Legislature, or of the Executive (when the Legislature cannot be convened) against domestic Violence.

ARTICLE V

The Congress, whenever two thirds of both Houses shall deem it necessary, shall propose Amendments to this Constitution, or, on the Application of the Legislatures of two thirds of the several States, shall call a Convention for proposing Amendments, which, in either Case, shall be valid to all Intents and Purposes, as Part of this Constitution, when ratified by the Legislatures of three fourths of the several States, or by Conventions in three fourths thereof, as the one or the other Mode of Ratification may be proposed by the Congress; Provided that no Amendment which may be made prior to the Year One thousand eight hundred and eight shall in any Manner affect the first and fourth Clauses in the Ninth Section of the first Article; and that no State, without its Consent, shall be deprived of its equal Suffrage in the Senate.

ARTICLE VI

All Debts contracted and Engagements entered into, before the Adoption of this Constitution, shall be as valid against the United States under this Constitution, as under the Confederation.

This Constitution, and the Laws of the United States which shall be made in Pursuance thereof; and all Treaties made, or which shall be made, under the Authority of the United States, shall be the supreme Law of the Land; and the Judges in every State shall be bound thereby, any Thing in the Constitution or Laws of any State to the Contrary notwithstanding.

The Senators and Representatives before mentioned, and the Members of the several State Legislatures, and all executive and judicial Officers, both of the United States and of the Several States, shall be bound by Oath or Affirmation, to support this Constitution; but no religious Test shall ever be required as a Qualification to any Office or public Trust under the United States.

ARTICLE VII

The Ratification of the Conventions of nine States, shall be sufficient for the Establishment of this Constitution between the States so ratifying the Same.

Amendment I [1791].

Congress shall make no law respecting an establishment of religion, or prohibiting the free exercise thereof; or abridging the freedom of speech, or the press; or the right of the people peaceably to assemble, and to petition the Government for a redress of grievances.

Amendment II [1791].

A well regulated Militia, being necessary to the security for a free State, the right of the people to keep and bear Arms, shall not be infringed.

Amendment III [1791].

No Soldier shall, in time of peace be quartered in any house, without the consent of the Owner, nor in time of war, but in a manner to be prescribed by law.

Amendment IV [1791].

The right of the people to be secure in their persons, houses, papers, and effects, against unreasonable searches and seizures, shall not be violated, and no Warrants shall issue, but upon probable cause, supported by Oath or Affirmation, and particularly describing the place to be searched, and the persons or things to be seized.

Amendment V [1791].

No person shall be held to answer for a capital, or otherwise infamous crime, unless on a presentment or indictment of a Grand Jury, except in cases arising in the land or naval forces, or in the Militia, when in actual service in time of

War or public danger; nor shall any person be subject for the same offense to be twice put in jeopardy of life or limb; nor shall be compelled in any criminal case to be a witness against himself, nor be deprived of life, liberty, or property, without due process of law; nor shall private property be taken for public use, without just compensation.

Amendment VI [1791].

In all criminal prosecutions, the accused shall enjoy the right to a speedy and public trial, by an impartial jury of the State and district wherein the crime shall have been committed, which district shall have been previously ascertained by law, and to be informed of the nature and cause of the accusation; to be confronted with the Witnesses against him; to have compulsory process for obtaining witnesses in his favor, and to have the Assistance of counsel for his defence.

Amendment VII [1791].

In suits at common law, where the value in controversy shall exceed twenty dollars, the right of trial by jury shall be preserved, and no fact tried by a jury, shall be otherwise re-examined in any Court of the United States, than according to the rules of the common law.

Amendment VIII [1791].

Excessive bail shall not be required, no excessive fines imposed, nor cruel and unusual punishments inflicted.

Amendment IX [1791].

The enumeration in the Constitution, of certain rights, shall not be construed to deny or disparage others retained by the people.

Amendment X [1791].

The powers not delegated to the United States by the Constitution, nor prohibited by it to the States, are reserved to the States respectively, or to the people.

Amendment XI [1798].

The judicial power of the United States shall not be construed to extend to any suit in law or equity, commenced or prosecuted against one of the United States by Citizens of another State, or by Citizens or Subjects of any Foreign State.

Amendment XII [1804].

The Electors shall meet in their respective states and vote by ballot for President and Vice-President, one of whom, at least, shall not be an inhabitant of the same state with themselves; they shall name in their ballots the person voted for as President, and in distinct ballots the person voted for as Vice-President, and they shall make distinct lists of all persons voted for as President, and of all persons voted for as Vice-President, and of the number of votes for each, which lists they shall sign and certify, and transmit sealed to the seat of the government of the United States, directed to the President of the Senate;—The President of the Senate shall, in the presence of the Senate and House of Representatives, open all the certificates and the votes shall then be counted;—The person having the greatest number of votes for President, shall be the President, if such number be a majority of the whole number of Electors appointed; and if no person have such majority, then from the persons having the highest numbers not exceeding three on the list of those voted for as President, the House of Representatives shall choose immediately, by ballot, the President. But in choosing the President, the votes shall be taken by states, the representation from each state having one vote; a quorum for this purpose shall consist of a member or members from two-thirds of the states, and a majority of all the states shall be necessary to a choice. And if the House of Representatives shall not choose a President whenever the right of choice shall devolve upon them, before the fourth day of March next following, then the Vice-President shall act as President, as in the case of the death or other constitutional disability of the President. The person having the greatest number of votes as Vice-President, shall be the Vice-President, if such number be a majority of the whole number of Electors appointed, and if no person have a majority, then from the two highest numbers on the list, the Senate shall choose the Vice-President; a quorum for the purpose shall consist of two-thirds of the whole number of Senators, and a majority of the whole number shall be necessary to a choice. But no person constitutionally ineligible to the office of President shall be eligible to that of the Vice-President of the United States.

Amendment XIII [1865].

Section 1. Neither slavery nor involuntary servitude, except as a punishment for crime whereof the party shall have been duly convicted, shall exist within the United States, or any place subject to their jurisdiction.

Section 2. Congress shall have power to enforce this article by appropriate legislation.

Amendment XIV [1868].

Section 1. All persons born or naturalized in the United States, and subject to the jurisdiction thereof, are citizens of the United States and of the State wherein they reside. No State shall make or enforce any law which shall abridge the privileges or immunities of citizens of the United States; nor shall any State deprive any person of life, liberty, or property, without due process of law; nor deny to any person within its jurisdiction the equal protection of the laws.

Section 2. Representatives shall be appointed among the several States according to their respective numbers, counting the whole number of persons in each State, excluding Indians not taxed. But when the right to vote at any election for the choice of electors for President and Vice President of the United States, Representatives in Congress, the Executive and Judicial officers of a State, or the members of the Legislature thereof, is denied to any of the male inhabitants of such State, being twenty-one years of age, and citizens of the United States, or in any way abridged, except for participation in rebellion, or other crime, the basis of representation therein shall be reduced in the proportion which the number of such male citizens shall bear the whole number of male citizens twenty-one years of age in such State.

Section 3. No person shall be a Senator or Representative in Congress, or elector of President and Vice President, or hold any office, civil or military, under the United States, or under any State, who, having previously taken an oath, as a member of Congress, or as an officer of the United States, or as a member of any State legislature, or as an executive or judicial officer of any State, to support the Constitution of the United States, shall have engaged in insurrection or rebellion against the same, or given aid or comfort to the enemies thereof. But Congress may by a vote of two-thirds of each House, remove such disability.

Section 4. The validity of the public debt of the United States, authorized by law, including debts incurred for payment of pensions and bounties for services in suppressing insurrection or rebellion, shall not be questioned. But neither the United States nor any State shall assume or pay any debt or obligation incurred in aid of insurrection of rebellion against the United States, or any claim for the loss or emancipation of any slave; but all such debts, obligations and claims shall be held illegal and void.

Section 5. The Congress shall have power to enforce, by appropriate legislation, the provisions of this article.

Amendment XV [1870].

Section 1. The right of citizens of the United States to vote shall not be denied or abridged by the United States or by any State on account of race, color, or previous condition of servitude.

Section 2. The Congress shall have power to enforce this article by appropriate legislation.

Amendment XVI [1913].

The Congress shall have power to lay and collect taxes on incomes, from whatever source derived, without apportionment among the several States, and without regard to any census or enumeration.

Amendment XVII [1913].

The Senate of the United States shall be composed of two Senators from each State, elected by the people thereof, for six years; and each Senator shall have one vote. The electors in each State shall have the qualifications requisite for electors of the most numerous branch of the State legislatures.

When vacancies happen in the representation of any State in the Senate, the executive authority of each State shall issue writs of election to fill such vacancies; *Provided,* That the legislature of any State may empower the executive thereof to make temporary appointments until the people fill the vacancies by election as the legislature may direct.

This amendment shall not be construed as to affect the election or term of any Senator chosen before it becomes valid as part of the Constitution.

Amendment XVIII [1919].

Section 1. After one year from the ratification of this article the manufacture, sale, or transportation of intoxicating liquors within, the importation thereof into, or the exportation thereof from the United States and all territory subject to the jurisdiction thereof for beverage purposes is hereby prohibited.

Section 2. The Congress and the several States shall have concurrent power to enforce this article by appropriate legislation.

Section 3. This article shall be inoperative unless it shall have been ratified as an amendment to the Constitution by the legislatures of the several States, as provided in the Constitution, within seven years from the date of the submission hereof to the States by the Congress.

Amendment XIX [1920].

The right of citizens of the United States to vote shall not be denied or abridged by the United States or by any State on account of sex.

Congress shall have power to enforce this article by appropriate legislation.

Amendment XX [1933].

Section 1. The terms of the President and Vice President shall end at noon on the 20th day of January, and the terms of Senators and Representatives at noon on the 3d day of January, of the years in which such terms would have ended if this article had not been ratified; and the terms of their successors shall then begin.

Section 2. The Congress shall assemble at least once in every year, and such meeting shall begin at noon on the 3d day of January, unless they shall by law appoint a different day.

Section 3. If, at the time fixed for the beginning of the term of the President, the President elect shall have died, the Vice President elect shall become President. If a President shall not have been chosen before the time fixed for the beginning of his term, or if the President elect shall have failed to qualify, then the Vice President elect shall act as President until a President shall have qualified; and the Congress may by law provide for the case wherein neither a President elect nor a Vice President elect shall have qualified, declaring who shall then act as President, or the manner in which one who is to act shall be selected, and such person shall act accordingly until a President or Vice President shall have qualified.

Section 4. The Congress may by law provide for the case of the death of any of the persons from whom the House of Representatives may choose a President whenever the right of choice shall have devolved upon them, and for the case of the death of any of the persons from whom the Senate may choose a Vice President whenever the right of choice shall have devolved upon them.

Section 5. Sections 1 and 2 shall take effect on the 15th day of October following the ratification of this article.

Section 6. This article shall be inoperative unless it shall have been ratified as an amendment to the Constitution by the legislatures of three-fourths of the several States within seven years from the date of its submission.

Amendment XXI [1933].

Section 1. The eighteenth article of amendment to the Constitution of the United States is hereby repealed.

Section 2. The transportation or importation into any State, Territory, or possession of the United States for delivery or use therein of intoxicating liquors, in violation of the laws thereof, is hereby prohibited.

Section 3. This article shall be inoperative unless it shall have been ratified as an amendment to the Constitution by conventions in the several States, as provided in the Constitution, within seven years from the date of the submission hereof to the States by the Congress.

Amendment XXII [1951].

Section 1. No person shall be elected to the office of the President more than twice, and no person who has held the office of President, or acted as President, for more than two years of a term to which some other person was elected President shall be elected to the office of the President more than once. But this Article shall not apply to any person holding the office of President when this Article was proposed by the Congress, and shall not prevent any person who may be holding the office of President, or acting as President, during the term within which this Article becomes operative from holding the office of President, or acting as President during the remainder of such term.

Section 2. This article shall be inoperative unless it shall have been ratified as an amendment to the Constitution by the legislatures of three-fourths of the several States within seven years from the date of its submission to the States by the Congress.

Amendment XXIII [1961].

Section 1. The District constituting the seat of Government of the United States shall appoint in such manner as the Congress may direct:

A number of electors of President and Vice President equal to the whole number of Senators and Representatives in Congress to which the District would be entitled if it were a State, but in no event more than the least populous State; they shall be in addition to those appointed by the States, but they shall be considered, for the purposes of the election of President and Vice President, to be electors appointed by a State; and they shall meet in the District and perform such duties as provided by the twelfth article of amendment.

Section 2. The Congress shall have power to enforce this article by appropriate legislation.

Amendment XXIV [1964].

Section 1. The right of citizens of the United States to vote in any primary or other election for President or Vice President, for electors for President or Vice President, or for Senator or Representative in Congress, shall not be denied or abridged by the United States or any State by reason of failure to pay any poll tax or other tax.

Section 2. The Congress shall have power to enforce this article by appropriate legislation.

Amendment XXV [1967].

Section 1. In case of the removal of the President from office or of his death or resignation, the Vice President shall become President.

Section 2. Whenever there is a vacancy in the office of the Vice President, the President shall nominate a Vice President who shall take office upon confirmation by a majority vote of both Houses of Congress.

Section 3. Whenever the President transmits to the President pro tempore of the Senate and the Speaker of the House of Representatives his written declaration that he is unable to discharge the powers and duties of his office, and until he transmits to them a written declaration to the contrary, such powers and duties shall be discharged by the Vice President as Acting President.

Section 4. Whenever the Vice President and a majority of either the principal officers of the executive departments or of such other body as Congress may by law provide, transmit to the President pro tempore of the Senate and the Speaker of the House of Representatives their written declaration that the President is unable to discharge the powers and duties of his office, the Vice President shall immediately assume the powers and duties of the office as Acting President.

Thereafter, when the President transmits to the President pro tempore of the Senate and the Speaker of the House of Representatives his written declaration that no inability exists, he shall resume the powers and duties of his office unless the Vice President and a majority of either the principal officers of the executive department or of such other body as Congress may by law provide, transmit within four days to the President pro tempore of the Senate and the Speaker of the House of Representatives their written declaration that the President is unable to discharge the powers and duties of his office. Thereupon Congress shall decide the issue, assembling within forty-eight hours for that purpose if not in session. If the Congress, within twenty-one days after receipt of the latter written declaration, or, if Congress is not in session, within twenty-one days after Congress is required to assemble, determines by two-thirds vote of both Houses that the President is unable to discharge the powers and duties of his office, the Vice President shall continue to discharge the same as Acting President; otherwise, the President shall resume the powers and duties of his office.

Amendment XXVI [1971].   **Section 1.** The right of citizens of the United States, who are eighteen years of age or older, to vote shall not be denied or abridged by the United States or by any State on account of age.

Section 2. The Congress shall have power to enforce this article by appropriate legislation.

Amendment XXVII [1992].   No law, varying the compensation for the services of the Senators and Representatives, shall take effect, until an election of Representatives shall have intervened.

Appendix B

Uniform Commercial Code (Selected Provisions)

ARTICLE 1

GENERAL PROVISIONS

PART 1   Short Title, Construction, Application and Subject Matter of the Act

§ 1-101.   Short Title.

This Act shall be known and may be cited as Uniform Commercial Code.

§ 1-102.   Purposes; Rules of Construction; Variation by Agreement.

(1) This Act shall be liberally construed and applied to promote its underlying purposes and policies.

(2) Underlying purposes and policies of this Act are

  (a) to simplify, clarify and modernize the law governing commercial transactions;

  (b) to permit the continued expansion of commercial practices through custom, usage and agreement of the parties;

  (c) to make uniform the law among the various jurisdictions.

(3) The effect of provisions of this Act may be varied by agreement, except as otherwise provided in this Act and except that the obligations of good faith, diligence, reasonableness and care prescribed by this Act may not be disclaimed by agreement but the parties may by agreement determine the standards by which the performance of such obligations is to be measured if such standards are not manifestly unreasonable.

(4) The presence in certain provisions of this Act of the words "unless otherwise agreed" or words of similar import does not imply that the effect of other provisions may not be varied by agreement under subsection (3).

(5) In this Act unless the context otherwise requires

  (a) words in the singular number include the plural, and in the plural include the singular;

  (b) words of the masculine gender include the feminine and the neuter, and when the sense so indicates words of the neuter gender may refer to any gender.

§ 1-103.   Supplementary General Principles of Law Applicable.

Unless displaced by the particular provisions of this Act, the principles of law and equity, including the law merchant and the law relative to capacity to contract, principal and agent, estoppel, fraud, misrepresentation, duress, coercion, mistake, bankruptcy, or other validating or invalidating cause shall supplement its provisions.

§ 1-104.   Construction Against Implicit Repeal.

This Act being a general act intended as a unified coverage of its subject matter, no part of it shall be deemed to be impliedly repealed by subsequent legislation if such construction can reasonably be avoided.

§ 1-105.   Territorial Application of the Act; Parties' Power to Choose Applicable Law.

(1) Except as provided hereafter in this section, when a transaction bears a reasonable relation to this state and also to another state or nation the parties may agree that the law either of this state or of such other state or nation shall govern their rights and duties. Failing such agreement this Act applies to transactions bearing an appropriate relation to this state.

(2) Where one of the following provisions of this Act specifies the applicable law, that provision governs and a contrary agreement is effective only to the extent permitted by the law (including the conflict of laws rules) so specified:

Rights of creditors against sold goods. Section 2–402.

Applicability of the Article on Leases. Sections 2A–105 and 2A–106.

Applicability of the Article on Bank Deposits and Collections. Section 4–102.

Governing law in the Article on Funds Transfers. Section 4A–507.

Letters of Credit, Section 5–116.
Bulk sales subject to the Article on Bulk Sales. Section 6–103.

Applicability of the Article on Investment Securities. Section 8–106.

Law governing perfection, the effect of perfection or non-perfection, and the priority of security interests and agricultural liens. Sections 9–301 through 9–307.

As amended in 1972, 1987, 1988, 1989, 1994, 1995, and 1999.

§ 1-106.   Remedies to Be Liberally Administered.

(1) The remedies provided by this Act shall be liberally administered to the end that the aggrieved party may be put in as good a position as if the other party had fully performed but neither consequential or special nor penal damages may be had except as specifically provided in this Act or by other rule of law.

(2) Any right or obligation declared by this Act is enforceable by action unless the provision declaring it specifies a different and limited effect.

§ 1-107.   Waiver or Renunciation of Claim or Right After Breach.

Any claim or right arising out of an alleged breach can be discharged in whole or in part without consideration by a written waiver or renunciation signed and delivered by the aggrieved party.

§ 1-108.   Severability.

If any provision or clause of this Act or application thereof to any person or circumstances is held invalid, such invalidity shall not affect other provisions or applications of the Act which can be given effect without the invalid provision or application, and to this end the provisions of this Act are declared to be severable.

§ 1-109.   Section Captions.

Section captions are parts of this Act.

PART 2   General Definitions and Principles of Interpretation

§ 1-201.   General Definitions.

Subject to additional definitions contained in the subsequent Articles of this Act which are applicable to specific Articles or Parts thereof, and unless the context otherwise requires, in this Act:

(1) "Action" in the sense of a judicial proceeding includes recoupment, counterclaim, set-off, suit in equity and any other proceedings in which rights are determined.

(2) "Aggrieved party" means a party entitled to resort to a remedy.

(3) "Agreement" means the bargain of the parties in fact as found in their language or by implication from other circumstances including course of dealing or usage of trade or course of performance as provided in this Act (Sections 1–205 and 2–208). Whether an agreement has legal consequences is determined by the provisions of this Act, if applicable; otherwise by the law of contracts (Section 1–103). (Compare "Contract".)

(4) "Bank" means any person engaged in the business of banking.

(5) "Bearer" means the person in possession of an instrument, document of title, or certificated security payable to bearer or indorsed in blank.

(6) "Bill of lading" means a document evidencing the receipt of goods for shipment issued by a person engaged in the business of transporting or forwarding goods, and includes an airbill. "Airbill" means a document serving for air transportation as a

bill of lading does for marine or rail transportation, and includes an air consignment note or air waybill.

(7) "Branch" includes a separately incorporated foreign branch of a bank.

(8) "Burden of establishing" a fact means the burden of persuading the triers of fact that the existence of the fact is more probable than its non-existence.

(9) "Buyer in ordinary course of business" means a person that buys goods in good faith, without knowledge that the sale violates the rights of another person in the goods, and in the ordinary course from a person, other than a pawnbroker, in the business of selling goods of that kind. A person buys goods in the ordinary course if the sale to the person comports with the usual or customary practices in the kind of business in which the seller is engaged or with the seller's own usual or customary practices. A person that sells oil, gas, or other minerals at the wellhead or minehead is a person in the business of selling goods of that kind. A buyer in ordinary course of business may buy for cash, by exchange of other property, or on secured or unsecured credit, and may acquire goods or documents of title under a pre-existing contract for sale. Only a buyer that takes possession of the goods or has a right to recover the goods from the seller under Article 2 may be a buyer in ordinary course of business. A person that acquires goods in a transfer in bulk or as security for or in total or partial satisfaction of a money debt is not a buyer in ordinary course of business.

(10) "Conspicuous": A term or clause is conspicuous when it is so written that a reasonable person against whom it is to operate ought to have noticed it. A printed heading in capitals (as: NON-NEGOTIABLE BILL OF LADING) is conspicuous. Language in the body of a form is "conspicuous" if it is in larger or other contrasting type or color. But in a telegram any stated term is "conspicuous". Whether a term or clause is "conspicuous" or not is for decision by the court.

(11) "Contract" means the total legal obligation which results from the parties' agreement as affected by this Act and any other applicable rules of law. (Compare "Agreement".)

(12) "Creditor" includes a general creditor, a secured creditor, a lien creditor and any representative of creditors, including an assignee for the benefit of creditors, a trustee in bankruptcy, a receiver in equity and an executor or administrator of an insolvent debtor's or assignor's estate.

(13) "Defendant" includes a person in the position of defendant in a cross-action or counterclaim.

(14) "Delivery" with respect to instruments, documents of title, chattel paper, or certificated securities means voluntary transfer of possession.

(15) "Document of title" includes bill of lading, dock warrant, dock receipt, warehouse receipt or order for the delivery of goods, and also any other document which in the regular course of business or financing is treated as adequately evidencing that the person in possession of it is entitled to receive, hold and dispose of the document and the goods it covers. To be a document of title a document must purport to be issued by or addressed to a bailee and purport to cover goods in the bailee's possession which are either identified or are fungible portions of an identified mass.

(16) "Fault" means wrongful act, omission or breach.

(17) "Fungible" with respect to goods or securities means goods or securities of which any unit is, by nature or usage of trade, the equivalent of any other like unit. Goods which are not fungible shall be deemed fungible for the purposes of this Act to the extent that under a particular agreement or document unlike units are treated as equivalents.

(18) "Genuine" means free of forgery or counterfeiting.

(19) "Good faith" means honesty in fact in the conduct or transaction concerned.

(20) "Holder" with respect to a negotiable instrument, means the person in possession if the instrument is payable to bearer or, in the cases of an instrument payable to an identified person, if the identified person is in possession. "Holder" with respect to a document of title means the person in possession if the goods are deliverable to bearer or to the order of the person in possession.

(21) To "honor" is to pay or to accept and pay, or where a credit so engages to purchase or discount a draft complying with the terms of the credit.

(22) "Insolvency proceedings" includes any assignment for the benefit of creditors or other proceedings intended to liquidate or rehabilitate the estate of the person involved.

(23) A person is "insolvent" who either has ceased to pay his debts in the ordinary course of business or cannot pay his debts as they become due or is insolvent within the meaning of the federal bankruptcy law.

(24) "Money" means a medium of exchange authorized or adopted by a domestic or foreign government and includes a monetary unit of account established by an intergovernmental organization or by agreement between two or more nations.

(25) A person has "notice" of a fact when

   (a) he has actual knowledge of it; or

   (b) he has received a notice or notification of it; or

   (c) from all the facts and circumstances known to him at the time in question he has reason to know that it exists.

A person "knows" or has "knowledge" of a fact when he has actual knowledge of it. "Discover" or "learn" or a word or phrase of similar import refers to knowledge rather than to reason to know. The time and circumstances under which a notice or notification may cease to be effective are not determined by this Act.

(26) A person "notifies" or "gives" a notice or notification to another by taking such steps as may be reasonably required to inform the other in ordinary course whether or not such other

actually comes to know of it. A person "receives" a notice or notification when

(a) it comes to his attention; or

(b) it is duly delivered at the place of business through which the contract was made or at any other place held out by him as the place for receipt of such communications.

(27) Notice, knowledge or a notice or notification received by an organization is effective for a particular transaction from the time when it is brought to the attention of the individual conducting that transaction, and in any event from the time when it would have been brought to his attention if the organization had exercised due diligence. An organization exercises due diligence if it maintains reasonable routines for communicating significant information to the person conducting the transaction and there is reasonable compliance with the routines. Due diligence does not require an individual acting for the organization to communicate information unless such communication is part of his regular duties or unless he has reason to know of the transaction and that the transaction would be materially affected by the information.

(28) "Organization" includes a corporation, government or governmental subdivision or agency, business trust, estate, trust, partnership or association, two or more persons having a joint or common interest, or any other legal or commercial entity.

(29) "Party", as distinct from "third party", means a person who has engaged in a transaction or made an agreement within this Act.

(30) "Person" includes an individual or an organization (See Section 1–102).

(31) "Presumption" or "presumed" means that the trier of fact must find the existence of the fact presumed unless and until evidence is introduced which would support a finding of its non-existence.

(32) "Purchase" includes taking by sale, discount, negotiation, mortgage, pledge, lien, issue or re-issue, gift or any other voluntary transaction creating an interest in property.

(33) "Purchaser" means a person who takes by purchase.

(34) "Remedy" means any remedial right to which an aggrieved party is entitled with or without resort to a tribunal.

(35) "Representative" includes an agent, an officer of a corporation or association, and a trustee, executor or administrator of an estate, or any other person empowered to act for another.

(36) "Rights" includes remedies.

(37) "Security interest" means an interest in personal property or fixtures which secures payment or performance of an obligation. The term also includes any interest of a consignor and a buyer of accounts, chattel paper, a payment intangible, or a promissory note in a transaction that is subject to Article 9. The special property interest of a buyer of goods on identification of those goods to a contract for sale under Section 2–401 is not a "security interest", but a buyer may also acquire a "security interest" by complying with Article 9. Except as otherwise provided in Section 2–505, the right of a seller or lessor of goods under Article 2 or 2A to retain or acquire possession of the goods is not a "security interest", but a seller or lessor may also acquire a "security interest" by complying with Article 9. The retention or reservation of title by a seller of goods notwithstanding shipment or delivery to the buyer (Section 2–401) is limited in effect to a reservation of a "security interest".

Whether a transaction creates a lease or security interest is determined by the facts of each case; however, a transaction creates a security interest if the consideration the lessee is to pay the lessor for the right to possession and use of the goods is an obligation for the term of the lease not subject to termination by the lessee, and

(a) the original term of the lease is equal to or greater than the remaining economic life of the goods,

(b) the lessee is bound to renew the lease for the remaining economic life of the goods or is bound to become the owner of the goods,

(c) the lessee has an option to renew the lease for the remaining economic life of the goods for no additional consideration or nominal additional consideration upon compliance with the lease agreement, or

(d) the lessee has an option to become the owner of the goods for no additional consideration or nominal additional consideration upon compliance with the lease agreement.

A transaction does not create a security interest merely because it provides that

(a) the present value of the consideration the lessee is obligated to pay the lessor for the right to possession and use of the goods is substantially equal to or is greater than the fair market value of the goods at the time the lease is entered into,

(b) the lessee assumes risk of loss of the goods, or agrees to pay taxes, insurance, filing, recording, or registration fees, or service or maintenance costs with respect to the goods,

(c) the lessee has an option to renew the lease or to become the owner of the goods,

(d) the lessee has an option to renew the lease for a fixed rent that is equal to or greater than the reasonably predictable fair market rent for the use of the goods for the term of the renewal at the time the option is to be performed, or

(e) the lessee has an option to become the owner of the goods for a fixed price that is equal to or greater than the reasonably predictable fair market value of the goods at the time the option is to be performed.

For purposes of this subsection (37):

(x) Additional consideration is not nominal if (i) when the option to renew the lease is granted to the lessee the rent is stated to be the fair market rent for the use of the goods for the term of the renewal determined at the time the option is to be performed, or (ii) when the option to become the owner of the goods is granted to the lessee the price is stated to be the fair market value of the goods determined at the time the option is to be performed. Additional consideration is nominal if it is less than the lessee's reasonably predictable cost of performing under the lease agreement if the option is not exercised;

(y) "Reasonably predictable" and "remaining economic life of the goods" are to be determined with reference to the facts and circumstances at the time the transaction is entered into; and

(z) "Present value" means the amount as of a date certain of one or more sums payable in the future, discounted to the date certain. The discount is determined by the interest rate specified by the parties if the rate is not manifestly unreasonable at the time the transaction is entered into; otherwise, the discount is determined by a commercially reasonable rate that takes into account the facts and circumstances of each case at the time the transaction was entered into.

(38) "Send" in connection with any writing or notice means to deposit in the mail or deliver for transmission by any other usual means of communication with postage or cost of transmission provided for and properly addressed and in the case of an instrument to an address specified thereon or otherwise agreed, or if there be none to any address reasonable under the circumstances. The receipt of any writing or notice within the time at which it would have arrived if properly sent has the effect of a proper sending.

(39) "Signed" includes any symbol executed or adopted by a party with present intention to authenticate a writing.

(40) "Surety" includes guarantor.

(41) "Telegram" includes a message transmitted by radio, teletype, cable, any mechanical method of transmission, or the like.

(42) "Term" means that portion of an agreement which relates to a particular matter.

(43) "Unauthorized" signature means one made without actual, implied or apparent authority and includes a forgery.

(44) "Value". Except as otherwise provided with respect to negotiable instruments and bank collections (Sections 3–303, 4–210 and 4–211) a person gives "value" for rights if he acquires them

(a) in return for a binding commitment to extend credit or for the extension of immediately available credit whether or not drawn upon and whether or not a chargeback is provided for in the event of difficulties in collection; or

(b) as security for or in total or partial satisfaction of a preexisting claim; or

(c) by accepting delivery pursuant to a preexisting contract for purchase; or

(d) generally, in return for any consideration sufficient to support a simple contract.

(45) "Warehouse receipt" means a receipt issued by a person engaged in the business of storing goods for hire.

(46) "Written" or "writing" includes printing, typewriting or any other intentional reduction to tangible form.

§1–202.   Prima Facie Evidence by Third Party Documents.

A document in due form purporting to be a bill of lading, policy or certificate of insurance, official weigher's or inspector's certificate, consular invoice, or any other document authorized or required by the contract to be issued by a third party shall be prima facie evidence of its own authenticity and genuineness and of the facts stated in the document by the third party.

§ 1–203.   Obligation of Good Faith.

Every contract or duty within this Act imposes an obligation of good faith in its performance or enforcement.

§ 1–204.   Time; Reasonable Time; "Seasonably".

(1) Whenever this Act requires any action to be taken within a reasonable time, any time which is not manifestly unreasonable may be fixed by agreement.

(2) What is a reasonable time for taking any action depends on the nature, purpose and circumstances of such action.

(3) An action is taken "seasonably" when it is taken at or within the time agreed or if no time is agreed at or within a reasonable time.

§ 1–205.   Course of Dealing and Usage of Trade.

(1) A course of dealing is a sequence of previous conduct between the parties to a particular transaction which is fairly to be regarded as establishing a common basis of understanding for interpreting their expressions and other conduct.

(2) A usage of trade is any practice or method of dealing having such regularity of observance in a place, vocation or trade as to justify an expectation that it will be observed with respect to the transaction in question. The existence and scope of such a usage are to be proved as facts. If it is established that such a usage is embodied in a written trade code or similar writing the interpretation of the writing is for the court.

(3) A course of dealing between parties and any usage of trade in the vocation or trade in which they are engaged or of which they are or should be aware give particular meaning to and supplement or qualify terms of an agreement.

(4) The express terms of an agreement and an applicable course of dealing or usage of trade shall be construed wherever reasonable as consistent with each other; but when such construction is unreasonable express terms control both course of dealing and usage of trade and course of dealing controls usage trade.

(5) An applicable usage of trade in the place where any part of performance is to occur shall be used in interpreting the agreement as to that part of the performance.

(6) Evidence of a relevant usage of trade offered by one party is not admissible unless and until he has given the other party such notice as the court finds sufficient to prevent unfair surprise to the latter.

§ 1–206. Statute of Frauds for Kinds of Personal Property Not Otherwise Covered.

(1) Except in the cases described in subsection (2) of this section a contract for the sale of personal property is not enforceable by way of action or defense beyond five thousand dollars in amount or value of remedy unless there is some writing which indicates that a contract for sale has been made between the parties at a defined or stated price, reasonably identifies the subject matter, and is signed by the party against whom enforcement is sought or by his authorized agent.
(2) Subsection (1) of this section does not apply to contracts for the sale of goods (Section 2–201) nor of securities (Section 8–113) nor to security agreements (Section 9–203).

As amended in 1994.

§ 1–207. Performance or Acceptance Under Reservation of Rights.

(1) A party who with explicit reservation of rights performs or promises performance or assents to performance in a manner demanded or offered by the other party does not thereby prejudice the rights reserved. Such words as "without prejudice", "under protest" or the like are sufficient.
(2) Subsection (1) does not apply to an accord and satisfaction.

As amended in 1990.

§ 1–208. Option to Accelerate at Will.

A term providing that one party or his successor in interest may accelerate payment or performance or require collateral or additional collateral "at will" or "when he deems himself insecure" or in words of similar import shall be construed to mean that he shall have power to do so only if he in good faith believes that the prospect of payment or performance is impaired. The burden of establishing lack of good faith is on the party against whom the power has been exercised.

§ 1–209. Subordinated Obligations.

An obligation may be issued as subordinated to payment of another obligation of the person obligated, or a creditor may subordinate his right to payment of an obligation by agreement with either the person obligated or another creditor of the person obligated. Such a subordination does not create a security interest as against either the common debtor or a subordinated creditor. This section shall be construed as declaring the law as it existed prior to the enactment of this section and not as modifying it. Added 1966.

Note: *This new section is proposed as an optional provision to make it clear that a subordination agreement does not create a security interest unless so intended.*

ARTICLE 2

SALES

PART 1   **Short Title, General Construction and Subject Matter**

§ 2–101. Short Title.

This Article shall be known and may be cited as Uniform Commercial Code—Sales.

§ 2–102. Scope; Certain Security and Other Transactions Excluded From This Article.

Unless the context otherwise requires, this Article applies to transactions in goods; it does not apply to any transaction which although in the form of an unconditional contract to sell or present sale is intended to operate only as a security transaction nor does this Article impair or repeal any statute regulating sales to consumers, farmers or other specified classes of buyers.

§ 2–103. Definitions and Index of Definitions.

(1) In this Article unless the context otherwise requires
 (a) "Buyer" means a person who buys or contracts to buy goods.
 (b) "Good faith" in the case of a merchant means honesty in fact and the observance of reasonable commercial standards of fair dealing in the trade.
 (c) "Receipt" of goods means taking physical possession of them.
 (d) "Seller" means a person who sells or contracts to sell goods.
 (2) Other definitions applying to this Article or to specified Parts thereof, and the sections in which they appear are:
  "Acceptance". Section 2–606.
  "Banker's credit". Section 2–325.
  "Between merchants". Section 2–104.
  "Cancellation". Section 2–106(4).
  "Commercial unit". Section 2–105.
  "Confirmed credit". Section 2–325.
  "Conforming to contract". Section 2–106.
  "Contract for sale". Section 2–106.
  "Cover". Section 2–712.
  "Entrusting". Section 2–403.

"Financing agency". Section 2–104.

"Future goods". Section 2–105.

"Goods". Section 2–105.

"Identification". Section 2–501.

"Installment contract". Section 2–612.

"Letter of Credit". Section 2–325.

"Lot". Section 2–105

"Merchant". Section 2–104.

"Overseas". Section 2–323.

"Person in position of seller". Section 2–707.

"Present sale". Section 2–106.

"Sale". Section 2–106.

"Sale on approval". Section 2–326.

"Sale or return". Section 2–326.

"Termination". Section 2–106.

(3) The following definitions in other Articles apply to this Article:

"Check". Section 3–104.

"Consignee". Section 7–102.

"Consignor". Section 7–102.

"Consumer goods". Section 9–109.

"Dishonor". Section 3–507.

"Draft". Section 3–104.

(4) In addition Article 1 contains general definitions and principles of construction and interpretation applicable throughout this Article.

As amended in 1994 and 1999.

§ 2–104.   Definitions: "Merchant"; "Between Merchants"; "Financing Agency".

(1) "Merchant" means a person who deals in goods of the kind or otherwise by his occupation holds himself out as having knowledge or skill peculiar to the practices or goods involved in the transaction or to whom such knowledge or skill may be attributed by his employment of an agent or broker or other intermediary who by his occupation holds himself out as having such knowledge or skill.

(2) "Financing agency" means a bank, finance company or other person who in the ordinary course of business makes advances against goods or documents of title or who by arrangement with either the seller or the buyer intervenes in ordinary course to make or collect payment due or claimed under the contract for sale, as by purchasing or paying the seller's draft or making advances against it or by merely taking it for collection whether or not documents of title accompany the draft. "Financing agency" includes also a bank or other person who similarly intervenes between persons who are in the position of seller and buyer in respect to the goods (Section 2–707).

(3) "Between merchants" means in any transaction with respect to which both parties are chargeable with the knowledge or skill of merchants.

§ 2–105.   Definitions: Transferability; "Goods"; "Future" Goods; "Lot"; "Commercial Unit".

(1) "Goods" means all things (including specially manufactured goods) which are movable at the time of identification to the contract for sale other than the money in which the price is to be paid, investment securities (Article 8) and things in action. "Goods" also includes the unborn young of animals and growing crops and other identified things attached to realty as described in the section on goods to be severed from realty (Section 2–107).

(2) Goods must be both existing and identified before any interest in them can pass. Goods which are not both existing and identified are "future" goods. A purported present sale of future goods or of any interest therein operates as a contract to sell.

(3) There may be a sale of a part interest in existing identified goods.

(4) An undivided share in an identified bulk of fungible goods is sufficiently identified to be sold although the quantity of the bulk is not determined. Any agreed proportion of such a bulk or any quantity thereof agreed upon by number, weight or other measure may to the extent of the seller's interest in the bulk be sold to the buyer who then becomes an owner in common.

(5) "Lot" means a parcel or a single article which is the subject matter of a separate sale or delivery, whether or not it is sufficient to perform the contract.

(6) "Commercial unit" means such a unit of goods as by commercial usage is a single whole for purposes of sale and division of which materially impairs its character or value on the market or in use. A commercial unit may be a single article (as a machine) or a set of articles (as a suite of furniture or an assortment of sizes) or a quantity (as a bale, gross, or carload) or any other unit treated in use or in the relevant market as a single whole.

§ 2–106.   Definitions: "Contract"; "Agreement"; "Contract for Sale"; "Sale"; "Present Sale"; "Conforming" to Contract; "Termination"; "Cancellation".

(1) In this Article unless the context otherwise requires "contract" and "agreement" are limited to those relating to the present or future sale of goods. "Contract for sale" includes both a present sale of goods and a contract to sell goods at a future time. A "sale" consists in the passing of title from the seller to the buyer for a price (Section 2–401). A "present sale" means a sale which is accomplished by the making of the contract.

(2) Goods or conduct including any part of a performance are "conforming" or conform to the contract when they are in accordance with the obligations under the contract.

(3) "Termination" occurs when either party pursuant to a power created by agreement or law puts an end to the contract

otherwise than for its breach. On "termination" all obligations which are still executory on both sides are discharged but any right based on prior breach or performance survives.

(4) "Cancellation" occurs when either party puts an end to the contract for breach by the other and its effect is the same as that of "termination" except that the cancelling party also retains any remedy for breach of the whole contract or any unperformed balance.

§ 2–107. Goods to Be Severed From Realty: Recording.

(1) A contract for the sale of minerals or the like (including oil and gas) or a structure or its materials to be removed from realty is a contract for the sale of goods within this Article if they are to be severed by the seller but until severance a purported present sale thereof which is not effective as a transfer of an interest in land is effective only as a contract to sell.

(2) A contract for the sale apart from the land of growing crops or other things attached to realty and capable of severance without material harm thereto but not described in subsection (1) or of timber to be cut is a contract for the sale of goods within this Article whether the subject matter is to be severed by the buyer or by the seller even though it forms part of the realty at the time of contracting, and the parties can by identification effect a present sale before severance.

(3) The provisions of this section are subject to any third party rights provided by the law relating to realty records, and the contract for sale may be executed and recorded as a document transferring an interest in land and shall then constitute notice to third parties of the buyer's rights under the contract for sale.

As amended in 1972.

PART 2 Form, Formation and Readjustment of Contract

§ 2–201. Formal Requirements; Statute of Frauds.

(1) Except as otherwise provided in this section a contract for the sale of goods for the price of $500 or more is not enforceable by way of action or defense unless there is some writing sufficient to indicate that a contract for sale has been made between the parties and signed by the party against whom enforcement is sought or by his authorized agent or broker. A writing is not insufficient because it omits or incorrectly states a term agreed upon but the contract is not enforceable under this paragraph beyond the quantity of goods shown in such writing.

(2) Between merchants if within a reasonable time a writing in confirmation of the contract and sufficient against the sender is received and the party receiving it has reason to know its con-

tents, its satisfies the requirements of subsection (1) against such party unless written notice of objection to its contents is given within ten days after it is received.

(3) A contract which does not satisfy the requirements of subsection (1) but which is valid in other respects is enforceable

(a) if the goods are to be specially manufactured for the buyer and are not suitable for sale to others in the ordinary course of the seller's business and the seller, before notice of repudiation is received and under circumstances which reasonably indicate that the goods are for the buyer, has made either a substantial beginning of their manufacture or commitments for their procurement; or

(b) if the party against whom enforcement is sought admits in his pleading, testimony or otherwise in court that a contract for sale was made, but the contract is not enforceable under this provision beyond the quantity of goods admitted; or

(c) with respect to goods for which payment has been made and accepted or which have been received and accepted (Sec. 2–606).

§ 2–202. Final Written Expression: Parol or Extrinsic Evidence.

Terms with respect to which the confirmatory memoranda of the parties agree or which are otherwise set forth in a writing intended by the parties as a final expression of their agreement with respect to such terms as are included therein may not be contradicted by evidence of any prior agreement or of a contemporaneous oral agreement but may be explained or supplemented

(a) by course of dealing or usage of trade (Section 1–205) or by course of performance (Section 2–208); and

(b) by evidence of consistent additional terms unless the court finds the writing to have been intended also as a complete and exclusive statement of the terms of the agreement.

§ 2–203. Seals Inoperative.

The affixing of a seal to a writing evidencing a contract for sale or an offer to buy or sell goods does not constitute the writing a sealed instrument and the law with respect to sealed instruments does not apply to such a contract or offer.

§ 2–204. Formation in General.

(1) A contract for sale of goods may be made in any manner sufficient to show agreement, including conduct by both parties which recognizes the existence of such a contract.

(2) An agreement sufficient to constitute a contract for sale may be found even though the moment of its making is undetermined.

(3) Even though one or more terms are left open a contract for sale does not fail for indefiniteness if the parties have intended to make a contract and there is a reasonably certain basis for giving an appropriate remedy.

§ 2–205.   Firm Offers.

An offer by a merchant to buy or sell goods in a signed writing which by its terms gives assurance that it will be held open is not revocable, for lack of consideration, during the time stated or if no time is stated for a reasonable time, but in no event may such period of irrevocability exceed three months; but any such term of assurance on a form supplied by the offeree must be separately signed by the offeror.

§ 2–206.   Offer and Acceptance in Formation of Contract.

(1) Unless other unambiguously indicated by the language or circumstances

(a) an offer to make a contract shall be construed as inviting acceptance in any manner and by any medium reasonable in the circumstances;

(b) an order or other offer to buy goods for prompt or current shipment shall be construed as inviting acceptance either by a prompt promise to ship or by the prompt or current shipment of conforming or nonconforming goods, but such a shipment of non-conforming goods does not constitute an acceptance if the seller seasonably notifies the buyer that the shipment is offered only as an accommodation to the buyer.

(2) Where the beginning of a requested performance is a reasonable mode of acceptance an offeror who is not notified of acceptance within a reasonable time may treat the offer as having lapsed before acceptance.

§ 2–207.   Additional Terms in Acceptance or Confirmation.

(1) A definite and seasonable expression of acceptance or a written confirmation which is sent within a reasonable time operates as an acceptance even though it states terms additional to or different from those offered or agreed upon, unless acceptance is expressly made conditional on assent to the additional or different terms.

(2) The additional terms are to be construed as proposals for addition to the contract. Between merchants such terms become part of the contract unless:

(a) the offer expressly limits acceptance to the terms of the offer;

(b) they materially alter it; or

(c) notification of objection to them has already been given or is given within a reasonable time after notice of them is received.

(3) Conduct by both parties which recognizes the existence of a contract is sufficient to establish a contract for sale although the writings of the parties do not otherwise establish a contract. In such case the terms of the particular contract consist of those terms on which the writings of the parties agree, together with any supplementary terms incorporated under any other provisions of this Act.

§ 2–208.   Course of Performance or Practical Construction.

(1) Where the contract for sale involves repeated occasions for performance by either party with knowledge of the nature of the performance and opportunity for objection to it by the other, any course of performance accepted or acquiesced in without objection shall be relevant to determine the meaning of the agreement.

(2) The express terms of the agreement and any such course of performance, as well as any course of dealing and usage of trade, shall be construed whenever reasonable as consistent with each other; but when such construction is unreasonable, express terms shall control course of performance and course of performance shall control both course of dealing and usage of trade (Section 1–205).

(3) Subject to the provisions of the next section on modification and waiver, such course of performance shall be relevant to show a waiver or modification of any term inconsistent with such course of performance.

§ 2–209.   Modification, Rescission and Waiver.

(1) An agreement modifying a contract within this Article needs no consideration to be binding.

(2) A signed agreement which excludes modification or rescission except by a signed writing cannot be otherwise modified or rescinded, but except as between merchants such a requirement on a form supplied by the merchant must be separately signed by the other party.

(3) The requirements of the statute of frauds section of this Article (Section 2–201) must be satisfied if the contract as modified is within its provisions.

(4) Although an attempt at modification or rescission does not satisfy the requirements of subsection (2) or (3) it can operate as a waiver.

(5) A party who has made a waiver affecting an executory portion of the contract may retract the waiver by reasonable notification received by the other party that strict performance will be required of any term waived, unless the retraction would be unjust in view of a material change of position in reliance on the waiver.

§ 2–210.   Delegation of Performance; Assignment of Rights.

(1) A party may perform his duty through a delegate unless otherwise agreed or unless the other party has a substantial interest in having his original promisor perform or control the acts required by the contract. No delegation of performance relieves the party delegating of any duty to perform or any liability for breach.

(2) Except as otherwise provided in Section 9–406, unless otherwise agreed, all rights of either seller or buyer can be assigned except where the assignment would materially change the duty of the other party, or increase materially the burden or risk imposed on him by his contract, or impair materially his chance of obtaining return performance. A right to damages for breach of the whole contract or a right arising out of the assignor's due performance of his entire obligation can be assigned despite agreement otherwise.

(3) The creation, attachment, perfection, or enforcement of a security interest in the seller's interest under a contract is not a transfer that materially changes the duty of or increases materially the burden or risk imposed on the buyer or impairs materially the buyer's chance of obtaining return performance within the purview of subsection (2) unless, and then only to the extent that, enforcement actually results in a delegation of material performance of the seller. Even in that event, the creation, attachment, perfection, and enforcement of the security interest remain effective, but (i) the seller is liable to the buyer for damages caused by the delegation to the extent that the damages could not reasonably by prevented by the buyer, and (ii) a court having jurisdiction may grant other appropriate relief, including cancellation of the contract for sale or an injunction against enforcement of the security interest or consummation of the enforcement.

(4) Unless the circumstances indicate the contrary a prohibition of assignment of "the contract" is to be construed as barring only the delegation to the assignee of the assignor's performance.

(5) An assignment of "the contract" or of "all my rights under the contract" or an assignment in similar general terms is an assignment of rights and unless the language or the circumstances (as in an assignment for security) indicate the contrary, it is a delegation of performance of the duties of the assignor and its acceptance by the assignee constitutes a promise by him to perform those duties. This promise is enforceable by either the assignor or the other party to the original contract.

(6) The other party may treat any assignment which delegates performance as creating reasonable grounds for insecurity and may without prejudice to his rights against the assignor demand assurances from the assignee (Section 2–609).

As amended in 1999.

PART 3   General Obligation and Construction of Contract

§ 2–301.   General Obligations of Parties.

The obligation of the seller is to transfer and deliver and that of the buyer is to accept and pay in accordance with the contract.

§ 2–302.   Unconscionable Contract or Clause.

(1) If the court as a matter of law finds the contract or any clause of the contract to have been unconscionable at the time it was made the court may refuse to enforce the contract, or it may enforce the remainder of the contract without the unconscionable clause, or it may so limit the application of any unconscionable clause as to avoid any unconscionable result.

(2) When it is claimed or appears to the court that the contract or any clause thereof may be unconscionable the parties shall be afforded a reasonable opportunity to present evidence as to its commercial setting, purpose and effect to aid the court in making the determination.

§ 2–303.   Allocations or Division of Risks.

Where this Article allocates a risk or a burden as between the parties "unless otherwise agreed", the agreement may not only shift the allocation but may also divide the risk or burden.

§ 2–304.   Price Payable in Money, Goods, Realty, or Otherwise.

(1) The price can be made payable in money or otherwise. If it is payable in whole or in part in goods each party is a seller of the goods which he is to transfer.

(2) Even though all or part of the price is payable in an interest in realty the transfer of the goods and the seller's obligations with reference to them are subject to this Article, but not the transfer of the interest in realty or the transferor's obligations in connection therewith.

§ 2–305.   Open Price Term.

(1) The parties if they so intend can conclude a contract for sale even though the price is not settled. In such a case the price is a reasonable price at the time for delivery if

(a) nothing is said as to price; or

(b) the price is left to be agreed by the parties and they fail to agree; or

(c) the price is to be fixed in terms of some agreed market or other standard as set or recorded by a third person or agency and it is not so set or recorded.

(2) A price to be fixed by the seller or by the buyer means a price for him to fix in good faith.

(3) When a price left to be fixed otherwise than by agreement of the parties fails to be fixed through fault of one party the other may at his option treat the contract as cancelled or himself fix a reasonable price.

(4) Where, however, the parties intend not to be bound unless the price be fixed or agreed and it is not fixed or agreed there is no contract. In such a case the buyer must return any goods already received or if unable so to do must pay their reasonable value at the time of delivery and the seller must return any portion of the price paid on account.

§ 2–306. Output, Requirements and Exclusive Dealings.

(1) A term which measures the quantity by the output of the seller or the requirements of the buyer means such actual output or requirements as may occur in good faith, except that no quantity unreasonably disproportionate to any stated estimate or in the absence of a stated estimate to any normal or otherwise comparable prior output or requirements may be tendered or demanded.

(2) A lawful agreement by either the seller or the buyer for exclusive dealing in the kind of goods concerned imposes unless otherwise agreed an obligation by the seller to use best efforts to supply the goods and by the buyer to use best efforts to promote their sale.

§ 2–307. Delivery in Single Lot or Several Lots.

Unless otherwise agreed all goods called for by a contract for sale must be tendered in a single delivery and payment is due only on such tender but where the circumstances give either party the right to make or demand delivery in lots the price if it can be apportioned may be demanded for each lot.

§ 2–308. Absence of Specified Place for Delivery.

Unless otherwise agreed

(a) the place for delivery of goods is the seller's place of business or if he has none his residence; but

(b) in a contract for sale of identified goods which to the knowledge of the parties at the time of contracting are in some other place, that place is the place for their delivery; and

(c) documents of title may be delivered through customary banking channels.

§ 2–309. Absence of Specific Time Provisions; Notice of Termination.

(1) The time for shipment or delivery or any other action under a contract if not provided in this Article or agreed upon shall be a reasonable time.

(2) Where the contract provides for successive performances but is indefinite in duration it is valid for a reasonable time but unless otherwise agreed may be terminated at any time by either party.

(3) Termination of a contract by one party except on the happening of an agreed event requires that reasonable notification be received by the other party and an agreement dispensing with notification is invalid if its operation would be unconscionable.

§ 2–310. Open Time for Payment or Running of Credit; Authority to Ship Under Reservation.

Unless otherwise agreed

(a) payment is due at the time and place at which the buyer is to receive the goods even though the place of shipment is the place of delivery; and

(b) if the seller is authorized to send the goods he may ship them under reservation, and may tender the documents of title, but the buyer may inspect the goods after their arrival before payment is due unless such inspection is inconsistent with the terms of the contract (Section 2–513); and

(c) if delivery is authorized and made by way of documents of title otherwise than by subsection (b) then payment is due at the time and place at which the buyer is to receive the documents regardless of where the goods are to be received; and

(d) where the seller is required or authorized to ship the goods on credit the credit period runs from the time of shipment but post-dating the invoice or delaying its dispatch will correspondingly delay the starting of the credit period.

§ 2–311. Options and Cooperation Respecting Performance.

(1) An agreement for sale which is otherwise sufficiently definite (subsection (3) of Section 2–204) to be a contract is not made invalid by the fact that it leaves particulars of performance to be specified by one of the parties. Any such specification must be made in good faith and within limits set by commercial reasonableness.

(2) Unless otherwise agreed specifications relating to assortment of the goods are at the buyer's option and except as otherwise provided in subsections (1)(c) and (3) of Section 2–319 specifications or arrangements relating to shipment are at the seller's option.

(3) Where such specification would materially affect the other party's performance but is not seasonably made or where one party's cooperation is necessary to the agreed performance of the other but is not seasonably forthcoming, the other party in addition to all other remedies

(a) is excused for any resulting delay in his own performance; and

(b) may also either proceed to perform in any reasonable manner or after the time for a material part of his own performance treat the failure to specify or to cooperate as a breach by failure to deliver or accept the goods.

§ 2–312. Warranty of Title and Against Infringement; Buyer's Obligation Against Infringement.

(1) Subject to subsection (2) there is in a contract for sale a warranty by the seller that

(a) the title conveyed shall be good, and its transfer rightful; and

b) the goods shall be delivered free from any security interest or other lien or encumbrance of which the buyer at the time of contracting has no knowledge.

(2) A warranty under subsection (1) will be excluded or modified only by specific language or by circumstances which give the buyer reason to know that the person selling does not claim title in himself or that he is purporting to sell only such right or title as he or a third person may have.

(3) Unless otherwise agreed a seller who is a merchant regularly dealing in goods of the kind warrants that the goods shall be delivered free of the rightful claim of any third person by way of infringement or the like but a buyer who furnishes specifications to the seller must hold the seller harmless against any such claim which arises out of compliance with the specifications.

§ 2-313.   Express Warranties by Affirmation, Promise, Description, Sample.

(1) Express warranties by the seller are created as follows:

(a) Any affirmation of fact or promise made by the seller to the buyer which relates to the goods and becomes part of the basis of the bargain creates an express warranty that the goods shall conform to the affirmation or promise.

(b) Any description of the goods which is made part of the basis of the bargain creates an express warranty that the goods shall conform to the description.

(c) Any sample or model which is made part of the basis of the bargain creates an express warranty that the whole of the goods shall conform to the sample or model.

(2) It is not necessary to the creation of an express warranty that the seller use formal words such as "warrant" or "guarantee" or that he have a specific intention to make a warranty, but an affirmation merely of the value of the goods or a statement purporting to be merely the seller's opinion or commendation of the goods does not create a warranty.

§ 2-314.   Implied Warranty: Merchantability; Usage of Trade.

(1) Unless excluded or modified (Section 2–316), a warranty that the goods shall be merchantable is implied in a contract for their sale if the seller is a merchant with respect to goods of that kind. Under this section the serving for value of food or drink to be consumed either on the premises or elsewhere is a sale.

(2) Goods to be merchantable must be at least such as

(a) pass without objection in the trade under the contract description; and

(b) in the case of fungible goods, are of fair average quality within the description; and

(c) are fit for the ordinary purposes for which such goods are used; and

(d) run, within the variations permitted by the agreement, of even kind, quality and quantity within each unit and among all units involved; and

(e) are adequately contained, packaged, and labeled as the agreement may require; and

(f) conform to the promises or affirmations of fact made on the container or label if any.

(3) Unless excluded or modified (Section 2–316) other implied warranties may arise from course of dealing or usage of trade.

§ 2-315.   Implied Warranty: Fitness for Particular Purpose.

Where the seller at the time of contracting has reason to know any particular purpose for which the goods are required and that the buyer is relying on the seller's skill or judgment to select or furnish suitable goods, there is unless excluded or modified under the next section an implied warranty that the goods shall be fit for such purpose.

§ 2-316.   Exclusion or Modification of Warranties.

(1) Words or conduct relevant to the creation of an express warranty and words or conduct tending to negate or limit warranty shall be construed wherever reasonable as consistent with each other; but subject to the provisions of this Article on parol or extrinsic evidence (Section 2–202) negation or limitation is inoperative to the extent that such construction is unreasonable.

(2) Subject to subsection (3), to exclude or modify the implied warranty of merchantability or any part of it the language must mention merchantability and in case of a writing must be conspicuous, and to exclude or modify any implied warranty of fitness the exclusion must be by a writing and conspicuous. Language to exclude all implied warranties of fitness is sufficient if it states, for example, that "There are no warranties which extend beyond the description on the face hereof."

(3) Notwithstanding subsection (2)

(a) unless the circumstances indicate otherwise, all implied warranties are excluded by expressions like "as is", "with all faults" or other language which in common understanding calls the buyer's attention to the exclusion of warranties and makes plain that there is no implied warranty; and

(b) when the buyer before entering into the contract has examined the goods or the sample or model as fully as he desired or has refused to examine the goods there is no implied warranty with regard to defects which an examination ought in the circumstances to have revealed to him; and

(c) an implied warranty can also be excluded or modified by course of dealing or course of performance or usage of trade.

(4) Remedies for breach of warranty can be limited in accordance with the provisions of this Article on liquidation or limitation of damages and on contractual modification of remedy (Sections 2–718 and 2–719).

§ 2–317.   Cumulation and Conflict of Warranties Express or Implied.

Warranties whether express or implied shall be construed as consistent with each other and as cumulative, but if such construction is unreasonable the intention of the parties shall determine which warranty is dominant. In ascertaining that intention the following rules apply:

(a) Exact or technical specifications displace an inconsistent sample or model or general language of description.

(b) A sample from an existing bulk displaces inconsistent general language of description.

(c) Express warranties displace inconsistent implied warranties other than an implied warranty of fitness for a particular purpose.

§ 2–318.   Third Party Beneficiaries of Warranties Express or Implied.

Note: If this Act is introduced in the Congress of the United States this section should be omitted. (States to select one alternative.)

Alternative A   A seller's warranty whether express or implied extends to any natural person who is in the family or household of his buyer or who is a guest in his home if it is reasonable to expect that such person may use, consume or be affected by the goods and who is injured in person by breach of the warranty. A seller may not exclude or limit the operation of this section.

Alternative B   A seller's warranty whether express or implied extends to any natural person who may reasonably be expected to use, consume or be affected by the goods and who is injured in person by breach of the warranty. A seller may not exclude or limit the operation of this section.

Alternative C   A seller's warranty whether express or implied extends to any person who may reasonably be expected to use, consume or be affected by the goods and who is injured by breach of the warranty. A seller may not exclude or limit the operation of this section with respect to injury to the person of an individual to whom the warranty extends.

As amended 1966.

§ 2–319.   F.O.B. and F.A.S. Terms.

(1) Unless otherwise agreed the term F.O.B. (which means "free on board") at a named place, even though used only in connection with the stated price, is a delivery term under which

(a) when the term is F.O.B. the place of shipment, the seller must at that place ship the goods in the manner provided in this Article (Section 2–504) and bear the expense and risk of putting them into the possession of the carrier; or

(b) when the term is F.O.B. the place of destination, the seller must at his own expense and risk transport the goods to that place and there tender delivery of them in the manner provided in this Article (Section 2–503);

(c) when under either (a) or (b) the term is also F.O.B. vessel, car or other vehicle, the seller must in addition at his own expense and risk load the goods on board. If the term is F.O.B. vessel the buyer must name the vessel and in an appropriate case the seller must comply with the provisions of this Article on the form of bill of lading (Section 2–323).

(2) Unless otherwise agreed the term F.A.S. vessel (which means "free alongside") at a named port, even though used only in connection with the stated price, is a delivery term under which the seller must

(a) at his own expense and risk deliver the goods alongside the vessel in the manner usual in that port or on a dock designated and provided by the buyer; and

(b) obtain and tender a receipt for the goods in exchange for which the carrier is under a duty to issue a bill of lading.

(3) Unless otherwise agreed in any case falling within subsection (1)(a) or (c) or subsection (2) the buyer must seasonably give any needed instructions for making delivery, including when the term is F.A.S. or F.O.B. the loading berth of the vessel and in an appropriate case its name and sailing date. The seller may treat the failure of needed instructions as a failure of cooperation under this Article (Section 2–311). He may also at his option move the goods in any reasonable manner preparatory to delivery or shipment.

(4) Under the term F.O.B. vessel or F.A.S. unless otherwise agreed the buyer must make payment against tender of the required documents and the seller may not tender nor the buyer demand delivery of the goods in substitution for the documents.

§ 2–320.   C.I.F. and C. & F. Terms.

(1) The term C.I.F. means that the price includes in a lump sum the cost of the goods and the insurance and freight to the named destination. The term C. & F. or C.F. means that the price so includes cost and freight to the named destination.

(2) Unless otherwise agreed and even though used only in connection with the stated price and destination, the term C.I.F. destination or its equivalent requires the seller at his own expense and risk to

(a) put the goods into the possession of a carrier at the port for shipment and obtain a negotiable bill or bills of lading covering the entire transportation to the named destination; and

(b) load the goods and obtain a receipt from the carrier (which may be contained in the bill of lading) showing that the freight has been paid or provided for; and

(c) obtain a policy or certificate of insurance, including any war risk insurance, of a kind and on terms then current at the port of shipment in the usual amount, in the currency of the contract, shown to cover the same goods covered by the bill of lading and providing for payment of loss to the order of the buyer or for the account of whom it may concern; but the seller may add to the price the amount of the premium for any such war risk insurance; and

(d) prepare an invoice of the goods and procure any other documents required to effect shipment or to comply with the contract; and

(e) forward and tender with commercial promptness all the documents in due form and with any indorsement necessary to perfect the buyer's rights.

(3) Unless otherwise agreed the term C. & F. or its equivalent has the same effect and imposes upon the seller the same obligations and risks as a C.I.F. term except the obligation as to insurance.

(4) Under the term C.I.F. or C. & F. unless otherwise agreed the buyer must make payment against tender of the required documents and the seller may not tender nor the buyer demand delivery of the goods in substitution for the documents.

§ 2-321.   C.I.F. or C. & F.: "Net Landed Weights"; "Payment on Arrival"; Warranty of Condition on Arrival.

Under a contract containing a term C.I.F. or C. & F.

(1) Where the price is based on or is to be adjusted according to "net landed weights", "delivered weights", "out turn" quantity or quality or the like, unless otherwise agreed the seller must reasonably estimate the price. The payment due on tender of the documents called for by the contract is the amount so estimated, but after final adjustment of the price a settlement must be made with commercial promptness.

(2) An agreement described in subsection (1) or any warranty of quality or condition of the goods on arrival places upon the seller the risk of ordinary deterioration, shrinkage and the like in transportation but has no effect on the place or time of identification to the contract for sale or delivery or on the passing of the risk of loss.

(3) Unless otherwise agreed where the contract provides for payment on or after arrival of the goods the seller must before payment allow such preliminary inspection as is feasible; but if the goods are lost delivery of the documents and payment are due when the goods should have arrived.

§ 2-322.   Delivery "Ex-Ship".

(1) Unless otherwise agreed a term for delivery of goods "ex-ship" (which means from the carrying vessel) or in equivalent language is not restricted to a particular ship and requires delivery from a ship which has reached a place at the named port of destination where goods of the kind are usually discharged.

(2) Under such a term unless otherwise agreed

(a) the seller must discharge all liens arising out of the carriage and furnish the buyer with a direction which puts the carrier under a duty to deliver the goods; and

(b) the risk of loss does not pass to the buyer until the goods leave the ship's tackle or are otherwise properly unloaded.

§ 2-323.   Form of Bill of Lading Required in Overseas Shipment; "Overseas".

(1) Where the contract contemplates overseas shipment and contains a term C.I.F. or C. & F. or F.O.B. vessel, the seller unless otherwise agreed must obtain a negotiable bill of lading stating that the goods have been loaded on board or, in the case of a term C.I.F. or C. & F., received for shipment.

(2) Where in a case within subsection (1) a bill of lading has been issued in a set of parts, unless otherwise agreed if the documents are not to be sent from abroad the buyer may demand tender of the full set; otherwise only one part of the bill of lading need be tendered. Even if the agreement expressly requires a full set

(a) due tender of a single part is acceptable within the provisions of this Article on cure of improper delivery (subsection (1) of Section 2–508); and

(b) even though the full set is demanded, if the documents are sent from abroad the person tendering an incomplete set may nevertheless require payment upon furnishing an indemnity which the buyer in good faith deems adequate.

(3) A shipment by water or by air or a contract contemplating such shipment is "overseas" insofar as by usage of trade or agreement it is subject to the commercial, financing or shipping practices characteristic of international deep water commerce.

§ 2-324.   "No Arrival, No Sale" Term.

Under a term "no arrival, no sale" or terms of like meaning, unless otherwise agreed,

(a) the seller must properly ship conforming goods and if they arrive by any means he must tender them on arrival but he assumes no obligation that the goods will arrive unless he has caused the non-arrival; and

(b) where without fault of the seller the goods are in part lost or have so deteriorated as no longer to conform to the contract or arrive after the contract time, the buyer may proceed as if there had been casualty to identified goods (Section 2–613).

§ 2-325.   "Letter of Credit" Term; "Confirmed Credit".

(1) Failure of the buyer seasonably to furnish an agreed letter of credit is a breach of the contract for sale.

(2) The delivery to seller of a proper letter of credit suspends the buyer's obligation to pay. If the letter of credit is dishonored, the seller may on seasonable notification to the buyer require payment directly from him.

(3) Unless otherwise agreed the term "letter of credit" or "banker's credit" in a contract for sale means an irrevocable credit issued by a financing agency of good repute and, where the shipment is overseas, of good international repute. The

term "confirmed credit" means that the credit must also carry the direct obligation of such an agency which does business in the seller's financial market.

§ 2–326.   Sale on Approval and Sale or Return; Rights of Creditors.

(1) Unless otherwise agreed, if delivered goods may be returned by the buyer even though they conform to the contract, the transaction is

(a) a "sale on approval" if the goods are delivered primarily for use, and

(b) a "sale or return" if the goods are delivered primarily for resale.

(2) Goods held on approval are not subject to the claims of the buyer's creditors until acceptance; goods held on sale or return are subject to such claims while in the buyer's possession.

(3) Any "or return" term of a contract for sale is to be treated as a separate contract for sale within the statute of frauds section of this Article (Section 2–201) and as contradicting the sale aspect of the contract within the provisions of this Article or on parol or extrinsic evidence (Section 2–202).

As amended in 1999.

§ 2–327.   Special Incidents of Sale on Approval and Sale or Return.

(1) Under a sale on approval unless otherwise agreed

(a) although the goods are identified to the contract the risk of loss and the title do not pass to the buyer until acceptance; and

(b) use of the goods consistent with the purpose of trial is not acceptance but failure seasonably to notify the seller of election to return the goods is acceptance, and if the goods conform to the contract acceptance of any part is acceptance of the whole; and

(c) after due notification of election to return, the return is at the seller's risk and expense but a merchant buyer must follow any reasonable instructions.

(2) Under a sale or return unless otherwise agreed

(a) the option to return extends to the whole or any commercial unit of the goods while in substantially their original condition, but must be exercised seasonably; and

(b) the return is at the buyer's risk and expense.

§ 2–328.   Sale by Auction.

(1) In a sale by auction if goods are put up in lots each lot is the subject of a separate sale.

(2) A sale by auction is complete when the auctioneer so announces by the fall of the hammer or in other customary manner. Where a bid is made while the hammer is falling in acceptance of a prior bid the auctioneer may in his discretion reopen the bidding or declare the goods sold under the bid on which the hammer was falling.

(3) Such a sale is with reserve unless the goods are in explicit terms put up without reserve. In an auction with reserve the auctioneer may withdraw the goods at any time until he announces completion of the sale. In an auction without reserve, after the auctioneer calls for bids on an article or lot, that article or lot cannot be withdrawn unless no bid is made within a reasonable time. In either case a bidder may retract his bid until the auctioneer's announcement of completion of the sale, but a bidder's retraction does not revive any previous bid.

(4) If the auctioneer knowingly receives a bid on the seller's behalf or the seller makes or procures such as bid, and notice has not been given that liberty for such bidding is reserved, the buyer may at his option avoid the sale or take the goods at the price of the last good faith bid prior to the completion of the sale. This subsection shall not apply to any bid at a forced sale.

PART 4   Title, Creditors and Good Faith Purchasers

§ 2–401.   Passing of Title; Reservation for Security; Limited Application of This Section.

Each provision of this Article with regard to the rights, obligations and remedies of the seller, the buyer, purchasers or other third parties applies irrespective of title to the goods except where the provision refers to such title. Insofar as situations are not covered by the other provisions of this Article and matters concerning title became material the following rules apply:

(1) Title to goods cannot pass under a contract for sale prior to their identification to the contract (Section 2–501), and unless otherwise explicitly agreed the buyer acquires by their identification a special property as limited by this Act. Any retention or reservation by the seller of the title (property) in goods shipped or delivered to the buyer is limited in effect to a reservation of a security interest. Subject to these provisions and to the provisions of the Article on Secured Transactions (Article 9), title to goods passes from the seller to the buyer in any manner and on any conditions explicitly agreed on by the parties.

(2) Unless otherwise explicitly agreed title passes to the buyer at the time and place at which the seller completes his performance with reference to the physical delivery of the goods, despite any reservation of a security interest and even though a document of title is to be delivered at a different time or place; and in particular and despite any reservation of a security interest by the bill of lading

(a) if the contract requires or authorizes the seller to send the goods to the buyer but does not require him to deliver them at destination, title passes to the buyer at the time and place of shipment; but

(b) if the contract requires delivery at destination, title passes on tender there.

(3) Unless otherwise explicitly agreed where delivery is to be made without moving the goods,

(a) if the seller is to deliver a document of title, title passes at the time when and the place where he delivers such documents; or

(b) if the goods are at the time of contracting already identified and no documents are to be delivered, title passes at the time and place of contracting.

(4) A rejection or other refusal by the buyer to receive or retain the goods, whether or not justified, or a justified revocation of acceptance revests title to the goods in the seller. Such revesting occurs by operation of law and is not a "sale".

§ 2–402.   Rights of Seller's Creditors Against Sold Goods.

(1) Except as provided in subsections (2) and (3), rights of unsecured creditors of the seller with respect to goods which have been identified to a contract for sale are subject to the buyer's rights to recover the goods under this Article (Sections 2–502 and 2–716).

(2) A creditor of the seller may treat a sale or an identification of goods to a contract for sale as void if as against him a retention of possession by the seller is fraudulent under any rule of law of the state where the goods are situated, except that retention of possession in good faith and current course of trade by a merchant-seller for a commercially reasonable time after a sale or identification is not fraudulent.

(3) Nothing in this Article shall be deemed to impair the rights of creditors of the seller

(a) under the provisions of the Article on Secured Transactions (Article 9); or

(b) where identification to the contract or delivery is made not in current course of trade but in satisfaction of or as security for a pre-existing claim for money, security or the like and is made under circumstances which under any rule of law of the state where the goods are situated would apart from this Article constitute the transaction a fraudulent transfer or voidable preference.

§ 2–403.   Power to Transfer; Good Faith Purchase of Goods; "Entrusting".

(1) A purchaser of goods acquires all title which his transferor had or had power to transfer except that a purchaser of a limited interest acquires rights only to the extent of the interest purchased. A person with voidable title has power to transfer a good title to a good faith purchaser for value. When goods have been delivered under a transaction of purchase the purchaser has such power even though

(a) the transferor was deceived as to the identity of the purchaser, or

(b) the delivery was in exchange for a check which is later dishonored, or

(c) it was agreed that the transaction was to be a "cash sale", or

(d) the delivery was procured through fraud punishable as larcenous under the criminal law.

(2) Any entrusting of possession of goods to a merchant who deals in goods of that kind gives him power to transfer all rights of the entruster to a buyer in ordinary course of business.

(3) "Entrusting" includes any delivery and any acquiescence in retention of possession regardless of any condition expressed between the parties to the delivery or acquiescence and regardless of whether the procurement of the entrusting or the possessor's disposition of the goods have been such as to be larcenous under the criminal law.

(4) The rights of other purchasers of goods and of lien creditors are governed by the Articles on Secured Transactions (Article 9), Bulk Transfers (Article 6) and Documents of Title (Article 7).

As amended in 1988.

PART 5   Performance

§ 2–501.   Insurable Interest in Goods; Manner of Identification of Goods.

(1) The buyer obtains a special property and an insurable interest in goods by identification of existing goods as goods to which the contract refers even though the goods so identified are non-conforming and he has an option to return or reject them. Such identification can be made at any time and in any manner explicitly agreed to by the parties. In the absence of explicit agreement identification occurs

(a) when the contract is made if it is for the sale of goods already existing and identified;

(b) if the contract is for the sale of future goods other than those described in paragraph (c), when goods are shipped, marked or otherwise designated by the seller as goods to which the contract refers;

(c) when the crops are planted or otherwise become growing crops or the young are conceived if the contract is for the sale of unborn young to be born within twelve months after contracting or for the sale of crops to be harvested within twelve months or the next normal harvest season after contracting whichever is longer.

(2) The seller retains an insurable interest in goods so long as title to or any security interest in the goods remains in him and where the identification is by the seller alone he may until default or insolvency or notification to the buyer that the identification is final substitute other goods for those identified.

(3) Nothing in this section impairs any insurable interest recognized under any other statute or rule of law.

§ 2–502.   Buyer's Right to Goods on Seller's Insolvency.

(1) Subject to subsections (2) and (3) and even though the goods have not been shipped a buyer who has paid a part or all of the price of goods in which he has a special property under the provisions of the immediately preceding section may on making and keeping good a tender of any unpaid portion of their price recover them from the seller if:

(a) in the case of goods bought for personal, family, or household purposes, the seller repudiates or fails to deliver as required by the contract; or

(b) in all cases, the seller becomes insolvent within ten days after receipt of the first installment on their price.

(2) The buyer's right to recover the goods under subsection (1)(a) vests upon acquisition of a special property, even if the seller had not then repudiated or failed to deliver.

(3) If the identification creating his special property has been made by the buyer he acquires the right to recover the goods only if they conform to the contract for sale.

As amended in 1999.

§ 2–503.   Manner of Seller's Tender of Delivery.

(1) Tender of delivery requires that the seller put and hold conforming goods at the buyer's disposition and give the buyer any notification reasonably necessary to enable him to take delivery. The manner, time and place for tender are determined by the agreement and this Article, and in particular

(a) tender must be at a reasonable hour, and if it is of goods they must be kept available for the period reasonably necessary to enable the buyer to take possession; but

(b) unless otherwise agreed the buyer must furnish facilities reasonably suited to the receipt of the goods.

(2) Where the case is within the next section respecting shipment tender requires that the seller comply with its provisions.

(3) Where the seller is required to deliver at a particular destination tender requires that he comply with subsection (1) and also in any appropriate case tender documents as described in subsections (4) and (5) of this section.

(4) Where goods are in the possession of a bailee and are to be delivered without being moved

(a) tender requires that the seller either tender a negotiable document of title covering such goods or procure acknowledgment by the bailee of the buyer's right to possession of the goods; but

(b) tender to the buyer of a non-negotiable document of title or of a written direction to the bailee to deliver is sufficient tender unless the buyer seasonably objects, and receipt by the bailee of notification of the buyer's rights fixes those rights as against the bailee and all third persons; but risk of loss of the goods and of any failure by the bailee to honor the non-

negotiable document of title or to obey the direction remains on the seller until the buyer has had a reasonable time to present the document or direction, and a refusal by the bailee to honor the document or to obey the direction defeats the tender.

(5) Where the contract requires the seller to deliver documents

(a) he must tender all such documents in correct form, except as provided in this Article with respect to bills of lading in a set (subsection (2) of Section 2–323); and

(b) tender through customary banking channels is sufficient and dishonor of a draft accompanying the documents constitutes non-acceptance or rejection.

§ 2–504.   Shipment by Seller.

Where the seller is required or authorized to send the goods to the buyer and the contract does not require him to deliver them at a particular destination, then unless otherwise agreed he must

(a) put the goods in the possession of such a carrier and make such a contract for their transportation as may be reasonable having regard to the nature of the goods and other circumstances of the case; and

(b) obtain and promptly deliver or tender in due form any document necessary to enable the buyer to obtain possession of the goods or otherwise required by the agreement or by usage of trade; and

(c) promptly notify the buyer of the shipment.

Failure to notify the buyer under paragraph (c) or to make a proper contract under paragraph (a) is a ground for rejection only if material delay or loss ensues.

§ 2–505.   Seller's Shipment under Reservation.

(1) Where the seller has identified goods to the contract by or before shipment:

(a) his procurement of a negotiable bill of lading to his own order or otherwise reserves in him a security interest in the goods. His procurement of the bill to the order of a financing agency or of the buyer indicates in addition only the seller's expectation of transferring that interest to the person named.

(b) a non-negotiable bill of lading to himself or his nominee reserves possession of the goods as security but except in a case of conditional delivery (subsection (2) of Section 2–507) a non-negotiable bill of lading naming the buyer as consignee reserves no security interest even though the seller retains possession of the bill of lading.

(2) When shipment by the seller with reservation of a security interest is in violation of the contract for sale it constitutes an improper contract for transportation within the preceding section but impairs neither the rights given to the buyer by shipment and identification of the goods to the contract nor the seller's powers as a holder of a negotiable document.

§ 2–506.   Rights of Financing Agency.

(1) A financing agency by paying or purchasing for value a draft which relates to a shipment of goods acquires to the extent of the payment or purchase and in addition to its own rights under the draft and any document of title securing it any rights of the shipper in the goods including the right to stop delivery and the shipper's right to have the draft honored by the buyer.

(2) The right to reimbursement of a financing agency which has in good faith honored or purchased the draft under commitment to or authority from the buyer is not impaired by subsequent discovery of defects with reference to any relevant document which was apparently regular on its face.

§ 2–507.   Effect of Seller's Tender; Delivery on Condition.

(1) Tender of delivery is a condition to the buyer's duty to accept the goods and, unless otherwise agreed, to his duty to pay for them. Tender entitles the seller to acceptance of the goods and to payment according to the contract.

(2) Where payment is due and demanded on the delivery to the buyer of goods or documents of title, his right as against the seller to retain or dispose of them is conditional upon his making the payment due.

§ 2–508.   Cure by Seller of Improper Tender or Delivery; Replacement.

(1) Where any tender or delivery by the seller is rejected because non-conforming and the time for performance has not yet expired, the seller may seasonably notify the buyer of his intention to cure and may then within the contract time make a conforming delivery.

(2) Where the buyer rejects a non-conforming tender which the seller had reasonable grounds to believe would be acceptable with or without money allowance the seller may if he seasonably notifies the buyer have a further reasonable time to substitute a conforming tender.

§ 2–509.   Risk of Loss in the Absence of Breach.

(1) Where the contract requires or authorizes the seller to ship the goods by carrier

(a) if it does not require him to deliver them at a particular destination, the risk of loss passes to the buyer when the goods are duly delivered to the carrier even though the shipment is under reservation (Section 2–505); but

(b) if it does require him to deliver them at a particular destination and the goods are there duly tendered while in the possession of the carrier, the risk of loss passes to the buyer when the goods are there duly so tendered as to enable the buyer to take delivery.

(2) Where the goods are held by a bailee to be delivered without being moved, the risk of loss passes to the buyer

(a) on his receipt of a negotiable document of title covering the goods; or

(b) on acknowledgment by the bailee of the buyer's right to possession of the goods; or

(c) after his receipt of a non-negotiable document of title or other written direction to deliver, as provided in subsection (4)(b) of Section 2–503.

(3) In any case not within subsection (1) or (2), the risk of loss passes to the buyer on his receipt of the goods if the seller is a merchant; otherwise the risk passes to the buyer on tender of delivery.

(4) The provisions of this section are subject to contrary agreement of the parties and to the provisions of this Article on sale on approval (Section 2–327) and on effect of breach on risk of loss (Section 2–510).

§ 2–510.   Effect of Breach on Risk of Loss.

(1) Where a tender or delivery of goods so fails to conform to the contract as to give a right of rejection the risk of their loss remains on the seller until cure or acceptance.

(2) Where the buyer rightfully revokes acceptance he may to the extent of any deficiency in his effective insurance coverage treat the risk of loss as having rested on the seller from the beginning.

(3) Where the buyer as to conforming goods already identified to the contract for sale repudiates or is otherwise in breach before risk of their loss has passed to him, the seller may to the extent of any deficiency in his effective insurance coverage treat the risk of loss as resting on the buyer for a commercially reasonable time.

§ 2–511.   Tender of Payment by Buyer; Payment by Check.

(1) Unless otherwise agreed tender of payment is a condition to the seller's duty to tender and complete any delivery.

(2) Tender of payment is sufficient when made by any means or in any manner current in the ordinary course of business unless the seller demands payment in legal tender and gives any extension of time reasonably necessary to procure it.

(3) Subject to the provisions of this Act on the effect of an instrument on an obligation (Section 3–310), payment by check is conditional and is defeated as between the parties by dishonor of the check on due presentment.

As amended in 1994.

§ 2–512.   Payment by Buyer Before Inspection.

(1) Where the contract requires payment before inspection non-conformity of the goods does not excuse the buyer from so making payment unless

(a) the non-conformity appears without inspection; or

(b) despite tender of the required documents the circumstances would justify injunction against honor under this Act (Section 5–109(b)).

(2) Payment pursuant to subsection (1) does not constitute an acceptance of goods or impair the buyer's right to inspect or any of his remedies.

As amended in 1995.

§ 2–513. Buyer's Right to Inspection of Goods.

(1) Unless otherwise agreed and subject to subsection (3), where goods are tendered or delivered or identified to the contract for sale, the buyer has a right before payment or acceptance to inspect them at any reasonable place and time and in any reasonable manner. When the seller is required or authorized to send the goods to the buyer, the inspection may be after their arrival.

(2) Expenses of inspection must be borne by the buyer but may be recovered from the seller if the goods do not conform and are rejected.

(3) Unless otherwise agreed and subject to the provisions of this Article on C.I.F. contracts (subsection (3) of Section 2–321), the buyer is not entitled to inspect the goods before payment of the price when the contract provides

(a) for delivery "C.O.D." or on other like terms; or

(b) for payment against documents of title, except where such payment is due only after the goods are to become available for inspection.

(4) A place or method of inspection fixed by the parties is presumed to be exclusive but unless otherwise expressly agreed it does not postpone identification or shift the place for delivery or for passing the risk of loss. If compliance becomes impossible, inspection shall be as provided in this section unless the place or method fixed was clearly intended as an indispensable condition failure of which avoids the contract.

§ 2–514. When Documents Deliverable on Acceptance; When on Payment.

Unless otherwise agreed documents against which a draft is drawn are to be delivered to the drawee on acceptance of the draft if it is payable more than three days after presentment; otherwise, only on payment.

§ 2–515. Preserving Evidence of Goods in Dispute.

In furtherance of the adjustment of any claim or dispute

(a) either party on reasonable notification to the other and for the purpose of ascertaining the facts and preserving evidence has the right to inspect, test and sample the goods including such of them as may be in the possession or control of the other; and

(b) the parties may agree to a third party inspection or survey to determine the conformity or condition of the goods and may agree that the findings shall be binding upon them in any subsequent litigation or adjustment.

PART 6   Breach, Repudiation and Excuse

§ 2–601. Buyer's Rights on Improper Delivery.

Subject to the provisions of this Article on breach in installment contracts (Section 2–612) and unless otherwise agreed under the sections on contractual limitations of remedy (Sections 2–718 and 2–719), if the goods or the tender of delivery fail in any respect to conform to the contract, the buyer may

(a) reject the whole; or

(b) accept the whole; or

(c) accept any commercial unit or units and reject the rest.

§ 2–602. Manner and Effect of Rightful Rejection.

(1) Rejection of goods must be within a reasonable time after their delivery or tender. It is ineffective unless the buyer seasonably notifies the seller.

(2) Subject to the provisions of the two following sections on rejected goods (Sections 2–603 and 2–604),

(a) after rejection any exercise of ownership by the buyer with respect to any commercial unit is wrongful as against the seller; and

(b) if the buyer has before rejection taken physical possession of goods in which he does not have a security interest under the provisions of this Article (subsection (3) of Section 2–711), he is under a duty after rejection to hold them with reasonable care at the seller's disposition for a time sufficient to permit the seller to remove them; but

(c) the buyer has no further obligations with regard to goods rightfully rejected.

(3) The seller's rights with respect to goods wrongfully rejected are governed by the provisions of this Article on Seller's remedies in general (Section 2–703).

§ 2–603. Merchant Buyer's Duties as to Rightfully Rejected Goods.

(1) Subject to any security interest in the buyer (subsection (3) of Section 2–711), when the seller has no agent or place of business at the market of rejection a merchant buyer is under a duty after rejection of goods in his possession or control to follow any reasonable instructions received from the seller with respect to the goods and in the absence of such instructions to make reasonable efforts to sell them for the seller's account if they are perishable or threaten to decline in value speedily.

Instructions are not reasonable if on demand indemnity for expenses is not forthcoming.

(2) When the buyer sells goods under subsection (1), he is entitled to reimbursement from the seller or out of the proceeds for reasonable expenses of caring for and selling them, and if the expenses include no selling commission then to such commission as is usual in the trade or if there is none to a reasonable sum not exceeding ten per cent on the gross proceeds.

(3) In complying with this section the buyer is held only to good faith and good faith conduct hereunder is neither acceptance nor conversion nor the basis of an action for damages.

§ 2–604. Buyer's Options as to Salvage of Rightfully Rejected Goods.

Subject to the provisions of the immediately preceding section on perishables if the seller gives no instructions within a reasonable time after notification of rejection the buyer may store the rejected goods for the seller's account or reship them to him or resell them for the seller's account with reimbursement as provided in the preceding section. Such action is not acceptance or conversion.

§ 2–605. Waiver of Buyer's Objections by Failure to Particularize.

(1) The buyer's failure to state in connection with rejection a particular defect which is ascertainable by reasonable inspection precludes him from relying on the unstated defect to justify rejection or to establish breach

(a) where the seller could have cured it if stated seasonally; or

(b) between merchants when the seller has after rejection made a request in writing for a full and final written statement of all defects on which the buyer proposes to rely.

(2) Payment against documents made without reservation of rights precludes recovery of the payment for defects apparent on the face of the documents.

§ 2–606. What Constitutes Acceptance of Goods.

(1) Acceptance of goods occurs when the buyer

(a) after a reasonable opportunity to inspect the goods signifies to the seller that the goods are conforming or that he will take or retain them in spite of their nonconformity; or

(b) fails to make an effective rejection (subsection (1) of Section 2–602), but such acceptance does not occur until the buyer has had a reasonable opportunity to inspect them; or

(c) does any act inconsistent with the seller's ownership; but if such act is wrongful as against the seller it is an acceptance only if ratified by him.

(2) Acceptance of a part of any commercial unit is acceptance of that entire unit.

§ 2–607. Effect of Acceptance; Notice of Breach; Burden of Establishing Breach After Acceptance; Notice of Claim or Litigation to Person Answerable Over.

(1) The buyer must pay at the contract rate for any goods accepted.

(2) Acceptance of goods by the buyer precludes rejection of the goods accepted and if made with knowledge of a non-conformity cannot be revoked because of it unless the acceptance was on the reasonable assumption that the non-conformity would be seasonably cured but acceptance does not of itself impair any other remedy provided by this Article for non-conformity.

(3) Where a tender has been accepted

(a) the buyer must within a reasonable time after he discovers or should have discovered any breach notify the seller of breach or be barred from any remedy; and

(b) if the claim is one for infringement or the like (subsection (3) of Section 2–312) and the buyer is sued as a result of such a breach he must so notify the seller within a reasonable time after he receives notice of the litigation or be barred from any remedy over for liability established by the litigation.

(4) The burden is on the buyer to establish any breach with respect to the goods accepted.

(5) Where the buyer is sued for breach of a warranty or other obligation for which his seller is answerable over

(a) he may give his seller written notice of the litigation. If the notice states that the seller may come in and defend and that if the seller does not do so he will be bound in any action against him by his buyer by any determination of fact common to the two litigations, then unless the seller after seasonable receipt of the notice does come in and defend he is so bound.

(b) if the claim is one for infringement or the like (subsection (3) of Section 2–312) the original seller may demand in writing that his buyer turn over to him control of the litigation including settlement or else be barred from any remedy over and if he also agrees to bear all expense and to satisfy any adverse judgment, then unless the buyer after seasonable receipt of the demand does turn over control the buyer is so barred.

(6) The provisions of subsections (3), (4) and (5) apply to any obligation of a buyer to hold the seller harmless against infringement or the like (subsection (3) of Section 2–312).

§ 2–608. Revocation of Acceptance in Whole or in Part.

(1) The buyer may revoke his acceptance of a lot or commercial unit whose non-conformity substantially impairs its value to him if he has accepted it

(a) on the reasonable assumption that its nonconformity would be cured and it has not been seasonably cured; or

(b) without discovery of such non-conformity if his acceptance was reasonably induced either by the difficulty of discovery before acceptance or by the seller's assurances.

(2) Revocation of acceptance must occur within a reasonable time after the buyer discovers or should have discovered the ground for it and before any substantial change in condition of the goods which is not caused by their own defects. It is not effective until the buyer notifies the seller of it.

(3) A buyer who so revokes has the same rights and duties with regard to the goods involved as if he had rejected them.

§ 2–609.   Right to Adequate Assurance of Performance.

(1) A contract for sale imposes an obligation on each party that the other's expectation of receiving due performance will not be impaired. When reasonable grounds for insecurity arise with respect to the performance of either party the other may in writing demand adequate assurance of due performance and until he receives such assurance may if commercially reasonable suspend any performance for which he has not already received the agreed return.

(2) Between merchants the reasonableness of grounds for insecurity and the adequacy of any assurance offered shall be determined according to commercial standards.

(3) Acceptance of any improper delivery or payment does not prejudice the party's right to demand adequate assurance of future performance.

(4) After receipt of a justified demand failure to provide within a reasonable time not exceeding thirty days such assurance of due performance as is adequate under the circumstances of the particular case is a repudiation of the contract.

§ 2–610.   Anticipatory Repudiation.

When either party repudiates the contract with respect to a performance not yet due the loss of which will substantially impair the value of the contract to the other, the aggrieved party may

(a) for a commercially reasonable time await performance by the repudiating party; or

(b) resort to any remedy for breach (Section 2–703 or Section 2–711), even though he has notified the repudiating party that he would await the latter's performance and has urged retraction; and

(c) in either case suspend his own performance or proceed in accordance with the provisions of this Article on the seller's right to identify goods to the contract notwithstanding breach or to salvage unfinished goods (Section 2–704).

§ 2–611.   Retraction of Anticipatory Repudiation.

(1) Until the repudiating party's next performance is due he can retract his repudiation unless the aggrieved party has since the repudiation cancelled or materially changed his position or otherwise indicated that he considers the repudiation final.

(2) Retraction may be by any method which clearly indicates to the aggrieved party that the repudiating party intends to perform, but must include any assurance justifiably demanded under the provisions of this Article (Section 2–609).

(3) Retraction reinstates the repudiating party's rights under the contract with due excuse and allowance to the aggrieved party for any delay occasioned by the repudiation.

§ 2–612.   "Installment Contract"; Breach.

(1) An "installment contract" is one which requires or authorizes the delivery of goods in separate lots to be separately accepted, even though the contract contains a clause "each delivery is a separate contract" or its equivalent.

(2) The buyer may reject any installment which is non-conforming if the non-conformity substantially impairs the value of that installment and cannot be cured or if the non-conformity is a defect in the required documents; but if the non-conformity does not fall within subsection (3) and the seller gives adequate assurance of its cure the buyer must accept that installment.

(3) Whenever non-conformity or default with respect to one or more installments substantially impairs the value of the whole contract there is a breach of the whole. But the aggrieved party reinstates the contract if he accepts a non-conforming installment without seasonably notifying of cancellation or if he brings an action with respect only to past installments or demands performance as to future installments.

§ 2–613.   Casualty to Identified Goods.

Where the contract requires for its performance goods identified when the contract is made, and the goods suffer casualty without fault of either party before the risk of loss passes to the buyer, or in a proper case under a "no arrival, no sale" term (Section 2–324) then

(a) if the loss is total the contract is avoided; and

(b) if the loss is partial or the goods have so deteriorated as no longer to conform to the contract the buyer may nevertheless demand inspection and at his option either treat the contract as voided or accept the goods with due allowance from the contract price for the deterioration or the deficiency in quantity but without further right against the seller.

§ 2–614.   Substituted Performance.

(1) Where without fault of either party the agreed berthing, loading, or unloading facilities fail or an agreed type of carrier becomes unavailable or the agreed manner of delivery otherwise becomes commercially impracticable but a commercially reasonable substitute is available, such substitute performance must be tendered and accepted.

(2) If the agreed means or manner of payment fails because of domestic or foreign governmental regulation, the seller may

withhold or stop delivery unless the buyer provides a means or manner of payment which is commercially a substantial equivalent. If delivery has already been taken, payment by the means or in the manner provided by the regulation discharges the buyer's obligation unless the regulation is discriminatory, oppressive or predatory.

§ 2–615. Excuse by Failure of Presupposed Conditions.

Except so far as a seller may have assumed a greater obligation and subject to the preceding section on substituted performance:

(a) Delay in delivery or non-delivery in whole or in part by a seller who complies with paragraphs (b) and (c) is not a breach of his duty under a contract for sale if performance as agreed has been made impracticable by the occurrence of a contingency the nonoccurrence of which was a basic assumption on which the contract was made or by compliance in good faith with any applicable foreign or domestic governmental regulation or order whether or not it later proves to be invalid.

(b) Where the causes mentioned in paragraph (a) affect only a part of the seller's capacity to perform, he must allocate production and deliveries among his customers but may at his option include regular customers not then under contract as well as his own requirements for further manufacture. He may so allocate in any manner which is fair and reasonable.

(c) The seller must notify the buyer seasonably that there will be delay or non-delivery and, when allocation is required under paragraph (b), of the estimated quota thus made available for the buyer.

§ 2–616. Procedure on Notice Claiming Excuse.

(1) Where the buyer receives notification of a material or indefinite delay or an allocation justified under the preceding section he may by written notification to the seller as to any delivery concerned, and where the prospective deficiency substantially impairs the value of the whole contract under the provisions of this Article relating to breach of installment contracts (Section 2–612), then also as to the whole,

(a) terminate and thereby discharge any unexecuted portion of the contract; or

(b) modify the contract by agreeing to take his available quota in substitution.

(2) If after receipt of such notification from the seller the buyer fails so to modify the contract within a reasonable time not exceeding thirty days the contract lapses with respect to any deliveries affected.

(3) The provisions of this section may not be negated by agreement except in so far as the seller has assumed a greater obligation under the preceding section.

PART 7 Remedies

§ 2–701. Remedies for Breach of Collateral Contracts Not Impaired.

Remedies for breach of any obligation or promise collateral or ancillary to a contract for sale are not impaired by the provisions of this Article.

§ 2–702. Seller's Remedies on Discovery of Buyer's Insolvency.

(1) Where the seller discovers the buyer to be insolvent he may refuse delivery except for cash including payment for all goods theretofore delivered under the contract, and stop delivery under this Article (Section 2–705).

(2) Where the seller discovers that the buyer has received goods on credit while insolvent he may reclaim the goods upon demand made within ten days after the receipt, but if misrepresentation of solvency has been made to the particular seller in writing within three months before delivery the ten day limitation does not apply. Except as provided in this subsection the seller may not base a right to reclaim goods on the buyer's fraudulent or innocent misrepresentation of solvency or of intent to pay.

(3) The seller's right to reclaim under subsection (2) is subject to the rights of a buyer in ordinary course or other good faith purchaser under this Article (Section 2–403). Successful reclamation of goods excludes all other remedies with respect to them.

§ 2–703. Seller's Remedies in General.

Where the buyer wrongfully rejects or revokes acceptance of goods or fails to make a payment due on or before delivery or repudiates with respect to a part or the whole, then with respect to any goods directly affected and, if the breach is of the whole contract (Section 2–612), then also with respect to the whole undelivered balance, the aggrieved seller may

(a) withhold delivery of such goods;

(b) stop delivery by any bailee as hereafter provided (Section 2–705);

(c) proceed under the next section respecting goods still unidentified to the contract;

(d) resell and recover damages as hereafter provided (Section 2–706);

(e) recover damages for non-acceptance (Section 2–708) or in a proper case the price (Section 2–709);

(f) cancel.

§ 2–704. Seller's Right to Identify Goods to the Contract Notwithstanding Breach or to Salvage Unfinished Goods.

(1) An aggrieved seller under the preceding section may

(a) identify to the contract conforming goods not already identified if at the time he learned of the breach they are in his possession or control;

(b) treat as the subject of resale goods which have demonstrably been intended for the particular contract even though those goods are unfinished.

(2) Where the goods are unfinished an aggrieved seller may in the exercise of reasonable commercial judgment for the purposes of avoiding loss and of effective realization either complete the manufacture and wholly identify the goods to the contract or cease manufacture and resell for scrap or salvage value or proceed in any other reasonable manner.

§ 2–705.   Seller's Stoppage of Delivery in Transit or Otherwise.

(1) The seller may stop delivery of goods in the possession of a carrier or other bailee when he discovers the buyer to be insolvent (Section 2–702) and may stop delivery of carload, truckload, planeload or larger shipments of express or freight when the buyer repudiates or fails to make a payment due before delivery or if for any other reason the seller has a right to withhold or reclaim the goods.

(2) As against such buyer the seller may stop delivery until

(a) receipt of the goods by the buyer; or

(b) acknowledgment to the buyer by any bailee of the goods except a carrier that the bailee holds the goods for the buyer; or

(c) such acknowledgment to the buyer by a carrier by reshipment or as warehouseman; or

(d) negotiation to the buyer of any negotiable document of title covering the goods.

(3) (a) To stop delivery the seller must so notify as to enable the bailee by reasonable diligence to prevent delivery of the goods.

(b) After such notification the bailee must hold and deliver the goods according to the directions of the seller but the seller is liable to the bailee for any ensuing charges or damages.

(c) If a negotiable document of title has been issued for goods the bailee is not obliged to obey a notification to stop until surrender of the document.

(d) A carrier who has issued a non-negotiable bill of lading is not obliged to obey a notification to stop received from a person other than the consignor.

§ 2–706.   Seller's Resale Including Contract for Resale.

(1) Under the conditions stated in Section 2–703 on seller's remedies, the seller may resell the goods concerned or the undelivered balance thereof. Where the resale is made in good faith and in a commercially reasonable manner the seller may recover the difference between the resale price and the contract price together with any incidental damages allowed under the provisions of this Article (Section 2–710), but less expenses saved in consequence of the buyer's breach.

(2) Except as otherwise provided in subsection (3) or unless otherwise agreed resale may be at public or private sale including sale by way of one or more contracts to sell or of identification to an existing contract of the seller. Sale may be as a unit or in parcels and at any time and place and on any terms but every aspect of the sale including the method, manner, time, place and terms must be commercially reasonable. The resale must be reasonably identified as referring to the broken contract, but it is not necessary that the goods be in existence or that any or all of them have been identified to the contract before the breach.

(3) Where the resale is at private sale the seller must give the buyer reasonable notification of his intention to resell.

(4) Where the resale is at public sale

(a) only identified goods can be sold except where there is a recognized market for a public sale of futures in goods of the kind; and

(b) it must be made at a usual place or market for public sale if one is reasonably available and except in the case of goods which are perishable or threaten to decline in value speedily the seller must give the buyer reasonable notice of the time and place of the resale; and

(c) if the goods are not to be within the view of those attending the sale the notification of sale must state the place where the goods are located and provide for their reasonable inspection by prospective bidders; and

(d) the seller may buy.

(5) A purchaser who buys in good faith at a resale takes the goods free of any rights of the original buyer even though the seller fails to comply with one or more of the requirements of this section.

(6) The seller is not accountable to the buyer for any profit made on any resale. A person in the position of a seller (Section 2–707) or a buyer who has rightfully rejected or justifiably revoked acceptance must account for any excess over the amount of his security interest, as hereinafter defined (subsection (3) of Section 2–711).

§ 2–707.   "Person in the Position of a Seller".

(1) A "person in the position of a seller" includes as against a principal an agent who has paid or become responsible for the price of goods on behalf of his principal or anyone who otherwise holds a security interest or other right in goods similar to that of a seller.

(2) A person in the position of a seller may as provided in this Article withhold or stop delivery (Section 2–705) and resell (Section 2–706) and recover incidental damages (Section 2–710).

§ 2–708.   Seller's Damages for Non-Acceptance or Repudiation.

(1) Subject to subsection (2) and to the provisions of this Article with respect to proof of market price (Section 2–723), the measure of damages for non-acceptance or repudiation by the buyer is the difference between the market price at the time and place for tender and the unpaid contract price together with any incidental damages provided in this Article (Section 2–710), but less expenses saved in consequence of the buyer's breach.

(2) If the measure of damages provided in subsection (1) is inadequate to put the seller in as good a position as performance would have done then the measure of damages is the profit (including reasonable overhead) which the seller would have made from full performance by the buyer, together with any incidental damages provided in this Article (Section 2–710), due allowance for costs reasonably incurred and due credit for payments or proceeds of resale.

§ 2–709.   Action for the Price.

(1) When the buyer fails to pay the price as it becomes due the seller may recover, together with any incidental damages under the next section, the price

(a) of goods accepted or of conforming goods lost or damaged within a commercially reasonable time after risk of their loss has passed to the buyer; and

(b) of goods identified to the contract if the seller is unable after reasonable effort to resell them at a reasonable price or the circumstances reasonably indicate that such effort will be unavailing.

(2) Where the seller sues for the price he must hold for the buyer any goods which have been identified to the contract and are still in his control except that if resale becomes possible he may resell them at any time prior to the collection of the judgment. The net proceeds of any such resale must be credited to the buyer and payment of the judgment entitles him to any goods not resold.

(3) After the buyer has wrongfully rejected or revoked acceptance of the goods or has failed to make a payment due or has repudiated (Section 2–610), a seller who is held not entitled to the price under this section shall nevertheless be awarded damages for non-acceptance under the preceding section.

§ 2–710.   Seller's Incidental Damages.

Incidental damages to an aggrieved seller include any commercially reasonable charges, expenses or commissions incurred in stopping delivery, in the transportation, care and custody of goods after the buyer's breach, in connection with return or resale of the goods or otherwise resulting from the breach.

§ 2–711.   Buyer's Remedies in General; Buyer's Security Interest in Rejected Goods.

(1) Where the seller fails to make delivery or repudiates or the buyer rightfully rejects or justifiably revokes acceptance then with respect to any goods involved, and with respect to the whole if the breach goes to the whole contract (Section 2–612), the buyer may cancel and whether or not he has done so may in addition to recovering so much of the price as has been paid

(a) "cover" and have damages under the next section as to all the goods affected whether or not they have been identified to the contract; or

(b) recover damages for non-delivery as provided in this Article (Section 2–713).

(2) Where the seller fails to deliver or repudiates the buyer may also

(a) if the goods have been identified recover them as provided in this Article (Section 2–502); or

(b) in a proper case obtain specific performance or replevy the goods as provided in this Article (Section 2–716).

(3) On rightful rejection or justifiable revocation of acceptance a buyer has a security interest in goods in his possession or control for any payments made on their price and any expenses reasonably incurred in their inspection, receipt, transportation, care and custody and may hold such goods and resell them in like manner as an aggrieved seller (Section 2–706).

§ 2–712.   "Cover"; Buyer's Procurement of Substitute Goods.

(1) After a breach within the preceding section the buyer may "cover" by making in good faith and without unreasonable delay any reasonable purchase of or contract to purchase goods in substitution for those due from the seller.

(2) The buyer may recover from the seller as damages the difference between the cost of cover and the contract price together with any incidental or consequential damages as hereinafter defined (Section 2–715), but less expenses saved in consequence of the seller's breach.

(3) Failure of the buyer to effect cover within this section does not bar him from any other remedy.

§ 2–713.   Buyer's Damages for Non-Delivery or Repudiation.

(1) Subject to the provisions of this Article with respect to proof of market price (Section 2–723), the measure of damages for non-delivery or repudiation by the seller is the difference between the market price at the time when the buyer learned of the breach and the contract price together with any incidental and consequential damages provided in this Article (Section 2–715), but less expenses saved in consequence of the seller's breach.

(2) Market price is to be determined as of the place for tender or, in cases of rejection after arrival or revocation of acceptance, as of the place of arrival.

§ 2–714.   Buyer's Damages for Breach in Regard to Accepted Goods.

(1) Where the buyer has accepted goods and given notification (subsection (3) of Section 2–607) he may recover as damages for any non-conformity of tender the loss resulting in the ordi-

nary course of events from the seller's breach as determined in any manner which is reasonable.

(2) The measure of damages for breach of warranty is the difference at the time and place of acceptance between the value of the goods accepted and the value they would have had if they had been as warranted, unless special circumstances show proximate damages of a different amount.

(3) In a proper case any incidental and consequential damages under the next section may also be recovered.

§ 2–715.   Buyer's Incidental and Consequential Damages.

(1) Incidental damages resulting from the seller's breach include expenses reasonably incurred in inspection, receipt, transportation and care and custody of goods rightfully rejected, any commercially reasonable charges, expenses or commissions in connection with effecting cover and any other reasonable expense incident to the delay or other breach.

(2) Consequential damages resulting from the seller's breach include

(a) any loss resulting from general or particular requirements and needs of which the seller at the time of contracting had reason to know and which could not reasonably be prevented by cover or otherwise; and

(b) injury to person or property proximately resulting from any breach of warranty.

§ 2–716.   Buyer's Right to Specific Performance or Replevin.

(1) Specific performance may be decreed where the goods are unique or in other proper circumstances.

(2) The decree for specific performance may include such terms and conditions as to payment of the price, damages, or other relief as the court may deem just.

(3) The buyer has a right of replevin for goods identified to the contract if after reasonable effort he is unable to effect cover for such goods or the circumstances reasonably indicate that such effort will be unavailing or if the goods have been shipped under reservation and satisfaction of the security interest in them has been made or tendered. In the case of goods bought for personal, family, or household purposes, the buyer's right of replevin vests upon acquisition of a special property, even if the seller had not then repudiated or failed to deliver.

As amended in 1999.

§ 2–717.   Deduction of Damages From the Price.

The buyer on notifying the seller of his intention to do so may deduct all or any part of the damages resulting from any breach of the contract from any part of the price still due under the same contract.

§ 2–718.   Liquidation or Limitation of Damages; Deposits.

(1) Damages for breach by either party may be liquidated in the agreement but only at an amount which is reasonable in the light of the anticipated or actual harm caused by the breach, the difficulties of proof of loss, and the inconvenience or nonfeasibility of otherwise obtaining an adequate remedy. A term fixing unreasonably large liquidated damages is void as a penalty.

(2) Where the seller justifiably withholds delivery of goods because of the buyer's breach, the buyer is entitled to restitution of any amount by which the sum of his payments exceeds

(a) the amount to which the seller is entitled by virtue of terms liquidating the seller's damages in accordance with subsection (1), or

(b) in the absence of such terms, twenty per cent of the value of the total performance for which the buyer is obligated under the contract or $500, whichever is smaller.

(3) The buyer's right to restitution under subsection (2) is subject to offset to the extent that the seller establishes

(a) a right to recover damages under the provisions of this Article other than subsection (1), and

(b) the amount or value of any benefits received by the buyer directly or indirectly by reason of the contract.

(4) Where a seller has received payment in goods their reasonable value or the proceeds of their resale shall be treated as payments for the purposes of subsection (2); but if the seller has notice of the buyer's breach before reselling goods received in part performance, his resale is subject to the conditions laid down in this Article on resale by an aggrieved seller (Section 2–706).

§ 2–719.   Contractual Modification or Limitation of Remedy.

(1) Subject to the provisions of subsections (2) and (3) of this section and of the preceding section on liquidation and limitation of damages,

(a) the agreement may provide for remedies in addition to or in substitution for those provided in this Article and may limit or alter the measure of damages recoverable under this Article, as by limiting the buyer's remedies to return of the goods and repayment of the price or to repair and replacement of nonconforming goods or parts; and

(b) resort to a remedy as provided is optional unless the remedy is expressly agreed to be exclusive, in which case it is the sole remedy.

(2) Where circumstances cause an exclusive or limited remedy to fail of its essential purpose, remedy may be had as provided in this Act.

(3) Consequential damages may be limited or excluded unless the limitation or exclusion is unconscionable. Limitation of consequential damages for injury to the person in the case of consumer goods is prima facie unconscionable

but limitation of damages where the loss is commercial is not.

§ 2–720. Effect of "Cancellation" or "Rescission" on Claims for Antecedent Breach.

Unless the contrary intention clearly appears, expressions of "cancellation" or "rescission" of the contract or the like shall not be construed as a renunciation or discharge of any claim in damages for an antecedent breach.

§ 2–721. Remedies for Fraud.

Remedies for material misrepresentation or fraud include all remedies available under this Article for non-fraudulent breach. Neither rescission or a claim for rescission of the contract for sale nor rejection or return of the goods shall bar or be deemed inconsistent with a claim for damages or other remedy.

§ 2–722. Who Can Sue Third Parties for Injury to Goods.

Where a third party so deals with goods which have been identified to a contract for sale as to cause actionable injury to a party to that contract

(a) a right of action against the third party is in either party to the contract for sale who has title to or a security interest or a special property or an insurable interest in the goods; and if the goods have been destroyed or converted a right of action is also in the party who either bore the risk of loss under the contract for sale or has since the injury assumed that risk as against the other;

(b) if at the time of the injury the party plaintiff did not bear the risk of loss as against the other party to the contract for sale and there is no arrangement between them for disposition of the recovery, his suit or settlement is, subject to his own interest, as a fiduciary for the other party to the contract;

(c) either party may with the consent of the other sue for the benefit of whom it may concern.

§ 2–723. Proof of Market Price: Time and Place.

(1) If an action based on anticipatory repudiation comes to trial before the time for performance with respect to some or all of the goods, any damages based on market price (Section 2–708 or Section 2–713) shall be determined according to the price of such goods prevailing at the time when the aggrieved party learned of the repudiation.

(2) If evidence of a price prevailing at the times or places described in this Article is not readily available the price prevailing within any reasonable time before or after the time described or at any other place which in commercial judgment or under usage of trade would serve as a reasonable substitute for the one described may be used, making any proper allowance for the cost of transporting the goods to or from such other place.

(3) Evidence of a relevant price prevailing at a time or place other than the one described in this Article offered by one party is not admissible unless and until he has given the other party such notice as the court finds sufficient to prevent unfair surprise.

§ 2–724. Admissibility of Market Quotations.

Whenever the prevailing price or value of any goods regularly bought and sold in any established commodity market is in issue, reports in official publications or trade journals or in newspapers or periodicals of general circulation published as the reports of such market shall be admissible in evidence. The circumstances of the preparation of such a report may be shown to affect its weight but not its admissibility.

§ 2–725. Statute of Limitations in Contracts for Sale.

(1) An action for breach of any contract for sale must be commenced within four years after the cause of action has accrued. By the original agreement the parties may reduce the period of limitation to not less than one year but may not extend it.

(2) A cause of action accrues when the breach occurs, regardless of the aggrieved party's lack of knowledge of the breach. A breach of warranty occurs when tender of delivery is made, except that where a warranty explicitly extends to future performance of the goods and discovery of the breach must await the time of such performance the cause of action accrues when the breach is or should have been discovered.

(3) Where an action commenced within the time limited by subsection (1) is so terminated as to leave available a remedy by another action for the same breach such other action may be commenced after the expiration of the time limited and within six months after the termination of the first action unless the termination resulted from voluntary discontinuance or from dismissal for failure or neglect to prosecute.

(4) This section does not alter the law on tolling of the statute of limitations nor does it apply to causes of action which have accrued before this Act becomes effective.

ARTICLE 2 AMENDMENTS (EXCERPTS)[1]

PART I Short Title, General Construction and Subject Matter

§ 2–103. Definitions and Index of Definitions.

* * * *

(1) In this article unless the context otherwise requires

* * * *

(b) "Conspicuous", with reference to a term, means so written, displayed, or presented that a reasonable person against which it is to operate ought to have noticed it. A term in an electronic record intended to evoke a response by an electronic agent is conspicuous if it is presented in a form that would enable a reasonably configured electronic agent to take it into account or react to it without review of the record by an individual. Whether a term is "conspicuous" or not is a decision for the court. Conspicuous terms include the following:

(i) for a person:

(A) a heading in capitals equal to or greater in size than the surrounding text, or in contrasting type, font, or color to the surrounding text of the same or lesser size;

(B) language in the body of a record or display in larger type than the surrounding text, or in contrasting type, font, or color to the surrounding text of the same size, or set off from surrounding text of the same size by symbols or other marks that call attention to the language; and

(ii) for a person or an electronic agent, a term that is so placed in a record or display that the person or electronic agent cannot proceed without taking action with respect to the particular term.

(c) "Consumer" means an individual who buys or contracts to buy goods that, at the time of contracting, are intended by the individual to be used primarily for personal, family, or household purposes.

(d) "Consumer contract" means a contract between a merchant seller and a consumer.

* * * *

(j) "Good faith" means honesty in fact and the observance of reasonable commercial standards of fair dealing.

(k) "Goods" means all things that are movable at the time of identification to a contract for sale. The term includes future goods, specially manufactured goods, the unborn young of animals, growing crops, and other identified things attached to realty as described in Section 2–107. The term does not include information, the money in which the price is to be paid, investment securities under Article 8, the subject matter of foreign exchange transactions, and choses in action.

* * * *

(m) "Record" means information that is inscribed on a tangible medium or that is stored in an electronic or other medium and is retrievable in perceivable form.

(n) "Remedial promise" means a promise by the seller to repair or replace the goods or to refund all or part of the price upon the happening of a specified event.

* * * *

(p) "Sign" means, with present intent to authenticate or adopt a record,

(i) to execute or adopt a tangible symbol; or

(ii) to attach to or logically associate with the record an electronic sound, symbol, or process.

* * * *

PART 2   Form, Formation, Terms and Readjustment of Contract; Electronic Contracting

§ 2–201.   Formal Requirements; Statute of Frauds.

(1) A contract for the sale of goods for the price of $5,000 or more is not enforceable by way of action or defense unless there is some record sufficient to indicate that a contract for sale has been made between the parties and signed by the party against whom which enforcement is sought or by the party's authorized agent or broker. A record is not insufficient because it omits or incorrectly states a term agreed upon but the contract is not enforceable under this subsection beyond the quantity of goods shown in the record.

(2) Between merchants if within a reasonable time a record in confirmation of the contract and sufficient against the sender is received and the party receiving it has reason to know its contents, it satisfies the requirements of subsection (1) against such party the recipient unless notice of objection to its contents is given in a record within 10 days after it is received.

(3) A contract which does not satisfy the requirements of subsection (1) but which is valid in other respects is enforceable

(a) if the goods are to be specially manufactured for the buyer and are not suitable for sale to others in the ordinary course of the seller's business and the seller, before notice of repudiation is received and under circumstances which reasonably indicate that the goods are for the buyer, has made either a substantial beginning of their manufacture or commitments for their procurement; or

(b) if the party against whom which enforcement is sought admits in the party's pleading, or in the party's testimony or otherwise under oath that a contract for sale was made, but the contract is not enforceable under this paragraph beyond the quantity of goods admitted; or

(c) with respect to goods for which payment has been made and accepted or which have been received and accepted (Sec. 2–606).

(4) A contract that is enforceable under this section is not rendered unenforceable merely because it is not capable of being

performed within one year or any other applicable period after its making.

* * * *

§ 2–207.   Terms of Contract; Effect of Confirmation.

If (i) conduct by both parties recognizes the existence of a contract although their records do not otherwise establish a contract, (ii) a contract is formed by an offer and acceptance, or (iii) a contract formed in any manner is confirmed by a record that contains terms additional to or different from those in the contract being confirmed, the terms of the contract, subject to Section 2–202, are:

(a) terms that appear in the records of both parties;

(b) terms, whether in a record or not, to which both parties agree; and

(c) terms supplied or incorporated under any provision of this Act.

* * * *

PART 3   General Obligation and Construction of Contract

* * * *

§ 2–312.   Warranty of Title and Against Infringement; Buyer's Obligation Against Infringement.

(1) Subject to subsection (2) there is in a contract for sale a warranty by the seller that

(a) the title conveyed shall be good, good and its transfer rightful and shall not, because of any colorable claim to or interest in the goods, unreasonably expose the buyer to litigation; and

(b) the goods shall be delivered free from any security interest or other lien or encumbrance of which the buyer at the time of contracting has no knowledge.

(2) Unless otherwise agreed a seller that is a merchant regularly dealing in goods of the kind warrants that the goods shall be delivered free of the rightful claim of any third person by way of infringement or the like but a buyer that furnishes specifications to the seller must hold the seller harmless against any such claim that arises out of compliance with the specifications.

(3) A warranty under this section may be disclaimed or modified only by specific language or by circumstances that give the buyer reason to know that the seller does not claim title, that the seller is purporting to sell only the right or title as the seller or a third person may have, or that the seller is selling subject to any claims of infringement or the like.

§ 2–313.   Express Warranties by Affirmation, Promise, Description, Sample; Remedial Promise.

(1) In this section, "immediate buyer" means a buyer that enters into a contract with the seller.

* * * *

(4) Any remedial promise made by the seller to the immediate buyer creates an obligation that the promise will be performed upon the happening of the specified event.

§ 2–313A.   Obligation to Remote Purchaser Created by Record Packaged with or Accompanying Goods.

(1) This section applies only to new goods and goods sold or leased as new goods in a transaction of purchase in the normal chain of distribution. In this section:

(a) "Immediate buyer" means a buyer that enters into a contract with the seller.

(b) "Remote purchaser" means a person that buys or leases goods from an immediate buyer or other person in the normal chain of distribution.

(2) If a seller in a record packaged with or accompanying the goods makes an affirmation of fact or promise that relates to the goods, provides a description that relates to the goods, or makes a remedial promise, and the seller reasonably expects the record to be, and the record is, furnished to the remote purchaser, the seller has an obligation to the remote purchaser that:

(a) the goods will conform to the affirmation of fact, promise or description unless a reasonable person in the position of the remote purchaser would not believe that the affirmation of fact, promise or description created an obligation; and

(b) the seller will perform the remedial promise.

(3) It is not necessary to the creation of an obligation under this section that the seller use formal words such as "warrant" or "guarantee" or that the seller have a specific intention to undertake an obligation, but an affirmation merely of the value of the goods or a statement purporting to be merely the seller's opinion or commendation of the goods does not create an obligation.

(4) The following rules apply to the remedies for breach of an obligation created under this section:

(a) The seller may modify or limit the remedies available to the remote purchaser if the modification or limitation is furnished to the remote purchaser no later than the time of purchase or if the modification or limitation is contained in the record that contains the affirmation of fact, promise or description.

(b) Subject to a modification or limitation of remedy, a seller in breach is liable for incidental or consequential damages under Section 2–715, but the seller is not liable for lost profits.

(c) The remote purchaser may recover as damages for breach of a seller's obligation arising under subsection (2) the loss resulting in the ordinary course of events as determined in any manner that is reasonable.

(5) An obligation that is not a remedial promise is breached if the goods did not conform to the affirmation of fact, promise or description creating the obligation when the goods left the seller's control.

§ 2–313B. Obligation to Remote Purchaser Created by Communication to the Public.

(1) This section applies only to new goods and goods sold or leased as new goods in a transaction of purchase in the normal chain of distribution. In this section:

(a) "Immediate buyer" means a buyer that enters into a contract with the seller.

(b) "Remote purchaser" means a person that buys or leases goods from an immediate buyer or other person in the normal chain of distribution.

(2) If a seller in advertising or a similar communication to the public makes an affirmation of fact or promise that relates to the goods, provides a description that relates to the goods, or makes a remedial promise, and the remote purchaser enters into a transaction of purchase with knowledge of and with the expectation that the goods will conform to the affirmation of fact, promise, or description, or that the seller will perform the remedial promise, the seller has an obligation to the remote purchaser that:

(a) the goods will conform to the affirmation of fact, promise or description unless a reasonable person in the position of the remote purchaser would not believe that the affirmation of fact, promise or description created an obligation; and

(b) the seller will perform the remedial promise.

(3) It is not necessary to the creation of an obligation under this section that the seller use formal words such as "warrant" or "guarantee" or that the seller have a specific intention to undertake an obligation, but an affirmation merely of the value of the goods or a statement purporting to be merely the seller's opinion or commendation of the goods does not create an obligation.

(4) The following rules apply to the remedies for breach of an obligation created under this section:

(a) The seller may modify or limit the remedies available to the remote purchaser if the modification or limitation is furnished to the remote purchaser no later than the time of purchase. The modification or limitation may be furnished as part of the communication that contains the affirmation of fact, promise or description.

(b) Subject to a modification or limitation of remedy, a seller in breach is liable for incidental or consequential damages under Section 2–715, but the seller is not liable for lost profits.

(c) The remote purchaser may recover as damages for breach of a seller's obligation arising under subsection (2) the loss resulting in the ordinary course of events as determined in any manner that is reasonable.

(5) An obligation that is not a remedial promise is breached if the goods did not conform to the affirmation of fact, promise or description creating the obligation when the goods left the seller's control.

* * * *

§ 2–316.   Exclusion or Modification of Warranties.

* * * *

(2) Subject to subsection (3), to exclude or modify the implied warranty of merchantability or any part of it in a consumer contract the language must be in a record, be conspicuous and state "The seller undertakes no responsibility for the quality of the goods except as otherwise provided in this contract," and in any other contract the language must mention merchantability and in case of a record must be conspicuous. Subject to subsection (3), to exclude or modify the implied warranty of fitness the exclusion must be in a record and be conspicuous. Language to exclude all implied warranties of fitness in a consumer contract must state "The seller assumes no responsibility that the goods will be fit for any particular purpose for which you may be buying these goods, except as otherwise provided in the contract," and in any other contract the language is sufficient if it states, for example, that "There are no warranties which extend beyond the description on the face hereof." Language that satisfies the requirements of this subsection for the exclusion and modification of a warranty in a consumer contract also satisfies the requirements for any other contract.

(3) Notwithstanding subsection (2):

(a) unless the circumstances indicate otherwise, all implied warranties are excluded by expressions like "as is", "with all faults" or other language which in common understanding calls the buyer's attention to the exclusion of warranties, makes plain that there is no implied warranty, and in a consumer contract evidenced by a record is set forth conspicuously in the record; and

(b) when the buyer before entering into the contract has examined the goods or the sample or model as fully as desired or has refused to examine the goods after a demand by the seller there is no implied warranty with regard to defects which an examination ought in the circumstances to have revealed to the buyer; and

(c) an implied warranty can also be excluded or modified by course of dealing or course of performance or usage of trade.

* * * *

§ 2–318. Third Party Beneficiaries of Warranties Express or Implied.

(1) In this section:

(a) "Immediate buyer" means a buyer that enters into a contract with the seller.

(b) "Remote purchaser" means a person that buys or leases goods from an immediate buyer or other person in the normal chain of distribution.

Alternative A to subsection (2) (2) A seller's warranty whether express or implied to an immediate buyer, a seller's remedial promise to an immediate buyer, or a seller's obligation to a remote purchaser under Section 2–313A or 2–313B extends to any natural person who is in the family or household of the immediate buyer or the remote purchaser or who is a guest in the home of either if it is reasonable to expect that the person may use, consume or be affected by the goods and who is injured in person by breach of the warranty, remedial promise or obligation. A seller may not exclude or limit the operation of this section.

Alternative B to subsection (2) (2) A seller's warranty whether express or implied to an immediate buyer, a seller's remedial promise to an immediate buyer, or a seller's obligation to a remote purchaser under Section 2–313A or 2–313B extends to any natural person who may reasonably be expected to use, consume or be affected by the goods and who is injured in person by breach of the warranty, remedial promise or obligation. A seller may not exclude or limit the operation of this section.

Alternative C to subsection (2) (2) A seller's warranty whether express or implied to an immediate buyer, a seller's remedial promise to an immediate buyer, or a seller's obligation to a remote purchaser under Section 2–313A or 2–313B extends to any person that may reasonably be expected to use, consume or be affected by the goods and that is injured by breach of the warranty, remedial promise or obligation. A seller may not exclude or limit the operation of this section with respect to injury to the person of an individual to whom the warranty, remedial promise or obligation extends.

* * * *

PART 5 Performance

* * * *

§ 2–502. Buyer's Right to Goods on Seller's Insolvency.

(1) Subject to subsections (2) and (3) and even though the goods have not been shipped a buyer who that has paid a part or all of the price of goods in which the buyer has a special property under the provisions of the immediately preceding section may on making and keeping good a tender of any unpaid portion of their price recover them from the seller if:

(a) in the case of goods bought by a consumer, the seller repudiates or fails to deliver as required by the contract; or

(b) in all cases, the seller becomes insolvent within ten days after receipt of the first installment on their price.

(2) The buyer's right to recover the goods under subsection (1) vests upon acquisition of a special property, even if the seller had not then repudiated or failed to deliver.

(3) If the identification creating the special property has been made by the buyer, the buyer acquires the right to recover the goods only if they conform to the contract for sale.

* * * *

§ 2–508. Cure by Seller of Improper Tender or Delivery; Replacement.

(1) Where the buyer rejects goods or a tender of delivery under Section 2–601 or 2–612 or except in a consumer contract justifiably revokes acceptance under Section 2–608(1)(b) and the agreed time for performance has not expired, a seller that has performed in good faith, upon seasonable notice to the buyer and at the seller's own expense, may cure the breach of contract by making a conforming tender of delivery within the agreed time. The seller shall compensate the buyer for all of the buyer's reasonable expenses caused by the seller's breach of contract and subsequent cure.

(2) Where the buyer rejects goods or a tender of delivery under Section 2–601 or 2–612 or except in a consumer contract justifiably revokes acceptance under Section 2–608(1)(b) and the agreed time for performance has expired, a seller that has performed in good faith, upon seasonable notice to the buyer and at the seller's own expense, may cure the breach of contract, if the cure is appropriate and timely under the circumstances, by making a tender of conforming goods. The seller shall compensate the buyer for all of the buyer's reasonable expenses caused by the seller's breach of contract and subsequent cure.

§ 2–509. Risk of Loss in the Absence of Breach.

(1) Where the contract requires or authorizes the seller to ship the goods by carrier

(a) if it does not require the seller to deliver them at a particular destination, the risk of loss passes to the buyer when the goods are delivered to the carrier even though the shipment is under reservation (Section 2–505); but

(b) if it does require the seller to deliver them at a particular destination and the goods are there tendered while in the possession of the carrier, the risk of loss passes to the buyer when the goods are there so tendered as to enable the buyer to take delivery.

(2) Where the goods are held by a bailee to be delivered without being moved, the risk of loss passes to the buyer

(a) on the buyer's receipt of a negotiable document of title covering the goods; or

(b) on acknowledgment by the bailee to the buyer of the buyer's right to possession of the goods; or

(c) after the buyer's receipt of a non-negotiable document of title or other direction to deliver in a record, as provided in subsection (4)(b) of Section 2–503.

(3) In any case not within subsection (1) or (2), the risk of loss passes to the buyer on the buyer's receipt of the goods.

* * * *

§ 2–513. Buyer's Right to Inspection of Goods.

* * * *

(3) Unless otherwise agreed, the buyer is not entitled to inspect the goods before payment of the price when the contract provides

(a) for delivery on terms that under applicable course of performance, course of dealing, or usage of trade are interpreted to preclude inspection before payment; or

(b) for payment against documents of title, except where such payment is due only after the goods are to become available for inspection.

* * * *

PART 6 Breach, Repudiation and Excuse

* * * *

§ 2–605. Waiver of Buyer's Objections by Failure to Particularize.

(1) The buyer's failure to state in connection with rejection a particular defect or in connection with revocation of acceptance a defect that justifies revocation precludes the buyer from relying on the unstated defect to justify rejection or revocation of acceptance if the defect is ascertainable by reasonable inspection

(a) where the seller had a right to cure the defect and could have cured it if stated seasonably; or

(b) between merchants when the seller has after rejection made a request in a record for a full and final statement in record form of all defects on which the buyer proposes to rely.

(2) A buyer's payment against documents tendered to the buyer made without reservation of rights precludes recovery of the payment for defects apparent on the face of the documents.

* * * *

§ 2–607. Effect of Acceptance; Notice of Breach; Burden of Establishing Breach After Acceptance; Notice of Claim or Litigation to Person Answerable Over.

(3) Where a tender has been accepted

(a) the buyer must within a reasonable time after the buyer discovers or should have discovered any breach notify the seller; however, failure to give timely notice bars the buyer from a remedy only to the extent that the seller is prejudiced by the failure and

(b) if the claim is one for infringement or the like (subsection (3) of Section 2–312) and the buyer is sued as a result of such a breach the buyer must so notify the seller within a reasonable time after the buyer receives notice of the litigation or be barred from any remedy over for liability established by the litigation.

* * * *

§ 2–608. Revocation of Acceptance in Whole or in Part.

* * * *

(4) If a buyer uses the goods after a rightful rejection or justifiable revocation of acceptance, the following rules apply:

(a) Any use by the buyer that is unreasonable under the circumstances is wrongful as against the seller and is an acceptance only if ratified by the seller.

(b) Any use of the goods that is reasonable under the circumstances is not wrongful as against the seller and is not an acceptance, but in an appropriate case the buyer shall be obligated to the seller for the value of the use to the buyer.

* * * *

§ 2–612. "Installment Contract"; Breach.

* * * *

(2) The buyer may reject any installment which is non-conforming if the non-conformity substantially impairs the value of that installment to the buyer or if the non-conformity is a defect in the required documents; but if the non-conformity does not fall within subsection (3) and the seller gives adequate assurance of its cure the buyer must accept that installment.

(3) Whenever non-conformity or default with respect to one or more installments substantially impairs the value of the whole contract there is a breach of the whole. But the aggrieved party reinstates the contract if the party accepts a non-conforming installment without seasonably notifying of cancellation or if the party brings an action with respect only to past installments or demands performance as to future installments.

* * * *

PART 7   Remedies

§ 2–702.   Seller's Remedies on Discovery of Buyer's Insolvency.

* * * *

(2) Where the seller discovers that the buyer has received goods on credit while insolvent the seller may reclaim the goods upon demand made within a reasonable time after the buyer's receipt of the goods. Except as provided in this subsection the seller may not base a right to reclaim goods on the buyer's fraudulent or innocent misrepresentation of solvency or of intent to pay.

* * * *

§ 2–705.   Seller's Stoppage of Delivery in Transit or Otherwise.

(1) The seller may stop delivery of goods in the possession of a carrier or other bailee when the seller discovers the buyer to be insolvent (Section 2–702) or when the buyer repudiates or fails to make a payment due before delivery or if for any other reason the seller has a right to withhold or reclaim the goods.

* * * *

§ 2–706.   Seller's Resale Including Contract for Resale.

(1) In an appropriate case involving breach by the buyer, the seller may resell the goods concerned or the undelivered balance thereof. Where the resale is made in good faith and in a commercially reasonable manner the seller may recover the difference between the contract price and the resale price together with any incidental or consequential damages allowed under the provisions of this Article (Section 2–710), but less expenses saved in consequence of the buyer's breach.

* * * *

§ 2–708.   Seller's Damages for Non-Acceptance or Repudiation.

(1) Subject to subsection (2) and to the provisions of this Article with respect to proof of market price (Section 2–723)

(a) the measure of damages for non-acceptance by the buyer is the difference between the contract price and the market price at the time and place for tender together with any incidental or consequential damages provided in this Article (Section 2–710), but less expenses saved in consequence of the buyer's breach; and

(b) the measure of damages for repudiation by the buyer is the difference between the contract price and the market price at the place for tender at the expiration of a commercially reasonable time after the seller learned of the repudiation, but no later than the time stated in paragraph (a), together with any incidental or consequential damages provided in this Article (Section 2–710), but less expenses saved in consequence of the buyer's breach.

(2) If the measure of damages provided in subsection (1) or in Section 2–706 is inadequate to put the seller in as good a position as performance would have done then the measure of damages is the profit (including reasonable overhead) which the seller would have made from full performance by the buyer, together with any incidental or consequential damages provided in this Article (Section 2–710).

§ 2–709.   Action for the Price.

(1) When the buyer fails to pay the price as it becomes due the seller may recover, together with any incidental or consequential damages under the next section, the price

(a) of goods accepted or of conforming goods lost or damaged within a commercially reasonable time after risk of their loss has passed to the buyer; and

(b) of goods identified to the contract if the seller is unable after reasonable effort to resell them at a reasonable price or the circumstances reasonably indicate that such effort will be unavailing.

* * * *

* * * *

* * * *

§ 2–710.   Seller's Incidental and Consequential Damages.

(1) Incidental damages to an aggrieved seller include any commercially reasonable charges, expenses or commissions incurred in stopping delivery, in the transportation, care and custody of goods after the buyer's breach, in connection with return or resale of the goods or otherwise resulting from the breach.

(2) Consequential damages resulting from the buyer's breach include any loss resulting from general or particular requirements and needs of which the buyer at the time of contracting had reason to know and which could not reasonably be prevented by resale or otherwise.

(3) In a consumer contract, a seller may not recover consequential damages from a consumer.

* * * *

§ 2-713.   Buyer's Damages for Non-Delivery or Repudiation.

(1) Subject to the provisions of this Article with respect to proof of market price (Section 2–723), if the seller wrongfully fails to deliver or repudiates or the buyer rightfully rejects or justifiably revokes acceptance

(a) the measure of damages in the case of wrongful failure to deliver by the seller or rightful rejection or justifiable revocation of acceptance by the buyer is the difference between the market price at the time for tender under the contract and the contract price together with any incidental or consequential damages provided in this Article (Section 2–715), but less expenses saved in consequence of the seller's breach; and

(b) the measure of damages for repudiation by the seller is the difference between the market price at the expiration of a commercially reasonable time after the buyer learned of the repudiation, but no later than the time stated in paragraph (a), and the contract price together with any incidental or consequential damages provided in this Article (Section 2–715), but less expenses saved in consequence of the seller's breach.

* * * *

§ 2-725.   Statute of Limitations in Contracts for Sale.

(1) Except as otherwise provided in this section, an action for breach of any contract for sale must be commenced within the later of four years after the right of action has accrued under subsection (2) or (3) or one year after the breach was or should have been discovered, but no longer than five years after the right of action accrued. By the original agreement the parties may reduce the period of limitation to not less than one year but may not extend it; however, in a consumer contract, the period of limitation may not be reduced.

(2) Except as otherwise provided in subsection (3), the following rules apply:

(a) Except as otherwise provided in this subsection, a right of action for breach of a contract accrues when the breach occurs, even if the aggrieved party did not have knowledge of the breach.

(b) For breach of a contract by repudiation, a right of action accrues at the earlier of when the aggrieved party elects to treat the repudiation as a breach or when a commercially reasonable time for awaiting performance has expired.

(c) For breach of a remedial promise, a right of action accrues when the remedial promise is not performed when due.

(d) In an action by a buyer against a person that is answerable over to the buyer for a claim asserted against the buyer, the buyer's right of action against the person answerable over accrues at the time the claim was originally asserted against the buyer.

(3) If a breach of a warranty arising under Section 2–312, 2–313(2), 2–314, or 2–315, or a breach of an obligation other than a remedial promise arising under Section 2–313A or 2–313B, is claimed the following rules apply:

(a) Except as otherwise provided in paragraph (c), a right of action for breach of a warranty arising under Section 2–313(2), 2–314 or 2–315 accrues when the seller has tendered delivery to the immediate buyer, as defined in Section 2–313, and has completed performance of any agreed installation or assembly of the goods.

(b) Except as otherwise provided in paragraph (c), a right of action for breach of an obligation other than a remedial promise arising under Section 2–313A or 2–313B accrues when the remote purchaser, as defined in sections 2–313A and 2–313B, receives the goods.

(c) Where a warranty arising under Section 2–313(2) or an obligation other than a remedial promise arising under 2–313A or 2–313B explicitly extends to future performance of the goods and discovery of the breach must await the time for performance the right of action accrues when the immediate buyer as defined in Section 2–313 or the remote purchaser as defined in Sections 2–313A and 2–313B discovers or should have discovered the breach.

(d) A right of action for breach of warranty arising under Section 2–312 accrues when the aggrieved party discovers or should have discovered the breach. However, an action for breach of the warranty of non-infringement may not be commenced more than six years after tender of delivery of the goods to the aggrieved party.

* * * *

ARTICLE 2A

LEASES

PART I   General Provisions

§ 2A-101. Short Title.

This Article shall be known and may be cited as the Uniform Commercial Code—Leases.

§ 2A-102. Scope.

This Article applies to any transaction, regardless of form, that creates a lease.

§ 2A-103. Definitions and Index of Definitions.

(1) In this Article unless the context otherwise requires:

(a) "Buyer in ordinary course of business" means a person who in good faith and without knowledge that the sale to him [or her] is in violation of the ownership rights or security interest or leasehold interest of a third party in the goods buys in ordinary course from a person in the business of selling goods of that kind but does not include a pawnbroker. "Buying" may be for cash or by exchange of other property or on secured or unsecured credit and includes receiving goods or documents of title under a pre-existing contract for sale but does not include a transfer in bulk or as security for or in total or partial satisfaction of a money debt.

(b) "Cancellation" occurs when either party puts an end to the lease contract for default by the other party.

(c) "Commercial unit" means such a unit of goods as by commercial usage is a single whole for purposes of lease and division of which materially impairs its character or value on the market or in use. A commercial unit may be a single article, as a machine, or a set of articles, as a suite of furniture or a line of machinery, or a quantity, as a gross or carload, or any other unit treated in use or in the relevant market as a single whole.

(d) "Conforming" goods or performance under a lease contract means goods or performance that are in accordance with the obligations under the lease contract.

(e) "Consumer lease" means a lease that a lessor regularly engaged in the business of leasing or selling makes to a lessee who is an individual and who takes under the lease primarily for a personal, family, or household purpose [, if the total payments to be made under the lease contract, excluding payments for options to renew or buy, do not exceed $_____].

(f) "Fault" means wrongful act, omission, breach, or default.

(g) "Finance lease" means a lease with respect to which:

(i) the lessor does not select, manufacture or supply the goods;

(ii) the lessor acquires the goods or the right to possession and use of the goods in connection with the lease; and

(iii) one of the following occurs:

(A) the lessee receives a copy of the contract by which the lessor acquired the goods or the right to possession and use of the goods before signing the lease contract;

(B) the lessee's approval of the contract by which the lessor acquired the goods or the right to possession and use of the goods is a condition to effectiveness of the lease contract;

(C) the lessee, before signing the lease contract, receives an accurate and complete statement designating the promises and warranties, and any disclaimers of warranties, limitations or modifications of remedies, or liquidated damages, including those of a third party, such as the manufacturer of the goods, provided to the lessor by the person supplying the goods in connection with or as part of the contract by which the lessor acquired the goods or the right to possession and use of the goods; or

(D) if the lease is not a consumer lease, the lessor, before the lessee signs the lease contract, informs the lessee in writing (a) of the identity of the person supplying the goods to the lessor, unless the lessee has selected that person and directed the lessor to acquire the goods or the right to possession and use of the goods from that person, (b) that the lessee is entitled under this Article to any promises and warranties, including those of any third party, provided to the lessor by the person supplying the goods in connection with or as part of the contract by which the lessor acquired the goods or the right to possession and use of the goods, and (c) that the lessee may communicate with the person supplying the goods to the lessor and receive an accurate and complete statement of those promises and warranties, including any disclaimers and limitations of them or of remedies.

(h) "Goods" means all things that are movable at the time of identification to the lease contract, or are fixtures (Section 2A–309), but the term does not include money, documents, instruments, accounts, chattel paper, general intangibles, or minerals or the like, including oil and gas, before extraction. The term also includes the unborn young of animals.

(i) "Installment lease contract" means a lease contract that authorizes or requires the delivery of goods in separate lots to be separately accepted, even though the lease contract contains a clause "each delivery is a separate lease" or its equivalent.

(j) "Lease" means a transfer of the right to possession and use of goods for a term in return for consideration, but a sale, including a sale on approval or a sale or return, or retention or creation of a security interest is not a lease. Unless the context clearly indicates otherwise, the term includes a sublease.

(k) "Lease agreement" means the bargain, with respect to the lease, of the lessor and the lessee in fact as found in their language or by implication from other circumstances including course of dealing or usage of trade or course of performance as provided in this Article. Unless the context clearly indicates otherwise, the term includes a sublease agreement.

(l) "Lease contract" means the total legal obligation that results from the lease agreement as affected by this Article and any other applicable rules of law. Unless the context clearly indicates otherwise, the term includes a sublease contract.

(m) "Leasehold interest" means the interest of the lessor or the lessee under a lease contract.

(n) "Lessee" means a person who acquires the right to possession and use of goods under a lease. Unless the context clearly indicates otherwise, the term includes a sublessee.

(o) "Lessee in ordinary course of business" means a person who in good faith and without knowledge that the lease to him [or her] is in violation of the ownership rights or security interest or leasehold interest of a third party in the goods, leases in ordinary course from a person in the business of selling or leasing goods of that kind but does not include a pawnbroker. "Leasing" may be for cash or by exchange of other property or on secured or unsecured credit and includes receiving goods or documents of title under a pre-existing lease contract but does not include a transfer in bulk or as security for or in total or partial satisfaction of a money debt.

(p) "Lessor" means a person who transfers the right to possession and use of goods under a lease. Unless the context clearly indicates otherwise, the term includes a sublessor.

(q) "Lessor's residual interest" means the lessor's interest in the goods after expiration, termination, or cancellation of the lease contract.

(r) "Lien" means a charge against or interest in goods to secure payment of a debt or performance of an obligation, but the term does not include a security interest.

(s) "Lot" means a parcel or a single article that is the subject matter of a separate lease or delivery, whether or not it is sufficient to perform the lease contract.

(t) "Merchant lessee" means a lessee that is a merchant with respect to goods of the kind subject to the lease.

(u) "Present value" means the amount as of a date certain of one or more sums payable in the future, discounted to the date certain. The discount is determined by the interest rate specified by the parties if the rate was not manifestly unreasonable at the time the transaction was entered into; otherwise, the discount is determined by a commercially reasonable rate that takes into account the facts and circumstances of each case at the time the transaction was entered into.

(v) "Purchase" includes taking by sale, lease, mortgage, security interest, pledge, gift, or any other voluntary transaction creating an interest in goods.

(w) "Sublease" means a lease of goods the right to possession and use of which was acquired by the lessor as a lessee under an existing lease.

(x) "Supplier" means a person from whom a lessor buys or leases goods to be leased under a finance lease.

(y) "Supply contract" means a contract under which a lessor buys or leases goods to be leased.

(z) "Termination" occurs when either party pursuant to a power created by agreement or law puts an end to the lease contract otherwise than for default.

(2) Other definitions applying to this Article and the sections in which they appear are:

"Accessions". Section 2A–310(1).
"Construction mortgage". Section 2A–309(1)(d).
"Encumbrance". Section 2A–309(1)(e).
"Fixtures". Section 2A–309(1)(a).
"Fixture filing". Section 2A–309(1)(b).
"Purchase money lease". Section 2A–309(1)(c).

(3) The following definitions in other Articles apply to this Article:

"Accounts". Section 9–106.
"Between merchants". Section 2–104(3).
"Buyer". Section 2–103(1)(a).
"Chattel paper". Section 9–105(1)(b).
"Consumer goods". Section 9–109(1).

"Document". Section 9–105(1)(f).
"Entrusting". Section 2–403(3).
"General intangibles". Section 9–106.
"Good faith". Section 2–103(1)(b).
"Instrument". Section 9–105(1)(i).
"Merchant". Section 2–104(1).
"Mortgage". Section 9–105(1)(j).
"Pursuant to commitment". Section 9–105(1)(k).
"Receipt". Section 2–103(1)(c).
"Sale". Section 2–106(1).
"Sale on approval". Section 2–326.
"Sale or return". Section 2–326.
"Seller". Section 2–103(1)(d).

(4) In addition Article 1 contains general definitions and principles of construction and interpretation applicable throughout this Article.

As amended in 1990 and 1999.

§ 2A–104. Leases Subject to Other Law.

(1) A lease, although subject to this Article, is also subject to any applicable:

(a) certificate of title statute of this State: (list any certificate of title statutes covering automobiles, trailers, mobile homes, boats, farm tractors, and the like);

(b) certificate of title statute of another jurisdiction (Section 2A–105); or

(c) consumer protection statute of this State, or final consumer protection decision of a court of this State existing on the effective date of this Article.

(2) In case of conflict between this Article, other than Sections 2A–105, 2A–304(3), and 2A–305(3), and a statute or decision referred to in subsection (1), the statute or decision controls.

(3) Failure to comply with an applicable law has only the effect specified therein.

As amended in 1990.

§ 2A–105. Territorial Application of Article to Goods Covered by Certificate of Title.

Subject to the provisions of Sections 2A–304(3) and 2A–305(3), with respect to goods covered by a certificate of title issued under a statute of this State or of another jurisdiction, compliance and the effect of compliance or noncompliance with a certificate of title statute are governed by the law (including the conflict of laws rules) of the jurisdiction issuing the certificate until the earlier of (a) surrender of the certificate, or (b) four months after the goods are removed from that jurisdiction and thereafter until a new certificate of title is issued by another jurisdiction.

§ 2A-106. Limitation on Power of Parties to Consumer Lease to Choose Applicable Law and Judicial Forum.

(1) If the law chosen by the parties to a consumer lease is that of a jurisdiction other than a jurisdiction in which the lessee resides at the time the lease agreement becomes enforceable or within 30 days thereafter or in which the goods are to be used, the choice is not enforceable.

(2) If the judicial forum chosen by the parties to a consumer lease is a forum that would not otherwise have jurisdiction over the lessee, the choice is not enforceable.

§ 2A-107. Waiver or Renunciation of Claim or Right After Default.

Any claim or right arising out of an alleged default or breach of warranty may be discharged in whole or in part without consideration by a written waiver or renunciation signed and delivered by the aggrieved party.

§ 2A-108. Unconscionability.

(1) If the court as a matter of law finds a lease contract or any clause of a lease contract to have been unconscionable at the time it was made the court may refuse to enforce the lease contract, or it may enforce the remainder of the lease contract without the unconscionable clause, or it may so limit the application of any unconscionable clause as to avoid any unconscionable result.

(2) With respect to a consumer lease, if the court as a matter of law finds that a lease contract or any clause of a lease contract has been induced by unconscionable conduct or that unconscionable conduct has occurred in the collection of a claim arising from a lease contract, the court may grant appropriate relief.

(3) Before making a finding of unconscionability under subsection (1) or (2), the court, on its own motion or that of a party, shall afford the parties a reasonable opportunity to present evidence as to the setting, purpose, and effect of the lease contract or clause thereof, or of the conduct.

(4) In an action in which the lessee claims unconscionability with respect to a consumer lease:

(a) If the court finds unconscionability under subsection (1) or (2), the court shall award reasonable attorney's fees to the lessee.

(b) If the court does not find unconscionability and the lessee claiming unconscionability has brought or maintained an action he [or she] knew to be groundless, the court shall award reasonable attorney's fees to the party against whom the claim is made.

(c) In determining attorney's fees, the amount of the recovery on behalf of the claimant under subsections (1) and (2) is not controlling.

§ 2A-109. Option to Accelerate at Will.

(1) A term providing that one party or his [or her] successor in interest may accelerate payment or performance or require collateral or additional collateral "at will" or "when he [or she] deems himself [or herself] insecure" or in words of similar import must be construed to mean that he [or she] has power to do so only if he [or she] in good faith believes that the prospect of payment or performance is impaired.

(2) With respect to a consumer lease, the burden of establishing good faith under subsection (1) is on the party who exercised the power; otherwise the burden of establishing lack of good faith is on the party against whom the power has been exercised.

PART 2   Formation and Construction of Lease Contract

§ 2A-201. Statute of Frauds.

(1) A lease contract is not enforceable by way of action or defense unless:

(a) the total payments to be made under the lease contract, excluding payments for options to renew or buy, are less than $1,000; or

(b) there is a writing, signed by the party against whom enforcement is sought or by that party's authorized agent, sufficient to indicate that a lease contract has been made between the parties and to describe the goods leased and the lease term.

(2) Any description of leased goods or of the lease term is sufficient and satisfies subsection (1)(b), whether or not it is specific, if it reasonably identifies what is described.

(3) A writing is not insufficient because it omits or incorrectly states a term agreed upon, but the lease contract is not enforceable under subsection (1)(b) beyond the lease term and the quantity of goods shown in the writing.

(4) A lease contract that does not satisfy the requirements of subsection (1), but which is valid in other respects, is enforceable:

(a) if the goods are to be specially manufactured or obtained for the lessee and are not suitable for lease or sale to others in the ordinary course of the lessor's business, and the lessor, before notice of repudiation is received and under circumstances that reasonably indicate that the goods are for the lessee, has made either a substantial beginning of their manufacture or commitments for their procurement;

(b) if the party against whom enforcement is sought admits in that party's pleading, testimony or otherwise in court that a lease contract was made, but the lease contract is not enforceable under this provision beyond the quantity of goods admitted; or

(c) with respect to goods that have been received and accepted by the lessee.

(5) The lease term under a lease contract referred to in subsection (4) is:

(a) if there is a writing signed by the party against whom enforcement is sought or by that party's authorized agent specifying the lease term, the term so specified;

(b) if the party against whom enforcement is sought admits in that party's pleading, testimony, or otherwise in court a lease term, the term so admitted; or

(c) a reasonable lease term.

§ 2A–202. Final Written Expression: Parol or Extrinsic Evidence.

Terms with respect to which the confirmatory memoranda of the parties agree or which are otherwise set forth in a writing intended by the parties as a final expression of their agreement with respect to such terms as are included therein may not be contradicted by evidence of any prior agreement or of a contemporaneous oral agreement but may be explained or supplemented:

(a) by course of dealing or usage of trade or by course of performance; and

(b) by evidence of consistent additional terms unless the court finds the writing to have been intended also as a complete and exclusive statement of the terms of the agreement.

§ 2A–203. Seals Inoperative.

The affixing of a seal to a writing evidencing a lease contract or an offer to enter into a lease contract does not render the writing a sealed instrument and the law with respect to sealed instruments does not apply to the lease contract or offer.

§ 2A–204. Formation in General.

(1) A lease contract may be made in any manner sufficient to show agreement, including conduct by both parties which recognizes the existence of a lease contract.

(2) An agreement sufficient to constitute a lease contract may be found although the moment of its making is undetermined.

(3) Although one or more terms are left open, a lease contract does not fail for indefiniteness if the parties have intended to make a lease contract and there is a reasonably certain basis for giving an appropriate remedy.

§ 2A–205. Firm Offers.

An offer by a merchant to lease goods to or from another person in a signed writing that by its terms gives assurance it will be held open is not revocable, for lack of consideration, during the time stated or, if no time is stated, for a reasonable time, but in no event may the period of irrevocability exceed 3 months. Any such term of assurance on a form supplied by the offeree must be separately signed by the offeror.

§ 2A–206. Offer and Acceptance in Formation of Lease Contract.

(1) Unless otherwise unambiguously indicated by the language or circumstances, an offer to make a lease contract must be construed as inviting acceptance in any manner and by any medium reasonable in the circumstances.

(2) If the beginning of a requested performance is a reasonable mode of acceptance, an offeror who is not notified of acceptance within a reasonable time may treat the offer as having lapsed before acceptance.

§ 2A–207. Course of Performance or Practical Construction.

(1) If a lease contract involves repeated occasions for performance by either party with knowledge of the nature of the performance and opportunity for objection to it by the other, any course of performance accepted or acquiesced in without objection is relevant to determine the meaning of the lease agreement.

(2) The express terms of a lease agreement and any course of performance, as well as any course of dealing and usage of trade, must be construed whenever reasonable as consistent with each other; but if that construction is unreasonable, express terms control course of performance, course of performance controls both course of dealing and usage of trade, and course of dealing controls usage of trade.

(3) Subject to the provisions of Section 2A–208 on modification and waiver, course of performance is relevant to show a waiver or modification of any term inconsistent with the course of performance.

§ 2A–208. Modification, Rescission and Waiver.

(1) An agreement modifying a lease contract needs no consideration to be binding.

(2) A signed lease agreement that excludes modification or rescission except by a signed writing may not be otherwise modified or rescinded, but, except as between merchants, such a requirement on a form supplied by a merchant must be separately signed by the other party.

(3) Although an attempt at modification or rescission does not satisfy the requirements of subsection (2), it may operate as a waiver.

(4) A party who has made a waiver affecting an executory portion of a lease contract may retract the waiver by reasonable notification received by the other party that strict performance will be required of any term waived, unless the retraction would be unjust in view of a material change of position in reliance on the waiver.

§ 2A–209. Lessee under Finance Lease as Beneficiary of Supply Contract.

(1) The benefit of the supplier's promises to the lessor under the supply contract and of all warranties, whether express or implied, including those of any third party provided in connection with or as part of the supply contract, extends to the lessee to the extent of the lessee's leasehold interest under a finance lease related to the supply contract, but is subject to the terms warranty and of the supply contract and all defenses or claims arising therefrom.

(2) The extension of the benefit of supplier's promises and of warranties to the lessee (Section 2A–209(1)) does not: (i) modify the rights and obligations of the parties to the supply contract, whether arising therefrom or otherwise, or (ii) impose any duty or liability under the supply contract on the lessee.

(3) Any modification or rescission of the supply contract by the supplier and the lessor is effective between the supplier and the lessee unless, before the modification or rescission, the supplier has received notice that the lessee has entered into a finance lease related to the supply contract. If the modification or rescission is effective between the supplier and the lessee, the lessor is deemed to have assumed, in addition to the obligations of the lessor to the lessee under the lease contract, promises of the supplier to the lessor and warranties that were so modified or rescinded as they existed and were available to the lessee before modification or rescission.

(4) In addition to the extension of the benefit of the supplier's promises and of warranties to the lessee under subsection (1), the lessee retains all rights that the lessee may have against the supplier which arise from an agreement between the lessee and the supplier or under other law.

As amended in 1990.

§ 2A–210. Express Warranties.

(1) Express warranties by the lessor are created as follows:

(a) Any affirmation of fact or promise made by the lessor to the lessee which relates to the goods and becomes part of the basis of the bargain creates an express warranty that the goods will conform to the affirmation or promise.

(b) Any description of the goods which is made part of the basis of the bargain creates an express warranty that the goods will conform to the description.

(c) Any sample or model that is made part of the basis of the bargain creates an express warranty that the whole of the goods will conform to the sample or model.

(2) It is not necessary to the creation of an express warranty that the lessor use formal words, such as "warrant" or "guarantee," or that the lessor have a specific intention to make a warranty, but an affirmation merely of the value of the goods or a statement purporting to be merely the lessor's opinion or commendation of the goods does not create a warranty.

§ 2A–211. Warranties Against Interference and Against Infringement; Lessee's Obligation Against Infringement.

(1) There is in a lease contract a warranty that for the lease term no person holds a claim to or interest in the goods that arose from an act or omission of the lessor, other than a claim by way of infringement or the like, which will interfere with the lessee's enjoyment of its leasehold interest.

(2) Except in a finance lease there is in a lease contract by a lessor who is a merchant regularly dealing in goods of the kind a warranty that the goods are delivered free of the rightful claim of any person by way of infringement or the like.

(3) A lessee who furnishes specifications to a lessor or a supplier shall hold the lessor and the supplier harmless against any claim by way of infringement or the like that arises out of compliance with the specifications.

§ 2A–212. Implied Warranty of Merchantability.

(1) Except in a finance lease, a warranty that the goods will be merchantable is implied in a lease contract if the lessor is a merchant with respect to goods of that kind.

(2) Goods to be merchantable must be at least such as

(a) pass without objection in the trade under the description in the lease agreement;

(b) in the case of fungible goods, are of fair average quality within the description;

(c) are fit for the ordinary purposes for which goods of that type are used;

(d) run, within the variation permitted by the lease agreement, of even kind, quality, and quantity within each unit and among all units involved;

(e) are adequately contained, packaged, and labeled as the lease agreement may require; and

(f) conform to any promises or affirmations of fact made on the container or label.

(3) Other implied warranties may arise from course of dealing or usage of trade.

§ 2A–213. Implied Warranty of Fitness for Particular Purpose.

Except in a finance of lease, if the lessor at the time the lease contract is made has reason to know of any particular purpose for which the goods are required and that the lessee is relying on the lessor's skill or judgment to select or furnish suitable goods, there is in the lease contract an implied warranty that the goods will be fit for that purpose.

§ 2A–214. Exclusion or Modification of Warranties.

(1) Words or conduct relevant to the creation of an express warranty and words or conduct tending to negate or limit a warranty must be construed wherever reasonable as consistent

with each other; but, subject to the provisions of Section 2A–202 on parol or extrinsic evidence, negation or limitation is inoperative to the extent that the construction is unreasonable.

(2) Subject to subsection (3), to exclude or modify the implied warranty of merchantability or any part of it the language must mention "merchantability", be by a writing, and be conspicuous. Subject to subsection (3), to exclude or modify any implied warranty of fitness the exclusion must be by a writing and be conspicuous. Language to exclude all implied warranties of fitness is sufficient if it is in writing, is conspicuous and states, for example, "There is no warranty that the goods will be fit for a particular purpose".

(3) Notwithstanding subsection (2), but subject to subsection (4),

(a) unless the circumstances indicate otherwise, all implied warranties are excluded by expressions like "as is" or "with all faults" or by other language that in common understanding calls the lessee's attention to the exclusion of warranties and makes plain that there is no implied warranty, if in writing and conspicuous;

(b) if the lessee before entering into the lease contract has examined the goods or the sample or model as fully as desired or has refused to examine the goods, there is no implied warranty with regard to defects that an examination ought in the circumstances to have revealed; and

(c) an implied warranty may also be excluded or modified by course of dealing, course of performance, or usage of trade.

(4) To exclude or modify a warranty against interference or against infringement (Section 2A–211) or any part of it, the language must be specific, be by a writing, and be conspicuous, unless the circumstances, including course of performance, course of dealing, or usage of trade, give the lessee reason to know that the goods are being leased subject to a claim or interest of any person.

§ 2A–215. Cumulation and Conflict of Warranties Express or Implied.

Warranties, whether express or implied, must be construed as consistent with each other and as cumulative, but if that construction is unreasonable, the intention of the parties determines which warranty is dominant. In ascertaining that intention the following rules apply:

(a) Exact or technical specifications displace an inconsistent sample or model or general language of description.

(b) A sample from an existing bulk displaces inconsistent general language of description.

(c) Express warranties displace inconsistent implied warranties other than an implied warranty of fitness for a particular purpose.

§ 2A–216. Third-Party Beneficiaries of Express and Implied arranties.

Alternative A   A warranty to or for the benefit of a lessee under this Article, whether express or implied, extends to any natural person who is in the family or household of the lessee or who is a guest in the lessee's home if it is reasonable to expect that such person may use, consume, or be affected by the goods and who is injured in person by breach of the warranty. This section does not displace principles of law and equity that extend a warranty to or for the benefit of a lessee to other persons. The operation of this section may not be excluded, modified, or limited, but an exclusion, modification, or limitation of the warranty, including any with respect to rights and remedies, effective against the lessee is also effective against any beneficiary designated under this section.

Alternative B   A warranty to or for the benefit of a lessee under this Article, whether express or implied, extends to any natural person who may reasonably be expected to use, consume, or be affected by the goods and who is injured in person by breach of the warranty. This section does not displace principles of law and equity that extend a warranty to or for the benefit of a lessee to other persons. The operation of this section may not be excluded, modified, or limited, but an exclusion, modification, or limitation of the warranty, including any with respect to rights and remedies, effective against the lessee is also effective against the beneficiary designated under this section.

Alternative C   A warranty to or for the benefit of a lessee under this Article, whether express or implied, extends to any person who may reasonably be expected to use, consume, or be affected by the goods and who is injured by breach of the warranty. The operation of this section may not be excluded, modified, or limited with respect to injury to the person of an individual to whom the warranty extends, but an exclusion, modification, or limitation of the warranty, including any with respect to rights and remedies, effective against the lessee is also effective against the beneficiary designated under this section.

§ 2A–217. Identification.

Identification of goods as goods to which a lease contract refers may be made at any time and in any manner explicitly agreed to by the parties. In the absence of explicit agreement, identification occurs:

(a) when the lease contract is made if the lease contract is for a lease of goods that are existing and identified;

(b) when the goods are shipped, marked, or otherwise designated by the lessor as goods to which the lease contract refers, if the lease contract is for a lease of goods that are not existing and identified; or

(c) when the young are conceived, if the lease contract is for a lease of unborn young of animals.

§ 2A–218. Insurance and Proceeds.

(1) A lessee obtains an insurable interest when existing goods are identified to the lease contract even though the goods identified are nonconforming and the lessee has an option to reject them.

(2) If a lessee has an insurable interest only by reason of the lessor's identification of the goods, the lessor, until default or insolvency or notification to the lessee that identification is final, may substitute other goods for those identified.

(3) Notwithstanding a lessee's insurable interest under subsections (1) and (2), the lessor retains an insurable interest until an option to buy has been exercised by the lessee and risk of loss has passed to the lessee.

(4) Nothing in this section impairs any insurable interest recognized under any other statute or rule of law.

(5) The parties by agreement may determine that one or more parties have an obligation to obtain and pay for insurance covering the goods and by agreement may determine the beneficiary of the proceeds of the insurance.

§ 2A–219. Risk of Loss.

(1) Except in the case of a finance lease, risk of loss is retained by the lessor and does not pass to the lessee. In the case of a finance lease, risk of loss passes to the lessee.

(2) Subject to the provisions of this Article on the effect of default on risk of loss (Section 2A–220), if risk of loss is to pass to the lessee and the time of passage is not stated, the following rules apply:

(a) If the lease contract requires or authorizes the goods to be shipped by carrier

(i) and it does not require delivery at a particular destination, the risk of loss passes to the lessee when the goods are duly delivered to the carrier; but

(ii) if it does require delivery at a particular destination and the goods are there duly tendered while in the possession of the carrier, the risk of loss passes to the lessee when the goods are there duly so tendered as to enable the lessee to take delivery.

(b) If the goods are held by a bailee to be delivered without being moved, the risk of loss passes to the lessee on acknowledgment by the bailee of the lessee's right to possession of the goods.

(c) In any case not within subsection (a) or (b), the risk of loss passes to the lessee on the lessee's receipt of the goods if the lessor, or, in the case of a finance lease, the supplier, is a merchant; otherwise the risk passes to the lessee on tender of delivery.

§ 2A–220. Effect of Default on Risk of Loss.

(1) Where risk of loss is to pass to the lessee and the time of passage is not stated:

(a) If a tender or delivery of goods so fails to conform to the lease contract as to give a right of rejection, the risk of their loss remains with the lessor, or, in the case of a finance lease, the supplier, until cure or acceptance.

(b) If the lessee rightfully revokes acceptance, he [or she], to the extent of any deficiency in his [or her] effective insurance coverage, may treat the risk of loss as having remained with the lessor from the beginning.

(2) Whether or not risk of loss is to pass to the lessee, if the lessee as to conforming goods already identified to a lease contract repudiates or is otherwise in default under the lease contract, the lessor, or, in the case of a finance lease, the supplier, to the extent of any deficiency in his [or her] effective insurance coverage may treat the risk of loss as resting on the lessee for a commercially reasonable time.

§ 2A–221. Casualty to Identified Goods.

If a lease contract requires goods identified when the lease contract is made, and the goods suffer casualty without fault of the lessee, the lessor or the supplier before delivery, or the goods suffer casualty before risk of loss passes to the lessee pursuant to the lease agreement or Section 2A–219, then:

(a) if the loss is total, the lease contract is avoided; and

(b) if the loss is partial or the goods have so deteriorated as to no longer conform to the lease contract, the lessee may nevertheless demand inspection and at his [or her] option either treat the lease contract as avoided or, except in a finance lease that is not a consumer lease, accept the goods with due allowance from the rent payable for the balance of the lease term for the deterioration or the deficiency in quantity but without further right against the lessor.

PART 3   Effect of Lease Contract

§ 2A–301. Enforceability of Lease Contract.

Except as otherwise provided in this Article, a lease contract is effective and enforceable according to its terms between the parties, against purchasers of the goods and against creditors of the parties.

§ 2A–302. Title to and Possession of Goods.

Except as otherwise provided in this Article, each provision of this Article applies whether the lessor or a third party has title to the goods, and whether the lessor, the lessee, or a third party has possession of the goods, notwithstanding any statute or rule of law that possession or the absence of possession is fraudulent.

§ 2A–303. Alienability of Party's Interest Under Lease Contract or of Lessor's Residual Interest in Goods; Delegation of Performance; Transfer of Rights.

(1) As used in this section, "creation of a security interest" includes the sale of a lease contract that is subject to Article 9, Secured Transactions, by reason of Section 9–109(a)(3).

(2) Except as provided in subsections (3) and Section 9–407, a provision in a lease agreement which (i) prohibits the voluntary or involuntary transfer, including a transfer by sale, sublease, creation or enforcement of a security interest, or attachment,

levy, or other judicial process, of an interest of a party under the lease contract or of the lessor's residual interest in the goods, or (ii) makes such a transfer an event of default, gives rise to the rights and remedies provided in subsection (4), but a transfer that is prohibited or is an event of default under the lease agreement is otherwise effective.

(3) A provision in a lease agreement which (i) prohibits a transfer of a right to damages for default with respect to the whole lease contract or of a right to payment arising out of the transferor's due performance of the transferor's entire obligation, or (ii) makes such a transfer an event of default, is not enforceable, and such a transfer is not a transfer that materially impairs the propsect of obtaining return performance by, materially changes the duty of, or materially increases the burden or risk imposed on, the other party to the lease contract within the purview of subsection (4).

(4) Subject to subsection (3) and Section 9–407:

(a) if a transfer is made which is made an event of default under a lease agreement, the party to the lease contract not making the transfer, unless that party waives the default or otherwise agrees, has the rights and remedies described in Section 2A–501(2);

(b) if paragraph (a) is not applicable and if a transfer is made that (i) is prohibited under a lease agreement or (ii) materially impairs the prospect of obtaining return performance by, materially changes the duty of, or materially increases the burden or risk imposed on, the other party to the lease contract, unless the party not making the transfer agrees at any time to the transfer in the lease contract or otherwise, then, except as limited by contract, (i) the transferor is liable to the party not making the transfer for damages caused by the transfer to the extent that the damages could not reasonably be prevented by the party not making the transfer and (ii) a court having jurisdiction may grant other appropriate relief, including cancellation of the lease contract or an injunction against the transfer.

(5) A transfer of "the lease" or of "all my rights under the lease", or a transfer in similar general terms, is a transfer of rights and, unless the language or the circumstances, as in a transfer for security, indicate the contrary, the transfer is a delegation of duties by the transferor to the transferee. Acceptance by the transferee constitutes a promise by the transferee to perform those duties. The promise is enforceable by either the transferor or the other party to the lease contract.

(6) Unless otherwise agreed by the lessor and the lessee, a delegation of performance does not relieve the transferor as against the other party of any duty to perform or of any liability for default.

(7) In a consumer lease, to prohibit the transfer of an interest of a party under the lease contract or to make a transfer an event of default, the language must be specific, by a writing, and conspicuous.

As amended in 1990 and 1999.

§ 2A–304. Subsequent Lease of Goods by Lessor.

(1) Subject to Section 2A–303, a subsequent lessee from a lessor of goods under an existing lease contract obtains, to the extent of the leasehold interest transferred, the leasehold interest in the goods that the lessor had or had power to transfer, and except as provided in subsection (2) and Section 2A–527(4), takes subject to the existing lease contract. A lessor with voidable title has power to transfer a good leasehold interest to a good faith subsequent lessee for value, but only to the extent set forth in the preceding sentence. If goods have been delivered under a transaction of purchase the lessor has that power even though:

(a) the lessor's transferor was deceived as to the identity of the lessor;

(b) the delivery was in exchange for a check which is later dishonored;

(c) it was agreed that the transaction was to be a "cash sale"; or

(d) the delivery was procured through fraud punishable as larcenous under the criminal law.

(2) A subsequent lessee in the ordinary course of business from a lessor who is a merchant dealing in goods of that kind to whom the goods were entrusted by the existing lessee of that lessor before the interest of the subsequent lessee became enforceable against that lessor obtains, to the extent of the leasehold interest transferred, all of that lessor's and the existing lessee's rights to the goods, and takes free of the existing lease contract.

(3) A subsequent lessee from the lessor of goods that are subject to an existing lease contract and are covered by a certificate of title issued under a statute of this State or of another jurisdiction takes no greater rights than those provided both by this section and by the certificate of title statute.

As amended in 1990.

§ 2A–305. Sale or Sublease of Goods by Lessee.

(1) Subject to the provisions of Section 2A–303, a buyer or sublessee from the lessee of goods under an existing lease contract obtains, to the extent of the interest transferred, the leasehold interest in the goods that the lessee had or had power to transfer, and except as provided in subsection (2) and Section 2A–511(4), takes subject to the existing lease contract. A lessee with a voidable leasehold interest has power to transfer a good leasehold interest to a good faith buyer for value or a good faith sublessee for value, but only to the extent set forth in the preceding sentence. When goods have been delivered under a transaction of lease the lessee has that power even though:

(a) the lessor was deceived as to the identity of the lessee;

(b) the delivery was in exchange for a check which is later dishonored; or

(c) the delivery was procured through fraud punishable as larcenous under the criminal law.

(2) A buyer in the ordinary course of business or a sublessee in the ordinary course of business from a lessee who is a merchant dealing in goods of that kind to whom the goods were entrusted by the lessor obtains, to the extent of the interest transferred, all of the lessor's and lessee's rights to the goods, and takes free of the existing lease contract.

(3) A buyer or sublessee from the lessee of goods that are subject to an existing lease contract and are covered by a certificate of title issued under a statute of this State or of another jurisdiction takes no greater rights than those provided both by this section and by the certificate of title statute.

§ 2A–306. Priority of Certain Liens Arising by Operation of Law.

If a person in the ordinary course of his [or her] business furnishes services or materials with respect to goods subject to a lease contract, a lien upon those goods in the possession of that person given by statute or rule of law for those materials or services takes priority over any interest of the lessor or lessee under the lease contract or this Article unless the lien is created by statute and the statute provides otherwise or unless the lien is created by rule of law and the rule of law provides otherwise.

§ 2A–307. Priority of Liens Arising by Attachment or Levy on, Security Interests in, and Other Claims to Goods.

(1) Except as otherwise provided in Section 2A–306, a creditor of a lessee takes subject to the lease contract.

(2) Except as otherwise provided in subsection (3) and in Sections 2A–306 and 2A–308, a creditor of a lessor takes subject to the lease contract unless the creditor holds a lien that attached to the goods before the lease contract became enforceable.

(3) Except as otherwise provided in Sections 9–317, 9–321, and 9–323, a lessee takes a leasehold interest subject to a security interest held by a creditor of the lessor.

As amended in 1990 and 1999.

§ 2A–308. Special Rights of Creditors.

(1) A creditor of a lessor in possession of goods subject to a lease contract may treat the lease contract as void if as against the creditor retention of possession by the lessor is fraudulent under any statute or rule of law, but retention of possession in good faith and current course of trade by the lessor for a commercially reasonable time after the lease contract becomes enforceable is not fraudulent.

(2) Nothing in this Article impairs the rights of creditors of a lessor if the lease contract (a) becomes enforceable, not in current course of trade but in satisfaction of or as security for a pre-existing claim for money, security, or the like, and (b) is made under circumstances which under any statute or rule of law apart from this Article would constitute the transaction a fraudulent transfer or voidable preference.

(3) A creditor of a seller may treat a sale or an identification of goods to a contract for sale as void if as against the creditor retention of possession by the seller is fraudulent under any statute or rule of law, but retention of possession of the goods pursuant to a lease contract entered into by the seller as lessee and the buyer as lessor in connection with the sale or identification of the goods is not fraudulent if the buyer bought for value and in good faith.

§ 2A–309. Lessor's and Lessee's Rights When Goods Become Fixtures.

(1) In this section:

(a) goods are "fixtures" when they become so related to particular real estate that an interest in them arises under real estate law;

(b) a "fixture filing" is the filing, in the office where a mortgage on the real estate would be filed or recorded, of a financing statement covering goods that are or are to become fixtures and conforming to the requirements of Section 9–502(a) and (b);

(c) a lease is a "purchase money lease" unless the lessee has possession or use of the goods or the right to possession or use of the goods before the lease agreement is enforceable;

(d) a mortgage is a "construction mortgage" to the extent it secures an obligation incurred for the construction of an improvement on land including the acquisition cost of the land, if the recorded writing so indicates; and

(e) "encumbrance" includes real estate mortgages and other liens on real estate and all other rights in real estate that are not ownership interests.

(2) Under this Article a lease may be of goods that are fixtures or may continue in goods that become fixtures, but no lease exists under this Article of ordinary building materials incorporated into an improvement on land.

(3) This Article does not prevent creation of a lease of fixtures pursuant to real estate law.

(4) The perfected interest of a lessor of fixtures has priority over a conflicting interest of an encumbrancer or owner of the real estate if:

(a) the lease is a purchase money lease, the conflicting interest of the encumbrancer or owner arises before the goods become fixtures, the interest of the lessor is perfected by a fixture filing before the goods become fixtures or within ten days thereafter, and the lessee has an interest of record in the real estate or is in possession of the real estate; or

(b) the interest of the lessor is perfected by a fixture filing before the interest of the encumbrancer or owner is of record, the lessor's interest has priority over any conflicting interest of a predecessor in title of the encumbrancer or owner, and the lessee has an interest of record in the real estate or is in possession of the real estate.

(5) The interest of a lessor of fixtures, whether or not perfected, has priority over the conflicting interest of an encumbrancer or owner of the real estate if:

(a) the fixtures are readily removable factory or office machines, readily removable equipment that is not primarily used or leased for use in the operation of the real estate, or readily removable replacements of domestic appliances that are goods subject to a consumer lease, and before the goods become fixtures the lease contract is enforceable; or

(b) the conflicting interest is a lien on the real estate obtained by legal or equitable proceedings after the lease contract is enforceable; or

(c) the encumbrancer or owner has consented in writing to the lease or has disclaimed an interest in the goods as fixtures; or

(d) the lessee has a right to remove the goods as against the encumbrancer or owner. If the lessee's right to remove terminates, the priority of the interest of the lessor continues for a reasonable time.

(6) Notwithstanding paragraph (4)(a) but otherwise subject to subsections (4) and (5), the interest of a lessor of fixtures, including the lessor's residual interest, is subordinate to the conflicting interest of an encumbrancer of the real estate under a construction mortgage recorded before the goods become fixtures if the goods become fixtures before the completion of the construction. To the extent given to refinance a construction mortgage, the conflicting interest of an encumbrancer of the real estate under a mortgage has this priority to the same extent as the encumbrancer of the real estate under the construction mortgage.

(7) In cases not within the preceding subsections, priority between the interest of a lessor of fixtures, including the lessor's residual interest, and the conflicting interest of an encumbrancer or owner of the real estate who is not the lessee is determined by the priority rules governing conflicting interests in real estate.

(8) If the interest of a lessor of fixtures, including the lessor's residual interest, has priority over all conflicting interests of all owners and encumbrancers of the real estate, the lessor or the lessee may (i) on default, expiration, termination, or cancellation of the lease agreement but subject to the agreement and this Article, or (ii) if necessary to enforce other rights and remedies of the lessor or lessee under this Article, remove the goods from the real estate, free and clear of all conflicting interests of all owners and encumbrancers of the real estate, but the lessor or lessee must reimburse any encumbrancer or owner of the real estate who is not the lessee and who has not otherwise agreed for the cost of repair of any physical injury, but not for any diminution in value of the real estate caused by the absence of the goods removed or by any necessity of replacing them. A person entitled to reimbursement may refuse permission to remove until the party seeking removal gives adequate security for the performance of this obligation.

(9) Even though the lease agreement does not create a security interest, the interest of a lessor of fixtures, including the lessor's residual interest, is perfected by filing a financing statement as a fixture filing for leased goods that are or are to become fixtures in accordance with the relevant provisions of the Article on Secured Transactions (Article 9).

As amended in 1990 and 1999.

§ 2A–310. Lessor's and Lessee's Rights When Goods Become Accessions.

(1) Goods are "accessions" when they are installed in or affixed to other goods.

(2) The interest of a lessor or a lessee under a lease contract entered into before the goods became accessions is superior to all interests in the whole except as stated in subsection (4).

(3) The interest of a lessor or a lessee under a lease contract entered into at the time or after the goods became accessions is superior to all subsequently acquired interests in the whole except as stated in subsection (4) but is subordinate to interests in the whole existing at the time the lease contract was made unless the holders of such interests in the whole have in writing consented to the lease or disclaimed an interest in the goods as part of the whole.

(4) The interest of a lessor or a lessee under a lease contract described in subsection (2) or (3) is subordinate to the interest of

(a) a buyer in the ordinary course of business or a lessee in the ordinary course of business of any interest in the whole acquired after the goods became accessions; or

(b) a creditor with a security interest in the whole perfected before the lease contract was made to the extent that the creditor makes subsequent advances without knowledge of the lease contract.

(5) When under subsections (2) or (3) and (4) a lessor or a lessee of accessions holds an interest that is superior to all interests in the whole, the lessor or the lessee may (a) on default, expiration, termination, or cancellation of the lease contract by the other party but subject to the provisions of the lease contract and this Article, or (b) if necessary to enforce his [or her] other rights and remedies under this Article, remove the goods from the whole, free and clear of all interests in the whole, but he [or she] must reimburse any holder of an interest in the whole who is not the lessee and who has not otherwise agreed for the cost of repair of any physical injury but not for any diminution in value of the whole caused by the absence of the goods removed or by any necessity for replacing them. A

person entitled to reimbursement may refuse permission to remove until the party seeking removal gives adequate security for the performance of this obligation.

§ 2A–311. Priority Subject to Subordination.

Nothing in this Article prevents subordination by agreement by any person entitled to priority.

As added in 1990.

PART 4   Performance of Lease Contract: Repudiated, Substituted and Excused

§ 2A–401. Insecurity: Adequate Assurance of Performance.

(1) A lease contract imposes an obligation on each party that the other's expectation of receiving due performance will not be impaired.

(2) If reasonable grounds for insecurity arise with respect to the performance of either party, the insecure party may demand in writing adequate assurance of due performance. Until the insecure party receives that assurance, if commercially reasonable the insecure party may suspend any performance for which he [or she] has not already received the agreed return.

(3) A repudiation of the lease contract occurs if assurance of due performance adequate under the circumstances of the particular case is not provided to the insecure party within a reasonable time, not to exceed 30 days after receipt of a demand by the other party.

(4) Between merchants, the reasonableness of grounds for insecurity and the adequacy of any assurance offered must be determined according to commercial standards.

(5) Acceptance of any nonconforming delivery or payment does not prejudice the aggrieved party's right to demand adequate assurance of future performance.

§ 2A–402. Anticipatory Repudiation.

If either party repudiates a lease contract with respect to a performance not yet due under the lease contract, the loss of which performance will substantially impair the value of the lease contract to the other, the aggrieved party may:

  (a) for a commercially reasonable time, await retraction of repudiation and performance by the repudiating party;

  (b) make demand pursuant to Section 2A–401 and await assurance of future performance adequate under the circumstances of the particular case; or

  (c) resort to any right or remedy upon default under the lease contract or this Article, even though the aggrieved party has notified the repudiating party that the aggrieved party would await the repudiating party's performance and assurance and has urged retraction. In addition, whether or not the aggrieved party is pur-

suing one of the foregoing remedies, the aggrieved party may suspend performance or, if the aggrieved party is the lessor, proceed in accordance with the provisions of this Article on the lessor's right to identify goods to the lease contract notwithstanding default or to salvage unfinished goods (Section 2A–524).

§ 2A–403. Retraction of Anticipatory Repudiation.

(1) Until the repudiating party's next performance is due, the repudiating party can retract the repudiation unless, since the repudiation, the aggrieved party has cancelled the lease contract or materially changed the aggrieved party's position or otherwise indicated that the aggrieved party considers the repudiation final.

(2) Retraction may be by any method that clearly indicates to the aggrieved party that the repudiating party intends to perform under the lease contract and includes any assurance demanded under Section 2A–401.

(3) Retraction reinstates a repudiating party's rights under a lease contract with due excuse and allowance to the aggrieved party for any delay occasioned by the repudiation.

§ 2A–404. Substituted Performance.

(1) If without fault of the lessee, the lessor and the supplier, the agreed berthing, loading, or unloading facilities fail or the agreed type of carrier becomes unavailable or the agreed manner of delivery otherwise becomes commercially impracticable, but a commercially reasonable substitute is available, the substitute performance must be tendered and accepted.

(2) If the agreed means or manner of payment fails because of domestic or foreign governmental regulation:

  (a) the lessor may withhold or stop delivery or cause the supplier to withhold or stop delivery unless the lessee provides a means or manner of payment that is commercially a substantial equivalent; and

  (b) if delivery has already been taken, payment by the means or in the manner provided by the regulation discharges the lessee's obligation unless the regulation is discriminatory, oppressive, or predatory.

§ 2A–405. Excused Performance.

Subject to Section 2A–404 on substituted performance, the following rules apply:

  (a) Delay in delivery or nondelivery in whole or in part by a lessor or a supplier who complies with paragraphs (b) and (c) is not a default under the lease contract if performance as agreed has been made impracticable by the occurrence of a contingency the nonoccurrence of which was a basic assumption on which the lease contract was made or by compliance in good faith with any applicable foreign or domestic governmental regulation or order, whether or not the regulation or order later proves to be invalid.

(b) If the causes mentioned in paragraph (a) affect only part of the lessor's or the supplier's capacity to perform, he [or she] shall allocate production and deliveries among his [or her] customers but at his [or her] option may include regular customers not then under contract for sale or lease as well as his [or her] own requirements for further manufacture. He [or she] may so allocate in any manner that is fair and reasonable.

(c) The lessor seasonably shall notify the lessee and in the case of a finance lease the supplier seasonably shall notify the lessor and the lessee, if known, that there will be delay or nondelivery and, if allocation is required under paragraph (b), of the estimated quota thus made available for the lessee.

§ 2A–406. Procedure on Excused Performance.

(1) If the lessee receives notification of a material or indefinite delay or an allocation justified under Section 2A–405, the lessee may by written notification to the lessor as to any goods involved, and with respect to all of the goods if under an installment lease contract the value of the whole lease contract is substantially impaired (Section 2A–510):

(a) terminate the lease contract (Section 2A–505(2)); or

(b) except in a finance lease that is not a consumer lease, modify the lease contract by accepting the available quota in substitution, with due allowance from the rent payable for the balance of the lease term for the deficiency but without further right against the lessor.

(2) If, after receipt of a notification from the lessor under Section 2A–405, the lessee fails so to modify the lease agreement within a reasonable time not exceeding 30 days, the lease contract lapses with respect to any deliveries affected.

§ 2A–407. Irrevocable Promises: Finance Leases.

(1) In the case of a finance lease that is not a consumer lease the lessee's promises under the lease contract become irrevocable and independent upon the lessee's acceptance of the goods.

(2) A promise that has become irrevocable and independent under subsection (1):

(a) is effective and enforceable between the parties, and by or against third parties including assignees of the parties, and

(b) is not subject to cancellation, termination, modification, repudiation, excuse, or substitution without the consent of the party to whom the promise runs.

(3) This section does not affect the validity under any other law of a covenant in any lease contract making the lessee's promises irrevocable and independent upon the lessee's acceptance of the goods.

As amended in 1990.

PART 5   Default

A. In General
§ 2A–501. Default: Procedure.

(1) Whether the lessor or the lessee is in default under a lease contract is determined by the lease agreement and this Article.

(2) If the lessor or the lessee is in default under the lease contract, the party seeking enforcement has rights and remedies as provided in this Article and, except as limited by this Article, as provided in the lease agreement.

(3) If the lessor or the lessee is in default under the lease contract, the party seeking enforcement may reduce the party's claim to judgment, or otherwise enforce the lease contract by self-help or any available judicial procedure or nonjudicial procedure, including administrative proceeding, arbitration, or the like, in accordance with this Article.

(4) Except as otherwise provided in Section 1–106(1) or this Article or the lease agreement, the rights and remedies referred to in subsections (2) and (3) are cumulative.

(5) If the lease agreement covers both real property and goods, the party seeking enforcement may proceed under this Part as to the goods, or under other applicable law as to both the real property and the goods in accordance with that party's rights and remedies in respect of the real property, in which case this Part does not apply.

As amended in 1990.

§ 2A–502. Notice After Default.

Except as otherwise provided in this Article or the lease agreement, the lessor or lessee in default under the lease contract is not entitled to notice of default or notice of enforcement from the other party to the lease agreement.

§ 2A–503. Modification or Impairment of Rights and Remedies.

(1) Except as otherwise provided in this Article, the lease agreement may include rights and remedies for default in addition to or in substitution for those provided in this Article and may limit or alter the measure of damages recoverable under this Article.

(2) Resort to a remedy provided under this Article or in the lease agreement is optional unless the remedy is expressly agreed to be exclusive. If circumstances cause an exclusive or limited remedy to fail of its essential purpose, or provision for an exclusive remedy is unconscionable, remedy may be had as provided in this Article.

(3) Consequential damages may be liquidated under Section 2A–504, or may otherwise be limited, altered, or excluded unless the limitation, alteration, or exclusion is unconscionable. Limitation, alteration, or exclusion of consequential damages for injury to the person in the case of consumer goods is prima facie unconscionable but limitation, alteration, or exclusion

of damages where the loss is commercial is not prima facie unconscionable.

(4) Rights and remedies on default by the lessor or the lessee with respect to any obligation or promise collateral or ancillary to the lease contract are not impaired by this Article.

As amended in 1990.

§ 2A–504. Liquidation of Damages.

(1) Damages payable by either party for default, or any other act or omission, including indemnity for loss or diminution of anticipated tax benefits or loss or damage to lessor's residual interest, may be liquidated in the lease agreement but only at an amount or by a formula that is reasonable in light of the then anticipated harm caused by the default or other act or omission.

(2) If the lease agreement provides for liquidation of damages, and such provision does not comply with subsection (1), or such provision is an exclusive or limited remedy that circumstances cause to fail of its essential purpose, remedy may be had as provided in this Article.

(3) If the lessor justifiably withholds or stops delivery of goods because of the lessee's default or insolvency (Section 2A–525 or 2A–526), the lessee is entitled to restitution of any amount by which the sum of his [or her] payments exceeds:

(a) the amount to which the lessor is entitled by virtue of terms liquidating the lessor's damages in accordance with subsection (1); or

(b) in the absence of those terms, 20 percent of the then present value of the total rent the lessee was obligated to pay for the balance of the lease term, or, in the case of a consumer lease, the lesser of such amount or $500.

(4) A lessee's right to restitution under subsection (3) is subject to offset to the extent the lessor establishes:

(a) a right to recover damages under the provisions of this Article other than subsection (1); and

(b) the amount or value of any benefits received by the lessee directly or indirectly by reason of the lease contract.

§ 2A–505. Cancellation and Termination and Effect of Cancellation, Termination, Rescission, or Fraud on Rights and Remedies.

(1) On cancellation of the lease contract, all obligations that are still executory on both sides are discharged, but any right based on prior default or performance survives, and the cancelling party also retains any remedy for default of the whole lease contract or any unperformed balance.

(2) On termination of the lease contract, all obligations that are still executory on both sides are discharged but any right based on prior default or performance survives.

(3) Unless the contrary intention clearly appears, expressions of "cancellation," "rescission," or the like of the lease contract may not be construed as a renunciation or discharge of any claim in damages for an antecedent default.

(4) Rights and remedies for material misrepresentation or fraud include all rights and remedies available under this Article for default.

(5) Neither rescission nor a claim for rescission of the lease contract nor rejection or return of the goods may bar or be deemed inconsistent with a claim for damages or other right or remedy.

§ 2A–506. Statute of Limitations.

(1) An action for default under a lease contract, including breach of warranty or indemnity, must be commenced within 4 years after the cause of action accrued. By the original lease contract the parties may reduce the period of limitation to not less than one year.

(2) A cause of action for default accrues when the act or omission on which the default or breach of warranty is based is or should have been discovered by the aggrieved party, or when the default occurs, whichever is later. A cause of action for indemnity accrues when the act or omission on which the claim for indemnity is based is or should have been discovered by the indemnified party, whichever is later.

(3) If an action commenced within the time limited by subsection (1) is so terminated as to leave available a remedy by another action for the same default or breach of warranty or indemnity, the other action may be commenced after the expiration of the time limited and within 6 months after the termination of the first action unless the termination resulted from voluntary discontinuance or from dismissal for failure or neglect to prosecute.

(4) This section does not alter the law on tolling of the statute of limitations nor does it apply to causes of action that have accrued before this Article becomes effective.

§ 2A–507. Proof of Market Rent: Time and Place.

(1) Damages based on market rent (Section 2A–519 or 2A–528) are determined according to the rent for the use of the goods concerned for a lease term identical to the remaining lease term of the original lease agreement and prevailing at the times specified in Sections 2A–519 and 2A–528.

(2) If evidence of rent for the use of the goods concerned for a lease term identical to the remaining lease term of the original lease agreement and prevailing at the times or places described in this Article is not readily available, the rent prevailing within any reasonable time before or after the time described or at any other place or for a different lease term which in commercial judgment or under usage of trade would serve as a reasonable substitute for the one described may be

used, making any proper allowance for the difference, including the cost of transporting the goods to or from the other place.

(3) Evidence of a relevant rent prevailing at a time or place or for a lease term other than the one described in this Article offered by one party is not admissible unless and until he [or she] has given the other party notice the court finds sufficient to prevent unfair surprise.

(4) If the prevailing rent or value of any goods regularly leased in any established market is in issue, reports in official publications or trade journals or in newspapers or periodicals of general circulation published as the reports of that market are admissible in evidence. The circumstances of the preparation of the report may be shown to affect its weight but not its admissibility.

As amended in 1990.

B. Default by Lessor

§ 2A–508. Lessee's Remedies.

(1) If a lessor fails to deliver the goods in conformity to the lease contract (Section 2A–509) or repudiates the lease contract (Section 2A–402), or a lessee rightfully rejects the goods (Section 2A–509) or justifiably revokes acceptance of the goods (Section 2A–517), then with respect to any goods involved, and with respect to all of the goods if under an installment lease contract the value of the whole lease contract is substantially impaired (Section 2A–510), the lessor is in default under the lease contract and the lessee may:

(a) cancel the lease contract (Section 2A–505(1));

(b) recover so much of the rent and security as has been paid and is just under the circumstances;

(c) cover and recover damages as to all goods affected whether or not they have been identified to the lease contract (Sections 2A–518 and 2A–520), or recover damages for nondelivery (Sections 2A–519 and 2A–520);

(d) exercise any other rights or pursue any other remedies provided in the lease contract.

(2) If a lessor fails to deliver the goods in conformity to the lease contract or repudiates the lease contract, the lessee may also:

(a) if the goods have been identified, recover them (Section 2A–522); or

(b) in a proper case, obtain specific performance or replevy the goods (Section 2A–521).

(3) If a lessor is otherwise in default under a lease contract, the lessee may exercise the rights and pursue the remedies provided in the lease contract, which may include a right to cancel the lease, and in Section 2A–519(3).

(4) If a lessor has breached a warranty, whether express or implied, the lessee may recover damages (Section 2A–519(4)).

(5) On rightful rejection or justifiable revocation of acceptance, a lessee has a security interest in goods in the lessee's possession or control for any rent and security that has been paid and any expenses reasonably incurred in their inspection, receipt, transportation, and care and custody and may hold those goods and dispose of them in good faith and in a commercially reasonable manner, subject to Section 2A–527(5).

(6) Subject to the provisions of Section 2A–407, a lessee, on notifying the lessor of the lessee's intention to do so, may deduct all or any part of the damages resulting from any default under the lease contract from any part of the rent still due under the same lease contract.

As amended in 1990.

§ 2A–509. Lessee's Rights on Improper Delivery; Rightful Rejection.

(1) Subject to the provisions of Section 2A–510 on default in installment lease contracts, if the goods or the tender or delivery fail in any respect to conform to the lease contract, the lessee may reject or accept the goods or accept any commercial unit or units and reject the rest of the goods.

(2) Rejection of goods is ineffective unless it is within a reasonable time after tender or delivery of the goods and the lessee seasonably notifies the lessor.

§ 2A–510. Installment Lease Contracts: Rejection and Default.

(1) Under an installment lease contract a lessee may reject any delivery that is nonconforming if the nonconformity substantially impairs the value of that delivery and cannot be cured or the nonconformity is a defect in the required documents; but if the nonconformity does not fall within subsection (2) and the lessor or the supplier gives adequate assurance of its cure, the lessee must accept that delivery.

(2) Whenever nonconformity or default with respect to one or more deliveries substantially impairs the value of the installment lease contract as a whole there is a default with respect to the whole. But, the aggrieved party reinstates the installment lease contract as a whole if the aggrieved party accepts a nonconforming delivery without seasonably notifying of cancellation or brings an action with respect only to past deliveries or demands performance as to future deliveries.

§ 2A–511. Merchant Lessee's Duties as to Rightfully Rejected Goods.

(1) Subject to any security interest of a lessee (Section 2A–508(5)), if a lessor or a supplier has no agent or place of business at the market of rejection, a merchant lessee, after rejection of goods in his [or her] possession or control, shall follow any reasonable instructions received from the lessor or the supplier with respect to the goods. In the absence of those instructions, a merchant lessee shall make reasonable efforts to sell, lease, or otherwise dispose of the goods for the lessor's account if they threaten to decline in value speedily.

Instructions are not reasonable if on demand indemnity for expenses is not forthcoming.

(2) If a merchant lessee (subsection (1)) or any other lessee (Section 2A–512) disposes of goods, he [or she] is entitled to reimbursement either from the lessor or the supplier or out of the proceeds for reasonable expenses of caring for and disposing of the goods and, if the expenses include no disposition commission, to such commission as is usual in the trade, or if there is none, to a reasonable sum not exceeding 10 percent of the gross proceeds.

(3) In complying with this section or Section 2A–512, the lessee is held only to good faith. Good faith conduct hereunder is neither acceptance or conversion nor the basis of an action for damages.

(4) A purchaser who purchases in good faith from a lessee pursuant to this section or Section 2A–512 takes the goods free of any rights of the lessor and the supplier even though the lessee fails to comply with one or more of the requirements of this Article.

§ 2A–512. Lessee's Duties as to Rightfully Rejected Goods.

(1) Except as otherwise provided with respect to goods that threaten to decline in value speedily (Section 2A–511) and subject to any security interest of a lessee (Section 2A–508(5)):

(a) the lessee, after rejection of goods in the lessee's possession, shall hold them with reasonable care at the lessor's or the supplier's disposition for a reasonable time after the lessee's seasonable notification of rejection;

(b) if the lessor or the supplier gives no instructions within a reasonable time after notification of rejection, the lessee may store the rejected goods for the lessor's or the supplier's account or ship them to the lessor or the supplier or dispose of them for the lessor's or the supplier's account with reimbursement in the manner provided in Section 2A–511; but

(c) the lessee has no further obligations with regard to goods rightfully rejected.

(2) Action by the lessee pursuant to subsection (1) is not acceptance or conversion.

§ 2A–513. Cure by Lessor of Improper Tender or Delivery; Replacement.

(1) If any tender or delivery by the lessor or the supplier is rejected because nonconforming and the time for performance has not yet expired, the lessor or the supplier may seasonably notify the lessee of the lessor's or the supplier's intention to cure and may then make a conforming delivery within the time provided in the lease contract.

(2) If the lessee rejects a nonconforming tender that the lessor or the supplier had reasonable grounds to believe would be acceptable with or without money allowance, the lessor or the supplier may have a further reasonable time to substitute a conforming tender if he [or she] seasonably notifies the lessee.

§ 2A–514. Waiver of Lessee's Objections.

(1) In rejecting goods, a lessee's failure to state a particular defect that is ascertainable by reasonable inspection precludes the lessee from relying on the defect to justify rejection or to establish default:

(a) if, stated seasonably, the lessor or the supplier could have cured it (Section 2A–513); or

(b) between merchants if the lessor or the supplier after rejection has made a request in writing for a full and final written statement of all defects on which the lessee proposes to rely.

(2) A lessee's failure to reserve rights when paying rent or other consideration against documents precludes recovery of the payment for defects apparent on the face of the documents.

§ 2A–515. Acceptance of Goods.

(1) Acceptance of goods occurs after the lessee has had a reasonable opportunity to inspect the goods and

(a) the lessee signifies or acts with respect to the goods in a manner that signifies to the lessor or the supplier that the goods are conforming or that the lessee will take or retain them in spite of their nonconformity; or

(b) the lessee fails to make an effective rejection of the goods (Section 2A–509(2)).

(2) Acceptance of a part of any commercial unit is acceptance of that entire unit.

§ 2A–516. Effect of Acceptance of Goods; Notice of Default; Burden of Establishing Default after Acceptance; Notice of Claim or Litigation to Person Answerable Over.

(1) A lessee must pay rent for any goods accepted in accordance with the lease contract, with due allowance for goods rightfully rejected or not delivered.

(2) A lessee's acceptance of goods precludes rejection of the goods accepted. In the case of a finance lease, if made with knowledge of a nonconformity, acceptance cannot be revoked because of it. In any other case, if made with knowledge of a nonconformity, acceptance cannot be revoked because of it unless the acceptance was on the reasonable assumption that the nonconformity would be seasonably cured. Acceptance does not of itself impair any other remedy provided by this Article or the lease agreement for nonconformity.

(3) If a tender has been accepted:

(a) within a reasonable time after the lessee discovers or should have discovered any default, the lessee shall notify the lessor and the supplier, if any, or be barred from any remedy against the party notified;

(b) except in the case of a consumer lease, within a reasonable time after the lessee receives notice of litigation for infringement or the like (Section 2A–211) the lessee shall notify the lessor or be barred from any remedy over for liability established by the litigation; and

(c) the burden is on the lessee to establish any default.

(4) If a lessee is sued for breach of a warranty or other obligation for which a lessor or a supplier is answerable over the following apply:

(a) The lessee may give the lessor or the supplier, or both, written notice of the litigation. If the notice states that the person notified may come in and defend and that if the person notified does not do so that person will be bound in any action against that person by the lessee by any determination of fact common to the two litigations, then unless the person notified after seasonable receipt of the notice does come in and defend that person is so bound.

(b) The lessor or the supplier may demand in writing that the lessee turn over control of the litigation including settlement if the claim is one for infringement or the like (Section 2A–211) or else be barred from any remedy over. If the demand states that the lessor or the supplier agrees to bear all expense and to satisfy any adverse judgment, then unless the lessee after seasonable receipt of the demand does turn over control the lessee is so barred.

(5) Subsections (3) and (4) apply to any obligation of a lessee to hold the lessor or the supplier harmless against infringement or the like (Section 2A–211).

As amended in 1990.

§ 2A–517. Revocation of Acceptance of Goods.

(1) A lessee may revoke acceptance of a lot or commercial unit whose nonconformity substantially impairs its value to the lessee if the lessee has accepted it:

(a) except in the case of a finance lease, on the reasonable assumption that its nonconformity would be cured and it has not been seasonably cured; or

(b) without discovery of the nonconformity if the lessee's acceptance was reasonably induced either by the lessor's assurances or, except in the case of a finance lease, by the difficulty of discovery before acceptance.

(2) Except in the case of a finance lease that is not a consumer lease, a lessee may revoke acceptance of a lot or commercial unit if the lessor defaults under the lease contract and the default substantially impairs the value of that lot or commercial unit to the lessee.

(3) If the lease agreement so provides, the lessee may revoke acceptance of a lot or commercial unit because of other defaults by the lessor.

(4) Revocation of acceptance must occur within a reasonable time after the lessee discovers or should have discovered the ground for it and before any substantial change in condition of the goods which is not caused by the nonconformity. Revocation is not effective until the lessee notifies the lessor.

(5) A lessee who so revokes has the same rights and duties with regard to the goods involved as if the lessee had rejected them.

As amended in 1990.

§ 2A–518. Cover; Substitute Goods.

(1) After a default by a lessor under the lease contract of the type described in Section 2A–508(1), or, if agreed, after other default by the lessor, the lessee may cover by making any purchase or lease of or contract to purchase or lease goods in substitution for those due from the lessor.

(2) Except as otherwise provided with respect to damages liquidated in the lease agreement (Section 2A–504) or otherwise determined pursuant to agreement of the parties (Sections 1–102(3) and 2A–503), if a lessee's cover is by lease agreement substantially similar to the original lease agreement and the new lease agreement is made in good faith and in a commercially reasonable manner, the lessee may recover from the lessor as damages (i) the present value, as of the date of the commencement of the term of the new lease agreement, of the rent under the new lease agreement applicable to that period of the new lease term which is comparable to the then remaining term of the original lease agreement minus the present value as of the same date of the total rent for the then remaining lease term of the original lease agreement, and (ii) any incidental or consequential damages, less expenses saved in consequence of the lessor's default.

(3) If a lessee's cover is by lease agreement that for any reason does not qualify for treatment under subsection (2), or is by purchase or otherwise, the lessee may recover from the lessor as if the lessee had elected not to cover and Section 2A–519 governs.

As amended in 1990.

§ 2A–519. Lessee's Damages for Non-Delivery, Repudiation, Default, and Breach of Warranty in Regard to Accepted Goods.

(1) Except as otherwise provided with respect to damages liquidated in the lease agreement (Section 2A–504) or otherwise determined pursuant to agreement of the parties (Sections 1–102(3) and 2A–503), if a lessee elects not to cover or a lessee elects to cover and the cover is by lease agreement that for any reason does not qualify for treatment under Section 2A–518(2), or is by purchase or otherwise, the measure of damages for non-delivery or repudiation by the lessor or for rejection or revocation of acceptance by the lessee is the present value, as of

the date of the default, of the then market rent minus the present value as of the same date of the original rent, computed for the remaining lease term of the original lease agreement, together with incidental and consequential damages, less expenses saved in consequence of the lessor's default.

(2) Market rent is to be determined as of the place for tender or, in cases of rejection after arrival or revocation of acceptance, as of the place of arrival.

(3) Except as otherwise agreed, if the lessee has accepted goods and given notification (Section 2A–516(3)), the measure of damages for non-conforming tender or delivery or other default by a lessor is the loss resulting in the ordinary course of events from the lessor's default as determined in any manner that is reasonable together with incidental and consequential damages, less expenses saved in consequence of the lessor's default.

(4) Except as otherwise agreed, the measure of damages for breach of warranty is the present value at the time and place of acceptance of the difference between the value of the use of the goods accepted and the value if they had been as warranted for the lease term, unless special circumstances show proximate damages of a different amount, together with incidental and consequential damages, less expenses saved in consequence of the lessor's default or breach of warranty.

As amended in 1990.

§ 2A–520. Lessee's Incidental and Consequential Damages.

(1) Incidental damages resulting from a lessor's default include expenses reasonably incurred in inspection, receipt, transportation, and care and custody of goods rightfully rejected or goods the acceptance of which is justifiably revoked, any commercially reasonable charges, expenses or commissions in connection with effecting cover, and any other reasonable expense incident to the default.

(2) Consequential damages resulting from a lessor's default include:

(a) any loss resulting from general or particular requirements and needs of which the lessor at the time of contracting had reason to know and which could not reasonably be prevented by cover or otherwise; and

(b) injury to person or property proximately resulting from any breach of warranty.

§ 2A–521. Lessee's Right to Specific Performance or Replevin.

(1) Specific performance may be decreed if the goods are unique or in other proper circumstances.

(2) A decree for specific performance may include any terms and conditions as to payment of the rent, damages, or other relief that the court deems just.

(3) A lessee has a right of replevin, detinue, sequestration, claim and delivery, or the like for goods identified to the lease contract if after reasonable effort the lessee is unable to effect cover for those goods or the circumstances reasonably indicate that the effort will be unavailing.

§ 2A–522. Lessee's Right to Goods on Lessor's Insolvency.

(1) Subject to subsection (2) and even though the goods have not been shipped, a lessee who has paid a part or all of the rent and security for goods identified to a lease contract (Section 2A–217) on making and keeping good a tender of any unpaid portion of the rent and security due under the lease contract may recover the goods identified from the lessor if the lessor becomes insolvent within 10 days after receipt of the first installment of rent and security.

(2) A lessee acquires the right to recover goods identified to a lease contract only if they conform to the lease contract.

C. Default by Lessee

§ 2A–523. Lessor's Remedies.

(1) If a lessee wrongfully rejects or revokes acceptance of goods or fails to make a payment when due or repudiates with respect to a part or the whole, then, with respect to any goods involved, and with respect to all of the goods if under an installment lease contract the value of the whole lease contract is substantially impaired (Section 2A–510), the lessee is in default under the lease contract and the lessor may:

(a) cancel the lease contract (Section 2A–505(1));

(b) proceed respecting goods not identified to the lease contract (Section 2A–524);

(c) withhold delivery of the goods and take possession of goods previously delivered (Section 2A–525);

(d) stop delivery of the goods by any bailee (Section 2A–526);

(e) dispose of the goods and recover damages (Section 2A–527), or retain the goods and recover damages (Section 2A–528), or in a proper case recover rent (Section 2A–529)

(f) exercise any other rights or pursue any other remedies provided in the lease contract.

(2) If a lessor does not fully exercise a right or obtain a remedy to which the lessor is entitled under subsection (1), the lessor may recover the loss resulting in the ordinary course of events from the lessee's default as determined in any reasonable manner, together with incidental damages, less expenses saved in consequence of the lessee's default.

(3) If a lessee is otherwise in default under a lease contract, the lessor may exercise the rights and pursue the remedies provided in the lease contract, which may include a right to cancel the lease. In addition, unless otherwise provided in the lease contract:

(a) if the default substantially impairs the value of the lease contract to the lessor, the lessor may exercise the rights and pursue the remedies provided in subsections (1) or (2); or

(b) if the default does not substantially impair the value of the lease contract to the lessor, the lessor may recover as provided in subsection (2).

As amended in 1990.

§ 2A–524. Lessor's Right to Identify Goods to Lease Contract.

(1) After default by the lessee under the lease contract of the type described in Section 2A–523(1) or 2A–523(3)(a) or, if agreed, after other default by the lessee, the lessor may:

(a) identify to the lease contract conforming goods not already identified if at the time the lessor learned of the default they were in the lessor's or the supplier's possession or control; and

(b) dispose of goods (Section 2A–527(1)) that demonstrably have been intended for the particular lease contract even though those goods are unfinished.

(2) If the goods are unfinished, in the exercise of reasonable commercial judgment for the purposes of avoiding loss and of effective realization, an aggrieved lessor or the supplier may either complete manufacture and wholly identify the goods to the lease contract or cease manufacture and lease, sell, or otherwise dispose of the goods for scrap or salvage value or proceed in any other reasonable manner.

As amended in 1990.

§ 2A–525. Lessor's Right to Possession of Goods.

(1) If a lessor discovers the lessee to be insolvent, the lessor may refuse to deliver the goods.

(2) After a default by the lessee under the lease contract of the type described in Section 2A–523(1) or 2A–523(3)(a) or, if agreed, after other default by the lessee, the lessor has the right to take possession of the goods. If the lease contract so provides, the lessor may require the lessee to assemble the goods and make them available to the lessor at a place to be designated by the lessor which is reasonably convenient to both parties. Without removal, the lessor may render unusable any goods employed in trade or business, and may dispose of goods on the lessee's premises (Section 2A–527).

(3) The lessor may proceed under subsection (2) without judicial process if that can be done without breach of the peace or the lessor may proceed by action.

As amended in 1990.

§ 2A–526. Lessor's Stoppage of Delivery in Transit or Otherwise.

(1) A lessor may stop delivery of goods in the possession of a carrier or other bailee if the lessor discovers the lessee to be insolvent and may stop delivery of carload, truckload, plane-load, or larger shipments of express or freight if the lessee repudiates or fails to make a payment due before delivery, whether for rent, security or otherwise under the lease contract, or for any other reason the lessor has a right to withhold or take possession of the goods.

(2) In pursuing its remedies under subsection (1), the lessor may stop delivery until

(a) receipt of the goods by the lessee;

(b) acknowledgment to the lessee by any bailee of the goods, except a carrier, that the bailee holds the goods for the lessee; or

(c) such an acknowledgment to the lessee by a carrier via reshipment or as warehouseman.

(3) (a) To stop delivery, a lessor shall so notify as to enable the bailee by reasonable diligence to prevent delivery of the goods.

(b) After notification, the bailee shall hold and deliver the goods according to the directions of the lessor, but the lessor is liable to the bailee for any ensuing charges or damages.

(c) A carrier who has issued a nonnegotiable bill of lading is not obliged to obey a notification to stop received from a person other than the consignor.

§ 2A–527. Lessor's Rights to Dispose of Goods.

(1) After a default by a lessee under the lease contract of the type described in Section 2A–523(1) or 2A–523(3)(a) or after the lessor refuses to deliver or takes possession of goods (Section 2A–525 or 2A–526), or, if agreed, after other default by a lessee, the lessor may dispose of the goods concerned or the undelivered balance thereof by lease, sale, or otherwise.

(2) Except as otherwise provided with respect to damages liquidated in the lease agreement (Section 2A–504) or otherwise determined pursuant to agreement of the parties (Sections 1–102(3) and 2A–503), if the disposition is by lease agreement substantially similar to the original lease agreement and the new lease agreement is made in good faith and in a commercially reasonable manner, the lessor may recover from the lessee as damages (i) accrued and unpaid rent as of the date of the commencement of the term of the new lease agreement, (ii) the present value, as of the same date, of the total rent for the then remaining lease term of the original lease agreement minus the present value, as of the same date, of the rent under the new lease agreement applicable to that period of the new lease term which is comparable to the then remaining term of the original lease agreement, and (iii) any incidental damages allowed under Section 2A–530, less expenses saved in consequence of the lessee's default.

(3) If the lessor's disposition is by lease agreement that for any reason does not qualify for treatment under subsection (2), or is by sale or otherwise, the lessor may recover from the lessee as if the lessor had elected not to dispose of the goods and Section 2A–528 governs.

(4) A subsequent buyer or lessee who buys or leases from the lessor in good faith for value as a result of a disposition under this section takes the goods free of the original lease contract and any rights of the original lessee even though the lessor fails to comply with one or more of the requirements of this Article.

(5) The lessor is not accountable to the lessee for any profit made on any disposition. A lessee who has rightfully rejected or justifiably revoked acceptance shall account to the lessor for any excess over the amount of the lessee's security interest (Section 2A–508(5)).

As amended in 1990.

§ 2A–528. Lessor's Damages for Non-acceptance, Failure to Pay, Repudiation, or Other Default.

(1) Except as otherwise provided with respect to damages liquidated in the lease agreement (Section 2A–504) or otherwise determined pursuant to agreement of the parties (Section 1–102(3) and 2A–503), if a lessor elects to retain the goods or a lessor elects to dispose of the goods and the disposition is by lease agreement that for any reason does not qualify for treatment under Section 2A–527(2), or is by sale or otherwise, the lessor may recover from the lessee as damages for a default of the type described in Section 2A–523(1) or 2A–523(3)(a), or if agreed, for other default of the lessee, (i) accrued and unpaid rent as of the date of the default if the lessee has never taken possession of the goods, or, if the lessee has taken possession of the goods, as of the date the lessor repossesses the goods or an earlier date on which the lessee makes a tender of the goods to the lessor, (ii) the present value as of the date determined under clause (i) of the total rent for the then remaining lease term of the original lease agreement minus the present value as of the same date of the market rent as the place where the goods are located computed for the same lease term, and (iii) any incidental damages allowed under Section 2A–530, less expenses saved in consequence of the lessee's default.

(2) If the measure of damages provided in subsection (1) is inadequate to put a lessor in as good a position as performance would have, the measure of damages is the present value of the profit, including reasonable overhead, the lessor would have made from full performance by the lessee, together with any incidental damages allowed under Section 2A–530, due allowance for costs reasonably incurred and due credit for payments or proceeds of disposition.

As amended in 1990.

§ 2A–529. Lessor's Action for the Rent.

(1) After default by the lessee under the lease contract of the type described in Section 2A–523(1) or 2A–523(3)(a) or, if agreed, after other default by the lessee, if the lessor complies with subsection (2), the lessor may recover from the lessee as damages:

(a) for goods accepted by the lessee and not repossessed by or tendered to the lessor, and for conforming goods lost or damaged within a commercially reasonable time after risk of loss passes to the lessee (Section 2A–219), (i) accrued and unpaid rent as of the date of entry of judgment in favor of the lessor (ii) the present value as of the same date of the rent for the then remaining lease term of the lease agreement, and (iii) any incidental damages allowed under Section 2A–530, less expenses saved in consequence of the lessee's default; and

(b) for goods identified to the lease contract if the lessor is unable after reasonable effort to dispose of them at a reasonable price or the circumstances reasonably indicate that effort will be unavailing, (i) accrued and unpaid rent as of the date of entry of judgment in favor of the lessor, (ii) the present value as of the same date of the rent for the then remaining lease term of the lease agreement, and (iii) any incidental damages allowed under Section 2A–530, less expenses saved in consequence of the lessee's default.

(2) Except as provided in subsection (3), the lessor shall hold for the lessee for the remaining lease term of the lease agreement any goods that have been identified to the lease contract and are in the lessor's control.

(3) The lessor may dispose of the goods at any time before collection of the judgment for damages obtained pursuant to subsection (1). If the disposition is before the end of the remaining lease term of the lease agreement, the lessor's recovery against the lessee for damages is governed by Section 2A–527 or Section 2A–528, and the lessor will cause an appropriate credit to be provided against a judgment for damages to the extent that the amount of the judgment exceeds the recovery available pursuant to Section 2A–527 or 2A–528.

(4) Payment of the judgment for damages obtained pursuant to subsection (1) entitles the lessee to the use and possession of the goods not then disposed of for the remaining lease term of and in accordance with the lease agreement.

(5) After default by the lessee under the lease contract of the type described in Section 2A–523(1) or Section 2A–523(3)(a) or, if agreed, after other default by the lessee, a lessor who is held not entitled to rent under this section must nevertheless be awarded damages for non-acceptance under Sections 2A–527 and 2A–528.

As amended in 1990.

§ 2A–530. Lessor's Incidental Damages.

Incidental damages to an aggrieved lessor include any commercially reasonable charges, expenses, or commissions incurred in stopping delivery, in the transportation, care and custody of goods after the lessee's default, in connection with return or disposition of the goods, or otherwise resulting from the default.

§ 2A–531. Standing to Sue Third Parties for Injury to Goods.

(1) If a third party so deals with goods that have been identified to a lease contract as to cause actionable injury to a party to the lease contract (a) the lessor has a right of action against the third party, and (b) the lessee also has a right of action against the third party if the lessee:

(i) has a security interest in the goods;

(ii) has an insurable interest in the goods; or

(iii) bears the risk of loss under the lease contract or has since the injury assumed that risk as against the lessor and the goods have been converted or destroyed.

(2) If at the time of the injury the party plaintiff did not bear the risk of loss as against the other party to the lease contract and there is no arrangement between them for disposition of the recovery, his [or her] suit or settlement, subject to his [or her] own interest, is as a fiduciary for the other party to the lease contract.

(3) Either party with the consent of the other may sue for the benefit of whom it may concern.

§ 2A–532. Lessor's Rights to Residual Interest.

In addition to any other recovery permitted by this Article or other law, the lessor may recover from the lessee an amount that will fully compensate the lessor for any loss of or damage to the lessor's residual interest in the goods caused by the default of the lessee.

As added in 1990.

REVISED ARTICLE 3

NEGOTIABLE INSTRUMENTS

PART I   General Provisions and Definitions

§ 3–101.   Short Title.

This Article may be cited as Uniform Commercial Code–Negotiable Instruments.

§ 3–102.   Subject Matter.

(a) This Article applies to negotiable instruments. It does not apply to money, to payment orders governed by Article 4A, or to securities governed by Article 8.

(b) If there is conflict between this Article and Article 4 or 9, Articles 4 and 9 govern.

(c) Regulations of the Board of Governors of the Federal Reserve System and operating circulars of the Federal Reserve Banks supersede any inconsistent provision of this Article to the extent of the inconsistency.

§ 3–103.   Definitions.

(a) In this Article:

(1) "Acceptor" means a drawee who has accepted a draft.

(2) "Drawee" means a person ordered in a draft to make payment.

(3) "Drawer" means a person who signs or is identified in a draft as a person ordering payment.

(4) "Good faith" means honesty in fact and the observance of reasonable commercial standards of fair dealing.

(5) "Maker" means a person who signs or is identified in a note as a person undertaking to pay.

(6) "Order" means a written instruction to pay money signed by the person giving the instruction. The instruction may be addressed to any person, including the person giving the instruction, or to one or more persons jointly or in the alternative but not in succession. An authorization to pay is not an order unless the person authorized to pay is also instructed to pay.

(7) "Ordinary care" in the case of a person engaged in business means observance of reasonable commercial standards, prevailing in the area in which the person is located, with respect to the business in which the person is engaged. In the case of a bank that takes an instrument for processing for collection or payment by automated means, reasonable commercial standards do not require the bank to examine the instrument if the failure to examine does not violate the bank's prescribed procedures and the bank's procedures do not vary unreasonably from general banking usage not disapproved by this Article or Article 4.

(8) "Party" means a party to an instrument.

(9) "Promise" means a written undertaking to pay money signed by the person undertaking to pay. An acknowledgment of an obligation by the obligor is not a promise unless the obligor also undertakes to pay the obligation.

(10) "Prove" with respect to a fact means to meet the burden of establishing the fact (Section 1–201(8)).

(11) "Remitter" means a person who purchases an instrument from its issuer if the instrument is payable to an identified person other than the purchaser.

(b) [Other definitions' section references deleted.]

(c) [Other definitions' section references deleted.]

(d) In addition, Article 1 contains general definitions and principles of construction and interpretation applicable throughout this Article.

§ 3–104.   Negotiable Instrument.

(a) Except as provided in subsections (c) and (d), "negotiable instrument" means an unconditional promise or order to pay a fixed amount of money, with or without interest or other charges described in the promise or order, if it:

(1) is payable to bearer or to order at the time it is issued or first comes into possession of a holder;

(2) is payable on demand or at a definite time; and

(3) does not state any other undertaking or instruction by the person promising or ordering payment to do any act in addition to the payment of money, but the promise or order may contain (i) an undertaking or power to give, maintain, or protect collateral to secure payment, (ii) an authorization or power to the holder to confess judgment or realize on or dispose of collateral, or (iii) a waiver of the benefit of any law intended for the advantage or protection of an obligor.

(b) "Instrument" means a negotiable instrument.

(c) An order that meets all of the requirements of subsection (a), except paragraph (1), and otherwise falls within the definition of "check" in subsection (f) is a negotiable instrument and a check.

(d) A promise or order other than a check is not an instrument if, at the time it is issued or first comes into possession of a holder, it contains a conspicuous statement, however expressed, to the effect that the promise or order is not negotiable or is not an instrument governed by this Article.

(e) An instrument is a "note" if it is a promise and is a "draft" if it is an order. If an instrument falls within the definition of both "note" and "draft," a person entitled to enforce the instrument may treat it as either.

(f) "Check" means (i) a draft, other than a documentary draft, payable on demand and drawn on a bank or (ii) a cashier's check or teller's check. An instrument may be a check even though it is described on its face by another term, such as "money order."

(g) "Cashier's check" means a draft with respect to which the drawer and drawee are the same bank or branches of the same bank.

(h) "Teller's check" means a draft drawn by a bank (i) on another bank, or (ii) payable at or through a bank.

(i) "Traveler's check" means an instrument that (i) is payable on demand, (ii) is drawn on or payable at or through a bank, (iii) is designated by the term "traveler's check" or by a substantially similar term, and (iv) requires, as a condition to payment, a countersignature by a person whose specimen signature appears on the instrument.

(j) "Certificate of deposit" means an instrument containing an acknowledgment by a bank that a sum of money has been received by the bank and a promise by the bank to repay the sum of money. A certificate of deposit is a note of the bank.

§ 3–105.   Issue of Instrument.

(a) "Issue" means the first delivery of an instrument by the maker or drawer, whether to a holder or nonholder, for the purpose of giving rights on the instrument to any person.

(b) An unissued instrument, or an unissued incomplete instrument that is completed, is binding on the maker or drawer, but nonissuance is a defense. An instrument that is conditionally issued or is issued for a special purpose is binding on the maker or drawer, but failure of the condition or special purpose to be fulfilled is a defense.

(c) "Issuer" applies to issued and unissued instruments and means a maker or drawer of an instrument.

§ 3–106.   Unconditional Promise or Order.

(a) Except as provided in this section, for the purposes of Section 3–104(a), a promise or order is unconditional unless it states (i) an express condition to payment, (ii) that the promise or order is subject to or governed by another writing, or (iii) that rights or obligations with respect to the promise or order are stated in another writing. A reference to another writing does not of itself make the promise or order conditional.

(b) A promise or order is not made conditional (i) by a reference to another writing for a statement of rights with respect to collateral, prepayment, or acceleration, or (ii) because payment is limited to resort to a particular fund or source.

(c) If a promise or order requires, as a condition to payment, a countersignature by a person whose specimen signature appears on the promise or order, the condition does not make the promise or order conditional for the purposes of Section 3–104(a). If the person whose specimen signature appears on an instrument fails to countersign the instrument, the failure to countersign is a defense to the obligation of the issuer, but the failure does not prevent a transferee of the instrument from becoming a holder of the instrument.

(d) If a promise or order at the time it is issued or first comes into possession of a holder contains a statement, required by applicable statutory or administrative law, to the effect that the rights of a holder or transferee are subject to claims or defenses that the issuer could assert against the original payee, the promise or order is not thereby made conditional for the purposes of Section 3–104(a); but if the promise or order is an instrument, there cannot be a holder in due course of the instrument.

§ 3–107.   Instrument Payable in Foreign Money.

Unless the instrument otherwise provides, an instrument that states the amount payable in foreign money may be paid in the foreign money or in an equivalent amount in dollars calculated by using the current bank-offered spot rate at the place of payment for the purchase of dollars on the day on which the instrument is paid.

§ 3–108.   Payable on Demand or at Definite Time.

(a) A promise or order is "payable on demand" if it (i) states that it is payable on demand or at sight, or otherwise indicates that it is payable at the will of the holder, or (ii) does not state any time of payment.

(b) A promise or order is "payable at a definite time" if it is payable on elapse of a definite period of time after sight or acceptance or at a fixed date or dates or at a time or times readily ascertainable at the time the promise or order is issued, subject to rights of (i) prepayment, (ii) acceleration, (iii) extension at the option of the holder, or (iv) extension to a further definite time at the option of the maker or acceptor or automatically upon or after a specified act or event.

(c) If an instrument, payable at a fixed date, is also payable upon demand made before the fixed date, the instrument is payable on demand until the fixed date and, if demand for payment is not made before that date, becomes payable at a definite time on the fixed date.

§ 3–109.   Payable to Bearer or to Order.

(a) A promise or order is payable to bearer if it:

(1) states that it is payable to bearer or to the order of bearer or otherwise indicates that the person in possession of the promise or order is entitled to payment;

(2) does not state a payee; or

(3) states that it is payable to or to the order of cash or otherwise indicates that it is not payable to an identified person.

(b) A promise or order that is not payable to bearer is payable to order if it is payable (i) to the order of an identified person or (ii) to an identified person or order. A promise or order that is payable to order is payable to the identified person.

(c) An instrument payable to bearer may become payable to an identified person if it is specially indorsed pursuant to Section 3–205(a). An instrument payable to an identified person may become payable to bearer if it is indorsed in blank pursuant to Section 3–205(b).

§ 3–110.   Identification of Person to Whom Instrument Is Payable.

(a) The person to whom an instrument is initially payable is determined by the intent of the person, whether or not authorized, signing as, or in the name or behalf of, the issuer of the instrument. The instrument is payable to the person intended by the signer even if that person is identified in the instrument by a name or other identification that is not that of the intended person. If more than one person signs in the name or behalf of the issuer of an instrument and all the signers do not intend the same person as payee, the instrument is payable to any person intended by one or more of the signers.

(b) If the signature of the issuer of an instrument is made by automated means, such as a check-writing machine, the payee of the instrument is determined by the intent of the person who supplied the name or identification of the payee, whether or not authorized to do so.

(c) A person to whom an instrument is payable may be identified in any way, including by name, identifying number, office, or account number. For the purpose of determining the holder of an instrument, the following rules apply:

(1) If an instrument is payable to an account and the account is identified only by number, the instrument is payable to the person to whom the account is payable. If an instrument is payable to an account identified by number and by the name of a person, the instrument is payable to the named person, whether or not that person is the owner of the account identified by number.

(2) If an instrument is payable to:

(i) a trust, an estate, or a person described as trustee or representative of a trust or estate, the instrument is payable to the trustee, the representative, or a successor of either, whether or not the beneficiary or estate is also named;

(ii) a person described as agent or similar representative of a named or identified person, the instrument is payable to the represented person, the representative, or a successor of the representative;

(iii) a fund or organization that is not a legal entity, the instrument is payable to a representative of the members of the fund or organization; or

(iv) an office or to a person described as holding an office, the instrument is payable to the named person, the incumbent of the office, or a successor to the incumbent.

(d) If an instrument is payable to two or more persons alternatively, it is payable to any of them and may be negotiated, discharged, or enforced by any or all of them in possession of the instrument. If an instrument is payable to two or more persons not alternatively, it is payable to all of them and may be negotiated, discharged, or enforced only by all of them. If an instrument payable to two or more persons is ambiguous as to whether it is payable to the persons alternatively, the instrument is payable to the persons alternatively.

§ 3–111.   Place of Payment.

Except as otherwise provided for items in Article 4, an instrument is payable at the place of payment stated in the instrument. If no place of payment is stated, an instrument is payable at the address of the drawee or maker stated in the instrument. If no address is stated, the place of payment is the place of business of the drawee or maker. If a drawee or maker has more than one place of business, the place of payment is any place of business of the drawee or maker chosen by the person entitled to enforce the instrument. If the drawee or maker has no place of business, the place of payment is the residence of the drawee or maker.

§ 3–112.   Interest.

(a) Unless otherwise provided in the instrument, (i) an instrument is not payable with interest, and (ii) interest on an interest-bearing instrument is payable from the date of the instrument.

(b) Interest may be stated in an instrument as a fixed or variable amount of money or it may be expressed as a fixed or variable rate or rates. The amount or rate of interest may be stated or described in the instrument in any manner and may require reference to information not contained in the instrument. If an instrument provides for interest, but the amount of interest payable cannot be ascertained from the description, interest is payable at the judgment rate in effect at the place of payment of the instrument and at the time interest first accrues.

§ 3–113.   Date of Instrument.

(a) An instrument may be antedated or postdated. The date stated determines the time of payment if the instrument is payable at a fixed period after date. Except as provided in Section 4–401(c), an instrument payable on demand is not payable before the date of the instrument.

(b) If an instrument is undated, its date is the date of its issue or, in the case of an unissued instrument, the date it first comes into possession of a holder.

§ 3–114.   Contradictory Terms of Instrument.

If an instrument contains contradictory terms, typewritten terms prevail over printed terms, handwritten terms prevail over both, and words prevail over numbers.

§ 3–115.   Incomplete Instrument.

(a) "Incomplete instrument" means a signed writing, whether or not issued by the signer, the contents of which show at the time of signing that it is incomplete but that the signer intended it to be completed by the addition of words or numbers.

(b) Subject to subsection (c), if an incomplete instrument is an instrument under Section 3–104, it may be enforced according to its terms if it is not completed, or according to its terms as augmented by completion. If an incomplete instrument is not an instrument under Section 3–104, but, after completion, the requirements of Section 3–104 are met, the instrument may be enforced according to its terms as augmented by completion.

(c) If words or numbers are added to an incomplete instrument without authority of the signer, there is an alteration of the incomplete instrument under Section 3–407.

(d) The burden of establishing that words or numbers were added to an incomplete instrument without authority of the signer is on the person asserting the lack of authority.

§ 3–116.   Joint and Several Liability; Contribution.

(a) Except as otherwise provided in the instrument, two or more persons who have the same liability on an instrument as makers, drawers, acceptors, indorsers who indorse as joint payees, or anomalous indorsers are jointly and severally liable in the capacity in which they sign.

(b) Except as provided in Section 3–419(e) or by agreement of the affected parties, a party having joint and several liability who pays the instrument is entitled to receive from any party having the same joint and several liability contribution in accordance with applicable law.

(c) Discharge of one party having joint and several liability by a person entitled to enforce the instrument does not affect the right under subsection (b) of a party having the same joint and several liability to receive contribution from the party discharged.

§ 3–117.   Other Agreements Affecting Instrument.

Subject to applicable law regarding exclusion of proof of contemporaneous or previous agreements, the obligation of a party to an instrument to pay the instrument may be modified, supplemented, or nullified by a separate agreement of the obligor and a person entitled to enforce the instrument, if the instrument is issued or the obligation is incurred in reliance on the agreement or as part of the same transaction giving rise to the agreement. To the extent an obligation is modified, supplemented, or nullified by an agreement under this section, the agreement is a defense to the obligation.

§ 3–118.   Statute of Limitations.

(a) Except as provided in subsection (e), an action to enforce the obligation of a party to pay a note payable at a definite time must be commenced within six years after the due date or dates stated in the note or, if a due date is accelerated, within six years after the accelerated due date.

(b) Except as provided in subsection (d) or (e), if demand for payment is made to the maker of a note payable on demand, an action to enforce the obligation of a party to pay the note must be commenced within six years after the demand. If no demand for payment is made to the maker, an action to enforce the note is barred if neither principal nor interest on the note has been paid for a continuous period of 10 years.

(c) Except as provided in subsection (d), an action to enforce the obligation of a party to an unaccepted draft to pay the draft must be commenced within three years after dishonor of the draft or 10 years after the date of the draft, whichever period expires first.

(d) An action to enforce the obligation of the acceptor of a certified check or the issuer of a teller's check, cashier's check, or traveler's check must be commenced within three years after demand for payment is made to the acceptor or issuer, as the case may be.

(e) An action to enforce the obligation of a party to a certificate of deposit to pay the instrument must be commenced within six years after demand for payment is made to the maker, but if the instrument states a due date and the maker is not required to pay before that date, the six-year period begins when a demand for payment is in effect and the due date has passed.

(f) An action to enforce the obligation of a party to pay an accepted draft, other than a certified check, must be commenced (i) within six years after the due date or dates stated in the draft or acceptance if the obligation of the acceptor is payable at a definite time, or (ii) within six years after the date of the acceptance if the obligation of the acceptor is payable on demand.

(g) Unless governed by other law regarding claims for indemnity or contribution, an action (i) for conversion of an instrument, for money had and received, or like action based on conversion, (ii) for breach of warranty, or (iii) to enforce an obligation, duty, or right arising under this Article and not governed by this section must be commenced within three years after the [cause of action] accrues.

§ 3–119.   Notice of Right to Defend Action.

In an action for breach of an obligation for which a third person is answerable over pursuant to this Article or Article 4, the defendant may give the third person written notice of the litigation, and the person notified may then give similar notice to any other person who is answerable over. If the notice states (i) that the person notified may come in and defend and (ii) that failure to do so will bind the person notified in an action later brought by the person giving the notice as to any determination of fact common to the two litigations, the person notified is so bound unless after seasonable receipt of the notice the person notified does come in and defend.

PART 2   Negotiation, Transfer, and Indorsement

§ 3–201.   Negotiation.

(a) "Negotiation" means a transfer of possession, whether voluntary or involuntary, of an instrument by a person other than the issuer to a person who thereby becomes its holder.

(b) Except for negotiation by a remitter, if an instrument is payable to an identified person, negotiation requires transfer of possession of the instrument and its indorsement by the holder. If an instrument is payable to bearer, it may be negotiated by transfer of possession alone.

§ 3–202.   Negotiation Subject to Rescission.

(a) Negotiation is effective even if obtained (i) from an infant, a corporation exceeding its powers, or a person without capacity, (ii) by fraud, duress, or mistake, or (iii) in breach of duty or as part of an illegal transaction.

(b) To the extent permitted by other law, negotiation may be rescinded or may be subject to other remedies, but those reme-

dies may not be asserted against a subsequent holder in due course or a person paying the instrument in good faith and without knowledge of facts that are a basis for rescission or other remedy.

§ 3–203.   Transfer of Instrument; Rights Acquired by Transfer.

(a) An instrument is transferred when it is delivered by a person other than its issuer for the purpose of giving to the person receiving delivery the right to enforce the instrument.

(b) Transfer of an instrument, whether or not the transfer is a negotiation, vests in the transferee any right of the transferor to enforce the instrument, including any right as a holder in due course, but the transferee cannot acquire rights of a holder in due course by a transfer, directly or indirectly, from a holder in due course if the transferee engaged in fraud or illegality affecting the instrument.

(c) Unless otherwise agreed, if an instrument is transferred for value and the transferee does not become a holder because of lack of indorsement by the transferor, the transferee has a specifically enforceable right to the unqualified indorsement of the transferor, but negotiation of the instrument does not occur until the indorsement is made.

(d) If a transferor purports to transfer less than the entire instrument, negotiation of the instrument does not occur. The transferee obtains no rights under this Article and has only the rights of a partial assignee.

§ 3–204.   Indorsement.

(a) "Indorsement" means a signature, other than that of a signer as maker, drawer, or acceptor, that alone or accompanied by other words is made on an instrument for the purpose of (i) negotiating the instrument, (ii) restricting payment of the instrument, or (iii) incurring indorser's liability on the instrument, but regardless of the intent of the signer, a signature and its accompanying words is an indorsement unless the accompanying words, terms of the instrument, place of the signature, or other circumstances unambiguously indicate that the signature was made for a purpose other than indorsement. For the purpose of determining whether a signature is made on an instrument, a paper affixed to the instrument is a part of the instrument.

(b) "Indorser" means a person who makes an indorsement.

(c) For the purpose of determining whether the transferee of an instrument is a holder, an indorsement that transfers a security interest in the instrument is effective as an unqualified indorsement of the instrument.

(d) If an instrument is payable to a holder under a name that is not the name of the holder, indorsement may be made by the holder in the name stated in the instrument or in the holder's name or both, but signature in both names may be required by a person paying or taking the instrument for value or collection.

§ 3–205.   Special Indorsement; Blank Indorsement; Anomalous Indorsement.

(a) If an indorsement is made by the holder of an instrument, whether payable to an identified person or payable to bearer, and the indorsement identifies a person to whom it makes the instrument payable, it is a "special indorsement." When specially indorsed, an instrument becomes payable to the identified person and may be negotiated only by the indorsement of that person. The principles stated in Section 3–110 apply to special indorsements.

(b) If an indorsement is made by the holder of an instrument and it is not a special indorsement, it is a "blank indorsement." When indorsed in blank, an instrument becomes payable to bearer and may be negotiated by transfer of possession alone until specially indorsed.

(c) The holder may convert a blank indorsement that consists only of a signature into a special indorsement by writing, above the signature of the indorser, words identifying the person to whom the instrument is made payable.

(d) "Anomalous indorsement" means an indorsement made by a person who is not the holder of the instrument. An anomalous indorsement does not affect the manner in which the instrument may be negotiated.

§ 3–206.   Restrictive Indorsement.

(a) An indorsement limiting payment to a particular person or otherwise prohibiting further transfer or negotiation of the instrument is not effective to prevent further transfer or negotiation of the instrument.

(b) An indorsement stating a condition to the right of the indorsee to receive payment does not affect the right of the indorsee to enforce the instrument. A person paying the instrument or taking it for value or collection may disregard the condition, and the rights and liabilities of that person are not affected by whether the condition has been fulfilled.

(c) If an instrument bears an indorsement (i) described in Section 4–201(b), or (ii) in blank or to a particular bank using the words "for deposit," "for collection," or other words indicating a purpose of having the instrument collected by a bank for the indorser or for a particular account, the following rules apply:

(1) A person, other than a bank, who purchases the instrument when so indorsed converts the instrument unless the amount paid for the instrument is received by the indorser or applied consistently with the indorsement.

(2) A depositary bank that purchases the instrument or takes it for collection when so indorsed converts the instrument unless the amount paid by the bank with respect to the instrument is received by the indorser or applied consistently with the indorsement.

(3) A payor bank that is also the depositary bank or that takes the instrument for immediate payment over the counter from a person other than a collecting bank converts the instrument unless the proceeds of the instrument are received by the indorser or applied consistently with the indorsement.

(4) Except as otherwise provided in paragraph (3), a payor bank or intermediary bank may disregard the indorsement and is not liable if the proceeds of the instrument are not received by the indorser or applied consistently with the indorsement.

(d) Except for an indorsement covered by subsection (c), if an instrument bears an indorsement using words to the effect that payment is to be made to the indorsee as agent, trustee, or other fiduciary for the benefit of the indorser or another person, the following rules apply:

(1) Unless there is notice of breach of fiduciary duty as provided in Section 3–307, a person who purchases the instrument from the indorsee or takes the instrument from the indorsee for collection or payment may pay the proceeds of payment or the value given for the instrument to the indorsee without regard to whether the indorsee violates a fiduciary duty to the indorser.

(2) A subsequent transferee of the instrument or person who pays the instrument is neither given notice nor otherwise affected by the restriction in the indorsement unless the transferee or payor knows that the fiduciary dealt with the instrument or its proceeds in breach of fiduciary duty.

(e) The presence on an instrument of an indorsement to which this section applies does not prevent a purchaser of the instrument from becoming a holder in due course of the instrument unless the purchaser is a converter under subsection (c) or has notice or knowledge of breach of fiduciary duty as stated in subsection (d).

(f) In an action to enforce the obligation of a party to pay the instrument, the obligor has a defense if payment would violate an indorsement to which this section applies and the payment is not permitted by this section.

§ 3–207.   Reacquisition.

Reacquisition of an instrument occurs if it is transferred to a former holder, by negotiation or otherwise. A former holder who reacquires the instrument may cancel indorsements made after the reacquirer first became a holder of the instrument. If the cancellation causes the instrument to be payable to the reacquirer or to bearer, the reacquirer may negotiate the instrument. An indorser whose indorsement is canceled is discharged, and the discharge is effective against any subsequent holder.

PART 3   Enforcement of Instruments

§ 3–301.   Person Entitled to Enforce Instrument.

"Person entitled to enforce" an instrument means (i) the holder of the instrument, (ii) a nonholder in possession of the instrument who has the rights of a holder, or (iii) a person not in possession of the instrument who is entitled to enforce the instrument pursuant to Section 3–309 or 3–418(d). A person may be a person entitled to enforce the instrument even though the person is not the owner of the instrument or is in wrongful possession of the instrument.

§ 3–302.   Holder in Due Course.

(a) Subject to subsection (c) and Section 3–106(d), "holder in due course" means the holder of an instrument if:

(1) the instrument when issued or negotiated to the holder does not bear such apparent evidence of forgery or alteration or is not otherwise so irregular or incomplete as to call into question its authenticity; and

(2) the holder took the instrument (i) for value, (ii) in good faith, (iii) without notice that the instrument is overdue or has been dishonored or that there is an uncured default with respect to payment of another instrument issued as part of the same series, (iv) without notice that the instrument contains an unauthorized signature or has been altered, (v) without notice of any claim to the instrument described in Section 3–306, and (vi) without notice that any party has a defense or claim in recoupment described in Section 3–305(a).

(b) Notice of discharge of a party, other than discharge in an insolvency proceeding, is not notice of a defense under subsection (a), but discharge is effective against a person who became a holder in due course with notice of the discharge. Public filing or recording of a document does not of itself constitute notice of a defense, claim in recoupment, or claim to the instrument.

(c) Except to the extent a transferor or predecessor in interest has rights as a holder in due course, a person does not acquire rights of a holder in due course of an instrument taken (i) by legal process or by purchase in an execution, bankruptcy, or creditor's sale or similar proceeding, (ii) by purchase as part of a bulk transaction not in ordinary course of business of the transferor, or (iii) as the successor in interest to an estate or other organization.

(d) If, under Section 3–303(a)(1), the promise of performance that is the consideration for an instrument has been partially performed, the holder may assert rights as a holder in due course of the instrument only to the fraction of the amount payable under the instrument equal to the value of the partial performance divided by the value of the promised performance.

(e) If (i) the person entitled to enforce an instrument has only a security interest in the instrument and (ii) the person obliged to pay the instrument has a defense, claim in recoupment, or claim to the instrument that may be asserted against the person who granted the security interest, the person entitled to enforce the instrument may assert rights as a holder in due course only to an amount payable under the instrument which, at the time of enforcement of the instrument, does not exceed the amount of the unpaid obligation secured.

(f) To be effective, notice must be received at a time and in a manner that gives a reasonable opportunity to act on it.

(g) This section is subject to any law limiting status as a holder in due course in particular classes of transactions.

§ 3–303.   Value and Consideration.

(a) An instrument is issued or transferred for value if:

(1) the instrument is issued or transferred for a promise of performance, to the extent the promise has been performed;

(2) the transferee acquires a security interest or other lien in the instrument other than a lien obtained by judicial proceeding;

(3) the instrument is issued or transferred as payment of, or as security for, an antecedent claim against any person, whether or not the claim is due;

(4) the instrument is issued or transferred in exchange for a negotiable instrument; or

(5) the instrument is issued or transferred in exchange for the incurring of an irrevocable obligation to a third party by the person taking the instrument.

(b) "Consideration" means any consideration sufficient to support a simple contract. The drawer or maker of an instrument has a defense if the instrument is issued without consideration. If an instrument is issued for a promise of performance, the issuer has a defense to the extent performance of the promise is due and the promise has not been performed. If an instrument is issued for value as stated in subsection (a), the instrument is also issued for consideration.

§ 3–304.   Overdue Instrument.

(a) An instrument payable on demand becomes overdue at the earliest of the following times:

(1) on the day after the day demand for payment is duly made;

(2) if the instrument is a check, 90 days after its date; or

(3) if the instrument is not a check, when the instrument has been outstanding for a period of time after its date which is unreasonably long under the circumstances of the particular case in light of the nature of the instrument and usage of the trade.

(b) With respect to an instrument payable at a definite time the following rules apply:

(1) If the principal is payable in installments and a due date has not been accelerated, the instrument becomes overdue upon default under the instrument for nonpayment of an installment, and the instrument remains overdue until the default is cured.

(2) If the principal is not payable in installments and the due date has not been accelerated, the instrument becomes overdue on the day after the due date.

(3) If a due date with respect to principal has been accelerated, the instrument becomes overdue on the day after the accelerated due date.

(c) Unless the due date of principal has been accelerated, an instrument does not become overdue if there is default in payment of interest but no default in payment of principal.

§ 3–305. Defenses and Claims in Recoupment.

(a) Except as stated in subsection (b), the right to enforce the obligation of a party to pay an instrument is subject to the following:

(1) a defense of the obligor based on (i) infancy of the obligor to the extent it is a defense to a simple contract, (ii) duress, lack of legal capacity, or illegality of the transaction which, under other law, nullifies the obligation of the obligor, (iii) fraud that induced the obligor to sign the instrument with neither knowledge nor reasonable opportunity to learn of its character or its essential terms, or (iv) discharge of the obligor in insolvency proceedings;

(2) a defense of the obligor stated in another section of this Article or a defense of the obligor that would be available if the person entitled to enforce the instrument were enforcing a right to payment under a simple contract; and

(3) a claim in recoupment of the obligor against the original payee of the instrument if the claim arose from the transaction that gave rise to the instrument; but the claim of the obligor may be asserted against a transferee of the instrument only to reduce the amount owing on the instrument at the time the action is brought.

(b) The right of a holder in due course to enforce the obligation of a party to pay the instrument is subject to defenses of the obligor stated in subsection (a)(1), but is not subject to defenses of the obligor stated in subsection (a)(2) or claims in recoupment stated in subsection (a)(3) against a person other than the holder.

(c) Except as stated in subsection (d), in an action to enforce the obligation of a party to pay the instrument, the obligor may not assert against the person entitled to enforce the instrument a defense, claim in recoupment, or claim to the instrument (Section 3–306) of another person, but the other person's claim to the instrument may be asserted by the obligor if the other person is joined in the action and personally asserts the claim against the person entitled to enforce the instrument. An obligor is not obliged to pay the instrument if the person seeking enforcement of the instrument does not have rights of a holder in due course and the obligor proves that the instrument is a lost or stolen instrument.

(d) In an action to enforce the obligation of an accommodation party to pay an instrument, the accommodation party may assert against the person entitled to enforce the instrument any defense or claim in recoupment under subsection (a) that the accommodated party could assert against the person entitled to enforce the instrument, except the defenses of discharge in insolvency proceedings, infancy, and lack of legal capacity.

§ 3–306. Claims to an Instrument.

A person taking an instrument, other than a person having rights of a holder in due course, is subject to a claim of a property or possessory right in the instrument or its proceeds, including a claim to rescind a negotiation and to recover the instrument or its proceeds. A person having rights of a holder in due course takes free of the claim to the instrument.

§ 3–307. Notice of Breach of Fiduciary Duty.

(a) In this section:

(1) "Fiduciary" means an agent, trustee, partner, corporate officer or director, or other representative owing a fiduciary duty with respect to an instrument.

(2) "Represented person" means the principal, beneficiary, partnership, corporation, or other person to whom the duty stated in paragraph (1) is owed.

(b) If (i) an instrument is taken from a fiduciary for payment or collection or for value, (ii) the taker has knowledge of the fiduciary status of the fiduciary, and (iii) the represented person makes a claim to the instrument or its proceeds on the basis that the transaction of the fiduciary is a breach of fiduciary duty, the following rules apply:

(1) Notice of breach of fiduciary duty by the fiduciary is notice of the claim of the represented person.

(2) In the case of an instrument payable to the represented person or the fiduciary as such, the taker has notice of the breach of fiduciary duty if the instrument is (i) taken in payment of or as security for a debt known by the taker to be the personal debt of the fiduciary, (ii) taken in a transaction known by the taker to be for the personal benefit of the fiduciary, or (iii) deposited to an account other than an account of the fiduciary, as such, or an account of the represented person.

(3) If an instrument is issued by the represented person or the fiduciary as such, and made payable to the fiduciary personally, the taker does not have notice of the breach of fiduciary duty unless the taker knows of the breach of fiduciary duty.

(4) If an instrument is issued by the represented person or the fiduciary as such, to the taker as payee, the taker has notice of the breach of fiduciary duty if the instrument is (i) taken in payment of or as security for a debt known by the taker to be the personal debt of the fiduciary, (ii) taken in a transaction known by the taker to be for the personal benefit of the fiduciary, or (iii) deposited to an account other than an account of the fiduciary, as such, or an account of the represented person.

§ 3–308. Proof of Signatures and Status as Holder in Due Course.

(a) In an action with respect to an instrument, the authenticity of, and authority to make, each signature on the instrument is admitted unless specifically denied in the pleadings. If the validity of a signature is denied in the pleadings, the burden of establishing validity is on the person claiming validity, but the signature is presumed to be authentic and authorized unless the action is to enforce the liability of the purported signer and the signer is dead or incompetent at the time of trial of the issue of validity of the signature. If an action to enforce the instrument is brought against a person as the undisclosed principal of a person who signed the instrument as a party to the instrument, the plaintiff has the burden of establishing that the defendant is liable on the instrument as a represented person under Section 3–402(a).

(b) If the validity of signatures is admitted or proved and there is compliance with subsection (a), a plaintiff producing the instrument is entitled to payment if the plaintiff proves entitlement to enforce the instrument under Section 3–301, unless the defendant proves a defense or claim in recoupment. If a defense or claim in recoupment is proved, the right to payment of the plaintiff is subject to the defense or claim, except to the extent the plaintiff proves that the plaintiff has rights of a holder in due course which are not subject to the defense or claim.

§ 3–309. Enforcement of Lost, Destroyed, or Stolen Instrument.

(a) A person not in possession of an instrument is entitled to enforce the instrument if (i) the person was in possession of the instrument and entitled to enforce it when loss of possession occurred, (ii) the loss of possession was not the result of a transfer by the person or a lawful seizure, and (iii) the person cannot reasonably obtain possession of the instrument because the instrument was destroyed, its whereabouts cannot be determined, or it is in the wrongful possession of an unknown person or a person that cannot be found or is not amenable to service of process.

(b) A person seeking enforcement of an instrument under subsection (a) must prove the terms of the instrument and the person's right to enforce the instrument. If that proof is made, Section 3–308 applies to the case as if the person seeking enforcement had produced the instrument. The court may not enter judgment in favor of the person seeking enforcement unless it finds that the person required to pay the instrument is adequately protected against loss that might occur by reason of a claim by another person to enforce the instrument. Adequate protection may be provided by any reasonable means.

§ 3–310. Effect of Instrument on Obligation for Which Taken.

(a) Unless otherwise agreed, if a certified check, cashier's check, or teller's check is taken for an obligation, the obligation is discharged to the same extent discharge would result if an amount of money equal to the amount of the instrument were taken in payment of the obligation. Discharge of the obligation does not affect any liability that the obligor may have as an indorser of the instrument.

(b) Unless otherwise agreed and except as provided in subsection (a), if a note or an uncertified check is taken for an obligation, the obligation is suspended to the same extent the obligation would be discharged if an amount of money equal to the amount of the instrument were taken, and the following rules apply:

(1) In the case of an uncertified check, suspension of the obligation continues until dishonor of the check or until it is paid or certified. Payment or certification of the check results in discharge of the obligation to the extent of the amount of the check.

(2) In the case of a note, suspension of the obligation continues until dishonor of the note or until it is paid. Payment of the note results in discharge of the obligation to the extent of the payment.

(3) Except as provided in paragraph (4), if the check or note is dishonored and the obligee of the obligation for which the instrument was taken is the person entitled to enforce the instrument, the obligee may enforce either the instrument or the obligation. In the case of an instrument of a third person which is negotiated to the obligee by the obligor, discharge of the obligor on the instrument also discharges the obligation.

(4) If the person entitled to enforce the instrument taken for an obligation is a person other than the obligee, the obligee may not enforce the obligation to the extent the obligation is suspended. If the obligee is the person entitled to enforce the instrument but no longer has possession of it because it was lost, stolen, or destroyed, the obligation may not be enforced to the extent of the amount payable on the instrument, and to that extent the obligee's rights against the obligor are limited to enforcement of the instrument.

(c) If an instrument other than one described in subsection (a) or (b) is taken for an obligation, the effect is (i) that stated in subsection (a) if the instrument is one on which a bank is liable as maker or acceptor, or (ii) that stated in subsection (b) in any other case.

§ 3–311. Accord and Satisfaction by Use of Instrument.

(a) If a person against whom a claim is asserted proves that (i) that person in good faith tendered an instrument to the claimant as full satisfaction of the claim, (ii) the amount of the claim was unliquidated or subject to a bona fide dispute, and (iii) the claimant obtained payment of the instrument, the following subsections apply.

(b) Unless subsection (c) applies, the claim is discharged if the person against whom the claim is asserted proves that the instrument or an accompanying written communication contained a conspicuous statement to the effect that the instrument was tendered as full satisfaction of the claim.

(c) Subject to subsection (d), a claim is not discharged under subsection (b) if either of the following applies:

(1) The claimant, if an organization, proves that (i) within a reasonable time before the tender, the claimant sent a conspicuous statement to the person against whom the claim is asserted that communications concerning disputed debts, including an instrument tendered as full satisfaction of a debt, are to be sent to a designated person, office, or place, and (ii) the instrument or accompanying communication was not received by that designated person, office, or place.

(2) The claimant, whether or not an organization, proves that within 90 days after payment of the instrument, the claimant tendered repayment of the amount of the instrument to the person against whom the claim is asserted. This paragraph does not apply if the claimant is an organization that sent a statement complying with paragraph (1)(i).

(d) A claim is discharged if the person against whom the claim is asserted proves that within a reasonable time before collection of the instrument was initiated, the claimant, or an agent of the claimant having direct responsibility with respect to the disputed obligation, knew that the instrument was tendered in full satisfaction of the claim.

§ 3–312.   Lost, Destroyed, or Stolen Cashier's Check, Teller's Check, or Certified Check.*

(a) In this section:

(1) "Check" means a cashier's check, teller's check, or certified check.

(2) "Claimant" means a person who claims the right to receive the amount of a cashier's check, teller's check, or certified check that was lost, destroyed, or stolen.

(3) "Declaration of loss" means a written statement, made under penalty of perjury, to the effect that (i) the declarer lost possession of a check, (ii) the declarer is the drawer or payee of the check, in the case of a certified check, or the remitter or payee of the check, in the case of a cashier's check or teller's check, (iii) the loss of possession was not the result of a transfer by the declarer or a lawful seizure, and (iv) the declarer cannot reasonably obtain possession of the check because the check was destroyed, its whereabouts cannot be determined, or it is in the wrongful possession of an unknown person or a person that cannot be found or is not amenable to service of process.

(4) "Obligated bank" means the issuer of a cashier's check or teller's check or the acceptor of a certified check.

(b) A claimant may assert a claim to the amount of a check by a communication to the obligated bank describing the check with reasonable certainty and requesting payment of the amount of the check, if (i) the claimant is the drawer or payee of a certified check or the remitter or payee of a cashier's check or teller's check, (ii) the communication contains or is accompanied by a declaration of loss of the claimant with respect to the check, (iii) the communication is received at a time and in a manner affording the bank a reasonable time to act on it before the check is paid, and (iv) the claimant provides reasonable identification if requested by the obligated bank. Delivery of a declaration of loss is a warranty of the truth of the statements made in the declaration. If a claim is asserted in compliance with this subsection, the following rules apply:

(1) The claim becomes enforceable at the later of (i) the time the claim is asserted, or (ii) the 90th day following the date of the check, in the case of a cashier's check or teller's check, or the 90th day following the date of the acceptance, in the case of a certified check.

(2) Until the claim becomes enforceable, it has no legal effect and the obligated bank may pay the check or, in the case of a teller's check, may permit the drawee to pay the check. Payment to a person entitled to enforce the check discharges all liability of the obligated bank with respect to the check.

(3) If the claim becomes enforceable before the check is presented for payment, the obligated bank is not obliged to pay the check.

(4) When the claim becomes enforceable, the obligated bank becomes obliged to pay the amount of the check to the claimant if payment of the check has not been made to a person entitled to enforce the check. Subject to Section 4–302(a)(1), payment to the claimant discharges all liability of the obligated bank with respect to the check.

(c) If the obligated bank pays the amount of a check to a claimant under subsection (b)(4) and the check is presented for payment by a person having rights of a holder in due course, the claimant is obliged to (i) refund the payment to the obligated bank if the check is paid, or (ii) pay the amount of the check to the person having rights of a holder in due course if the check is dishonored.

(d) If a claimant has the right to assert a claim under subsection (b) and is also a person entitled to enforce a cashier's check, teller's check, or certified check which is lost, destroyed, or stolen, the claimant may assert rights with respect to the check either under this section or Section 3–309.

Added in 1991.

PART 4   Liability of Parties

§ 3–401.   Signature.

(a) A person is not liable on an instrument unless (i) the person signed the instrument, or (ii) the person is represented by an agent or representative who signed the instrument and the signature is binding on the represented person under Section 3–402.

(b) A signature may be made (i) manually or by means of a device or machine, and (ii) by the use of any name, including a trade or assumed name, or by a word, mark, or symbol executed or adopted by a person with present intention to authenticate a writing.

§ 3–402.   Signature by Representative.

(a) If a person acting, or purporting to act, as a representative signs an instrument by signing either the name of the represented person or the name of the signer, the represented person is bound by the signature to the same extent the represented person would be bound if the signature were on a simple contract. If the represented person is bound, the signature of the representative is the "authorized signature of the represented person" and the represented person is liable on the instrument, whether or not identified in the instrument.

(b) If a representative signs the name of the representative to an instrument and the signature is an authorized signature of the represented person, the following rules apply:

(1) If the form of the signature shows unambiguously that the signature is made on behalf of the represented person who is identified in the instrument, the representative is not liable on the instrument.

(2) Subject to subsection (c), if (i) the form of the signature does not show unambiguously that the signature is made in a representative capacity or (ii) the represented person is not identified in the instrument, the representative is liable on the instrument to a holder in due course that took the instrument without notice that the representative was not intended to be liable on the instrument. With respect to any other person, the representative is liable on the instrument unless the representative proves that the original parties did not intend the representative to be liable on the instrument.

(c) If a representative signs the name of the representative as drawer of a check without indication of the representative status and the check is payable from an account of the represented person who is identified on the check, the signer is not liable on the check if the signature is an authorized signature of the represented person.

§ 3–403.   Unauthorized Signature.

(a) Unless otherwise provided in this Article or Article 4, an unauthorized signature is ineffective except as the signature of the unauthorized signer in favor of a person who in good faith pays the instrument or takes it for value. An unauthorized signature may be ratified for all purposes of this Article.

(b) If the signature of more than one person is required to constitute the authorized signature of an organization, the signature of the organization is unauthorized if one of the required signatures is lacking.

(c) The civil or criminal liability of a person who makes an unauthorized signature is not affected by any provision of this Article which makes the unauthorized signature effective for the purposes of this Article.

§ 3–404.   Impostors; Fictitious Payees.

(a) If an impostor, by use of the mails or otherwise, induces the issuer of an instrument to issue the instrument to the impostor, or to a person acting in concert with the impostor, by impersonating the payee of the instrument or a person authorized to act for the payee, an indorsement of the instrument by any person in the name of the payee is effective as the indorsement of the payee in favor of a person who, in good faith, pays the instrument or takes it for value or for collection.

(b) If (i) a person whose intent determines to whom an instrument is payable (Section 3–110(a) or (b)) does not intend the person identified as payee to have any interest in the instrument, or (ii) the person identified as payee of an instrument is a fictitious person, the following rules apply until the instrument is negotiated by special indorsement:

(1) Any person in possession of the instrument is its holder.

(2) An indorsement by any person in the name of the payee stated in the instrument is effective as the indorsement of the payee in favor of a person who, in good faith, pays the instrument or takes it for value or for collection.

(c) Under subsection (a) or (b), an indorsement is made in the name of a payee if (i) it is made in a name substantially similar to that of the payee or (ii) the instrument, whether or not indorsed, is deposited in a depositary bank to an account in a name substantially similar to that of the payee.

(d) With respect to an instrument to which subsection (a) or (b) applies, if a person paying the instrument or taking it for value or for collection fails to exercise ordinary care in paying or taking the instrument and that failure substantially contributes to loss resulting from payment of the instrument, the person bearing the loss may recover from the person failing to exercise ordinary care to the extent the failure to exercise ordinary care contributed to the loss.

§ 3–405.   Employer's Responsibility for Fraudulent Indorsement by Employee.

(a) In this section:

(1) "Employee" includes an independent contractor and employee of an independent contractor retained by the employer.

(2) "Fraudulent indorsement" means (i) in the case of an instrument payable to the employer, a forged indorsement purporting to be that of the employer, or (ii) in the case of an instrument with respect to which the employer is the issuer, a forged indorsement purporting to be that of the person identified as payee.

(3) "Responsibility" with respect to instruments means authority (i) to sign or indorse instruments on behalf of the employer, (ii) to process instruments received by the employer for bookkeeping purposes, for deposit to an account, or for other disposition, (iii) to prepare or process instruments for issue in the name of the employer, (iv) to supply information determining the names or addresses of payees of instruments to be issued in the name of the employer, (v) to control the disposition of

instruments to be issued in the name of the employer, or (vi) to act otherwise with respect to instruments in a responsible capacity. "Responsibility" does not include authority that merely allows an employee to have access to instruments or blank or incomplete instrument forms that are being stored or transported or are part of incoming or outgoing mail, or similar access.

(b) For the purpose of determining the rights and liabilities of a person who, in good faith, pays an instrument or takes it for value or for collection, if an employer entrusted an employee with responsibility with respect to the instrument and the employee or a person acting in concert with the employee makes a fraudulent indorsement of the instrument, the indorsement is effective as the indorsement of the person to whom the instrument is payable if it is made in the name of that person. If the person paying the instrument or taking it for value or for collection fails to exercise ordinary care in paying or taking the instrument and that failure substantially contributes to loss resulting from the fraud, the person bearing the loss may recover from the person failing to exercise ordinary care to the extent the failure to exercise ordinary care contributed to the loss.

(c) Under subsection (b), an indorsement is made in the name of the person to whom an instrument is payable if (i) it is made in a name substantially similar to the name of that person or (ii) the instrument, whether or not indorsed, is deposited in a depositary bank to an account in a name substantially similar to the name of that person.

§ 3–406. Negligence Contributing to Forged Signature or Alteration of Instrument.

(a) A person whose failure to exercise ordinary care substantially contributes to an alteration of an instrument or to the making of a forged signature on an instrument is precluded from asserting the alteration or the forgery against a person who, in good faith, pays the instrument or takes it for value or for collection.

(b) Under subsection (a), if the person asserting the preclusion fails to exercise ordinary care in paying or taking the instrument and that failure substantially contributes to loss, the loss is allocated between the person precluded and the person asserting the preclusion according to the extent to which the failure of each to exercise ordinary care contributed to the loss.

(c) Under subsection (a), the burden of proving failure to exercise ordinary care is on the person asserting the preclusion. Under subsection (b), the burden of proving failure to exercise ordinary care is on the person precluded.

§ 3–407. Alteration.

(a) "Alteration" means (i) an unauthorized change in an instrument that purports to modify in any respect the obligation of a party, or (ii) an unauthorized addition of words or numbers or other change to an incomplete instrument relating to the obligation of a party.

(b) Except as provided in subsection (c), an alteration fraudulently made discharges a party whose obligation is affected by the alteration unless that party assents or is precluded from asserting the alteration. No other alteration discharges a party, and the instrument may be enforced according to its original terms.

(c) A payor bank or drawee paying a fraudulently altered instrument or a person taking it for value, in good faith and without notice of the alteration, may enforce rights with respect to the instrument (i) according to its original terms, or (ii) in the case of an incomplete instrument altered by unauthorized completion, according to its terms as completed.

§ 3–408. Drawee Not Liable on Unaccepted Draft.

A check or other draft does not of itself operate as an assignment of funds in the hands of the drawee available for its payment, and the drawee is not liable on the instrument until the drawee accepts it.

§ 3–409. Acceptance of Draft; Certified Check.

(a) "Acceptance" means the drawee's signed agreement to pay a draft as presented. It must be written on the draft and may consist of the drawee's signature alone. Acceptance may be made at any time and becomes effective when notification pursuant to instructions is given or the accepted draft is delivered for the purpose of giving rights on the acceptance to any person.

(b) A draft may be accepted although it has not been signed by the drawer, is otherwise incomplete, is overdue, or has been dishonored.

(c) If a draft is payable at a fixed period after sight and the acceptor fails to date the acceptance, the holder may complete the acceptance by supplying a date in good faith.

(d) "Certified check" means a check accepted by the bank on which it is drawn. Acceptance may be made as stated in subsection (a) or by a writing on the check which indicates that the check is certified. The drawee of a check has no obligation to certify the check, and refusal to certify is not dishonor of the check.

§ 3–410. Acceptance Varying Draft.

(a) If the terms of a drawee's acceptance vary from the terms of the draft as presented, the holder may refuse the acceptance and treat the draft as dishonored. In that case, the drawee may cancel the acceptance.

(b) The terms of a draft are not varied by an acceptance to pay at a particular bank or place in the United States, unless the acceptance states that the draft is to be paid only at that bank or place.

(c) If the holder assents to an acceptance varying the terms of a draft, the obligation of each drawer and indorser that does not expressly assent to the acceptance is discharged.

§ 3–411.   Refusal to Pay Cashier's Checks, Teller's Checks, and Certified Checks.

(a) In this section, "obligated bank" means the acceptor of a certified check or the issuer of a cashier's check or teller's check bought from the issuer.

(b) If the obligated bank wrongfully (i) refuses to pay a cashier's check or certified check, (ii) stops payment of a teller's check, or (iii) refuses to pay a dishonored teller's check, the person asserting the right to enforce the check is entitled to compensation for expenses and loss of interest resulting from the nonpayment and may recover consequential damages if the obligated bank refuses to pay after receiving notice of particular circumstances giving rise to the damages.

(c) Expenses or consequential damages under subsection (b) are not recoverable if the refusal of the obligated bank to pay occurs because (i) the bank suspends payments, (ii) the obligated bank asserts a claim or defense of the bank that it has reasonable grounds to believe is available against the person entitled to enforce the instrument, (iii) the obligated bank has a reasonable doubt whether the person demanding payment is the person entitled to enforce the instrument, or (iv) payment is prohibited by law.

§ 3–412.   Obligation of Issuer of Note or Cashier's Check.

The issuer of a note or cashier's check or other draft drawn on the drawer is obliged to pay the instrument (i) according to its terms at the time it was issued or, if not issued, at the time it first came into possession of a holder, or (ii) if the issuer signed an incomplete instrument, according to its terms when completed, to the extent stated in Sections 3–115 and 3–407. The obligation is owed to a person entitled to enforce the instrument or to an indorser who paid the instrument under Section 3–415.

§ 3–413.   Obligation of Acceptor.

(a) The acceptor of a draft is obliged to pay the draft (i) according to its terms at the time it was accepted, even though the acceptance states that the draft is payable "as originally drawn" or equivalent terms, (ii) if the acceptance varies the terms of the draft, according to the terms of the draft as varied, or (iii) if the acceptance is of a draft that is an incomplete instrument, according to its terms when completed, to the extent stated in Sections 3–115 and 3–407. The obligation is owed to a person entitled to enforce the draft or to the drawer or an indorser who paid the draft under Section 3–414 or 3–415.

(b) If the certification of a check or other acceptance of a draft states the amount certified or accepted, the obligation of the acceptor is that amount. If (i) the certification or acceptance does not state an amount, (ii) the amount of the instrument is subsequently raised, and (iii) the instrument is then negotiated to a holder in due course, the obligation of the acceptor is the amount of the instrument at the time it was taken by the holder in due course.

§ 3–414.   Obligation of Drawer.

(a) This section does not apply to cashier's checks or other drafts drawn on the drawer.

(b) If an unaccepted draft is dishonored, the drawer is obliged to pay the draft (i) according to its terms at the time it was issued or, if not issued, at the time it first came into possession of a holder, or (ii) if the drawer signed an incomplete instrument, according to its terms when completed, to the extent stated in Sections 3–115 and 3–407. The obligation is owed to a person entitled to enforce the draft or to an indorser who paid the draft under Section 3–415.

(c) If a draft is accepted by a bank, the drawer is discharged, regardless of when or by whom acceptance was obtained.

(d) If a draft is accepted and the acceptor is not a bank, the obligation of the drawer to pay the draft if the draft is dishonored by the acceptor is the same as the obligation of an indorser under Section 3–415(a) and (c).

(e) If a draft states that it is drawn "without recourse" or otherwise disclaims liability of the drawer to pay the draft, the drawer is not liable under subsection (b) to pay the draft if the draft is not a check. A disclaimer of the liability stated in subsection (b) is not effective if the draft is a check.

(f) If (i) a check is not presented for payment or given to a depositary bank for collection within 30 days after its date, (ii) the drawee suspends payments after expiration of the 30-day period without paying the check, and (iii) because of the suspension of payments, the drawer is deprived of funds maintained with the drawee to cover payment of the check, the drawer to the extent deprived of funds may discharge its obligation to pay the check by assigning to the person entitled to enforce the check the rights of the drawer against the drawee with respect to the funds.

§ 3–415.   Obligation of Indorser.

(a) Subject to subsections (b), (c), and (d) and to Section 3–419(d), if an instrument is dishonored, an indorser is obliged to pay the amount due on the instrument (i) according to the terms of the instrument at the time it was indorsed, or (ii) if the indorser indorsed an incomplete instrument, according to its terms when completed, to the extent stated in Sections 3–115 and 3–407. The obligation of the indorser is owed to a person entitled to enforce the instrument or to a subsequent indorser who paid the instrument under this section.

(b) If an indorsement states that it is made "without recourse" or otherwise disclaims liability of the indorser, the indorser is not liable under subsection (a) to pay the instrument.

(c) If notice of dishonor of an instrument is required by Section 3–503 and notice of dishonor complying with that section is not given to an indorser, the liability of the indorser under subsection (a) is discharged.

(d) If a draft is accepted by a bank after an indorsement is made, the liability of the indorser under subsection (a) is discharged.

(e) If an indorser of a check is liable under subsection (a) and the check is not presented for payment, or given to a depositary bank for collection, within 30 days after the day the indorsement was made, the liability of the indorser under subsection (a) is discharged.

As amended in 1993.

§ 3-416.   Transfer Warranties.

(a) A person who transfers an instrument for consideration warrants to the transferee and, if the transfer is by indorsement, to any subsequent transferee that:

(1) the warrantor is a person entitled to enforce the instrument;

(2) all signatures on the instrument are authentic and authorized;

(3) the instrument has not been altered;

(4) the instrument is not subject to a defense or claim in recoupment of any party which can be asserted against the warrantor; and

(5) the warrantor has no knowledge of any insolvency proceeding commenced with respect to the maker or acceptor or, in the case of an unaccepted draft, the drawer.

(b) A person to whom the warranties under subsection (a) are made and who took the instrument in good faith may recover from the warrantor as damages for breach of warranty an amount equal to the loss suffered as a result of the breach, but not more than the amount of the instrument plus expenses and loss of interest incurred as a result of the breach.

(c) The warranties stated in subsection (a) cannot be disclaimed with respect to checks. Unless notice of a claim for breach of warranty is given to the warrantor within 30 days after the claimant has reason to know of the breach and the identity of the warrantor, the liability of the warrantor under subsection (b) is discharged to the extent of any loss caused by the delay in giving notice of the claim.

(d) A [cause of action] for breach of warranty under this section accrues when the claimant has reason to know of the breach.

§ 3-417.   Presentment Warranties.

(a) If an unaccepted draft is presented to the drawee for payment or acceptance and the drawee pays or accepts the draft, (i) the person obtaining payment or acceptance, at the time of presentment, and (ii) a previous transferor of the draft, at the time of transfer, warrant to the drawee making payment or accepting the draft in good faith that:

(1) the warrantor is, or was, at the time the warrantor transferred the draft, a person entitled to enforce the draft or

authorized to obtain payment or acceptance of the draft on behalf of a person entitled to enforce the draft;

(2) the draft has not been altered; and

(3) the warrantor has no knowledge that the signature of the drawer of the draft is unauthorized.

(b) A drawee making payment may recover from any warrantor damages for breach of warranty equal to the amount paid by the drawee less the amount the drawee received or is entitled to receive from the drawer because of the payment. In addition, the drawee is entitled to compensation for expenses and loss of interest resulting from the breach. The right of the drawee to recover damages under this subsection is not affected by any failure of the drawee to exercise ordinary care in making payment. If the drawee accepts the draft, breach of warranty is a defense to the obligation of the acceptor. If the acceptor makes payment with respect to the draft, the acceptor is entitled to recover from any warrantor for breach of warranty the amounts stated in this subsection.

(c) If a drawee asserts a claim for breach of warranty under subsection (a) based on an unauthorized indorsement of the draft or an alteration of the draft, the warrantor may defend by proving that the indorsement is effective under Section 3–404 or 3–405 or the drawer is precluded under Section 3–406 or 4–406 from asserting against the drawee the unauthorized indorsement or alteration.

(d) If (i) a dishonored draft is presented for payment to the drawer or an indorser or (ii) any other instrument is presented for payment to a party obliged to pay the instrument, and (iii) payment is received, the following rules apply:

(1) The person obtaining payment and a prior transferor of the instrument warrant to the person making payment in good faith that the warrantor is, or was, at the time the warrantor transferred the instrument, a person entitled to enforce the instrument or authorized to obtain payment on behalf of a person entitled to enforce the instrument.

(2) The person making payment may recover from any warrantor for breach of warranty an amount equal to the amount paid plus expenses and loss of interest resulting from the breach.

(e) The warranties stated in subsections (a) and (d) cannot be disclaimed with respect to checks. Unless notice of a claim for breach of warranty is given to the warrantor within 30 days after the claimant has reason to know of the breach and the identity of the warrantor, the liability of the warrantor under subsection (b) or (d) is discharged to the extent of any loss caused by the delay in giving notice of the claim.

(f) A [cause of action] for breach of warranty under this section accrues when the claimant has reason to know of the breach.

§ 3-418.   Payment or Acceptance by Mistake.

(a) Except as provided in subsection (c), if the drawee of a draft pays or accepts the draft and the drawee acted on the mistaken belief that (i) payment of the draft had not been stopped pursuant to Section 4–403 or (ii) the signature of the drawer of the draft was authorized, the drawee may recover the amount of the draft from the person to whom or for whose benefit payment was made or, in the case of acceptance, may revoke the acceptance. Rights of the drawee under this subsection are not affected by failure of the drawee to exercise ordinary care in paying or accepting the draft.

(b) Except as provided in subsection (c), if an instrument has been paid or accepted by mistake and the case is not covered by subsection (a), the person paying or accepting may, to the extent permitted by the law governing mistake and restitution, (i) recover the payment from the person to whom or for whose benefit payment was made or (ii) in the case of acceptance, may revoke the acceptance.

(c) The remedies provided by subsection (a) or (b) may not be asserted against a person who took the instrument in good faith and for value or who in good faith changed position in reliance on the payment or acceptance. This subsection does not limit remedies provided by Section 3–417 or 4–407.

(d) Notwithstanding Section 4–215, if an instrument is paid or accepted by mistake and the payor or acceptor recovers payment or revokes acceptance under subsection (a) or (b), the instrument is deemed not to have been paid or accepted and is treated as dishonored, and the person from whom payment is recovered has rights as a person entitled to enforce the dishonored instrument.

§ 3–419.   Instruments Signed for Accommodation.

(a) If an instrument is issued for value given for the benefit of a party to the instrument ("accommodated party") and another party to the instrument ("accommodation party") signs the instrument for the purpose of incurring liability on the instrument without being a direct beneficiary of the value given for the instrument, the instrument is signed by the accommodation party "for accommodation."

(b) An accommodation party may sign the instrument as maker, drawer, acceptor, or indorser and, subject to subsection (d), is obliged to pay the instrument in the capacity in which the accommodation party signs. The obligation of an accommodation party may be enforced notwithstanding any statute of frauds and whether or not the accommodation party receives consideration for the accommodation.

(c) A person signing an instrument is presumed to be an accommodation party and there is notice that the instrument is signed for accommodation if the signature is an anomalous indorsement or is accompanied by words indicating that the signer is acting as surety or guarantor with respect to the obligation of another party to the instrument. Except as provided in Section 3–605, the obligation of an accommodation party to pay the instrument is not affected by the fact that the person enforcing

the obligation had notice when the instrument was taken by that person that the accommodation party signed the instrument for accommodation.

(d) If the signature of a party to an instrument is accompanied by words indicating unambiguously that the party is guaranteeing collection rather than payment of the obligation of another party to the instrument, the signer is obliged to pay the amount due on the instrument to a person entitled to enforce the instrument only if (i) execution of judgment against the other party has been returned unsatisfied, (ii) the other party is insolvent or in an insolvency proceeding, (iii) the other party cannot be served with process, or (iv) it is otherwise apparent that payment cannot be obtained from the other party.

(e) An accommodation party who pays the instrument is entitled to reimbursement from the accommodated party and is entitled to enforce the instrument against the accommodated party. An accommodated party who pays the instrument has no right of recourse against, and is not entitled to contribution from, an accommodation party.

§ 3–420.   Conversion of Instrument.

(a) The law applicable to conversion of personal property applies to instruments. An instrument is also converted if it is taken by transfer, other than a negotiation, from a person not entitled to enforce the instrument or a bank makes or obtains payment with respect to the instrument for a person not entitled to enforce the instrument or receive payment. An action for conversion of an instrument may not be brought by (i) the issuer or acceptor of the instrument or (ii) a payee or indorsee who did not receive delivery of the instrument either directly or through delivery to an agent or a co-payee.

(b) In an action under subsection (a), the measure of liability is presumed to be the amount payable on the instrument, but recovery may not exceed the amount of the plaintiff's interest in the instrument.

(c) A representative, other than a depositary bank, who has in good faith dealt with an instrument or its proceeds on behalf of one who was not the person entitled to enforce the instrument is not liable in conversion to that person beyond the amount of any proceeds that it has not paid out.

PART 5   Dishonor

§ 3–501.   Presentment.

(a) "Presentment" means a demand made by or on behalf of a person entitled to enforce an instrument (i) to pay the instrument made to the drawee or a party obliged to pay the instrument or, in the case of a note or accepted draft payable at a bank, to the bank, or (ii) to accept a draft made to the drawee.

(b) The following rules are subject to Article 4, agreement of the parties, and clearing-house rules and the like:

(1) Presentment may be made at the place of payment of the instrument and must be made at the place of payment if the instrument is payable at a bank in the United States; may be made by any commercially reasonable means, including an oral, written, or electronic communication; is effective when the demand for payment or acceptance is received by the person to whom presentment is made; and is effective if made to any one of two or more makers, acceptors, drawees, or other payors.

(2) Upon demand of the person to whom presentment is made, the person making presentment must (i) exhibit the instrument, (ii) give reasonable identification and, if presentment is made on behalf of another person, reasonable evidence of authority to do so, and (. . .) sign a receipt on the instrument for any payment made or surrender the instrument if full payment is made.

(3) Without dishonoring the instrument, the party to whom presentment is made may (i) return the instrument for lack of a necessary indorsement, or (ii) refuse payment or acceptance for failure of the presentment to comply with the terms of the instrument, an agreement of the parties, or other applicable law or rule.

(4) The party to whom presentment is made may treat presentment as occurring on the next business day after the day of presentment if the party to whom presentment is made has established a cut-off hour not earlier than 2 P.M. for the receipt and processing of instruments presented for payment or acceptance and presentment is made after the cut-off hour.

§ 3–502. Dishonor.

(a) Dishonor of a note is governed by the following rules:

(1) If the note is payable on demand, the note is dishonored if presentment is duly made to the maker and the note is not paid on the day of presentment.

(2) If the note is not payable on demand and is payable at or through a bank or the terms of the note require presentment, the note is dishonored if presentment is duly made and the note is not paid on the day it becomes payable or the day of presentment, whichever is later.

(3) If the note is not payable on demand and paragraph (2) does not apply, the note is dishonored if it is not paid on the day it becomes payable.

(b) Dishonor of an unaccepted draft other than a documentary draft is governed by the following rules:

(1) If a check is duly presented for payment to the payor bank otherwise than for immediate payment over the counter, the check is dishonored if the payor bank makes timely return of the check or sends timely notice of dishonor or nonpayment under Section 4–301 or 4–302, or becomes accountable for the amount of the check under Section 4–302.

(2) If a draft is payable on demand and paragraph (1) does not apply, the draft is dishonored if presentment for payment is duly made to the drawee and the draft is not paid on the day of presentment.

(3) If a draft is payable on a date stated in the draft, the draft is dishonored if (i) presentment for payment is duly made to the drawee and payment is not made on the day the draft becomes payable or the day of presentment, whichever is later, or (ii) presentment for acceptance is duly made before the day the draft becomes payable and the draft is not accepted on the day of presentment.

(4) If a draft is payable on elapse of a period of time after sight or acceptance, the draft is dishonored if presentment for acceptance is duly made and the draft is not accepted on the day of presentment.

(c) Dishonor of an unaccepted documentary draft occurs according to the rules stated in subsection (b)(2), (3), and (4), except that payment or acceptance may be delayed without dishonor until no later than the close of the third business day of the drawee following the day on which payment or acceptance is required by those paragraphs.

(d) Dishonor of an accepted draft is governed by the following rules:

(1) If the draft is payable on demand, the draft is dishonored if presentment for payment is duly made to the acceptor and the draft is not paid on the day of presentment.

(2) If the draft is not payable on demand, the draft is dishonored if presentment for payment is duly made to the acceptor and payment is not made on the day it becomes payable or the day of presentment, whichever is later.

(e) In any case in which presentment is otherwise required for dishonor under this section and presentment is excused under Section 3–504, dishonor occurs without presentment if the instrument is not duly accepted or paid.

(f) If a draft is dishonored because timely acceptance of the draft was not made and the person entitled to demand acceptance consents to a late acceptance, from the time of acceptance the draft is treated as never having been dishonored.

§ 3–503. Notice of Dishonor.

(a) The obligation of an indorser stated in Section 3–415(a) and the obligation of a drawer stated in Section 3–414(d) may not be enforced unless (i) the indorser or drawer is given notice of dishonor of the instrument complying with this section or (ii) notice of dishonor is excused under Section 3–504(b).

(b) Notice of dishonor may be given by any person; may be given by any commercially reasonable means, including an oral, written, or electronic communication; and is sufficient if it reasonably identifies the instrument and indicates that the instrument has been dishonored or has not been paid or accepted. Return of an instrument given to a bank for collection is sufficient notice of dishonor.

(c) Subject to Section 3–504(c), with respect to an instrument taken for collection by a collecting bank, notice of dishonor must be given (i) by the bank before midnight of the next banking day following the banking day on which the bank receives notice of dishonor of the instrument, or (ii) by any other person within 30 days following the day on which the person receives notice of dishonor. With respect to any other instrument, notice of dishonor must be given within 30 days following the day on which dishonor occurs.

§ 3–504.   Excused Presentment and Notice of Dishonor.

(a) Presentment for payment or acceptance of an instrument is excused if (i) the person entitled to present the instrument cannot with reasonable diligence make presentment, (ii) the maker or acceptor has repudiated an obligation to pay the instrument or is dead or in insolvency proceedings, (iii) by the terms of the instrument presentment is not necessary to enforce the obligation of indorsers or the drawer, (iv) the drawer or indorser whose obligation is being enforced has waived presentment or otherwise has no reason to expect or right to require that the instrument be paid or accepted, or (v) the drawer instructed the drawee not to pay or accept the draft or the drawee was not obligated to the drawer to pay the draft.

(b) Notice of dishonor is excused if (i) by the terms of the instrument notice of dishonor is not necessary to enforce the obligation of a party to pay the instrument, or (ii) the party whose obligation is being enforced waived notice of dishonor. A waiver of presentment is also a waiver of notice of dishonor.

(c) Delay in giving notice of dishonor is excused if the delay was caused by circumstances beyond the control of the person giving the notice and the person giving the notice exercised reasonable diligence after the cause of the delay ceased to operate.

§ 3–505.   Evidence of Dishonor.

(a) The following are admissible as evidence and create a presumption of dishonor and of any notice of dishonor stated:

(1) a document regular in form as provided in subsection (b) which purports to be a protest;

(2) a purported stamp or writing of the drawee, payor bank, or presenting bank on or accompanying the instrument stating that acceptance or payment has been refused unless reasons for the refusal are stated and the reasons are not consistent with dishonor;

(3) a book or record of the drawee, payor bank, or collecting bank, kept in the usual course of business which shows dishonor, even if there is no evidence of who made the entry.

(b) A protest is a certificate of dishonor made by a United States consul or vice consul, or a notary public or other person authorized to administer oaths by the law of the place where dishonor occurs. It may be made upon information satisfactory to that person. The protest must identify the instrument and certify either that presentment has been made or, if not made, the reason why it was not made, and that the instrument has been dishonored by nonacceptance or nonpayment. The protest may also certify that notice of dishonor has been given to some or all parties.

PART 6   Discharge and Payment

§ 3–601.   Discharge and Effect of Discharge.

(a) The obligation of a party to pay the instrument is discharged as stated in this Article or by an act or agreement with the party which would discharge an obligation to pay money under a simple contract.

(b) Discharge of the obligation of a party is not effective against a person acquiring rights of a holder in due course of the instrument without notice of the discharge.

§ 3–602.   Payment.

(a) Subject to subsection (b), an instrument is paid to the extent payment is made (i) by or on behalf of a party obliged to pay the instrument, and (ii) to a person entitled to enforce the instrument. To the extent of the payment, the obligation of the party obliged to pay the instrument is discharged even though payment is made with knowledge of a claim to the instrument under Section 3–306 by another person.

(b) The obligation of a party to pay the instrument is not discharged under subsection (a) if:

(1) a claim to the instrument under Section 3–306 is enforceable against the party receiving payment and (i) payment is made with knowledge by the payor that payment is prohibited by injunction or similar process of a court of competent jurisdiction, or (ii) in the case of an instrument other than a cashier's check, teller's check, or certified check, the party making payment accepted, from the person having a claim to the instrument, indemnity against loss resulting from refusal to pay the person entitled to enforce the instrument; or

(2) the person making payment knows that the instrument is a stolen instrument and pays a person it knows is in wrongful possession of the instrument.

§ 3–603.   Tender of Payment.

(a) If tender of payment of an obligation to pay an instrument is made to a person entitled to enforce the instrument, the effect of tender is governed by principles of law applicable to tender of payment under a simple contract.

(b) If tender of payment of an obligation to pay an instrument is made to a person entitled to enforce the instrument and the tender is refused, there is discharge, to the extent of the amount of the tender, of the obligation of an indorser or accommodation party having a right of recourse with respect to the obligation to which the tender relates.

(c) If tender of payment of an amount due on an instrument is made to a person entitled to enforce the instrument, the obligation of the obligor to pay interest after the due date on the amount tendered is discharged. If presentment is required with respect to an instrument and the obligor is able and ready to pay on the due date at every place of payment stated in the instrument, the obligor is deemed to have made tender of payment on the due date to the person entitled to enforce the instrument.

§ 3–604. Discharge by Cancellation or Renunciation.

(a) A person entitled to enforce an instrument, with or without consideration, may discharge the obligation of a party to pay the instrument (i) by an intentional voluntary act, such as surrender of the instrument to the party, destruction, mutilation, or cancellation of the instrument, cancellation or striking out of the party's signature, or the addition of words to the instrument indicating discharge, or (ii) by agreeing not to sue or otherwise renouncing rights against the party by a signed writing.

(b) Cancellation or striking out of an indorsement pursuant to subsection (a) does not affect the status and rights of a party derived from the indorsement.

§ 3–605. Discharge of Indorsers and Accommodation Parties.

(a) In this section, the term "indorser" includes a drawer having the obligation described in Section 3–414(d).

(b) Discharge, under Section 3–604, of the obligation of a party to pay an instrument does not discharge the obligation of an indorser or accommodation party having a right of recourse against the discharged party.

(c) If a person entitled to enforce an instrument agrees, with or without consideration, to an extension of the due date of the obligation of a party to pay the instrument, the extension discharges an indorser or accommodation party having a right of recourse against the party whose obligation is extended to the extent the indorser or accommodation party proves that the extension caused loss to the indorser or accommodation party with respect to the right of recourse.

(d) If a person entitled to enforce an instrument agrees, with or without consideration, to a material modification of the obligation of a party other than an extension of the due date, the modification discharges the obligation of an indorser or accommodation party having a right of recourse against the person whose obligation is modified to the extent the modification causes loss to the indorser or accommodation party with respect to the right of recourse. The loss suffered by the indorser or accommodation party as a result of the modifica-

tion is equal to the amount of the right of recourse unless the person enforcing the instrument proves that no loss was caused by the modification or that the loss caused by the modification was an amount less than the amount of the right of recourse.

(e) If the obligation of a party to pay an instrument is secured by an interest in collateral and a person entitled to enforce the instrument impairs the value of the interest in collateral, the obligation of an indorser or accommodation party having a right of recourse against the obligor is discharged to the extent of the impairment. The value of an interest in collateral is impaired to the extent (i) the value of the interest is reduced to an amount less than the amount of the right of recourse of the party asserting discharge, or (ii) the reduction in value of the interest causes an increase in the amount by which the amount of the right of recourse exceeds the value of the interest. The burden of proving impairment is on the party asserting discharge.

(f) If the obligation of a party is secured by an interest in collateral not provided by an accommodation party and a person entitled to enforce the instrument impairs the value of the interest in collateral, the obligation of any party who is jointly and severally liable with respect to the secured obligation is discharged to the extent the impairment causes the party asserting discharge to pay more than that party would have been obliged to pay, taking into account rights of contribution, if impairment had not occurred. If the party asserting discharge is an accommodation party not entitled to discharge under subsection (e), the party is deemed to have a right to contribution based on joint and several liability rather than a right to reimbursement. The burden of proving impairment is on the party asserting discharge.

(g) Under subsection (e) or (f), impairing value of an interest in collateral includes (i) failure to obtain or maintain perfection or recordation of the interest in collateral, (ii) release of collateral without substitution of collateral of equal value, (iii) failure to perform a duty to preserve the value of collateral owed, under Article 9 or other law, to a debtor or surety or other person secondarily liable, or (iv) failure to comply with applicable law in disposing of collateral.

(h) An accommodation party is not discharged under subsection (c), (d), or (e) unless the person entitled to enforce the instrument knows of the accommodation or has notice under Section 3–419(c) that the instrument was signed for accommodation.

(i) A party is not discharged under this section if (i) the party asserting discharge consents to the event or conduct that is the basis of the discharge, or (ii) the instrument or a separate agreement of the party provides for waiver of discharge under this section either specifically or by general language indicating that parties waive defenses based on suretyship or impairment of collateral.

ADDENDUM TO REVISED ARTICLE 3

Notes to Legislative Counsel

1. If revised Article 3 is adopted in your state, the reference in Section 2–511 to Section 3–802 should be changed to Section 3–310.

2. If revised Article 3 is adopted in your state and the Uniform Fiduciaries Act is also in effect in your state, you may want to consider amending Uniform Fiduciaries Act § 9 to conform to Section 3–307(b)(2)(iii) and (4)(iii). See Official Comment 3 to Section 3–307.

REVISED ARTICLE 9

SECURED TRANSACTIONS

PART 1   General Provisions

[Subpart 1. Short Title, Definitions, and General Concepts]

§ 9–101.   Short Title.

This article may be cited as Uniform Commercial Code—Secured Transactions.

§ 9–102.   Definitions and Index of Definitions.

(a) In this article:

(1) "Accession" means goods that are physically united with other goods in such a manner that the identity of the original goods is not lost.

(2) "Account", except as used in "account for", means a right to payment of a monetary obligation, whether or not earned by performance, (i) for property that has been or is to be sold, leased, licensed, assigned, or otherwise disposed of, (ii) for services rendered or to be rendered, (iii) for a policy of insurance issued or to be issued, (iv) for a secondary obligation incurred or to be incurred, (v) for energy provided or to be provided, (vi) for the use or hire of a vessel under a charter or other contract, (vii) arising out of the use of a credit or charge card or information contained on or for use with the card, or (viii) as winnings in a lottery or other game of chance operated or sponsored by a State, governmental unit of a State, or person licensed or authorized to operate the game by a State or governmental unit of a State. The term includes health-care insurance receivables. The term does not include (i) rights to payment evidenced by chattel paper or an instrument, (ii) commercial tort claims, (iii) deposit accounts, (iv) investment property, (v) letter-of-credit rights or letters of credit, or (vi) rights to payment for money or funds advanced or sold, other than rights arising out of the use of a credit or charge card or information contained on or for use with the card.

(3) "Account debtor" means a person obligated on an account, chattel paper, or general intangible. The term does not include persons obligated to pay a negotiable instrument, even if the instrument constitutes part of chattel paper.

(4) "Accounting", except as used in "accounting for", means a record:

(A) authenticated by a secured party;

(B) indicating the aggregate unpaid secured obligations as of a date not more than 35 days earlier or 35 days later than the date of the record; and

(C) identifying the components of the obligations in reasonable detail.

(5) "Agricultural lien" means an interest, other than a security interest, in farm products:

(A) which secures payment or performance of an obligation for:

(i) goods or services furnished in connection with a debtor's farming operation; or

(ii) rent on real property leased by a debtor in connection with its farming operation;

(B) which is created by statute in favor of a person that:

(i) in the ordinary course of its business furnished goods or services to a debtor in connection with a debtor's farming operation; or

(ii) leased real property to a debtor in connection with the debtor's farming operation; and

(C) whose effectiveness does not depend on the person's possession of the personal property.

(6) "As-extracted collateral" means:

(A) oil, gas, or other minerals that are subject to a security interest that:

(i) is created by a debtor having an interest in the minerals before extraction; and

(ii) attaches to the minerals as extracted; or

(B) accounts arising out of the sale at the wellhead or minehead of oil, gas, or other minerals in which the debtor had an interest before extraction.

(7) "Authenticate" means:

(A) to sign; or

(B) to execute or otherwise adopt a symbol, or encrypt or similarly process a record in whole or in part, with the present intent of the authenticating person to identify the person and adopt or accept a record.

(8) "Bank" means an organization that is engaged in the business of banking. The term includes savings banks, savings and loan associations, credit unions, and trust companies.

(9) "Cash proceeds" means proceeds that are money, checks, deposit accounts, or the like.

(10) "Certificate of title" means a certificate of title with respect to which a statute provides for the security interest in question to be indicated on the certificate as a condition or result of the security interest's obtaining priority over the rights of a lien creditor with respect to the collateral.

(11) "Chattel paper" means a record or records that evidence both a monetary obligation and a security interest in specific goods, a security interest in specific goods and software used in the goods, a security interest in specific goods and license of software used in the goods, a lease of specific goods, or a lease of specific goods and license of software used in the goods. In this paragraph, "monetary obligation" means a monetary obligation secured by the goods or owed under a lease of the goods and includes a monetary obligation with respect to software used in the goods. The term does not include (i) charters or other contracts involving the use or hire of a vessel or (ii) records that evidence a right to payment arising out of the use of a credit or charge card or information contained on or for use with the card. If a transaction is evidenced by records that include an instrument or series of instruments, the group of records taken together constitutes chattel paper.

(12) "Collateral" means the property subject to a security interest or agricultural lien. The term includes:

(A) proceeds to which a security interest attaches;

(B) accounts, chattel paper, payment intangibles, and promissory notes that have been sold; and

(C) goods that are the subject of a consignment.

(13) "Commercial tort claim" means a claim arising in tort with respect to which:

(A) the claimant is an organization; or

(B) the claimant is an individual and the claim:

(i) arose in the course of the claimant's business or profession; and

(ii) does not include damages arising out of personal injury to or the death of an individual.

(14) "Commodity account" means an account maintained by a commodity intermediary in which a commodity contract is carried for a commodity customer.

(15) "Commodity contract" means a commodity futures contract, an option on a commodity futures contract, a commodity option, or another contract if the contract or option is:

(A) traded on or subject to the rules of a board of trade that has been designated as a contract market for such a contract pursuant to federal commodities laws; or

(B) traded on a foreign commodity board of trade, exchange, or market, and is carried on the books of a commodity intermediary for a commodity customer.

(16) "Commodity customer" means a person for which a commodity intermediary carries a commodity contract on its books.

(17) "Commodity intermediary" means a person that:

(A) is registered as a futures commission merchant under federal commodities law; or

(B) in the ordinary course of its business provides clearance or settlement services for a board of trade that has been designated as a contract market pursuant to federal commodities law.

(18) "Communicate" means:

(A) to send a written or other tangible record;

(B) to transmit a record by any means agreed upon by the persons sending and receiving the record; or

(C) in the case of transmission of a record to or by a filing office, to transmit a record by any means prescribed by filing-office rule.

(19) "Consignee" means a merchant to which goods are delivered in a consignment.

(20) "Consignment" means a transaction, regardless of its form, in which a person delivers goods to a merchant for the purpose of sale and:

(A) the merchant:

(i) deals in goods of that kind under a name other than the name of the person making delivery;

(ii) is not an auctioneer; and

(iii) is not generally known by its creditors to be substantially engaged in selling the goods of others;

(B) with respect to each delivery, the aggregate value of the goods is $1,000 or more at the time of delivery;

(C) the goods are not consumer goods immediately before delivery; and

(D) the transaction does not create a security interest that secures an obligation.

(21) "Consignor" means a person that delivers goods to a consignee in a consignment.

(22) "Consumer debtor" means a debtor in a consumer transaction.

(23) "Consumer goods" means goods that are used or bought for use primarily for personal, family, or household purposes.

(24) "Consumer goods transaction" means a consumer transaction in which:

(A) an individual incurs an obligation primarily for personal, family, or household purposes; and

(B) a security interest in consumer goods secures the obligation.

(25) "Consumer obligor" means an obligor who is an individual and who incurred the obligation as part of a transaction entered into primarily for personal, family, or household purposes.

(26) "Consumer transaction" means a transaction in which (i) an individual incurs an obligation primarily for personal, family, or household purposes, (ii) a security interest secures the obligation, and (iii) the collateral is held or acquired primarily for personal, family, or household purposes. The term includes consumer-goods transactions.

(27) "Continuation statement" means an amendment of a financing statement which:

(A) identifies, by its file number, the initial financing statement to which it relates; and

(B) indicates that it is a continuation statement for, or that it is filed to continue the effectiveness of, the identified financing statement.

(28) "Debtor" means:

(A) a person having an interest, other than a security interest or other lien, in the collateral, whether or not the person is an obligor;

(B) a seller of accounts, chattel paper, payment intangibles, or promissory notes; or

(C) a consignee.

(29) "Deposit account" means a demand, time, savings, passbook, or similar account maintained with a bank. The term does not include investment property or accounts evidenced by an instrument.

(30) "Document" means a document of title or a receipt of the type described in Section 7–201(2).

(31) "Electronic chattel paper" means chattel paper evidenced by a record or records consisting of information stored in an electronic medium.

(32) "Encumbrance" means a right, other than an ownership interest, in real property. The term includes mortgages and other liens on real property.

(33) "Equipment" means goods other than inventory, farm products, or consumer goods.

(34) "Farm products" means goods, other than standing timber, with respect to which the debtor is engaged in a farming operation and which are:

(A) crops grown, growing, or to be grown, including:

(i) crops produced on trees, vines, and bushes; and

(ii) aquatic goods produced in aquacultural operations;

(B) livestock, born or unborn, including aquatic goods produced in aquacultural operations;

(C) supplies used or produced in a farming operation; or

(D) products of crops or livestock in their unmanufactured states.

(35) "Farming operation" means raising, cultivating, propagating, fattening, grazing, or any other farming, livestock, or aquacultural operation.

(36) "File number" means the number assigned to an initial financing statement pursuant to Section 9–519(a).

(37) "Filing office" means an office designated in Section 9–501 as the place to file a financing statement.

(38) "Filing-office rule" means a rule adopted pursuant to Section 9–526.

(39) "Financing statement" means a record or records composed of an initial financing statement and any filed record relating to the initial financing statement.

(40) "Fixture filing" means the filing of a financing statement covering goods that are or are to become fixtures and satisfying Section 9–502(a) and (b). The term includes the filing of a financing statement covering goods of a transmitting utility which are or are to become fixtures.

(41) "Fixtures" means goods that have become so related to particular real property that an interest in them arises under real property law.

(42) "General intangible" means any personal property, including things in action, other than accounts, chattel paper, commercial tort claims, deposit accounts, documents, goods, instruments, investment property, letter-of-credit rights, letters of credit, money, and oil, gas, or other minerals before extraction. The term includes payment intangibles and software.

(43) "Good faith" means honesty in fact and the observance of reasonable commercial standards of fair dealing.

(44) "Goods" means all things that are movable when a security interest attaches. The term includes (i) fixtures, (ii) standing timber that is to be cut and removed under a conveyance or contract for sale, (iii) the unborn young of animals, (iv) crops grown, growing, or to be grown, even if the crops are produced on trees, vines, or bushes, and (v) manufactured homes. The term also includes a computer program embedded in goods and any supporting information provided in connection with a transaction relating to the program if (i) the program is associated with the goods in such a manner that it customarily is considered part of the goods, or (ii) by becoming the owner of the goods, a person acquires a right to use the program in connection with the goods. The term does not include a computer program embedded in goods that consist solely of the medium in which the program is embedded. The term also does not include accounts, chattel paper, commercial tort claims, deposit accounts, documents, general intangibles, instruments, investment property, letter-of-credit rights, letters of credit, money, or oil, gas, or other minerals before extraction.

(45) "Governmental unit" means a subdivision, agency, department, county, parish, municipality, or other unit of the government of the United States, a State, or a foreign country. The term includes an organization having a separate corporate existence if the organization is eligible to issue debt on which interest is exempt from income taxation under the laws of the United States.

(46) "Health-care-insurance receivable" means an interest in or claim under a policy of insurance which is a right to payment of a monetary obligation for health-care goods or servies provided.

(47) "Instrument" means a negotiable instrument or any other writing that evidences a right to the payment of a monetary obligation, is not itself a security agreement or lease, and is of a type that in ordinary course of business is transferred by delivery with any necessary indorsement or assignment. The term does not include (i) investment property, (ii) letters of credit, or (iii) writings that evidence a right to payment arising out of the use of a credit or charge card or information contained on or for use with the card.

(48) "Inventory" means goods, other than farm products, which:

(A) are leased by a person as lessor;

(B) are held by a person for sale or lease or to be furnished under a contract of service;

(C) are furnished by a person under a contract of service; or

(D) consist of raw materials, work in process, or materials used or consumed in a business.

(49) "Investment property" means a security, whether certificated or uncertificated, security entitlement, securities account, commodity contract, or commodity account.

(50) "Jurisdiction of organization", with respect to a registered organization, means the jurisdiction under whose law the organization is organized.

(51) "Letter-of-credit right" means a right to payment or performance under a letter of credit, whether or not the beneficiary has demanded or is at the time entitled to demand payment or performance. The term does not include the right of a beneficiary to demand payment or performance under a letter of credit.

(52) "Lien creditor" means:

(A) a creditor that has acquired a lien on the property involved by attachment, levy, or the like;

(B) an assignee for benefit of creditors from the time of assignment;

(C) a trustee in bankruptcy from the date of the filing of the petition; or

(D) a receiver in equity from the time of appointment.

(53) "Manufactured home" means a structure, transportable in one or more sections, which, in the traveling mode, is eight body feet or more in width or 40 body feet or more in length, or, when erected on site, is 320 or more square feet, and which is built on a permanent chassis and designed to be used as a dwelling with or without a permanent foundation when connected to the required utilities, and includes the plumbing, heating, air-conditioning, and electrical systems contained therein. The term includes any structure that meets all of the requirements of this paragraph except the size requirements and with respect to which the manufacturer voluntarily files a certification required by the United States Secretary of Housing and Urban Development and complies with the standards established under Title 42 of the United States Code.

(54) "Manufactured-home transaction" means a secured transaction:

(A) that creates a purchase-money security interest in a manufactured home, other than a manufactured home held as inventory; or

(B) in which a manufactured home, other than a manufactured home held as inventory, is the primary collateral.

(55) "Mortgage" means a consensual interest in real property, including fixtures, which secures payment or performance of an obligation.

(56) "New debtor" means a person that becomes bound as debtor under Section 9–203(d) by a security agreement previously entered into by another person.

(57) "New value" means (i) money, (ii) money's worth in property, services, or new credit, or (iii) release by a transferee of an interest in property previously transferred to the transferee. The term does not include an obligation substituted for another obligation.

(58) "Noncash proceeds" means proceeds other than cash proceeds.

(59) "Obligor" means a person that, with respect to an obligation secured by a security interest in or an agricultural lien on the collateral, (i) owes payment or other performance of the obligation, (ii) has provided property other than the collateral to secure payment or other performance of the obligation, or (iii) is otherwise accountable in whole or in part for payment or other performance of the obligation. The term does not include issuers or nominated persons under a letter of credit.

(60) "Original debtor", except as used in Section 9–310(c), means a person that, as debtor, entered into a security agreement to which a new debtor has become bound under Section 9–203(d).

(61) "Payment intangible" means a general intangible under which the account debtor's principal obligation is a monetary obligation.

(62) "Person related to", with respect to an individual, means:

(A) the spouse of the individual;

(B) a brother, brother-in-law, sister, or sister-in-law of the individual;

(C) an ancestor or lineal descendant of the individual or the individual's spouse; or

(D) any other relative, by blood or marriage, of the individual or the individual's spouse who shares the same home with the individual.

(63) "Person related to", with respect to an organization, means:

(A) a person directly or indirectly controlling, controlled by, or under common control with the organization;

(B) an officer or director of, or a person performing similar functions with respect to, the organization;

(C) an officer or director of, or a person performing similar functions with respect to, a person described in subparagraph (A);

(D) the spouse of an individual described in subparagraph (A), (B), or (C); or

(E) an individual who is related by blood or marriage to an individual described in subparagraph (A), (B), (C), or (D) and shares the same home with the individual.

(64) "Proceeds", except as used in Section 9–609(b), means the following property:

(A) whatever is acquired upon the sale, lease, license, exchange, or other disposition of collateral;

(B) whatever is collected on, or distributed on account of, collateral;

(C) rights arising out of collateral;

(D) to the extent of the value of collateral, claims arising out of the loss, nonconformity, or interference with the use of, defects or infringement of rights in, or damage to, the collateral; or (E) to the extent of the value of collateral and to the extent payable to the debtor or the secured party, insurance payable by reason of the loss or nonconformity of, defects or infringement of rights in, or damage to, the collateral.

(65) "Promissory note" means an instrument that evidences a promise to pay a monetary obligation, does not evidence an order to pay, and does not contain an acknowledgment by a bank that the bank has received for deposit a sum of money or funds.

(66) "Proposal" means a record authenticated by a secured party which includes the terms on which the secured party is willing to accept collateral in full or partial satisfaction of the obligation it secures pursuant to Sections 9–620, 9–621, and 9–622.

(67) "Public-finance transaction" means a secured transaction in connection with which:

(A) debt securities are issued;

(B) all or a portion of the securities issued have an initial stated maturity of at least 20 years; and

(C) the debtor, obligor, secured party, account debtor or other person obligated on collateral, assignor or assignee of a secured obligation, or assignor or assignee of a security interest is a State or a governmental unit of a State.

(68) "Pursuant to commitment", with respect to an advance made or other value given by a secured party, means pursuant to the secured party's obligation, whether or not a subsequent event of default or other event not within the secured party's control has relieved or may relieve the secured party from its obligation.

(69) "Record", except as used in "for record", "of record", "record or legal title", and "record owner", means information that is inscribed on a tangible medium or which is stored in an electronic or other medium and is retrievable in perceivable form.

(70) "Registered organization" means an organization organized solely under the law of a single State or the United States and as to which the State or the United States must maintain a public record showing the organization to have been organized.

(71) "Secondary obligor" means an obligor to the extent that:

(A) the obligor's obligation is secondary; or

(B) the obligor has a right of recourse with respect to an obligation secured by collateral against the debtor, another obligor, or property of either.

(72) "Secured party" means:

(A) a person in whose favor a security interest is created or provided for under a security agreement, whether or not any obligation to be secured is outstanding;

(B) a person that holds an agricultural lien;

(C) a consignor;

(D) a person to which accounts, chattel paper, payment intangibles, or promissory notes have been sold;

(E) a trustee, indenture trustee, agent, collateral agent, or other representative in whose favor a security interest or agricultural lien is created or provided for; or

(F) a person that holds a security interest arising under Section 2–401, 2–505, 2–711(3), 2A–508(5), 4–210, or 5–118.

(73) "Security agreement" means an agreement that creates or provides for a security interest.

(74) "Send", in connection with a record or notification, means:

(A) to deposit in the mail, deliver for transmission, or transmit by any other usual means of communication, with postage or cost of transmission provided for, addressed to any address reasonable under the circumstances; or

(B) to cause the record or notification to be received within the timce that it would have been received if properly sent under subparagraph (A).

(75) "Software" means a computer program and any supporting information provided in connection with a transaction relating to the program. The term does not include a computer program that is included in the definition of goods.

(76) "State" means a State of the United States, the District of Columbia, Puerto Rico, the United States Virgin Islands, or any territory or insular possession subject to the jurisdiction of the United States.

(77) "Supporting obligation" means a letter-of-credit right or secondary obligation that supports the payment or performance of an account, chattel paper, a document, a general intangible, an instrument, or investment property.

(78) "Tangible chattel paper" means chattel paper evidenced by a record or records consisting of information that is inscribed on a tangible medium.

(79) "Termination statement" means an amendment of a financing statement which:

(A) identifies, by its file number, the initial financing statement to which it relates; and

(B) indicates either that it is a termination statement or that the identified financing statement is no longer effective.

(80) "Transmitting utility" means a person primarily engaged in the business of:

(A) operating a railroad, subway, street railway, or trolley bus;

(B) transmitting communications electrically, electromagnetically, or by light;

(C) transmitting goods by pipeline or sewer; or

(D) transmitting or producing and transmitting electricity, steam, gas, or water.

(b) The following definitions in other articles apply to this article:

"Applicant." Section 5–102
"Beneficiary." Section 5–102
"Broker." Section 8–102
"Certificated security." Section 8–102
"Check." Section 3–104
"Clearing corporation." Section 8–102
"Contract for sale." Section 2–106
"Customer." Section 4–104
"Entitlement holder." Section 8–102
"Financial asset." Section 8–102
"Holder in due course." Section 3–302
"Issuer" (with respect to a letter of credit or letter-of-credit right). Section 5–102
"Issuer" (with respect to a security). Section 8–201
"Lease." Section 2A–103
"Lease agreement." Section 2A–103
"Lease contract." Section 2A–103
"Leasehold interest." Section 2A–103
"Lessee." Section 2A–103
"Lessee in ordinary course of business." Section 2A–103
"Lessor." Section 2A–103
"Lessor's residual interest." Section 2A–103
"Letter of credit." Section 5–102
"Merchant." Section 2–104
"Negotiable instrument." Section 3–104
"Nominated person." Section 5–102
"Note." Section 3–104
"Proceeds of a letter of credit." Section 5–114
"Prove." Section 3–103
"Sale." Section 2–106
"Securities account." Section 8–501
"Securities intermediary." Section 8–102
"Security." Section 8–102
"Security certificate." Section 8–102
"Security entitlement." Section 8–102
"Uncertificated security." Section 8–102

(c) Article 1 contains general definitions and principles of construction and interpretation applicable throughout this article.

Amended in 1999 and 2000.

§ 9–103.   Purchase-Money Security Interest; Application of Payments; Burden of Establishing.

(a) In this section:

(1) "purchase-money collateral" means goods or software that secures a purchase-money obligation incurred with respect to that collateral; and

(2) "purchase-money obligation" means an obligation of an obligor incurred as all or part of the price of the collateral or for value given to enable the debtor to acquire rights in or the use of the collateral if the value is in fact so used.

(b) A security interest in goods is a purchase-money security interest:

(1) to the extent that the goods are purchase-money collateral with respect to that security interest;

(2) if the security interest is in inventory that is or was purchase-money collateral, also to the extent that the security interest secures a purchase-money obligation incurred with respect to other inventory in which the secured party holds or held a purchase-money security interest; and

(3) also to the extent that the security interest secures a purchase-money obligation incurred with respect to software in which the secured party holds or held a purchase-money security interest.

(c) A security interest in software is a purchase-money security interest to the extent that the security interest also secures a purchase-money obligation incurred with respect to goods in which the secured party holds or held a purchase-money security interest if:

(1) the debtor acquired its interest in the software in an integrated transaction in which it acquired an interest in the goods; and

(2) the debtor acquired its interest in the software for the principal purpose of using the software in the goods.

(d) The security interest of a consignor in goods that are the subject of a consignment is a purchase-money security interest in inventory.

(e) In a transaction other than a consumer-goods transaction, if the extent to which a security interest is a purchase-money security interest depends on the application of a payment to a particular obligation, the payment must be applied:

(1) in accordance with any reasonable method of application to which the parties agree;

(2) in the absence of the parties' agreement to a reasonable method, in accordance with any intention of the obligor manifested at or before the time of payment; or

(3) in the absence of an agreement to a reasonable method and a timely manifestation of the obligor's intention, in the following order:

(A) to obligations that are not secured; and

(B) if more than one obligation is secured, to obligations secured by purchase-money security interests in the order in which those obligations were incurred.

(f) In a transaction other than a consumer-goods transaction, a purchase-money security interest does not lose its status as such, even if:

(1) the purchase-money collateral also secures an obligation that is not a purchase-money obligation;

(2) collateral that is not purchase-money collateral also secures the purchase-money obligation; or

(3) the purchase-money obligation has been renewed, refinanced, consolidated, or restructured.

(g) In a transaction other than a consumer-goods transaction, a secured party claiming a purchase-money security interest has the burden of establishing the extent to which the security interest is a purchase-money security interest.

(h) The limitation of the rules in subsections (e), (f), and (g) to transactions other than consumer-goods transactions is intended to leave to the court the determination of the proper rules in consumer-goods transactions. The court may not infer from that limitation the nature of the proper rule in consumer-goods transactions and may continue to apply established approaches.

§ 9-104.   Control of Deposit Account.

(a) A secured party has control of a deposit account if:

(1) the secured party is the bank with which the deposit account is maintained;

(2) the debtor, secured party, and bank have agreed in an authenticated record that the bank will comply with instructions originated by the secured party directing disposition of the funds in the deposit account without further consent by the debtor; or

(3) the secured party becomes the bank's customer with respect to the deposit account.

(b) A secured party that has satisfied subsection (a) has control, even if the debtor retains the right to direct the disposition of funds from the deposit account.

§ 9-105.   Control of Electronic Chattel Paper.

A secured party has control of electronic chattel paper if the record or records comprising the chattel paper are created, stored, and assigned in such a manner that:

(1) a single authoritative copy of the record or records exists which is unique, identifiable and, except as otherwise provided in paragraphs (4), (5), and (6), unalterable;

(2) the authoritative copy identifies the secured party as the assignee of the record or records;

(3) the authoritative copy is communicated to and maintained by the secured party or its designated custodian;

(4) copies or revisions that add or change an identified assignee of the authoritative copy can be made only with the participation of the secured party;

(5) each copy of the authoritative copy and any copy of a copy is readily identifiable as a copy that is not the authoritative copy; and

(6) any revision of the authoritative copy is readily identifiable as an authorized or unauthorized revision.

§ 9-106.   Control of Investment Property.

(a) A person has control of a certificated security, uncertificated security, or security entitlement as provided in Section 8–106.

(b) A secured party has control of a commodity contract if:

(1) the secured party is the commodity intermediary with which the commodity contract is carried; or

(2) the commodity customer, secured party, and commodity intermediary have agreed that the commodity intermediary will apply any value distributed on account of the commodity contract as directed by the secured party without further consent by the commodity customer.

(c) A secured party having control of all security entitlements or commodity contracts carried in a securities account or commodity account has control over the securities account or commodity account.

§ 9-107.   Control of Letter-of-Credit Right.

A secured party has control of a letter-of-credit right to the extent of any right to payment or performance by the issuer or any nominated person if the issuer or nominated person has consented to an assignment of proceeds of the letter of credit under Section 5–114(c) or otherwise applicable law or practice.

§ 9-108.   Sufficiency of Description.

(a) Except as otherwise provided in subsections (c), (d), and (e), a description of personal or real property is sufficient, whether or not it is specific, if it reasonably identifies what is described.

(b) Except as otherwise provided in subsection (d), a description of collateral reasonably identifies the collateral if it identifies the collateral by:

(1) specific listing;

(2) category;

(3) except as otherwise provided in subsection (e), a type of collateral defined in [the Uniform Commercial Code];

(4) quantity;

(5) computational or allocational formula or procedure; or

(6) except as otherwise provided in subsection (c), any other method, if the identity of the collateral is objectively determinable.

(c) A description of collateral as "all the debtor's assets" or "all the debtor's personal property" or using words of similar import does not reasonably identify the collateral.

(d) Except as otherwise provided in subsection (e), a description of a security entitlement, securities account, or commodity account is sufficient if it describes:

(1) the collateral by those terms or as investment property; or

(2) the underlying financial asset or commodity contract.

(e) A description only by type of collateral defined in [the Uniform Commercial Code] is an insufficient description of:

(1) a commercial tort claim; or

(2) in a consumer transaction, consumer goods, a security entitlement, a securities account, or a commodity account.

[Subpart 2. Applicability of Article]

§ 9-109.   Scope.

(a) Except as otherwise provided in subsections (c) and (d), this article applies to:

(1) a transaction, regardless of its form, that creates a security interest in personal property or fixtures by contract;

(2) an agricultural lien;

(3) a sale of accounts, chattel paper, payment intangibles, or promissory notes;

(4) a consignment;

(5) a security interest arising under Section 2–401, 2–505, 2–711(3), or 2A–508(5), as provided in Section 9–110; and

(6) a security interest arising under Section 4–210 or 5–118.

(b) The application of this article to a security interest in a secured obligation is not affected by the fact that the obligation is itself secured by a transaction or interest to which this article does not apply.

(c) This article does not apply to the extent that:

(1) a statute, regulation, or treaty of the United States preempts this article;

(2) another statute of this State expressly governs the creation, perfection, priority, or enforcement of a security interest created by this State or a governmental unit of this State;

(3) a statute of another State, a foreign country, or a governmental unit of another State or a foreign country, other than a statute generally applicable to security interests, expressly governs creation, perfection, priority, or enforcement of a security interest created by the State, country, or governmental unit; or

(4) the rights of a transferee beneficiary or nominated person under a letter of credit are independent and superior under Section 5–114.

(d) This article does not apply to:

(1) a landlord's lien, other than an agricultural lien;

(2) a lien, other than an agricultural lien, given by statute or other rule of law for services or materials, but Section 9–333 applies with respect to priority of the lien;

(3) an assignment of a claim for wages, salary, or other compensation of an employee;

(4) a sale of accounts, chattel paper, payment intangibles, or promissory notes as part of a sale of the business out of which they arose;

(5) an assignment of accounts, chattel paper, payment intangibles, or promissory notes which is for the purpose of collection only;

(6) an assignment of a right to payment under a contract to an assignee that is also obligated to perform under the contract;

(7) an assignment of a single account, payment intangible, or promissory note to an assignee in full or partial satisfaction of a preexisting indebtedness;

(8) a transfer of an interest in or an assignment of a claim under a policy of insurance, other than an assignment by or to a health-care provider of a health-care-insurance receivable and any subsequent assignment of the right to payment, but Sections 9–315 and 9–322 apply with respect to proceeds and priorities in proceeds;

(9) an assignment of a right represented by a judgment, other than a judgment taken on a right to payment that was collateral;

(10) a right of recoupment or set-off, but:

(A) Section 9–340 applies with respect to the effectiveness of rights of recoupment or set-off against deposit accounts; and

(B) Section 9–404 applies with respect to defenses or claims of an account debtor;

(11) the creation or transfer of an interest in or lien on real property, including a lease or rents thereunder, except to the extent that provision is made for:

(A) liens on real property in Sections 9–203 and 9–308;

(B) fixtures in Section 9–334;

(C) fixture filings in Sections 9–501, 9–502, 9–512, 9–516, and 9–519; and

(D) security agreements covering personal and real property in Section 9–604;

(12) an assignment of a claim arising in tort, other than a commercial tort claim, but Sections 9–315 and 9–322 apply with respect to proceeds and priorities in proceeds; or

(13) an assignment of a deposit account in a consumer transaction, but Sections 9–315 and 9–322 apply with respect to proceeds and priorities in proceeds.

§ 9–110. Security Interests Arising under Article 2 or 2A.

A security interest arising under Section 2–401, 2–505, 2–711(3), or 2A–508(5) is subject to this article. However, until the debtor obtains possession of the goods:

(1) the security interest is enforceable, even if Section 9–203(b)(3) has not been satisfied;

(2) filing is not required to perfect the security interest;

(3) the rights of the secured party after default by the debtor are governed by Article 2 or 2A; and

(4) the security interest has priority over a conflicting security interest created by the debtor.

PART 2 Effectiveness of Security Agreement; Attachment of Security Interest; Rights of Parties to Security Agreement

[Subpart 1. Effectiveness and Attachment]

§ 9–201. General Effectiveness of Security Agreement.

(a) Except as otherwise provided in [the Uniform Commercial Code], a security agreement is effective according to its terms between the parties, against purchasers of the collateral, and against creditors.

(b) A transaction subject to this article is subject to any applicable rule of law which establishes a different rule for consumers and [insert reference to (i) any other statute or regulation that regulates the rates, charges, agreements, and practices for loans, credit sales, or other extensions of credit and (ii) any consumer-protection statute or regulation].

(c) In case of conflict between this article and a rule of law, statute, or regulation described in subsection (b), the rule of law, statute, or regulation controls. Failure to comply with a statute or regulation described in subsection (b) has only the effect the statute or regulation specifies.

(d) This article does not:

(1) validate any rate, charge, agreement, or practice that violates a rule of law, statute, or regulation described in subsection (b); or

(2) extend the application of the rule of law, statute, or regulation to a transaction not otherwise subject to it.

§ 9–202.   Title to Collateral Immaterial.

Except as otherwise provided with respect to consignments or sales of accounts, chattel paper, payment intangibles, or promissory notes, the provisions of this article with regard to rights and obligations apply whether title to collateral is in the secured party or the debtor.

§ 9–203.   Attachment and Enforceability of Security Interest; Proceeds; Supporting Obligations; Formal Requisites.

(a) A security interest attaches to collateral when it becomes enforceable against the debtor with respect to the collateral, unless an agreement expressly postpones the time of attachment.

(b) Except as otherwise provided in subsections (c) through (i), a security interest is enforceable against the debtor and third parties with respect to the collateral only if:

(1) value has been given;

(2) the debtor has rights in the collateral or the power to transfer rights in the collateral to a secured party; and

(3) one of the following conditions is met:

(A) the debtor has authenticated a security agreement that provides a description of the collateral and, if the security interest covers timber to be cut, a description of the land concerned;

(B) the collateral is not a certificated security and is in the possession of the secured party under Section 9–313 pursuant to the debtor's security agreement;

(C) the collateral is a certificated security in registered form and the security certificate has been delivered to the secured party under Section 8–301 pursuant to the debtor's security agreement; or

(D) the collateral is deposit accounts, electronic chattel paper, investment property, or letter-of-credit rights, and the secured party has control under Section 9–104, 9–105, 9–106, or 9–107 pursuant to the debtor's security agreement.

(c) Subsection (b) is subject to Section 4–210 on the security interest of a collecting bank, Section 5–118 on the security interest of a letter-of-credit issuer or nominated person, Section 9–110 on a security interest arising under Article 2 or 2A, and Section 9–206 on security interests in investment property.

(d) A person becomes bound as debtor by a security agreement entered into by another person if, by operation of law other than this article or by contract:

(1) the security agreement becomes effective to create a security interest in the person's property; or

(2) the person becomes generally obligated for the obligations of the other person, including the obligation secured under the security agreement, and acquires or succeeds to all or substantially all of the assets of the other person.

(e) If a new debtor becomes bound as debtor by a security agreement entered into by another person:

(1) the agreement satisfies subsection (b)(3) with respect to existing or after-acquired property of the new debtor to the extent the property is described in the agreement; and

(2) another agreement is not necessary to make a security interest in the property enforceable.

(f) The attachment of a security interest in collateral gives the secured party the rights to proceeds provided by Section 9–315 and is also attachment of a security interest in a supporting obligation for the collateral.

(g) The attachment of a security interest in a right to payment or performance secured by a security interest or other lien on personal or real property is also attachment of a security interest in the security interest, mortgage, or other lien.

(h) The attachment of a security interest in a securities account is also attachment of a security interest in the security entitlements carried in the securities account.

(i) The attachment of a security interest in a commodity account is also attachment of a security interest in the commodity contracts carried in the commodity account.

§ 9–204.   After-Acquired Property; Future Advances.

(a) Except as otherwise provided in subsection (b), a security agreement may create or provide for a security interest in after-acquired collateral.

(b) A security interest does not attach under a term constituting an after-acquired property clause to:

(1) consumer goods, other than an accession when given as additional security, unless the debtor acquires rights in them within 10 days after the secured party gives value; or

(2) a commercial tort claim.

(c) A security agreement may provide that collateral secures, or that accounts, chattel paper, payment intangibles, or promissory notes are sold in connection with, future advances or other value, whether or not the advances or value are given pursuant to commitment.

§ 9–205. Use or Disposition of Collateral Permissible.

(a) A security interest is not invalid or fraudulent against creditors solely because:

(1) the debtor has the right or ability to:

(A) use, commingle, or dispose of all or part of the collateral, including returned or repossessed goods;

(B) collect, compromise, enforce, or otherwise deal with collateral;

(C) accept the return of collateral or make repossessions; or

(D) use, commingle, or dispose of proceeds; or

(2) the secured party fails to require the debtor to account for proceeds or replace collateral.

(b) This section does not relax the requirements of possession if attachment, perfection, or enforcement of a security interest depends upon possession of the collateral by the secured party.

§ 9–206. Security Interest Arising in Purchase or Delivery of Financial Asset.

(a) A security interest in favor of a securities intermediary attaches to a person's security entitlement if:

(1) the person buys a financial asset through the securities intermediary in a transaction in which the person is obligated to pay the purchase price to the securities intermediary at the time of the purchase; and

(2) the securities intermediary credits the financial asset to the buyer's securities account before the buyer pays the securities intermediary.

(b) The security interest described in subsection (a) secures the person's obligation to pay for the financial asset.

(c) A security interest in favor of a person that delivers a certificated security or other financial asset represented by a writing attaches to the security or other financial asset if:

(1) the security or other financial asset:

(A) in the ordinary course of business is transferred by delivery with any necessary indorsement or assignment; and

(B) is delivered under an agreement between persons in the business of dealing with such securities or financial assets; and

(2) the agreement calls for delivery against payment.

(d) The security interest described in subsection (c) secures the obligation to make payment for the delivery.

[Subpart 2. Rights and Duties]

§ 9–207. Rights and Duties of Secured Party Having Possession or Control of Collateral.

(a) Except as otherwise provided in subsection (d), a secured party shall use reasonable care in the custody and preservation of collateral in the secured party's possession. In the case of chattel paper or an instrument, reasonable care includes taking necessary steps to preserve rights against prior parties unless otherwise agreed.

(b) Except as otherwise provided in subsection (d), if a secured party has possession of collateral:

(1) reasonable expenses, including the cost of insurance and payment of taxes or other charges, incurred in the custody, preservation, use, or operation of the collateral are chargeable to the debtor and are secured by the collateral;

(2) the risk of accidental loss or damage is on the debtor to the extent of a deficiency in any effective insurance coverage;

(3) the secured party shall keep the collateral identifiable, but fungible collateral may be commingled; and

(4) the secured party may use or operate the collateral:

(A) for the purpose of preserving the collateral or its value;

(B) as permitted by an order of a court having competent jurisdiction; or

(C) except in the case of consumer goods, in the manner and to the extent agreed by the debtor.

(c) Except as otherwise provided in subsection (d), a secured party having possession of collateral or control of collateral under Section 9–104, 9–105, 9–106, or 9–107:

(1) may hold as additional security any proceeds, except money or funds, received from the collateral;

(2) shall apply money or funds received from the collateral to reduce the secured obligation, unless remitted to the debtor; and

(3) may create a security interest in the collateral.

(d) If the secured party is a buyer of accounts, chattel paper, payment intangibles, or promissory notes or a consignor:

(1) subsection (a) does not apply unless the secured party is entitled under an agreement:

(A) to charge back uncollected collateral; or

(B) otherwise to full or limited recourse against the debtor or a secondary obligor based on the nonpayment or other default of an account debtor or other obligor on the collateral; and

(2) subsections (b) and (c) do not apply.

§ 9–208. Additional Duties of Secured Party Having Control of Collateral.

(a) This section applies to cases in which there is no outstanding secured obligation and the secured party is not committed to make advances, incur obligations, or otherwise give value.

(b) Within 10 days after receiving an authenticated demand by the debtor:

(1) a secured party having control of a deposit account under Section 9–104(a)(2) shall send to the bank with which the deposit account is maintained an authenticated statement that

releases the bank from any further obligation to comply with instructions originated by the secured party;

(2) a secured party having control of a deposit account under Section 9–104(a)(3) shall:

(A) pay the debtor the balance on deposit in the deposit account; or

(B) transfer the balance on deposit into a deposit account in the debtor's name;

(3) a secured party, other than a buyer, having control of electronic chattel paper under Section 9–105 shall:

(A) communicate the authoritative copy of the electronic chattel paper to the debtor or its designated custodian;

(B) if the debtor designates a custodian that is the designated custodian with which the authoritative copy of the electronic chattel paper is maintained for the secured party, communicate to the custodian an authenticated record releasing the designated custodian from any further obligation to comply with instructions originated by the secured party and instructing the custodian to comply with instructions originated by the debtor; and

(C) take appropriate action to enable the debtor or its designated custodian to make copies of or revisions to the authoritative copy which add or change an identified assignee of the authoritative copy without the consent of the secured party;

(4) a secured party having control of investment property under Section 8–106(d)(2) or 9–106(b) shall send to the securities intermediary or commodity intermediary with which the security entitlement or commodity contract is maintained an authenticated record that releases the securities intermediary or commodity intermediary from any further obligation to comply with entitlement orders or directions originated by the secured party; and

(5) a secured party having control of a letter-of-credit right under Section 9–107 shall send to each person having an unfulfilled obligation to pay or deliver proceeds of the letter of credit to the secured party an authenticated release from any further obligation to pay or deliver proceeds of the letter of credit to the secured party.

§ 9–209.   Duties of Secured Party If Account Debtor Has Been Notified of Assignment.

(a) Except as otherwise provided in subsection (c), this section applies if:

(1) there is no outstanding secured obligation; and

(2) the secured party is not committed to make advances, incur obligations, or otherwise give value.

(b) Within 10 days after receiving an authenticated demand by the debtor, a secured party shall send to an account debtor that has received notification of an assignment to the secured party as assignee under Section 9–406(a) an authenticated record that releases the account debtor from any further obligation to the secured party.

(c) This section does not apply to an assignment constituting the sale of an account, chattel paper, or payment intangible.

§ 9–210.   Request for Accounting; Request Regarding List of Collateral or Statement of Account.

(a) In this section:

(1) "Request" means a record of a type described in paragraph (2), (3), or (4).

(2) "Request for an accounting" means a record authenticated by a debtor requesting that the recipient provide an accounting of the unpaid obligations secured by collateral and reasonably identifying the transaction or relationship that is the subject of the request.

(3) "Request regarding a list of collateral" means a record authenticated by a debtor requesting that the recipient approve or correct a list of what the debtor believes to be the collateral securing an obligation and reasonably identifying the transaction or relationship that is the subject of the request.

(4) "Request regarding a statement of account" means a record authenticated by a debtor requesting that the recipient approve or correct a statement indicating what the debtor believes to be the aggregate amount of unpaid obligations secured by collateral as of a specified date and reasonably identifying the transaction or relationship that is the subject of the request.

(b) Subject to subsections (c), (d), (e), and (f), a secured party, other than a buyer of accounts, chattel paper, payment intangibles, or promissory notes or a consignor, shall comply with a request within 14 days after receipt:

(1) in the case of a request for an accounting, by authenticating and sending to the debtor an accounting; and

(2) in the case of a request regarding a list of collateral or a request regarding a statement of account, by authenticating and sending to the debtor an approval or correction.

(c) A secured party that claims a security interest in all of a particular type of collateral owned by the debtor may comply with a request regarding a list of collateral by sending to the debtor an authenticated record including a statement to that effect within 14 days after receipt.

(d) A person that receives a request regarding a list of collateral, claims no interest in the collateral when it receives the request, and claimed an interest in the collateral at an earlier time shall comply with the request within 14 days after receipt by sending to the debtor an authenticated record:

(1) disclaiming any interest in the collateral; and

(2) if known to the recipient, providing the name and mailing address of any assignee of or successor to the recipient's interest in the collateral.

(e) A person that receives a request for an accounting or a request regarding a statement of account, claims no interest in the obligations when it receives the request, and claimed an interest in the obligations at an earlier time shall comply with the request within 14 days after receipt by sending to the debtor an authenticated record:

(1) disclaiming any interest in the obligations; and

(2) if known to the recipient, providing the name and mailing address of any assignee of or successor to the recipient's interest in the obligations.

(f) A debtor is entitled without charge to one response to a request under this section during any six-month period. The secured party may require payment of a charge not exceeding $25 for each additional response.

As amended in 1999.

PART 3 Perfection and Priority

[Subpart 1. Law Governing Perfection and Priority]

§ 9–301. Law Governing Perfection and Priority of Security Interests.

Except as otherwise provided in Sections 9–303 through 9–306, the following rules determine the law governing perfection, the effect of perfection or nonperfection, and the priority of a security interest in collateral:

(1) Except as otherwise provided in this section, while a debtor is located in a jurisdiction, the local law of that jurisdiction governs perfection, the effect of perfection or nonperfection, and the priority of a security interest in collateral.

(2) While collateral is located in a jurisdiction, the local law of that jurisdiction governs perfection, the effect of perfection or nonperfection, and the priority of a possessory security interest in that collateral.

(3) Except as otherwise provided in paragraph (4), while negotiable documents, goods, instruments, money, or tangible chattel paper is located in a jurisdiction, the local law of that jurisdiction governs:

(A) perfection of a security interest in the goods by filing a fixture filing;

(B) perfection of a security interest in timber to be cut; and

(C) the effect of perfection or nonperfection and the priority of a nonpossessory security interest in the collateral.

(4) The local law of the jurisdiction in which the wellhead or minehead is located governs perfection, the effect of perfection or nonperfection, and the priority of a security interest in as-extracted collateral.

§ 9–302. Law Governing Perfection and Priority of Agricultural Liens.

While farm products are located in a jurisdiction, the local law of that jurisdiction governs perfection, the effect of perfection or nonperfection, and the priority of an agricultural lien on the farm products.

§ 9–303. Law Governing Perfection and Priority of Security Interests in Goods Covered by a Certificate of Title.

(a) This section applies to goods covered by a certificate of title, even if there is no other relationship between the jurisdiction under whose certificate of title the goods are covered and the goods or the debtor.

(b) Goods become covered by a certificate of title when a valid application for the certificate of title and the applicable fee are delivered to the appropriate authority. Goods cease to be covered by a certificate of title at the earlier of the time the certificate of title ceases to be effective under the law of the issuing jurisdiction or the time the goods become covered subsequently by a certificate of title issued by another jurisdiction.

(c) The local law of the jurisdiction under whose certificate of title the goods are covered governs perfection, the effect of perfection or nonperfection, and the priority of a security interest in goods covered by a certificate of title from the time the goods become covered by the certificate of title until the goods cease to be covered by the certificate of title.

§ 9–304. Law Governing Perfection and Priority of Security Interests in Deposit Accounts.

(a) The local law of a bank's jurisdiction governs perfection, the effect of perfection or nonperfection, and the priority of a security interest in a deposit account maintained with that bank.

(b) The following rules determine a bank's jurisdiction for purposes of this part:

(1) If an agreement between the bank and the debtor governing the deposit account expressly provides that a particular jurisdiction is the bank's jurisdiction for purposes of this part, this article, or [the Uniform Commercial Code], that jurisdiction is the bank's jurisdiction.

(2) If paragraph (1) does not apply and an agreement between the bank and its customer governing the deposit account expressly provides that the agreement is governed by the law of a particular jurisdiction, that jurisdiction is the bank's jurisdiction.

(3) If neither paragraph (1) nor paragraph (2) applies and an agreement between the bank and its customer governing the deposit account expressly provides that the deposit account is maintained at an office in a particular jurisdiction, that jurisdiction is the bank's jurisdiction.

(4) If none of the preceding paragraphs applies, the bank's jurisdiction is the jurisdiction in which the office identified in an account statement as the office serving the customer's account is located.

(5) If none of the preceding paragraphs applies, the bank's jurisdiction is the jurisdiction in which the chief executive office of the bank is located.

§ 9–305.   Law Governing Perfection and Priority of Security Interests in Investment Property.

(a) Except as otherwise provided in subsection (c), the following rules apply:

(1) While a security certificate is located in a jurisdiction, the local law of that jurisdiction governs perfection, the effect of perfection or nonperfection, and the priority of a security interest in the certificated security represented thereby.

(2) The local law of the issuer's jurisdiction as specified in Section 8–110(d) governs perfection, the effect of perfection or nonperfection, and the priority of a security interest in an uncertificated security.

(3) The local law of the securities intermediary's jurisdiction as specified in Section 8–110(e) governs perfection, the effect of perfection or nonperfection, and the priority of a security interest in a security entitlement or securities account.

(4) The local law of the commodity intermediary's jurisdiction governs perfection, the effect of perfection or nonperfection, and the priority of a security interest in a commodity contract or commodity account.

(b) The following rules determine a commodity intermediary's jurisdiction for purposes of this part:

(1) If an agreement between the commodity intermediary and commodity customer governing the commodity account expressly provides that a particular jurisdiction is the commodity intermediary's jurisdiction for purposes of this part, this article, or [the Uniform Commercial Code], that jurisdiction is the commodity intermediary's jurisdiction.

(2) If paragraph (1) does not apply and an agreement between the commodity intermediary and commodity customer governing the commodity account expressly provides that the agreement is governed by the law of a particular jurisdiction, that jurisdiction is the commodity intermediary's jurisdiction.

(3) If neither paragraph (1) nor paragraph (2) applies and an agreement between the commodity intermediary and commodity customer governing the commodity account expressly provides that the commodity account is maintained at an office in a particular jurisdiction, that jurisdiction is the commodity intermediary's jurisdiction.

(4) If none of the preceding paragraphs applies, the commodity intermediary's jurisdiction is the jurisdiction in which the office identified in an account statement as the office serving the commodity customer's account is located.

(5) If none of the preceding paragraphs applies, the commodity intermediary's jurisdiction is the jurisdiction in which the chief executive office of the commodity intermediary is located.

(c) The local law of the jurisdiction in which the debtor is located governs:

(1) perfection of a security interest in investment property by filing;

(2) automatic perfection of a security interest in investment property created by a broker or securities intermediary; and

(3) automatic perfection of a security interest in a commodity contract or commodity account created by a commodity intermediary.

§ 9–306.   Law Governing Perfection and Priority of Security Interests in Letter-of-Credit Rights.

(a) Subject to subsection (c), the local law of the issuer's jurisdiction or a nominated person's jurisdiction governs perfection, the effect of perfection or nonperfection, and the priority of a security interest in a letter-of-credit right if the issuer's jurisdiction or nominated person's jurisdiction is a State.

(b) For purposes of this part, an issuer's jurisdiction or nominated person's jurisdiction is the jurisdiction whose law governs the liability of the issuer or nominated person with respect to the letter-of-credit right as provided in Section 5–116.

(c) This section does not apply to a security interest that is perfected only under Section 9–308(d).

§ 9–307.   Location of Debtor.

(a) In this section, "place of business" means a place where a debtor conducts its affairs.

(b) Except as otherwise provided in this section, the following rules determine a debtor's location:

(1) A debtor who is an individual is located at the individual's principal residence.

(2) A debtor that is an organization and has only one place of business is located at its place of business.

(3) A debtor that is an organization and has more than one place of business is located at its chief executive office.

(c) Subsection (b) applies only if a debtor's residence, place of business, or chief executive office, as applicable, is located in a jurisdiction whose law generally requires information concerning the existence of a nonpossessory security interest to be made generally available in a filing, recording, or registration system as a condition or result of the security interest's obtaining priority over the rights of a lien creditor with respect to the collateral. If subsection (b) does not apply, the debtor is located in the District of Columbia.

(d) A person that ceases to exist, have a residence, or have a place of business continues to be located in the jurisdiction specified by subsections (b) and (c).

(e) A registered organization that is organized under the law of a State is located in that State.

(f) Except as otherwise provided in subsection (i), a registered organization that is organized under the law of the United Statesand a branch or agency of a bank that is not organized under the law of the United States or a State are located:

(1) in the State that the law of the United States designates, if the law designates a State of location;

(2) in the State that the registered organization, branch, or agency designates, if the law of the United States authorizes the registered organization, branch, or agency to designate its State of location; or

(3) in the District of Columbia, if neither paragraph (1) nor paragraph (2) applies.

(g) A registered organization continues to be located in the jurisdiction specified by subsection (e) or (f) notwithstanding:

(1) the suspension, revocation, forfeiture, or lapse of the registered organization's status as such in its jurisdiction of organization; or

(2) the dissolution, winding up, or cancellation of the existence of the registered organization.

(h) The United States is located in the District of Columbia.

(i) A branch or agency of a bank that is not organized under the law of the United States or a State is located in the State in which the branch or agency is licensed, if all branches and agencies of the bank are licensed in only one State.

(j) A foreign air carrier under the Federal Aviation Act of 1958, as amended, is located at the designated office of the agent upon which service of process may be made on behalf of the carrier.

(k) This section applies only for purposes of this part.

[Subpart 2. Perfection]

§ 9–308. When Security Interest or Agricultural Lien Is Perfected; Continuity of Perfection.

(a) Except as otherwise provided in this section and Section 9–309, a security interest is perfected if it has attached and all of the applicable requirements for perfection in Sections 9–310 through 9–316 have been satisfied. A security interest is perfected when it attaches if the applicable requirements are satisfied before the security interest attaches.

(b) An agricultural lien is perfected if it has become effective and all of the applicable requirements for perfection in Section 9–310 have been satisfied. An agricultural lien is perfected when it becomes effective if the applicable requirements are satisfied before the agricultural lien becomes effective.

(c) A security interest or agricultural lien is perfected continuously if it is originally perfected by one method under this article and is later perfected by another method under this article, without an intermediate period when it was unperfected.

(d) Perfection of a security interest in collateral also perfects a security interest in a supporting obligation for the collateral.

(e) Perfection of a security interest in a right to payment or performance also perfects a security interest in a security interest, mortgage, or other lien on personal or real property securing the right.

(f) Perfection of a security interest in a securities account also perfects a security interest in the security entitlements carried in the securities account.

(g) Perfection of a security interest in a commodity account also perfects a security interest in the commodity contracts carried in the commodity account.

Legislative Note: Any statute conflicting with subsection (e) must be made expressly subject to that subsection.

§ 9–309. Security Interest Perfected upon Attachment.

The following security interests are perfected when they attach:

(1) a purchase-money security interest in consumer goods, except as otherwise provided in Section 9–311(b) with respect to consumer goods that are subject to a statute or treaty described in Section 9–311(a);

(2) an assignment of accounts or payment intangibles which does not by itself or in conjunction with other assignments to the same assignee transfer a significant part of the assignor's outstanding accounts or payment intangibles;

(3) a sale of a payment intangible;

(4) a sale of a promissory note;

(5) a security interest created by the assignment of a health-care-insurance receivable to the provider of the health-care goods or services;

(6) a security interest arising under Section 2–401, 2–505, 2–711(3), or 2A–508(5), until the debtor obtains possession of the collateral;

(7) a security interest of a collecting bank arising under Section 4–210;

(8) a security interest of an issuer or nominated person arising under Section 5–118;

(9) a security interest arising in the delivery of a financial asset under Section 9–206(c);

(10) a security interest in investment property created by a broker or securities intermediary;

(11) a security interest in a commodity contract or a commodity account created by a commodity intermediary;

(12) an assignment for the benefit of all creditors of the transferor and subsequent transfers by the assignee thereunder; and

(13) a security interest created by an assignment of a beneficial interest in a decedent's estate; and

(14) a sale by an individual of an account that is a right to payment of winnings in a lottery or other game of chance.

§ 9–310.   When Filing Required to Perfect Security Interest or Agricultural Lien; Security Interests and Agricultural Liens to Which Filing Provisions Do Not Apply.

(a) Except as otherwise provided in subsection (b) and Section 9–312(b), a financing statement must be filed to perfect all security interests and agricultural liens.

(b) The filing of a financing statement is not necessary to perfect a security interest:

(1) that is perfected under Section 9–308(d), (e), (f), or (g);

(2) that is perfected under Section 9–309 when it attaches;

(3) in property subject to a statute, regulation, or treaty described in Section 9–311(a);

(4) in goods in possession of a bailee which is perfected under Section 9–312(d)(1) or (2);

(5) in certificated securities, documents, goods, or instruments which is perfected without filing or possession under Section 9–312(e), (f), or (g);

(6) in collateral in the secured party's possession under Section 9–313;

(7) in a certificated security which is perfected by delivery of the security certificate to the secured party under Section 9–313;

(8) in deposit accounts, electronic chattel paper, investment property, or letter-of-credit rights which is perfected by control under Section 9–314;

(9) in proceeds which is perfected under Section 9–315; or

(10) that is perfected under Section 9–316.

(c) If a secured party assigns a perfected security interest or agricultural lien, a filing under this article is not required to continue the perfected status of the security interest against creditors of and transferees from the original debtor.

§ 9–311.   Perfection of Security Interests in Property Subject to Certain Statutes, Regulations, and Treaties.

(a) Except as otherwise provided in subsection (d), the filing of a financing statement is not necessary or effective to perfect a security interest in property subject to:

(1) a statute, regulation, or treaty of the United States whose requirements for a security interest's obtaining priority over the rights of a lien creditor with respect to the property preempt Section 9–310(a);

(2) [list any certificate-of-title statute covering automobiles, trailers, mobile homes, boats, farm tractors, or the like, which provides for a security interest to be indicated on the certificate as a condition or result of perfection, and any non-Uniform Commercial Code central filing statute]; or

(3) a certificate-of-title statute of another jurisdiction which provides for a security interest to be indicated on the certificate as a condition or result of the security interest's obtaining priority over the rights of a lien creditor with respect to the property.

(b) Compliance with the requirements of a statute, regulation, or treaty described in subsection (a) for obtaining priority over the rights of a lien creditor is equivalent to the filing of a financing statement under this article. Except as otherwise provided in subsection (d) and Sections 9–313 and 9–316(d) and (e) for goods covered by a certificate of title, a security interest in property subject to a statute, regulation, or treaty described in subsection (a) may be perfected only by compliance with those requirements, and a security interest so perfected remains perfected notwithstanding a change in the use or transfer of possession of the collateral.

(c) Except as otherwise provided in subsection (d) and Section 9–316(d) and (e), duration and renewal of perfection of a security interest perfected by compliance with the requirements prescribed by a statute, regulation, or treaty described in subsection (a) are governed by the statute, regulation, or treaty. In other respects, the security interest is subject to this article.

(d) During any period in which collateral subject to a statute specified in subsection (a)(2) is inventory held for sale or lease by a person or leased by that person as lessor and that person is in the business of selling goods of that kind, this section does not apply to a security interest in that collateral created by that person.

Legislative Note: This Article contemplates that perfection of a security interest in goods covered by a certificate of title occurs upon receipt by appropriate State officials of a properly tendered application for a certificate of title on which the security interest is to be indicated, without a relation back to an earlier time. States whose certificate-of-title statutes provide for perfection at a different time or contain a relation-back provision should amend the statutes accordingly.

§ 9–312.   Perfection of Security Interests in Chattel Paper, Deposit Accounts, Documents, Goods Covered by Documents, Instruments, Investment Property, Letter-of-Credit Rights, and Money; Perfection by Permissive Filing; Temporary Perfection without Filing or Transfer of Possession.

(a) A security interest in chattel paper, negotiable documents, instruments, or investment property may be perfected by filing.

(b) Except as otherwise provided in Section 9–315(c) and (d) for proceeds:

(1) a security interest in a deposit account may be perfected only by control under Section 9–314;

(2) and except as otherwise provided in Section 9–308(d), a security interest in a letter-of-credit right may be perfected only by control under Section 9–314; and

(3) a security interest in money may be perfected only by the secured party's taking possession under Section 9–313.

(c) While goods are in the possession of a bailee that has issued a negotiable document covering the goods:

(1) a security interest in the goods may be perfected by perfecting a security interest in the document; and

(2) a security interest perfected in the document has priority over any security interest that becomes perfected in the goods by another method during that time.

(d) While goods are in the possession of a bailee that has issued a nonnegotiable document covering the goods, a security interest in the goods may be perfected by:

(1) issuance of a document in the name of the secured party;

(2) the bailee's receipt of notification of the secured party's interest; or

(3) filing as to the goods.

(e) A security interest in certificated securities, negotiable documents, or instruments is perfected without filing or the taking of possession for a period of 20 days from the time it attaches to the extent that it arises for new value given under an authenticated security agreement.

(f) A perfected security interest in a negotiable document or goods in possession of a bailee, other than one that has issued a negotiable document for the goods, remains perfected for 20 days without filing if the secured party makes available to the debtor the goods or documents representing the goods for the purpose of:

(1) ultimate sale or exchange; or

(2) loading, unloading, storing, shipping, transshipping, manufacturing, processing, or otherwise dealing with them in a manner preliminary to their sale or exchange.

(g) A perfected security interest in a certificated security or instrument remains perfected for 20 days without filing if the secured party delivers the security certificate or instrument to the debtor for the purpose of:

(1) ultimate sale or exchange; or

(2) presentation, collection, enforcement, renewal, or registration of transfer.

(h) After the 20-day period specified in subsection (e), (f), or (g) expires, perfection depends upon compliance with this article.

§ 9–313.   When Possession by or Delivery to Secured Party Perfects Security Interest without Filing.

(a) Except as otherwise provided in subsection (b), a secured party may perfect a security interest in negotiable documents, goods, instruments, money, or tangible chattel paper by taking possession of the collateral. A secured party may perfect a security interest in certificated securities by taking delivery of the certificated securities under Section 8–301.

(b) With respect to goods covered by a certificate of title issued by this State, a secured party may perfect a security interest in the goods by taking possession of the goods only in the circumstances described in Section 9–316(d).

(c) With respect to collateral other than certificated securities and goods covered by a document, a secured party takes possession of collateral in the possession of a person other than the debtor, the secured party, or a lessee of the collateral from the debtor in the ordinary course of the debtor's business, when:

(1) the person in possession authenticates a record acknowledging that it holds possession of the collateral for the secured party's benefit; or

(2) the person takes possession of the collateral after having authenticated a record acknowledging that it will hold possession of collateral for the secured party's benefit.

(d) If perfection of a security interest depends upon possession of the collateral by a secured party, perfection occurs no earlier than the time the secured party takes possession and continues only while the secured party retains possession.

(e) A security interest in a certificated security in registered form is perfected by delivery when delivery of the certificated security occurs under Section 8–301 and remains perfected by delivery until the debtor obtains possession of the security certificate.

(f) A person in possession of collateral is not required to acknowledge that it holds possession for a secured party's benefit.

(g) If a person acknowledges that it holds possession for the secured party's benefit:

(1) the acknowledgment is effective under subsection (c) or Section 8–301(a), even if the acknowledgment violates the rights of a debtor; and

(2) unless the person otherwise agrees or law other than this article otherwise provides, the person does not owe any duty to the secured party and is not required to confirm the acknowledgment to another person.

(h) A secured party having possession of collateral does not relinquish possession by delivering the collateral to a person other than the debtor or a lessee of the collateral from the debtor in the ordinary course of the debtor's business if the person was instructed before the delivery or is instructed contemporaneously with the delivery:

(1) to hold possession of the collateral for the secured party's benefit; or

(2) to redeliver the collateral to the secured party.

(i) A secured party does not relinquish possession, even if a delivery under subsection (h) violates the rights of a debtor. A person to which collateral is delivered under subsection (h) does not owe any duty to the secured party and is not required to confirm the delivery to another person unless the person otherwise agrees or law other than this article otherwise provides.

§ 9–314.   Perfection by Control.

(a) A security interest in investment property, deposit accounts, letter-of-credit rights, or electronic chattel paper may be perfected by control of the collateral under Section 9–104, 9–105, 9–106, or 9–107.

(b) A security interest in deposit accounts, electronic chattel paper, or letter-of-credit rights is perfected by control under Section 9–104, 9–105, or 9–107 when the secured party obtains control and remains perfected by control only while the secured party retains control.

(c) A security interest in investment property is perfected by control under Section 9–106 from the time the secured party obtains control and remains perfected by control until:

(1) the secured party does not have control; and

(2) one of the following occurs:

(A) if the collateral is a certificated security, the debtor has or acquires possession of the security certificate;

(B) if the collateral is an uncertificated security, the issuer has registered or registers the debtor as the registered owner; or

(C) if the collateral is a security entitlement, the debtor is or becomes the entitlement holder.

§ 9–315.   Secured Party's Rights on Disposition of Collateral and in Proceeds.

(a) Except as otherwise provided in this article and in Section 2–403(2):

(1) a security interest or agricultural lien continues in collateral notwithstanding sale, lease, license, exchange, or other disposition thereof unless the secured party authorized the disposition free of the security interest or agricultural lien; and

(2) a security interest attaches to any identifiable proceeds of collateral.

(b) Proceeds that are commingled with other property are identifiable proceeds:

(1) if the proceeds are goods, to the extent provided by Section 9–336; and

(2) if the proceeds are not goods, to the extent that the secured party identifies the proceeds by a method of tracing, including application of equitable principles, that is permitted under law other than this article with respect to commingled property of the type involved.

(c) A security interest in proceeds is a perfected security interest if the security interest in the original collateral was perfected.

(d) A perfected security interest in proceeds becomes unperfected on the 21st day after the security interest attaches to the proceeds unless:

(1) the following conditions are satisfied:

(A) a filed financing statement covers the original collateral;

(B) the proceeds are collateral in which a security interest may be perfected by filing in the office in which the financing statement has been filed; and

(C) the proceeds are not acquired with cash proceeds;

(2) the proceeds are identifiable cash proceeds; or

(3) the security interest in the proceeds is perfected other than under subsection (c) when the security interest attaches to the proceeds or within 20 days thereafter.

(e) If a filed financing statement covers the original collateral, a security interest in proceeds which remains perfected under subsection (d)(1) becomes unperfected at the later of:

(1) when the effectiveness of the filed financing statement lapses under Section 9–515 or is terminated under Section 9–513; or

(2) the 21st day after the security interest attaches to the proceeds.

§ 9–316.   Continued Perfection of Security Interest Following Change in Governing Law.

(a) A security interest perfected pursuant to the law of the jurisdiction designated in Section 9–301(1) or 9–305(c) remains perfected until the earliest of:

(1) the time perfection would have ceased under the law of that jurisdiction;

(2) the expiration of four months after a change of the debtor's location to another jurisdiction; or

(3) the expiration of one year after a transfer of collateral to a person that thereby becomes a debtor and is located in another jurisdiction.

(b) If a security interest described in subsection (a) becomes perfected under the law of the other jurisdiction before the earliest time or event described in that subsection, it remains perfected thereafter. If the security interest does not become perfected under the law of the other jurisdiction before the earliest time or event, it becomes unperfected and is deemed never to have been perfected as against a purchaser of the collateral for value.

(c) A possessory security interest in collateral, other than goods covered by a certificate of title and as-extracted collateral consisting of goods, remains continuously perfected if:

(1) the collateral is located in one jurisdiction and subject to a security interest perfected under the law of that jurisdiction;

(2) thereafter the collateral is brought into another jurisdiction; and

(3) upon entry into the other jurisdiction, the security interest is perfected under the law of the other jurisdiction.

(d) Except as otherwise provided in subsection (e), a security interest in goods covered by a certificate of title which is perfected by any method under the law of another jurisdiction when the goods become covered by a certificate of title from this State remains perfected until the security interest would have become unperfected under the law of the other jurisdiction had the goods not become so covered.

(e) A security interest described in subsection (d) becomes unperfected as against a purchaser of the goods for value and is deemed never to have been perfected as against a purchaser of the goods for value if the applicable requirements for perfection under Section 9–311(b) or 9–313 are not satisfied before the earlier of:

(1) the time the security interest would have become unperfected under the law of the other jurisdiction had the goods not become covered by a certificate of title from this State; or

(2) the expiration of four months after the goods had become so covered.

(f) A security interest in deposit accounts, letter-of-credit rights, or investment property which is perfected under the law of the bank's jurisdiction, the issuer's jurisdiction, a nominated person's jurisdiction, the securities intermediary's jurisdiction, or the commodity intermediary's jurisdiction, as applicable, remains perfected until the earlier of:

(1) the time the security interest would have become unperfected under the law of that jurisdiction; or

(2) the expiration of four months after a change of the applicable jurisdiction to another jurisdiction.

(g) If a security interest described in subsection (f) becomes perfected under the law of the other jurisdiction before the earlier of the time or the end of the period described in that subsection, it remains perfected thereafter. If the security interest does not become perfected under the law of the other jurisdiction before the earlier of that time or the end of that period, it becomes unperfected and is deemed never to have been perfected as against a purchaser of the collateral for value.

[Subpart 3. Priority]

§ 9–317. Interests That Take Priority over or Take Free of Security Interest or Agricultural Lien.

(a) A security interest or agricultural lien is subordinate to the rights of:

(1) a person entitled to priority under Section 9–322; and

(2) except as otherwise provided in subsection (e), a person that becomes a lien creditor before the earlier of the time:

(A) the security interest or agricultural lien is perfected; or

(B) one of the conditions specified in Section 9–203(b)(3) is met and a financing statement covering the collateral is filed.

(b) Except as otherwise provided in subsection (e), a buyer, other than a secured party, of tangible chattel paper, documents, goods, instruments, or a security certificate takes free of a security interest or agricultural lien if the buyer gives value and receives delivery of the collateral without knowledge of the security interest or agricultural lien and before it is perfected.

(c) Except as otherwise provided in subsection (e), a lessee of goods takes free of a security interest or agricultural lien if the lessee gives value and receives delivery of the collateral without knowledge of the security interest or agricultural lien and before it is perfected.

(d) A licensee of a general intangible or a buyer, other than a secured party, of accounts, electronic chattel paper, general intangibles, or investment property other than a certificated security takes free of a security interest if the licensee or buyer gives value without knowledge of the security interest and before it is perfected.

(e) Except as otherwise provided in Sections 9–320 and 9–321, if a person files a financing statement with respect to a purchase-money security interest before or within 20 days after the debtor receives delivery of the collateral, the security interest takes priority over the rights of a buyer, lessee, or lien creditor which arise between the time the security interest attaches and the time of filing.

As amended in 2000.

§ 9–318. No Interest Retained in Right to Payment That Is Sold; Rights and Title of Seller of Account or Chattel Paper with Respect to Creditors and Purchasers.

(a) A debtor that has sold an account, chattel paper, payment intangible, or promissory note does not retain a legal or equitable interest in the collateral sold.

(b) For purposes of determining the rights of creditors of, and purchasers for value of an account or chattel paper from, a debtor that has sold an account or chattel paper, while the buyer's security interest is unperfected, the debtor is deemed to have rights and title to the account or chattel paper identical to those the debtor sold.

§ 9–319. Rights and Title of Consignee with Respect to Creditors and Purchasers.

(a) Except as otherwise provided in subsection (b), for purposes of determining the rights of creditors of, and purchasers for value of goods from, a consignee, while the goods are in the possession of the consignee, the consignee is deemed to have rights and title to the goods identical to those the consignor had or had power to transfer.

(b) For purposes of determining the rights of a creditor of a consignee, law other than this article determines the rights and title of a consignee while goods are in the consignee's possession if, under this part, a perfected security interest held by the consignor would have priority over the rights of the creditor.

§ 9–320. Buyer of Goods.

(a) Except as otherwise provided in subsection (e), a buyer in ordinary course of business, other than a person buying farm products from a person engaged in farming operations, takes free of a security interest created by the buyer's seller, even if the security interest is perfected and the buyer knows of its existence.

(b) Except as otherwise provided in subsection (e), a buyer of goods from a person who used or bought the goods for use primarily for personal, family, or household purposes takes free of a security interest, even if perfected, if the buyer buys:

(1) without knowledge of the security interest;

(2) for value;

(3) primarily for the buyer's personal, family, or household purposes; and

(4) before the filing of a financing statement covering the goods.

(c) To the extent that it affects the priority of a security interest over a buyer of goods under subsection (b), the period of effectiveness of a filing made in the jurisdiction in which the seller is located is governed by Section 9–316(a) and (b).

(d) A buyer in ordinary course of business buying oil, gas, or other minerals at the wellhead or minehead or after extraction takes free of an interest arising out of an encumbrance.

(e) Subsections (a) and (b) do not affect a security interest in goods in the possession of the secured party under Section 9–313.

§ 9–321.   Licensee of General Intangible and Lessee of Goods in Ordinary Course of Business.

(a) In this section, "licensee in ordinary course of business" means a person that becomes a licensee of a general intangible in good faith, without knowledge that the license violates the rights of another person in the general intangible, and in the ordinary course from a person in the business of licensing general intangibles of that kind. A person becomes a licensee in the ordinary course if the license to the person comports with the usual or customary practices in the kind of business in which the licensor is engaged or with the licensor's own usual or customary practices.

(b) A licensee in ordinary course of business takes its rights under a nonexclusive license free of a security interest in the general intangible created by the licensor, even if the security interest is perfected and the licensee knows of its existence.

(c) A lessee in ordinary course of business takes its leasehold interest free of a security interest in the goods created by the lessor, even if the security interest is perfected and the lessee knows of its existence.

§ 9–322.   Priorities among Conflicting Security Interests in and Agricultural Liens on Same Collateral.

(a) Except as otherwise provided in this section, priority among conflicting security interests and agricultural liens in the same collateral is determined according to the following rules:

(1) Conflicting perfected security interests and agricultural liens rank according to priority in time of filing or perfection. Priority dates from the earlier of the time a filing covering the collateral is first made or the security interest or agricultural lien is first perfected, if there is no period thereafter when there is neither filing nor perfection.

(2) A perfected security interest or agricultural lien has priority over a conflicting unperfected security interest or agricultural lien.

(3) The first security interest or agricultural lien to attach or become effective has priority if conflicting security interests and agricultural liens are unperfected.

(b) For the purposes of subsection (a)(1):

(1) the time of filing or perfection as to a security interest in collateral is also the time of filing or perfection as to a security interest in proceeds; and

(2) the time of filing or perfection as to a security interest in collateral supported by a supporting obligation is also the time of filing or perfection as to a security interest in the supporting obligation.

(c) Except as otherwise provided in subsection (f), a security interest in collateral which qualifies for priority over a conflicting security interest under Section 9–327, 9–328, 9–329, 9–330, or 9–331 also has priority over a conflicting security interest in:

(1) any supporting obligation for the collateral; and

(2) proceeds of the collateral if:

(A) the security interest in proceeds is perfected;

(B) the proceeds are cash proceeds or of the same type as the collateral; and

(C) in the case of proceeds that are proceeds of proceeds, all intervening proceeds are cash proceeds, proceeds of the same type as the collateral, or an account relating to the collateral.

(d) Subject to subsection (e) and except as otherwise provided in subsection (f), if a security interest in chattel paper, deposit accounts, negotiable documents, instruments, investment property, or letter-of-credit rights is perfected by a method other than filing, conflicting perfected security interests in proceeds of the collateral rank according to priority in time of filing.

(e) Subsection (d) applies only if the proceeds of the collateral are not cash proceeds, chattel paper, negotiable documents, instruments, investment property, or letter-of-credit rights.

(f) Subsections (a) through (e) are subject to:

(1) subsection (g) and the other provisions of this part;

(2) Section 4–210 with respect to a security interest of a collecting bank;

(3) Section 5–118 with respect to a security interest of an issuer or nominated person; and

(4) Section 9–110 with respect to a security interest arising under Article 2 or 2A.

(g) A perfected agricultural lien on collateral has priority over a conflicting security interest in or agricultural lien on the same collateral if the statute creating the agricultural lien so provides.

§ 9–323. Future Advances.

(a) Except as otherwise provided in subsection (c), for purposes of determining the priority of a perfected security interest under Section 9–322(a)(1), perfection of the security interest dates from the time an advance is made to the extent that the security interest secures an advance that:

(1) is made while the security interest is perfected only:

(A) under Section 9–309 when it attaches; or

(B) temporarily under Section 9–312(e), (f), or (g); and

(2) is not made pursuant to a commitment entered into before or while the security interest is perfected by a method other than under Section 9–309 or 9–312(e), (f), or (g).

(b) Except as otherwise provided in subsection (c), a security interest is subordinate to the rights of a person that becomes a lien creditor to the extent that the security interest secures an advance made more than 45 days after the person becomes a lien creditor unless the advance is made:

(1) without knowledge of the lien; or

(2) pursuant to a commitment entered into without knowledge of the lien.

(c) Subsections (a) and (b) do not apply to a security interest held by a secured party that is a buyer of accounts, chattel paper, payment intangibles, or promissory notes or a consignor.

(d) Except as otherwise provided in subsection (e), a buyer of goods other than a buyer in ordinary course of business takes free of a security interest to the extent that it secures advances made after the earlier of:

(1) the time the secured party acquires knowledge of the buyer's purchase; or

(2) 45 days after the purchase.

(e) Subsection (d) does not apply if the advance is made pursuant to a commitment entered into without knowledge of the buyer's purchase and before the expiration of the 45-day period.

(f) Except as otherwise provided in subsection (g), a lessee of goods, other than a lessee in ordinary course of business, takes the leasehold interest free of a security interest to the extent that it secures advances made after the earlier of:

(1) the time the secured party acquires knowledge of the lease; or

(2) 45 days after the lease contract becomes enforceable.

(g) Subsection (f) does not apply if the advance is made pursuant to a commitment entered into without knowledge of the lease and before the expiration of the 45-day period.

As amended in 1999.

§ 9–324. Priority of Purchase-Money Security Interests.

(a) Except as otherwise provided in subsection (g), a perfected purchase-money security interest in goods other than inventory or livestock has priority over a conflicting security interest in the same goods, and, except as otherwise provided in Section 9–327, a perfected security interest in its identifiable proceeds also has priority, if the purchase-money security interest is perfected when the debtor receives possession of the collateral or within 20 days thereafter.

(b) Subject to subsection (c) and except as otherwise provided in subsection (g), a perfected purchase-money security interest in inventory has priority over a conflicting security interest in the same inventory, has priority over a conflicting security interest in chattel paper or an instrument constituting proceeds of the inventory and in proceeds of the chattel paper, if so provided in Section 9–330, and, except as otherwise provided in Section 9–327, also has priority in identifiable cash proceeds of the inventory to the extent the identifiable cash proceeds are received on or before the delivery of the inventory to a buyer, if:

(1) the purchase-money security interest is perfected when the debtor receives possession of the inventory;

(2) the purchase-money secured party sends an authenticated notification to the holder of the conflicting security interest;

(3) the holder of the conflicting security interest receives the notification within five years before the debtor receives possession of the inventory; and

(4) the notification states that the person sending the notification has or expects to acquire a purchase-money security interest in inventory of the debtor and describes the inventory.

(c) Subsections (b)(2) through (4) apply only if the holder of the conflicting security interest had filed a financing statement covering the same types of inventory:

(1) if the purchase-money security interest is perfected by filing, before the date of the filing; or

(2) if the purchase-money security interest is temporarily perfected without filing or possession under Section 9–312(f), before the beginning of the 20-day period thereunder.

(d) Subject to subsection (e) and except as otherwise provided in subsection (g), a perfected purchase-money security interest in livestock that are farm products has priority over a conflicting security interest in the same livestock, and, except as otherwise provided in Section 9–327, a perfected security interest in their identifiable proceeds and identifiable products in their unmanufactured states also has priority, if:

(1) the purchase-money security interest is perfected when the debtor receives possession of the livestock;

(2) the purchase-money secured party sends an authenticated notification to the holder of the conflicting security interest;

(3) the holder of the conflicting security interest receives the notification within six months before the debtor receives possession of the livestock; and

(4) the notification states that the person sending the notification has or expects to acquire a purchase-money security interest in livestock of the debtor and describes the livestock.

(e) Subsections (d)(2) through (4) apply only if the holder of the conflicting security interest had filed a financing statement covering the same types of livestock:

(1) if the purchase-money security interest is perfected by filing, before the date of the filing; or

(2) if the purchase-money security interest is temporarily perfected without filing or possession under Section 9–312(f), before the beginning of the 20-day period thereunder.

(f) Except as otherwise provided in subsection (g), a perfected purchase-money security interest in software has priority over a conflicting security interest in the same collateral, and, except as otherwise provided in Section 9–327, a perfected security interest in its identifiable proceeds also has priority, to the extent that the purchase-money security interest in the goods in which the software was acquired for use has priority in the goods and proceeds of the goods under this section.

(g) If more than one security interest qualifies for priority in the same collateral under subsection (a), (b), (d), or (f):

(1) a security interest securing an obligation incurred as all or part of the price of the collateral has priority over a security interest securing an obligation incurred for value given to enable the debtor to acquire rights in or the use of collateral; and

(2) in all other cases, Section 9–322(a) applies to the qualifying security interests.

§ 9–325.   Priority of Security Interests in Transferred Collateral.

(a) Except as otherwise provided in subsection (b), a security interest created by a debtor is subordinate to a security interest in the same collateral created by another person if:

(1) the debtor acquired the collateral subject to the security interest created by the other person;

(2) the security interest created by the other person was perfected when the debtor acquired the collateral; and

(3) there is no period thereafter when the security interest is unperfected.

(b) Subsection (a) subordinates a security interest only if the security interest:

(1) otherwise would have priority solely under Section 9–322(a) or 9–324; or

(2) arose solely under Section 2–711(3) or 2A–508(5).

§ 9–326.   Priority of Security Interests Created by New Debtor.

(a) Subject to subsection (b), a security interest created by a new debtor which is perfected by a filed financing statement that is effective solely under Section 9–508 in collateral in which a new debtor has or acquires rights is subordinate to a security interest in the same collateral which is perfected other than by a filed financing statement that is effective solely under Section 9–508.

(b) The other provisions of this part determine the priority among conflicting security interests in the same collateral perfected by filed financing statements that are effective solely under Section 9–508. However, if the security agreements to which a new debtor became bound as debtor were not entered into by the same original debtor, the conflicting security interests rank according to priority in time of the new debtor's having become bound.

§ 9–327.   Priority of Security Interests in Deposit Account.

The following rules govern priority among conflicting security interests in the same deposit account:

(1) A security interest held by a secured party having control of the deposit account under Section 9–104 has priority over a conflicting security interest held by a secured party that does not have control.

(2) Except as otherwise provided in paragraphs (3) and (4), security interests perfected by control under Section 9–314 rank according to priority in time of obtaining control.

(3) Except as otherwise provided in paragraph (4), a security interest held by the bank with which the deposit account is maintained has priority over a conflicting security interest held by another secured party.

(4) A security interest perfected by control under Section 9–104(a)(3) has priority over a security interest held by the bank with which the deposit account is maintained.

§ 9–328.   Priority of Security Interests in Investment Property.

The following rules govern priority among conflicting security interests in the same investment property:

(1) A security interest held by a secured party having control of investment property under Section 9–106 has priority over a security interest held by a secured party that does not have control of the investment property.

(2) Except as otherwise provided in paragraphs (3) and (4), conflicting security interests held by secured parties each of which has control under Section 9–106 rank according to priority in time of:

(A) if the collateral is a security, obtaining control;

(B) if the collateral is a security entitlement carried in a securities account and:

(i) if the secured party obtained control under Section 8–106(d)(1), the secured party's becoming the person for which the securities account is maintained;

(ii) if the secured party obtained control under Section 8–106(d)(2), the securities intermediary's agreement to comply with the secured party's entitlement orders with respect to security entitlements carried or to be carried in the securities account; or

(iii) if the secured party obtained control through another person under Section 8–106(d)(3), the time on which priority would be based under this paragraph if the other person were the secured party; or

(C) if the collateral is a commodity contract carried with a commodity intermediary, the satisfaction of the requirement for control specified in Section 9–106(b)(2) with respect to commodity contracts carried or to be carried with the commodity intermediary.

(3) A security interest held by a securities intermediary in a security entitlement or a securities account maintained with the securities intermediary has priority over a conflicting security interest held by another secured party.

(4) A security interest held by a commodity intermediary in a commodity contract or a commodity account maintained with the commodity intermediary has priority over a conflicting security interest held by another secured party.

(5) A security interest in a certificated security in registered form which is perfected by taking delivery under Section 9–313(a) and not by control under Section 9–314 has priority over a conflicting security interest perfected by a method other than control.

(6) Conflicting security interests created by a broker, securities intermediary, or commodity intermediary which are perfected without control under Section 9–106 rank equally.

(7) In all other cases, priority among conflicting security interests in investment property is governed by Sections 9–322 and 9–323.

§ 9–329. Priority of Security Interests in Letter-of-Credit Right.

The following rules govern priority among conflicting security interests in the same letter-of-credit right:

(1) A security interest held by a secured party having control of the letter-of-credit right under Section 9–107 has priority to the extent of its control over a conflicting security interest held by a secured party that does not have control.

(2) Security interests perfected by control under Section 9–314 rank according to priority in time of obtaining control.

§ 9–330. Priority of Purchaser of Chattel Paper or Instrument.

(a) A purchaser of chattel paper has priority over a security interest in the chattel paper which is claimed merely as proceeds of inventory subject to a security interest if:

(1) in good faith and in the ordinary course of the purchaser's business, the purchaser gives new value and takes possession of the chattel paper or obtains control of the chattel paper under Section 9–105; and

(2) the chattel paper does not indicate that it has been assigned to an identified assignee other than the purchaser.

(b) A purchaser of chattel paper has priority over a security interest in the chattel paper which is claimed other than merely as proceeds of inventory subject to a security interest if the purchaser gives new value and takes possession of the chattel paper or obtains control of the chattel paper under Section 9–105 in good faith, in the ordinary course of the purchaser's business, and without knowledge that the purchase violates the rights of the secured party.

(c) Except as otherwise provided in Section 9–327, a purchaser having priority in chattel paper under subsection (a) or (b) also has priority in proceeds of the chattel paper to the extent that:

(1) Section 9–322 provides for priority in the proceeds; or

(2) the proceeds consist of the specific goods covered by the chattel paper or cash proceeds of the specific goods, even if the purchaser's security interest in the proceeds is unperfected.

(d) Except as otherwise provided in Section 9–331(a), a purchaser of an instrument has priority over a security interest in the instrument perfected by a method other than possession if the purchaser gives value and takes possession of the instrument in good faith and without knowledge that the purchase violates the rights of the secured party.

(e) For purposes of subsections (a) and (b), the holder of a purchase-money security interest in inventory gives new value for chattel paper constituting proceeds of the inventory.

(f) For purposes of subsections (b) and (d), if chattel paper or an instrument indicates that it has been assigned to an identified secured party other than the purchaser, a purchaser of the chattel paper or instrument has knowledge that the purchase violates the rights of the secured party.

§ 9–331. Priority of Rights of Purchasers of Instruments, Documents, and Securities under Other Articles; Priority of Interests in Financial Assets and Security Entitlements under Article 8.

(a) This article does not limit the rights of a holder in due course of a negotiable instrument, a holder to which a negotiable document of title has been duly negotiated, or a protected purchaser of a security. These holders or purchasers take priority over an earlier security interest, even if perfected, to the extent provided in Articles 3, 7, and 8.

(b) This article does not limit the rights of or impose liability on a person to the extent that the person is protected against the assertion of a claim under Article 8.

(c) Filing under this article does not constitute notice of a claim or defense to the holders, or purchasers, or persons described in subsections (a) and (b).

§ 9–332. Transfer of Money; Transfer of Funds from Deposit Account.

(a) A transferee of money takes the money free of a security interest unless the transferee acts in collusion with the debtor in violating the rights of the secured party.

(b) A transferee of funds from a deposit account takes the funds free of a security interest in the deposit account unless the transferee acts in collusion with the debtor in violating the rights of the secured party.

§ 9–333. Priority of Certain Liens Arising by Operation of Law.

(a) In this section, "possessory lien" means an interest, other than a security interest or an agricultural lien:

(1) which secures payment or performance of an obligation for services or materials furnished with respect to goods by a person in the ordinary course of the person's business;

(2) which is created by statute or rule of law in favor of the person; and

(3) whose effectiveness depends on the person's possession of the goods.

(b) A possessory lien on goods has priority over a security interest in the goods unless the lien is created by a statute that expressly provides otherwise.

§ 9–334.   Priority of Security Interests in Fixtures and Crops.

(a) A security interest under this article may be created in goods that are fixtures or may continue in goods that become fixtures. A security interest does not exist under this article in ordinary building materials incorporated into an improvement on land.

(b) This article does not prevent creation of an encumbrance upon fixtures under real property law.

(c) In cases not governed by subsections (d) through (h), a security interest in fixtures is subordinate to a conflicting interest of an encumbrancer or owner of the related real property other than the debtor.

(d) Except as otherwise provided in subsection (h), a perfected security interest in fixtures has priority over a conflicting interest of an encumbrancer or owner of the real property if the debtor has an interest of record in or is in possession of the real property and:

(1) the security interest is a purchase-money security interest;

(2) the interest of the encumbrancer or owner arises before the goods become fixtures; and

(3) the security interest is perfected by a fixture filing before the goods become fixtures or within 20 days thereafter.

(e) A perfected security interest in fixtures has priority over a conflicting interest of an encumbrancer or owner of the real property if:

(1) the debtor has an interest of record in the real property or is in possession of the real property and the security interest:

(A) is perfected by a fixture filing before the interest of the encumbrancer or owner is of record; and

(B) has priority over any conflicting interest of a predecessor in title of the encumbrancer or owner;

(2) before the goods become fixtures, the security interest is perfected by any method permitted by this article and the fixtures are readily removable:

(A) factory or office machines;

(B) equipment that is not primarily used or leased for use in the operation of the real property; or

(C) replacements of domestic appliances that are consumer goods;

(3) the conflicting interest is a lien on the real property obtained by legal or equitable proceedings after the security interest was perfected by any method permitted by this article; or

(4) the security interest is:

(A) created in a manufactured home in a manufactured-home transaction; and

(B) perfected pursuant to a statute described in Section 9–311(a)(2).

(f) A security interest in fixtures, whether or not perfected, has priority over a conflicting interest of an encumbrancer or owner of the real property if:

(1) the encumbrancer or owner has, in an authenticated record, consented to the security interest or disclaimed an interest in the goods as fixtures; or

(2) the debtor has a right to remove the goods as against the encumbrancer or owner.

(g) The priority of the security interest under paragraph (f)(2) continues for a reasonable time if the debtor's right to remove the goods as against the encumbrancer or owner terminates.

(h) A mortgage is a construction mortgage to the extent that it secures an obligation incurred for the construction of an improvement on land, including the acquisition cost of the land, if a recorded record of the mortgage so indicates. Except as otherwise provided in subsections (e) and (f), a security interest in fixtures is subordinate to a construction mortgage if a record of the mortgage is recorded before the goods become fixtures and the goods become fixtures before the completion of the construction. A mortgage has this priority to the same extent as a construction mortgage to the extent that it is given to refinance a construction mortgage.

(i) A perfected security interest in crops growing on real property has priority over a conflicting interest of an encumbrancer or owner of the real property if the debtor has an interest of record in or is in possession of the real property.

(j) Subsection (i) prevails over any inconsistent provisions of the following statutes:

[List here any statutes containing provisions inconsistent with subsection (i).]

Legislative Note: States that amend statutes to remove provisions inconsistent with subsection (i) need not enact subsection (j).

§ 9–335.   Accessions.

(a) A security interest may be created in an accession and continues in collateral that becomes an accession.

(b) If a security interest is perfected when the collateral becomes an accession, the security interest remains perfected in the collateral.

(c) Except as otherwise provided in subsection (d), the other provisions of this part determine the priority of a security interest in an accession.

(d) A security interest in an accession is subordinate to a security interest in the whole which is perfected by compliance with the requirements of a certificate-of-title statute under Section 9–311(b).

(e) After default, subject to Part 6, a secured party may remove an accession from other goods if the security interest in the accession has priority over the claims of every person having an interest in the whole.

(f) A secured party that removes an accession from other goods under subsection (e) shall promptly reimburse any holder of a security interest or other lien on, or owner of, the whole or of the other goods, other than the debtor, for the cost of repair of any physical injury to the whole or the other goods. The secured party need not reimburse the holder or owner for any diminution in value of the whole or the other goods caused by the absence of the accession removed or by any necessity for replacing it. A person entitled to reimbursement may refuse permission to remove until the secured party gives adequate assurance for the performance of the obligation to reimburse.

§ 9–336. Commingled Goods.

(a) In this section, "commingled goods" means goods that are physically united with other goods in such a manner that their identity is lost in a product or mass.

(b) A security interest does not exist in commingled goods as such. However, a security interest may attach to a product or mass that results when goods become commingled goods.

(c) If collateral becomes commingled goods, a security interest attaches to the product or mass.

(d) If a security interest in collateral is perfected before the collateral becomes commingled goods, the security interest that attaches to the product or mass under subsection (c) is perfected.

(e) Except as otherwise provided in subsection (f), the other provisions of this part determine the priority of a security interest that attaches to the product or mass under subsection (c).

(f) If more than one security interest attaches to the product or mass under subsection (c), the following rules determine priority:

(1) A security interest that is perfected under subsection (d) has priority over a security interest that is unperfected at the time the collateral becomes commingled goods.

(2) If more than one security interest is perfected under subsection (d), the security interests rank equally in proportion to the value of the collateral at the time it became commingled goods.

§ 9–337. Priority of Security Interests in Goods Covered by Certificate of Title.

If, while a security interest in goods is perfected by any method under the law of another jurisdiction, this State issues a certificate of title that does not show that the goods are subject to the security interest or contain a statement that they may be subject to security interests not shown on the certificate:

(1) a buyer of the goods, other than a person in the business of selling goods of that kind, takes free of the security interest if the buyer gives value and receives delivery of the goods after issuance of the certificate and without knowledge of the security interest; and

(2) the security interest is subordinate to a conflicting security interest in the goods that attaches, and is perfected under Section 9–311(b), after issuance of the certificate and without the conflicting secured party's knowledge of the security interest.

§ 9–338. Priority of Security Interest or Agricultural Lien Perfected by Filed Financing Statement Providing Certain Incorrect Information.

If a security interest or agricultural lien is perfected by a filed financing statement providing information described in Section 9–516(b)(5) which is incorrect at the time the financing statement is filed:

(1) the security interest or agricultural lien is subordinate to a conflicting perfected security interest in the collateral to the extent that the holder of the conflicting security interest gives value in reasonable reliance upon the incorrect information; and

(2) a purchaser, other than a secured party, of the collateral takes free of the security interest or agricultural lien to the extent that, in reasonable reliance upon the incorrect information, the purchaser gives value and, in the case of chattel paper, documents, goods, instruments, or a security certificate, receives delivery of the collateral.

§ 9–339. Priority Subject to Subordination.

This article does not preclude subordination by agreement by a person entitled to priority.

[Subpart 4. Rights of Bank]

§ 9–340. Effectiveness of Right of Recoupment or Set-Off against Deposit Account.

(a) Except as otherwise provided in subsection (c), a bank with which a deposit account is maintained may exercise any right of recoupment or set-off against a secured party that holds a security interest in the deposit account.

(b) Except as otherwise provided in subsection (c), the application of this article to a security interest in a deposit account does not affect a right of recoupment or set-off of the secured party as to a deposit account maintained with the secured party.

(c) The exercise by a bank of a set-off against a deposit account is ineffective against a secured party that holds a security interest in the deposit account which is perfected by control under Section 9–104(a)(3), if the set-off is based on a claim against the debtor.

§ 9–341. Bank's Rights and Duties with Respect to Deposit Account.

Except as otherwise provided in Section 9–340(c), and unless the bank otherwise agrees in an authenticated record, a bank's rights and duties with respect to a deposit account maintained with the bank are not terminated, suspended, or modified by:

(1) the creation, attachment, or perfection of a security interest in the deposit account;

(2) the bank's knowledge of the security interest; or

(3) the bank's receipt of instructions from the secured party.

§ 9–342.   Bank's Right to Refuse to Enter into or Disclose Existence of Control Agreement.

This article does not require a bank to enter into an agreement of the kind described in Section 9–104(a)(2), even if its customer so requests or directs. A bank that has entered into such an agreement is not required to confirm the existence of the agreement to another person unless requested to do so by its customer.

PART 4   Rights of Third Parties

§ 9–401.   Alienability of Debtor's Rights.

(a) Except as otherwise provided in subsection (b) and Sections 9–406, 9–407, 9–408, and 9–409, whether a debtor's rights in collateral may be voluntarily or involuntarily transferred is governed by law other than this article.

(b) An agreement between the debtor and secured party which prohibits a transfer of the debtor's rights in collateral or makes the transfer a default does not prevent the transfer from taking effect.

§ 9–402.   Secured Party Not Obligated on Contract of Debtor or in Tort.

The existence of a security interest, agricultural lien, or authority given to a debtor to dispose of or use collateral, without more, does not subject a secured party to liability in contract or tort for the debtor's acts or omissions.

§ 9–403.   Agreement Not to Assert Defenses against Assignee.

(a) In this section, "value" has the meaning provided in Section 3–303(a).

(b) Except as otherwise provided in this section, an agreement between an account debtor and an assignor not to assert against an assignee any claim or defense that the account debtor may have against the assignor is enforceable by an assignee that takes an assignment:

(1) for value;

(2) in good faith;

(3) without notice of a claim of a property or possessory right to the property assigned; and

(4) without notice of a defense or claim in recoupment of the type that may be asserted against a person entitled to enforce a negotiable instrument under Section 3–305(a).

(c) Subsection (b) does not apply to defenses of a type that may be asserted against a holder in due course of a negotiable instrument under Section 3–305(b).

(d) In a consumer transaction, if a record evidences the account debtor's obligation, law other than this article requires that the record include a statement to the effect that the rights of an assignee are subject to claims or defenses that the account debtor could assert against the original obligee, and the record does not include such a statement:

(1) the record has the same effect as if the record included such a statement; and

(2) the account debtor may assert against an assignee those claims and defenses that would have been available if the record included such a statement.

(e) This section is subject to law other than this article which establishes a different rule for an account debtor who is an individual and who incurred the obligation primarily for personal, family, or household purposes.

(f) Except as otherwise provided in subsection (d), this section does not displace law other than this article which gives effect to an agreement by an account debtor not to assert a claim or defense against an assignee.

§ 9–404.   Rights Acquired by Assignee; Claims and Defenses against Assignee.

(a) Unless an account debtor has made an enforceable agreement not to assert defenses or claims, and subject to subsections (b) through (e), the rights of an assignee are subject to:

(1) all terms of the agreement between the account debtor and assignor and any defense or claim in recoupment arising from the transaction that gave rise to the contract; and

(2) any other defense or claim of the account debtor against the assignor which accrues before the account debtor receives a notification of the assignment authenticated by the assignor or the assignee.

(b) Subject to subsection (c) and except as otherwise provided in subsection (d), the claim of an account debtor against an assignor may be asserted against an assignee under subsection (a) only to reduce the amount the account debtor owes.

(c) This section is subject to law other than this article which establishes a different rule for an account debtor who is an individual and who incurred the obligation primarily for personal, family, or household purposes.

(d) In a consumer transaction, if a record evidences the account debtor's obligation, law other than this article requires that the record include a statement to the effect that the account debtor's recovery against an assignee with respect to claims and defenses against the assignor may not exceed amounts paid by the account debtor under the record, and the record does not include such a statement, the extent to which a claim of an account debtor against the assignor may be asserted against an assignee is determined as if the record included such a statement.

(e) This section does not apply to an assignment of a health-care-insurance receivable.

§ 9–405. Modification of Assigned Contract.

(a) A modification of or substitution for an assigned contract is effective against an assignee if made in good faith. The assignee acquires corresponding rights under the modified or substituted contract. The assignment may provide that the modification or substitution is a breach of contract by the assignor. This subsection is subject to subsections (b) through (d).

(b) Subsection (a) applies to the extent that:

(1) the right to payment or a part thereof under an assigned contract has not been fully earned by performance; or

(2) the right to payment or a part thereof has been fully earned by performance and the account debtor has not received notification of the assignment under Section 9–406(a).

(c) This section is subject to law other than this article which establishes a different rule for an account debtor who is an individual and who incurred the obligation primarily for personal, family, or household purposes.

(d) This section does not apply to an assignment of a health-care-insurance receivable.

§ 9–406. Discharge of Account Debtor; Notification of Assignment; Identification and Proof of Assignment; Restrictions on Assignment of Accounts, Chattel Paper, Payment Intangibles, and Promissory Notes Ineffective.

(a) Subject to subsections (b) through (i), an account debtor on an account, chattel paper, or a payment intangible may discharge its obligation by paying the assignor until, but not after, the account debtor receives a notification, authenticated by the assignor or the assignee, that the amount due or to become due has been assigned and that payment is to be made to the assignee. After receipt of the notification, the account debtor may discharge its obligation by paying the assignee and may not discharge the obligation by paying the assignor.

(b) Subject to subsection (h), notification is ineffective under subsection (a):

(1) if it does not reasonably identify the rights assigned;

(2) to the extent that an agreement between an account debtor and a seller of a payment intangible limits the account debtor's duty to pay a person other than the seller and the limitation is effective under law other than this article; or

(3) at the option of an account debtor, if the notification notifies the account debtor to make less than the full amount of any installment or other periodic payment to the assignee, even if:

(A) only a portion of the account, chattel paper, or payment intangible has been assigned to that assignee;

(B) a portion has been assigned to another assignee; or

(C) the account debtor knows that the assignment to that assignee is limited.

(c) Subject to subsection (h), if requested by the account debtor, an assignee shall seasonably furnish reasonable proof that the assignment has been made. Unless the assignee complies, the account debtor may discharge its obligation by paying the assignor, even if the account debtor has received a notification under subsection (a).

(d) Except as otherwise provided in subsection (e) and Sections 2A–303 and 9–407, and subject to subsection (h), a term in an agreement between an account debtor and an assignor or in a promissory note is ineffective to the extent that it:

(1) prohibits, restricts, or requires the consent of the account debtor or person obligated on the promissory note to the assignment or transfer of, or the creation, attachment, perfection, or enforcement of a security interest in, the account, chattel paper, payment intangible, or promissory note; or

(2) provides that the assignment or transfer or the creation, attachment, perfection, or enforcement of the security interest may give rise to a default, breach, right of recoupment, claim, defense, termination, right of termination, or remedy under the account, chattel paper, payment intangible, or promissory note.

(e) Subsection (d) does not apply to the sale of a payment intangible or promissory note.

(f) Except as otherwise provided in Sections 2A–303 and 9–407 and subject to subsections (h) and (i), a rule of law, statute, or regulation that prohibits, restricts, or requires the consent of a government, governmental body or official, or account debtor to the assignment or transfer of, or creation of a security interest in, an account or chattel paper is ineffective to the extent that the rule of law, statute, or regulation:

(1) prohibits, restricts, or requires the consent of the government, governmental body or official, or account debtor to the assignment or transfer of, or the creation, attachment, perfection, or enforcement of a security interest in the account or chattel paper; or

(2) provides that the assignment or transfer or the creation, attachment, perfection, or enforcement of the security interest may give rise to a default, breach, right of recoupment, claim, defense, termination, right of termination, or remedy under the account or chattel paper.

(g) Subject to subsection (h), an account debtor may not waive or vary its option under subsection (b)(3).

(h) This section is subject to law other than this article which establishes a different rule for an account debtor who is an individual and who incurred the obligation primarily for personal, family, or household purposes.

(i) This section does not apply to an assignment of a health-care-insurance receivable.

(j) This section prevails over any inconsistent provisions of the following statutes, rules, and regulations:

[List here any statutes, rules, and regulations containing provisions inconsistent with this section.]

Legislative Note: States that amend statutes, rules, and regulations to remove provisions inconsistent with this section need not enact subsection (j).

As amended in 1999 and 2000.

§ 9–407. Restrictions on Creation or Enforcement of Security Interest in Leasehold Interest or in Lessor's Residual Interest.

(a) Except as otherwise provided in subsection (b), a term in a lease agreement is ineffective to the extent that it:

(1) prohibits, restricts, or requires the consent of a party to the lease to the assignment or transfer of, or the creation, attachment, perfection, or enforcement of a security interest in an interest of a party under the lease contract or in the lessor's residual interest in the goods; or

(2) provides that the assignment or transfer or the creation, attachment, perfection, or enforcement of the security interest may give rise to a default, breach, right of recoupment, claim, defense, termination, right of termination, or remedy under the lease.

(b) Except as otherwise provided in Section 2A–303(7), a term described in subsection (a)(2) is effective to the extent that there is:

(1) a transfer by the lessee of the lessee's right of possession or use of the goods in violation of the term; or

(2) a delegation of a material performance of either party to the lease contract in violation of the term.

(c) The creation, attachment, perfection, or enforcement of a security interest in the lessor's interest under the lease contract or the lessor's residual interest in the goods is not a transfer that materially impairs the lessee's prospect of obtaining return performance or materially changes the duty of or materially increases the burden or risk imposed on the lessee within the purview of Section 2A–303(4) unless, and then only to the extent that, enforcement actually results in a delegation of material performance of the lessor.

As amended in 1999.

§ 9–408. Restrictions on Assignment of Promissory Notes, Health-Care-Insurance Receivables, and Certain General Intangibles Ineffective.

(a) Except as otherwise provided in subsection (b), a term in a promissory note or in an agreement between an account debtor and a debtor which relates to a health-care-insurance receivable or a general intangible, including a contract, permit, license, or franchise, and which term prohibits, restricts, or requires the consent of the person obligated on the promissory note or the account debtor to, the assignment or transfer of, or creation, attachment, or perfection of a security interest in, the promissory note, health-care-insurance receivable, or general intangible, is ineffective to the extent that the term:

(1) would impair the creation, attachment, or perfection of a security interest; or

(2) provides that the assignment or transfer or the creation, attachment, or perfection of the security interest may give rise to a default, breach, right of recoupment, claim, defense, termination, right of termination, or remedy under the promissory note, health-care-insurance receivable, or general intangible.

(b) Subsection (a) applies to a security interest in a payment intangible or promissory note only if the security interest arises out of a sale of the payment intangible or promissory note.

(c) A rule of law, statute, or regulation that prohibits, restricts, or requires the consent of a government, governmental body or official, person obligated on a promissory note, or account debtor to the assignment or transfer of, or creation of a security interest in, a promissory note, health-care-insurance receivable, or general intangible, including a contract, permit, license, or franchise between an account debtor and a debtor, is ineffective to the extent that the rule of law, statute, or regulation:

(1) would impair the creation, attachment, or perfection of a security interest; or

(2) provides that the assignment or transfer or the creation, attachment, or perfection of the security interest may give rise to a default, breach, right of recoupment, claim, defense, termination, right of termination, or remedy under the promissory note, health-care-insurance receivable, or general intangible.

(d) To the extent that a term in a promissory note or in an agreement between an account debtor and a debtor which relates to a health-care-insurance receivable or general intangible or a rule of law, statute, or regulation described in subsection (c) would be effective under law other than this article but is ineffective under subsection (a) or (c), the creation, attachment, or perfection of a security interest in the promissory note, health-care-insurance receivable, or general intangible:

(1) is not enforceable against the person obligated on the promissory note or the account debtor;

(2) does not impose a duty or obligation on the person obligated on the promissory note or the account debtor;

(3) does not require the person obligated on the promissory note or the account debtor to recognize the security interest, pay or render performance to the secured party, or accept payment or performance from the secured party;

(4) does not entitle the secured party to use or assign the debtor's rights under the promissory note, health-care-insurance receivable, or general intangible, including any related information or materials furnished to the debtor in the transaction

giving rise to the promissory note, health-care-insurance receivable, or general intangible;

(5) does not entitle the secured party to use, assign, possess, or have access to any trade secrets or confidential information of the person obligated on the promissory note or the account debtor; and

(6) does not entitle the secured party to enforce the security interest in the promissory note, health-care-insurance receivable, or general intangible.

(e) This section prevails over any inconsistent provisions of the following statutes, rules, and regulations:

[List here any statutes, rules, and regulations containing provisions inconsistent with this section.]

Legislative Note: States that amend statutes, rules, and regulations to remove provisions inconsistent with this section need not enact subsection (e).

As amended in 1999.

§ 9–409.   Restrictions on Assignment of Letter-of-Credit Rights Ineffective.

(a) A term in a letter of credit or a rule of law, statute, regulation, custom, or practice applicable to the letter of credit which prohibits, restricts, or requires the consent of an applicant, issuer, or nominated person to a beneficiary's assignment of or creation of a security interest in a letter-of-credit right is ineffective to the extent that the term or rule of law, statute, regulation, custom, or practice:

(1) would impair the creation, attachment, or perfection of a security interest in the letter-of-credit right; or

(2) provides that the assignment or the creation, attachment, or perfection of the security interest may give rise to a default, breach, right of recoupment, claim, defense, termination, right of termination, or remedy under the letter-of-credit right.

(b) To the extent that a term in a letter of credit is ineffective under subsection (a) but would be effective under law other than this article or a custom or practice applicable to the letter of credit, to the transfer of a right to draw or otherwise demand performance under the letter of credit, or to the assignment of a right to proceeds of the letter of credit, the creation, attachment, or perfection of a security interest in the letter-of-credit right:

(1) is not enforceable against the applicant, issuer, nominated person, or transferee beneficiary;

(2) imposes no duties or obligations on the applicant, issuer, nominated person, or transferee beneficiary; and

(3) does not require the applicant, issuer, nominated person, or transferee beneficiary to recognize the security interest, pay or render performance to the secured party, or accept payment or other performance from the secured party.

As amended in 1999.

PART 5   Filing

[Subpart 1. Filing Office; Contents and Effectiveness of Financing Statement]

§ 9–501.   Filing Office.

(a) Except as otherwise provided in subsection (b), if the local law of this State governs perfection of a security interest or agricultural lien, the office in which to file a financing statement to perfect the security interest or agricultural lien is:

(1) the office designated for the filing or recording of a record of a mortgage on the related real property, if:

(A) the collateral is as-extracted collateral or timber to be cut; or

(B) the financing statement is filed as a fixture filing and the collateral is goods that are or are to become fixtures; or

(2) the office of [ ] [or any office duly authorized by [ ]], in all other cases, including a case in which the collateral is goods that are or are to become fixtures and the financing statement is not filed as a fixture filing.

(b) The office in which to file a financing statement to perfect a security interest in collateral, including fixtures, of a transmitting utility is the office of [ ]. The financing statement also constitutes a fixture filing as to the collateral indicated in the financing statement which is or is to become fixtures.

Legislative Note: The State should designate the filing office where the brackets appear. The filing office may be that of a governmental official (e.g., the Secretary of State) or a private party that maintains the State's filing system.

§ 9–502.   Contents of Financing Statement; Record of Mortgage as Financing Statement; Time of Filing Financing Statement.

(a) Subject to subsection (b), a financing statement is sufficient only if it:

(1) provides the name of the debtor;

(2) provides the name of the secured party or a representative of the secured party; and

(3) indicates the collateral covered by the financing statement.

(b) Except as otherwise provided in Section 9–501(b), to be sufficient, a financing statement that covers as-extracted collateral or timber to be cut, or which is filed as a fixture filing and covers goods that are or are to become fixtures, must satisfy subsection (a) and also:

(1) indicate that it covers this type of collateral;

(2) indicate that it is to be filed [for record] in the real property records;

(3) provide a description of the real property to which the collateral is related [sufficient to give constructive notice of a

mortgage under the law of this State if the description were contained in a record of the mortgage of the real property]; and

(4) if the debtor does not have an interest of record in the real property, provide the name of a record owner.

(c) A record of a mortgage is effective, from the date of recording, as a financing statement filed as a fixture filing or as a financing statement covering as-extracted collateral or timber to be cut only if:

(1) the record indicates the goods or accounts that it covers;

(2) the goods are or are to become fixtures related to the real property described in the record or the collateral is related to the real property described in the record and is as-extracted collateral or timber to be cut;

(3) the record satisfies the requirements for a financing statement in this section other than an indication that it is to be filed in the real property records; and

(4) the record is [duly] recorded.

(d) A financing statement may be filed before a security agreement is made or a security interest otherwise attaches.

Legislative Note: Language in brackets is optional. Where the State has any special recording system for real property other than the usual grantor-grantee index (as, for instance, a tract system or a title registration or Torrens system) local adaptations of subsection (b) and Section 9–519(d) and (e) may be necessary. See, e.g., Mass. Gen. Laws Chapter 106, Section 9–410.

§ 9–503.   Name of Debtor and Secured Party.

(a) A financing statement sufficiently provides the name of the debtor:

(1) if the debtor is a registered organization, only if the financing statement provides the name of the debtor indicated on the public record of the debtor's jurisdiction of organization which shows the debtor to have been organized;

(2) if the debtor is a decedent's estate, only if the financing statement provides the name of the decedent and indicates that the debtor is an estate;

(3) if the debtor is a trust or a trustee acting with respect to property held in trust, only if the financing statement:

(A) provides the name specified for the trust in its organic documents or, if no name is specified, provides the name of the settlor and additional information sufficient to distinguish the debtor from other trusts having one or more of the same settlors; and

(B) indicates, in the debtor's name or otherwise, that the debtor is a trust or is a trustee acting with respect to property held in trust; and

(4) in other cases:

(A) if the debtor has a name, only if it provides the individual or organizational name of the debtor; and

(B) if the debtor does not have a name, only if it provides the names of the partners, members, associates, or other persons comprising the debtor.

(b) A financing statement that provides the name of the debtor in accordance with subsection (a) is not rendered ineffective by the absence of:

(1) a trade name or other name of the debtor; or

(2) unless required under subsection (a)(4)(B), names of partners, members, associates, or other persons comprising the debtor.

(c) A financing statement that provides only the debtor's trade name does not sufficiently provide the name of the debtor.

(d) Failure to indicate the representative capacity of a secured party or representative of a secured party does not affect the sufficiency of a financing statement.

(e) A financing statement may provide the name of more than one debtor and the name of more than one secured party.

§ 9–504.   Indication of Collateral.

A financing statement sufficiently indicates the collateral that it covers if the financing statement provides:

(1) a description of the collateral pursuant to Section 9–108; or

(2) an indication that the financing statement covers all assets or all personal property.

As amended in 1999.

§ 9–505.   Filing and Compliance with Other Statutes and Treaties for Consignments, Leases, Other Bailments, and Other Transactions.

(a) A consignor, lessor, or other bailor of goods, a licensor, or a buyer of a payment intangible or promissory note may file a financing statement, or may comply with a statute or treaty described in Section 9–311(a), using the terms "consignor", "consignee", "lessor", "lessee", "bailor", "bailee", "licensor", "licensee", "owner", "registered owner", "buyer", "seller", or words of similar import, instead of the terms "secured party" and "debtor".

(b) This part applies to the filing of a financing statement under subsection (a) and, as appropriate, to compliance that is equivalent to filing a financing statement under Section 9–311(b), but the filing or compliance is not of itself a factor in determining whether the collateral secures an obligation. If it is determined for another reason that the collateral secures an obligation, a security interest held by the consignor, lessor, bailor, licensor, owner, or buyer which attaches to the collateral is perfected by the filing or compliance.

§ 9–506.   Effect of Errors or Omissions.

(a) A financing statement substantially satisfying the requirements of this part is effective, even if it has minor errors or omissions, unless the errors or omissions make the financing statement seriously misleading.

(b) Except as otherwise provided in subsection (c), a financing statement that fails sufficiently to provide the name of the debtor in accordance with Section 9–503(a) is seriously misleading.

(c) If a search of the records of the filing office under the debtor's correct name, using the filing office's standard search logic, if any, would disclose a financing statement that fails sufficiently to provide the name of the debtor in accordance with Section 9–503(a), the name provided does not make the financing statement seriously misleading.

(d) For purposes of Section 9–508(b), the "debtor's correct name" in subsection (c) means the correct name of the new debtor.

§ 9–507.   Effect of Certain Events on Effectiveness of Financing Statement.

(a) A filed financing statement remains effective with respect to collateral that is sold, exchanged, leased, licensed, or otherwise disposed of and in which a security interest or agricultural lien continues, even if the secured party knows of or consents to the disposition.

(b) Except as otherwise provided in subsection (c) and Section 9–508, a financing statement is not rendered ineffective if, after the financing statement is filed, the information provided in the financing statement becomes seriously misleading under Section 9–506.

(c) If a debtor so changes its name that a filed financing statement becomes seriously misleading under Section 9–506:

(1) the financing statement is effective to perfect a security interest in collateral acquired by the debtor before, or within four months after, the change; and

(2) the financing statement is not effective to perfect a security interest in collateral acquired by the debtor more than four months after the change, unless an amendment to the financing statement which renders the financing statement not seriously misleading is filed within four months after the change.

§ 9–508.   Effectiveness of Financing Statement If New Debtor Becomes Bound by Security Agreement.

(a) Except as otherwise provided in this section, a filed financing statement naming an original debtor is effective to perfect a security interest in collateral in which a new debtor has or acquires rights to the extent that the financing statement would have been effective had the original debtor acquired rights in the collateral.

(b) If the difference between the name of the original debtor and that of the new debtor causes a filed financing statement that is effective under subsection (a) to be seriously misleading under Section 9–506:

(1) the financing statement is effective to perfect a security interest in collateral acquired by the new debtor before, and within four months after, the new debtor becomes bound under Section 9B–203(d); and

(2) the financing statement is not effective to perfect a security interest in collateral acquired by the new debtor more than four months after the new debtor becomes bound under Section 9–203(d) unless an initial financing statement providing the name of the new debtor is filed before the expiration of that time.

(c) This section does not apply to collateral as to which a filed financing statement remains effective against the new debtor under Section 9–507(a).

§ 9–509.   Persons Entitled to File a Record.

(a) A person may file an initial financing statement, amendment that adds collateral covered by a financing statement, or amendment that adds a debtor to a financing statement only if:

(1) the debtor authorizes the filing in an authenticated record or pursuant to subsection (b) or (c); or

(2) the person holds an agricultural lien that has become effective at the time of filing and the financing statement covers only collateral in which the person holds an agricultural lien.

(b) By authenticating or becoming bound as debtor by a security agreement, a debtor or new debtor authorizes the filing of an initial financing statement, and an amendment, covering:

(1) the collateral described in the security agreement; and

(2) property that becomes collateral under Section 9–315(a)(2), whether or not the security agreement expressly covers proceeds.

(c) By acquiring collateral in which a security interest or agricultural lien continues under Section 9–315(a)(1), a debtor authorizes the filing of an initial financing statement, and an amendment, covering the collateral and property that becomes collateral under Section 9–315(a)(2).

(d) A person may file an amendment other than an amendment that adds collateral covered by a financing statement or an amendment that adds a debtor to a financing statement only if:

(1) the secured party of record authorizes the filing; or

(2) the amendment is a termination statement for a financing statement as to which the secured party of record has failed to file or send a termination statement as required by Section 9–513(a) or (c), the debtor authorizes the filing, and the termination statement indicates that the debtor authorized it to be filed.

(e) If there is more than one secured party of record for a financing statement, each secured party of record may authorize the filing of an amendment under subsection (d).

As amended in 2000.

§ 9–510.   Effectiveness of Filed Record.

(a) A filed record is effective only to the extent that it was filed by a person that may file it under Section 9–509.

(b) A record authorized by one secured party of record does not affect the financing statement with respect to another secured party of record.

(c) A continuation statement that is not filed within the six-month period prescribed by Section 9–515(d) is ineffective.

§ 9–511.   Secured Party of Record.

(a) A secured party of record with respect to a financing statement is a person whose name is provided as the name of the secured party or a representative of the secured party in an initial financing statement that has been filed. If an initial financing statement is filed under Section 9–514(a), the assignee named in the initial financing statement is the secured party of record with respect to the financing statement.

(b) If an amendment of a financing statement which provides the name of a person as a secured party or a representative of a secured party is filed, the person named in the amendment is a secured party of record. If an amendment is filed under Section 9–514(b), the assignee named in the amendment is a secured party of record.

(c) A person remains a secured party of record until the filing of an amendment of the financing statement which deletes the person.

§ 9–512.   Amendment of Financing Statement.

[Alternative A]

(a) Subject to Section 9–509, a person may add or delete collateral covered by, continue or terminate the effectiveness of, or, subject to subsection (e), otherwise amend the information provided in, a financing statement by filing an amendment that:

(1) identifies, by its file number, the initial financing statement to which the amendment relates; and

(2) if the amendment relates to an initial financing statement filed [or recorded] in a filing office described in Section 9–501(a)(1), provides the information specified in Section 9–502(b).

[Alternative B]

(a) Subject to Section 9–509, a person may add or delete collateral covered by, continue or terminate the effectiveness of, or, subject to subsection (e), otherwise amend the information provided in, a financing statement by filing an amendment that:

(1) identifies, by its file number, the initial financing statement to which the amendment relates; and

(2) if the amendment relates to an initial financing statement filed [or recorded] in a filing office described in Section 9–501(a)(1), provides the date [and time] that the initial financing statement was filed [or recorded] and the information specified in Section 9–502(b).

[End of Alternatives]

(b) Except as otherwise provided in Section 9–515, the filing of an amendment does not extend the period of effectiveness of the financing statement.

(c) A financing statement that is amended by an amendment that adds collateral is effective as to the added collateral only from the date of the filing of the amendment.

(d) A financing statement that is amended by an amendment that adds a debtor is effective as to the added debtor only from the date of the filing of the amendment.

(e) An amendment is ineffective to the extent it:

(1) purports to delete all debtors and fails to provide the name of a debtor to be covered by the financing statement; or

(2) purports to delete all secured parties of record and fails to provide the name of a new secured party of record.

Legislative Note: States whose real-estate filing offices require additional information in amendments and cannot search their records by both the name of the debtor and the file number should enact Alternative B to Sections 9–512(a), 9–518(b), 9–519(f), and 9–522(a).

§ 9–513.   Termination Statement.

(a) A secured party shall cause the secured party of record for a financing statement to file a termination statement for the financing statement if the financing statement covers consumer goods and:

(1) there is no obligation secured by the collateral covered by the financing statement and no commitment to make an advance, incur an obligation, or otherwise give value; or

(2) the debtor did not authorize the filing of the initial financing statement.

(b) To comply with subsection (a), a secured party shall cause the secured party of record to file the termination statement:

(1) within one month after there is no obligation secured by the collateral covered by the financing statement and no commitment to make an advance, incur an obligation, or otherwise give value; or

(2) if earlier, within 20 days after the secured party receives an authenticated demand from a debtor.

(c) In cases not governed by subsection (a), within 20 days after a secured party receives an authenticated demand from a debtor, the secured party shall cause the secured party of record for a financing statement to send to the debtor a termination statement for the financing statement or file the termination statement in the filing office if:

(1) except in the case of a financing statement covering accounts or chattel paper that has been sold or goods that are the subject of a consignment, there is no obligation secured by the collateral covered by the financing statement and no commitment to make an advance, incur an obligation, or otherwise give value;

(2) the financing statement covers accounts or chattel paper that has been sold but as to which the account debtor or other person obligated has discharged its obligation;

(3) the financing statement covers goods that were the subject of a consignment to the debtor but are not in the debtor's possession; or

(4) the debtor did not authorize the filing of the initial financing statement.

(d) Except as otherwise provided in Section 9–510, upon the filing of a termination statement with the filing office, the financing statement to which the termination statement relates ceases to be effective. Except as otherwise provided in Section 9–510, for purposes of Sections 9–519(g), 9–522(a), and 9–523(c), the filing with the filing office of a termination statement relating to a financing statement that indicates that the debtor is a transmitting utility also causes the effectiveness of the financing statement to lapse.

As amended in 2000.

§ 9–514.   Assignment of Powers of Secured Party of Record.

(a) Except as otherwise provided in subsection (c), an initial financing statement may reflect an assignment of all of the secured party's power to authorize an amendment to the financing statement by providing the name and mailing address of the assignee as the name and address of the secured party.

(b) Except as otherwise provided in subsection (c), a secured party of record may assign of record all or part of its power to authorize an amendment to a financing statement by filing in the filing office an amendment of the financing statement which:

(1) identifies, by its file number, the initial financing statement to which it relates;

(2) provides the name of the assignor; and

(3) provides the name and mailing address of the assignee.

(c) An assignment of record of a security interest in a fixture covered by a record of a mortgage which is effective as a financing statement filed as a fixture filing under Section 9–502(c) may be made only by an assignment of record of the mortgage in the manner provided by law of this State other than [the Uniform Commercial Code].

§ 9–515.   Duration and Effectiveness of Financing Statement; Effect of Lapsed Financing Statement.

(a) Except as otherwise provided in subsections (b), (e), (f), and (g), a filed financing statement is effective for a period of five years after the date of filing.

(b) Except as otherwise provided in subsections (e), (f), and (g), an initial financing statement filed in connection with a public-finance transaction or manufactured-home transaction is effective for a period of 30 years after the date of filing if it indicates that it is filed in connection with a public-finance transaction or manufactured-home transaction.

(c) The effectiveness of a filed financing statement lapses on the expiration of the period of its effectiveness unless before the lapse a continuation statement is filed pursuant to subsection (d). Upon lapse, a financing statement ceases to be effective and any security interest or agricultural lien that was perfected by the financing statement becomes unperfected, unless the security interest is perfected otherwise. If the security interest or agricultural lien becomes unperfected upon lapse, it is deemed never to have been perfected as against a purchaser of the collateral for value.

(d) A continuation statement may be filed only within six months before the expiration of the five-year period specified in subsection (a) or the 30-year period specified in subsection (b), whichever is applicable.

(e) Except as otherwise provided in Section 9–510, upon timely filing of a continuation statement, the effectiveness of the initial financing statement continues for a period of five years commencing on the day on which the financing statement would have become ineffective in the absence of the filing. Upon the expiration of the five-year period, the financing statement lapses in the same manner as provided in subsection (c), unless, before the lapse, another continuation statement is filed pursuant to subsection (d). Succeeding continuation statements may be filed in the same manner to continue the effectiveness of the initial financing statement.

(f) If a debtor is a transmitting utility and a filed financing statement so indicates, the financing statement is effective until a termination statement is filed.

(g) A record of a mortgage that is effective as a financing statement filed as a fixture filing under Section 9–502(c) remains effective as a financing statement filed as a fixture filing until the mortgage is released or satisfied of record or its effectiveness otherwise terminates as to the real property.

§ 9–516.   What Constitutes Filing; Effectiveness of Filing.

(a) Except as otherwise provided in subsection (b), communication of a record to a filing office and tender of the filing fee or acceptance of the record by the filing office constitutes filing.

(b) Filing does not occur with respect to a record that a filing office refuses to accept because:

(1) the record is not communicated by a method or medium of communication authorized by the filing office;

(2) an amount equal to or greater than the applicable filing fee is not tendered;

(3) the filing office is unable to index the record because:

(A) in the case of an initial financing statement, the record does not provide a name for the debtor;

(B) in the case of an amendment or correction statement, the record:

(i) does not identify the initial financing statement as required by Section 9–512 or 9–518, as applicable; or

(ii) identifies an initial financing statement whose effectiveness has lapsed under Section 9–515;

(C) in the case of an initial financing statement that provides the name of a debtor identified as an individual or an amendment that provides a name of a debtor identified as an individual which was not previously provided in the financing statement to which the record relates, the record does not identify the debtor's last name; or

(D) in the case of a record filed [or recorded] in the filing office described in Section 9–501(a)(1), the record does not provide a sufficient description of the real property to which it relates;

(4) in the case of an initial financing statement or an amendment that adds a secured party of record, the record does not provide a name and mailing address for the secured party of record;

(5) in the case of an initial financing statement or an amendment that provides a name of a debtor which was not previously provided in the financing statement to which the amendment relates, the record does not:

(A) provide a mailing address for the debtor;

(B) indicate whether the debtor is an individual or an organization; or

(C) if the financing statement indicates that the debtor is an organization, provide:

(i) a type of organization for the debtor;

(ii) a jurisdiction of organization for the debtor; or

(iii) an organizational identification number for the debtor or indicate that the debtor has none;

(6) in the case of an assignment reflected in an initial financing statement under Section 9–514(a) or an amendment filed under Section 9–514(b), the record does not provide a name and mailing address for the assignee; or

(7) in the case of a continuation statement, the record is not filed within the six-month period prescribed by Section 9–515(d).

(c) For purposes of subsection (b):

(1) a record does not provide information if the filing office is unable to read or decipher the information; and

(2) a record that does not indicate that it is an amendment or identify an initial financing statement to which it relates, as required by Section 9–512, 9–514, or 9–518, is an initial financing statement.

(d) A record that is communicated to the filing office with tender of the filing fee, but which the filing office refuses to accept for a reason other than one set forth in subsection (b), is effective as a filed record except as against a purchaser of the collateral which gives value in reasonable reliance upon the absence of the record from the files.

§ 9–517.   Effect of Indexing Errors.

The failure of the filing office to index a record correctly does not affect the effectiveness of the filed record.

§ 9–518.   Claim Concerning Inaccurate or Wrongfully Filed Record.

(a) A person may file in the filing office a correction statement with respect to a record indexed there under the person's name if the person believes that the record is inaccurate or was wrongfully filed.

[Alternative A]

(b) A correction statement must:

(1) identify the record to which it relates by the file number assigned to the initial financing statement to which the record relates;

(2) indicate that it is a correction statement; and

(3) provide the basis for the person's belief that the record is inaccurate and indicate the manner in which the person believes the record should be amended to cure any inaccuracy or provide the basis for the person's belief that the record was wrongfully filed.

[Alternative B]

(b) A correction statement must:

(1) identify the record to which it relates by:

(A) the file number assigned to the initial financing statement to which the record relates; and

(B) if the correction statement relates to a record filed [or recorded] in a filing office described in Section 9–501(a)(1), the date [and time] that the initial financing statement was filed [or recorded] and the information specified in Section 9–502(b);

(2) indicate that it is a correction statement; and

(3) provide the basis for the person's belief that the record is inaccurate and indicate the manner in which the person believes the record should be amended to cure any inaccuracy or provide the basis for the person's belief that the record was wrongfully filed.

[End of Alternatives]

(c) The filing of a correction statement does not affect the effectiveness of an initial financing statement or other filed record.

Legislative Note: States whose real-estate filing offices require additional information in amendments and cannot search their records by both the name of the debtor and the file number should enact Alternative B to Sections 9–512(a), 9–518(b), 9–519(f), and 9–522(a).

[Subpart 2. Duties and Operation of Filing Office]

§ 9–519.   Numbering, Maintaining, and Indexing Records; Communicating Information Provided in Records.

(a) For each record filed in a filing office, the filing office shall:

(1) assign a unique number to the filed record;

(2) create a record that bears the number assigned to the filed record and the date and time of filing;

(3) maintain the filed record for public inspection; and

(4) index the filed record in accordance with subsections (c), (d), and (e).

(b) A file number [assigned after January 1, 2002,] must include a digit that:

(1) is mathematically derived from or related to the other digits of the file number; and

(2) aids the filing office in determining whether a number communicated as the file number includes a single-digit or transpositional error.

(c) Except as otherwise provided in subsections (d) and (e), the filing office shall:

(1) index an initial financing statement according to the name of the debtor and index all filed records relating to the initial financing statement in a manner that associates with one another an initial financing statement and all filed records relating to the initial financing statement; and

(2) index a record that provides a name of a debtor which was not previously provided in the financing statement to which the record relates also according to the name that was not previously provided.

(d) If a financing statement is filed as a fixture filing or covers as-extracted collateral or timber to be cut, [it must be filed for record and] the filing office shall index it:

(1) under the names of the debtor and of each owner of record shown on the financing statement as if they were the mortgagors under a mortgage of the real property described; and

(2) to the extent that the law of this State provides for indexing of records of mortgages under the name of the mortgagee, under the name of the secured party as if the secured party were the mortgagee thereunder, or, if indexing is by description, as if the financing statement were a record of a mortgage of the real property described.

(e) If a financing statement is filed as a fixture filing or covers as-extracted collateral or timber to be cut, the filing office shall index an assignment filed under Section 9–514(a) or an amendment filed under Section 9–514(b):

(1) under the name of the assignor as grantor; and

(2) to the extent that the law of this State provides for indexing a record of the assignment of a mortgage under the name of the assignee, under the name of the assignee.

[Alternative A]

(f) The filing office shall maintain a capability:

(1) to retrieve a record by the name of the debtor and by the file number assigned to the initial financing statement to which the record relates; and

(2) to associate and retrieve with one another an initial financing statement and each filed record relating to the initial financing statement.

[Alternative B]

(f) The filing office shall maintain a capability:

(1) to retrieve a record by the name of the debtor and:

(A) if the filing office is described in Section 9–501(a)(1), by the file number assigned to the initial financing statement to

which the record relates and the date [and time] that the record was filed [or recorded]; or

(B) if the filing office is described in Section 9–501(a)(2), by the file number assigned to the initial financing statement to which the record relates; and

(2) to associate and retrieve with one another an initial financing statement and each filed record relating to the initial financing statement.

[End of Alternatives]

(g) The filing office may not remove a debtor's name from the index until one year after the effectiveness of a financing statement naming the debtor lapses under Section 9–515 with respect to all secured parties of record.

(h) The filing office shall perform the acts required by subsections (a) through (e) at the time and in the manner prescribed by filing-office rule, but not later than two business days after the filing office receives the record in question.

[(i) Subsection[s] [(b)] [and] [(h)] do[es] not apply to a filing office described in Section 9–501(a)(1).]

Legislative Notes:

1. States whose filing offices currently assign file numbers that include a verification number, commonly known as a "check digit," or can implement this requirement before the effective date of this Article should omit the bracketed language in subsection (b).

2. In States in which writings will not appear in the real property records and indices unless actually recorded the bracketed language in subsection (d) should be used.

3. States whose real-estate filing offices require additional information in amendments and cannot search their records by both the name of the debtor and the file number should enact Alternative B to Sections 9–512(a), 9–518(b), 9–519(f), and 9–522(a).

4. A State that elects not to require real-estate filing offices to comply with either or both of subsections (b) and (h) may adopt an applicable variation of subsection (i) and add "Except as otherwise provided in subsection (i)," to the appropriate subsection or subsections.

§ 9–520. Acceptance and Refusal to Accept Record.

(a) A filing office shall refuse to accept a record for filing for a reason set forth in Section 9–516(b) and may refuse to accept a record for filing only for a reason set forth in Section 9–516(b).

(b) If a filing office refuses to accept a record for filing, it shall communicate to the person that presented the record the fact of and reason for the refusal and the date and time the record would have been filed had the filing office accepted it. The communication must be made at the time and in the manner prescribed by filing-office rule but [, in the case of a filing office described in Section 9–501(a)(2),] in no event more than two business days after the filing office receives the record.

(c) A filed financing statement satisfying Section 9–502(a) and (b) is effective, even if the filing office is required to refuse to accept it for filing under subsection (a). However, Section 9–338 applies to a filed financing statement providing information described in Section 9–516(b)(5) which is incorrect at the time the financing statement is filed.

(d) If a record communicated to a filing office provides information that relates to more than one debtor, this part applies as to each debtor separately.

Legislative Note: A State that elects not to require real-property filing offices to comply with subsection (b) should include the bracketed language.

§ 9–521.   Uniform Form of Written Financing Statement and Amendment.

(a) A filing office that accepts written records may not refuse to accept a written initial financing statement in the following form and format except for a reason set forth in Section 9–516(b):

[NATIONAL UCC FINANCING STATEMENT (FORM UCC1)(REV. 7/29/98)]

[NATIONAL UCC FINANCING STATEMENT ADDENDUM (FORM UCC1Ad)(REV. 07/29/98)]

(b) A filing office that accepts written records may not refuse to accept a written record in the following form and format except for a reason set forth in Section 9–516(b):

[NATIONAL UCC FINANCING STATEMENT AMENDMENT (FORM UCC3)(REV. 07/29/98)]

[NATIONAL UCC FINANCING STATEMENT AMENDMENT ADDENDUM (FORM UCC3Ad)(REV. 07/29/98)]

§ 9–522.   Maintenance and Destruction of Records.

[Alternative A]

(a) The filing office shall maintain a record of the information provided in a filed financing statement for at least one year after the effectiveness of the financing statement has lapsed under Section 9–515 with respect to all secured parties of record. The record must be retrievable by using the name of the debtor and by using the file number assigned to the initial financing statement to which the record relates.

[Alternative B]

(a) The filing office shall maintain a record of the information provided in a filed financing statement for at least one year after the effectiveness of the financing statement has lapsed under Section 9–515 with respect to all secured parties of record. The record must be retrievable by using the name of the debtor and:

(1) if the record was filed [or recorded] in the filing office described in Section 9–501(a)(1), by using the file number assigned to the initial financing statement to which the record relates and the date [and time] that the record was filed [or recorded]; or

(2) if the record was filed in the filing office described in Section 9–501(a)(2), by using the file number assigned to the initial financing statement to which the record relates.

[End of Alternatives]

(b) Except to the extent that a statute governing disposition of public records provides otherwise, the filing office immediately may destroy any written record evidencing a financing statement. However, if the filing office destroys a written record, it shall maintain another record of the financing statement which complies with subsection (a).

Legislative Note: States whose real-estate filing offices require additional information in amendments and cannot search their records by both the name of the debtor and the file number should enact Alternative B to Sections 9–512(a), 9–518(b), 9–519(f), and 9–522(a).

§ 9–523.   Information from Filing Office; Sale or License of Records.

(a) If a person that files a written record requests an acknowledgment of the filing, the filing office shall send to the person an image of the record showing the number assigned to the record pursuant to Section 9–519(a)(1) and the date and time of the filing of the record. However, if the person furnishes a copy of the record to the filing office, the filing office may instead:

(1) note upon the copy the number assigned to the record pursuant to Section 9–519(a)(1) and the date and time of the filing of the record; and

(2) send the copy to the person.

(b) If a person files a record other than a written record, the filing office shall communicate to the person an acknowledgment that provides:

(1) the information in the record;

(2) the number assigned to the record pursuant to Section 9–519(a)(1); and

(3) the date and time of the filing of the record.

(c) The filing office shall communicate or otherwise make available in a record the following information to any person that requests it:

(1) whether there is on file on a date and time specified by the filing office, but not a date earlier than three business days before the filing office receives the request, any financing statement that:

(A) designates a particular debtor [or, if the request so states, designates a particular debtor at the address specified in the request];

(B) has not lapsed under Section 9–515 with respect to all secured parties of record; and

(C) if the request so states, has lapsed under Section 9–515 and a record of which is maintained by the filing office under Section 9–522(a);

(2) the date and time of filing of each financing statement; and

(3) the information provided in each financing statement.

(d) In complying with its duty under subsection (c), the filing office may communicate information in any medium. However, if requested, the filing office shall communicate information by issuing [its written certificate] [a record that can be admitted into evidence in the courts of this State without extrinsic evidence of its authenticity].

(e) The filing office shall perform the acts required by subsections (a) through (d) at the time and in the manner prescribed by filing-office rule, but not later than two business days after the filing office receives the request.

(f) At least weekly, the [insert appropriate official or governmental agency] [filing office] shall offer to sell or license to the public on a nonexclusive basis, in bulk, copies of all records filed in it under this part, in every medium from time to time available to the filing office.

Legislative Notes:
1. States whose filing office does not offer the additional service of responding to search requests limited to a particular address should omit the bracketed language in subsection (c)(1)(A).
2. A State that elects not to require real-estate filing offices to comply with either or both of subsections (e) and (f) should specify in the appropriate subsection(s) only the filing office described in Section 9–501(a)(2).

§ 9–524.   Delay by Filing Office.

Delay by the filing office beyond a time limit prescribed by this part is excused if:

(1) the delay is caused by interruption of communication or computer facilities, war, emergency conditions, failure of equipment, or other circumstances beyond control of the filing office; and

(2) the filing office exercises reasonable diligence under the circumstances.

§ 9–525.   Fees.

(a) Except as otherwise provided in subsection (e), the fee for filing and indexing a record under this part, other than an initial financing statement of the kind described in subsection (b), is [the amount specified in subsection (c), if applicable, plus]:

(1) $[X] if the record is communicated in writing and consists of one or two pages;

(2) $[2X] if the record is communicated in writing and consists of more than two pages; and

(3) $[1/2X] if the record is communicated by another medium authorized by filing-office rule.

(b) Except as otherwise provided in subsection (e), the fee for filing and indexing an initial financing statement of the following kind is [the amount specified in subsection (c), if applicable, plus]:

(1) $———— if the financing statement indicates that it is filed in connection with a public-finance transaction;

(2) $———— if the financing statement indicates that it is filed in connection with a manufactured-home transaction.

[Alternative A]
(c) The number of names required to be indexed does not affect the amount of the fee in subsections (a) and (b).

[Alternative B]
(c) Except as otherwise provided in subsection (e), if a record is communicated in writing, the fee for each name more than two required to be indexed is $————.

[End of Alternatives]

(d) The fee for responding to a request for information from the filing office, including for [issuing a certificate showing] [communicating] whether there is on file any financing statement naming a particular debtor, is:

(1) $———— if the request is communicated in writing; and

(2) $———— if the request is communicated by another medium authorized by filing-office rule.

(e) This section does not require a fee with respect to a record of a mortgage which is effective as a financing statement filed as a fixture filing or as a financing statement covering as-extracted collateral or timber to be cut under Section 9–502(c). However, the recording and satisfaction fees that otherwise would be applicable to the record of the mortgage apply.

Legislative Notes:
1. To preserve uniformity, a State that places the provisions of this section together with statutes setting fees for other services should do so without modification.
2. A State should enact subsection (c), Alternative A, and omit the bracketed language in subsections (a) and (b) unless its indexing system entails a substantial additional cost when indexing additional names.

As amended in 2000.

§ 9–526.   Filing-Office Rules.

(a) The [insert appropriate governmental official or agency] shall adopt and publish rules to implement this article. The filing-office rules must be[:

(1) consistent with this article[; and

(2) adopted and published in accordance with the [insert any applicable state administrative procedure act]].

(b) To keep the filing-office rules and practices of the filing office in harmony with the rules and practices of filing offices in other jurisdictions that enact substantially this part, and to keep the technology used by the filing office compatible with the technology used by filing offices in other jurisdictions that enact substantially this part, the [insert appropriate governmental official or agency], so far as is consistent with the purposes, policies, and provisions of this article, in adopting, amending, and repealing filing-office rules, shall:

(1) consult with filing offices in other jurisdictions that enact substantially this part; and

(2) consult the most recent version of the Model Rules promulgated by the International Association of Corporate Administrators or any successor organization; and

(3) take into consideration the rules and practices of, and the technology used by, filing offices in other jurisdictions that enact substantially this part.

§ 9–527.   Duty to Report.

The [insert appropriate governmental official or agency] shall report [annually on or before ———] to the [Governor and Legislature] on the operation of the filing office. The report must contain a statement of the extent to which:

(1) the filing-office rules are not in harmony with the rules of filing offices in other jurisdictions that enact substantially this part and the reasons for these variations; and

(2) the filing-office rules are not in harmony with the most recent version of the Model Rules promulgated by the International Association of Corporate Administrators, or any successor organization, and the reasons for these variations.

PART 6   Default

[Subpart 1. Default and Enforcement of Security Interest]

§ 9–601.   Rights after Default; Judicial Enforcement; Consignor or Buyer of Accounts, Chattel Paper, Payment Intangibles, or Promissory Notes.

(a) After default, a secured party has the rights provided in this part and, except as otherwise provided in Section 9–602, those provided by agreement of the parties. A secured party:

(1) may reduce a claim to judgment, foreclose, or otherwise enforce the claim, security interest, or agricultural lien by any available judicial procedure; and

(2) if the collateral is documents, may proceed either as to the documents or as to the goods they cover.

(b) A secured party in possession of collateral or control of collateral under Section 9–104, 9–105, 9–106, or 9–107 has the rights and duties provided in Section 9–207.

(c) The rights under subsections (a) and (b) are cumulative and may be exercised simultaneously.

(d) Except as otherwise provided in subsection (g) and Section 9–605, after default, a debtor and an obligor have the rights provided in this part and by agreement of the parties.

(e) If a secured party has reduced its claim to judgment, the lien of any levy that may be made upon the collateral by virtue of

an execution based upon the judgment relates back to the earliest of:

(1) the date of perfection of the security interest or agricultural lien in the collateral;

(2) the date of filing a financing statement covering the collateral; or

(3) any date specified in a statute under which the agricultural lien was created.

(f) A sale pursuant to an execution is a foreclosure of the security interest or agricultural lien by judicial procedure within the meaning of this section. A secured party may purchase at the sale and thereafter hold the collateral free of any other requirements of this article.

(g) Except as otherwise provided in Section 9–607(c), this part imposes no duties upon a secured party that is a consignor or is a buyer of accounts, chattel paper, payment intangibles, or promissory notes.

§ 9–602.   Waiver and Variance of Rights and Duties.

Except as otherwise provided in Section 9–624, to the extent that they give rights to a debtor or obligor and impose duties on a secured party, the debtor or obligor may not waive or vary the rules stated in the following listed sections:

(1) Section 9–207(b)(4)(C), which deals with use and operation of the collateral by the secured party;

(2) Section 9–210, which deals with requests for an accounting and requests concerning a list of collateral and statement of account;

(3) Section 9–607(c), which deals with collection and enforcement of collateral;

(4) Sections 9–608(a) and 9–615(c) to the extent that they deal with application or payment of noncash proceeds of collection, enforcement, or disposition;

(5) Sections 9–608(a) and 9–615(d) to the extent that they require accounting for or payment of surplus proceeds of collateral;

(6) Section 9–609 to the extent that it imposes upon a secured party that takes possession of collateral without judicial process the duty to do so without breach of the peace;

(7) Sections 9–610(b), 9–611, 9–613, and 9–614, which deal with disposition of collateral;

(8) Section 9–615(f), which deals with calculation of a deficiency or surplus when a disposition is made to the secured party, a person related to the secured party, or a secondary obligor;

(9) Section 9–616, which deals with explanation of the calculation of a surplus or deficiency;

(10) Sections 9–620, 9–621, and 9–622, which deal with acceptance of collateral in satisfaction of obligation;

(11) Section 9–623, which deals with redemption of collateral;

(12) Section 9–624, which deals with permissible waivers; and

(13) Sections 9–625 and 9–626, which deal with the secured party's liability for failure to comply with this article.

§ 9–603. Agreement on Standards Concerning Rights and Duties.

(a) The parties may determine by agreement the standards measuring the fulfillment of the rights of a debtor or obligor and the duties of a secured party under a rule stated in Section 9–602 if the standards are not manifestly unreasonable.

(b) Subsection (a) does not apply to the duty under Section 9–609 to refrain from breaching the peace.

§ 9–604. Procedure If Security Agreement Covers Real Property or Fixtures.

(a) If a security agreement covers both personal and real property, a secured party may proceed:

(1) under this part as to the personal property without prejudicing any rights with respect to the real property; or

(2) as to both the personal property and the real property in accordance with the rights with respect to the real property, in which case the other provisions of this part do not apply.

(b) Subject to subsection (c), if a security agreement covers goods that are or become fixtures, a secured party may proceed:

(1) under this part; or

(2) in accordance with the rights with respect to real property, in which case the other provisions of this part do not apply.

(c) Subject to the other provisions of this part, if a secured party holding a security interest in fixtures has priority over all owners and encumbrancers of the real property, the secured party, after default, may remove the collateral from the real property.

(d) A secured party that removes collateral shall promptly reimburse any encumbrancer or owner of the real property, other than the debtor, for the cost of repair of any physical injury caused by the removal. The secured party need not reimburse the encumbrancer or owner for any diminution in value of the real property caused by the absence of the goods removed or by any necessity of replacing them. A person entitled to reimbursement may refuse permission to remove until the secured party gives adequate assurance for the performance of the obligation to reimburse.

§ 9–605. Unknown Debtor or Secondary Obligor.

A secured party does not owe a duty based on its status as secured party:

(1) to a person that is a debtor or obligor, unless the secured party knows:

(A) that the person is a debtor or obligor;

(B) the identity of the person; and

(C) how to communicate with the person; or

(2) to a secured party or lienholder that has filed a financing statement against a person, unless the secured party knows:

(A) that the person is a debtor; and

(B) the identity of the person.

§ 9–606. Time of Default for Agricultural Lien.

For purposes of this part, a default occurs in connection with an agricultural lien at the time the secured party becomes entitled to enforce the lien in accordance with the statute under which it was created.

§ 9–607. Collection and Enforcement by Secured Party.

(a) If so agreed, and in any event after default, a secured party:

(1) may notify an account debtor or other person obligated on collateral to make payment or otherwise render performance to or for the benefit of the secured party;

(2) may take any proceeds to which the secured party is entitled under Section 9–315;

(3) may enforce the obligations of an account debtor or other person obligated on collateral and exercise the rights of the debtor with respect to the obligation of the account debtor or other person obligated on collateral to make payment or otherwise render performance to the debtor, and with respect to any property that secures the obligations of the account debtor or other person obligated on the collateral;

(4) if it holds a security interest in a deposit account perfected by control under Section 9–104(a)(1), may apply the balance of the deposit account to the obligation secured by the deposit account; and

(5) if it holds a security interest in a deposit account perfected by control under Section 9–104(a)(2) or (3), may instruct the bank to pay the balance of the deposit account to or for the benefit of the secured party.

(b) If necessary to enable a secured party to exercise under subsection (a)(3) the right of a debtor to enforce a mortgage nonjudicially, the secured party may record in the office in which a record of the mortgage is recorded:

(1) a copy of the security agreement that creates or provides for a security interest in the obligation secured by the mortgage; and

(2) the secured party's sworn affidavit in recordable form stating that:

(A) a default has occurred; and

(B) the secured party is entitled to enforce the mortgage nonjudicially.

(c) A secured party shall proceed in a commercially reasonable manner if the secured party:

(1) undertakes to collect from or enforce an obligation of an account debtor or other person obligated on collateral; and

(2) is entitled to charge back uncollected collateral or otherwise to full or limited recourse against the debtor or a secondary obligor.

(d) A secured party may deduct from the collections made pursuant to subsection (c) reasonable expenses of collection and enforcement, including reasonable attorney's fees and legal expenses incurred by the secured party.

(e) This section does not determine whether an account debtor, bank, or other person obligated on collateral owes a duty to a secured party.

As amended in 2000.

§ 9–608. Application of Proceeds of Collection or Enforcement; Liability for Deficiency and Right to Surplus.

(a) If a security interest or agricultural lien secures payment or performance of an obligation, the following rules apply:

(1) A secured party shall apply or pay over for application the cash proceeds of collection or enforcement under Section 9–607 in the following order to:

(A) the reasonable expenses of collection and enforcement and, to the extent provided for by agreement and not prohibited by law, reasonable attorney's fees and legal expenses incurred by the secured party;

(B) the satisfaction of obligations secured by the security interest or agricultural lien under which the collection or enforcement is made; and

(C) the satisfaction of obligations secured by any subordinate security interest in or other lien on the collateral subject to the security interest or agricultural lien under which the collection or enforcement is made if the secured party receives an authenticated demand for proceeds before distribution of the proceeds is completed.

(2) If requested by a secured party, a holder of a subordinate security interest or other lien shall furnish reasonable proof of the interest or lien within a reasonable time. Unless the holder complies, the secured party need not comply with the holder's demand under paragraph (1)(C).

(3) A secured party need not apply or pay over for application noncash proceeds of collection and enforcement under Section 9–607 unless the failure to do so would be commercially unreasonable. A secured party that applies or pays over for application noncash proceeds shall do so in a commercially reasonable manner.

(4) A secured party shall account to and pay a debtor for any surplus, and the obligor is liable for any deficiency.

(b) If the underlying transaction is a sale of accounts, chattel paper, payment intangibles, or promissory notes, the debtor is not entitled to any surplus, and the obligor is not liable for any deficiency.

As amended in 2000.

§ 9–609. Secured Party's Right to Take Possession after Default.

(a) After default, a secured party:

(1) may take possession of the collateral; and

(2) without removal, may render equipment unusable and dispose of collateral on a debtor's premises under Section 9–610.

(b) A secured party may proceed under subsection (a):

(1) pursuant to judicial process; or

(2) without judicial process, if it proceeds without breach of the peace.

(c) If so agreed, and in any event after default, a secured party may require the debtor to assemble the collateral and make it available to the secured party at a place to be designated by the secured party which is reasonably convenient to both parties.

§ 9–610. Disposition of Collateral after Default.

(a) After default, a secured party may sell, lease, license, or otherwise dispose of any or all of the collateral in its present condition or following any commercially reasonable preparation or processing.

(b) Every aspect of a disposition of collateral, including the method, manner, time, place, and other terms, must be commercially reasonable. If commercially reasonable, a secured party may dispose of collateral by public or private proceedings, by one or more contracts, as a unit or in parcels, and at any time and place and on any terms.

(c) A secured party may purchase collateral:

(1) at a public disposition; or

(2) at a private disposition only if the collateral is of a kind that is customarily sold on a recognized market or the subject of widely distributed standard price quotations.

(d) A contract for sale, lease, license, or other disposition includes the warranties relating to title, possession, quiet enjoyment, and the like which by operation of law accompany a voluntary disposition of property of the kind subject to the contract.

(e) A secured party may disclaim or modify warranties under subsection (d):

(1) in a manner that would be effective to disclaim or modify the warranties in a voluntary disposition of property of the kind subject to the contract of disposition; or

(2) by communicating to the purchaser a record evidencing the contract for disposition and including an express disclaimer or modification of the warranties.

(f) A record is sufficient to disclaim warranties under subsection (e) if it indicates "There is no warranty relating to title, possession, quiet enjoyment, or the like in this disposition" or uses words of similar import.

§ 9–611. Notification before Disposition of Collateral.

(a) In this section, "notification date" means the earlier of the date on which:

(1) a secured party sends to the debtor and any secondary obligor an authenticated notification of disposition; or

(2) the debtor and any secondary obligor waive the right to notification.

(b) Except as otherwise provided in subsection (d), a secured party that disposes of collateral under Section 9–610 shall send to the persons specified in subsection (c) a reasonable authenticated notification of disposition.

(c) To comply with subsection (b), the secured party shall send an authenticated notification of disposition to:

(1) the debtor;

(2) any secondary obligor; and

(3) if the collateral is other than consumer goods:

(A) any other person from which the secured party has received, before the notification date, an authenticated notification of a claim of an interest in the collateral;

(B) any other secured party or lienholder that, 10 days before the notification date, held a security interest in or other lien on the collateral perfected by the filing of a financing statement that:

(i) identified the collateral;

(ii) was indexed under the debtor's name as of that date; and

(iii) was filed in the office in which to file a financing statement against the debtor covering the collateral as of that date; and

(C) any other secured party that, 10 days before the notification date, held a security interest in the collateral perfected by compliance with a statute, regulation, or treaty described in Section 9–311(a).

(d) Subsection (b) does not apply if the collateral is perishable or threatens to decline speedily in value or is of a type customarily sold on a recognized market.

(e) A secured party complies with the requirement for notification prescribed by subsection (c)(3)(B) if:

(1) not later than 20 days or earlier than 30 days before the notification date, the secured party requests, in a commercially reasonable manner, information concerning financing statements indexed under the debtor's name in the office indicated in subsection (c)(3)(B); and

(2) before the notification date, the secured party:

(A) did not receive a response to the request for information; or

(B) received a response to the request for information and sent an authenticated notification of disposition to each secured party or other lienholder named in that response whose financing statement covered the collateral.

§ 9–612. Timeliness of Notification before Disposition of Collateral.

(a) Except as otherwise provided in subsection (b), whether a notification is sent within a reasonable time is a question of fact.

(b) In a transaction other than a consumer transaction, a notification of disposition sent after default and 10 days or more before the earliest time of disposition set forth in the notification is sent within a reasonable time before the disposition.

§ 9–613. Contents and Form of Notification before Disposition of Collateral: General.

Except in a consumer-goods transaction, the following rules apply:

(1) The contents of a notification of disposition are sufficient if the notification:

(A) describes the debtor and the secured party;

(B) describes the collateral that is the subject of the intended disposition;

(C) states the method of intended disposition;

(D) states that the debtor is entitled to an accounting of the unpaid indebtedness and states the charge, if any, for an accounting; and

(E) states the time and place of a public disposition or the time after which any other disposition is to be made.

(2) Whether the contents of a notification that lacks any of the information specified in paragraph (1) are nevertheless sufficient is a question of fact.

(3) The contents of a notification providing substantially the information specified in paragraph (1) are sufficient, even if the notification includes:

(A) information not specified by that paragraph; or

(b) minor errors that are not seriously misleading.

(4) A particular phrasing of the notification is not required.

(5) The following form of notification and the form appearing in Section 9–614(3), when completed, each provides sufficient information:

NOTIFICATION OF DISPOSITION
OF COLLATERAL

To: [*Name of debtor, obligor, or other person to which the notification is sent*]

From: [*Name, address, and telephone number of secured party*]

Name of Debtor(s): [*Include only if debtor(s) are not an addressee*]

[*For a public disposition:*]

We will sell [or lease or license, *as applicable*] the [*describe collateral*] [to the highest qualified bidder] in public as follows:

Day and Date: _____

Time: _____

Place: _____

[*For a private disposition:*]

We will sell [or lease or license, *as applicable*] the [*describe collateral*] privately sometime after [*day and date*].

You are entitled to an accounting of the unpaid indebtedness secured by the property that we intend to sell [or lease or license *as applicable*] [for a charge of $_____]. You may request an accounting by calling us at [*telephone number*].

[End of Form]

As amended in 2000.

§ 9–614.   Contents and Form of Notification before Disposition of Collateral: Consumer-Goods Transaction.

In a consumer-goods transaction, the following rules apply:

(1) A notification of disposition must provide the following information:

(A) the information specified in Section 9–613(1);

(B) a description of any liability for a deficiency of the person to which the notification is sent;

(C) a telephone number from which the amount that must be paid to the secured party to redeem the collateral under Section 9–623 is available; and

(D) a telephone number or mailing address from which additional information concerning the disposition and the obligation secured is available.

(2) A particular phrasing of the notification is not required.

(3) The following form of notification, when completed, provides sufficient information:

[*Name and address of secured party*]

[*Date*]

NOTICE OF OUR PLAN TO SELL PROPERTY

[*Name and address of any obligor who is also a debtor*]

Subject: [*Identification of Transaction*]

We have your [*describe collateral*], because you broke promises in our agreement.

[*For a public disposition:*]

We will sell [*describe collateral*] at public sale. A sale could include a lease or license. The sale will be held as follows:

Date:_____

Time: _____

Place: _____

You may attend the sale and bring bidders if you want.

[*For a private disposition:*]

We will sell [*describe collateral*] at private sale sometime after [*date*]. A sale could include a lease or license.

The money that we get from the sale (after paying our costs) will reduce the amount you owe. If we get less money than you owe, you [*will or will not, as applicable*] still owe us the difference. If we get more money than you owe, you will get the extra money, unless we must pay it to someone else. You can get the property back at any time before we sell it by paying us the full amount you owe (not just the past due payments), including our expenses. To learn the exact amount you must pay, call us at [*telephone number*].

If you want us to explain to you in writing how we have figured the amount that you owe us, you may call us at [*telephone number*] [*or write us at* [*secured party's address*]] and request a written explanation. [We will charge you $_____ for the explanation if we sent you another written explanation of the amount you owe us within the last six months.]

If you need more information about the sale call us at [*telephone number*] [*or write us at* [*secured party's address*]].

We are sending this notice to the following other people who have an interest in [*describe collateral*] or who owe money under your agreement:

[*Names of all other debtors and obligors, if any*]

[End of Form]

(4) A notification in the form of paragraph (3) is sufficient, even if additional information appears at the end of the form.

(5) A notification in the form of paragraph (3) is sufficient, even if it includes errors in information not required by paragraph (1), unless the error is misleading with respect to rights arising under this article.

(6) If a notification under this section is not in the form of paragraph (3), law other than this article determines the effect of including information not required by paragraph (1).

§ 9–615.   Application of Proceeds of Disposition; Liability for Deficiency and Right to Surplus.

(a) A secured party shall apply or pay over for application the cash proceeds of disposition under Section 9–610 in the following order to:

(1) the reasonable expenses of retaking, holding, preparing for disposition, processing, and disposing, and, to the extent provided for by agreement and not prohibited by law, reasonable attorney's fees and legal expenses incurred by the secured party;

(2) the satisfaction of obligations secured by the security interest or agricultural lien under which the disposition is made;

(3) the satisfaction of obligations secured by any subordinate security interest in or other subordinate lien on the collateral if:

(A) the secured party receives from the holder of the subordinate security interest or other lien an authenticated demand for proceeds before distribution of the proceeds is completed; and

(B) in a case in which a consignor has an interest in the collateral, the subordinate security interest or other lien is senior to the interest of the consignor; and

(4) a secured party that is a consignor of the collateral if the secured party receives from the consignor an authenticated demand for proceeds before distribution of the proceeds is completed.

(b) If requested by a secured party, a holder of a subordinate security interest or other lien shall furnish reasonable proof of the interest or lien within a reasonable time. Unless the holder does so, the secured party need not comply with the holder's demand under subsection (a)(3).

(c) A secured party need not apply or pay over for application noncash proceeds of disposition under Section 9–610 unless the failure to do so would be commercially unreasonable. A secured party that applies or pays over for application noncash proceeds shall do so in a commercially reasonable manner.

(d) If the security interest under which a disposition is made secures payment or performance of an obligation, after making the payments and applications required by subsection (a) and permitted by subsection (c):

(1) unless subsection (a)(4) requires the secured party to apply or pay over cash proceeds to a consignor, the secured party shall account to and pay a debtor for any surplus; and

(2) the obligor is liable for any deficiency.

(e) If the underlying transaction is a sale of accounts, chattel paper, payment intangibles, or promissory notes:

(1) the debtor is not entitled to any surplus; and

(2) the obligor is not liable for any deficiency.

(f) The surplus or deficiency following a disposition is calculated based on the amount of proceeds that would have been realized in a disposition complying with this part to a transferee other than the secured party, a person related to the secured party, or a secondary obligor if:

(1) the transferee in the disposition is the secured party, a person related to the secured party, or a secondary obligor; and

(2) the amount of proceeds of the disposition is significantly below the range of proceeds that a complying disposition to a person other than the secured party, a person related to the secured party, or a secondary obligor would have brought.

(g) A secured party that receives cash proceeds of a disposition in good faith and without knowledge that the receipt violates the rights of the holder of a security interest or other lien that is not subordinate to the security interest or agricultural lien under which the disposition is made:

(1) takes the cash proceeds free of the security interest or other lien;

(2) is not obligated to apply the proceeds of the disposition to the satisfaction of obligations secured by the security interest or other lien; and

(3) is not obligated to account to or pay the holder of the security interest or other lien for any surplus.

As amended in 2000.

§ 9–616. Explanation of Calculation of Surplus or Deficiency.

(a) In this section:

(1) "Explanation" means1 a writing that:

(A) states the amount of the surplus or deficiency;

(B) provides an explanation in accordance with subsection (c) of how the secured party calculated the surplus or deficiency;

(C) states, if applicable, that future debits, credits, charges, including additional credit service charges or interest, rebates, and expenses may affect the amount of the surplus or deficiency; and

(D) provides a telephone number or mailing address from which additional information concerning the transaction is available.

(2) "Request" means a record:

(A) authenticated by a debtor or consumer obligor;

(B) requesting that the recipient provide an explanation; and

(C) sent after disposition of the collateral under Section 9–610.

(b) In a consumer-goods transaction in which the debtor is entitled to a surplus or a consumer obligor is liable for a deficiency under Section 9–615, the secured party shall:

(1) send an explanation to the debtor or consumer obligor, as applicable, after the disposition and:

(A) before or when the secured party accounts to the debtor and pays any surplus or first makes written demand on the consumer obligor after the disposition for payment of the deficiency; and

(B) within 14 days after receipt of a request; or

(2) in the case of a consumer obligor who is liable for a deficiency, within 14 days after receipt of a request, send to the consumer obligor a record waiving the secured party's right to a deficiency.

(c) To comply with subsection (a)(1)(B), a writing must provide the following information in the following order:

(1) the aggregate amount of obligations secured by the security interest under which the disposition was made, and, if the amount reflects a rebate of unearned interest or credit service charge, an indication of that fact, calculated as of a specified date:

(A) if the secured party takes or receives possession of the collateral after default, not more than 35 days before the secured party takes or receives possession; or

(B) if the secured party takes or receives possession of the collateral before default or does not take possession of the collateral, not more than 35 days before the disposition;

(2) the amount of proceeds of the disposition;

(3) the aggregate amount of the obligations after deducting the amount of proceeds;

(4) the amount, in the aggregate or by type, and types of expenses, including expenses of retaking, holding, preparing for disposition, processing, and disposing of the collateral, and attorney's fees secured by the collateral which are known to the secured party and relate to the current disposition;

(5) the amount, in the aggregate or by type, and types of credits, including rebates of interest or credit service charges, to which the obligor is known to be entitled and which are not reflected in the amount in paragraph (1); and

(6) the amount of the surplus or deficiency.

(d) A particular phrasing of the explanation is not required. An explanation complying substantially with the requirements of subsection (a) is sufficient, even if it includes minor errors that are not seriously misleading.

(e) A debtor or consumer obligor is entitled without charge to one response to a request under this section during any six-month period in which the secured party did not send to the debtor or consumer obligor an explanation pursuant to subsection (b)(1). The secured party may require payment of a charge not exceeding $25 for each additional response.

§ 9–617.   Rights of Transferee of Collateral.

(a) A secured party's disposition of collateral after default:

(1) transfers to a transferee for value all of the debtor's rights in the collateral;

(2) discharges the security interest under which the disposition is made; and

(3) discharges any subordinate security interest or other subordinate lien [other than liens created under [cite acts or statutes providing for liens, if any, that are not to be discharged]].

(b) A transferee that acts in good faith takes free of the rights and interests described in subsection (a), even if the secured party fails to comply with this article or the requirements of any judicial proceeding.

(c) If a transferee does not take free of the rights and interests described in subsection (a), the transferee takes the collateral subject to:

(1) the debtor's rights in the collateral;

(2) the security interest or agricultural lien under which the disposition is made; and

(3) any other security interest or other lien.

§ 9–618.   Rights and Duties of Certain Secondary Obligors.

(a) A secondary obligor acquires the rights and becomes obligated to perform the duties of the secured party after the secondary obligor:

(1) receives an assignment of a secured obligation from the secured party;

(2) receives a transfer of collateral from the secured party and agrees to accept the rights and assume the duties of the secured party; or

(3) is subrogated to the rights of a secured party with respect to collateral.

(b) An assignment, transfer, or subrogation described in subsection (a):

(1) is not a disposition of collateral under Section 9–610; and

(2) relieves the secured party of further duties under this article.

§ 9–619.   Transfer of Record or Legal Title.

(a) In this section, "transfer statement" means a record authenticated by a secured party stating:

(1) that the debtor has defaulted in connection with an obligation secured by specified collateral;

(2) that the secured party has exercised its post-default remedies with respect to the collateral;

(3) that, by reason of the exercise, a transferee has acquired the rights of the debtor in the collateral; and

(4) the name and mailing address of the secured party, debtor, and transferee.

(b) A transfer statement entitles the transferee to the transfer of record of all rights of the debtor in the collateral specified in the statement in any official filing, recording, registration, or certificate-of-title system covering the collateral. If a transfer statement is presented with the applicable fee and request form to the official or office responsible for maintaining the system, the official or office shall:

(1) accept the transfer statement;

(2) promptly amend its records to reflect the transfer; and

(3) if applicable, issue a new appropriate certificate of title in the name of the transferee.

(c) A transfer of the record or legal title to collateral to a secured party under subsection (b) or otherwise is not of itself a disposition of collateral under this article and does not of itself relieve the secured party of its duties under this article.

§ 9–620.   Acceptance of Collateral in Full or Partial Satisfaction of Obligation; Compulsory Disposition of Collateral.

(a) Except as otherwise provided in subsection (g), a secured party may accept collateral in full or partial satisfaction of the obligation it secures only if:

(1) the debtor consents to the acceptance under subsection (c);

(2) the secured party does not receive, within the time set forth in subsection (d), a notification of objection to the proposal authenticated by:

(A) a person to which the secured party was required to send a proposal under Section 9–621; or

(B) any other person, other than the debtor, holding an interest in the collateral subordinate to the security interest that is the subject of the proposal;

(3) if the collateral is consumer goods, the collateral is not in the possession of the debtor when the debtor consents to the acceptance; and

(4) subsection (e) does not require the secured party to dispose of the collateral or the debtor waives the requirement pursuant to Section 9–624.

(b) A purported or apparent acceptance of collateral under this section is ineffective unless:

(1) the secured party consents to the acceptance in an authenticated record or sends a proposal to the debtor; and

(2) the conditions of subsection (a) are met.

(c) For purposes of this section:

(1) a debtor consents to an acceptance of collateral in partial satisfaction of the obligation it secures only if the debtor agrees to the terms of the acceptance in a record authenticated after default; and

(2) a debtor consents to an acceptance of collateral in full satisfaction of the obligation it secures only if the debtor agrees

to the terms of the acceptance in a record authenticated after default or the secured party:

(A) sends to the debtor after default a proposal that is unconditional or subject only to a condition that collateral not in the possession of the secured party be preserved or maintained;

(B) in the proposal, proposes to accept collateral in full satisfaction of the obligation it secures; and

(C) does not receive a notification of objection authenticated by the debtor within 20 days after the proposal is sent.

(d) To be effective under subsection (a)(2), a notification of objection must be received by the secured party:

(1) in the case of a person to which the proposal was sent pursuant to Section 9–621, within 20 days after notification was sent to that person; and

(2) in other cases:

(A) within 20 days after the last notification was sent pursuant to Section 9–621; or

(B) if a notification was not sent, before the debtor consents to the acceptance under subsection (c).

(e) A secured party that has taken possession of collateral shall dispose of the collateral pursuant to Section 9–610 within the time specified in subsection (f) if:

(1) 60 percent of the cash price has been paid in the case of a purchase-money security interest in consumer goods; or

(2) 60 percent of the principal amount of the obligation secured has been paid in the case of a non-purchase-money security interest in consumer goods.

(f) To comply with subsection (e), the secured party shall dispose of the collateral:

(1) within 90 days after taking possession; or

(2) within any longer period to which the debtor and all secondary obligors have agreed in an agreement to that effect entered into and authenticated after default.

(g) In a consumer transaction, a secured party may not accept collateral in partial satisfaction of the obligation it secures.

§ 9–621.   Notification of Proposal to Accept Collateral.

(a) A secured party that desires to accept collateral in full or partial satisfaction of the obligation it secures shall send its proposal to:

(1) any person from which the secured party has received, before the debtor consented to the acceptance, an authenticated notification of a claim of an interest in the collateral;

(2) any other secured party or lienholder that, 10 days before the debtor consented to the acceptance, held a security interest in or other lien on the collateral perfected by the filing of a financing statement that:

(A) identified the collateral;

(B) was indexed under the debtor's name as of that date; and

(C) was filed in the office or offices in which to file a financing statement against the debtor covering the collateral as of that date; and

(3) any other secured party that, 10 days before the debtor consented to the acceptance, held a security interest in the collateral perfected by compliance with a statute, regulation, or treaty described in Section 9–311(a).

(b) A secured party that desires to accept collateral in partial satisfaction of the obligation it secures shall send its proposal to any secondary obligor in addition to the persons described in subsection (a).

§ 9–622.   Effect of Acceptance of Collateral.

(a) A secured party's acceptance of collateral in full or partial satisfaction of the obligation it secures:

(1) discharges the obligation to the extent consented to by the debtor;

(2) transfers to the secured party all of a debtor's rights in the collateral;

(3) discharges the security interest or agricultural lien that is the subject of the debtor's consent and any subordinate security interest or other subordinate lien; and

(4) terminates any other subordinate interest.

(b) A subordinate interest is discharged or terminated under subsection (a), even if the secured party fails to comply with this article.

§ 9–623.   Right to Redeem Collateral.

(a) A debtor, any secondary obligor, or any other secured party or lienholder may redeem collateral.

(b) To redeem collateral, a person shall tender:

(1) fulfillment of all obligations secured by the collateral; and

(2) the reasonable expenses and attorney's fees described in Section 9–615(a)(1).

(c) A redemption may occur at any time before a secured party:

(1) has collected collateral under Section 9–607;

(2) has disposed of collateral or entered into a contract for its disposition under Section 9–610; or

(3) has accepted collateral in full or partial satisfaction of the obligation it secures under Section 9–622.

§ 9–624.   Waiver.

(a) A debtor or secondary obligor may waive the right to notification of disposition of collateral under Section 9–611 only by an agreement to that effect entered into and authenticated after default.

(b) A debtor may waive the right to require disposition of collateral under Section 9–620(e) only by an agreement to that effect entered into and authenticated after default.

(c) Except in a consumer-goods transaction, a debtor or secondary obligor may waive the right to redeem collateral under Section 9–623 only by an agreement to that effect entered into and authenticated after default.

[Subpart 2. Noncompliance with Article]

§ 9–625.   Remedies for Secured Party's Failure to Comply with Article.

(a) If it is established that a secured party is not proceeding in accordance with this article, a court may order or restrain collection, enforcement, or disposition of collateral on appropriate terms and conditions.

(b) Subject to subsections (c), (d), and (f), a person is liable for damages in the amount of any loss caused by a failure to comply with this article. Loss caused by a failure to comply may include loss resulting from the debtor's inability to obtain, or increased costs of, alternative financing.

(c) Except as otherwise provided in Section 9–628:

(1) a person that, at the time of the failure, was a debtor, was an obligor, or held a security interest in or other lien on the collateral may recover damages under subsection (b) for its loss; and

(2) if the collateral is consumer goods, a person that was a debtor or a secondary obligor at the time a secured party failed to comply with this part may recover for that failure in any event an amount not less than the credit service charge plus 10 percent of the principal amount of the obligation or the time-price differential plus 10 percent of the cash price.

(d) A debtor whose deficiency is eliminated under Section 9–626 may recover damages for the loss of any surplus. However, a debtor or secondary obligor whose deficiency is eliminated or reduced under Section 9–626 may not otherwise recover under subsection (b) for noncompliance with the provisions of this part relating to collection, enforcement, disposition, or acceptance.

(e) In addition to any damages recoverable under subsection (b), the debtor, consumer obligor, or person named as a debtor in a filed record, as applicable, may recover $500 in each case from a person that:

(1) fails to comply with Section 9–208;

(2) fails to comply with Section 9–209;

(3) files a record that the person is not entitled to file under Section 9–509(a);

(4) fails to cause the secured party of record to file or send a termination statement as required by Section 9–513(a) or (c);

(5) fails to comply with Section 9–616(b)(1) and whose failure is part of a pattern, or consistent with a practice, of noncompliance; or

(6) fails to comply with Section 9–616(b)(2).

(f) A debtor or consumer obligor may recover damages under subsection (b) and, in addition, $500 in each case from a person that, without reasonable cause, fails to comply with a request under Section 9–210. A recipient of a request under Section 9–210 which never claimed an interest in the collateral or obligations that are the subject of a request under that section has a

reasonable excuse for failure to comply with the request within the meaning of this subsection.

(g) If a secured party fails to comply with a request regarding a list of collateral or a statement of account under Section 9–210, the secured party may claim a security interest only as shown in the list or statement included in the request as against a person that is reasonably misled by the failure.

As amended in 2000.

§ 9–626.   Action in Which Deficiency or Surplus Is in Issue.

(a) In an action arising from a transaction, other than a consumer transaction, in which the amount of a deficiency or surplus is in issue, the following rules apply:

(1) A secured party need not prove compliance with the provisions of this part relating to collection, enforcement, disposition, or acceptance unless the debtor or a secondary obligor places the secured party's compliance in issue.

(2) If the secured party's compliance is placed in issue, the secured party has the burden of establishing that the collection, enforcement, disposition, or acceptance was conducted in accordance with this part.

(3) Except as otherwise provided in Section 9–628, if a secured party fails to prove that the collection, enforcement, disposition, or acceptance was conducted in accordance with the provisions of this part relating to collection, enforcement, disposition, or acceptance, the liability of a debtor or a secondary obligor for a deficiency is limited to an amount by which the sum of the secured obligation, expenses, and attorney's fees exceeds the greater of:

(A) the proceeds of the collection, enforcement, disposition, or acceptance; or

(B) the amount of proceeds that would have been realized had the noncomplying secured party proceeded in accordance with the provisions of this part relating to collection, enforcement, disposition, or acceptance.

(4) For purposes of paragraph (3)(B), the amount of proceeds that would have been realized is equal to the sum of the secured obligation, expenses, and attorney's fees unless the secured party proves that the amount is less than that sum.

(5) If a deficiency or surplus is calculated under Section 9–615(f), the debtor or obligor has the burden of establishing that the amount of proceeds of the disposition is significantly below the range of prices that a complying disposition to a person other than the secured party, a person related to the secured party, or a secondary obligor would have brought.

(b) The limitation of the rules in subsection (a) to transactions other than consumer transactions is intended to leave to the court the determination of the proper rules in consumer transactions. The court may not infer from that limitation the nature of the proper rule in consumer transactions and may continue to apply established approaches.

§ 9–627. Determination of Whether Conduct Was Commercially Reasonable.

(a) The fact that a greater amount could have been obtained by a collection, enforcement, disposition, or acceptance at a different time or in a different method from that selected by the secured party is not of itself sufficient to preclude the secured party from establishing that the collection, enforcement, disposition, or acceptance was made in a commercially reasonable manner.

(b) A disposition of collateral is made in a commercially reasonable manner if the disposition is made:

(1) in the usual manner on any recognized market;

(2) at the price current in any recognized market at the time of the disposition; or

(3) otherwise in conformity with reasonable commercial practices among dealers in the type of property that was the subject of the disposition.

(c) A collection, enforcement, disposition, or acceptance is commercially reasonable if it has been approved:

(1) in a judicial proceeding;

(2) by a bona fide creditors' committee;

(3) by a representative of creditors; or

(4) by an assignee for the benefit of creditors.

(d) Approval under subsection (c) need not be obtained, and lack of approval does not mean that the collection, enforcement, disposition, or acceptance is not commercially reasonable.

§ 9–628. Nonliability and Limitation on Liability of Secured Party; Liability of Secondary Obligor.

(a) Unless a secured party knows that a person is a debtor or obligor, knows the identity of the person, and knows how to communicate with the person:

(1) the secured party is not liable to the person, or to a secured party or lienholder that has filed a financing statement against the person, for failure to comply with this article; and

(2) the secured party's failure to comply with this article does not affect the liability of the person for a deficiency.

(b) A secured party is not liable because of its status as secured party:

(1) to a person that is a debtor or obligor, unless the secured party knows:

(A) that the person is a debtor or obligor;

(B) the identity of the person; and

(C) how to communicate with the person; or

(2) to a secured party or lienholder that has filed a financing statement against a person, unless the secured party knows:

(A) that the person is a debtor; and

(B) the identity of the person.

(c) A secured party is not liable to any person, and a person's liability for a deficiency is not affected, because of any act or omission arising out of the secured party's reasonable belief that a transaction is not a consumer-goods transaction or a consumer transaction or that goods are not consumer goods, if the secured party's belief is based on its reasonable reliance on:

(1) a debtor's representation concerning the purpose for which collateral was to be used, acquired, or held; or

(2) an obligor's representation concerning the purpose for which a secured obligation was incurred.

(d) A secured party is not liable to any person under Section 9–625(c)(2) for its failure to comply with Section 9–616.

(e) A secured party is not liable under Section 9–625(c)(2) more than once with respect to any one secured obligation.

PART 7   Transition

§ 9–701. Effective Date.

This [Act] takes effect on July 1, 2001.

§ 9–702. Savings Clause.

(a) Except as otherwise provided in this part, this [Act] applies to a transaction or lien within its scope, even if the transaction or lien was entered into or created before this [Act] takes effect.

(b) Except as otherwise provided in subsection (c) and Sections 9–703 through 9–709:

(1) transactions and liens that were not governed by [former Article 9], were validly entered into or created before this [Act] takes effect, and would be subject to this [Act] if they had been entered into or created after this [Act] takes effect, and the rights, duties, and interests flowing from those transactions and liens remain valid after this [Act] takes effect; and

(2) the transactions and liens may be terminated, completed, consummated, and enforced as required or permitted by this [Act] or by the law that otherwise would apply if this [Act] had not taken effect.

(c) This [Act] does not affect an action, case, or proceeding commenced before this [Act] takes effect.

As amended in 2000.

§ 9–703. Security Interest Perfected before Effective Date.

(a) A security interest that is enforceable immediately before this [Act] takes effect and would have priority over the rights of a person that becomes a lien creditor at that time is a perfected security interest under this [Act] if, when this [Act] takes effect, the applicable requirements for enforceability and perfection under this [Act] are satisfied without further action.

(b) Except as otherwise provided in Section 9–705, if, immediately before this [Act] takes effect, a security interest is enforceable and would have priority over the rights of a person that becomes a lien creditor at that time, but the applicable requirements for enforceability or perfection under this [Act] are not satisfied when this [Act] takes effect, the security interest:

(1) is a perfected security interest for one year after this [Act] takes effect;

(2) remains enforceable thereafter only if the security interest becomes enforceable under Section 9–203 before the year expires; and

(3) remains perfected thereafter only if the applicable requirements for perfection under this [Act] are satisfied before the year expires.

§ 9–704.   Security Interest Unperfected before Effective Date.

A security interest that is enforceable immediately before this [Act] takes effect but which would be subordinate to the rights of a person that becomes a lien creditor at that time:

(1) remains an enforceable security interest for one year after this [Act] takes effect;

(2) remains enforceable thereafter if the security interest becomes enforceable under Section 9–203 when this [Act] takes effect or within one year thereafter; and

(3) becomes perfected:

(A) without further action, when this [Act] takes effect if the applicable requirements for perfection under this [Act] are satisfied before or at that time; or

(B) when the applicable requirements for perfection are satisfied if the requirements are satisfied after that time.

§ 9–705.   Effectiveness of Action Taken before Effective Date.

(a) If action, other than the filing of a financing statement, is taken before this [Act] takes effect and the action would have resulted in priority of a security interest over the rights of a person that becomes a lien creditor had the security interest become enforceable before this [Act] takes effect, the action is effective to perfect a security interest that attaches under this [Act] within one year after this [Act] takes effect. An attached security interest becomes unperfected one year after this [Act] takes effect unless the security interest becomes a perfected security interest under this [Act] before the expiration of that period.

(b) The filing of a financing statement before this [Act] takes effect is effective to perfect a security interest to the extent the filing would satisfy the applicable requirements for perfection under this [Act].

(c) This [Act] does not render ineffective an effective financing statement that, before this [Act] takes effect, is filed and satisfies the applicable requirements for perfection under the law of the jurisdiction governing perfection as provided in [former Section 9–103]. However, except as otherwise provided in subsections (d) and (e) and Section 9–706, the financing statement ceases to be effective at the earlier of:

(1) the time the financing statement would have ceased to be effective under the law of the jurisdiction in which it is filed; or

(2) June 30, 2006.

(d) The filing of a continuation statement after this [Act] takes effect does not continue the effectiveness of the financing statement filed before this [Act] takes effect. However, upon the timely filing of a continuation statement after this [Act] takes effect and in accordance with the law of the jurisdiction governing perfection as provided in Part 3, the effectiveness of a financing statement filed in the same office in that jurisdiction before this [Act] takes effect continues for the period provided by the law of that jurisdiction.

(e) Subsection (c)(2) applies to a financing statement that, before this [Act] takes effect, is filed against a transmitting utility and satisfies the applicable requirements for perfection under the law of the jurisdiction governing perfection as provided in [former Section 9–103] only to the extent that Part 3 provides that the law of a jurisdiction other than the jurisdiction in which the financing statement is filed governs perfection of a security interest in collateral covered by the financing statement.

(f) A financing statement that includes a financing statement filed before this [Act] takes effect and a continuation statement filed after this [Act] takes effect is effective only to the extent that it satisfies the requirements of Part 5 for an initial financing statement.

§ 9–706.   When Initial Financing Statement Suffices to Continue Effectiveness of Financing Statement.

(a) The filing of an initial financing statement in the office specified in Section 9–501 continues the effectiveness of a financing statement filed before this [Act] takes effect if:

(1) the filing of an initial financing statement in that office would be effective to perfect a security interest under this [Act];

(2) the pre-effective-date financing statement was filed in an office in another State or another office in this State; and

(3) the initial financing statement satisfies subsection (c).

(b) The filing of an initial financing statement under subsection (a) continues the effectiveness of the pre-effective-date financing statement:

(1) if the initial financing statement is filed before this [Act] takes effect, for the period provided in [former Section 9–403] with respect to a financing statement; and

(2) if the initial financing statement is filed after this [Act] takes effect, for the period provided in Section 9–515 with respect to an initial financing statement.

(c) To be effective for purposes of subsection (a), an initial financing statement must:

(1) satisfy the requirements of Part 5 for an initial financing statement;

(2) identify the pre-effective-date financing statement by indicating the office in which the financing statement was filed

and providing the dates of filing and file numbers, if any, of the financing statement and of the most recent continuation statement filed with respect to the financing statement; and

(3) indicate that the pre-effective-date financing statement remains effective.

§ 9–707.   Amendment of Pre-Effective-Date Financing Statement.

(a) In this section, "Pre-effective-date financing statement" means a financing statement filed before this [Act] takes effect.
(b) After this [Act] takes effect, a person may add or delete collateral covered by, continue or terminate the effectiveness of, or otherwise amend the information provided in, a pre-effective-date financing statement only in accordance with the law of the jurisdiction governing perfection as provided in Part 3. However, the effectiveness of a pre-effective-date financing statement also may be terminated in accordance with the law of the jurisdiction in which the financing statement is filed.
(c) Except as otherwise provided in subsection (d), if the law of this State governs perfection of a security interest, the information in a pre-effective-date financing statement may be amended after this [Act] takes effect only if:

(1) the pre-effective-date financing statement and an amendment are filed in the office specified in Section 9–501;

(2) an amendment is filed in the office specified in Section 9–501 concurrently with, or after the filing in that office of, an initial financing statement that satisfies Section 9–706(c); or

(3) an initial financing statement that provides the information as amended and satisfies Section 9–706(c) is filed in the office specified in Section 9–501.
(d) If the law of this State governs perfection of a security interest, the effectiveness of a pre-effective-date financing statement may be continued only under Section 9–705(d) and (f) or 9–706.
(e) Whether or not the law of this State governs perfection of a security interest, the effectiveness of a pre-effective-date financing statement filed in this State may be terminated after

this [Act] takes effect by filing a termination statement in the office in which the pre-effective-date financing statement is filed, unless an initial financing statement that satisfies Section 9–706(c) has been filed in the office specified by the law of the jurisdiction governing perfection as provided in Part 3 as the office in which to file a financing statement.

As amended in 2000.

§ 9–708.   Persons Entitled to File Initial Financing Statement or Continuation Statement.

A person may file an initial financing statement or a continuation statement under this part if:

(1) the secured party of record authorizes the filing; and

(2) the filing is necessary under this part:

(A) to continue the effectiveness of a financing statement filed before this [Act] takes effect; or

(B) to perfect or continue the perfection of a security interest.

As amended in 2000.

§ 9–709.   Priority.

(a) This [Act] determines the priority of conflicting claims to collateral. However, if the relative priorities of the claims were established before this [Act] takes effect, [former Article 9] determines priority.
(b) For purposes of Section 9–322(a), the priority of a security interest that becomes enforceable under Section 9–203 of this [Act] dates from the time this [Act] takes effect if the security interest is perfected under this [Act] by the filing of a financing statement before this [Act] takes effect which would not have been effective to perfect the security interest under [former Article 9]. This subsection does not apply to conflicting security interests each of which is perfected by the filing of such a financing statement.

Glossary

A

Absolute privilege Existing in courtrooms and legislative hearings, this is additional protection that allows anyone speaking there, such as a witness in a trial, to say anything at all and never be sued for defamation. (Chapter 6)

Acceptance A secured party's retention of the collateral as full or partial satisfaction of the debt. (Chapter 13)

Accounts Any right to receive payment for goods sold or leased, other than rights covered by chattel paper or instruments. (Chapter 13)

Accredited investor Under the Securities Act of 1933, an accredited investor is an institution (such as a bank or insurance company) or any individual with a net worth of more than $1 million or an annual income of more than $200,000. (Chapter 19)

Acquit To find the defendant not guilty of the crime for which he was tried. (Chapter 7)

Act of State doctrine A rule requiring American courts to abstain from cases if a court order would interfere with the ability of the President or Congress to conduct foreign policy. (Chapter 8)

Actual malice In cases of defamation against a public figure or public official, the prosecution can win only if they prove actual malice—that the defendant knew the statement was false or acted with reckless disregard of the truth. (Chapter 6)

Actus reus The guilty act. The prosecution must show that a criminal defendant committed some proscribed act. In a murder prosecution, taking another person's life is the actus reus. (Chapter 7)

Adjudicate To hold a formal hearing in a disputed matter and issue an official decision. (Chapter 4)

Administrative agencies Created by Congress or a state legislature, these agencies oversee all aspects of commerce. These agencies include the Federal Communications Commission (FCC), the Federal Trade Commission (FTC), and the Bureau of U.S. Citizenship and Immigration Services (USCIS). (Chapter 1)

Administrative law Concerns all agencies, boards, commissions, and other entities created by a federal or state legislature and charged with investigating, regulating, and adjudicating a particular industry or issue. (Chapter 1)

Administrative law judge (ALJ) In an adjudicate hearing, one who is employed by the agency but is expected to be impartial in his or her rulings. (Chapter 4)

Affidavit A written statement signed under oath. (Chapter 7)

Affirm A decision by an appellate court to uphold the judgment of a lower court. (Chapter 3)

Affirmative action A plan introduced in a workplace for the purpose of either remedying the effects of past discrimination or achieving equitable representation of minorities and women. (Chapter 15)

After-acquired property Items that a debtor obtains after making a security agreement with the secured party. (Chapter 13)

Age Discrimination in Employment Act (ADEA) of 1967 Prohibits age discrimination against employees or job applicants who are at least 40 years old. (Chapter 15)

Agent A person who acts for a principal. (Chapter 7, 14)

Alternative dispute resolution Any method of resolving a legal conflict other than litigation, such as: negotiation, arbitration, mediation, mini-trials, and summary jury trials. (Chapter 3)

Annual report Each year, public companies must send their shareholders an annual report that contains detailed financial data. (Chapter 18)

Anticybersquatting Consumer Protection Act Permits both trademark owners and famous people to sue anyone who registers their name as a domain name in "bad faith." (Chapter 22)

Antitrust laws Laws that make it illegal to destroy competition and capture an entire market. (Chapter 8)

Apparent authority A situation in which conduct of a principal causes a third party to believe that the principal consents to have an act done on his behalf by a person purporting to act for him when, in fact, that person is not acting for the principal. (Chapter 14)

Appellant The party who appeals a lower court decision to a higher court. (Chapter 3)

Appellate court Any court in a state or federal system that reviews cases that have already been tried. (Chapter 3)

Appellee The party opposing an appeal from a lower court to a higher court. (Chapter 3)

Arbitration A form of alternative dispute resolution in which the parties hire a neutral third party to hear their respective arguments, receive evidence, and then make a binding decision. (Chapter 3, 16)

Arson Malicious use of fire or explosives to damage or destroy real estate or personal property. (Chapter 7)

Assault An intentional act that causes the plaintiff to fear an imminent battery. (Chapter 6)

Assignee The party who receives an assignment of contract rights from a party to the contract. (Chapter 10)

Assignment The act by which a party transfers contract rights to a third person. (Chapter 10)

Assignor The party who assigns contract rights to a third person. (Chapter 10)

Assumption of risk A special rule that holds that one who voluntarily enters an obviously dangerous situation cannot complain if he or she is injured. (Chapter 6)

Attachment A court order seizing property of a party to a civil action, so that there will be sufficient assets available to pay the judgment. (Chapter 5, 13)

Authenticate To sign a document or to use any symbol or encryption method that identifies the person and clearly indicates he or she is adopting the record as his or her own. (Chapter 13)

Authorized and issued stock Stock that has been approved by the corporation's charter and subsequently sold. (Chapter 18)

Authorized and unissued stock Stock that has been approved by the corporation's charter, but has not yet been sold. (Chapter 18)

B

Bailee A person who rightfully possesses goods belonging to another. (Chapter 23)

Bailment Giving possession and control of personal property to another person. (Chapter 23)

Bailor One who creates a bailment by delivering goods to another. (Chapter 23)

Battery The intentional touching of another person in a way that is unwanted or offensive. (Chapter 6)

Berne Convention Requires member countries to provide automatic copyright protection to any works created in another member country. (Chapter 22)

Bilateral contract A binding agreement in which each party has made a promise to the other. (Chapter 9)

Bilateral mistake Error occurring when both parties negotiate based on the same factual error. (Chapter 10)

Bill A proposed statute that has been submitted for consideration to Congress or a state legislature. (Chapter 4)

Bill of Rights A list of 10 amendments added to the Constitution in 1791 that guaranteed many liberties directly to individual citizens. (Chapter 5)

Blue sky laws State securities laws. (Chapter 19)

Bona fide occupational qualification A job requirement that would otherwise be discriminatory is permitted in situations in which it is essential to the position in question. (Chapter 15)

Bonds Long-term debt secured by some of the issuing company's assets. (Chapter 18)

Brief The written legal argument that an attorney files with an appeal court. (Chapter 3)

Buildings Real property such as houses, office buildings, and factories. (Chapter 23)

Burden of proof The allocation of which party must prove its case. In a civil case, the plaintiff has the burden of proof to persuade the factfinder of every element of her case. In a criminal case, the government has the burden of proof. (Chapter 3)

Business judgment rule A common law rule that protects managers from liability if they are acting without a conflict of interest, and make informed decisions that have a rational business purpose. (Chapter 18)

Buyer in ordinary course of business Someone who buys goods in good faith from a seller who routinely deals in such goods. (Chapter 13)

Bylaws A document that specifies the organizational rules of a corporation or other organization, such as the date of the annual meeting and the required number of directors. (Chapter 18)

C

Capacity The legal ability to enter into a contract. (Chapter 10)

Categorical imperative Based on the Golden Rule, this concept was introduced by German philosopher Immanuel Kant and centers on the belief that an individual should not do something unless he or she would be willing for everyone else to do it also. (Chapter 2)

Cease and desist order Command given to the violator to stop the offending activity. (Chapter 24)

***Certiorari,* writ of** Formal notice from the United States Supreme Court that it will accept a case for review. (Chapter 3)

Challenge for cause An attorney's request, during voir dire, to excuse a prospective juror because of apparent bias. (Chapter 3)

Chattel paper Any writing that indicates two things: (1) a debtor owes money and (2) a secured party has a security interest in specific goods. The most common chattel paper is a document indicating a consumer sale on credit. (Chapter 13)

Check An instrument in which the drawer orders the drawee bank to pay money to the payee. (Chapter 11)

Chicago School A theory of antitrust law first developed at the University of Chicago. Adherents to this theory believe that antitrust enforcement should focus on promoting efficiency and should not generally be concerned about the size or number of competitors in any market. (Chapter 20)

Children's Online Privacy Protection Act of 1998 (COPPA) Prohibits Internet operators from collecting information from children under 13 without parental permission. It also requires sites to disclose how they will use any information they acquire. (Chapter 21)

Civil law The large body of law concerning the rights and duties between parties. It is distinguished from criminal law, which concerns behavior outlawed by a government. (Chapter 1)

Class action A method of litigating a civil lawsuit in which one or more plaintiffs (or occasionally defendants) seek to represent an entire group of people with similar claims against a common opponent. (Chapter 3)

Classification The process by which the Customs Service decides what label to attach to imported merchandise, and therefore what level of tariff to impose. (Chapter 8)

Clayton Act Prohibits mergers that are anticompetitive. (Chapter 20)

Close corporation A corporation with a small number of shareholders. Its stock is not publicly traded. (Chapter 17)

Closing A meeting at which property is actually sold. (Chapter 23)

Collateral The property subject to a security interest. (Chapter 13)

Collateral promise A promise to pay the debt of another person, as a favor to the debtor. (Chapter 10)

Collective bargaining Contract negotiations between an employer and a union. (Chapter 16)

Collective bargaining unit The precisely defined group of employees who are represented by a particular union. (Chapter 16)

Comity A doctrine that requires a court to abstain from hearing a case out of respect for another court that also has jurisdiction. International comity demands that an American court refuse to hear a case in which a foreign court shares jurisdiction if there is a conflict between the laws and if it is more logical for the foreign court to take the case. (Chapter 8)

Commerce clause One of the powers granted by Article I, §8 of the Constitution, it gives Congress exclusive power to regulate international commerce and concurrent power with the states to regulate domestic commerce. (Chapter 5)

Commercial impracticability After the creation of a contract, an entirely unforeseen event occurs which makes enforcement of the contract extraordinarily unfair. (Chapter 17)

Commercial paper Instruments such as checks and promissory notes that contain a promise to pay money. Commercial paper includes both negotiable and non-negotiable instruments. (Chapter 11)

Commercial speech Communication, such as television advertisements, that has the dominant theme of proposing a commercial transaction. (Chapter 5)

Common law Judge-made law, that is, the body of all decisions made by appellate courts over the years. (Chapter 1, 4)

Common stock Certificates that reflect ownership in a corporation. Owners of this equity security are last in line for corporate pay-outs such as dividends and liquidation proceeds. (Chapter 18)

Comparative negligence state A state in which a plaintiff may generally recover even if she is partially negligent. (Chapter 6)

Compensatory damages Those that flow directly from the contract. (Chapter 6, 10)

Complaint A pleading, filed by the plaintiff, providing a short statement of the claim. (Chapter 3)

Concerted action Tactics, such as a strike, used by a union to gain a bargaining advantage. (Chapter 16)

Concurrent estates When two or more people own real property at the same time. (Chapter 23)

Confiscation Expropriation without adequate compensation of property owned by foreigners. (Chapter 8)

Consent order An agreement entered into by a wrongdoer and an administrative agency (such as the Securities and Exchange Commission or the Federal Trade Commission) in which the wrongdoer agrees not to violate the law in the future. (Chapter 24)

Consequential damages Those resulting from the unique circumstances of this injured party. (Chapter 10)

Consideration In contract law, something of legal value that has been bargained for and given in exchange by the parties. (Chapter 9, 13)

Constitution of the United States Drafted in 1787 by the Framers, or the Founding Fathers, this document is a series of compromises about power, and of the separation of power, within government. (Chapter 5)

Consumer report Any communication about a consumer's creditworthiness, character, general reputation, or lifestyle that is considered as a factor in establishing credit, obtaining insurance, securing a job, acquiring a government license, or for any other legitimate business need. (Chapter 24)

Contract A legally enforceable promise or set of promises. (Chapter 9)

Contributory negligence A rule of tort law that permits a negligent defendant to escape liability if she can demonstrate that the plaintiff's own conduct contributed in any way to the plaintiff's harm. (Chapter 6)

Control security Stock owned by any officer or director of the issuer, or by any shareholder who holds more than 10 percent of a class of stock of the issuer. (Chapter 19)

Controlling the Assault of Non-Solicited Pornography and Marketing Act (CAN-SPAM) A federal statute regulating spam. (Chapter 21)

Cookie A small computer file that identifies the user of a computer. Internet sites typically place cookies on a computer's hard drive to track visitors to their site. (Chapter 21)

Copyright Under federal law, the holder of a copyright owns a particular expression of an idea, but not the idea itself. This ownership right applies to creative activities such as literature, music, drama, and software. (Chapter 22)

Counter-claim A claim made by the defendant against the plaintiff. (Chapter 3)

Countervailing duties A tariff imposed by the United States on subsidized goods. (Chapter 8)

Covenant A promise by either the landlord or the tenant to do something or refrain from doing something. (Chapter 23)

Criminal Conduct that society has outlawed. (Chapter 7)

Criminal law Rules that permit a government to punish certain behavior by fine or imprisonment. (Chapter 1)

Criminal negligence Gross deviations from reasonable conduct. (Chapter 7)

Cross-examination During a hearing, for a lawyer to question an opposing witness. (Chapter 3)

D

Damages (1) The harm that a plaintiff complains of at trial, such as an injury to her person, or money lost because of a contract breach. (2) Money awarded by a trial court for injury suffered. (Chapter 14)

De novo The power of an appellate court or appellate agency to make a new decision in a matter under appeal, entirely ignoring the findings and conclusions of the lower court or agency official. (Chapter 4)

Debentures Long-term, unsecured debt, typically issued by a corporation. (Chapter 18)

Debtor A person who owes money or some other obligation to another party. (Chapter 13)

Deed A document proving ownership of the land. (Chapter 23)

Defamation The act of injuring someone's reputation by stating something false about her to a third person. *Libel* is defamation done either in writing or by broadcast. *Slander* is defamation done orally. (Chapter 6, 14)

Default The failure to perform an obligation, such as the failure to pay money when due. (Chapter 13)

Default judgment Court order awarding one party everything it requested because the opposing party failed to respond in time. (Chapter 3)

Delegation The act by which a party to a contract transfers duties to a third person who is not a party to the contract. (Chapter 10)

Deponent The person being questioned in a deposition. (Chapter 3)

Deterrence Using punishment, such as imprisonment, to discourage criminal behavior. (Chapter 7)

Digital Millennium Copyright Act Provides that it is illegal to delete copyright information, such as the name of the author or the title of the article; it is illegal to circumvent encryption or scrambling devices that protect copyrighted works; and it is illegal to distribute tools and technologies used to circumvent encryption devices. (Chapter 22)

Direct examination During a hearing, for a lawyer to question his own witness. (Chapter 3)

Directed verdict The decision by a court to instruct a jury that it must find in favor of a particular party because, in the judge's opinion, no reasonable person could disagree on the outcome. (Chapter 3)

Disabled person Someone with a physical or mental impairment that substantially limits a major life activity, or someone who is regarded as having such an impairment. (Chapter 15)

Disaffirmance The act of notifying the other party to a contract that the party giving the notice refuses to be bound by the agreement. (Chapter 9)

Discharge (1) A party to a contract has no more duties. (2) A party to an instrument is released from liability. (Chapter 13)

Disclaimer A statement that a particular warranty does not apply. (Chapter 11)

Discovery A stage in litigation, after all pleadings have been served, in which each party seeks as much relevant information as possible about the opposing party's case. (Chapter 3)

Dissociation A dissociation occurs when a partner leaves a partnership. (Chapter 17)

Doctrine of precedent Requires that the judges decide current cases based on previous rulings. (Chapter 1)

Documents of title The proof of ownership retained by someone who ships or stores goods. (Chapter 13)

Domestic corporation A corporation is a domestic corporation in the state in which it was formed. (Chapter 18)

Donee A person who receives a gift. (Chapter 23)

Donor A person who makes a gift to another. (Chapter 23)

Double jeopardy A criminal defendant may be prosecuted only once for a particular criminal offense. (Chapter 7)

Draft The drawer of this instrument orders someone else to pay money. Checks are the most common form of draft. The drawer of a check orders a bank to pay money. (Chapter 8, 11)

Dram act/dram shop laws Acts in many states making liquor stores, bars, and restaurants liable for serving drinks to intoxicated customers who later cause harm. (Chapter 6)

Drawee The person who pays a draft. In the case of a check, the bank is the drawee. (Chapter 11)

Drawer The person who issues a draft. (Chapter 11)

Due Process Clause Part of the Fifth Amendment. Procedural due process ensures that before depriving anyone of liberty or property, the government must go through procedures which ensure that the deprivation is fair. Substantive due process holds that certain rights, such as privacy, are so fundamental that the government may not eliminate them. (Chapter 7)

Dumping Selling merchandise at one price in the domestic market and at a cheaper, unfair price in an international market. (Chapter 8)

Duress (1) A criminal defense in which the defendant shows that she committed the wrongful act because a third person threatened her with imminent physical harm. (2) An improper threat made to force another party to enter into a contract. (Chapter 7)

Duty of care Requires officers and directors to act in the best interests of the corporation and to use the same care that an ordinarily prudent person would in the management of her own assets. (Chapter 18)

Duty of fair representation Requires that a union represent all members fairly, impartially, and in good faith. (Chapter 16)

Duty of loyalty Prohibits managers from making a decision that benefits them at the expense of the corporation. (Chapter 18)

E

Easement The right to enter land belonging to another and make a limited use of it, without taking anything away. (Chapter 23)

Economic Espionage Act of 1996 Makes it a criminal offense to steal (or attempt to steal) trade secrets for the benefit of someone other than the owner, including for the benefit of any foreign government. (Chapter 22)

Electronic Communications Privacy Act of 1986 (ECPA) A federal statute that prohibits unauthorized interception or disclosure of wire and electronic communications or unauthorized access to stored communications. Permits employers to monitor workers' telephone calls and e-mail messages if (1) the employee consents, (2) the monitoring occurs in the ordinary course of business, or (3) in the case of e-mail, the employer provides the e-mail system. (Chapter 15, 21)

Element A fact that a party to a lawsuit must prove in order to prevail. (Chapter 6)

Embezzlement Fraudulent conversion of property already in the defendant's possession. (Chapter 7)

Eminent domain The power of the government to take private property for public use. (Chapter 5, 23)

Employee at will A worker whose job does not have a specified duration. (Chapter 15)

Enabling legislation A statute authorizing the creation of a new administrative agency and specifying its powers and duties. (Chapter 4)

Entrapment A criminal defense in which the defendant demonstrates that the government induced him to break the law. (Chapter 7)

Equal Credit Opportunity Act (ECOA) Prohibits any creditor from discriminating against a borrower because of race, color, religion, national origin, sex, marital status, age (as long as the borrower is old enough to enter into a legal contract), or because the borrower is receiving welfare. (Chapter 24)

Equal Pay Act Passed in 1963, this states that an employee may not be paid at a lesser rate than employees of the opposite sex for equal work. (Chapter 15)

Equal Protection Clause Part of the Fourteenth Amendment, it generally requires the government to treat equally situated people the same. (Chapter 5)

Equity The broad powers of a court to fashion a remedy where justice demands it and no common law remedy exists. An injunction is an example of an equitable remedy. (Chapter 1)

Error of law A mistake made by a trial judge that concerns a legal issue as opposed to a factual matter. Permitting too many leading questions is a legal error; choosing to believe one witness rather than another is a factual matter. (Chapter 3)

Estate The legal entity that holds title to assets after the owner dies and before the property is distributed. (Chapter 23)

Ethics The study of how people ought to act. (Chapter 2)

Evidence, rules of Law governing the proof offered during a trial or formal hearing. These rules limit the questions that may be asked of witnesses and the introduction of physical objects. (Chapter 3)

Exclusionary rule In a criminal trial, a ban on the use of evidence obtained in violation of the Constitution. (Chapter 7)

Exclusive dealing agreement A potential violation of §1 of the Sherman Act, in which a distributor or retailer agrees with a supplier not to carry the products of any other supplier. (Chapter 20)

Exculpatory clause A contract provision that attempts to release one party from liability in the event the other party is injured. (Chapter 9)

Executed contract A binding agreement in which all parties have fulfilled all obligations. (Chapter 9)

Executory contract A binding agreement in which one or more of the parties has not fulfilled its obligations. (Chapter 9)

Exhaustion of remedies A principle of administrative law that no party may appeal an agency action to a court until she has utilized all available appeals within the agency itself. (Chapter 4)

Expectation interest A remedy in a contract case that puts the injured party in the position he would have been in had both sides fully performed. (Chapter 10)

Export To transport goods or services out of a country. (Chapter 8)

Express authority Conduct of a principal that, reasonably interpreted, causes the agent to believe that the principal desires him to do a specific act. (Chapter 14)

Express contract A binding agreement in which the parties explicitly state all important terms. (Chapter 9)

Express warranty A guarantee, created by the words or actions of the seller, that goods will meet certain standards. (Chapter 11)

Expropriation A government's seizure of property or companies owned by foreigners. (Chapter 8)

Externality An economics term used to describe the situation in which people do not bear the full cost of their decisions. (Chapter 25)

F

Fair Labor Standards Act (FLSA) Passed in 1938, this act regulates wages and limits child labor. (Chapter 15)

Fair use doctrine Permits limited use of copyrighted material without permission of the author for purposes such as criticism, comment, news reporting, scholarship, or research. (Chapter 22)

False imprisonment The intentional restraint of another person without reasonable cause and without her consent. (Chapter 6)

Family Entertainment and Copyright Act Makes it a criminal offense to use a camcorder to film a movie in the theater. This statute also establishes criminal penalties for willful copyright infringement that involves distributing software, music, or film on a computer network. (Chapter 22)

Family and Medical Leave Act Passed in 1993 by Congress, this guarantees both men and women up to 12 weeks of unpaid leave each year for childbirth, adoption, or medical emergencies for themselves or a family member. (Chapter 15)

Federal Insecticide, Fungicide, and Rodenticide Act (FIFRA) Requires manufacturers to register all pesticides with the EPA. (Chapter 25)

Federal question jurisdiction One of the two main types of civil cases that a United States district court has the power to hear. It involves a federal statute or a constitutional provision. (Chapter 3)

Fee simple absolute The greatest possible ownership right in real property, including the right to possess, use, and dispose of the property in any lawful manner. (Chapter 23)

Felony The most serious crimes, typically those for which the defendant could be imprisoned for more than a year. (Chapter 7)

Fiduciary duty An obligation to behave in a trustworthy and confidential fashion toward the object of that duty. (Chapter 14)

Financing statement A document that a secured party files to give the general public notice that the secured party has a secured interest in the collateral. (Chapter 13)

Fixtures Goods that are attached to real estate. (Chapter 13, 23)

Foreign corporation A corporation formed in another state. (Chapter 18)

Foreign Corrupt Practices Act (FCPA) Makes it illegal for an American businessperson to give "anything of value" to any foreign official in order to influence an official decision. (Chapter 8)

Foreign Sovereign Immunity Act A federal statute that protects other nations from suit in courts of the United States, except under specified circumstances. (Chapter 8)

Framers The drafters of the Constitution of the United States; another term used for the Founding Fathers. (Chapter 5)

Fraud Deception of another person to obtain money or property from her. (Chapter 7, 21)

Freehold estate The present right to possess property and to use it in any lawful manner. (Chapter 23)

Frustration of purpose After the creation of a contract, an entirely unforeseen event occurs that eliminates the value of the contract for one of the parties. (Chapter 17)

Fundamental rights In constitutional law, those rights that are so basic that any governmental interference with them is suspect and likely to be unconstitutional. (Chapter 5)

G

GATT See General Agreement on Tariffs and Trade. (Chapter 8)

General deterrence See Deterrence. (Chapter 7)

General intangibles Potential sources of income such as copyrights, patents, trademarks, goodwill and certain other rights to payment. (Chapter 13)

Gift A voluntary transfer of property from one person to another without consideration. (Chapter 23)

Gift *causa mortis* A gift made in contemplation of approaching death. (Chapter 23)

Goods Anything movable, except for money, securities, and certain legal rights. (Chapter 8, 13)

Government securities Include any security issued or guaranteed by federal or state government. (Chapter 19)

Gramm-Leach-Bliley Privacy Act of 1999 (GLB) Requires banks and other financial institutions to disclose to consumers any non-public information they wish to reveal to third parties. (Chapter 21)

Grant Occurs when a landowner expressly intends to convey an easement to someone else. (Chapter 23)

Grantee The person who receives property, or some interest in it, from the owner. (Chapter 23)

Grantor (1) An owner who conveys property, or some interest in it. (2) Someone who creates a trust. (Chapter 23)

Grievance A formal complaint with a company, notifying management that the union claims a contract violation. (Chapter 16)

H

Hacking Gaining unauthorized access to a computer system. (Chapter 21)

Harmless error A ruling made by a trial court which an appeals court determines was legally wrong but not fatal to the decision. (Chapter 3)

Holder in due course Someone who has given value for an instrument, in good faith, without notice of outstanding claims or other defenses. (Chapter 11)

Horizontal agreement or merger An agreement or merger between two potential competitors. (Chapter 20)

I

Identity Theft and Assumption Deterrence Act of 1998 This statute prohibits the use of false identification to commit fraud or other crime and it also permits the victim to seek restitution in court. (Chapter 21)

Illusory promise An apparent promise that is unenforceable because the promisor makes no firm commitment. (Chapter 9)

Implied authority When a principal directs an agent to undertake a transaction, the agent has the right to do acts that are incidental to it, usually accompany it, or are reasonably necessary to accomplish it. (Chapter 14)

Implied contract A binding agreement created not by explicit language but by the informal words and conduct of the parties. (Chapter 9)

Implied warranty Guarantees created by the Uniform Commercial Code and imposed on the seller of goods. (Chapter 11)

Import To transport goods or services into a country. (Chapter 8)

Import ban When particular goods are flatly prohibited. (Chapter 8)

In camera "In the judge's chambers," meaning that the judge does something out of view of the jury and the public. (Chapter 3)

Incidental damages The relatively minor costs, such as storage and advertising, that the injured party suffered when responding to a contract breach. (Chapter 17)

Incorporation When rights explicitly guaranteed at one level are incorporated into rights that apply at other levels. (Chapter 5)

Indemnification A promise to pay someone else's obligations. (Chapter 14)

Independent contractor Someone who undertakes tasks for others and whose work is not closely controlled. (Chapter 14)

Indictment The government's formal charge that a defendant has committed a crime. (Chapter 7)

Indorsement The signature of the payee. (Chapter 12)

Initial public offering (IPO) A company's first public sale of securities. (Chapter 19)

Injunction A court order that a person either do or stop doing something. (Chapter 1)

Insane If a defendant is found to have been insane at the time of the crime, he or she will be declared not guilty and will generally be committed to a mental institution. (Chapter 7)

Integrated contract A writing that the parties intend as the complete and final expression of their agreement. (Chapter 10)

Intentional tort An act deliberately performed that violates a legally imposed duty and injures someone. (Chapter 6)

Inter vivos gift A gift made "during life," that is, when the donor is not under any fear of impending death. (Chapter 23)

Interest A legal right in something, such as ownership or a mortgage or a tenancy. (Chapter 10)

Intermediary agent Someone who hires subagents for the principal. (Chapter 14)

International comity In the event of a conflict, this requires one court to respect the other legal system and decline to hear a suit if it would more logically be resolved in the foreign country. (Chapter 8)

Inventory Goods that the seller is holding for sale or lease in the ordinary course of its business. (Chapter 13)

Issuer The maker of a promissory note or the drawer of a draft. (Chapter 11)

J

Joint tenancy Upon the death of one joint tenant (owner), his interest passes to the surviving joint tenants, not to his heirs. (Chapter 23)

Joint venture A partnership for a limited purpose. (Chapter 17, 20)

Judgment *non obstante verdicto* (JNOV) "Judgment notwithstanding the verdict." A trial judge overturns the verdict of the jury and enters a judgment in favor of the opposing party. (Chapter 3)

Judicial activism The willingness shown by certain courts (and not by others) to decide issues of public policy, such as constitutional questions (free speech, equal protection, etc.) and matters of contract fairness (promissory estoppel, unconscionability, etc.). (Chapter 5, 9)

Judicial restraint A court's preference to abstain from adjudicating major social issues and to leave such matters to legislatures. (Chapter 5, 9)

Judicial review The power of the judicial system to examine, interpret, and even nullify actions taken by another branch of government. (Chapter 5)

Jurisdiction The power of a court to hear a particular dispute, civil or criminal, and to make a binding decision. (Chapter 3)

Jurisprudence The study of the purposes and philosophies of the law, as opposed to particular provisions of the law. (Chapter 1)

Justification A criminal defense in which the defendant establishes that he broke the law to avoid a greater harm. (Chapter 6)

L

Labor-Management Relations Act Passed in 1947, this prohibits union abuses such as coercing employees to join. It also outlaws secondary boycotts. (Chapter 16)

Labor-Management Reporting and Disclosure Act (LMRDA) Passed in 1959, LMRDA, also known as the Landrum-Griffin Act, requires union leadership to make certain financial disclosures and guarantees free speech and fair elections within a union. (Chapter 16)

Larceny Taking personal property with the intention of preventing the owner from ever using it. (Chapter 7)

Lease A contract creating a landlord-tenant relationship. (Chapter 23)

Letter of credit A commercial device used to guarantee payment in international trade, usually between parties that have not previously worked together. (Chapter 8)

Libel See Defamation. (Chapter 6)

License To grant permission to another person (1) to make or sell something or (2) to enter on property. (Chapter 23)

Lien A security interest created by rule of law, often based on labor that the secured party has expended on the collateral. (Chapter 23)

Life estate An ownership interest in real property entitling the holder to use the property during his lifetime, but which terminates upon his death. (Chapter 23)

Limited liability limited partnership In a limited liability limited partnership, the general partner is not personally liable for the debts of the partnership. (Chapter 17)

Limited partnership A partnership with two types of partners: (1) limited partners who have no personal liability for the debts of the enterprise nor any right to manage the business, and (2) general partners who are responsible for management and personally liable for all debts. (Chapter 17)

Liquidated damages A contract clause specifying how much a party must pay upon breach. (Chapter 10)

Litigation The process of resolving disputes through formal court proceedings. (Chapter 3)

Litigator A lawyer who handles court cases. (Chapter 3)

M

Maker The issuer of a promissory note. (Chapter 11)

Material Important or significant. Information that would affect a person's decision if he knew it. (Chapter 19)

Mediation The process of using a neutral person to aid in the settlement of a legal dispute. A mediator's decision is non-binding. (Chapter 3)

Memorandum A supporting argument that is submitted with a motion. (Chapter 3)

Mens rea Guilty state of mind. (Chapter 7)

Merchant One who routinely deals in the particular goods involved, or who appears to have special knowledge or skill in those goods, or who uses agents with special knowledge or skill in those goods. (Chapter 12)

Mini-trial A form of alternative dispute resolution in which the parties present short versions of their cases to a panel of three "judges." (Chapter 3)

Minor A person under the age of 18. (Chapter 9, 15)

Minute book Records of shareholder meetings and directors's meetings are kept in the corporation's minute book. (Chapter 18)

Misdemeanor A less serious crime, typically one for which the maximum penalty is incarceration for less than a year, often in a jail, as opposed to a prison. (Chapter 7)

Misrepresentation A factually incorrect statement made during contract negotiations. (Chapter 9)

Mitigation One party acts to minimize its losses when the other party breaches a contract. (Chapter 10)

Modify An appellate court order changing a lower court ruling. (Chapter 3)

Money laundering Taking the proceeds of certain criminal acts and either 1) using the money to promote crime, or 2) attempting to conceal the source of the money. (Chapter 7)

Monopolization A company acquires or maintains a monopoly through the commission of unacceptably aggressive acts. A violation of §2 of the Sherman Act. (Chapter 20)

Mortgage A security interest in real property. (Chapter 23)

Mortgagee A creditor who obtains a security interest in real property, typically in exchange for money given to the mortgagor to buy the property. (Chapter 23)

Mortgagor A debtor who gives a mortgage (security interest) in real property to a creditor, typically in exchange for money used to buy the property. (Chapter 23)

Motion A formal request that a court take some specified step during litigation. A motion to compel discovery is a request that a trial judge order the other party to respond to discovery. (Chapter 3)

Motion to compel answers to interrogatories A formal request that the court order the other party to supply more complete answers. (Chapter 3)

Motion to dismiss A request that the court terminate a case without permitting it to go further. (Chapter 3)

Motion for a protective order A request that the court limit the discovery of the other party by decreasing the number of depositions. (Chapter 3)

Motion to suppress A request that the court exclude evidence because it was obtained in violation of the Constitution. (Chapter 7)

Multinational enterprise A corporation that is doing business in more than one country simultaneously. (Chapter 8)

N

NAFTA See North American Free Trade Agreement. (Chapter 8)

National Environmental Policy Act of 1969 (NEPA) Requires all federal agencies to prepare an environmental impact statement (EIS) for every major federal action significantly affecting the quality of the human environment. (Chapter 25)

National Labor Relations Act (NLRA) Passed in 1935, the NLRA, also known that the Wagner Act, ensures the right of workers to form unions and encourages management and unions to bargain collectively and productively. (Chapter 16)

National Labor Relations Board (NLRB) The administrative agency charged with overseeing labor law. (Chapter 16)

National security letter (NSL) Issued by the FBI, these letters are demands of communications firms, such as Internet service providers and telephone companies, to furnish the government with customer records and never divulge to anyone what it has done. (Chapter 7)

Nationalization A government's seizure of property or companies. (Chapter 8)

Negligence per se Violation of a standard of care set by statute. Driving while intoxicated is illegal; thus, if a drunk driver injures a pedestrian, he has committed negligence per se. (Chapter 6)

Negotiation An instrument that has been transferred to the holder by someone other than the issuer. (Chapter 12)

Norris-LaGuardia Act Passed by Congress in 1932, this prohibits federal court injunctions in nonviolent labor disputes. (Chapter 16)

Note An unconditional, written promise that the maker of the instrument will pay a specific amount of money on demand or at a definite time. When issued by a corporation, a note refers to short-term debt, typically payable within five years. (Chapter 11, 18)

Novation If there is an existing contract between A and B, a novation occurs when A agrees to release B from all liability on the contract in return for C's willingness to accept B's liability. (Chapter 10, 18)

O

Obligee The party to a contract who is entitled to receive performance from the other party. (Chapter 10)

Obligor The party to a contract who is required to do something for the benefit of the other party. (Chapter 10, 13)

Ocean Dumping Act of 1972 Prohibits the dumping of wastes in ocean water without a permit from the EPA. (Chapter 25)

Occupational Safety and Health Act of 1970 (OSHA) A federal statute that regulates safety standards in the workplace for many industries. (Chapter 7, 15)

Offeree The party in contract negotiations who receives the first offer. (Chapter 9)

Offeror The party in contract negotiations who makes the first offer. (Chapter 9)

Oil Pollution Act of 1990 Passed in response to the *Exxon Valdez* oil spill, this statute sets design standards for ships operating in U.S. waters. (Chapter 25)

Oppression When one party uses its superior power to force a contract on the weaker party. (Chapter 10)

P

Paris Convention for the Protection of Industrial Property (Paris Convention) Requires each member country to grant to citizens of other member countries the same rights under patent law as its own citizens enjoy. (Chapter 22)

Parol evidence Written or oral evidence, outside the language of a contract, offered by one party to clarify interpretation of the agreement. (Chapter 10)

Partially disclosed principal If the third party in an agency relationship knows that the agent is acting for a principal, but does not know the identity of the principal, that principal is partially disclosed. (Chapter 14)

Partnership An association of two or more persons to carry on as co-owners of a business for profit. (Chapter 17)

Partnership at will A partnership that has no fixed duration. A partner has the right to resign from the partnership at any time. (Chapter 17)

Partnership by estoppel If a person who is not a partner implies that he is a partner or does not object when other people imply it, he is liable as if he really were a partner. (Chapter 17)

Patent The right to the exclusive use of an invention for 20 years. (Chapter 22)

Patent Law Treaty Requires that countries use the same standards for the form and content of patent applications (whether submitted on paper or electronically). (Chapter 22)

Payee Someone who is owed money under the terms of an instrument. (Chapter 11)

***Per se* violation of an antitrust law** An automatic breach. Courts will generally not consider mitigating factors. (Chapter 20)

Peremptory challenge During voir dire, a request by one attorney that a prospective juror be excused for an unstated reason. (Chapter 3)

Perfection A series of steps a secured party must take to protect its rights in collateral against people other than the debtor. (Chapter 13)

Personal property All property other than real property. (Chapter 23)

Personal satisfaction contract A contract in which the promisee makes a personal, subjective evaluation of the promisor's performance. (Chapter 11)

Phishing Type of fraud in which an individual sends an e-mail directing the recipient to enter personal information on a Website that is an illegal imitation of a legitimate site. (Chapter 21)

Plea bargain An agreement between prosecution and defense that the defendant will plead guilty to a reduced charge, and the prosecution will recommend to the judge a relatively lenient sentence. (Chapter 7)

Pleadings The documents that begin a lawsuit: the complaint, the answer, the counter-claim and reply. (Chapter 3)

Precedent An earlier case that decided the same legal issue as that presently in dispute, and which therefore will control the outcome of the current case. (Chapter 1, 4)

Predatory pricing A violation of §2 of the Sherman Act in which a company lowers its prices below cost to drive competitors out of business. (Chapter 20)

Preemption The doctrine, based on the Supremacy Clause, by which any federal statute takes priority whenever (1) a state statute conflicts or (2) there is no conflict but Congress indicated an intention to control the issue involved. (Chapter 5)

Preferred stock Owners of preferred stock have a right to receive dividends and liquidation proceeds of the company before common shareholders. (Chapter 18)

Preponderance of the evidence The level of proof that a plaintiff must meet to prevail in a civil lawsuit. It means that the plaintiff must offer evidence that, in sum, is slightly more persuasive than the defendant's evidence. (Chapter 3)

Prima facie "At first sight." A fact or conclusion that is presumed to be true unless someone presents evidence to disprove it. (Chapter 15)

Principal In an agency relationship, the principal is the person for whom the agent is acting. (Chapter 14)

Private law Refers to the rights and duties between individuals that they themselves have created, for example, by entering into a contract or employment relationship. (Chapter 1)

Probable cause In a search and seizure case, it means that the information available indicates that it is more likely than not that a search will uncover particular criminal evidence. (Chapter 7)

Procedural due process *See* Due Process Clause. (Chapter 5)

Procedural law The rules establishing how the legal system itself is to operate in a particular kind of case. (Chapter 1)

Proceeds Anything that a debtor obtains from the sale or disposition of collateral. Normally, proceeds refers to cash obtained from the sale of the secured property. (Chapter 13)

Product liability The potential responsibility that a manufacturer or seller has for injuries caused by defective goods. (Chapter 11)

Professional corporation A form of organization that permits professionals (such as doctors, lawyers, and accountants) to incorporate. Shareholders are not personally liable for the torts of other shareholders, or for the contract debts of the organization. (Chapter 17)

Profit The right to enter land belonging to another and take something away, such as minerals or timber. (Chapter 23)

Promissory estoppel A doctrine in which a court may enforce a promise made by the defendant even when there is no contract, if the defendant knew that the plaintiff was likely to rely on the promise, the plaintiff did in fact rely, and enforcement of it is the only way to avoid injustice. (Chapter 9)

Promissory note The maker of the instrument promises to pay a specific amount of money. (Chapter 11)

Promoter The person who creates a corporation by raising capital and undertaking the legal steps necessary for formation. (Chapter 18)

Promulgate To issue a new rule. (Chapter 4)

Proof of claim A simple form stating the name of the creditor and the amount of the claim. (Chapter 13)

Prospectus Under the Securities Act of 1933, an issuer must provide this document to anyone who purchases a security in a public transaction. The prospectus contains detailed information about the issuer and its business, a description of the stock, and audited financial statements. (Chapter 19)

Provisional patent application (PPA) The PPA is a simpler, shorter, cheaper application that gives inventors the opportunity to show their ideas to potential investors without incurring the full expense of a patent application. (Chapter 22)

Proxy (1) A person whom the shareholder designates to vote in his place. (2) The written form (typically a card) that the shareholder uses to appoint a designated voter. (Chapter 18)

Proxy statement When a public company seeks proxy votes from its shareholders, it must include a proxy statement. This statement contains information about the company, such as a detailed description of management compensation. (Chapter 18)

Public law refers to the rights and obligations of governments as they deal with the nation's citizens, for example, by taxing individuals, zoning neighborhoods, and regulating advertisements. (Chapter 1)

Public policy rule Prohibits an employer from firing a worker for a reason that violates basic social rights, duties, or responsibilities. (Chapter 15)

Puffery A statement that a reasonable person would realize is a sales pitch, representing the exaggerated opinion of the seller. (Chapter 10)

Purchase money security interest A security interest taken by the person who sells the collateral to the debtor, or by a person who advances money so that the debtor may buy the collateral. (Chapter 13)

Q

Qualified privilege Exists when two people have a legitimate need to exchange information; protects the parties from defamation. (Chapter 6)

Quantum meruit "As much as she deserves." The damages awarded in a quasi-contract case. (Chapter 9)

Quasi-contract A legal fiction in which, to avoid injustice, the court awards damages as if a contract had existed, although one did not. (Chapter 9)

Quid pro quo "This for that." A type of sexual harassment that occurs if any aspect of a job is made contingent upon sexual activity. (Chapter 15)

Quorum The number of voters that must be present for a meeting to count. (Chapter 18)

Quota A limit on the quantity of a particular good that may enter a nation. (Chapter 8)

R

Racketeer Influenced and Corrupt Organizations Act (RICO) A law passed by Congress to prevent gangsters from taking money they earned illegally and investing it into legitimate businesses. (Chapter 7)

Racketeering acts Any of a long list of specialized crimes including embezzlement, arson, mail fraud, and wire fraud. (Chapter 7)

Ratification When someone accepts the benefit of an unauthorized transaction or fails to repudiate it once he has learned of it, he is then bound by it. (Chapter 8, 14)

Real property Land, together with certain things associated with it, such as buildings, subsurface rights, air rights, plant life and fixtures. (Chapter 23)

Reasonable doubt The level of proof that the government must meet to convict the defendant in a criminal case. The factfinder must be persuaded to a very high degree of certainty that the defendant did what the government alleges. (Chapter 3)

Reciprocal dealing agreement An agreement under which Company *A* will purchase from Company *B* only if Company *B* also buys from Company *A*. These agreements are rule of reason violations of the Sherman Act. (Chapter 20)

Record Information written on paper or stored in an electronic or other medium. (Chapter 13)

Record date To vote at a shareholders meeting, a shareholder must own stock on the record date. (Chapter 13, 18)

Red herring A preliminary prospectus. (Chapter 19)

Reformation The process by which a court rewrites a contract to ensure its accuracy or viability. (Chapter 10)

Refusal to deal An agreement among competitors that they will not trade with a particular supplier or buyer. Such an agreement is a rule of reason violation of the Sherman Act. (Chapter 20)

Registration statement A document filed with the Securities and Exchange Commission under the Securities Act of 1933 by an issuer seeking to sell securities in a public transaction. (Chapter 19)

Reliance interest A remedy in a contract case that puts the injured party in the position he would have been in had the parties never entered into a contract. (Chapter 10, 19)

Remand The power of an appellate court to return a case to a lower court for additional action. (Chapter 3)

Rent Compensation the tenant pays the landlord for use of the premises. (Chapter 23)

Repatriation of profits Occurs when an investing company pulls its earnings out of a foreign country and takes them back home. (Chapter 8)

Reply A pleading, filed by the plaintiff in response to a defendant's counter-claim. (Chapter 3)

Repossess A secured party takes collateral because the debtor has defaulted on payments. (Chapter 13)

Res ipsa loquitur A doctrine of tort law holding that the facts may imply negligence when the defendant had exclusive control of the thing that caused the harm, the accident would not normally have occurred without negligence, and the plaintiff played no role in causing the injury. (Chapter 6)

Resale price maintenance A per se violation of the Sherman Act in which a manufacturer enters into an agreement with retailers about the prices they will charge. (Chapter 20)

Rescind To cancel a contract. (Chapter 9, 10, 14)

Rescission Means to "undo" a contract and put the parties where they were before they made the agreement. (Chapter 11)

Reservation Occurs when an owner sells land but keeps some right to enter the property. (Chapter 23)

Respondeat superior "Let the master answer." A principle of liability that holds that the master (the principal) is liable for the agent's misbehavior whether or not the principal was at fault. (Chapter 14)

Restitution Restoring an injured party to its original position. (Chapter 9)

Restitution interest A remedy in a contract case that returns to the injured party a benefit that he has conferred on the other party, which it would be unjust to leave with that person. (Chapter 10)

Restricted security Any stock purchased in a private offering (such as one under Regulation D). (Chapter 19)

Retribution Giving a criminal defendant the punishment he deserves. (Chapter 7)

Reverse The power of an appellate court to overrule a lower court and grant judgment for the party that had lost in the lower court. (Chapter 3)

Rule of reason violation An action that breaches the antitrust laws only if it has an anticompetitive impact. (Chapter 20)

S

Scienter In a case of securities fraud, the plaintiff must prove that the defendant acted willfully, knowingly, or recklessly. (Chapter 19)

Secured party The person or company that holds that security interest. (Chapter 13)

Securities Act of 1933 Requires that, before offering or selling securities, the issuer must register the securities with the SEC, unless the securities qualify for an exemption. (Chapter 19)

Security Any transaction in which the buyer (1) invests money in a common enterprise and (2) expects to earn a profit predominantly from the efforts of others. (Chapter 19)

Security agreement A contract in which the debtor gives a security interest to the secured party. (Chapter 13)

Security interest An interest in personal property or fixtures that secures the performance of some obligation. (Chapter 13)

Self-dealing Occurs when a manager makes a decision benefiting either himself or another company with which he has a relationship. (Chapter 18)

Servant An agent whose work is closely controlled by the principal. (Chapter 14)

Sexual harassment Unwanted sexual advances, comments or touching, sufficiently severe to violate Title VII of the 1964 Civil Rights Act. (Chapter 15)

Sherman Act A statute that controls anticompetitive conduct that harms the American market. (Chapter 8)

Shilling A seller at auction either bids on his own goods or agrees to cross-bid with a group of other sellers. (Chapter 21)

Short-term notes High-quality negotiable notes or drafts that are due within nine months of issuance and are not sold to the general public. (Chapter 19)

Signatory A person, company, or nation that has signed a legal document, such as a contract, agreement, or treaty. (Chapter 8)

Single-recovery principle Requires a court to settle the matter once and for all, by awarding a lump sum for past and future expenses. (Chapter 6)

Sit-down strike Illegal striking tactic in which union members stop working but remain at their job posts, physically blocking replacement workers from taking their places. (Chapter 16)

Slander See Defamation. (Chapter 6)

Social Security A federal system that originated in 1935; currently pays benefits to workers who are retired, disabled, or temporarily unemployed and to the spouses and children of disabled or deceased workers. (Chapter 15)

Sole proprietorship An unincorporated business owned by a single person. (Chapter 17)

Sovereign Refers to the recognized political power whom citizens obey. In the United States, the federal and all of the state governments are sovereigns. (Chapter 1)

Sovereign immunity Holds that the courts of one nation lack the jurisdiction (power) to hear suits against foreign governments. (Chapter 8)

Spam Unsolicited commercial or bulk e-mail. ("To spam" is to send such e-mail.) (Chapter 21)

Specific deterrence See Deterrence. (Chapter 7)

Spyware A computer program that slips onto your computer without your permission—through e-mails, Internet downloads, or software installations. (Chapter 21)

Stakeholders Anyone who is affected by the activities of a corporation, such as employees, customers, creditors, suppliers, shareholders, and neighbors. (Chapter 18)

Stare decisis "Let the decision stand." A basic principle of the common law, it means that precedent is usually binding. (Chapter 1)

Statute A law passed by a legislative body, such as Congress. (Chapter 1)

Statute of frauds This law provides that certain contracts are not enforceable unless in writing. (Chapter 10)

Statute of limitations A statute that determines the period within which a particular kind of lawsuit must be filed. (Chapter 10, 18)

Strict liability A tort doctrine holding to a very high standard all those who engage in ultrahazardous activity (e.g., using explosives) or who manufacture certain products. (Chapter 6)

Strike The ultimate weapon of a labor union, it occurs when all or most employees of a particular plant or employer walk off the job and refuse to work. (Chapter 16)

Subcontracting A manufacturer, rather than producing all parts of a product and then assembling them, contracts for other companies, frequently overseas, to make some of the parts. (Chapter 16)

Subpoena An order to appear, issued by a court or government body. (Chapter 4)

Subpoena *duces tecum* An order to produce certain documents or things before a court or government body. (Chapter 4)

Substantive due process See Due Process Clause. (Chapter 5)

Substantive law Rules that establish the rights of parties. For example, the prohibition against slander is substantive law, as opposed to procedural law. (Chapter 1)

Summary judgment The power of a trial court to terminate a lawsuit before a trial has begun, on the grounds that no essential facts are in dispute. (Chapter 3)

Summary jury trial A form of alternative dispute resolution in which a small panel of jurors hears shortened, summarized versions of the evidence. (Chapter 3)

Supremacy Clause From Article VI of the Constitution, it declares that federal statutes and treaties take priority over any state law, if there is a conflict between the two or, even absent a conflict, if Congress manifests an intent to preempt the field. (Chapter 5)

Surplus A sum greater than the debt. (Chapter 13)

Surprise When the weaker party did not fully understand the consequences of its agreement. (Chapter 10)

T

Takings Clause Part of the Fifth Amendment, it ensures that when any governmental unit takes private property for public use, it must compensate the owner. (Chapter 5)

Tariff A duty imposed on imported goods by the government of the importing nation. (Chapter 8)

Tenancy in common Occurs when the owners have an equal interest in the entire property. (Chapter 23)

Tenancy by the entirety A form of joint ownership available only to married couples. If one member of the couple dies, the property goes automatically to the survivor. Creditors cannot attach the property, nor can one owner sell the property without the other's permission. (Chapter 23)

Tender offer A public offer to buy a block of stock directly from shareholders. (Chapter 18)

Term partnership When the partners agree in advance on the duration of a partnership. (Chapter 17)

Termination statement A document indicating that it no longer claims a security interest in the collateral. (Chapter 13)

Third party beneficiary Someone who is not a party to a contract but stands to benefit from it. (Chapter 11)

Title examination Occurs after parties have agreed to terms and signed a contract. The buyer's lawyer, or someone he or she hires, searches through the local land registry for all documents that relate to the property. (Chapter 23)

Title VII of the Civil Rights Act of 1964 Prohibits employers from discriminating on the basis of race, color, religion, sex, or national origin. More specifically, it prohibits (1) discrimination in the workplace, (2) sexual harassment, and (3) discrimination because of pregnancy. It also permits employers to develop affirmative action plans. (Chapter 15)

Tort A civil wrong, committed in violation of a duty that the law imposes. (Chapter 6)

Trade secret A formula, device, process, method, or compilation of information that, when used in business, gives the owner an advantage over competitors who do not know it. (Chapter 22)

Trademark Any combination of words and symbols that a business uses to identify its products or services and that federal law will protect. (Chapter 22)

Transaction value The price actually paid for merchandise when it was sold for export to the United States (plus shipping and other minor costs). (Chapter 8)

Treasury stock Stock that has been bought back by its issuing corporation. (Chapter 18)

Trial court Any court in a state or federal system that holds formal hearings to determine the facts in a civil or criminal case. (Chapter 3)

True impossibility Means that something has happened making it utterly impossible to do what the promisor said he would do. (Chapter 11)

Tying arrangement A violation of the Sherman and Clayton Acts in which a seller requires that two distinct products be purchased together. The seller uses its significant power in the market for the tying product to shut out a substantial part of the market for the tied product. (Chapter 20)

U

Ultrahazardous activity Conduct that is lawful yet unusual and much more likely to cause injury than normal commercial activity. (Chapter 6, 7)

Unconscionable contract An agreement that a court refuses to enforce because it is fundamentally unfair as a result of unequal bargaining power by one party. (Chapter 9)

Undisclosed principal If a third party in an agency relationship does not know that the agent is acting for a principal, that principal is undisclosed. (Chapter 14)

Unenforceable agreement Occurs when the parties intend to form a valid bargain but a court declares that some rule of law prevents enforcing it. (Chapter 9)

Unilateral contract A binding agreement in which one party has made an offer that the other can accept only by action, not words. (Chapter 9)

Unilateral mistake When only one party enters a contract under a mistaken assumption. (Chapter 10)

Utilitarianism The philosophy that all decisions should be evaluated according to how much happiness they create. (Chapter 2)

V

Valid contract A contract that satisfies all the law's requirements. (Chapter 9)

Value The holder has *already* done something in exchange for the instrument. (Chapter 12)

Vengeance After a serious crime has occurred, society's desire to see the perpetrator suffer; related to the idea of retribution. (Chapter 7)

Vertical agreement or merger An agreement or merger between two companies at different stages of the production process, such as when a company acquires one of its suppliers or distributors. (Chapter 20)

Veto When the president opposes a bill that has passed through both houses; a veto means that the bill will not become law. (Chapter 4)

Void agreement An agreement that neither party may legally enforce, usually because the purpose of the bargain was illegal or because one of the parties lacked capacity to make it. (Chapter 9)

Voidable contract An agreement that, because of some defect, may be terminated by one party, such as a minor, but not by both parties. (Chapter 9)

Voir dire The process of selecting a jury. Attorneys for the parties and the judge may inquire of prospective jurors whether they are biased or incapable of rendering a fair and impartial verdict. (Chapter 3)

W

Warrant Written permission from a neutral official to conduct a search; the warrant must specify with reasonable certainty the place to be searched and the items to be seized. (Chapter 7)

Warranty A guarantee that goods will meet certain standards. (Chapter 11)

Whipsaw strike Occurs when a union is simultaneously bargaining with various employers. (Chapter 16)

Whistleblower Someone who discloses wrongful behavior. (Chapter 15)

Workers' compensation statutes Ensure that employees receive payment for injuries incurred at work. (Chapter 15)

Writ An order from a government compelling someone to do a particular thing. (Chapter 1)

Writ of *certiorari* A petition filed by a party who wants the Supreme Court to hear a case and review the ruling made by a lower court. (Chapter 3)

Wrongful discharge Prohibits an employer from firing a worker for a bad reason. (Chapter 15)

Zoning statutes State laws that permit local communities to regulate building and land use. (Chapter 23)

Table of Cases

Note: Bold page references indicate a discussion of the case. Cases shown in color are new to this edition. Page ranges with "n" indicate footnote citations.

Index

G

Supplemental Business Case Studies

from

Business Ethics
Fifth Edition

by

Marianne M. Jennings

8A

Advertising Content

Ads sell products. But how much can the truth be stretched? Are ads ever irresponsible by encouraging harmful behavior?

CASE 8.1

Joe Camel: The Cartoon Character Who Sold Cigarettes and Nearly Felled an Industry

Old Joe Camel, originally a member of a circus that passed through Winston-Salem, North Carolina, each year, was adopted by R.J. Reynolds (RJR) marketers in 1913 as the symbol for a brand being changed from "Red Kamel" to "Camel." In the late 1980s, RJR revived Old Joe with a new look in the form of a cartoon. He became the camel with a "Top Gun" flier jacket, sunglasses, a smirk, and a lot of appeal to young people.

In December 1991, the *Journal of the American Medical Association (JAMA)* published three surveys that found that the cartoon character Joe Camel reached children very effectively. Of children between the ages of 3 and 6 who were surveyed, 51.1 percent recognized Joe Camel as being associated with Camel cigarettes.[1] The 6-year-olds were as familiar with Joe Camel as they were with the Mickey Mouse logo for the Disney Channel. The surveys also established that 97.7 percent of students between the ages of 12 and 19 had seen Old Joe and 58 percent thought the ads he was used in were cool. Camel was identified by 33 percent of the students who smoke as their favorite brand.[2]

Before the survey results appeared in *JAMA*, the American Cancer Society, the American Heart Association, and the American Lung Association had petitioned the FTC to ban the ads as "one of the most egregious examples in recent history of tobacco advertising that targets children."[3]

[1] Kathleen Deveny, "Joe Camel Ads Reach Children, Research Finds," The Wall Street Journal, December 11, 1991, p. B1.
[2] Walecia Konrad, "I'd Toddle a Mile for a Camel," Business Week, December 23, 1991, p. 34. While the studies and their methodology have been questioned, their impact was made before the challenges and questions were raised.
[3] Deveny, "Joe Camel Ads Reach Children," p. B1.

In 1990, Camel shipments rose 11.3 percent. Joe Camel helped RJR take its Camel cigarettes from 2.7 to 3.1 percent of the market.[4]

Michael Pertschuk, former FTC head and co-director of the Advocacy Institute, an antismoking group, said, "These are the first studies to give us hard evidence, proving what everybody already knows is true: These ads target kids. I think this will add impetus to the movement to further limit tobacco advertising.[5] Joe Tye, founder of Stop Teenage Addictions to Tobacco, stated, "There is a growing body of evidence that teen smoking is increasing. And it's 100 percent related to Camel."[6]

A researcher who worked on the December 1991 *JAMA* study, Dr. Joseph R. DiFranza, stated, "We're hoping this information leads to a complete ban of cigarette advertising."[7] Dr. John Richards summarized the study as follows, "The fact is that the ad is reaching kids, and it is changing their behavior."[8]

RJR spokesman David Fishel responded to the allegations with sales evidence: "We can track 98 percent of Camel sales; and they're not going to youngsters. It's simply not in our best interest for young people to smoke, because that opens the door for the government to interfere with our product."[9] At the time the survey results were published, RJR, along with other manufacturers and the Tobacco Institute, began a multimillion-dollar campaign with billboards and bumper stickers to discourage children from smoking but announced it had no intention of abandoning Joe Camel. The Tobacco Institute publishes a free popular pamphlet called "Tobacco: Helping Youth Say No."

Former U.S. Surgeon General Antonia Novello was very vocal in her desire to change alcohol and cigarette advertising. In March 1992, she called for the withdrawal of the Joe Camel ad campaign: "In years past, R.J. Reynolds would have us walk a mile for a Camel. Today it's time that we invite old Joe Camel himself to take a hike."[10] The AMA's executive vice president, Dr. James S. Todd, concurred:

This is an industry that kills 400,000 per year, and they have got to pick up new customers. We believe the company is directing its ads to the children who are 3, 6 and 9 years old.[11]

Cigarette sales are, in fact, declining 3 percent per year in the United States.

The average Camel smoker is 35 years old, responded an RJR spokeswoman: "Just because children can identify our logo doesn't mean they will use our product."[12] Since the introduction of Joe Camel, however, Camel's share of the under-eighteen market has climbed to 33 percent from 5 percent. Among 18- to 25-year-olds, Camel's market share has climbed to 7.9 percent from 4.4 percent.

---

[4] Konrad, "I'd Toddle a Mile for a Camel," p. 34.

[5] Deveny, "Joe Camel Ads Reach Children," p. B6.

[6] Laura Bird, "Joe Smooth for President," Adweek's Marketing Week, May 20, 1991, p. 21.

[7] Konrad, "I'd Toddle a Mile for a Camel," p. 34.

[8] "Camels for Kids," Time, December 23, 1991, p. 52.

[9] Id.

[10] William Chesire, "Don't Shoot: It's Only Joe Camel," Arizona Republic, March 15, 1992, p. C1.

[11] Id.

[12] Konrad, "I'd Toddle a Mile for a Camel," p. 34.

The Centers for Disease Control reported in March 1992 that smokers between the ages of 12 and 18 prefer Marlboro, Newport, or Camel cigarettes, the three brands with the most extensive advertising.[13]

Teenagers throughout the country were wearing Joe Camel T-shirts. Brown & Williamson, the producer of Kool cigarettes, began testing a cartoon character for its ads, a penguin wearing sunglasses and Day-Glo sneakers. Company spokesman Joseph Helewicz stated that the ads are geared to smokers between 21 and 35 years old. Helewicz added that cartoon advertisements for adults are not new and cited the Pillsbury Doughboy and the Pink Panther as effective advertising images.

In mid-1992, then-Surgeon General Novello, along with the American Medical Association, began a campaign called "Dump the Hump" to pressure the tobacco industry to stop ad campaigns that teach kids to smoke. In 1993, the FTC staff recommended a ban on the Joe Camel ads. In 1994, then-Surgeon General Joycelyn Elders blamed the tobacco industry's $4 billion in ads for increased smoking rates among teens. RJR's tobacco division chief, James W. Johnston, responded, "I'll be damned if I'll pull the ads."[14] RJR put together a team of lawyers and others it referred to as in-house censors to control Joe's influence. A campaign to have Joe wear a bandana was nixed, as was one for a punker Joe with pink hair.[15]

In 1994, RJR CEO James Johnston testified before a Congressional panel on the Joe Camel controversy and stated, "We do not market to children and will not," and added, "We do not survey anyone under the age of 18."[16]

As health issues related to smokers continued to expand, along with product liability litigation and state attorneys' general pursuit of compensation for their states' health system costs of smokers, more information about the Joe Camel campaign was discovered. Lawyers in a California suit against RJR discovered charts from a presentation at a September 30, 1974 Hilton Head, South Carolina, retreat of RJR top executives and board.[17] The charts offered the following information:

Company	Brand	Share of 14- to 24-year-old market
Philip Morris	Marlboro	33%
Brown & Williamson	Kool	17%
Reynolds	Winston	14%
Reynolds	Salem	9%[18]

[13] "Selling Death," Mesa Tribune, March 16, 1992, p. A8.

[14] Anna White, "Joe Camel's World Tour," The New York Times, April 23, 1997, p. A21.

[15] Melanie Wells and Chris Woodyard, "FTC Says Joe Camel Tobacco Icon Targeted Young," USA Today, May 29, 1991, p. 1A.

[16] Milo Geyelin, "Reynolds Aimed Specifically to Lure Young Smokers Years Ago, Data Suggest," The Wall Street Journal, January 15, 1998, p. A4.

[17] Doug Levy and Melanie Wells, "Papers: RJR Did Court Teens," USA Today, January 15, 1998, pp. 1A, 1B.

[18] Eben Shapiro, "FTC Staff Recommends Ban of Joe Camel Campaign," The Wall Street Journal, August 11, 1994, pp. B1, B8.

RJR's then-vice president of marketing, C.A. Tucker, said, "As this 14–24 age group matures, they will account for a key share of total cigarette volume for at least the next 25 years."[19] The meeting then produced a plan for increasing RJR's presence among the under-35 age group which included sponsoring NASCAR auto racing. Another memo described plans to study "the demographics and smoking behavior of 14- to 17-year-olds."[20]

Internal documents about targeting young people were damaging. A 1981 RJR internal memo on marketing surveys cautioned research personnel to tally underage smokers as "age 18."[21] A 1981 Philip Morris internal document indicated information about smoking habits in children as young as 15 was important because "today's teenager is tomorrow's potential regular customer."[22] Other Philip Morris documents from the 1980s expressed concerns that Marlboro sales would soon decline because teenage smoking rates were falling.[23]

A 1987 marketing survey in France and Canada by RJR before it launched the Joe Camel campaign showed that the cartoon image with its fun and humor attracted attention. One 1987 internal document uses the phrase "young adult smokers"[24] and notes a target campaign to the competition's "male Marlboro smokers ages 13–24."[25]

A 1997 survey of 534 teens by *USA Today* revealed the following:

Ad	Have seen ad	Liked ad
Joe Camel	95%	65%
Marlboro Man	94%	44%[26]
Budweiser Frogs	99%	92%

Marlboro was the brand smoked by most teens in the survey. The survey found 28 percent of teens between the ages of 13 and 18 smoke—an increase of 4 percent since 1991.[27] In 1987, Camels were the cigarette of choice for 3 percent of teenagers when Joe Camel debuted. By 1993, the figure had climbed to 16 percent.[28]

In early 1990, the Federal Trade Commission (FTC) began an investigation of RJR and its Joe Camel ads to determine whether underage smokers were illegally targeted

[19] Bruce Horovitz and Doug Levy, "Tobacco Firms Try to Sow Seeds of Self-Regulation," USA Today, May 16, 1996, pp. 1B, 2B.

[20] Bruce Ingersoll, "Joe Camel Ads Illegally Target Kids, FTC Says," The Wall Street Journal, May 29, 1997, pp. B1, B8.

[21] Geyelin, "Reynolds Aimed Specifically to Lure Young Smokers Years Ago," p. A4.

[22] Suein L. Hwang, Timothy Noah, and Laurie McGinley, "Philip Morris Has Its Own Youth-Smoking Plan," The Wall Street Journal, May 16, 1996, pp. B1, B4.

[23] Barry Meier, "Tobacco Executives Wax Penitent Before House Panel in Hopes of Preserving Accord," The New York Times, January 30, 1998, p. A15.

[24] Wells and Woodyard, "FTC Says Joe Camel Tobacco Icon Targeted Young," p. 1A.

[25] Id.

[26] "Joe Camel Shills to Kids," USA Today, June 2, 1997, p. 12A.

[27] Id.

[28] Alan Kline, "Joe Camel is One Species the Government Wants Extinct," Washington Times, June 8, 1997, p. 10.

by the ten-year Joe Camel Campaign.[29] The FTC had dismissed a complaint in 1994, but did not have the benefits of the newly discovered internal memos.[30]

By late 1997, RJR began phasing out Joe Camel.[31] New Camel ads feature men and women in their 20s, with a healthy look, in clubs and swimming pools with just a dromedary logo somewhere in the ad. Joe continued as a youth icon. A "Save Joe Camel" Web site developed and Joe Camel paraphernalia brought top dollar. A Joe Camel shower curtain sold for $200. RJR also vowed not to feature the Joe Camel character on non-tobacco items such as T-shirts. The cost of the abandonment was estimated at $250 million.[32]

Philip Morris proposed its own plan to halt youth smoking in 1996, which includes no vending machine ads, no billboard ads, no tobacco ads in magazines with 15 percent or more of youth subscribers, and limits on sponsorships to events (rodeos, motor sports) where 75 percent or more of attendees are adults.[33, 34]

It was also in 1997 that the combined pressure from Congress, the state attorneys general, and ongoing class action suits produced what came to be known as "the tobacco settlement." The tobacco settlement in all of its various forms bars outdoor advertising, the use of human images (Marlboro man) and cartoon characters, and vending-machine sales. This portion of the settlement was advocated by those who were concerned that teenagers would be attracted to cigarette smoking via these ads and that cigarettes were readily available in machines.[35]

While the governmental suits were settled, those suits focused simply on reimbursement for government program costs in treating smokers for their health issues related to smoking. The private litigation has not ended. A Florida jury, after finding tobacco companies guilty of fraud and conspiracy, issued a damage award of $144 billion against several companies. The bulk of the award consisted of punitive damages. The total losses to date are as follows:

$144 billion—verdict in Florida class action suit

$40 billion—settlement of Florida, Texas, and Minnesota suits

$206 billion—settlement of suits by 46 states and 5 territories

$3.4 billion—settlement of Mississippi Medicaid suit

The Florida judgment would be allocated among the tobacco companies as follows:

Phillip Morris—50%, or $73.96 billion

Lorillard—10%, or $16.25 billion

Brown & Williamson—13%, or $17.59 billion

[29] Doug Levy, "Blowing Smoke?" USA Today, January 15, 1998, pp. 1B, 2B.
[30] Shapiro, "FTC Staff Recommends Ban of Joe Camel Campaign," pp. B1, B8.
[31] "Smokin' Joe Camel Near His Last Gasp," Time, June 9, 1997, p. 47.
[32] Maria Mallory, "That's One Angry Camel," Business Week, March 7, 1994, pp. 94, 95.
[33] Horovitz and Levy, "Tobacco Firms Try to Sow Seeds of Self-Regulation," pp. 1B, 2B.
[34] Gary Rausch, "Tobacco Firms Unite to Curb Teen Smoking," Mesa Tribune, June 24, 1991, pp. B1, B6.
[35] Meier, "Tobacco Executives Wax Penitent Before House Panel," p. A15.

R.J. Reynolds—24%, or $36.28 billion

The annual sales of the companies are as follows:

Phillip Morris—$19.6 billion

R.J. Reynolds—$7.5 billion

Brown & Williamson—not available

Lorillard—$4.0 billion

Liggett—$423 million[36]

Since the time of the tobacco settlement and the Joe Camel ad campaign, the industry has changed in some ways, but in other ways remains unbowed by the events described here. For example, in 2002, Philip Morris was poised to introduce a new cigarette that was designed to save lives. If left unattended, the cigarette would extinguish itself, thus eliminating the tremendous fire risk that results from smokers falling asleep while their cigarettes are still burning. Nonextinguished cigarettes are the leading cause of fire fatalities in the United States. The cigarette was to be released under the company's Merit brand.

However, a company scientist, Michael Lee Watkins, told his superiors that the cigarettes were, in fact, a greater fire risk than conventional cigarettes, because chunks of them fell off onto smokers and nearby objects. He was fired, and Philip Morris released the Merit cigarette with special advertising emphasizing its safety. The Justice Department got wind, as it were, of the problem from Dr. Watkins, and has filed suit against Morris and other tobacco companies for deception as well as for the safety issues related to the cigarettes. Dr. Watkins has agreed to serve as a witness for the government.

Philip Morris indicates that Dr. Watkins was fired for failing to attend meetings, for speaking negatively of his colleagues, and for failing to document his research.

Philip Morris says that Dr. Watkins was correct in that chunks of the Merit safety cigarette did tend to fall off, thereby creating a different fire hazard, but the company fixed that problem by substituting a different paper before Merit was released to the market.

The suit is but one part of the legal and regulatory quagmire the tobacco companies once again find themselves in. New York passed a statute, soon to take effect, which requires that cigarettes sold in the state be "self-extinguishing" according to rules and guidelines contained in the statute. At least seven other states have similar legislation pending. Canadian health authorities are also working on fire-safe cigarette requirements.

Customers have complained about being burned when chunks of the new cigarettes fall off onto them and their clothing. The test cigarettes appeared in New York in June 2004, and the problems with them continue. The Justice Department litigation also continues, with depositions and document production.

---

[36] Rick Bragg and Sarah Kershaw, "Juror Says a 'Sense of Mission' Led to Huge Tobacco Damages," *The New York Times*, July 16, 2000, pp. A1, A16.

However, there are positive signs from the industry. In the summer of 2004, Philip Morris launched a massive ad campaign directed at children and teens, warning them not to begin smoking. The company ran radio and television ads directing kids and parents to a Web site for help on peer pressure, smoking, and talking about the dangers of smoking. The company also inserted multipage glossy pamphlet inserts, titled "Raising Kids Who Don't Smoke: Peer Pressure & Smoking," in major magazines. The pamphlets tell parents, "Talk to your kids about not smoking. They'll listen."

Discussion Questions

1. Suppose you were the executive in charge of marketing for R.J. Reynolds. Would you have recommended an alternative to the Joe Camel character? What if RJR insisted on the Joe Camel ad?

2. Suppose you work with a pension fund that has a large investment in RJR. Would you consider selling your RJR holdings?

3. Do you agree with the statement that identification of the logo does not equate with smoking or with smoking Camels? Do regulators agree? Did the Joe Camel ads generate market growth?

4. What effect will RJR's voluntary action have on the regulatory trend?

5. Anti-tobacco activist Alan Blum said, "This business of saying 'Oh, my God, they went after kids' is ex post facto rationalization for not having done anything. It's not as if we on the do-good side didn't know that." Is he right?

6. What do you make of Philip Morris's problems with the fire-safe cigarette? What do you make of its new antismoking ad campaign targeted at children and teens? Is it significant that the company with the highest percentage of the youth market undertook the campaign to prevent kids from smoking?

Sources

Beatty, Sally Goll, "Marlboro's Billboard Man May Soon Ride into the Sunset," *The Wall Street Journal*, July 1, 1997, pp. B1, B6.

Boot, Max, "Turning a Camel into a Scapegoat," *The Wall Street Journal*, June 4, 1997, p. A19.

Burger, Katrina, "Joe Cashes In," *Forbes*, August 11, 1997, p. 39.

Dagnoli, Judann, "RJR Aims New Ads at Young Smokers," *Advertising Age*, July 11, 1988, pp. 2–3.

Horovitz, Bruce, and Melanie Wells, "How Ad Images Shape Habits," *USA Today*, January 31–February 2, 1997, pp. 1A, 2A.

Lippert, Barbara, "Camel's Old Joe Poses the Question: What Is Sexy?" *Adweek's Marketing Week*, October 3, 1988, p. 55.

"March against Smoking Joe," *Arizona Republic*, June 22, 1992, p. A3.

Martinez, Barbara, "Antismoking Ads Aim to Gross Out Teens," *The Wall Street Journal*, March 31, 1997, pp. B1, B5.

O'Connell, Vanessa, "U.S. Suit Alleges Philip Morris Hid Cigarette-Fire Risk," *The Wall Street Journal*, April 23, 2004, pp. A1, A8.

CASE 8.2

Alcohol Advertising: The College Focus

The mix is unquestionably there. Alcohol ads mix youth, fun, and enticing activities like scuba diving and skiing. Anheuser-Busch's Bud Light ads have Spuds MacKenzie, the "Party Animal" dog. Stroh's has its Swedish Bikini Team. Beer companies sponsor large promotions of their products on the beaches during college spring break weeks.[37]

In 1991, then-U.S. Surgeon General Antonia Novello asked the industry to voluntarily cut ads that attract minors. Novello stated, "I must call for industry's voluntary elimination of the types of alcohol advertising that appeal to youth on the bases of certain life-style appeals, sexual appeals, sports appeal, or risky activities, as well as advertising with the more blatant youth appeals of cartoon characters and youth slang."[38] A 1991 survey revealed that 10.6 million of the 20.7 million students in grades seven through twelve had had at least one drink in the last year.[39] Of the drinking group, 8 million drank weekly, 5.4 million had drinking binges, and one-half million had five or more drinks in a row at least once a week.[40]

Industry officials maintain that they are very active in and financially supportive of programs for alcohol-use education, including Mothers against Drunk Driving.

Anheuser-Busch spends $20 million of its $260 million ad budget on a campaign that features the slogan "Know when to say when." Miller Brewing Company runs a thirty-second television ad with the slogan "Think when you drink" as part of the $8 million per year that it spends to promote responsible drinking.

During spring breaks in 1991 and 1992, Miller and Anheuser-Busch did not use their multistory inflatable beer cans on popular beaches in Florida, Texas, and Mexico. In Daytona Beach, Florida, Miller put billboards along the highways with the slogan "Good beer is properly aged. You should be too." Miller's manager for alcohol and consumer issues, John Shafer, explained, "It's just good business sense to make sure we're on the right side of these issues."[41]

Patricia Taylor, a director at the Center for Science in the Public Interest, responded to the efforts by saying: "The beer companies are spending hundreds of millions every

---

[37] The industry promoted products with multi-story inflatable beer cans. Jeffrey Zbar, "Spring Break, Inflatable Beer Bottles Gone but Other Marketers Move In," Advertising Age, April 1, 1991, p. 16.

[38] Hilary Sout, "Surgeon General Wants to Age Alcohol Ads," The Wall Street Journal, November 5, 1991, p. B1.

[39] Julia Flynn Siler, "It Isn't Miller Time Yet, and This Bud's Not for You," Business Week, June 24, 1991, p. 52.

[40] Id.

[41] Id.

year to present a very positive image of drinking. That overwhelms all attempts to talk about the other side of the issue."[42]

Novello ordered new studies of the link between alcohol advertising and underage drinking. She also urged the industry to drop advertising meant to appeal to young people.[43] Anheuser-Busch created a campaign with ads in trade magazines and posters for stores to remind retailers not to sell beer to underage buyers. Novello responded, "These ads may be a stronger influence on students than they realize."[44]

Late in 1996, Anheuser-Busch announced that it would stop advertising its beer on MTV. Anheuser-Busch spent $534 million on advertising in 1995, with MTV spending equaling $2 million of that total budget. However, television is known as the best method for reaching Generation X buyers. The ads were shifted to VH1. Coors has never advertised on MTV, stating, "We don't like to walk the fine line." Miller Brewing Company continues its MTV ads.

In 1998, the American Academy of Pediatrics and the American Public Health Association joined together to launch a campaign to ask Anheuser-Busch to stop using frogs, lizards, and other amphibians in its ads. The posters for these two groups trace beer ads from Spuds MacKenzie to Frank and Louis, the lizards, and ask, "Fed up with beer ads that look like cartoons?" The posters liken the animals to Joe Camel. The two groups also ran a presentation to shareholders at Anheuser-Busch's 1998 annual meeting. They were joined by Mothers Against Drunk Driving, the Marin Institute, and the Center on Alcohol Advertising.

Anheuser-Busch issued a response to the campaign noting that drunk-driving fatalities involving teens and underage drinking have both declined since 1982, and that Anheuser-Busch has spent $200 million since that time on education programs designed to halt underage drinking. Also, Anheuser-Busch did voluntarily abandon, in 1997, the frogs that refrained "Bud-weis-er."

Because of concerns about liability as well as concerns about image, the notion of college-student spring break marketing has been downplayed during the past five years by U.S. businesses. Many U.S. businesses, for reasons of costs springing from damages to property and others from liability for alcohol-induced accidents, have declined to market their products or facilities to the spring-break crowd.

To fill the void, U.S. companies have begun to use Mexico, Amsterdam, and the Caribbean as liability-free spring-break areas and are intensely marketing these sites to college students. StudentSpringBreak.com encourages students to take a trip to Amsterdam, a "pot-smoker's paradise." It also notes, "Your yearly intake of alcohol could happen in one small week in Cancun, Mexico, on spring break." Hotels and travel agencies sell $179 passes for seven bars with one all-you-can-drink-night in each one.[45]

Cancun, Jamaica, Mazatlan, Acapulco, the Bahamas, Cabo San Lucas, and Amsterdam now top Miami, Fort Lauderdale, Daytona Beach, and South Padre Island. The drinking age in the U.S. locations is 21, but it is only 18 in the travel destinations abroad.

---

[42] Id.

[43] Stuart Elliott, "A Rising Tide of Rhetoric over Warnings on Alcohol," *The New York Times,* April 2, 1991, p. D18.

[44] Id.

[45] Donna Leinwand, "Alcohol-Soaked Spring Break Lures Students Abroad," *USA Today,* January 6, 2003, pp. 1A, 2A.

Discussion Questions

1. Suppose you were an officer of a brewery whose advertising campaign targets young adults (18–21). Would you change the campaign?

2. Wouldn't your ads appeal to various groups regardless of their focus?

3. Would it be censorship for the government to control the content of your ads?

4. Are campaigns on responsible drinking sufficient?

5. Do beer companies' ads attempt to encourage underage people to drink?

6. Is the international strategy a means of circumventing the law? Is it a means of avoiding social responsibility as well as liability?

Sources

Balu, Rekha, "Anheuser-Busch Amphibian Ads Called Cold-Blooded by Doctors," *The Wall Street Journal*, April 10, 1998, p. B6.

Buck, Rinker, "Ode to Miller Beer," *Adweek's Marketing Week*, May 27, 1991, p. 16.

Colford, Steven W., "FTC May Crash Beer Promos' Campus Party," *Advertising Age*, March 25, 1991, pp. 3–4.

Horovitz, Bruce, "Brewer to Stop Ads on MTV," *USA Today*, December 23, 1996, p. 1A.

Wells, Melanie, "Budweiser Frogs Will be Put Out to Pasture," *USA Today*, January 14, 1997, pp. 1B, 8B.

Yang, Catherine, and Stan Crock, "The Spirited Brawl Ahead Over Liquor Ads on TV," *Business Week*, December 16, 1996, p. 47.

CASE 8.3

The Obligation to Screen? The Obligation to Reject: *Soldier of Fortune* Classifieds[46]

Soldier of Fortune (SOF) is a national magazine focused on guns and military clothing and aimed at "professional adventurers." In its large classified advertising section, individuals and companies offer guns, gun-related products, gun and equipment repairs, employment opportunities, and personal services.

Some of the classified ads printed between 1975, the magazine's debut, and 1984 offered services under such titles as "Mercenary for Hire," "Bounty Hunter," "High-Risk Contracts," "Dirty Work," "Mechanic," and "Do Anything, Anywhere at the Right

[46] Adapted from M. Jennings, *Legal Environment of Business*, 2d ed., PWS Kent, Boston, 1991, pp. 229–231.

Price." During this period, *SOF* ran 2,000 classified ads, about three dozen of which had titles like these.

Various media, including the Associated Press, United Press International, *Rocky Mountain News, Denver Post, Time*, and *Newsweek*, reported links between *SOF* classified ads and crimes or criminal plots. These connections were made directly to five specific *SOF* ads and alleged with four others. Law enforcement officials contacted *SOF* staffers in investigating two crimes linked to personal service ads in the magazine.

Nature of *SOF* Ads

Dr. Park Dietz, a forensic psychiatrist, concluded from his study of the ads that the average *SOF* subscriber—a male who owns camouflage clothing and more than one gun—would understand some phrases in *SOF's* classified ads as solicitations for illegal activity given the ads' context. At that time, *SOF* contained display ads for semi-automatic rifles and books with titles such as *How to Kill*, along with articles on "Harassing the Bear, New Afghan Tactics Stall Soviet Victory," "Pipestone Canyon, Summertime in 'Nam and the Dyin' Was Easy," and "Night Raiders on Russia's Border."

Dietz suggested that the *SOF* personal service ads carry the connotation of criminal activity because of the nature of the magazine. He noted that the same ads would not carry that connotation if they appeared in *Esquire* or *Vanity Fair*.

The Hearn Ad

In September, October, and November of 1984, *SOF* ran the following ad:

EX-MARINES-67–69 'Nam Vets, Ex-DI, weapons specialist—jungle warfare, pilot, M.E., high risk assignments, U.S. or overseas. [Phone number]

"Ex-DI" means ex-drill instructor; "M.E." means multiengine planes; and "high risk assignments" means work as a bodyguard or security specialist.

The ad was placed by John Wayne Hearn, who said he wanted to recruit Vietnam veterans for work as bodyguards and security men for executives. Hearn's partner said they also hoped to train troops for South American countries. Hearn said he did not place the ad with an intent to solicit criminal employment but that 90 percent of the responses to the ad sought his participation in illegal activities, such as beatings, kidnappings, jailbreaks, bombings, and murders. His only lawful inquiry was from a Lebanese oil conglomerate seeking bodyguards; Hearn received a commission to place seven men with it.

Robert Black contacted Hearn through the *SOF* ad. Between 1982 and 1984, Black had asked at least four friends or coworkers in Bryan, Texas, to kill his wife, Sandra Black, or help him kill her. Initially, Black discussed bodyguard work with Hearn, and then their conversations focused on Black's gun collection. In October 1984, Hearn traveled to Texas from his Atlanta home to see Black's collection. During the visit, Black told Hearn his plans for murdering his wife. After Hearn returned to Atlanta, Black repeatedly called him. In a conversation with Debbie Bannister, Hearn's girlfriend, Black offered Hearn $10,000 to kill Black's wife. Bannister then communicated the offer to Hearn.

Hearn had no previous criminal record, but on January 6, 1985, he killed Bannister's sister. On February 2, he murdered Bannister's husband, and nineteen days later, he killed Sandra Black. He was convicted of the murders and sentenced to concurrent life terms.

The Victims' Suit against *SOF*

Sandra Black's mother, Marjorie Eimann, and her son, Gary Wayne Black, sued *SOF* for negligence in publishing Hearn's ad. The trial court awarded Eimann and Black $9.4 million in damages.

An appellate court reversed the decision, saying:

Given the pervasiveness of advertising in our society and the important role it plays, we decline to impose on publishers the obligation to reject all ambiguous advertisements for products or services that might pose a threat of harm. The burden on a publisher to avoid liability from suits of this type is too great.[47]

Other Cases of Ad Liability

SOF was sued again over a classified ad after Douglas Norwood was ambushed, assaulted, shot, and finally killed by a car bomb late in 1985. Each of his assailants had been hired through the following *SOF* ads:

GUN FOR HIRE: 37-year-old professional mercenary desires jobs. Vietnam Veteran. Discreet and very private. Bodyguard, courier, and other special skills. All jobs considered. [Phone number]

GUN FOR HIRE: Nam sniper instructor. SWAT. Pistol, rifle, security specialist, bodyguard, courier plus. All jobs considered. Privacy guaranteed. Mike [Phone number].[48]

The case was settled out of court in 1987.

In another case, Richard Braun was shot and killed outside his Atlanta home by an experienced mercenary, Richard Savage, who had been hired by Braun's business associate, Bruce Gastwirth, through an ad in *Soldier of Fortune*. Savage's ad began with the words "Gun for Hire." Braun's sons sued the magazine and were awarded $4.3 million. The amount was later reduced in a settlement of the case.[49]

The Association of Newspaper Classified Advertising Managers, Inc. (ANCAM) has the following policy:

Advertisements containing statements that injure the health of readers, directly or indirectly, are not acceptable.

Another ANCAM section provides:

Any advertisement fostering the evasion or violation of any law or making a direct or indirect offer of any article or service that violates a city, state or federal statute is unacceptable.[50]

---

[47] Eimann v. Soldier of Fortune Magazine, Inc., *880 F.2d 830 (5th Cir. 1989), cert. denied, 493 U.S. 1024 (1990).*

[48] Norwood v. Soldier of Fortune Magazine, *651 F.Supp 1397 (W.D. Anc. 1987).*

[49] "Military Magazine Gets Jury Judgment Reduced," The Wall Street Journal, *March 1, 1993, p. B3.*

[50] Don Tomlinson, "Choosing Social Responsibility Over Law: The Soldier of Fortune Classified Advertising Cases," Business & Professional Ethics Journal 9, *1990, pp. 79–96.*

Discussion Questions

1. Assume that you are *SOF's* new director of display and classified advertising. You know *SOF* was relieved of any liability for Sandra Black's death, so it is not obligated to check or reject ads. Your conscience, however, remains troubled as you review ads with such language as "high-risk assignment" and "bounty hunter." As you think about the Black case, you rationalize that Hearn was on a murder spree and Black was simply a victim of his sudden violence. On the other hand, Hearn would never have known Black if his classified ad had not brought a call from Robert Black. Further, only five to ten ads of over a total of 2,000 classifieds have resulted in crimes or criminal plots. You discuss this dilemma over lunch with your senior staff member, who responds: "Yes, but we could have prevented those crimes by not running the ads."

   Screening the ads will take time, private detectives, and an assumption of liability the law does not require you to make. Will you change *SOF's* ad policy? Will you conduct ad background checks?

2. Does this dilemma present conflicting moral standards?

3. To whom do you owe your loyalty in making your decision?

4. Should *SOF* feel morally responsible for Sandra Black's death?

5. Is the appellate court's decision not to impose liability on *SOF* an application of utilitarianism?

6. Should the decision on advertising policy be different following Sandra Black's murder?

7. William L. Prosser, a legal scholar, has stated, "Nearly all human acts . . . carry some recognizable possibility of harm to another." Why do we allow recovery for some of those harmful acts and not others?

8. *Soldier of Fortune* stopped accepting personal service ads in 1986. Is that an appropriate and ethical resolution?

CASE 8.4

Hollywood Ads

Actress Demi Moore starred in the 1995 movie entitled *The Scarlet Letter*, which was based on Nathaniel Hawthorne's book of the same name. Hollywood Pictures ran the following quote from a *Time* magazine review: "'Scarlet Letter' Gets What It Always Needed: Demi Moore." The actual review by *Time* magazine read: "Stuffy old *Scarlet Letter* gets what it always needed: Demi Moore and a happier ending." A *Time* spokesman noted that the statement was clearly ironic. In the same review, the *Time* critic, Richard Corliss, referred to the movie as "revisionist slog" and gave it an "F."

An ad for the 1995 movie *Seven* quoted *Entertainment Weekly* as calling it a "masterpiece." The actual review read, "The credits sequence . . . is a small masterpiece of dementia."

A movie industry observer stated in response to these examples, "The practice of fudging critics' quotes [in ads] is common." However, there is more than simple "fudging." Ads for the movie *Thirteen Days* included the descriptive phrases "by-the-numbers recreation" and "close to perfect" in order to reflect what producers touted as the strength of the film—its historical accuracy. But the ads also included pictures of the Spruance-class destroyer and F-15 jet fighters. Neither of these defense systems was available in 1962, the time of the movie, which is a depiction of the 13-day Cuban missile crisis during the Kennedy administration. These systems were not developed until the 1970s.

The movie studios pulled the ads after they had run for one weekend. They also pulled those ads that showed the movie's star, Kevin Costner, walking with the actors who played John and Robert Kennedy because that scene was not a part of the movie.

In 2001, ads by Sony Studios had theater critic David Manning proclaiming that *The Animal*, starring Rob Schneider and ex-"Survivor" Colleen Haskell, was "another winner." Mr. Manning also gave a favorable review of Sony's *A Knight's Tale*. However, David Manning is fictitious. He is a critic created out of whole cloth by young marketing staff members at Sony.[51]

....

Discussion Questions

1. Is the practice of fudging quotes ethical? Should Hollywood Pictures have pulled the *Scarlet Letter* ads?

2. How accurate should movie ads be? How historically authentic?

3. Is the practice of making up critics to provide quotes on movies ethical?

[51] *"Ads for Missile Crisis Movie Are Pulled Because of Errors,"* The New York Times, *January 13, 2001, p. A8.*

9A

Contract Relations

The law of contracts is detailed, but ethical discussions center on the fairness of treatment and the balance of the agreement.

CASE 9.1

Intel and Pentium: What to Do When the Chips Are Down

Intel, which makes components used in 80 percent of all personal computers sold, introduced the powerful Pentium chip in 1993. Intel had spent $1 billion developing the chip and the cost of producing it was estimated to be between $50 and $150 each. When the Pentium chip was finally rolled out, Intel shipped 4 million of the chips to computer manufacturers, including IBM.

In July 1994, Intel discovered a flaw in the "floating-point unit" of the chip, which is the section that completes complex calculations quickly.[1]

The flaw caused errors in division calculations involving numbers with more than eight digits to the right of the decimal, such as in this type of equation:[2]

$$\frac{4{,}195{,}835}{3{,}145{,}727} \times 3{,}145{,}727 = 4{,}195{,}835$$

Pentium-equipped computers computed the answer, in error, as 4,195,579. Before introducing the Pentium chip, Intel had run 1 trillion tests on it. Those tests showed that the Pentium chip would produce an error once every 27,000 years, making the chance of an average user getting an error one in 9 billion.

In November, Thomas Nicely, a mathematician at Lynchburg College in Virginia, discovered the Pentium calculations flaw described above. On Thanksgiving Day 1994, Intel publicly acknowledged the flaw in the Pentium chip, and the next day its stock fell from 65⅛ to 63⅞. Intel stated that the problem had been corrected but flawed chips were still being shipped because a three-month production schedule was just ending.

[1] *Evan Ramstad, "Pentium: a Cautionary Tale,"* Arizona Republic, *December 21, 1994, p. C1.*
[2] *Janice Castro, "When the Chips Are Down,"* Time, *December 26, 1994, p. 126.*

Intel initially offered to replace the chips but only for users who ran complicated calculations as part of their jobs. The replacement offer carried numerous conditions.[3]

On December 12, 1994, IBM announced that it would stop all shipments of its personal computers because its own tests indicated that the Pentium flaw was far more frequent than Intel had indicated.[4] IBM's tests concluded that computer users working on spreadsheets for as little as fifteen minutes per day could produce a mistake every twenty-four days. Intel's then-CEO Andrew Grove called IBM's reaction "unwarranted." No other computer manufacturer adopted IBM's position. IBM's chief of its personal computing division, G. Richard Thoman, emphasized that IBM had little choice: "It is absolutely critical for this industry to grow, that people trust that our products work right."[5] Following the IBM announcement, Intel's stock price dropped 6.5 percent, and trading had to be halted temporarily.

On December 20, 1994, CEO Grove announced that Intel would replace all Pentium chips:

> We were dealing with a consumer community that was upset with us. That they were upset with us—it has finally dawned on us—is because we were telling them what's good for them. . . . I think we insulted them.[6]

Replacing the chips could have cost up to $360 million. Intel offered to send owners a new chip that they could install or to have service firms replace chips for customers who were uncomfortable doing it themselves.

Robert Sombric, the data processing manager for the city of Portsmouth, New Hampshire, found Intel's decision to continue selling flawed chips for months inexcusable: "I treat the city's money just as if it were my own. And I'm telling you: I wouldn't buy one of these things right now until we really know the truth about it."[7,8]

Following the replacement announcement, Intel's stock rose $3.44 to $61.25. One market strategist praised the replacement program: "It's about time. It's very clear they were fighting a losing battle, both in public relations as well as user confidence."[9-11]

Grove responded that Intel's delay in offering replacements was based on concerns about precedent. "If we live by an uncompromising standard that demands perfection, it will be bad for everybody,"[12] he said. He also acknowledged that Intel had agreed to sell the flawed Pentium chips to a jewelry manufacturer.[13]

---

[3] James Overstreet, "Pentium Jokes Fly, but Sales Stay Strong," USA Today, December 7, 1994, p. 1B.

[4] Ira Sager and Robert D. Hof, "Bare Knuckles at Big Blue," Business Week, December 26, 1994, pp. 60–62.

[5] Bart Ziegler and Don Clark, "Computer Giants' War over Flaw in Pentium Jolts the PC Industry," The Wall Street Journal, December 13, 1994, pp. A1, A11.

[6] Jim Carlton and Stephen Kreider Yoder, "Humble Pie: Intel to Replace Its Pentium Chips," The Wall Street Journal, December 21, 1994, pp. B1, B9.

[7] Jim Carlton and Scott McCartney, "Corporations Await More Information; Will Consumers Balk?" The Wall Street Journal, December 14, 1994, pp. B1, B5.

[8] Stephen Kreider Yoder, "The Pentium Proposition: To Buy or Not to Buy," The Wall Street Journal, December 14, 1994, p. B1.

[9] Carlton and Kreider Yoder, "Humble Pie: Intel to Replace Its Pentium Chips," pp. B1, B9.

[10] "Intel Eats Crow, Replaces Pentiums," Mesa Tribune, December 21, 1994, p. F1.

[11] Catalina Ortiz, "Intel to Replace Flawed Pentium Chips," Arizona Republic, December 21, 1994, pp. A1, A8.

[12] Ziegler and Clark, "Computer Giants' War over Flaw in Pentium Jolts the PC Industry," pp. A1, A11.

[13] Otis Port, "A Chip on Your Shoulder—or Your Cuffs," Business Week, January 23, 1995, p. 8.

By December 16, 1994, ten lawsuits in three states involving eighteen law firms had been filed against Intel for the faulty chips. Chip replacement demands by customers, however, were minimal.

Intel's internal employee newsletter had an April 1, 1995 edition that spoofed the infamous chip.[14] A spoof form provided in the newsletter required customers with Pentium chips to submit a 5,000-word essay on "Why My Pentium Should Be Replaced."

In 1997, Intel launched two new products: Pentium Pro and Pentium II. A new potential bug, again affecting only intensive engineering and scientific mathematical operations, was uncovered. Intel, however, published the list of bugs with technical information and remedies for both of the new processors. One analyst commented on the new approach, "They have learned a lot since then. You can't approach the consumer market with an engineering mindset."[15]

Discussion Questions

1. Should Intel have disclosed the flaw in the Pentium chip when it first discovered it in July 1994?

2. Should Intel have issued an immediate recall? Why do you think the company didn't do that? Discuss what analysis their executives missed by applying the models you learned in Unit 1.

3. Was it ethical to offer limited replacement of the chip?

4. A joke about Intel's Pentium chip (source unknown) circulated on the Internet:

Top Ten Reasons to Buy a Pentium-Equipped Computer

10. Your current computer is too accurate.

9. You want to get into the Guinness Book of World Records as "owner of most expensive paperweight."

8. Math errors add zest to life.

7. You need an alibi for the IRS.

6. You want to see what all the fuss is about.

5. You've always wondered what it would be like to be a plaintiff.

4. The "Intel Inside" logo matches your decor perfectly.

3. You no longer have to worry about CPU overheating.

2. You got a great deal from the Jet Propulsion Laboratory.

And, the number one reason to buy a Pentium-equipped computer: It'll probably work.[16]

Based on this circulating joke, discuss the long-term impact of this chip and Intel's decisions on how to handle it on Intel.

[14] Richard B. Schmitt, "Flurry of Lawsuits Filed against Intel over Pentium Flaw," The Wall Street Journal, December 16, 1994, p. B3.
[15] James Kim, "Intel Proactive With Potential Buy," USA Today, May 6, 1997, p. 1B.
[16] From memo furnished to author by Intel employee at the time of the Intel chip problems.

5. Assume that you are an Intel manager invited to the 1994 post-Thanksgiving meeting on how to respond to the public revelation of the flawed chips. You believe the failure to offer replacements will damage the company over the long term. Further, you feel strongly that providing a replacement is a balanced and ethical thing to do. However, CEO Grove disagrees. How would you persuade him to offer replacements to all purchasers?

6. If you could not persuade Grove to replace the chips, would you stay at the company?

7. Has the Pentium incident caused long-term damage to the computer industry?

8. Consider the following analysis (from "Intel Eats Crow, Replaces Pentium," *Mesa Tribune*, December 21, 1994, p. F1):

Regarding your article "Bare Knuckles at Big Blue" (News: Analysis & Commentary, Dec. 26), future generations of business school students will study Intel Corp.'s response to the problems with the Pentium chip as a classic case study in how to transform a technical problem into a public-relations nightmare.

Intel's five-point plan consisted of:

1) Initially deny that the problem exists;

2) When irrefutable evidence is presented that the problem exists, downplay its significance;

3) Agree to only replace items for people who can demonstrate extreme hardship;

4) Continue running your current ad campaign extolling the virtues of the product as if nothing has happened;

5) Count the short-term profits.[17]

List other companies discussed in this book or in other readings that followed this same five-point pattern.

CASE 9.2
....
Hidden Car Rental Fees

During the 1980s, there were six major players in the global rental car market with the following dollar amounts of market share:

Share	(in billions)
Hertz	$4.0
Avis	3.2
Budget	2.5
National	2.5
Alamo	0.6
Dollar	0.5
Other	2.5[18]

---

[17] "Intel Eats Crow, Replaces Pentiums," p. F1.

[18] Matthew L. Wald, "Hertz to New York: Pay More," The New York Times, *January 19, 1992, p. F10.*

The competition in the industry was fierce. The companies offered customers various promotions, discounts, special rates, and other offers and the result was that customers were often confused by the variety of rates and rental plans. All the national firms have daily, weekend, and weekly rates. Some firms offer unlimited free mileage, while others offer 100 free miles with a charge for each additional mile.[19] The rates were almost impossible to compare.

When customers finally did decide on a company and rent cars, they were surprised by the additional charges that seemed to mount at the counter as they signed the paperwork for the car rental. The rental companies added extra charges for a second driver; a child seat; remote dropoff; and insurance, including collision/damage waiver (CDW), liability, personal effects, and personal accident coverage. CDW is the money-maker for the smaller rental agencies, which offer lower base rental rates and make their profits through extras such as CDW. These companies maintain that without CDW, which 90 percent of their customers take, they could not compete or survive, and prices would have to go up. Indeed, by 1992, prices at all car rental companies had risen an average of 12 percent.[20]

The CDW fees were expensive but consumers often paid the fees because of fears about what would happen if they had an accident in a rental car. A National Car Rental customer in Boston who paid nine dollars a day on top of the sixty-dollar-per-day rental fee in 1987 said, "It's expensive, but I figure you get in a crack-up and you're going to get nailed if you don't have it."[21] Nearly all insured drivers are covered by their own auto policies when they rent cars and the CDW is often double coverage but the pitch by rental agents at the counters did produce the 90 percent customer buy-in to CDW.

In 1988, regulatory and legislative bodies began investigating and challenging car rental practices.[22] Various types of regulations and challenges to the rental car industry practices popped up around the country. Some states took the position that because there was so much insurance coverage being sold at rental car counters that rental car agents should be licensed as insurance agents. Investigations found that some renters who refused CDW had been told no cars were available. Others had $1,000 to $3,000 frozen on their credit cards because they did not take CDW.[23] In 1989, several states considered legislation to ban CDWs. California passed a law that limited the waiver fee to nine dollars per day and required disclosure to the customer about its purposes (including disclosure in ads). New York and Illinois limited charges for car damage to $100 and $200, respectively, which effectively eliminated the need for most renters to buy CDW. In August 1988, a U.S. district court in New York ordered Hertz Corporation to refund $13 million to customers after the company pleaded guilty to criminal charges in connection with overcharging customers to repair vehicles that had been damaged but for which there was no CDW.[24] On September 4, 1988, the National

---

[19] Michael Katz, "FTC Forces Car Rental Firms to Reveal All," The Wall Street Journal, August 14, 1992, pp. B1, B2.
[20] James S. Hirsch, "Rental Car Firms Jack up Their Prices," The Wall Street Journal, November 4, 1992, pp. B1, B13.
[21] Corie Brown, "Cracking Down on a Costly Car-Rental Option," Business Week, November 30, 1987, p. 135.
[22] Jonathan Dahl and Christopher Winans, "States, Car-Rental Firms Collide over Damage Waivers," The Wall Street Journal, August 14, 1989, p. B1.
[23] Taylor, "Why Car Rentals Drive You Nuts," p. 74.
[24] Wald, "Hertz to New York," p. F10.

Association of Attorneys General appointed a task force headed by Kansas Attorney General Bob Stephan to study deceptive and unfair practices in the car rental industry.[25]

In August 1988, the Federal Trade Commission (FTC) cited both large and small companies for using deceptive practices in advertising. Clinton Krislov, a Chicago lawyer who represented consumers in class action lawsuits against rental agencies in Chicago and Des Moines, observed:

> This is sort of like trying to judge an ugly contest among frogs. There are, I suppose, some pockets of honesty in this business, but. . . .[26]

The FTC also proposed a regulation that would require the use of a standard rental contract and disclosure in all ads of full rental charges, including those for gas, collision protection, and repairs. The regulation would also limit charges for collisions and theft to $100.[27] The regulation did not pass, but the FTC focus on car rental industry practices continued.

In 1992, the FTC charged Dollar Rent-A-Car Systems, Inc., and Value Rent-A-Car, Inc., with failure to fully disclose information on charges to customers. Both Dollar and Value settled with the FTC in 1993 by agreeing to disclose more information in their ads.[28]

Under greater scrutiny and regulatory supervision, the companies began implementing new strategies to compensate for the lost earnings from the add-ons that were now either prohibited or declined as consumers began to understand their rights. They also began to rent to customers who were less likely to have an accident and started screening processes and restrictions on rentals. For example, during the late 1980s and early 1990s, companies refused to rent to or added a surcharge of ten to fifteen dollars a day on drivers between the ages of 21 and 25.[29-31] National began screening renters in New York City and Florida for driving-while-intoxicated (DWI) convictions or suspended or revoked licenses. Some firms charge an additional twenty-five dollars for more than one driver and have raised dropoff and refueling fees.[32-35] In 1995, Avis and Hertz reinstated mileage charges for certain renters in certain areas.[36] In 1997, Budget began charging $30–$100 for no-shows on their reservations.[37] A ban on under-age 25

---

[25] David Jones, "Illinois Moves to Ban Rental Car Waivers," National Underwriter, July 11, 1988, pp. 3, 79.

[26] Alex Taylor, III, "Why Car Rentals Drive You Nuts," Fortune, August 31, 1987, p. 74.

[27] Earl Golz, "Hidden Auto Rental Charges, Fees Can Take You for a Ride," Mesa Tribune, February 21, 1989, p. D1.

[28] Katz, "FTC Forces Car Rental Firms to Reveal All," pp. B1, B2.

[29] Susan Brink, Edward C. Baig, Steven D. Kaye, and Margaret Mannix, "A Pox on Young Drivers," U.S. News & World Report, March 29, 1993, p. 63.

[30] James S. Hirsch, "Auto Renters Hit the Brakes on Under-25s," The Wall Street Journal, March 16, 1993, p. B1.

[31] Lisa Miller, "Young Drivers Can Rent Cars, New York Rules," The Wall Street Journal, March 28, 1997, pp. B1, B2.

[32] "Car-Rental Firms Make Extra Drivers Costly," The Wall Street Journal, November 10, 1992, p. B1.

[33] Jonathan Dahl, "Rental Counters Reject Drivers without Good Records," The Wall Street Journal, October 23, 1992, p. B1.

[34] James S. Hirsch, "'Do-Not-Rent' Lists Tag Bad Drivers," The Wall Street Journal, September 15, 1993, p. B1.

[35] Matthew L. Wald, "Car-Rental Computers Rejecting High-Risk Drivers," The New York Times, September 9, 1993, pp. A1, A9.

[36] Lisa Miller, "Car Rental Industry Promises That Things Will Improve. Really," The Wall Street Journal, July 17, 1997, pp. A1, A8.

[37] Donna Rosato, "Budget Rent-A-Car to Charge No-Shows," USA Today, July 3, 1997, p. 1B.

drivers is in effect in the industry, with the exception of New York, where a judge has ruled such age-based distinctions to be a form of discrimination.[38, 39]

Competition became even more intense and the industry restructured. Dollar and Thrifty combined into one publicly held company, Dollar Thrifty. National and Alamo are now owned by Republic Industries.

In 1996, a new car rental company, Enterprise Rent-A-Car, became the nation's largest rental car company, focusing not on airports but on small towns and the need for rentals when the family car is in the shop. Enterprise holds 20 percent of the $15 billion U.S. market.[40] The price of an Enterprise rental is 30 percent below Avis or Hertz, and most of the company's fees are paid by warranty policies or insurance coverage (in the case of an accident).[41]

Discussion Questions

1. Assume you are the public affairs vice president for one of the top six rental car companies. Would you change any of your policies with respect to CDW?

2. Would you change your advertising to disclose CDW charges?

3. Would you instruct your counter agents to explain that the CDW coverage may be duplicative?

4. Would you change any of the other extra charges typical in the industry (that is, would you revamp your pricing policy)? Would such a change hurt or help your ability to compete? What do you think car rental executives missed in analyzing their contract charges, disclosures, and advertising? Apply the ethical models and determine whether the practices they were using were ethical.

5. Do you see practices in this industry that regulators may tackle in the future? Would you voluntarily change any of these practices? Recall the regulatory cycle that you studied in Unit 7 and apply it and the George Fisher guidelines on leadership to this case.

6. Is it significant that Enterprise, with its different charges, captured the market?

Sources

Bryant, Adam, "GM Agrees to Sell Car Rental Unit," *The New York Times*, April 5, 1995, pp. C1, C2.

Jacobson, Gianna, "Enterprise's Unconventional Path," *The New York Times*, January 23, 1997, pp. C1, C6.

---

[38] Miller, "Young Drivers Can Rent Cars, New York Rules," pp. B1, B2.
[39] Noelle Knox, "Cars Available! But With More Strings Attached," The New York Times, January 11, 1998, p. BU6.
[40] Brian O'Reilly, "The Rent-A-Car Jocks Who Made Enterprise #1," Fortune, October 28, 1996, pp. 126–128.
[41] Matthew L. Wald, "Hertz Ends 'Drop Charges' on One-Way Rentals," The New York Times, October 15, 1992, pp. C1, C10.

CASE 9.3

Thinning Diet Industry

Oprah Winfrey started a diet craze when she appeared on her television show in 1988 in her size-ten Calvin Klein jeans and boasted of losing sixty-seven pounds by using Sandoz Nutrition Corporation's Optifast Program. The preventive medicine center at Philadelphia's Graduate Hospital got 500 calls about Optifast on the day of Oprah's announcement. Since then, the diet industry has grown 15 percent per year with total annual revenues topping $3 billion. The major competitors in 1992, at the height of the diet market, were:

Weight Watchers International	$1.3 billion
Nutri/System, Inc.	$764 million
Diet Center, Inc.	$275 million
Thompson Medical Company (Slim-Fast)	$260 million
Sandoz Nutrition (Optifast)	$120 million[42]

Diet programs are sold through celebrity endorsements and before-and-after ads. Lynn Redgrave has represented Weight Watchers; Susan Saint James has appeared for Diet Center; and Christina Ferrara, Tommy Lasorda, Kathie Lee Gifford, Whoopie Goldberg, and others have endorsed Slim-Fast and Ultra Slim-Fast. Nutri/System has relied on radio disc jockeys to use its programs and then tell listeners about their weight losses.

The CEO of Weight Watchers likened the diet craze to the excesses of the 1980s on Wall Street: everything is more and more extreme.[43] By mid-year 1990, Representative Ron Wyden of Oregon, chair of the House Small Business Subcommittee, asked industry representatives to explain their hard-sell tactics. Wyden's hearings revealed that fully 90 percent of those who lose weight rapidly on the quick-loss programs regain the lost weight and often more within two years. Wyden asked why employees of these programs were referred to as weight loss specialists when in fact they had no expertise and were really sales personnel. Weight Watchers CEO Charles Berger testified:

Without touching on the issue of greed, some companies in our field have overpromised quick weight loss. And the promises have grown increasingly excessive.[44]

Just before the House hearings, nineteen women sued Nutri/System and Jenny Craig, Inc., in Dade County (Miami), Florida, for gallbladder damage allegedly caused by the programs' diets. Seventeen of the women had had their gallbladders removed after participating in the Nutri/System program, even though they had no previous diagnosis of gallbladder difficulties.

In response to the suits and in the hearings, Nutri/System stated that obese people are vulnerable to a variety of ailments, including gallbladder disease. The company

[42] Kathleen Deveny, "Blame It on Dashed Hopes (and Oprah): Disillusioned Dieters Shun Liquid Meals," The Wall Street Journal, October 13, 1992, pp. B1, B11.
[43] Julie Johnson, "Bringing Sanity to the Diet Craze," Time, May 21, 1990, p. 74.
[44] Id.

labeled the suits "without merit" and "a carefully orchestrated" campaign by the lawyers for the nineteen women.

Nutri/System was forced into Chapter 11 bankruptcy but emerged in 1993 under new ownership and a new weight loss philosophy that included encouraging the use of exercise equipment in its facilities.

A marketing consultant has observed about the diet industry:

> There is such a market for faddish nutritional services that even if you lose some customers you'll get new ones. To some extent in this industry, a lot more depends on how good your marketing is than your product.[45]

In 1991, the Federal Trade Commission (FTC) charged Optifast 70, Medifast 70, and Ultrafast with making marketing claims that were deceptive and "unsubstantiated hype."[46] The agency called the statement "you'll have all you need to control your weight for the rest of your life" unsubstantiated.[47] The FTC also announced it was investigating other diet programs. Representative Wyden said the FTC's complaints against the three companies were only "the tail of the elephant; the real test is whether these standards will be applied throughout the industry."[48]

By mid-1992, the FTC completed its investigation of misleading advertising by more than a dozen diet chains and promulgated guidelines for such advertising.[49] Before-and-after testimonials must include pictures of typical clients, not just the most successful ones, and claims of keeping the weight off must be documented. The FTC's guidelines were the result of the National Institutes of Health's findings that virtually all dieters regain two thirds of their weight within a year and all of it within five years.[50]

As the FTC was promulgating these rules, the Food and Drug Administration (FDA) announced that it would decide whether phenylpropanolamine, an amphetamine-like stimulant, could continue to be used in appetite-suppressant products, such as Acutrim and Dexatrim. Further, lawsuits based in product liability on the inherent dangers of these diet pills (including wrongful death actions) are pending around the country.[51]

Meanwhile, Oprah Winfrey announced that she would never again use a liquid diet, and an Alabama jury awarded $15 million to the mother of a 23-year-old bride-to-be who died of heart failure after losing twenty-one pounds in six weeks under the supervision of the Physicians' Weight Loss Center.

Several sociological issues surround weight loss. Susie Orbach, author of *Fat Is a Feminist Issue*, observes that 50 million Americans begin diets every year: "When I started working in this field 22 years ago, eating problems affected a limited group,

[45] Alix Freedman and Udayan Gupta, "Lawsuits May Trim Diet Firms," The Wall Street Journal, March 23, 1990, p. B1.

[46] Jeanne Saddler, "Three Diet Firms Settle False Ad Case; Two Others Vow to Fight FTC Charges," The Wall Street Journal, October 1, 1993, p. B8.

[47] Molly O'Neill, "Five Diet Companies Ask U.S. for Uniform Rules on Ads," The New York Times, August 25, 1992, pp. C1, C2.

[48] Jeanne Saddler, "FTC Targets Thin Claims of Liquid Diets," The Wall Street Journal, October 17, 1991, pp. B1, B6.

[49] Mike Snider, "FTC Weighs Claims of Diet Program Ads," USA Today, March 26, 1993, p. 1D.

[50] Mike Snider, "FTC Cites Diet Firms for False Claims," USA Today, October 1, 1993, p. 1D.

[51] Joseph Weber, "The Diet Business Takes It on the Chin," Business Week, April 16, 1990, pp. 86–87.

women in their 30s and 40s. Now, we know from studies that girls of 9 and women of 60 are all obsessed with the way they look."[52]

The top two companies in the diet industry—Jenny Craig and Weight Watchers—were cited by the FTC in October 1993 for falsely advertising the success of their programs.[53] Three other companies (Diet Center, Nutri/System, and Physicians' Weight Loss Centers of America) settled with the FTC by agreeing to (1) not misrepresent program performance in ads, (2) gather and make available supporting data, and (3) include disclosures that most weight loss is temporary and say whether a testimonial is typical or not.[54]

The New York City Department of Consumer Affairs was the first in the nation to issue "truth-in-dieting" regulations for diet centers, violations of which carry a $500 fine:

1. Centers must post a prominent Weight-Loss Consumer Bill of Rights sign in every room where a sales presentation is made. The sign informs consumers there may be serious health problems associated with rapid weight loss and that only lifestyle changes, such as healthy eating and exercise, promote permanent weight loss.
2. All centers must also give every potential client a palm-size Consumer Bill of Rights card.
3. All centers must inform potential clients of hidden costs of products or laboratory tests that may be part of the program.
4. All centers must tell dieters the expected duration of the program.

The FTC actions against false advertising led to a 15 percent reduction in diet industry revenues in 1994.[55, 56]

In 1997, just as the industry was recovering, the American Society of Bariatric Physicians released a list of its concerns about the industry's usage of obesity drugs such as Redux and fen-Phen along with promises of permanent weight loss.[57] The presence of the new prescription obesity drugs produced new weight-loss clinics focusing entirely on the pills and prescriptions, with a total of 18 million monthly prescriptions in 1996 given, in many cases, not to the clinically obese but to those seeking to lose five to ten pounds.[58, 59]

A 1997 study found the presence of heart valve damage among users of fen-Phen and the FDA withdrew the diet drugs from the market.[60] Those who had been using the diet drugs began litigation. By 2000, American Home Products had agreed to a $4.8 billion settlement with 11,000 class action litigants.[61] Since the time of the FDA ban on

---

[52] Larry Armstrong and Maria Mallory, "The Diet Business Starts Sweating," Business Week, June 22, 1992, pp. 32–33.
[53] Amy Barrett, "How Can Jenny Craig Keep on Gaining?" Business Week, April 12, 1993, pp. 52–53.
[54] Keith L. Alexander, "A Health Kick at Weight Watchers," Business Week, January 16, 1995, p. 36.
[55] Weber, "The Diet Business Takes It on the Chin," pp. 86–87.
[56] Ellen Neuborne, "Weight-Loss Programs Going Hungry," USA Today, July 28, 1994, pp. 1C, 2C.
[57] Laura Johannes, "New Diet-Drug Data Spark More Controversy," The Wall Street Journal, October 1, 1997, pp. B1, B12.
[58] Robert Langreth and Laura Johannes, "Redux Diet Pill Receives a Boost in New Study," The Wall Street Journal, April 1, 1998, pp. B1, B4.
[59] Gina Kolata, "Companies Recall 2 Top Diet Drugs at F.D.A.'s Urging," The Wall Street Journal, September 16, 1997, p. A1.
[60] Jeanne Saddler, "Diet Firms' Weight-Loss Claims Are Being Investigated by FTC," The Wall Street Journal, March 26, 1993, pp. B1, B5.
[61] Steve Sternberg, "Lawsuits: Drug Development's Big Side Effect," USA Today, January 12, 2000, p. 10D.

the drugs, those companies with alternative diet drugs without as much risk have had a difficult time selling even prescription drugs. Sales of anti-obesity drugs reached almost $500 million in 1996, but by 1998 had fallen to $28.8 million, a level at which they remain.[62] There are still cases pending involving those who did not settle with the class as part of the nationwide litigation. For example, a jury awarded Gloria Lopez, a cafeteria supervisor who took Pondimin, the fenfluramine portion of fen-Phen, for five months and lost ten pounds, $54 million because her aortic valve was damaged and will eventually require replacement.[63]

Diet centers relying on the two drugs have also been named in the litigation and many, based solely on the prescription approach, have closed.[64, 65] Customers who have become plaintiffs are complaining about the lack of warnings given to them by these diet centers.

In early 1998, a study of 1,072 people, sponsored by the parent company of the manufacturers of Redux and Pondimin, found only a 6.5 to 7.3 percent rate of heart valve problems in patients who took the drugs, as opposed to a 4.5 percent rate in patients who took the dummy pill. A cardiologist labeled the difference in rates "not statistically significant." However, the FDA ban remained and the litigation continued.[66]

New products for weight reduction that speed up metabolism and suppress appetite continue to come to market. Metabolife International, Inc., ran an aggressive Web-based campaign to counter negative media reports about side effects for its Metabolife dietary supplement that the company says speeds up metabolism and reduces the appetite.[67] In 2002, the FDA began an investigation of Metabolife and other products with the ingredient called Ephedra, also known as ma huang, an herbal supplement, which is very common in many weight-loss products. Metabolife sales peaked at $1 billion in the late 1990s. In 1999, more than 12 million people used products containing Ephedra, but the FDA became concerned when at least 70 deaths and more than 1,400 adverse events were linked to Ephedra. Adverse effects included high blood pressure, insomnia, nervousness, tremors, headaches, seizures, heart attacks, and strokes.[68] Baltimore Orioles pitcher, Steve Bechler, 23, died in 2003, a death rumored to be caused by his taking Ephedra. The Ephedra Industry Council (created by Metabolife) released information indicating that in many of these cases the problem was not Ephedra but rather the poor-quality manufacturing and production involved in cheap dietary pills and products. The Rand Institute conducted a study of Ephedra to determine whether these effects are caused by Ephedra and, if so, how extensive they are.

In the meantime, the FDA discovered that Metabolife failed to turn over 13,000 health complaints about Ephedra products and the lawsuits began to erupt all over the country. In 2004, the largest jury verdict to date of $7.4 million was awarded by a Texas jury to a woman who suffered a stroke and brain damage after taking Metabolife. The

[62] Dana Canedy, "Predecessors' Woes Make Diet Drug a Tough Sell," The New York Times, April 11, 1998, p. B1.

[63] Margaret Cronin Fisk, "Fen-Phen Jury Awards $56 Million," National Law Journal, April 23, 2001, p. A10.

[64] "A Bill of Rights for Dieters," Shape, November 1993, p. 30.

[65] Freedman and Gupta, "Lawsuits May Trim Diet Firms," pp. B1, B2.

[66] Kolata, "Companies Recall 2 Top Diet Drugs at F.D.A.'s Urging," p. A1.

[67] Bruce Orwall, "Diet-Pill Maker Battles a Report Before It Airs," The Wall Street Journal, October 6, 1999, pp. B1, B4.

[68] http://www.cnn.com/2002/HEALTH/diet.fitness/08/15/ephedra.investigatio/.

herbal stimulant is now banned by the FDA. Michael Ellis, the founder and CEO of Metabolife, was indicted in July 2004 for lying to the FDA and also for income tax evasion.[69] The indictment charges Ellis and Metabolife, Inc. with six counts of making false, fictitious, and fraudulent representations to the FDA and two counts of corruptly endeavoring to influence, obstruct, and impede proceedings being conducted by the FDA concerning the regulation of dietary supplements containing Ephedra.

Ellis, who is a former police officer, was convicted of a misdemeanor drug charge related to the production of methamphetamine. Metabolife founder Michael Blevins was charged at the same time when the two were working out of a home to produce at least 50 pounds of methamphetamine. Ellis served probation for his guilty plea, but Blevins did prison time. Through his lawyer, Ellis responded to the FDA's criminal charges, "The government has concocted a hypertechnical violation by taking statements to a regulatory agency out of context."[70]

....

Discussion Questions

1. Assume that you get a part-time job as a "weight counselor" with a quick-weight-loss program. Would you have any ethical constraints in performing your job?

2. Don't people just want to lose weight quickly? What if you told them they would gain it back and face health risks but they decided to go forward anyway? Would you and your product be adhering to a proper moral standard of full disclosure and freedom of choice?

3. Does the diet industry make money from temporary motivation? Or does the diet industry provide only temporary motivation?

4. Are the weight-loss ads misleading?

5. Weight Watchers, which posted a $50 million loss in 1994, has begun a new program emphasizing health foods, heart disease prevention, and exercise. Will this type of program avoid the ethical issues of rapid-weight-loss programs?

6. Given the Redux and fen-Phen problems, what can be safely concluded about the diet industry? What would be an ethical approach to running a weight-loss clinic?

7. Do you think there is a conflict with the 1998 study's sponsorship? What precautions should those professors conducting the study take?

8. What do you learn about the industry from Metabolife, the ban, the suits, and the indictment?

....

Sources

Hellmich, Nanci, "Heart Valve Damage Prompts Withdrawal," *USA Today*, September 16, 1997, p. 1A.

Hellmich, Nanci, "Withdrawal of Drugs Leaves Dieters in Quandary," *USA Today*, September 22, 1997, p. 6D.

---

[69] http://www.cbsnews.com/stories/2004/07/23/health/main631424.shtml.

[70] http://story.news.yahoo.com/news?tmpl=story&u=/ap/20040723/ap_on_he_me/metabolife&e=1&ncid=.

Hilts, Philip J., "Medicine Remains as Much Art as Science," *The New York Times*, September 21, 1997, p. WK5.

Janofsky, Michael, "Hearing for Franchisees in Nutri/System Buyout," *The New York Times*, May 11, 1993, p. C6.

Johannes, Laura, and Steve Secklow, "Heart-Valve Problem That Felled Diet Pills Had Arisen Previously," *The Wall Street Journal*, December 11, 1997, p. A1.

Schroder, Michael, "The Diet Business Is Getting a Lot Skinnier," *Business Week*, June 24, 1991, pp. 132–134.

Sternberg, Steve, "Study: No Heart Damage From Diet Drug," *USA Today*, April 1, 1998, p. 1A.

CASE 9.4

Sears and High-Cost Auto Repairs

In 1991, the California Department of Consumer Affairs began investigating Sears Auto Repair Centers. Sears' automotive unit, with 850 repair shops nationwide, generated 9 percent of the merchandise group's $19.4 billion in revenues. It was one of the fastest growing and most profitable divisions of Sears over the previous two years.

In the California investigation, agents posed as customers at thirty-three of the seventy-two Sears automotive repair shops located from Los Angeles to Sacramento. They found that they were overcharged 90 percent of the time by an average of $223. In the first phase of the investigation, the agents took thirty-eight cars with worn-out brakes but no other mechanical problems to twenty-seven Sears shops between December 1990 and December 1991. In thirty-four of the cases, the agents were told that their cars needed additional work. At the Sears shop in Concord, a San Francisco suburb, the agent was overcharged $585 to replace the front brake pads, front and rear springs, and control-arm bushings. Sears advertised brake jobs at prices of $48 and $58.[71]

In the second phase of the investigation, Sears was notified of the investigation and ten shops were targeted. In seven of those cases, the agents were overcharged. No springs and shocks were sold in these cases, but the average overcharge was $100 per agent.

Up until 1990, Sears had paid its repair center service advisors by the hour rather than by the amount of work.[72] But in February 1990, Sears instituted an incentive compensation policy under which employees were paid based on the amount of repairs customers authorized.[73] Service advisors also had to meet sales quotas on specific auto parts; those who did not meet the quotas often had their hours reduced or were assigned to work in other departments in the Sears stores. California regulators

---

[71] James R. Healey, "Shops under Pressure to Boost Profits," *USA Today*, July 14, 1992, p. 1A.
[72] Gregory A. Patterson, "Distressed Shoppers, Disaffected Workers Prompt Stores to Alter Sales Commissions," The Wall Street Journal, *July 1, 1992, pp. B1, B4.*
[73] James R. Healey, "Sears Auto Cuts Commissions," *USA Today*, June 23, 1992, p. 2B.

said the number of consumer complaints they received about Sears shops increased dramatically after the commission structure was implemented.

The California Department of Consumer Affairs charged all seventy-two Sears automotive shops in the state with fraud, false advertising, and failure to clearly state parts and labor on invoices.

Jim Conran, the director of the consumer affairs department, stated:

This is a flagrant breach of the trust and confidence the people of California have placed in Sears for generations. Sears has used trust as a marketing tool, and we don't believe they've lived up to that trust. The violation of the faith that was placed in Sears cannot be allowed to continue, and for past violations of law, a penalty must be paid.[74]

Dick Schenkkan, a San Francisco lawyer representing Sears, charged that Conran issued the complaint in response to bipartisan legislative efforts to cut his agency's funding because of a state budget crunch and claimed, "He is garnering as much publicity as he can as quickly as he can. If you wanted to embark on a massive publicity campaign to demonstrate how aggressive you are and how much need there is for your services in the state, what better target than a big, respected business that would guarantee massive press coverage?"[75]

Richard Kessel, the executive director of the New York State Consumer Protection Board, stated that he also had "some real problems" with Sears' policy of paying people by commission. "If that's the policy," Kessel said, "that in my mind could certainly lead to abuses in car repairs."[76]

Immediately following the issuing of the California complaint, Sears said that the state's investigation was "very seriously flawed and simply does not support the allegations. The service we recommend and the work we perform are in accordance with the highest industry standards."[77]

It then ran the following ad:

With over two million automotive customers serviced last year in California alone, mistakes may have occurred. However, Sears wants you to know that we would never intentionally violate the trust customers have shown in our company for 105 years.

Ten days after the complaint was announced, the chairman of Sears, Edward A. Brennan, announced that Sears was eliminating the commission-based pay structure for employees who propose auto repairs.[78] He conceded that the pay structure may have created an environment in which mistakes were made because of rigid attention to goals. Brennan announced the compensation system would be replaced with one in which customer satisfaction would now be the primary factor in determining service personnel rewards, shifting the emphasis away from quantity to quality. An outside firm would be hired to conduct unannounced shopping audits of Sears auto centers to be certain the hard sells were eliminated. Further, Brennan said, the sales quotas on

---

[74] Lawrence M. Fisher, "Accusation of Fraud at Sears," *The New York Times, June 12, 1992, pp. C2, C12.*
[75] Id.
[76] Id.
[77] Tung Yin, "Sears Is Accused of Billing Fraud at Auto Centers," *The Wall Street Journal, June 12, 1992, p. B1.*
[78] Lawrence M. Fisher, "Sears' Auto Centers to Halt Commissions," *The New York Times, June 23, 1992, p. C1.*

parts would be discontinued. While he did not admit to any scheme to recommend unnecessary repairs, he emphasized that the system encouraged mistakes and he accepted full responsibility for the policies. "The buck stops with me," he said.[79]

Sears auto repair customers filed class action lawsuits in California, and a New Jersey undercover investigation produced similar findings of overcharging. New Jersey officials found that 100 percent of the Sears stores in its investigation recommended unneeded work compared to 16 percent of stores not owned by Sears.[80] On June 25, 1992, Sears ran a full-page ad in all major newspapers throughout the country. The ad, a letter signed by Brennan, had the following text:

An Open Letter to Sears Customers:

You may have heard recent allegations that some Sears Auto Centers in California and New Jersey have sold customers parts and services they didn't need. We take such charges very seriously, because they strike at the core of our company—our reputation for trust and integrity.

We are confident that our Auto Center customers' satisfaction rate is among the highest in the industry. But after an extensive review, we have concluded that our incentive compensation and goal-setting program inadvertently created an environment in which mistakes have occurred. We are moving quickly and aggressively to eliminate that environment.

To guard against such things happening in the future, we're taking significant action:

We have eliminated incentive compensation and goal-setting systems for automotive service advisors—the folks who diagnose problems and recommend repairs to you. We have replaced these practices with a new non-commission program designed to achieve even higher levels of customer satisfaction. Rewards will now be based on customer satisfaction.

We're augmenting our own quality control efforts by retaining an independent organization to conduct ongoing, unannounced "shopping audits" of our automotive services to ensure that company policies are being met.

We have written to all state attorneys general, inviting them to compare our auto repair standards and practices with those of their states in order to determine whether differences exist.

And we are helping to organize and fund a joint industry-consumer-government effort to review current auto repair practices and recommend uniform industry standards.

We're taking these actions so you'll continue to come to Sears with complete confidence. However, one thing we will never change is our commitment to customer safety. Our policy of preventive maintenance—recommending replacement of worn parts before they fail—has been criticized by the California Bureau of Automotive Repair as constituting unneeded repairs. We don't see it that way. We recommend preventive maintenance because that's what our customers want, and because it makes for safer cars on the road. In fact, 75 percent of the consumers we talked to in a nationwide survey last weekend told us that auto repair centers should recommend replacement parts for preventive maintenance. As always, no work will ever be performed without your approval.

---

[79] Gregory A. Patterson, "Sears' Brennan Accepts Blame for Auto Flap," *The Wall Street Journal, June 23, 1992, p. B1.*
[80] Jennifer Steinhauer, "Time to Call a Sears Repairman," *The New York Times, January 15, 1998, pp. B1, B2.*

We understand that when your car needs service, you look for, above all, someone you can trust. And when trust is at stake, you can't merely react, we must overreact.

We at Sears are totally committed to maintaining your confidence. You have my word on it.

Ed Brennan
Chairman and Chief Executive Officer
Sears, Roebuck and Co.[81]

On September 2, 1992, Sears agreed to pay $8 million to resolve the consumer affairs agency claims on overcharging in California. The $8 million included reimbursement costs, new employee training, and coupons for discounts at the service center. Another $15 million in fines was paid in 41 other states to settle class action suits.[82, 83]

In December 1992, Sears fired John T. Lundegard, the director of its automotive operations. Sears indicated that Lundegard's termination was not related to the controversy surrounding the auto centers.

Sears recorded a net loss of $3.9 billion despite $52.3 billion in sales in 1992—the worst performance ever by the retailer in its 108-year history and its first loss since 1933. Its Allstate Insurance division was reeling from damage claims for Hurricane Andrew in the Gulf Coast and Hurricane Iniki in Hawaii ($1.25 billion). Auto center revenue dropped $80 million in the last quarter of 1992, and Sears paid out a total of $27 million to settle state overcharging claims. Moody's downgraded Sears debt following the loss announcement.

In 1994, Sears partially reinstated its sales-incentive practices in its auto centers. Service advisors must earn at least 40 percent of their total pay in commissions on the sale and installation of tires, batteries, shock absorbers, and struts. Not included on commission scales are brakes and front-end alignments (the core of the 1992 problems). Earnings in auto centers have not yet returned to pre-1992 levels.

Discussion Questions

1. What temptations did the employee compensation system present?

2. If you had been a service advisor, would you have felt comfortable recommending repairs that were not immediately necessary but would be eventually?

3. What will the complaints cost Sears, regardless of their eventual disposition?

4. Did Brennan acknowledge moral responsibility for the overcharges?

5. Does it matter whether the overcharges were intentional or part of business incentives?

---

[81] "Open Letter," Arizona Republic, June 25, 1992, p. A9.
[82] Barnaby J. Feder, "Sears Post First Loss Since 1933," The New York Times, October 23, 1992, p. C1.
[83] "Sears Gets Handed a Huge Repair Bill," Business Week, September 14, 1992, p. 38.

6. A public relations expert has said of the Sears debacle: "Don't make the Sears mistake. When responding to a crisis, tell the public what happened and why. Apologize with no crossed fingers. Then say what you're going to do to make sure it doesn't happen again."[84] What are the ethical standards in this public relations formula?

7. What will be the likely results of the incentive reinstatement?

8. There are some who have expressed concerns about the ethical culture at Sears. While incentive systems may have created the auto center fraud problems, consider the following dilemmas involving Sears since the time of its auto center fraud cases:

- Montgomery Ward obtained an order from a federal court prohibiting Sears from hiring employees away from Wards as it works its way through Chapter 11 bankruptcy. The order was based on an e-mail sent from Sears' regional vice president, Mary Conway, in which Sears managers are instructed to "be predatory" about hiring away Montgomery Ward managers.

- A class action civil suit was filed in Atlanta against Sears by consumers who allege that Sears sold them used batteries as new. One of the plaintiffs in the suit alleges that an investigator purchased one hundred "new" batteries from Sears in 1995 (in thirty-two states) and that seventy-eight of them showed signs of previous usage. A Sears internal auto-center document explains that the high allowances the centers must give customers on returns of batteries cuts into profits and induces the sale of used batteries to compensate. (Sears denies the allegation and attributes it to disgruntled former employees and not understanding that a nick does not necessarily mean a battery is used.)[85]

- Sears admitted to "flawed legal judgment" when it made repayment agreements with its credit card customers who were already in bankruptcy, a practice in violation of creditors' rights and priorities. Sears agreed to refund the amounts collected from the 2,700 customers who were put into the program. Sears warned the refunds could have a "material effect" on earnings. The announcement caused a drop in Sears' stock price of 3⅞. Sears included the following notice to its credit card customers:

NOTICE: If you previously filed for personal bankruptcy under Chapter 7 and entered into a reaffirmation agreement with Sears, you may be a member of a Settlement Class in a proposed class action settlement. For information, please call 1-800-529-4500. There are deadlines as early as October 8, 1997 applicable to the settlement.

Sears entered a guilty plea to criminal fraud charges in connection with the bankruptcy issues and agreed to pay a $60 million fine, the largest in the history of bankruptcy fraud cases.[86] The company also settled with the fifty state attorneys general, which included $40 million in state fines, $12 million for state shareholder suits, and a write-off of the $126 million owed by the cardholders involved which was forgiven as part of the settlement.[87]

---

[84] Nat B. Read, "Sears PR Debacle Shows How Not to Handle a Crisis," The Wall Street Journal, January 11, 1993, p. A14.
[85] There were questions and investigations surrounding Exide Corporation, Sears battery supplier. The questions related to the quality of the batteries and Exide at one point announced that it expected to face criminal indictment for certain of its business practices. Keith Bradsher, "Exide Says Indictment Is Likely Over Its Car Battery Sales to Sears," The New York Times, January 11, 2001, pp. B1, B7.
[86] Joseph B. Cahill, "Sears Agrees to Plead Guilty to Charges of Criminal Fraud in Credit-Card Case," The Wall Street Journal, February 10, 1999, p. B2.
[87] Id.

Sears also settled the class action suit on the bankruptcy issue by agreeing to pay $36 million in cash and issuing $118 million in coupons to those cardholders affected by its conduct with regard to bankruptcy customers. Sears did not admit any wrongdoing as part of the settlement but indicated the action was taken "to avoid the litigation."[88] Sears spent $56 million in legal and administrative costs in handling the bankruptcy cases.

Sears has been struggling to find its market niche for some time. In 2001, it was forced to close eighty-nine stores as it watched its competitor, Montgomery Ward, close its doors for good.[89] In 2004, Kmart purchased Sears.

Discussion Questions

1. What do you believe creates Sears' culture?

2. Sears' stock price and earnings fell. What lesson is there in these consequences?

3. Compute the total costs of the bankruptcy cases to Sears.

Sources

Berner, Robert, "Sears Faces Controversy Over Car Batteries," *The Wall Street Journal*, August 26, 1997, p. B2.

Berner, Robert, and JoAnn S. Lublin, "Sears Is Told It Can't Shop for Ward Brass," *The Wall Street Journal*, August 13, 1997, pp. B1, B6.

Conlin, Michelle, "Sears: The Turnaround Is For Real," *Forbes*, December 15, 1997.

Flynn, Julia, Christina Del Valle, and Russell Mitchell, "Did Sears Take Other Customers for a Ride?" *Business Week*, August 3, 1992, pp. 24–25.

Fuchsberg, Gilbert, "Sears Reinstates Sales Incentives in Some Centers," *The Wall Street Journal*, March 7, 1994, p. B1.

Miller, James, "Sears Roebuck Expects Loss in Third Period," *The Wall Street Journal*, September 8, 1992, p. A3.

Patterson, Gregory A., "Sears Debt of $11 Billion Is Downgraded," *The Wall Street Journal*, December 11, 1992, p. A3.

"Sears Roebuck Fires Head of Its Auto Unit," *The Wall Street Journal*, December 21, 1992, p. B6.

Stevenson, Richard W., "Sears' Crisis: How Did It Do?" *The New York Times*, June 17, 1992, p. C1.

Woodyard, Chris, "Sears to Refund Millions to Bankrupt Customers," *USA Today*, April 11–13, 1997, p. 1A.

---

[88] Leslie Kaufman, "Sears Settles Suit on Raising of Its Credit Card Rates," The New York Times, *March 11, 1999, p. C2.*
[89] Amy Merrick, "Sears to Shut 89 Stores and Report Big Changes," The Wall Street Journal, *January 5, 2001, p. A4.*

Magazine Contests: The Disclosure of Odds

Investigations of American Family Publishers and Publishers Clearing House centered on the mailings sent by the companies that included the term "finalist" on the envelope and whether the materials stated clearly enough that "no purchase is required." The "finalist" notification is mailed with subscription information for the purchase of subscriptions to magazines. Most people (99 percent) who send in their entries do order magazines.

Twenty-four states investigated Publishers Clearing House and American Family Publishers in twenty-one states. The Florida Attorney General filed suit against Publishers Clearing House as well as Ed McMahon and Dick Clark, their celebrity spokespersons, for deceptive practices.

One mailing from American Family Publishers includes the following:[90]

So please accept our invitation as soon as you receive it. Once you do, you'll experience the thrill of winning—and that's guaranteed.

The investigation in the various states revealed that many senior citizens were subscribing to between twenty and thirty magazines with the hope of collecting prizes they believed were theirs. Some of the language used in the 200 million mailings included the following:

John Doe, it's down to a 2 person race for $11,000,000—you and one other person in— (state's name placed here) were issued one of two winning numbers.

We have reserved an $11,000,000 sum in your name.

Are you willing to risk letting your alternative take it all?

These statements were in bold while disclaimers establishing that the win was not all that certain were in fine print. The language printed in bold caused many to buy yet another subscription with the hope of winning.

American Family Publishers (the company with the mailings that read "YOU MAY ALREADY BE A WINNER" on the outside of the envelope) agreed to pay $1.25 million to settle allegations in thirty-two states plus the District of Columbia regarding deceptive sales practices. Lawsuits against Dick Clark and Ed McMahon, the spokesmen for the company, were settled.

The settlement requires American Family to establish a toll-free telephone number for information requests as well as a Web site. Consumers must also be given information about getting off American Family mailing lists. Finally, American Family must stop using two mail addresses for the entries. Those who were simply entering the contest were instructed to use one address, while those who were subscribing and entering were told to send their envelope to another address. The two-address system

---

[90] Tom Loury, "Settlement Won't End American Family Woes," *USA Today*, March 20, 1998, pp. 1B, 2B.

led many to believe that an accompanying subscription was a key in collecting the prize described in the bold print.

Discussion Questions

1. Do you think there was deception in any of the practices?

2. What is the role of regulators in this situation?

3. Have the companies taken advantage of potential customers?

CASE 9.6

McDonald's and the Disappearing Dodge Viper Game Pieces

Jerome P. Jacobson was the marketing mastermind who managed McDonald's customer games such as Monopoly and Who Wants to Be a Millionaire. Though not an employee of McDonald's, Mr. Jacobson was a principal at Simon Marketing, which made and handled the distribution of the game materials and pieces.

Being in a position of security and trust, Mr. Jacobson was able to skim off winning game pieces before they were distributed to McDonald's and then to the customers. Beginning in 1995, Mr. Jacobson, or "Uncle Jerry," as he was known, operated a ring of at least eight people who conspired to take the trips, cars, and large prizes McDonald's games offered. They are alleged to have netted $13 million from obtaining the winning game pieces.

The FBI uncovered the prize network when it began working on an anonymous tip from someone who indicated that "Uncle Jerry" might be fixing the McDonald's games. The FBI tracked closely those who were claiming the prizes and then set up a series of wiretaps that eventually led to the disclosure of the ring. The agents were able to follow members of the ring to their clandestine meetings, one of which was held in, ironically, Fair Play, South Carolina.[91] In some of the wiretaps the agents listened as the participants argued over how to split the proceeds. In other meetings they simply discussed ways to push McDonald's to pay their prizes more quickly.[92] With McDonald's cooperation in providing the names of winners for all their contests, the FBI was able to uncover the network of Uncle Jerry. McDonald's cooperated with the FBI in what would eventually become a sting operation.

What the FBI uncovered with this information and cooperation was a complex organizational structure headed by Uncle Jerry, who was based out of Lawrenceville, Georgia. Jacobson would embezzle the game pieces and then sell them to individuals around the country. These individuals would become recruiters who would ask friends

[91] David Stout, "8 Charged with Rigging McDonald's Promotional Games," The New York Times, August 22, 2001, p. A14.
[92] Gary Fields and Shirley Leung, "Eight People Arrested, Charged with Bilking McDonald's Contests," The Wall Street Journal, August 22, 2001, pp. A3, A8.

SECTION A. CONTRACT RELATIONS

unit 9

section A

501

and relatives to buy pieces and claim the prizes. Some of these individuals actually mortgaged their homes in order to be able to buy the winning pieces from the recruiters. When they claimed their prizes, and they were mostly the big prizes such as a Dodge Viper and the millionaire tickets, they would pay a portion to the recruiters. The recruiters would then give a portion of their proceeds to Uncle Jerry. No one is certain where the informant fits in the organization, but he was able to supply the FBI with several names of those who were eventually arrested.

In order to right the wrong to its customers, McDonald's ran a $10 million prize giveaway weekend over the Labor Day weekend from August 30 through September 2, 2001.[93] McDonald's ended its contract with Simon Marketing at the same time. It was a 25-year relationship and McDonald's was responsible for 77 percent of Simon's revenues.[94]

Discussion Questions

1. Although an accounting firm was hired to supervise Jacobson and his distribution, apparently Jacobson operated without any checks. What does this factor and the case teach about internal controls?

2. What is the significance of the informant's work and tip?

3. When the FBI approached McDonald's, it knew that its games and image would be tarnished. Why do you think McDonald's cooperated?

4. Why did McDonald's run the $10 million Labor Day weekend game?

5. Mr. Jacobson met some of his recruiters when he worked as a police officer. Do you think their skills in law enforcement helped them evade authorities and detection for as long as they did?

[93] Bruce Horovitz, "Games Scandal Tarnishes Golden Arches," USA Today, August 22, 2001, p. 1B.
[94] Gary Strauss, "Informant Key to Unlocking Scam Behind the Golden Arches," USA Today, August 24, 2001, pp. 1B, 2B.

9 B

Product Safety

Only a manufacturer knows the results of its safety tests on a product. Only the manufacturer can correct defects or recall dangerous products. The decision to act on safety tests or recall a product is costly. The only "earnings" on recalls are the preservation of the company's reputation.

CASE 9.7

Tylenol: The Product and Its Packaging Safety

In 1982, 23-year-old Diane Elsroth died after taking a Tylenol capsule laced with cyanide. Within five days of her death, seven more people died from taking tainted Tylenol purchased from stores in the Chicago area.

Tylenol generated $525 million per year for McNeil Consumer Products, Inc., a subsidiary of Johnson & Johnson. The capsule form of the pain reliever represented 30 percent of Tylenol sales. McNeil's marketing studies indicated that consumers found the capsules easy to swallow and believed, without substantiation, that Tylenol in capsule form worked faster than Tylenol tablets.

The capsules' design, however, meant they could be taken apart, tainted, and then restored to the packaging without evidence of tampering. After the Chicago poisonings, which were never solved, McNeil and Johnson & Johnson executives were told at a meeting that processes for sealing the capsules had been greatly improved, but no one could give the assurance that they were tamperproof.

The executives realized that abandoning the capsule would give their competitors, Bristol-Myers (Excedrin) and American Home Products (Anacin), a market advantage, plus the cost would be $150 million just for 1982. Jim Burke, CEO of Johnson & Johnson, told the others that without a tamperproof package for the capsules, they would risk the survival of not only Tylenol but Johnson & Johnson. The executives decided to abandon the capsule.

Frank Young, a Food and Drug Administration commissioner, stated at the time, "This is a matter of Johnson & Johnson's own business judgment, and represents a responsible action under tough circumstances."[95]

Johnson & Johnson quickly developed "caplets"—tablets in the shape of a capsule—then offered consumers a coupon for a bottle of the new caplets if they turned in their capsules. Within five days of the announcement of the capsule recall and caplets offer, 200,000 consumers had responded. Johnson & Johnson had eliminated a key product in its line—one that customers clearly preferred—in the interest of safety. Otto Lerbinger of Boston University's College of Communication cited Johnson & Johnson as a "model of corporate social responsibility for its actions."[96]

President Ronald Reagan, addressing a group of business executives, said, "Jim Burke, of Johnson & Johnson, you have our deepest admiration. In recent days you have lived up to the very highest ideals of corporate responsibility and grace under pressure."[97]

Within one year of the Tylenol poisonings, Johnson & Johnson regained its 40 percent market share for Tylenol. While many attribute the regain of market share to tamperproof packaging, the other companies had moved to that form as well. However, it is interesting to note that McNeil was able to have its new product and packaging on the shelves within weeks of the fatal incidents. There had been some preparation for the change prior to the fatalities, but the tragedy was the motivation for the change to safer packaging and product forms.

McNeil continues to enjoy the goodwill from the rapid response to the poisonings. Even as new issues with Tylenol have developed, McNeil seems to be given the benefit of the doubt because of the goodwill and reputational capital it purchased with the capsule recalls.[98]

On December 21, 1994, the *Journal of the American Medical Association* published the results of a five-and-one-half-year study showing that moderate overdoses of acetaminophen (known most widely by the brand name Tylenol) led to liver damage in ten patients.[99, 100] The damage occurred even in patients who did not drink and was most pronounced in those who did drink or had not been eating. Further, the study by Dr. David Whitcomb at the University of Pittsburgh medical school found that taking one pill of acetaminophen per day for a year may double the risk of kidney failure.[101]

The American Association of Poison Control Centers for 1996 shows 31,511 cases of inappropriate exposure to pediatric acetaminophen products.[102] There were minor effects in 631 children and life-threatening permanent effects in six. Adult deaths from overexposure are put at 100, more than cocaine deaths (hospital statistics are not included).

Tylenol is a stunning source of revenue for McNeil and Johnson & Johnson, with revenue of $1.3 billion per year. In 1993, acetaminophen accounted for 48 percent of

[95] "Drug Firm Pulls All Its Capsules off the Market," Arizona Republic, February 18, 1986, p. A2.

[96] Pat Guy and Clifford Glickman, "J & J Uses Candor in Crisis," USA Today, February 12, 1986, p. 2B.

[97] "The Tylenol Rescue," Newsweek, March 3, 1986, p. 52.

[98] "Legacy of Tampering," Arizona Republic, September 29, 1992, p. A1.

[99] "Acetaminophen Overdoses Linked to Liver Damage," Mesa Tribune, December 21, 1994, p. A12.

[100] Doug Levy, "Acetaminophen Overuse Can Lead to Liver Damage," USA Today, December 22, 1994, p. 1D.

[101] "Second Tylenol Study Links Heavy Use to Kidney Risk," Arizona Republic, December 22, 1994, p. A6.

[102] Thomas Easton and Stephan Herrera, "J & J's Dirty Little Secret," Forbes, January 12, 1998, pp. 42–44.

the total $2.9 billion in sales of all over-the-counter drugs. Tylenol made up 70 percent of all acetaminophen sales. Advil's total sales, the next highest amount, trailed at less than $400,000,000.

Plaintiffs who claimed they were victims of overdose and the lack of effective warnings have not been successful against Johnson & Johnson.[103] The product labels before current modification read "Gentle on an infant's stomach," and Tylenol's ad slogan was, "Nothing's safer."

Patients combining Tylenol with alcohol have produced 200 cases of liver damage in the past twenty years, with fatality in 20 percent of those cases. The level of alcohol among these cases was multiple drinks every day.

In 1997, Tylenol added a new label to its infant Tylenol, "Taking more than the recommended dose . . . could cause serious health risks," because of liver damage in children.[104]

....

Discussion Questions

1. Was the risk small that there would be other poisonings of Tylenol capsules?

2. Were the shareholders' interests ignored in the decision to take a $150 million dollar write-off and a possible loss of $525 million in annual sales by abandoning the capsules?

3. Suppose that you were a Tylenol competitor. Would you have continued selling your capsules?

4. Was Burke's action a long-term decision? Did it take into account the interests of all stakeholders?

5. What financial arguments could be made against the decision to abandon the capsule?

6. Were the risks appropriately balanced in this case?

7. Following the poisonings, the federal government developed packaging regulations for nonprescription drugs. Should manufacturers have developed the tamperproof packaging on their own?

8. General Robert Wood Johnson, the CEO of Johnson & Johnson from 1932 to 1963, wrote a credo for his company that states the company's first responsibility is to the people who use its products and services; the second responsibility is to its employees; the third to the community and its environment; and the fourth to the stockholders.[105] Johnson and his successors have believed that if the credo's first three responsibilities are met, the stockholders will be well served. Does Johnson & Johnson follow its credo?

9. If you were a manufacturer of acetaminophen, how would you respond to the study results published in 1994? What action would you take?

10. How would you handle the resulting litigation?

11. Did the warning take too long?

---

[103] Deborah Sharp, "Alcohol-Tylenol Death Goes to Trial in Florida," USA Today, March 24, 1997, p. 3A.
[104] Richard Cole, "Tylenol Agrees to Warning on Labels of Risk to Children," Arizona Republic, October 19, 1997, p. A5.
[105] Brief History of Johnson & Johnson, 1992 (company pamphlet).

....

CASE 9.8

Ford and Its Pinto and GM and Its Malibu: The Repeating Exploding Gas Tank Problem

The Ford Pinto

In 1968, Ford began designing a subcompact automobile that ultimately became the Pinto. Lee Iacocca, then a Ford vice president, conceived the idea of a subcompact car and was its moving force. Ford's objective was to build a car weighing 2,000 pounds or less to sell for no more than $2,000. At that time, prices for gasoline were increasing, and the American auto industry was losing competitive ground to the small vehicles of Japanese and German manufacturers.

The Pinto was a rush project. Ordinarily, auto manufacturers work to blend the engineering concerns with the style preferences of consumers that they determine from marketing surveys. As a result, the placement of the Pinto fuel tank was dictated by style, not engineering. The preferred practice in Europe and Japan was to locate the gas tank over the rear axle in subcompacts because a small vehicle has less "crush space" between the rear axle and the bumper than larger cars.[106] The Pinto's styling, however, required the tank to be placed behind the rear axle, leaving only nine to ten inches of "crush space"—far less than in any other American automobile or Ford overseas subcompact. In addition, the Pinto's bumper was little more than a chrome strip, less substantial than the bumper of any other American car produced then or later. The Pinto's rear structure also lacked reinforcing longitudinal side members, known as "hat sections," and horizontal cross members running between them, such as those in larger cars produced by Ford. The result of these style-driven changes was that the Pinto was less crush resistant than other vehicles. But, there was one more problem, which was that the Pinto's differential housing had an exposed flange and bolt heads. These resulting protrusions meant that a gas tank driven forward against the differential by a rear impact would be punctured.[107]

Pinto prototypes were built and tested. Ford tested these prototypes, as well as two production Pintos, to determine the integrity of the fuel system in rear-end accidents. It also tested to see if the Pinto would meet a proposed federal regulation requiring all automobiles manufactured in 1972 to be able to withstand a twenty-mile-per-hour fixed-barrier impact and those made after January 1, 1973, to withstand a thirty-mile-per-hour fixed-barrier impact without significant fuel spillage.[108]

The crash tests revealed that the Pinto's fuel system as designed could not meet the proposed twenty-mile-per-hour standard. When mechanical prototypes were struck from the rear with a moving barrier at twenty-one miles per hour, the fuel tanks were driven forward and punctured, causing fuel leakage in excess of the proposed

---

[106] Rachel Dardis and Claudia Zent, "The Economics of the Pinto Recall," Journal of Consumer Affairs, Winter 1982, pp. 261–277.
[107] Id.
[108] Id.

regulation standard. A production Pinto crashing at twenty-one miles per hour into a fixed barrier resulted in the fuel neck being torn from the gas tank and the tank being punctured by a bolt head on the differential housing. In at least one test, spilled fuel entered the driver's compartment through gaps resulting from the separation of the seams joining the rear wheel wells to the floor pan.

Ford tested other vehicles, including modified or reinforced mechanical Pinto prototypes, that proved safe at speeds at which the Pinto failed. Vehicles in which rubber bladders had been installed in the tank and were then crashed into fixed barriers at twenty-one miles per hour had no leakage from punctures in the gas tank. Vehicles with fuel tanks installed above rather than behind the rear axle passed the fuel system integrity test at thirty-one miles per hour against a fixed barrier. A Pinto with two longitudinal hat sections added to firm up the rear structure passed a twenty-mile-per-hour fixed-barrier test with no fuel leakage.[109]

The vulnerability of the Pinto's fuel tank at speeds of twenty and thirty miles per hour in fixed-barrier tests could have been remedied inexpensively, but Ford produced and sold the Pinto without doing anything to fix the defects. Among the design changes that could have been made were side and cross members at $2.40 and $1.80 per car, respectively; a shock-absorbent "flak suit" to protect the tank at $4; a tank within a tank and placement of the tank over the axle at $5.08 to $5.79; a nylon bladder within the tank at $5.25 to $8; placement of the tank over the axle surrounded with a protective barrier at $9.59 per car; imposition of a protective shield between the differential housing and the tank at $2.35; improvement and reinforcement of the bumper at $2.60; and addition of eight inches of crush space at a cost of $6.40. Equipping the car with a reinforced rear structure, smooth axle, improved bumper, and additional crush space at a total of $15.30 would have made the fuel tank safe when hit from the rear by a vehicle the size of a Ford Galaxie. If, in addition, a bladder or tank within a tank had been used or if the tank had been protected with a shield, the tank would have been safe in a rear-end collision of forty to forty-five miles per hour. If the tank had been located over the rear axle, it would have been safe in a rear impact at fifty miles per hour or more.[110]

As the Pinto approached actual production, the engineers responsible for the components of the project "signed off" to their immediate supervisors, who in turn "signed off" to their superiors, and so on up the chain of command until the entire project was approved for release by the lead engineers, and ultimately, Iacocca. The Pinto crash tests results were known to these decision makers when they decided to go forward with production.

At an April 1971 product review meeting, a report by Ford engineers on the financial impact of a proposed federal standard on fuel system integrity and the cost savings that would accrue from deferring even minimal "fixes" of the Pinto was discussed.

In 1969, the chief assistant research engineer in charge of cost-weight evaluation of the Pinto and the chief chassis engineer in charge of crash testing the early prototype both expressed concern about the integrity of the Pinto's fuel system and complained about management's unwillingness to deviate from the design if the change would cost money.

---

[109] Grimshaw v. Ford Motor Co., *174 Cal. Rptr. 378 (1981).*
[110] Id.

J. C. Echold, Ford's director of automotive safety, studied the issue of gas tank design in anticipation of government regulations requiring modification. His study, "Fatalities Associated with Crash Induced Fuel Leakage and Fires," included the following cost–benefit analysis:

> The total benefit is shown to be just under $50 million, while the associated cost is $137 million. Thus, the cost is almost three times the benefits, even using a number of highly favorable benefit assumptions.[111]

Benefits

Savings—180 burn deaths, 180 serious burn injuries, 2,100 burned vehicles

Unit cost—$200,000 per death, $67,000 per injury, $700 per vehicle

Total benefits—(180 × $200,000) + (180 × $67,000) + (2,100 × $700) = $49.15 million

Costs

Sales—11 million cars, 1.5 million light trucks

Unit cost—$11 per car, $11 per truck

Total costs—(11,000,000 × $11) + (1,500,000 × $11) = $137 million

Ford's unit cost of $200,000 for one life was based on a National Highway Traffic Safety Administration calculation developed as shown in Table 9.1.

Despite the concerns of the engineers and the above report, Ford went forward with production of the Pinto without any design change or any of the proposed modifications. Shortly after the release of the car, significant mechanical issues were recurring, with complaints by vehicle owners as well as a number of fiery rear-end collisions. One of the most public cases happened in 1971 when the Gray family purchased a 1972 Pinto hatchback (the 1972 models were made available in the Fall of 1971) manufactured by Ford in October 1971. The Grays had trouble with the car from the outset. During the first few months of ownership, they had to return the car to the dealer for repairs a number of times. The problems included excessive gas and oil consumption, down-shifting of the automatic transmission, lack of power, and occasional stalling. It was later learned that the stalling and excessive fuel consumption were caused by a heavy carburetor float.

On May 28, 1972, Mrs. Gray, accompanied by 13-year-old Richard Grimshaw, set out in the Pinto from Anaheim for Barstow to meet Mr. Gray. The Pinto was then six months old and had been driven approximately 3,000 miles. Mrs. Gray stopped in San Bernardino for gasoline, then got back onto Interstate 15 and proceeded toward Barstow at sixty to sixty-five miles per hour. As she approached the Route 30 off ramp where traffic was congested, she moved from the outside fast lane into the middle lane. The Pinto then suddenly stalled and coasted to a halt. It was later established that the carburetor float had become so saturated with gasoline that it sank, opening the float chamber and causing the engine to flood. The driver of the vehicle immediately behind

---

[111] Ralph Drayton, "One Manufacturer's Approach to Automobile Safety Standards," CTLA News, February 8, 1968, p. 11.

TABLE 9.1 Ford's Unit Cost of $200,000 for One Life

Component	1971 costs
Future productivity losses	
Direct	$132,000
Indirect	41,300
Medical costs	
Hospital	700
Other	425
Property damage	1,500
Insurance administration	4,700
Legal and court	3,000
Employer losses	1,000
Victim's pain and suffering	10,000
Funeral	900
Assets (lost consumption)	5,000
Miscellaneous accident cost	200
Total per family	$200,725[112]

Mrs. Gray's car was able to swerve and pass it, but the driver of a 1962 Ford Galaxie was unable to avoid hitting the Pinto. The Galaxie had been traveling from fifty to fifty-five miles per hour but had slowed to between twenty-eight and thirty-seven miles per hour at the time of impact.[113]

The Pinto burst into flames that engulfed its interior. According to one expert, the impact of the Galaxie had driven the Pinto's gas tank forward and caused it to be punctured by the flange or one of the bolts on the differential housing so that fuel sprayed from the punctured tank and entered the passenger compartment through gaps opening between the rear wheel well sections and the floor pan. By the time the Pinto came to rest after the collision, both occupants had been seriously burned. When they emerged from the vehicle, their clothing was almost completely burned off. Mrs. Gray died a few days later of congestive heart failure as a result of the burns. Grimshaw survived, only through heroic medical measures. He underwent numerous and extensive surgeries and skin grafts, some occurring over the ten years after the collision. He lost parts of several fingers on his left hand and his left ear, and his face required many skin grafts.[114]

As Ford continued to litigate Mrs. Gray's lawsuit and thousands of other rear-impact Pinto suits, damages reaching $6 million had been awarded to plaintiffs by 1980. In 1979, Indiana filed criminal charges against Ford for reckless homicide.

[112] Mark Dowie, "Pinto Madness," Mother Jones, September/October 1977, p. 28.
[113] "Who Pays for the Damage?" Time, January 21, 1980, p. 61.
[114] Adapted from Grimshaw v. Ford Motor Co., 174 Cal. Rptr. 348 (1981).

Discussion Questions

1. Calculate the total cost if all the "fixes" for the Pinto gas tank problem had been done.

2. What was management's position on the fixes?

3. Using the decision models you have learned, list some of the analysis questions and issues management missed in making its decision to go forward with production without any design changes.

4. Did the Pinto design violate any laws?

5. Was Ford simply answering a public demand for a small, fuel-efficient, and inexpensive auto?

6. Don't all automobiles present the potential for injuries? Do we assume risks in driving and buying an automobile?

7. If you had been one of the engineers who was concerned, what would you have done differently? Do you think there was anything you could do? What if you resigned as Dr. LiCari at Beech-Nut did (Case 5.16)? Could you then notify a government agency?

8. In 1996, Ford issued a recall on 8.7 million vehicles because a joint investigation with NHTSA revealed the ignition in certain cars could short circuit and cause a fire. Ford ran full-page ads in major newspapers. The ad from *The Wall Street Journal*, May 8, 1996, p. B7, is reproduced below:

T.J. Wagner   Ford Motor Company
Vice President   Dearborn, MI 48121

Customer Communication & Satisfaction

To Our Ford, Lincoln and Mercury Owners:

As I am sure you have read, Ford Motor Company recently announced a program to voluntarily recall 8.7 million vehicles to replace ignition switches. You should know that at the time we announced the recall, the actual number of complaints which may be related to the ignition switch in question was less than two hundredths of one percent of that total. We regret the inconvenience this has caused the customers who have placed their trust in our products.

Q: *What happened?*

A: Following an intensive investigation in cooperation with the U.S. National Highway Traffic Safety Administration and Transport Canada, we determined that the ignition switch in a very small percentage of certain models could develop a short circuit—creating the potential for overheating, smoke, and possibly fire in the steering column of the vehicle. The factors that contribute to this are a manufacturing process change to the ignition switch in combination with the electrical load through the switch.

Q: *What vehicles are affected by this voluntary recall?*

A: The following model year vehicles are affected:

- 1988 Ford EXP.
- 1988–1990 Ford Escort.

- 1988–1992 Ford Mustang, Thunderbird, Tempo, and Mercury Cougar and Topaz.
- 1993 Ford Mustang, Thunderbird, Tempo, and Mercury Cougar and Topaz models built prior to October 1992.
- 1988–1989 Ford Crown Victoria, Mercury Grand Marquis and Lincoln Town Car.
- 1988–1991 Ford Aerostar, Ford Bronco full-size sport utility and Ford F-Series light truck.

Q: *What should I do?*

A: If you own one of these vehicles, you will receive a letter from us instructing you to take your vehicle to the Ford or Lincoln/Mercury dealer of your choice and have the switch replaced free of charge. However, you do not have to wait for our letter. You may contact your dealer and arrange to have the switch replaced immediately if you choose, free of charge.

Q: *How long will it take?*

A: The repair procedure should take about one hour. But please contact your dealer in advance to schedule a time that is convenient for you.

Q: *What if I need additional help?*

A: You may contact your dealer anytime, or call our Ford Ignition Switch Recall Customer Information Line at 1-800-323-8400.

We're in business because people believe in our products. We make improvements because we believe we can make our products better. And at times we'll take a major step like this to make sure that people who buy a Ford, Lincoln or Mercury vehicle know that they bought more than a vehicle, they bought a company and a dealer organization that stands behind the cars and trucks they build and sell. This is our *Quality is Job 1* promise to you. Thank you for your patience and support.

What was different about Ford's conduct in this case? Has Ford had an ethical cultural change on product safety? Why did Ford voluntarily agree to fix almost 9 million vehicles?

The Chevrolet (GM) Malibu

On July 9, 1999, a Los Angeles jury awarded Patricia Anderson, her four children, and friend, Jo Tigner, $107 million in actual damages and $4.8 billion in punitive damages from General Motors in a lawsuit the six brought against GM because they were trapped and burned in their Chevrolet Malibu when it exploded on impact following a rear-end collision.[115]

Coleman Thorton, the jury foreman, explaining the large verdict said, "GM has no regard for the people in their cars, and they should be held responsible for it." Richard Shapiro, an attorney for GM said, "We're very disappointed. This was a very sympathetic case. The people who were injured were innocent in this matter. They were the victims of a drunk driver."[116]

---

[115] Ann W. O'Neill, Henry Weinstein, and Eric Malnic, "Jury Orders GM to Pay Record Sum," Arizona Republic, July 10, 1999, pp. A1, A2.
[116] Id.

The accident occurred on Christmas Eve 1993 and was the result of a drunk driver striking the Anderson Malibu at 70 mph. The driver's blood alcohol level was .20, but the defense lawyers noted they were not permitted to disclose to the jury that the driver of the auto that struck the Malibu was drunk.

The discovery process in the case uncovered a 1973 internal "value analysis" memo on "post-collision fuel-tank fires" written by a low-level GM engineer, Edward C. Ivey, in which he calculated the value of preventing fuel-fed fires. Mr. Ivey used a figure of $200,000 for the cost of a fatality and noted that there are 500 fatalities per year in GM auto fuel fire accidents. The memo also stated that his analysis must be read in the context of "it is really impossible to put a value on human life." Mr. Ivey wrote, using an estimate of $200,000 as the value of human life, that the cost of these explosions to GM would be $2.40 per car. After an in-house lawyer discovered the memo in 1981, he wrote:

> Obviously Ivey is not an individual whom we would ever, in any conceivable situation, want identified to the plaintiffs in a post-collision fuel-fed fire case, and the documents he generated are undoubtedly some of the potentially most harmful and most damaging were they ever to be produced.[117]

In the initial cases brought against GM, the company's defense was that the engineer's thinking was his own and did not reflect company policy. However, when the 1981 lawyer commentary was found as part of discovery in a Florida case in 1998, GM lost that line of defense. In the Florida case in which a 13-year-old boy was burned to death in a 1983 Oldsmobile Cutlass station wagon, the jury awarded his family $33 million.

The two documents have become the center of each case. Judge Ernest G. Williams of Los Angeles Superior Court, who upheld the verdict in the $4.9 billion LA case but reduced the damages, wrote in his opinion:

> The court finds that clear and convincing evidence demonstrated that defendants' fuel tank was placed behind the axle of the automobiles of the make and model here in order to maximize profits—to the disregard of public safety.[118]

Currently, there are 100 such cases pending around the country. The suits center around GM's mid-size "A-cars," which include the Malibu, Buick Century, Oldsmobile Cutlass, and Pontiac Grand Prix. Approximately 7.5 million cars are equipped with this gas tank design. On appeal, the Los Angeles verdict was reduced from $4.9 billion (total) to $1.2 billion.[119]

....

Discussion Questions

1. Why do you think the drunk driver was not held responsible for the Los Angeles accident?

2. If you had found the 1973 memo, what would you have done with it?

3. If you had read the 1973 memo prior to the time the Malibu was released for production and to the market, what would you have done with it?

---

[117] Milo Geyelin, "How an Internal Memo Written 26 Years Ago Is Costing GM Dearly," *The Wall Street Journal*, September 29, 1999, pp. A1, A6.
[118] Id.
[119] Margaret A. Jacobs, "BMW Decision Used to Whittle Punitive Awards," *The Wall Street Journal*, September 13, 1999, p. B2.

4. What happens over time when memos such as this engineer's discussion are concealed?

5. What did the GM managers miss in ignoring the engineer's concerns? Why do you think they said he was acting on his own? If an employee writes a memo about the company's product is the employee ever acting on his or her own?

6. Offer some general lessons from these two cases for business managers and for yourself when you enter the business world.

CASE 9.9

ATVs: Danger on Wheels

Honda Motor Company, Ltd.; Yamaha Motor Company, Ltd.; Suzuki Motors Company, Ltd.; Kawasaki Heavy Industries, Ltd.; and Polaris Industries all made various types of motorcycles and all-terrain vehicles (ATVs) during the late 1970s and 1980s. Honda was the leading seller of ATVs, offering a full range of three-wheel models. It even made a very small three-wheel ATV for children ages four through ten that it advertised at the height of the market in the mid-1980s. The fat-wheeled vehicles that look like large tricycles were advertised as able to conquer all land surfaces with great ease. Suzuki's ads said its ATV would "embarrass the wind."[120]

The ATV was introduced in 1977 by Honda; several other manufacturers entered the market in the following year. Yamaha and Kawasaki ATVs were larger in size and motor capacity and carried higher price tags than Honda's.

In 1978, based on a complaint from the National Association of Emergency Room Physicians (NAERP) and the American Neurological Society (ANS), the Consumer Product Safety Commission began investigating ATVs and their use and misuse. The commission's reports, which incorporated information from NAERP and ANS, found that:

1. ATV accidents were increasing dramatically:[121]
   Of all the fatalities over the five-year period, 165 involved children ages eleven and younger, while 47 percent of the total involved children ages sixteen and younger.[122]

	ATV-related emergency room admissions	**Deaths from ATV accidents**
1982	8,600	26
1983	26,900	85
1984	63,900	153
1985	85,900	246
1986	86,400	268

[120] Frederick M. Maynard, "Peril in the Path of All-Terrain Vehicles," Business and Society Review, Winter 1987, pp. 48–52.
[121] Daniel B. Moskowitz, "Why ATVs Could Land in a Heap of Trouble," Business Week, November 30, 1987, p. 38. The numbers do vary in press releases and according to various groups.
[122] James Bolger, "The High Gravity Risk of ATV's," Safety & Health, November 1987, pp. 48–49.

2. Of all ATV-related injuries, 90 percent involved people under the age of thirty and 70 percent involved those under the age of eighteen.

3. In some areas, ATV-related injuries accounted for 45 percent of all emergency care on weekends.

4. Ninety percent of all injuries happened to experienced ATV riders (those who had logged more than twenty-five hours of riding time).

5. Leg injuries were common, with spiral fractures being the most frequent form.

6. Many injuries requiring emergency care were leg burns caused by riders holding their legs too close to ATV engines.

Dr. Ralph R. Fine, codirector of the National Spinal Cord Injury Statistical Center, testified before a House committee about his concerns: "We were seeing a disproportionate number of spinal cord injuries resulting from three wheeler or ATV crashes. These are dangerously deceptive, deceptively dangerous vehicles."[123]

Honda was aware of the report and submitted a study to the Consumer Product Safety Commission that showed the accidents with injuries happened when ATVs were misused.[124] Referred to in the Honda report as "hotdogging," misuse included driving too fast, climbing hills at ninety-degree angles, going through rapidly moving water, and using ramps for jumping.[125]

Between 1982 and 1986, there were more than 50,000 ATV-related injuries. By 1986, 2.1 million ATVs at an average price of $2,000 each were in use. Between 1982 and 1988, 858 people were killed in ATV accidents, many of them young children. A Consumer Product Safety Commission report concluded, "Children under 12 years of age are unable to operate any size ATV safely."[126] State attorneys general began efforts to regulate ATV use in 1986. Texas Assistant Attorney General Stephen Gardner stated, "These are killer machines. They should not be allowed."[127] The CPSC tried to have the industry sales to sixteen-year-olds and younger banned, but was unsuccessful.[128]

After the report, Yamaha introduced a four-wheel ATV, including one model with two seats. Yamaha also undertook a dealer education program and issued an instruction manual with the vehicles to encourage responsible operation.[129]

Roy Janson of the American All-Terrain Vehicle Association, a subsidiary of the American Motorcyclist Association, stated at congressional hearings on ATVs:

Problems result primarily from how a vehicle is used rather than from its design. When ATVs are used as intended, they present no unreasonable risk to their operators. The major problems related to three-wheel ATV injuries are the failure of users to wear proper safety equipment while operating ATVs and using these vehicles in areas not recommended for

[123] "Public Safety: All-Terrain Vehicles," National Safety and Health News, August 1985, pp. 78–80.

[124] Jeff Riggenbach, "Regulation Not Needed; Danger Is Exaggerated," USA Today, November 6, 1986, p. 10A.

[125] "Safety Group Targets Use of ATVs by Young Riders," Mesa Tribune, November 20, 1986, p. A4.

[126] Randolph Schmid, "Safety Panel Tackles All-Terrain Cycle Issue," Phoenix Gazette, November 19, 1986, p. A14.

[127] Moskowitz, "Why ATVs Could Land in a Heap of Trouble," p. 38.

[128] "ATV Makers Warned to Halt Sales to Children or Face Ban," Mesa Tribune, October 2, 1986, p. A2.

[129] Alan R. Isley, "Industry Is Emphasizing Safety," USA Today, November 6, 1986, p. 1B.

ATV recreation. User education and information programs are clearly the most effective means for addressing the problems relating to misuse.[130]

In 1980, major nationally franchised rental centers ceased renting ATVs because of liability concerns.

In 1986, the Consumer Product Safety Commission published proposed ATV regulations that included these key provisions:

1. No ATVs below certain size limits would be manufactured. ATV riders would have to weigh at least 100 pounds and be at least sixteen years old.
2. All ATVs would have four wheels.
3. All manufacturers would undertake educational ad campaigns on the use and dangers of ATVs. No promotional advertising would be permitted in any media form.

While the proposed regulations were being debated, ATV accidents continued to climb steadily. Of particular concern was the marked increase in severe injuries, such as spinal cord and head injuries, to children six to ten years of age. At the same time, some manufacturers continued to provide studies to the Consumer Product Safety Commission indicating misuse, not design, was the primary cause of ATV accidents.

By 1987, the Association of Trial Lawyers of America had established a clearinghouse for the exchange of information on ATV claims, and over 400 lawsuits had been filed. Three fourths of the suits were being settled for a typical payment of $1 million.

Because of increased, widely publicized objections from consumer groups, as well as a call for action from the American Academy of Pediatrics, the commission recalled three-wheel ATVs in May 1988 and halted their manufacture.[131] Meanwhile, manufacturers accelerated production of four-wheel vehicles. After judicial review of the commission's order and agreements were reached with the five manufacturers, the commission withdrew the recall but successfully implemented the ban on future sales.[132]

Some consumer groups, however, still felt a recall was necessary. James Florio, a Congressman from New Jersey, said, "How can anyone truly concerned with safety in effect say 'tough luck' to people who currently own these unsafe vehicles?"[133]

However, the manufacturers did agree to take the following steps:

- Offer cash incentives to encourage owners of ATVs purchased after December 30, 1987, to enroll in training programs.
- Revise warning labels and owner's manuals to outline the dangers of vehicle operation.
- Set up a consumer telephone hotline.
- Restrict sales of ATVs with engine displacements greater than ninety cubic centimeters displacement (CCD) to people sixteen years or older; children under twelve years would not be permitted to operate vehicles with engines greater than seventy CCD.

---

[130] *"Public Safety,"* p. 79.
[131] *"We Need Regulation of Dangerous ATVs,"* USA Today, November 14, 1986, p. 10A.
[132] *"ATV Makers Agree to Warnings, Vehicle Ban,"* Arizona Business Gazette, May 9, 1988, Law 3.
[133] *"Outlawing a Three-Wheeler,"* Time, January 11, 1988, p. 59.

- Scrap a provision in the preliminary agreement that would have required ATV purchasers to sign a form acknowledging the risks of operating the vehicle.[134]

Honda sent out the following "Safety Alert"[135] to owners of its ATVs in January 1988:

The Consumer Product Safety Commission has concluded that all-terrain vehicles (ATVs) may present a risk of death or severe injury in certain circumstances. While accidents may occur for many reasons:

- Over 900 people, including many children, have died in accidents associated with ATVs since 1982.
- Many people have become severely paralyzed or suffered severe internal injuries as a result of accidents associated with ATVs.
- Thousands of people have been treated in hospital emergency rooms every month for injuries received while riding an ATV.

Because of this, the United States government has filed a lawsuit against all manufacturers and distributors of ATVs asking the court to declare that ATVs are hazardous and to order the manufacturers and distributors to take actions to protect ATV riders. The distributors, while contesting the validity of the allegations made by the government, are presently engaged in discussions with the government to resolve these issues without litigation.

You should be aware that an ATV is not a toy and may be dangerous to operate. An ATV handles different [sic] from other vehicles, including motorcycles and cars. According to the Consumer Product Safety Commission, an ATV can roll over on the rider or violently throw the rider without warning, and even hitting a small rock, bump, or hole at low speed can upset the ATV.

To avoid death or severe personal injury:

Never drive an ATV without proper instruction. *Take a training course.* Beginning drivers should receive training from a certified instructor. . . .

- *Never* lend your ATV to anyone who has not taken a training course or has not been driving an ATV for at least a year.
- *Always* follow these age recommendations:
  - A child under 12 years old should never drive an ATV with engine size 70 CCD or greater.
  - A child under 16 years old should never drive an ATV with engine size greater than 90 CCD.
- *Never* allow a child under 16 years old to drive an ATV without adult supervision. Children need to be observed carefully because not all children have the strength, size, skills, or judgment needed to drive an ATV safely.
- *Never* drive an ATV after consuming alcohol or drugs.
- *Never* carry a passenger on an ATV; carrying a passenger may upset the balance of the ATV and may cause it to go out of control.
- *Never* drive an ATV on pavement. The vehicle is not designed to be used on paved surfaces and may be difficult to control.

[134] Matt DeLorenzo, "ATV Companies Agree to Warn, Train Owners," Automotive News, *March 21, 1988, p. 58.*
[135] *Reprinted with permission of Honda Motor Company, Ltd.*

- *Never* drive an ATV on a public road, even a dirt or gravel one, because you may not be able to avoid colliding with other vehicles. Also, driving on a public road with an ATV may be against the law.
- *Never* attempt to do "wheelies," jumps, or other stunts.
- *Never* drive an ATV without a good helmet and goggles. You should also wear boots, gloves, heavy trousers, and a long-sleeve shirt.
- *Never* drive an ATV at excessive speeds.
- *Always* be extremely careful when driving an ATV, especially when approaching hills, turns, and obstacles and when driving on unfamiliar or rough terrain.
- *Always* read the owner's manual carefully and follow the operating procedures described.

Discussion Questions

1. Is the ATV too dangerous to be sold?

2. Are the warnings and the ban on future ATV sales sufficient?

3. If you were in marketing for one of the five firms, could you continue your sales efforts?

4. Should the three-wheel ATV have been recalled?

5. Is the cost of a recall just too high?

CASE 9.10

E. coli, Jack-in-the-Box, and Cooking Temperatures

On January 11, 1993, young Michael Nole and his family ate dinner at a Jack-in-the-Box restaurant in Tacoma, Washington, where Michael enjoyed his $2.69 "Kid's Meal." The next day, Michael was admitted to Children's Hospital and Medical Center in Seattle with severe stomach cramps and bloody diarrhea. Several days later, Michael died of kidney and heart failure.[136]

At the same time, 300 other people in Idaho, Nevada, and Washington who had eaten at Jack-in-the-Box restaurants were poisoned with *E. coli* bacteria, the cause of Michael's death. By the end of the outbreak, more than 600 people nationwide were affected.[137]

Jack-in-the-Box, based in San Diego, was not in the best financial health, having just restructured $501 million in debt. The outbreak of poisonings came at a difficult time for the company.

Federal guidelines require that meat be cooked to an internal temperature of 140 degrees Fahrenheit. Jack-in-the-Box followed those guidelines. In May 1992 and

---

[136] Catherine Yang and Amy Barrett, "In a Stew over Tainted Meat," *Business Week*, April 12, 1993, p. 36.

[137] Fred Bayles, "Meat Safety," *USA Today*, October 8, 1997, p. 1A.

September 1992, the state of Washington notified all restaurants, including Jack-in-the-Box, of new regulations requiring hamburgers to be cooked to 155 degrees Fahrenheit. The change would increase restaurants' costs because cooking to 155 degrees slows delivery of food to customers and increases energy costs.

At a news conference one week after the poisonings, Jack-in-the-Box president Robert J. Nugent criticized state authorities for not notifying the company of the 155-degree rule. A week later, the company found the notifications, which it had misplaced, and issued a statement.

After the Jack-in-the-Box poisonings, the federal government recommended that all states increase their cooking temperature requirements to 155 degrees. Burger King cooks to 160 degrees; Hardee's, Wendy's, and Taco Bell to 165 degrees. The U.S. Agriculture Department also changed its meat inspection standards.[138, 139]

The poisonings cut sales at Jack-in-the-Box by 20 percent.[140] Three store managers were laid off, and the company's plan to build five new restaurants was put on hold until sales picked up. Jack-in-the-Box scrapped 20,000 pounds of hamburger patties produced at meat plants where the bacteria was suspected to have originated. It also changed meat suppliers and added extra meat inspections of its own at an expected cost of $2 million a year.[141]

Consumer groups advocated a 160-degree internal temperature for cooking and a requirement that the meat no longer be pink or red inside.

A class action law suit brought by plaintiffs with minor *E. coli* effects was settled for $12 million. Two other suits, brought on behalf of children who went into comas, were settled for $3 million and $15.6 million, respectively.[142] All of the suits were settled by the end of 1997, most of the settlements coming from a pool of $100 million established by the company's ten insurers.[143]

Discussion Questions

1. In 1993, Jack-in-the-Box adopted tougher standards for its meat suppliers than those required by the federal government so that suppliers test more frequently for *E. coli*. Could Jack-in-the-Box have done more before the outbreak occurred?

2. The link between cooking to a 155-degree internal temperature and the destruction of *E. coli* bacteria had been publicly known for five years at the time of the outbreak. The federal Centers for Disease Control tests showed Jack-in-the-Box hamburgers were cooked to 120 degrees. Should Jack-in-the-Box have increased cooking temperatures voluntarily and sooner?

[138] Richard Gibson and Scott Kilman, "Tainted Hamburger Incident Heats Up Debate over U.S. Meat-Inspection System," The Wall Street Journal, February 12, 1993, pp. B1, B7.

[139] Martin Tolchin, "Clinton Orders Hiring of 160 Meat Inspectors," The New York Times, February 12, 1993, p. A11.

[140] Ronald Grover, Dori Jones Yang, and Laura Holson, "Boxed in at Jack-in-the-Box," Business Week, February 15, 1993, p. 40.

[141] Adam Bryant, "Foodmaker Cancels Expansion," The New York Times, February 15, 1993, p. C3.

[142] "Jack-in-the-Box Ends E-Coli Suits," National Law Journal, November 17, 1997, p. A8.

[143] Bob Van Voris, "Jack in the Box Ends E-Coli Suits," National Law Journal, November 17, 1997.

3. What does the misplacement of the state health department notices on cooking temperature say about the culture at Jack-in-the-Box?

4. Are there moral issues involved in deciding what temperature to cook meat to?

5. A plaintiff's lawyer praised Jack-in-the-Box saying, "They paid out in a way that made everybody walking away from the settlement table think they had been treated fairly." What do we learn about the company from this statement?

9c

Product Social Issues

Sometimes the product is legal, the quality is good, and yet the product does have its issues. In this section, the issues are ones of social responsibility.

CASE 9.11

The Mommy Doll

Villy Nielsen, APS, a Danish toy company, introduced the Mommy-To-Be doll in the United States. The doll, named Judith, looks like it is pregnant. When its belly is removed, a baby is revealed inside that can be popped out. Once the baby is removed, the doll's original stomach pops into place. The new stomach is flat and instantly restores Judith's youthful figure.

Teenage girls are intrigued by the doll, and call it "neat." However, Diane Welsh, the president of the New York chapter of the National Organization for Women, stated, "A doll that magically becomes pregnant and unpregnant is an irresponsible toy. We need to understand having a child is a very serious business. We have enough unwanted children in this world."[144]

Mommy-To-Be comes with Charles, her husband, and baby accessories. An eleven-year-old shopper said of the doll, "I don't think she looks like a mommy. . . . She looks like a teenager."[145]

Discussion Questions

1. Is the doll a socially responsible toy?

2. Would you carry the doll if you owned a toy store?

3. Would you want your children to have the doll?

[144] "Mommy Doll Makes Birth a Snap," Mesa Tribune, May 9, 1992, p. A7.
[145] Id.

CASE 9.12
Rock Music Warning Labels

In the summer of 1985, Tipper Gore, the wife of then-Senator Albert Gore of Tennessee, and Susan Baker, the wife of former U.S. Treasury Secretary James Baker, formed a citizens' group called the Parents Music Resource Center (PMRC). The group's concern was that rock music advocates "aggressive and hostile rebellion, the abuse of drugs and alcohol, irresponsible sexuality, sexual perversions, violence and involvement in the occult." Gore began the group after she listened to the song "Darling Nikki" from her eleven-year-old daughter's *Purple Rain* album by Prince. The song is about a girl masturbating as she looks at a magazine. Gore then discovered Sheena Easton singing about "genital arousal," Judas Priest singing about oral sex at gunpoint, and the lyrics in Motley Crue's top-selling *Shout at the Devil* album, describing killing a person and watching his face turn blue.

PMRC's strategy was to work with record companies to reach a mutually agreeable solution to the problem. PMRC met with the Recording Industry Association of America to request a ratings system for records, similar to that used for movies, and a requirement that printed lyrics be included with all records so that disc jockeys would know what they are sending out over the airwaves. In the first month after PMRC was organized, it received over 10,000 letters of support and inquiry. PMRC maintains a database with the following information:

- Teenagers listen to their music four to six hours per day for a total of 10,000 hours between grades seven and twelve.
- Of all violent crimes, 70 percent are committed by youths under the age of seventeen.
- Teenage suicide has increased by 300 percent since 1955.
- U.S. teenage pregnancy rates are the highest in the world.[146]

When PMRC failed to reach an agreement with the record industry, congressional hearings were held on a proposed bill to require labeling on records. Susan Baker and Tipper Gore testified, as did musicians Frank Zappa, former member of the Mothers of Invention, and Dee Snider of Twisted Sister. Zappa stated, "Putting labels on albums is the equivalent of treating dandruff by decapitation."[147]

Though nothing came of the hearings, by 1990 bills were pending in thirty-five state legislatures to require labeling of records. PMRC backed state groups lobbying for the legislation.[148] In Arizona, a reporter for *New Times* asked a sponsor of a labeling bill, Senator Jan Brewer, to read some of the objectionable lyrics. The reporter recorded the reading, set it to music, and played the tape over the speakers in the Capitol.[149]

In May 1990, with the state legislative debates on the label requirements still in progress, the Recording Industry Association of America introduced a uniform label

---

[146] William A. Henry, "Did the Music Say Do It?" Time, July 30, 1990, p. 65.
[147] "Musicians Mock Senators' Wives at Hearing," Mesa Tribune, September 20, 1995, p. A4.
[148] "Record Firm to Back Stores with Legal Aid," Mesa Tribune, June 5, 1990, p. A2.
[149] Ed Foster, "Music-Label Bill Shelved," Arizona Republic, March 24, 1990, p. A1.

for albums with explicit lyrics and expressed hope that its voluntary use by industry members would halt the passage of legislation.[150] The black-and-white label appears in the lower right-hand corner of the album and reads: "Parental Advisory—Explicit Lyrics."[151] The label is to be used on albums with lyrics relating to sex, violence, suicide, drug abuse, bigotry, or satanic worship. Use of the label is the decision of the record company and the artist.[152]

The PMRC and the National Parent and Teacher Association endorsed the warning system and asked state legislators to consider dropping proposed label legislation.[153]

Controversy continued to surround rock music lyrics. In the summer of 1990, parents of a teenager who committed suicide sued the rock group Judas Priest, alleging that its lyrics resulted in murderous mind control and the death of their son.[154] Their subliminal persuasion argument was unsuccessful.[155]

By 1995, the record industry's then ten-year-old warning label program was reviewed with the conclusion that parents don't know what the explicit-lyrics labels are.[156] A meeting between the Recording Industry Association of America and the National Association of Recording Merchandisers resulted in new plans to help the system work better.[157] The provisions included:

- Display signs in stores explaining the "Parental Advisory Explicit Lyrics" logo.[158]
- Ensure that record companies use the correct size (1-inch by ½-inch) and placement (lower right) on the record's permanent packaging.
- Alert reviewers of each record's sticker status.
- Encourage inclusion of a record's warning label in ads and promotional materials.

The attention to gangsta rap music also resulted in increased attention to lyrics. Recording company MCA was targeted in 1996 for marketing "death and degradation." MCA refused to make changes other than complying with warning labels and called Mr. William Bennett, a former secretary of education and author, a "warden of morality." Wal-Mart refused to stock explicit lyric music.

In late November 1997, the Senate began exploring the effects of music on children. One parent testified that his 15-year-old son committed suicide after listening to the Marilyn Manson album, *Antichrist Superstar*.

The issues of rock music, lyrics, and artists' rights had its usual cycle of relative quiet between 1997 and 2000. However, during the presidential election of 2000, the issues again surfaced because Mr. Gore was running for president and his wife Tipper again was in the news along with the issues that concerned her. In addition, George W. Bush chose Dick Cheney as his running mate. Mr. Cheney is married to Dr. Lynne

[150] "Warning: Rock Music Ahead," Time, May 21, 1990, p. 69.

[151] Robert M. Andrews, "Records Get Uniform Warning Tag," Arizona Republic, May 10, 1990, p. A1.

[152] Carrie White, "Rating Rock Music," Mesa Tribune, December 12, 1995, p. D1.

[153] "Record Firm to Back Stores with Legal Aid," p. A2.

[154] David Stout, "Senate Hearing Is Told Lyrics Led to Suicide," The New York Times, November 7, 1997, p. A1.

[155] Henry, "Did the Music Say Do It?" p. 65.

[156] Edna Gundersen, "Explicit Lyrics Warning Just Aren't Sticking," USA Today, October 25, 1995, p. 1D.

[157] Julia Malone, "Washington Wives Use Influence to Target Sex, Drugs in Rock Music," Christian Science Monitor, August 23, 1995, pp. 1, 36.

[158] "MCA 'Peddling Filth,' Critics Say," Arizona Republic, December 11, 1996, p. A7.

Cheney, who was the head of the Council on Humanities for Presidents Reagan and Bush, holds a PhD in literature, and is a resident scholar at the American Enterprise Institute.

During the presidential campaign of 2000, both Mrs. Cheney and Mrs. Gore became vocal about the lyrics of rock star Eminem. Eminem released his "The Marshall Mathers LP," which became the fastest-selling release ever, selling 5.2 million copies in two months. The album sold 8 million copies in nine months.[159] Mrs. Cheney stunned Congress when she read lyrics from Eminem's song, most too crude to reproduce here, but which included phrases such as:

Beat your bitches [sic] ass while your kids stare in silence

Went up inside the First National Bank broke, and left rich

Walking bio-hazard causing wreckage

His lyrics were described by various critics and commentators:

"Vile and full of frightening calls to violence." Jim Fouratt, *Billboard*

"In the hands of a more capable artist (say, Frank Zappa or Richard Pryor), this vitriol might be taken to such an extreme to make it a subversive farce; in Em's ego-fueled tirade, it's merely sickeningly offensive . . . about as funny as kiddie porn . . ." *Sonic Net.com*

"The first great pop record of the 21st Century . . . A-minus for artistry, D-plus for moral responsibility." *Entertainment Weekly*

"Crude, hostile, bigoted lyrics." Michael Medved, *USA Today*[160]

....

Discussion Questions

1. What are the ethical issues in the production of songs with explicit lyrics?

2. Will voluntary regulation work for the recording industry?

3. If you were a record producer, would your company sign artists who sing explicit lyrics?

4. If you were a record producer, would you feel an obligation to do more than put a warning label on albums with explicit lyrics?

5. You have just been informed that a teenager committed suicide while listening to the music of one of the artists your company produces. The music suggested suicide as an alternative to unhappiness. Would you feel morally responsible for the suicide? Should the artist feel morally responsible?

6. Does the reemergence of Eminem establish that rock music lyrics will always be an issue? Is there a danger that the bar is lowered with each discussion? For example, in this edition of the book, the Eminem lyrics are simply too crude to include whereas the lyrics from the last round could be included. Is this decline evidence of a decline in the social responsibility of record companies and artists?

[159] Edna Gundersen, "Eminem: What's With This Guy?" *USA Today,* July 27, 2000, p. 1D.
[160] Mim Udovitch, "Visible Man," *New York Times Magazine,* February 18, 2001, pp. 9–10.

....

CASE 9.13

Stem-Cell Research

During the summer of 2001, there was extensive debate over stem-cell research because President George W. Bush was faced with the decision of whether to allow federal funding for the extraction of stem cells from human embryos.

Stem-cell research has strong advocates in the medical and scientific community because of their belief that the research holds great potential for cures for Alzheimer's disease, cancer, spinal cord injuries, Parkinson's, diabetes, and a range of other related illnesses.[161] The advocates had strong support from Mrs. Nancy Reagan, wife of President Ronald Reagan, who had suffered from Alzheimer's for nearly a decade, and Christopher Reeve, a Hollywood actor with a spinal cord injury. Ron Reagan, Mr. Reagan's son, spoke at the Democrat National Convention in 2004 urging the delegates to support embryonic stem-cell research and to vote for John Kerry for president to ensure that the research developed with federal funding.

However, stem-cell research has its strong opponents among those who believe that life begins at conception and that the "harvesting" of stem cells from embryos is the taking of life, and that encouraging such research is likely to result in the creation of human embryos for purposes of harvesting the cells. These opponents tout adult stem-cell research as an alternative that has been pursued with some success and a solution that avoids what they see as a moral dilemma. They also fear the likelihood of the slippery slope to cloning.[162] Indeed, the House voted to ban human cloning during this time period because of concerns that any federal funding that would be approved might lead to further experimentation.[163] Richard M. Doerflinger, of the U.S. Conference of Catholic Bishops, has called the research "grotesque," and said, "Those who have become accustomed to destroying 'spare' embryos for research now think nothing of taking the next horrible step, creating human life for the purpose of destroying it."[164]

During the time of the debate, the media revealed that the Jones Institute, a private fertility clinic in Norfolk, Virginia, was mixing eggs and sperm to create human embryos.[165]

Mr. Bush, as a compromise position on a hotly debated issue, approved limited federal funding for lines of research on stem cells that were already "harvested." His reasoning was that the cells should not be thrown away.

While the public continued its debate, biotech businesses were gearing up for what they felt would be the new direction for medical research and treatment. For example, Advanced Cell Technology, Inc. began acquiring eggs from female donors for purposes

---

[161] Robert P. George, "Don't Destroy Human Life," The Wall Street Journal, July 30, 2001, p. A16.

[162] David Baltimore, "Don't Impede Medical Progress," The Wall Street Journal, July 30, 2001, p. A16.

[163] Sheryl Gay Stolberg, "House Backs Ban on Human Cloning for Any Objective," The New York Times, August 1, 2001, pp. A1, A11.

[164] Laurie McGinley, "Nancy Reagan Urges GOP to Back Stem-Cell Research," The Wall Street Journal, July 12, 2001, p. B2.

[165] Sheryl Gay Stolberg, "Bioethicists Find Themselves the Ones Being Scrutinized," The New York Times, August 2, 2001, pp. A1, A14.

of future research.[166] Later in 2001, Advanced Cell Technology announced that it has successfully cloned a human embryo.[167]

Universities such as Georgetown and Michigan, with extensive cancer research programs, stand to benefit substantially from federal research dollars. Upon President Bush's announcement of his partial approval, biotech stocks soared.

....

Discussion Questions

1. Is it ethical for the Jones Institute to create embryos? What of Advanced Cell Technology's cloning?

2. One bioethicist has questioned the role of bioethicists in the debate, raising the question, "Are we being ethical even as we say what is ethical?" What if they are funded by hospitals, biotech companies, and pharmaceutical firms in their research or at their colleges and universities?

3. Is stem-cell research a moral issue that breaks down along religious lines or are there implications for each side's position?

4. Pope John Paul II, believed to suffer from Parkinson's, has taken a strong position against stem-cell research and indicated, "The end never justifies the means."[168] What does he mean? Are businesses using this rationalization?

5. Would you work for a company that creates human embryos? That conducts stem-cell research? Why or why not? Be sure to refer to Unit 8 for a sample of a shareholder proposal on embryonic stem-cell research.

[166] "Cloning of Embryos for Research Raises Ethics Questions," The Wall Street Journal, July 12, 2001, p. B2.
[167] Sheryl Gay Stolberg, "Cloning Executive Presses Senate," The New York Times, December 5, 2001, p. A22.
[168] Robert A. Sirico, "No Compromise on Stem Cells," The Wall Street Journal, July 11, 2001, p. A16.